Cor

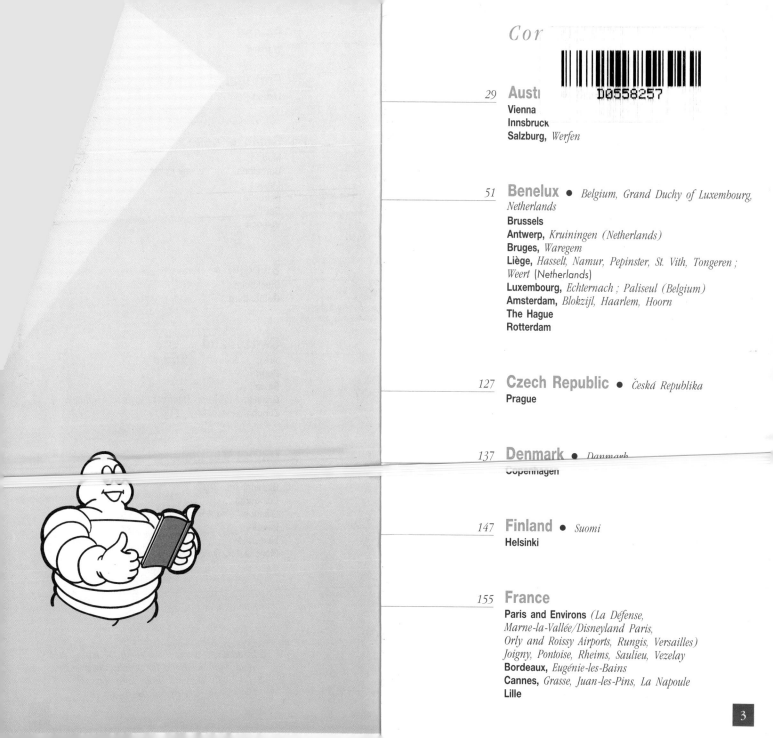

29 **Aust**
Vienna
Innsbruck
Salzburg, *Werfen*

51 **Benelux** • *Belgium, Grand Duchy of Luxembourg, Netherlands*
Brussels
Antwerp, *Kruiningen (Netherlands)*
Bruges, *Waregem*
Liège, *Hasselt, Namur, Pepinster, St. Vith, Tongeren ; Weert* (Netherlands)
Luxembourg, *Echternach ; Paliseul (Belgium)*
Amsterdam, *Blokzijl, Haarlem, Hoorn*
The Hague
Rotterdam

127 **Czech Republic** • *Česká Republika*
Prague

137 **Denmark** • *Danmark*
Copenhagen

147 **Finland** • *Suomi*
Helsinki

155 **France**
Paris and Environs *(La Défense, Marne-la-Vallée/Disneyland Paris, Orly and Roissy Airports, Rungis, Versailles) Joigny, Pontoise, Rheims, Saulieu, Vezelay*
Bordeaux, *Eugénie-les-Bains*
Cannes, *Grasse, Juan-les-Pins, La Napoule*
Lille

Lyons, *Annecy, Chagny, Fleurie Mionnay, Montrond-les-Bains, Roanne, St-Bonnet-le-Froid, Valence, Vienne, Vonnas*
Marseilles, *Les Baux-de-Provence, Carry-le-Rouet*
Monaco (Principality of)
Nice, *St-Martin-du-Var, Vence*
Strasbourg, *Illhaeusern, Lembach, Marlenheim*
Valley of the Loire : Tours, *Amboise, Bracieux, Onzain, Romorantin-Lanthenay*

273 **Germany** • *Deutschland*
Berlin
Cologne, *Bergisch-Gladbach, Bad Laasphe, Wittlich*
Dresden
Düsseldorf, *Essen-Kettwig, Grevenbroich*
Frankfurt on Main, *Eltville, Mannheim, Stromberg, Wertheim*
Leipzig
Hamburg
Hanover
Munich, *Aschau*
Stuttgart, *Baiersbronn, Öhringen*

349 **Greece** • *Elláda*
Athens

357 **Hungary** • *Magyarország*
Budapest

367 **Ireland,** *Republic of*
Dublin

377 **Italy** • *Italia*
Rome, *Baschi*
Florence
Milan, *Abbiategrasso, Bergamo, Canneto sull' Oglio, Erbusco, Ranco, Soriso*
Naples, *Island of Capri, Sant'Agata sui Due Golfi*
Palermo *(Sicily)*
Taormina *(Sicily)*
Turin, *Costigliole d'Asti*
Venice, *Padova, Verona*

449 **Norway** • *Norge*
Oslo

457 **Poland**
Warsaw

465 **Portugal**
Lisbon

479 **Spain** • *España*
Madrid
Barcelona, *San Celoni, Rosa*
Málaga
Marbella
Sevilla
Valencia

525 **Sweden** • *Sverige*
Stockholm
Gothenburg

539 **Switzerland**
Suisse – Schweiz – Svizzera
Berne
Basle
Geneva, *Lausanne, Montreux, Vufflens-le-Château*
Zürich

563 **United Kingdom**
London, *Bray-on-Thames, Oxford, Reading*
Birmingham, *Bristol*
Edinburgh
Glasgow, *Ullapool*
Leeds
Liverpool
Manchester, *Longridge*

In addition to those situated in the main cities, restaurants renowned for their excellent cuisine will be found in the towns printed in light type in the list above.

Dear Reader

With the aim of giving the maximum amount of information in a limited number of pages Michelin has adopted a system of symbols which is renowned the world over.
Failing this system the present publication would run to six volumes.
Judge for yourselves by comparing the descriptive text below with the equivalent extract from the Guide in symbol form.

La Résidence (Paul), 09 18 21 32 43, Fax 09 18 21 32 49, lake, « Flowered garden », BX **a**
March-November – **Meals** *(closed Sunday)* 350/650 – 75 – **25 rm** 500/800.
Spec. Goujonnettes de sole, Poulet aux écrevisses, Profiteroles.
Wines. Vouvray, Bourgueil.

This demonstration clearly shows that each entry contains a great deal of information. The symbols are easily learnt and to know them will enable you to understand the Guide and to choose those establishments that you require.

A very comfortable hotel where you will enjoy a pleasant stay and be tempted to prolong your visit.
The excellence of the cuisine, which is personally supervised by the proprietor Mr Paul, is worth a detour on your journey.
The hotel is in a quiet secluded setting, away from built-up areas.
To reserve phone 21 32 43 ; the Fax number is 21 32 49.
The hotel affords a fine view of the lake ; in good weather it is possible to eat out of doors.
The hotel is enhanced by an attractive flowered garden and has an indoor swimming pool and a private tennis court. Smoking is not allowed in certain areas of the hotel. Direct dialling telephone in room.
Parking facilities, under cover, are available to hotel guests.
The hotel accepts payment by American [illegible] and Japan Credit Bureau credit cards.
Letters giving the location of the hotel on the town plan : BX **a**.
The hotel is open from March to November but the restaurant closes every Sunday.
The set meal prices range from 350 F for the lowest to 650 F for the highest.
The cost of continental breakfast served in the bedroom is 75 F.
25 bedroomed hotel. The charges vary from 500 F for a single to 800 F for the best double or twin bedded room.
Included for the gourmet are some culinary specialities, recommended by the hotelier : Strips of deep-fried sole fillets, Chicken with crayfish, Choux pastry balls filled with ice cream and covered with chocolate sauce. In addition to the best quality wines you will find many of the local wines worth sampling : Vouvray, Bourgueil.

This revised edition from
Michelin Tyre Company's Tourism Department
offers you a selection
of hotels and restaurants
in the main European cities.
The latter have been chosen for
their business or tourist interest.

In addition
the guide indicates establishments,
located in other towns,
renowned for the excellence of their cuisine.

We hope that the guide will help you
with your choice of hotel or restaurant
and prove useful for your sightseeing.
Have an enjoyable stay.

Hotels, Restaurants

Categories, standard of comfort

	XXXXX	*Luxury in the traditional style*
	XXXX	*Top class comfort*
	XXX	*Very comfortable*
	XX	*Comfortable*
	X	*Quite comfortable*
M		*In its class, hotel with modern amenities*

Atmosphere and setting

...	*Pleasant hotels*
XXXXX ... X	*Pleasant restaurants*
« Park »	*Particularly attractive feature*
	Very quiet or quiet secluded hotel
	Quiet hotel
sea,	*Exceptional view, Panoramic view*
	Interesting or extensive view

Cuisine

	Exceptional cuisine in the country, worth a special journey
	Excellent cooking : worth a detour
	A very good restaurant in its category
Meals	*Good food at moderate prices*

Hotel facilities

30 rm	*Number of rooms*
	Lift (elevator) – Television in room
	Non-smoking areas
	Air conditioning
	Telephone in room: direct dialling for outside calls
	Minitel – modem point in the bedrooms
	Tennis court(s) – Outdoor or indoor swimming pool
	Sauna – Exercise room
	Garden – Beach with bathing facilities
	Meals served in garden or on terrace
	Garage – Car park
	Bedrooms accessible to disabled people
150	*Equipped conference room : maximum capacity*
	Dogs are not allowed
without rest.	*The hotel has no restaurant*

Prices

These prices are given in the currency of the country in question. Valid for 1997 the rates shown should only vary if the cost of living changes to any great extent.

Meals

Meals 130/260	*Set meal prices*
Meals a la carte 160/290	*"a la carte" meal prices*
b.i.	*House wine included*
	Table wine available by the carafe

Hotels

30 rm 305/500	*Lowest price for a comfortable single and highest price for the best double room.*
30 rm 345/580	*Price includes breakfast*

Breakfast

55	*Price of breakfast*

Credit cards

AE GB JCB VISA	*Credit cards accepted*

Service and Taxes

Except in Finland, Greece and Spain, prices shown are inclusive, that is to say service and V.A.T. included. In the U.K. and Ireland, **s** *= service only included,* **t** *= V.A.T. only included. In Italy, when not included, a percentage for service is shown after the meal prices, eg. (16 %).*

Town Plans

Main conventional signs

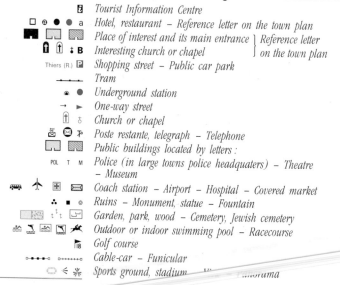

	Tourist Information Centre
a	*Hotel, restaurant – Reference letter on the town plan*
	Place of interest and its main entrance } *Reference letter on the town plan*
B	*Interesting church or chapel* } *Reference letter on the town plan*
Thiers (R.)	*Shopping street – Public car park*
	Tram
	Underground station
	One-way street
	Church or chapel
	Poste restante, telegraph – Telephone
	Public buildings located by letters :
POL T M	*Police (in large towns police headquaters) – Theatre – Museum*
	Coach station – Airport – Hospital – Covered market
	Ruins – Monument, statue – Fountain
	Garden, park, wood – Cemetery, Jewish cemetery
	Outdoor or indoor swimming pool – Racecourse
18	*Golf course*
	Cable-car – Funicular
	Sports ground, stadium – View – Panorama

Names shown on the street plans are in the language of the country to conform to local signposting.

Sights

★★★	*Worth a journey*
★★	*Worth a detour*
★	*Interesting*

*Avec cette nouvelle édition,
les Services de Tourisme du Pneu Michelin
vous proposent une sélection
d'hôtels et restaurants
des principales villes d'Europe,
choisies en raison
de leur vocation internationale
sur le plan des affaires et du tourisme.*

*Vous y trouverez également les grandes tables
situées hors de ces grandes villes.*

*Nous vous souhaitons d'agréables séjours
et espérons que ce guide
vous aidera utilement
pour le choix d'un hôtel,
d'une bonne table
et pour la visite des principales curiosités.*

Hôtels, Restaurants

Classe et confort

	Grand luxe et tradition
	Grand confort
	Très confortable
	Bon confort
	Assez confortable
M	*Dans sa catégorie, hôtel d'équipement moderne*

L'agrément

...	*Hôtels agréables*
...	*Restaurants agréables*
« Park »	*Élément particulièrement agréable*
	Hôtel très tranquille, ou isolé et tranquille
	Hôtel tranquille
sea,	*Vue exceptionnelle, panorama*
	Vue intéressante ou étendue

La table

	Une des meilleures tables du pays, vaut le voyage
	Table excellente, mérite un détour
	Une très bonne table dans sa catégorie
Meals	*Repas soignés à prix modérés*

L'installation

30 rm	*Nombre de chambres*
	Ascenseur – Télévision dans la chambre
	Non-fumeurs
	Air conditionné
	Téléphone dans la chambre direct avec l'extérieur
	Prise Modem – Minitel dans la chambre
	Tennis – Piscine : de plein air ou couverte
	Sauna – Salle de remise en forme
	Jardin – Plage aménagée
	Repas servis au jardin ou en terrasse
	Garage – Parc à voitures
	Chambres accessibles aux handicapés physiques
150	*Salles de conférences : capacité maximum*
	Accès interdit aux chiens
without rest.	*L'hôtel n'a pas de restaurant*

Les prix

Les prix sont indiqués dans la monnaie du pays. Établis pour l'année 1997, ils ne doivent être modifiés que si le coût de la vie subit des variations importantes.

Au restaurant

Meals 130/260	*Prix des repas à prix fixes*
Meals à la carte 160/290	*Prix des repas à la carte*
b.i.	*Boisson comprise*
	Vin de table en carafe

A l'hôtel

30 rm 305/500	*Prix minimum pour une chambre d'une personne et maximum pour la plus belle chambre occupée par deux personnes*
30 rm 345/580	*Prix des chambres petit déjeuner compris*

Petit déjeuner

55	*Prix du petit déjeuner*

Cartes de crédit

MC AE GB JCB VISA	*Cartes de crédit acceptées*

Service et taxes

A l'exception de la Finlande, de la Grèce et de l'Espagne, les prix indiqués sont nets. Au Royaume Uni et en Irlande, **s** *= service compris,* **t** *= T.V.A. comprise. En Italie, le service est parfois compté en supplément aux prix des repas. Ex. : (16 %).*

Les Plans

Principaux signes conventionnels

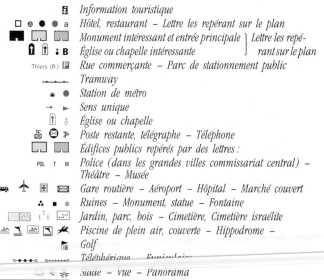

Information touristique

a — *Hôtel, restaurant – Lettre les repérant sur le plan*

Monument intéressant et entrée principale } *Lettre les repérant sur le plan*

B — *Église ou chapelle intéressante* } *Lettre les repérant sur le plan*

Thiers (R.) — *Rue commerçante – Parc de stationnement public*

Tramway

Station de métro

Sens unique

Église ou chapelle

Poste restante, télégraphe – Téléphone

Édifices publics repérés par des lettres :

POL T M — *Police (dans les grandes villes commissariat central) – Théâtre – Musée*

Gare routière – Aéroport – Hôpital – Marché couvert

Ruines – Monument, statue – Fontaine

Jardin, parc, bois – Cimetière, Cimetière israélite

Piscine de plein air, couverte – Hippodrome – Golf

Téléphérique – Funiculaire

Stade – Vue – Panorama

Les indications portées sur les plans sont dans la langue du pays, en conformité avec la dénomination locale.

Les curiosités

★★★ *Vaut le voyage*

★★ *Mérite un détour*

★ *Intéressante*

Mit dieser Neuauflage
präsentieren Ihnen die
Michelin-Touristikabteilungen
eine Auswahl von Hotels und Restaurants
in europäischen Großstädten
von internationaler Bedeutung
für Geschäftsreisende und Touristen.

Besonders gute Restaurants
in der näheren Umgebung
dieser Städte wurden ebenfalls
aufgenommen.

Wir wünschen einen angenehmen
Aufenthalt
und hoffen, daß Ihnen dieser Führer
bei der Wahl eines Hotels,
eines Restaurants
und beim Besuch der
Hauptsehenswürdigkeiten
gute Dienste leisten wird.

Hotels, Restaurants

Klasseneinteilung und Komfort

		Großer Luxus und Tradition
		Großer Komfort
		Sehr komfortabel
		Mit gutem Komfort
		Mit Standard-Komfort
M		*Moderne Einrichtung*

Annehmlichkeiten

...	*Angenehme Hotels*
...	*Angenehme Restaurants*
« Park »	*Besondere Annehmlichkeit*
	Sehr ruhiges oder abgelegenes und ruhiges Hotel
	Ruhiges Hotel
sea,	*Reizvolle Aussicht, Rundblick*
	Interessante oder weite Sicht

Küche

	Eine der besten Küchen des Landes : eine Reise wert
	Eine hervorragende Küche : verdient einen Umweg
	Eine sehr gute Küche : verdient Ihre besondere Beachtung
Meals	*Sorgfältig zubereitete preiswerte Mahlzeiten*

Einrichtung

30 rm	*Anzahl der Zimmer*
	Fahrstuhl – Fernsehen im Zimmer
	Nichtraucher – Klimaanlage
	Zimmertelefon mit direkter Außenverbindung
	Minitel Anschluß im Zimmer
	Tennis – Freibad – Hallenbad
	Sauna – Fitneßraum
	Garten – Strandbad
	Garten-, Terrassenrestaurant
	Garage – Parkplatz
	Für Körperbehinderte leicht zugängliche Zimmer
150	*Konferenzräume mit Höchstkapazität*
	Hunde sind unerwünscht
without rest.	*Hotel ohne Restaurant*

Die Preise

Die Preise sind in der jeweiligen Landeswährung angegeben. Sie gelten für das Jahr 1997 und ändern sich nur bei starken Veränderungen der Lebenshaltungskosten.

Im Restaurant

Meals 130/260	*Feste Menupreise*
Meals à la carte 160/290	*Mahlzeiten "a la carte"*
b.i.	*Getränke inbegriffen*
	Preiswerter Wein in Karaffen

Im Hotel

30 rm 305/500	*Mindestpreis für ein Einzelzimmer und Höchstpreis für das schönste Doppelzimmer für zwei Personen.*
30 rm 345/580	*Zimmerpreis inkl. Frühstück*

Frühstück

55	*Preis des Frühstücks*

Kreditkarten

MC AE GB JCB VISA	*Akzeptierte Kreditkarten*

Bedienungsgeld und Gebühren

Mit Ausnahme von Finnland, Griechenland und Spanien sind die angegebenen Preise Inklusivpreise. In den Kapiteln über Großbritannien und Irland bedeutet s = Bedienungsgeld inbegriffen, t = MWSt inbegriffen. In Italien wird für die Bedienung gelegentlich ein Zuschlag zum Preis der Mahlzeit erhoben, zB (16 %).

Stadtpläne

Erklärung der wichtigsten Zeichen

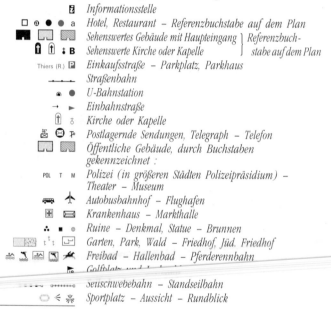

Informationsstelle
Hotel, Restaurant – Referenzbuchstabe auf dem Plan
Sehenswertes Gebäude mit Haupteingang } *Referenzbuchstabe auf dem Plan*
Sehenswerte Kirche oder Kapelle
Thiers (R.) *Einkaufsstraße – Parkplatz, Parkhaus*
Straßenbahn
U-Bahnstation
Einbahnstraße
Kirche oder Kapelle
Postlagernde Sendungen, Telegraph – Telefon
Öffentliche Gebäude, durch Buchstaben gekennzeichnet :
POL T M *Polizei (in größeren Städten Polizeipräsidium) – Theater – Museum*
Autobusbahnhof – Flughafen
Krankenhaus – Markthalle
Ruine – Denkmal, Statue – Brunnen
Garten, Park, Wald – Friedhof, Jüd. Friedhof
Freibad – Hallenbad – Pferderennbahn
Golfplatz und [illegible]
Seilschwebebahn – Standseilbahn
Sportplatz – Aussicht – Rundblick

Die Angaben auf den Stadtplänen erfolgen, übereinstimmend mit der örtlichen Beschilderung, in der Landessprache.

Sehenswürdigkeiten

★★★ *Eine Reise wert*
★★ *Verdient einen Umweg*
★ *Sehenswert*

この改訂版ガイドブックはミシュラン・タイヤ社観光部がおとどけするものです。

ビジネスに、観光に、国際的な拠点ヨーロッパ主要都市が誇る自慢のホテルとレストランを、そして郊外にたたずむ名うてのレストランをあわせて、御紹介いたします。

このガイドブックが、より快適なホテル、味わい深いレストランやあこがれの地と出逢うきっかけとなり、皆さまの旅をより素晴らしいものにするお手伝いができれば幸いです。

ホテル　レストラン

等級と快適さ

- 豪華で伝統的様式
- トップクラス
- たいへん快適
- 快適
- 割に快適
- M 等級内での近代的設備のホテル

居心地

- 居心地よいホテル
- 居心地よいレストラン
- « Park » 特に魅力的な特徴
- 大変静かなホテルまたは人里離れた静かなホテル
- 静かなホテル
- sea, 見晴らしがよい展望（例：海）、パノラマ
- 素晴らしい風景

料理

- 最上の料理、出かける価値あり
- 素晴らしい料理、寄り道の価値あり
- 等級内では大変おいしい料理
- Meals 手頃な値段でおいしい料理

設備

30 rm ルームナンバー

エレベーター、室内テレビ

非喫煙室

空調設備

室内に電話あり、外線直通

ミニテル/モデムの回線付き

テニスコート。屋外プール。屋内プール。

サウナ。トレーニングルーム。

くつろげる庭。整備された海水浴場

食事が庭またはテラスでできる。

駐車場、パーキング。

体の不自由な方のための設備あり

会議又は研修会の出来るホテル

犬の連れ込みおことわり

without rest. レストランの無いホテル

料金

料金は1997年のその国の貨幣単位で示してありますが、物価の変動などで変わる場合もあります。

レストラン

Meals 130/260
Meals a la carte 160/290 定食、ア・ラ・カルトそれぞれの最低料金と最高料金。

b.i. 飲食付

デカンター入りテーブルワイン有ります。

ホテル

30 rm 305/500 一人部屋の最低料金と二人部屋の最高料金。

30 rm 345/580 朝食代は含まれています

朝食

55 朝食代

クレジット・カード

クレジット・カード使用可

サービス料と税金

フィンランド、ギリシャ、スペイン以外の国に関しては正価料金。英国及びアイルランドでは、 **s.**：サービス料込み、**t.**：付加価 値税込み、を意味する。イタリアでは、サービス料が料金に加算されることがある。例：(16%)

地 図

主な記号

	ツーリストインフォメーション
a	ホテル・レストラン ― 地図上での目印番号
	興味深い歴史的建造物と、その中央入口 } 地図上での目印番号
B	興味深い教会または聖堂 } 地図上での目印番号
Thiers (R.) P	商店街　公共駐車場
	路面電車
	地下鉄駅
	一方通行路
	教会または聖堂 ―局留郵便、電報 ― 電話
	公共建造物、記号は下記の通り
POL T M	警察（大都市では、中央警察書） ―劇場 ― 美術観、博物館
	長距離バス発着所 ― 空港 ― 病院 ― 屋内市場
	庭園、公園、森林 ― 墓地 ― ユダヤ教の墓地
9	屋外プール、屋内プール ― 競馬場 ― ゴルフ場
	ロープウェイ ― ケーブルカー
	・スタジアム ― 風景 ― パノラマ

地図上の名称は、地方の標識に合わせてその国の言葉で表記されています。

名 所

★★★　出かける価値あり

★★　立ち寄る価値あり

★　興味深い

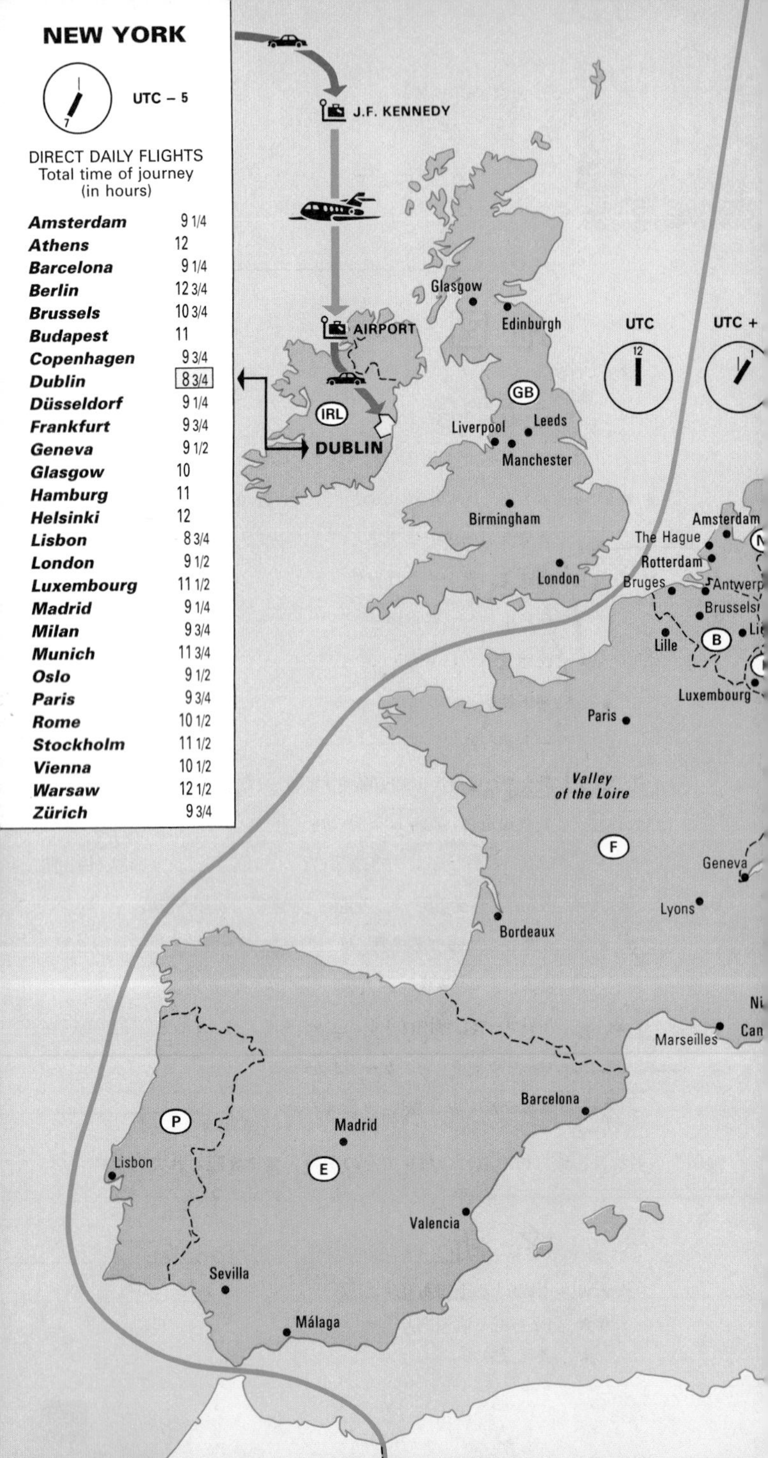

NEW YORK

UTC – 5

DIRECT DAILY FLIGHTS
Total time of journey
(in hours)

Amsterdam	9 1/4
Athens	12
Barcelona	9 1/4
Berlin	12 3/4
Brussels	10 3/4
Budapest	11
Copenhagen	9 3/4
Dublin	8 3/4
Düsseldorf	9 1/4
Frankfurt	9 3/4
Geneva	9 1/2
Glasgow	10
Hamburg	11
Helsinki	12
Lisbon	8 3/4
London	9 1/2
Luxembourg	11 1/2
Madrid	9 1/4
Milan	9 3/4
Munich	11 3/4
Oslo	9 1/2
Paris	9 3/4
Rome	10 1/2
Stockholm	11 1/2
Vienna	10 1/2
Warsaw	12 1/2
Zürich	9 3/4

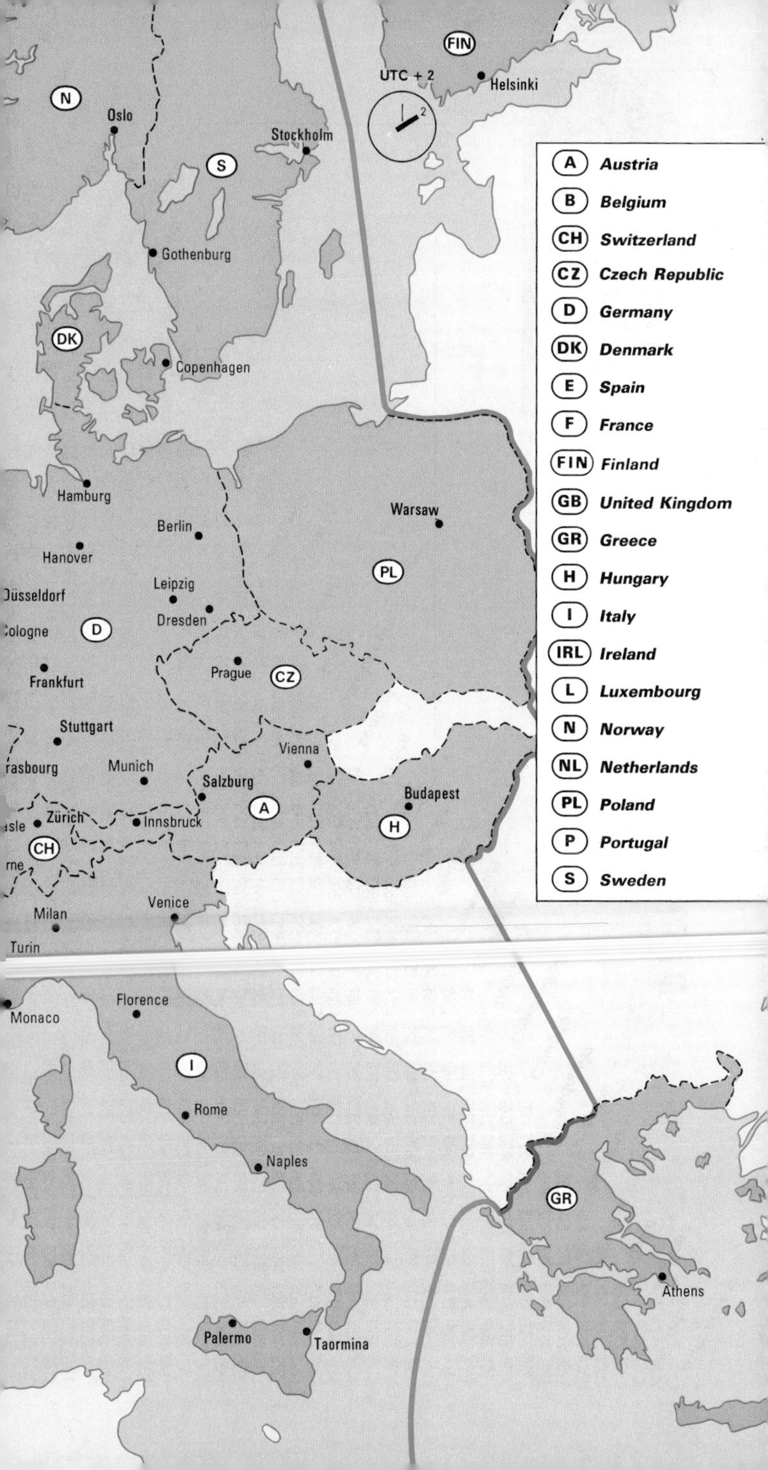
FIN
UTC + 2
Helsinki
N
Oslo
S
Stockholm
Gothenburg
DK
Copenhagen
Hamburg
Berlin
Warsaw
Hanover
PL
Leipzig
Düsseldorf
Dresden
Cologne
D
Prague
CZ
Frankfurt
Stuttgart
Vienna
Strasbourg
Munich
Salzburg
Budapest
A
Zürich
Innsbruck
H
Basle
CH
Berne
Venice
Milan
Turin
Monaco
Florence
I
Rome
Naples
GR
Athens
Palermo
Taormina
A Austria
B Belgium
CH Switzerland
CZ Czech Republic
D Germany
DK Denmark
E Spain
F France
FIN Finland
GB United Kingdom
GR Greece
H Hungary
I Italy
IRL Ireland
L Luxembourg
N Norway
NL Netherlands
PL Poland
P Portugal
S Sweden

DISTANCES BY ROAD

(in kilometres)

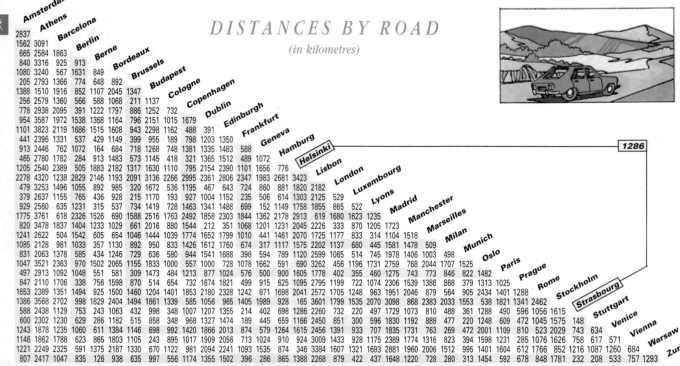

	Amsterdam	Athens	Barcelona	Berlin	Berne	Bordeaux	Brussels	Budapest	Cologne	Copenhagen	Dublin	Edinburgh	Frankfurt	Geneva	Hamburg	Helsinki	Lisbon	London	Luxembourg	Lyons	Madrid	Manchester	Marseilles	Milan	Munich	Oslo	Paris	Prague	Rome	Stockholm	Strasbourg	Stuttgart	Venice	Vienna	Warsaw
Athens	2837																																		
Barcelona	1562	3091																																	
Berlin	665	2584	1863																																
Berne	840	3316	925	913																															
Bordeaux	1080	3240	567	1631	849																														
Brussels	205	2793	1366	774	648	892																													
Budapest	1388	1510	1916	852	1107	2045	1347																												
Cologne	256	2579	1360	566	588	1068	211	1137																											
Copenhagen	778	2938	2095	391	1222	1797	886	1252	732																										
Dublin	954	3587	1972	1538	1368	1164	796	2151	1015	1679																									
Edinburgh	1101	3823	2119	1686	1515	1608	943	2298	1162	488	391																								
Frankfurt	441	2396	1331	537	429	1149	399	955	189	798	1203	1350																							
Geneva	913	2446	762	1072	164	684	718	1268	748	1381	1335	1483	588																						
Hamburg	465	2780	1782	284	913	1483	573	1145	418	321	1365	1512	489	1072																					
Helsinki	1205	2540	2389	505	1883	2182	1317	1630	1110	795	2154	2390	1101	1656	776																				
Lisbon	2278	4320	1238	2829	2146	1193	2091	3136	2266	2995	2361	2806	2347	1983	2681	3423																			
London	479	3253	1496	1055	892	985	320	1672	536	1195	467	643	724	860	881	1820	2182																		
Luxembourg	379	2637	1155	765	436	928	215	1170	193	927	1004	1152	235	506	614	1303	2125	529																	
Lyons	929	2560	635	1231	315	537	734	1419	728	1463	1341	1488	699	152	1149	1758	1855	865	522																
Madrid	1775	3761	618	2326	1526	690	1588	2516	1763	2492	1858	2303	1844	1362	2178	2913	619	1680	1623	1235															
Manchester	820	3478	1837	1404	1233	1029	661	2016	880	1544	212	351	1068	1201	1231	2045	2226	333	870	1205	1723														
Marseilles	1241	2622	504	1542	605	654	1046	1444	1039	1774	1652	1799	1010	441	1461	2070	1725	1177	833	314	1104	1518													
Milan	1085	2128	981	1033	357	1130	892	950	833	1426	1612	1760	674	317	1117	1575	2202	1137	680	445	1581	1478	509												
Munich	831	2063	1378	585	434	1246	729	636	580	944	1541	1688	398	594	789	1120	2599	1065	514	745	1978	1406	1003	498											
Oslo	1047	3521	2363	970	1502	2065	1155	1833	1000	557	1000	728	1078	1662	591	690	3262	456	1196	1731	2759	768	2044	1707	1525										
Paris	497	2913	1092	1048	551	581	309	1473	484	1213	877	1024	576	500	900	1605	1778	402	355	460	1275	743	773	846	822	1482									
Prague	847	2110	1706	338	756	1598	870	514	654	732	1674	1821	499	915	625	1095	2795	1199	722	1074	2306	1539	1386	868	379	1313	1025								
Rome	1653	2389	1351	1494	925	1500	1460	1204	1401	1853	2180	2328	1242	871	1698	2041	2572	1705	1248	963	1951	2046	879	564	905	2434	1401	1288							
Stockholm	1386	3568	2702	998	1829	2404	1494	1861	1339	585	1056	965	1405	1989	928	165	3601	1799	1535	2070	3098	868	2383	2033	1553	538	1821	1341	2462						
Strasbourg	588	2438	1129	753	243	1063	432	998	348	1007	1207	1355	214	402	698	1286	2260	732	220	497	1729	1073	810	488	361	1288	490	596	1056	1615					
Stuttgart	600	2302	1230	629	286	1182	515	858	348	968	1327	1474	189	445	659	1166	2450	851	300	596	1830	1192	888	477	220	1248	609	472	1045	1575	148				
Venice	1243	1878	1235	1060	611	1384	1146	698	992	1420	1866	2013	874	579	1264	1615	2456	1391	933	707	1835	1731	763	269	472	2001	1109	810	523	2029	743	634			
Vienna	1146	1862	1788	623	865	1803	1105	243	895	1017	1909	2056	713	1024	910	924	3009	1433	928	1175	2389	1774	1316	823	394	1598	1231	285	1076	1626	758	617	571		
Warsaw	1221	2249	2325	591	1375	2187	1330	670	1122	981	2094	2241	1093	1535	874	346	3384	1607	1321	1693	2881	1960	2006	1512	995	1401	1604	612	1766	852	1216	1087	1260	684	
Zurich	807	2417	1047	835	126	938	635	997	556	1174	1355	1502	396	286	865	1388	2268	879	422	437	1648	1220	728	280	313	1454	592	678	848	1781	232	208	533	757	1293

Helsinki – Strasbourg: 1286

AIR LINKS *(in hours)*

3 1/2 not daily

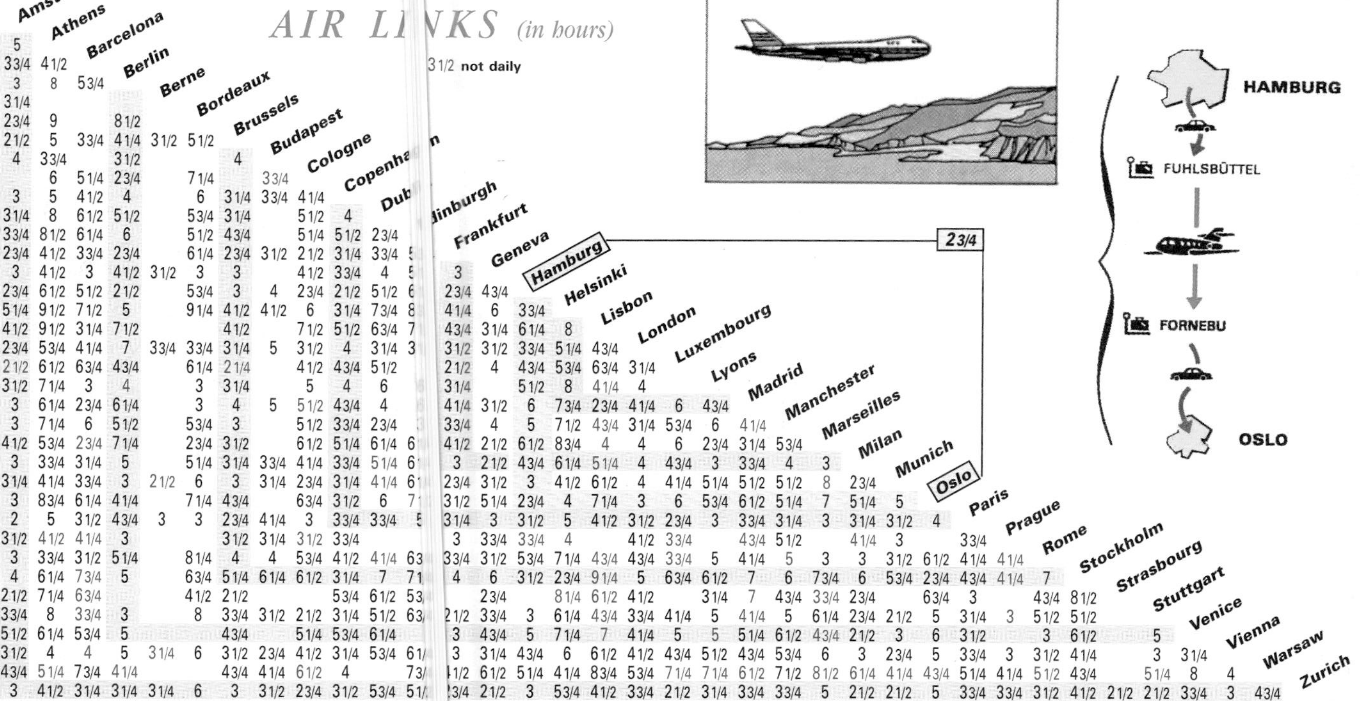

	Amsterdam	Athens	Barcelona	Berlin	Berne	Bordeaux	Brussels	Budapest	Cologne	Copenhagen	Dublin	Edinburgh	Frankfurt	Geneva	Hamburg	Helsinki	Lisbon	London	Luxembourg	Lyons	Madrid	Manchester	Marseilles	Milan	Munich	Oslo	Paris	Prague	Rome	Stockholm	Strasbourg	Stuttgart	Venice	Vienna	Warsaw
Athens	5																																		
Barcelona	3 3/4	4 1/2																																	
Berlin	3	8	5 3/4																																
Berne	3 1/4																																		
Bordeaux	2 3/4	9		8 1/2																															
Brussels	2 1/2	5	3 3/4	4 1/4	3 1/2	5 1/2																													
Budapest	4	3 3/4		3 1/2			4																												
Cologne		6	5 1/4	2 3/4		7 1/4		3 3/4																											
Copenhagen	3	5	4 1/2	4		6	3 1/4	3 3/4	4 1/4																										
Dublin	3 1/4	8	6 1/2	5 1/2		5 3/4	3 1/4		5 1/2	4																									
Edinburgh	3 3/4	8 1/2	6 1/4	6		5 1/2	4 3/4		5 1/4	5 1/2	2 3/4																								
Frankfurt	2 3/4	4 1/2	3 3/4	2 3/4		6 1/4	2 3/4	3 1/2	2 1/2	3 1/4	3 3/4	[illegible]																							
Geneva	3	4 1/2	3	4 1/2	3 1/2	3	3		4 1/2	3 3/4	4	[illegible]	3																						
Hamburg	2 3/4	6 1/2	5 1/2	2 1/2		5 3/4	3	4	2 3/4	2 1/2	5 1/2	[illegible]	2 3/4	4 3/4																					
Helsinki	5 1/4	9 1/2	7 1/2	5		9 1/4	4 1/2	4 1/2	6	3 1/4	7 3/4	[illegible]	4 1/4	6	3 3/4																				
Lisbon	4 1/2	9 1/2	3 1/4	7 1/2			4 1/2		7 1/2	5 1/2	6 3/4	[illegible]	4 3/4	3 1/4	6 1/4	8																			
London	2 3/4	5 3/4	4 1/4	7	3 3/4	3 3/4	3 1/4	5	3 1/2	4	3 1/4	[illegible]	3 1/2	3 1/2	3 3/4	5 1/4	4 3/4																		
Luxembourg	2 1/2	6 1/2	6 3/4	4 3/4		6 1/4	2 1/4		4 1/2	4 3/4	5 1/2		2 1/2	4	4 3/4	5 3/4	6 3/4	3 1/4																	
Lyons	3 1/2	7 1/4	3	4		3	3 1/4		5	4	6		3 1/4		5 1/2	8	4 1/4	4																	
Madrid	3	6 1/4	2 3/4	6 1/4		3	4	5	5 1/2	4 3/4	4		4 1/4	3 1/2	6	7 3/4	2 3/4	4 1/4	6	4 3/4															
Manchester	3	7 1/4	6	5 1/2		5 3/4	3		5 1/2	3 3/4	2 3/4	[illegible]	3 3/4	4	5	7 1/2	4 3/4	3 1/4	5 3/4	6	4 1/4														
Marseilles	4 1/2	5 3/4	2 3/4	7 1/4		2 3/4	3 1/2		6 1/2	5 1/4	6 1/4	[illegible]	4 1/2	2 1/2	6 1/2	8 3/4	4	4	6	2 3/4	3 1/4	5 3/4													
Milan	3	3 3/4	3 1/4	5		5 1/4	3 1/4	3 3/4	4 1/4	3 3/4	5 1/4	[illegible]	3	2 1/2	4 3/4	6 1/4	5 1/4	4	4 3/4	3	3 3/4	4	3												
Munich	3 1/4	4 1/4	3 3/4	3	2 1/2	6	3	3 1/4	2 3/4	3 1/4	4 1/4	[illegible]	2 3/4	3 1/2	3	4 1/2	6 1/2	4	4 1/4	5 1/4	5 1/2	5 1/2	8	2 3/4											
Oslo	3	8 3/4	6 1/4	4 1/4		7 1/4	4 3/4		6 3/4	3 1/2	6	[illegible]	3 1/2	5 1/4	2 3/4	4	7 1/4	3	6	5 3/4	6 1/2	5 1/4	7	5 1/4	5										
Paris	2	5	3 1/2	4 3/4	3	3	2 3/4	4 1/4	3	3 3/4	3 3/4	[illegible]	3 1/4	3	3 1/2	5	4 1/2	3 1/2	2 3/4	3	3 3/4	3 1/4	3	3 1/4	3 1/2	4									
Prague	3 1/2	4 1/2	4 1/4	3			3 1/2	3 1/4	3 1/2	3 3/4			3	3 3/4	3 3/4	4		4 1/2	3 3/4		4 3/4	5 1/2		4 1/4	3		3 3/4								
Rome	3	3 3/4	3 1/2	5 1/4		8 1/4	4	4	5 3/4	4 1/2	4 1/4	[illegible]	3 3/4	3 1/2	5 3/4	7 1/4	4 3/4	4 3/4	3 3/4	5	4 1/4	5	3	3	3 1/2	6 1/2	4 1/4	4 1/4							
Stockholm	4	6 1/4	7 3/4	5		6 3/4	5 1/4	6 1/4	6 1/2	3 1/4	7	[illegible]	4	6	3 1/2	2 3/4	9 1/4	5	6 3/4	6 1/2	7	6	7 3/4	6	5 3/4	2 3/4	4 3/4	4 1/4	7						
Strasbourg	2 1/2	7 1/4	6 3/4			4 1/2	2 1/2			5 3/4	6 1/2	[illegible]		2 3/4		8 1/4	6 1/2	4 1/2		3 1/4	7	4 3/4	3 3/4	2 3/4		6 3/4	3		4 3/4	8 1/2					
Stuttgart	3 3/4	8	3 3/4	3		8	3 3/4	3 1/2	2 1/2	3 1/4	5 1/2	[illegible]	2 1/2	3 3/4	3	6 1/4	4 3/4	3 3/4	4 1/4	5	4 1/4	5	6 1/4	2 3/4	2 1/2	5	3 1/4	3	5 1/2	5 1/2					
Venice	5 1/2	6 1/4	5 3/4	5			4 3/4		5 1/4	5 3/4	6 1/4		3	4 3/4	5	7 1/4	7	4 1/4	5	5	5 1/4	6 1/2	4 3/4	2 1/2	3	6	3 1/2		3	6 1/2		5			
Vienna	3 1/2	4	4	5	3 1/4	6	3 1/2	2 3/4	4 1/2	3 1/4	5 3/4	[illegible]	3	3 1/4	4 3/4	6	6 1/2	4 1/2	4 3/4	5 1/2	4 3/4	5 3/4	6	3	2 3/4	5	3 3/4	3	3 1/2	4 1/4		3	3 1/4		
Warsaw	4 3/4	5 1/4	7 3/4	4 1/4			4 3/4	4 1/4	6 1/2	4		[illegible]	4 1/2	6 1/2	5 1/4	4 1/4	8 3/4	5 3/4	7 1/4	7 1/4	6 1/2	7 1/2	8 1/2	6 1/4	4 1/4	4 3/4	5 1/4	4 1/4	5 1/2	4 3/4		5 1/4	8	4	
Zurich	3	4 1/2	3 1/4	3 1/4	3 1/4	6	3	3 1/2	2 3/4	3 1/2	5 3/4	[illegible]	2 3/4	2 1/2	3	5 3/4	4 1/2	3 3/4	2 1/2	3 1/4	3 3/4	3 3/4	5	2 1/2	2 1/2	5	3 3/4	3 3/4	3 1/2	4 1/2	2 1/2	2 1/2	3 3/4	3	4 3/4

Austria

Österreich

VIENNA

INNSBRUCK – SALZBURG

PRACTICAL INFORMATION

LOCAL CURRENCY

Austrian Schilling; *100 ATS = 9.15 USD ($) (Jan. 97)*

TOURIST INFORMATION

In Vienna: *Österreich-Information, 1040 Wien, Margaretenstr. 1, ✆ (01) 5 87 20 00, Fax 588 66 20*
Niederösterreich-Information, 1010 Wien, Fischhof 3/3, ✆ (01) 5 33 31 14, Fax 533 100 60 60

Austrian National Holiday: *26 October*

AIRLINES

AUSTRIAN SWISSAIR: *1010 Wien, Kärtner Ring 18, ✆ (01) 5 05 57 57, Fax 505 14 34*

AIR FRANCE: *1010 Wien, Kärntner Str. 49, ✆ (01) 5 14 18 18, Fax 513 94 26*

BRITISH AIRWAYS: *1010 Wien, Kärntner Ring 10, ✆ (01) 505 76 91, Fax 504 20 84*

DEUTSCHE LUFTHANSA: *1060 Wien, Maria Hilfer Str. 123, ✆ (01) 5 99 11 99, Fax 599 11 40*

JAPAN AIRLINES: *1010 Wien, Kärntner Str. 11, ✆ (01) 512 75 22, Fax 512 75 54*

FOREIGN EXCHANGE

Hotels, restaurants and shops do not always accept foreign currencies and it is wise, therefore, to change money and cheques at the banks and exchange offices which are found in the larger stations, airports and at the frontier.

SHOPPING and BANK HOURS

Shops are open from 9am to 6pm, but often close for a lunch break. They are closed Saturday afternoon, Sunday and Bank Holidays (except the shops in railway stations). Branch offices of banks are open from Monday to Friday between 8am and 12.30pm (in Salzburg 12am) and from 1.30pm to 3pm (in Salzburg 2pm to 4.30pm), Thursday to 5.30pm (only in Vienna).
In the index of street names those printed in red are where the principal shops are found.

BREAKDOWN SERVICE

ÖAMTC: *See addresses in the text of each city.*

ARBÖ: *in Vienna: Mariahilfer Str. 180, ✆ (01) 8 91 21, Fax (01) 89 12 12 36*
in Salzburg: Münchner Bundesstr. 9, ✆ (0662) 43 83 81, in Innsbruck: Stadlweg 7, ✆ (0512) 34 51 23
In Austria the ÖAMTC (emergency number ✆ 120) and the ARBÖ (emergency number ✆ 123) make a special point of assisting foreign motorists. They have motor patrols covering main roads.

TIPPING

Service is generally included in hotel and restaurant bills. But in Austria, it is usual to give more than the expected tip in hotels, restaurants and cafés. Taxi-drivers, porters, barbers and theatre attendants also expect tips.

SPEED LIMITS

The speed limit in built up areas (indicated by place name signs at the beginning and end of such areas) is 50 km/h - 31 mph; on motorways 130 km/h - 80 mph and on all other roads 100 km/h - 62 mph.

SEAT BELTS

The wearing of seat belts in Austria is compulsory for drivers and all passengers.

VIENNA

(WIEN) *Austria* 987 ⑩ 426 ⑫ – *pop. 1 640 000 – alt. 156 m.* – ✪ *1.*

Budapest 208 ④ *– München 435* ⑦ *– Praha 292* ① *– Salzburg 292* ⑦ *– Zagreb 362* ⑥*.*

Tourist-information, ✉ A-1010, Kärtner Str. 38, ☎ 513 88 92 – ÖAMTC, ✉ A-1010, Schubertring 1, ☎ 71 19 90, Fax 7 13 18 07.

18 Freudenau 65a, ☎ 2 18 95 64 – 9 At Wienerberg ☎ 661 23 70 00, Fax 661 23 77 89

Wien-Schwechat by ③, ☎ 711 10 and 711 10 22 31, Air Terminal, at Stadtpark (HY) *☎ 72 35 34*

☎ 58 00 29 89. – Exhibition Centre, Messeplatz 1, ☎ 727 20.

HOFBURG★★★ FGY

Imperial Palace of the Habsburgs (Kaiserpalast der Habsburger) : Swiss Court – Royal Chapel – Amalienhof – Stallburg – Leopold Wing – Ballhausplatz – Imperial Chancellery – Spanish Riding School – Neue Burg – Josefsplatz – Michaelerplatz – In der Burg – Capuchins Crypt – Church of the Augustinians. Art Collections : Imperial Treasury★★★ – Imperial Apartments★★ – Austrian National Library (Great Hall★ – Frescoes★★) – Collection of Court Porcelain and Silver★★ – Collection of Arms and Armour★★ – Collection of Old Musical Instruments★ – Albertina (Dürer Collection★) – Museum of Ephesian Sculpture (Reliefs of Ephesus★★).

BUILDINGS AND MONUMENTS

St Stephen's Cathedral★★★ (Stephansdom) GY *– Schönbrunn★★★ (Apartments★★★, Park★★, Gloriette★★, Coach Room★★)* AS *– Upper and Lower Belvedere★★ (Oberes und Unteres Belvedere) (Terraced Gardens and Art Collections★)* HZ *and* DV *– Opera★ (Staatsoper)★* GY *– Church of St Charles★★ (Karlskirche)* GZ *– Church of St Michael (Michaeler Kirche)* GY *– Church of the Minor Friars (Minoritenkirche)* FY *– Church of the Teutonic Order (Deutschordenskirche) (Altarpiece★, Treasure★)* GY **E** *– Church of the Jesuits (Jesuitenkirche)* HY **H** *– Church of Our Lady of the River Bank (Maria am Gestade)* GX *– Church of the Faithful Virgin (Maria Treu)* [illegible] *Otto Wagner★* GZ **Q** *– Pavilion of the Secession★* GZ **S**.

STREETS, SQUARES, PARKS

The Tour of the Ring★ – The Old Town (Altstadt)★ – Kärntner Straße GY *– Graben (Plague Column)* GY *– Am Hof (Column to the Virgin)* GY *– Herrengasse★* GY *– Maria-Theresien-Platz* FY *– Prater★ (Giant Wheel, ≤★)* BR *– Oberlaapark★* BS *– Donner Fountain (Donnerbrunnen)★* GY **Y** *– Heldenplatz* FY *– Burggarten* GY *– Volksgarten* FY *– Rathausplatz* FY.

IMPORTANT MUSEUMS *(Hofburg and Belvedere see above)*

Museum of Fine Arts★★★ (Kunsthistorisches Museum) FY *– Historical Museum of the City of Vienna★★ (Historisches Museum der Stadt Wien)* GZ **M6** *– Austrian Folklore Museum★★ (Österreichisches Museum für Volkskunde)* AR **M7** *– Gallery of Painting and Fine Arts★ (Gemäldegalerie der Akademie der Bildenden Künste)* GZ **M9** *– Natural History Museum★ (Naturhistorisches Museum)* FY **M1** *– Birthplace of Schubert (Schubert-Museum)* BR **M16** *– Austrian Museum of Applied Arts★ (Österreichisches Museum für angewandte Kunst)* HY **M10** *– Clock Museum (Uhrenmuseum der Stadt Wien)* GY **M3**.

EXCURSIONS

Danube Tower★★ (Donauturm) BR *– Leopoldsberg ≤★★* AR *– Kahlenberg ≤★* AR *– Klosterneuburg Abbey (Stift Klosterneuburg) (Altarpiece by Nicolas of Verdun★)* AR *– Grinzing★* AR *– Baden★* AS *– Vienna Woods★ (Wienerwald)* AS.

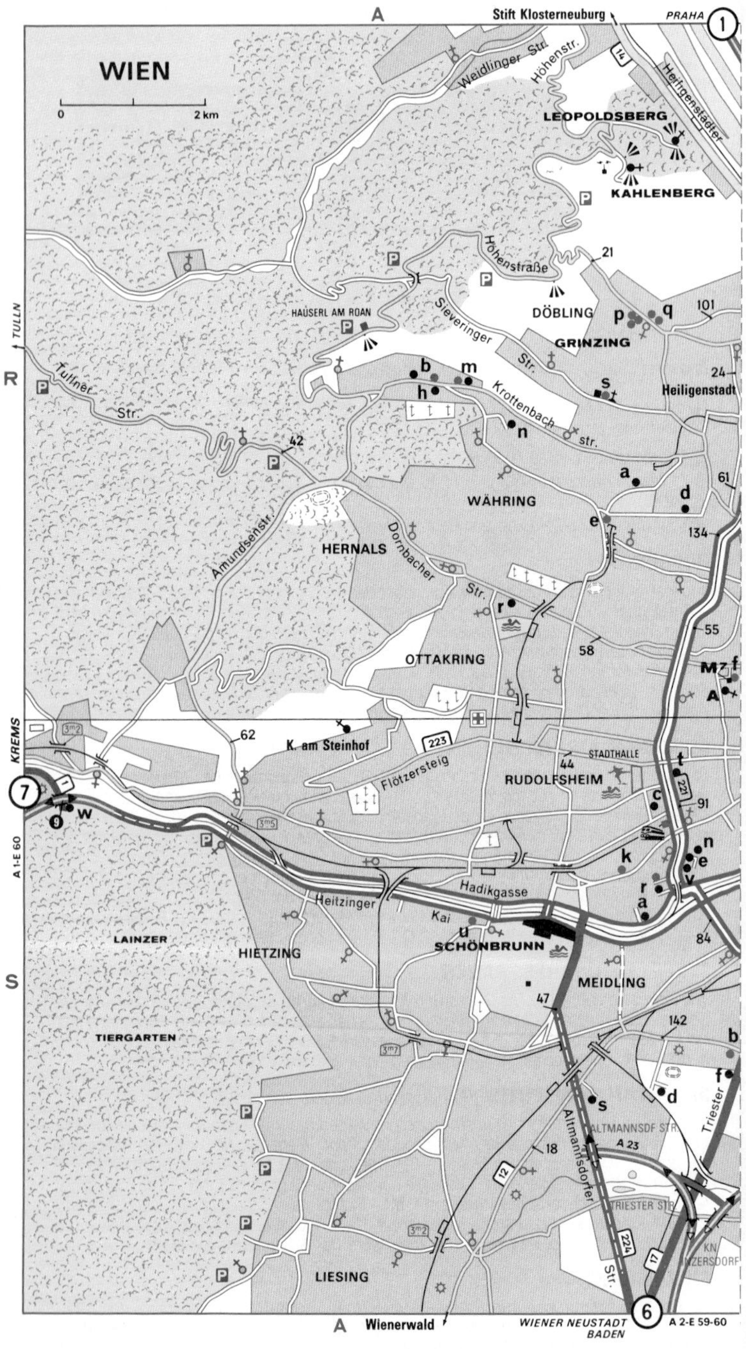
WIEN
0
2 km
A
Stift Klosterneuburg
PRAHA
1
LEOPOLDSBERG
KAHLENBERG
Höhenstraße
DÖBLING
GRINZING
Heiligenstadt
HAUSERL AM ROAN
Sieveringer Str.
Krottenbach str.
TULLN
R
Tullner Str.
WÄHRING
HERNALS
Amundsenstr.
Dornbacher Str.
OTTAKRING
KREMS
K. am Steinhof
STADTHALLE
RUDOLFSHEIM
Flötzersteig
7
A1-E 60
Heitzinger Kai
Hadikgasse
SCHÖNBRUNN
LAINZER
HIETZING
MEIDLING
S
TIERGARTEN
Altmannsdorfer Str.
ALTMANNSDF STR.
A 23
TRIESTER STR.
Triester
LIESING
A
Wienerwald
WIENER NEUSTADT
BADEN
6
A 2-E 59-60

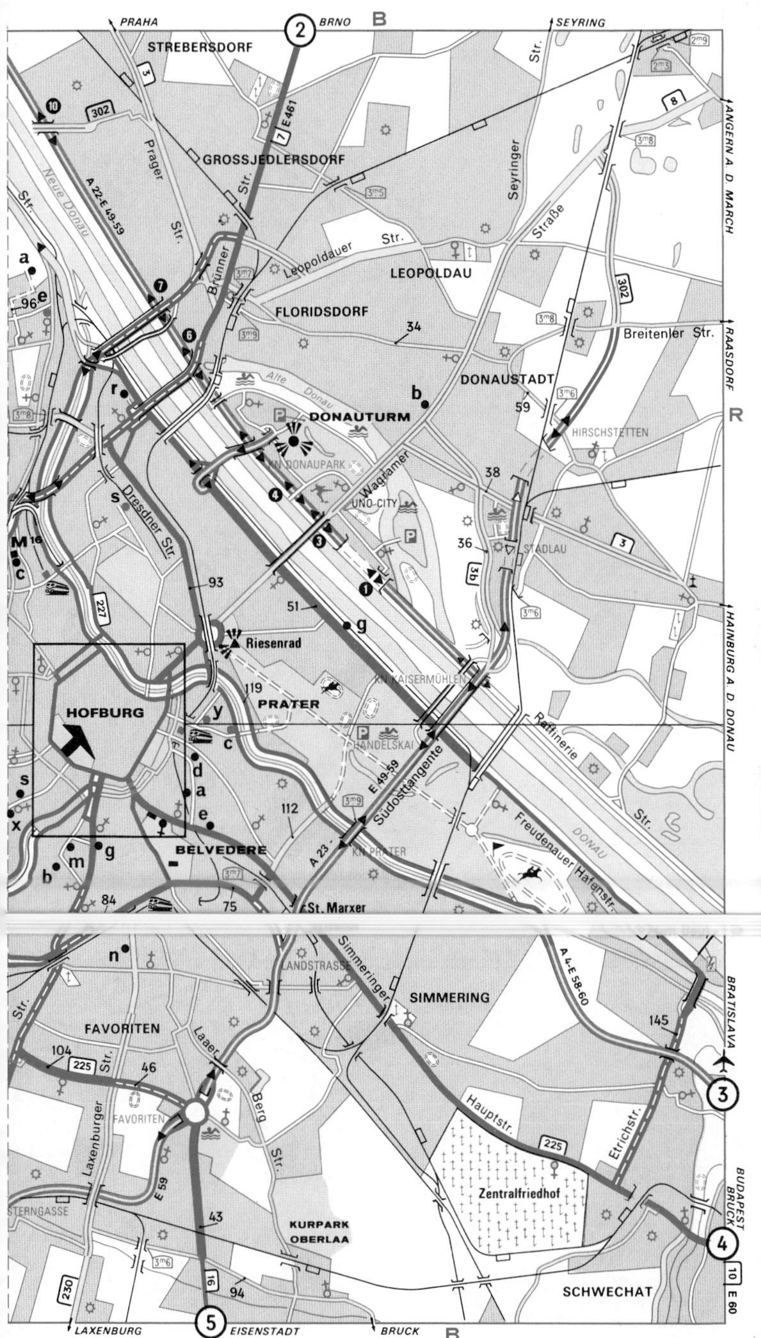
PRAHA
BRNO
SEYRING
STREBERSDORF
GROSSJEDLERSDORF
LEOPOLDAU
FLORIDSDORF
DONAUSTADT
DONAUTURM
HIRSCHSTETTEN
STADLAU
UNO-CITY
Riesenrad
HOFBURG
PRATER
HANDELSKAI
BELVEDERE
St. Marxer
LANDSTRASSE
SIMMERING
FAVORITEN
Zentralfriedhof
KURPARK OBERLAA
SCHWECHAT
LAXENBURG
EISENSTADT
BRUCK
ANGERN A. D. MARCH
RAASDORF
HAINBURG A. D. DONAU
BRATISLAVA
BUDAPEST BRUCK
Breitenler Str.
Leopoldauer Str.
Brünner Str.
Prager Str.
Seyringer Straße
Wagramer
Dresdner Str.
Neue Donau
Alte Donau
Südosttangente
Freudenauer Hafenstr.
Raffinerie Str.
Simmeringer Hauptstr.
Etrichstr.
Laaer Berg Str.
Laxenburger Str.
STERNGASSE
A 22-E 49-59
E 49-59
A 4-E 58-60
E 59
E 461
E 60
DONAU

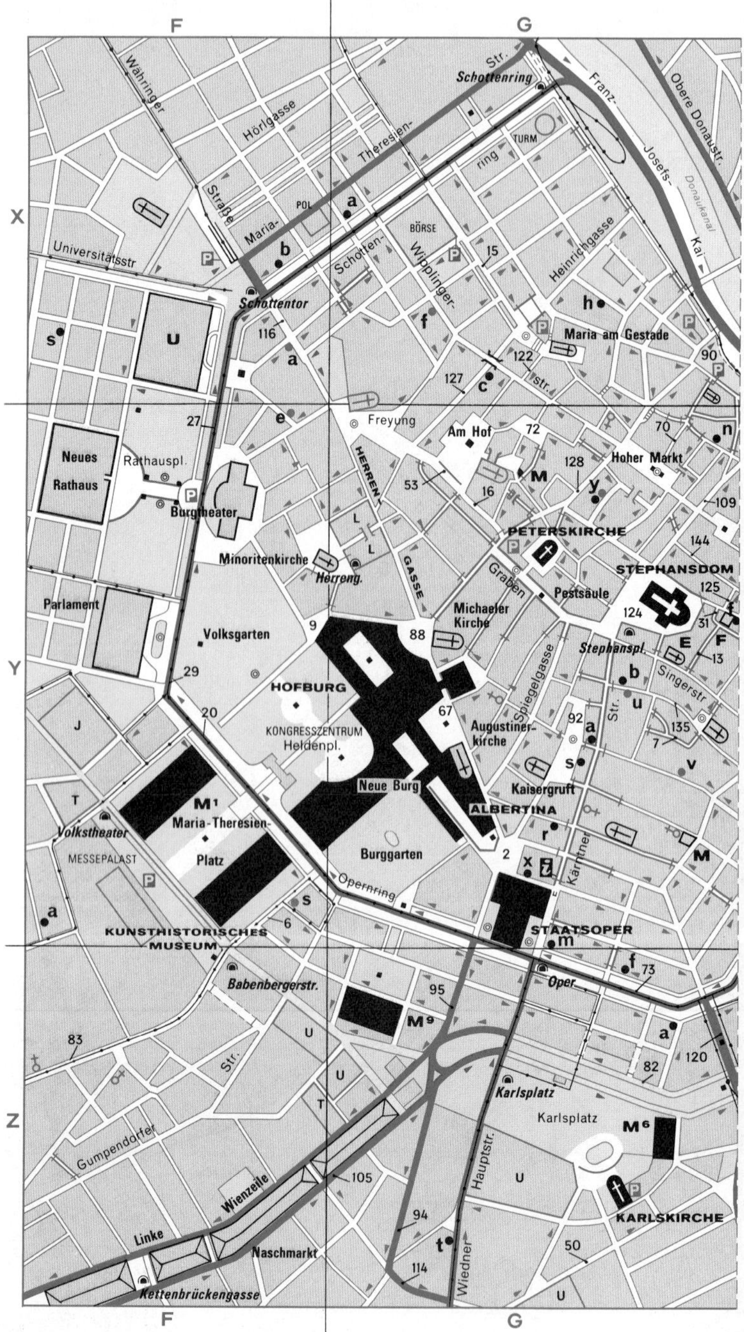
F
G
X
Y
Z
Schottenring
Franz-Josefs-Kai
Obere Donaustr.
Donaukanal
Währinger Straße
Hörlgasse
Theresien-
TURM
ring
Maria-
POL
BÖRSE
Schotten-
Wipplinger-
Heinrichgasse
Universitätsstr
Schottentor
U
Maria am Gestade
Freyung
Am Hof
HERREN
GASSE
Neues Rathaus
Rathauspl.
Burgtheater
Minoritenkirche
Herreng.
Hoher Markt
PETERSKIRCHE
STEPHANSDOM
Graben
Pestsäule
Parlament
Volksgarten
Michaeler Kirche
Stephanspl.
Singerstr
Spiegelgasse
HOFBURG
KONGRESSZENTRUM
Heldenpl.
Augustiner-kirche
Neue Burg
Kaisergruft
ALBERTINA
Volkstheater
MESSEPALAST
Maria-Theresien-Platz
Burggarten
Opernring
Kärntner Str.
STAATSOPER
KUNSTHISTORISCHES MUSEUM
Babenbergerstr.
Oper
Karlsplatz
Gumpendorfer Str.
Wienzeile
Linke
Naschmarkt
Kettenbrückengasse
Wiedner Hauptstr.
KARLSKIRCHE

WIEN

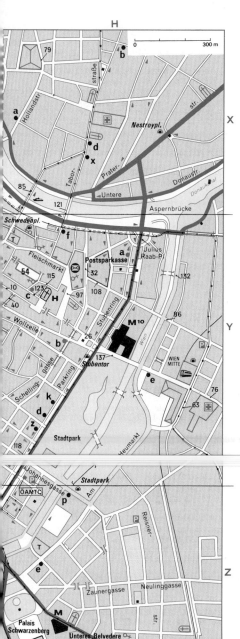

Street	Grid	No.
Babenbergerstr.	FY	6
Graben	GY	
Kärntner Straße	GY	
Landstraßer Hauptstr	HY	76
Mariahilfer Str.	FZ	83
Rotenturmstraße	GY	109
Stephansplatz	GY	124
Tuchlauben	GY	128
Wollzeile	GY	144
Albertinaplatz	GY	2
Ballgasse	GY	7
Ballhausplatz	FY	9
Bäckerstr	HY	10
Blutgasse	GY	13
Börsegasse	GX	15
Bognergasse	GY	16
Breitenfurter Str.	AS	18
Burgring	FY	20
Cobenzlgasse	AR	21
Döblinger Hauptstr.	AR	24
Dr. Karl-Lueger-Platz	HY	26
Dr. Karl-Lueger-Ring	FY	27
Dr. Renner-Ring	FY	29
Domgasse	GY	31
Dominikanerbastei	HY	32
Donaufelder Str.	BR	34
Donaustadtstr.	BR	36
Erzherzog-Karl-Str.	BR	38
Essiggasse	HY	40
Exelbergstr.	AR	42
Favoritenstr.	BS	43
Gablenzgasse	AS	44
Grenzackerstr.	BS	46
Grünbergstr.	AS	47
Gußhausstr	GZ	50
Handelskai	BR	51
Heidenschuß	GY	53
Heiligenkreuzerhof	HY	54
Hernalser Gürtel	AR	55
Hernalser Hauptstr.	AR	58
Hirschstettner Str.	BR	59
Hohe Warte	AR	61
Huttelbergstr.	AS	62
Invalidenstr	HY	63
Josefsplatz	GY	67
Judengasse	GY	70
Judenplatz	GY	72
Kärntner Ring	GZ	73
Landstraßer Gürtel	BS	75
Leopoldsgasse	HX	79
Lothringerstr	GZ	82
Margareten Gürtel	ABS	84
Marienbrücke	HX	85
Marxergasse	HY	86
Michaelerplatz	GY	88
Morzinplatz	GX	90
Neubau Gürtel	AR	91
Neuer Markt	GY	92
Nordbahnstr.	BR	93
[illegible]	[illegible]	[illegible]
[illegible]	[illegible]	[illegible]
Pfarrplatz	BR	96
Postgasse	HY	97
Prinz-Eugen-Str.	HZ	99
Probusgasse	AR	101
Raxstr.	BS	104
Rechte Wienzeile	GZ	105
Rennweg	HZ	107
Rosenbursenstr	HY	108
Schlachthausgasse	BS	112
Schleifmühlgasse	GZ	114
Schönlaterngasse	HY	115
Schottengasse	FX	116
Schubertring	HY	118
Schüttelstr.	BR	119
Schwarzenbergplatz	GZ	120
Schwedenbrücke	HX	121
Schwertgasse	GX	122
Sonnenfelsgasse	HY	123
Strobelgasse	GY	125
Tiefer Graben	GX	127
Vordere Zollamtsstr.	HY	132
Währinger Gürtel	AR	134
Weihburggasse	GY	135
Weiskirchnerstr	HY	137
Wienerbergstr.	AS	142
Zinnergasse	BS	145

North is at the top on all town plans.

Town Centre, city districts (Stadtbezirke) 1 - 9 :

Imperial, Kärntner Ring 16, ✉ A-1015, ✆ 50 11 00, Telex 112630, Fax 50110410, « Converted 19C palace » - |‡| ⇜ rm ▤ TV ✆ - 🏃 100. AE ⊙ E VISA JCB ✻ GZ a
Imperial (booking essential) *(dinner only)* **Meals** à la carte 530/890 - ***Café Imperial :*** **Meals** à la carte 350/600 - **128 rm** ☕ 4890/8480 - 22 suites.

ANA Grand Hotel M, Kärtner Ring 9, ✉ A-1010, ✆ 51 58 00, Telex 115760, Fax 5151313 - |‡| ⇜ rm ▤ TV ✆ 🚗 - 🏃 300. AE ⊙ E VISA JCB. ✻ rest GZ f
Le ciel *(closed Sunday and August)* **Meals** 390 (lunch) and à la carte 530/750 - ***Unkai*** (Japanese cuisine) *(closed Monday lunch)* **Meals** 220 (lunch) and 450/1020 - **205 rm** ☕ 3700/7500 - 11 suites.

Sacher, Philharmonikerstr. 4, ✉ A-1010, ✆ 5 14 56, Telex 112520, Fax 51457810, « Collection of valuable furniture and paintings » - |‡| ⇜ rm ▤ TV ✆. AE ⊙ E VISA JCB. ✻ rest GY x
Meals 450 (lunch) and à la carte 560/760 - **108 rm** ☕ 2640/6400 - 3 suites.

Bristol, Kärntner Ring 1, ✉ A-1015, ✆ 51 51 60, Fax 51516550 - |‡| ⇜ rm ▤ TV ✆ - 🏃 180. AE ⊙ E VISA JCB. ✻ rest GYZ m
Meals (see also Korso below) - ***Rôtisserie Sirk :*** **Meals** à la carte 470/770 - **141 rm** ☕ 3690/8380 - 11 suites.

Plaza Wien M, Schottenring 11, ✉ A-1010, ✆ 31 39 00, Telex 135859, Fax 31390160, Massage, Fб, ≘s - |‡| ⇜ rm ▤ TV ✆ ♿ 🚗 - 🏃 150. AE ⊙ E VISA JCB. ✻ rest GX a
Meals (see La Scala below) - **218 rm** ☕ 2840/4470 - 36 suites.

Hotel im Palais Schwarzenberg, Schwarzenbergplatz 9, ✉ A-1030, ✆ 7 98 45 15, Telex 136124, Fax 7894714, « Converted 1727 baroque palace, park », 🪑, 🎾 - |‡| TV ✆ P - 🏃 200. AE ⊙ E VISA JCB. ✻ rest HZ
Meals 390 (lunch) and à la carte 530/830 - **44 rm** ☕ 3070/7640 - 6 suites.

Vienna Hilton, Landstraßer Hauptstr. 2 (near Stadtpark), ✉ A-1030, ✆ 71 70 00, Fax 7130691, ≤ - |‡| ⇜ rm ▤ TV ✆ 🚗 - 🏃 660. AE ⊙ E VISA JCB HY e
Arcadia : **Meals** à la carte 360/560 - ***Terminal Pub :*** **Meals** à la carte 190/280 - **600 rm** ☕ 3460/4820 - 25 suites.

Vienna Marriott Hotel, Parkring 12a, ✉ A-1010, ✆ 51 51 80, Fax 515186722, Massage, Fб, ≘s, 🏊 - |‡| ⇜ rm ▤ TV ✆ ♿ 🚗 - 🏃 600. ✻ rest HY d
310 rm - 7 suites.

Inter-Continental, Johannesgasse 28, ✉ A-1037, ✆ 71 12 20, Telex 131235, Fax 7134489, ≤, Fб, ≘s - |‡| ⇜ rm ▤ TV ♿ 🚗 - 🏃 1100. AE ⊙ E VISA JCB. ✻ rest HZ p
Vier Jahreszeiten *(closed Saturday and Sunday)* **Meals** 490 (buffet lunch) and à la carte 470/750 - ***Brasserie :*** **Meals** à la carte 280/540 - **460 rm** ☕ 2870/4920 - 25 suites.

Renaissance Penta Vienna Hotel M (former imperial riding school with modern hotel wing), Ungargasse 60, ✉ A-1030, ✆ 71 17 50, Telex 112529, Fax 711758145, Massage, ≘s, 🏊, 🪑 - |‡| ⇜ rm ▤ TV ✆ ♿ 🚗 - 🏃 500. AE ⊙ E VISA JCB. ✻ rest BS a
Meals 350 (buffet lunch) and à la carte 310/530 - **342 rm** ☕ 3000/3600.

Holiday Inn Crowne Plaza Vienna M, Handelskai 269, ✉ A-1020, ✆ 7 27 77, Telex 133318, Fax 72777199, ⛱, Fб, ≘s, 🏊 (heated), 🎾 - |‡| ⇜ rm ▤ TV ✆ ♿ P - 🏃 300. AE ⊙ E VISA JCB. ✻ rest BR g
Meals 295 (buffet) and à la carte 380/615 - **367 rm** ☕ 1950/3250.

Radisson SAS-Palais Hotel, Parkring 16, ✉ A-1010, ✆ 51 51 70, Fax 5122216, ≘s - |‡| ⇜ rm ▤ TV ♿ 🚗 - 🏃 300. AE ⊙ E VISA JCB. ✻ rest HY z
Le siècle *(closed Saturday, Sunday and Bank Holidays)* **Meals** 340 (buffet lunch) and à la carte 480/760 - ***Palais Café :*** **Meals** à la carte 270/470 - **245 rm** ☕ 2560/5080 - 42 suites.

Ambassador, Neuer Markt 5, ✉ A-1015, ✆ 5 14 66, Fax 5132999 - |‡| TV. AE ⊙ E VISA JCB GY s
Meals à la carte 350/690 - **105 rm** ☕ 1770/4940.

Das Triest M, Wiedner Hauptstr. 12, ✉ A-1040, ✆ 58 91 80, Fax 5891818, ⛱, « Modern interior design », Fб, ≘s - |‡| ⇜ rm ▤ TV ✆ 🚗 - 🏃 60. AE ⊙ E VISA JCB. ✻ rest GZ t
Meals *(closed lunch Saturday and Sunday)* 165/255 (lunch) and à la carte 275/525 - **73 rm** ☕ 2100/2600 - 7 suites.

Hotel de France, Schottenring 3, ✉ A-1010, ✆ 31 36 80, Telex 114360, Fax 3195969, ≘s - |‡| ⇜ rm TV ♿ - 🏃 120 FX b
216 rm - 10 suites.

Arcotel Hotel Wimberger M, Neubaugürtel 34, A-1070, 52 16 50, Fax 52165810, – rm rm – 600. AE E VISA JCB AS t
Meals 290 (buffet lunch) and à la carte 335/590 – **225 rm** 2200/2600 – 13 suites.

Biedermeier, Landstraßer Hauptstr. 28 (at Sünnhof), A-1030, 71 67 10, Telex 111039, Fax 71671503, , « Bedrooms furnished in the Biedermeier style » – rm – 100. AE E VISA JCB BS d
Meals à la carte 323/535 – **203 rm** 1900/2400 – 11 suites.

Kaiserin Elisabeth without rest, Weihburggasse 3, A-1010, 5 15 26, Telex 112422, Fax 51526 – . AE E VISA JCB GY b
63 rm 1350/2450.

City-Central without rest, Taborstr. 8a, A-1020, 21 10 50, Fax 21105140 – . AE E VISA HX x
58 rm 1680/2280.

Stefanie, Taborstr. 12, A-1020, 21 15 00, Telex 134589, Fax 21150160, – rm – 70. AE E VISA JCB HX d
Meals à la carte 320/430 – **131 rm** 1480/2480.

K. u. K. Hotel Maria Theresia without rest, Kirchberggasse 6 - 8, A-1070, 5 21 23, Telex 111530, Fax 5212370 – rm – 40. AE E VISA JCB FY a
123 rm 1730/2600.

Sofitel Belvedere, Am Heumarkt 35-37, A-1030, 71 61 60, Telex 111822, Fax 71616844 – rm – 30. AE E VISA JCB. rest HZ e
Meals à la carte 220/475 – **211 rm** 1990/3300.

K u. K Palais Hotel without rest, Rudolfsplatz 11, A-1010, 5 33 13 53, Telex 134049, Fax 533135370 – rm – 40. AE E VISA JCB GX h
66 rm 1680/2290.

Astron Suite Hotel M without rest, Mariahilfer Str. 78, A-1070, 5 24 56 00, Fax 524560015, – . AE E VISA JCB BS x
54 rm 1320/2080.

Kummer, Mariahilfer Str. 71a, A-1070, 5 88 95, Telex 111417, Fax 5878133 – rm . AE E VISA JCB BS s
Meals à la carte 280/400 – **100 rm** 1495/2200.

Erzherzog Rainer, Wiedner Hauptstr. 27, A-1040, 50 11 10, Fax 50111350 – rm rest – 50. AE E VISA JCB BS g
Meals à la carte 240/600 – **84 rm** 1380/2380.

Astoria (19C period house with typical interior), Führichgasse 1, A-1015, 51 57 70, Fax 5157782 – – 20. AE E VISA JCB GY r
Meals *(closed Saturday - Sunday and July - August)* à la carte 370/580 – **108 rm** 1700/2700.

Lassalle M without rest, Engerthstr. 173, A-1020, 21 31 50, Fax 21315100, – – 40. AE E VISA JCB. rest BR r
[illegible]

Arkadenhof M without rest, Viriotgasse 5, A-1090, 3 10 08 37, Fax 3107686 – – 30. AE E VISA JCB BR c
45 rm 1380/1880.

Rathauspark without rest, Rathausstr. 17, A-1010, 40 41 20, Fax 40412761 – – 20. AE E VISA JCB FX s
117 rm 1340/2400.

Europa, Neuer Markt 3, A-1015, 51 59 40, Telex 112292, Fax 5138138 – rm . AE E VISA JCB. rest GY a
Meals à la carte 380/590 – **102 rm** 1700/2700.

Alba Palace, Margaretenstr. 92, A-1050, 54 68 60, Telex 114321, Fax 5468686, – – 100. AE E VISA JCB BS b
Meals à la carte 300/480 – **117 rm** 1390/2600.

Mercure Nestroy M without rest, Rotensterngasse 12, A-1020, 21 14 00, Fax 211407, – – 50. AE E VISA HX b
62 rm 1650/2300 – 7 suites.

President, Wallgasse 23, A-1060, 5 99 90, Fax 5967646, – – 50. AE E VISA AS v
Meals *(closed Sunday and Monday)* à la carte 240/460 – **77 rm** 1350/2350.

Tigra without rest, Tiefer Graben 14 - 18, A-1010, 53 39 64 10, Fax 5339645 – rm . AE E VISA GX c
58 rm 1280/1850.

Amadeus without rest, Wildpretmarkt 5, ✉ A-1010, ℘ 5 33 87 38, Fax 533873838 – AE VISA GY y
closed 22 to 27 December – **30 rm** 1090/1950.

Mercure Europaplatz M, Matrosengasse 6, ✉ A-1060, ℘ 59 90 10, Fax 5976900 – rm – 70. AE VISA JCB AS n
Meals à la carte 300/530 – **211 rm** 1550/2400 – 6 suites.

Am Parkring, Parkring 12, ✉ A-1015, ℘ 51 48 00, Fax 5148040, ≤ Vienna – . AE VISA JCB. HY k
Meals *(closed Sunday and Monday dinner)* à la carte 350/510 – **65 rm** 1720/2600 – 7 suites.

Alba-Accadia, Margaretenstr. 53, ✉ A-1050, ℘ 58 85 00, Telex 113264, Fax 58850899, , – – 30. AE VISA JCB BS m
Meals à la carte 300/480 – **104 rm** 1430/2600.

König von Ungarn, Schulerstr. 10, ✉ A-1010, ℘ 5 15 84, Fax 515848 – rm – 15 GY f
33 rm.

Capricorno without rest, Schwedenplatz 3, ✉ A-1010, ℘ 53 33 10 40, Fax 53376714 – . AE VISA HY f
46 rm 1380/2280.

Mercure Wien City without rest, Hollandstr. 3, ✉ A-1020, ℘ 21 31 30, Fax 21313230 – rm . AE VISA JCB HX a
63 rm 1490/1960.

Mercure, Fleischmarkt 1a, ✉ A-1010, ℘ 53 46 00, Fax 53460232 – rm . AE VISA GY n
Meals à la carte 305/485 – **154 rm** 1630/2150.

Artis without rest, Rennweg 51, ✉ A-1030, ℘ 7 13 25 21, Telex 131797, Fax 7145930 – – 50. AE VISA BS e
168 rm 1200/1890.

Ibis, Mariahilfer Gürtel 22, ✉ A-1060, ℘ 5 99 98, Telex 133833, Fax 5979090 – rm – 60. AE VISA AS e
Meals à la carte 230/330 – **341 rm** 1110/1325.

Steirereck, Rasumofskygasse 2 / Ecke Weißgerberlände, ✉ A-1030, ℘ 7 13 31 68, Fax 71351682 – . AE VISA BS c
closed Saturday, Sunday and Bank Holidays – **Meals** *(outstanding wine list, tour of the wine-cellar possible)* (booking essential) 395/(lunch) and à la carte 620/880
Spec. Fenchelsuppe mit Hummer, Wildente mit Quittenrotkraut und Topinambursauce, Apfel-Mohn-Torte mit Preiselbeeren.

Korso - Hotel Bristol, Kärntner Ring 1, ✉ A-1015, ℘ 51 51 65 46, Fax 51516550 – . AE VISA JCB. GYZ m
closed Saturday lunch and August – **Meals** 420 (lunch) and à la carte 690/955.

La Scala - Hotel Plaza Wien, Schottenring 11, ✉ A-1010, ℘ 31 39 01 50, Fax 31390160 – . AE VISA JCB. GX a
closed Saturday lunch, Sunday and Bank Holidays – **Meals** 295 (lunch) and à la carte 400/840.

Drei Husaren, Weihburggasse 4, ✉ A-1010, ℘ 51 21 09 20, Fax 512109218 – AE VISA JCB GY u
closed 24 to 27 December – **Meals** 425 (lunch) and à la carte 610/915.

Gottfried, Untere Viaduktgasse 45/Marxergasse, ✉ A-1030, ℘ 7 13 82 56, Fax 7138257 – AE VISA JCB BRS y
closed Saturday lunch, Sunday, Monday and Bank Holidays – **Meals** *(booking essential)* (outstanding wine list) 330 (lunch) and à la carte 470/680
Spec. Lachsforelle mit Hollerblütenvinaigrette, Gebratene Gänsestopfleber mit eingelegten Dörrmarillen, Weißer Pfirsich in Huflattichhonig glasiert.

Selina, Laudongasse 13, ✉ A-1080, ℘ 4 05 64 04, Fax 4080459 – AE VISA JCB AR f
closed Saturday June-July, Sunday and Bank Holidays – **Meals** *(booking essential)* 620 and à la carte 460/670
Spec. Schaumsuppe von Meeresfischen mit Safran und Vermouth, Beiriedschnitte mit Rahm-Blattspinat und Grammeltascherln, Topfen-Kaiserschmarr'n mit karamelisierten Walnüssen.

Grotta Azzurra (Italian rest.), Babenberger Str. 5, ✉ A-1010, ℘ 58 61 04 40, Fax 586104415 – AE VISA FY s
closed 24 to 27 December – **Meals** 270 (lunch) and à la carte 390/580.

Steirer Stub'n, Wiedner Hauptstr. 111, ✉ A-1050, ℘ 5 44 43 49, Fax 5440888 – . AE VISA BS k
closed Sunday – **Meals** *(booking essential)* à la carte 370/530.

XX **Walter Bauer**, Sonnenfelsgasse 17, ✉ A-1010, ✆ 5 12 98 71, Fax 5129871 – AE
closed Saturday lunch, Sunday, Monday and 19 July - 18 August – **Meals** (booking essential) à la carte 340/680. HY c

XX **Kupferdachl**, Schottengasse 7 (entrance Mölker Bastei), ✉ A-1010, ✆ 5 33 93 81, Fax 53393814 – AE ① E VISA FX a
closed Christmas – **Meals** à la carte 345/595.

XX **Schubertstüberln**, Schreyvogelgasse 4, ✉ A-1010, ✆ 5 33 71 87, Fax 5353546, 🏠 – AE ① E VISA FXY e
closed Saturday and Sunday – **Meals** à la carte 330/580.

XX **Salut**, Wildpretmarkt 3, ✉ A-1010, ✆ 5 33 13 22 – AE ① E VISA GY y
closed Sunday and Bank Holidays – **Meals** 220/600 and à la carte 445/580.

XX **Plachutta**, Wollzeile 38, ✉ A-1010, ✆ 5 12 15 77, Fax 512157720, 🏠 – ▤. E VISA
closed 26 July to 9 August – **Meals** à la carte 345/550. HY b

X **Fadinger**, Wipplingerstr. 29, ✉ A-1010, ✆ 5 33 43 41 GX f
closed Saturday and Sunday – **Meals** (booking essential) à la carte 270/500.

X **Zum Kuckuck**, Himmelpfortgasse 15, ✉ A-1010, ✆ 5 12 84 70, Fax 7741855 – AE ① E VISA GY v
closed Sunday – **Meals** 250 (lunch) and à la carte 395/600.

X **Hedrich**, Stubenring 2, ✉ A-1010, ✆ 5 12 95 88 HY a
closed Friday - Sunday, Bank Holidays and August – **Meals** à la carte 280/495.

City districts (Stadtbezirke) 10 - 15 :

Holiday Inn [M], Triester Str. 72, ✉ A-1100, ✆ 6 05 30, Fax 60530580, ≤, 🏠 – |$| ⇔ ▤ [TV] ♿ 🚗 – 🔬 240. AE ① E VISA JCB AS f
Meals *(closed Saturday and Sunday lunch)* 225 (buffet) and à la carte – **172 rm** ☕ 1850/3050 – 9 suites.

Renaissance Wien, Ullmannstr. 71, ✉ A-1150, ✆ 8 50 40, Fax 8504100, 🏋, 🏊, ☐ – |$| ⇔ rm ▤ [TV] ♿ 🚗 – 🔬 200. AE ① E VISA JCB AS a
Orangerie : **Meals** a la carte 360/675 – ***Allegro :*** **Meals** 375/480 (buffet only) – **307 rm** ☕ 1890/3280 – 3 suites.

Gartenhotel Altmannsdorf 🔇, Hoffingergasse 26, ✉ A-1120, ✆ 8 04 75 27, Fax 804752751, 🏠, Park, 🏊 – |$| ⇔ rm [TV] ☎ 🚗 – 🔬 60. AE ① E VISA AS s
Meals à la carte 290/460 – **95 rm** ☕ 1300/1850.

Trend Hotel Bosei [M] 🔇, Gutheil-Schoder-Gasse 9, ✉ A-1100, ✆ 66 10 60, Fax 6610699 – |$| ⇔ rm [TV] ☎ Ⓟ – 🔬 150. AE ① E VISA AS d
Meals à la carte 270/420 – **184 rm** ☕ 1320/2400 – 8 suites.

Trend Hotel Favorita [M], Laxenburger Str. 8, ✉ A-1100, ✆ 60 14 60, Fax 60146720, 🏊 – |$| [TV] ☎ 🚗 – 🔬 150. AE ① E VISA. ✗ rest BS n
Meals à la carte 230/570 – **161 rm** ☕ 1320/1700 – 4 suites.

Austrotel, Felberstr. 4, ✉ A-1150, ✆ 98 11 10, Fax 98111930, 🏊 – |$| ⇔ rm [TV] ☎ ♿ 🚗 – 🔬 180. AE ① E VISA AS c
Meals à la carte 280/410 – **250 rm** ☕ 1760/3900.

Reither without rest, Graumanngasse 16, ✉ A-1150, ✆ 8 93 68 41, Fax 8936835, 🏊, ☐ – |$| ⇔ [TV] ☎ 🚗. AE ① E VISA AS r
closed 22 to 27 December – **50 rm** ☕ 1100/2280.

XXX **Altwienerhof** with rm, Herklotzgasse 6, ✉ A-1150, ✆ 8 92 60 00, Fax 89260008, « Winter garden, courtyard-terrace » – |$| [TV] ☎. AE ① E VISA AS r
✿ *closed 1 to 24 January* – **Meals** *(closed Saturday lunch and Sunday)* (outstanding wine list) 298 (lunch) and à la carte 480/695 – **23 rm** ☕ 650/1400
Spec. Pralinen von der Gänseleber, Jakobsmuscheln mit Kardamon, Gebackenes Stubenküken mit Erdäpfelsalat.

XX Windows of Vienna, Wienerbergstr. 7, ✉ A-1100, ✆ 6 07 94 80, Fax 6072267, ✳ Vienna – |$| ▤ 🚗 AS b

XX **Vikerl's Lokal**, Würfelgasse 4, ✉ A-1150, ✆ 8 94 34 30, Fax 8924183 AS k
closed Sunday dinner and Monday, 3 weeks July to August – **Meals** à la carte 285/490.

XX **Hietzinger Bräu**, Auhofstr. 1, ✉ A-1130, ✆ 87 77 08 70, Fax 877708722, 🏠 – ▤. E VISA AS u
closed mid July - mid August – **Meals** *(mainly boiled beef dishes)* (booking essential) à la carte 355/545.

City districts (Stadtbezirke) 16 - 19 :

Modul, Peter-Jordan-Str. 78, ✉ A-1190, ✆ 4 76 60, Fax 47660117, 🏠 – ▤ [TV] ☎ 🚗 – 🔬 200 AR a
Cottage : **40 rm** – 25 suites.

Landhaus Fuhrgassl-Huber without rest, Rathstr. 24, A-1190, 4 40 30 33, Fax 4402714, « Country house atmosphere », – AR m
22 rm.

Gartenhotel Glanzing without rest, Glanzinggasse 23, A-1190, 47 04 27 20, Fax 470427214, AE VISA AR n
18 rm 1180/2200.

Clima Villenhotel, Nussberggasse 2c, A-1190, 37 15 16 (Hotel) 37 16 61 (Rest.), Telex 115670, Fax 371392, « Rest. Bockkeller, vaulted cellar with Tyrolian farmhouse furniture », – 30. AE VISA BR a
Meals *(closed Sunday)* à la carte 360/630 – **30 rm** 1300/2500.

Jäger without rest, Hernalser Hauptstr. 187, A-1170, 48 66 62 00, Fax 48666208 – VISA AR r
18 rm 950/1600.

Celtes without rest, Celtesgasse 1a, A-1190, 4 40 41 51, Fax 4404152116 – AR b
12 rm.

Park-Villa without rest, Hasenauerstr. 12, A-1190, 3 19 10 05, Fax 319100541, – AR d
21 rm.

Schild without rest, Neustift am Walde 97, A-1190, 44 04 04 40, Fax 4404000, – AE VISA AR h
32 rm 810/1480.

Eckel, Sieveringer Str. 46, A-1190, 3 20 32 18, Fax 3206660, – AE VISA
closed Sunday, Monday, Bank Holidays, 10 to 25 August and 22 December - 15 January – **Meals** à la carte 330/685. AR s

Plachutta with rm, Heiligenstädter Str. 179, A-1190, 37 41 25, Fax 37412520, – VISA BR e
closed 22 July - 11 August – **Meals** *(mainly boiled beef dishes)* à la carte 370/590 – **4 rm** 760/1180.

Sailer, Gersthofer Str. 14, A-1180, 47 92 12 12, Fax 47921214, – AR e
closed Sunday dinner – **Meals** 175 (lunch) and à la carte 400/550.

City district (Stadtbezirk) 22 :

Trend Hotel Donauzentrum, Wagramer Str. 83, A-1220, 20 35 54 50, Fax 2035545183, – rm – 40. AE VISA BR b
Meals 160 (lunch) and à la carte 210/380 – **137 rm** 1320/2200.

Mraz u. Sohn, Wallensteinstr. 59, A-1200, 330 45 94, Fax 3501536 – VISA BR s
closed Saturday - Sunday, 24 December - 2 January and 3 weeks August – **Meals** à la carte 400/625.

Heurigen and Buschen-Schänken (wine gardens)

– *(mostly self-service, hot and cold dishes from buffet, prices according to weight of chosen meals, therefore not shown below. Buschen-Schänken sell their own wines only)* :

Oppolzer, Himmelstr. 22, A-1190, 32 24 16, Fax 322416, « Garden » –
closed Sunday, Bank Holidays and Christmas – **Meals** (dinner only) à la carte 190/300. AR p

Altes Preßhaus, Cobenzlgasse 15, A-1190, 3 20 23 93, Fax 320234285, « Old vaulted wine cellar with wine press » – AE VISA JCB AR p
closed January and February – **Meals** (dinner only) 300/450 (buffet) and à la carte 190/370.

Wolff, Rathstr. 44, A-1190, 4 40 23 35, Fax 4401403, « Terraced garden »
Meals (buffet only). AR m

Fuhrgassl Huber, Neustift am Walde 68, A-1190, 4 40 14 05, Fax 4402730, (wine-garden with Viennese Schrammelmusik), « Courtyard-terrace » – VISA AR b
Meals (buffet).

Kirchenstöckl, Cobenzlgasse 3, A-1190, 32 66 62, Fax 4403917, – AE VISA AR p
closed Sunday – **Meals** (dinner only) à la carte 205/375.

Grinzinger Hauermandl, Cobenzlgasse 20, A-1190, 32 30 27, Fax 320571322, – AE VISA AR q
closed Sunday – **Meals** (dinner only) à la carte 260/380.

Grinzinger Weinbottich, Cobenzlgasse 28, A-1190, 32 42 37, Fax 32071322, – AE VISA AR q
closed Monday – **Meals** (dinner only) à la carte 255/350.

at Auhof motorway station *W : 8 km :*

Novotel Wien-West, Am Auhof, ✉ A-1140, ☎ (01) 97 92 54 20, Fax 9794140, (heated), – rm ▤ TV ☎ ♿ P – 180. AE ⓓ E VISA AS w
Meals 210 (buffet lunch) and à la carte 190/410 – **115 rm** 1155/1410.

at Perchtoldsdorf *A-2380 SW : 13 km by B12 and Breitenfurter Str.* AS :

XXX **Jahreszeiten**, Hochstr. 17, ✉ A-2380, ☎ (01) 8 65 31 29, Fax 865312973 – ▤. AE ⓓ E VISA
closed Saturday lunch, Sunday dinner, Monday, 2 weeks at Easter and mid July - mid August – **Meals** 330 (lunch) and à la carte 560/695
Spec. Lasagne von Hummer mit grünem Spargel, Hausgebeizter Lachs auf Trüffelnudeln mit Roter Butter, Nougatknöderl in Caramelsauce mit Zitronensorbet.

at Vienna-Schwechat Airport ③ *: 20 km :*

Sofitel Wien Airport M, at the airport, ✉ A-1300, ☎ 70 15 10, Fax 7062828 – rm TV ♿ P – 300. AE ⓓ E VISA JCB
Meals à la carte 360/510 – **142 rm** 2530/2760.

Novotel Wien Airport, at the airport, ✉ A-1300, ☎ 70 10 70, Fax 7073239, – rm TV ☎ ♿ P – 20. AE ⓓ E VISA JCB
Meals à la carte 170/350 – **183 rm** 1600/2000.

XXX **Le Gourmet**, Terminal 2, first floor, ✉ A-1300, ☎ 70 07 26 72, Fax 700713563 – AE ⓓ E VISA JCB
Meals à la carte 420/590.

INNSBRUCK *6020 Austria* 426 G 7, 987 ⑩ – *pop. 120 000 – alt. 580 m – Wintersport : 580/2300 m 3 7 – 0512.*

See : *Maria-Theresien-Strasse* ★ CZ ≤ ★★ *on the Nordkette, Belfry (Stadtturm)* CZ B ✲ ★ *over the city – Little Golden Roof (Goldenes Dachl)* ★ CZ – *Helblinghaus* ★ CZ – *Hofburg* ★ CZ – *Hofkirche* CZ *(Maximilian's Mausoleum* ★, *Silver Chapel* ★★*) – Tyrol Museum of Popular Art (Tiroler Volkskunstmuseum)* ★★ CDZ – *"Ferdinandeum" Tyrol Museum (Tiroler Landesmuseum "Ferdinandeum")* ★ DZ**M2** – *Wilten Basilica* ★ AY.

Envir. : *Hafelekar* ✲ ★★ – *Upland Tour (Mittelgebirge)* ★★ *(Hall in Tirol* ★, *Volders* ★, *Igls* ★, *– Elbögen road* ★★*) – The Stubaital* ★.

Innsbruck-Igls, Lans (05222)77165 ; Innsbruck-Igls, Rinn (05223)8177.

Innsbruck Information, Burggraben 3, ☎ 5356, Fax 535643.

ÖAMTC, *Andechsstr. 81, ☎ 3320120, Fax 491612.*

Wien 733 – München 140 – Salzburg 164.

Plans on following pages

Europa-Tyrol, Südtiroler Platz 2, ☎ 59 31, Fax 587800, – rm TV – 200. AE ⓓ E VISA JCB. rest DZ a
Meals à la carte 340/650 – **122 rm** 1750/2900 – 6 suites.

Holiday Inn, Salurner Str. 15, ☎ 5 93 50, Telex 534267, Fax 5935220, – rm TV – 350. AE ⓓ E VISA JCB CDZ b
Guggeryllis : **Meals** à la carte 300/510 – **176 rm** 1500/2600 – 4 suites.

Goldener Adler, Herzog-Friedrich-Str. 6, ☎ 58 63 34, Fax 584409, « 14C Tyrolian inn » – TV ☎. AE ⓓ E VISA CZ c
Meals à la carte 315/580 – **37 rm** 1080/1600.

Central, Gilmstr. 5, ☎ 59 20, Telex 533824, Fax 580310, – TV ☎ – 30. AE ⓓ E VISA DZ d
Meals à la carte 195/410 – **87 rm** 1250/2100.

Maria Theresia without rest, Maria Theresienstr. 31, ☎ 59 33, Telex 533300, Fax 575619 – TV ☎. AE ⓓ E VISA JCB CZ g
103 rm 1200/2200.

Romantik Hotel Schwarzer Adler, Kaiserjägerstr. 2, ☎ 58 71 09, Fax 561697 – rm TV ☎ – 40. AE ⓓ E VISA DZ e
Meals *(closed Sunday and Bank Holidays)* à la carte 310/550 – **26 rm** 1100/2100.

Neue Post, Maximilianstr. 15, ☎ 5 94 76, Fax 581818 – TV ☎ P. AE ⓓ E VISA JCB CZ v
Meals *(closed Sunday and November)* à la carte 215/400 – **60 rm** 1100/2600.

Alpotel Tirol, Innrain 13, ☎ 57 79 31, Fax 57793115, – TV ☎ ♿ – 50. AE ⓓ E VISA CZ f
Meals *(closed Saturday lunch, Sunday and Bank Holidays)* 290/610 and à la carte 270/540 – **73 rm** 900/1780.

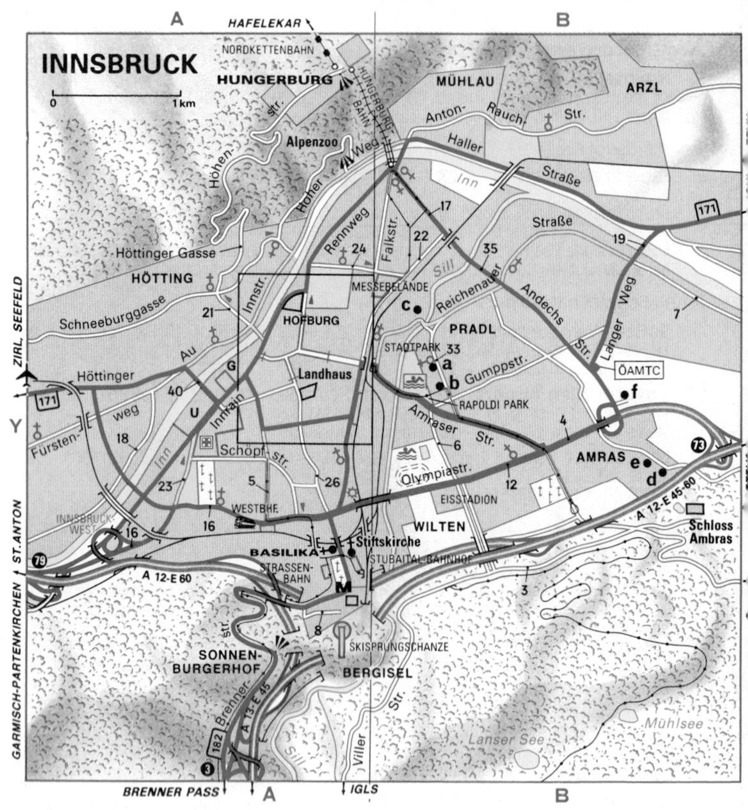

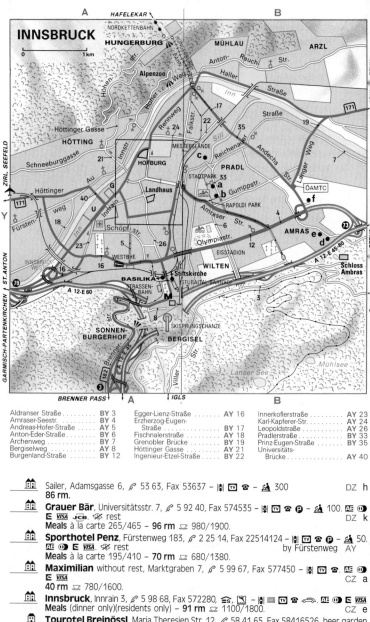

Aldranser Straße	BY	3
Amraser-Seestr.	BY	4
Andreas-Hofer-Straße	AY	5
Anton-Eder-Straße	BY	6
Archenweg	BY	7
Bergiselweg	AY	8
Burgenland-Straße	BY	12
Egger-Lienz-Straße	AY	16
Erzherzog-Eugen-Straße	BY	17
Fischnalerstraße	AY	18
Grenobler Brücke	BY	19
Höttinger Gasse	AY	21
Ingenieur-Etzel-Straße	BY	22
Innerkoflerstraße	AY	23
Karl-Kapferer-Str.	AY	24
Leopoldstraße	AY	26
Pradlerstraße	BY	33
Prinz-Eugen-Straße	BY	35
Universitäts-Brücke	AY	40

[hotel] Sailer, Adamsgasse 6, ☎ 53 63, Fax 53637 – [lift] [TV] ☎ – [conference] 300 — DZ h
86 rm.

[hotel] **Grauer Bär**, Universitätsstr. 7, ☎ 5 92 40, Fax 574535 – [lift] [TV] ☎ [P] – [conference] 100. AE ⓓ E VISA JCB. ✻ rest — DZ k
Meals à la carte 265/465 – **96 rm** ☐ 980/1900.

[hotel] **Sporthotel Penz**, Fürstenweg 183, ☎ 2 25 14, Fax 22514124 – [lift] [TV] ☎ [P] – [conference] 50. AE ⓓ E VISA. ✻ rest — by Fürstenweg AY
Meals à la carte 195/410 – **70 rm** ☐ 680/1380.

[hotel] **Maximilian** without rest, Marktgraben 7, ☎ 5 99 67, Fax 577450 – [lift] [TV] ☎. AE ⓓ E VISA — CZ a
40 rm ☐ 780/1600.

[hotel] **Innsbruck**, Innrain 3, ☎ 5 98 68, Fax 572280, [sauna], [pool] – [lift] [air] [TV] ☎ [garage]. AE ⓓ E VISA — CZ e
Meals (dinner only)(residents only) – **91 rm** ☐ 1100/1800.

[hotel] **Tourotel Breinössl**, Maria Theresien Str. 12, ☎ 58 41 65, Fax 58416526, beer garden – [lift] [no smoking] rm [TV] ☎ [P]. AE ⓓ E VISA — CZ p
Meals à la carte 170/300 – **40 rm** ☐ 950/1440.

[hotel] **Weißes Rößl** [quiet], Kiebachgasse 8, ☎ 58 30 57, Fax 5830575, [terrace] – [lift] [TV] ☎. AE E VISA JCB — CZ n
closed 2 weeks April and November – **Meals** *(closed Sunday and Bank Holidays)* à la carte 200/410 – **14 rm** ☐ 850/1500.

INNSBRUCK

Adolf Pichler-Platz . . . . CZ 2
Bozner Platz . . . . DZ 10
Burggraben . . . . CZ 14
Domplatz . . . . CZ 15
Herzog-Friedrich-Straße . . . . CZ 20
Ingenieur-Etzel-Straße . . . . DZ 22
Landhausplatz . . . . CZ 25
Leopoldstraße . . . . CZ 26
Meinhardstr. . . . . DZ 28
Meraner Straße . . . . CZ 30
Pfarrgasse . . . . CZ 32
Stiftgasse . . . . CZ 37
Südbahnstraße . . . . DZ 38

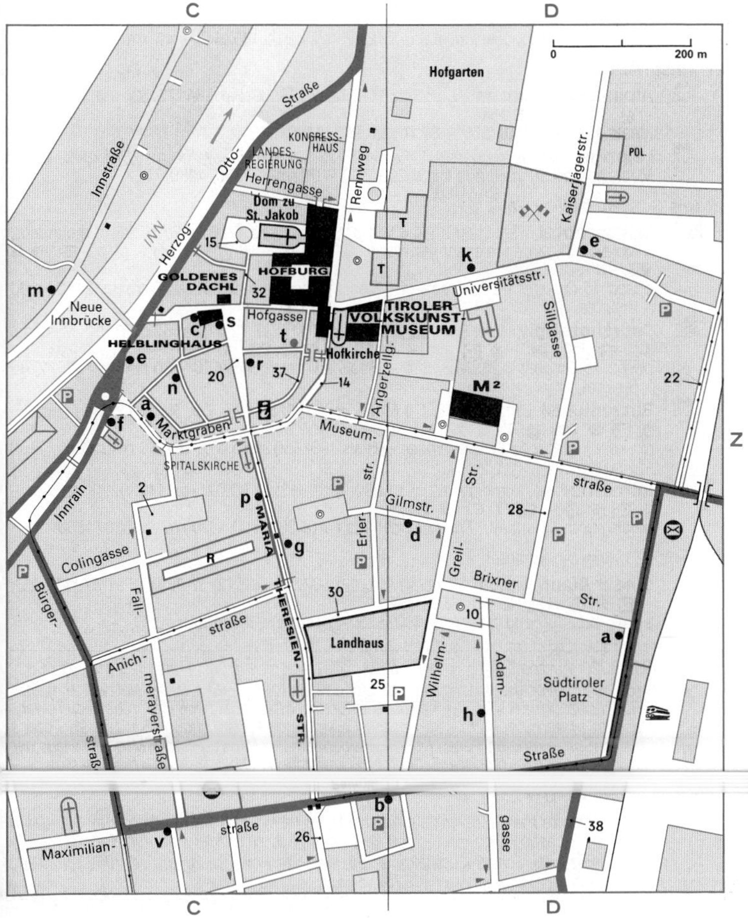

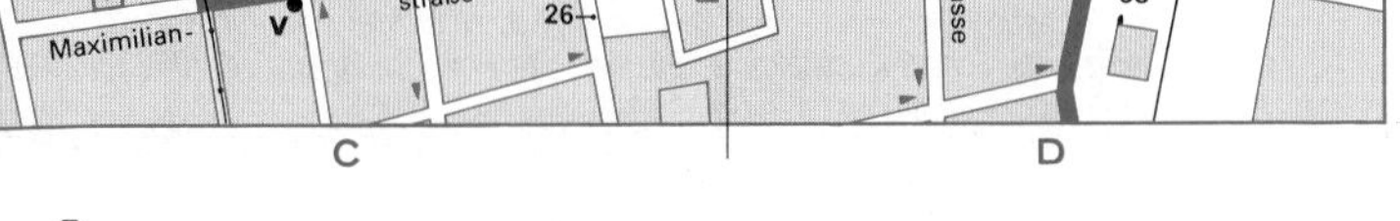

Weisses Kreuz, Herzog-Friedrich-Str.31, 5 94 79, Fax 5947990, « 15C Tyrolian inn » – CZ r
Meals à la carte 205/405 – **39 rm** 710/1380.

Mondschein without rest, Mariahilfstr. 6, 2 27 84, Fax 2278490 – CZ m
35 rm 700/1400.

Altstadtstüberl, Riesengasse 11, 58 23 47, Fax 583495 – CZ t
closed Sunday and Bank Holidays – **Meals** à la carte 310/450.

at Innsbruck-Amras :

Austrotel Innsbruck, Bernhard-Höfel-Str. 16, 34 43 33, Telex 533292, Fax 344428, – 200. BY f
Meals à la carte180/430 – **135 rm** 1380/2090.

Kapeller, Phillipine-Welser-Str. 96, ✆ 34 31 06, Fax 34310668 – 50. AE VISA JCB BY e
Meals *(closed Monday lunch, Sunday and Bank Holidays)* 250/480 and à la carte 275/520 – **36 rm** 700/1650.

Bierwirt, Bichlweg 2, ✆ 34 21 43, Fax 3421435, « Cosy lounge », – 80. VISA
Meals *(closed Saturday lunch and Sunday)* à la carte 185/415 – **47 rm** 650/1100.

at Innsbruck-Pradl :

Alpinpark, Pradler Str. 28, ✆ 34 86 00, Telex 533509, Fax 364172, – – 30. AE VISA BY a
Meals à la carte 210/500 – **87 rm** 850/1480.

Leipzigerhof, Defreggerstr. 13, ✆ 34 35 25, Fax 394357 – rm . AE VISA
Meals *(closed Sunday)* à la carte 200/390 – **60 rm** 650/1250. BY b

at Igls *S : 4 km by Viller Str.* AB :

Schlosshotel, Viller Steig 2, ✉ 6080, ✆ (0512) 37 72 17, Fax 37721798, < mountains, « Mansion in garden, elegant installation », – – 15. AE VISA. rest
closed 15 October - 21 December – **Meals** à la carte 400/600 – **20 rm** 2150/4000 – 6 suites.

Sporthotel Igls, Hilber Str. 17, ✉ 6080, ✆ (051) 237 72 41, Fax 378679, , Massage, – – 50. AE VISA. rest
closed 15 October - 21 December – **Meals** à la carte 345/650 – **80 rm** 1370/2740 – 6 suites.

Batzenhäusl, Lanserstr. 12, ✉ 6080, ✆ (0512) 3 86 18, Fax 386187, – . AE VISA
closed 15 October to 15 December – **Meals** 190/350 and à la carte – **30 rm** 800/1100 – 3 suites.

Römerhof, Römerstr. 62, ✉ 6080, ✆ (0512) 37 89 02, Fax 37890220, – – 15. AE VISA
Meals *(closed Monday - Friday lunch)* à la carte 260/650 – **20 rm** 850/1600.

at Lans *SE : 6km by Aldranser Str.* BY :

Wilder Mann with rm, Römerstr. 12, ✉ 6072, ✆ (0512) 37 96 96, Fax 379139, – – 40. AE VISA
Meals 320/380 and à la carte 300/525 – **14 rm** 980/1660.

SALZBURG *5020. Austria* 426 L 5, 420 W 23, 987 – *pop. 140 000 – alt. 425 m –* *0662.*

See : *< ** over the town (from the Mönchsberg)* X *and < ** (from Hettwer Bastei)* Y *– Hohensalzburg ** X, Z: < ** (from the Kuenburg Bastion), ** (from the Reck Tower), Museum (Burgmuseum)* – St. Peter's Churchyard (Petersfriedhof)** Z – St. Peter's Church (Stiftskirche St. Peter)** Z – Residenz** Z – Natural History Museum (Haus der Natur)** Y **M2** – Franciscan's Church (Franziskanerkirche)* Z **A** – Getreidegasse* Y – Mirabell Gardens (Mirabellgarten)* V (Grand Staircase ** of the castle) – Baroque-museum* V **M 3** – Dom* Z.*

Envir. : *Road to the Gaisberg (Gaisbergstraße)** (<*) by ① – Untersberg* by ②: 10 km (with) – Castle Hellbrunn (Schloß Hellbrunn) * by Nonntaler Hauptstraße X.*

Salzburg-Wals, Schloß Klessheim, ✆ 85 08 51 ; Hof (① : 20 km), ✆ (06229) 23 90 ; St. Lorenz (① : 29 km), ✆ (06232) 38 35.

Innsbrucker Bundesstr. 95 (by ③), ✆ 85 12 23 - City Air Terminal, Südtiroler Platz (Autobus Station) V – Lastenstraße.

Exhibition Centre (Messegelände), Linke Glanzeile 65, ✆ 3 45 66.

Tourist Information, Mozartplatz 5, ✆ 88 98 73 30, Fax 8898732.

ÖAMTC, *Alpenstr. 102 (by ②), ✆ 6 26 61 60, Fax 62661622.*

Wien 292 ① – Innsbruck 177 ③ – München 140 ③.

Plans on following pages

Österreichischer Hof, Schwarzstr. 5, ✆ 8 89 77, Telex 633590, Fax 8897714, « Salzach-side setting, terrace with < old town and castle » – rm – 70. AE VISA JCB Y b
Zirbelzimmer : **Meals** à la carte 460/710 – ***Salzach-Grill :*** **Meals** à la carte 250/500 – **120 rm** 2200/5900 – 7 suites.

Sheraton, Auerspergstr. 4, ✆ 88 99 90, Telex 632518, Fax 881776, « Terrace in spa gardens », entrance to the spa facilities – rm – 120. AE VISA JCB. rest V s
Meals *(closed Sunday dinner - Monday)* à la carte 480/660 – **163 rm** 2500/5400 – 9 suites.

SALZBURG

Auerspergstraße . . . . V 3
Bürglsteinstraße . . . . X 5
Erzabt-Klotz-Str. . . . . X 9
Gstättengasse . . . . X 12
Kaiserschützenstr. . . . . V 20
Nonntaler Hauptstr. . . . . X 29
Späthgasse . . . . X 37

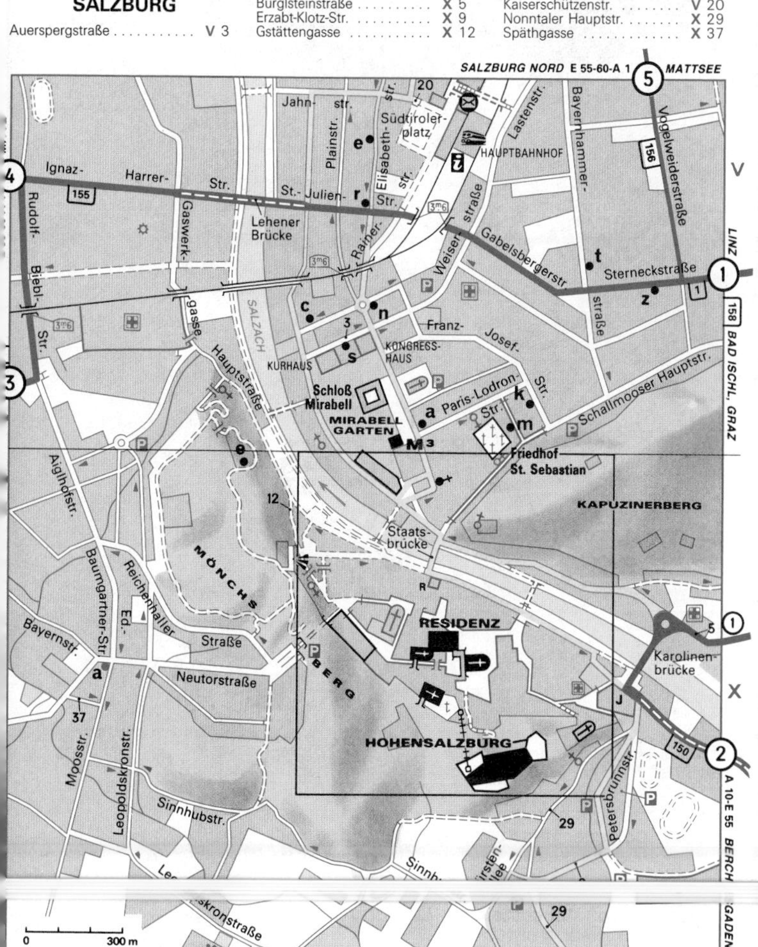

Altstadt Radisson SAS, Judengasse 15, ☎ 8 48 57 10, Fax 8485716, « Modernised 14C nobleman's house, antique furnishings » – rm – 35. AE VISA JCB. rest Y s
Meals à la carte 340/560 – **60 rm** 3220/6405 – 16 suites.

Bristol, Makartplatz 4, ☎ 87 35 57(Hotel) 87 84 17(Rest.), Telex 633337, Fax 8735576 – rm – 60. AE VISA JCB Y a
closed early January - end March – **Meals** *(closed Sunday except Festival)* à la carte 300/560 – **64 rm** 2800/5215 – 9 suites.

Holiday Inn Crowne Plaza-Pitter, Rainerstr. 6, ☎ 8 89 78, Fax 878893, – rm – 160. AE VISA JCB. rest V n
Rainerstube *(dinner only)* **Meals** à la carte 380/510 – ***Auersberg :*** **Meals** à la carte 260/470 – **186 rm** 1900/4800 – 6 suites.

Ramada Hotel Salzburg, Fanny-von-Lehnert-Str. 7, ☎ 4 68 80, Telex 632695, Fax 4688298, Massage, – rm – 810. AE VISA JCB by Kaiserschützenstraße V
Meals à la carte 260/380 – **257 rm** 2370/2720.

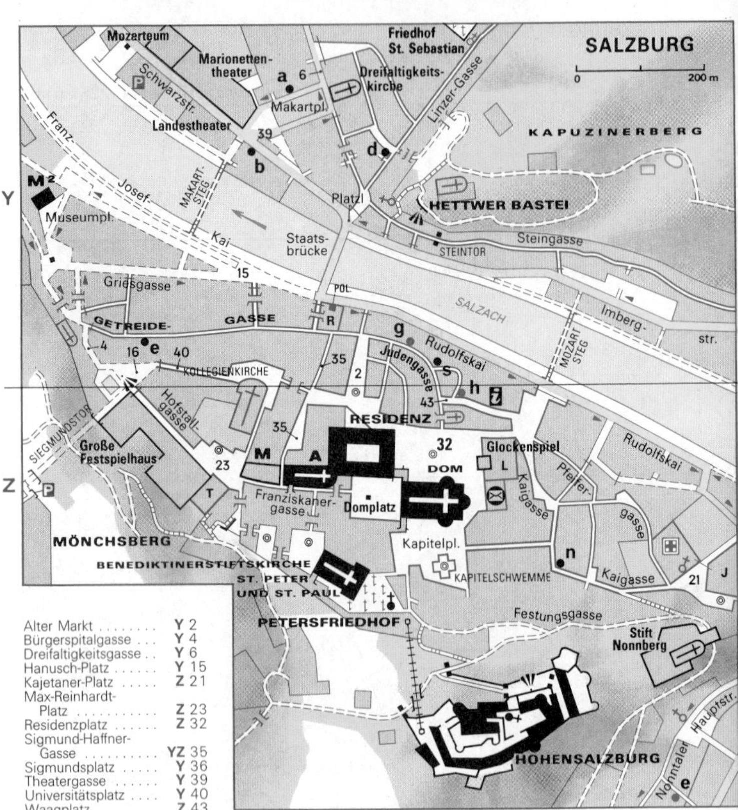

Alter Markt	Y 2
Bürgerspitalgasse	Y 4
Dreifaltigkeitsgasse	Y 6
Hanusch-Platz	Y 15
Kajetaner-Platz	Z 21
Max-Reinhardt-Platz	Z 23
Residenzplatz	Z 32
Sigmund-Haffner-Gasse	YZ 35
Sigmundsplatz	Y 36
Theatergasse	Y 39
Universitätsplatz	Y 40
Waagplatz	Z 43

Goldener Hirsch, Getreidegasse 37, ✆ 8 08 40, Telex 632967, Fax 843349, « 15C nobleman's house, tastefully furnished » – |‡| ⇔ rm ▤ TV – 🏛 20. AE ⓓ E VISA JCB — Y e
Meals à la carte 400/710 – **71 rm** ☐ 2490/5280 – 3 suites.

Schloß Mönchstein 🐎, Mönchsberg Park 26, ✆ 8 48 55 50, Fax 848559, ≤ Salzburg and surroundings, ☂, « Small castle with elegant, stylish furnishings, wedding chapel, park », ☀, 🎾 – |‡| TV 🚗 P – 🏛 30. AE ⓓ E JCB. ✻ rest — X e
Meals à la carte 520/860 – **17 rm** ☐ 2200/6200.

Rosenberger, Bessarabierstr. 94, ✆ 4 35 54 60, Fax 43951095, ≘s – |‡| ⇔ rm TV ♿ 🚗 P – 🏛 360 — by (4)
120 rm.

Dorint-Hotel, Sterneckstr. 20, ✆ 88 20 31, Fax 8820319, ≘s – |‡| ⇔ rm ▤ rest TV ♿ 🚗 – 🏛 150. AE ⓓ E VISA. ✻ rest — V
Meals à la carte 220/420 – **140 rm** ☐ 1530/2010.

Carlton without rest, Markus-Sittikus-Str. 3, ✆ 88 21 91, Fax 87478447, ≘s – |‡| ⇔ TV ☎ 🚗 P. AE ⓓ E VISA JCB — V
39 rm ☐ 1710/2830 – 13 suites.

Austrotel, Mirabellplatz 8, ✆ 88 16 88, Telex 632361, Fax 881687 – |‡| ⇔ rm TV ☎ – 🏛 25. AE ⓓ E VISA — V
Meals *(closed Sunday - Monday)* à la carte 300/415 – **74 rm** ☐ 1700/2600.

Mercure, Bayerhamerstr. 14, ✆ 8 81 43 80, Fax 871111411, ☂ – |‡| ⇔ rm TV ☎ ♿ 🚗 P – 🏛 90. AE ⓓ E VISA JCB — V
Meals à la carte 260/360 – **121 rm** ☐ 1400/2100.

Novotel Salzburg City, Franz-Josef-Str. 26, ✆ 88 20 41, Telex 632886, Fax 874240 ≘s – |‡| ⇔ rm TV ☎ ♿ 🚗 P – 🏛 110. AE ⓓ E VISA — V
Meals (dinner only) à la carte 230/380 – **140 rm** ☐ 1365/2260.

Zum Hirschen without rest, St.-Julien-Str. 21, 88 90 30, Fax 8890358, Massage, – . V r
64 rm 815/1750.

Kasererbräu without rest, Kaigasse 33, 84 24 06, Fax 84244551, – . Z n
closed 3 February - 16 March – **43 rm** 1120/2640.

Kasererhof without rest, Alpenstr. 6, 6 39 65, Telex 633477, Fax 6396550, – . by ②
closed February – **53 rm** 1610/3660.

Wolf-Dietrich, Wolf-Dietrich-Str. 7, 87 12 75, Fax 882320, , – . V m
closed early February - mid March – **Meals** *(closed Sunday)* (dinner only) à la carte 210/405 – **29 rm** 920/2175.

Hohenstauffen without rest, Elisabethstr. 19, 8 77 66 90, Fax 87219351 – . V e
31 rm 800/2065.

Fuggerhof without rest, Eberhard-Fugger-Str. 9, 6 41 29 00, Fax 6412904, , , , – . by Bürglsteinstr. X
closed 20 December - 26 January – **20 rm** 980/2400.

Gablerbräu, Linzer Gasse 9, 8 89 65, Telex 631067, Fax 8896555, – – 25. Y d
Meals à la carte 180/430 – **52 rm** 1070/1740.

K+K Restaurant am Waagplatz, Waagplatz 2 (1st floor), 84 21 56, Fax 84215633, , « Medieval dinner with period performance in the Freysauff-Keller (by arrangement) » – Z h
closed Sunday January to Easter – **Meals** (booking essential) à la carte 315/480.

Riedenburg, Neutorstr. 31, 83 08 15, – . X a
closed Monday lunch, Sunday and 2 weeks June – **Meals** à la carte 365/510.

Zum Mohren, Judengasse 9, 84 23 87, Fax 50179 – Y g
closed Sunday, Bank Holidays and mid June - mid July – **Meals** (booking essential) à la carte 220/410.

at Salzburg-Aigen *by Bürglsteinstr.* X :

Rosenvilla without rest, Höfelgasse 4, A-5026, 62 17 65, Fax 6252308 – .
15 rm 1150/ 2200.

Doktorwirt, Glaser Str. 9, A-5026, 62 29 73, Fax 62171724, , , (heated), – – 25. . rest
closed 10 to 26 February and end October - end November – **Meals** *(closed Monday)* à la carte 200/400 – **39 rm** 850/1950.

Gasthof Schloß Aigen, Schwarzenbergpromenade 37, A-5026, 62 12 84, Fax 621284, – .
closed Thursday lunch, Wednesday, early January - early February and 2 to 8 September [illegible]

at Salzburg-Liefering *by* ④ :

Brandstätter, Münchner Bundesstr. 69, A-5020, 43 45 35, Fax 43453590, , , , – – 40. rest
closed 22 to 27 December – **Meals** *(closed 2 to 16 January and Sunday except saison)* (booking essential) à la carte 295/600 – **34 rm** 785/2300
Spec. Lauwarmer Kalbsbrustsalat mit Gemüsevinaigrette, Kalbssalonbeuscherl mit Semmelknödel, Bauernente im Rohr gebraten.

at Salzburg-Maria Plain *by Plainstr.* V :

Maria Plain (17C inn), Plainbergweg 41, A-5101, 4 50 70 10, Fax 45070119, « Garden with » – – 40.
closed 1 week July – **Meals** *(closed Tuesday - Wednesday, except Festival)* à la carte 260/380 – **27 rm** 880/1300 – 5 suites.

at Salzburg-Nonntal

Purzelbaum (Bistro-rest.), Zugallistr. 7, A-5020, 84 88 43, –
closed Monday lunch, Sunday and 2 weeks July – **Meals** (booking essential for dinner) à la carte 420/550. Z e

at Salzburg-Parsch *by Bürglsteinstr.* X :

Villa Pace , Sonnleitenweg 9, A-5020, 6 41 50 10, Fax 6415015, town and Hohensalzburg, , , (heated), – rm . . rest
closed October - March – **Meals** *(closed Monday lunch and Sunday, except Festival)* (booking essential) à la carte 430/570 – **15 rm** 2450/7100 – 5 suites.

on the Heuberg *NE : 3 km by ① – alt. 565 m*

Schöne Aussicht, Heuberg 3, ✉ A-5023 *Salzburg*, ☎ (0662) 64 06 08, Fax 6406082, « Garden with ≤ Salzburg and Alps », – – 30.
closed November - March – **Meals** *(dinner only)* a la carte 265/480 – **28 rm** 830/2200.

on the Gaisberg *by ① :*

Vitalhotel Kobenzl, Gaisberg 11, alt. 750 m, ✉ A-5020 Salzburg, ☎ (0662) 64 15 10, Telex 633833, Fax 642238, « Beautiful panoramic location with ≤ Salzburg and Alps », Massage, – – 40. rest
Meals à la carte 320/600 – **40 rm** 1650/4400 – 5 suites.

Romantik-Hotel Gersberg Alm, Gersberg 37, alt. 800 m, ✉ A-5023 Salzburg-Gnigl, ☎ (0662) 64 12 57, Fax 644278, – – 55.
Meals à la carte 300/485 – **40 rm** 1230/3710.

near Airport *by ③ :*

Radisson-SAS-Airport-Center-Hotel, Bundesstr. 4, ✉ A-5073 Salzburg-Wals, ☎ (0662) 8 58 10, Fax 85814000 – rm – 90.
Meals à la carte 230/455 – **152 rm** 1205/2300.

Airporthotel, Loigstr. 20a, ✉ A-5020 Salzburg-Loig, ☎ (0662) 85 00 20, Telex 633634, Fax 85002044, – rm – 25.
Meals (residents only) – **32 rm** 1200/1960.

at Anif *② : 7 km*

Friesacher, ✉ A-5081, ☎ (06246) 89 77, Fax 897749, – – 25
closed 2 to 22 January – **Meals** *(closed Wednesday)* à la carte 180/410 – **54 rm** 720/1610.

Point Hotel, Berchtesgadener Str. 364, ✉ A-5081, ☎ (06246) 74 25 60, Fax 74256443, Massage, (heated), (indoor) – rm – 100. rest
Meals à la carte 235/450 – **62 rm** 1430/2254.

at Elixhausen *N : 8 km by ⑤ :*

Romantik-Hotel Gmachl, Dorfstr. 14, ✉ A-5161, ☎ (0662) 48 02 12, Fax 48021272, (indoor court), (indoor) – rm – 40.
closed 1 - 14 July – **Meals** *(closed Monday lunch and Sunday dinner)* à la carte 270/470 – **50 rm** 1100/2150 – 3 suites.

at Hallwang-Söllheim *by ①, and Linzer Bundesstraße : 7 km :*

Pfefferschiff, Söllheim 3, ✉ A-5023, ☎ (0662) 66 12 42, Fax 661841, – .
closed Sunday - Monday, end June - mid July and 1 week September – **Meals** à la carte 440/670
Spec. Sulz vom Kalbsbries und Beuscherl, Wallerfilet mit Pesto auf geschmorten Tomaten, Waldviertler Beiried mit Speckknödel.

at Hof *① : 20 km :*

Schloß Fuschl (former 15C hunting seat with 3 guesthouses), ✉ A-5322, ☎ (06229) 2 25 30, Telex 633454, Fax 2253531, ≤, Massage, – – 100. rest
Meals à la carte 450/800 – **84 rm** 2800/5900 – 12 suites.

Jagdhof am Fuschlsee (former 18C farmhouse with guesthouse), ✉ A-5322, ☎ (06229) 2 37 20, Telex 633454, Fax 2372413, ≤, – – 90. rest
Meals à la carte 245/400 – **54 rm** 950/1800.

at Fuschl am See *① : 26 km :*

Ebner's Waldhof, Seepromenade, ✉ A-5330, ☎ (06226) 2 64, Fax 644, ≤, Massage, – – 60. rest
closed 3 weeks March - April and November - 15 December – **Meals** (booking essential) à la carte 290/480 – **75 rm** 1025/2480.

at Mondsee ① : *28 km (by motorway A 1)*

Seehof ⚘, (SE : 7 km), ✉ A-5311 *Loibichl*, ✆ (06232) 50 31, Fax 503151, ≤, « Garden-terrace », Massage, ≦s, ▲e, ☶, ✂ – ⇹ rest ▣ ⇔ ⓟ – 🔺 15
closed mid September - mid May – **Meals** à la carte 370/515 – **35 rm** ☐ 3600/5720 – 4 suites.

Landhaus Eschlböck-Plomberg with rm, (S : 5 km), ✉ A-5310 *St. Lorenz-Plomberg*, ✆ (06232) 35 72, Fax 316620, ≤, 🏠, ≦s, ▲e, ☶ boat landing place – ⇹ rest ▣ ☎ ⓟ. AE ⓘ E VISA
Meals *(closed September - May Tuesday and Wednesday)* (booking essential) à la carte 400/700 – **12 rm** ☐ 1000/3050.

at Werfen *S : 42 km by ② and A 10 :*

Karl-Rudolf Obauer with rm, Markt 46, ✉ A-5450, ✆ (06468) 21 20, Fax 21212, 🏠 – ▣ ☎ ⓟ. AE
✿✿ **Meals** (booking essential) 380/800 and à la carte 520/780 – **8 rm** ☐ 850/1600
Spec. Forellestrudel "Obauer", Gefüllte Taube mit Semmel und Pilzen, Nachspeisenvariation "Obauer".

Benelux

Belgium

BRUSSELS – ANTWERP – BRUGES – LIÈGE

Grand Duchy of Luxembourg

LUXEMBOURG

Netherlands

AMSTERDAM – The HAGUE – ROTTERDAM

PRACTICAL INFORMATION

LOCAL CURRENCY

Belgian Franc: *100 BEF = 3,12 USD ($) (Jan. 97) can also be used in Luxembourg*

Dutch Florin: *100 NLG = 57,35 USD ($) (Jan. 97)*

TOURIST INFORMATION

Telephone numbers and addresses of Tourist Offices are given in the text of each city under **ℹ**.

National Holiday: *In Belgium: 21 July, in Netherlands: 30 April, in Luxembourg: 23 June.*

AIRLINES

SABENA : *rue Marché-aux-Herbes 110, 1000 Bruxelles, ☏ (02) 723 89 40, 70, Grand-Rue, L-1660 Luxembourg, ☏ 22 12 12, Weteringschans 26, 1017 SG Amsterdam, ☏ (020) 626 29 66.*

LUXAIR : *Luxembourg Airport, L-2987 Luxembourg, ☏ 4 79 81.*

KLM : *avenue Marnix 28, 1050 Bruxelles, ☏ (02) 507 70 70, 1, Airport Findel, Air terminal (office 327), L-1110 Luxembourg, ☏ 42 48 42, Amsterdamseweg 55, 1182 GP Amsterdam, ☏ (020) 649 91 23.*

FOREIGN EXCHANGE

In Belgium, *banks close at 4.30pm and weekends;*

in the Netherlands, *banks close at 5.00pm and weekends, Schiphol Airport exchange offices open daily from 6.30am to 11.30pm.*

TRANSPORT

Taxis: *may be hailed in the street, at taxi ranks or called by telephone.*

Bus, tramway: *practical for long and short distances and good for sightseeing.*

Brussels has a **Métro** *(subway) network. In each station complete information and plans will be found.*

POSTAL SERVICES

Post offices open Monday to Friday from 9am to 5pm in Benelux.

SHOPPING

Shops and boutiques are generally open from 9am to 7pm in Belgium and Luxembourg, and from 9am to 6pm in the Netherlands. The main shopping areas are:

in Brussels: *Rue Neuve, Porte de Namur, Avenue Louise - Also Brussels antique market on Saturday from 9am to 3pm, and Sunday from 9am to 1pm (around place du Grand-Sablon) - Flower and Bird market (Grand-Place) on Sunday morning.*

in Luxembourg: *Grand'Rue and around Place d'Armes - Station Quarter.*

in Amsterdam: *Kalverstraat, Leidsestraat, Nieuwendijk, P.C. Hoofstraat and Utrechtsestraat. Second-hand goods and antiques. Amsterdam Flea Market (near Waterlooplein).*

BREAKDOWN SERVICE

24 hour assistance:

Belgium: *TCB, Brussels ☏ (02) 233 22 11 – VTB-VAB, Antwerp ☏ (0 3) 253 63 63 – RACB, Brussels ☏ (0 2) 287 09 00.*

Luxembourg: *ACL ☏ 45 00 451.*

Netherlands: *ANWB, The Hague ☏ (0 70) 314 71 47 – KNAC, The Hague ☏ (0 70) 383 16 12.*

TIPPING

In Benelux, prices include service and taxes.

SPEED LIMITS – SEAT BELTS

In Belgium and Luxembourg, the maximum speed limits are 120 km/h-74 mph on motorways and dual carriageways, 90 km/h-56 mph on all other roads and 50 km/h-31 mph in built-up areas. In the Netherlands, 100/120 km/h-62/74 mph on motorways and "autowegen", 80 km/h-50 mph on other roads and 50 km/h-31 mph in built-up areas. In each country, the wearing of seat belts is compulsory for driver and passengers.

BRUSSELS

(BRUXELLES - BRUSSEL) *1000 Région de Bruxelles-Capitale – Brussels Hoofdstedelijk Gewest* 213 ⑱ *and* 409 G 3– ⑫ S – *Pop. 951 580* – ✪ *2.*

Paris 308 – Amsterdam 204 – Düsseldorf 222 – Lille 116 – Luxembourg 219.

ℹ *(closed Sundays except in Summer) (T.I.B.) Town Hall (Hôtel de Ville), Grand'Place,* ✉ *1000* ☎ *513 89 40, Fax 514 45 38 – Office de Promotion du Tourisme (O.P.T.) r. Marché-aux-Herbes 61,* ✉ *1000,* ☎ *504 02 22, Fax 513 69 50 – Vlaams Commissariaat-Generaal voor Toerisme (V.C.G.T.), Grasmarkt 61,* ✉ *1000,* ☎ *504 03 00, Fax 513 88 03.*

18 9 *at Tervuren SE : 14 km, Château de Ravenstein* ☎ *(0 2) 767 58 01, Fax (0 2) 767 28 41 –* 18 *at Melsbroek NE : 14 km, Steenwagenstraat 11* ☎ *(0 2) 751 82 05, Fax (0 2) 751 84 25 –* 18 *at Anderlecht, Sports Area of la Pede, r. Scholle 1* ☎ *(0 2) 521 16 87, Fax (0 2) 521 51 56 –* 9 *at Watermael-Boitsfort, chaussée de la Hulpe 53a* ☎ *(0 2) 672 22 22, Fax (0 2) 675 34 81 –* 9 *at Overijse SE : 16 km, Gemslaan 55* ☎ *(0 2) 687 50 30, Fax (0 2) 687 37 68 –* 9 *at Itterbeek W : 8 km, J.M. van Lierdelaan 28 b* ☎ *(0 2) 567 00 38, Fax (0 2) 569 01 98 –* 18 *at Kampenhout NE : 20 km, Wildersedreef 56* ☎ *(016) 65 12 16, Fax (0 16) 65 16 80 –* 9 *at Duisburg E : 18 km, Hertswegenstraat 39* ☎ *(0 2) 767 97 52.*

✈ *Sabena office, r. Marché-aux-Herbes 110,* ✉ *1000,* ☎ *723 89 40, direct railway line* ☎ [illegible]

🚘 ☎ *203 36 40 and 203 28 80.*

See : *Atomium*★ *(Heysel) – National basilica of Koekelberg*★ *– Place Royale*★ KZ *– Market Square*★★★ *(Grand-Place)* JY *– Monnaie Theatre*★ JY *– St-Hubert Arcades*★★ JY *– Erasmus House*★★ *(Anderlecht) – Gauchie House*★ *(Etterbeek)* HS **W** *– Castle and park*★★ *(Gaasbeek, SW : 12 km) – Royal Plant Houses*★★ *(Laeken) – Horta Museum*★★ *(St-Gilles)* EFU **M**[10] *– Van Buuren House*★ *(Uccle)* EFV **M**[13] *– Old England*★ KZ **B** *– Sts-Michaels and Gudule Cathedral*★★ KY *– Church of N.-D. de la Chapelle*★ JZ *– Church of N.-D. du Sablon*★ JZ *– Cambre Abbey*★★ *(Ixelles)* FGV *– Church of Sts-Pierre and Guidon*★ *(Anderlecht) – Royal Museums of Belgian Fine Arts*★★★ KZ *– Florist De Backer*★ KY **F**[1] *– Grand et Petit Sablon*★★ JZ *– Rue des Bouchers*★ JY *– Manneken Pis*★★ JZ.

Museums : *Ancien Art*★★★ KZ*– Royal Museum of Art and History*★★★ HS **M**[7] *– Modern Art*★★ KZ **M**[1] *– Belgian Centre of Comic Strips*★★ KY **M**[5] *– Autoworld*★★ HS **M**[23] *– Natural Science (Royal Institute)*★★ GS **M**[9] *– Musical Instruments*★★ JZ **M**[2] *– Meunier*★ *(Ixelles)* FV **M**[12] *– Ixelles Municipal Museum*★★ FGT **M**[11] *– Charlier*★ FR **M**[21] *– Bibliotheca Wittockiana*★ *(Woluwé-St-Pierre) – Royal Museum of Central Africa*★★ *(Tervuren).*

BRUXELLES BRUSSEL

Louise (Galerie) .... FS 161
Midi (Bd du) .... ES

Baudouin (Bd) .... EQ 16
Bienfaiteurs (Pl. des) .... GQ 21
Brabançonne (Av. de la) . GR 28
Edouard de Thibault (Av.). HS 72
Europe (Bd de l') .... ES 89
Frans Courtens (Av.) .... HQ 102
Frère-Orban (Sq.) .... FR 104

Froissart (R.) .... GS 106
Gén. Eisenhower (Av.) ... GQ 108
Hal (Porte de) .... ES 114
Henri Jaspar (Av.) .... ES 117
Herbert Hoover (Av.) .... HR 118
Industrie (Quai de l') .... ER 126
Jan Stobbaerts (Av.) ..... GQ 133

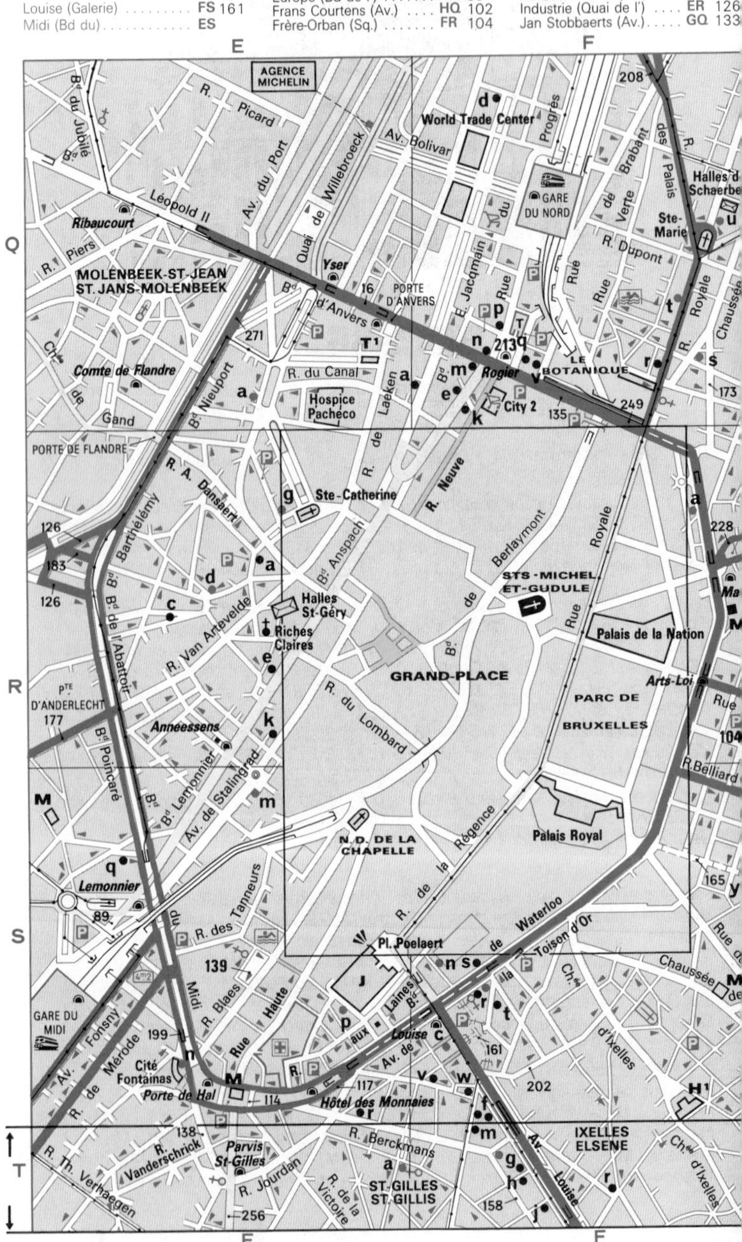

Jardin Botanique (Bd du) . FQ 135
Jean Volders (Av.) . . . . . . ET 138
Jeu de Balle (Pl. du) . . . . . ES 139
Livourne (R. de) . . . . FT 158
Luxembourg (R. de) . . . . . FS 165
Marie-Louise (Sq.) . . . . . . GR 171
Méridien (R. du) . . . . FQ 173
Mons (Chée de) . . . . ER 177
Nerviens (Av. des) . . . . . . GS 181
Ninove (Chée de) . . . . ER 183
Palmerston (Av.) . . . . GR 187
Porte de Hal (Av. de la) . . ES 199
Prince Royal (R. du) . . . . . FS 202
Reine (Av. de la) . . . . FQ 208
Rogier (Pl.) . . . . FQ 213
Roi Vainqueur (Pl. du) . . . HS 216
Saint-Antoine (Pl.) . . . . GT 220
Scailquin (R.) . . . . FR 228
Victoria Regina (Av) . . . . . FQ 249
Waterloo (Chée de) . . . . . ET 256
9e de Ligne (Bd du) . . . . . EQ 271

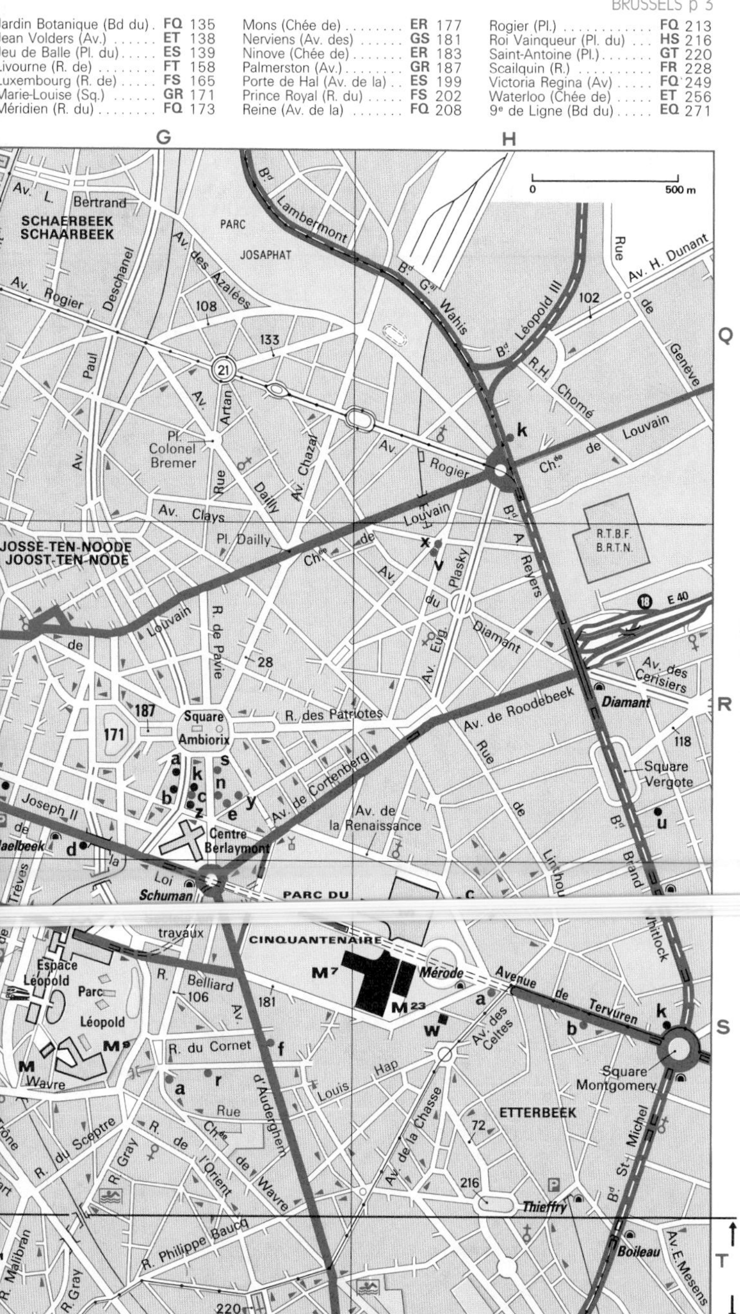

BRUXELLES
BRUSSEL

Américaine (R.) . . . . FU 8
Auguste Rodin (Av.) . . . . . . GU 12
Besme (Av.) . . . . EV 18
Boendael (Drève de). . . . . . GX 22
Cambre (Bd de la) . . . . GV 33
Coccinelles (Av. des) . . . . . HX 40
Congo (Av. du) . . . . GV 48
Copernic (R.) . . . . FX 51
Doronée (R.) . . . . FV 61
Dries . . . . HX 63
Emile de Beco (Av.) . . . . . GU 79
Emile De Mot (Av.) . . . . . GV 81
Eperons d'Or (Av. des) . . . . GU 85
Everard (av.) . . . . EV 91
Hippodrome (Av. de l') . . . . GU 120

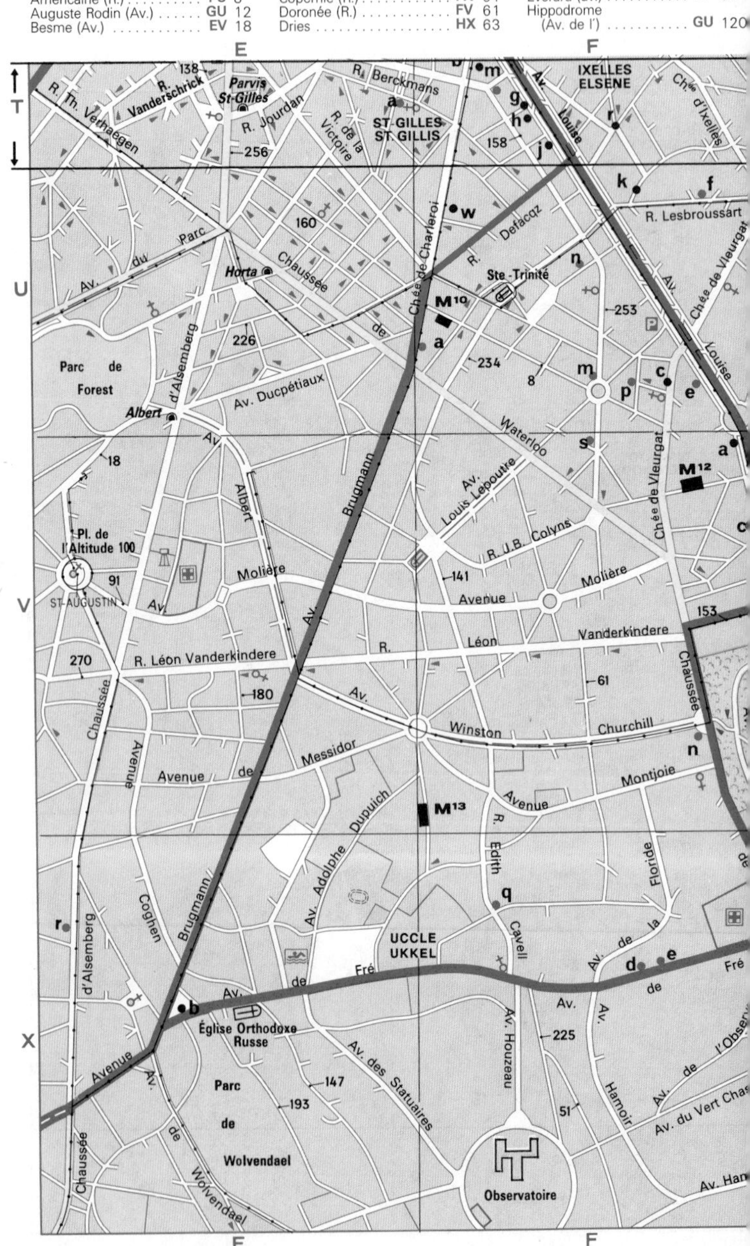

Invalides (Bd des) . . . . HV 127
Jean Volders (Av.) . . . . ET 138
Jos Stallaert (R.) . . . . FV 141
Juliette Wytsman (R.) . . . . GU 145
Kamerdelle (Av.) . . . . EX 147
Legrand (Av.) . . . . FV 153
Livourne (R. de) . . . . FT 158
Louis Morichar (Pl.) . . . . . EU 160
Mutualité (R. de la) . . . . . EV 180
Nouvelle (Av.) . . . . GU 184
Paul Stroobant (Av.) . . . . . EX 193
Saint-Antoine (Pl.) . . . . . . GT 220
Saisons (Av. des) . . . . GV 223
Saturne (Av. de) . . . . FX 225
Savoie (R. de) . . . . EU 226
Tabellion (R. de) . . . . FU 234
Washington (R.) . . . . FU 253
Waterloo (Chée de) . . . . . ET 256
2e Rég. de Lanciers (Av. du) . . . . GHU 265
7 Bonniers (Av. des) . . . . EV 270

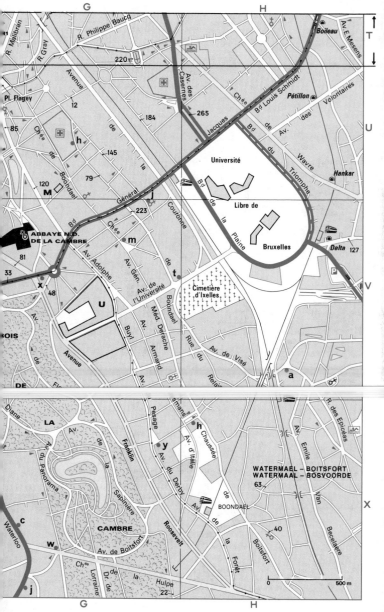

BRUXELLES BRUSSEL

Adolphe Max (Bd) ..... **JY** 3
Anspach (Bd) .... **JY**
Beurre (Rue au) .... **JY** 19
Etuve (R. de l') .... **JZ** 88
Fripiers (R. des) .... **JY** 105
Grand Sablon (Pl. du) ... **KZ** 112
Ixelles (Chée d') .... **KZ** 129
Marché-aux-Herbes (R. du) .... **JY** 168
Marché-aux-Poulets (R. du) .... **JY** 169
Midi (R. du) .... **JYZ**
Neuve (Rue) .... **JY**
Reine (Galerie de la) .... **JY** 210
Roi (Galerie du) .... **KY** 214
Toison d'Or (Av. de la) .. **KZ** 238

Albertine (Pl. de l') ..... **KZ** 4
Assaut (R. d') .... **KY** 10
Baudet (R.) .... **KZ** 15
Bortier (Galerie) .... **JZ** 23
Bouchers (Petite rue des) . **JY** 24
Bouchers (R. des) .... **JY** 25
Bourse (Pl. de la) .... **JY** 27
Briques (Quai aux) ...... **JY** 29
Chêne (R. du) .... **JZ** 39
Colonies (R. des) .... **KY** 43
Comédiens (R. des) ..... **KY** 45
Commerce (R. du) ...... **KZ** 46
Croix-de-Fer (R. de la) .... **KY** 52
Duquesnoy (Rue) .... **JYZ** 66
Ernest Allard (R.) .... **JZ** 87
Europe (Carr. de l') ..... **KY** 90
Fossé-aux-Loups (R. du) .... **JKY** 99
Impératrice (Bd de l') ... **KY** 124

Joseph Lebeau (R.) ...... **JZ** 142
Laeken (R. de) .... **JY** 151
Louvain (R. de) .... **KY** 163
Mercier (R. du Card.) .... **KY** 172
Montagne (Rue de la) .... **KY** 178
Musée (Pl. du) .... **KZ** 179
Nord (Passage du) .... **JY** 182
Petit Sablon (Sq. du) .... **KZ** 195
Presse (R. de la) .... **KY** 201
Princes (Galeries des) .... **JY** 205
Ravenstein (R.) .... **KZ** 207
Rollebeek (R. de) .... **JZ** 217
Ruysbroeck (R. de) ...... **KZ** 219
Ste-Catherine (Pl.) ...... **JY** 221
Sainte-Gudule (Pl.) ...... **KY** 222
Trône (R. du) .... **KZ** 241
Ursulines (R. des) .... **JZ** 243
Waterloo (Bd de) .... **KZ** 255
6 Jeunes Hommes (R. des) .... **KZ** 268

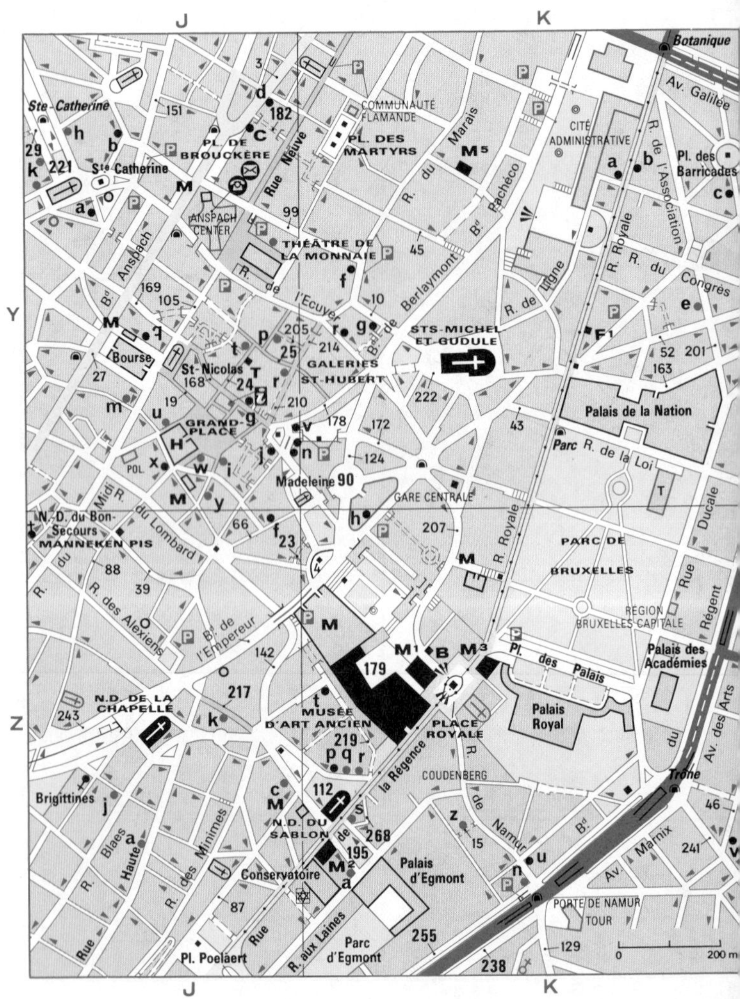

Alphabetical listing of hotels and restaurants

A

19 Abbaye de Rouge Cloître (L')
24 Abbey
18 Adrienne Atomium
17 Agenda (L')
18 Alain Cornelis
13 Alban Chambon (L') (at Métropole H.)
21 Albert Premier
25 Alfa Rijckendael
16 Alfa Sablon
24 Aloyse Kloos
22 Amandier (L')
22 Amici miei
14 Amigo
25 André D'Haese
16 Anecdote (L')
23 Arconati (Host. d')
13 Arctia
13 Arenberg
20 Argus
25 Arlecchino (L') (at Aub. de Waterloo H.)
15 Armes de Bruxelles (Aux)
15 Astrid
14 Astrid « Chez Pierrot »
14 Atelier (L')
[illegible] Atlas
20 Aub. de Boendael (L')
25 Aub. Napoléon
26 Aub. Saint-Pierre (L')
25 Aub. de Waterloo

B

18 Baguettes Impériales (Les)
26 Barbay
25 Barbizon
20 Béarnais (Le)
20 Beau-Site
13 Bedford
16 Belle Maraîchère (La)
22 Bellini (Le)
19 Belson
14 Bernard
22 Blue Elephant
25 Boetfort
25 Bois Savanes
20 Brasserie Mareboeuf (La)
22 Brasseries Georges
17 Bristol Stéphanie
18 Brouette (La)
19 Bruneau
23 Butterfly (The)
24 Bijgaarden (De)

C

22 Cadre Noir (Le)
19 Cambrils
20 Capital
15 Carrefour de l'Europe
16 Casa Manolo
21 Cascade
16 Castello Banfi
18 Centenaire (Le)
24 Chalet Rose
13 Chambord
16 « Chez Marius » En Provence
22 Cité du Dragon (La)
19 Citronnelle (La)
14 City Garden
19 Claude Dupont
16 Clef des Champs (La)
17 Clubhouse
13 Comme Chez Soi
18 Comtes de Flandre (Les) (at Sheraton Towers H.)
17 Conrad
22 County House
20 Couvert d'Argent (Le)

D

21 Dames Tarine (Les)
21 Diplomat
15 Dixseptième (Le)
18 Dome (Le)
14 Dorint
16 Duc d'Arenberg (Au)

E

16 Écailler du Palais Royal (L')
22 Entre-Temps (L')
18 Erasme
14 Euroflat
14 Europa
14 Eurovillage
19 Evergreen

F

15 Falstaff Gourmand
19 Fierlant (De)
20 Flagrant Délice (Le)
19 Fontaine de Jade (La)
21 Forcado (Le)
16 François
22 Frères Romano (Les)

G

13 George V
24 Gosset
25 Green Park
18 Grignotière (La)
24 Groenendaal

H

16 Hilton
22 Hoef (De)
23 Holiday Inn Airport
21 Holiday Inn City Centre
21 Hugo's (at Royal Crown Gd H. Mercure)

I – J – K

23 Ibis Airport
15 Ibis off Grand'Place
15 Ibis Ste-Catherine
20 Inada
14 In 't Spinnekopke
25 Istas
21 I Trulli
14 Jardin d'Espagne (Le)
14 J et B
13 Jolly Atlanta
16 Jolly du Grand Sablon
24 Kasteel Gravenhof
15 Kelderke ('t)
25 Koen van Loven

L

23 Lambeau
21 Lambermont
16 Larmes du Tigre (Les)
20 Leopold
25 Lien Zana
16 Lola
16 Loup-Galant (Le)
18 Lychee

M

16 Maison du Bœuf (at Hilton H.)
15 Maison du Cygne (La)
20 Maison Félix
17 Maison de Maître (La) (at Conrad H.)
22 Maison de Thaïlande (La)
21 Mamounia (La)
21 Manos
21 Manos Stephanie
15 Matignon
17 Mayfair
19 Mercure
14 Méridien (Le)
26 Met (De)
13 Métropole
24 Michel
18 Ming Dynasty
19 Momotaro
23 Mon Manège à Toi
23 Montgomery
20 Mosaïque (La)
20 Mövenpick Cadettt
23 Mucha (Le)
14 Mykonos

N – O

14 New Charlemagne
21 New Siru
23 Novotel Airport
15 Novotel off Grand'Place
15 Ogenblik (L')
24 Oude Pastorie (D')

P – Q

18 Paix (La)
20 Pagode d'Or (La)
21 Palace
14 Pappa e Citti
19 Park

26 Parkhof
20 Perles de Pluie (Les)
26 Philippe Verbaeys
13 Plaza (Le)
24 Plezanten Hof (De)
17 Porte des Indes (La)
13 Président Centre
18 Président Nord
18 Président World Trade Center
18 Prince de Liège (Le)
15 Quatre Saisons (Les) (at Royal Windsor H.)
13 Queen Anne

R

13 Radisson SAS
23 Rainbow Airport
23 Relais Delbeccha
23 Relais de la Woluwe (Le)
17 Renaissance
22 Rives du Gange (Les)
25 Roland Debuyst
14 Roma
15 Roue d'Or (La)
21 Royal Crown Gd H. Mercure
13 Royal Embassy
14 Royal Windsor

S

13 Sabina
18 Saint-Guidon
24 Saint-Sébastien (Le)
[illegible]
13 Sea Grill (at Radisson SAS H.)
19 Serpolet (Le)
26 Sheraton Airport
17 Sheraton Towers
15 Sirène d'Or (La)
23 Sodehotel La Woluwe
20 Sofitel
23 Sofitel Airport
13 Sofitel Astoria
17 Stanhope
19 Stirwen
26 Stockmansmolen
26 Stoveke ('t)

T

17 Tagawa
17 Taishin (at Mayfair H.)
14 Takesushi
15 Taverne du Passage
24 Terborght
15 Tête d'Or (La)
23 Trois Couleurs (Des)
22 Trois Tilleuls (Host. des)
17 Truffe Noire (La)
16 Truite d'Argent et H. Welcome (La)
21 Tulip Inn Delta

U – V

21 Ultieme Hallucinatie (De)
18 Ustel
26 Val Joli (Le)
22 Vieux Boitsfort (Au)
23 Vignoble de Margot (Le)
22 Villa d'Este
17 Villa Lorraine

W – Y – Z

24 Waerboom
22 Willy et Marianne
20 Yen

Starred establishments

✿✿✿

19	XXXX	Bruneau	13	XXX	Comme Chez Soi

✿✿

24	XXXXX	Bijgaarden (De)	19	XXX	Claude Dupont
13	XXXX	Sea Grill (at Radisson SAS H.)	16	XXX	Écailler du Palais Royal (L'

✿

17	XXXXX	Villa Lorraine	15	XXX	Les 4 Saisons (at Royal Windsor H.)
25	XXXX	Barbizon	17	XXX	Truffe Noire (La)
16	XXXX	Maison du Bœuf (at Hilton H.)	24	XX	Aloyse Kloos
17	XXXX	Maison de Maître (La) (at Conrad H.)	18	XX	Baguettes Impériales (Les
24	XXXX	Michel	18	XX	Grignotière (La)
23	XXX	Des 3 Couleurs	19	XX	Stirwen
25	XXX	André D'Haese	23	XX	Vignoble de Margot (Le
			22	XX	Villa d'Este

Establishments according to style of cuisine

Buffets

18 Adrienne Atomium *Q. Atomium*
14 Atelier (L') *Q. de l'Europe*
17 Café Wiltcher's (at Conrad H.) *Q. Louise*
17 Renaissance *Q. Léopold*

Grill

20 Aub. de Boendael (L') *Ixelles Q. Boondael*
25 Aub. Napoléon *Env. at Meise*
22 Hoef (De) *Uccle*

Pub rest – Brasseries

20 Brasserie Marebœuf (La) *Ixelles, Q. Boondael*
22 Brasseries Georges *Uccle*
20 Capital *Ixelles Q. Bascule*
22 Entre-Temps (L') *Watermael-Boitsfort*
18 Erasme *Anderlecht*
25 Istas *Env. at Overijse*
24 Kasteel Gravenhof *Env. at Dworp*
15 Kelderke ('t) *Q. Grand'Place*
25 Lien Zana *Env. at Schepdaal*
26 Met (De) *Env. at Vilvoorde*
21 New Siru *St-Josse-ten-Noode Q. Botanique*
18 Paix (La) *Anderlecht*
15 Roue d'Or (La) *Q. Grand'Place*
26 Sheraton Airport *Env. at Zaventem*
26 Stockmansmolen *Env. at Zaventem*
15 Taverne du Passage *Q. Grand'Place*

Seafood – Oyster bar

16 Belle Maraîchère (La) *Q. Ste-Catherine*
22 Brasseries Georges *Uccle*
22 Cadre Noir (Le) *Schaerbeek Q. Meiser*
16 Écailler du Palais Royal (L') *Q. des Sablons*
16 François *Q. Ste-Catherine*
13 Sea Grill (at Radisson SAS H.)
15 Sirène d'Or (La) *Q. Ste-Catherine*
26 Stoveke ('t) *Env. at Strombeek-Bever*
16 Truite d'Argent and H. Welcome (La) *Q. Ste-Catherine*

Asian

17 Renaissance *Q. Léopold*

Chinese

22 Cité du Dragon (La) *Uccle*
18 Lychee *Q. Atomium*
19 Fontaine de Jade (La) *Etterbeek Q. Cinquantenaire*
18 Ming Dynasty *Q. Atomium*

Greek

14 Mykonos *Q. de l'Europe*

Indian

17 Porte des Indes (La) *Q. Louise*
22 Rives du Gange (Les) *Watermael-Boitsfort*

Italian

22 Amici miei *Schaerbeek Q. Meiser*
25 Arlecchino (L') (at Aub. de Waterloo H.) *Env. at Sint-Genesius-Rode*
16 Castello Banfi *Q. des Sablons*
21 I Trulli *St-Gilles Q. Louise*
23 Mucha (Le) *Woluwé-St-Pierre*
14 Pappa e Citti *Q. de l'Europe*
14 Roma
19 San Daniele *Ganshoren*

Japanese

19 Momotaro Etterbeek *Q. Cinquantenaire*
17 Tagawa *Q. Louise*
17 Taishin (at Mayfair H.) *Q. Louise*
14 Takesushi *Q. de l'Europe*

Moroccan

21 Mamounia (La) *St-Gilles*

Portuguese

21 Forcado (Le) *St-Gilles*

Scandinavian

13 Atrium *(at Radisson SAS H.)*
17 Bristol Stéphanie *Q. Louise*

Spanish

16 Casa Manolo *Q. Palais de Justice*
14 Jardin d'Espagne (Le) *Q. de l'Europe*

Thaï

22 Blue Elephant *Uccle*
25 Bois Savanes *Env. at Sint-Genesius-Rode*
16 Larmes du Tigre (Les) *Q. Palais de Justice*
22 Maison de Thaïlande (La) *Watermael-Boitsfort*
20 Perles de Pluie (Les) *Ixelles Q. Louise*

Vietnamese

18 Baguettes Impériales (Les) *Q. Atomium*
19 Citronnelle (La) *Auderghem*
20 Pagode d'Or (La) *Ixelles Q. Boondael*
20 Yen *Ixelles*

BRUXELLES (BRUSSEL)

Radisson SAS, r. Fossé-aux-Loups 47, ✉ 1000, ✆ 227 31 31 and 227 31 70 (rest), Telex 22202, Fax 223 18 18, « Patio with remains of 12C City enclosure wall », – 25-380. AE VISA JCB. rest KY f
Meals see rest *Sea Grill* below – **Atrium** *(partly Scandinavian cuisine) Lunch 975* - a la carte 1100/1650 – 750 – **275 rm** 4500/14000, 6 suites.

Sofitel Astoria, r. Royale 103, ✉ 1000, ✆ 217 62 90, Fax 217 11 50, « Early 20C residence, Belle Epoque style » – – 25-180. AE E VISA JCB. KY b
Meals *Le Palais Royal (closed Saturday lunch, Sunday dinner and 15 July-15 August)* 1500/2600 – 850 – **106 rm** 12000, 14 suites.

Le Plaza, bd. A. Max 118, ✉ 1000, ✆ 227 67 00, Fax 227 67 20 – rm – 25-800. AE E VISA JCB. rest FQ e
Meals a la carte approx. 1100 – **186 rm** 5900/6900, 6 suites.

Métropole, pl. de Brouckère 31, ✉ 1000, ✆ 217 23 00, Telex 21234, Fax 218 02 20, « Late 19C hall and lounges », – – 25-400. AE E VISA JCB JY c
Meals see rest *L'Alban Chambon* below – **405 rm** 7500/12000, 5 suites.

Bedford, r. Midi 135, ✉ 1000, ✆ 512 78 40, Telex 24059, Fax 514 17 59 – – 25-200. AE E VISA ER k
Meals *Lunch 1100* – 1100 – **298 rm** 6500/7700.

Jolly Atlanta, bd A. Max 7, ✉ 1000, ✆ 217 01 20, Telex 21475, Fax 217 37 58 – rest – 25-50. AE E VISA. rest JY d
Meals (residents only) – **235 rm** 6000/8950, 6 suites.

Président Centre without rest, r. Royale 160, ✉ 1000, ✆ 219 00 65, Telex 26784, Fax 218 09 10 – . AE E VISA JCB. KY a
73 rm 4900/5900.

Royal Embassy without rest, bd Anspach 159, ✉ 1000, ✆ 512 81 00, Fax 514 30 97, – . AE E VISA. ER e
54 rm 3800/4300.

Arctia without rest, r. Arenberg 18, ✉ 1000, ✆ 548 18 11, Fax 548 18 20, – – 25-80. AE E VISA JCB KY r
95 rm 4500/6900, 5 suites.

Arenberg, r. Assaut 15, ✉ 1000, ✆ 511 07 70, Fax 514 19 76 – rest – 25-90. AE E VISA JCB. KY g
Meals a la carte 1000/1300 – **155 rm** 6000/7000.

Chambord without rest, r. Namur 82, ✉ 1000, ✆ 548 99 10, Fax 514 08 47 – . AE E VISA JCB. KZ u
69 rm 3400/6000.

Queen Anne without rest, bd E. Jacqmain 110, ✉ 1000, ✆ 217 16 00, Telex 22676, Fax 217 18 38 – . AE E VISA EFQ a
60 rm 2750/3400.

George V without rest, [illegible]
. E VISA ER c
17 rm 2400.

Sabina without rest, r. Nord 78, ✉ 1000, ✆ 218 26 37, Fax 219 32 39 – . AE E VISA JCB KY c
24 rm 1800/2300.

Sea Grill - (at Radisson SAS H.), r. Fossé-aux-Loups 47, ✉ 1000, ✆ 227 31 20, Fax 219 62 62, Seafood – . AE E VISA JCB. KY f
closed Saturday lunch, Sunday, 30 March-6 April and 20 July-17 August – **Meals** *Lunch 1650* – a la carte 2200/2700
Spec. Bar de ligne en croûte de sel marin, Manchons de crabe royal tièdis au beurre de persil plat, Homard à la presse.

L'Alban Chambon - (at Métropole H.), pl. de Brouckère 21, ✉ 1000, ✆ 217 76 50, Fax 218 02 20, « Late 19C atmosphere » – . AE E VISA JCB. JY c
closed Saturday, Sunday and Bank Holidays – **Meals** *Lunch 1450 b.i.* – a la carte 1700/2300.

Comme Chez Soi (Wynants), pl. Rouppe 23, ✉ 1000, ✆ 512 29 21, Fax 511 80 52, « Belle Epoque atmosphere with Horta decor » – . AE E VISA ES m
closed Sunday, Monday, 29 June-28 July and Christmas-New Year – **Meals** (booking essential) *Lunch 1975* – 4750, a la carte 2700/3300
Spec. Filets de sole, mousseline aux crevettes grises et Riesling, Dodine de caneton au Chambertin, Effeuillées aux fruits rouges et chocolat blanc pour "Jessica".

XX **Roma,** r. Princes 14, ✉ 1000, ✆ 219 01 94, Fax 218 34 30, Italian cuisine – ▤. AE ⓓ E VISA JY e
closed Saturday lunch, Sunday, Bank Holidays and mid July-mid August – **Meals** *Lunch 990* – a la carte 1200/2300.

XX **Astrid "Chez Pierrot",** r. Presse 21, ✉ 1000, ✆ 217 38 31, Fax 217 38 31 – AE ⓓ E VISA JCB KY e
closed Sunday, Easter week and 15 July-15 August – **Meals** *Lunch 850* – 950/1500.

XX **J and B,** r. Baudet 5, ✉ 1000, ✆ 512 04 84, Fax 511 79 30 – ▤. AE ⓓ E VISA JCB KZ z
closed Saturday lunch, Sunday dinner and 21 July-7 August – **Meals** *Lunch 725* – 995/1425.

XX **Bernard** 1st floor, r. Namur 93, ✉ 1000, ✆ 512 88 21, Fax 502 21 77 – ▤. AE ⓓ E VISA JCB KZ n
closed Saturday and Sunday – **Meals** (lunch only July-August) 900 b.i./2750 b.i..

X **In 't Spinnekopke,** pl. du Jardin aux Fleurs 1, ✉ 1000, ✆ 511 86 95, Fax 513 24 97, 🏠, Partly regional cuisine, open until 11 p.m., « Typical ancient Brussels pub » – ▤. AE ⓓ E VISA ER d
Meals *Lunch 295* – a la carte 800/1350.

Quartier de l'Europe

Dorint M, bd Charlemange 11, ✉ 1000, ✆ 231 09 09, Fax 230 33 71, Fā, ≘s – |‡| ⇔ ▤ TV ☎ ♿ 🚗 – 🏛 25-150. AE ⓓ E VISA JCB GR c
Meals *Lunch 990* – a la carte 1100/1700 – ☕ 600 – **205 rm** 7800, 2 suites.

Europa, r. Loi 107, ✉ 1040, ✆ 230 13 33, Telex 26310, Fax 230 36 82, Fā – |‡| ⇔ ▤ TV ☎ 🚗 P – 🏛 25-350. AE ⓓ E VISA JCB. ⛌ GR d
Meals *Lunch 990 b.i.* – 990/1650 – ☕ 780 – **236 rm** 9500/10500, 4 suites.

Eurovillage M, bd Charlemagne 80, ✉ 1000, ✆ 230 85 55, Fax 230 56 35, 🏠, ≘s – |‡| ⇔ ▤ TV ☎ 🚗 – 🏛 25-120. AE ⓓ E GR a
Meals *(closed August) Lunch 700* – a la carte 1100/1450 – **80 rm** ☕ 5250/6500.

Euroflat without rest, bd Charlemagne 50, ✉ 1000, ✆ 230 00 10, Telex 21120, Fax 230 36 83, ≘s – |‡| TV ☎ 🚗 – 🏛 25-80. AE ⓓ E VISA JCB. ⛌ GR b
121 rm ☕ 5700/6500, 12 suites.

New Charlemagne without rest, bd Charlemagne 25, ✉ 1000, ✆ 230 21 35, Telex 22772, Fax 230 25 10 – |‡| ⇔ TV ☎ 🚗 – 🏛 30-60. AE ⓓ E VISA GR k
☕ 525 – **66 rm** 3200/4900.

City Garden without rest, r. Joseph II 59, ✉ 1000, ✆ 282 82 82, Fax 230 64 37 – |‡| ⇔ TV ☎ 🚗. AE ⓓ E VISA JCB. ⛌ GR
94 rm ☕ 6000/6500, 2 suites.

XX **Le Jardin d'Espagne,** r. Archimède 65, ✉ 1000, ✆ 736 34 49, Fax 735 17 45, 🏠, Partly Spanish cuisine – AE E VISA GR s
closed Saturday lunch and Sunday – **Meals** *Lunch 950* – 950/1250.

XX **Pappa e Citti,** r. Franklin 18, ✉ 1000, ✆ 732 61 10, Fax 732 57 40, 🏠, Italian cuisine – AE E VISA JCB. ⛌ GR e
closed Saturday, Sunday, Bank Holidays, 7 to 31 August and 24 December-3 January – **Meals** a la carte 1200/1750.

X **L'Atelier,** r. Franklin 28, ✉ 1000, ✆ 734 91 40, Fax 735 35 98, Buffets – AE ⓓ E VISA
closed Bank Holidays, weekends, 2 August-1 September and 24 December-5 January – **Meals** *Lunch 770* – 980/1200. GR y

X **Takesushi,** bd Charlemagne 21, ✉ 1000, ✆ 230 56 27, 🏠, Japanese cuisine – AE ⓓ E VISA GR z
closed Saturday and Sunday lunch – **Meals** a la carte 1500/1900.

X **Mykonos,** r. Archimède 63, ✉ 1000, ✆ 735 17 59, 🏠, Greek cuisine – ⓓ E VISA
closed Saturday lunch, Sunday, 1 week Easter, first 2 weeks September and late December – **Meals** – a la carte 900/1450. GR r

Quartier Grand'Place (Ilot Sacré)

Royal Windsor, r. Duquesnoy 5, ✉ 1000, ✆ 505 55 55, Telex 62905, Fax 505 55 00, Fā, ≘s – |‡| ⇔ ▤ TV ☎ 🚗 – 🏛 25-250. AE ⓓ E VISA JCB JYZ
Meals see rest *Les 4 Saisons* below – ☕ **264 rm** ☕ 11450/15450, 11 suites.

Amigo, r. Amigo 1, ✉ 1000, ✆ 547 47 47, Telex 21618, Fax 513 52 77, « Collection of works of art » – |‡| ▤ rm TV ☎ 🚗 – 🏛 25-200. AE ⓓ E VISA JCB. ⛌ rest
Meals *Lunch 1460 b.i.* – 1460 b.i./1740 b.i. – **171 rm** ☕ 6700/9000, 7 suites. JY

Le Méridien M, Carrefour de l'Europe 3, ✉ 1000, ✆ 548 42 11 and 548 47 16 (rest), Fax 548 40 80, ≤, Fā – |‡| ⇔ ▤ TV ☎ ♿ 🚗 – 🏛 25-200. AE ⓓ E VISA
Meals *L'Epicerie* *Lunch 1395* - a la carte 1300/1650 – ☕ 850 – **212 rm** ☕ 11000/12000, 12 suites. KZ

Carrefour de l'Europe, r. Marché-aux-Herbes 110, ✉ 1000, ℘ 504 94 00, Fax 504 95 00 – 25-150. AE ① E VISA. JKY n
Meals 1000/1900 – **58 rm** 8500/9500, 5 suites.

Novotel off Grand'Place, r. Marché-aux-Herbes 120, ✉ 1000, ℘ 514 33 33, Fax 511 77 23 – 25. AE ① E VISA JCB JKY n
Meals (open until midnight) a la carte approx. 1100 – 460 – **136 rm** 5600/6500.

Le Dixseptième without rest, r. Madeleine 25, ✉ 1000, ℘ 502 57 44, Fax 502 64 24, « Elegant town house » – 25. AE ① E VISA JCB. JY j
16 rm 5800/10600, 7 suites.

Ibis off Grand'Place without rest, r. Marché-aux-Herbes 100, ✉ 1000, ℘ 514 40 40, Fax 514 50 67 – 25-120. AE ① E VISA JCB JKY v
173 rm 4100/4400.

Matignon, r. Bourse 10, ✉ 1000, ℘ 511 08 88, Fax 513 69 27 – AE ① E VISA JY q
Meals *(closed Monday and 15 January-20 February)* – a la carte approx. 1000 – **22 rm** 2500/3100.

La Maison du Cygne, Grand'Place 9, ✉ 1000, ℘ 511 82 44, Fax 514 31 48, « Former 17C guildhouse » – AE ① E VISA JCB JY w
closed Saturday lunch, Sunday, first 3 weeks August and late December – **Meals** *Lunch 1400* – a la carte 1350/2000.

Les 4 Saisons - (at Royal Windsor H.), 1st floor, r. Homme Chrétien 2, ✉ 1000, ℘ 505 55 55, Telex 62905, Fax 505 55 00 – AE ① E VISA JCB JYZ f
closed Saturday lunch and 19 July-17 August – **Meals** *Lunch 1490* – 1690/2290, – a la carte 2000/2800
Spec. Terrine de foie d'oie au naturel, Sole pochée à la crème d'écrevisses et duxelles, Filet d'agneau gratiné au fromage de brebis et salpicon d'abats au jus.

Aux Armes de Bruxelles, r. Bouchers 13, ✉ 1000, ℘ 511 55 98, Fax 514 33 81, Brussels atmosphere, open until 11 p.m. – AE ① E VISA JCB JY t
closed Monday and 15 June-15 July – **Meals** *Lunch 495* – 995/1695.

La Tête d'Or, r. Tête d'Or 9, ✉ 1000, ℘ 511 02 01, Fax 502 44 91, « Ancient Brussels residence » – AE ① E VISA JY u
closed Saturday and Sunday – **Meals** 990/1495.

Falstaff Gourmand, r. Pierres 38, ✉ 1000, ℘ 512 17 61, Fax 512 17 61, Open until 11 p.m ; – AE ① E VISA JCB JY m
closed Sunday dinner, Monday, Bank Holidays and last 3 weeks July – **Meals** *Lunch 495* – a la carte 1050/1400.

L'Ogenblik, Galerie des Princes 1, ✉ 1000, ℘ 511 61 51, Fax 513 41 58, Open until midnight, « Ancient pub interior" – AE ① E VISA JCB JY p
closed Sunday – **Meals** a la carte 1700/2400.

La Roue d'Or, r. Chapeliers 26, ✉ 1000, ℘ 514 25 54, Fax 512 30 81, Open until midnight, « Typical ancient Brussels pub » – AE ① E VISA JY y
closed Saturday, Sunday and 19 July-19 August – **Meals** *Lunch 325* – a la carte 1100/

't Kelderke, Grand'Place 15, ✉ 1000, ℘ 513 73 44, Fax 512 30 81, Brussels atmosphere, open until 2 a.m., « Pub in a vaulted cellar » – AE ① E VISA JY i
Meals *Lunch 275* – a la carte 800/1200.

Taverne du Passage, Galerie de la Reine 30, ✉ 1000, ℘ 512 37 32, Fax 511 08 82, Brussels atmosphere, open until midnight – AE ① E VISA JY r
closed Wednesday and Thursday in June and July – **Meals** a la carte 950/1400.

Quartier Ste-Catherine (Marché-aux-Poissons)

Atlas without rest, r. Vieux Marché-aux-Grains 30, ✉ 1000, ℘ 502 60 06, Fax 502 69 35 – 40. AE ① E VISA ER a
83 rm 4900, 5 suites.

Astrid M without rest, pl. du Samedi 11, ✉ 1000, ℘ 219 31 19, Fax 219 31 70 – 25-120. AE ① E VISA JY b
100 rm 3000/5500.

Ibis Ste-Catherine without rest, r. Joseph Plateau 2, ✉ 1000, ℘ 513 76 20, Fax 514 22 14 – 25-80. AE ① E VISA JCB JY a
235 rm 3550/3800.

La Sirène d'Or, pl. Ste-Catherine 1a, ✉ 1000, ℘ 513 51 98, Fax 502 13 05, Seafood – AE ① E VISA JCB ER g
closed Sunday, Monday, first 3 weeks September and 24 December-1 January – **Meals** *Lunch 950* – 950/1500.

La Truite d'Argent and H. Welcome with rm, quai au Bois-à-Brûler 23, ✉ 1000, ☎ 219 95 46, Fax 217 18 87, – rest. JY h
Meals (Seafood, open until 11.30 p.m.) *(closed Saturday lunch and Sunday except Bank Holidays, 10 to 18 August and Christmas-13 January)* Lunch 980 – 1540 – 250 – **6 rm** 2300/3200.

François, quai aux Briques 2, ✉ 1000, ☎ 511 60 89, Fax 512 06 67, Oyster bar, seafood – . JY k
closed Monday – **Meals** Lunch 995 – a la carte 1600/2400.

La Belle Maraîchère, pl. Ste-Catherine 11, ✉ 1000, ☎ 512 97 59, Fax 513 76 91, Seafood – . JY k
closed Wednesday and Thursday – **Meals** Lunch 950 – 950/1700.

Le Loup-Galant, quai aux Barques 4, ✉ 1000, ☎ 219 99 98, Fax 219 99 98, –
closed Saturday lunch, Sunday, Monday dinner, Bank Holidays, 1 week Easter, 1 to 15 August and 24 to 31 December – **Meals** Lunch 450 – 1000 b.i./1390. EQ a

Quartier des Sablons

Jolly du Grand Sablon M, r. Bodenbroek 2, ✉ 1000, ☎ 512 88 00, Telex 20397, Fax 512 67 66 – – 25-100. KZ p
Meals (Residents only) – **195 rm** 7800/10200, 6 suites.

Alfa Sablon M without rest, r. Paille 4, ✉ 1000, ☎ 513 60 40, Fax 511 81 41, – . KZ t
28 rm 8600, 4 suites.

L'Écailler du Palais Royal (Basso), r. Bodenbroek 18, ✉ 1000, ☎ 512 87 51, Fax 511 99 50, Seafood – . KZ r
closed Sunday, Bank Holidays, 28 March-5 April and 1 to 30 August – **Meals** a la carte 2700/3000
Spec. Bouillabaisse de poissons des côtes du Nord, Tronçon de turbot aux herbes aromatiques, Homard au Sauvignon.

Au Duc d'Arenberg, pl. du Petit Sablon 9, ✉ 1000, ☎ 511 14 75, Fax 512 92 92, « Collection of modern paintings » – KZ a
closed Sunday, Bank Holidays and last week December – **Meals** Lunch 1450 – a la carte 1950/2350.

"Chez Marius" En Provence, pl. du Petit Sablon 1, ✉ 1000, ☎ 511 12 08, Fax 512 27 89 – KZ s
closed Sunday, Bank Holidays and 15 July-15 August – **Meals** Lunch 850 – 1100/2000.

Castello Banfi, r. Bodenbroek 12, ✉ 1000, ☎ 512 87 94, Fax 512 87 94, Partly Italian cuisine – . KZ q
closed Sunday dinner, Monday, 1 week Easter, last 3 weeks August and late December – **Meals** Lunch 950 – 1595.

Lola, pl. du Grand Sablon 33, ✉ 1000, ☎ 514 24 60, Open until 11.30 p.m. – . JZ c
Meals a la carte 850/1400.

La Clef des Champs, r. Rollebeek 23, ✉ 1000, ☎ 512 11 93, Fax 513 89 49, – . JZ k
closed Sunday and Monday – **Meals** 990/1250.

Quartier Palais de Justice

Hilton, bd de Waterloo 38, ✉ 1000, ☎ 504 11 11, Telex 22744, Fax 504 21 11, ≤ *town*, – – 45-600. FS s
Meals see rest ***Maison du Bœuf*** below – ***Café d'Egmont*** Lunch 1040 - 1040 – 640 – **421 rm** 9500/12900, 7 suites.

Maison du Bœuf - (at Hilton H.), 1st floor, bd de Waterloo 38, ✉ 1000, ☎ 504 11 11, Telex 22744, Fax 504 21 11, ≤ – . FS s
Meals Lunch 1650 – a la carte approx. 2600
Spec. Fantaisie de crevettes de la mer du Nord, Train de côtes de bœuf américain rôti en croûte de sel, Tartare de la Maison du Bœuf.

L'anecdote, r. Grand Cerf 16, ✉ 1000, ☎ 511 72 42, Fax 512 17 35 – FS n
closed Sunday, Bank Holidays and 21 July-16 August – **Meals** Lunch 570 – 690/1080.

Les Larmes du Tigre, r. Wynants 21, ✉ 1000, ☎ 512 18 77, Fax 502 10 03, Thai cuisine – ES p
closed Saturday lunch – **Meals** Lunch 395 – a la carte 900/1300.

Casa Manolo, r. Haute 165, ✉ 1000, ☎ 513 21 68, Fax 513 35 24, Partly Spanish cuisine, open until midnight – JZ a
closed Wednesday – **Meals** Lunch 325 – a la carte 900/1450.

Quartier Léopold *(see also at Ixelles)*

Stanhope, r. Commerce 9, ✉ 1000, ✆ 506 91 11, Fax 512 17 08, « Town house with walled terrace », – AE E VISA JCB. KZ v
Meals *(closed Saturday, Sunday and Bank Holidays)* Lunch 1350 – a la carte 1450/2600 – **35 rm** 9500/12500, 15 suites.

Renaissance M, r. Parnasse 19, ✉ 1050, ✆ 505 29 29, Fax 505 22 55, – – 25-360. AE E VISA JCB. GS e
Meals (buffet with partly Asian cuisine, open until 11 p.m.) *Lunch 790* – a la carte approx. 1300 – 650 – **238 rm** 8000/9000, 19 suites.

Quartier Louise *(see also at Ixelles and at St-Gilles)*

Conrad, av. Louise 71, ✉ 1050, ✆ 542 42 42, Fax 542 42 00, « Hotel complex around an early 20C mansion », – – 25-650. AE E VISA JCB FS f
Meals see rest ***La Maison de Maître*** below – ***Café Wiltcher's*** (buffet, open until 11 p.m.) *Lunch 1050* - a la carte approx. 1600 – 900 – **254 rm** 13000/14000, 15 suites.

Bristol Stéphanie M, av. Louise 91, ✉ 1050, ✆ 543 33 11, Telex 25558, Fax 538 03 07, – – 25-215. AE E VISA JCB
Meals (Scandinavian cuisine) *(closed Saturday lunch, Sunday dinner and 19 July-19 August)* *Lunch 990* – 1195/1395 – 540 – **139 rm** 7950/9950, 2 suites. FT g

Mayfair, av. Louise 381, ✉ 1050, ✆ 649 98 00, Fax 649 22 49 – – 30-60. AE E VISA JCB. rest FV a
Meals see rest ***Taishin*** below – ***Louis XVI*** *(closed Saturday)* *Lunch 380* - a la carte approx. 1300 – 580 – **97 rm** 8200, 2 suites.

Clubhouse without rest, r. Blanche 4, ✉ 1000, ✆ 537 92 10, Fax 537 00 18 – – 30. AE E VISA JCB FT h
80 rm 5400/6900, 1 suite.

L'Agenda without rest, r. Florence 6, ✉ 1000, ✆ 539 00 31, Fax 539 00 63 – AE E VISA JCB FT j
300 – **38 rm** 3300/3600.

La Maison de Maître - (at Conrad H.), av. Louise 71, ✉ 1050, ✆ 542 47 16, Fax 542 48 42 – AE E VISA JCB FS f
closed Saturday lunch, Sunday, Bank Holidays and 1 to 20 August – **Meals** *Lunch 1350* – 1650/2550, – a la carte 2450/3100
Spec. Cappuccino de champignons des bois aux langoustines (15 September-1 March), Bar de ligne en croûte de sel, beurre nantais à la citronelle, Poularde en demi-deuil, cuite en vessie.

La Porte des Indes, av. Louise 455, ✉ 1050, ✆ 647 86 51, Fax 640 30 59, Indian cuisine, « Exotic decor » – AE E VISA FV c
closed Sunday lunch – **Meals** *Lunch 650* – a la carte 1150/1950.

Taishin - (at Mayfair H.), av. Louise 381, ✉ 1050, ✆ 647 84 04, Japanese cuisine – AE E VISA JCB. FV a
closed Sunday – **Meals** *Lunch 450* – 1500/3000.

Tagawa, av. Louise 279, ✉ 1050, ✆ 640 50 95, Fax [illegible], Japanese cuisine – AE E VISA JCB. FU e
closed Saturday lunch, Sunday, Bank Holidays, 23 December-3 January and after 8.30 p.m. – **Meals** *Lunch 390* – a la carte 1050/1900.

Quartier Bois de la Cambre

Villa Lorraine (Van de Casserie), av. du Vivier d'Oie 75, ✉ 1000, ✆ 374 31 63, Fax 372 01 95, « Terrace » – AE E VISA JCB GX w
closed Sunday and 3 weeks July – **Meals** *Lunch 1750* – 3000, a la carte 2650/3650
Spec. Nage d'écrevisses à l'orge perlé (April-December), Rouget-barbet au cresson et tapenade, Râble de lièvre clouté aux truffes (15 October-10 January).

La Truffe Noire, bd de la Cambre 12, ✉ 1000, ✆ 640 44 22, Fax 647 97 04, « Elegant interior » – AE E VISA GV x
closed Saturday lunch, Sunday, 1 week Easter, last 2 weeks August and 1 to 9 January – **Meals** *Lunch 1975 b.i.* – 2100, a la carte approx. 3200
Spec. Carpaccio aux truffes, Truffe à la croque au sel et ses grillettes, St-Pierre aux poireaux et truffes.

Quartier Botanique, Gare du Nord *(see also at St-Josse-ten-Noode)*

Sheraton Towers, pl. Rogier 3, ✉ 1210, ✆ 224 31 11, Telex 26887, Fax 224 34 56, – – 25-600. AE E VISA JCB FQ n
Meals see rest ***Les Comtes de Flandre*** below – ***Crescendo*** (open until 11 p.m.) *Lunch 650* - a la carte 1050/1650 – 750 – **464 rm** 8450/9450, 42 suites.

Président World Trade Center, bd E. Jacqmain 180, ✉ 1000, ☎ 203 20 20, Fax 203 24 40, ... - 25-350. AE ⓓ E VISA JCB FQ d
Meals (lunch only) 990/1290 - **286 rm** 7500/8500, 16 suites.

Le Dome with annex Le Dome II Ⓜ, bd du Jardin Botanique 12, ✉ 1000, ☎ 218 06 80, Fax 218 41 12, ... - 25-100. AE ⓓ E VISA JCB FQ m
Meals *(closed Sunday)* Lunch 650 - a la carte 900/1500 - **125 rm** 7000/8400.

Président Nord without rest, bd A. Max 107, ✉ 1000, ☎ 219 00 60, Telex 61417, Fax 218 12 69 - ... AE ⓓ E VISA JCB. FQ k
63 rm 3900/5900.

Les Comtes de Flandre - (at Sheraton Towers H.), pl. Rogier 3, ✉ 1210, ☎ 224 31 11, Telex 26887, Fax 224 34 56 - ... AE ⓓ E VISA JCB FQ n
closed Saturday, Sunday and August - **Meals** Lunch 1250 - 1950.

Quartier Atomium (Centenaire - Trade Mart - Laeken)

Les Baguettes Impériales (Mme Ma), av. J. Sobieski 70, ✉ 1020, ☎ 479 67 32, Fax 479 67 32, ..., Partly Vietnamese cuisine, « Terrace » - ... AE ⓓ E VISA.
closed Tuesday, Sunday dinner, 2 weeks Easter and August - **Meals** a la carte 1800/2500
Spec. Mï au homard, Mangue chaude à la crème de soja, Pigeonneau farci aux nids d'hirondelle.

Ming Dynasty, av. de l'Esplanade BP 9, ✉ 1020, ☎ 475 23 45, Fax 475 23 50, Chinese cuisine, open until 11 p.m. - ... AE ⓓ E VISA
closed Saturday lunch, Sunday and mid July-mid August - **Meals** Lunch 750 - a la carte 950/1500.

Le Centenaire, av. J. Sobieski 84, ✉ 1020, ☎ 478 66 23, Fax 478 66 23 - AE ⓓ E VISA JCB
closed Sunday, Monday, July and Christmas-New Year - **Meals** Lunch 695 - 995/1550.

Lychee, r. De Wand 118, ✉ 1020, ☎ 268 19 14, Fax 268 19 14, Chinese cuisine, open until 11 p.m. - ... AE ⓓ E VISA
closed 15 July-15 August - **Meals** Lunch 325 - a la carte approx. 1000.

Adrienne Atomium, Square Atomium, ✉ 1020, ☎ 478 30 00, Fax (0 10) 68 80 41, ※ *town*, Buffets - AE ⓓ E VISA
closed Sunday and July - **Meals** Lunch 690 - 840.

ANDERLECHT

Le Prince de Liège, chaussée de Ninove 664, ✉ 1070, ☎ 522 16 00, Fax 520 81 85 - ... - 25. AE ⓓ E VISA
Meals *(closed Sunday dinner and 10 July-7 August)* Lunch 545 - 845/1325 - **32 rm** 1950/2950.

Ustel, Square de l'Aviation 6, ✉ 1070, ☎ 520 60 53, Fax 520 33 28 - ... - 30. AE E VISA. ES c
Meals *(closed Saturday lunch, Sunday and July)* Lunch 325 - a la carte 950/1250 - **64 rm** 3600/4300.

Erasme, rte de Lennik 790, ✉ 1070, ☎ 523 62 82, Fax 523 62 83, ... rest ... - 25-80. AE ⓓ E VISA
closed 1 to 15 August - **Meals** (Pub rest) Lunch 395 - a la carte approx. 900 - **52 rm** 2950

Saint-Guidon 2nd floor, av. Théo Verbeeck 2 (in the Constant Vanden Stock stadium), ✉ 1070, ☎ 520 55 36, Fax 523 38 27 - ... - 25-500. ⓓ E VISA JCB.
closed Saturday, Sunday, Bank Holidays, first league match days, July and Christmas-New Year - **Meals** (lunch only) 1295/2000 b.i..

Alain Cornelis, av. Paul Janson 82, ✉ 1070, ☎ 523 20 83, Fax 523 20 83, ... - AE ⓓ E VISA
closed Saturday lunch, Sunday, Bank Holidays, 20 July-18 August and 24 December-5 January - **Meals** Lunch 870 - a la carte approx. 1700.

La Brouette, bd Prince de Liège 61, ✉ 1070, ☎ 522 51 69, Fax 522 51 69 - AE ⓓ E VISA
closed Saturday lunch, Sunday dinner, Monday and July
Meals Lunch 850 - 990/1600.

La Paix r. Ropsy-Chaudron 49 (opposite the slaughterhouse), ✉ 1070, ☎ 523 09 58 Fax 520 10 39, Pub rest - AE E VISA
closed Saturday, Sunday and last 3 weeks July - **Meals** (lunch only except Friday) a la carte 1000/1400.

AUDERGHEM (OUDERGEM)

La Grignotière (Chanson), chaussée de Wavre 2041, ✉ 1160, ☎ 672 81 85 Fax 672 81 85 - AE ⓓ E VISA
closed Sunday, Monday, Bank Holidays and August - **Meals** Lunch 1350 - 1750/1900
Spec. St-Jacques grillées aux orties et jus de truffes (October-March), Filet de sandre rôti et ragoût de lentilles aux saveurs balsamiques, Pigeonneau à la sauge, mousseline de pois frais (21 March- 21 June).

L'Abbaye de Rouge Cloître, r. Rouge Cloître 8, 1160, 672 45 25, Fax 660 12 01, « On the edge of a forest » – – 25-45. AE E VISA
closed Saturday, Sunday dinner and 22 December-6 January – **Meals** *Lunch 890* – 890.

La Citronnelle, chaussée de Wavre 1377, 1160, 672 98 43, Fax 672 98 43, Vietnamese cuisine – AE E VISA
closed Monday, Saturday lunch and last 2 weeks August – **Meals** *Lunch 420* – a la carte approx. 900.

ETTERBEEK

Stirwen, chaussée St-Pierre 15, 1040, 640 85 41, Fax 648 43 08 – AE E VISA JCB
closed Saturday lunch, Sunday, 2 weeks August and 2 weeks December – **Meals** *Lunch 950* – a la carte 1650/2450 GS a
Spec. Tête de veau ravigote, Joue de bœuf braisée à la bourguignonne, Fricassée de chipirons à la basquaise.

Quartier Cinquantenaire (Montgomery)

Park without rest, av. de l'Yser 21, 1040, 735 74 00, Fax 735 19 67, – – 25. AE E VISA JCB HS c
51 rm 6100/7500.

Le Serpolet, av. de Tervuren 59, 1040, 736 17 01, Fax 736 67 85, – AE E VISA HS b
closed Saturday lunch and dinner Sunday and Monday – **Meals** – 995/1750.

La Fontaine de Jade, av. de Tervuren 5, 1040, 736 32 10, Fax 732 46 86, Chinese cuisine, open until 11 p.m. – AE E VISA HS a
closed Tuesday – **Meals** *Lunch 680* – 950/1750.

Momotaro, av. d'Auderghem 106, 1040, 734 06 64, Fax 734 64 18, Japanese cuisine with sushi-bar – AE E VISA. GS f
closed Sunday and 4 to 17 August – **Meals** *Lunch 395* – a la carte 900/1500.

EVERE

Belson without rest, chaussée de Louvain 805, 1140, 705 20 30, Fax 705 20 43 – – 25. AE E VISA JCB.
625 – **131 rm** 3650/8700, 3 suites.

Mercure, av. J. Bordet 74, 1140, 726 73 35, Telex 65460, Fax 726 82 95, – – 25-120. AE E VISA JCB
Meals *(closed lunch Saturday and Sunday)* – a la carte approx. 1200 – 560 – **113 rm** 4100/5750, 7 suites.

Evergreen without rest, av. V. Day 1, 1140, 726 70 15, Fax 726 62 60 – . AE E VISA
20 rm 2200/3350.

FOREST (VORST)

De Fierlant without rest, r. De Fierlant 67, 1190, 538 60 70, Fax 538 91 99 –
closed 23 December-5 January – **40 rm** 2000/2300.

GANSHOREN

Bruneau, av. Broustin 75, 1083, 427 69 78, Fax 425 97 26, « Terrace » – . AE E VISA
closed holiday Thursdays, Tuesday dinner, Wednesday, 31 July-27 August and 1 to 10 February – **Meals** *Lunch 1975* – 2950/4250, a la carte 2500/3200
Spec. Coussinet de raie aux pinces de homard, Jalousie de ris de veau croustillant, Aile de poulette de Bresse Belle-Alliance.

Claude Dupont, av. Vital Riethuisen 46, 1083, 426 00 00, Fax 426 65 40 – AE E VISA
closed Monday, Tuesday and early July-early August – **Meals** *Lunch 1775* – 2175 a la carte 1900/2700
Spec. Petitenage d'écrevisses à l'émulsion de cerfeuil (June-January), Les poissons de la mer du Nord en bouillabaisse, Canette des bois aux pêches (June-September).

San Daniele, av. Charles-Quint 6, 1083, 426 79 23, Fax 426 92 14, Partly Italian cuisine – . AE E VISA JCB
closed Sunday, Monday dinner and 15 July-15 August – **Meals** a la carte 1250/2100.

Cambrils 1st floor, av. Charles-Quint 365, 1083, 465 35 82, Fax 465 76 63, – . AE E VISA
closed dinner Monday and Thursday, Sunday and 15 July-15 August – **Meals** *Lunch 890* – 890/1190.

IXELLES (ELSENE)

Yen, r. Lesbroussart 49, ✉ 1050, ✆ 649 07 47, Vietnamese cuisine, open until 11 p.m. – AE ⓓ E VISA. FU f
closed Sunday – **Meals** *Lunch 320* – a la carte 800/1150.

Quartier Boondael (University)

Le Couvert d'Argent, pl. Marie-José 9, ✉ 1050, ✆ 648 45 45, Fax 648 22 28, « Elegant pavilion in garden » – P. AE ⓓ E VISA JCB GX y
closed Sunday and Monday – **Meals** *Lunch 990* – 990/2200.

L'Aub. de Boendael, square du Vieux Tilleul 12, ✉ 1050, ✆ 672 70 55, Fax 660 75 82, Grill rest, Rustic – P. AE ⓓ E VISA HX h
closed Saturday, Sunday, Bank Holidays, 26 July-17 August and 20 December-4 January – **Meals** 1375 b.i..

La Pagode d'Or, chaussée de Boondael 332, ✉ 1050, ✆ 649 06 56, Fax 646 54 75, Vietnamese cuisine, open until 11 p.m. – AE ⓓ E VISA. GV m
Meals *Lunch 350* – 890/1350.

La Brasserie Marebœuf, av. de la Couronne 445, ✉ 1050, ✆ 648 99 06, Fax 648 38 30, Open until midnight – AE ⓓ E VISA GHV t
closed Sunday – **Meals** *Lunch 550* – 895.

Quartier Bascule

Capital M, chaussée de Vleurgat 191, ✉ 1050, ✆ 646 64 20, Fax 646 33 14, – rest TV – 25-40. AE ⓓ E VISA JCB. rm FU c
Meals (Pub-rest) *Lunch 480* – a la carte 1100/1550 – **62 rm** 3600/3900.

La Mosaïque, r. Forestière 23, ✉ 1050, ✆ 649 02 35, Fax 647 11 49, – P. AE ⓓ E VISA FU p
closed Saturday lunch, Sunday, Bank Holidays, 30 March-6 April, 15 August-7 September and 24 to 30 December – **Meals** *Lunch 1200 b.i.* – 1350/1700.

Le Flagrant Délice, pl. Leemans 10, ✉ 1050, ✆ 538 40 21, Fax 534 32 70 – AE ⓓ E VISA. FU m
closed Sunday and Monday – **Meals** *Lunch 1100* – a la carte 2000/2600.

Maison Félix 1st floor, r. Washington 149 (square Henri Michaux), ✉ 1050, ✆ 345 66 93, Fax 344 92 85 – AE ⓓ E VISA. FV s
closed Sunday, Monday, last 2 weeks July and first week January – **Meals** *Lunch 900* – 1500/1900.

Quartier Léopold *(see also at Bruxelles)*

Leopold, r. Luxembourg 35, ✉ 1050, ✆ 511 18 28, Fax 514 19 39, – TV – 25-60. AE ⓓ E VISA. FS y
Meals ***Les Anges*** *(closed Saturday lunch and Sunday)* *Lunch 1300* - a la carte 1500/2000 – **88 rm** 4450/5650.

Quartier Louise *(see also at Bruxelles and at St-Gilles)*

Sofitel without rest, av. de la Toison d'Or 40, ✉ 1050, ✆ 514 22 00, Fax 514 57 44 – TV – 25-120. AE ⓓ E VISA JCB FS t
750 – **171 rm** 12000.

Mövenpick Cadettt M, r. Paul Spaak 15, ✉ 1000, ✆ 645 61 11, Fax 646 63 44, – TV – 25-40. AE ⓓ E VISA JCB FU k
Meals (open until 11 p.m.) a la carte approx. 1100 – 500 – **128 rm** 5250.

Beau-Site without rest, r. Longue Haie 76, ✉ 1000, ✆ 640 88 89, Fax 640 16 11 – TV. AE ⓓ E VISA FT r
38 rm 3450/3950.

Argus without rest, r. Capitaine Crespel 6, ✉ 1050, ✆ 514 07 70, Fax 514 12 22 – TV. AE ⓓ E VISA – **41 rm** 3200/3500. FS t

Les Perles de Pluie, r. Châtelain 25, ✉ 1050, ✆ 649 67 23, Fax 644 07 60, Thai cuisine, open until 11 p.m. – AE ⓓ E VISA FU r
closed Saturday lunch – **Meals** *Lunch 450* – 890/1250.

MOLENBEEK-ST-JEAN (SINT-JANS-MOLENBEEK)

Le Béarnais, bd Louis Mettewie 318, ✉ 1080, ✆ 411 51 51, Fax 410 70 81 – AE ⓓ E VISA
closed Sunday, Monday dinner and last week July-first week August – **Meals** *Lunch 1090* – a la carte approx. 1900.

ST-GILLES (SINT-GILLIS)

Inada, r. Source 73, ✉ 1060, ✆ 538 01 13, Fax 538 01 13 – AE ⓓ E VISA ET a
closed Saturday lunch, Sunday, Monday, Bank Holidays and 15 July-August – **Meals** *Lunch 720* – a la carte 1550/2450.

XX **Le Forcado,** chaussée de Charleroi 192, ✉ 1060, ✆ 537 92 20, Fax 537 92 20, 余, Portuguese cuisine – ▤. AE ⓓ E VISA EFU a
closed Sunday, Bank Holidays, carnival week and August – **Meals** a la carte approx. 1300.

X **La Mamounia,** av. Porte de Hal 9, ✉ 1060, ✆ 537 73 22, Fax 539 39 59, Moroccan cuisine, open until 11 p.m. – AE ⓓ E VISA JCB ES n
closed Monday except Bank Holidays and 15 July-15 August – **Meals** *Lunch 495* – 745/1295.

Quartier Louise *(see also at Bruxelles and at Ixelles)*

Holiday Inn City Centre, chaussée de Charleroi 38, ✉ 1060, ✆ 533 66 66, Fax 538 90 14 – ▤ ☎ – 25-250. AE ⓓ E VISA. FT m
Meals a la carte 1000/1400 – 600 – **201 rm** 7300.

Manos Stephanie without rest, chaussée de Charleroi 28, ✉ 1060, ✆ 539 02 50, Fax 537 57 29, « Mansion with particular atmosphere » – ▤ ☎. AE ⓓ E VISA JCB FS f
48 rm 6450/7850, 7 suites.

Manos without rest, chaussée de Charleroi 102, ✉ 1060, ✆ 537 96 82, Fax 539 36 55, – ☎ – 25. AE ⓓ E VISA JCB FU w
500 – **35 rm** 3600/5500, 3 suites.

Cascade Ⓜ without rest, r. Berckmans 128, ✉ 1060, ✆ 538 88 30, Fax 538 92 79 – ▤ ☎ – 25. AE ⓓ E VISA. ES r
80 rm 2800/7000.

Tulip Inn Delta, chaussée de Charleroi 17, ✉ 1060, ✆ 539 01 60, Telex 63225, Fax 537 90 11 – ☎ – 25-100. AE ⓓ E VISA JCB. FS w
Meals *Lunch 445* – a la carte approx. 900 – **246 rm** 5500/6500.

Diplomat without rest, r. Jean Stas 32, ✉ 1060, ✆ 537 42 50, Fax 539 33 79 – ☎. AE ⓓ E VISA JCB. FS v
68 rm 5500/6500.

XX **I Trulli,** r. Jourdan 18, ✉ 1060, ✆ 538 98 20, Fax 537 79 30, 余, Partly Italian cuisine, open until midnight – AE ⓓ E VISA JCB FS c
closed Sunday, 11 to 31 July and 22 December-1 January – **Meals** *Lunch 445* – a la carte 1450/2050.

ST-JOSSE-TEN-NOODE (SINT-JOOST-TEN-NODE)

Quartier Botanique *(see also at Bruxelles)*

Royal Crown Gd H. Mercure, r. Royale 250, ✉ 1210, ✆ 220 66 11, Fax 217 84 44, – ▤ ☎ Ⓟ – 25-350. AE ⓓ E VISA JCB FQ r
Meals see rest ***Hugo's*** below – 650 – **304 rm** 7000/9000, 5 suites.

Palace, r. Gineste 3, ✉ 1210, ✆ 203 62 00, Fax 203 55 55 – ▤ ☎ – 25-450. AE ⓓ E VISA JCB. FQ v
Meals ***Le Temps Présent*** *(closed August) Lunch 750* - a la carte 1000/1500 – **359 rm** 6400/7400, 1 suite.

New Siru, pl. Rogier 1, ✉ 1210, ✆ 203 35 80, Telex 21722, Fax 203 33 03, « Each room decorated by a contemporary Belgian artist » – ▤ rest ☎ – 25-100. AE FQ p
Meals (Brasserie) *(closed Sunday and Bank Holidays) Lunch* [illegible] – a la carte approx. 1200 –
101 rm 2900/5900.

Albert Premier without rest, pl. Rogier 20, ✉ 1210, ✆ 203 31 25, Telex 27111, Fax 203 43 31 – ☎ – 25-60. AE ⓓ E VISA FQ q
285 rm 2500/3500.

XXX **Hugo's** - (at Royal Crown Gd H. Mercure), r. Royale 250, ✉ 1210, ✆ 220 66 11, Fax 217 84 44 – ▤ Ⓟ. AE ⓓ E VISA JCB FQ r
closed Saturday, Sunday and mid July-mid August – **Meals** *Lunch 1000* – a la carte 1400/2500.

XX **De Ultieme Hallucinatie,** r. Royale 316, ✉ 1210, ✆ 217 06 14, Fax 217 72 40, « Art Nouveau interior » – Ⓟ. AE ⓓ E VISA. FQ t
closed Saturday lunch, Sunday, Bank Holidays and 20 July-18 August – **Meals** *Lunch 950* – 1450/2750 b.i..

X **Les Dames Tartine,** chaussée de Haecht 58, ✉ 1210, ✆ 218 45 49, Fax 218 45 49 – AE ⓓ E VISA. FQ s
closed Saturday lunch, Sunday and Monday – **Meals** *Lunch 750* – 990.

SCHAERBEEK (SCHAARBEEK)

Quartier Meiser

Lambermont (with annex) without rest, bd Lambermont 322, ✉ 1030, ✆ 242 55 95, Fax 215 36 13 – ☎. AE ⓓ E VISA
69 rm 3400/3900.

XX **Le Cadre Noir,** av. Milcamps 158, ✉ 1030, ☎ 734 14 45, Seafood – AE ⓓ E VISA HR v
closed Saturday lunch, Sunday dinner and Monday – **Meals** 885/1280.

X **Amici miei,** bd. Gén. Wahis 248, ✉ 1030, ☎ 705 49 80, Fax 705 29 65, Italian cuisine – AE ⓓ E VISA HQ k
closed Saturday lunch, Sunday and late July-early August – **Meals** a la carte 1000/1450.

UCCLE (UKKEL)

County House, square des Héros 2, ✉ 1180, ☎ 375 44 20, Fax 375 31 22 – rest TV ☎ – 25-140. AE ⓓ E VISA. EX b
Meals a la carte approx. 1500 – **83 rm** 4200/5800, 16 suites.

XXX **Les Frères Romano,** av. de Fré 182, ✉ 1180, ☎ 374 70 98, Fax 374 04 18, – P. AE ⓓ E VISA FX d
closed Sunday, Bank Holidays and last 3 weeks August – **Meals** *Lunch 975* – a la carte approx. 1600.

XX **L'Amandier,** av. de Fré 184, ✉ 1180, ☎ 374 03 95, Fax 374 86 92, , Open until 11 p.m., « Terrace overlooking a garden » – AE ⓓ E VISA FX e
closed Saturday lunch – **Meals** a la carte 1250/1650.

XX **Villa d'Este,** r. Etoile 142, ✉ 1180, ☎ 376 48 48, , « Terrace » – P. AE ⓓ E VISA
closed Sunday dinner, Monday, July and late December – **Meals** *Lunch 990* – 990/1600 a la carte 1750/2200
Spec. Sole farcie aux poireaux, Fricassée de coquelet à la moutarde de Meaux, Suprême de turbotin au basilic (21 March-21 September).

XX **La Cité du Dragon,** chaussée de Waterloo 1024, ✉ 1180, ☎ 375 80 80, Fax 375 69 77, , Chinese cuisine, open until 11 p.m., « Exotic garden with fountains » – P. AE ⓓ E VISA GX c
Meals *Lunch 565* – a la carte approx. 1000.

XX **Blue Elephant,** chaussée de Waterloo 1120, ✉ 1180, ☎ 374 49 62, Fax 375 44 68, Thaï cuisine, « Exotic decor » – P. AE ⓓ E VISA GX
closed Saturday lunch – **Meals** *Lunch 850* – a la carte 1050/1650.

XX **Willy et Marianne,** chaussée d'Alsemberg 705, ✉ 1180, ☎ 343 60 09 – AE ⓓ E VISA EX
closed Tuesday dinner, Wednesday, 2 weeks carnival and 2 weeks July – **Meals** *Lunch 450* – 995.

X **De Hoef,** r. Edith Cavell 218, ✉ 1180, ☎ 374 34 17, Fax 375 30 84, , Grill rest, « 17C inn » – AE ⓓ E VISA FX c
closed 10 to 31 July – **Meals** *Lunch 395* – 795.

X **Brasseries Georges,** av. Winston Churchill 259, ✉ 1180, ☎ 347 21 00, Fax 344 02 45, , Oyster bar, open until midnight – . AE ⓓ E VISA FV r
Meals a la carte 1100/1450.

WATERMAEL-BOITSFORT (WATERMAAL-BOSVOORDE)

XX **Host. des 3 Tilleuls** with rm, Berensheide 8, ✉ 1170, ☎ 672 30 14, Fax 673 65 52 – TV ☎ . AE ⓓ E VISA JCB. rm
Meals *(closed Sunday and 15 July-15 August)* 1100 – **7 rm** 3250/4350.

XX **Les Rives du Gange** with rm, av. de la Fauconnerie 1, ✉ 1170, ☎ 672 16 01 Telex 62661, Fax 672 43 30, – TV ☎. AE ⓓ E VISA
Meals (Indian cuisine, open until 11.30 p.m.) *Lunch 595* – 990 – **19 rm** 2480/3480.

XX **Au Vieux Boitsfort,** pl. Bischoffsheim 9, ✉ 1170, ☎ 672 23 32, Fax 660 22 94, – AE ⓓ E VISA JCB
closed Saturday lunch and Sunday – **Meals** 1390/2390.

XX **Le Bellini,** pl. Eug. Keym 4, ✉ 1170, ☎ 673 83 83, Fax 662 07 07 – AE ⓓ E VISA
closed Saturday lunch, Sunday dinner, Monday, 2 weeks August, Christmas and New Year – **Meals** *Lunch 690* – 1000/1500. HV

X **L'Entre-Temps,** r. Philippe Dewolfs 7, ✉ 1170, ☎ 672 87 20, Fax 672 87 20, , Brasserie – AE ⓓ E VISA
closed Tuesday dinner, Wednesday and 21 July-15 August – **Meals** *Lunch 490* – a la carte 900/1250.

X **La Maison de Thaïlande,** r. Middelbourg 22, ✉ 1170, ☎ 672 26 57, Fax 672 26 57, , Thaï cuisine – AE ⓓ E VISA
closed lunch Saturday and Sunday, Tuesday and July – **Meals** *Lunch 720* – a la carte approx. 1000.

WOLUWÉ-ST-LAMBERT (SINT-LAMBRECHTS-WOLUWE)

Sodehotel La Woluwe M, av. E. Mounier 5, ✉ 1200, ℘ 775 21 11, Fax 770 47 80, – | TV ☎ – 25-200. AE VISA
Meals *Le Lidrus* *Lunch 1175* - a la carte approx. 1500 – 595 – **112 rm** 3800/8200, 8 suites.

Lambeau M without rest, av. Lambeau 150, ✉ 1200, ℘ 732 51 70, Fax 732 54 90 – TV ☎. AE VISA HR u
24 rm 1900/3100.

Mon Manège à Toi, r. Neerveld 1, ✉ 1200, ℘ 770 02 38, Fax 762 95 80, « Floral garden » – P. AE VISA
closed Saturday, Sunday, Bank Holidays, 7 to 31 July and 24 December-1 January – **Meals** a la carte approx. 2100.

Le Relais de la Woluwe, av. Georges Henri 1, ✉ 1200, ℘ 762 66 36, Fax 762 18 55, « Terrace and garden » – 25-80. AE VISA.
closed Saturday lunch, Sunday and 22 December-1 January – **Meals** 1650 b.i..

The Butterfly, chaussée de Stockel 294, ✉ 1200, ℘ 763 22 16, Fax 763 22 16 – AE VISA
closed Monday dinner and Tuesday – **Meals** *Lunch 495* – 950/1280.

WOLUWÉ-ST-PIERRE (SINT-PIETERS-WOLUWE)

Montgomery M, av. de Tervuren 134, ✉ 1150, ℘ 741 85 11, Fax 741 85 00, – | TV ☎ – 25. AE VISA JCB. HS k
Meals *(closed weekends, Bank Holidays, 21 July-17 August and 22 December-4 January)* *Lunch 1050* – 1790 – 450 – **61 rm** 9600/12300, 2 suites.

Des 3 Couleurs (Tourneur), av. de Tervuren 453, ✉ 1150, ℘ 770 33 21, Fax 770 80 45, « Terrace » – AE VISA
closed Saturday lunch, Sunday dinner, and mid August-mid September – **Meals** 2000, a la carte approx. 2100
Spec. Cassolette de langoustines aux petits légumes, sauce Champagne, Saumon Liliane, Crêpe Normande.

Le Vignoble de Margot 1st floor, r. Paul Wemaere 2, ✉ 1150, ℘ 779 23 23, Fax 779 05 45 – . AE VISA
closed Saturday lunch, Sunday, 21 July-16 August and 23 December-2 January – **Meals** *Lunch 695 b.i.* – 1395/2295, a la carte 1800/2300
Spec. Risotto de langoustines poêlées, Poularde à la broche, Croustillant d'amandes.

Le Mucha, av. Jules Dujardin 23, ✉ 1150, ℘ 770 24 14, Fax 770 24 14, , Partly Italian cuisine, open until 11 p.m. – AE VISA
closed Sunday and 1 to 23 September – **Meals** *Lunch 460* – 850/1250.

BRUSSELS ENVIRONS

at Diegem *Brussels-Zaventem motorway Diegem exit* C *Machelen pop. 11 516 – ✉ 1831 Diegem – 02 :*

Holiday Inn Airport, Holidaystraat 7 ℘ 720 58 65, Telex 24285, Fax 720 41 45, , , – | TV ☎ P – 25-400. AE VISA JCB. rest
[illegible] **310 rm** 8000

Sofitel Airport, Bessenveldstraat 15 ℘ 725 11 60, Fax 721 43 45, , , – TV ☎ P – 25-300. AE VISA.
Meals *Lunch 895* – a la carte 1150/1700 – 750 – **125 rm** 9500.

Novotel Airport, Olmenstraat ℘ 725 30 50, Fax 721 39 58, , – | TV ☎ P – 25-200. AE VISA JCB. rest
Meals (open until midnight) a la carte 900/1250 – 460 – **205 rm** 5150.

Rainbow Airport M, Berkenlaan 4 ℘ 721 77 77, Fax 721 55 96, – | TV ☎ P – 25-60. AE VISA JCB.
Meals *(closed Saturday and Sunday)* a la carte approx. 1000 – **100 rm** 4700.

Ibis Airport, Bessenveldstraat 17 ℘ 725 43 21, Fax 725 40 40, – | rest TV ☎ P – 25-60. AE VISA JCB. rest
Meals *Lunch 555* – 695 – **95 rm** 3100.

at Dilbeek *W : 7 km – pop. 37 418 – ✉ 1700 Dilbeek – 02 :*

Relais Delbeccha, Bodegemstraat 158 ℘ 569 44 30, Fax 569 75 30, , – TV ☎ P – 25-120. AE VISA.
closed Sunday dinner – **Meals** *Lunch 1025* – a la carte 1450/1800 – 450 – **12 rm** 3250/4025.

Host. d'Arconati with rm, d'Arconatistraat 77 ℘ 569 35 00, Fax 569 35 04, , « Floral terrace », – TV ☎ P – 60. AE VISA
Meals *(closed Sunday dinner, Monday, Tuesday, February and 1 week July)* *Lunch 975* – 1775 – **4 rm** *(closed February)* 2000/3000.

at Dworp *(Tourneppe) S : 16 km © Beersel pop. 22 715 – ✉ 1653 Dworp – ☎ 0 2 :*

Kasteel Gravenhof, Alsembergsesteenweg 676 ☎ 380 44 99, Fax 380 40 60, « Woodland setting, lake », – 25-120. AE ① E VISA JCB
Meals (Pub rest) *Lunch 625* – a la carte approx. 1200 – ☐ 420 – **24 rm** 4850.

at Grimbergen *N : 11 km – pop. 32 628 – ✉ 1850 Grimbergen – ☎ 0 2 :*

Abbey, Kerkeblokstraat 5 ☎ 270 08 88, Fax 270 81 88, – rest – 30-200. AE ① E VISA. rm
closed July – **Meals 't Wit Paard** *(closed Saturday and Sunday) Lunch 1250* - a la carte 1800/2200 – ☐ 400 – **28 rm** 4800/5500.

at Groot-Bijgaarden *NW : 7 km © Dilbeek pop. 37 418 – ✉ 1702 Groot-Bijgaarden – ☎ 0 2 :*

Waerboom, Jozef Mertensstraat 140 ☎ 463 15 00, Fax 463 10 30, – – 25-270. AE ① E VISA.
closed mid July-mid August – **Meals** (residents only) – **34 rm** ☐ 2950/4100.

Gosset M, Alfons Gossetlaan 52 ☎ 466 21 30, Fax 466 18 50, – – 25-200. AE ① E VISA. rm
closed 23 December-2 January – **Meals** *Lunch 350* – a la carte 1100/1600 – **48 rm** ☐ 3250/4100.

De Bijgaarden, I. Van Beverenstraat 20 (near castle) ☎ 466 44 85, Fax 463 08 11, ←, – AE ① E VISA
closed Saturday lunch, Sunday, 30 March-7 April, 11 August-1 September and 1 January dinner-4 January – **Meals** *Lunch 1975* – 3250/4250, – a la carte 3000/3750
Spec. Carpaccio de foie gras d'oie et salade de pourpier à l'huile de truffes blanches, Turbot "château" rôti et béarnaise de homard, Canette de barbarie à la presse (January-mid October).

Michel (Coppens), Schepen Gossetlaan 31 ☎ 466 65 91, Fax 466 90 07, – P. AE ① E VISA
closed Sunday, Monday and August – **Meals** *Lunch 1580* – 2350, a la carte 1900/2750
Spec. Pieds de porc et épinards aux langoustines poêlées, Bar de ligne en terre d'argile, Pigeonneau aux raviolis de pois et ail doux (March-June).

at Hoeilaart *SE : 13 km – pop. 9 666 – ✉ 1560 Hoeilaart – ☎ 0 2 :*

Groenendaal, Groenendaalsesteenweg 145 (at Groenendaal) ☎ 657 94 47, Fax 657 20 30, – – 25. AE ① E VISA JCB
Meals *(closed Saturday lunch and Sunday dinner) Lunch 790* – a la carte approx. 1600 – **8 rm** ☐ 3500/4500.

Aloyse Kloos, Terhulpsesteenweg 2 (at Groenendaal) ☎ 657 37 37, – P. E VISA
closed Sunday dinner, Monday, 2 weeks Easter and August – **Meals** *Lunch 1450* – 2200, a la carte 1900/2300
Spec. Saumon mariné aux truffes, Ecrevisses à la luxembourgeoise (July-December), Mignardises de cailles aux morilles.

at Huizingen *S : 12 km © Beersel pop. 22 715 – ✉ 1654 Huizingen – ☎ 0 2 :*

Terborght, Oud Dorp 16 (near E 19 - exit 15) ☎ 380 10 10, Fax 380 10 97, « Rustic » – P. AE ① E VISA.
closed dinner Sunday and Tuesday, Monday, carnival and 15 July-15 August – **Meals** *Lunch 950* – 1750/2400 b.i..

at Kobbegem *NW : 11 km © Asse pop. 27 507 – ✉ 1730 Kobbegem – ☎ 0 2 :*

Chalet Rose, Brusselsesteenweg 331 ☎ 452 60 41, Fax 452 26 75, – P. AE ① E VISA
closed Sunday dinner, Monday and July – **Meals** *Lunch 1275* – a la carte 1200/1950.

De Plezanten Hof, Broekstraat 2 ☎ 452 89 39, Fax 452 99 11, – P. AE ① E VISA
closed dinner Tuesday and Sunday, Wednesday, carnival week and 3 weeks August – **Meals** *Lunch 1150* – 1500/2500.

at Kraainem *E : 12 km – pop. 12 795 – ✉ 1950 Kraainem – ☎ 0 2 :*

d'Oude Pastorie, Pastoorkesweg 1 (Park Jourdain) ☎ 720 63 46, Fax 720 63 46, « Lakeside setting in park » – P. AE ① E VISA.
closed Monday dinner, Thursday, 31 March-7 April and 14 August-8 September – **Meals** *Lunch 1200* – a la carte approx. 1700.

at Linkebeek *S : 12 km – pop. 4 663 – ✉ 1630 Linkebeek – ☎ 0 2 :*

Le Saint-Sébastien, r. Station 90 ☎ 380 54 90, Fax 380 54 41, – P. ① E VISA
closed Monday and September – **Meals** *Lunch 750* – 1150/1450.

at Machelen *NE : 12 km – pop. 11 516 – ✉ 1830 Machelen – ☎ 0 2 :*

XXX **André D'Haese,** Heirbaan 210 ☎ 253 54 56, Fax 253 47 65, « Modern interior, terrace with landscaped garden » – P. AE E VISA JCB.
closed Saturday lunch, Sunday, Bank Holidays, 1 week after Easter, last 2 weeks July and late December – **Meals** *Lunch 1300* – 2250/2900, – a la carte 2200/2600
Spec. Lotte et foie gras d'oie fumé aux haricots verts et tomates séchées, Filet de St-Pierre poêlé tout céleri, Ris de veau braisé à brun Zingara.

at Meise *N : 14 km – pop. 17 755 – ✉ 1860 Meise – ☎ 0 2 :*

XXX **Aub. Napoléon,** Bouchoutlaan 1 ☎ 269 30 78, Fax 269 79 98, Grill rest – P. AE E VISA
closed August – **Meals** *Lunch 1450* – a la carte 1650/2300.

XXX **Koen Van Loven,** Brusselsesteenweg 11 ☎ 270 05 77, Fax 270 05 46, – 25-150. AE E VISA.
closed Sunday dinner, Monday, 8 to 16 February and 29 March-13 April – **Meals** *Lunch 1175* – 1495/1795.

at Melsbroek *NE : 14 km C Steenokkerzeel pop. 10 134 – ✉ 1820 Melsbroek – ☎ 0 2 :*

XXX **Boetfort,** Sellaerstraat 42 ☎ 751 64 00, Fax 751 62 00, « 17C mansion, park » – P – 25-40. AE E VISA.
closed Wednesday dinner, Saturday lunch, Sunday and carnival week – **Meals** *Lunch 1200* – 1500/1950.

at Nossegem *E : 13 km C Zaventem pop. 26 535 – ✉ 1930 Nossegem – ☎ 0 2 :*

XX **Roland Debuyst,** Leuvensesteenweg 614 ☎ 757 05 59, Fax 759 50 08, – P. AE E VISA
closed Saturday lunch, Sunday, Monday dinner, and August – **Meals** *Lunch 1250* – 1850/2190.

at Overijse *SE : 16 km – pop. 23 469 – ✉ 3090 Overijse – ☎ 0 2 :*

XXXX **Barbizon** (Deluc), Welriekendedreef 95 (at Jezus-Eik) ☎ 657 04 62, Fax 657 40 66, « Terrace and garden » – P. AE E VISA
closed Tuesday, Wednesday, February and 29 July-20 August – **Meals** *Lunch 1750* – 2585/3250, – a la carte 2300/2800
Spec. Vinaigrette de homard et tomate au corail, Bar aux huîtres hachées, rosotto au safran, Croustillant de ris de veau aux carottes, cumin et petits oignons.

X **Istas,** Brusselsesteenweg 652 (at Jezus-Eik) ☎ 657 05 11, Fax 657 05 11, Pub rest – P. E VISA
closed Wednesday, Thursday and August – **Meals** a la carte 800/1200.

at Schepdaal *W : 12 km C Dilbeek pop. 37 418 – ✉ 1703 Schepdaal – ☎ 0 2 :*

Lien Zana, Ninoofsesteenweg 1022 ☎ 569 65 25, Fax 569 64 64, – rest TV P – 25. AE E VISA
closed 21 July-15 August – **Meals** (Pub-rest) *Lunch 350* – a la carte approx. 900 – **27 rm** 2400/4000.

at Sint-Genesius-Rode *(Rhode-St-Genèse) S : 13 km – pop. 18 014 – ✉ 1640 Sint-Genesius-Rode – ☎ 0 2 :*

Aub. de Waterloo, chaussée de Waterloo 212 ☎ 358 35 80, Fax 358 38 06 – TV P – 25-80. AE E VISA
Meals see rest ***L'Arlecchino*** below – **84 rm** 2150/6450.

XX **L'Arlecchino** - (at Aub. de Waterloo H.), chaussée de Waterloo 212 ☎ 358 34 16, Fax 358 28 96, Italian cuisine, with Trattoria – P. AE E VISA
Meals – 800/1580 b.i.

X **Bois Savanes,** chaussée de Waterloo 208 ☎ 358 37 78, Thaï cuisine – P. AE E VISA
closed lunch Monday and Tuesday and first 3 weeks August – **Meals** *Lunch 495* – a la carte approx. 1100.

at Sint-Pieters-Leeuw *SO : 13 km – pop. 29 627 – ✉ 1600 Sint-Pieters-Leeuw – ☎ 0 2 :*

Green Park M, V. Nonnemanstraat 15 ☎ 331 19 70, Fax 331 03 11, « Lakeside setting », – TV P – 25-100. AE E VISA JCB
closed July – **Meals** *(closed Friday) Lunch 450* – a la carte 1200/1550 – **18 rm** 3650/4150.

at Strombeek-Bever *N : 9 km C Grimbergen pop. 32 628 – ✉ 1853 Strombeek-Bever – ☎ 0 2 :*

Alfa Rijckendael M, Luitberg 1 ☎ 267 41 24 and 267 55 00 (rest), Telex 20140, Fax 267 94 01, – TV P – 25-40. AE E VISA
Meals *(closed Wednesday) Lunch 880* – a la carte 1250/2050 – **49 rm** 4900.

XX **Val Joli,** Leestbeekstraat 16 ☎ 460 65 43, Fax 460 04 00, ☂, « Terrace and garden » – P. AE E VISA
closed Monday, Tuesday, 2 weeks June and 2 weeks November – **Meals** 990.

XX **'t Stoveke,** Jetsestraat 52 ☎ 267 67 25, ☂, Seafood – AE ⓓ E VISA
closed Sunday, Monday, 3 weeks June, Christmas and New Year – **Meals** Lunch 1190 – 1720/2300.

at Vilvoorde (Vilvorde) N : 17 km – pop. 33 346 – ✉ 1800 Vilvoorde – ☎ 0 2 :

XX **Barbay,** Romeinsesteenweg 220 (SW : 4 km at Koningslo) ☎ 267 00 45, Fax 267 00 45, ☂ – AE ⓓ E VISA
closed Saturday lunch, Sunday and 15 July-7 August – **Meals** Lunch 895 – a la carte 1200/1700.

XX **De Met** 1st floor, Grote Markt 7 ☎ 253 30 00, Fax 253 31 00, Partly pub rest, « Former covered market, Art Deco style » – 🏛 25-400. AE E VISA
closed Wednesday dinner, Saturday lunch and Sunday – **Meals** Lunch 1375 b.i. – a la carte approx. 2000.

at Vlezenbeek W : 11 km C Sint-Pieters-Leeuw pop. 29 627 – ✉ 1602 Vlezenbeek – ☎ 0 2 :

XX **Philippe Verbaeys,** Dorp 49 ☎ 569 05 25, ☂ – AE ⓓ E VISA
closed Sunday dinner and Monday – **Meals** Lunch 490 – 990/1490.

at Wemmel N : 12 km – pop. 13 761 – ✉ 1780 Wemmel – ☎ 0 2 :

XX **Parkhof,** Parklaan 7 ☎ 460 42 89, Fax 460 25 10, ☂, « Terrace » – P. AE ⓓ E VISA JCB
closed Wednesday, Thursday and late September-early October – **Meals** Lunch 850 – 1100/1900.

at Wezembeek-Oppem E : 11 km – pop. 13 613 – ✉ 1970 Wezembeek-Oppem – ☎ 0 2 :

XX **L'Aub. Saint-Pierre,** Sint-Pietersplein 8 ☎ 731 21 79, Fax 731 28 28, ☂ – AE ⓓ E VISA
closed Saturday lunch, Sunday, Bank Holidays, 15 July-15 August and 24 December-3 January – **Meals** Lunch 1490 – a la carte 1350/1700.

at Zaventem Brussels-Zaventem airport motorway – pop. 26 535 – ✉ 1930 Zaventem – ☎ 0 2 :

🏨 **Sheraton Airport,** at airport ☎ 725 10 00, Telex 27085, Fax 725 11 55, Fō – ▮ ⇔ ▤ TV ☎ ♿ 🚗 – 🏛 25-600. AE ⓓ E VISA JCB. ⚘ rest
Meals ***Concorde*** Lunch 1375 - a la carte 1850/2250 *Lindbergh Taverne* (open until 11.30 p.m.) Lunch 690 - a la carte approx. 1000 – ☕ 790 – **297 rm** 10900/11900, 2 suites.

XX **Stockmansmolen** 1st floor, H. Henneaulaan 164 ☎ 725 34 34, Fax 725 75 05, Partly pub rest, « Former watermill » – P. AE ⓓ E VISA
closed Saturday, Sunday and 21 July-15 August – **Meals** Lunch 1675 – 2700.

The hotels have entered into certain undertakings towards the readers of this Guide.
Make it plain that you have the most recent Guide.

ANTWERP (ANTWERPEN) 2000 212 ⑮ and 409 G 2 - ⑧ S – pop. 459 072 – ☎ 0 3.

See : Around the Market Square and the Cathedral★★★ : Market Square★ (Grote Markt) FY Vlaaikensgang★ FY, Cathedral★★★ FY and its tower★★★ FY – Butchers' House★ (Vleeshuis) : Musical instruments★ FY **D** – Rubens' House★★ (Rubenshuis) GZ – Interior★ of St. James' Church (St-Jacobskerk) GY - Hendrik Conscience Place★ GY – St. Charles Borromeo's Church★ (St-Carolus Borromeuskerk) GY – St. Paul's Church (St-Pauluskerk) interior★ FY – Zoo★★ (Dierentuin) DEU – Zurenborg Quater★ EV – The port (Haven) ⛴ FY.

Museums : Maritime "Steen"★ (Nationaal Scheepvaartmuseum Steen) FY – Etnographic Museum★ FY **M**[1] – Plantin-Moretus★★★ FZ – Mayer Van den Bergh★★ : Mad Meg★★ (Dulle Griet) GZ – Rockox House★ (Rockoxhuis) GY **M**[4] – Royal Art Gallery★★★ (Koninklijk Museum voor Schone Kunsten) CV **M**[5] – Museum of Photography★ CV **M**[6] – Open-air Museum of Sculpture Middelheim★ (Openluchtmuseum voor Beeldhouwkunst).

18 9 at Kapellen N : 15,5 km, G. Capiaulei 2 ☎ (0 3) 666 84 56, - 18 at Aartselaar S : 10 km Kasteel Cleydael ☎ (0 3) 887 00 79 - 18 at Wommelgem E : 10 km, Uilenbaan 15 ☎ (0 3) 355 14 30 - 18 9 at Broechem E : 13 km, Kasteel Bossenstein ☎ (0 3) 485 64 46.

ℹ (closed Sunday except April-October) Grote Markt 15 ☎ 232 01 03, Fax 231 19 37 - Tourist association of the province, (closed Saturday and Sunday) Karel Oomsstraat 11 ✉ 2018, ☎ 216 28 10, Fax 237 83 65.

Brussels 48 – Amsterdam 159 – Luxembourg 261 – Rotterdam 103.

ANTWERPEN

Groenplaats	FZ	
Klapdorp	GY	
Meir	GZ	
Nationalestr.	FZ	
Paardenmarkt	GY	
Schoenmarkt	FZ	
Gildekamerstr.	FY	69
Handschoenmarkt	FY	82
Korte Gasthuisstr.	GZ	112
Maria Pijpelinckxstr.	GZ	127
Oude Koornmarkt	FYZ	147
Repenstr.	FY	168
Rosier	FZ	172
Sint-Jansvliet	FZ	184
Sint-Rochusstr.	FZ	189
Steenhouwersvest	FZ	193
Twaalf Maandenstr.	GZ	199
Veemarkt	FY	201
Vleeshouwersstr.	FY	205
Vrijdagmarkt	FZ	213
Wisselstr.	FY	214
Zirkstr.	FY	216
Zwartzusterstr.	FY	217

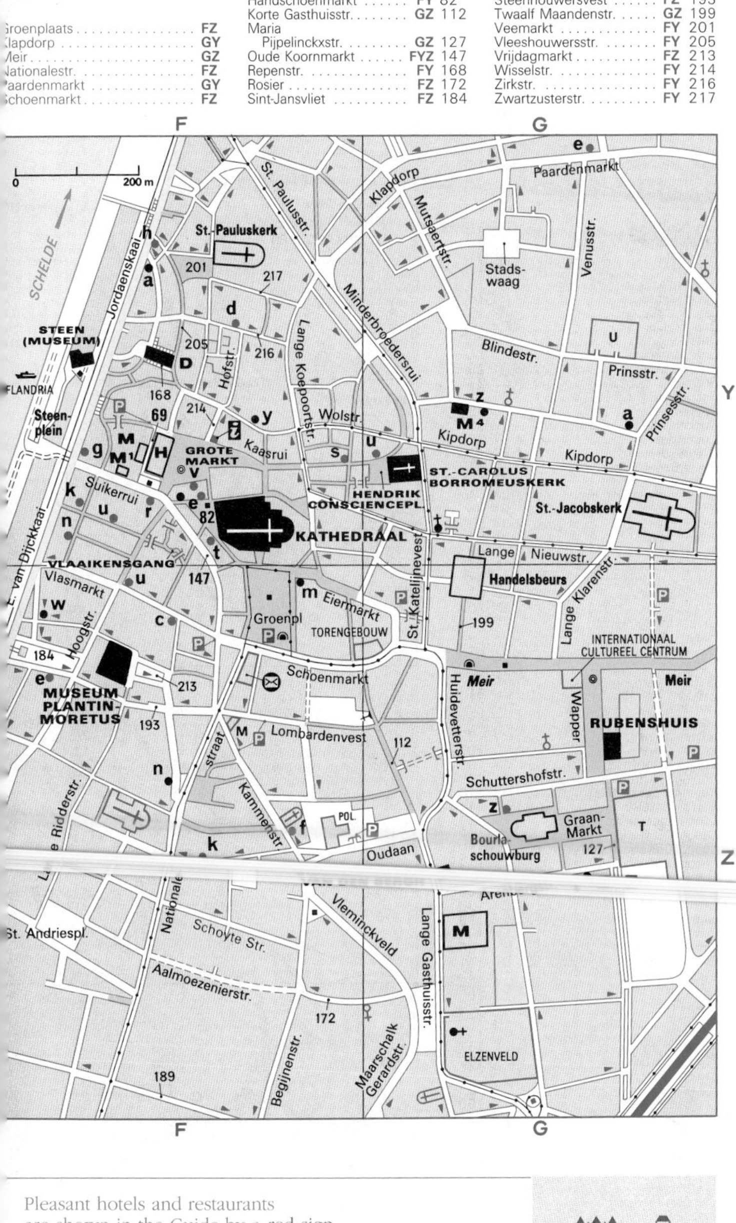

Pleasant hotels and restaurants
are shown in the Guide by a red sign.
Please send us the names
of any where you have enjoyed your stay.
Your Michelin Guide will be even better.

ANTWERPEN

Street	Grid	No.
Carnotstr.	EU	
Dambruggestr.	ETU	39
Gemeentestr.	DU	63
de Keyserlei	DU	103
Leysstr.	DU	123
Offerandestr.	EU	136
Pelikaanstr.	DU	151
Quellinstr.	DU	165
Turnhoutsebaan (BORGERHOUT)	EU	
van Aerdtstr.	DT	3
Amsterdamstr.	DT	4
Ankerrui	DT	6
Ballaerstr.	DV	12
Bolivarplaats	CV	15
Borsbeekbrug	EX	16
van Breestr.	DV	19
Brialmontlei	DV	21
Britselei	DV	22
Broederminstr.	CV	24
Brouwersvliet	DT	25
Brusselstr.	CV	27
Cassiersstr.	DT	31
Charlottalei	DV	33
Cockerillkaai	CV	36
Cuperusstr.	EV	37
Diksmuidelaan	EX	43
Emiel Banningstr.	CV	51
Emiel Vloorsstr.	CX	52
Emile Verhaerenlaan	CT	54
Erwtenstr.	ET	55
van Eycklei	DV	57
Falconplein	DT	58
Franklin Rooseveltpl.	DU	60
Gén. Armstrongweg	CX	64
Gérard Le Grellelaan	DX	66
de Gerlachekaai	CV	67
Gitschotellei	EX	70
Graaf van Egmontstr.	CV	72
Haantjeslei	CDV	79
Halenstr.	ET	81
Hessenplein	DT	84
Jan de Voslei	CX	90
Jan van Gentstr.	CV	91
Jezusstr.	DU	96
Justitiestr.	DV	97
Kasteelpleinstr.	DV	102
Kloosterstr.	CU	105
Kol. Silvertopstr.	CX	106
Koningin Astridplein	DEU	109
Koningin Elisabethlei	DX	110
Korte Winkelstr.	DTU	114
Lange Lobroekstr.	ET	117
Lange Winkelstr.	DT	118
Léopold de Waelplein	CV	120
Léopold de Waelstr.	CV	121
Londenstr.	DT	124
Maria-Henriettalei	DV	129
Mercatorstr.	DEV	130
Namenstr.	CV	133
van den Nestlei	EV	135
Ommeganckstr.	EU	138
Orteliuskaai	DT	141
Osystr.	DU	142
Oude Leeuwenrui	DT	148
Plantinkaai	CU	153
Ploegstr.	EU	154
Pluvierstr.	CU	156
Posthofbrug	EX	157
Prins Albertlei	DX	159
Provinciestr.	EUV	162
Pyckestr.	CX	163
Quinlen Matsijslei	DUV	166
Rolwagenstr.	EV	171
Schijnpoortweg	ET	174
van Schoonhovestr.	DEU	175
Simonsstr.	DEV	178
Sint-Bernardse steenweg	CX	180
Sint-Gummarusstr.	DT	181
Sint-Jansplein	DT	183
Sint-Jozefsstr.	DV	186
Sint-Michielskaai	CU	187
Stuivenbergplein	ET	196
Viaduct Dam	ET	202
Visestr.	ET	204
Volkstr.	CV	207
Vondelstr.	DT	208

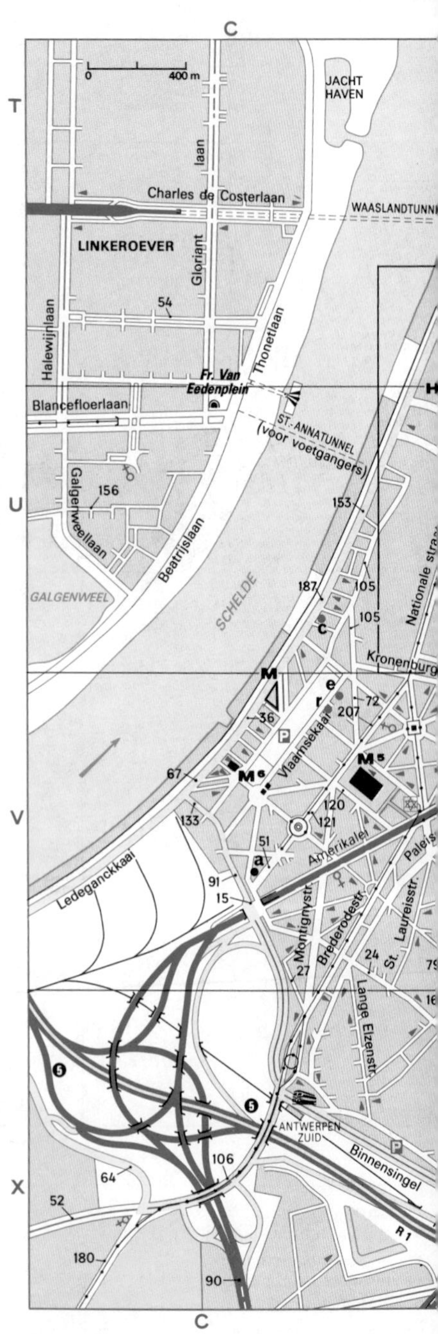

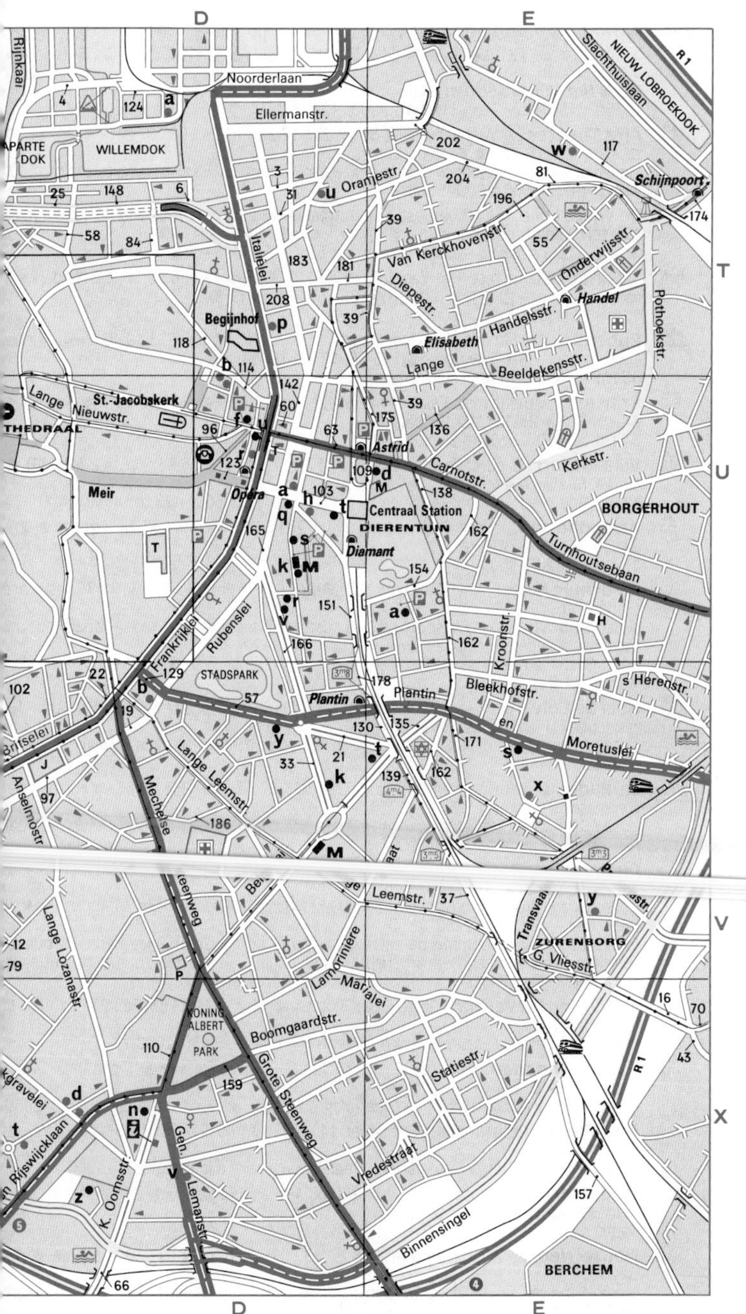
D
E
T
U
V
X
Noorderlaan
Ellermanstr.
WILLEMDOK
APARTE DOK
Rijnkaai
NIEUW LOBROEKDOK
Slachthuislaan
R1
Oranjestr.
Van Kerckhovenstr.
Schijnpoort
Onderwijsstr.
Diepestr.
Handel
Handelsstr.
Italiëlei
Begijnhof
Elisabeth
Lange Beeldekensstr.
Potthoekstr.
Lange Nieuwstr.
St.-Jacobskerk
THEDRAAL
Meir
Opera
Astrid
Carnotstr.
Kerkstr.
Centraal Station
DIERENTUIN
BORGERHOUT
Diamant
Turnhoutsebaan
Frankrijklei
Rubenslei
STADSPARK
Plantin
Kroonstr.
Bleekhofstr.
s Herenstr.
Moretuslei
Lange Leemstr.
Mechelse steenweg
Anselmostr.
Leemstr.
Lange Lozanastr.
Lamorinière
Marialei
Transvaal
ZURENBORG
G. Vliesstr.
KONING ALBERT PARK
Boomgaardstr.
Grote Steenweg
Statiestr.
Gen. Lemanstr.
K. Oomsstr.
Rijswijcklaan
Vredestraat
Binnensingel
BERCHEM

Old Antwerp

Hilton [M], Groenplaats ☎ 204 12 12, Fax 204 12 13, « Facade of an early 20C department store », [gym], [lift] - [lift] [no smoking] [air] [TV] ☎ [garage] - [seminar] 30-1000. AE Ⓓ E VISA JCB. [no dogs] rest FZ n
Meals ***Het Vijfde Seizoen*** *(closed Saturday lunch and late July-early August)* *Lunch 1275* - 1550/1750 - [breakfast] 725 - **199 rm** 4900, 12 suites.

Alfa Theater [M], Arenbergstraat 30 ☎ 231 17 20, Fax 233 88 58, [lift] - [lift] [no smoking] [air] [TV] ☎ - [seminar] 25-50. AE Ⓓ E VISA. [no dogs] rest GZ
Meals *(closed Saturday lunch, Sunday and Bank Holidays)* *Lunch 590* – a la carte approx. 1300 - **122 rm** [breakfast] 3400/5800, 5 suites.

De Witte Lelie [quiet] without rest, Keizerstraat 16 ☎ 226 19 66, Fax 234 00 19, « Typical 17C terraced houses, patio » - [lift] [TV] ☎ [garage]. AE Ⓓ E VISA JCB GY
closed 22 December-3 January - **7 rm** [breakfast] 6500/15000, 3 suites.

't Sandt without rest, Het Zand 17 ☎ 232 93 90, Fax 232 56 13, « 19C residence in rococo style » - [lift] [TV] ☎ [garage] - [seminar] 25-150. AE Ⓓ E VISA FZ
13 rm [breakfast] 4500/8000, 1 suite.

Rubens [M] [quiet] without rest, Oude Beurs 29 ☎ 222 48 48, Fax 225 19 40, « Floral inner courtyard » - [lift] [TV] ☎ [P] - [seminar] 25-50. AE Ⓓ E VISA. [no dogs] FY
35 rm [breakfast] 4500/9000, 1 suite.

Prinse [quiet] without rest, Keizerstraat 63 ☎ 226 40 50, Fax 225 11 48 - [lift] [no smoking] [TV] ☎ [disabled] [garage] - [seminar] 25-150. AE E VISA. [no dogs] GY
34 rm [breakfast] 3700/5100, 1 suite.

Villa Mozart, Handschoenmarkt 3 ☎ 231 30 31, Fax 231 56 85, [terrace], [lift] - [lift] [TV] ☎ AE Ⓓ E VISA JCB FY
Meals (Pub rest) *Lunch 920* – a la carte 1200/1550 – [breakfast] 500 – **25 rm** 3500/5400.

Antigone without rest, Jordaenskaai 11 ☎ 231 66 77, Fax 231 37 74 - [lift] [TV] ☎ [P] - [seminar] 30. AE Ⓓ E VISA. [no dogs] FY
18 rm [breakfast] 3200/3500.

't Fornuis (Segers), Reyndersstraat 24 ☎ 233 62 70, Fax 233 99 03, « 17C residence, rustic interior » - AE Ⓓ E VISA. [no dogs] FZ
closed Saturday, Sunday, last 3 weeks August and Christmas-New Year – **Meals** (booking essential) a la carte 2150/2950
Spec. Sole à la rhubarbe, Galettes aux épices et au crabe frais, Ris de veau rôti au chou vert et truffes.

Huis De Colvenier, St-Antoniusstraat 8 ☎ 226 65 73, Fax 227 13 14, [terrace], « Late 19C residence » - [air] [P]. AE Ⓓ E VISA FZ
closed Saturday lunch, Sunday dinner, Monday, 10 to 16 February and 20 July-15 August – **Meals** *Lunch 1200* – a la carte 2000/2600.

La Rade 1st floor, E. Van Dijckkaai 8 ☎ 233 37 37, Fax 233 49 63, « Former 19C freemason's lodge » - AE Ⓓ E VISA FY
closed Saturday lunch, Sunday, Bank Holidays, 10 to 16 February and 7 to 27 July – **Meals** *Lunch 1450* – a la carte 2350/3000.

De Kerselaar (Michiels), Grote Pieter Potstraat 22 ☎ 233 59 69, Fax 233 11 49 – [air] AE Ⓓ E VISA JCB. [no dogs] FY
closed lunch Saturday and Monday, Sunday, 21 March-1 April and 4 to 19 August – **Meals** *Lunch 1350* – a la carte 2150/2550
Spec. Tourteau et pomme de terre à la crème de caviar et fines herbes, Poularde fermière farcie aux cèpes et artichauts, Gâteau chaud au chocolat, orangettes et sauce pistachée.

't Silveren Claverblat, Grote Pieter Potstraat 16 ☎ 231 33 88, Fax 231 31 46 – AE Ⓓ E VISA FY
closed Tuesday and Saturday lunch – **Meals** *Lunch 1000* – 1450/2000.

P. Preud'homme, Suikerrui 28 ☎ 233 42 00, Fax 226 08 96, [terrace], Open until 11 p.m. – [air]. AE Ⓓ E VISA JCB. [no dogs] FY
closed February and Tuesday October-May – **Meals** *Lunch 1200* – a la carte 1450/2150

Het Nieuwe Palinghuis, St-Jansvliet 14 ☎ 231 74 45, Fax 231 50 53, Seafood – [air] AE Ⓓ E VISA FZ
closed Monday, Tuesday and June – **Meals** *Lunch 1150* – a la carte 1300/1900.

De Gulden Beer, Grote Markt 14 ☎ 226 08 41, Fax 232 52 09, [terrace], Partly Italian cuisine – [air]. AE Ⓓ E VISA JCB. [no dogs] FY
Meals *Lunch 950* – 1400/1800.

Neuze Neuze, Wijngaardstraat 19 ☎ 232 27 97, Fax 225 27 38 – AE Ⓓ E VISA JCB FY
closed Saturday lunch, Sunday and mid-July-early August – **Meals** *Lunch 1000* – a la carte 1600/2500.

In de Schaduw van de Kathedraal, Handschoenmarkt 17 232 40 14, Fax 226 88 14, , Mussels in season – . FY e
closed Monday lunch Easter-October, Monday dinner, Tuesday and 8 January-8 February – **Meals** *Lunch 995* – a la carte 1700/2050.

De Matelote (Garnich), Haarstraat 9 231 32 07, Fax 231 08 13, Seafood – . FY u
closed lunch Saturday and Monday, Sunday, Bank Holidays, July and 1 to 15 January – **Meals** a la carte 2200/2600
Spec. Saumon mariné, sauce au caviar, Barbue aux épinards, moutarde et fromage blanc, Bar vapeur, vinaigrette tiède tomatée et ciboule.

Zirk, Zirkstraat 29 225 25 86, Fax 226 51 77 – . FY d
closed Saturday lunch, Sunday, Monday, first 2 weeks February and last 2 weeks August – **Meals** *Lunch 1200* – a la carte 2000/2300.

De Perelaer, Kammenstraat 75 233 42 73, Fax 226 28 51, « 16C residence » – . FZ f
closed lunch Saturday and Monday, Sunday and 28 July-14 August – **Meals** *Lunch 1100* – 1650/1950.

De Manie, H. Conscienceplein 3 232 64 38, Fax 232 64 38, – GY u
closed Wednesday, Sunday and 17 August-3 September – **Meals** a la carte approx. 1500.

Rooden Hoed, Oude Koornmarkt 25 233 28 44, Mussels in season, Antwerp atmosphere – . FY t
Meals *Lunch 875* – a la carte approx. 1300.

Don Carlos, St-Michielskaai 34 216 40 46, Partly Spanish cuisine – CU c
closed Monday – **Meals** (dinner only) a la carte approx. 1200.

Town Centre

Park Lane [M], Van Eycklei 32, 2018, 285 85 85 and 285 85 80 (rest), Fax 285 85 86, , , , – – 25-450. . DV y
Meals ***Longchamps*** *(closed Saturday lunch, Sunday and Bank Holidays)* *Lunch 1100* - a la carte 1500/2000 – **166 rm** 7950/10400, 12 suites.

Carlton, Quinten Matsijslei 25, 2018, 231 15 15, Telex 31072, Fax 225 30 90, – – 25-100. . rest DU v
Meals *(closed dinner Friday and Sunday, Saturday lunch, first 3 weeks August and late December)* *Lunch 575* – a la carte approx. 1400 – **127 rm** 5700/6700, 1 suite.

Alfa De Keyser [M], De Keyserlei 66, 2018, 234 01 35, Fax 232 39 70, , , – – 25-160. . rest DU t
Meals *(closed Saturday lunch and Sunday)* *Lunch 665* – a la carte 1200/1600 – 500 – **120 rm** 5100/6200, 3 suites.

Hylitt [M] without rest, De Keyserlei 28 (access by Appelmansstraat), 2018, 202 68 00, Fax 202 68 90 – . . DU q
550 – **24 rm** 3500/4500, 56 suites.

[illegible] – 25. DV k
80 rm 6500/8000.

Switel, Copernicuslaan 2, 2018, 231 67 80, Fax 233 02 90, , , , – – 25-1000. EU a
Meals – a la carte approx. 1400 – 575 – **308 rm** 5500, 2 suites.

Residence without rest, Molenbergstraat 9 232 76 75, Fax 233 73 28 – – 40. . DU f
400 – **48 rm** 2500/4500.

Alfa Empire without rest, Appelmansstraat 31, 2018, 231 47 55, Fax 233 40 60 – . DU s
400 – **70 rm** 3900/4700.

Astoria [M] without rest, Korte Herentalsestraat 5, 2018, 227 31 30, Fax 227 31 34, , – . DU r
66 rm 3600/4500.

Colombus without rest, Frankrijklei 4 233 03 90, Fax 226 09 46, , – . . DU u
32 rm 3250/3800.

Alfa Congress, Plantin en Moretuslei 136, 2018, 235 30 00, Fax 235 52 31 – – 25-120. . rest EV s
Meals *(closed Saturday, Sunday and Bank Holidays)* *Lunch 800* – a la carte approx. 1400 – **66 rm** 2500/3600.

Ambassador without rest, Belgiëlei 8, ✉ 2018, ☏ 281 41 61, Fax 239 55 16 – |♦| TV ☎ 🚗. AE ⓓ E VISA. ✻ DEV
☕ 300 – **77 rm** 3500.

Atlanta without rest, Koningin Astridplein 14, ✉ 2018, ☏ 203 09 19, Fax 226 37 37 – |♦| ✻ TV ☎ – 🏛 30. AE ⓓ E VISA DEU c
60 rm ☕ 3500.

Eden without rest, Lange Herentalsestraat 25, ✉ 2018, ☏ 233 06 08, Fax 233 12 28 – |♦| TV ☎ 🚗. AE ⓓ E VISA. ✻ DU k
66 rm ☕ 2750/3750.

Corum, Italiëlei 177 ☏ 232 23 44, Fax 232 24 41, 🍴 – ▤. AE ⓓ E VISA DT p
closed Saturday lunch, Sunday, Monday and last 3 weeks July – **Meals** *Lunch 1250* – a la carte approx. 2100.

De Barbarie, Van Breestraat 4, ✉ 2018, ☏ 232 81 98, Fax 231 26 78, 🍴 – AE E VISA JCB DV b
closed Saturday lunch, Sunday, Monday and first 2 weeks September – **Meals** *Lunch 1450* – a la carte 2000/2400.

De Lepeleer, Lange St-Annastraat 10 ☏ 225 19 31, Fax 231 31 24, « Several small houses in a 16C cul-de-sac » – Ⓟ. AE ⓓ E VISA DU t
closed Saturday lunch, Sunday, Bank Holidays and 21 July-16 August – **Meals** *Lunch 1500 b.i.* – 2700 b.i..

De Zeste, Lange Dijkstraat 36, ✉ 2060, ☏ 233 45 49, Fax 232 34 18 – ▤. AE ⓓ E VISA DT
closed Sunday – **Meals** *Lunch 1200* – 1950.

Fouquets, De Keyserlei 17, ✉ 2018, ☏ 232 62 09, Fax 226 16 88, 🍴, Open until 11 p.m. – ▤. AE ⓓ E VISA DU
closed first 3 weeks August – **Meals** *Lunch 690* – a la carte 1000/1500.

Blue Phoenix, Frankrijklei 14 ☏ 233 33 77, Fax 233 88 46, Chinese cuisine – ▤. AE E VISA. ✻ DU
closed Monday, Saturday lunch and August – **Meals** *Lunch 800* – 800/2000.

't Peerd, Paardenmarkt 53 ☏ 231 98 25, Fax 231 59 40, 🍴 – ▤. AE ⓓ E VISA
closed Tuesday dinner, Wednesday, 2 weeks Easter and 4 to 19 September – **Meals** *Lunch 990* – a la carte 1300/2050.

't Lammeke, Lange Lobroekstraat 51 (opposite the slaughterhouse), ✉ 2060, ☏ 236 79 86, Fax 271 05 16, 🍴 – ▤. AE ⓓ E VISA ET v
closed lunch Saturday and Sunday and 15 July-15 August – **Meals** *Lunch 1075* – 875/1475.

Yamayu Santatsu, Ossenmarkt 19 ☏ 234 09 49, Fax 234 09 49, Japanese cuisine – ▤. AE ⓓ E VISA DTU
closed Sunday lunch, Monday and first 2 weeks August – **Meals** *Lunch 420* – 1500/1700.

South Quarter

Holiday Inn Crowne Plaza, G. Legrellelaan 10, ✉ 2020, ☏ 237 29 00, Telex 33843, Fax 216 02 96, 🍴, 🏋, ♨, 🏊 – |♦| ✻ ▤ TV ☎ Ⓟ – 🏛 25-800. AE ⓓ E VISA JCB
Meals *Lunch 995* – a la carte approx. 1300 – ☕ 575 – **258 rm** 5995, 4 suites.

Sofitel, Desguinlei 94, ✉ 2018, ☏ 244 82 11, Fax 216 47 12, 🍴, 🏋, ♨ – |♦| ✻ ▤ TV ☎ 🚗 Ⓟ – 🏛 25-600. AE ⓓ E VISA. ✻ rest DX
Meals ***Tiffany's*** *(closed Saturday lunch and July-August)* *Lunch 1300* - a la carte 1000/1800 – ☕ 650 – **215 rm** 6500, 5 suites.

Firean 🐚 without rest, Karel Oomsstraat 6, ✉ 2018, ☏ 237 02 60, Fax 238 11 68, « Period residence, Art Deco style » – |♦| ▤ TV ☎ 🚗. AE ⓓ E VISA JCB. ✻ DX
closed 2 to 25 August and 20 December-3 January – **15 rm** ☕ 4100/5700.

Industrie Ⓜ without rest, Emiel Banningstraat 52 ☏ 238 66 00, Fax 238 86 88 – TV ☎. AE ⓓ E VISA. ✻ CV
13 rm ☕ 2700/3700.

Vateli, Van Putlei 31, ✉ 2018, ☏ 238 72 52, Fax 238 25 88 – ▤ Ⓟ. AE ⓓ E VISA. ✻
closed Saturday lunch, Sunday, Bank Holidays and last 2 weeks July – **Meals** *Lunch 1450 b.i.* – 2500 b.i. DX

Loncin, Markgravelei 127, ✉ 2018, ☏ 248 29 89, Fax 248 38 66, 🍴, Open until midnight – ▤. ⓓ E VISA. ✻ DX
closed Tuesday October-April and Wednesday – **Meals** *Lunch 1700 b.i.* – a la carte 2050/2400.

Liang's Garden, Markgravelei 141, ✉ 2018, ☏ 237 22 22, Fax 248 38 34, Chinese cuisine – ▤. AE ⓓ E VISA DX
closed Sunday and 2 weeks July – **Meals** *Lunch 950* – a la carte 1150/1750.

Kommilfoo, Vlaamse Kaai 17 ☏ 237 30 00, Fax 237 30 00 – ▤. AE ⓓ E VISA CV
closed Saturday lunch and Sunday – **Meals** *Lunch 1100* – a la carte 1450/1850.

De Poterne, Desguinlei 186, ✉ 2018, ☏ 238 28 24, Fax 248 59 67 – AE ⓓ E VISA
closed Saturday lunch, Sunday, 1 to 16 August and 31 December-2 January – **Meals** *Lunch 1350* – a la carte approx. 2000. DX

Suburbs

North – *2030 – 03 :*

Novotel, Luithagen-Haven 6 542 03 20, Fax 541 70 93, – 25-180. AE E VISA
Meals (open until midnight) *Lunch 1095* – a la carte 1000/1550 – 425 – **119 rm** 3500.

at Borgerhout *E : 3 km C Antwerpen – 2140 Borgerhout – 03 :*

Holiday Inn, Luitenant Lippenslaan 66 235 91 91, Fax 235 08 96, – 25-230. AE E VISA
Meals – a la carte approx. 1300 – 550 – **201 rm** 2400/4950, 3 suites.

at Deurne *NE : 3 km C Antwerpen – 2100 Deurne – 03 :*

De Violin, Bosuil 1 324 34 04, Fax 326 33 20, « Small farmhouse » – AE E VISA.
closed Sunday, Monday dinner and 20 August-9 September – **Meals** *Lunch 1495 b.i.* – a la carte approx. 2000.

Périgord, Turnhoutsebaan 273 325 52 00, Fax 325 52 00 – AE E VISA.
closed Tuesday, Wednesday, Saturday lunch, 1 week carnival and July – **Meals** *Lunch 900* – 1435/2800.

at Ekeren *N : 11 km C Antwerpen – 2180 Ekeren – 03 :*

Hof de Bist, Veltwijcklaan 258 664 61 30, Fax 664 67 24, – AE E VISA
closed Sunday, Monday, Tuesday and August – **Meals** *Lunch 2500 b.i.* – 2000.

at Merksem *N : 2 km C Antwerpen – 2170 Merksem – 03 :*

Maritime, Bredabaan 978 646 22 23, Fax 646 22 71, Seafood – AE E VISA.
closed Monday – **Meals** *Lunch 995* – a la carte approx. 2000.

at Wilrijk *S : 6 km C Antwerpen – 2610 Wilrijk – 03 :*

Schans XV, Moerelei 155 828 45 64, Fax 828 93 29, « Early 20C redoubt » – AE E VISA.
closed Thursday dinner, Saturday lunch, Sunday, Bank Holidays, 2 weeks February and 2 weeks late July – **Meals** *Lunch 995 b.i.* – a la carte 1800/2500.

Environs

at Aartselaar *S : 10 km – pop. 14 488 – 2630 Aartselaar – 03 :*

Kasteel Solhof without rest, Baron Van Ertbornstraat 116 877 30 00, Fax 877 31 31, « Terrace in public park », – 25. AE E VISA.
600 – **24 rm** 4800/6000.

Host. Kasteelhoeve Groeninghe with rm, Kontichsesteenweg 78 457 95 86, Fax 458 13 68, « Restored Flemish farm », – 25-150. AE E VISA.
closed 3 to 17 August and 21 to 31 December – **Meals** *(closed Saturday lunch, Sunday*

Kasteel Cleydael with rm, Cleydaellaan 36 (W : direction Hemiksem) 887 05 04, Fax 887 20 18, « Restored moated feudal castle » – 25-60. AE E VISA.
closed Sunday, Monday, Bank Holidays, 20 July-19 August and 21 December-4 January – **Meals** *Lunch 1750* – a la carte 2100/2450 – **6 rm** 5500/6500, 1 suite.

Villa Verde, Kleistraat 175 887 56 85, Fax 887 22 56, – AE E VISA.
closed Saturday lunch, Sunday dinner, Monday, 20 July-11 August and 1 to 15 January – **Meals** *Lunch 1100* – 1700/2450.

at Boechout *SE : 9 km – pop. 11 586 – 2530 Boechout – 03 :*

De Schone van Boskoop (Keersmaekers), Appelkantstraat 10 454 19 31, Fax 454 19 31, « Terrace with ornamental pool » – AE E VISA.
closed Sunday, Monday, 1 week April, 3 weeks August and first week January – **Meals** *Lunch 1500* – a la carte 2400/3100
Spec. Carpaccio de St-Jacques à la crème de caviar, Ravioli de foie gras, pied de porc et truffes, Homard en 2 assiettes.

at Brasschaat *N : 11 km – pop. 36 688 – 2930 Brasschaat – 03 :*

Halewijn, Donksesteenweg 212 (Ekeren-Donk) 647 20 10, Fax 647 08 95, – AE E VISA
closed Monday – **Meals** a la carte 1100/1850.

at Kapellen *N : 15,5 km – pop. 25 290 – ✉ 2950 Kapellen – ☎ 0 3 :*

XXX ✿ **De Bellefleur** (Buytaert), Antwerpsesteenweg 253 ✆ 664 67 19, Fax 665 02 01, « Veranda surrounded by floral gardens » – P. AE O E VISA
closed Saturday lunch, Sunday, Monday and July – **Meals** *Lunch 1750 b.i.* – 3750 b.i., a la carte 2800/3150
Spec. Ragoût d'écrevisses et champignons, Lotte rôtie, sauce hollandaise à la moutarde, Poularde de Malines au gros sel.

at Kontich *S : 12 km – pop. 19 373 – ✉ 2550 Kontich – ☎ 0 3 :*

XXX **Carême,** Koningin Astridlaan 114 ✆ 457 63 04, Fax 457 93 02, – ▤ P. AE O E VISA
closed Saturday lunch, Sunday, Monday and July – **Meals** *Lunch 1095* – 1650/2350.

at Ranst *E : 12 km – pop. 16 982 – ✉ 2520 Ranst – ☎ 0 3 :*

XX **Ten Schawijcke,** Schawijkplasweg 14 ✆ 353 92 32, Fax 353 92 32, « Restored farmhouse manor, rustic » – P. AE O E VISA.
closed Monday, Tuesday and 15 August-15 September – **Meals** 1100/1950.

at Schoten *NE : 10 km – pop. 31 794 – ✉ 2900 Schoten – ☎ 0 3 :*

XX **Kleine Barreel,** Bredabaan 1147 ✆ 645 85 84, Fax 645 85 03 – ▤ P. AE O E VISA JCB.
Meals *Lunch 1175* – 1175/1650.

XX **Uilenspiegel,** Brechtsebaan 277 (3 km on N 115) ✆ 651 61 45, Fax 652 08 08, « Terrace and garden » – P. AE E VISA
closed Monday, Tuesday, 2 weeks July and 2 weeks January – **Meals** *Lunch 975* – 1395/1950

at Wijnegem *E : 10 km – pop. 8 554 – ✉ 2110 Wijnegem – ☎ 0 3 :*

XXX **Ter Vennen,** Merksemsebaan 278 ✆ 326 20 60, Fax 326 38 47, « Terrace » – P. AE O E VISA
Meals *Lunch 1675* – a la carte 2100/2700.

Kruiningen *Zeeland (Netherlands) C Reimerswaal pop. 20 341* 211 *E 14 and* 408 *D 7*
☎ 0 113 – 56 km.

Le Manoir , Zandweg 2 (W : 1 km), ✉ 4416 NA, ✆ 38 17 53, Fax 38 17 63, ←, – TV ☎ P. AE O E VISA
closed 1 to 21 January – **Meals** see rest ***Inter Scaldes*** below – ☕ 13 – **10 rm** 325/450, 2 suites.

XXXX ✿✿ **Inter Scaldes** (Mme Boudeling) - at Le Manoir H., Zandweg 2 (W : 1 km), ✉ 4416 NA ✆ 38 17 53, Fax 38 17 63, , « Terrace-veranda overlooking an English-style garden » – P. AE O E VISA
closed Monday, Tuesday, first week October and 1 to 21 January – **Meals** *Lunch 100* – a la carte 170/196
Spec. Homard fumé, sauce au caviar, Bar légèrement fumé à la tomate, basilic et olive (May-November), Turbot en robe de truffes et son beurre.

BRUGES *(BRUGGE) 8000 West-Vlaanderen* 213 ③ *and* 409 *C 2 – pop. 116 273 – ☎ 0 50.*

See : *Procession of the Holy Blood★★★ (Heilig Bloedprocessie) – Historic centre and canals★★★ (Historisch centrum en grachten) – Market square★★ (Markt) AU, Belfry and Halles★★★ (Belfort en Hallen) ←★★ from the top AU – Market-town★★ (Burg) AU – Basilica of the Holy Blood★ (Basiliek van het Heilig Bloed) : low Chapel★ or St. Basiles Chapel (beneden- of St-Basiliuskapel)* AU **B** – *Chimney of the "Brugse Vrije"★ in the Palace of the "Brugse Vrije"* AU **S** – *Rosery quay (Rozenhoedkaai) ←★★* AU **63** – *Dijver ←★★* AU – *St. Boniface bridge (Bonifatiusbrug) : site★★* AU – *Beguinage★★ (Begijnhof)* AV – *Trips on the canals★★★ (Boottocht)* AU – *Church of Our Lady★ (O.-L.-Vrouwekerk) : tower★★, statue of the Madonna★★, tombstone★★ of Mary of Burgundy★★* AV **N.**

Museums : *Groeninge★★★ (Stedelijk Museum voor Schone Kunsten)* AU – *Memling★★ (St. John's Hospital)* AV – *Gruuthuse★ : bust of Charles the Fifth★ (borstbeeld van Karel V)* AU **M¹** – *Brangwyn★* AU **M⁴** – *Folklore★ (Museum voor Volkskunde)* DY **M².**

Envir : *Zedelgem : baptismal font★ in the St. Lawrence's church SW : 10,5 km – Damme★ NE : 7 km.*

18 9 *at Sijsele NE : 7 km, Doornstraat 16 ✆ (0 50) 33 35 72, Fax (0 50) 35 89 25.*

Burg 11 ✆ 44 86 86, Fax 44 86 00 and at railway station, Stationsplein – Tourist association of the province, Kasteel Tillegem ✉ 8200 Sint-Michiels, ✆ 38 02 96, Fax 38 02 9.

Brussels 96 – Ghent 45 – Lille 72 – Ostend 28.

Plans on following pages

Town Centre

Holiday Inn Crowne Plaza, Burg 10 34 58 34, Fax 34 56 15, « Interesting medieval remains and objects in basement », – 25-400. AE E VISA JCB. AU a
Meals **'t Kapittel** *(closed Wednesday dinner, Saturday lunch and Sunday)* Lunch 995 b.i. - 1250 b.i./2155 b.i. – 620 – **93 rm** 6200/7600, 3 suites.

Sofitel, Boeveriestraat 2 34 09 71, Fax 34 40 53, – 25-200. AE E VISA CZ b
Meals – 950/1600 b.i. – 500 – **155 rm** 5700/6700.

De Tuilerieën without rest, Dijver 7 34 36 91, Fax 34 04 00, – 25-45. AE E VISA JCB AU c
closed 2 weeks December – **24 rm** 6950/11950, 1 suite.

Relais Oud Huis Amsterdam without rest, Spiegelrei 3 34 18 10, Telex 83121, Fax 33 88 91, « 17C residence, former Dutch trading post », – 25. AE E VISA JCB AT d
25 rm 3950/6250.

De Orangerie without rest, Kartuizerinnenstraat 10 34 16 49, Fax 33 30 16, « Period canalside residence » – AE E VISA JCB AU e
closed 2 weeks February – **19 rm** 5950/8950.

Die Swaene, Steenhouwersdijk 1 34 27 98, Fax 33 66 74, « Stylish furnishings », – 30. AE E VISA JCB AU p
Meals *(closed Wednesday, Thursday lunch and 3 to 19 January)* Lunch 1150 – 1850/2250 – **19 rm** 5500/6800, 2 suites.

Park without rest, Vrijdagmarkt 5 33 33 64, Fax 33 47 63 – – 25-250. AE E VISA CY j
86 rm 4200/5400.

de' Medici, Potterierei 15 33 98 33, Fax 33 07 64, « Modern style », – 25-60. AE E VISA JCB. rest CX g
Meals (dinner only) *(closed Sunday and Monday)* 850/1650 – ***Koto*** (Japanese cuisine, teppan-yaki) Lunch 690 - 1280/2780 – **80 rm** 3800/5000.

Acacia M without rest, Korte Zilverstraat 3a 34 44 11, Fax 33 88 17, – 25-40. AE E VISA JCB. AU n
34 rm 3450/5450, 2 suites.

Karos without rest, Hoefijzerlaan 37 34 14 48, Fax 34 00 91, AE E VISA BY f
closed 2 January-15 February – **60 rm** 2900/4800.

Prinsenhof without rest, Ontvangersstraat 9 34 26 90, Fax 34 23 21 – AE E VISA JCB CY s
16 rm 3400/6700.

Pandhotel without rest, Pandreitje 16 34 06 66, Fax 34 05 56, « Opulent interior » – AE E VISA JCB AU q
24 rm 3890/7290.

Alfa Dante, Coupure 29a 34 01 94, Fax 34 35 39, – – 25-60. AE
closed February – **Meals** (vegetarian cuisine) *(closed Sunday dinner, Monday, Tuesday and after 8.30 p.m.)* a la carte 950/1350 – **20 rm** 3150/4650.

Novotel Centrum, Katelijnestraat 65b 33 75 33, Telex 81799, Fax 33 65 56, – – 50-400. AE E VISA JCB AV h
Meals – a la carte 800/1250 – 425 – **126 rm** 3750/4100.

Portinari without rest, 't Zand 15 34 10 34, Fax 34 41 80 – – 25-80. AE E VISA JCB CY k
closed 2 to 25 January – **40 rm** 3000/4500.

Jan Brito without rest, Freren Fonteinstraat 1 33 06 01, Fax 33 06 52, « Gabled façades 16, 17 and 18C interior », – AE E VISA JCB. AU j
18 rm 3200/5900.

De Castillion, Heilige Geeststraat 1 34 30 01, Fax 33 94 75, – – 25-50. AE E VISA JCB. rest AU r
Meals *(closed Sunday dinner and lunch Monday and Tuesday except Bank Holidays)* Lunch 1250 – 1250/1975 – **20 rm** 3500/5500.

Bryghia without rest, Oosterlingenplein 4 33 80 59, Fax 34 14 30 – AE E VISA JCB. AT t
closed 4 January- 27 February – **18 rm** 2800/4500.

Hansa without rest, N. Desparsstraat 11 33 84 44, Fax 33 42 05 – AE E VISA JCB. AT k
20 rm 3500/3800.

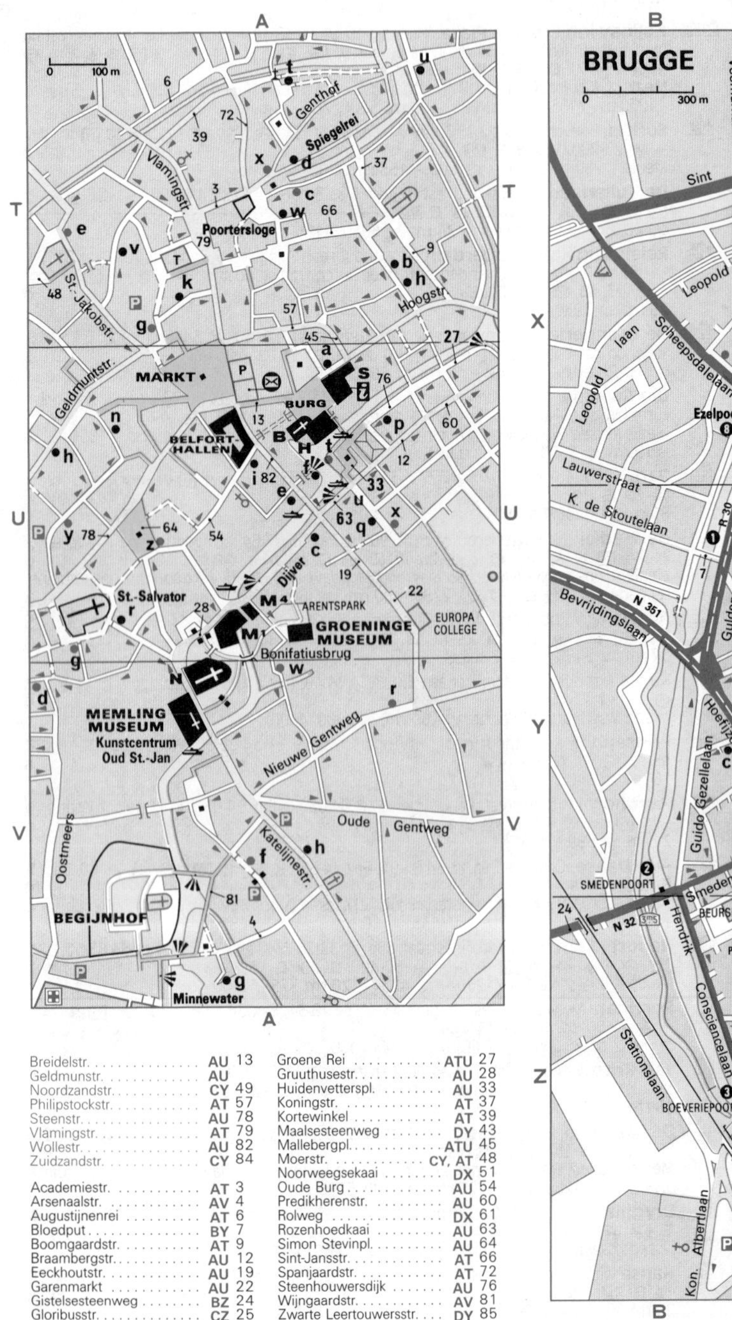

Breidelstr.	AU	13
Geldmunstr.	AU	
Noordzandstr.	CY	49
Philipstockstr.	AT	57
Steenstr.	AU	78
Vlamingstr.	AT	79
Wollestr.	AU	82
Zuidzandstr.	CY	84
Academiestr.	AT	3
Arsenaalstr.	AV	4
Augustijnenrei	AT	6
Bloedput	BY	7
Boomgaardstr.	AT	9
Braambergstr.	AU	12
Eeckhoutstr.	AU	19
Garenmarkt	AU	22
Gistelsesteenweg	BZ	24
Gloribusstr.	CZ	25
Groene Rei	ATU	27
Gruuthusestr.	AU	28
Huidenvetterspl.	AU	33
Koningstr.	AT	37
Kortewinkel	AT	39
Maalsesteenweg	DY	43
Mallebergpl.	ATU	45
Moerstr.	CY, AT	48
Noorweegsekaai	DX	51
Oude Burg	AU	54
Predikherenstr.	AU	60
Rolweg	DX	61
Rozenhoedkaai	AU	63
Simon Stevinpl.	AU	64
Sint-Jansstr.	AT	66
Spanjaardstr.	AT	72
Steenhouwersdijk	AU	76
Wijngaardstr.	AV	81
Zwarte Leertouwersstr.	DY	85

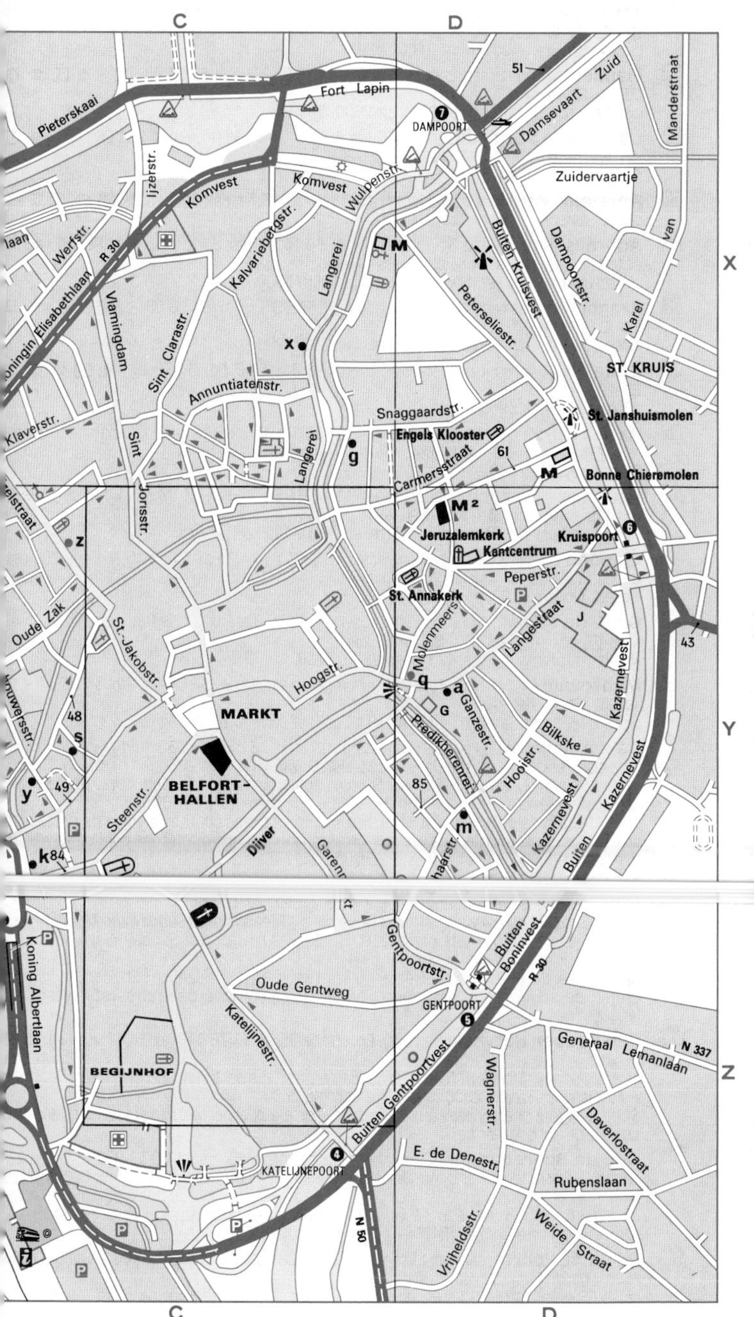

C
D
Pieterskaai
Fort Lapin
DAMPOORT
Damsevaart Zuid
Manderstraat
Zuidervaartje
Komvest
Wulpenstr.
Werfstr.
R 30
Kalvariebergstr.
Langerei
Buiten Kruisvest
Dampoortstr.
Van
Karel
Koningin Elisabethlaan
Vlamingdam
Sint Clarastr.
Peterseliestr.
ST. KRUIS
St. Janshuismolen
Annuntiatenstr.
Snaggaardstr.
Klaverstr.
Sint
Engels Klooster
Bonne Chieremolen
Carmersstraat
Jorisstr.
Jeruzalemkerk
Kruispoort
Kantcentrum
Peperstr.
St. Annakerk
Oude Zak
St.-Jakobstr.
Molenmeers
Langestraat
Kazernevest
Hoogstr.
MARKT
Ganzestr.
Predikherenrei
Bilkske
Hooistr.
BELFORT-HALLEN
Steenstr.
Dijver
Buiten Kazernevest
Gentpoortstr.
Buiten Boninvest
Koning Albertlaan
Oude Gentweg
Katelijnestr.
GENTPOORT
Generaal Lemanlaan
N 337
BEGIJNHOF
Wagnerstr.
Buiten Gentpoortvest
Daverlostraat
KATELIJNEPOORT
E. de Denestr.
Rubenslaan
N 50
Vrijheldsstr.
Weide Straat
X
Y
Z

Ter Duinen without rest, Langerei 52 ℘ 33 04 37, Fax 34 42 16 – |‡| ▤ TV ☎ ⇔ P. AE ① E VISA JCB. ✻ CX
closed January – **20 rm** ☐ 2400/3950.

Flanders without rest, Langestraat 38 ℘ 33 88 89, Fax 33 93 45, ⊠ – |‡| TV ☎ P AE ① E VISA JCB DY
closed 4 to 29 January – **16 rm** ☐ 2600/3950.

Gd H. Oude Burg without rest, Oude Burg 5 ℘ 44 51 11, Fax 44 51 00, ⌂ – |‡| TV ☎ ⇔ – 🔬 25-180. AE ① E VISA JCB AU
138 rm ☐ 2500/4750.

Anselmus without rest, Riddersstraat 15 ℘ 34 13 74, Fax 34 19 16 – TV ☎. AE E VISA AT
closed January – **10 rm** ☐ 2700/3000.

Adornes without rest, St-Annarei 26 ℘ 34 13 36, Fax 34 20 85, ≤, « Period vaulted cellars » – |‡| TV ☎ ⇔. AE E VISA JCB AT
closed January-14 February – **20 rm** ☐ 2600/3600.

Aragon without rest, Naaldenstraat 24 ℘ 33 35 33, Fax 34 28 05 – |‡| TV ☎ ⇔. AE ① E VISA JCB AT
closed January-13 February – **18 rm** ☐ 2250/4200.

Biskajer without rest, Biskajersplein 4 ℘ 34 15 06, Fax 34 39 11 – |‡| TV ☎. AE ① E VISA AT
17 rm ☐ 2800/3950.

Azalea without rest, Wulfhagestraat 43 ℘ 33 14 78, Fax 33 97 00, « Canalside terrace » – |‡| TV ☎ ⇔. AE ① E VISA JCB CY
25 rm ☐ 2800/4100.

Patritius without rest, Riddersstraat 11 ℘ 33 84 54, Fax 33 96 34, ⌂ – |‡| TV ☎ ⇔ P – 🔬 25. AE ① E VISA JCB AT
closed January-15 February – **16 rm** ☐ 2000/4000.

Egmond without rest, Minnewater 15 ℘ 34 14 45, Fax 34 29 40, « Early 20C residence in garden », ⌂ – TV ☎ P. ✻ AV
closed January – **8 rm** ☐ 3200/3600.

Gd H. du Sablon, Noordzandstraat 21 ℘ 33 39 02, Fax 33 39 08, « Early 20C hall » – |‡| TV ☎ – 🔬 25-100. AE ① E VISA AU
Meals (residents only) – **42 rm** ☐ 2800/3700.

Montovani without rest, Schouwvegerstraat 11 ℘ 34 53 66, Fax 34 53 67 – TV ☎. AE ① E VISA. ✻ BY
closed 16 to 31 January – **13 rm** ☐ 1600/2900.

XXXX ✿✿✿ **De Karmeliet** (Van Hecke), Langestraat 19 ℘ 33 82 59, Fax 33 10 11, ⌂, « Ancient patrician residence, terrace » – P. AE ① E VISA JCB DY
closed Sunday lunch June-August, Sunday dinner, Monday, 22 June-7 July and 3 weeks January – **Meals** Lunch 2100 – 2600/3500, – a la carte 2950/3400
Spec. Suprêmes de pigeon rôtis, saucisson de ses cuisses confites au pied de porc, sauce aux épices, Tuile sucrée et salée aux grosses langoustines et chicons confits, Ravioli à la vanille et pommes caramélisées en chaud-froid.

XXX ✿ **De Snippe** (Huysentruyt) with rm, Nieuwe Gentweg 53 ℘ 33 70 70, Fax 33 76 62, « 18C residence with murals » – |‡| TV ☎ P. AE ① E VISA AV
closed 6 to 21 February and 2 weeks November – **Meals** *(closed Sunday and Monday lunch)* Lunch 1950 b.i. – 2500, a la carte 2600/2900 – **9 rm** *(closed Sunday November-April)* ☐ 4500/7000
Spec. Foie d'oie au gros sel et anguilles rissolées au balsamico, St-Jacques grillées à la crème de salsifis et caviar, Loup de mer à la persillade de truffes et chicons aux langoustines.

XXX ✿ **Den Gouden Harynck** (Serruys), Groeninge 25 ℘ 33 76 37, Fax 34 42 70 – P. AE ① E VISA AUV
closed Sunday, Monday, 1 week after Easter, last 2 weeks July and last week December – **Meals** Lunch 1200 – 2000, a la carte approx. 2600
Spec. Langoustines grillées aux herbes, St-Pierre aux asperges et verjus, Pigeonneau en croûte de sel à la vanille.

XXX **Duc de Bourgogne** with rm, Huidenvettersplein 12 ℘ 33 20 38, Fax 34 40 37, ≤ canals, « Rustic decor and murals of late medieval style » – ▤ rest TV ☎. AE ① E VISA JCB AU
closed 8 to 31 July and 3 to 31 January – **Meals** *(closed Monday and Tuesday lunch)* Lunch 1250 – a la carte approx. 2400 – **10 rm** ☐ 3600/5200.

XXX **De Witte Poorte,** Jan Van Eyckplein 6 ℘ 33 08 83, Fax 34 55 60, ⌂, « Vaulted dining room, garden » – AE ① E VISA JCB AT
closed Sunday and Monday except Bank Holidays, 2 weeks February and last 2 weeks June – **Meals** Lunch 1100 – 1750/2050.

XXX **Den Braamberg,** Pandreitje 11 ☎ 33 73 70, Fax 33 99 73 – AE E VISA JCB AU u
closed Thursday, Sunday, 15 to 31 July and 1 to 10 January – **Meals** *Lunch 1700 b.i.* – a la carte 1650/2550.

XXX **'t Pandreitje,** Pandreitje 6 ☎ 33 11 90, Fax 34 00 70 – AE ⓓ E VISA JCB AU x
closed Wednesday, Sunday, 10 to 16 February, 30 June-13 July and 27 October-2 November – **Meals** *Lunch 1450* – 1650/2150.

XX **'t Stil Ende,** Scheepsdalelaan 12 ☎ 33 92 03, Fax 33 26 22, 🏞 – AE ⓓ E VISA JCB. ⚘ BX a
closed Saturday lunch, Sunday dinner, Monday and late July-early August – **Meals** *Lunch 950* – 1500/1950.

XX **'t Bourgoensche Cruyce** ⚘ with rm, Wollestraat 43 ☎ 33 79 26, Fax 34 19 68, ≤ *canals and old Flemish houses* – |♦| ▤ rest ▣ ☎. AE ⓓ E VISA AU f
closed 1 to 9 July and 18 November-10 December – **Meals** *(closed Tuesday and Wednesday) Lunch 1750 b.i.* – 1800 – **8 rm** ☐ 3400/4400.

XX **Hermitage** (Dryepondt), Ezelstraat 18 ☎ 34 41 73 – ⓓ E VISA JCB CY z
✿ *closed Sunday, Monday and 15 July-15 August* – **Meals** (dinner only) (booking essential) a la carte approx. 2400
Spec. Terrine de foie gras d'oie, Ris de veau sauce aux truffes, Turbot aux lentilles, gingembre et cardamone.

XX **De Lotteburg,** Goezeputstraat 43 ☎ 33 75 35, Fax 33 04 04, 🏞, Seafood – AE ⓓ E VISA JCB. ⚘ AV d
closed Monday, Tuesday, last week January-first week February and last week July-first week August – **Meals** *Lunch 1395 b.i.* – 1595/1895.

XX **Kardinaalshof,** St-Salvatorskerkhof 14 ☎ 34 16 91, Fax 34 20 62, Seafood – AE ⓓ E VISA AUV g
closed Thursday lunch Wednesday and first 2 weeks July – **Meals** *Lunch 1100* – 1100/1875.

XX **Patrick Devos,** Zilverstraat 41 ☎ 33 55 66, Fax 33 58 67, « Belle Epoque interior, patio » – AE ⓓ E VISA JCB. ⚘ AU y
closed Sunday, 21 July-8 August and 24 to 31 December – **Meals** *Lunch 900* – 1500/2200.

XX **Spinola,** Spinolarei 1 ☎ 34 17 85, Fax 34 13 71, « Rustic » – AE ⓓ E VISA AT c
closed Sunday, Monday lunch and 1 to 15 July – **Meals** a la carte 1400/1800.

XX **Tanuki,** Oude Gentweg 1 ☎ 34 75 12, Fax 34 75 12, Japanese cuisine – ▤. AE E VISA JCB. ⚘ AV f
closed Monday and Tuesday – **Meals** *Lunch 430* – 1390/1900.

X **Bhavani,** Simon Stevinplein 5 ☎ 33 90 25, Fax 34 89 52, 🏞, Indian cuisine, open until 11 p.m. – AE ⓓ E VISA JCB AU z
Meals *Lunch 650* – 850/1300.

X **Brasserie Raymond,** Eiermarkt 5 ☎ 33 78 48, Fax 33 78 48, 🏞, Open until 11.30 p.m. – AE ⓓ E VISA JCB AT g
closed Tuesday, 3 to 14 March, 1 to 15 July and 11 to 18 November – **Meals** *Lunch 475* – a la carte 800/1450.

X **René,** St-Jacobstraat 58 ☎ 34 12 24 – AE E VISA JCB. ⚘ AT e

Suburbs

North-West – ✉ *8000* – ☎ *0 50 :*

XX **De Gouden Korenhalm,** Oude Oostendsesteenweg 79 (Sint-Pieters) ☎ 31 33 93, Fax 31 18 96, 🏞, « Typical Flemish farmhouse » – ⓟ. AE ⓓ E VISA
closed Monday, late February and late August – **Meals** *Lunch 995* – 1420/1850.

South – ✉ *8200* – ☎ *0 50 :*

🏨 **Novotel Zuid,** Chartreuseweg 20 (Sint-Michiels) ☎ 40 21 40, Telex 81507, Fax 40 21 41, 🏞, ⛱, 🌳 – |♦| ⇆ ▤ rest ▣ ☎ ♿ ⓟ – 🏛 25-200. AE ⓓ E VISA. ⚘ rest
Meals *Lunch 500* – a la carte 950/1350 – ☐ 425 – **101 rm** 3350/3750.

XXX **Casserole** (Hotel school), Groene-Poortdreef 17 (Sint-Michiels) ☎ 40 30 30, Fax 40 30 35, 🏞, « Garden setting » – ⓟ. AE ⓓ E VISA. ⚘
closed Saturday, Sunday and School Holidays – **Meals** (lunch only) *Lunch 950* – a la carte approx. 1400.

South-West – ✉ *8200* – ☎ *0 50 :*

🏨 **Host. Pannenhuis** ⚘, Zandstraat 2 ☎ 31 19 07, Fax 31 77 66, ≤, 🏞, « Terrace and garden » – ▣ ☎ ⓟ – 🏛 25. AE ⓓ E VISA JCB
Meals *(closed Tuesday dinner, Wednesday, 15 January-2 February and 3 to 25 July) Lunch 1250* – 1250/1650 – **18 rm** *(closed 15 January-2 February)* ☐ 3250/3950.

XX **Herborist** with rm, De Watermolen 15 (by N 32 : 6 km, then on the right after E 40 St-Andries) 38 76 00, « Inn with country atmosphere », – TV P. AE E VISA
closed Sunday dinner, Monday, 26 March-6 April, 26 June-6 July, 26 September-6 October and 26 December-6 January – **Meals** *Lunch 1750 b.i.* – 2950 b.i./3650 b.i. – **4 rm** 3150/4250.

at Sint-Kruis *E : 6 km* C *Bruges* – *8310 Sint-Kruis* – *0 50 :*

Wilgenhof without rest, Polderstraat 151 36 27 44, Fax 36 28 21, , « An area of reclaimed land (polder) », – TV P. AE E VISA JCB
closed last week January – **6 rm** 2500/4100.

XXX **Ronnie Jonkman,** Maalsesteenweg 438 36 07 67, Fax 35 76 96, , « Terraces » – P. AE E VISA JCB
closed Sunday, Monday, 1 to 15 April, 1 to 15 July and 1 to 15 October – **Meals** *Lunch 1750 b.i.* – a la carte 2150/2750.

Environs

at Hertsberge *S by N 50 : 12,5 km* C *Oostkamp pop. 20 882* – *8020 Hertsberge* – *0 50 :*

XXX **Manderley,** Kruisstraat 13 27 80 51, , « Terrace and garden » – P. AE E VISA
closed Thursday dinner September-May, Sunday dinner, Monday, first week October and last 3 weeks January – **Meals** *Lunch 1200* – 1700/2100.

at Ruddervoorde *S by N 50 : 12 km* C *Oostkamp pop. 20 882* – *8020 Ruddervoorde* – *0 50 :*

XXX **Host. Leegendael** with rm, Kortrijkstraat 498 (N 50) 27 76 99, Fax 27 58 80, « Period residence, country atmosphere » – TV P. AE E VISA
closed 17 to 27 February and 16 August-16 September – **Meals** *(closed dinner Tuesday and Sunday, Wednesday and Saturday lunch) Lunch 990* – a la carte 1600/2200 – **6 rm** 1750/2550.

at Varsenare *W : 6,5 km* C *Jabbeke pop. 13 058* – *8490 Varsenare* – *0 50 :*

XXXX **Manoir Stuivenberg** with rm, Gistelsteenweg 27 38 15 02, Fax 38 28 92, , TV P. AE E VISA.
Meals *(closed Sunday and Monday dinner) Lunch 1485* – 1895/2350 – **7 rm** 4450/6500, 1 suite.

at Waardamme *S by N 50 : 11 km* C *Oostkamp pop. 20 882* – *8020 Waardamme* – *0 50 :*

XXX **Ter Talinge,** Rooiveldstraat 46 27 90 61, Fax 28 00 52, , « Terrace » – P. AE E VISA
closed Wednesday, Thursday, 19 February-7 March and 22 August-5 September – **Meals** *Lunch 1100* – a la carte 1250/1700.

at Zedelgem *SW : 10,5 km* – *pop. 21 195* – *8210 Zedelgem* – *0 50 :*

Zuidwege without rest, Torhoutsesteenweg 128 20 13 39, Fax 20 17 39 – TV P – 25. AE E VISA.
closed 23 December-5 January – **17 rm** 1850/2550.

XX **Ter Leepe,** Torhoutsesteenweg 168 20 01 97, Fax 20 88 54 – P. AE E VISA
closed Wednesday dinner, Sunday, carnival and 20 to 31 July – **Meals** *Lunch 1300 b.i.* – a la carte approx. 1500.

Waregem *8790 West-Vlaanderen* 213 ⑮ *and* 409 D 3 – *pop. 35 610* – *0 56* – *47 km.*

XXXX **'t Oud Konijntje** (Mmes Desmedt), Bosstraat 53 (S : 2 km near E 17) 60 19 37, Fax 60 92 12, , « Floral terrace » – P. AE E VISA
closed dinner Thursday and Sunday, Friday, 22 July-13 August and 22 December-4 January – **Meals** *Lunch 1500* – a la carte 2300/2700
Spec. Mosaïque de foie d'oie et foie de canard, Suprême de bar légèrement fumé et vinaigrette au jus de truffes, Poêlée de selle, langue et ris d'agneau au chou fondant et risotto de poireaux.

Pleasant hotels and restaurants
are shown in the Guide by a red sign.
Please send us the names
of any where you have enjoyed your stay.
Your Michelin Guide will be even better.

XXXXX ... X

LIÈGE 4000 213 ㉒ and 409 J 4 ⑰ N – pop. 192 393 – ✪ 0 4.

See : *Citadel* ≤** DW – *Cointe Park* ≤* CX – *Old town*** – *Palace of the Prince-Bishops** : *court of honour*** EY – *The Perron** (*market cross*) EY **A** – *Baptismal font**** of *St. Bartholomew's church* FY – *Treasury*** of *St. Paul's Cathedral : reliquary of Charles the Bold*** EZ – *St. James church*** : *vaults of the nave*** EZ – *Altarpiece** in the *St. Denis church* EY – *Church of St. John : Wooden Calvary statues** EY – *Aquarium** FZ **D**.

Museums : *Provincial Museum of Life in Wallonia*** EY – *Religious and Roman Art Museum** FY **M**5 – *Curtius and Glass Museum** : *evangelistary of Notger****, *collection of glassware** FY **M**1 – *Arms** FY **M**3 – *Ansembourg** FY **M**2.

Envir : *Blégny-Trembleur*** NE : 20 km – *Baptismal font** in the *church** of St. Severin SW : 27 km – *Visé* N : 17 km, *Reliquary of St. Hadelin** in the collegiate church.

r. Bernalmont 2 ℘ 227 44 66, Fax 227 91 92 – at Angleur S : 7,5 km, rte du Condroz 541 ℘ (0 4) 336 20 21, Fax (0 4) 337 20 26 – at Gomzé-Andoumont SE : 18 km, r. Gomzé 30 ℘ (0 4) 360 92 07, Fax (0 4) 360 92 06.

℘ 342 52 14.

En Féronstrée 92 ℘ 221 92 21, Fax 221 92 22 and (closed Sunday October-April) Gare des Guillemins ℘ 252 44 19 – Tourist association of the province (closed Sunday), bd de la Sauvenière 77 ℘ 222 42 10, Fax 222 10 92.

Brussels 97 – Amsterdam 242 – Antwerp 119 – Cologne 122 – Luxembourg 159.

Plans on following pages

Bedford M, quai St-Léonard 36 ℘ 228 81 11, Fax 227 45 75, « Inner garden » – AE VISA. rm — DW g
Meals (open until 11 p.m.) *Lunch 1050* – a la carte approx. 900 – **149 rm** 3250/3800.

Michel Germeau, r. Vennes 151 (Fétinne), ✉ 4020, ℘ 343 72 42, Fax 344 03 86, « Early 20C mansion » – AE VISA — DX y
closed Monday, 17 to 24 February, 4 to 19 August and 1 to 8 December – **Meals** *Lunch 1050* – 1350/1650.

Old town

Mercure, bd de la Sauveniere 100 ℘ 221 77 11, Fax 221 77 01 – 25-100. AE VISA JCB. — EY t
Meals *Lunch 700* – a la carte approx. 1400 – **105 rm** 4500/4975.

Au Vieux Liège, quai Goffe 41 ℘ 223 77 48, Fax 223 78 60, « 16C residence » – AE VISA — FY a
closed Wednesday dinner, Sunday, Bank Holidays, 1 week Easter and mid July-mid August – **Meals** *Lunch 1250* – 1250/1600.

Chez Max, pl. de la République Française 12 ℘ 222 08 59, Fax 222 90 02, Oyster bar, open until 11 p.m., « Elegant brasserie decorated by Luc Genot » – AE VISA JCB
closed Saturday lunch and Sunday – **Meals** *Lunch 990* – a la carte 1400/1800. — EY a

Robert Lesenne, r. Boucherie 9 ℘ 222 07 93, Fax 222 92 33 – AE VISA — FY m
closed Saturday lunch, Sunday and August – **Meals** 1250.

Le Shanghai 1st floor, Galeries Cathédrale 104 ℘ 222 22 63, Fax 223 00 50, Chinese cuisine – AE VISA — EZ r

As Ouhes, pl. du Marché 21 ℘ 223 32 25, Fax 222 30 19, Oyster bar – AE VISA
closed Sunday and last 2 weeks July – **Meals** *Lunch 400* – 1000 b.i./1350 b.i.. — EY e

Enoteca, r. Casquette 5 ℘ 222 24 64, Fax 222 34 31
VISA — EY g
closed Saturday lunch, Sunday and Bank Holidays – **Meals** *Lunch 590* – 1090.

Lalo's Bar, r. Madeleine 18 ℘ 223 22 57, Fax 223 22 57, Italian cuisine, open until 11.30 p.m. – VISA JCB — EY d
closed Saturday lunch, Sunday and 21 July-15 August – **Meals** *Lunch 395* – 800/1250.

Guillemins

L'Héliport, bd Frère-Orban ℘ 252 13 21, ≤, – AE VISA — CX b
closed Sunday, Monday dinner and July – **Meals** – 1290.

La Maison Thaïe, bd d'Avroy 180 ℘ 222 00 91, Fax 221 05 21, Thaï cuisine – AE VISA
closed Tuesday and Saturday lunch – **Meals** a la carte approx. 1000. — CX d

Le Duc d'Anjou, r. Guillemins 127 ℘ 252 28 58, Mussels in season, open until 11.30 p.m. – AE VISA – **Meals** 795. — CX n

Outremeuse

Holiday Inn without rest, Esplanade de l'Europe 2, ✉ 4020, ℘ 342 60 20, Fax 343 48 10, ≤, – 25-50. AE VISA JCB — DX a
214 rm 5250/6600, 5 suites.

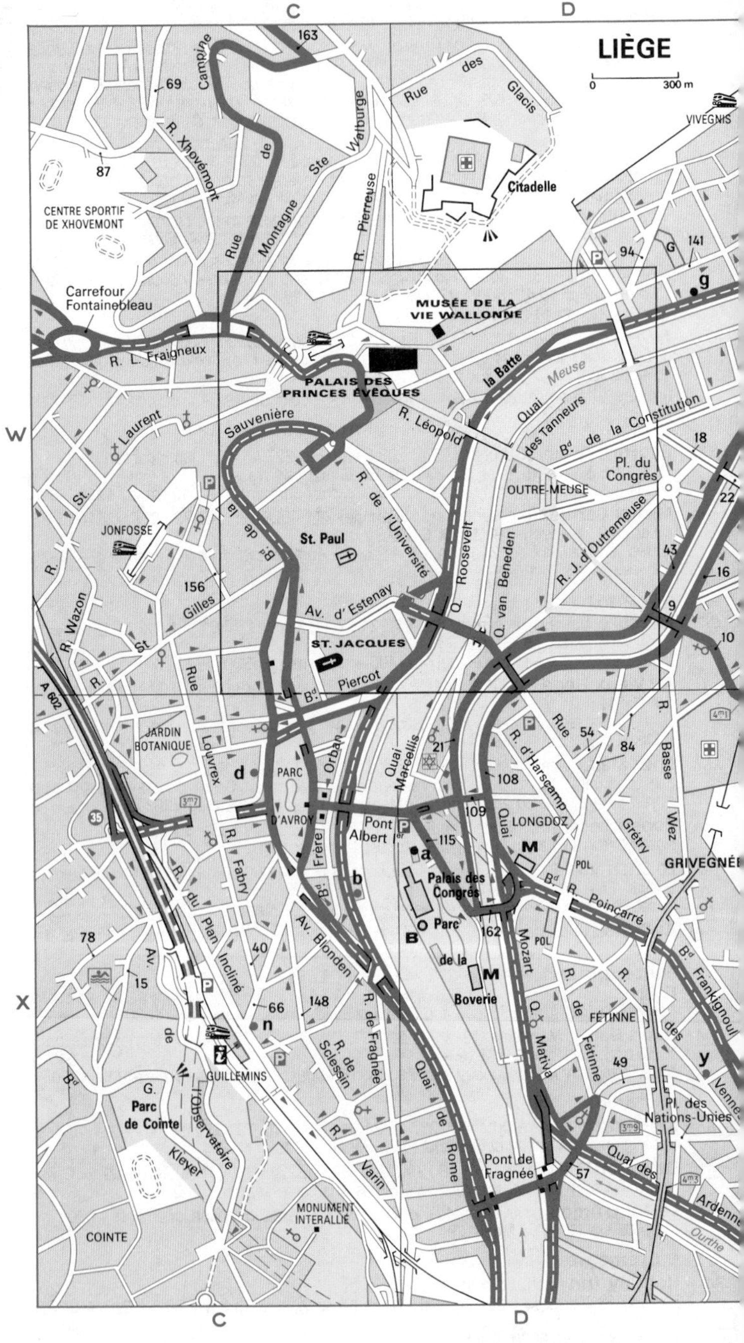

LIÈGE
0
300 m
C
D
W
X
CENTRE SPORTIF DE XHOVEMONT
Carrefour Fontainebleau
R. L. Fraigneux
R. Xhovémont
Rue de Campine
Montagne Ste Walburge
R. Pierreuse
Rue des Glacis
Citadelle
VIVEGNIS
MUSÉE DE LA VIE WALLONNE
PALAIS DES PRINCES ÉVÊQUES
la Batte
Quai des Tanneurs
Meuse
Bd de la Constitution
R. Léopold
Sauvenière
Bd de la Sauvenière
R. de l'Université
St. Paul
Av. d'Estenay
ST. JACQUES
Bd Piercot
Q. Roosevelt
Q. van Beneden
R. J. d'Outremeuse
OUTRE-MEUSE
Pl. du Congrès
St. Laurent
JONFOSSE
St. Gilles
R. Wazon
A 602
JARDIN BOTANIQUE
Rue Louvrex
PARC D'AVROY
Bd Frère Orban
Quai Marcellis
Pont Albert Ier
Palais des Congrès
Parc de la Boverie
R. d'Harscamp
LONGDOZ
Quai Mozart
Rue Grétry
R. Basse Wez
GRIVEGNÉE
Bd R. Poincarré
Bd Frankignoul
R. Fabry
R. du Plan Incliné
Av. Blonden
R. de Fragnée
R. de Sclessin
Av. Rogier
Quai de Rome
Q. Mativa
R. de Fétinne
FÉTINNE
R. des Vennes
Pl. des Nations-Unies
Quai des Ardennes
Ourthe
Pont de Fragnée
GUILLEMINS
Bd de l'Observatoire
Parc de Cointe
Kleyer
R. Varin
MONUMENT INTERALLIÉ
COINTE
POL.
M
a
b
d
g
n
y
B
G
163
69
87
94
141
18
22
43
16
9
10
156
21
54
84
108
109
115
162
35
78
15
40
66
148
49
57

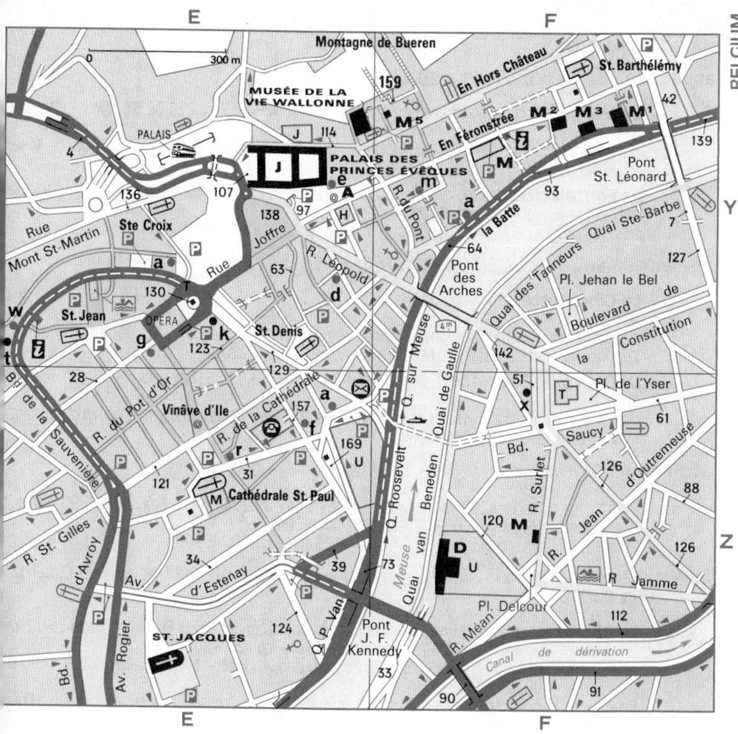

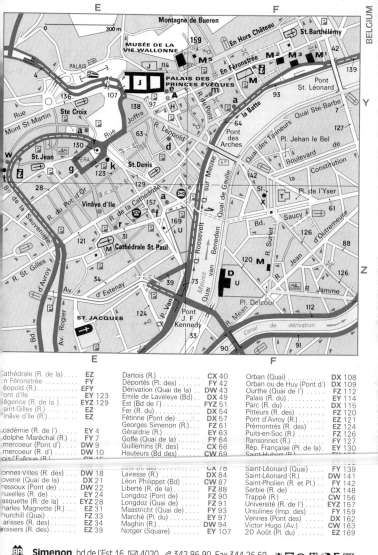

Cathédrale (R. de la) .... EZ
En Féronstrée .... FY
Léopold (R.) .... EFY
Pont d'Ile .... EY 123
Régence (R. de la) .... EYZ 129
Saint-Gilles (R.) .... EZ
Vinâve d'Ile (R.) .... EZ

Académie (R. de l') .... EY 4
Adolphe Maréchal (R.) .. FY 7
Amercoeur (Pont d') .... DW 9
Amercoeur (R. d') .... DW 10
Bois-l'Évêque (R.) ....

Bonnes-Villes (R. des) ... DW 18
Boverie (Quai de la) .... DX 21
Bressoux (Pont de) .... DW 22
Bruxelles (R. de) .... EY 24
Casquette (R. de la) .... EYZ 28
Charles Magnette (R.) ... EZ 31
Churchill (Quai) .... FZ 33
Clarisses (R. des) .... EZ 34
Croisiers (R. des) .... EZ 39

Dartois (R.) .... CX 40
Déportés (Pl. des) .... FY 42
Dérivation (Quai de la) .. DW 43
Emile de Laveleye (Bd) .. DX 49
Est (Bd de l') .... FYZ 51
Fer (R. du) .... DX 54
Fétinne (Pont de) .... DX 57
Georges Simenon (R.) ... FZ 61
Gérardrie (R.) .... EY 63
Goffe (Quai de la) .... FY 64
Guillemins (R. des) .... CX 66
Hauteurs (Bd des) .... CW 69
.... CX 78
Lairesse (R.) .... DX 84
Léon Philippet (Bd) .... CW 87
Liberté (R. de la) .... FZ 88
Longdoz (Pont de) .... FZ 90
Longdoz (Quai de) .... FZ 91
Maastricht (Quai de) .... FY 93
Marché (Pl. du) .... EY 97
Maghin (R.) .... DW 94
Notger (Square) .... EY 107

Orban (Quai) .... DX 108
Orban ou de Huy (Pont d') DX 109
Ourthe (Quai de l') .... FZ 112
Palais (R. du) .... EY 114
Parc (R. du) .... DX 115
Pitteurs (R. des) .... FZ 120
Pont d'Avroy (R.) .... EZ 121
Prémontrés (R. des) .... EZ 124
Puits-en-Soc (R.) .... FZ 126
Ransonnet (R.) .... FY 127
Rép. Française (Pl. de la) . EY 130
Saint-Hubert (R.) ....
Saint-Léonard (Quai) .... FY 139
Saint-Léonard (R.) .... DW 141
Saint-Pholien (R. et Pl.) .. FY 142
Serbie (R. de) .... CX 148
Trappé (R.) .... CW 156
Université (R. de l') .... EYZ 157
Ursulines (Imp. des) .... FY 159
Vennes (Pont des) .... DX 162
Victor Hugo (Av.) .... CW 163
20 Août (Pl. du) .... EZ 169

Simenon, bd de l'Est 16, ✉ 4020, ☎ 342 86 90, Fax 344 26 69 – 🛗 📺 ☎. AE ⓓ E VISA
Meals (Pub rest, lunch only) *(closed 24 December-2 January) Lunch 220* – a la carte approx. 800 – ☕ 280 – **11 rm** 2000. FZ x

Suburbs

at Chênée *E : 7,5 km* 🄲 *Liège* – ✉ *4032 Chênée* – ☎ *0 4 :*

XXX **Le Gourmet,** r. Large 91 ☎ 365 87 97, Fax 365 38 12, 🌳, « Winter garden » – Ⓟ. AE ⓓ E VISA
closed Monday dinner, Wednesday, Saturday lunch, last 2 weeks July-first 2 weeks August and first week January – **Meals** *Lunch 990* – 990/1500.

XX **Le Vieux Chênée,** r. Gravier 45 ☎ 367 00 92, Fax 367 59 15 – AE ⓓ E VISA
closed Thursday except Bank Holidays and 2 weeks July – **Meals** *Lunch 890* – a la carte 1050/1550.

Environs

at Ans *NW : 4 km – pop. 27781 – ✉ 4430 Ans – ☎ 04 :*

XX **Le Marguerite,** r. Walthère Jamar 171 ✆ 226 43 46, Fax 226 38 35, 余 – AE ⓓ E VISA JCB
closed Saturday lunch, Sunday, Monday, last 3 weeks July and late December – **Meals** *Lunch 980* – 1450.

XX **La Fontaine de Jade,** r. Yser 321 ✆ 246 49 72, Fax 263 69 53, Chinese cuisine, open until 11 p.m. – ▤. AE ⓓ E VISA
closed Tuesday – **Meals** *Lunch 450* – a la carte 800/1150.

at Flémalle *SW : 14 km* C *Flémalle pop. 26633 – ✉ 4400 Flémalle-Haute – ☎ 04 :*

XXX **La Ciboulette,** chaussée de Chokier 96 ✆ 275 19 65, Fax 275 05 81, 余 – AE ⓓ E VISA
closed Monday, Saturday lunch, dinner Sunday and Wednesday, 30 July-14 August and 29 December-12 January – **Meals** *Lunch 1200* – 1200/2200.

XX **Le Gourmet Gourmand,** Grand-Route 411 ✆ 233 07 56, Fax 233 19 21, 余 – AE ⓓ E VISA
closed Saturday lunch, Monday, dinner Tuesday, Wednesday and mid July-mid August – **Meals** *Lunch 1250* – 1500/1650.

at Herstal *NE : 8 km – pop. 36841 – ✉ 4040 Herstal – ☎ 04 :*

Post ⛺, r. Hurbise (by motorway E 40 exit 34) ✆ 264 64 00, Fax 248 06 90, 余, – |♦| ▤ rest TV ☎ P – 🏛 25-60. AE ⓓ E VISA
Meals *Lunch 800* – a la carte 950/1450 – **93 rm** ☕ 2800/5900.

at Neuville-en-Condroz *S : 18 km* C *Neupré pop. 9239 – ✉ 4121 Neuville-en-Condroz ☎ 04 :*

XXXX ✿ **Le Chêne Madame** (Mme Tilkin), av. de la Chevauchée 70 (in Rognacs wood SE : 2 km) ✆ 371 41 27, Fax 371 29 43, « Country Inn » – P. AE ⓓ E VISA
closed Monday, dinner Sunday and Thursday and August – **Meals** *Lunch 1090* – 1690 b.i. a la carte 1700/2500
Spec. Rôti d'agneau de Pauillac aux herbes, cuit en croûte de sel, Salade de lapereau à l'huile de noix, Gibiers en saison.

Hasselt *3500 Limburg* 213 ⑨ *and* 409 I 3 *– pop. 67486 – ☎ 0 11 – 42 km.*

at Stevoort *by N 2 : 5 km to Kermt, then road on the left* C *Hasselt – ✉ 3512 Stevoort – ☎ 0 11*

XXXXX ✿✿ **Scholteshof** (Souvereyns) ⛺ with rm, Kermtstraat 130 ✆ 25 02 02, Fax 25 43 28, 余, « 18C farmhouse with vines, kitchen garden, orchard and English style gardens », – TV ☎ P – 🏛 25-60. AE ⓓ E VISA
closed 14 to 31 July and 3 weeks January – **Meals** *(closed Wednesday) Lunch 2650 b.i.* 3450/4750, – a la carte 3750/4600 – ☕ 600 – **11 rm** 2900/5800, 7 suites
Spec. Raviolis de légumes et homard avec carpaccio de cabillaud à la coriandre, Pièce de bœuf piquée de truffes et olives noires, Soufflé au fromage blanc à la verveine et aux fruits rouges.

Namur *5000 Namur* 213 ⑳ 214 ⑤ *and* 409 H 4 *– pop. 105014 – ☎ 0 81 – 61 km.*

at Lives-sur-Meuse *E : 9 km* C *Namur – ✉ 5101 Lives-sur-Meuse – ☎ 0 81 :*

XXXX ✿✿ **La Bergerie** (Lefevere), r. Mosanville 100 ✆ 58 06 13, Fax 58 19 39, ≤, « Overlooking the valley, terrace and garden with ornamental fountain » – ▤ P. AE ⓓ VISA
closed Monday, Tuesday and late February-early March – **Meals** *Lunch 1750 b.i.* – a la carte 2500/3000
Spec. Truite de notre vivier au Bleu, Agneau rôti "Bergerie", Le gâteau de crêpes soufflées

Pepinster *4860 Liège* 213 ㉓ *and* 409 K 4 *– pop. 9127 – ☎ 0 87 – 26 km.*

XXX ✿✿ **Host. Lafarque** ⛺ with rm, Chemin des Douys 20 (W : 4 km by N 61, locality Goffontaine) ✆ 46 06 51, Fax 46 97 28, ≤, 余, « Park », – TV ☎ P. AE ⓓ E VISA ✻ rm
closed Monday, Tuesday, 3 weeks March and 1 week September – **Meals** *Lunch 1550* a la carte 2500/3000 – ☕ 400 – **6 rm** 3000/3950
Spec. Fondant de sandre et homard gratiné au Champagne, Ravioli de radis noir aux truffes (December-March), Fantaisie de lapereau aux épices de pain d'épices.

St-Vith *4780 Liège* 214 ⑨ *and* 409 L 5 *- pop. 8 807 - ☎ 0 80 - 78 km.*

XXX ✿✿ **Zur Post** (Pankert) with rm, Hauptstr. 39 ✆ 22 80 27, Fax 22 93 10 - TV ☎. AE E VISA. ✈ rest
closed Sunday dinner, Monday, Tuesday lunch, first 2 weeks July and January - **Meals** *Lunch 1450* - a la carte approx. 2500 - ☕ 500 - **8 rm** 1800/3300
Spec. Fond d'artichaut farci d'une poêlée de foie d'oie aux épinards, Croustade de loup de mer et jeune fenouil au vinaigre balsamique et huile de noisettes, Cochon de lait en cocotte aux éclats de truffes et champignons sauvages (February-15 September).

Tongeren *3700 Limburg* 213 ㉒ *and* 409 J 3 *- pop. 29 788 - ☎ 0 12 - 19 km.*

at Vliermaal *N : 5 km* C *Kortessem pop. 7 903 - ✉ 3724 Vliermaal - ☎ 0 12 :*

XXXXX ✿✿ **Clos St. Denis** (Denis), Grimmertingenstraat 24 ✆ 23 60 96, Fax 26 32 07, « 17C farmhouse manor, shaded terrace and garden » - P. AE ⓓ E VISA. ✈
closed Monday, Tuesday, 2 to 8 April, 16 to 30 July, 29 October-4 November and 23 December-6 January - **Meals** *Lunch 1500* - a la carte 2600/3700
Spec. Jarret de veau confit et foie de canard mariné aux truffes façon mille-feuille, Tarte fine de tomates confites et filets de rouget-barbet à la tapenade, Carpaccio de canard landais au basilic.

Weert *Limburg (Netherlands)* 211 O 15 *and* 408 I 8 *- pop. 41 683 - ☎ 0 495 - 90 km.*

✿✿ **Host. E. Mertens** Wilhelminasingel 80, ✉ 6001 GV, ✆ 53 10 57, Fax 54 45 96, - 🛗 TV ☎ 🚗 - 🏛 25. AE E VISA. ✈
closed Saturday lunch and Sunday - **Meals** ***l'Auberge*** *Lunch 65* - a la carte 114/130 - **14 rm** ☕ 145/235
Spec. St-Jacques marinées et escabèche de queues de langoustines au citron vert (October-April), Selle et carré d'agneau régional au saupiquet de son jarret (April-June), Gâteau de noisettes caramélisées au parfait de grains de café, crème au Whiskey.

LUXEMBOURG

(LËTZEBUERG) 215 E 4 *and* 409 L 7 – *pop. 75 377.*

Amsterdam 391 – Bonn 190 – Brussels 219 – Ettelbrück 30.

ℹ *(closed Sunday except April-October) pl. d'Armes.* ✉ *2011,* ☎ *22 28 09, Fax 47 48 18 – Air Terminus gare centrale,* ✉ *1010,* ☎ *40 08 08 20, Fax 40 08 08 30.*

⛳18 *Hoehenhof (Senningerberg) near Airport, rte de Trèves 1,* ✉ *2633,* ☎ *34 00 90, Fax 34 83 91.*

✈ *Arrival and departure information* ☎ *47 98 23 11 and 47 98 23 15. Findel by E 44 : 6 km* ☎ *40 08 08 – Air Terminal : pl. de la Gare* ☎ *48 11 99.*

See : *Site★★ – Old Luxembourg★★* G *: Place de la Constitution ⩽★★* F*, Plateau St. Esprit ⩽★★* G*, Chemin de la Corniche★★, ⩽★★* G*, The Bock cliff ⩽★★, Bock Casemates★★* G*, Boulevard Victor Thorn ⩽★* G *121, Grand-Ducal Palace★* G*, Cathedral of Our Lady★ (Notre-Dame)* F *– Grand-Duchess Charlotte Bridge★* DY *– The Trois Glands ⩽★ (Three Acorns)* DY.

Museum : *National Museum of Art and History★, Gallo Romain section★, Luxembourg life section (decorative arts and folk traditions)★★* G **M1**.

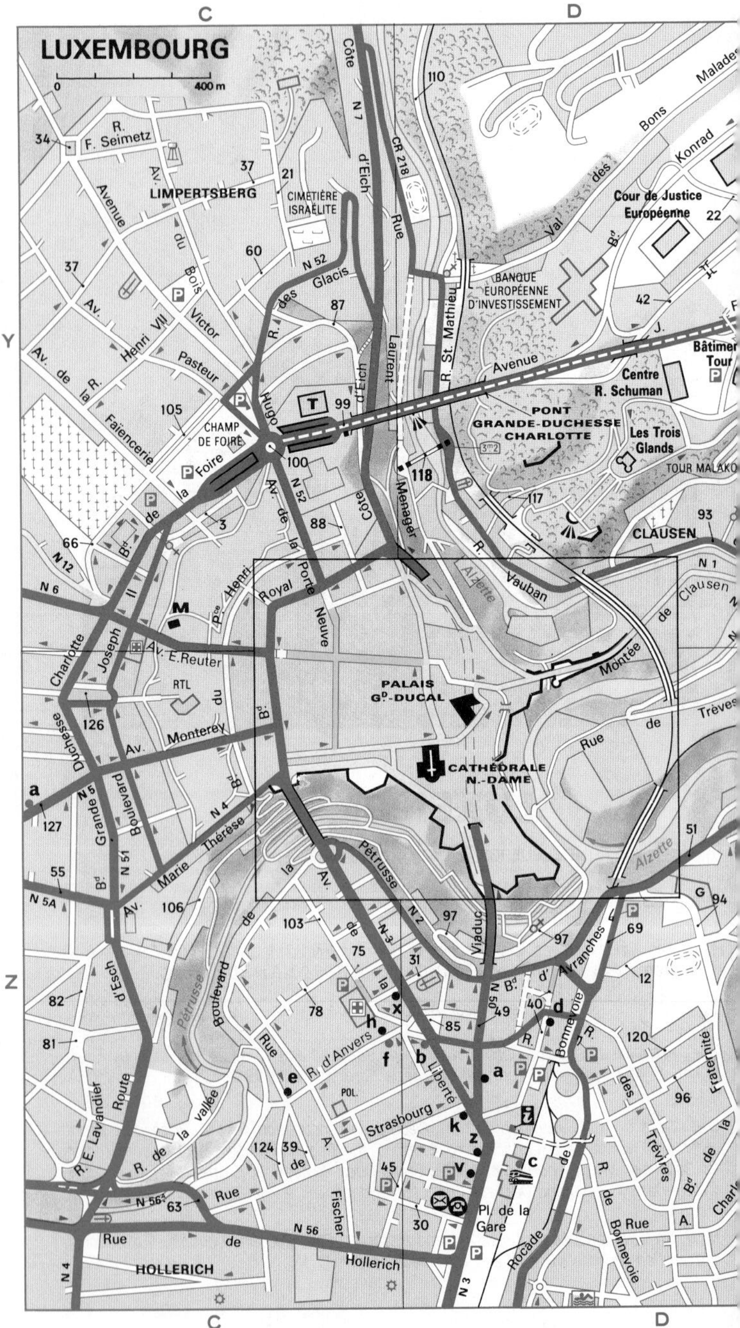
LUXEMBOURG
0
400 m
LIMPERTSBERG
CIMETIÈRE ISRAÉLITE
BANQUE EUROPÉENNE D'INVESTISSEMENT
Cour de Justice Européenne
Centre R. Schuman
PONT GRANDE-DUCHESSE CHARLOTTE
Les Trois Glands
TOUR MALAKO
CHAMP DE FOIRE
CLAUSEN
PALAIS Gᴰ-DUCAL
CATHÉDRALE N.-DAME
RTL
HOLLERICH
Pl. de la Gare
POL.

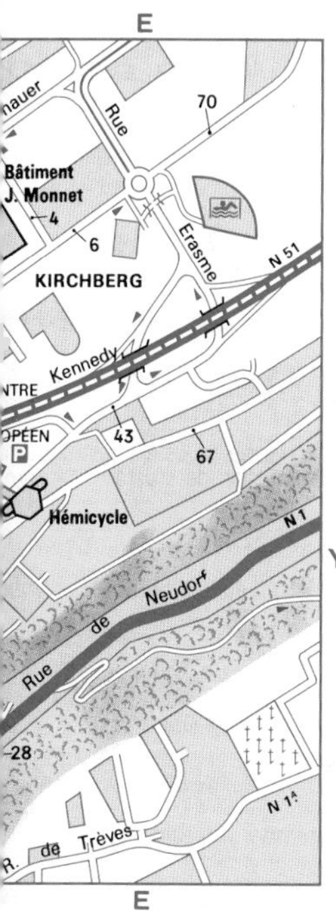

Capucins (R. des) ..... F
Chimay (R.) .... F 24
Curé (R. du) .... F
Fossé (R. du) .... F 46
Gare (Av. de la) .... DZ 49
Grand-Rue .... F
Liberté (Av. de la) ..... CDZ
Philippe II (R.) .... F 91
Porte-Neuve (Av. de la) . CY
Strasbourg (R. de) ..... CDZ

Adames (R.) .... CY 3
Albert Wehrer (R.) ..... EY 4
Alcide de Gasperi (R.) .. EY 6
Aldringen (R.) .... F 7
Athénée (R. de l') ..... F 9
Auguste Lumière (R.) .. DZ 12
Bains (R. des) .... F 13
Boucherie (R. de la) ... G 15
Bruxelles (Pl. de) ...... F 16
Cerisiers (R. des) ...... CY 21
Charles-Léon Hammes (R.) .... DY 22
Clairefontaine (Pl.) ..... FG 27
Clausen (R. de) .... EY 28
Commerce (R. du) ..... CDZ 30
Dicks (R.) .... CDZ 31
Eau (R. de l') .... G 33
Edouard André (Square) .... CY 34
Ermesinde (R.) .... CY 37
Etats-Unis (R. des) ..... CZ 39
Fort Neipperg (R. du) .. DZ 40
Fort Niedergrünewald (R. du) .... DY 42
Fort Thüngen (R. du) ... EY 43
Fort Wedell (R. du) .... CDZ 45
Franklin-Roosevelt (Bd) . F 48
Général Patton (Bd du) .... DZ 51
Guillaume (Av.) .... CZ 55
Guillaume II (R.) .... F 58
Guillaume Schneider (R.) .... CY 60
Jean Baptiste Merkels (R.) .... CZ 63
Jean Ulveling (Bd) .... FG 64
J.P. Probst (R.) .... CY 66
Jules Wilhem (R.) ..... EY 67
Laboratoire (R. du) .... DZ 69
Léon Hengen (R.) ..... EY 70
Marché (Pl. du) ...... G 72
Marché aux Herbes (R. du) .... FG 73
Martyrs (Pl. des) ...... CZ 75
Michel Rodange (R.) .. CZ 78
Nancy (Pl. de) .... CZ 81
Nassau (R. de) .... CZ 82
Notre-Dame (R.) ...... F 84
Paris (Pl. de) .... DZ 85
Paul Eyschen (R.) ..... CY 87
Pescatore (Av.) .... CY 88
Pfaffenthal (Montée de) .... FG 90
Pierre de Mansfeld (Allée) .... DY 93
Pierre et Marie Curie (R.) .... DZ 94
Pierre Hentges (R.) .... DZ 96
Prague (R. de) .... DZ 97
Robert Schuman (Bd) . CY 99
Robert Schuman (Rond-Point) .... CY 100
Sainte-Zithe (R.) ...... CZ 103
Scheffer (Allée) .... CY 105
Semois (R. de la) ..... CZ 106
Sigefroi (R.) .... G 108
Sostène Weis (R.) ..... G 109
Stavelot (R. de) .... DY 110
Théâtre (Pl. du) ...... F 114
Tour Jacob (Av. de la) .... EY 115
Trois Glands (R. des) .... DY 117
Vauban (Pont) .... DY 118
Verger (R. du) .... DZ 120
Victor Thorn (Bd) ..... G 121
Willy Georgen (R.) .... F 123
Wilson (R.) .... CZ 124
Winston Churchill (Pl.) . CZ 126
10 Septembre (Av. du) .... CZ 127

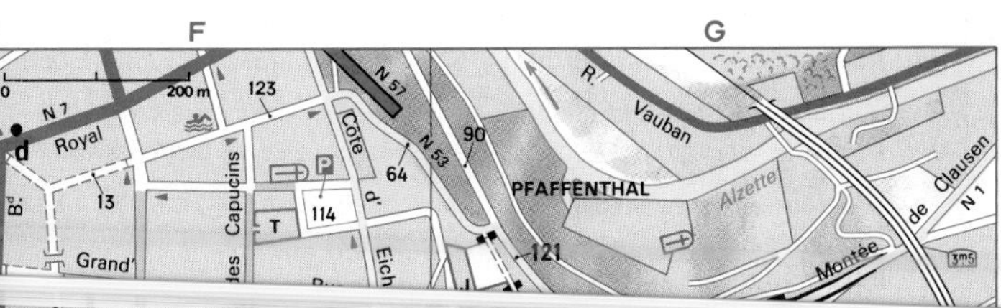

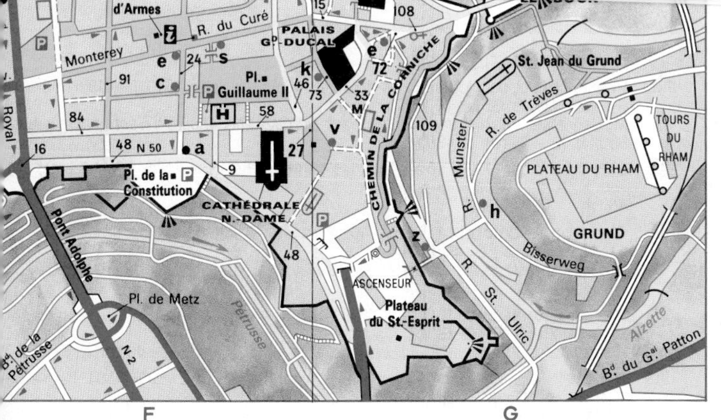

Luxembourg-Centre

Le Royal, bd Royal 12, 2449, 241 61 61, Fax 22 59 48, , , , – 25-350. . F
Meals *Le Jardin* *Lunch 1080* - a la carte approx. 1300 – **210 rm** 9200/10200, 15 suit

Gd H. Cravat, bd Roosevelt 29, 2450, 22 19 75, Telex 2846, Fax 22 67 11 – rest – 25. . rest F
Meals (Pub-rest) 950/1300 – **58 rm** 5600/7200.

Rix without rest, bd Royal 20, 2449, 47 16 66, Fax 22 75 35 – . F
closed 20 December-5 January – **20 rm** 4280/6280.

Clairefontaine (Tintinger), pl. de Clairefontaine 9, 1341, 46 22 11, Fax 47 08 2 – . G
closed Saturday lunch, Sunday, 10 to 15 February, 1 to 5 April, 15 to 31 August, 3 8 November and 24 to 28 December – **Meals** *Lunch 1750* – 2560, a la carte appr 2200
Spec. Variation de foie gras maison, Poularde de Bresse en vessie, sauce Albufera (autum Mille-feuille de homard, son risotto au Champagne et infusion de crustacés (autum **Wines** Pinot gris, Riesling.

St-Michel (Glauben) 1st floor, r. Eau 32, 1449, 22 32 15, Fax 46 25 93, « In t old city, rustic interior » – G
closed Saturday lunch, Sunday, Bank Holidays, 28 July-11 August and 24 Decembe 5 January – **Meals** *Lunch 1750* – a la carte 2250/2700
Spec. Mille-feuille de canard au foie gras, Filet de sandre gratiné à la moëlle, Soupière poularde au coulis de truffes (January-late March). **Wines** Riesling Koëppchen, Pinot g

Speltz, r. Chimay 8, 1333, 47 49 50, Fax 47 46 77, – F
closed Saturday, Sunday, Bank Holidays, 29 March-6 April, 2 to 17 August and 24 Dece ber-4 January – **Meals** 1350.

La Lorraine 1st floor, pl. d'Armes 7, 1136, 47 14 36, Fax 47 09 64, , Oys bar and Seafood – . F
closed Saturday lunch, Sunday and 15 August-8 September – **Meals** a la carte 180 2650.

Jan Schneidewind "Am Pays", r. Curé 20, 1368, 22 26 18, Fax 46 24 40, Seafood – . F
closed Saturday lunch, February and late December – **Meals** *Lunch 1480* – 1480/2280

Poêle d'Or, r. Marché-aux-Herbes 20, 1728, 22 26 06, Fax 22 26 05, Open u 11 p.m. – G
closed Monday dinner and Tuesday – **Meals** *Lunch 990* – a la carte approx. 1300.

L'Océan, r. Louvigny 7, 1946, 22 88 66, Fax 22 88 67, Oyster bar and Seafo – F
closed Sunday dinner, Monday, 13 to 20 May and 31 August-14 September – **Meals** a carte 1550/2000.

Luxembourg-Grund

Kamakura, r. Münster 4, 2160, 47 06 04, Fax 46 73 30, Japanese cuisine – . G
closed Sunday – **Meals** *Lunch 360* – 755/960.

Luxembourg-Station

President, pl. de la Gare 32, 1024, 48 61 61, Telex 1510, Fax 48 61 80 – – 40. . rest DZ
Meals (dinner only) *(closed Sunday, Bank Holidays and August-1 September)* a la ca 800/1500 – **35 rm** 4800/6400.

City without rest, r. Strasbourg 1, 2561, 29 11 22, Fax 29 11 33 – – 25-100. DZ
35 rm 3000/5300.

Christophe Colomb, r. Anvers 10, 1130, 408 41 41, Fax 40 84 08, – rest . CZ
Meals (Pub-rest) *(closed Saturday and Sunday)* *Lunch 330* – a la carte 850/1300 – **24** 3400/3800.

International, pl. de la Gare 20, 1616, 48 59 11, Fax 49 32 27 – – 25-50. . rm DZ
Meals *(closed 23 December-11 January)* *Lunch 950* – 950/1395 – **48 rm** 3800/50

Arcotel without rest, 1st floor, av. de la Gare 43, 1611, 49 40 01, Fax 40 56 – . . DZ
30 rm 4800.

Central Molitor, av. de la Liberté 28, ⊠ 1930, ℘ 48 99 11, Fax 48 33 82 – ⫿ ▤ rest TV ☎ ⇔. AE ⓓ E VISA CDZ x
Meals (lunch only) *(closed Saturday, last week July-first 2 weeks August and late December-early January)* *Lunch 340* – 800 – **36 rm** ☐ 3500/4600.

Marco Polo without rest, r. Fort Neipperg 27, ⊠ 2230, ℘ 406 41 41, Fax 40 48 84 – ⫿ TV ☎ ⇔. AE ⓓ E VISA DZ d
18 rm ☐ 3400/3800.

Aub. Le Châtelet (annex - 9 rm), bd de la Pétrusse 2, ⊠ 2320, ℘ 40 21 01, Fax 40 36 66 – ⫿ TV ☎ P. AE ⓓ E VISA CZ e
Meals *(closed Saturday, Sunday, Bank Holidays and 20 December-5 January)* a la carte approx. 1100 – **29 rm** ☐ 3500/3900.

Cordial 1st floor, pl. de Paris 1, ⊠ 2314, ℘ 48 85 38, Fax 40 77 76 – E VISA DZ b
closed Friday, Saturday lunch, 7 to 14 February, 19 to 24 May and 15 July-15 August – **Meals** *Lunch 1450* – 1450/2600.

Italia with rm, r. Anvers 15, ⊠ 1130, ℘ 48 66 26, Fax 48 08 07, , Partly Italian cuisine – TV ☎. AE ⓓ E VISA CZ f
Meals a la carte 950/1800 – **20 rm** ☐ 2500/3100.

Suburbs

Airport *NE : 8 km :*

Sheraton Aérogolf ⓢ, rte de Trèves 1, ⊠ 1019, ℘ 34 05 71, Telex 2662, Fax 34 02 17 – ⫿ ⇸ ▤ TV ☎ P – 25-120. AE ⓓ E VISA. ⊘ rest
Meals ***Le Montgolfier*** (open until midnight) *Lunch 975* - a la carte 1000/1650 – ☐ 575 – **137 rm** 6300/9000, 8 suites.

Ibis, rte de Trèves, ⊠ 2632, ℘ 43 88 01, Fax 43 88 02, ←, – ⫿ ▤ TV ☎ P – 25-80. AE ⓓ E VISA
Meals *Lunch 380* – 730 – **120 rm** ☐ 2900/3900.

Trust Inn without rest, r. Neudorf 679, ⊠ 2220, ℘ 42 30 51, Fax 42 30 56 – ▤ TV ☎ P. AE ⓓ E VISA
7 rm ☐ 2000/2800.

Le Grimpereau, r. Cents 140, ⊠ 1319, ℘ 43 67 87, Fax 42 60 26, – P. AE E VISA. ⊘
closed Tuesday July-15 September, Monday, 1 week carnival, first 3 weeks August and All Saints' week – **Meals** *Lunch 1250* – 1250/1950.

at Belair Ⓒ *Luxembourg :*

Parc Belair Ⓜ ⓢ, av. du X Septembre 109, ⊠ 2551, ℘ 44 23 23, Fax 44 44 84, ←, – ⫿ ⇸ ▤ rest TV ☎ ⇔ – 25-60. AE ⓓ E VISA
Meals *(dinner only except Sunday)* a la carte 900/1300 – **45 rm** ☐ 5900/6400, 7 suites.

Astoria, av. du X Septembre 44, ⊠ 2550, ℘ 44 62 23, Fax 45 82 96, – ▤ – 25. AE ⓓ E VISA CZ a
closed Saturday, dinner Sunday and Monday and 26 December-2 January – **Meals** a la carte 1800/2150.

[illegible] 70, ⊠ [illegible], ℘ 44 27 66, Fax 37 91 73, Thaï cuisine – AE ⓓ E VISA. ⊘
closed Monday, Saturday lunch and 15 August-4 September – **Meals** *Lunch 650* – a la carte approx. 1300.

at Dommeldange *(Dummeldéng) N : 5,5 km* Ⓒ *Luxembourg :*

Inter.Continental ⓢ, r. Jean Engling, ⊠ 1466, ℘ 4 37 81, Telex 3754, Fax 43 60 95, ←, , – ⫿ ⇸ ▤ TV ☎ P – 25-360. AE ⓓ E VISA. ⊘ rest
Meals ***Les Continents*** *(closed lunch Saturday and Sunday, August and first 2 weeks January)* *Lunch 1450* - a la carte 1650/2200 – ***Café Stiffchen*** (open until 11.30 p.m.) *Lunch 980* - a la carte 1100/1600 – ☐ 620 – **324 rm** 6700/8950, 15 suites.

Parc, rte d'Echternach 120, ⊠ 1453, ℘ 43 56 43, Fax 43 69 03, , , , , – ⫿ TV ☎ ♿ P – 40-1500. AE ⓓ E VISA
Meals (open until 11.30 p.m.) a la carte 850/1300 – **218 rm** ☐ 3800/4600, 3 suites.

Host. du Grünewald, rte d'Echternach 10, ⊠ 1453, ℘ 43 18 82 and 42 03 14 (rest), Fax 42 06 46 and 42 03 14 (rest), – ⫿ ▤ rest TV ☎ P – 25-40. AE ⓓ E VISA. ⊘ rest
Meals *(closed Saturday lunch, Sunday, Bank Holidays and 1 to 22 January)* *Lunch 1590* – a la carte 1700/2450 – **26 rm** ☐ 3900/4900, 2 suites.

at Gasperich *(Gaasperech) S : 4 km* Ⓒ *Luxembourg :*

Inn Side Ⓜ, r. Henri Schnadt 1 (Cloche d'Or), ⊠ 2530, ℘ 49 00 06, Fax 49 06 80, , « Design », , – ⫿ ⇸ ▤ rest TV ☎ ♿ ⇔ – 25-200. AE ⓓ E VISA
Meals (buffets) *Lunch 900* – a la carte approx. 1500 – **158 rm** ☐ 4700/5300.

Upland of Kirchberg *(Kiirchbierg)* :

Sofitel M, r. Fort Niedergrünewald 6 (European Centre), ✉ 2015, ☎ 43 77 6 Fax 43 86 58 – rest EY
Meals *Brasserie Europa* a la carte approx. 1200 – 750 – **100 rm** 8500/9000, 4 suite

Europlaza, r. Fort Niedergrünewald 6 (European Centre), ✉ 2015, ☎ 43 77 61, – 25-300. rest EY
Meals *(open until 11 p.m.) Lunch 820* – a la carte approx. 1100 – **257 rm** 6500/750 3 suites.

at the skating-rink of Kockelscheuer *(Kockelscheier) S by N 31* :

Patin d'Or (Berring), rte de Bettembourg 40, ✉ 1899, ☎ 22 64 99, Fax 40 40 11 –
closed Saturday, Sunday, Bank Holidays and late December-early January – **Meals** 200 a la carte 2300/2700
Spec. Terrine de foie d'oie et artichauts en gelée de petits légumes truffés, Dos de b rôti à la peau au jus de clams, Pigeon au polenta, épinards et navets aigres-doux. **Win** Pinot gris, Riesling Koëppchen.

at Limpertsberg *(Lampertsbierg)* C *Luxembourg* :

Bouzonviller, r. A. Unden 138, ✉ 2652, ☎ 47 22 59, Fax 46 43 89, ←, –
closed Saturday, Sunday, 1 to 22 August and 23 December-2 January – **Meals** *Lunch 16* – a la carte approx. 2100.

at Rollingergrund *(Rolléngergronn)* C *Luxembourg* :

Sieweburen, r. Septfontaines 36, ✉ 2534, ☎ 44 23 56, Fax 44 23 53, ←, « Woodland setting », –
closed late December – **Meals** (Pub rest) *(closed Wednesday) Lunch 340* – a la carte 900/13 – **14 rm** 2500/3700.

Environs

at Bridel *(Briddel) by N 12 : 7 km* C *Kopstal pop. 2 974* :

Le Rondeau, r. Luxembourg 82, ✉ 8140, ☎ 33 94 73, Fax 33 37 46 –
closed Monday dinner, Tuesday, last 3 weeks August and first 2 weeks January – **Mea** *Lunch 900* – 980/1900.

at Hesperange *(Hesper) SE : 5,5 km – pop. 9 918* :

L'Agath (Steichen) with rm, rte de Thionville 274 (Howald), ✉ 5884, ☎ 48 86 8 Fax 48 55 05, – 60.
closed Saturday lunch, Sunday dinner, Monday, mid July-early August and late Decembe early January – **Meals** *Lunch 1600* – 1850, a la carte 2100/2600 – **5 rm** 2200/330
Spec. Raviolis de homard et bisque légère, Goujonnettes de sole safranées, Côtes d'agne en croûte d'herbes à la provençale. **Wines** Riesling, Pinot gris.

Klein, rte de Thionville 432, ✉ 5886, ☎ 36 08 42, Fax 36 08 43 –
closed Sunday dinner and Monday – **Meals** *Lunch 1400* – 1650/2500.

at Strassen *(Strossen) W : 4 km – pop. 4 919* :

L'Olivier with apartments, rte d'Arlon 140, ✉ 8008, ☎ 31 36 66, Fax 31 36 27 – – 25-350.
Meals see rest ***La Cime*** below – **42 rm** 2990/3790, 4 suites.

La Cime - (at L'Olivier H.), rte d'Arlon 140a, ✉ 8008, ☎ 31 88 13, Fax 31 36 27,
Meals *Lunch 990* – a la carte 1300/1650.

Le Nouveau Riquewihr, rte d'Arlon 373, ✉ 8011, ☎ 31 99 80, Fax 31 97 05, –
closed Sunday, 24, 25, 26, 31 December and 1 January – **Meals** *Lunch 980* – a la carte appr 1300.

at Walferdange *(Walfer) N : 5 km – pop. 5 818* :

Moris M, pl. des Martyrs, ✉ 7201, ☎ 33 01 05, Fax 33 30 70, – rest – 50.
Meals *(closed Monday) Lunch 750* – a la carte 1050/1800 – **23 rm** 2700/3700.

l'Etiquette, rte de Diekirch 50, ✉ 7220, ☎ 33 51 67, Fax 33 51 69, –
Meals 750/1600.

Echternach *(Iechternach)* 215 D 6 *and* 409 M 6 *– pop. 4 211 – 35 km.*

at Geyershaff *(Geieschhaff) SW : 6,5 km by E 27* C *Bech pop. 787 :*

XXX **La Bergerie** (Phal), ✉ 6251, ☎ 79 04 64, Fax 79 07 71, ≤, terrace, « Floral country setting » – P. AE ① E VISA
✿✿ *closed Sunday dinner, Monday and 15 January-early March* – **Meals** *Lunch 1800* – a la carte 2350/2650
Spec. Minute d'esturgeon fumé au beurre citronné, Ballottine de pintade truffée, Soufflé chaud aux framboises. **Wines** Pinot gris, Riesling.

Paliseul *6850 Luxembourg belge (Belgium)* 214 ⑯ *and* 409 I 6 *– pop. 4 863 –* ☎ *0 61 – 94 km.*

XXX **Au Gastronome** (Libotte) with rm, r. Bouillon 2 (Paliseul-Gare) ☎ 53 30 64, Fax 53 38 91, « Floral garden with pool » – ▤ TV ☎ P. AE ① E VISA
✿✿ *closed Sunday dinner and Monday except Bank Holidays, last week June-first week July and January-7 February* – **Meals** *Lunch 1200* – a la carte 2150/2800 – ☕ 350 – **9 rm** 3000/4000
Spec. Jambonnettes de grenouilles au coulis de persil et aux croquettes d'ail, Dos de turbot au four à l'ail et à la coriandre, sauce hollandaise au cresson, Cochon de lait rôti au miel, sauce aux épices.

AMSTERDAM

Noord-Holland **210** J 8, **211** J 8 *and* **408** G 4 – ㉑ S – *Pop. 722 230* – ☎ *20.*

Brussels 204 – Düsseldorf 227 – The Hague 60 – Luxembourg 419 – Rotterdam 76.

Stationsplein, ✉ 1012 AB ☎ 06-34 03 40 66, Fax 625 28 69.

18 *Bauduinlaan 35 ✉ 1165 NE at Halfweg (W : 6 km) ☎ (0 20) 497 78 66, Fax (0 20) 497 59 66*

9 *Zwarte Laantje 4 ✉ 1099 CE at Duivendrecht (S : 5 km) ☎ (0 20) 694 36 50, Fax (0 20) 663 46 21* – 9 *Buikslotermurdÿk 41 ✉ 1027 AC ☎ (0 20) 632 56 50, Fax (0 20) 634 35 06.*

✈ *at Schiphol SW : 9,5 km ☎ (0 20) 601 91 11.*

See: *Old Amsterdam★★★ – The canals★★★ (Grachten) : Boat trips★ (Rondvaart) – Dam : Royal Palace★ (Koninklijk Paleis)* LY, *pulpit★ in the New Church★ (Nieuwe Kerk)* LY – *Beguine Convent★★ (Begijnhof)* LY – *Flower market★ (Bloemenmarkt)* LY – *Cromhout Houses★ (Cromhouthuizen) – Reguliersgracht ≤★ – Keizersgracht ≤★ – ≤ from the sluice bridge Oudezijds Kolk-Oudezijds Voorburgwal* MX – *Groenburgwal ≤★* LMY – *Thin Bridge★ (Magere Brug)* MZ – *Artis★ (Zoological Garden) – Westerkerk★* KX.

Museums: *Amsterdam Historical Museum★★ (Amsterdams Historisch Museum)* LY – *Madame Tussaud's Scenerama★ : wax museum* LY **M1** – *Rijksmuseum★★★* KZ – *Vincent van Gogh National Museum★★★ (Rijksmuseum) – Municipal★★ (Stedelijk Museum) : Modern Art – Amstelkringmuseum "Our Dear Lord in the Attic"★ (Museum Amstelkring Ons' Lieve Heer op Solder) : clandestine chapel* MX **M4** – *Rembrandt's House★ (Rembrandthuis) : works by the master* MY **M5** – *Jewish Museum★ (Joods Historisch Museum)* MY **M6** – *Allard Pierson★ : antiquities* LY **M7** – *Tropical Museum★ (Tropenmuseum) – Netherlands Maritime History Museum★ (Nederlands Scheepvaart Museum) – Anne Frank's House★★* KX **M8**.

Casino, Max Euweplein 62, ✉ 1017 MB (near Leidseplein) ☎ 620 10 06, Fax 620 36 66.

AMSTERDAM
0
200 m
J
K
X
Y
Z
Westerstr.
Anjeliersstr.
Egelantiersstr.
Egelantiers gracht
Nieuwe Leliestr.
Bloem gracht
Rozengracht
Laurier- straat
Laurier gracht
Elandsstr.
Elands gracht
Runstr.
Raamstr.
Leidse gracht
Leidsestraat
Leidseplein
Westerkerk
Raadhuis straat
Hartenstr.
Wolvenstr.
Kerkstr.
Lelie gracht
PRINSEN GRACHT
KEIZERS GRACHT
HEREN GRACHT
Marnixstr.
Lijnbaans gracht
Singelgracht
Nassau kade
Kostverlorenvaart
Hendrikstraat
2e Hugo de Grootstr.
Fr.
Hugo de Groot gracht
Da Costa gracht
de Clercqstr.
Bilderdijkstr.
Kinkerstr.
J. v. Lennep straat
Jacob van Lennep kanaal
Bosboom Toussaintstr.
Overtoom
1e Constantijn Huygensstr.
Vondel straat
Vondelpark
Stadhouders kade
Wetering schans
Hooftstr.
P. C.
Paulus Potterstr.
RIJKSMUSEU
Paradiso
CASINO
POL.
S 105
S 100
S 106
S 109
110
88
6
M8
M
U
J
T
a
b
c
d
f
k
m
n
p
q
s
t
u
v
x

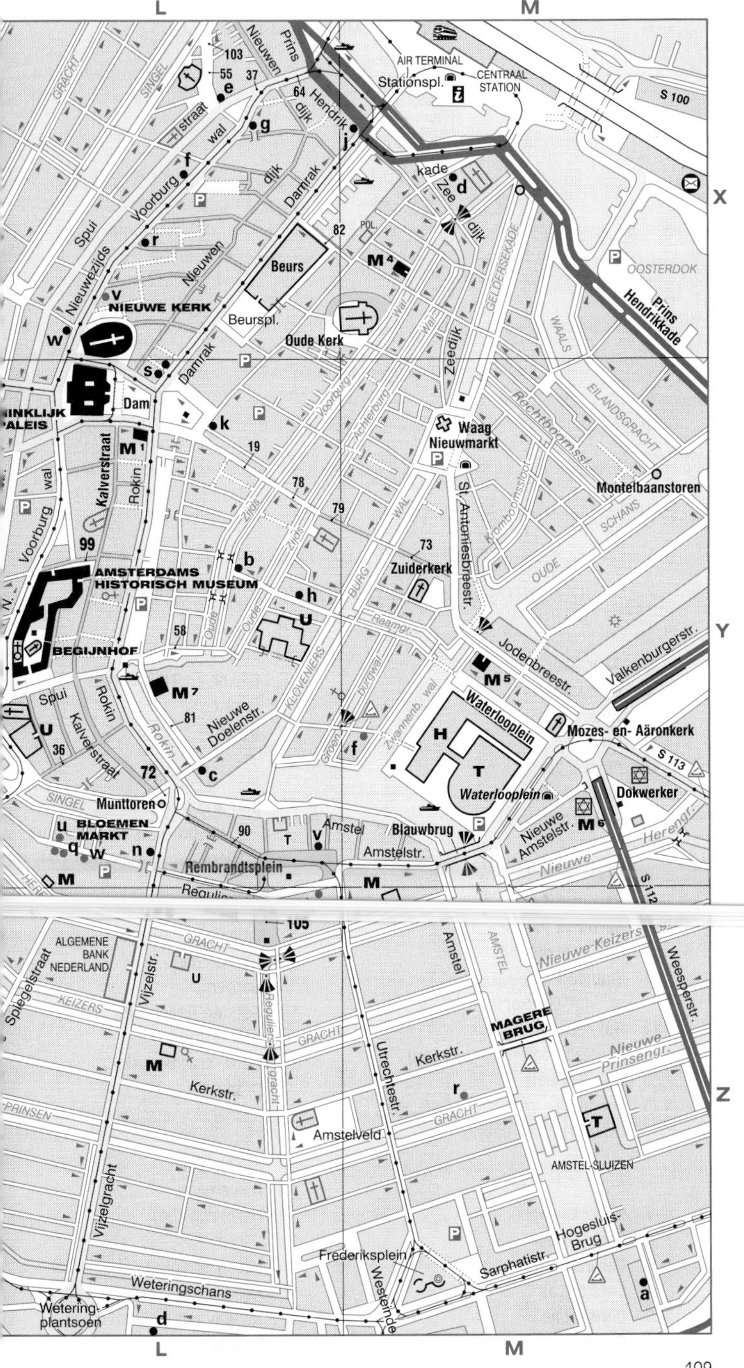
L
M
X
Y
Z
AIR TERMINAL
Stationspl.
CENTRAAL STATION
Beurs
Beurspl.
NIEUWE KERK
Oude Kerk
Dam
AMSTERDAMS HISTORISCH MUSEUM
BEGIJNHOF
Waag Nieuwmarkt
Montelbaanstoren
Zuiderkerk
Waterlooplein
Mozes- en- Aäronkerk
Dokwerker
Munttoren
BLOEMEN MARKT
Rembrandtsplein
Blauwbrug
Amstelstr.
ALGEMENE BANK NEDERLAND
MAGERE BRUG
Amstelveld
AMSTEL-SLUIZEN
Frederiksplein
Sarphatistr.
Hogesluis-Brug
Weteringschans
Wetering-plantsoen
OOSTERDOK
Prins Hendrikkade
Damrak
Rokin
Kalverstraat
Spui
Vijzelstr.
Vijzelgracht
Utrechtsestr.
Weesperstr.
Jodenbreestr.
Valkenburgerstr.
St. Antoniesbreestr.
Zeedijk
Nieuwe Doelenstr.
Kerkstr.
Spiegelstraat

STREET INDEX TO AMSTERDAM TOWN PLAN

van Baerlestr. JZ 6
Damrak LX
Damstr. LY 19
Heiligeweg LY 36
Kalverstr. LY
Kinkerstr. JY
Leidsestr. KYZ
Nieuwendijk LX
P.C. Hooftstr. KZ
Raadhuisstr. KXY
Reguliersbreestr. LY 90
Rokin LY
Rozengracht JKY
Spui LY
Utrechtsestr. MZ

Amstel MYZ
Amstelstr. MY
Amstelveld LMZ
Angeliersstr. KX
Beursplein LX
Bilderdijkstr. JY
Blauwbrug MY
Bosboom Toussaintstr. JYZ
de Clerscstr. JY
Constantijn Huygensstr. (1e) JZ
Dam LY
Egelantiersstr. KX
Elandsgracht KY
Elandsstr. JKY
Frederik Hendrikstr. JX
Frederikspl. MZ
Hartenstr. KY
Hekelveld LX 37
Hogesluis-Brug MZ
Hugo de Grootstr. (2e) JX
Jodenbreestr. MY
Kattengat LX 55
Kerkstr. KLZ
Langebrugsteeg LY 58
Laurierstr. JKY
Leidseplein KZ
Magerebrug MZ
Marnixstr. JXY
Martelaarsgracht LX 64
Muntplein LY 72
Nassaukade JXY
Nieuwe Amstelstr. MY
Nieuwe Doelenstr. LY
Nieuwe Hoogstr. MY 73
Nieuwe Leliestr. KX
Nieuwe Spiegelstr. LZ
Nieuwezijds Voorburgwal LXY
Nieuwendijk LX
Nieuwmarkt MY
Oude Doelenstr. LY 78
Oude Hoogstr. LMY 79
Oude Turfmarkt LY 81
Oudebrugsteeg LMX 82
Paulus Potterstr. KZ
Prins Hendrikkade LMX
Raamstr. KY
Reestraat KY 8
Reguliersdwarsstr. LY
Rembrandtsplein LMY
Runstr. KY
Sint-Antoniesbreestr. MY
Sint-Luciensteeg LY 9
Spuistr. LX
Stadhouderskade KZ
Stationsplein MX
Stromarkt LX 1
Thorbeckepl. LZ 1
Valkenburgerstr. MY
Vijzelgracht LZ
Vijzelstr. LZ
Vondelstr. JZ
Waterlooplein MY
Weesperstr. MZ
Westeinde MZ
Westermarkt KX 1
Westerstr. KX
Wetering-plantsoen LZ
Wetering-schans KLZ
Wolvenstr. KY
Zeedijk MX

Alphabetical listing of hotels and restaurants

A

11 Aker (De)
8 Ambassade
7 American
7 Amstel
8 Amsterdam
8 Asterisk
10 Aujourd'hui

B

7 Barbizon Centre
7 Barbizon Palace
10 Beddington's
9 Blauwe Parade (De) (at Die Port van Cleve H.)
12 Bokkedoorms (De) (at Haarlem/Overveen)
9 Bols Taverne
10 Bordewijk
11 Brasserie Van Baerle

C – D

7 Canal Crown
8 Canal House
8 Caransa
10 Casaló (La)
8 Christophe
10 Ciel Bleu (at Okura H.)
8 Cok City
10 Cok Hotels
8 Dikker en Thijs Fenice
11 Dorint
9 Dynasty

E – F – G

9 Edo and Kyo (at Gd H. Krasnapolsky H.)
8 Estheréa
7 Europe
8 Excelsior (at Europe H.)
11 Galaxy
10 Garage (Le)
10 Garden
9 Gouden Reael (De)
11 Grand Hotel
7 Gd H. Krasnapolsky
7 Grand (The)

H

10 Haesje Claes
11 Halvemaan
11 Herbergh (De)
10 Hilton
12 Hilton Schiphol
11 Holiday Inn
7 Holiday Inn Crowne Plaza
9 Hosokawa

I – J

9 Indrapura
12 Jagershuis ('t)
7 Jolly Carlton
11 Jonge Dikkert (De)

K – L

12 Kaatje bij de Sluis (at Blokzijl)
12 Kampje (Het)
11 Keyzer
12 Klein Paardenburg
10 Lairesse
9 Lonny's

M – N

9 Manchurian
10 Mangerie de Kersentuin (at Garden H.)
7 Marriott
10 Memphis
11 Mercure Airport
10 Mercure a/d Amstel
10 Meridien Apollo (Le)
11 Novotel

O – P – Q – R

9 Oesterbar (De)
10 Okura
12 Oude Rosmolen (De) (at Hoorn)
12 Paardenburg
9 Pêcheur (Le)
8 Port van Cleve (Die)
7 Pulitzer
9 Quatre Canetons (Les)
8 Radèn Mas
7 Radisson SAS
7 Renaissance
11 Résidence Fontaine Royale (at Grand Hotel)
8 Rive (La) (at Amstel H.)
11 Rosarium

S – T

9 Sancerre
9 Sea Palace
9 Sichuan Food
7 Sofitel
9 Swarte Schaep ('t)
7 Swissôtel Ascot
9 Tom Yam
10 Toro
9 Tout Court
9 Treasure
8 Tulip Inn
9 Tuynhuys (Het)

V – W – Y – Z

8 Vermeer (at Barbizon Palace H.)
7 Victoria
10 Villa Borgmann
8 Vondel
8 Vijff Vlieghen (D')
8 Wiechmann

Establishments according to style of cuisine

Pub rest – Brasseries

7 American *Centre*
7 Amstel Bar and Brasserie (The) (at Amstel H.) *Centre*
9 Bols Taverne *Centre*
10 Brasserie Camelia (at Okura H.) *South and West Q.*
7 Brasserie Reflet (at GD H. Krasnapolsky H.) *Centre*
11 Brasserie Van Baerle *South and West Q.*
7 Café Barbizon (at Barbizon Palace H *Centre*
7 Café Roux (at The Grand H.) *Centre*
10 Le Garage *South and West Q.*
11 Keyser *South and West Q.*

Seafood – Oyster bar

9 Oesterbar (De) *Centre*
9 Pêcheur (Le) *Centre*
11 Pescadou (Le) *Env. at Amstelveen*

Asian

9 Sea Palace *Centre*

Chinese

9 Sichuan Food *Centre*
9 Treasure *Centre*

Dutch regional

7 Dorrius (at Holiday Inn Crowne Plaza H.) *Centre*
8 Roode Leeuw (De) (at Amsterdam H.) *Centre*

Indonesian

9 Indrapura *Centre*
9 Lonny's *Centre*
8 Radèn Mas *Centre*

Italian

7 Caruso (at Jolly Carlton H.) *Centre*
10 Roberto's (at Hilton H.) *South and West Q.*

Japanese

9 Edo and Kyo (at Gd H. Krasnapolsky H.) *Centre*
9 Hosokawa *Centre*
10 Sazanka (at Okura H.) *South and West Q.*
10 Yamazato (at Okura H.) *South and West Q.*

Oriental

9 Dynasty *Centre*
9 Manchurian *Centre*

Swiss

7 Swissôtel Ascot *Centre*

Thaï

9 Tom Yam *Centre*

Centre

Amstel, Prof. Tulpplein 1, ✉ 1018 GX, ☎ 622 60 60, Telex 11004, Fax 622 58 08, – – 25-180. AE E VISA JCB. MZ a
Meals see rest ***La Rive*** below – ***The Amstel Bar and Brasserie*** (open until 11.30 p.m.) a la carte approx. 70 – 39 – **62 rm** 825/875, 17 suites.

The Grand, O.Z. Voorburgwal 197, ✉ 1012 EX, ☎ 555 31 11, Fax 555 32 22, « Historic building, authentic Art Nouveau lounges, inner garden », – rest – 25-320. AE E VISA JCB. LY b
Meals ***Café Roux*** (open until 11 p.m.) a la carte approx. 45 – 38 – **155 rm** 545/645, 11 suites.

Europe, Nieuwe Doelenstraat 2, ✉ 1012 CP, ☎ 531 17 77, Fax 531 17 78, – – 25-250. AE E VISA JCB LY c
Meals see rest ***Excelsior*** below – ***Le Relais*** (open until midnight) 40/50 – 35 – **96 rm** 420/820, 5 suites.

Barbizon Palace, Prins Hendrikkade 59, ✉ 1012 AD, ☎ 556 45 64, Fax 624 33 53, – rest – 25-300. AE E VISA JCB. rest
Meals see rest ***Vermeer*** below – ***Café Barbizon*** (open until 11 p.m.) *Lunch 48* – a la carte 44/77 – 33 – **265 rm** 375/510, 3 suites. MX d

Gd H. Krasnapolsky, Dam 9, ✉ 1012 JS, ☎ 554 91 11, Fax 622 86 07, « 19C winter garden », – – 25-750. AE E VISA JCB LY k
Meals see rest ***Edo and Kyo*** below – ***Brasserie Reflet*** (dinner only until 11 p.m.) a la carte approx. 45 – 30 – **415 rm** 350, 14 suites.

Radisson SAS M, Rusland 17, ✉ 1012 CK, ☎ 623 12 31, Telex 10365, Fax 520 82 00, « Patio with 18C presbytery », – – 25-150. AE E VISA JCB. LY h
Meals ***De Palmboom*** 58 – 33 – **246 rm** 375/400, 1 suite.

Holiday Inn Crowne Plaza, N.Z. Voorburgwal 5, ✉ 1012 RC, ☎ 620 05 00, Fax 620 11 73, – rm – 25-260. AE E VISA JCB
Meals ***Dorrius*** (Partly Dutch regional cooking, dinner only until 11 p.m.) a la carte 49/79 – 43 – **268 rm** 393/469, 2 suites. LX g

Marriott, Stadhouderskade 21, ✉ 1054 ES, ☎ 607 55 55, Fax 607 55 11, – – 25-360. AE E VISA. KZ f
Meals (dinner only until 11 p.m.) *(closed Sunday and Monday)* 30/50 – 34 – **387 rm** 495, 5 suites.

Victoria, Damrak 1, ✉ 1012 LG, ☎ 623 42 55, Telex 16625, Fax 625 29 97, – – 30-150. AE E VISA JCB. LMX j
Meals a la carte 43/80 – 30 – **286 rm** 395/455, 19 suites.

Pulitzer, Prinsengracht 323, ✉ 1016 GZ, ☎ 523 52 35, Fax 627 67 53, « 24 terraced canalside houses from 17 and 18C », – – 25-150. AE E VISA JCB. rest KY m
Meals ***De Goudsbloem*** (dinner only) *(closed 27 to 30 December)* a la carte approx. 80 – **230 rm** 455, 2 suites.

Renaissance, Kattengat 1, ✉ 1012 SZ, ☎ 621 22 23, Fax 627 52 45, « Contemporary
Meals a la carte 43/60 – 33 – **405 rm** 350/535, 6 suites. LX e

Barbizon Centre, Stadhouderskade 7, ✉ 1054 ES, ☎ 685 13 51, Telex 12601, Fax 685 16 11, – – 25-200. AE E VISA JCB. rest
Meals *Lunch 45* – a la carte 65/82 – 33 – **236 rm** 485, 2 suites. KZ p

Jolly Carlton M, Vijzelstraat 4, ✉ 1017 HK, ☎ 622 22 66 and 623 83 20 (rest), Fax 626 61 83 – – 25-200. AE E VISA JCB. LY n
Meals ***Caruso*** (Italian cuisine, dinner only until 11 p.m.) *(closed Monday)* a la carte 50/80 – 30 – **219 rm** 300/400.

American, Leidsekade 97, ✉ 1017 PN, ☎ 624 53 22, Fax 625 32 36, – – 70-160. AE E VISA. KZ q
Meals (Art Deco style pub rest, open until midnight) *Lunch 29* – a la carte 65/82 – 30 – **185 rm** 575, 3 suites.

Swissôtel Ascot, Damrak 95, ✉ 1012 LP, ☎ 626 00 66 – – 25-60. AE E VISA JCB. rest LXY s
Meals (Swiss cuisine) *Lunch 37* – a la carte approx. 60 – 28 – **109 rm** 360/460.

Sofitel, N.Z. Voorburgwal 67, ✉ 1012 RE, ☎ 627 59 00, Fax 623 89 32, – – 25-60. AE E VISA. rest LX r
Meals (dinner only) a la carte 58/74 – 30 – **148 rm** 360/399.

Canal Crown without rest, Herengracht 519, ✉ 1017 BV, ☎ 420 00 55, Fax 420 09 93 – . AE E VISA LZ c
25 – **57 rm** 175/350.

Ambassade without rest, Herengracht 341, ✉ 1016 AZ, ☎ 626 23 33, Fax 624 53 2… – AE VISA KY
46 rm 240/305, 6 suites.

Canal House without rest, Keizersgracht 148, ✉ 1015 CX, ☎ 622 51 8… Fax 624 13 17, « Antique furniture », – AE E VISA. KX
26 rm 225/265.

Estheréa without rest, Singel 305, ✉ 1012 WJ, ☎ 624 51 46, Fax 623 90 01 – AE E VISA JCB. LY
75 rm 325/375.

Caransa without rest, Rembrandtsplein 19, ✉ 1017 CT, ☎ 622 94 55, Fax 622 27 7… – 25-200. AE E VISA JCB LY
25 – **66 rm** 300/390.

Tulip Inn, Spuistraat 288, ✉ 1012 VX, ☎ 420 45 45, Fax 420 43 00, – AE E VISA JCB LY
Meals *Lunch 35* – 43 – **208 rm** 220/275.

Cok City without rest, N.Z. Voorburgwal 50, ✉ 1012 SC, ☎ 422 00 11, Fax 420 03 5… – AE E VISA JCB. LX
106 rm 250.

Die Port van Cleve, N.Z. Voorburgwal 178, ✉ 1012 SJ, ☎ 624 48 60, Fax 622 02 4… – 25-50. AE E VISA JCB. LX
Meals see rest ***De Blauwe Parade*** below – **116 rm** 182/287.

Dikker en Thijs Fenice, Prinsengracht 444, ✉ 1017 EK, ☎ 626 77 21, Fax 625 89 8… – 25. AE E VISA KZ
De Prinsenkelder (dinner only until midnight) a la carte approx. 60 – **25 rm** 250/45…

Amsterdam, Damrak 93, ✉ 1012 LP, ☎ 555 06 66, Fax 620 47 16 – AE E VISA JCB LXY
Meals ***De Roode Leeuw*** (Dutch regional cooking) *Lunch 38* - 50 – **80 rm** 199/350.

Wiechmann without rest, Prinsengracht 328, ✉ 1016 HX, ☎ 626 33 21, Fax 626 89 6… – KY
38 rm 250.

Asterisk without rest, Den Texstraat 16, ✉ 1017 ZA, ☎ 626 23 96, Fax 638 27 90 E VISA LZ
29 rm 149/185.

Vondel without rest, Vondelstraat 28, ✉ 1054 GE, ☎ 612 01 20, Fax 685 43 21, – 25. AE E VISA. JZ
25 – **38 rm** 255/310.

La Rive - (at Amstel H.), Prof. Tulpplein 1, ✉ 1018 GX, ☎ 622 60 60, Telex 1100… Fax 622 58 08, « Amstel-side setting », – AE E VISA JCB. MZ
closed lunch Saturday and Sunday – **Meals** *Lunch 50* – 125/175, – a la carte 133/165
Spec. Filet de rouget en persillade de jambon sec, crème de thon étuvée au mélang… d'herbes (April-September), Langoustines sous croûte de pommes de terre et tombé… d'épinards, Noix de ris de veau grillées et gratin de macaronis au Vieux Hollande.

Vermeer - (at Barbizon Palace H.), Prins Hendrikkade 59, ✉ 1012 AD, ☎ 556 48 8… Fax 624 33 53 – AE E VISA JCB. MX
closed Saturday lunch, Sunday, 13 July-11 August and 26 December-5 January – **Meal…** *Lunch 50* – 85/125, – a la carte 98/122
Spec. Tartare de veau aux truffes et parmesan, Baudroie grillée au paprika et fondu… d'aubergines, Soufflé au mascarpone et basilic.

Excelsior - (at Europe H.), Nieuwe Doelenstraat 2, ✉ 1012 CP, ☎ 531 17 7… Fax 531 17 78, Open until 11 p.m., – AE E VISA JCB LY
closed Saturday lunch – **Meals** *Lunch 65* – 75/170 b.i..

D'Vijff Vlieghen, Spuistraat 294, ✉ 1012 VX, ☎ 624 83 69, Fax 623 64 04, « Typic… 17C houses » – AE E VISA JCB LY
closed 24 to 30 December and 1 January – **Meals** (dinner only until midnight) a la cart… 75/97.

Radèn Mas, Stadhouderskade 6, ✉ 1054 ES, ☎ 685 40 41, Fax 685 39 81, Indonesia… cuisine, open until 11 p.m., « Exotic decor » – AE E VISA JCB. JKZ
Meals *Lunch 33* – 55/99.

Christophe (Royer), Leliegracht 46, ✉ 1015 DH, ☎ 625 08 07, Fax 638 91 32 – E VISA KX
closed Sunday, Monday and early January – **Meals** (dinner only) 85/105, – a la cart… 110/133
Spec. Fondant d'aubergine au cumin, Ris de veau rôti au romarin et citron confit, Figu… fraîches rôties et glace au thym.

XXX **De Blauwe Parade** - (at Die Port van Cleve H.), N.Z. Voorburgwal 178, ✉ 1012 SJ, ☎ 624 48 60, Fax 622 02 40, « Delftware » - AE ⓓ E VISA JCB. ✻ LX w
closed 2 weeks February - **Meals** *Lunch 40* - 43.

XXX **Dynasty,** Reguliersdwarsstraat 30, ✉ 1017 BM, ☎ 626 84 00, Fax 622 30 38, ⛱, Oriental cuisine, « Terrace » - ▤. AE ⓓ E VISA. ✻ LY q
closed Tuesday and January - **Meals** (dinner only until 11 p.m.) a la carte approx. 80.

XX **Het Tuynhuys,** Reguliersdwarsstraat 28, ✉ 1017 BM, ☎ 627 66 03, Fax 627 66 03, ⛱, « Terrace » - ▤. AE ⓓ E VISA LY q
Meals *Lunch 55* - 58/79.

XX **'t Swarte Schaep** 1st floor, Korte Leidsedwarsstraat 24, ✉ 1017 RC, ☎ 622 30 21, Fax 624 82 68, Open until 11 p.m., « 17C Dutch interior » - ▤. AE ⓓ E VISA JCB KZ n
closed 30 April, 25, 26 and 31 December and 1 January - **Meals** *Lunch 55* - 75/90.

XX **Les Quatre Canetons,** Prinsengracht 1111, ✉ 1017 JJ, ☎ 624 63 07, Fax 638 45 99 - AE ⓓ E VISA JCB MZ r
closed Saturday lunch and Sunday - **Meals** *Lunch 60* - a la carte 92/114.

XX **Tout Court,** Runstraat 13, ✉ 1016 GJ, ☎ 625 86 37, Fax 625 44 11 - AE ⓓ E VISA KY s
closed first week January - **Meals** (dinner only until 11.30 p.m.) 50/88.

XX **Indrapura,** Rembrandtsplein 42, ✉ 1017 CV, ☎ 623 73 29, Fax 624 90 78, Indonesian cuisine - ▤. AE ⓓ E VISA JCB. ✻ LYZ h
Meals (dinner only until 11 p.m.) a la carte 47/82.

XX **Sichuan Food,** Reguliersdwarsstraat 35, ✉ 1017 BK, ☎ 626 93 27, Fax 627 72 81, Chinese cuisine - ▤. AE ⓓ E VISA. ✻ LY u
✿ *closed 31 December* - **Meals** (dinner only until 11 p.m., booking essential) a la carte 58/78
Spec. Dim Sum, Canard laqué à la pékinoise, Huîtres sautées maison.

XX **Bols Taverne,** Rozengracht 106, ✉ 1016 NH, ☎ 624 57 52, Fax 620 41 94, ⛱ - ▤. AE ⓓ E VISA JCB JKY b
closed Sunday, Bank Holidays except Christmas and New Year and mid July-mid August - **Meals** *Lunch 50* - 59/69.

XX **De Oesterbar,** Leidseplein 10, ✉ 1017 PT, ☎ 623 29 88, Fax 623 21 99, Seafood, open until 1 a.m. - ▤. AE ⓓ E VISA. ✻ KZ t
closed Christmas and 31 December - **Meals** a la carte 83/104.

XX **Manchurian,** Leidseplein 10a, ✉ 1017 PT, ☎ 623 13 30, Fax 626 21 05, Oriental cuisine - ▤. AE ⓓ E VISA. ✻ KZ t
Meals 43/90.

XX **Le Pêcheur,** Reguliersdwarsstraat 32, ✉ 1017 BM, ☎ 624 31 21, Fax 624 31 21, ⛱, Seafood, open until 11 p.m. - AE ⓓ E VISA JCB. ✻ LY w
closed Sunday - **Meals** *Lunch 48* - 48/62.

XX **Hosokawa,** Max Euweplein 22, ✉ 1017 MB, ☎ 638 80 86, Fax 638 22 19, Japanese cuisine, teppan-yaki - AE ⓓ E VISA JCB KZ u
Meals (dinner only) 85/120.

XX **Treasure,** N.Z. Voorburgwal 115, ✉ 1012 RH, ☎ 626 09 15, Fax 640 12 12, Chinese cuisine, open until 11.30 p.m. - ▤. AE E VISA JCB. ✻ LX v
closed Wednesday - **Meals** a la carte 43/71.

XX **Sancerre,** Reestraat 28, ✉ 1016 DN, ☎ 627 87 94, Fax 623 87 49 - AE ⓓ E VISA JCB. ✻ KY a
Meals (dinner only) 58/90.

XX **Lonny's,** Rozengracht 46, ✉ 1016 ND, ☎ 623 89 50, Fax 615 78 83, Indonesian cuisine, « Exotic decor » - ▤. AE ⓓ E VISA JCB KXY d
Meals (dinner only until 11 p.m.) 55/95.

XX **Sea Palace,** Oosterdokskade 8, ✉ 1011 AE, ☎ 626 47 77, Fax 620 42 66, Asian cuisine, open until 11 p.m., « Floating restaurant with ≤ town » - ▤. AE ⓓ E VISA JCB. ✻
Meals a la carte approx. 50.

X **Tom Yam,** Staalstraat 22, ✉ 1011 JM, ☎ 622 95 33, Fax 693 25 44, Thaï cuisine - ▤. AE ⓓ E VISA JCB MY f
Meals (dinner only) 43/70.

X **De Gouden Reael,** Zandhoek 14, ✉ 1013 KT, ☎ 623 38 83, « 17C house on old harbour site » - AE ⓓ E VISA. ✻
closed Sunday and last week December - **Meals** *Lunch 55* - 55/70.

X **Edo and Kyo** - (at Gd H. Krasnapolsky H.), Dam 9, ✉ 1012 JS, ☎ 554 60 96, Fax 639 30 47, Japanese cuisine, open until 11 p.m. - AE ⓓ E VISA JCB. ✻ LY k
Meals *Lunch 45* - 65/100.

✗ **Haesje Claes,** Spuistraat 273, ⊠ 1012 VR, ℘ 624 99 98, Fax 627 48 17, Amsterdam atmosphere – AE ⓓ E VISA JCB. ✻ LY x
Meals *Lunch 25* – 25/45.

✗ **Bordewijk,** Noordermarkt 7, ⊠ 1015 MV, ℘ 624 38 99, Fax 420 66 03, 余 – AE E VISA
closed Monday, 22 July-14 August and 27 December-3 January – **Meals** (dinner only) a la carte 65/85.

South and West Quarters

Okura, Ferdinand Bolstraat 333, ⊠ 1072 LH, ℘ 678 71 11, Telex 16182, Fax 671 23 44, Ⅰ₅, ≘s, ⊠, ⚓ – |‡| ⇆ ▤ [TV] ☎ ⇔ [P] – 🏛 25-650. AE ⓓ E VISA JCB. ✻
Meals see rest ***Ciel Bleu*** and ***Yamazato*** below – ***Sazanka*** *(closed lunch Saturday and Sunday)* (Japanese cuisine, teppan-yaki) *Lunch 38* - 50/145 – ***Brasserie Le Camelia*** *Lunch 41* - 51/61 – ☕ 39 – **358 rm** 375/540, 12 suites.

Le Meridien Apollo, Apollolaan 2, ⊠ 1077 BA, ℘ 673 59 22, Fax 570 57 44, 余, « Terrace with ≤ canal », ⚓ – |‡| ⇆ ▤ rm [TV] ☎ [P] – 🏛 25-200. AE ⓓ E VISA JCB
Meals (open until 11 p.m.) *Lunch 55* – a la carte 59/75 – ☕ 33 – **226 rm** 395/470, 2 suites

Garden, Dijsselhofplantsoen 7, ⊠ 1077 BJ, ℘ 664 21 21, Fax 679 93 56 – |‡| ⇆ [TV] ☎ [P] – 🏛 25-150. AE ⓓ E VISA JCB
Meals see rest ***Mangerie De Kersentuin*** below – ☕ 35 – **96 rm** 225/495, 2 suites.

Hilton, Apollolaan 138, ⊠ 1077 BG, ℘ 678 07 80, Fax 662 66 88, 余, ⚓ – |‡| ⇆ ▤ rest [TV] ☎ [P] – 🏛 25-350. AE ⓓ E VISA JCB. ✻
Meals ***Roberto's*** (Italian cuisine) a la carte approx. 80 – ☕ 38 – **268 rm** 445/615, 3 suites.

Mercure a/d Amstel [M], Joan Muyskenweg 10, ⊠ 1096 CJ, ℘ 665 81 81, Fax 694 87 35, Ⅰ₅, ≘s – |‡| ⇆ ▤ rm [TV] ☎ ♿ [P] – 🏛 25-450. AE ⓓ E VISA. ✻
Meals a la carte approx. 75 – ☕ 28 – **178 rm** ☕ 240.

Memphis without rest, De Lairessestraat 87, ⊠ 1071 NX, ℘ 673 31 41, Fax 673 73 12 – |‡| ⇆ [TV] ☎ – 🏛 25-60. AE ⓓ E VISA. ✻
☕ 28 – **74 rm** 295/370.

Toro 🌿 without rest, Koningslaan 64, ⊠ 1075 AG, ℘ 673 72 23, Fax 675 00 31, « Waterside terrace, overlooking the park » – |‡| [TV] ☎. AE ⓓ E VISA. ✻
22 rm ☕ 180/220.

Lairesse without rest, De Lairessestraat 7, ⊠ 1071 NR, ℘ 671 95 96, Fax 671 17 56 – |‡| [TV] ☎. AE ⓓ E VISA JCB
34 rm ☕ 190/310.

Cok Hotels without rest, Koninginneweg 34, ⊠ 1075 CZ, ℘ 664 61 11, Fax 664 53 04 – |‡| [TV] ☎ ♿ – 🏛 25-80. AE ⓓ E VISA JCB. ✻
159 rm ☕ 150/300.

Villa Borgmann 🌿 without rest, Koningslaan 48, ⊠ 1075 AE, ℘ 673 52 52, Fax 676 25 80 – |‡| [TV] ☎. AE ⓓ E VISA JCB
15 rm ☕ 175/225.

La Casaló 🌿 without rest, Amsteldijk 862, ⊠ 1079 LN, ℘ 642 36 80, Fax 644 74 09, ≤, « Floating hotel on the Amstel » – [TV] ☎. AE ⓓ E VISA
4 rm ☕ 275.

✗✗✗ **Ciel Bleu** - (at Okura H.), 23th floor, Ferdinand Bolstraat 333, ⊠ 1072 LH, ℘ 678 71 11, Telex 16182, Fax 671 23 44, ≤ town, ⚓ – ▤ [P]. AE ⓓ E VISA JCB. ✻
Meals (dinner only) 75/118.

✗✗ **Le Garage,** Ruysdaelstraat 54, ⊠ 1071 XE, ℘ 679 71 76, Fax 662 22 49, Open until 11 p.m., « Artistic atmosphere in a contemporary and cosmopolitan brasserie » – AE ⓓ E VISA JCB
closed lunch Saturday and Sunday and Bank Holidays – **Meals** *Lunch 40* – 58/70.

✗✗ **Mangerie De Kerstentuin** - (at Garden H.), Dijsselhofplantsoen 7, ⊠ 1077 BJ, ℘ 664 21 21, Fax 679 93 56 – ▤. AE ⓓ E VISA JCB. ✻
closed Sunday, 31 December and 1 January – **Meals** (dinner only until 11 p.m.) 53/73.

✗✗ **Aujourd'hui,** C. Krusemanstraat 15, ⊠ 1075 NB, ℘ 679 08 77, Fax 676 76 27, 余 – AE ⓓ E VISA JCB
closed Saturday, Sunday and last 3 weeks August – **Meals** *Lunch 55* – a la carte approx. 90

✗✗ **Yamazato** - (at Okura H.), Ferdinand Bolstraat 333, ⊠ 1072 LH, ℘ 678 71 11, Telex 16182, Fax 671 23 44, Japanese cuisine, ⚓ – ▤ [P]. AE ⓓ E VISA JCB. ✻
Meals *Lunch 30* – 30/150.

✗✗ **Beddington's,** Roelof Hartstraat 6, ⊠ 1071 VH, ℘ 676 52 01, Fax 671 74 29 – AE ⓓ E VISA JCB. ✻
closed lunch Saturday and Monday, Sunday and 22 December-4 January – **Meals** *Lunch 55* – 65/80.

Keyzer, Van Baerlestraat 96, ✉ 1071 BB, ☎ 671 14 41, Fax 673 73 53, Pub rest, open until 11.30 p.m. – AE E VISA JCB.
closed Sunday and Bank Holidays – **Meals** *Lunch 40* – 60.

Brasserie Van Baerle, Van Baerlestraat 158, ✉ 1071 BG, ☎ 679 15 32, Fax 671 71 96, Pub rest – AE E VISA
closed Saturday and 25 December-1 January – **Meals** *Lunch 45* – 45/68.

Buitenveldert (RAI)

Holiday Inn, De Boelelaan 2, ✉ 1083 HJ, ☎ 646 23 00, Fax 646 47 90 – – 25-350. AE E VISA JCB
Meals (open until 11 p.m.) 55/70 – 32 – **261 rm** 360/460, 2 suites.

Novotel, Europaboulevard 10, ✉ 1083 AD, ☎ 541 11 23, Telex 13375, Fax 646 28 23 – – 25-225. AE E VISA
Meals (open until midnight) *Lunch 28* – 43 – 28 – **598 rm** 260/275, 2 suites.

Halvemaan, van Leyenberghlaan 320 (Gijsbrecht van Aemstelpark), ✉ 1082 GM, ☎ 644 03 48, Fax 644 17 77, « Terrace with private lake » – AE E VISA.
closed Saturday, Sunday and 24 December-first week January – **Meals** *Lunch 55* – 95/125, – a la carte 99/116
Spec. Terre et mer au jus de gingembre et soja, Ris de veau meunière et ravioli de ragoût de rognon de veau, Crème brûlée de pamplemousse au poire concassé et miel.

Rosarium, Amstelpark 1, ✉ 1083 HZ, ☎ 644 40 85, Fax 646 60 04, « Floral park » – – 300. AE E VISA
closed Sunday – **Meals** *Lunch 43* – 60.

North

Galaxy, Distelkade 21, ✉ 1031 XP, ☎ 634 43 66, Telex 18607, Fax 636 03 45 – rest – 25-250. AE E VISA JCB
Meals *Lunch 24* – a la carte 43/63 – **280 rm** 215/250.

Suburbs

by motorway The Hague (A 4) – *0 20 :*

Mercure Airport, Oude Haagseweg 20, ✉ 1066 BW, ☎ 617 90 05, Fax 615 90 27 – – 25-250. AE E VISA JCB. rest
Meals *Lunch 40* – 43/65 – 28 – **151 rm** 225/300.

at Sloten *SW : 14 km* [C] *Amsterdam – 0 20 :*

De Aker, Akersluis 8, ✉ 1066 EZ, ☎ 669 09 33, Fax 669 14 29, – AE E VISA
closed lunch Saturday and Sunday – **Meals** *Lunch 38* – a la carte approx. 65.

Environs

at Amstelveen *S : 11 km – pop. 74 359 – 0 20.*

Plein 1960 nr 2, ✉ 1181 ZM, ☎ 547 51 11, Fax 647 02 88

[illegible] (S : 2.5 km direction Uithoorn), ✉ 1187 XC, ☎ 645 55 58, Fax 641 21 21 – [illegible]
Meals see rest ***Résidence Fontaine Royale*** below, shuttle service – **81 rm** 175/300, 10 suites.

De Jonge Dikkert, Amsterdamseweg 104a, ✉ 1182 HG, ☎ 641 13 78, Fax 645 91 62, « 17C windmill » – AE E VISA
closed lunch Saturday and Sunday – **Meals** *Lunch 58* – 58/68.

Résidence Fontaine Royale - (at Grand Hotel), Dr Willem Dreesweg 1 (S : 2 km, direction Uithoorn), ✉ 1185 VA, ☎ 640 15 01, Fax 640 16 61, – – 25-225. AE E VISA.
Meals *Lunch 30* – a la carte 61/81.

Le Pescadou, Amsterdamseweg 448, ✉ 1181 BW, ☎ 647 04 43, Fax 647 04 43, Seafood – AE E VISA JCB
closed lunch Saturday and Sunday and 22 December-1 January – **Meals** *Lunch 40* – a la carte 65/90.

at Badhoevedorp *SW : 15 km* [C] *Haarlemmermeer pop. 104 275 – 0 20 :*

Dorint, Sloterweg 299, ✉ 1171 VB, ☎ 658 81 11, Fax 659 71 01, – – 25-150. AE E VISA JCB. rest
Meals *Lunch 40* – a la carte 55/97 – 30 – **198 rm** 315/370.

De Herbergh, Sloterweg 259, ✉ 1171 CP, ☎ 659 26 00, Fax 659 83 90, – rest AE E VISA
Meals *Lunch 50* – a la carte approx. 60 – 17 – **15 rm** 150/175.

at Ouderkerk aan de Amstel *S : 10 km* *Amstelveen pop. 74 359 – 0 20*

't Jagershuis, Amstelzijde 2, ✉ 1184 VA, ℘ 496 20 20, Fax 496 45 41, ≤, « Inn with Amstel-side terrace », – TV ☎ P – 30. AE ⓓ E VISA JCB
Meals *(closed lunch Saturday and Sunday) Lunch 58* – a la carte approx. 75 – 25 – **12 rm** 150/315.

Paardenburg, Amstelzijde 55, ✉ 1184 TZ, ℘ 496 12 10, Fax 496 40 17, , « 19C murals, riverside terrace » – P. AE ⓓ E VISA JCB
Meals *Lunch 60* – 60/100.

Klein Paardenburg, Amstelzijde 59, ✉ 1184 TZ, ℘ 496 13 35, – AE ⓓ E VISA
closed Sunday and 25 December-3 January – **Meals** *Lunch 68* – 95.

Het Kampje, Kerkstraat 56, ✉ 1191 JE, ℘ 496 19 43, Fax 496 57 01, – AE E VISA JCB
closed Saturday, Sunday, 26 April-16 May and 24 December-7 January – **Meals** *Lunch 4C* – 50/60.

at Schiphol *(international airport) SW : 15 km* *Haarlemmermeer pop. 104 275 – 0 20 – Casino, Schiphol airport – Central Terminal ℘ (0 23) 571 80 44, Fax (0 23) 571 62 26*

Hilton Schiphol, Herbergierstraat 1, ✉ 1118 ZK, ℘ 603 45 67, Fax 648 09 17, – TV ☎ P – 25-110. AE ⓓ E VISA JCB
Meals (open until 11.30 p.m.) *(closed Saturday, Sunday and July-August)* – a la carte 60/88 – 38 – **265 rm** 475/535, 1 suite.

Blokzijl *Overijssel* *Brederwiede pop. 12 023* 210 *P 6 and* 408 *I 3 – 0 527 – 102 km.*

Kaatje bij de Sluis , Brouwerstraat 20, ✉ 8356 DV, ℘ 29 18 33, Fax 29 18 36, ≤, , « Terrace and garden along an intersection of canals », , – TV ☎ P AE ⓓ E VISA
closed Monday, Tuesday, February and 28 December-7 January – **Meals** *(closed Monday, Tuesday and Saturday lunch)* – 99, a la carte 100/180 – 33 – **8 rm** 205/265
Spec. Carpaccio de hareng au caviar, Canard sauvage aux betteraves et olives (August-November), Choucroute au foie d'oie sauté (September-April).

Haarlem *Noord-Holland* 210 *H 8,* 211 *H 8 and* 408 *E 4 – pop. 148 908 – 0 23 – 24 km.*

at Overveen *W : 4 km* *Bloemendaal pop. 16 735 – 0 23 :*

De Bokkedoorns, Zeeweg 53 (W : 2,5 km), ✉ 2051 EB, ℘ 526 36 00, Fax 527 31 43, , « Terrace, ≤ lake surrounded by wooded dunes » – P. AE ⓓ E VISA.
closed Monday, Saturday lunch, 30 April lunch, 5 and 24 December and 29 December-5 January – **Meals** *Lunch 65* – a la carte approx. 145
Spec. Tartare de St-Jacques et ragoût de homard, Waterzooï de turbot, Pigeon rôti, tapenade aux amandes et truffes.

Hoorn *Noord-Holland* 210 *M 2 and* 408 *G 4 – pop. 61 374 – 0 229 – 43 km.*

De Oude Rosmolen (Fonk), Duinsteeg 1, ✉ 1621 ER, ℘ 21 47 52, Fax 21 49 38 – AE ⓓ E VISA
closed Thursday, 2 weeks February, 10 to 29 August and 28 December-8 January – **Meals** (dinner only, booking essential) 110/150, – a la carte 100/128
Spec. Profiteroles à la mousse de foie gras, Ris de veau à la financière, Pâtisseries maison

WHEN IN **EUROPE** *NEVER BE WITHOUT :*
Michelin Main Road Maps ;
Michelin Regional Maps ;
Michelin Detailed Maps ;
Michelin Red Guides :
Benelux, Deutschland, España Portugal, France, Great Britain and Ireland, Italia, Suisse
(Hotels and restaurants listed with symbols ; preliminary pages in English)

Michelin Green Guides :
Austria, England : The West Country, France, Germany, Great Britain, Greece, Ireland, Italy, London, Netherlands, Portugal, Rome, Scotland, Spain, Switzerland, Atlantic Coast, Auvergne Rhône Valley, Brittany, Burgundy Jura, Châteaux of the Loire, Disneyland Paris, Dordogne, Flanders Picardy and the Paris region, French Riviera, Ile-de-France, Normandy, Paris, Provence, Pyrénées Roussillon Gorges du Tarn
(sights and touring programmes described fully in English ; town plans).

NETHERLANDS

he HAGUE *(Den HAAG or 's-GRAVENHAGE) Zuid-Holland* 211 *F 10 - ① ② and* 408 *D 5 - pop. 442 937 - ☎ 0 70.*

See : *Binnenhof★ : The Knight's Room★ (Ridderzaal)* JY *– Court pool (Hofvijver)* ≤★ HJY *– Lange Voorhout★* HJX *– Madurodam★★ – Scheveningen★★.*

Museums : *Mauritshuis★★★* JY *– Prince William V art gallery★ (Schilderijengalerij Prins Willem V)* HY **M²** *– Panorama Mesdag★* HX *– Mesdag★ – Municipal★★ (Gemeentehuis) – Bredius★* JY.

18 at Rijswijk SE : 5 km, Delftweg 59, ✉ 2289 AL, ℘ (0 70) 319 24 24 - 18 at Wassenaar NE : 11 km, Groot Haesebroekseweg 22, ✉ 2243 EC, ℘ (0 70) 517 96 07 and 9 Hoge Klei 1, ✉ 2243 XZ, ℘ (0 70) 511 78 46.

✈ Amsterdam-Schiphol NE : 37 km ℘ (0 20) 601 91 11 – Rotterdam-Zestienhoven SE : 17 km ℘ (0 10) 446 34 44.

Kon. Julianaplein 30, ✉ 2595 AA, ℘ 0 6-34 03 50 51, Fax 347 21 02.

Amsterdam 55 – Brussels 182 – Rotterdam 24 – Delft 13.

Plan on next page

Centre

Des Indes, Lange Voorhout 54, ✉ 2514 EG, ℘ 363 29 32, Fax 356 28 63, « Late 19C residence » – – 25-60. AE D E VISA JCB. rm JX s
Meals *Le Restaurant* *Lunch 55* - 65/100 – 38 – **70 rm** 320/525, 6 suites.

Holiday Inn Crowne Plaza Promenade, van Stolkweg 1, ✉ 2585 JL, ℘ 352 51 61, Fax 354 10 46, ≤, , « Collection of modern Dutch paintings » – rest – 25-400. AE D E VISA JCB
Meals (open until midnight) *Lunch 43* – a la carte 60/78 – 35 – **93 rm** 355/395, 4 suites.

Carlton Ambassador , Sophialaan 2, ✉ 2514 JP, ℘ 363 03 63, Fax 360 05 35, « Dutch and English style interior » – – 25-120. AE D E VISA JCB HX c
Meals *Lunch 40* – 43/50 – 34 – **70 rm** 345/385, 10 suites.

Sofitel, Koningin Julianaplein 35, ✉ 2595 AA, ℘ 381 49 01, Fax 382 59 27 – – 25-100. AE D E VISA. rest
Meals 50 – 30 – **143 rm** 250/295.

Bel Air, Johan de Wittlaan 30, ✉ 2517 JR, ℘ 352 53 54, Fax 353 52 53, – – 25-250. AE D E VISA JCB. rest
Meals *Lunch 38* – a la carte 46/77 – 23 – **348 rm** 250/280, 2 suites.

Mercure Central without rest, Spui 180, ✉ 2511 BW, ℘ 363 67 00, Fax 363 93 98, – – 25-110. AE D E VISA JCB. rm JZ v
24 – **156 rm** 195/205, 3 suites.

Corona, Buitenhof 42, ✉ 2513 AH, ℘ 363 79 30, Fax 361 57 85, – rest – 30-100. AE D E VISA JCB HY v
Meals (Brasserie) *Lunch 53 b.i.* – 45/50 – 25 – **26 rm** 240/285.

Parkhotel without rest, Molenstraat 53, ✉ 2513 BJ, ℘ 362 43 71, Fax 361 45 25 – – 25-100. AE D E VISA HY a
114 rm 160/275.

Novotel, Hofweg 5, ✉ 2511 AA, ℘ [illegible] – 25-100. AE D E VISA HJY e
Meals a la carte approx. 55 – 23 – **104 rm** 210, 2 suites.

Paleis without rest, Molenstraat 26, ✉ 2513 BL, ℘ 362 46 21, Fax 361 45 33, – . AE D E VISA JCB HY r
20 – **20 rm** 155/175.

De Hoogwerf, Zijdelaan 20, ✉ 2594 BV, ℘ 347 55 14, Fax 381 95 96, , « 17C farmhouse, garden » – AE D E VISA JCB.
closed Sunday and Bank Holidays except Christmas – **Meals** *Lunch 45* – 55/125.

Da Roberto, Noordeinde 196, ✉ 2514 GS, ℘ 346 49 77, Fax 362 52 86, Italian cuisine – . AE D E VISA HX k
closed Sunday – **Meals** *Lunch 55* – a la carte approx. 90.

Royal Dynasty, Noordeinde 123, ✉ 2514 GG, ℘ 365 25 98, Fax 365 25 22, Asian cuisine – . AE D E VISA. HX k
closed Monday – **Meals** *Lunch 30* – 50/68.

't Ganzenest (Visbeen), Groenewegje 115, ✉ 2515 LP, ℘ 389 67 09, Fax 380 07 41 – AE D E VISA. JZ r
closed Monday, Tuesday, Easter, Whitsun, 3 weeks August and first week January – **Meals** (dinner only) 55/90, – a la carte 72/90
Spec. Carpaccio de thon mariné à la vinaigrette de soja, Crème de moules au concombre et à la coriandre (September-February), Filet d'agneau poché aux raviolis de ris d'agneau, ragoût de girolles, truffes et fèves fraîches (May-August).

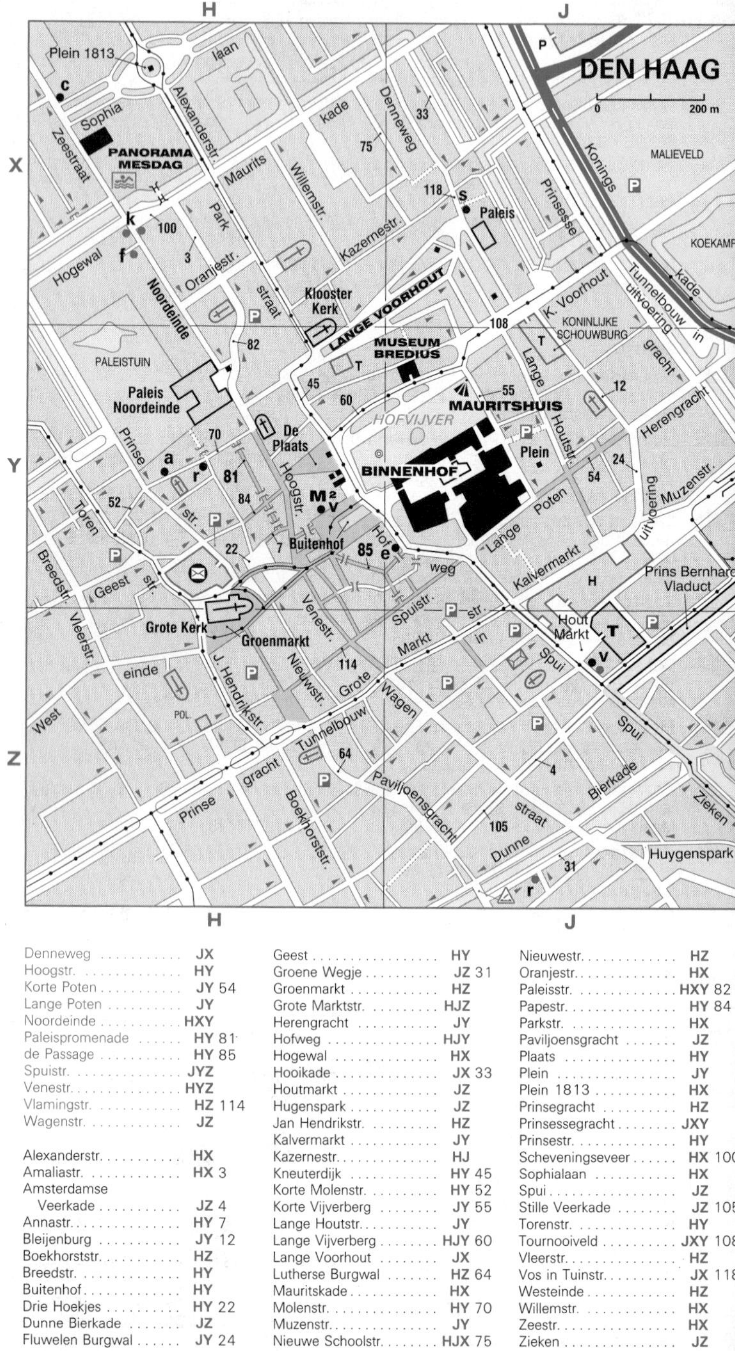

Denneweg	JX	
Hoogstr.	HY	
Korte Poten	JY	54
Lange Poten	JY	
Noordeinde	HXY	
Paleispromenade	HY	81
de Passage	HY	85
Spuistr.	JYZ	
Venestr.	HYZ	
Vlamingstr.	HZ	114
Wagenstr.	JZ	
Alexanderstr.	HX	
Amaliastr.	HX	3
Amsterdamse Veerkade	JZ	4
Annastr.	HY	7
Bleijenburg	JY	12
Boekhorststr.	HZ	
Breedstr.	HY	
Buitenhof	HY	
Drie Hoekjes	HY	22
Dunne Bierkade	JZ	
Fluwelen Burgwal	JY	24
Geest	HY	
Groene Wegje	JZ	31
Groenmarkt	HZ	
Grote Marktstr.	HJZ	
Herengracht	JY	
Hofweg	HJY	
Hogewal	HX	
Hooikade	JX	33
Houtmarkt	JZ	
Hugenspark	JZ	
Jan Hendrikstr.	HZ	
Kalvermarkt	JY	
Kazernestr.	HJ	
Kneuterdijk	HY	45
Korte Molenstr.	HY	52
Korte Vijverberg	JY	55
Lange Houtstr.	JY	
Lange Vijverberg	HJY	60
Lange Voorhout	JX	
Lutherse Burgwal	HZ	64
Mauritskade	HX	
Molenstr.	HY	70
Muzenstr.	JY	
Nieuwe Schoolstr.	HJX	75
Nieuwestr.	HZ	
Oranjestr.	HX	
Paleisstr.	HXY	82
Papestr.	HY	84
Parkstr.	HX	
Paviljoensgracht	JZ	
Plaats	HY	
Plein	JY	
Plein 1813	HX	
Prinsegracht	HZ	
Prinsessegracht	JXY	
Prinsestr.	HY	
Scheveningseveer	HX	10C
Sophialaan	HX	
Spui	JZ	
Stille Veerkade	JZ	105
Torenstr.	HY	
Tournooiveld	JXY	108
Vleerstr.	HZ	
Vos in Tuinstr.	JX	118
Westeinde	HZ	
Willemstr.	HX	
Zeestr.	HX	
Zieken	JZ	

La Grande Bouffe, Maziestraat 10, ✉ 2514 GT, 360 27 23 – AE E VISA HX f
closed Saturday lunch, Sunday, Monday, 16 February-3 March and 27 July-25 August – **Meals** *Lunch 45* – 55/68.

Shirasagi, Spui 170, ✉ 2511 BW, 346 47 00, Fax 346 26 01, Japanese cuisine – AE E VISA JCB. JZ v
closed lunch Saturday, Sunday and Monday and 31 December-2 January – **Meals** 45/135.

Scheveningen 's-Gravenhage – *0 70 – Seaside resort★★ – Casino Kurhaus, Kurhausweg 1, ✉ 2507 RT, 351 26 21, Fax 354 31 83.*

Gevers Deijnootweg 1134, ✉ 2586 BX, 0-6 34 03 50 51, Fax 352 04 26

Kurhaus, Gevers Deijnootplein 30, ✉ 2586 CK, 416 26 36, Fax 416 26 46, « Former late 19C concert hall » – 35-480. AE E VISA JCB. rest
Meals see rest ***Kandinsky*** below – ***Kurzaal*** (buffets) 53/63 – 40 – **233 rm** 390/490, 8 suites.

Carlton Beach, Gevers Deijnootweg 201, ✉ 2586 HZ, 354 14 14, Fax 352 00 20, – 30-250. AE E VISA.
Meals (open until midnight) 50/90 – 33 – **183 rm** 245/290.

Europa, Zwolsestraat 2, ✉ 2587 VJ, 351 26 51, Fax 350 64 73, – 25-450. AE E VISA JCB. rest
Meals (open until 11 p.m.) *Lunch 30* – a la carte approx. 75 – 33 – **173 rm** 240/280, 1 suite.

Kandinsky - (at Kurhaus H.), Gevers Deijnootplein 30, ✉ 2586 CK, 416 26 34, Fax 416 26 46, – . AE E VISA.
closed Saturday lunch and Sunday – **Meals** (dinner only July-August) *Lunch 55* – 90.

Seinpost, Zeekant 60, ✉ 2586 AD, 355 52 50, Fax 355 50 93, Seafood – . AE E VISA
closed Sunday and Bank Holidays – **Meals** *Lunch 58* – 63/68 b.i..

Radèn Mas, Gevers Deijnootplein 125, ✉ 2586 CR, 354 54 32, Fax 354 54 32, Partly Indonesian cuisine – . AE E VISA JCB.
Meals *Lunch 30* – 48/95.

China Delight, Dr Lelykade 116, ✉ 2583 CN, 355 54 50, Fax 354 66 52, Chinese cuisine – . E VISA JCB
Meals *Lunch 30* – a la carte 49/104.

Bali, Badhuisweg 1, ✉ 2587 CA, 350 24 34, Fax 354 03 63, Indonesian cuisine – . AE E VISA.
Meals (dinner only) 55/85.

Environs

Leidschendam *E : 6 km – pop. 34 387 – 0 70 :*

Green Park, Weigelia 22, ✉ 2262 AB, 320 92 80, Fax 327 49 07, – rest – 25-200. AE E VISA JCB
Meals *Lunch 40* – 45/60 – **92 rm** 250/290, 5 suites.

Villa Rozenrust, Veursestraatweg 104, ✉ 2265 CG, 327 74 60, Fax 327 50 62, « Terrace » – . AE E VISA
closed Saturday lunch, Sunday and 28 July-17 August – **Meals** *Lunch 65* – 98/110, – a la carte approx. 100
Spec. Dégustation de 2 carpaccio, Tagliatelle au foie d'oie sauté, Cailles aux truffes et abricots.

Voorburg *E : 5 km – pop. 39 671 – 0 70 :*

Savelberg, Oosteinde 14, ✉ 2271 EH, 387 20 81, Fax 387 77 15, « 17C residence with terrace in public park » – 35. AE E VISA JCB
closed 28 December-12 January – **Meals** *(closed Saturday lunch, Sunday and Monday) Lunch 58* – a la carte 94/126 – **14 rm** 250/350.

Mövenpick Cadettt, Stationsplein 8, ✉ 2275 AZ, 337 37 37, Fax 337 37 00, – 25-160. AE E VISA JCB
Meals (buffets) *Lunch 30* – 43 – 18 – **120 rm** 149/189.

Villa la Ruche, Prinses Mariannelaan 71, ✉ 2275 BB, 386 01 10, Fax 386 50 64 – . AE E VISA
closed Sunday and 27 December-5 January – **Meals** *Lunch 45* – 50/80.

Papermoon, Herenstraat 175, ✉ 2271 CE, 387 31 61, Fax 386 80 36, – . VISA.
closed Monday, 1 week July and first week January – **Meals** (dinner only) 43/58.

at Wassenaar *NE : 11 km – pop. 25 830 – 0 70 :*

Aub. de Kieviet, Stoeplaan 27, ✉ 2243 CX, ☎ 511 92 32, Fax 511 09 69, « Floral terrace » – 25-50. AE VISA JCB
Lunch 45 – 55/65 – 30 – **23 ch** 235/410, 1 suite.

ROTTERDAM *Zuid-Holland 211 G 11 - ㊴ ㊵ and 408 E 6 ㉕ N – pop. 598 239 – 0 10*

Casino JY, Weena 624 ✉ 3012 CN, ☎ 414 77 99, Fax 414 92 33.

See : *Lijnbaan★ JKY – St. Laurence Church (Grote- of St-Laurenskerk) : interior★ KY – Euromast★ (Tower) ★★, ★ JZ – The harbour★★ KZ – Willemsbrug★★ – Erasmusbrug★★ KZ – Delftse Poort (building)★ JY* **R** *– World Trade Center★ KY* **A** *– The Netherlands architectural institute★ JZ* **B** *– Boompjes★ KZ – Willemswerf (building)★ KY*

Museums : *History Museum Het Schielandshuis★ KY* **M⁴** *– Boymans-van Beuningen★★★ J – History "De Dubbelde Palmboom"★.*

Envir : *SE : 7 km, Kinderdijk Windmils★★.*

18 at Capelle aan den IJssel E : 8 km, 's Gravenweg 311, ✉ 2905 LB, ☎ (0 10) 442 21 09 Fax (0 10) 442 24 85 - 9 at Rhoon SW : 11 km, Veerweg 2a, ✉ 3161 EX, ☎ (0 10) 501 80 58.

Zestienhoven ☎ 446 34 44.

Europoort to Hull : North Sea Ferries ☎ (0 181) 25 55 00, Fax (0 181) 25 52 1 (information) and 25 55 55 (reservations).

Coolsingel 67, ✉ 3012 AC, ☎ 0 6-34 03 40 65, Fax 413 01 24 and – Central Station Stationsplein 1, ✉ 3013 AJ, ☎ 0-6-34 03 40 65.

Amsterdam 76 – The Hague 24 – Antwerp 103 – Brussels 148 – Utrecht 57.

Plan opposite

Centre

Parkhotel M, Westersingel 70, ✉ 3015 LB, ☎ 436 36 11, Fax 436 42 12, – rest – 25-70. AE VISA JCB. JZ
Meals *Lunch 43* – a la carte 70/100 – 30 – **187 rm** 265/315, 2 suites.

Hilton, Weena 10, ✉ 3012 CM, ☎ 414 40 44, Fax 411 88 84 – rest – 25-365. AE VISA JCB KY
Meals a la carte 51/70 – 36 – **246 rm** 395/445, 8 suites.

Holiday Inn City Centre, Schouwburgplein 1, ✉ 3012 CK, ☎ 433 38 00 Fax 414 54 82 – – 25-300. AE VISA. JY
Meals (dinner only July-August and weekends) 47/55 – 33 – **98 rm** 240/380, 2 suites

Atlanta, Aert van Nesstraat 4, ✉ 3012 CA, ☎ 411 04 20, Fax 413 53 20 – – 25-250. AE VISA KY
Meals (dinner only) 40/90 – 28 – **164 rm** 200/265.

New York, Koninginnehoofd 1, ✉ 3072 AD, ☎ 439 05 00, Fax 484 27 01, « Former head office of the Holland-America Line maritime company » – 25-120. AE VISA. rm KZ
Meals (open until 11 p.m.) *Lunch 35* – a la carte 43/63 – 15 – **72 rm** 135/250.

Inntel, Leuvehaven 80, ✉ 3011 EA, ☎ 413 41 39, Fax 413 32 22, – rest – 25-220. AE VISA KZ
Meals *Lunch 40* – 43 – 25 – **150 rm** 225/260.

Scandia, Willemsplein 1, ✉ 3016 DN, ☎ 413 47 90, Fax 412 78 90, – rest – 25-70. AE VISA JCB. KZ
closed 21 December-2 January – **Meals** *Lunch 25* – 40 – **104 rm** 135/200.

Pax without rest, Schiekade 658, ✉ 3032 AK, ☎ 466 33 44, Fax 467 52 78 – AE VISA JCB
45 rm 135/250.

Van Walsum, Mathenesserlaan 199, ✉ 3014 HC, ☎ 436 32 75, Fax 436 44 10 – AE VISA JCB. rest JZ
closed 22 December-2 January – **Meals** (dinner residents only) – **25 rm** 100/160.

Parkheuvel (Helder), Heuvellaan 21, ✉ 3016 GL, ☎ 436 07 66, Fax 436 71 40, « Terrace and maritime trade » – AE VISA JZ
closed Sunday and 27 December-2 January – **Meals** *Lunch 73* – 93, a la carte 98/132
Spec. Rouget à la ratatouille de champignons, courgette et anguille fumée, Turbot à la mousseline d'anchois, ragoût de champignons et jus de veau, Volaille rôtie aux pommes de terre et oignons grelots (July-September).

Old Dutch, Rochussenstraat 20, ✉ 3015 EK, ☎ 436 03 44, Fax 436 78 26, – AE VISA. JZ
closed Saturday mid June-mid September, Sunday and Bank Holidays – **Meals** *Lunch 53* – a la carte 73/100.

ROTTERDAM

ursplein . . . . KY 9
nnenweg . . . . JY
tersloot . . . . KY 13
olsingel . . . . KY
ogstr. . . . . KY
rel Doormanstr. . . . . JY
rte Hoogstr. . . . . KY 46
rte Lijnbaan . . . . JY 48
nbaan . . . . JKY
adhuispl. . . . . KY 93

Aert van Nesstr. . . . . JKY 4
Binnenwegpl. . . . . KY 10
Delftsepl . . . . JY 21
Delftsestr. . . . . JY 22
G.J. de Jonghweg . . . . JZ 25
Grotekerkpl. . . . . KY 30
Haagseveer . . . . KY 33
Jonker Fransstr. . . . . KY 39
Keizerstr. . . . . KY 40
Kruiskade . . . . JKY 51
Kruisplein . . . . JY 52
Nieuwestr. . . . . KY 70

van Oldenbarnevelt-plaats . . . . JKY 72
Pompenburg . . . . KY 78
Posthoornstr. . . . . KY 79
Regentessebrug . . . . KY 82
Scheepstimmermanslaan KZ 85
Schouwburgplein . . . . . . JY 88
Veerhaven . . . . KZ 102
Veerkade . . . . KZ 103
van Vollenhovenstr. . . . . KZ 107
Westewagenstr. . . . . KY 110
Wijnbrug . . . . KY 112
Witte de Withstr. . . . . . . KZ 112

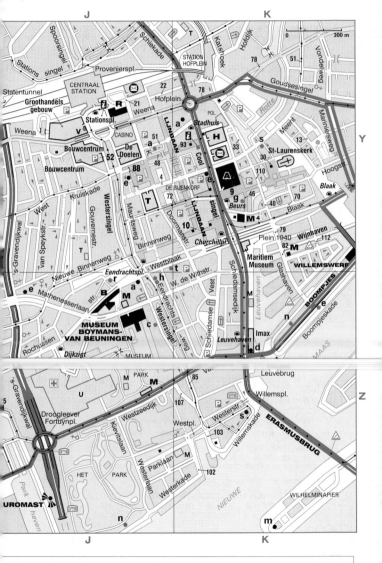

Don't get lost, use **Michelin Maps** which are kept up to date.

XXX **Radèn Mas** 1st floor, Kruiskade 72, ✉ 3012 EH, ☎ 411 72 44, Fax 411 97 11, Indonesian cuisine, « Exotic decor » – ▤. AE ⓓ E VISA JCB. ✻ JY
Meals *Lunch 33* – a la carte approx. 80.

XX **Brasserie La Vilette,** Westblaak 160, ✉ 3012 KM, ☎ 414 86 92, Fax 414 33 91 –
AE ⓓ E VISA JCB JKY
closed Sunday, 21 July-10 August and 24 December-4 January – **Meals** *Lunch 55* – 55/7

XX **de Castellane,** Eendrachtsweg 22, ✉ 3012 LB, ☎ 414 11 59, Fax 214 08 97,
« Terrace » – AE ⓓ E VISA JZ
closed Saturday lunch, Sunday, Bank Holidays, 4 to 23 August and 22 December-4 January – **Meals** *Lunch 50* – a la carte 85/103.

XX **World Trade Center** 23rd floor, Beursplein 37, ✉ 3011 AA, ☎ 405 44 6
Fax 405 51 20, ※ *city* – ▤ P. AE ⓓ E VISA JCB KY
closed Saturday lunch, Sunday, 21 July-8 August and 27 December-1 January – **Meals** *Lunch 53* – 63/83.

XX **Brancatelli,** Boompjes 264, ✉ 3011 XD, ☎ 411 41 51, Fax 404 57 34, Italian cuisine, open until 11 p.m. – ▤. AE ⓓ E VISA JCB KZ
Meals *Lunch 60* – a la carte approx. 75.

XX **Boompjes,** Boompjes 701, ✉ 3011 XZ, ☎ 413 60 70, Fax 413 70 87, ≤ Nieuwe Maas (Meuse), 余 – ▤. AE ⓓ E VISA KZ
Meals *Lunch 53* – 70/85.

X **De Engel** (de Blijker), Eendrachtsweg 19, ✉ 3012 LB, ☎ 413 82 56, Fax 412 51 96
AE ⓓ E VISA. ✻ JZ
Meals (dinner only until 11.30 p.m.) 55/73, – a la carte 70/85
Spec. Cabillaud rôti sur ratatouille au lard frit, Lapin de garenne aux artichauts, toma et céleri-rave, Ananas glacé, crème à la vanille.

X **Engels,** Stationsplein 45, ✉ 3013 AK, ☎ 411 95 50, Fax 413 94 21, Multinational cuisines, open until 11 p.m. – ▤ P – 🏠 25-800. AE ⓓ E VISA JCB JY
Meals 40/48.

X **Anak Mas,** Meent 72a, ✉ 3011 JN, ☎ 414 84 87, Fax 412 44 74, Indonesian cuisine
▤. AE ⓓ E VISA JCB KY
closed Sunday – **Meals** (dinner only until 11 p.m.) 43.

Suburbs

Airport *N : 2,5 km* C *Rotterdam* – ☎ *0 10 :*

🏨 **Airport,** Vliegveldweg 59, ✉ 3043 NT, ☎ 462 55 66, Fax 462 22 66, 余 – |≡| ⇔
☎ ♿ P – 🏠 25-425. AE ⓓ E VISA JCB
Meals 50 – ☐ 23 – **97 rm** 195/240, 1 suite.

at Hillegersberg *NE : 10 km* C *Rotterdam* – ☎ *0 10 :*

X **Mangerie Lommerrijk,** Straatweg 99, ✉ 3054 AB, ☎ 422 00 11, Fax 422 64 96,
余, Pub rest – ▤ P – 🏠 250. AE ⓓ E VISA
closed Monday and 24 and 31 December – **Meals** *Lunch 35* – a la carte 52/70.

at Kralingen *E : 2 km* C *Rotterdam* – ☎ *0 10 :*

🏨 **Novotel Brainpark,** K.P. van der Mandelelaan 150 (near A 16), ✉ 3062 M
☎ 453 07 77, Fax 453 15 03 – |≡| ⇔ ▤ TV ☎ ♿ P – 🏠 25-400. AE ⓓ E VISA
Meals (open until 11 p.m.) a la carte approx. 55 – ☐ 23 – **196 rm** 175.

XXX **In den Rustwat,** Honingerdijk 96, ✉ 3062 NX, ☎ 413 41 10, Fax 404 85 40, 余, « 1 residence » – ▤ P. AE ⓓ E VISA
closed Saturday lunch and Sunday – **Meals** *Lunch 63* – 89/110.

at Ommoord *NE : 10 km* C *Rotterdam* – ☎ *0 10 :*

XX **Keizershof,** Martin Luther Kingweg 7, ✉ 3069 EW, ☎ 455 13 33, Fax 456 80 23,
– P – 🏠 30. AE ⓓ E VISA
closed 28 July-18 August – **Meals** 43/79.

Europoort zone *W : 25 km* – ☎ *0 181 :*

🏨 **De Beer Europoort,** Europaweg 210 (N 15), ✉ 3198 LD, ☎ 26 23 77, Fax 26 29 2
≤, 余, 🏊, ✂ – |≡| TV ☎ P – 🏠 25-180. AE ⓓ E VISA
Meals *Lunch 45* – a la carte approx. 65 – **78 rm** ☐ 150/190.

Environs

at Capelle aan den IJssel *E : 8 km – pop. 60 500* – ☎ *0 10 :*

🏨 **Barbizon** M, Barbizonlaan 2 (near A 20), ✉ 2908 MA, ☎ 456 44 55, Fax 456 78 58,
余 – |≡| ⇔ TV ☎ P – 🏠 30-250. AE ⓓ E VISA JCB. ✻
Meals 43 – ☐ 32 – **100 rm** 245/275, 1 suite.

at Rhoon *S : 10 km* *Albrandswaard pop. 15 141 – 0 10 :*

XXX **Het Kasteel van Rhoon,** Dorpsdijk 63, ✉ 3161 KD, ✆ 501 88 96, Fax 501 24 18, ≤, « Situated in the outbuildings of the mansion » – P. AE ① E VISA
closed 25 and 26 December – **Meals** *Lunch 70 b.i.* – 68/98.

at Schiedam *W : 6 km – pop. 73 480 – 0 10 :*

Buitenhavenweg 9, ✉ 3113 BC, ✆ 473 30 00, Fax 473 66 95

Novotel, Hargalaan 2 (near A 20), ✉ 3118 JA, ✆ 471 33 22, Fax 470 06 56, – P – 25-200. AE ① E VISA
Meals (open until 11 p.m.) a la carte approx. 55 – 23 – **133 rm** 169.

XXX **La Duchesse,** Maasboulevard 9, ✉ 3114 HB, ✆ 426 46 26, Fax 473 25 01, ≤ Nieuwe Maas (Meuse), – P. AE ① E VISA JCB
closed Saturday lunch, Sunday and 31 December – **Meals** *Lunch 55* – a la carte 103/120.

XXX **Aub. Hosman Frères** 1st floor, Korte Dam 10, ✉ 3111 BG, ✆ 426 40 96, Fax 473 00 08, Collection of alcoholic spirits – . AE ① E VISA
closed Sunday and Monday – **Meals** *Lunch 50* – a la carte approx. 85.

X **Orangerie Duchesse,** Maasboulevard 9, ✉ 3114 HB, ✆ 426 46 26, Fax 473 25 01, ≤ Nieuwe Maas (Meuse), – P. AE ① E VISA JCB
closed 25, 26 and 31 December – **Meals** (dinner only) 55.

Czech Republic

Česká Republika

PRACTICAL INFORMATION

LOCAL CURRENCY

Crown : *100 CRT = 3.66 US $ (Jan. 97)*

National Holiday in the Czech Republic : *28 October.*

PRICES

Prices may change if goods and service costs in the Czech Republic are revised and it is therefore always advisable to confirm rates with the hotelier when making a reservation.

FOREIGN EXCHANGE

It is strongly advised against changing money other than in banks, exchange offices or authorised offices such as large hotels, tourist offices, etc... Banks are usually open on weekdays from 8am to 5pm. Some exchange offices in the old city are open 24 h. a day.

HOTEL RESERVATIONS

In case of difficulties in finding a room through our hotel selection, it is always possible to apply to AVE Wilsonova 8, Prague 2, ☎ 24 22 35 21. CEDOK Na příkopě 18, Prague 1 ☎ 24 19 76 15.

POSTAL SERVICES

Post offices are open from 8am to 6pm on weekdays and 12 on Saturdays.
The **General Post Office** *is open 24 hours a day : Jindřišska 14, Prague 1, ☎ 24 22 85 88.*

SHOPPING IN PRAGUE

In the index of street names, those printed in red are where the principal shops are found. Typical goods to be bought include embroidery, puppets, glass, porcelain, ceramics... Shops are generally open from 9am to 7pm.

TIPPING

Hotel, restaurant and café bills include service in the total charge but it is up to you to tip the staff.

CAR HIRE

The international car hire companies have branches in Prague. Your hotel porter should be able to give details and help you with your arrangements.

BREAKDOWN SERVICE

A 24 hour – breakdown service is operated by YELLOW ANGELS, Limuzská 12, Prague 10, ☎ 77 34 55, and ADOS Assistance ☎ 67 31 07 13.

SPEED LIMITS - SEAT BELTS - MOTORWAYS TAX

The maximum permitted speed on motorways is 110 km/h - 68 mph, 90 km/h - 56 mph on other roads and 60 km/h - 37 mph in built up areas except where a lower speed limit is indicated.
The wearing of seat belts is compulsory for drivers and passengers.
Driving on motorways is subject to the purchase of a single rate annual road tax obtainable from frontier posts and tourist offices.
In the Czech Republic, drivers must not drink alcoholic beverage at all.

PRAGUE

(PRAHA) *Česká Republika* 976 F 3 – *Pop. 1 214 600* – ✆ 2.

Berlin 344 – Dresden 152 – Munich 384 – Nurnberg 287 – Wroclaw 272 – Vienna 291.

Prague Information Service : Na Příkope 20 (main office), Staroměstské nám 1, and Main Railway Station ✆ 187
CEDOK : Na příkopě 18, Prague 1 ✆ 24 19 71 11, Fax 232 16 56.

Golf Club Praha, Motol-Praha 5, ✆ 651 24 64
Ruzyně (Prague Airport) NW 20 km, by road nº 7 ✆ 36 77 60.
Bus to airport : ČSA Bus at airlines Terminal V. Celnici 5 ✆ 20 10 43 10.
CZECH AIRLINES (ČESKÉ AEROLINIE) V. Celnici 5, PRAGUE 1 ✆ 20 10 41 11.

See: *Castle District★★★ (Hradčany)* ABY : *Prague Castle★★★ (Pražský Hrad)* BY, *St Vitus' Cathedral★★★ (Katedrála sv. Víta)* BY, *Royal Palace★★ (Královský palác)* BY, *St George's Basilica and Convent★★ (National Gallery's Collection of Old Czech Art* [illegible] *Jiří/Jiřský Klašter)* BY, *Hradčany Square★ (Hradčanské náměstí)* AY **37**, *Schwarzenberg Palace★ (Schwarzenberský Palác)* ABY **P4**, *Loretto★★ (Loreta)* AY, *Strahov Monastery★★ (Strahovský Klášter)* AY – *Lesser Town★★★ (Malá Strana)* BY : *Charles Bridge★★★ (Karlův Most)* BCY, *Lesser Town Square★★ (Malostranské náměstí)* BY, *St Nicholas Church★★★ (Sv. Mikuláš)* BY, *Nerudova Street★★ (Nerudova)* BY, *Wallenstein Palace★★ (Valdštejnský Palác)* BY – *Old Town★★★ (Staré Město)* CY : *Old Town Square★★★ (Staroměstské náměstí)* CY, *Astronomical Clock★★ (Orloj)* CY **B**, *Old Town Hall – Extensive view★★★ (Staroměstská radnice)* CY **B**, *St Nicolas'★ (Sv. Mikuláš)* CY, *Týn Church★ (Týnský chrám)* CY, *Jewish Quarter★★★ (Josefov)* CY, *Old-New Synagogue★★ (Staronová Synagóga)* CY, *Old Jewish Cemetery★★ (Starý židovský hřbitov)* CY **V**, *St Agnes Convent★★ (National Gallery's Collection of 19 C Czech Painting and Sculpture) (Anežský klášter)* CY, *Celetná Street★★ (Celetná)* CDY, *Powder Tower★ (Prašná Brána)* DY, *House of the black Madonna★ (Dům u černe Matky boží)* CDY **E**, *Municipal House★★ (Obecní Dům)* DY **F** – *New Town★★★ (Nové Město)* CDZ : *Wenceslas Square★★★ (Václavské náměstí)* CDYZ.

Museums: *National Gallery★★★ (Národní Galérie)* AY, *National Museum★ (Národní muzeum)* DZ, *National Theatre★★ (Národní divadlo)* CZ, *Decorative Arts Museum★ (Umělecko průmyslové muzeum)* CY **M¹**, *City Museum★ (Prague model★★) (Muzeum hlavního města Prahy)* DY **M²**, *Vila America★ (Dvořák Museum)* DZ.

Outskirts: *Karlštejn Castle SW : 30 km* ET – *Konopiště Castle SW : 40 km* FT.

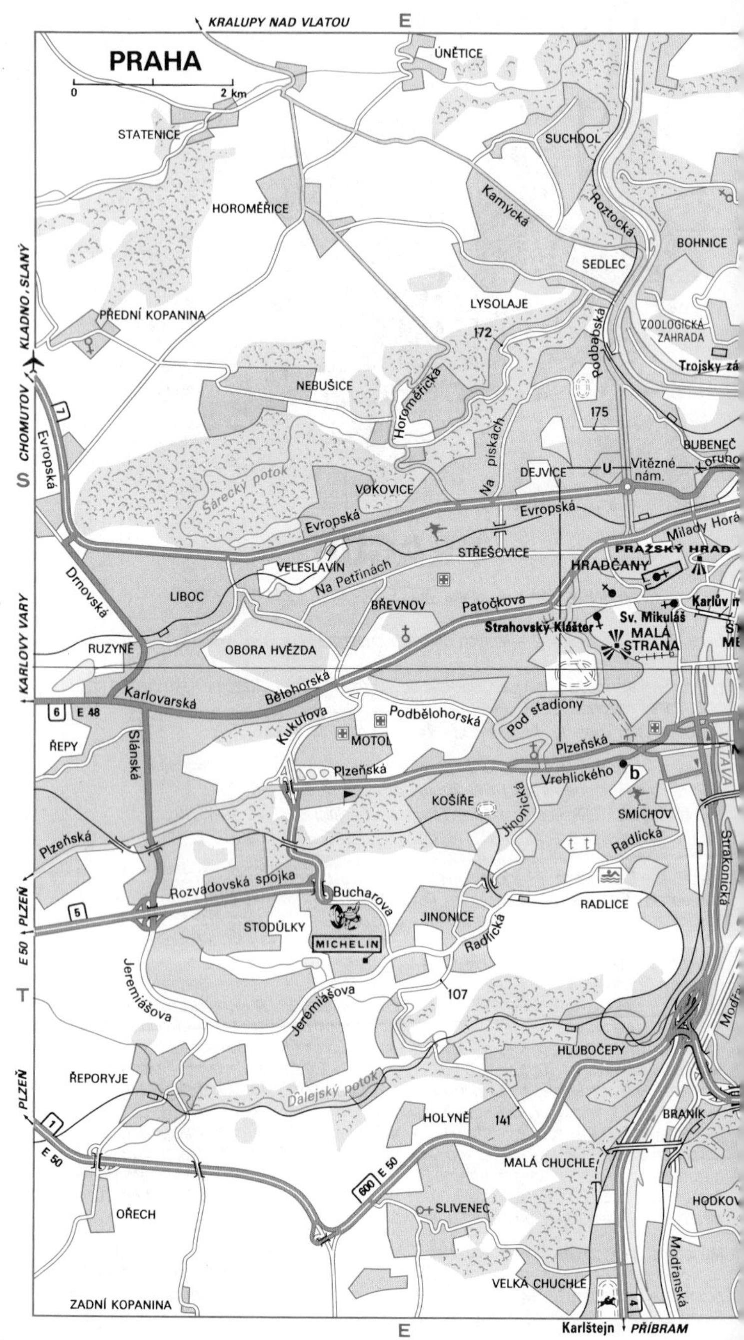

KRALUPY NAD VLATOU
E
PRAHA
0
2 km
ÚNĚTICE
STATENICE
SUCHDOL
HOROMĚŘICE
Kamýcká
Roztocká
BOHNICE
SEDLEC
KLADNO, SLANÝ
LYSOLAJE
PŘEDNÍ KOPANINA
Podbabská
ZOOLOGICKÁ ZAHRADA
172
Trojský zá
NEBUŠICE
Horoměřická
175
CHOMUTOV
7
Evropská
Na pískách
BUBENEČ
Šárecký potok
DEJVICE
Vítězné nám.
S
VOKOVICE
Evropská
Evropská
Milady Horá
VELESLAVÍN
STŘEŠOVICE
PRAŽSKÝ HRAD
Na Petřinách
HRADČANY
Drnovská
LIBOC
BŘEVNOV
Patočkova
Karlův m
KARLOVY VARY
Sv. Mikuláš
Strahovský Klášter
MALÁ STRANA
RUZYNĚ
OBORA HVĚZDA
Bělohorská
Karlovarská
Pod stadiony
6
E 48
Kukulova
Podbělohorská
ŘEPY
Slánská
MOTOL
Plzeňská
Plzeňská
Vrchlického
b
VLTAVA
KOŠÍŘE
Jinonická
SMÍCHOV
Plzeňská
Radlická
Strakonická
PLZEŇ
Rozvadovská spojka
Bucharova
5
RADLICE
STODŮLKY
JINONICE
E 50
MICHELIN
Radlická
Jeremiášova
T
107
Jeremiášova
HLUBOČEPY
ŘEPORYJE
Dalejský potok
PLZEŇ
1
HOLYNĚ
141
BRANÍK
E 50
MALÁ CHUCHLE
600
E 50
OŘECH
SLIVENEC
HODKOV
Modřanská
VELKÁ CHUCHLE
4
ZADNÍ KOPANINA
Karlštejn
PŘÍBRAM
E

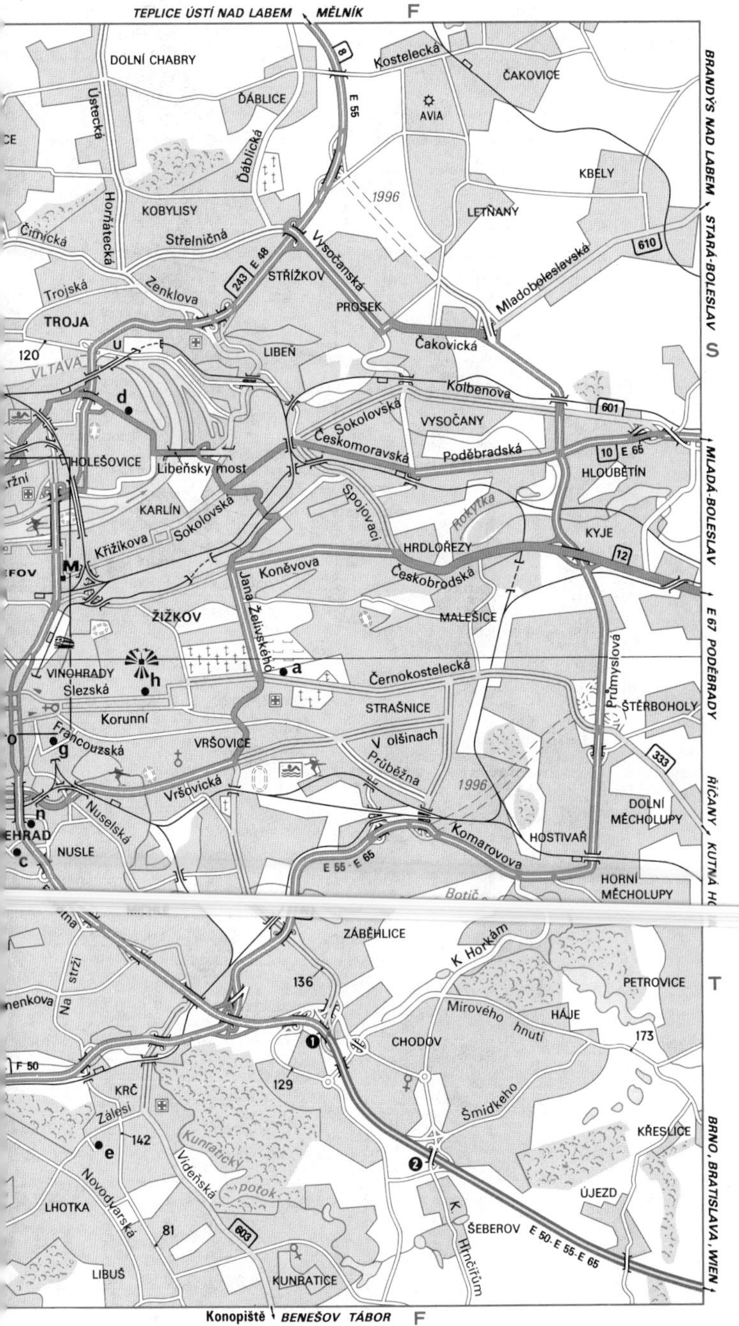
TEPLICE ÚSTÍ NAD LABEM
MĚLNÍK
F
BRANDÝS NAD LABEM
STARÁ-BOLESLAV
S
MLADÁ-BOLESLAV
E 67 PODĚBRADY
ŘÍČANY
KUTNÁ H
T
BRNO, BRATISLAVA, WIEN
Konopiště
BENEŠOV TÁBOR
F
DOLNÍ CHABRY
ĎÁBLICE
Kostelecká
ČAKOVICE
AVIA
KBELY
LETŇANY
KOBYLISY
Střelničná
STŘÍŽKOV
Vysočanská
PROSEK
Mladoboleslavská
Čakovická
TROJA
Trojská
Zenklova
LIBEŇ
VLTAVA
Kolbenova
VYSOČANY
Sokolovská
Českomoravská
Poděbradská
HLOUBĚTÍN
HOLEŠOVICE
Libeňský most
KARLÍN
Spojovací
Rokytka
KYJE
Křižíkova
HRDLOŘEZY
Koněvova
Českobrodská
ŽIŽKOV
MALEŠICE
Jana Želivského
VINOHRADY
Slezská
Černokostelecká
Průmyslová
STRAŠNICE
ŠTĚRBOHOLY
Korunní
Francouzská
VRŠOVICE
V olšinach
Průběžná
Vršovická
Nuselská
NUSLE
DOLNÍ MĚCHOLUPY
HOSTIVAŘ
Komarovova
HORNÍ MĚCHOLUPY
Botič
ZÁBĚHLICE
K Horkám
PETROVICE
Mírového hnutí
HÁJE
CHODOV
Šmidkeho
KRČ
Zálesí
KŘESLICE
Kunratický potok
Vídeňská
Novodvorská
LHOTKA
ŠEBEROV
K Hrnčířům
ÚJEZD
LIBUŠ
KUNRATICE
Ústecká
Ďáblická
Čimická
Horňátecká
1996
E 55
E 48
E 65
E 55 - E 65
E 50 - E 55 - E 65
F 50
8
243
610
601
10
12
333
603
120
136
129
142
81
173
Na strži
U
M
a
c
d
e
g
h
n

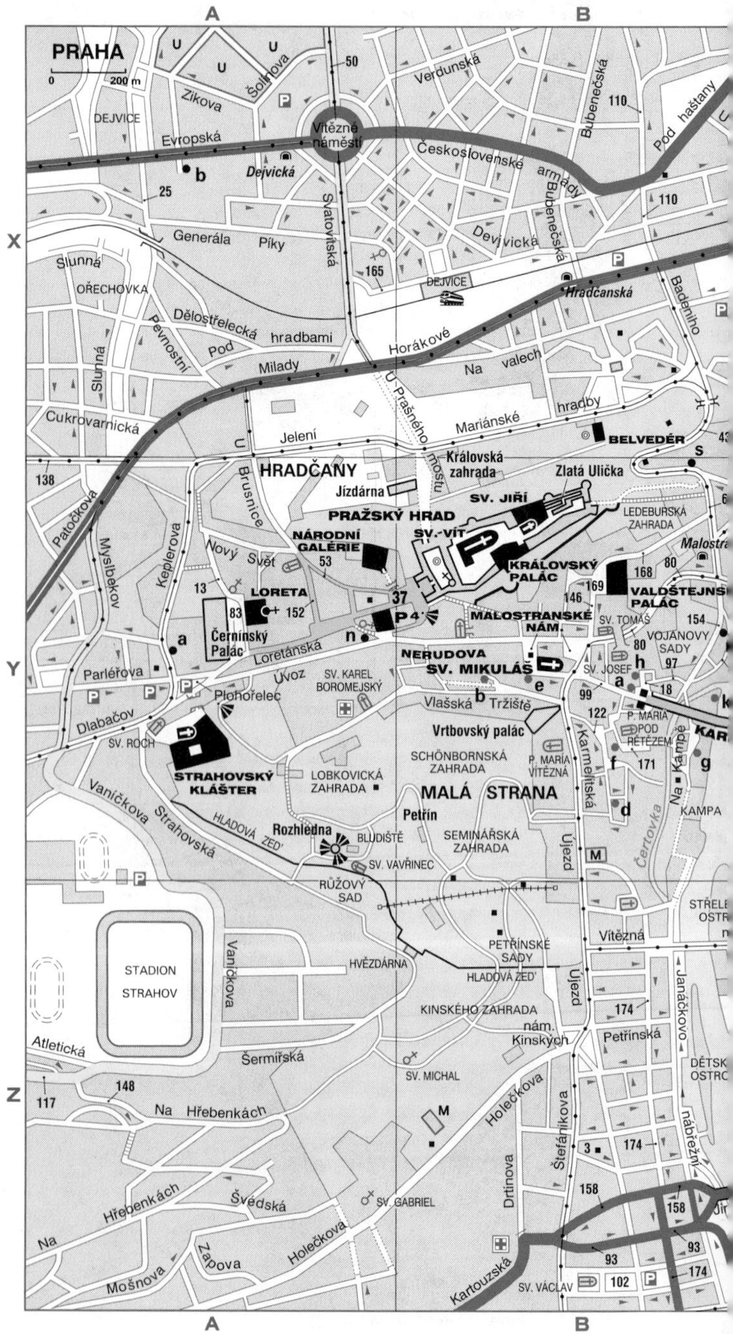
PRAHA
0
200 m
A
B
X
Y
Z
DEJVICE
Evropská
Vítězné náměstí
Dejvická
Zikova
Šolínova
Verdunská
Bubenečská
Pod kaštany
Československé armády
Generála Píky
Svatovítská
Dejvická
Hradčanská
Slunná
OŘECHOVKA
Dělostřelecká
Pevnostní
Pod hradbami
Milady Horákové
Na valech
Badeniho
Cukrovarnická
Jelení
Mariánské hradby
U Prašného mostu
BELVEDÉR
Královská zahrada
HRADČANY
Jízdárna
Zlatá Ulička
SV. JIŘÍ
PRAŽSKÝ HRAD
LEDEBURSKÁ ZAHRADA
NÁRODNÍ GALÉRIE
SV. VÍT
KRÁLOVSKÝ PALÁC
VALDŠTEJNSKÝ PALÁC
Nový Svět
Brusnice
Patočkova
Myslbekova
Keplerova
LORETA
Černínský Palác
MALOSTRANSKÉ NÁM.
SV. TOMÁŠ
VOJANOVY SADY
Loretánská
NERUDOVA
SV. MIKULÁŠ
SV. JOSEF
Parléřova
Úvoz
SV. KAREL BOROMEJSKÝ
Pohořelec
Vlašská
Tržiště
Dlabačov
Vrtbovský palác
P. MARIA POD ŘETĚZEM
SV. ROCH
STRAHOVSKÝ KLÁŠTER
SCHÖNBORNSKÁ ZAHRADA
P. MARIA VÍTĚZNÁ
Karmelitská
Na Kampě
LOBKOVICKÁ ZAHRADA
MALÁ STRANA
KAMPA
Vaníčkova
Strahovská
HLADOVÁ ZEĎ
Petřín
Rozhledna
BLUDIŠTĚ
SEMINÁŘSKÁ ZAHRADA
Čertovka
SV. VAVŘINEC
RŮŽOVÝ SAD
Újezd
PETŘÍNSKÉ SADY
Vítězná
HVĚZDÁRNA
HLADOVÁ ZEĎ
STADION STRAHOV
Vaníčkova
KINSKÉHO ZAHRADA
Janáčkovo nábřeží
nám. Kinských
Petřínská
Atletická
Šermířská
SV. MICHAL
Holečkova
Na Hřebenkách
Štefánikova
Drtinova
Hřebenkách
Švédská
SV. GABRIEL
Na Mošnova
Zapova
Holečkova
Kartouzská
SV. VÁCLAV
Malostranská
50
110
110
165
25
138
13
83
152
53
37
168
80
169
146
154
80
97
18
99
122
171
174
148
117
174
3
158
158
93
93
102
174
a
b
e
f
g
h
n
s
d

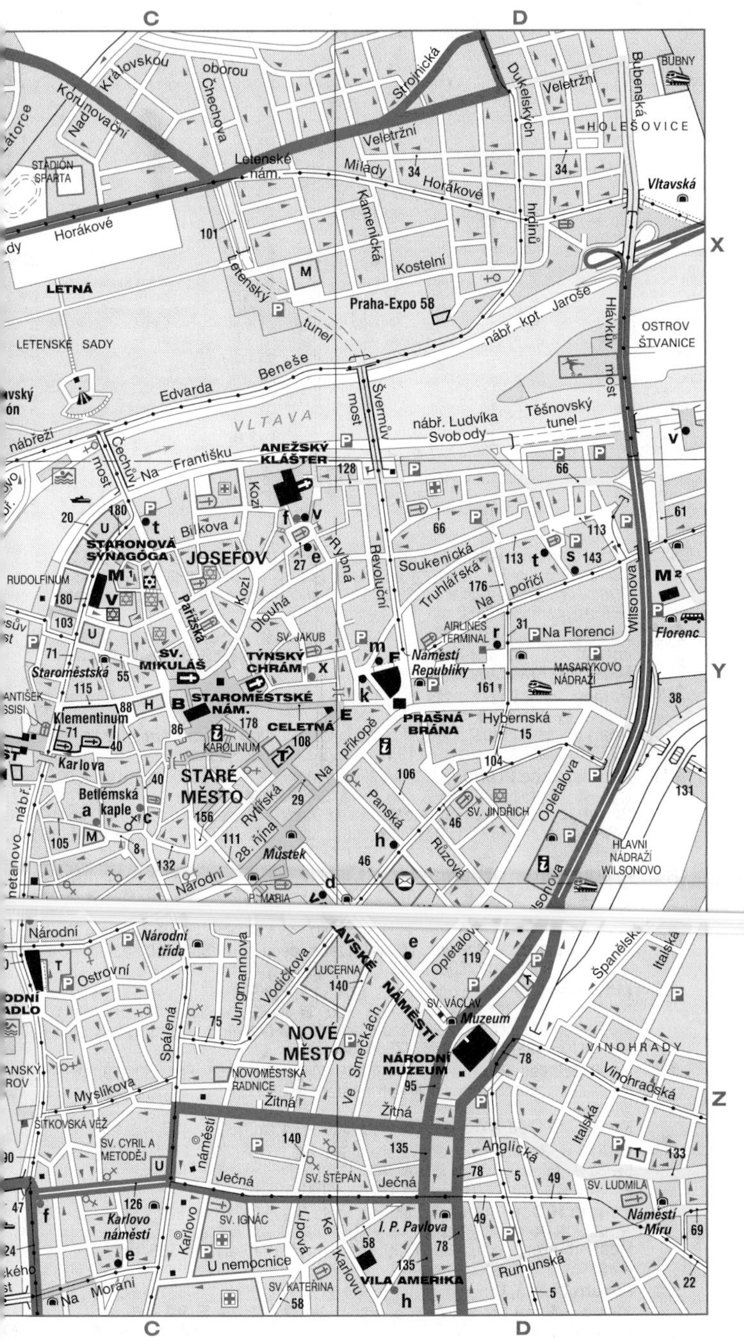
C
D
X
Y
Z
Korunovační
Nad Královskou
oborou
Čechova
Letenské nám.
STADIÓN SPARTA
Horákové
LETNÁ
Letenský tunel
Praha-Expo 58
LETENSKÉ SADY
Edvarda Beneše
nábř. kpt. Jaroše
VLTAVA
Strojnická
Veletržní
Dukelských hrdinů
Bubenská
BUBNY
HOLEŠOVICE
Vltavská
Milady Horákové
Kamenická
Kostelní
Hlávkův most
OSTROV ŠTVANICE
Těšnovský tunel
nábř. Ludvíka Svobody
Štefánikův most
Čechův most
Na Františku
ANEŽSKÝ KLÁŠTER
STARONOVÁ SYNAGÓGA
JOSEFOV
RUDOLFINUM
Bílkova
Kozí
Pařížská
Dlouhá
Rybná
Revoluční
Soukenická
Truhlářská
Na poříčí
Wilsonova
Florenc
Na Florenci
AIRLINES TERMINAL
Náměstí Republiky
MASARYKOVO NÁDRAŽÍ
SV. JAKUB
TÝNSKÝ CHRÁM
SV. MIKULÁŠ
Staroměstská
STAROMĚSTSKÉ NÁM.
Klementinum
CELETNÁ
PRAŠNÁ BRÁNA
Hybernská
KAROLINUM
Karlova
Betlémská kaple
STARÉ MĚSTO
Na příkopě
Panská
SV. JINDŘICH
Opletalova
Růžová
HLAVNÍ NÁDRAŽÍ WILSONOVO
Rytířská
28. října
Můstek
Národní
Národní třída
Ostrovní
Jungmannova
Vodičkova
LUCERNA
SV. VÁCLAV
Muzeum
NOVÉ MĚSTO
NÁRODNÍ MUZEUM
Spálená
Myslíkova
NOVOMĚSTSKÁ RADNICE
Žitná
Ve Smečkách
ŠITKOVSKÁ VĚŽ
SV. CYRIL A METODĚJ
Karlovo náměstí
Ječná
SV. ŠTĚPÁN
SV. IGNÁC
U nemocnice
Lipová
Ke Karlovu
I. P. Pavlova
VILA AMERIKA
SV. KATEŘINA
Na Moráni
VINOHRADY
Vinohradská
Italská
Španělská
Anglická
SV. LUDMILA
Náměstí Míru
Rumunská

STREET INDEX TO PRAHA TOWN PLAN

Street	Grid	No.
Celetná	CDY	
Na příkopě	CDY	
Národní	CZ	
Václavské náměstí	CDZ	
Arbesovo náměstí	BZ	3
Bělehradská	DZ	5
Betlémské náměstí	CY	8
Cihelná	BY	10
Černínská	AY	13
Dlážděná	DY	15
Dražického náměstí	BY	18
Dvořákovo nábřeží	CY	20
Francouzská	DY	22
Gymnasijní	AX	25
Haštalské náměstí	CY	27
Havířská	CY	29
Havlíčkova	DY	31
Heřmanova	DX	34
Hradčanské náměstí	AY	37
Husitská	DY	38
Husova	CY	40
Chotkova	BX	43
Jindřišská	DY	46
Jiráskovo náměstí	CZ	47
Jugoslávská	DZ	49
Jugoslávských partyzánů	AX	50
Kanovnická	AY	53
Kaprova	CY	55
Kateřinská	CDZ	58
Ke Štvanici	DY	61
Klárov	BY	63
Klimentská	DY	66
Korunní	DZ	69
Křižovnická	CY	71
Lazarská	CZ	75
Legerova	DZ	78
Letenská	BY	80
Libušská	FT	81
Loretánské náměstí	AY	83
Malé náměstí	CY	86
Mariánské náměstí	CY	88
Masarykovo nábřeží	CZ	90
Matoušova	BZ	93
Mezibranská	DZ	95
Míšeňská	BY	97
Mostecká	BY	99
Nad štolou	CX	101
náměstí 14. října	BZ	102
náměstí Jana Palacha	CY	103
náměstí Maxima Gorkého	DY	104
Náprstkova	CY	105
Nekázanka	DY	106
Novoveská	ET	107
Ovocný trh	CY	108
Pelléova	BX	110
Perlová	CY	111
Petrská	DY	113
Platnéřská	CY	115
Pod Stadiony	AZ	117
Politických vězňů	DZ	119
Povltavská	FS	120
Prokopská	BY	122
Rašínovo nábřeží	CZ	124
Resslova	CZ	1
Řásnovka	DY	1
Ryšaveho	FT	1
Seifertova	DY	1
Skořepka	CY	1
Slezská	DZ	1
Sokolská	DZ	1
Sporilovská	FT	1
Střešovická	AY	1
Štěpánská	DZ	1
Štěpařská	ET	1
Štúrova	FT	1
Těšnov	DY	1
Tomášská	BY	1
Turistiká	AZ	1
U Bruských Kasáren	BY	1
U kasáren	AY	1
U lužického semináře	BY	1
Uhelný trh	CY	1
V botanice	BZ	1
V celnici	DY	1
Václavkova	AX	1
Valdštejnská	BY	1
Valdštejnské náměstí	BY	1
Velkopřevorské náměstí	BY	1
V Šáreckém údolí	ES	1
Výstavní	FT	1
Zborovská	BZ	1
Zelená	ES	1
Zlatnická	DY	1
Železná	CY	1
17. listopadu	CY	1

Inter-Continental, Nám. Curieových 43, ✉ 110 00, ✆ 2488 1111, Fax 2488 1123, – rm – 250. AE ① E VISA JCB. CY
Primator : **Meals** (buffet lunch) 600/750 and a la carte (see also ***Zlatá Praha*** below
365 rm 6550/7350.

Savoy, Keplerova Ul. 6, ✉ 118 00, ✆ 2430 2430, Fax 2430 2128, « Elega installation », – rm – 30. AE ① E VISA JCB AY
Meals (see ***Hradčany*** below) – **60 rm** 7670/9100, 1 suite.

Palace, Panská 12, ✉ 111 21, ✆ 2409 3111, Fax 2422 1240 – rm – 80. AE ① E VISA JCB. rest DY
Meals (buffet lunch) 720/1020 and a la carte – ***Club Restaurant :*** **Meals** (dinner or 780/1020 and a la carte – **119 rm** 7380/8750, 5 suites.

Renaissance Prague, V Celnici 7, ✉ 110 00, ✆ 2182 2100, Fax 2182 2200, – rm – 245. AE ① E VISA JCB. DY
Potomac (✆ 2182 2431) **: Meals** *(closed Sunday)* (dinner only) 750/1000 and a la ca – ***Pavillion*** (✆ 2182 2431) **: Meals** (buffet lunch) 495/520 – ***U Korbele*** (✆ 2182 243 **Meals** 300/500 and a la carte – **298 rm** 6200/6800, 11 suites.

Prague Hilton Atrium, Pobřežní 1, ✉ 186 00, ✆ 2484 1111, Fax 2484 2378, – rm – 350. AE ① E VISA DX
Chez Louis : **Meals** (dinner only) 1050/1350 and a la carte – ***Praha :*** **Meals** 500/750 a dinner a la carte – ***Morava :*** **Meals** - Czech specialities - 550/700 and dinner a la ca – 350 – **766 rm** 7600/8250, 22 suites.

Mövenpick M, Mozartova 261/1, ✉ 151 33, ✆ 5715 1111, Fax 5715 3131, pa – 300. AE ① E VISA JCB. rest ET
Meals (buffet lunch) 450/900 and a la carte – ***Il Giardino :*** **Meals** (dinner only) 450 a a la carte – **404 rm** 4662/7668, 31 suites.

Hoffmeister, Pod Bruskou 9, ✉ 118 00, ✆ 561 8155, Fax 530 959, « Elega installation, collection of Adolf Hoffmeister's artwork » – rm . AE ① VISA JCB. BXY
Meals 550/1500 and a la carte – 300 – **34 rm** 5600/6400, 4 suites.

Grand H. Bohemia, Králodvorská 4, ✉ 110 00, ✆ 2480 4111, Fax 232 9545 – – 100. AE ① E VISA JCB DY
Meals a la carte 490/850 – **75 rm** 7800/10300, 3 suites.

Rogner H. Don Giovanni, Vinohradská 157a, ✉ 130 61, ✆ 6703 1111, Fax 6703 67 – rm – 200. AE E VISA. rest FT
Meals (buffet lunch) 490/1500 and dinner a la carte – **356 rm** 4310/54 44 suites.

Forum Praha, Kongresová 1, ✉ 140 69, ✆ 6119 1111, Fax 421 669, squash – rm – 290. AE ① E VISA JCB FT
Harmonie : **Meals** 600/1000 and a la carte – ***Ceska :*** **Meals** (buffet only) 620/68 **531 rm** 6250/8005.

Diplomat, Europská 15, ✉ 160 00, ℰ 2439 4111, Fax 2439 4215, – |‡| rm ▤ TV ☎ – 350. AE ⓓ E VISA JCB. rest AX b
Meals (buffet lunch) 380/430 and a la carte – **364 rm** ☐ 4472/6708, 18 suites.

Maximilian without rest., Haštalská 14, ✉ 110 00, ℰ 2180 6111, Fax 2180 6110 – |‡| ▤ TV ☎ – 60. AE ⓓ E VISA JCB CY e
71 rm ☐ 4608/5508, 1 suite.

U Krále Karla, ¿voz 4, ✉ 110 00, ℰ 538 805, Fax 538 811, « 17C Baroque house, antique furniture » – |‡| ▤ rm TV ☎. AE ⓓ E VISA AY n
Meals 240 (lunch) and a la carte 340/780 – **18 rm** ☐ 5000/5500.

Villa Voyta, K Novému Dvoru 124-54, ✉ 142 00, ℰ 472 5511, Fax 472 9426, – |‡| ▤ rm TV ☎ P. AE ⓓ E VISA JCB FT e
Meals 650/1200 and a la carte – **13 rm** ☐ 4100/5600.

Adria, Václavské Nám. 26, ✉ 110 00, ℰ 2108 1111, Fax 2108 1300 – |‡| ▤ TV ☎ – 70. AE ⓓ E VISA. CZ d
Meals 320/800 and a la carte – **61 rm** ☐ 4280/5680, 5 suites.

City H. Moran, Na Moráni 15, ✉ 120 00, ℰ 2491 5208, Fax 297 533 – |‡| TV ☎. AE ⓓ E VISA JCB. rest CZ e
Meals 350/750 and a la carte – **57 rm** ☐ 4900/5880.

Esplanade, Washingtonova 19, ✉ 110 00, ℰ 2421 1715, Fax 2422 9306, « Art Nouveau building » – |‡| ▤ rm TV ☎ P – 40. AE ⓓ E VISA JCB DZ f
Meals a la carte 400/800 – **68 rm** ☐ 5250/6890, 6 suites.

Jalta Praha, Václavské Nám. 45, ✉ 110 00, ℰ 2422 9133, Fax 2421 3866 – |‡| ▤ rest TV ☎ – 150. AE ⓓ E VISA JCB. DZ e
Meals 350/1900 and a la carte – **80 rm** ☐ 5600/6600, 5 suites.

Vyšehrad, Marie Cibulkové 29, ✉ 140 00, ℰ 436 002, Fax 435 774 – |‡| ▤ TV ☎. AE ⓓ E VISA JCB. FT c
Meals a la carte 300/500 – **26 rm** ☐ 5300/5900, 1 suite.

Paříž, U Obecního Domu 1, ✉ 110 00, ℰ 2422 2151, Fax 2422 5475, « Neo-Gothic and Art Nouveau architecture » – |‡| ▤ rest TV ☎ P – 55. AE ⓓ E VISA JCB. rest
Meals 550/650 and a la carte – **88 rm** ☐ 6219/6737, 4 suites. DY m

Alta, Ortenovo Nám. 22, ✉ 170 00, ℰ 800 252-9, Fax 6671 2011 – |‡| ▤ rest TV ☎ – 30. AE ⓓ E VISA JCB. rest FS d
Meals a la carte 350/400 – **82 rm** ☐ 2470/3090, 5 suites.

Ametyst, Jana Masaryka 11, ✉ 120 00, ℰ 2425 4185, Fax 2425 1315, – |‡| rm ▤ rest TV ☎ & – 35. AE ⓓ E VISA JCB FT g
Meals (buffet lunch) 460/500 and a la carte – ***Vienna :* Meals** a la carte 472/1282 – **84 rm** ☐ 4100/5200.

Sieber, Slezská 55, ✉ 130 00, ℰ 2425 0025, Fax 2425 0024 – |‡| TV ☎. AE ⓓ E VISA JCB. FT h
Meals (dinner only) a la carte 300/400 – **12 rm** ☐ 3580/3800.

U Páva, U Lužického Semináře 32, ✉ 110 00, ℰ 2451 0922, Fax 533 379 – ▤ rm TV ☎ P. AE ⓓ E VISA. rest BY m

Casa Marcello, Řásnovka 783, ✉ 110 00, ℰ 231 0260, Fax 231 3323, – TV ☎. AE ⓓ E VISA JCB. rest CY v
Meals - Italian - (buffet lunch) 250/600 and a la carte – **12 rm** ☐ 5100/7500, 4 suites.

Bílá Labuťv, Biskupská 9, ✉ 110 00, ℰ 2481 1382, Fax 232 2905 – |‡| TV ☎ & P. AE ⓓ E VISA JCB DY t
Meals 250/1400 and a la carte – **54 rm** ☐ 4200/4800.

Harmony, Na Poříčí 31, ✉ 110 00, ℰ 232 4595, Fax 231 0009 – |‡| TV ☎ &. AE ⓓ E VISA JCB DY s
Meals (buffet lunch) a la carte 250/700 – **51 rm** ☐ 2408/3341, 9 suites.

Union, Ostrcilovo Nám. 4, ✉ 128 00, ℰ 6121 4812, Fax 6121 4820 – |‡| TV ☎ P. AE ⓓ E VISA JCB. rest FT s
Meals 150/250 and a la carte – **57 rm** ☐ 2800/3380.

Zlatá Praha (at Intercontinental H.), Nám. Curieových 43, ✉ 110 00, ℰ 2488 1111, Fax 2488 1123, ≤ Prague – ▤. AE ⓓ E VISA JCB CY t
Meals 1200/1500 and a la carte.

Hradčany (at Savoy H.), Keplerova Ul. 6, ✉ 118 00, ℰ 2430 2430, Fax 2430 2128 – ▤. AE ⓓ E VISA JCB AY a
Meals 460/750 and a la carte.

La Perle de Prague (7th floor), Rašínovo Nábřeží 80, ✉ 120 00, ℰ 2198 4160, Fax 2198 4179, ≤ – ▤. AE ⓓ E VISA JCB CZ f
French rest – **Meals** 1100/1300 and a la carte.

XXX **Parnas,** Smetanovo Nábřeží 2, ✉ 110 00, ✆ 2422 7614, Fax 2422 8932, ≤ – AE E VISA
Meals (dinner booking essential) 690/1590 and a la carte. CZ

XXX **Klub Kampa,** Na Kampě 14, ✉ 110 00, ✆ 539 985 – AE ⓓ E VISA. ✻ BY
Meals (dinner only) a la carte 400/800.

XX **Flambée,** Betlém Palais, Husova 5, ✉ 110 00, ✆ 2424 8512, Fax 2424 8513, « 14
vaulted cellar » – Ⓟ. AE ⓓ E VISA JCB CY
Meals 900/8000 and a la carte.Javoslav Hynek (1/94)

XX **Pod Věží** with rm, Mostecká 2, ✉ 110 00, ✆ 533 710, Fax 531 859 – TV ☎ Ⓟ.
ⓓ E VISA BY
Meals a la carte 350/800 – **12 rm** 3900/5300.

XX **Vinárna V Zatisi,** Liliová 1, Betlémské Nám., ✉ 110 00, ✆ 2422 8977, Fax 2422 89
– AE E VISA CY
Meals 595/895 and a la carte.

XX **David,** Tržiště 21, Malá Strana, ✉ 110 00, ✆ 539 325, Fax 534 721 – AE ⓓ VISA JC
Meals (dinner booking essential) 450/750 and a la carte. BY

X **Bistrot de Marlène,** Plavecká 4, ✉ 120 00, ✆ 29 10 77, Fax 29 10 77 – AE
VISA ET
closed Saturday lunch, Sunday and 24 December-4 January – French rest – **Meals** (bookir
essential) a la carte 610/800.

X **Kampa Park,** Na Kampě 8b, ✉ 110 00, ✆ 5731 3493, Fax 5731 3495, ⛱, « Vltav
riverside setting, ≤ Charles Bridge » – AE ⓓ E VISA JCB BY
Meals (dinner booking essential) 450/850 and a la carte.

X **U Patrona,** Dražického Nám. 4, ✉ 110 00, ✆ 531 512, Fax 2422 8932 – AE E VIS
Meals 540/900 and a la carte. BY

X **La Provence,** Štupartská 9, ✉ 110 00, ✆ 232 4801, Fax 2481 6695, « Vaulted cellar
– AE E VISA CY
Meals - Mediterranean Bistro - (booking essential) a la carte 350/700.

X **Circle Line,** Malostranske Nám. 12, ✉ 110 00, ✆ 530 308, Fax 2422 8932, Vaulted cell
– AE E VISA BY
closed Sunday – **Meals** - Seafood - (dinner only) a la carte 715/1400.

LOCAL ATMOSPHERE AND CZECH CUISINE

XX **U Vladaře,** Maltézské Nám. 10, ✉ 118 00, ✆ 538 128, Fax 530 842, ⛱ – AE ⓓ
VISA JCB BY
Meals (buffet lunch) a la carte 400/750.

XX **U Červeného Kola,** Anežská 2, ✉ 110 00, ✆ 2481 1118, Fax 2481 1118, « Courtyar
terrace » – AE ⓓ E VISA JCB. ✻ CY
Meals 450/960 and a la carte.

XX **U Modre Kachnicky,** Nebovidská 6, ✉ 118 00, ✆ 2451 0217, Fax 2451 021
« 14C house with modern murals » – AE ⓓ VISA JCB BY
Meals (dinner booking essential) a la carte 390/660.

X **Hostinec U Kalicha,** Na Bojišti 12, ✉ 120 00, ✆ 291 945, Fax 290 701, Typical Pragu
beerhouse – AE ⓓ E VISA JCB DZ
Meals a la carte 270/510.

Denmark

Danmark

COPENHAGEN

PRACTICAL INFORMATION

LOCAL CURRENCY

Danish Kroner: *100 DKK = 16.83 USD ($) (Jan. 97)*

TOURIST INFORMATION

The telephone number and address of the Tourist Information office is given in the text under ℹ.

National Holiday in Denmark: *5 June.*

FOREIGN EXCHANGE

Banks are open between 9.30am and 4.00pm (6.00pm on Thursdays) on weekdays except Saturdays. The main banks in the centre of Copenhagen, the Central Station and the Airport have exchange facilities outside these hours.

AIRLINES

SAS: *Hamerichsgade 1, ☎ 32 32 68 08*

AIR FRANCE: *Ved Versterpot 6, ☎ 33 33 91 00*

BRITISH AIRWAYS: *Rådhuspladsen 16, ☎ 33 14 37 50*

LUFTHANSA: *V. Farimagsgade 7, ☎ 33 37 73 33*

UNITED AIRLINES: *V. Farimagsgade 1, ☎ 33 13 52 98*

MEALS

At lunchtime, follow the custom of the country and try the typical buffets of Scandinavian specialities.

At dinner, the a la carte and set menus will offer you more conventional cooking.

SHOPPING IN COPENHAGEN

Strøget (Department stores, exclusive shops, boutiques).

Kompagnistræde (Antiques). Shops are generally open from 10am to 8pm (Saturday 10am to 5pm).

See also in the index of street names, those printed in red are where the principal shops are found.

THEATRE BOOKINGS

Your hotel porter will be able to make your arrangements or direct you to Theatre Booking Agents.

CAR HIRE

The international car hire companies have branches in Copenhagen – Your hotel porter should be able to give details and help you with your arrangements.

TIPPING

In Denmark, all hotels and restaurants include a service charge. As for the taxis, there is no extra charge to the amount shown on the meter.

SPEED LIMITS

The maximum permitted speed in cities is 50 km/h - 31 mph, outside cities 80 km/h - 50 mph and 110 km/h - 68 mph on motorways. Cars towing caravans 70 km/h – 44 mph and buses 80 km/h – 50 mph also on motorways.

Local signs may indicate lower or permit higher limits. On the whole, speed should always be adjusted to prevailing circumstances. In case of even minor speed limit offences, drivers will be liable to heavy fines to be paid on the spot. If payment cannot be made, the car may be impounded.

SEAT BELTS

The wearing of seat belts is compulsory for drivers and all passengers except children under the age of 3 and taxi passengers.

COPENHAGEN

(KØBENHAVN) *Danmark* 985 Q 9 – *pop. 622 000, Greater Copenhagen 1 354 000.*

Berlin 385 – Hamburg 305 – Oslo 583 – Stockholm 630.

Copenhagen Tourist Information, Bernstorffsgade 1, ✉ *1577 V* ☏ *33 11 13 25, Fax 33 93 49 69.*

Dansk Golf Union 56 ☏ *43 45 55 55.*
Copenhagen/Kastrup SE : 10 km ☏ *31 54 17 01 – Air Terminal : main railway station.*
Motorail for Southern Europe : ☏ *33 14 17 01.*
Further information from the D S B, main railway station or tourist information centre (see below).

See : *Rosenborg Castle*★★★ *(Rosenborg Slot)* CX – *Amalienborg Palace*★★ *(Amalienborg)* DY – *Nyhavn*★★ *(canal)* DY – *Tivoli*★★ *: May to mid-september* BZ – *Christiansborg Palace*★ *(Christiansborg)* CZ – *Citadel*★ *(Kastellet)* DX – *Gråbrødretorv*★ CY **28** – *Little Mermaid*★ *(Den Lille Havfrue)* DX – *Marble Bridge*★ *(Marmorbroen)* CZ **50** – *Marble Church*★ *(Marmorkirken)* DY – *Kongens Nytorv*★ DX – *Round Tower*★ *(Rundetårn)* CY **E** – *Stock Exchange*★ *(Børsen)* CDZ – *Strøget*★ BCYZ – *Town Hall (Rådhuset)* BZ **H** : *Jens Olsen's astronomical clock*★ BZH.

Museums : *National Museum*★★★ *(Nationalmuseet)* CZ – *Ny Carlsberg Glyptotek*★★★*: art collection* BZ – *National Fine Arts Museum*★★ *(Statens Museum for Kunst)* CX – *Thorvaldsen Museum*★ *(Thorvaldsens Museum)* CZ **M¹**.

Outskirts : *Ordrupgård*★★*: art collection (Ordrupgårdsamlingen) N : 10 km* CX – *Louisiana Museum of Modern Art*★★ *(Museum for Moderne Kunst) N : 35 km* CX – *Dragør*★ *SW : 13 km* CZ – *Rungstedlund*★*: Karen Blixen Museum N : 25 km* CX – *Open-Air Museum*★ *(Frilandsmuseet) NW : 12 km* AX.

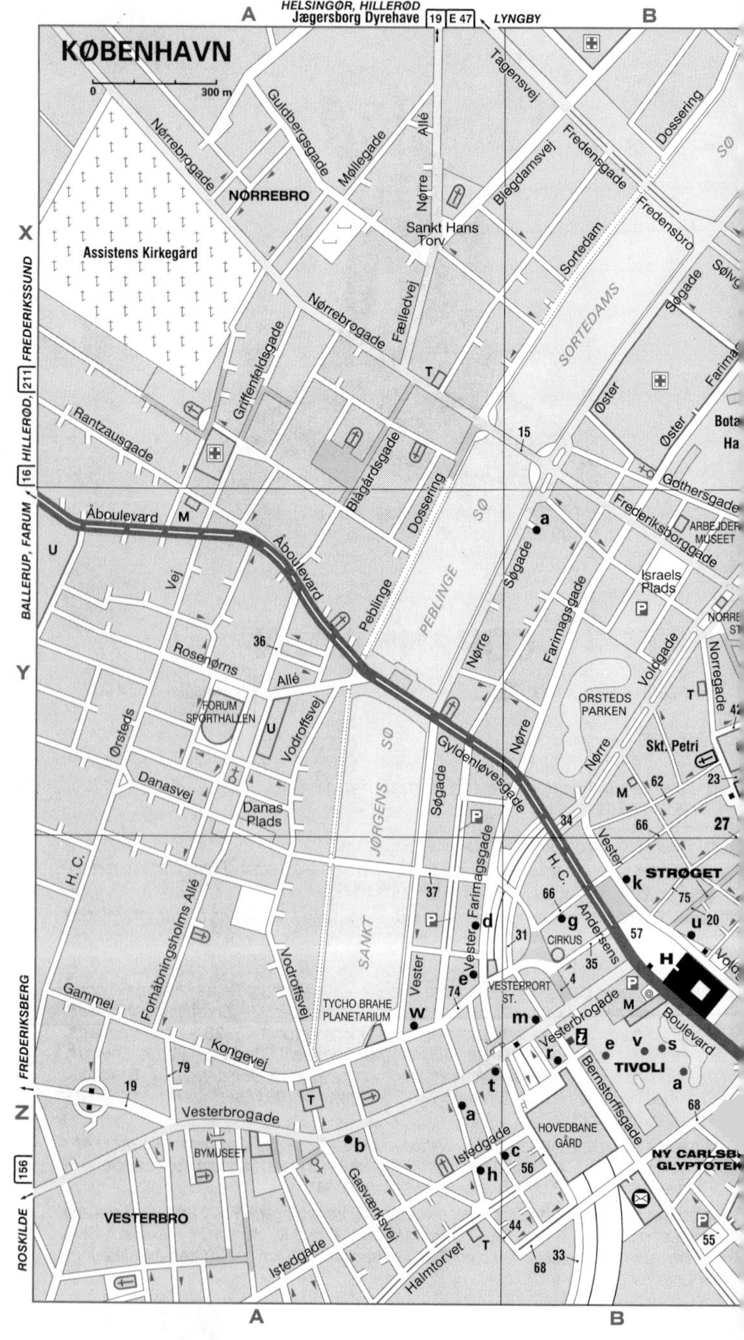
KØBENHAVN
0
300 m
HELSINGØR, HILLERØD
Jægersborg Dyrehave
19
E 47
LYNGBY
BALLERUP, FARUM
16
HILLERØD, 211 FREDERIKSSUND
FREDERIKSBERG
ROSKILDE
156
NØRREBRO
Assistens Kirkegård
Nørrebrogade
Guldbergsgade
Møllegade
Nørre Allé
Sankt Hans Torv
Fælledvej
Tagensvej
Blegdamsvej
Fredensgade
Fredensbro
Dossering
Sortedam
SORTEDAMS
Søgade
Øster
Griffenfeldsgade
Rantzausgade
Blågårdsgade
Dossering
Åboulevard
Peblinge
PEBLINGE
SØ
Søgade
Nørre
Farimagsgade
Gothersgade
Frederiksborggade
ARBEJDER MUSEET
Israels Plads
Voldgade
Norregade
ORSTEDS PARKEN
Skt. Petri
Rosenørns Allé
FORUM SPORTHALLEN
Vodroffsvej
Ørsteds
Danasvej
Danas Plads
JØRGENS
SANKT
Gyldenløvesgade
Søgade
Farimagsgade
Vester
H. C. Andersens Boulevard
STRØGET
CIRKUS
VESTERPORT ST.
Vesterbrogade
TIVOLI
Bernstorffsgade
HOVEDBANE GÅRD
NY CARLSB GLYPTOTEK
H. C.
Forhåbningsholms Allé
Gammel Kongevej
Vodroffsvej
TYCHO BRAHE PLANETARIUM
Vesterbrogade
BYMUSEET
VESTERBRO
Gasværksvej
Istedgade
Halmtorvet
Boulevard
A
B
X
Y
Z

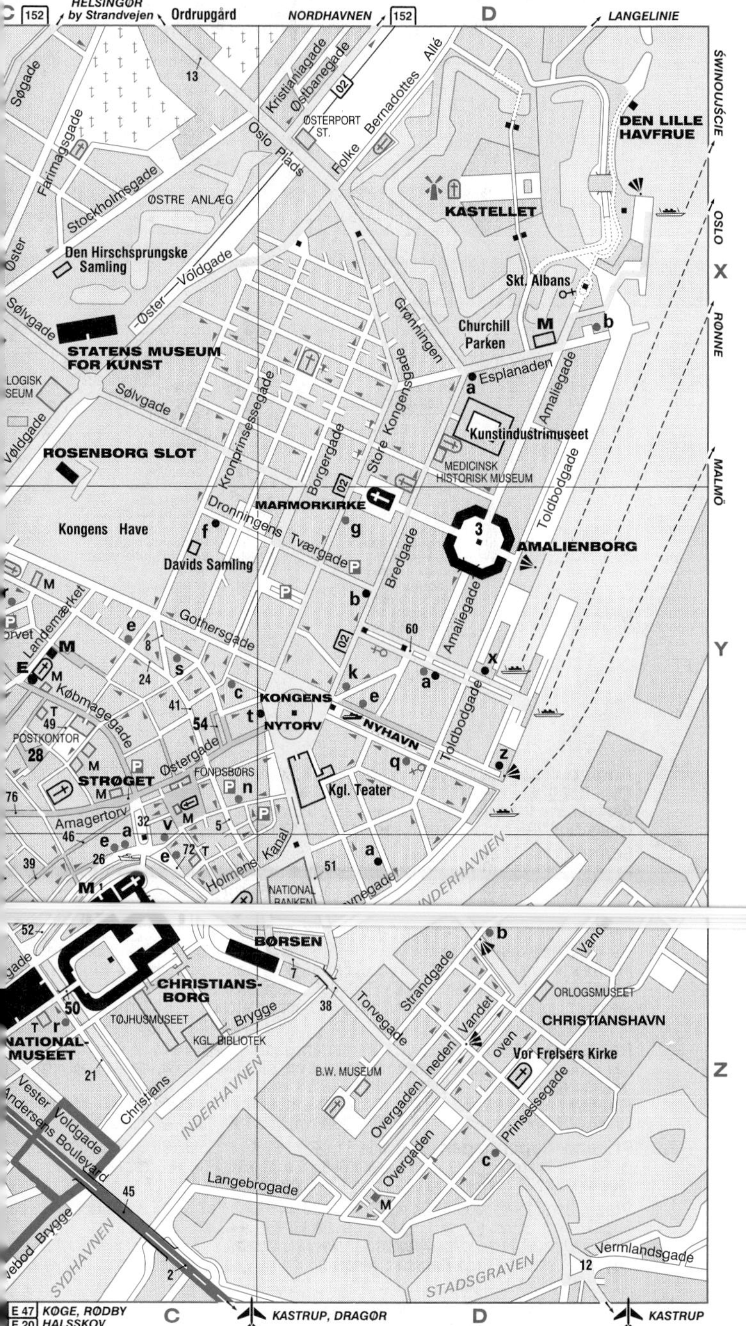

HELSINGØR by Strandvejen
Ordrupgård
NORDHAVNEN
LANGELINIE
ŚWINOUJŚCIE
OSLO
RØNNE
MALMÖ
DEN LILLE HAVFRUE
KASTELLET
ØSTERPORT ST.
Den Hirschsprungske Samling
STATENS MUSEUM FOR KUNST
ROSENBORG SLOT
Kongens Have
Davids Samling
MARMORKIRKE
AMALIENBORG
Kunstindustrimuseet
MEDICINSK HISTORISK MUSEUM
Churchill Parken
Skt. Albans
KONGENS NYTORV
NYHAVN
STRØGET
Kgl. Teater
FONDSBØRS
POSTKONTOR
NATIONAL BANKEN
BØRSEN
CHRISTIANSBORG
TØJHUSMUSEET
KGL. BIBLIOTEK
NATIONALMUSEET
ORLOGSMUSEET
CHRISTIANSHAVN
Vor Frelsers Kirke
B.W. MUSEUM
INDERHAVNEN
SYDHAVNEN
STADSGRAVEN
KØGE, RØDBY HALSSKOV
KASTRUP, DRAGØR
KASTRUP

STREET INDEX TO KØBENHAVN TOWN PLAN

Street	Grid	No.
Amagertorv (Strøget)	CY	
Bredgade	DY	
Frederiksberggade (Strøget)	BZ	20
Købmagergade	CY	
Nygade (Strøget)	CYZ	52
Nørre Voldgade	BY	
Store Kongensgade	DXY	
Vesterbrogade	ABZ	
Vimmelskaftet (Strøget)	CY	76
Østergade (Strøget)	CY	
Amager Boulevard	CZ	2
Amaliegade	DXY	
Amalienborg Plads	DY	3
Axeltorv	BZ	4
Bernstorffsgade	BZ	
Blegdamsvej	BX	
Blågårdsgåde	AX	
Borgergade	DXY	
Bremerholm	CY	5
Børsgade	DZ	7
Christan IX's Gade	CY	8
Christiansborg Slotsplads	CZ	9
Christians Brygge	CZ	
Christmas Møllers Plads	DZ	12
Dag Hammarskjölds Allé	CX	13
Danas Plads	AY	
Danasvej	AY	
Dronningens Tværgade	CDY	
Dronning Louises Bro	BX	15
Esplanaden	DX	
Farvergade	BZ	16
Fiolstræde	BY	17
Folke Bernadottes Allé	DX	
Forhåbningsholms Allé	AZ	
Fredensbro	BX	
Fredensgade	BX	
Frederiksberg Allé	AZ	19
Frederiksborggade	BY	
Frederiksholms Kanal	CZ	21
Frue Plads	BY	23
Fælledvej	AX	
Gammel Kongevej	AZ	
Gammel Mønt	CY	24
Gammel Strand	CZ	26
Gammeltorv	BYZ	27
Gasværksvej	AZ	
Gothersgade	BCY	
Griffenfeldsgade	AX	
Grønningen	DX	
Gråbrødretorv	CY	28
Guldbergsgade	AX	
Gyldenløvesgade	AY	
Halmtorvet	AZ	
Hambrosgade	CZ	30
Hammerichsgade	BZ	31
Havnegade	DZ	
H.C. Andersens Boulevard	BCZ	
H.C. Ørsteds Vej	AY	
Holmens Kanal	CDZ	
Højbro Plads	CY	32
Ingerslevsgade	BZ	33
Israels Plads	BY	
Istedgade	AZ	
Jarmers Plads	BY	34
Jernbanegade	BZ	35
Julius Thomsens Gade	AY	36
Kalvebod Brygge	CZ	
Kampmannsgade	AZ	37
Knippelsbro	DZ	38
Kompagnistræde	CZ	39
Kongens Nytorv	DY	
Kristen Bernikows Gade	CY	41
Kristianiagade	DX	
Kronprinsessegade	CXY	
Krystalgade	BCY	42
Kultorvet	CY	
Kvægtorvsgade	ABZ	44
Landemaerket	CY	
Langebro	CZ	45
Langebrogade	CDZ	
Læderstræde	CYZ	46
Løngangstræde	BZ	48
Løvstræde	CY	49
Marmorbroen	CZ	50
Møllegade	AX	
Niels Juels Gade	DZ	51
Nybrogade	CZ	52
Nyhavn	DY	
Nytorv	BZ	53
Nørre Allé	AX	
Nørrebrogade	AX	
Nørre Farimagsgade	BY	
Nørregade	BY	
Nørre Søgade	ABY	
Oslo Plads	DX	
Overgaden neden Vandet	DZ	
Overgaden oven Vandet	DZ	
Peblinge Dossering	AY	
Pistolstræde	CY	
Polititorvet	BZ	
Prinsessegade	DZ	
Rantzausgade	AX	
Reventlowsgade	BZ	
Rosenørns Allé	AY	
Rådhuspladsen	BZ	
Rådhusstræde	CZ	
Sankt Annæ Plads	DY	
Sankt Hans Torv	AX	
Sankt Peders Stræde	BY	
Skindergade	CY	
Sortedam Dossering	BX	
Stockholmsgade	CX	
Store Kannikestræde	CY	
Stormgade	CZ	
Strandgade	DZ	
Studiestræde	BYZ	
Sølvgade	BCX	
Sølvtorvet	CX	
Tagensvej	BX	
Tietgensgade	BZ	
Toldbodgade	DXY	
Torvegade	DZ	
Vandkunsten	CZ	
Webersgade	BX	
Ved Stranden	CZ	
Ved Vesterport	AZ	
Vermlandsgade	DZ	
Vester Farimagsgade	AZ	
Vestergade	BZ	
Vester Søgade	AYZ	
Vester Voldgade	BCZ	
Vindebrogade	CZ	
Vodroffsvej	AYZ	
Værnedamsvej	AZ	
Østbanegade	DX	
Øster Farimagsgade	BCX	
Øster Søgade	BCX	
Øster Voldgade	CX	
Aboulevard	AY	

Angleterre, Kongens Nytorv 34, ✉ 1050 K, ☎ 33 12 00 95, Fax 33 12 11 18, Fō, ≡ – |$| TV ☎ – 400. AE ① E VISA JCB. ✻ CDY
Restaurant D'Angleterre : **Meals** 225/395 and a la carte – ***Restaurant Wiinbla***
Meals 158/295 and a la carte – ☕ 120 – **130 rm** 1850/2300.

Scandic H. Copenhagen M, Vester Søgade 6, ✉ 1601 V, ☎ 33 14 35 3
Fax 33 32 12 23, ≤, ≋ – |$| ⇹ rm ▤ TV ☎ – 1200. AE ① E VISA JCB. ✻ re
Meals (buffet lunch) 175/500 and a la carte – **465 rm** ☕ 995/1950. AZ

Radisson SAS Scandinavia, Amager Boulevard 70, ✉ 2300 S, ☎ 33 11 23 2
Fax 31 57 01 93, ≤ Copenhagen, Fō, ≋, ⊠, squash – |$| ⇹ rm TV ☎ P – 18
AE ① E VISA JCB. ✻ rest by Amager Boulevard CZ
Mama's Papa's : **Meals** (buffet lunch) 185/245 and a la carte – ***Blue Elepha***
(☎ 33 11 15 00) **: Meals** - Thai - 350/495 and a la carte – ***Kyoto*** (☎ 33 32 16 7
Meals - Japanese - (dinner only) 170/300 and a la carte – **507 rm** ☕ 1745/20
35 suites.

Radisson SAS Royal ⚲, Hammerichsgade 1, ✉ 1611 V, ☎ 33 42 60 0
Fax 33 42 61 00, ≤, « Panoramic restaurant on 20th floor », Fō, ≋ – |$| ⇹ rm ▤
☎ ⇔ P – 250. AE ① E VISA JCB. ✻ rest BZ
Summit : **Meals** *(closed Sunday)* 245/450 and a la carte – ***Café Royal :*** **Meals** (buf
lunch) 195 and a la carte 119/405 – **263 rm** ☕ 1690/1990, 2 suites.

Phoenix Copenhagen, Bredgade 37, ✉ 1260 K, ☎ 33 95 95 00, Fax 33 33 98 3
|$| ⇹ rm ▤ rest TV ☎ ⇔ – 80. AE ① E VISA JCB. ✻ rest DY
Meals 135/275 and a la carte – ☕ 110 – **209 rm** 1090/2290, 3 suites.

Plaza, Bernstorffsgade 4, ✉ 1577 V, ☎ 33 14 92 62, Fax 33 93 93 62, « Library ba
– |$| ⇹ rm ▤ rm TV ☎ – 35. AE ① E VISA JCB. ✻ rest BZ
closed 20 to 28 December – ***Alexander Nevski :*** **Meals** *(closed July)* (dinner only) 268/3
and a la carte – ***Flora Danica :*** **Meals** (lunch only) a la carte approx. 172 – **87**
☕ 1550/2150, 6 suites.

Kong Frederik, Vester Voldgade 25, ✉ 1552 V, ☎ 33 12 59 02, Fax 33 93 59 1
|$| TV ☎ – 80. AE ① E VISA JCB. ✻ BZ
Meals 145/295 and a la carte – ☕ 100 – **110 rm** 1150/1450.

Kong Arthur, Nørre Søgade 11, 1370 K, 33 11 12 12, Fax 33 32 61 30, – rm – 50. BY a
Brochner (33 93 58 05) **: Meals** *(closed Sunday and Bank Holidays)* (dinner only) 185/265 and a la carte – ***Sticks 'n' Sushi*** (33 11 14 07) **: Meals** - Japanese - (closed Bank Holidays) (dinner only) 155/180 and a la carte – **107 rm** 980/1300.

Radisson SAS Falconer, Falkoner Allé 9, 2000 Frederiksberg C, 31 19 80 01 (changing to 38 19 50 01 from 7 October 1997), Fax 31 87 11 91, Copenhagen, – rm rm – 2000. by Gammel Kongevej AZ
Meals (buffet lunch) 185/350 and a la carte – **163 rm** 1150/1860, 3 suites.

Imperial, Vester Farimagsgade 9, 1606 V, 33 12 80 00, Fax 33 93 80 31 – rm – 100. AZ e
***Imperial Garden* : Meals** (dinner only) 295/450 and a la carte – ***Imperial Brasserie* : Meals** (buffet lunch) 250 and a la carte – **163 rm** 1160/2310.

Palace, Rådhuspladsen 57, 1550 V, 33 14 40 50, Fax 33 14 52 79, – rm – 50. rest BZ u
Meals (buffet lunch)/dinner a la carte 150/284 – **162 rm** 1325/1825.

Neptun, Sankt Annae Plads 14-20, 1250 K, 33 13 89 00, Fax 33 14 12 50 – rm rm – 40. DY a
closed 20 to 29 December – **Meals** *(closed Sunday and July)* 165/290 and a la carte – **117 rm** 1050/1640, 16 suites.

Sophie Amalie, Sankt Annae Plads 21, 1021 K, 33 13 34 00, Fax 33 12 57 17, – rest – 50. DY x
Meals 135/265 and a la carte – 90 – **134 rm** 805/990.

Copenhagen Crown without rest., Vesterbrogade 41, 1620 V, 31 21 21 66, Fax 31 21 00 66 – rm – 25. AZ b
78 rm 925/1190, 2 suites.

Copenhagen Star without rest., Colbj ! rnsensgade 13, 1652 V, 31 22 11 00, Fax 31 22 21 99 – rm – 25. ABZ c
132 rm 925/1190, 2 suites.

Ascot without rest., Studiestraede 61, 1554 V, 33 12 60 00, Fax 33 14 60 40, – – 50. BZ g
118 rm 810/1390, 32 suites.

City without rest., Peder Skrams Gade 24, 1054 K, 33 13 06 66, Fax 33 13 06 67 – DZ a
81 rm 775/1125.

71 Nyhavn, Nyhavn 71, 1051 K, 33 11 85 85, Fax 33 93 15 85, « Former warehouse » – rm rest DY z
Meals *(closed Sunday, July and Bank Holidays)* (dinner only) 245/282 and a la carte – **76 rm** 995/1560, 6 suites.

Mercur, Vester Farimagsgade 17, 1780 V, 33 12 57 11, Fax 33 12 57 17, – rm AZ d
Meals *(closed Sunday)* 145/470 and a la carte – **108 rm** 665/1600, 1 suite.

Christian IV without rest., Dronningens Tvaergade 45, 1302 K, 33 32 10 44, Fax 33 32 07 06 – CY f
closed 23 to 28 December – **42 rm** 790/980.

Esplanaden without rest., Bredgade 78, 1260 K, 33 91 32 00, Fax 33 91 32 39 – DX a
closed 20 to 29 December – **112 rm** 695/1000, 4 suites.

Komfort, Løngangstraede 27, 1468 K, 33 12 65 70, Fax 33 15 28 99 – rest BZ n
closed 22 to 30 December – **Meals** 98/158 and a la carte – **201 rm** 900/1200.

Absalon without rest., Helgolandsgade 15-19, 1653 V, 31 24 22 11 (changing to 33 24 22 11 from 13 May 1997), Fax 31 24 34 11 – AZ h
closed 21 December-5 January – **177 rm** 735/1100.

Danmark without rest., Vester Voldgade 89, 1552 V, 33 11 48 06, Fax 33 14 36 30 – BZ t
closed 20 December-2 January – **49 rm** 595/950, 2 suites.

Kong Hans Kaelder, Vingårdsstraede 6, 1070 K, 33 11 68 68, Fax 33 32 67 68, « Vaulted Gothic cellar » – CY n
closed Sunday, 28 March-2 April, 29 June-28 August and 23 December-2 January – **Meals** (booking essential) (dinner only) 395/865 and a la carte 375/800
Spec. Warm foie gras with a raspberry vinegar, Fried sole with orange and poppy seeds, Grilled lobster in the shell with ginger, garlic and lobster butter.

XX ✿✿ **Kommandanten,** Ny Adelgade 7, ✉ 1104 K, ✆ 33 12 09 90, Fax 33 93 12 23, « 17 town house, contemporary furnishings » – AE ◑ E VISA JCB CY
closed Saturday lunch, Sunday, 24 December-4 January and Bank Holidays – **Meals** (booking essential) 320/550 and a la carte 450/615
Spec. Norway lobster with artichoke salad and artichoke soufflé, Boiled oxtail, lobster and parsley potato purée, sauce lyonnaise, Selection of chocolate desserts.

XX ✿ **Nouvelle,** Gammel Strand 34 (1st floor), ✉ 1202 K, ✆ 33 13 50 18, Fax 33 32 07 9 – AE ◑ E VISA JCB CZ
closed Saturday lunch, Sunday, July, 23 December-first week January and Bank Holidays – **Meals** (booking essential) 250/485 and a la carte 405/475
Spec. Egg "Nouvelle" filled with lobster, mousseline sauce and sevruga caviar, Bornholm herrings served as appetisers, Hare in truffle sauce with apples, mild chilli and fried parsley root.

XX **Restaurationen,** Møntergade 19, ✉ 1116 K, ✆ 33 14 94 95 – AE ◑ E VISA
closed Sunday, Monday, July, 23 December-5 January and Bank Holidays – **Meals** (booking essential) (dinner only except December) 415. CY

XX ✿ **Era Ora,** Torvegade 62, ✉ 1400 K, ✆ 31 54 06 93, Fax 32 96 02 09, « Tasteful installation » – ⇔ ▤. AE ◑ E VISA JCB DZ
closed Sunday and 23 to 26 December – **Meals** - Italian - (booking essential) (dinner only) 385/500
Spec. Scallops perfumed with orange and oregano, Pappardelle with chestnuts and hare, Chocolate roll covered with a snow-white cream.

XX ✿ **Pierre André,** Ny Østergade 21, ✉ 1101 K, ✆ 33 16 17 19 – AE ◑ E VISA JCB
closed Saturday lunch, Sunday, 7 to 27 July and Bank Holidays – **Meals** (booking essential) 185/390 and a la carte 315/430 CY
Spec. Fricassée aux moules et coquille St. Jacques au curry, Noisettes de chevreuil au poivre, Poire Belle Hélène.

XX **Krogs,** Gammel Strand 38, ✉ 1202 K, ✆ 33 15 89 15, Fax 33 15 83 19, ⛱, 18C house – AE ◑ E VISA JCB CZ
closed Sunday and 22 to 26 December – **Meals** - Seafood - (booking essential) 178/42 and a la carte.

XX ☺ **Lumskebugten,** Esplanaden 21, ✉ 1263 K, ✆ 33 15 60 29, Fax 33 32 87 18, ⛱, « Mid 19C café-pavilion » – AE ◑ E VISA JCB DX
closed Saturday lunch, Sunday, Christmas, New Year and Bank Holidays – **Meals** 185/55 and a la carte 312/384.

XX **St. Gertruds Kloster,** Hauser Plads 32, ✉ 1127 K, ✆ 33 14 66 30, Fax 33 93 93 6 « Part 14C monastic cellars » – ▤. AE ◑ E VISA JCB CY
Meals (dinner only except December) 345/575 and a la carte.

XX **Leonore Christine,** Nyhavn 9 (1st floor), ✉ 1051 K, ✆ 33 13 50 40, Fax 33 13 50 4 18C house – AE ◑ E VISA JCB DY
closed 23 December-1 January – **Meals** 195/365 and a la carte.

X ☺ **Kanalen,** Christianshavn-Wilders Plads, ✉ 1403 K, ✆ 32 95 13 30, Fax 32 95 13 38, ⛱, « Canalside house » – Ⓟ. AE ◑ E VISA JCB DZ
closed Sunday – **Meals** (booking essential) 148/248 and a la carte 211/434.

X **Den Gyldne Fortun,** Ved Stranden 18, ✉ 1061 K, ✆ 33 12 20 11, Fax 33 93 35 – AE ◑ E VISA JCB CZ
closed lunch Saturday and Sunday, 23 to 31 March, 17 to 19 and 25 to 27 May and 22 December-2 January – **Meals** - Seafood - 175/295 and a la carte.

X **Den Sorte Ravn,** Nyhavn 14, ✉ 1051 K, ✆ 33 13 12 33, Fax 33 13 24 72 – ▤. AE ◑ E VISA JCB DY
closed Easter and 24 to 26 December – **Meals** 350 (dinner) and a la carte 328/460.

X **Els,** Store Strandstraede 3, ✉ 1255 K, ✆ 33 14 13 41, Fax 33 91 07 00, « 19C murals » – ▤. AE ◑ E VISA JCB DY
closed Sunday lunch – **Meals** 176/366 and a la carte.

X **Thorvaldsen,** Gammel Strand 34 (ground floor), ✉ 1202 K, ✆ 33 32 04 0 Fax 33 32 07 97, ⛱ – AE ◑ E VISA JCB CZ
closed dinner 10 October-31 March, Sunday, 23 December-first week January and Bank Holidays – **Meals** (booking essential) 175/225 and a la carte.

in Tivoli : *Vesterbrogade 3 ✉ 1620 V (Entrance fee payable)*

XXX **Divan 2,** ✆ 33 12 51 51, Fax 33 91 08 82, ≤, ⛱, « Floral decoration and terrace » AE ◑ E VISA JCB BZ
24 April-14 September – **Meals** 325/685 and a la carte.

XXX **Belle Terrasse,** ✆ 33 12 11 36, Fax 33 15 00 31, ≤, ⛱, « Floral decoration and terrace » – AE ◑ E VISA JCB BZ
25 April-14 September – **Meals** 295/545 and a la carte.

XX **Divan No. 1,** ✆ 33 11 42 42, Fax 33 11 74 07, ≤, 畬, « 19C pavilion » – AE ① E VISA JCB BZ v
24 April-14 September – **Meals** 165/495 and a la carte.

XX **La Crevette,** Bernstorffsgade 5, ✉ 1577 V, ✆ 33 14 68 47, Fax 33 14 60 06, ≤, 畬, « Terrace overlooking flowered garden » – AE ① E VISA JCB BZ e
24 April-14 September – **Meals** - Seafood - 295/395 and a la carte.

SMØRREBRØD

The following list of simpler restaurants and cafés/bars specialize in Danish open sandwiches and are generally open from 10.00am to 4.00pm.

X **Ida Davidsen,** St. Kongensgade 70, ✉ 1264 K, ✆ 33 91 36 55, Fax 33 11 36 55 – AE ① E VISA JCB DY g
closed Saturday, Sunday, July, Christmas-New Year and Bank Holidays – **Meals** (buffet lunch) a la carte 35/175.

X **Slotskaelderen-Hos Gitte Kik,** Fortunstraede 4, ✉ 1065 K, ✆ 33 11 15 37 – AE ① E VISA JCB CYZ v
closed Sunday, Monday and Bank Holidays – **Meals** (lunch only) a la carte 30/68.

X **Sankt Annae,** Sankt Annae Plads 12, ✉ 1250 K, ✆ 33 12 54 97 – ① E VISA JCB DY a
closed Saturday, Sunday and 3 weeks July – **Meals** (lunch only) a la carte 115/145.

X **Kanal Caféen,** Frederiksholms Kanal 18, ✉ 1220 K, ✆ 33 11 57 70, Fax 33 13 79 62, 畬 – AE ① E VISA JCB CZ r
closed Saturday, Sunday, Christmas-New Year and Bank Holidays – **Meals** (lunch only) 33/68 and a la carte.

at Hellerup *N : 7 ½ km by Østbanegade* DX *and Road 2 – ✉ 2900 Hellerup :*

Hellerup Parkhotel, Strandvejen 203, ✆ 39 62 40 44, Fax 39 62 56 57, Ⅎ₆, ≘s – |≑| ⇔ rm ▣ ☎ Ⓟ – 🔏 150. AE ① E VISA JCB. ⅋ rest
Meals (see ***Saison*** below) – **71 rm** ⊐ 895/1450.

XX **Saison** (at Hellerup Parkhotel), Strandvejen 203, ✆ 39 62 48 42, Fax 39 62 56 57 – Ⓟ. AE ① E VISA JCB
closed Sunday, 3 weeks July and Bank Holidays – **Meals** 235/515 and a la carte.

at Klampenborg *N : 12 km by Østbanegade* DX*, Road 2 and Road 152 (coast rd) – ✉ 2930 :*

X **Den Gule Cottage,** Staunings Plaene, Strandvejen 506, ✆ 39 64 06 91, Fax 39 64 27 77, ≤, 畬, « Thatched cottage beside the sea » – Ⓟ. AE ① E VISA JCB
Meals (booking essential) 225/380 and a la carte.

X **Den Røde Cottage,** Strandvejen 550, ✆ 39 90 46 14, Fax 39 90 86 14, 畬, « Small cottage in a clearing » – AE ① E VISA JCB
Meals (booking essential) 190/295 and a la carte.

at Søllerød *N : 20 km by Tagensvej* BX *and Road 19 – ✉ 2840 Holte :*

XXX ✿ **Søllerød Kro,** Søllerødvej 35, ✆ 45 80 25 05, Fax 45 80 22 70, 畬, « 17C thatched inn, terrace » – Ⓟ. AE ① E VISA JCB. ⅋
Meals 150/525 and a la carte 385/575
Spec. Poached oysters and smoked salmon, watercress and cucumber salad. Medallion of venison with a wild mushroom tartlet, blackcurrant sauce, iced coffee soufflé.

at Kastrup Airport *SE : 10 km by Amager Boulevard* CZ *– ✉ 2300 S :*

Radisson SAS Globetrotter Ⓜ, Engvej 171, *NW : 3 km by coastal rd* ✆ 31 55 14 33, Fax 31 55 81 45, Ⅎ₆, ≘s, ▧ – |≑| ⇔ rm ▣ ☎ Ⓟ – 🔏 360. AE ① E VISA JCB. ⅋ rest
Meals (buffet lunch) a la carte 225/432 – **197 rm** ⊐ 945/1460.

Dan Ⓜ, Kastruplundgade 15, Kastrup, ✉ 2770, *N : 2 ½ km by coastal rd* ✆ 32 51 14 00, Fax 32 51 37 01, 畬, ≘s – |≑| ⇔ rm ▤ rest ▣ ☎ Ⓟ – 🔏 120. AE ① E VISA JCB. ⅋ rest
Meals (buffet lunch) 168/265 and a la carte – **218 rm** ⊐ 795/1095, 10 suites.

Finland

Suomi

HELSINKI

PRACTICAL INFORMATION

LOCAL CURRENCY

Finnish Mark: *100 FIM = 21.54 USD ($) (Jan. 97)*

TOURIST INFORMATION

The Tourist Office is situated near the Market Square, Pohjoisesplanadi 19 ☏ 169 3757 and 174 088. Open from 2 May to 30 September, Monday to Friday 9am - 7pm, Saturday and Sunday 9am - 3pm, and from 1 October to 30 April, Monday to Friday 9am - 5pm and Saturday from 9am to 3pm. Hotel bookings are possible from a reservation board situated in airport arrival lounge and in main railway station; information also available free.

National Holiday in Finland: *6 December.*

FOREIGN EXCHANGE

Banks are open between 9.15am and 4.15pm on weekdays only. Exchange office at Helsinki-Vantaa airport and Helsinki harbour open daily between 6.30am and 11pm.

MEALS

At lunchtime, follow the custom of the country and try the typical buffets of Scandinavian specialities.

At dinner, the a la carte and set menus will offer you more conventionnal cooking. Booking is essential.

Many city centre restaurants are closed for a few days over the Midsummer Day period.

SHOPPING IN HELSINKI

Furs, jewelry, china, glass and ceramics, Finnish handicraft and wood.

In the index of street names, those printed in red are where the principal shops are found. Your hotel porter will be able to help you with information.

THEATRE BOOKINGS

A ticket service - Lippupalvelu, Mannerheimintie 5, is selling tickets for cinema, concert and theatre performances - Telephone 9700 4700, open Mon-Fri 9am to 6pm, Sat. 9am to 2pm.

CAR HIRE

The international car hire companies have branches in Helsinki city and at Vantaa airport. Your hotel porter should be able to help you with your arrangements.

TIPPING

Service is normally included in hotel and restaurant bills - Doormen, baggage porters etc. are generally given a gratuity; taxi drivers are usually not tipped.

SPEED LIMITS

The maximum permitted speed on motorways is 120 km/h - 74 mph (in winter 100 km/h - 62 mph), 80 km/h - 50 mph on other roads and 50 km/h - 31 mph in built-up areas.

SEAT BELTS

The wearing of seat belts in Finland is compulsory for drivers and for front and rear seat passengers.

HELSINKI

Finland 985 L 21 *– Pop. 491 777 –* ✪ *9.*

Lahti 103 – Tampere 176 – Turku 165.

ℹ *City Tourist Office Pohjoisesplanadi 19 ✆ 169 37 57, Fax 169 38 39 – Automobile and Touring Club of Finland: Autoliitto ✆ 694 00 22, Telex 124 839, Fax 693 25 78.*

⛳18 *Tali Manor ✆ 550 235.*

[illegible]
✆ 818 8114, Fax 818 40 92 – Air Terminal : Hotel Intercontinental, Mannerheimintie 46 – Finnair City Terminal : Asema – Aukio 3, ✆ 818 77 50, Fax 818 77 65.

⛴ *To Sweden, Estonia, Poland and boat excursions : contact the City Tourist Office (see below) – Car Ferry: Silja Line – Finnjet Line ✆ 180 41.*

See: *Senate Square★★★ (Senaatintori)* DY **53** *– Market Square★★ (Kauppatori* DY **26** *– Esplanadi★★* CDY **8/43** *– Railway Station★★ (Rautatiesema)* CX *– Finlandia Hall★★ (Finlandia-talo)* BX *– National Opera House★★ (Kansallisoopera)* BX *– Church in the Rock★★ (Temppeliaukion kirkko)* BX *– Ateneum Art Museum★★ (Ateneum, Suomen Taiteen Museo)* CY **M¹** *– National Museum★★ (Kansallismuseo)* BX **M²** *– Lutheran Cathedral★ (Tuomiokirkko)* DY *– Parliament House★ (Eduskuntatalo)* BX *– Amos Anderson Collection★ (Amos Andersinin taidemuseo)* BY **M⁴** *– Uspensky Cathedral★ (Uspenskin katedraali)* DY *– Cygnaeus home and collection★ (Cynaeuksen galleria)* DZ **B** *– Mannerheim home and collection★ (Mannerheim-museo)* DZ **M⁵** *– Olympic Stadium★ (Olympiastadion)* ✵★★ BX **21** *– Museum of Applied Arts★ (Taideteollisuusmuseo)* CZ **M⁶** *– Sibelius Monument★ (Sibelius-monumentti)* AX **S** *– Ice-breaker fleet★* DX.

Outskirts: *Fortress of Suomenlinna★★ by boat* DZ *– Seurasaari Open-Air Museum★★* BX *– Urho Kekkonen Museum★ (Urho Kekkosen museo)* BX.

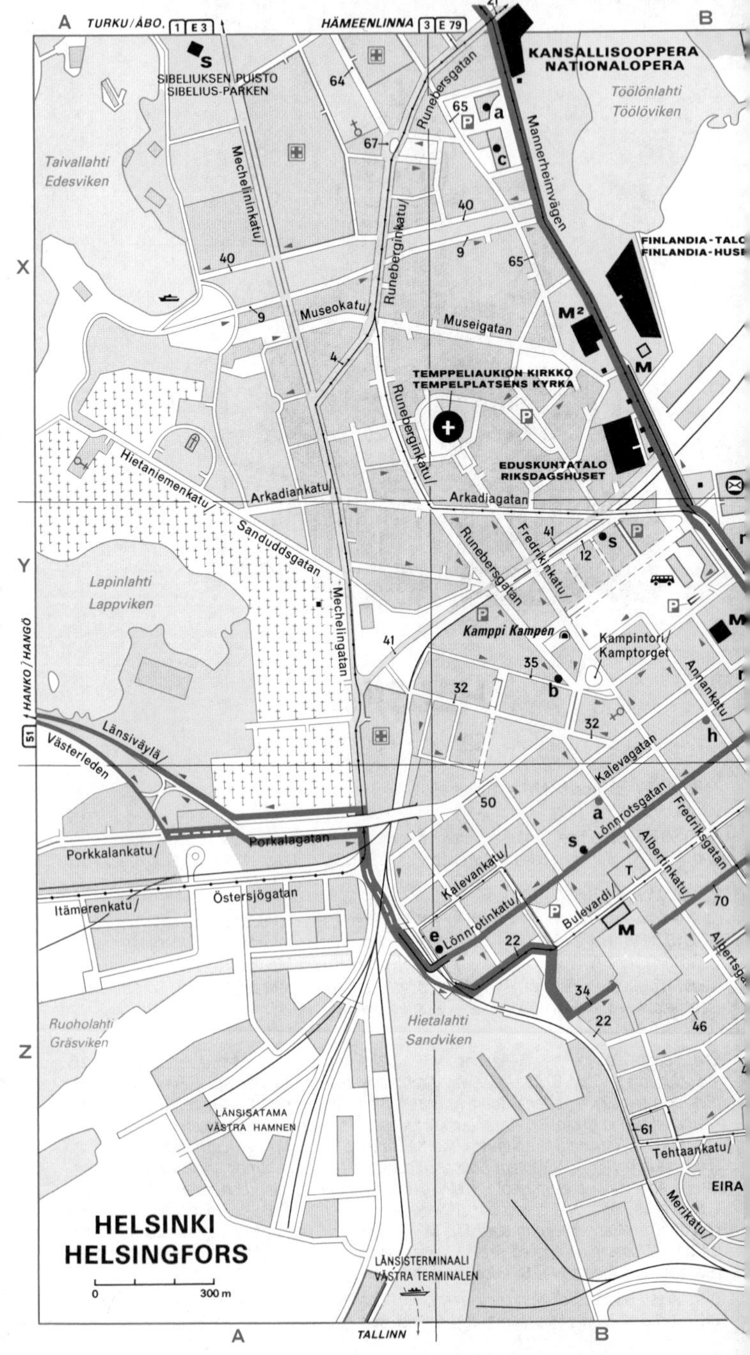
TURKU/ÅBO
1 E 3
HÄMEENLINNA
3 E 79
KANSALLISOOPPERA
NATIONALOPERA
Töölönlahti
Töölöviken
SIBELIUKSEN PUISTO
SIBELIUS-PARKEN
Taivallahti
Edesviken
Mechelininkatu
Runebergsgatan
Mannerheimvägen
Runeberginkatu
Museokatu
Museigatan
FINLANDIA-TALO
FINLANDIA-HUSET
TEMPPELIAUKION KIRKKO
TEMPELPLATSENS KYRKA
EDUSKUNTATALO
RIKSDAGSHUSET
Hietaniemenkatu
Sanduddsgatan
Arkadiankatu
Arkadiagatan
Fredrikinkatu
Lapinlahti
Lappviken
Mechelingatan
Kamppi Kampen
Kampintori/
Kamptorget
Annankatu
HANKO/HANGÖ
51
Länsiväylä
Västerleden
Kalevagatan
Lönnrotsgatan
Fredriksgatan
Albertinkatu
Porkalagatan
Porkkalankatu
Kalevankatu
Lönnrotinkatu
Bulevardi
Itämerenkatu
Östersjögatan
Albertsgatan
Ruoholahti
Gräsviken
Hietalahti
Sandviken
LÄNSISATAMA
VÄSTRA HAMNEN
Tehtaankatu
EIRA
Merikatu
HELSINKI
HELSINGFORS
0
300 m
LÄNSISTERMINAALI
VÄSTRA TERMINALEN
TALLINN

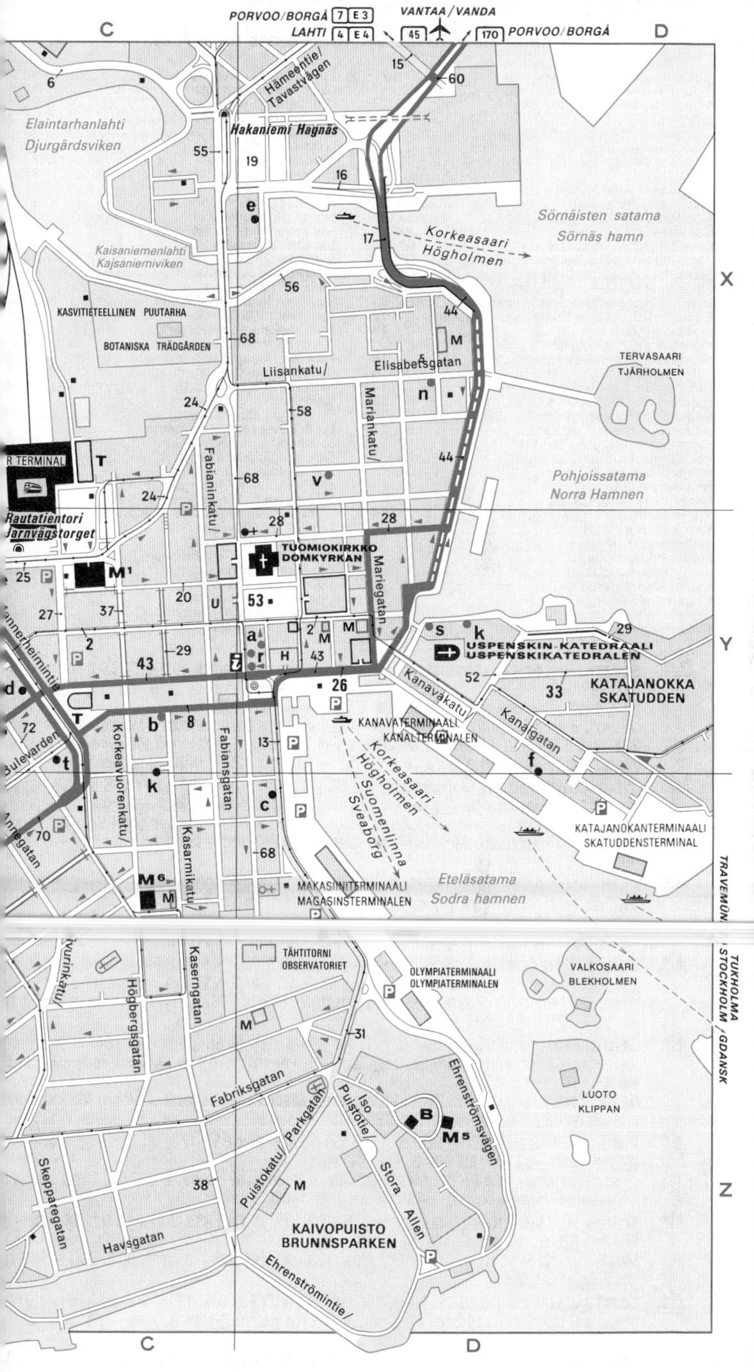
PORVOO/BORGÅ 7 E 3
LAHTI 4 E 4
VANTAA/VANDA
45
170 PORVOO/BORGÅ
C
D
Hämeentie/Tavastvägen
Hakaniemi Hagnäs
Eläintarhanlahti
Djurgårdsviken
Kaisaniemenlahti
Kajsaniemiviken
Sörnäisten satama
Sörnäs hamn
Korkeasaari
Högholmen
KASVITIETEELLINEN PUUTARHA
BOTANISKA TRÄDGÅRDEN
Liisankatu/
Elisabetsgatan
Mariankatu/
TERVASAARI
TJÄRHOLMEN
Pohjoissatama
Norra Hamnen
R TERMINAL
Rautatientori
Järnvägstorget
Fabianinkatu/
TUOMIOKIRKKO
DOMKYRKAN
Mariegatan
USPENSKIN-KATEDRAALI
USPENSKIKATEDRALEN
KATAJANOKKA
SKATUDDEN
Kanavakatu/
Kanalgatan
KANAVATERMINAALI
KANALTERMINALEN
Korkeasaari
Högholmen
Suomenlinna
Sveaborg
Mannerheimintie
Bulevarden
Annegatan
Korkeavuorenkatu/
Fabiansgatan
Kasarmikatu/
KATAJANOKANTERMINAALI
SKATUDDENSTERMINAL
Eteläsatama
Sodra hamnen
MAKASIINITERMINAALI
MAGASINSTERMINALEN
TRAVEMÜN
TUKHOLMA
STOCKHOLM
GDANSK
TÄHTITORNI
OBSERVATORIET
OLYMPIATERMINAALI
OLYMPIATERMINALEN
VALKOSAARI
BLEKHOLMEN
Kaserngatan
Högbergsgatan
Fabriksgatan
Iso Puistotie
Ehrenströmsvägen
LUOTO
KLIPPAN
Puistokatu/Parkgatan
Stora Allen
Skepparegatan
Havsgatan
KAIVOPUISTO
BRUNNSPARKEN
Ehrenströmintie/
X
Y
Z

STREET INDEX TO HELSINKI/HELSINGFORS TOWN PLAN

Aleksanterinkatu/Alexandersgatan .... CDY 2
Fabianinkatu/Fabiansgatan .... CXYZ
Keskuskatu/Centralgatan .... CY 27
Kluuvikatu/Glogatan .... CY 29
Mannerheimintie/Mannerheimvägen ...... BCXY
Mikonkatu/Mikaelsgatan .... CY 37
Pohjoisesplanadi/Norra esplanaden .... CDY 43

Albertinkatu/Albertsgatan .... BZ
Annankatu/Annegatan .... BCYZ
Arkadiankatu/Arkadiagatan .... ABX
Bulevardi/Bulevarden .... BCXY
Caloniuksenkatu/Caloniusgatan .... AX 4
Ehrenströmintie/Ehrenströmsvägen .... DZ
Eläintarhantie/Djurgårdsvägen .... CX 6
Eteläesplanadi/Södra esplanaden .... CY 8
Eteläinen Hesperiankatu/Södra Hesperiagatan .. ABX 9
Eteläinen Rautatiekatu/Södra Järnvägsgatan . BY 12
Eteläranta/Södra kajen .... DY 13
Fredrikinkatu/Fredriksgatan .... BYZ
Haapaniemenkatu/Aspnäsgatan .... DX 15
Hakaniemenranta/Hagnäskajen .... DX 16
Hakaniemen silta/Hagnäs bro .... DX 17
Hakaniemen tori/Hagnäs torg .... DX 19
Hallituskatu/Regeringsgatan .... CY 20
Helsinginkatu/Helsingegatan .... BX 21
Hietalahdenranta/Sandvikskajen .... BZ 22
Hietaniemenkatu/Sanduddsgatan .... AXY
Hämeentie/Tavastvägen .... DX
Iso Puistotie/Stora Allen .... DZ
Itämerenkatu/Östersjögatan .... AZ
Kaisaniemenkatu/Kajsaniemigatan .... CX 24
Kaivokatu/Brunnsgatan .... CY 25
Kalevankatu/Kalevagatan .... BYZ
Kampintori/Kamptorget .... BY
Kanavakatu/Kanalgatan .... DXY
Kasarmikatu/Kaserngatan .... CZ
Kauppatori/Salutorget .... DY 26
Kirkkokatu/Kyrkogatan .... DY 28
Korkeavuorenkatu/Högbergsgatan .... CYZ

Laivasillankatu/Skeppsbrogatan .... DZ 2
Laivastokatu/Maringatan .... DY 3
Laivurinkatu/Skepparegatan .... CZ
Lapinlahdenkatu/Lappviksgatan .... BY 3
Liisankatu/Elisabetsgatan .... DX
Luotsikatu/Lotsgatan .... DY 3
Länsiväylä/Västerleden .... AYZ
Lönnrotinkatu/Lönnrotsgatan .... BZ
Mallaskatu/Maltgatan .... BZ 3
Malminkatu/Malmgatan .... BY 3
Mariankatu/Mariegatan .... DXY
Mechelininkatu/Mechelingatan .... AXY
Merikatu/Havsgatan .... BCZ
Museokatu/Museigatan .... ABX
Neitsytpolku/Jungfrustigen .... CZ 3
Pohjoinen Hesperiankatu/Norra Hesperiagatan . ABX 4
Pohjoinen Rautatiekatu/Norra Järnvägsgatan . ABY 4
Pohjoisranta/Norra kajen .... DX 4
Porkkalankatu/Porkalagatan .... AZ
Puistokatu/Parkgatan .... DZ
Punavuorenkatu/Rödbergsgatan .... BZ 4
Pursimiehenkatu/Båtsmansgatan .... BZ 4
Ratakatu/Bangatan .... CZ 4
Rautatientori/Järnvägstorget .... CY
Runeberginkatu/Runebersgatan .... ABXY
Ruoholahdenkatu/Gräsviksgatan .... BZ 5
Satamakatu/Hamngatan .... DY 5
Senaatintori/Senatstorget .... DY 5
Siltasaarenkatu/Broholmsgatan .... CX 5
Siltavuorenranta/Brobergskajen .... DX 5
Snellmaninkatu/Snellmansgatan .... DX 5
Sörnäisten rantatie/Sörnäs strandväg .... DX 6
Tehtaankatu/Fabriksgatan .... BCDZ
Telakkakatu/Docksgatan .... BZ 6
Topeliuksenkatu/Topeliusgatan .... AX 6
Töölönkatu/Tölögatan .... BX 6
Töölöntori/Tölötorg .... AX 6
Unioninkatu/Unionsgatan .... DXYZ 6
Uudenmaankatu/Nylandsgatan .... BCZ 7
Yrjönkatu/Georgsgatan .... BCY 7

Strand Inter-Continental Ⓜ, John Stenbergin Ranta 4, ⊠ 00530, ☎ 39 35… Fax 393 5255, ≤, « Contemporary Finnish architecture and decor », ≘s, ☒ - |‡| ⇎ r… ▤ ☑ ☎ ♿ ⇔ - 🏛 300. AE ⓓ E VISA JCB. ✻ rest DX
closed 28 to 31 March and 24 to 26 December – ***Atrium Plaza :*** **Meals** (buffet lunc… 225 and a la carte – ***Pamir :*** **Meals** *(closed Saturday, Sunday and 20 June-mid Augus…* (dinner only) 395 and a la carte – ☕ 50 – **192 rm** 1290/1440, 8 suites.

Inter-Continental, Mannerheimintie 46, ⊠ 00260, ☎ 40 551, Fax 405 53255, ≤, … ≘s, ☒ - |‡| ⇎ rm ▤ ☑ ☎ ⇔ Ⓟ - 🏛 700. AE ⓓ E VISA JCB. ✻ rest BX
Galateia : **Meals** - Seafood - *(closed Saturday and Sunday)* (dinner only) 240/380 and la carte – ***Brasserie :*** **Meals** (buffet lunch) 95/250 and a la carte – ☕ 65 – **552 r…** 990/1400, 12 suites.

Radisson SAS H. Helsinki Ⓜ, Runeberginkatu 2, ⊠ 00100, ☎ 69 580, Fax 695 8710… ⅃ₐ, ≘s - |‡| ⇎ rm ▤ ☑ ☎ ♿ ⇔ - 🏛 250. AE ⓓ E VISA JCB. ✻ BY
Johan Ludvig : **Meals** *(closed Saturday lunch and Sunday)* (grill rest.) 125/270 and a la cart… – ***Ströget :*** **Meals** (buffet lunch) and a la carte 135/214 – **253 rm** ☕ 1140/1485, 7 suites

Sokos H. Hesperia, Mannerheimintie 50, ⊠ 00260, ☎ 43 101, Fax 431 0995, ⅃ₐ, ≘… ☒ - |‡| ⇎ rm ▤ ☑ ☎ ⇔ Ⓟ - 🏛 300. AE ⓓ E VISA JCB. ✻ rest BX
closed 22 December-2 January – ***Fransmanni :*** **Meals** 200/250 and a la carte – **372 r…** ☕ 990/1250, 4 suites.

Grand Marina, Katajanokanlaituri 7, ⊠ 00160, ☎ 16 661, Fax 664 764, « Converte… warehouse in contemporary style », ≘s - |‡| ⇎ rm ▤ ☑ ☎ ♿ ⇔ Ⓟ - 🏛 70. … ⓓ E VISA DYZ
Baltic Room : **Meals** 95/200 and a la carte – ***Bistro :*** **Meals** (buffet lunch) 42 and dinn… a la carte 85/250 – **446 rm** ☕ 790/940, 16 suites.

Palace, Eteläranta 10, ⊠ 00130, ☎ 134 56705, Fax 657 474, ≤, ≘s - |‡| ⇎ rm … ☑ ☎ ⇔ - 🏛 60. AE ⓓ E VISA. ✻ rest DZ
closed Christmas – ***La Vista :*** **Meals** - Italian - *(closed Bank Holidays)* 110/244 and a la car… – (see also ***Palace*** below) – **45 rm** ☕ 990/1400, 2 suites.

Sokos H. Klaus Kurki, Bulevardi 2, ⊠ 00120, ☎ 618 911, Fax 618 91234, ≘s - … ⇎ rm ☑ ☎. AE ⓓ E VISA JCB. ✻ rest CY
Meals *(closed Sunday and Bank Holidays)* 125 (dinner) and a la carte 118/200 – **132 r…** ☕ 780/1000, 2 suites.

Lord ⛭, Lönnrotinkatu 29, ⊠ 00180, ☎ 615 815, Fax 680 1315, « Part Jugendstil (A… Nouveau) building, fireplaces », ≘s - |‡| ⇎ rm ▤ rm ☑ ☎ ♿ ⇔ - 🏛 200. AE … E VISA. ✻ rest BZ
Meals *(closed Sunday and Bank Holidays)* 85/300 and a la carte – **47 rm** ☕ 650/800, 1 suit…

Arctia H. Marski, Mannerheimintie 10, ✉ 00100, ✆ 68 061, Fax 642 377, – rm – 300. AE ⓓ E VISA JCB. rest CY d
closed 24 to 26 December – ***Marskin Kellari :*** **Meals** *(closed Sunday lunch)* (buffet lunch) 150/200 and a la carte – **230 rm** 1050/1300, 6 suites.

Sokos H. Vaakuna, Asema-aukio 2, ✉ 00100, ✆ 131 181, Fax 131 18234, – rm. AE ⓓ E VISA JCB. rest BY n
10th Floor Dining : **Meals** *(closed Sunday)* (dinner only) a la carte 198/277 – ***Brasserie :*** **Meals** 112/202 – **262 rm** 960/1140, 10 suites.

Seaside, Ruoholahdenranta 3, ✉ 00180, ✆ 69 360, Fax 69 32123, – rm – 60. AE ⓓ E VISA. rest ABZ e
Meals 85/250 and a la carte – **280 rm** 640/940.

Ramada Presidentti, Eteläinen Rautatiekatu 4, ✉ 00100, ✆ 6911, Fax 694 7886, – rm – 400. AE ⓓ E VISA JCB. rest BY s
Meals a la carte 95/242 – 30 – **485 rm** 1070/1255, 5 suites.

Sokos H. Torni, Yrjönkatu 26, ✉ 00100, ✆ 131 131, Fax 131 1361, – rm – 35. AE ⓓ E VISA. rest BY r
closed 21 to 25 December – **Meals** *(closed Saturday lunch and Sunday)* 185/360 and a la carte – **152 rm** 960/1150.

Rivoli Jardin without rest., Kasarmikatu 40, ✉ 00130, ✆ 177 880, Fax 656 988, – . AE ⓓ E VISA CYZ k
closed Christmas – **53 rm** 790/900.

Sokos H. Pasila, Maistraatinportti 3, ✉ 00240, N : 3 km by Mannerheimintie ✆ 148 841, Fax 143 771, *squash* – – 120. AE ⓓ E VISA JCB. rest
closed 19 to 31 December – **Meals** 250 and a la carte – **246 rm** 660/800, 2 suites.

Cumulus Seurahuone, Kaivokatu 12, ✉ 00100, ✆ 69 141, Fax 691 4010, – rm – 60. AE ⓓ E VISA. rest CY e
Meals (buffet lunch) 150/200 and a la carte – **118 rm** 690/870.

Aurora, Helsinginkatu 50, ✉ 00530, NE : 2 km on Lahti road ✆ 770 100, Fax 770 10200, *squash* – rm – 220. AE ⓓ E VISA. rest
closed 23 to 26 December – **Meals** *(closed Sunday)* a la carte 102/170 – **70 rm** 440/520.

Savoy, Eteläesplanadi 14 (8th floor), ✉ 00130, ✆ 176 571, Fax 628 715, « Typical Finnish design dating from 1937 » – AE ⓓ E VISA CY b
closed Saturday and Sunday – **Meals** 170/400 and a la carte.

Palace (at Palace H.), Eteläranta 10 (10th floor), ✉ 00130, ✆ 134 561, Fax 657 474, harbour and city – . AE ⓓ E VISA DZ c
closed July lunch, Saturday, Sunday and Bank Holidays – **Meals** 210/470 and a la carte.

Alexander Nevski, Pohjoisesplanadi 17, ✉ 00170, ✆ 639 610, Fax 631 435 – . AE ⓓ E VISA DY r
closed lunch Sunday and July, midsummer and Christmas – **Meals** - Russian - 120/350 and a la carte.

[illegible] VISA DY r
closed Sunday and Bank Holidays except 15 May-15 September – **Meals** - Seafood - (booking essential) 100/300 and a la carte.

Sipuli, Kanavaranta 3 (2nd floor), ✉ 00160, ✆ 179 900, Fax 630 662, « Picture window Uspensky Cathedral (orthodox) » – AE ⓓ E VISA DY s
closed Saturday, Sunday and 20 June-3 August – **Meals** (booking essential) (dinner only) 192/255 and a la carte.

Svenska Klubben, Maurinkatu 6, ✉ 00170, ✆ 135 4706, Fax 135 4896, « Scottish style house » – AE ⓓ E VISA DX n
closed Sunday and 15 June-15 August – **Meals** 120/220 and a la carte.

Rivoli, Albertinkatu 38, ✉ 00180, ✆ 643 455, Fax 647 780 – . AE ⓓ E VISA BZ a
closed Saturday lunch, Saturday June-July, Sunday, Easter, midsummer and Christmas – **Meals** a la carte 152/226.

Amadeus, Sofiankatu 4, ✉ 00170, ✆ 626 676, Fax 636 064 – AE ⓓ E VISA DY a
closed Sunday, weekends in July and Bank Holidays – **Meals** - Brasserie - 150 (lunch) and dinner a la carte 216/290.

Kanavaranta, Kanavaranta 3E/F, ✉ 00160, ✆ 6222 633, Fax 6222 616, « Mid 19C harbour warehouse with nautical tavern » – . AE ⓓ E VISA DY k
closed lunch Monday, Saturday and 30 June-12 August and Sunday – **Meals** (booking essential) 180/295 and a la carte 165/244.

Safka, Vironkatu 8, ✉ 00170, ☎ 135 7287, Fax 278 3178 – AE ⓓ E V JCB DX
closed Monday dinner, Sunday, 28 to 31 March, July and 23 to 28 December – **Meals** (booking essential) 100/215 and dinner a la carte 150/215.

Lappi, Annankatu 22, ✉ 00100, ☎ 645 550, Fax 645 551, « Typical Finni atmosphere » – AE ⓓ E VISA BY
Meals - Finnish - (booking essential) 178/212 and a la carte.

at Vantaa *N : 19 km by A 137* – DX – *90 Helsinki :*

Sokos H. Vantaa Ⓜ, Hertaksentie 2 (near Tikkurila Railway Station), ✉ 013C ☎ 857 851, Fax 857 85555, ≘s, 18 – |‡| ⇜ rm ▤ TV ☎ ♿ ⇔ P – 🔬 95. AE (E VISA. ⚘ rest
closed Christmas – **Meals** a la carte 103/180 – **150 rm** ☐ 660/800, 8 suites.

Holiday Inn Garden Court Helsinki Airport ⛰, Rälssitie 2, ✉ 01510, (near t airport) ☎ 870 900, Fax 870 90101, ≘s – |‡| ⇜ rm TV ☎ ♿ P – 🔬 30. AE ⓓ E V JCB. ⚘
closed 23 to 26 December – **Meals** - Bistro - *(closed lunch Saturday, Sunday and Ba Holidays)* 150 and a la carte – **287 rm** ☐ 830/930.

Airport H. Rantasipi, Robert Huberin Tie 4, ✉ 01510, (near the airport) ☎ 8705 Fax 822 846, ≘s, ▣ – |‡| ⇜ rm TV ☎ ♿ P – 🔬 250. AE ⓓ E VISA. ⚘ rest
Meals *(closed Sunday lunch)* (buffet lunch) 95 and a la carte 150/240 – **276 r** ☐ 670/770, 4 suites.

France

PARIS AND ENVIRONS – BORDEAUX
CANNES – LILLE – LYONS
MARSEILLES – PRINCIPALITY OF MONACO
NICE – STRASBOURG
VALLEY OF THE LOIRE

PRACTICAL INFORMATION

LOCAL CURRENCY

French Franc: *100 FRF = 19.09 USD ($) (Jan. 97)*

TOURIST INFORMATION IN PARIS

Paris "Welcome" Office *(Office du Tourisme et des Congrès de Paris - Accueil de France): 127 Champs-Élysées, 8th, ✆ 01 49 52 53 54, Fax 01 49 52 53 00*

American Express *11 Rue Scribe, 9th, ✆ 01 47 77 79 79, Fax 01 47 77 78 75*

National Holiday in France: *14 July*

AIRLINES

AMERICAN AIRLINES: *109, rue Fg-St-Honoré, 8th, ✆ 01 42 89 05 22, Fax 01 42 99 99 95*

UNITED AIRLINES: *55 rue Raspail, Levallois Perret (92) ✆ 01 41 40 30 30*

T.W.A.: *6, rue Christophe-Colomb, 8th, ✆ 01 49 19 20 00, Fax 01 49 19 20 09*

DELTA AIRLINES: *4, rue Scribe, 9th, ✆ 01 47 68 92 92, Fax 01 47 68 52 82*

BRITISH AIRWAYS: *13 bd de la Madeleine, 1st, ✆ 01 47 78 14 14, Fax 01 78 53 34 43*

AIR FRANCE: *119 Champs-Élysées, 8th, ✆ 01 42 99 21 01, Fax 01 42 99 21 99*

AIR INTER: *119 Champs-Élysées, 8th, ✆ 01 47 23 59 58, Fax 01 47 23 74 58*

FOREIGN EXCHANGE OFFICES

Banks: *close at 5pm and at weekends*

Orly Airport: *daily 6.30am to 11.30pm*

Roissy-Charles de Gaulle Airport: *daily 7am to 11.30pm*

TRANSPORT IN PARIS

Taxis: *may be hailed in the street when showing the illuminated sign-available day and night at taxi ranks or called by telephone*

Bus-Métro (subway): *for full details see the Michelin Plan de Paris n° 11. The metro is quicker but the bus is good for sightseeing and practical for short distances.*

POSTAL SERVICES

Local post offices: *open Mondays to Fridays 8am to 7pm; Saturdays 8am to noon*

General Post Office: *52 rue du Louvre, 1st: open 24 hours*

SHOPPING IN PARIS

Department stores: *Boulevard Haussmann, Rue de Rivoli and Rue de Sèvres*

Exclusive shops and boutiques: *Faubourg St-Honoré, Rue de la Paix and Rue Royale, Avenue Montaigne.*

Antiques and second-hand goods: *Swiss Village (Avenue de la Motte Picquet), Louvre des Antiquaires (Place du Palais Royal), Flea Market (Porte Clignancourt).*

TIPPING

Service is generally included in hotel and restaurants bills. But you may choose to leave more than the expected tip to the staff. Taxi-drivers, porters, barbers and theatre or cinema attendants also expect a small gratuity.

BREAKDOWN SERVICE

Certain garages in central and outer Paris operate a 24 hour breakdown service. If you breakdown the police are usually able to help by indicating the nearest one.

SPEED LIMITS

The maximum permitted speed in built up areas is 50 km/h - 31 mph; on motorways the speed limit is 130 km/h - 80 mph and 110 km/h - 68 mph on dual carriageways. On all other roads 90 km/h - 56 mph.

SEAT BELTS

The wearing of seat belts is compulsory for drivers and passengers.

PARIS AND ENVIRONS

Maps: 10, 11, 12 G. Paris.

Map of arrondissements and districts	pp. 2 and 3
Maps	pp. 4 to 11
Sights	p. 12
Alphabetical list of hotels and restaurants	pp. 13 to 21
Hotels and restaurants of PARIS	pp. 23 to 62
Environs	pp. 63 to 68

Population: *Paris 2 152 333 ; Ile-de-France region : 10 651 000.*

Altitude: *Observatory : 60 m ; Place Concorde : 34 m*

Air Terminals – To Orly: *Esplanade des Invalides, 7th, ✆ 01 43 17 21 65*
To Charles de Gaulle *(Roissy): Palais des Congrès, Porte Maillot, 17th, ✆ 01 44 09 51 52*

Paris'Airports: *see Orly and Charles de Gaulle (Roissy)*

Railways, motorail: *information ✆ 01 36 35 35 35.*

ARRONDISSEMENT

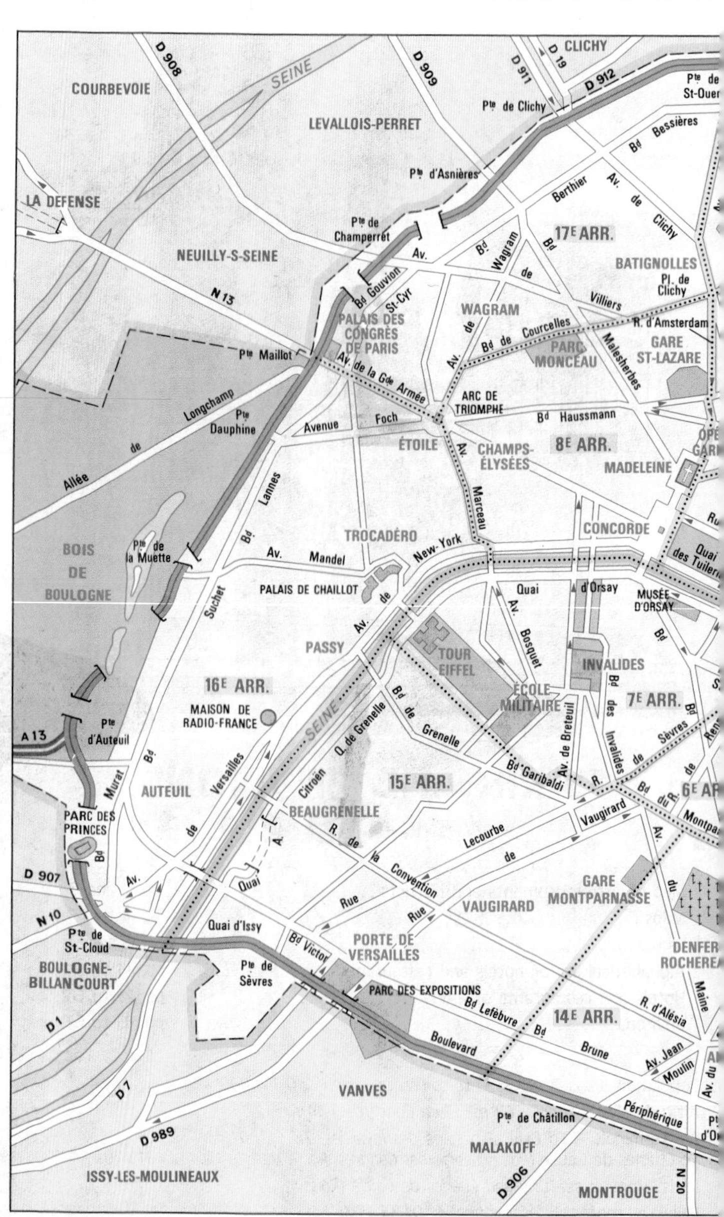

ND DISTRICTS

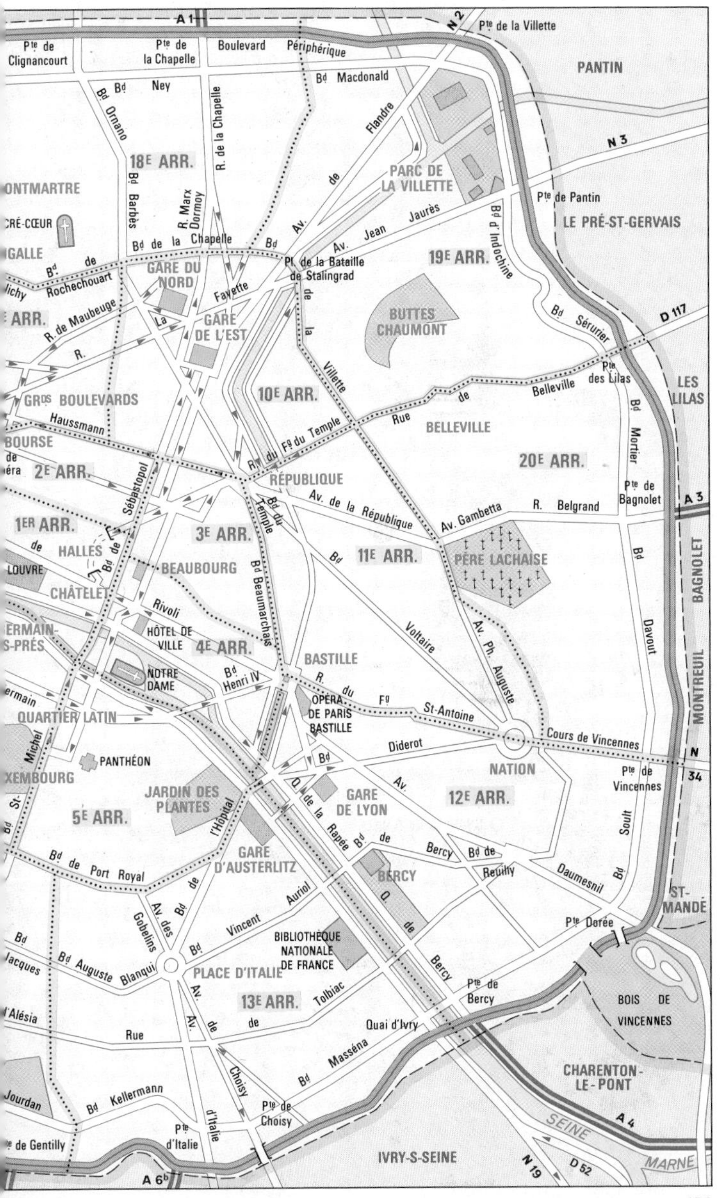

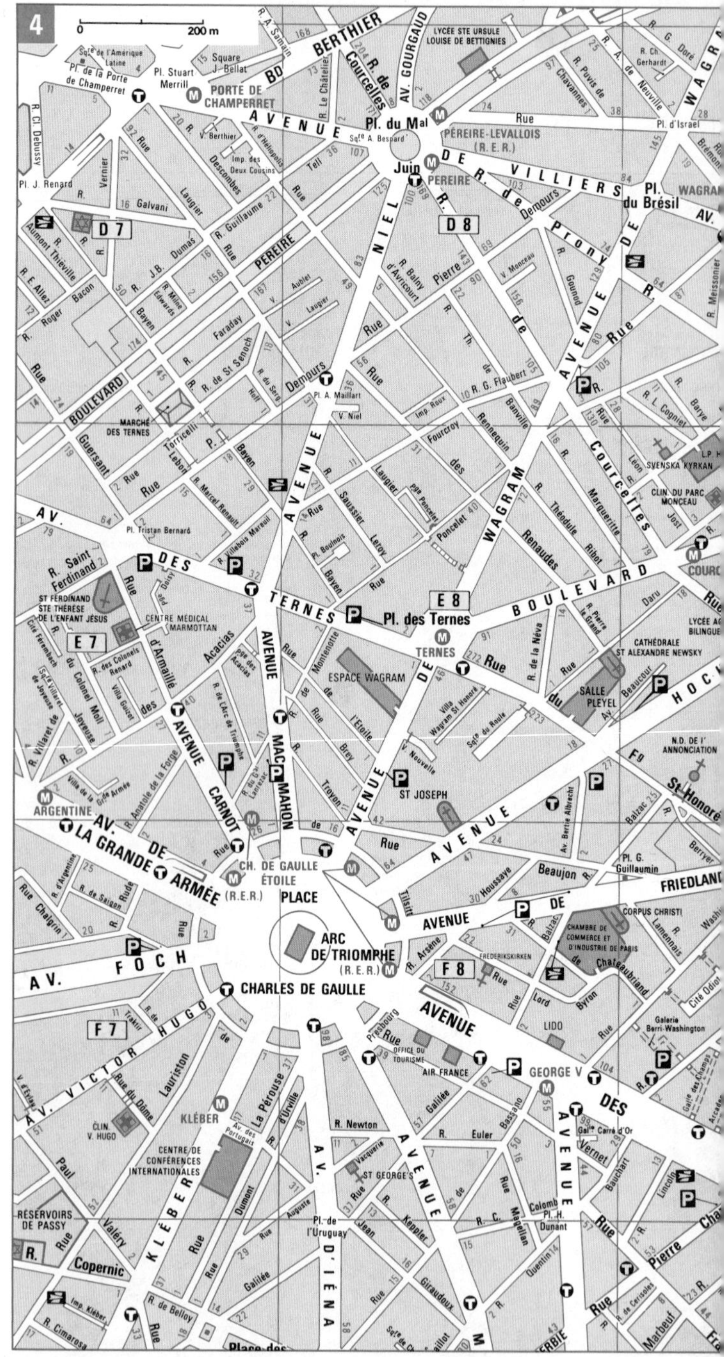
4
0
200 m
D 7
D 8
E 7
E 8
F 7
F 8
BD BERTHIER
R. de Courcelles
AV. GOURGAUD
LYCÉE STE URSULE LOUISE DE BETTIGNIES
Pl. Stuart Merrill
Square J. Bellat
Pl. de la Porte de Champerret
PORTE DE CHAMPERRET
Pl. du Mal Juin
PÉREIRE-LEVALLOIS (R.E.R.)
PEREIRE
AVENUE DE VILLIERS
Pl. d'Israel
Pl. du Brésil
AV. DE WAGRAM
R. de Prony
R. de Demours
AVENUE NIEL
PEREIRE
BOULEVARD
MARCHÉ DES TERNES
R. Bayen
R. Laugier
R. Poncelet
AVENUE DE WAGRAM
R. Pierre Demours
R. Fourcroy
R. Rennequin
R. Théodule Ribot
R. de Courcelles
SVENSKA KYRKAN
CLIN. DU PARC MONCEAU
AV. DES TERNES
Pl. des Ternes
TERNES
BOULEVARD DE COURCELLES
ST FERDINAND STE THÉRESE DE L'ENFANT JESUS
CENTRE MÉDICAL MARMOTTAN
R. d'Armaillé
R. des Acacias
ESPACE WAGRAM
R. de l'Étoile
R. du Fg St Honoré
SALLE PLEYEL
CATHÉDRALE ST ALEXANDRE NEWSKY
LYCÉE AG BILINGUE
N.D. DE L'ANNONCIATION
ST JOSEPH
AVENUE CARNOT
AVENUE MAC MAHON
AVENUE DE WAGRAM
AVENUE HOCHE
ARGENTINE
AV. DE LA GRANDE ARMÉE
CH. DE GAULLE ÉTOILE (R.E.R.)
PLACE CHARLES DE GAULLE
ARC DE TRIOMPHE (R.E.R.)
AV. FOCH
AVENUE DE FRIEDLAND
CORPUS CHRISTI
CHAMBRE DE COMMERCE ET D'INDUSTRIE DE PARIS
R. de Chateaubriand
FREDERIKSKIRKEN
R. Lord Byron
LIDO
Galerie Berri-Washington
AVENUE DES CHAMPS-ÉLYSÉES
OFFICE DU TOURISME
AIR FRANCE
GEORGE V
AV. VICTOR HUGO
CLIN. V. HUGO
KLÉBER
CENTRE DE CONFÉRENCES INTERNATIONALES
AVENUE KLÉBER
R. La Pérouse
AV. D'IÉNA
R. Newton
ST GEORGE'S
AVENUE MARCEAU
AVENUE GEORGE V
R. Galilée
R. Euler
R. Bassano
R. Vernet
R. Magellan
Pl. H. Dunant
R. Pierre Charron
R. Marbeuf
RÉSERVOIRS DE PASSY
R. Copernic
R. Paul Valéry
R. Lauriston
Pl. de l'Uruguay
R. Jean Giraudoux
R. Keppler
R. Quentin
R. de Belloy
R. Cimarosa
Imp. Kléber

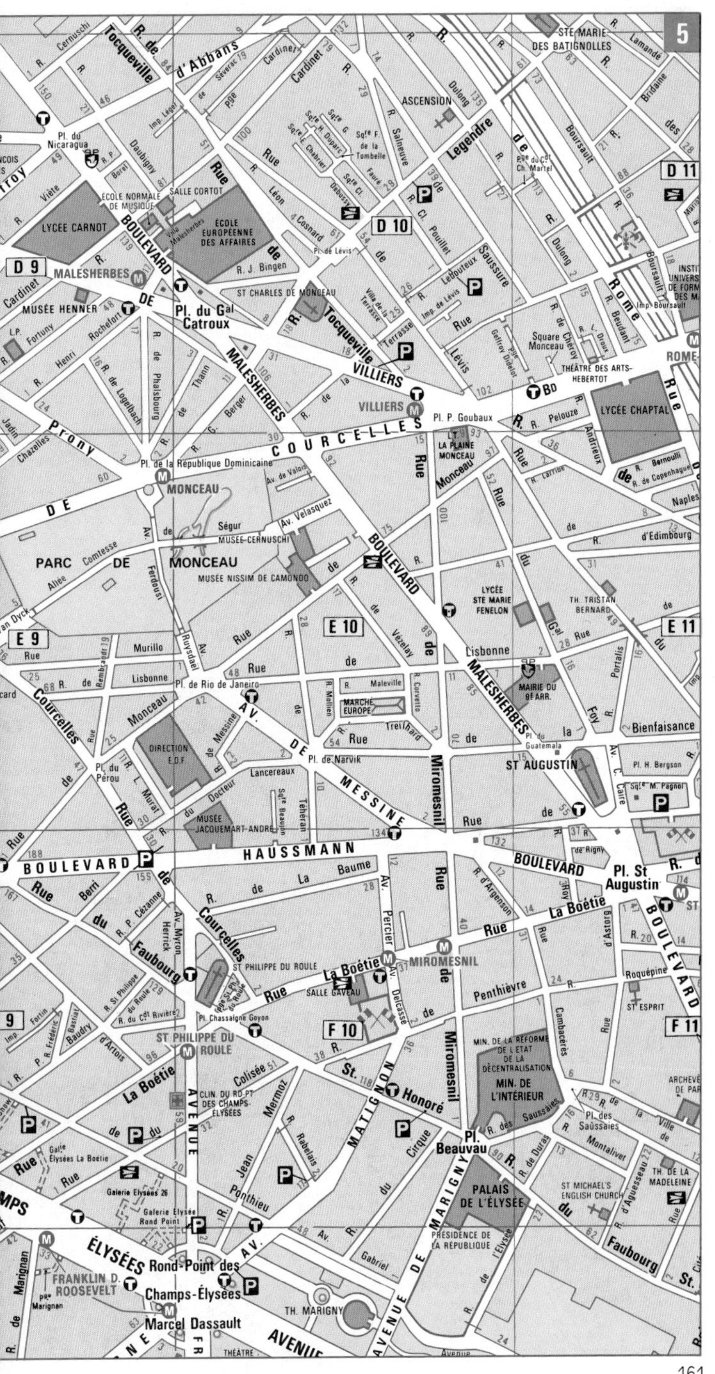
5
D 9
D 10
D 11
E 9
E 10
E 11
F 10
F 11
BOULEVARD DE MALESHERBES
COURCELLES
PARC DE MONCEAU
MUSÉE CERNUSCHI
MUSÉE NISSIM DE CAMONDO
LYCEE CARNOT
ÉCOLE EUROPÉENNE DES AFFAIRES
MALESHERBES
VILLIERS
MONCEAU
LYCÉE CHAPTAL
ST AUGUSTIN
BOULEVARD HAUSSMANN
MUSÉE JACQUEMART-ANDRÉ
DIRECTION E.D.F.
MIROMESNIL
ST PHILIPPE DU ROULE
MIN. DE L'INTÉRIEUR
PALAIS DE L'ÉLYSÉE
PRÉSIDENCE DE LA RÉPUBLIQUE
FRANKLIN D. ROOSEVELT
Rond-Point des Champs-Élysées
Marcel Dassault
TH. MARIGNY
AVENUE DE MARIGNY
ÉLYSÉES
Pl. St Augustin
Pl. Beauvau
MAIRIE DU 8E ARR.
LYCÉE STE MARIE FENELON
ASCENSION
STE MARIE DES BATIGNOLLES
Rue du Faubourg St-Honoré
Rue La Boétie
AVENUE MATIGNON
AV. DE MESSINE
Rue de Rome
Rue de Tocqueville
Rue de Lisbonne

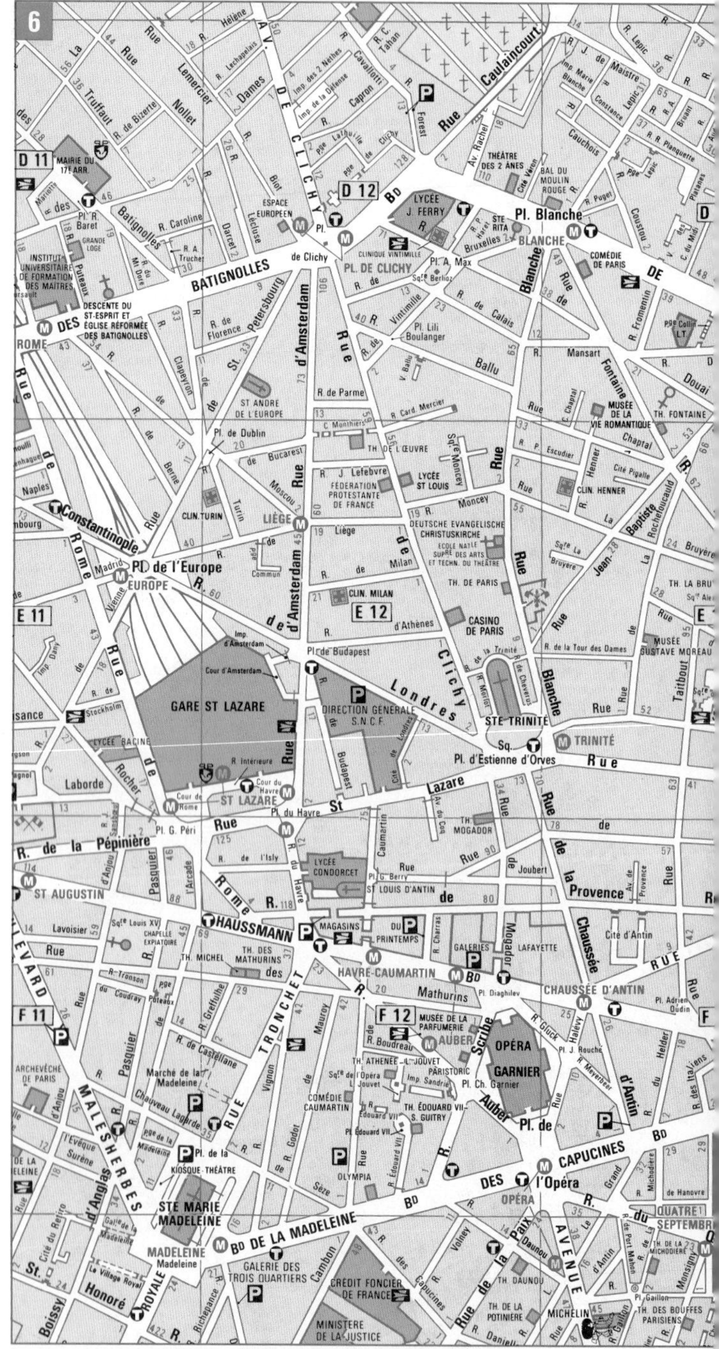

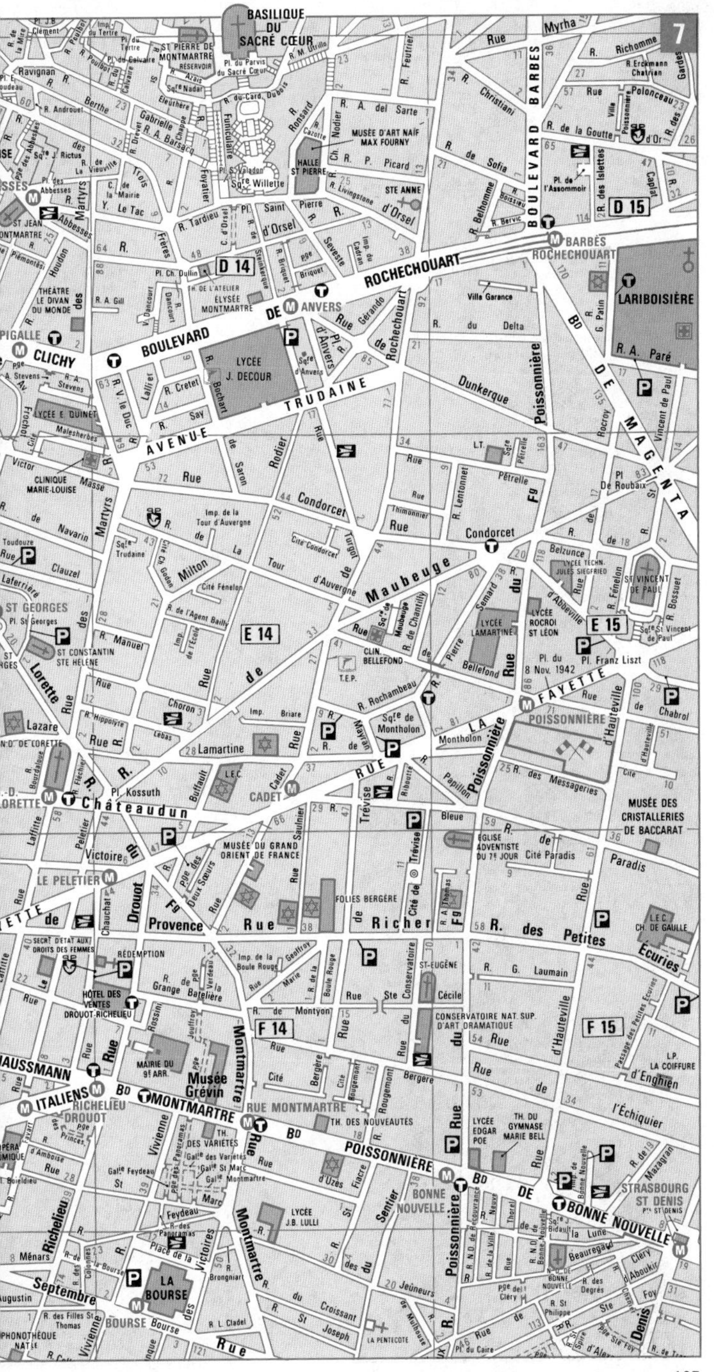

7
BASILIQUE DU SACRÉ CŒUR
ST PIERRE DE MONTMARTRE
RÉSERVOIR
Pl. du Parvis du Sacré Cœur
Pl. du Tertre
Pl. du Calvaire
Pl. J.B. Clément
R. Poulbot
Sq.re Nadar
R. Azaïs
R. du Card. Dubois
R. Ravignan
R. Androuet
R. Berthe
R. Gabrielle
R. Drevet
R. A. Barsacq
R. Chappe
Funiculaire
R. Foyatier
Pl. S. Valadon
Sq.re Willette
R. Ronsard
R. Cazotte
HALLE ST PIERRE
R. Ch. Nodier
R. A. del Sarte
MUSÉE D'ART NAÏF MAX FOURNY
R. P. Picard
R. Livingstone
STE ANNE
R. d'Orsel
R. Feutrier
R. Christiani
R. de Sofia
R. Belhomme
R. Boissieu
R. Bervic
BOULEVARD BARBÈS
Rue Myrha
R. Richomme
R. Erckmann Chatrian
Rue Polonceau
R. de la Goutte d'Or
Pl. de l'Assommoir
R. des Islettes
R. Caplat
D 15
BARBÈS ROCHECHOUART
LARIBOISIÈRE
R. A. Paré
R. G. Patin
R. Vincent de Paul
BD DE MAGENTA
R. Rocroy
ABBESSES
ST JEAN MONTMARTRE
R. des Abbesses
Sq.re J. Rictus
R. de la Vieuville
R. des Trois Frères
Pl. des Abbesses
C. de la Mairie
R. Yvonne Le Tac
R. Tardieu
R. Houdon
THÉATRE LE DIVAN DU MONDE
R. A. Gill
R. Steinkerque
R. Briquet
Pge Briquet
R. Seveste
Imp. du Cadran
D 14
Pl. Ch. Dullin
TH. DE L'ATELIER
ÉLYSÉE MONTMARTRE
BOULEVARD DE ROCHECHOUART
ANVERS
Rue Gérando
Pl. d'Anvers
Sq.re d'Anvers
Villa Garance
R. du Delta
R. Dunkerque
PIGALLE
CLICHY
LYCÉE J. DECOUR
R. Bochart
R. Lallier
R. Cretet
R. V. le Duc
R. Say
AVENUE TRUDAINE
LYCÉE E. QUINET
R. Frochot
R. Victor Massé
CLINIQUE MARIE-LOUISE
R. de Navarin
R. des Martyrs
R. Rodier
R. de Saron
Rue Condorcet
Cité Condorcet
R. Turgot
Rue Thimonnier
R. Lentonnet
Rue Pétrelle
Sq.re Pétrelle
Fg Poissonnière
Condorcet
Pl De Roubaix
R. de Belzunce
LYCÉE TECHN. JULES SIEGFRIED
ST VINCENT DE PAUL
R. Fénelon
R. Bossuet
Sq.re St Vincent de Paul
E 15
Imp. de la Tour d'Auvergne
R. de la Tour d'Auvergne
Sq.re Trudaine
Cité Ch. Godon
R. Milton
Cité Fénelon
R. Clauzel
R. Laferrière
ST GEORGES
Pl. St Georges
ST CONSTANTIN STE HÉLÈNE
R. Manuel
R. de l'Agent Bailly
Imp. de l'École
E 14
Rue de Maubeuge
Sq.re de Maubeuge
R. de Chantilly
R. Pierre Semard
LYCÉE LAMARTINE
LYCÉE ROCROI ST LÉON
R. d'Abbeville
Pl. du 8 Nov. 1942
Pl. Franz Liszt
Rue de Bellefond
CLIN. BELLEFOND
T.E.P.
R. Rochambeau
Sq.re de Montholon
Rue Montholon
RUE LA FAYETTE
POISSONNIÈRE
Rue de Chabrol
R. d'Hauteville
Rue de Lorette
R. Choron
Imp. Briare
R. Hippolyte Lebas
Lazare
N.D. DE LORETTE
Rue Lamartine
R. Mayran
R. Cadet
CADET
L.E.C.
R. Fléchier
R. Bourdaloue
Pl. Kossuth
Châteaudun
R. Buffault
R. Ribouté
R. de Trévise
R. Papillon
R. des Messageries
MUSÉE DES CRISTALLERIES DE BACCARAT
R. Bleue
ÉGLISE ADVENTISTE DU 7E JOUR
Cité Paradis
R. de Paradis
R. Laffitte
R. Le Peletier
R. Victoire
LE PELETIER
Pge des Deux Sœurs
MUSÉE DU GRAND ORIENT DE FRANCE
R. Saulnier
FOLIES BERGÈRE
Cité de Trévise
R. A. Thomas
Fg de Provence
Rue Richer
R. des Petites Écuries
L.E.C. CH. DE GAULLE
R. Chauchat
R. Drouot
SECR. D'ÉTAT AUX DROITS DES FEMMES
RÉDEMPTION
HÔTEL DES VENTES DROUOT-RICHELIEU
Imp. de la Boule Rouge
R. Geoffroy Marie
R. de la Boule Rouge
R. Grange Batelière
Pge Verdeau
Rue Ste Cécile
ST-EUGÈNE
R. du Conservatoire
R. G. Laumain
R. de Montyon
F 14
CONSERVATOIRE NAT. SUP. D'ART DRAMATIQUE
F 15
Passage des Petites Écuries
L.P. LA COIFFURE
R. d'Enghien
HAUSSMANN
R. Rossini
R. Jouffroy
MAIRIE DU 9E ARR.
Musée Grévin
Rue Montmartre
Cité Bergère
Cité Rougemont
Rue Bergère
R. de l'Échiquier
ITALIENS
RICHELIEU DROUOT
BD MONTMARTRE
RUE MONTMARTRE
TH. DES NOUVEAUTÉS
LYCÉE EDGAR POE
TH. DU GYMNASE MARIE BELL
BD POISSONNIÈRE
TH. DES VARIÉTÉS
Gal.ie des Variétés
Gal.ie St Marc
Gal.ie Montmartre
Gal.ie Feydeau
Pge des Panoramas
R. Vivienne
Pge des Princes
R. d'Amboise
R. Boïeldieu
OPÉRA COMIQUE
R. Favart
Rue d'Uzès
R. du Sentier
R. St Fiacre
BONNE NOUVELLE
BD DE BONNE NOUVELLE
R. de Mazagran
STRASBOURG ST DENIS
P.te ST DENIS
Imp. de Bonne Nouvelle
Sq.re Bidault
R. de la Lune
R. Beauregard
R. Thorel
R. Notre Dame de Recouvrance
R. de la Ville Neuve
R. N.D. de Bonne Nouvelle
N.D. DE BONNE NOUVELLE
R. des Degrés
R. de Cléry
R. d'Aboukir
R. Ste Foy
R. St Philippe
Pge de Cléry
LYCÉE J.B. LULLI
R. Feydeau
R. des Panoramas
Place de la Bourse
R. des Colonnes
R. Ménars
R. Richelieu
R. du Quatre Septembre
LA BOURSE
BOURSE
R. Brongniart
R. Notre Dame des Victoires
R. Montmartre
R. du Croissant
R. St Joseph
R. des Jeûneurs
R. du Mail
R. de Mulhouse
LA PENTECOTE
R. L. Cladel
R. des Filles St Thomas
PHONOTHÈQUE NAT.LE
R. Augustin
Rue de la Bourse
Pl. du Caire
Rue du Caire
Pge Ste Foy
R. d'Alexandrie
R. de la Lune
R. Ste Apolline
Rue St Denis

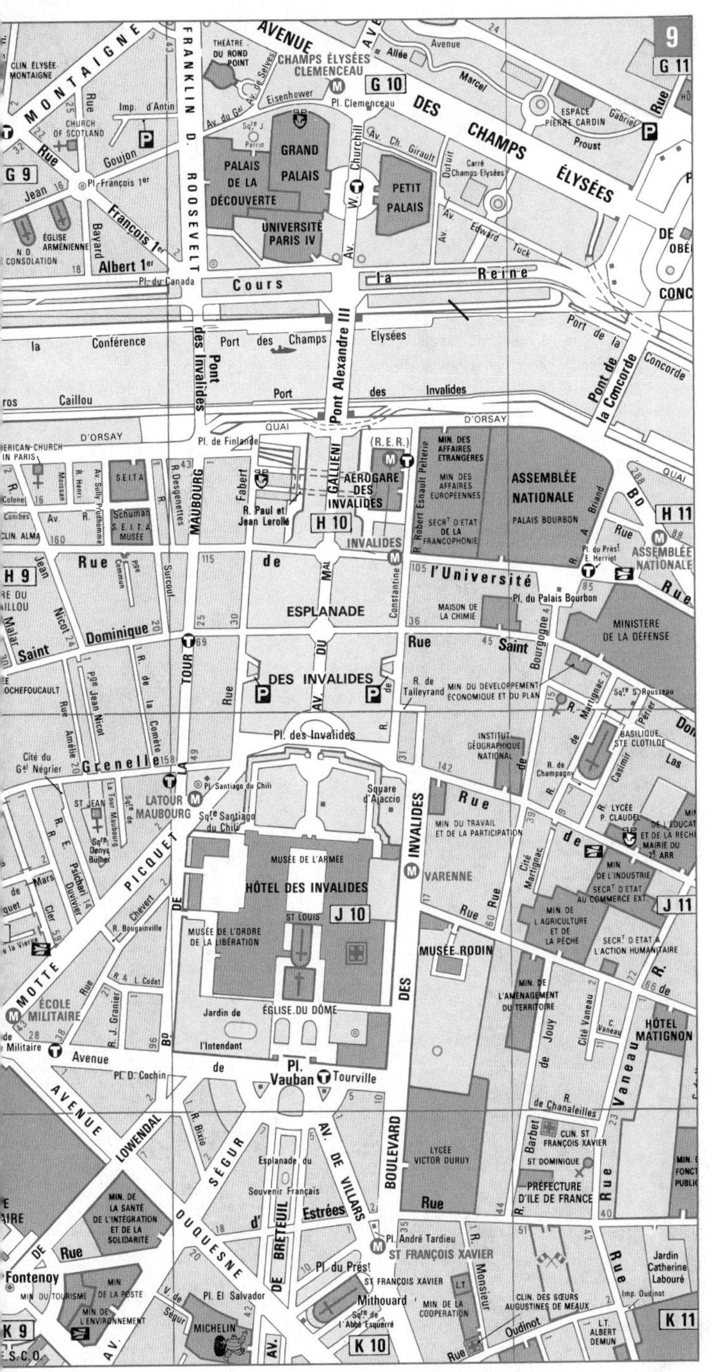
9
G 10
G 11
G 9
H 9
H 10
H 11
J 10
J 11
K 9
K 10
K 11
AVENUE CHAMPS ÉLYSÉES
DES CHAMPS ÉLYSÉES
CHAMPS ÉLYSÉES CLEMENCEAU
Pl. Clemenceau
GRAND PALAIS
PALAIS DE LA DÉCOUVERTE
PETIT PALAIS
UNIVERSITÉ PARIS IV
THÉATRE DU ROND POINT
ESPACE PIERRE CARDIN
Cours la Reine
Pont Alexandre III
Pont des Invalides
Pont de la Concorde
Port des Champs Elysées
Port des Invalides
QUAI D'ORSAY
ASSEMBLÉE NATIONALE
PALAIS BOURBON
MIN. DES AFFAIRES ETRANGÈRES
AÉROGARE DES INVALIDES
INVALIDES
ESPLANADE DES INVALIDES
Rue de l'Université
Rue Saint Dominique
Rue de Grenelle
Rue de Varenne
MINISTÈRE DE LA DÉFENSE
BASILIQUE STE CLOTILDE
INSTITUT GÉOGRAPHIQUE NATIONAL
MUSÉE DE L'ARMÉE
HÔTEL DES INVALIDES
ÉGLISE DU DÔME
MUSÉE RODIN
HÔTEL MATIGNON
LATOUR MAUBOURG
VARENNE
ÉCOLE MILITAIRE
BOULEVARD DES INVALIDES
Pl. Vauban
LYCÉE VICTOR DURUY
ST FRANÇOIS XAVIER
Pl. André Tardieu
PRÉFECTURE D'ILE DE FRANCE
AVENUE LOWENDAL
AV. DE SÉGUR
AV. DE VILLARS
MICHELIN
Fontenoy
Rue Oudinot
Jardin Catherine Labouré

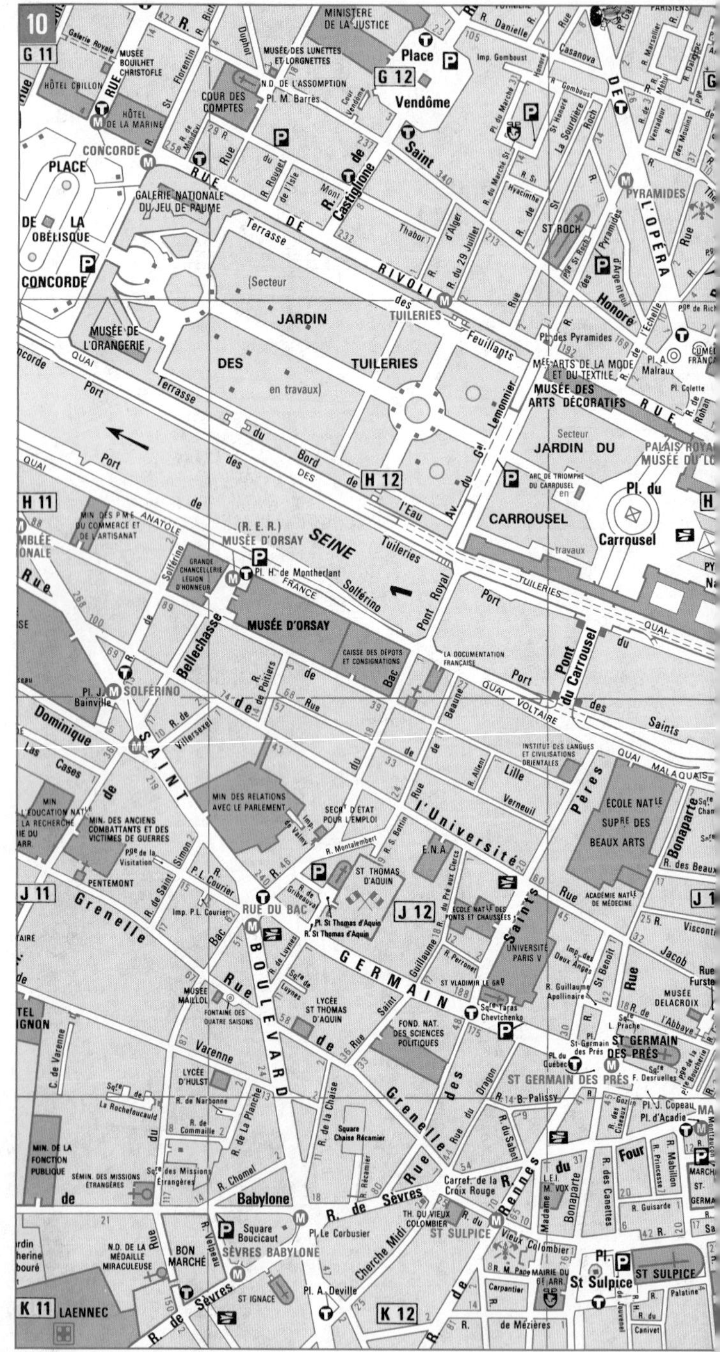
10
G 11
G 12
H 11
H 12
J 11
J 12
K 11
K 12
MINISTERE DE LA JUSTICE
Place Vendôme
MUSÉE DES LUNETTES ET LORGNETTES
N.D. DE L'ASSOMPTION
Pl. M. Barrès
COUR DES COMPTES
Galerie Royale
MUSÉE BOUILHET CHRISTOFLE
HÔTEL CRILLON
HÔTEL DE LA MARINE
CONCORDE
PLACE DE LA CONCORDE
OBÉLISQUE
GALERIE NATIONALE DU JEU DE PAUME
RUE DE RIVOLI
R. de Castiglione
Saint Honoré
Imp. Gomboust
ST ROCH
PYRAMIDES
L'OPÉRA
Pl. des Pyramides
Terrasse
JARDIN DES TUILERIES
(Secteur en travaux)
TUILERIES
Feuillants
MUSÉE DE L'ORANGERIE
Quai
Port de la Concorde
Terrasse du Bord de l'Eau
Port des Tuileries
QUAI DES TUILERIES
Av. du Gal Lemonnier
Mée ARTS DE LA MODE ET DU TEXTILE
MUSÉE DES ARTS DÉCORATIFS
Pl. A. Malraux
Pl. Colette
Secteur JARDIN DU CARROUSEL en travaux
ARC DE TRIOMPHE DU CARROUSEL
Pl. du Carrousel
PALAIS ROYAL
SEINE
Pont Royal
Pont du Carrousel
Quai Voltaire
QUAI ANATOLE FRANCE
MIN. DES P.M.E. DU COMMERCE ET DE L'ARTISANAT
ASSEMBLÉE NATIONALE
(R. E. R.) MUSÉE D'ORSAY
Pl. H. de Montherlant
GRANDE CHANCELLERIE LÉGION D'HONNEUR
MUSÉE D'ORSAY
CAISSE DES DÉPOTS ET CONSIGNATIONS
LA DOCUMENTATION FRANÇAISE
Port des Saints Pères
QUAI MALAQUAIS
Rue de Solférino
Rue de Bellechasse
Rue de Poitiers
Rue de Lille
Rue de Verneuil
Rue de l'Université
Rue du Bac
Rue de Beaune
R. Allent
Pl. J. Bainville
SOLFÉRINO
Rue Saint Dominique
R. de Villersexel
Las Cases
INSTITUT DES LANGUES ET CIVILISATIONS ORIENTALES
ÉCOLE NATLE SUPRE DES BEAUX ARTS
Rue Bonaparte
MIN. DES RELATIONS AVEC LE PARLEMENT
SECRT D'ÉTAT POUR L'EMPLOI
Imp. de Valmy
MIN. L'ÉDUCATION NATLE LA RECHERCHE
MIN. DES ANCIENS COMBATTANTS ET DES VICTIMES DE GUERRES
Pge de la Visitation
PENTEMONT
R. de Saint Simon
P.L. Courier
Imp. P.L. Courier
R. Montalembert
R. S. Bottin
E.N.A.
R. du Pré aux Clercs
ST THOMAS D'AQUIN
Pl. St Thomas d'Aquin
R. St Thomas d'Aquin
R. de Gribeauval
RUE DU BAC
ÉCOLE NATLE DES PONTS ET CHAUSSÉES
Rue des Saints Pères
ACADÉMIE NATLE DE MÉDECINE
R. des Beaux Arts
R. Visconti
Rue Jacob
Rue de Grenelle
BOULEVARD SAINT GERMAIN
R. de Luynes
Sqre de Luynes
LYCÉE ST THOMAS D'AQUIN
R. Perronet
ST VLADIMIR LE GRD
UNIVERSITÉ PARIS V
Imp. des Deux Anges
R. Guillaume Apollinaire
St Benoit
MUSÉE DELACROIX
Rue Furstenberg
R. de l'Abbaye
Sqre L. Prache
Pl. St-Germain des Prés
ST GERMAIN DES PRÉS
Pl. du Québec
Sqre F. Desruelles
Pge de la petite Boucherie
Sqre Taras Chevtchenko
FOND. NAT. DES SCIENCES POLITIQUES
MUSÉE MAILLOL
FONTAINE DES QUATRE SAISONS
Rue de Varenne
C. de Varenne
LYCÉE D'HULST
Sqre de La Rochefoucauld
R. de Narbonne
R. de Commaille
R. de La Planche
R. de la Chaise
Square Chaise Récamier
R. Récamier
Rue des Saints Pères
Rue du Dragon
R. du Sabot
R. B. Palissy
R. des Ciseaux
Pl. J. Copeau
Pl. d'Acadie
Rue du Four
R. Princesse
R. Mabillon
MIN. DE LA FONCTION PUBLIQUE
SÉMIN. DES MISSIONS ÉTRANGÈRES
Sqre des Missions Étrangères
R. Chomel
Rue de Babylone
R. de Sèvres
Carref. de la Croix Rouge
Rue de Rennes
L.E.I. Mt VOX
Rue Bonaparte
R. des Canettes
R. Guisarde
TH. DU VIEUX COLOMBIER
R. du Vieux Colombier
ST SULPICE
Madame
Square Boucicaut
SÈVRES BABYLONE
Pl. Le Corbusier
Cherche Midi
N.D. DE LA MÉDAILLE MIRACULEUSE
BON MARCHÉ
R. Velpeau
Rue du Bac
ST IGNACE
Pl. A. Deville
R. de Sèvres
LAENNEC
R. M. Pape Carpantier
MAIRIE DU 6E ARR.
Pl. St Sulpice
ST SULPICE
R. de Mézières
R. Palatine
R. du Canivet
Rue de Jouvenel
R. de Rennes

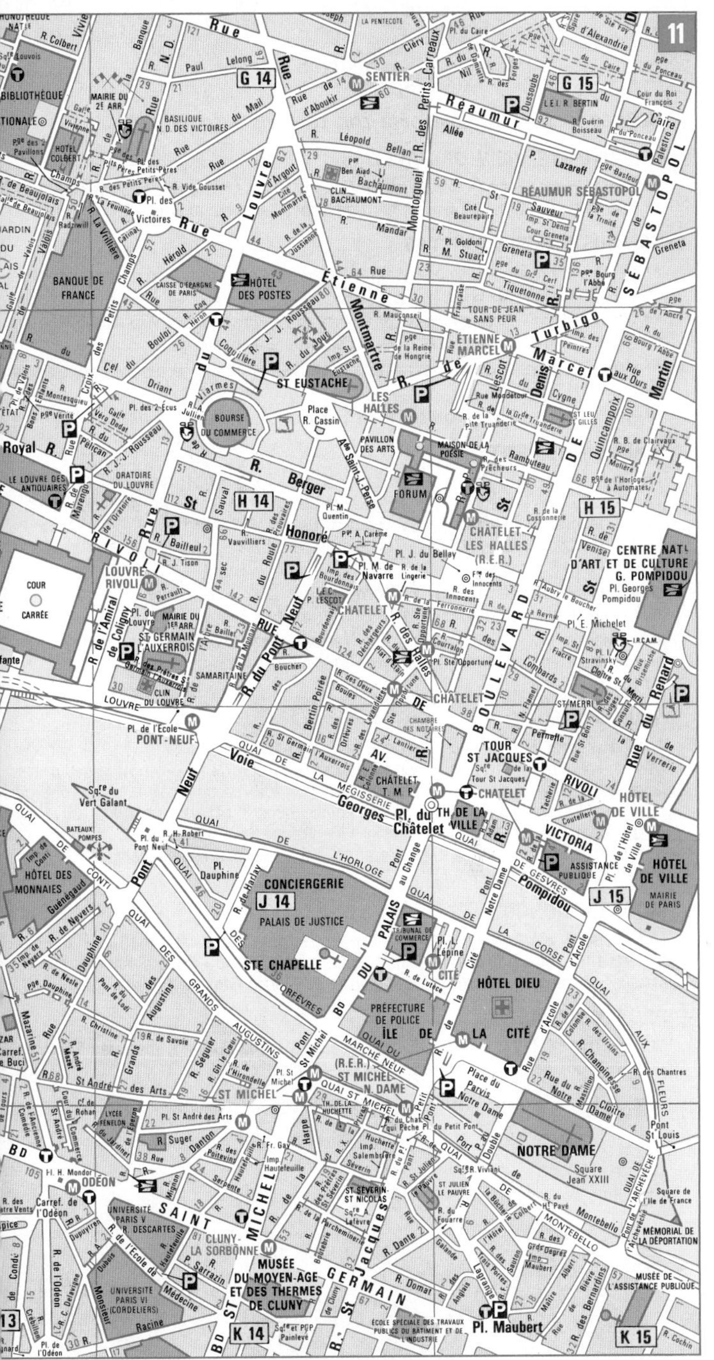

11
G 14
G 15
H 14
H 15
J 14
J 15
K 14
K 15
BIBLIOTHÈQUE NATIONALE
R. Colbert
MAIRIE DU 2E ARR.
BASILIQUE N.D. DES VICTOIRES
HÔTEL COLBERT
SENTIER
Rue Réaumur
Rue du Louvre
Rue Montorgueil
R. des Petits Carreaux
Rue de Cléry
R. d'Aboukir
R. Léopold Bellan
Allée
P. Lazareff
R. St Sauveur
RÉAUMUR SÉBASTOPOL
BD. DE SÉBASTOPOL
L.E.I. R. BERTIN
R. du Caire
Pl. du Caire
R. Dussoubs
R. Greneta
R. Tiquetonne
TOUR DE JEAN SANS PEUR
Rue Étienne Marcel
ÉTIENNE MARCEL
Rue de Turbigo
Rue St Denis
Rue St Martin
Rue Quincampoix
Rue aux Ours
R. Rambuteau
Pl. des Victoires
BANQUE DE FRANCE
R. Hérold
CAISSE D'EPARGNE DE PARIS
HÔTEL DES POSTES
R. J. J. Rousseau
R. du Bouloi
R. Coquillière
ST EUSTACHE
LES HALLES
Place R. Cassin
BOURSE DU COMMERCE
R. Berger
PAVILLON DES ARTS
MAISON DE LA POÉSIE
FORUM
CHÂTELET LES HALLES (R.E.R.)
R. de Viarmes
LE LOUVRE DES ANTIQUAIRES
ORATOIRE DU LOUVRE
Royal
Rue St Honoré
Rue de Rivoli
LOUVRE RIVOLI
COUR CARRÉE
MAIRIE DU 1ER ARR.
ST GERMAIN L'AUXERROIS
SAMARITAINE
R. du Pont Neuf
Pl. J. du Bellay
Pl. M. de Navarre
L.E.C. P. LESCOT
CHÂTELET
R. des Halles
R. de la Ferronnerie
R. des Lombards
R. St Merri
R. du Renard
CENTRE NATL D'ART ET DE CULTURE G. POMPIDOU
Pl. Georges Pompidou
Pl. E. Michelet
I.R.C.A.M.
Pl. I. Stravinsky
ST MERRI
TOUR ST JACQUES
Sq.re de la Tour St Jacques
Av. Victoria
CHÂTELET T. M. P.
TH. DE LA VILLE
Pl. du Châtelet
HÔTEL DE VILLE
MAIRIE DE PARIS
ASSISTANCE PUBLIQUE
Quai de Gesvres
Voie Georges Pompidou
Quai de la Mégisserie
Quai du Louvre
Pl. de l'École
PONT-NEUF
Pont Neuf
Sq.re du Vert Galant
Pl. Dauphine
Quai de l'Horloge
CONCIERGERIE
PALAIS DE JUSTICE
STE CHAPELLE
TRIBUNAL DE COMMERCE
Pl. L. Lépine
CITÉ
HÔTEL DIEU
PRÉFECTURE DE POLICE
ÎLE DE LA CITÉ
Quai de la Corse
Pont d'Arcole
Rue d'Arcole
Place du Parvis Notre Dame
NOTRE DAME
Square Jean XXIII
Quai aux Fleurs
Pont St Louis
Square de l'Île de France
MÉMORIAL DE LA DÉPORTATION
Quai de Conti
HÔTEL DES MONNAIES
Quai des Grands Augustins
Quai des Orfèvres
Bd du Palais
Pont St Michel
Quai St Michel
ST MICHEL
ST MICHEL N. DAME (R.E.R.)
Petit Pont
Sq.re R. Viviani
ST JULIEN LE PAUVRE
ST SÉVERIN ST NICOLAS
Quai de Montebello
Rue St Jacques
Rue de la Harpe
R. de la Huchette
TH. DE LA HUCHETTE
LYCÉE FÉNELON
Pl. St André des Arts
R. Danton
R. Suger
ODÉON
Carref. de l'Odéon
UNIVERSITÉ PARIS V R. DESCARTES
UNIVERSITÉ PARIS VI (CORDELIERS)
R. de l'École de Médecine
Rue Monsieur le Prince
Bd Saint Michel
Bd Saint Germain
CLUNY-LA SORBONNE
MUSÉE DU MOYEN-AGE ET DES THERMES DE CLUNY
Sq.re P. Painlevé
ÉCOLE SPÉCIALE DES TRAVAUX PUBLICS DU BATIMENT ET DE L'INDUSTRIE
Pl. Maubert
R. des Bernardins
MUSÉE DE L'ASSISTANCE PUBLIQUE
R. de la Bûcherie
R. Galande
R. Dante

Sights

How to make the most of a trip to Paris – some ideas :

A BIRD'S-EYE VIEW OF PARIS

★★★ *Eiffel Tower* J 7 – ★★★ *Montparnasse Tower* LM 11 – ★★★ *Notre-Dame Towers* K 15 – ★★★ *Sacré Cœur Dome* D 14 – ★★★ *Arc de Triomphe platform* F 8.

FAMOUS PARISIAN VISTAS

★★★ *Arc de Triomphe – Champs-Élysées – Place de la Concorde : ⩽ from the Rond Point on the Champs-Élysées* G 10.

★★ *The Madeleine – Place de la Concorde – Palais Bourbon (National Assembly) : ⩽ from the Obelisk in the middle of Place de la Concorde* G 11.

★★★ *The Trocadéro – Eiffel Tower – Ecole Militaire : ⩽ from the terrace of the Palais de Chaillot* H 7.

★★ *The Invalides – Grand and Petit Palais : ⩽ from Pont Alexandre III* H 10.

MAIN MONUMENTS

The Louvre★★★ *(Cour Carrée, Perrault's Colonnade, Pyramid)* H 13 – *Eiffel Tower*★★★ J 7 – *Notre-Dame Cathedral*★★★ K 15 – *Sainte-Chapelle*★★★ J 14 – *Arc de Triomphe*★★★ F 8 – *The Invalides*★★★ *(Napoleon's Tomb)* J 10 – *Palais-Royal*★★ H 13 – *The Opéra*★★ F 12 – *The Conciergerie*★★ J 14 – *The Panthéon*★★ L 14 – *Luxembourg*★★ *(Palace and Gardens)* KL 13.

Churches : *The Madeleine*★★ G 11 – *Sacré Cœur*★★ D 14 – *St-Germain-des-Prés*★★ J 13 – *St-Etienne-du-Mont*★★ – *St-Germain-l'Auxerrois*★★ H 14.

In the Marais : *Place des Vosges*★★ – *Hôtel Lamoignon*★★ – *Hôtel Guénégaud*★★ *(Museum of the Chase and of Nature)* – *Hôtel de Soubise*★★ *(Historical Museum of France) by* HJ 15.

MAIN MUSEUMS

The Louvre★★★ H 13 – *Musée d'Orsay*★★★ *(mid-19C to early 20C)* H 12 – *National Museum of Modern Art*★★★ *(Centre Georges-Pompidou)* H 15 – *Army Museum*★★★ *(Invalides)* J 10 – *Museum of Decorative Arts*★★ *(107 rue de Rivoli)* H 13 – *Hôtel de Cluny*★★ *(Museum of the Middle Ages and Roman Baths)* K 14 – *Rodin*★★ *(Hôtel de Biron)* J 10 – *Carnavalet*★★ *(History of Paris)* J 17 – *Picasso*★★ H 17 – *Cité de la Science et de l'Industrie*★★★ *(La Villette)* – *Marmottan*★★ *(Impressionist artists)* – *Orangerie*★★ *(from the Impressionists until 1930)* H 11.

MODERN MONUMENTS

La Défense★★ *(CNIT, Grande Arche)* – *Centre Georges-Pompidou*★★ H 15 – *Forum des Halles* H 14 – *Institut du Monde Arabe*★ – *Opéra de la Bastille* – *Bercy (Palais Omnisports, Ministry of Finance)* – *Bibliothèque Nationale de France François Mitterrand.*

PRETTY AREAS

Montmartre★★★ D 14 – *Ile St-Louis*★★ J 14 J 15 – *the Quays*★★ *(between Pont des Arts and Pont de Sully)* J 14 J 15 – *St Séverin district*★★ K 14.

K 14, G 10 : *Reference letters and numbers on the town plans.*

Use MICHELIN *Green Guide* Paris *for a well-informed visit.*

Alphabetical list (Hotels and restaurants)

A

29 Abbaye St-Germain
58 Abrial
61 Abricotel
44 Acadia
52 Agape (L')
49 Aiglon (L')
28 Aiguière (L')
55 Al Mounia
55 Alain Ducasse
44 Alba
31 Albe
44 Albert 1er
49 Alésia Montparnasse
53 Alexander
28 Alisier (L')
50 Alizé Grenelle
33 Allard
47 Allegro Nation
27 Allegro République
61 Allobroges (Les)
42 Alsace (L')
46 Alsaco Winstub (L')
28 Ambassade d'Auvergne
40 Ambassadeurs (Les)
43 Ambassador
28 Ambroisie (L')
28 Amognes (Les)
59 Amphyclès
52 Amuse Bouche (L')
48 Anacréon
42 Androuët
29 Angleterre
43 Anjou-Lafayette
29 Anjou-Normandie
59 Apicius
50 Apollinaire
36 Apollon
50 Apollon Montparnasse
42 Appart' (L')
31 Aramis St-Germain
40 Arc Élysée
39 Arcade (L')
50 Arès
50 Ariane Montparnasse
26 Armand Au Palais Royal
52 Armoise (L')
35 Arpège
32 Arrosée (L')
61 Arts (des)
28 Astier
37 Astor
41 Astor (L')
58 Astrid
33 Atelier Maître Albert
39 Atlantic H.
36 Aub. Bressane
32 Aub. des Deux Signes
59 Aub. des Dolomites
62 Aucune Idée ?
59 Augusta
44 Axel

B

60 Ballon des Ternes
57 Balmoral
53 Baltimore
37 Balzac
33 Balzar
36 Bamboche (Le)
57 Banville
28 Bascou (Au)
32 Bastide Odéon (La)
24 Baudelaire Opéra
60 Baumann Ternes
59 Béatilles (Les)
35 Beato
38 Beau Manoir
27 Beaubourg
34 Beaugency
50 Beaugrenelle St-Charles
56 Beaujolais d'Auteuil
27 Beauséjour
61 Beauvilliers
38 Bedford
27 Bel Air
34 Bellechasse
35 Bellecour (Le)
56 Bellini
30 Belloy St-Germain
28 Benoît
43 Bergère
34 Bersoly's

59 Beudant (Le)
48 Biche au Bois (A la)
59 Billy Gourmand
46 Bistro de Gala
33 Bistro de la Grille
46 Bistro des Deux Théâtres
60 Bistro du 17e
60 Bistrot d'à Côté Flaubert
32 Bistrot d'Alex
56 Bistrot de l'Étoile, 19 rue Lauriston
60 Bistrot de l'Étoile, 13 rue Troyon
62 Bistrot du 19e
28 Bistrot du Dôme 4th
52 Bistrot du Dôme 14th
42 Bistrot du Sommelier
45 Bistrot Papillon
43 Blanche Fontaine
64 Bleu Marine
42 Bœuf sur le Toit
28 Bofinger
36 Bon Accueil (Au)
26 Bonne Fourchette
33 Bookinistes (Les)
32 Bouchons de François Clerc (Les) 5th
59 Bouchons de François Clerc (Les) 17th
42 Boucoléon (Le)
33 Bouillon Racine
35 Boule d'Or (La)
34 Bourdonnais (La)
34 Bourgogne et Montana
60 Braisière (La)
45 Brasserie Café de la Paix
45 Brasserie Flo
43 Brébant
27 Bretonnerie
37 Bristol, 112 rue du faubourg St-Honoré, (Hotel)
40 Bristol, 112 rue du faubourg St-Honoré, (Rest.)
30 Buci (de)
56 Butte Chaillot (La)

C

34 Cadran (du)
26 Café Marly
33 Cafetière (La)
36 Calèche (La)
38 California
31 California H.
24 Cambon
32 Campagne et Provence
58 Campanile
35 Cantine des Gourmets (La)
42 Cap Vernet
44 Capucines
50 Carladez Cambronne
43 Carlton's H.
27 Caron de Beaumarchais
51 Caroubier (Le)
25 Carré des Feuillants
26 Cartes Postales (Les)
39 Castiglione
23 Castille
46 Catherine - Le Poitou (Chez)
26 Caveau du Palais
60 Caves Petrissans
34 Cayré
25 Céladon (Le)
50 Célébrités (Les)
44 Celte La Fayette
41 Cercle Ledoyen (Le)
52 Cévennes (Les)
34 Champ-de-Mars
36 Champ de Mars (Le)
45 Champagne-Mulhouse
58 Champerret-Héliopolis
57 Champerret-Villiers
28 Chardenoux
45 Charlot "Roi des Coquillages"
32 Chat Grippé (Le)
38 Château Frontenac
52 Château Poivre
38 Chateaubriand
45 Chateaubriant (Au)
50 Châtillon H.
52 Chaumière (La) 15th
62 Chaumière (La) 19th
51 Chen
67 Chesnoy (Le)
67 Chevalet (Le)
57 Cheverny
64 Cheyenne
36 Chez Eux (D')
41 Chiberta
62 Clair de la Lune (Au)
38 Claridge-Bellman
36 Clémentine
58 Clos Longchamp (Le)
31 Clos Médicis
40 Colisée
36 Collinot (Chez)
45 Comme Chez Soi
43 Commodore

63 Communautés (Les)
57 Concorde La Fayette
38 Concorde St-Lazare
39 Concortel
67 Connemara (Le)
55 Conti
52 Contre-Allée
41 Copenhague
64 Copthorne
25 Corbeille (La)
39 Cordélia
44 Corona
23 Costes
36 Côté 7eme (Du)
61 Cottage Marcadet
51 Coupole (La)
37 Crillon
61 Crimée
27 Croix de Malte
67 Cuisine Bourgeoise (La)
56 Cuisinier François (Le)

D

50 Daguerre
61 Damrémont
50 Delambre
60 Dessirier
46 Deux Canards (Aux)
51 Dînée (La)
63 Disneyland Hôtel
32 Dodin-Bouffant
51 Dôme (Le)
33 Dominique
56 Driver's (Le)
25 Drouant
51 Duc (Le)
33 Duc de Saint-Simon

E

61 Eden H.
23 Édouard VII et rest. Le Delmonico
54 Eiffel Kennedy
34 Eiffel Park H.
39 Élysée (de l')
40 Élysées (Les)
54 Élysées Bassano
39 Élysées Mermoz
38 Élysées-Ponthieu et Résidence
53 Élysées Régencia
53 Élysées Sablons
37 Élysées Star
35 Empereur (L')
27 Entre Ciel et Terre
32 Épi Dupin (L')
60 Epicure 108
52 Épopée (L')
51 Erawan
48 Escapade en Touraine (L')
24 Espadon
51 Etape (L')
48 Etchégorry
58 Étoile d'Or (L')
39 Étoile Friedland
54 Étoile Maillot
58 Étoile Park H.
58 Étoile Péreire
57 Étoile St-Ferdinand
62 Étrier (L')
28 Excuse (L')
46 Excuse Mogador (L')

F

26 Fabrice (Chez)
31 Familia
59 Faucher
55 Faugeron
24 Favart
42 Fenêtre sur Cour
42 Ferme des Mathurins
35 Ferme St-Simon
42 Fermette Marbeuf 1900 (La)
29 Fernandises (Les)
30 Ferrandi
35 Flamberge (La)
39 Flèche d'Or
30 Fleurie (de)
54 Floride Étoile
36 Florimond (Le)
36 Foc Ly
56 Fontaine d'Auteuil
36 Fontaine de Mars (La)
52 Fontana Rosa
40 Fortuny
34 France
48 Françoise (Chez)
43 Franklin
39 Franklin Roosevelt
44 Frantour Paris-Est
47 Frégate (La)
53 Frémiet

G

26 Gabriel (Chez)
39 Galiléo
53 Garden Élysée
52 Gastroquet (Le)
51 Gauloise (La)
25 Gaya Rive Droite
36 Gaya Rive Gauche
24 Gd H. de Besançon
27 Gd H. Prieuré
65 Gd Hôtel Mercure Orly
37 George V
26 Georges (Chez) 2d
60 Georges (Chez) 17th
41 Géorgiques (Les)
25 Gérard Besson
56 Géraud (Chez)
36 Gildo
55 Giulio Rebellato
36 Glénan (Les)
38 Golden Tulip St-Honoré
25 Goumard-Prunier
48 Gourmandise (La)
59 Graindorge
45 Grand Café Capucines
26 Grand Colbert (Le)
43 Grand Hôtel Inter-Continental
24 Grand Vefour
56 Grande Cascade (La)
30 Grands Hommes
45 Grange Batelière
41 Grenadin (Le)
32 Grilladin (Au)
26 Grille St-Honoré (A la)
28 Grizzli (Le)
58 Guy Savoy
60 Guyvonne (Chez)

H - I

54 Hameau de Passy
58 Harvey
41 Hédiard
49 Hilton 15th
64 Hilton
64 Hilton Orly
61 Holiday Inn 19th
64 Holiday Inn
65 Holiday Inn
54 Holiday Inn Garden Court
29 Holiday Inn Saint Germain des Pré
46 Holiday Inn Tolbiac
24 Horset Opéra (L')
43 Horset Pavillon (L')
65 Hyatt Regency
46 I Golosi
47 Ibis 13th
64 Ibis
65 Ibis
65 Ibis
67 Ibis
47 Ibis Bercy
63 Ibis La Défense
44 Ibis Lafayette
47 Ibis Porte d'Italie
59 Il Ristorante
60 Impatient (L')
32 Inagiku
41 Indra
23 Inter - Continental
50 Istria

J - K

48 Jacky (Chez)
31 Jacques Cagna
55 Jamin
41 Jardin (Le)
31 Jardin de Cluny
30 Jardin de l'Odéon
34 Jardins d'Eiffel (Les)
30 Jardins du Luxembourg
54 Jardins du Trocadéro (Les)
46 Jean (Chez)
48 Jean-Pierre Frelet
27 Jeu de Paume
32 Joséphine "Chez Dumonet"
35 Jules Verne
45 Julien
53 K. Palace
25 Kinugawa 1st
42 Kinugawa 8th
54 Kléber

L

56 Lac Hong
43 Lafayette
51 Lal Qila
37 Lancaster

40 Lasserre
29 Latitudes St-Germain
60 Laudrin (Chez)
61 Laumière (Le)
40 Laurent
40 Lavoisier-Malesherbes
35 Le Divellec
40 Ledoyen
29 Left Bank St-Germain
49 Lenox Montparnasse
34 Lenox Saint-Germain
60 Léon (Chez)
26 Lescure
39 Lido
50 Lilas Blanc
29 Littré
42 Lloyd's (Le)
34 Londres
23 Lotti
51 Lous Landès
23 Louvre (du)
24 Louvre St-Honoré
40 Lucas Carton
41 Luna (La)
27 Lutèce
29 Lutétia

M

29 Madison
57 Magellan
41 Maison Blanche
35 Maison de l'Amérique Latine (La)
32 Maître Paul (Chez)
53 Majestic
24 Malte Opéra
58 Manoir de Paris
31 Manoir St-Germain des Prés (Au)
24 Mansart
28 Maraîcher (Le)
41 Marcande (Le)
41 Marée (La)
67 Marée de Versailles (La)
62 Marie-Louise
59 Marines de Pétrus (Les)
56 Marius
42 Marius et Janette
31 Marronniers
48 Marronniers (Les)
32 Marty
54 Massenet
39 Mathurins
36 Maupertu (Le)
32 Mavrommatis
31 Maxim
64 Maxim's
39 Mayflower
47 Média
57 Mercédès
64 Mercure
64 Mercure
67 Mercure
47 Mercure Blanqui
57 Mercure Étoile
25 Mercure Galant
61 Mercure Montmartre
49 Mercure Montparnasse
44 Mercure Monty
39 Mercure Opéra Garnier
50 Mercure Paris XV
46 Mercure Pont de Bercy
49 Mercure Porte de Versailles
49 Mercure Tour Eiffel
46 Mercure Vincent Auriol
57 Meridien (Le)
49 Méridien Montparnasse
27 Méridional
23 Meurice
24 Meurice (Le)
48 Michel
58 Michel Rostang
51 Mille Colonnes
28 Miravile
44 Modern' Est
47 Modern H. Lyon
50 Modern H. Val Girard
33 Moissonnier
58 Monceau
58 Monceau Élysées
58 Monceau Étoile
28 Monde des Chimères (Le)
51 Moniage Guillaume
38 Montaigne
33 Montalembert
44 Monterosa
50 Montparnasse 25
45 Montréal
51 Morot Gaudry
44 Moulin
33 Moulin à Vent "Chez Henri"
34 Muguet
54 Murat
45 Muses (Les)

N

38 Napoléon
57 Neuville (de)
57 Neva
39 New Roblin et rest. le Mazagran
63 New-York
63 Newport Bay Club
39 Newton Opéra
55 Ngo (Chez)
60 Niçoise (La)
54 Nicolo
49 Nikko
24 Noailles (de)
23 Normandy
31 Notre Dame
47 Nouvel H.
63 Novotel
64 Novotel
65 Novotel
67 Novotel
46 Novotel Bercy
46 Novotel Gare de Lyon
63 Novotel La Défense
24 Novotel Les Halles
49 Novotel Porte d'Orléans
49 Novotel Vaugirard

O

32 O à la Bouche (L')
30 Odéon (de l')
30 Odéon H.
36 Oeillade (L')
46 Oenothèque (L')
36 Olivades (Les)
44 Opéra Cadet
23 Opéra Richepanse
40 Orangerie (L')
52 Os à Moelle (L')
47 Oulette (L')

P

36 P'tit Troquet (Le)
46 P'tite Tonkinoise (La)
52 P'tits Bouchons de François Clerc (Les)
43 Paix République
25 Palais Royal
33 Palanquin (Le)
61 Palma
30 Panthéon
53 Parc (Le)
31 Parc St-Séverin
31 Paris
47 Paris Bastille
67 Pascal Le Falher
54 Passy Eiffel
50 Pasteur
48 Paul (Chez)
56 Paul Chêne
35 Paul Minchelli
25 Pauline (Chez)
46 Pavillon Bastille
27 Pavillon de la Reine
51 Pavillon Montsouris
55 Pavillon Noura
61 Pavillon Puebla
65 Pavillon Trianon (Le)
52 Père Claude (Le)
53 Pergolèse
55 Pergolèse (Le)
28 Petit Bofinger (Le)
59 Petit Colombier (Le)
35 Petit Laurent (Le)
52 Petit Mâchon (Le)
48 Petit Marguery (Le)
52 Petit Plat (Le)
26 Petit Restaurant (Le)
45 Petit Riche (Au)
60 Petite Auberge (La)
56 Petite Tour (La)
59 Pétrus
26 Pharamond
51 Philippe Detourbe
42 Pichet (Le)
25 Pied de Cochon (Au)
25 Pierre " A la Fontaine Gaillon "
52 Pierre (Chez)
26 Pierre Au Palais Royal
41 Pierre Gagnaire
26 Pile ou Face
24 Place du Louvre
37 Plaza Athénée
40 Plaza Élysées
26 Poquelin (Le)
55 Port Alma
65 Potager du Roy (Le)
62 Poulbot Gourmet (Le)
26 Poule au Pot (La)
38 Powers
44 Pré (du)

56 Pré Catelan (Le)
47 Pressoir (Au)
30 Prince de Conti
37 Prince de Galles
44 Printania
32 Procope (Le)
55 Prunier-Traktir
28 Pyrénées Cévennes "Chez Philippe"

Q

57 Quality Inn Pierre
33 Quatre et Une Saveurs (Les)
38 Queen Elizabeth
39 Queen Mary
45 Quercy (Le)
48 Quincy (Le)

R

53 Raphaël
49 Raspail Montparnasse
35 Récamier
52 Régalade (La)
40 Régence
30 Régent (Le)
57 Regent's Garden
24 Régina
54 Régina de Passy
61 Regyn's Montmartre
46 Relais Beaujolais
34 Relais Bosquet
29 Relais Christine
55 Relais d'Auteuil
47 Relais de Lyon
51 Relais de Sèvres
62 Relais des Buttes
31 Relais Louis XIII
29 Relais Médicis
65 Relais Mercure
29 Relais St-Germain
28 Relais St-Paul (Le)
30 Relais St-Sulpice
63 Renaissance
65 Rescatore
54 Résidence Chambellan Morgane
44 Résidence du Pré
38 Résidence du Roy
54 Résidence Foch
30 Résidence Henri IV
54 Résidence Impériale
54 Résidence Marceau
39 Résidence Monceau
50 Résidence St-Lambert
47 Résidence Vert Galant
45 Rest. Opéra
48 Rhône (Le)
43 Richmond
23 Ritz
30 Rives de Notre-Dame (Les)
27 Rivoli Notre Dame
38 Rochester Champs-Élysées
61 Roma Sacré Coeur
32 Rond de Serviette (Le)
53 Rond-Point de Longchamp
56 Rosimar
60 Rôtisserie d'Armaillé (La)
33 Rôtisserie d'en Face
33 Rôtisserie du Beaujolais
25 Rôtisserie Monsigny
38 Royal Alma
54 Royal Élysées
38 Royal H.
58 Royal Magda
37 Royal Monceau
24 Royal St-Honoré
30 Royal St-Michel

S

26 Saint Amour (Le)
29 Sainte Beuve
45 Saintongeais (Le)
30 Saints-Pères (des)
37 San Régis
64 Santa Fé
41 Sarladais (Le)
25 Saudade
56 Scheffer (Le)
43 Scribe
36 Sédillot (Le)
30 Select
51 Senteurs de Provence (Aux)
63 Séquoia Lodge
54 Sévigné
31 Sèvres Azur
34 Sèvres Vaneau
64 Sheraton
42 Shozan
48 Sipario
47 Slavia

64 Sofitel
37 Sofitel Arc de Triomphe
38 Sofitel Champs-Élysées
65 Sofitel Château de Versailles
63 Sofitel CNIT
49 Sofitel Forum Rive Gauche
63 Sofitel La Défense
49 Sofitel Porte de Sèvres
31 Sorbonne (La)
59 Sormani (Le)
26 Soufflé (Le)
26 Souletin (Le)
60 Soupière (La)
56 Sous l'Olivier
28 Sousceyrac (A)
34 Splendid
57 Splendid Étoile
48 St-Amarante
31 St-Christophe
34 St-Germain
30 St-Germain-des-Prés
29 St-Grégoire
53 St-James Paris
44 St-Laurent
43 St-Pétersbourg
52 St-Vincent (Le)
27 Stella
24 Stendhal
42 Stresa
44 Suède
30 Sully St-Germain
42 Suntory
61 Super H.

T

45 Table d'Anvers (La)
36 Table d'Eiffel (La)
59 Table de Pierre (La)
28 Table Richelieu (La)
40 Taillevent
60 Taïra
36 Tan Dinh
56 Tang
41 Tante Louise (Chez)
48 Temps des Cerises (Le)
47 Terminus-Lyon
43 Terminus Nord, 12 boulevard Denain, (Hotel)
45 Terminus Nord, 23 rue de Dunkerque, (Rest.)
57 Ternes Arc de Triomphe
61 Terrass'H.
28 Thaï Elephant
36 Thoumieux
58 Tilsitt Étoile
33 Timbale St-Bernard (La)
59 Timgad
32 Timonerie (La)
42 Tong Yen
31 Tour d'Argent
52 Tour (de la)
50 Tour Eiffel Dupleix
44 Touraine Opéra
47 Touring Hôtel Magendie
34 Tourville (Le)
32 Toutoune (Chez)
47 Train Bleu
48 Traversière (Le)
37 Trémoille (La)
41 30 - Fauchon (Le)
65 Trianon Palace
44 Trinité Plaza
65 Trois Marches (Les)
47 Trou Gascon (Au)
60 Troyon (Le)
32 Truffière (La)
59 Truite Vagabonde (La)
55 Tsé-Yang
35 Turenne

U - V

54 Union H. Étoile
33 Valérie Tortu
34 Varenne (de)
26 Vaudeville
27 Verlain
37 Vernet
34 Verneuil St-Germain
62 Verrière d'Eric Frechon (La)
50 Versailles
65 Versailles (Le)
47 Viator
27 Victoire Suprême du Coeur
54 Victor Hugo
29 Victoria Palace
37 Vigny (de)
29 Villa (La)
30 Villa des Artistes
53 Villa Maillot
56 Villa Vinci

42 Village d'Ung et Li Lam
56 Vin et Marée
35 Vin sur Vin
24 Violet
55 Vivarois
24 Vivienne
25 Vong (Chez)

W

39 Waldorf Madeleine
46 Wally Le Saharien
38 Warwick
39 West-End
23 Westminster

Y - Z

32 Yugaraj
41 Yvan
26 Yvan sur Seine
51 Yves Quintard
55 Zébra Square
48 Zygomates (Les)

MICHELIN GREEN GUIDES in English

Austria	Germany	New York City
Belgium Luxemburg	Great Britain	Portugal
Brussels	Greece	Quebec
California	Ireland	Rome
Canada	Italy	Scotland
Chicago	London	Spain
England : The West Country	Mexico	Switzerland
France	Netherlands	Tuscany
	New England	Washington DC

HOTELS, RESTAURANTS

Listed by districts and arrondissements

(List of Hotels and Restaurants in alphabetical order, see pp 13 to 21)

12: These reference letters and numbers correspond to the squares on the Michelin Map of Paris no 10. Paris Atlas no 11. Map with street index no 12 and Map of Paris no 14.

onsult any of the above publications when looking for a car park nearest to a listed establishment.

Opéra, Palais-Royal, Halles, Bourse.

1st and 2nd arrondissements - 1st: ✉ 75001 - 2nd: ✉ 75002

Ritz, 15 pl. Vendôme (1st) ✆ 01 43 16 30 30, Fax 01 43 16 31 78, « Attractive pool and luxurious fitness centre » – 100. AE GB JCB. rest G 12
see ***Espadon*** below - ***Bar Vendôme*** (lunch only) **Meals** a la carte 350/500 – ☕ 180 – **142 rm** 3200/4300, 45 suites.

Meurice, 228 r. Rivoli (1st) ✆ 01 44 58 10 10, Fax 01 44 58 10 15 – rm rm – 100. AE GB JCB. rest G 12
Meals see ***Le Meurice*** below – ☕ 150 – **134 rm** 2750/3700, 46 suites.

Inter - Continental, 3 r. Castiglione (1st) ✆ 01 44 77 11 11, Fax 01 44 77 14 60, – rm – 500. AE GB JCB. rest G 12
Brasserie 234 Rivoli ✆ 01 44 77 10 40 **Meals** 130(lunch) and a la carte 180/250 – ***La Terrasse Fleurie*** ✆ 01 44 77 10 44 *(May-September)* **Meals** (lunch only) a la carte approx. 200 – ☕ 195 – **358 rm** 2500/3150, 87 suites.

Castille M, 37 r. Cambon (1st) ✆ 01 44 58 44 58, Fax 01 44 58 44 00, – rm – 30. AE GB JCB G 12
Il Cortile ✆ 01 44 58 45 67, Italian rest. *(closed Sunday)* **Meals** 195 and a la carte 190/320 – ☕ 120 – **86 rm** 1990/3200, 7 suites, 14 duplex.

Westminster, 13 r. Paix (2nd) ✆ 01 42 61 57 46, Fax 01 42 60 30 66 – rm rm – 60. AE GB JCB G 12
Meals see ***Le Céladon*** below – ☕ 110 – **84 rm** 1650/2500, 18 suites.

du Louvre, pl. A. Malraux (1st) ✆ 01 44 58 38 38, Fax 01 44 58 38 01, – – 100. AE GB JCB H 13
Brasserie Le Louvre : **Meals** 175(dinner) and a la carte 180/310 – ☕ 110 – **194 rm** 1350/1950, 5 suites.

Lotti, 7 r. Castiglione (1st) ✆ 01 42 60 37 34, Fax 01 40 15 93 56 – rm . AE GB JCB G 12
Meals 160/220 and a la carte 270/460 – ☕ 120 – **129 rm** 1410/3330.

Costes, 239 r. St-Honoré (1st) ✆ 01 42 44 50 00, Fax 01 42 44 50 01, « Elegant mansion tastefully decorated », – – 30. AE GB JCB
Meals a la carte 230/450 – ☕ 100 – **60 rm** 1500/3500. G 12

Edouard VII and rest. Le Delmonico, 39 av. Opéra (2nd) ✆ 01 42 61 56 90, Fax 01 42 61 47 73 – . AE GB G 13
Meals *(closed August, Saturday and Sunday)* 168 – ☕ 90 – **65 rm** 1300/1500, 4 suites.

Opéra Richepanse M without rest, 14 r. Richepanse (1st) ✆ 01 42 60 36 00, Fax 01 42 60 13 03 – . AE GB JCB G 12
☕ 65 – **35 rm** 1200/1400, 3 suites.

Normandy, 7 r. Échelle (1st) ✆ 01 42 60 30 21, Fax 01 42 60 45 81 – rm – 30. AE GB JCB H 13
L'Échelle *(closed Saturday and Sunday)* **Meals** 150/220 – ☕ 75 – **111 rm** 1265/1680, 4 suites.

Royal St-Honoré M without rest, 221 r. St-Honoré (1st) ✆ 01 42 60 32 79, Fax 01 42 60 47 44 – AE GB JCB G 1
90 – **67 rm** 1250/1950, 5 suites.

Régina, 2 pl. Pyramides (1st) ✆ 01 42 60 31 10, Fax 01 40 15 95 16, « "Art Nouveau" lobby » – rm – 30. AE GB JCB. rest H 1
Meals *(closed August, Saturday, Sunday and Bank Holidays)* 165 (lunch), 260/295 and a la carte 260/380 – 95 – **116 rm** 1600/2200, 14 suites.

Stendhal without rest, 22 r. D. Casanova (2nd) ✆ 01 44 58 52 52, Fax 01 44 58 52 0 – AE GB G 1
95 – **20 rm** 1350/1500.

L'Horset Opéra M without rest, 18 r. d'Antin (2nd) ✆ 01 44 71 87 00, Fax 01 42 66 55 54 – rm AE GB JCB G 1
80 – **54 rm** 990/1350.

Cambon M without rest, 3 r. Cambon (1st) ✆ 01 44 58 93 93, Fax 01 42 60 30 59 AE GB JCB G 1
80 – **42 rm** 1280/1680.

Mansart without rest, 5 r. Capucines (1st) ✆ 01 42 61 50 28, Fax 01 49 27 97 44 – AE GB JCB. G 1
50 – **57 rm** 830/1500.

Novotel Les Halles M, 8 pl. M.-de-Navarre (1st) ✆ 01 42 21 31 31, Fax 01 40 26 05 79, – rm – 120. AE GB JCB H 1
Meals 110 b.i. – 64 – **280 rm** 885/930, 5 suites.

de Noailles M without rest, 9 r. Michodière (2nd) ✆ 01 47 42 92 90, Fax 01 49 24 92 71, contemporary decor – AE GB JCB G 1
40 – **58 rm** 680/880.

Favart without rest, 5 r. Marivaux (2nd) ✆ 01 42 97 59 83, Fax 01 40 15 95 58 – AE GB JCB F 1
20 – **37 rm** 490/590.

Violet M without rest, 7 r. J. Lantier (1st) ✆ 01 42 33 45 38, Fax 01 40 28 03 56 – AE GB JCB. J 1
55 – **30 rm** 550/730.

Place du Louvre M without rest, 21 r. Prêtres-St-Germain-L'Auxerrois (1st) ✆ 01 42 33 78 68, Fax 01 42 33 09 95 – AE GB JCB H 1
40 – **20 rm** 496/812.

Malte Opéra without rest, 63 r. Richelieu (2nd) ✆ 01 44 58 94 94, Fax 01 42 86 88 1 – AE GB JCB. G 1
80 – **54 rm** 790/890, 5 duplex.

Louvre St-Honoré M without rest, 141 r. St-Honoré (1st) ✆ 01 42 96 23 23, Fax 01 42 96 21 61 – AE GB JCB H 1
45 – **40 rm** 496/862.

Gd H. de Besançon M without rest, 56 r. Montorgueil (2nd) ✆ 01 42 36 41 08, Fax 01 45 08 08 79 – rm AE GB JCB. G 1
40 – **20 rm** 550/650.

Baudelaire Opéra without rest, 61 r. Ste Anne (2nd) ✆ 01 42 97 50 62, Fax 01 42 86 85 85 – AE GB JCB G 1
38 – **24 rm** 480/650, 5 duplex.

Vivienne without rest, 40 r. Vivienne (2nd) ✆ 01 42 33 13 26, Fax 01 40 41 98 19 – GB F 1
40 – **44 rm** 360/500.

Espadon - Hôtel Ritz, 15 pl. Vendôme (1st) ✆ 01 43 16 30 30, Fax 01 43 16 31 78, – AE GB JCB. G 1
Meals 380 (lunch)/600 and a la carte 500/770
Spec. Foie gras de canard. Côte double de veau de lait et légumes de saison. Chariot de desserts.

Grand Vefour, 17 r. Beaujolais (1st) ✆ 01 42 96 56 27, Fax 01 42 86 80 71 « Pre-Revolutionary (late 18C) Café Style » – AE GB JCB. G 1
closed August, Saturday and Sunday – **Meals** 325 (lunch)/750 and a la carte 590/840
Spec. Saumon mi-cuit en terrine, lait fumé aux grains de pavot. Parmentier de queue de bœuf aux truffes. Sablé au basilic, fenouil confit et poivron rouge en sorbet (dessert).

Le Meurice - Hôtel Meurice, 228 r. Rivoli (1st) ✆ 01 44 58 10 50, Fax 01 44 58 10 1 – AE GB JCB. G 1
Meals 330 (lunch), 395 b.i./500 and a la carte 340/470
Spec. Foie gras de canard à la pulpe de raisin noir (autumn, winter). Langoustines frites en papillote. Canette bressane rôtie aux cèpes et navets aigres-doux (autumn).

XXXX ✿✿ **Drouant,** pl. Gaillon (2nd) ✆ 01 42 65 15 16, Fax 01 49 24 02 15, « Home of the Academie Goncourt since 1914 » – ▤. AE ⦶ GB G 13
Meals 290 (lunch)/650 and a la carte 520/700 - ***Café Drouant :*** **Meals** 200 and a la carte 250/360
Spec. Charlotte de langoustines aux aubergines confites. Turbot rôti en croûte d'argile, aux truffes et au persil simple. Quartier d'agneau des Pyrénées rôti à l'ail doux (season).

XXXX ✿✿ **Carré des Feuillants** (Dutournier), 14 r. Castiglione (1st) ✆ 01 42 86 82 82, Fax 01 42 86 07 71 – ▤. AE ⦶ GB JCB G 12
closed August, Saturday lunch and Sunday – **Meals** 285 (lunch)and a la carte 480/660
Spec. Homard breton (June-September). Langoustines pimentées rôties. Lièvre à la mode d'Aquitaine (October-November).

XXXX ✿✿ **Goumard-Prunier,** 9 r. Duphot (1st) ✆ 01 42 60 36 07, Fax 01 42 60 04 54 – ▤. AE ⦶ GB JCB G 12
closed Sunday and Monday – **Meals** - Seafood - 295 (lunch)/780 and a la carte 450/600
Spec. Ecrevisses à la nage façon Prunier (August-February). Bar de ligne grillé et petits artichauts confits aux épices. Turbot de ligne rôti à l'arête.

XXXX ✿✿ **Gérard Besson,** 5 r. Coq Héron (1st) ✆ 01 42 33 14 74, Fax 01 42 33 85 71 – ▤. AE ⦶ GB JCB H 14
closed Saturday (except dinner from 15 September to 15 June) and Sunday – **Meals** 280 (lunch)/520 and a la carte 450/680
Spec. Tartelette Lucullus. Gibier (season). Truffes (15 December-20 March).

XXX ✿ **Le Céladon** - Hôtel Westminster, 15 r. Daunou (2nd) ✆ 01 47 03 40 42, Fax 01 42 60 30 66 – ▤. AE ⦶ GB JCB G 12
closed August, Saturday, Sunday and Bank Holidays – **Meals** 240/350 and a la carte 370/490
Spec. Galette de homard à l'huile de pistache. Tronçon de turbot en cocotte au céleri rave et parfum de truffe. Poitrine de pigeonneau et foie gras en charlotte d'endives (October-April).

XXX **Pierre " A la Fontaine Gaillon ",** pl. Gaillon (2nd) ✆ 01 47 42 63 22, Fax 01 47 42 82 84, ☂ – ▤. AE ⦶ GB G 13
closed Saturday lunch and Sunday – **Meals** 165 and a la carte 210/390.

XXX ✿ **Mercure Galant,** 15 r. Petits-Champs (1st) ✆ 01 42 97 53 85, Fax 01 42 96 08 89 – AE GB G 13
closed Saturday lunch, Sunday and Bank Holidays – **Meals** 240/310 and a la carte 320/450
Spec. Salade de homard breton aux agrumes. Poissons. "Mille et une feuilles" (dessert).

XXX **Chez Vong,** 10 r. Grande-Truanderie (1st) ✆ 01 40 39 99 89, Fax 01 42 33 38 15 – ▤. AE ⦶ GB H 15
closed Sunday – **Meals** - Chinese and Vietnamese rest. - a la carte 190/300.

XXX **Au Pied de Cochon** (24 hr service), 6 r. Coquillière (1st) ✆ 01 40 13 77 00, Fax 01 40 13 77 09, brasserie – ▤. AE ⦶ GB H 14
Meals 178 and a la carte 160/350.

XXX **La Corbeille,** 154 r. Montmartre (2nd) ✆ 01 40 26 30 87, Fax 01 40 26 08 20 – ▤. GB G 14
closed August, Saturday lunch and Sunday – **Meals** 165/300 and a la carte 260/370.

XX **Chez Pauline,** 5 r. Villédo (1st) ✆ 01 42 96 20 70, Fax 01 49 27 99 89, bistro – AE ⦶ GB JCB G 13
closed Saturday (except dinner from October-April) and Sunday – **Meals** 220 and a la carte 290/410.

XX **Rôtisserie Monsigny,** 1 r. Monsigny (2nd) ✆ 01 42 96 16 61, Fax 01 42 97 40 97 – ▤. AE GB JCB G 13
closed 10 to 20 August and Saturday lunch – **Meals** 160 and a la carte 200/310 ♁.

XX **Palais Royal,** 110 Galerie de Valois - Jardin du Palais Royal (1st) ✆ 01 40 20 00 27, Fax 01 40 20 00 82, ☂ – AE ⦶ GB JCB G 13
closed 23 December-2 January, Saturday lunch and Sunday from September-May – **Meals** a la carte 190/320.

XX **Saudade,** 34 r. Bourdonnais (1st) ✆ 01 42 36 30 71, Fax 01 42 36 27 77 – ▤. AE GB. ✂ H 14
closed Sunday – **Meals** - Portuguese rest. - 129 (lunch)and a la carte 170/330.

XX **Kinugawa,** 9 r. Mont-Thabor (1st) ✆ 01 42 60 65 07, Fax 01 42 60 45 21 – ▤. AE ⦶ GB JCB. ✂ G 12
closed 22 December-6 January and Sunday – **Meals** - Japanese rest. - 150 (lunch), 245/700 and a la carte 250/370.

XX **Gaya Rive Droite,** 17 r. Duphot (1st) ✆ 01 42 60 43 03, Fax 01 42 60 04 54, « Attractive glazed tile panels » – ▤. AE GB G 12
closed Sunday – **Meals** - Seafood - a la carte 240/330.

XX ✿ **Pierre Au Palais Royal,** 10 r. Richelieu (1st) ✆ 01 42 96 09 17, Fax 01 42 96 09 6 – AE ⓓ GB H 1
closed August, Saturday, Sunday and Bank Holidays – **Meals** 195 and a la carte 250/38
Spec. Escalope de foie gras de canard chaud. Quenelles de brochet. Bœuf ficelle à l ménagère.

XX **Le Poquelin,** 17 r. Molière (1st) ✆ 01 42 96 22 19, Fax 01 42 96 05 72 – ▤. AE ⓓ GB JCB G 1
closed 1 to 20 August, Saturday lunch and Sunday – **Meals** 189 and a la carte 270/370

XX **Armand Au Palais Royal,** 4 r. Beaujolais (1st) ✆ 01 42 60 05 11, Fax 01 42 96 16 2 – AE GB JCB G 1
closed 3 to 31 August, Saturday lunch and Sunday – **Meals** 180 (lunch)/250.

XX **Chez Fabrice,** 38 r. Croix des Petits-Champs (1st) ✆ 01 40 20 06 46 – AE GB H 1
closed Saturday lunch and Sunday – **Meals** 125/185.

XX **Pile ou Face,** 52bis r. N.-D.-des-Victoires (2nd) ✆ 01 42 33 64 33, Fax 01 42 36 61 0 – ▤. AE GB G 1
closed August, 23 December-1 January, Saturday and Sunday – **Meals** 245 (lunch)/32 and a la carte 280/380.

XX **Pharamond,** 24 r. Grande-Truanderie (1st) ✆ 01 42 33 06 72, Fax 01 40 28 01 81, bistrot, « Fine 1900 decor » – AE ⓓ GB G 1
closed Monday lunch and Sunday – **Meals** 200 b.i./310 b.i. and a la carte 240/440.

XX **Vaudeville,** 29 r. Vivienne (2nd) ✆ 01 40 20 04 62, Fax 01 49 27 08 78, brasserie – AE ⓓ GB G 1
Meals a la carte 170/320.

XX **Le Grand Colbert,** 2 r. Vivienne (2nd) ✆ 01 42 86 87 88, Fax 01 42 86 82 65, brasserie – AE ⓓ GB G 1
closed 10 to 25 August – **Meals** 155 and a la carte 170/290 ♁.

XX **Bonne Fourchette,** 320 r. St-Honoré, in the backyard (1st) ✆ 01 42 60 45 27 – ▤ ⓓ GB. ✻ G 1
closed August, February Holidays, Sunday lunch and Saturday – **Meals** 125/165 and a la carte 230/300.

XX **Le Soufflé,** 36 r. Mont-Thabor (1st) ✆ 01 42 60 27 19, Fax 01 42 60 54 98 – ▤. AE ⓓ GB JCB G 1
closed Sunday – **Meals** 175/250 and a la carte 180/340.

XX **Chez Gabriel,** 123 r. St-Honoré (1st) ✆ 01 42 33 02 99 – ▤. AE ⓓ GB JCB. ✻ H 1
closed 8 to 25 August, 24 December-2 January, Sunday and Bank Holidays – **Meals** 175/220.

XX **Les Cartes Postales,** 7 r. Gomboust (1st) ✆ 01 42 61 02 93, Fax 01 42 61 02 93 – GB JCB G 1
closed Saturday lunch and Sunday – **Meals** (booking essential) 135/350 and a la carte 220/380.

X **A la Grille St-Honoré,** 15 pl. Marché St-Honoré (1st) ✆ 01 42 61 00 93 Fax 01 47 03 31 64 – ▤. AE ⓓ GB G 1
closed 1 to 26 August, Sunday and Monday – **Meals** 180 and a la carte 300/380.

X **Yvan sur Seine,** 26 quai Louvre (1st) ✆ 01 42 36 49 52 – ▤. AE ⓓ GB H 1
closed lunch Saturday and Sunday – **Meals** 98 (lunch)/138 and a la carte 190/280.

X **Café Marly,** 93 r. Rivoli - Cour Napoléon (1st) ✆ 01 49 26 06 60, Fax 01 49 26 07 06 ☂, « Original decor at the Louvre museum, terrace » – ▤. AE ⓓ GB H 1
Meals a la carte 180/280.

X **Caveau du Palais,** 19 pl. Dauphine (1st) ✆ 01 43 26 04 28, Fax 01 43 26 81 84 – AE GB J 1
closed Christmas-New Year and Sunday from October-April – **Meals** 184 b.i. and a la carte 200/350.

X **Le Saint Amour,** 8 r. Port Mahon (2nd) ✆ 01 47 42 63 82 – ▤. AE ⓓ GB JCB G 1
closed Saturday except dinner from 15 September-15 June, Sunday and Bank Holidays – **Meals** 165 and a la carte 230/340.

X **Le Petit Restaurant,** 50 r. Richelieu (1st) ✆ 01 40 15 97 39 – ▤. AE GB G 1
closed August, Saturday and Sunday – **Meals** 170 ♁.

X **Chez Georges,** 1 r. Mail (2nd) ✆ 01 42 60 07 11, bistro – ▤. AE GB G 1
closed 4 to 24 August and Sunday – **Meals** a la carte 200/330.

X **La Poule au Pot,** 9 r. Vauvilliers (1st) ✆ 01 42 36 32 96, bistro – GB. ✻ H 1
Meals (dinner only) 160 and a la carte 210/280.

X **Lescure,** 7 r. Mondovi (1st) ✆ 01 42 60 18 91, bistro – GB G 1
closed August, Saturday dinner and Sunday – **Meals** 105 and a la carte 90/200.

X **Le Souletin,** 6 r. Vrillière (1st) ✆ 01 42 61 43 78, bistro – GB G 1
closed Sunday and Bank Holidays – **Meals** a la carte 160/230.

Entre Ciel et Terre, 5 r. Hérold (1st) ✆ 01 45 08 49 84, no smoking rest. – GB G 14
closed August, Saturday and Sunday – **Meals** Vegetarian rest. 87 and a la carte 120/180.

Victoire Suprême du Coeur, 41 r. Bourdonnais (1st) ✆ 01 40 41 93 95, Fax 01 40 41 94 57 – GB H 14
closed 10 to 16 April, 15 to 31 August and Sunday – **Meals** - Vegetarian rest. - 65 (lunch)/82.

Bastille, République, Hôtel de Ville.

3rd, 4th and 11th arrondissements.
3rd: ✉ 75003
4th: ✉ 75004
11th: ✉ 75011

Pavillon de la Reine without rest, 28 pl. Vosges (3rd) ✆ 01 42 77 96 40, Fax 01 42 77 63 06 – AE GB JCB J 17
95 – **31 rm** 1600/1950, 14 suites, 10 duplex.

Jeu de Paume without rest, 54 r. St-Louis-en-l'Ile (4th) ✆ 01 43 26 14 18, Fax 01 40 46 02 76, « 17C tennis court » – 30. AE GB JCB K 16
80 – **32 rm** 895/1350.

Bretonnerie without rest, 22 r. Ste-Croix-de-la-Bretonnerie (4th) ✆ 01 48 87 77 63, Fax 01 42 77 26 78 – GB. J 16
closed 28 July-24 August – 50 – **27 rm** 650/780, 3 suites.

Bel Air M without rest, 5/7 r. Rampon (11th) ✆ 01 47 00 41 57, Fax 01 47 00 21 56 – AE GB JCB. G 17
45 – **48 rm** 540/610.

Caron de Beaumarchais M without rest, 12 r. Vieille-du-Temple (4th) ✆ 01 42 72 34 12, Fax 01 42 72 34 63 – AE GB JCB J 16
48 – **19 rm** 620/730.

Méridional without rest, 36 bd Richard-Lenoir (11th) ✆ 01 48 05 75 00, Fax 01 43 57 42 85 – AE GB JCB J 18
45 – **36 rm** 600.

Beaubourg without rest, 11 r. S. Le Franc (4th) ✆ 01 42 74 34 24, Fax 01 42 78 68 11 – AE GB. H 15
38 – **28 rm** 590/700.

Rivoli Notre Dame without rest, 19 r. Bourg Tibourg (4th) ✆ 01 42 78 47 39, Fax 01 40 29 07 00 – AE GB JCB. J 16
40 – **31 rm** 500/680.

Verlain without rest, 97 r. St-Maur (11th) ✆ 01 43 57 44 88, Fax 01 43 57 32 06 – AE GB JCB G 19
40 – **38 rm** 490/520.

Lutèce without rest, 65 r. St-Louis-en-l'Ile (4th) ✆ 01 43 26 23 52, Fax 01 43 29 60 25 – AE GB. K 16
45 – **23 rm** 830/850.

Stella M without rest, 14 r. Neuve St-Pierre (4th) ✆ 01 44 59 28 50, Fax 01 44 59 28 79 – AE GB JCB J 17
45 – **20 rm** 556/662.

Gd H. Prieuré without rest, 20 r. Grand Prieuré (11th) ✆ 01 47 00 74 14, Fax 01 49 23 06 64 – AE GB. G 17
30 – **32 rm** 300/360.

Allegro République M without rest, 39 r. J.-P. Timbaud (11th) ✆ 01 48 06 64 97, Fax 01 48 05 03 38 – AE GB G 18
35 – **42 rm** 365/420.

Croix de Malte M without rest, 5 r. Malte (11th) ✆ 01 48 05 09 36, Fax 01 43 57 02 54 – rm AE GB JCB H 17
45 – **29 rm** 470/535.

Beauséjour M without rest, 71 av. Parmentier (11th) ✆ 01 47 00 38 16, Fax 01 43 55 47 89 – AE GB JCB H 18
30 – **31 rm** 290/350.

XXXX L'Ambroisie (Pacaud), 9 pl. des Vosges (4th) ✆ 01 42 78 51 45 – AE GB. ✻ J 1
✻✻✻ *closed July, February Holidays, Sunday and Monday* – **Meals** a la carte 720/1 030
Spec. Charlotte de foie gras de canard landais au fenouil épicé. Noix de ris de veau clouté au romarin, poêlée d'artichauts aux zestes de citron. Dacquoise au praliné, giboulée d fruits rouges.

XXX **Miravile,** 72 quai Hôtel de Ville (4th) ✆ 01 42 74 72 22, Fax 01 42 74 67 55 – ▤. A GB J 1
closed 5 to 20 August, Saturday lunch and Sunday – **Meals** 240 and a la carte 290/42

XXX **Ambassade d'Auvergne,** 22 r. Grenier St-Lazare (3rd) ✆ 01 42 72 31 2 Fax 01 42 78 85 47 – ▤. AE GB H 1
Meals 160 and a la carte 190/340.

XX **Benoît,** 20 r. St-Martin (4th) ✆ 01 42 72 25 76, Fax 01 42 72 45 68, bistro J 1
✻ *closed August* – **Meals** 200 (lunch)and a la carte 330/470
Spec. Terrine de foie gras de canard. Steak de lotte au poivre. Aiguillette de bœuf mod aux carottes.

XX **Bofinger,** 5 r. Bastille (4th) ✆ 01 42 72 87 82, Fax 01 42 72 97 68, brasserie, « Bell Epoque decor » – AE ⓓ GB J 1
Meals 169 b.i. and a la carte 190/300.

XX **Pyrénées Cévennes "Chez Philippe",** 106 r. Folie-Méricourt (11th ✆ 01 43 57 33 78, Fax 01 43 57 66 17 – ▤. AE ⓓ GB G 1
closed August, Saturday and Sunday – **Meals** a la carte 230/350.

XX **A Sousceyrac** (Asfaux), 35 r. Faidherbe (11th) ✆ 01 43 71 65 30, Fax 01 40 09 79 7
✻ – ▤. AE ⓓ GB J 1
closed August, Saturday lunch and Sunday – **Meals** 175 b.i. and a la carte 240/340
Spec. Ris de veau aux pleurotes. Cassoulet. Lièvre à la royale "Gaston Richard" (season

XX **L'Excuse,** 14 r. Charles V (4th) ✆ 01 42 77 98 97, Fax 01 42 77 88 55 – AE GB J 1
closed 10 to 17 August and Sunday – **Meals** 165 (lunch)/185 and a la carte 280/400

XX **Thaï Elephant,** 43 r. Roquette (11th) ✆ 01 47 00 42 00, Fax 01 47 00 45 44, « Typic decor » – ▤. AE ⓓ GB J 1
closed Saturday lunch – **Meals** - Thai rest. - 150 (lunch), 275/300 and a la carte 190/27

XX **L'Alisier,** 26 r. Montmorency (3rd) ✆ 01 42 72 31 04, Fax 01 42 72 74 83 – GB ✻ H 1
closed August, Saturday and Sunday – **Meals** 185 and a la carte 250/400.

XX **L'Aiguière,** 37bis r. Montreuil (11th) ✆ 01 43 72 42 32, Fax 01 43 72 96 36 – ▤. AE ⓓ GB K 2
closed Saturday lunch and Sunday – **Meals** 135/248 and a la carte 260/380.

XX **Les Amognes,** 243 r. Fg St-Antoine (11th) ✆ 01 43 72 73 05 – GB K 2
closed 2 to 20 August, Monday lunch and Sunday – **Meals** 180.

XX **La Table Richelieu,** 276 bd Voltaire (11th) ✆ 01 43 72 31 23 – ▤. AE GB K 2
closed Saturday lunch and Monday – **Meals** 149 b.i./260 and a la carte 220/320.

XX **Chardenoux,** 1 r. J. Vallès (11th) ✆ 01 43 71 49 52, bistro, « Early 20C decor » – A ⓓ GB. ✻ K 2
closed August, Saturday lunch and Sunday – **Meals** a la carte 160/250.

X **Bistrot du Dôme,** 2 r. Bastille (4th) ✆ 01 48 04 88 44, Fax 01 48 04 00 59 – ▤. A GB J 1
Meals - Seafood - a la carte 170/270.

X **Au Bascou,** 38 r. Réaumur (3rd) ✆ 01 42 72 69 25, bistro – AE GB G 1
closed August, Saturday lunch and Sunday – **Meals** a la carte 180/240.

X **Le Petit Bofinger,** 6 r. Bastille (4th) ✆ 01 42 72 05 23, Fax 01 42 72 97 68 – ▤. A ⓓ GB J 1
Meals 89 b.i. (lunch)/128 b.i..

X **Le Grizzli,** 7 r. St-Martin (4th) ✆ 01 48 87 77 56, ✻, bistro – AE GB J 1
closed Sunday – **Meals** 120 (lunch)/155 and a la carte 160/250.

X **Astier,** 44 r. J.-P. Timbaud (11th) ✆ 01 43 57 16 35, bistro – GB G 1
closed 12 to 22 April, August, 15 to 31 December, Saturday, Sunday and Bank Holiday – **Meals** 135.

X **Le Maraîcher,** 5 r. Beautreillis (4th) ✆ 01 42 71 42 49 – GB K 1
closed 15 July-15 August, Christmas-New Year, Saturday lunch, Monday lunch and Sunda – **Meals** 180/285 and a la carte 190/260.

X **Le Monde des Chimères,** 69 r. St-Louis-en-l'Ile (4th) ✆ 01 43 54 45 27 Fax 01 43 29 84 88 – GB K 1
closed Sunday and Monday – **Meals** 89 (lunch)/160 and a la carte 250/390.

X **Le Relais St-Paul,** 33 r. F. Miron (4th) ✆ 01 48 87 34 20 – GB J 1
closed August, February Holidays, Saturday lunch and Sunday – **Meals** 90 (lunch)/135 an a la carte 180/240.

Anjou-Normandie, 13 r. Folie-Méricourt (11th) ☎ 01 47 00 30 59 – GB H 18
closed August, Saturday and Sunday – **Meals** (lunch only) 141/200 and a la carte 160/280.

Les Fernandises, 19 r. Fontaine au Roi (11th) ☎ 01 48 06 16 96, bistro – GB G 18
closed 4 to 25 August, Sunday and Monday – **Meals** 100 (lunch)/130 and a la carte 160/260.

Quartier Latin, Luxembourg, St-Germain-des-Prés.

5th and 6th arrondissements.
5th: ✉ 75005
6th: ✉ 75006

Lutétia, 45 bd Raspail (6th) ☎ 01 49 54 46 46, Fax 01 49 54 46 00 – ☎ – 300. AE GB K 12
see ***Le Paris*** below - - ***Brasserie Lutétia*** ☎ 01 49 54 46 76 **Meals** 180/295 – 130 – **225 rm** 1490/1900, 30 suites.

Relais Christine M without rest, 3 r. Christine (6th) ☎ 01 43 26 71 80, Fax 01 43 26 89 38 – rm ☎. AE GB JCB J 14
95 – **36 rm** 1630/2000, 15 duplex.

Relais St-Germain M without rest, 9 carrefour de l'Odéon (6th) ☎ 01 43 29 12 05, Fax 01 46 33 45 30, « Attractive interior » – kitchenette ☎. AE GB JCB K 13
22 rm 1280/1950.

Relais Médicis M without rest, 23 r. Racine (6th) ☎ 01 43 26 00 60, Fax 01 40 46 83 39, « Tasteful decor » – ☎. AE GB JCB K 13
16 rm 930/1480.

Holiday Inn Saint Germain des Prés M without rest, 92 r. Vaugirard (6th) ☎ 01 42 22 00 56, Fax 01 42 22 05 39 – rm ☎. AE GB JCB L 12
75 – **134 rm** 940/1030.

Abbaye St-Germain without rest, 10 r. Cassette (6th) ☎ 01 45 44 38 11, Fax 01 45 48 07 86 – ☎. AE GB. K 12
42 rm 950/1500, 4 duplex.

Left Bank St-Germain without rest, 9 r. Ancienne Comédie (6th) ☎ 01 43 54 01 70, Fax 01 43 26 17 14 – ☎. AE GB JCB. K 13
30 – **30 rm** 895/990.

Madison M without rest, 143 bd St-Germain (6th) ☎ 01 40 51 60 00, Fax 01 40 51 60 01 – ☎. AE GB JCB J 13
55 rm 760/1500.

Victoria Palace without rest, 6 r. Blaise-Desgoffe (6th) ☎ 01 45 49 70 00, Fax 01 45 49 23 75 – rm ☎. AE GB JCB L 11
95 – **76 rm** 840/2000, 3 suites.

Sainte Beuve M without rest, 9 r. Ste-Beuve (6th) ☎ 01 45 48 20 07, Fax 01 45 48 67 52 – ☎. AE GB JCB L 12
80 – **22 rm** 700/1550.

Angleterre without rest, 44 r. Jacob (6th) ☎ 01 42 60 34 72, Fax 01 42 60 16 93 – ☎. AE GB. J 13
50 – **24 rm** 630/1100, 3 suites.

Littré without rest, 9 r. Littré (6th) ☎ 01 45 44 38 68, Fax 01 45 44 88 13 – ☎ – 25. AE GB JCB. L 11
50 – **93 rm** 990/1000, 4 suites.

St-Grégoire M without rest, 43 r. Abbé Grégoire (6th) ☎ 01 45 48 23 23, Fax 01 45 48 33 95 – ☎. AE GB JCB. L 12
60 – **20 rm** 790/1390.

Latitudes St-Germain M without rest, 7-11 r. St-Benoit (6th) ☎ 01 42 61 53 53, Fax 01 49 27 09 33 – ☎. AE GB J 13
72 – **117 rm** 1060.

La Villa M without rest, 29 r. Jacob (6th) ☎ 01 43 26 60 00, Fax 01 46 34 63 63, « Contemporary decor » – rm ☎. AE GB J 13
80 – **29 rm** 900/1800, 3 suites.

St-Germain-des-Prés without rest, 36 r. Bonaparte (6th) ✆ 01 43 26 00
Fax 01 40 46 83 63 – 🛗 ▤ rm 📺 ☎. AE GB J
☕ 50 – **30 rm** 750/1300.

Les Rives de Notre-Dame M without rest, 15 quai St-Michel (5th) ✆ 01 43 54 81
Fax 01 43 26 27 09, ≤ – 🛗 ⚟ rm ▤ 📺 ☎. AE ① GB JCB J
☕ 85 – **10 rm** 950/2500.

Ferrandi without rest, 92 r. Cherche-Midi (6th) ✆ 01 42 22 97 40, Fax 01 45 44 89
– 🛗 ▤ 📺 ☎. AE ① GB JCB L
☕ 60 – **41 rm** 480/980.

Villa des Artistes M ⛰ without rest, 9 r. Grande Chaumière (6th) ✆ 01 43 26 60
Fax 01 43 54 73 70 – 🛗 ▤ 📺 ☎. AE ① GB JCB. ✻ L
59 rm ☕ 660/860.

Panthéon without rest, 19 pl. Panthéon (5th) ✆ 01 43 54 32 95, Fax 01 43 26 64
≤ – 🛗 ▤ 📺 ☎. AE ① GB JCB. ✻ L
closed 3 to 24 August – ☕ 45 – **34 rm** 680/780.

Grands Hommes without rest, 17 pl. Panthéon (5th) ✆ 01 46 34 19 6
Fax 01 43 26 67 32, ≤ – 🛗 ▤ 📺 ☎. AE ① GB JCB. ✻ L
☕ 45 – **32 rm** 680/780.

Le Régent M without rest, 61 r. Dauphine (6th) ✆ 01 46 34 59 80, Fax 01 40 51 05
– 🛗 ▤ 📺 ☎. AE ① GB JCB J
☕ 55 – **25 rm** 750/1000.

Résidence Henri IV M without rest, 50 r. Bernardins (5th) ✆ 01 44 41 31 8
Fax 01 46 33 93 22 – 🛗 kitchenette 📺 ☎. AE ① GB JCB. ✻ K
☕ 40 – **8 rm** 630/800, 5 suites.

de Buci M without rest, 6 r. Buci (6th) ✆ 01 43 26 89 22, Fax 01 46 33 80 31 – 🛗
☎ ♿. AE ① GB JCB. ✻ J
☕ 70 – **24 rm** 950/1300.

Odéon H. M without rest, 3 r. Odéon (6th) ✆ 01 43 25 90 67, Fax 01 43 25 55 98
🛗 ▤ 📺 ☎. AE ① GB JCB. ✻ K
☕ 55 – **33 rm** 706/1312.

de Fleurie without rest, 32 r. Grégoire de Tours (6th) ✆ 01 53 73 70 0
Fax 01 53 73 70 20 – 🛗 ▤ 📺 ☎. AE ① GB. ✻ K
☕ 50 – **29 rm** 650/1200.

Prince de Conti M without rest, 8 r. Guénégaud (6th) ✆ 01 44 07 30 4
Fax 01 44 07 36 34 – 🛗 ⚟ rm ▤ 📺 ☎ ♿. AE ① GB. ✻ J
☕ 60 – **26 rm** 750/990.

Relais St-Sulpice M ⛰ without rest, 3 r. Garancière (6th) ✆ 01 46 33 99 0
Fax 01 46 33 00 10 – 🛗 ▤ 📺 ☎ ♿. AE ① GB JCB. ✻ K
☕ 50 – **26 rm** 900/1200.

Jardins du Luxembourg M ⛰ without rest, 5 imp. Royer-Collard (5t
✆ 01 40 46 08 88, Fax 01 40 46 02 28 – 🛗 ⚟ rm ▤ 📺 ☎ ♿. AE ① GB JC
✻ L
☕ 50 – **25 rm** 780/820.

Belloy St-Germain M without rest, 2 r. Racine (6th) ✆ 01 46 34 26 5
Fax 01 46 34 66 18 – 🛗 📺 ☎. AE GB JCB K
☕ 50 – **50 rm** 450/910.

des Saints-Pères without rest, 65 r. Sts-Pères (6th) ✆ 01 45 44 50 0
Fax 01 45 44 90 83 – 🛗 ▤ 📺 ☎. AE GB. ✻ J
☕ 55 – **36 rm** 550/1250, 3 suites.

Sully St-Germain M without rest, 31 r. Écoles (5th) ✆ 01 43 26 56 0
Fax 01 43 29 74 42, 🏋 – 🛗 ▤ 📺 ☎. AE ① GB JCB. ✻ K
☕ 50 – **56 rm** 600/950.

Royal St-Michel M without rest, 3 bd St-Michel (5th) ✆ 01 44 07 06 0
Fax 01 44 07 36 25 – 🛗 ▤ 📺 ☎. AE ① GB JCB K
☕ 45 – **39 rm** 790/1160.

de l'Odéon without rest, 13 r. St-Sulpice (6th) ✆ 01 43 25 70 11, Fax 01 43 29 97 3
« 16C house » – 🛗 ▤ 📺 ☎. AE ① GB JCB K
☕ 55 – **29 rm** 660/950.

Select M without rest, 1 pl. Sorbonne (5th) ✆ 01 46 34 14 80, Fax 01 46 34 51 79
🛗 ▤ 📺 ☎. AE ① GB JCB K
☕ 40 – **67 rm** 650/890.

Jardin de l'Odéon M without rest, 7 r. Casimir Delavigne (6th) ✆ 01 46 34 23 9
Fax 01 43 25 28 12 – 🛗 📺 ☎ ♿. AE GB JCB K
☕ 50 – **41 rm** 606/1012.

Clos Médicis without rest, 56 r. Monsieur Le Prince (6th) 01 43 29 10 80, Fax 01 43 54 26 90 – rm . AE GB JCB K 14
65 – **38 rm** 790/990.

St-Christophe without rest, 17 r. Lacépède (5th) 01 43 31 81 54, Fax 01 43 31 12 54 – . AE GB L 15
50 – **31 rm** 650.

Au Manoir St-Germain des Prés without rest, 153 bd St-Germain (6th) 01 42 22 21 65, Fax 01 45 48 22 25 – rm . AE GB JCB J 12
40 – **32 rm** 750/990.

Aramis St-Germain without rest, 124 r. Rennes (6th) 01 45 48 03 75, Fax 01 45 44 99 29 – – 30. AE GB JCB. L 12
45 – **42 rm** 550/850.

Parc St-Séverin without rest, 22 r. Parcheminerie (5th) 01 43 54 32 17, Fax 01 43 54 70 71 – . AE GB JCB. K 14
50 – **27 rm** 500/1500.

Notre Dame without rest, 1 quai St-Michel (5th) 01 43 54 20 43, Fax 01 43 26 61 75, – . AE GB JCB K 14
40 – **23 rm** 590/790, 3 duplex.

Jardin de Cluny without rest, 9 r. Sommerard (5th) 01 43 54 22 66, Fax 01 40 51 03 36 – . AE GB JCB. K 14
50 – **40 rm** 665/800.

Marronniers without rest, 21 r. Jacob (6th) 01 43 25 30 60, Fax 01 40 46 83 56 – . GB. J 13
45 – **37 rm** 715/865.

Sèvres Azur without rest, 22 r. Abbé-Grégoire (6th) 01 45 48 84 07, Fax 01 42 84 01 55 – . AE GB JCB K 11-12
38 – **31 rm** 435/490.

Albe without rest, 1 r. Harpe (5th) 01 46 34 09 70, Fax 01 40 46 85 70 – rm . AE GB JCB. K 14
45 – **45 rm** 514/750.

Maxim without rest, 28 r. Censier (5th) 01 43 31 16 15, Fax 01 43 31 93 87 – . AE GB JCB. M 15
45 – **36 rm** 470/535.

Familia without rest, 11 r. Écoles (5th) 01 43 54 55 27, Fax 01 43 29 61 77 – . AE GB. K-L 15
35 – **30 rm** 370/490.

California H. without rest, 32 r. Écoles (5th) 01 46 34 12 90, Fax 01 46 34 75 52 – . AE GB K 14-15
45 – **44 rm** 520/700.

La Sorbonne without rest, 6 r. Victor Cousin (5th) 01 43 54 58 08, Fax 01 40 51 05 18 – rm . AE GB K 14
35 – **37 rm** 425/500.

Tour d'Argent (Terrail), 15 quai Tournelle (5th) 01 43 54 23 31, Fax 01 44 07 12 04, Notre-Dame, « Small museum showing the development of eating utensils. In the cellar : an illustrated history of wine » – . AE GB JCB K 16
closed Monday – **Meals** 395 (lunch)and a la carte 750/960
Spec. Quenelles de brochet "André Terrail". Caneton "Tour d'Argent". Crêpes "Belle Époque".

Jacques Cagna, 14 r. Grands Augustins (6th) 01 43 26 49 39, Fax 01 43 54 54 48, « Old Parisian house » – . AE GB JCB J 14
closed 3 to 24 August, 23 December-2 January, Saturday lunch and Sunday – **Meals** 270 (lunch)and a la carte 420/650
Spec. Lotte en cocotte à l'estragon. Poularde de Houdan en deux services. Gibier (season).

Paris - Hôtel Lutétia, 45 bd Raspail (6th) 01 49 54 46 90, Fax 01 49 54 46 00, « "Art Deco" decor » – . AE GB K 12
closed 26 July-24 August, Saturday and Sunday – **Meals** 260 (lunch), 360/565 and a la carte 400/480
Spec. Turbot cuit dans le sel de Guérande. Jarret de veau cuit en cocotte. Le "tout chocolat".

Relais Louis XIII (Martinez), 8 r. Grands Augustins (6th) 01 43 26 75 96, Fax 01 44 07 07 80, « Historical house, 16C cellar » – . AE GB JCB J 14
closed 3 to 25 August, Monday lunch and Sunday – **Meals** 195 (lunch)/250 and a la carte 260/370
Spec. Choux farcis au saumon légèrement fumé. Dos de Saint-Pierre, ravigote de pied de porc et ragoût de haricots tarbais. Millefeuille à la vanille.

XXX **Le Procope,** 13 r. Ancienne Comédie (6th) ✆ 01 40 46 79 00, Fax 01 40 46 79 (
« Former 18C literary café » – ▤. AE ⓓ GB K
Meals 106 (lunch)/185 and a la carte 170/350 ♨.

XX **Aub. des Deux Signes,** 46 r. Galande (5th) ✆ 01 43 25 46 56, Fax 01 46 33 20
« Medieval decor » – AE ⓓ GB JCB K
closed August, Saturday lunch and Sunday – **Meals** 150/230 and a la carte 300/42(

XX **Campagne et Provence,** 25 quai Tournelle (5th) ✆ 01 43 54 05
Fax 01 43 29 74 93 – ▤. GB. ✂ K
closed Monday lunch, Saturday lunch and Sunday – **Meals** 158 (lunch)and a la carte 200/3(

XX **Le Chat Grippé,** 87 r. Assas (6th) ✆ 01 43 54 70 00, Fax 01 43 26 42 05 – ▤. AE
JCB. ✂ LM
closed 20 July-20 August, Saturday lunch and Monday – **Meals** 160/200.

XX **Yugaraj,** 14 r. Dauphine (6th) ✆ 01 43 26 44 91, Fax 01 46 33 50 77 – ▤. AE ⓓ
JCB. ✂ J
Meals - Indian rest. - 130 (lunch), 180/220 and a la carte 230/260.

XX **La Truffière,** 4 r. Blainville (5th) ✆ 01 46 33 29 82, Fax 01 46 33 64 74 – ▤. AE ⓓ
closed Monday – **Meals** 98 (lunch), 140/198 ♨. L

XX **Dodin-Bouffant,** 25 r. F.-Sauton (5th) ✆ 01 43 25 25 14, Fax 01 43 29 52 61 – ▤.
ⓓ GB K
closed Saturday lunch and Sunday – **Meals** 180 b.i./245 b.i. and a la carte 240/410.

XX **Marty,** 20 av. Gobelins (5th) ✆ 01 43 31 39 51, Fax 01 43 37 63 70, brasserie – AE
GB JCB M
Meals 192/288 b.i. and a la carte 190/300.

XX **La Timonerie** (de Givenchy), 35 quai Tournelle (5th) ✆ 01 43 25 44 42 – GB
✿ *closed August, Monday lunch and Sunday* – **Meals** 250 (lunch)/350 K
Spec. Foie gras rôti sur pomme de terre séchée au four. Sandre rôti, choux et pomm
de terre en vinaigrette. Tarte fine au chocolat.

XX **Mavrommatis,** 42 r. Daubenton (5th) ✆ 01 43 31 17 17, Fax 01 43 36 13 08 – ▤.
✂ M
closed Monday – **Meals** - Greek rest. - 120 (lunch)/140 and a la carte 170/220.

XX **Bistrot d'Alex,** 2 r. Clément (6th) ✆ 01 43 54 09 53 – ▤. AE GB K
closed 24 December-2 January, Saturday lunch and Sunday – **Meals** 140/170 and a la car
160/270.

XX **Joséphine "Chez Dumonet",** 117 r. Cherche Midi (6th) ✆ 01 45 48 52
Fax 01 42 84 06 83, bistro – AE GB L
closed August, Saturday and Sunday – a la carte 210/560 - ***La Rôtisserie:*** ✆ 01 42 22 81
(closed July, Monday and Tuesday) **Meals** 150 b.i. and a la carte approx. 180.

XX **Le Rond de Serviette,** 97 r. Cherche-Midi (6th) ✆ 01 45 44 01 02, Fax 01 42 22 50
– ▤. AE ⓓ GB JCB L
closed 2 to 24 August, Saturday lunch and Sunday – **Meals** 132 b.i. (lunch), 168/250 b

XX **Chez Toutoune,** 5 r. Pontoise (5th) ✆ 01 43 26 56 81 – AE GB K
closed Monday lunch – **Meals** 118 (lunch)/180.

XX **L'Arrosée,** 12 r. Guisarde (6th) ✆ 01 43 54 66 59, Fax 01 43 54 66 59 – ▤. AE ⓓ
JCB. ✂ K
closed Saturday lunch and Sunday lunch – **Meals** 150/210 and a la carte 270/500.

XX **Chez Maître Paul,** 12 r. Monsieur-le-Prince (6th) ✆ 01 43 54 74 59, Fax 01 46 34 58
– AE ⓓ GB JCB K
closed Saturday lunch and Sunday in July-August – **Meals** 155/190 b.i. and a la car
180/340.

XX **Les Bouchons de François Clerc,** 12 r. Hôtel Colbert (5th) ✆ 01 43 54 15
Fax 01 46 34 68 07 – AE GB K
closed 13 to 20 August, Saturday lunch and Sunday – **Meals** 117 b.i. (lunch)/219.

XX **La Bastide Odéon,** 7 r. Corneille (6th) ✆ 01 43 26 03 65, Fax 01 44 07 28 93 – GB.
closed 3 to 25 August, Sunday and Monday – **Meals** 180. K

XX **Inagiku,** 14 r. Pontoise (5th) ✆ 01 43 54 70 07, Fax 01 40 51 74 44 – ▤. GB K
closed 1 to 15 August and Sunday – **Meals** - Japanese rest. - 88 (lunch), 148/248 and
la carte 230/320.

XX **L'O à la Bouche,** 157 bd Montparnasse (6th) ✆ 01 43 26 26 53, Fax 01 43 26 40 43 –
closed 17 to 23 March, 3 to 25 August, 1 to 9 January, Sunday and Monday – **Meals** 1
(lunch), 140/180. M

X **L'Épi Dupin,** 11 r. Dupin (6th) ✆ 01 42 22 64 56, Fax 01 42 22 30 42 – GB K
closed 1 to 25 August, Saturday and Sunday – **Meals** 153.

X **Au Grilladin,** 6 r. Mézières (6th) ✆ 01 45 48 30 38, Fax 01 45 48 30 38 – AE GB K
closed 26 July-26 August, 23 December-2 January, Monday lunch and Sunday – **Mea**
124/159 and a la carte 190/320.

Bouillon Racine, 3 r. Racine (6th) ✆ 01 44 32 15 60, Fax 01 44 32 15 61, brasserie, « "Art Nouveau" decor » – ▤. GB K 14
closed Sunday – **Meals** a la carte 150/250.

Les Bookinistes, 53 quai Grands Augustins (6th) ✆ 01 43 25 45 94, Fax 01 43 25 23 07 – ▤. AE GB JCB J 14
closed Sunday lunch and Saturday – **Meals** 160 and a la carte 200/260.

La Timbale St-Bernard, 16 r. Fossés St-Bernard (5th) ✆ 01 46 34 28 28, Fax 01 46 34 66 26 – AE ⓓ GB JCB K 15
closed 4 to 24 August, Saturday lunch and Sunday – **Meals** 98 (lunch), 168/250 b.i. and a la carte 170/250.

Le Palanquin, 12 r. Princesse (6th) ✆ 01 43 29 77 66 – GB K 13
closed Sunday – **Meals** - Vietnamese rest. - 70 (lunch), 105/148 and a la carte 150/210.

Moulin à Vent "Chez Henri", 20 r. Fossés-St-Bernard (5th) ✆ 01 43 54 99 37, bistrot – GB. ✻ K 15
closed August, Sunday and Monday – **Meals** a la carte 240/320.

Dominique, 19 r. Bréa (6th) ✆ 01 43 27 08 80, Fax 01 43 26 88 35 – AE ⓓ GB L 12
closed 20 July-20 August, Monday lunch and Sunday – **Meals** - Russian rest. - 150/180 b.i. and a la carte 190/300 ♁.

Rôtisserie d'en Face, 2 r. Christine (6th) ✆ 01 43 26 40 98, Fax 01 43 54 54 48 – ▤. AE ⓓ GB JCB – *closed Saturday lunch and Sunday* – **Meals** 159 (lunch)/210. J 14

Rôtisserie du Beaujolais, 19 quai Tournelle (5th) ✆ 01 43 54 17 47, Fax 01 44 07 12 04 – GB K 15
closed Monday – **Meals** a la carte 170/240.

Allard, 41 r. St-André-des-Arts (6th) ✆ 01 43 26 48 23, Fax 01 46 33 04 02, bistro – ▤. AE ⓓ GB JCB K 14
closed Sunday – **Meals** 150 (lunch)/200 and a la carte 240/420.

Moissonnier, 28 r. Fossés-St-Bernard (5th) ✆ 01 43 29 87 65, bistro – GB K 15
closed 1 August-2 September, February Holidays, Sunday dinner and Monday – **Meals** 150 and a la carte 180/290.

Atelier Maître Albert, 1 r. Maître Albert (5th) ✆ 01 46 33 13 78, Fax 01 44 07 01 86 – ▤. AE GB K 15
closed Monday lunch and Sunday – **Meals** 130 b.i. (lunch), 170/230 b.i..

Balzar, 49 r. Écoles (5th) ✆ 01 43 54 13 67, Fax 01 44 07 14 91, brasserie – ▤. AE GB
closed August – **Meals** a la carte 150/320.

La Cafetière, 21 r. Mazarine (6th) ✆ 01 46 33 76 90, Fax 01 43 25 76 90 – GB J 13
closed 3 to 24 August, 24 December-5 January and Sunday – **Meals** - Italian rest. - a la carte 180/220.

Valérie Tortu, 11 r. Grande Chaumière (6th) ✆ 01 46 34 07 58, Fax 01 46 34 06 84 – AE GB L 12
closed 10 to 30 August, Saturday lunch and Sunday – **Meals** 158 and a la carte 180/280.

Bistro de la Grille, 14 r. Mabillon (6th) ✆ 01 43 54 16 87, bistro – GB K 13
Meals 95 (lunch), 150/170 ♁.

Les Quatre et Une Saveurs, 72 r. Cardinal-Lemoine (5th) ✆ 01 43 26 88 80, Fax 01 43 26 90 07 – GB L 15
closed Monday – **Meals** - Vegetarian rest. - 120/130.

Faubourg-St-Germain, Invalides, École Militaire.

7th arrondissement.
7th: ✉ 75007

Montalembert Ⓜ, 3 r. Montalembert ✆ 01 45 49 68 68, Fax 01 45 49 69 49, 🍴, « Original decor » – |♿| ▤ 📺 ☎ – 🏛 25. AE ⓓ GB JCB J 12
Meals 170 (lunch), 215/300 and a la carte 220/370 – ☕ 100 – **51 rm** 1625/2080, 5 suites.

Duc de Saint-Simon 🐦 without rest, 14 r. St-Simon ✆ 01 44 39 20 20, Fax 01 45 48 68 25, « Tastefully furnished interior » – |♿| 📺 ☎. AE GB. ✻ J 11
☕ 70 – **29 rm** 1025/1425, 5 suites.

Cayré without rest, 4 bd Raspail ✆ 01 45 44 38 88, Fax 01 45 44 98 13 – rm AE GB JCB J 1
☐ 50 – **119 rm** 900.

Le Tourville M without rest, 16 av. Tourville ✆ 01 47 05 62 62, Fax 01 47 05 43 9 – TV ☎. AE GB J
☐ 60 – **30 rm** 890/1390.

Bellechasse M without rest, 8 r. Bellechasse ✆ 01 45 50 22 31, Fax 01 45 51 52 3 – rm TV ☎. AE GB JCB H 1
☐ 75 – **41 rm** 910.

La Bourdonnais, 111 av. La Bourdonnais ✆ 01 47 05 45 42, Fax 01 45 55 75 54 – TV ☎. AE GB JCB J
Meals see rest. ***La Cantine des Gourmets*** below – ☐ 40 – **57 rm** 510/690, 3 suite

Lenox Saint-Germain without rest, 9 r. Université ✆ 01 42 96 10 9 Fax 01 42 61 52 83 – TV ☎. AE GB JCB J 1
☐ 45 – **32 rm** 650/1100.

Splendid M without rest, 29 av. Tourville ✆ 01 45 51 29 29, Fax 01 44 18 94 60 – TV ☎. AE GB J
☐ 46 – **48 rm** 590/990.

Bourgogne et Montana without rest, 3 r. Bourgogne ✆ 01 45 51 20 2 Fax 01 45 56 11 98 – TV ☎. AE GB JCB H 1
☐ 70 – **28 rm** 690/930, 6 suites.

Les Jardins d'Eiffel M without rest, 8 r. Amélie ✆ 01 47 05 46 21, Fax 01 45 55 28 C – rm TV ☎. AE GB JCB H
☐ 60 – **80 rm** 700/960.

Eiffel Park H. M without rest, 17 bis r. Amélie ✆ 01 45 55 10 01, Fax 01 47 05 28 6 – TV ☎ – 25. AE GB JCB. J
☐ 55 – **36 rm** 650/695.

Verneuil St-Germain without rest, 8 r. Verneuil ✆ 01 42 60 82 14, Fax 01 42 61 40 3 – TV ☎. AE GB JCB. J 1
26 rm ☐ 700/950.

Muguet M without rest, 11 r. Chevert ✆ 01 47 05 05 93, Fax 01 45 50 25 37 – ☎. AE GB J
☐ 45 – **45 rm** 440/510.

du Cadran M without rest, 10 r. Champ-de-Mars ✆ 01 40 62 67 00, Fax 01 40 62 67 1 – TV ☎. AE GB. J
☐ 50 – **42 rm** 850/920.

Relais Bosquet without rest, 19 r. Champ-de-Mars ✆ 01 47 05 25 4 Fax 01 45 55 08 24 – TV ☎. AE GB J
☐ 53 – **40 rm** 760/810.

Sèvres Vaneau without rest, 86 r. Vaneau ✆ 01 45 48 73 11, Fax 01 45 49 27 74 rm TV ☎. AE GB JCB K 1
☐ 75 – **39 rm** 780/840.

St-Germain without rest, 88 r. Bac ✆ 01 49 54 70 00, Fax 01 45 48 26 89 – TV. GB. J 1
☐ 45 – **29 rm** 415/730.

de Varenne without rest, 44 r. Bourgogne ✆ 01 45 51 45 55, Fax 01 45 51 86 6 – TV ☎. AE GB J 1
☐ 46 – **24 rm** 560/710.

Beaugency without rest, 21 r. Duvivier ✆ 01 47 05 01 63, Fax 01 45 51 04 96 – ☎. AE GB J
☐ 40 – **30 rm** 600/700.

Bersoly's without rest, 28 r. Lille ✆ 01 42 60 73 79, Fax 01 49 27 05 55 – TV AE GB J 1
closed 11 to 24 August – ☐ 50 – **16 rm** 600/750.

Londres without rest, 1 r. Augereau ✆ 01 45 51 63 02, Fax 01 47 05 28 96 – TV AE GB JCB J
☐ 45 – **30 rm** 495/595.

France without rest, 102 bd La Tour Maubourg ✆ 01 47 05 40 49, Fax 01 45 56 96 7 – TV ☎. AE GB J
☐ 35 – **60 rm** 385/500.

Champ-de-Mars without rest, 7 r. Champ-de-Mars ✆ 01 45 51 52 3C Fax 01 45 51 64 36 – TV ☎. AE GB JCB. J
☐ 35 – **25 rm** 355/420.

L'Empereur without rest, 2 r. Chevert ✆ 01 45 55 88 02, Fax 01 45 51 88 54 – |♦| TV ☎. AE GB J 9
☐ 37 – **38 rm** 421/466.

Turenne without rest, 20 av. Tourville ✆ 01 47 05 99 92, Fax 01 45 56 06 04 – |♦| TV ☎. AE ① GB. ✻ J 9
☐ 38 – **34 rm** 320/525.

XXXX ✿ **Jules Verne,** Eiffel Tower : 2nd platform, lift in south leg ✆ 01 45 55 61 44, Fax 01 47 05 29 41, ← Paris – ▤. AE ① GB JCB. ✻ J 7
Meals 290 (lunch)/680 and a la carte 510/660
Spec. Petit pain soufflé aux gros tourteaux. Dos de turbot au jus de pommes vertes. Entrecôte de veau de Corrèze aux truffes.

XXXX ✿✿✿ **Arpège** (Passard), 84 r. Varenne ✆ 01 45 51 47 33, Fax 01 44 18 98 39 – ▤. AE ① GB JCB J 10
closed Sunday lunch and Saturday – **Meals** 320 (lunch)/690 and a la carte 480/680
Spec. Carpaccio de langoustines au caviar sevruga. Dragée de pigeonneau vendéen à l'hydromel. Tomate confite farcie aux douze saveurs (dessert).

XXXX ✿✿ **Le Divellec,** 107 r. Université ✆ 01 45 51 91 96, Fax 01 45 51 31 75 – ▤. AE ① GB JCB. ✻ H 10
closed Christmas-New Year, Sunday and Monday – **Meals** - Seafood - 290 (lunch)/390 (lunch) and a la carte 450/850
Spec. Huîtres spéciales frémies à la laitue de mer. Homard à la presse avec son corail. Escalope de turbot braisée aux truffes.

XXX ✿ **Paul Minchelli,** 54 bd La Tour Maubourg ✆ 01 47 05 89 86, Fax 01 45 56 03 84 – ▤. GB
closed August, 24 December-2 January, Sunday, Monday and Bank Holidays – **Meals** - Seafood - a la carte 430/550 J 9
Spec. Homard au miel et aux épices. Filet de bar au vert. Darnes de lotte pochée, riz noir et aïoli de pommes de terre (spring-summer).

XXX **La Flamberge,** 12 av. Rapp ✆ 01 47 05 91 37, Fax 01 45 50 31 27 – ▤. AE ① GB
closed August, 20 to 28 December, Saturday lunch and Sunday – **Meals** 270 b.i. and a la carte 280/410. H 8

XXX ✿ **La Cantine des Gourmets,** 113 av. La Bourdonnais ✆ 01 47 05 47 96, Fax 01 45 51 09 29 – ▤. AE GB J 9
Meals 240 b.i. (lunch), 320/420 and a la carte 340/480 🍷
Spec. Petits choux farcis de langoustines à la moëlle et fleur de sel. Volaille de Houdan pochée-poêlée, ravioles de foie gras. Chiboust à la vanille, petits farcis de clémentines.

XXX **La Boule d'Or,** 13 bd La Tour Maubourg ✆ 01 47 05 50 18, Fax 01 47 05 91 21 – ▤. AE ① GB JCB H 10
closed Saturday lunch – **Meals** 175/210.

XXX **Le Petit Laurent,** 38 r. Varenne ✆ 01 45 48 79 64, Fax 01 45 44 15 95 – AE ① GB J 11
closed August, Saturday lunch and Sunday – **Meals** 185/250 and a la carte 270/390.

XX ✿ **Le Bellecour** (Goutagny), 22 r. Surcouf ✆ 01 45 51 46 93, Fax 01 45 50 30 11 – ▤. AE ① GB H 9
closed August, Saturday except dinner from 15 September-15 July and Sunday – **Meals** 160 (lunch)/220
Spec. Truffière de Saint-Jacques (15 December-15 April). Quenelle de brochet "maison". Lièvre à la cuillère (15 October-15 January).

XX ✿ **Récamier** (Cantegrit), 4 r. Récamier ✆ 01 45 48 86 58, Fax 01 42 22 84 76, 🏖 – ▤. AE ① GB JCB K 12
closed Sunday – **Meals** 300 b.i. and a la carte 280/450
Spec. Oeufs en meurette. Mousse de brochet sauce Nantua. Sauté de bœuf bourguignon.

XX **La Maison de l'Amérique Latine,** 217 bd St-Germain ✆ 01 45 49 33 23, Fax 01 40 49 03 94, 🏖, « 18C mansion, terrace opening onto the garden » – AE ① GB. ✻ J 11
closed 4 to 25 August, Saturday, Sunday and Bank Holidays – **Meals** (closed dinner from November-April) 195 (lunch)and a la carte 300/340.

XX **Beato,** 8 r. Malar ✆ 01 47 05 94 27 – ▤. AE GB H 9
closed 25 July-25 August, 21 to 29 December, Sunday and Monday – **Meals** - Italian rest. - 145 (lunch)and a la carte 240/350 🍷.

XX **Ferme St-Simon,** 6 r. St-Simon ✆ 01 45 48 35 74, Fax 01 40 49 07 31 – ▤. AE ① GB J 11
closed 2 to 17 August, Saturday lunch and Sunday – **Meals** 170 (lunch)/190 and a la carte 250/340.

XX **Vin sur Vin,** 18 r. Monttessuy ✆ 01 47 05 14 20, Fax 01 47 05 05 55 – ▤. GB H 8
closed 2 to 17 August, 23 December-3 January, Monday lunch, Saturday lunch and Sunday – **Meals** a la carte 270/370.

XX **Les Glénan,** 54 r. Bourgogne ☎ 01 47 05 96 65 – ▤. AE GB JCB J 1(
closed August, February Holidays, Saturday and Sunday – **Meals** - Seafood - 200 b.i. an
a la carte 280/360.

XX **Le Bamboche,** 15 r. Babylone ☎ 01 45 49 14 40, Fax 01 45 49 14 44 – AE GB K 1
closed 11 to 24 August, Saturday and Sunday – **Meals** 190 and a la carte 280/380.

XX **Gildo,** 153 r. Grenelle ☎ 01 45 51 54 12, Fax 01 45 51 57 42 – ▤. AE GB J
closed 27 July-25 August, Monday lunch and Sunday – **Meals** - Italian rest. - 149 (lunch)an
a la carte 250/390.

XX **D'Chez Eux,** 2 av. Lowendal ☎ 01 47 05 52 55, Fax 01 45 55 60 74 – AE ⓓ GB J
closed August and Sunday – **Meals** 265 and a la carte 210/410.

XX **Foc Ly,** 71 av. Suffren ☎ 01 47 83 27 12, Fax 01 46 24 48 46 – ▤. AE GB K
closed Monday in July-August – **Meals** - Chinese and Thai rest. - 160 b.i. (dinner)and a l
carte 150/290.

XX **Tan Dinh,** 60 r. Verneuil ☎ 01 45 44 04 84, Fax 01 45 44 36 93 J 1
closed August and Sunday – **Meals** - Vietnamese rest. - a la carte 240/280.

XX **Le Champ de Mars,** 17 av. La Motte-Picquet ☎ 01 47 05 57 99, Fax 01 44 18 94 6
– AE ⓓ GB J
closed 20 July-20 August and Monday – **Meals** 118/198 and a la carte 180/310.

X **Gaya Rive Gauche,** 44 r. Bac ☎ 01 45 44 73 73, Fax 01 42 60 04 54 – AE GB J 1
closed August, Sunday lunch and Bank Holidays – **Meals** - Seafood - a la carte 270/34(

X **Le P'tit Troquet,** 28 r. Exposition ☎ 01 47 05 80 39, Fax 01 47 05 80 39, bistro
GB J
closed 3 to 25 August, Saturday lunch and Sunday – **Meals** 149 and a la carte approx
170.

X **Les Olivades,** 41 av. Ségur ☎ 01 47 83 70 09, Fax 01 42 73 04 75 – AE GB K
closed August, Saturday lunch and Sunday – **Meals** 159/210.

X **Thoumieux** with rm, 79 r. St-Dominique ☎ 01 47 05 49 75, Fax 01 47 05 36 96, bras
serie – ▤ rest TV ☎. AE GB H
Meals 72/150 b.i. and a la carte 180/260 – ☐ 35 – **10 rm** 550/600.

X **Le Maupertu,** 94 bd La Tour Maubourg ☎ 01 45 51 37 96 – GB J 1
closed 10 to 31 August, Saturday lunch and Sunday – **Meals** 135 and a la carte 200/25(

X **Clémentine,** 62 av. Bosquet ☎ 01 45 51 41 16, Fax 01 45 55 76 79 – AE GB J
closed 17 to 31 August, Saturday lunch and Sunday – **Meals** 139/180 and a la cart
180/270.

X **L'Oeillade,** 10 r. St-Simon ☎ 01 42 22 01 60 – ▤. GB J 1
closed 15 to 22 August and Saturday lunch – **Meals** 158 and a la carte 200/280.

X **Chez Collinot,** 1 r. P. Leroux ☎ 01 45 67 66 42 – GB K 1
closed August, Saturday except dinner from September-June and Sunday – **Meals** 13

X **La Fontaine de Mars,** 129 r. St-Dominique ☎ 01 47 05 46 44, Fax 01 47 05 11 1
☂, bistro – AE GB J
closed Sunday – **Meals** a la carte 180/270.

X **La Table d'Eiffel,** 39 av. La Motte-Picquet ☎ 01 45 55 90 20, Fax 01 44 18 36 73
AE ⓓ GB JCB H
Meals 175 b.i.

X **Le Sédillot,** 2 r. Sédillot ☎ 01 45 51 95 82, « Art Nouveau decor » – AE GB H
closed 9 to 17 August, Saturday and Sunday – **Meals** 85/150 and a la carte 180,
300 ♁.

X **La Calèche,** 8 r. Lille ☎ 01 42 60 24 76, Fax 01 47 03 31 10 – ▤. AE ⓓ GB JCB
closed 7 to 31 August, 24 December-1 January, Saturday and Sunday – **Meals** 100/17
and a la carte 180/290. J 1

X **Aub. Bressane,** 16 av. La Motte-Picquet ☎ 01 47 05 98 37 – ▤. AE GB H
closed 11 to 17 August and Saturday lunch – **Meals** 139 b.i. and a la carte 160/260.

X **Du Côté 7ème,** 29 r. Surcouf ☎ 01 47 05 81 65, bistro – AE GB JCB H 9-1
closed 12 to 20 August and Monday – **Meals** 180 b.i..

X **Le Florimond,** 19 av. La Motte-Picquet ☎ 01 45 55 40 38 – GB H
closed 5 to 20 August, Saturday lunch and Sunday – **Meals** 105/157 and a la cart
180/280.

X **Au Bon Accueil,** 14 r. Monttessuy ☎ 01 47 05 46 11 – GB H
closed August, 21 to 28 December, Saturday lunch and Sunday – **Meals** 120 (lunch)/13
and a la carte approx. 220.

X **Apollon,** 24 r. J. Nicot ☎ 01 45 55 68 47, Fax 01 47 05 13 60 H
closed Sunday – **Meals** - Greek rest. - 128/210 b.i. and a la carte 160/250.

Champs-Élysées, St-Lazare, Madeleine.

8th arrondissement.
8th: ✉ 75008

Plaza Athénée, 25 av. Montaigne ☎ 01 53 67 66 65, Fax 01 53 67 66 66, – rm – 30 - 100. AE ⓓ GB JCB. rest G 9
see rest. ***Régence*** below ***-Relais-Plaza*** ☎ 01 53 67 64 00 *(closed 4 to 24 August)* **Meals** 290 and a la carte 320/500 – ***La Cour Jardin*** (terrace) *(May-September)* **Meals** 400/500 – 160 – **163 rm** 2950/4650, 42 suites.

Crillon, 10 pl. Concorde ☎ 01 44 71 15 00, Fax 01 44 71 15 02, – rm – 30 - 60. AE ⓓ GB JCB G 11
see ***Les Ambassadeurs*** below ***-L'Obélisque*** ☎ 01 44 71 15 15 *(closed August and Bank Holidays)* **Meals** 270 and a la carte approx. 300 – 155 – **118 rm** 2900/4100, 45 suites.

Bristol, 112 r. Fg St-Honoré ☎ 01 53 43 43 00, Fax 01 53 43 43 01, – rm – 30 - 60. AE ⓓ GB JCB. F 10
Meals see ***Bristol*** below – 170 – **153 rm** 2500/3950, 41 suites.

George V, 31 av. George-V ☎ 01 47 23 54 00, Fax 01 47 20 40 00, – – 30 - 600. AE ⓓ GB JCB. rest G 8
Les Princes *(closed 1 to 15 January)* **Meals** 280/380 and a la carte 330/460 – ***Le Grill*** ☎ 01 47 23 60 80 *(closed August, February Holidays, Saturday and Sunday)* **Meals** 195 and a la carte 220/320 – 150 – **219 rm** 1800/3900, 39 suites.

Royal Monceau, 37 av. Hoche ☎ 01 42 99 88 00, Fax 01 42 99 89 90, « Pool and fitness centre » – rm – 25 - 100. AE ⓓ GB JCB. E 8
see ***Le Jardin*** below ***- Carpaccio*** ☎ 01 42 99 98 90, Italian rest. *(closed August)* **Meals** a la carte 300/420 – 145 – **180 rm** 2500/3500.

Prince de Galles, 33 av. George-V ☎ 01 53 23 77 77, Fax 01 53 23 78 78, – rm – 25 - 100. AE ⓓ GB JCB. G 8
Jardin des Cygnes : **Meals** 260/320 and a la carte 360/520 – 155 – **138 rm** 2295/3485, 30 suites.

Vernet, 25 r. Vernet ☎ 01 44 31 98 00, Fax 01 44 31 85 69 – . AE ⓓ GB JCB. rest F 8
see ***Les Élysées*** below – 120 – **54 rm** 1650/2300, 3 suites.

de Vigny M without rest, 9 r. Balzac ☎ 01 42 99 80 80, Fax 01 42 99 80 40, « Tasteful decor » – rm . AE ⓓ GB JCB F 8
90 – **25 rm** 1900/2200, 12 suites.

Lancaster, 7 r. Berri ☎ 01 40 76 40 76, Fax 01 40 76 40 00, – rm . AE ⓓ GB JCB F 9
Meals (residents only) a la carte approx. 280 – 120 – **52 rm** 1800/2650, 8 suites.

San Régis, 12 r. J. Goujon ☎ 01 44 95 16 16, Fax 01 45 61 05 48, « Tasteful decor » – . AE ⓓ GB JCB. G 9
Meals 200/250 (except weekends)and a la carte 290/400 – 110 – **34 rm** 1650/2850, 10 suites.

Astor M, 11 r. d'Astorg ☎ 01 53 05 05 05, Fax 01 53 05 05 30, – rm rm . AE ⓓ GB JCB F 11
Meals see ***L'Astor*** below – 120 – **130 rm** 1790/2950, 4 suites.

La Trémoille, 14 r. La Trémoille ☎ 01 47 23 34 20, Fax 01 40 70 01 08 – – 25. AE ⓓ GB JCB G 9
Meals *(closed Saturday, Sunday and Bank Holidays)* 220 and a la carte 220/350 – 100 – **104 rm** 1950/2240, 3 suites.

Élysées Star M without rest, 19 r. Vernet ☎ 01 47 20 41 73, Fax 01 47 23 32 15 – rm – 30. AE ⓓ GB JCB F 8
90 – **38 rm** 1700/1900.

Balzac M without rest, 6 r. Balzac ☎ 01 44 35 18 00, Fax 01 44 35 18 05 – . AE ⓓ GB JCB F 8
see ***Pierre Gagnaire*** below – 90 – **56 rm** 1850/2200, 14 suites.

Sofitel Arc de Triomphe, 14 r. Beaujon ☎ 01 53 89 50 50, Fax 01 53 89 50 51 – rm – 40. AE ⓓ GB JCB F 8
Le Clovis ☎ 01 53 89 50 53 *(closed August, Saturday, Sunday and Bank Holidays)* **Meals** 235/500 and a la carte 340/480 – 120 – **135 rm** 1800/2700.

Golden Tulip St-Honoré M, 218 r. Fg St-Honoré ✆ 01 49 53 03 03, Fax 01 40 75 02 0 – kitchenette ⇔ rm – 140. AE GB JCB E
Relais Vermeer (closed August, Saturday lunch and Sunday) **Meals** 180/220 – 11 – **54 rm** 1500/1800, 18 suites.

Château Frontenac without rest, 54 r. P. Charron ✆ 01 53 23 13 1 Fax 01 53 23 13 01 – – 25. AE GB. G
85 – **102 rm** 950/1450, 4 suites.

Bedford, 17 r. de l'Arcade ✆ 01 44 94 77 77, Fax 01 44 94 77 97 – – 5 AE GB. rest F 1
Meals *(closed 2 to 31 August, Saturday and Sunday)* (lunch only) 200 a la carte 230/35 – 70 – **137 rm** 800/980, 11 suites.

Warwick M, 5 r. Berri ✆ 01 45 63 14 11, Fax 01 45 63 75 81 – ⇔ rm – 30 - 110. AE GB JCB. rest F
La Couronne ✆ 01 45 61 82 08 *(closed August, Saturday lunch, Sunday and Bank Holidays)* **Meals** 250/400 and a la carte 280/410 – 110 – **147 rm** 2100/2670, 5 suite

California, 16 r. Berri ✆ 01 43 59 93 00, Fax 01 45 61 03 62, « Important collection of paintings » – ⇔ rm – 25 - 80. AE GB JCB F
Meals *(closed August, Saturday and Sunday)* (lunch only) 170 – 120 – **147 rm** 1800/2200, 13 duplex.

Résidence du Roy M without rest, 8 r. François 1er ✆ 01 42 89 59 5 Fax 01 40 74 07 92 – kitchenette – 25. AE GB JCB G
90, 28 suites 1260/1740, 4 studios, 3 duplex.

Concorde St-Lazare, 108 r. St-Lazare ✆ 01 40 08 44 44, Fax 01 42 93 01 20, « 19th century lobby, remarkable billiards room » – ⇔ rm – 25 - 150. AE GB JCB. rest E
Café Terminus : **Meals** 148/198 b.i. and a la carte approx. 230, – 105 – **295 rm** 1300/1900, 5 suites.

Napoléon without rest, 40 av. Friedland ✆ 01 47 66 02 02, Fax 01 47 66 82 33 – ⇔ rm – 30 - 60. AE GB JCB F
90 – **70 rm** 1250/1950, 32 suites.

Queen Elizabeth, 41 av. Pierre-1er-de-Serbie ✆ 01 53 57 25 25, Fax 01 53 57 25 2 – ⇔ rm – 30. AE GB JCB G
Meals *(closed August and Sunday)* (lunch only) 170 b.i./230 b.i. – 90 – **53 rm** 1200/1850, 12 suites.

Beau Manoir without rest, 6 r. de l'Arcade ✆ 01 42 66 03 07, Fax 01 42 68 03 0 « Attractive interior » – . AE GB JCB F 1
29 rm 995/1200, 3 suites.

Sofitel Champs-Élysées M, 8 r. J. Goujon ✆ 01 43 59 52 41, Fax 01 49 53 08 4 – ⇔ rm – 200. AE GB JCB G
Les Saveurs *(closed Saturday and Sunday from September-June)* **Meals** a la carte 220/310 – 85 – **40 rm** 1500/1800.

Claridge-Bellman, 37 r. François 1er ✆ 01 47 23 54 42, Fax 01 47 23 08 84 – . AE GB. G
Meals *(closed August, Saturday and Sunday)* a la carte 170/290 – 70 – **42 rm** 1150/1350.

Rochester Champs-Élysées M without rest, 92 r. La Boétie ✆ 01 43 59 96 1 Fax 01 42 56 01 38 – – 25. AE GB. F
85 – **90 rm** 880/1180.

Montaigne M without rest, 6 av. Montaigne ✆ 01 47 20 30 50, Fax 01 47 20 94 – . AE GB JCB G
95 – **29 rm** 1300/1850.

Royal H. M without rest, 33 av. Friedland ✆ 01 43 59 08 14, Fax 01 45 63 69 92 – ⇔ rm . AE GB JCB F
95 – **58 rm** 1650/1950.

Chateaubriand M without rest, 6 r. Chateaubriand ✆ 01 40 76 00 5 Fax 01 40 76 09 22 – ⇔ rm . AE GB JCB. F
65 – **28 rm** 1200/1500.

Royal Alma without rest, 35 r. J. Goujon ✆ 01 42 25 83 30, Fax 01 45 63 68 64 – . AE GB JCB. G
95 – **61 rm** 1380/1620, 3 suites.

Élysées-Ponthieu and Résidence without rest, 24 r. Ponthieu ✆ 01 53 89 58 5 Fax 01 53 89 59 59 – kitchenette ⇔ rm . AE GB JCB F
75 – **92 rm** 800/985, 6 suites.

Powers without rest, 52 r. François 1er ✆ 01 47 23 91 05, Fax 01 49 52 04 63 – . AE GB JCB G
65 – **53 rm** 826/1392.

Résidence Monceau without rest, 85 r. Rocher ✆ 01 45 22 75 11, Fax 01 45 22 30 88 – 🛗 TV ☎ ♿. AE ⓓ GB JCB. ✻ E 11
☕ 50 – **51 rm** 700/875.

Waldorf Madeleine M without rest, 12 bd Malesherbes ✆ 01 42 65 72 06, Fax 01 40 07 10 45 – 🛗 ⚡ rm ▤ TV ☎. AE ⓓ GB JCB F 11
☕ 50 – **45 rm** 1100/1400.

Concortel without rest, 19 r. Pasquier ✆ 01 42 65 45 44, Fax 01 42 65 18 33 – 🛗 ▤ TV ☎. AE ⓓ GB F 11
☕ 50 – **46 rm** 500/750.

Mathurins M without rest, 43 r. Mathurins ✆ 01 44 94 20 94, Fax 01 44 94 00 44 – 🛗 ▤ TV ☎ ♿ 🚗. AE ⓓ GB. ✻ F 11
☕ 65 – **33 rm** 1000/1200, 3 suites.

Castiglione, 40 r. Fg St-Honoré ✆ 01 44 94 25 25, Fax 01 42 65 12 27 – 🛗 ▤ TV ☎ – 🏛 80. AE ⓓ GB G 11
Meals 125/160 – ☕ 60 – **114 rm** 1250/1500.

New Roblin and rest. Le Mazagran, 6 r. Chauveau-Lagarde ✆ 01 44 71 20 80, Fax 01 42 65 19 49 – 🛗 ▤ TV ☎. AE ⓓ GB JCB. ✻ rest F 11
Meals *(closed Saturday, Sunday and Bank Holidays)* 89/155 🍷 – ☕ 60 – **77 rm** 700/900.

L'Arcade M without rest, 9 r. de l'Arcade ✆ 01 53 30 60 00, Fax 01 40 07 03 07 – 🛗 ▤ TV ☎ ♿ – 🏛 25. AE GB JCB F 11
☕ 55 – **37 rm** 770/940, 4 duplex.

de l'Élysée without rest, 12 r. Saussaies ✆ 01 42 65 29 25, Fax 01 42 65 64 28 – 🛗 ▤ TV ☎. AE ⓓ GB JCB. ✻ F 11
☕ 60 – **32 rm** 700/980.

West-End without rest, 7 r. Clément-Marot ✆ 01 47 20 30 78, Fax 01 47 20 34 42 – 🛗 TV ☎. AE ⓓ GB JCB G 9
☕ 60 – **54 rm** 700/1300.

Lido M without rest, 4 passage Madeleine ✆ 01 42 66 27 37, Fax 01 42 66 61 23 – 🛗 ▤ TV ☎. AE ⓓ GB JCB F 11
32 rm 830/980.

Étoile Friedland without rest, 177 r. Fg St-Honoré ✆ 01 45 63 64 65, Fax 01 45 63 88 96 – 🛗 ⚡ rm ▤ TV ☎ ♿. AE ⓓ GB JCB F 9
☕ 75 – **40 rm** 1300.

Queen Mary M without rest, 9 r. Greffulhe ✆ 01 42 66 40 50, Fax 01 42 66 94 92 – 🛗 ▤ TV ☎. AE GB JCB. ✻ F 12
☕ 69 – **36 rm** 725/895.

Galiléo without rest, 54 r. Galilée ✆ 01 47 20 66 06, Fax 01 47 20 67 17 – 🛗 ▤ TV ☎ ♿. GB. ✻ F 8
☕ 50 – **27 rm** 800/950.

Franklin Roosevelt without rest, 18 r. Clément-Marot ✆ 01 47 23 61 66, Fax 01 47 20 44 30 – 🛗 TV ☎. AE GB. ✻ G 9
☕ 55 – **45 rm** 795/895.

Élysées Mermoz M without rest, 30 r. J. Mermoz ✆ 01 42 25 75 30, Fax 01 45 62 87 10 – 🛗 ▤ TV ☎ ♿. AE ⓓ GB F 10
☕ 45 – **21 rm** 690/850, 5 suites.

Mercure Opéra Garnier M without rest, 4 r. de l'Isly ✆ 01 43 87 35 50, Fax 01 43 87 03 29 – 🛗 ⚡ rm ▤ TV ☎ ♿. AE ⓓ GB JCB F 12
☕ 58 – **141 rm** 790/850.

Flèche d'Or M without rest, 29 r. Amsterdam ✆ 01 48 74 06 86, Fax 01 48 74 06 04 – 🛗 ⚡ rm ▤ TV ☎ ♿. AE ⓓ GB E 12
☕ 35 – **61 rm** 750/850.

Cordélia without rest, 11 r. Greffulhe ✆ 01 42 65 42 40, Fax 01 42 65 11 81 – 🛗 ▤ rm TV ☎. AE ⓓ GB. ✻ F 11
☕ 50 – **30 rm** 740/850.

Atlantic H. without rest, 44 r. Londres ✆ 01 43 87 45 40, Fax 01 42 93 06 26 – 🛗 TV ☎. AE GB JCB. ✻ E 12
☕ 52 – **87 rm** 520/790.

Mayflower without rest, 3 r. Chateaubriand ✆ 01 45 62 57 46, Fax 01 42 56 32 38 – 🛗 TV ☎. AE GB F 9
☕ 50 – **24 rm** 656/962.

Newton Opéra without rest, 11 bis r. de l'Arcade ✆ 01 42 65 32 13, Fax 01 42 65 30 90 – 🛗 ▤ TV ☎. AE ⓓ GB F 11
☕ 50 – **31 rm** 690.

Fortuny without rest, 35 r. de l'Arcade ☎ 01 42 66 42 08, Fax 01 42 66 00 32 –
TV ☎. AE ⓓ GB JCB F
☕ 50 – **30 rm** 680/750.

Plaza Élysées without rest, 177 bd Haussmann ☎ 01 45 63 93 83, Fax 01 45 61 14
– TV ☎. AE ⓓ GB JCB F
☕ 40 – **41 rm** 685/790.

Arc Élysée M without rest, 45 r. Washington ☎ 01 45 63 69 33, Fax 01 45 63 76
– TV ☎ ♿. AE ⓓ GB JCB F
☕ 50 – **23 rm** 696/902.

L'Orangerie without rest, 9 r. Constantinople ☎ 01 45 22 07 51, Fax 01 45 22 16
– rm TV ☎. AE ⓓ GB JCB. E
☕ 35 – **29 rm** 450/550.

Colisée without rest, 6 r. Colisée ☎ 01 43 59 95 25, Fax 01 45 63 26 54 – TV
AE ⓓ GB JCB F
☕ 45 – **45 rm** 660/875.

Lavoisier-Malesherbes without rest, 21 r. Lavoisier ☎ 01 42 65 10 9
Fax 01 42 65 02 43 – TV ☎. GB. F
☕ 35 – **32 rm** 370/500.

Les Ambassadeurs - Hôtel Crillon, 10 pl. Concorde ☎ 01 44 71 16 1
Fax 01 44 71 15 02, « 18C decor » – . AE ⓓ GB JCB. G
Meals 340 (lunch)/630 and a la carte 440/700
Spec. Moelleux de pommes ratte, médaillons de homard à la civette. Suprême bar croustillant aux amandes douces. Tarte sablée au chocolat, glace vanille aux n caramélisées.

Taillevent (Vrinat), 15 r. Lamennais ☎ 01 44 95 15 01, Fax 01 42 25 95 18 – . AE
GB JCB. F
closed 26 July-25 August, Saturday, Sunday and Bank Holidays – **Meals** (booking essent a la carte 530/840
Spec. Boudin de homard à la nage. Ballotine d'agneau aux truffes. Millefeuille à la vani

Lasserre, 17 av. F.-D.-Roosevelt ☎ 01 43 59 53 43, Fax 01 45 63 72 23, « Retractal roof » – . AE GB. G
closed 3 August-1 September, Monday lunch and Sunday – **Meals** a la carte 600/80
Spec. Emincé de sandre sur flan d'endives caramélisées. Petits pâtés de ris de veau a pleurotes. Bavaroise aux griottes sauce chocolat.

Lucas Carton (Senderens), 9 pl. Madeleine ☎ 01 42 65 22 90, Fax 01 42 65 06
« Authentic 1900 decor » – . AE ⓓ GB JCB. G
closed 2 to 24 August, Saturday lunch and Sunday – **Meals** 395 (lunch)and a la carte 65 1200
Spec. Langoustines au vermicelle frit, œuf coque aux truffes. Pastilla de lapin au foie gr et ses côtelettes au romarin. Millefeuille d'arlettes aux oranges confites.

Ledoyen, carré Champs-Élysées (1st floor) ☎ 01 53 05 10 01, Fax 01 47 42 55 01, - s also rest. Le Cercle – P. AE ⓓ GB JCB. G
closed August, Saturday and Sunday – **Meals** 290 (lunch), 520/590 and a la carte 480/8
Spec. Truffe en feuilleté de pomme de terre (December-February). Turbot rôti à la biè de garde, oignons frits. Mousse chaude au cacao aux deux cuissons.

Laurent, 41 av. Gabriel ☎ 01 42 25 00 39, Fax 01 45 62 45 21, , « Pleasant sumr terrace » – AE ⓓ GB. G
closed Saturday lunch, Sunday and Bank Holidays – **Meals** 390 and a la carte 540/8
Spec. Langoustines croustillantes au basilic. Sole au plat, jeunes poireaux au gingemb Variation sur le chocolat.

Bristol - Hôtel Bristol, 112 r. Fg St-Honoré ☎ 01 53 43 43 40, Fax 01 53 43 43 01,
– . AE ⓓ GB JCB. F
Meals 360/580 and a la carte 530/770
Spec. Langoustines royales grillées au sel de Guérande. Ravioles de champignons a truffes. Pigeonneau du Lauragais doré à la broche.

Régence - Hôtel Plaza Athénée, 25 av. Montaigne ☎ 01 53 67 65 00, Fax 01 53 67 66
– . AE ⓓ GB JCB. G
closed 14 July-3 August – **Meals** 310 (lunch)/585 and a la carte 450/660
Spec. Marinière de coquillages et langoustines aux fettucini. Aiguillettes de Saint-Pierre curry. Ris de veau meunière au beurre salé et citron confit.

Les Élysées - Hôtel Vernet, 25 r. Vernet ☎ 01 44 31 98 98, Fax 01 44 31 85 69, « F glass roof » – . AE ⓓ GB JCB. F
closed 28 July-24 August, 22 to 28 December, Saturday, Sunday and Bank Holidays – **Me** 340 (lunch), 390/530 and a la carte 420/620
Spec. Epautre "comme un risotto", cuisses de grenouilles en persillade. Filets de roug poêlés à la tapenade. Chausson feuilleté au chocolat amer.

XXXX ✿✿ **Pierre Gagnaire** - Hôtel Balzac, 6 r. Balzac ✆ 01 44 35 18 25, Fax 01 44 35 18 37 – ▤. AE ⓓ GB F 8
closed 2 to 24 August, February Holidays, Sunday lunch and Saturday – **Meals** 450 (lunch), 480/1200 and a la carte 540/730
Spec. Tourtière de légumes de saison, mousseline d'olives noires de Nyons. Tronçon de sole de ligne braisé à la manzanilla, jus de coing à l'estragon. Coffre de pigeon aux bâtons de cannelle en cocotte, jus de cuisson lié au chocolat.

XXXX ✿ **L'Astor** - Hôtel Astor, 11 rue d'Astorg ✆ 01 53 05 05 05, Fax 01 53 05 05 30 – ▤. AE ⓓ GB JCB F 11
closed Saturday and Sunday – **Meals** 290 b.i. (lunch) and a la carte 250/400
Spec. Salade de pommes de terre truffées à la tomate confite et parmesan. Pigeonneau en cocotte, pommes croustillantes. Moelleux au chocolat.

XXXX ✿ **Chiberta,** 3 r. Arsène-Houssaye ✆ 01 45 63 77 90, Fax 01 45 62 85 08 – ▤. AE ⓓ GB JCB F 8
closed 1 August-1 September, 24 December-2 January, Saturday, Sunday and Bank Holidays – **Meals** 290 and a la carte 440/580
Spec. Salade de langoustines aux tomates et poivre de Sechuan. Saint-Pierre aux anchois et tapenade au basilic. Soufflé chaud aux noix, fondu au caramel.

XXXX ✿ **La Marée,** 1 r. Daru ✆ 01 43 80 20 00, Fax 01 48 88 04 04 – ▤. AE ⓓ GB E 8
closed Saturday lunch and Sunday – **Meals** - Seafood - a la carte 360/590
Spec. Belons au champagne (September-May). Langoustines poêlées aux carottes confites. Turbotin à la moutarde.

XXX **Maison Blanche,** 15 av. Montaigne ✆ 01 47 23 55 99, Fax 01 47 20 09 56, ≤, 🏠, « Contemporary decor » – ▤. AE GB G 9
closed August, 5 to 11 January, Saturday lunch and Sunday – **Meals** a la carte 370/550.

XXX ✿ **Le Jardin** - Hôtel Royal Monceau, 37 av. Hoche ✆ 01 42 99 98 70, Fax 01 42 99 89 94, 🏠 – ▤. AE ⓓ GB JCB. ✂ E 8
closed Saturday and Sunday – **Meals** 280/430 and a la carte 390/640
Spec. Langoustines rôties au poivre. Morue à la ratatouille de pommes de terre. Figues rôties dans leurs feuilles aux épices.

XXX ✿ **Copenhague,** 142 av. Champs-Élysées (1st floor) ✆ 01 44 13 86 26, Fax 01 42 25 83 10, 🏠 – ▤. AE ⓓ GB JCB. ✂ F 8
closed 4 to 31 August, 1 to 7 January, Saturday lunch, Sunday and Bank Holidays – **Meals** - Danish rest. - 240/270 and a la carte 280/430 - ***Flora Danica :*** **Meals** 165b.i./260 and a la carte 230/370
Spec. Filet de cabillaud poêlé, beurre safrané. Cotelette et mignon de renne aux airelles. Crêpes aux mures jaunes, glace vanille.

XXX **Le 30 - Fauchon,** 30 pl. Madeleine ✆ 01 47 42 56 58, Fax 01 47 42 96 02, 🏠 – ▤. AE ⓓ GB JCB F 12
closed Sunday – **Meals** 245 (dinner), 259/450 b.i. and a la carte 290/440.

XXX **Yvan,** 1bis r. J. Mermoz ✆ 01 43 59 18 40, Fax 01 42 89 30 95 – ▤. AE ⓓ GB F-G 10
closed Saturday lunch and Sunday – **Meals** 168 (dinner), 178/298 and a la carte 260/390.

XXX **Le Marcande,** 52 r. Miromesnil ✆ 01 42 65 19 14, Fax 01 40 76 03 27, 🏠 – AE GB F 10
closed 11 to 25 August, Saturday and Sunday – **Meals** 240 and a la carte 260/400.

XXX **Indra,** 10 r. Cdt-Rivière ✆ 01 43 59 46 40, Fax 01 44 07 31 19 – ▤. AE ⓓ GB F 9
closed Sunday – **Meals** - Indian rest. - 195 (lunch), 220/300 and a la carte 210/280.

XX **La Luna,** 69 r. Rocher ✆ 01 42 93 77 61, Fax 01 40 08 02 44 – ▤. AE GB E 11
closed Sunday – **Meals** - Seafood - a la carte 280/420.

XX **Les Géorgiques,** 36 av. George-V ✆ 01 40 70 10 49 – ▤. AE ⓓ GB JCB. ✂ G 8
closed Saturday lunch and Sunday – **Meals** 180 (lunch)/360 and a la carte 350/450.

XX **Chez Tante Louise,** 41 r. Boissy-d'Anglas ✆ 01 42 65 06 85, Fax 01 42 65 28 19 – ▤. AE ⓓ GB JCB F 11
closed August, Saturday and Sunday – **Meals** 190 and a la carte 240/340.

XX **Le Sarladais,** 2 r. Vienne ✆ 01 45 22 23 62, Fax 01 45 22 23 62 – ▤. AE GB E 11
closed August, Saturday lunch and Sunday – **Meals** 145 (dinner)/200 and a la carte 230/350.

XX **Le Grenadin,** 46 r. Naples ✆ 01 45 63 28 92, Fax 01 45 61 24 76 – ▤. AE GB
closed Saturday lunch and Sunday – **Meals** 200/330 and a la carte 270/420. E 11

XX **Le Cercle Ledoyen,** carré Champs-Élysées (ground floor) ✆ 01 53 05 10 02, Fax 01 47 42 55 01, 🏠 – ▤. AE ⓓ GB JCB. ✂ G 10
closed Sunday – **Meals** a la carte 220/270.

XX **Hédiard,** 21 pl. Madeleine ✆ 01 43 12 88 99, Fax 01 43 12 88 98 – ▤. AE ⓓ GB F 11
closed Sunday – **Meals** a la carte approx. 300.

XX **Bœuf sur le Toit,** 34 r. Colisée ✆ 01 43 59 83 80, Fax 01 45 63 45 40, brasserie – AE ⓓ GB F
Meals a la carte 180/300.

XX **La Fermette Marbeuf 1900,** 5 r. Marbeuf ✆ 01 53 23 08 00, Fax 01 53 23 08 « 1900 decor with original ceramics and stained glass windows » – ▤. AE ⓓ GB
Meals 178 and a la carte 220/330 ♁.

XX **Marius et Janette,** 4 av. George-V ✆ 01 47 23 41 88, Fax 01 47 23 07 19, – AE ⓓ GB JCB G
Meals - Seafood - 300 b.i./500 b.i. and a la carte 350/480.

XX **Androuët,** 41 r. Amsterdam ✆ 01 48 74 26 93, Fax 01 49 95 02 54 – ▤. AE GB E
closed Sunday – **Meals** - Cheese specialities - 175 (lunch), 195/250 and a la carte 22 350.

XX **Suntory,** 13 r. Lincoln ✆ 01 42 25 40 27, Fax 01 45 63 25 86 – ▤. AE ⓓ GB J F
closed Saturday lunch and Sunday – **Meals** - Japanese rest. - 135 (lunch), 395/630 an la carte 270/550.

XX **Le Lloyd's,** 23 r. Treilhard ✆ 01 45 63 21 23, Fax 01 45 63 36 83 – AE GB E
closed 24 December-2 January, Saturday and Sunday – **Meals** 185 (dinner)and a la ca 230/370.

XX **Shozan,** 11 r. de la Trémoille ✆ 01 47 23 37 32, Fax 01 47 23 67 30 – ▤. AE ⓓ JCB G
closed Saturday lunch and Sunday – **Meals** - French and Japanese rest. - 175 (lunch) a a la carte 280/410.

XX **Stresa,** 7 r. Chambiges ✆ 01 47 23 51 62 – ▤. AE ⓓ GB. G
closed August, 20 December-2 January, Saturday dinner and Sunday – **Meals** - Italian re - (booking essential) a la carte 220/370.

XX **Village d'Ung et Li Lam,** 10 r. J. Mermoz ✆ 01 42 25 99 79, Fax 01 42 25 12 06 ▤. AE ⓓ GB F
Meals - Chinese and Thai rest. - 98/159 and a la carte 160/210.

XX **Kinugawa,** 4 r. St-Philippe du Roule ✆ 01 45 63 08 07, Fax 01 42 60 45 21 – ▤. AE GB JCB. F
closed 22 December-6 January and Sunday – **Meals** - Japanese rest. - 150 (lunch), 245/7 and a la carte 250/370.

XX **Bistrot du Sommelier,** 97 bd Haussmann ✆ 01 42 65 24 85, Fax 01 53 75 23 2 ▤. AE GB F
closed 26 July-24 August, 24 December-2 January, Saturday and Sunday – **Meals** a la ca 280/330 ♁.

XX **Le Pichet,** 68 r. P. Charron ✆ 01 43 59 50 34, Fax 01 45 63 07 82 – ▤. AE GB GF
closed Saturday except dinner from September-May and Sunday – **Meals** a la car 260/470.

XX **L'Alsace** (24 hr service), 39 av. Champs-Élysées ✆ 01 53 93 97 00, Fax 01 53 93 97 , brasserie – ▤. AE ⓓ GB F
Meals 123 b.i. (dinner)/178 and a la carte 170/360 ♁.

XX **Tong Yen,** 1bis r. J. Mermoz ✆ 01 42 25 04 23, Fax 01 45 63 51 57 – ▤. AE GB F
closed 1 to 24 August – **Meals** - Chinese rest. - a la carte 180/340.

X **Ferme des Mathurins,** 17 r. Vignon ✆ 01 42 66 46 39 – ⓓ GB F
closed August, Sunday and Bank Holidays – **Meals** 160/210 and a la carte 180/320.

X **Fenêtre sur Cour,** 4 r. de l'Arcade ✆ 01 42 65 53 13, Fax 01 42 66 53 82 – GB F
closed 11 to 17 August, Saturday lunch and Sunday – **Meals** 160/250 b.i. and a la ca 230/320.

X **L'Appart',** 9 r. Colisée ✆ 01 53 75 16 34, Fax 01 53 76 15 39 – ▤. AE GB JCB
Meals 175 and a la carte 190/260.

X **Cap Vernet,** 82 av. Marceau ✆ 01 47 20 20 40, Fax 01 47 20 95 36, – ▤. AE JCB F
Meals a la carte 210/330.

X **Le Boucoléon,** 10 r. Constantinople ✆ 01 42 93 73 33 – GB JCB. E
closed August, Saturday lunch, Sunday and Bank Holidays – **Meals** 90/150.

Don't get lost, use Michelin Maps which are updated annually.

Opéra, Gare du Nord, Gare de l'Est, Grands Boulevards.

9th and 10th arrondissements.
9th: ✉ 75009
10th: ✉ 75010

Grand Hôtel Inter-Continental, 2 r. Scribe (9th) ☎ 01 40 07 32 32, Fax 01 42 66 12 51, – ⇅ ⇔ rm ▤ TV ☎ ♿ – 🚗 – 300. AE ⓓ GB JCB. ✻ rest see **Rest. Opéra** and **Brasserie Café de la Paix** below - **La Verrière** ☎ 01 40 07 31 00 *(closed August, 25 December-4 January, dinner Sunday and Monday)* **Meals** 195/275 – ☕ 120 – **492 rm** 1700/2800, 22 suites. F 12

Scribe, 1 r. Scribe (9th) ☎ 01 44 71 24 24, Fax 01 44 71 24 42 – ⇅ ⇔ rm ▤ TV ☎ ♿ – 50. AE ⓓ GB JCB. ✻ rest F 12
see **Les Muses** below - **Le Jardin des Muses :** **Meals** 98(lunch), 140 and a la carte 160/220 – ☕ 105 – **206 rm** 1600/2450, 11 suites.

Ambassador, 16 bd Haussmann (9th) ☎ 01 44 83 40 40, Fax 01 40 22 08 74 – ⇅ ⇔ rm ▤ TV ☎ – 110. AE ⓓ GB JCB F 13
Venantius ☎ 01 48 00 06 38 *(closed August, Saturday and Sunday)* **Meals** 180 (dinner), 220/280 and a la carte 300/460 – ☕ 122 – **289 rm** 1500/1800.

Commodore, 12 bd Haussmann (9th) ☎ 01 42 46 72 82, Fax 01 47 70 23 81 – ⇅ ⇔ rm TV ☎ – 25. AE ⓓ GB JCB F 13
Cancans (brasserie) **Meals** 89 – **Le Carvery** (lunch only) *(closed July, August, Saturday and Sunday)* **Meals** 220 – ☕ 95 – **157 rm** 1450/1650, 5 suites.

Terminus Nord M without rest, 12 bd Denain (10th) ☎ 01 42 80 20 00, Fax 01 42 80 63 89 – ⇅ ⇔ rm TV ☎ ♿ – 80. AE ⓓ GB JCB E 16
☕ 75 – **247 rm** 925/985.

Lafayette M without rest, 49 r. Lafayette (9th) ☎ 01 42 85 05 44, Fax 01 49 95 06 60 – ⇅ ⇔ rm TV ☎ ♿. AE ⓓ GB JCB F 14
☕ 75 – **96 rm** 875/940, 7 suites.

St-Pétersbourg, 33 r. Caumartin (9th) ☎ 01 42 66 60 38, Fax 01 42 66 53 54 – ⇅ ▤ rest TV ☎ – 25. AE ⓓ GB JCB. ✻ rest F 12
Le Relais *(closed August, Saturday and Sunday)* **Meals** 140 and a la carte 180/270 – ☕ 70 – **100 rm** 865/955.

Brébant, 32 bd Poissonnière (9th) ☎ 01 47 70 25 55, Fax 01 42 46 65 70 – ⇅ ▤ rest TV ☎ – 25 - 100. AE ⓓ GB JCB F 14
Vieux Pressoir : **Meals** 98/198 and a la carte 130/300 – ☕ 48 – **122 rm** 760/890.

L'Horset Pavillon, 38 r. Échiquier (10th) ☎ 01 42 46 92 75, Fax 01 42 47 03 97 – ⇅ ⇔ rm ▤ TV ☎. AE ⓓ GB JCB F 15
Meals *(closed Saturday, Sunday and Bank Holidays)* 85/165 b.i. and a la carte 180/320 – ☕ 80 – **92 rm** 850/950.

Franklin M without rest, 19 r. Buffault (9th) ☎ 01 42 80 27 27, Fax 01 48 78 13 04 – ⇅ ⇔ rm TV ☎. AE ⓓ GB JCB E 14
☕ 75 – **68 rm** 780/840.

Blanche Fontaine without rest, 34 r. Fontaine (9th) ☎ 01 45 26 72 32, Fax 01 42 81 05 52 – ⇅ TV ☎ 🚗. AE ⓓ GB JCB. ✻ D 13
☕ 40 – **45 rm** 466/540, 4 suites.

Carlton's H. without rest, 55 bd Rochechouart (9th) ☎ 01 42 81 91 00, Fax 01 42 81 97 04, « Rooftop panoramic terrace, ≤ Paris » – ⇅ ⇔ rm TV ☎. AE ⓓ GB JCB D 14
☕ 45 – **103 rm** 615/665.

Bergère without rest, 34 r. Bergère (9th) ☎ 01 47 70 34 34, Fax 01 47 70 36 36 – ⇅ ▤ TV ☎. AE ⓓ GB JCB. ✻ F 14
☕ 60 – **134 rm** 690/990.

Richmond without rest, 11 r. Helder (9th) ☎ 01 47 70 53 20, Fax 01 48 00 02 10 – ⇅ TV ☎. AE ⓓ GB JCB. ✻ F 13
☕ 40 – **58 rm** 660/820.

Anjou-Lafayette without rest, 4 r. Riboutté (9th) ☎ 01 42 46 83 44, Fax 01 48 00 08 97 – ⇅ TV ☎. AE ⓓ GB JCB E 14
☕ 40 – **39 rm** 480/620.

Paix République without rest, 2 bis bd St-Martin (10th) ☎ 01 42 08 96 95, Fax 01 42 06 36 30 – ⇅ TV ☎. AE ⓓ GB JCB. ✻ G 16
☕ 40 – **45 rm** 550/980.

Frantour Paris-Est M without rest, 4 r. 8 Mai 1945 (cour d'Honneur gare de l'Es
(10th) ✆ 01 44 89 27 00, Fax 01 44 89 27 49 – TV ☎ – 250. AE GB E
55 – **45 rm** 535/1035.

Touraine Opéra M without rest, 73 r. Taitbout (9th) ✆ 01 48 74 50 4
Fax 01 42 81 26 09 – rm TV ☎. AE GB JCB E
75 – **39 rm** 780/840.

Albert 1er M without rest, 162 r. Lafayette (10th) ✆ 01 40 36 82 4
Fax 01 40 35 72 52 – TV ☎. AE GB JCB. E
40 – **57 rm** 440/548.

Opéra Cadet M without rest, 24 r. Cadet (9th) ✆ 01 53 34 50 50, Fax 01 53 34 50 6
– TV ☎. AE GB JCB F
65 – **82 rm** 755/980, 3 suites.

Mercure Monty M without rest, 5 r. Montyon (9th) ✆ 01 47 70 26 1
Fax 01 42 46 55 10 – rm TV ☎ – 50. AE GB JCB F
60 – **71 rm** 595/710.

Corona without rest, 8 cité Bergère (9th) ✆ 01 47 70 52 96, Fax 01 42 46 83
– TV ☎. AE GB JCB F
45 – **56 rm** 570/690, 4 suites.

Trinité Plaza without rest, 41 r. Pigalle (9th) ✆ 01 42 85 57 00, Fax 01 45 26 41
– TV ☎. AE GB JCB E
30 – **42 rm** 570/660.

Résidence du Pré without rest, 15 r. P. Sémard (9th) ✆ 01 48 78 26 7
Fax 01 42 80 64 83 – TV ☎. AE GB. E
50 – **40 rm** 425/485.

du Pré without rest, 10 r. P. Sémard (9th) ✆ 01 42 81 37 11, Fax 01 40 23 98 28 –
TV ☎. AE GB. E
50 – **41 rm** 445/570.

Acadia M without rest, 4 r. Geoffroy Marie (9th) ✆ 01 40 22 99 99, Fax 01 40 22 01 8
– TV ☎. AE GB JCB. F
60 – **36 rm** 790/990.

Axel without rest, 15 r. Montyon (9th) ✆ 01 47 70 92 70, Fax 01 47 70 43 37 – r
TV ☎. AE GB JCB F
45 – **38 rm** 640/750.

Monterosa M without rest, 30 r. La Bruyère (9th) ✆ 01 48 74 87 9
Fax 01 42 81 01 12 – rm TV ☎. AE GB JCB E
32 – **36 rm** 400/600.

Printania without rest, 19 r. Château d'Eau (10th) ✆ 01 42 01 84 2
Fax 01 42 39 55 12 – TV ☎. AE GB. F
42 – **51 rm** 496/592.

Moulin M without rest, 39 r. Fontaine (9th) ✆ 01 42 81 93 25, Fax 01 40 16 09 90
rm TV ☎. AE GB JCB D
75 – **50 rm** 550/810.

Celte La Fayette without rest, 25 r. Buffault (9th) ✆ 01 49 95 09 4
Fax 01 49 95 01 88 – TV ☎. AE GB JCB E
51 – **50 rm** 530/680.

Capucines without rest, 6 r. Godot de Mauroy (9th) ✆ 01 47 42 25 0
Fax 01 42 68 05 05 – TV ☎. AE GB JCB F
38 – **45 rm** 550/600.

Modern' Est without rest, 91 bd Strasbourg (10th) ✆ 01 40 37 77 2
Fax 01 40 37 17 55 – TV ☎. GB. E
30 – **30 rm** 380/460.

Alba without rest, 34 ter r. La Tour d'Auvergne (9th) ✆ 01 48 78 80 2
Fax 01 42 85 23 13 – kitchenette TV ☎. AE GB JCB. E
40 – **24 rm** 450/700.

Ibis Lafayette without rest, 122 r. Lafayette (10th) ✆ 01 45 23 27 2
Fax 01 42 46 73 79 – rm TV ☎. AE GB E
40 – **70 rm** 410/455.

St-Laurent M without rest, 5 r. St-Laurent (10th) ✆ 01 42 09 59 7
Fax 01 42 09 83 50 – TV ☎. AE GB JCB EF
45 – **44 rm** 550/680.

Suède without rest, 106 bd Magenta (10th) ✆ 01 40 36 10 12, Fax 01 40 36 11 98
rm TV ☎. AE GB JCB E 15-
45 – **52 rm** 470/535.

Champagne-Mulhouse without rest, 87 bd Strasbourg (10th) ✆ 01 42 09 12 28, Fax 01 42 09 48 12 – ▮ ⇔ rm ▭ ☎. AE ⓓ GB JCB E 15
▭ 45 – **31 rm** 470/535.

Montréal without rest, 23 r. Godot-de-Mauroy (9th) ✆ 01 42 65 99 54, Fax 01 49 24 07 33 – ▮ ⇔ rm ▭ ☎. AE ⓓ GB JCB F 12
closed August – ▭ 35 – **14 rm** 285/600, 5 suites.

XXX ✿ **Rest. Opéra** - Grand Hôtel Inter-Continental, pl. Opéra (9th) ✆ 01 40 07 30 10, Fax 01 40 07 33 86, « Second Empire decor » – ▤. AE ⓓ GB JCB. ✗ F 12
closed August, Saturday, Sunday and Bank Holidays – **Meals** 240 (lunch)/350 b.i. and a la carte 390/600
Spec. Langoustines croustillantes, émulsion d'agrumes à l'huile d'olive. Bar grillé au jus de fenouil à l'anis étoilé. Dessert tout chocolat.

XXX ✿ **Les Muses** - Hôtel Scribe, 1 r. Scribe (9th) ✆ 01 44 71 24 26, Fax 01 44 71 24 64 – ▤. AE ⓓ GB JCB. ✗ F 12
closed August, Saturday, Sunday and Bank Holidays – **Meals** 230/290 and a la carte approx. 350
Spec. Parmentier de foie gras de canard chaud. Noisettes de biche poêlées, figues au foie gras et nouilles alsaciennes (October-February). Tarte au chocolat "Manjari", soupe d'oranges aux fleurs séchées.

XXX ✿ **La Table d'Anvers** (Conticini), 2 pl. Anvers (9th) ✆ 01 48 78 35 21, Fax 01 45 26 66 67 – ▤. AE GB D 14
closed Saturday lunch and Sunday – **Meals** 180 (lunch)/250 and a la carte 470/580
Spec. Homard en salade, œuf sucré et fleur de bananier. Rôti de lotte bardé à la coriandre. Monte-Cristo : "un tabac" (dessert).

XXX **Charlot "Roi des Coquillages",** 12 pl. Clichy (9th) ✆ 01 53 20 48 00, Fax 01 53 20 48 09 – ▤. AE ⓓ GB D 12
Meals - Seafood - 178 and a la carte 230/340.

XX **Au Chateaubriant,** 23 r. Chabrol (10th) ✆ 01 48 24 58 94, Fax 01 42 47 09 75, Collection of paintings – ▤. AE GB E 15
closed August, Sunday and Monday – **Meals** - Italian rest. - 159 and a la carte 280/330.

XX **Brasserie Café de la Paix** - Grand Hôtel Inter-Continental, 12 bd Capucines (9th) ✆ 01 40 07 30 20, Fax 01 40 07 33 86, ☂ – ▤. AE ⓓ GB JCB F 12
Meals 159 and a la carte 230/360 ♁.

XX **Julien,** 16 r. Fg St-Denis (10th) ✆ 01 47 70 12 06, Fax 01 42 47 00 65, « Belle Epoque brasserie » – ▤. AE ⓓ GB F 15
Meals a la carte 190/310.

XX **Grand Café Capucines** (24 hr service), 4 bd Capucines (9th) ✆ 01 43 12 19 00, Fax 01 43 12 19 09, brasserie, « Belle Epoque decor » – ▤. AE ⓓ GB F 13
Meals 178 and a la carte 170/360 ♁.

XX **Grange Batelière,** 16 r. Grange Batelière (9th) ✆ 01 47 70 85 15, Fax 01 47 70 85 15 – ▤. AE GB G 10
closed August, Saturday lunch, Sunday and Bank Holidays – **Meals** 185/300 and a la carte 250/360.

XX **Le Quercy,** 36 r. Condorcet (9th) ✆ 01 48 78 30 61 – AE ⓓ GB E 14
closed 1 August-1 September, Sunday and Bank Holidays – **Meals** 152 and a la carte 190/320.

XX **Bistrot Papillon,** 6 r. Papillon (9th) ✆ 01 47 70 90 03, Fax 01 48 24 05 59 – ▤. AE ⓓ GB E 15
closed 29 March-7 April, 4 to 25 August, Saturday and Sunday – **Meals** 140 and a la carte 210/310 ♁.

XX **Comme Chez Soi,** 20 r. Lamartine (9th) ✆ 01 48 78 00 02, Fax 01 42 85 09 78 – ▤. AE GB E 14
closed August, Saturday and Sunday – **Meals** 80/140 and a la carte 200/320.

XX **Au Petit Riche,** 25 r. Le Peletier (9th) ✆ 01 47 70 68 68, Fax 01 48 24 10 79, bistro, « Late 19C decor » – ▤. AE ⓓ GB JCB F 13
closed Sunday – **Meals** 160/350 b.i. and a la carte 190/270 ♁.

XX **Brasserie Flo,** 7 cour Petites-Écuries (10th) ✆ 01 47 70 13 59, Fax 01 42 47 00 80, « 1900 decor » – ▤. AE ⓓ GB F 15
Meals a la carte 170/280 ♁.

XX **Terminus Nord,** 23 r. Dunkerque (10th) ✆ 01 42 85 05 15, Fax 01 40 16 13 98, brasserie – ▤. AE ⓓ GB E 16
Meals a la carte 180/300.

XX **Le Saintongeais,** 62 r. Fg Montmartre (9th) ✆ 01 42 80 39 92 – AE ⓓ GB E 14
closed August, Saturday and Sunday – **Meals** 135 and a la carte 190/240.

XX **La P'tite Tonkinoise,** 56 r. Fg Poissonnière (10th) ✆ 01 42 46 85 98 – AE GB
closed 1 August-4 September, 22 December-5 January, Sunday and Monday – **Meal**
Vietnamese rest. - 133 (lunch) and a la carte 140/230. F

X **Wally Le Saharien,** 36 r. Rodier (9th) ✆ 01 42 85 51 90 – E
closed Monday lunch and Sunday – **Meals** - North African rest. - 240 and a la carte 160/2

X **I Golosi,** 6 r. Grange Batelière (9th) ✆ 01 48 24 18 63, Fax 01 45 23 18 96, « Veneti
decor » – ▤. GB F
closed August, Saturday dinner and Sunday – **Meals** - Italian rest - a la carte 170/23

X **L'Oenothèque,** 20 r. St-Lazare (9th) ✆ 01 48 78 08 76, Fax 01 40 16 10 27 –
GB E
closed 18 to 31 August, Saturday and Sunday – **Meals** a la carte 210/310.

X **Aux Deux Canards,** 8 r. Fg Poissonnière (10th) ✆ 01 47 70 03 23, Fax 01 44 83 02
– AE ⓓ GB JCB F
closed August, Saturday lunch and Sunday – **Meals** a la carte 160/240.

X **L'Alsaco Winstub,** 10 r. Condorcet (9th) ✆ 01 45 26 44 31 – AE GB E
closed August and Sunday – **Meals** 79 (lunch), 87/170 b.i. and a la carte 160/260.

X **Chez Jean,** 52 r. Lamartine (9th) ✆ 01 48 78 62 73, Fax 01 48 78 62 73, bistro
GB E
closed 2 to 24 August, 24 December-2 January, Saturday lunch and Sunday – **Meals** 1
b.i..

X **Bistro de Gala,** 45 r. Fg Montmarte (9th) ✆ 01 40 22 90 50 – ▤. AE ⓓ GB JC
closed Saturday lunch and Sunday – **Meals** 150 🌡. F

X **Relais Beaujolais,** 3 r. Milton (9th) ✆ 01 48 78 77 91, bistro – GB E
closed August, Saturday and Sunday – **Meals** 130 (lunch) and a la carte 160/290.

X **Bistro des Deux Théâtres,** 18 r. Blanche (9th) ✆ 01 45 26 41 43, Fax 01 48 74 08
– ▤. AE GB E
Meals 169 b.i.

X **Chez Catherine - Le Poitou,** 65 r. Provence (9th) ✆ 01 45 26 72 88, bistro – G
closed August, 3 to 13 January, Monday dinner, Saturday and Sunday – **Meals** a la car
150/220 🌡. F

X **L'Excuse Mogador,** 21 r. Joubert (9th) ✆ 01 42 81 98 19 – GB F
closed August, 25 to 31 December, Monday dinner, Saturday and Sunday – **Meals** 75/
and a la carte 100/170.

Bastille, Gare de Lyon, Place d'Italie, Bois de Vincennes.

12th and 13th arrondissements.
12th: ✉ 75012
13th: ✉ 75013

Novotel Gare de Lyon Ⓜ, 2 r. Hector Malo (12th) ✆ 01 44 67 60 0
Fax 01 44 67 60 60, ⛱ – ▮ ⇔ rm ▤ TV ☎ ♿ 🚗 – 🧑‍🏫 150. AE ⓓ GB JCB
Meals 133 🌡 – ☕ 64 – **253 rm** 780/820. L

Pavillon Bastille Ⓜ without rest, 65 r. Lyon (12th) ✆ 01 43 43 65 6
Fax 01 43 43 96 52 – ▮ ⇔ rm ▤ TV ☎ ♿. AE ⓓ GB JCB K
☕ 65 – **25 rm** 795/955.

Novotel Bercy, 86 r. Bercy (12th) ✆ 01 43 42 30 00, Fax 01 43 45 30 60, –
⇔ rm ▤ TV ☎ ♿ – 🧑‍🏫 30 - 60. AE ⓓ GB M
Meals 138 – ☕ 64 – **129 rm** 690/720.

Holiday Inn Tolbiac Ⓜ without rest, 21 r. Tolbiac (13th) ✆ 01 45 84 61 6
Fax 01 45 84 43 38 – ▮ ⇔ rm ▤ TV ☎ ♿ – 🧑‍🏫 25. AE ⓓ GB P
☕ 65 – **71 rm** 770.

Mercure Pont de Bercy without rest, 6 bd Vincent Auriol (13th) ✆ 01 45 82 48 0
Fax 01 45 82 19 16 – ▮ ⇔ rm ▤ TV ☎ ♿ – 🧑‍🏫 40. AE ⓓ GB M
☕ 60 – **89 rm** 650/690.

Mercure Vincent Auriol Ⓜ without rest, 178 bd Vincent Auriol (13t
✆ 01 44 24 01 01, Fax 01 44 24 07 07 – ▮ ⇔ rm TV ☎ ♿ – 🧑‍🏫 50. AE ⓓ GB N
☕ 62 – **70 rm** 680/785.

Mercure Blanqui without rest, 25 bd Blanqui (13th) ✆ 01 45 80 82 23, Fax 01 45 81 45 84 – rm. AE GB P 15
60 – **50 rm** 790.

Paris Bastille M without rest, 67 r. Lyon (12th) ✆ 01 40 01 07 17, Fax 01 40 01 07 27 – – 25. AE GB JCB K 18
70 – **37 rm** 766/956.

Allegro Nation M without rest, 33 av. Dr A. Netter (12th) ✆ 01 40 04 90 90, Fax 01 40 04 99 20 – . AE GB M 12
40 – **49 rm** 450/550.

Slavia without rest, 51 bd St-Marcel (13th) ✆ 01 43 37 81 25, Fax 01 45 87 05 03 – . AE GB. M 16
32 – **37 rm** 345/385, 6 suites.

Résidence Vert Galant, 43 r. Croulebarbe (13th) ✆ 01 44 08 83 50, Fax 01 44 08 83 69 – . AE GB JCB. rm N 15
Meals see rest. ***Etchegory*** below – 40 – **15 rm** 400/500.

Terminus-Lyon without rest, 19 bd Diderot (12th) ✆ 01 43 43 24 03, Fax 01 43 44 09 00 – . AE GB JCB. L 18
40 – **60 rm** 450/660.

Modern H. Lyon without rest, 3 r. Parrot (12th) ✆ 01 43 43 41 52, Fax 01 43 43 81 16 – . AE GB JCB. L 18
39 – **48 rm** 495/570.

Média without rest, 22 r. Reine Blanche (13th) ✆ 01 45 35 72 72, Fax 01 43 31 43 31 – . AE GB. M 15
closed August – 35 – **18 rm** 395/480, 3 duplex.

Ibis Bercy, 77 r. Bercy (12th) ✆ 01 43 42 91 91, Fax 01 43 42 34 79, – rm – 25 - 160. AE GB M 19
Meals 95 – 40 – **368 rm** 420/445.

Relais de Lyon without rest, 64 r. Crozatier (12th) ✆ 01 43 44 22 50, Fax 01 43 41 55 12 – . AE GB JCB. K 19
40 – **34 rm** 350/480.

Ibis Porte d'Italie M without rest, 25 av. Stephen Pichon (13th) ✆ 01 44 24 94 85, Fax 01 44 24 20 70 – rm . AE GB N 16
39 – **58 rm** 405/445.

Touring Hôtel Magendie M without rest, 2 r. Magendie (13th) ✆ 01 43 36 13 61, Fax 01 43 36 47 48 – . GB N 14
112 rm 325/395.

Ibis without rest, 177 r. Tolbiac (13th) ✆ 01 45 80 16 60, Fax 01 45 80 95 80 – rm . AE GB P 15
39 – **60 rm** 390/430.

Viator without rest, 1 r. Parrot (12th) ✆ 01 43 43 11 00, Fax 01 43 43 10 89 – . AE GB. L 18
35 – **45 rm** 320/370.

Nouvel H. without rest, 24 av. Bel Air (12th) ✆ 01 43 43 01 81, Fax 01 43 44 64 13 – . AE GB L 21
40 – **28 rm** 360/535.

Au Pressoir (Seguin), 257 av. Daumesnil (12th) ✆ 01 43 44 38 21, Fax 01 43 43 81 77 – . AE GB M 22
closed August, Saturday and Sunday – **Meals** 400 and a la carte 390/500
Spec. Salade de pommes de terre au foie gras. Assiette de fruits de mer tièdes (October-May). Lièvre à la royale (October-November).

Train Bleu, Gare de Lyon (12th) ✆ 01 43 43 09 06, Fax 01 43 43 97 96, brasserie, « Murals depicting the journey from Paris to the Mediterranean » – AE GB JCB
Meals (1st floor) 250 b.i. and a la carte 220/330. L 18

L'Oulette, 15 pl. Lachambeaudie (12th) ✆ 01 40 02 02 12, Fax 01 40 02 04 77, – AE GB N 20
closed Saturday lunch and Sunday – **Meals** 165/245 b.i. and a la carte 250/380.

Au Trou Gascon, 40 r. Taine (12th) ✆ 01 43 44 34 26, Fax 01 43 07 80 55 – . AE GB JCB M 21
closed 26 July-24 August, 28 December-4 January, Saturday lunch and Sunday – **Meals** (booking essential) 190 (lunch)/285 b.i. and a la carte 300/410
Spec. Chipirons sautés "façon pibales" (June-September). Petit pâté chaud de cèpes au jus de persil (season). Volaille de Chalosse rôtie.

La Frégate, 30 av. Ledru-Rollin (12th) ✆ 01 43 43 90 32 – . AE GB L 18
closed August, Saturday and Sunday – **Meals** - Seafood - 160/210 and a la carte 280/400.

XX **La Gourmandise,** 271 av. Daumesnil (12th) ☎ 01 43 43 94 41 – AE GB M 2
closed 6 to 27 August, Monday dinner and Sunday – **Meals** 145/199 b.i. and a la cart 250/370.

XX **Le Petit Marguery,** 9 bd Port-Royal (13th) ☎ 01 43 31 58 59, bistro – AE GB M 1
closed August, 24 December-3 January, Sunday and Monday – **Meals** 165 (lunch), 205 250.

XX **Le Traversière,** 40 r. Traversière (12th) ☎ 01 43 44 02 10, Fax 01 43 44 64 20 – GB JCB K 1
closed August, dinner Sunday and Monday – **Meals** 120 (lunch)/165 and a la carte 230 360 ♨.

XX **Les Marronniers,** 53 bis bd Arago (13th) ☎ 01 47 07 58 57, Fax 01 43 36 85 20 – AE GB N 1
closed August, February Holidays and Sunday – **Meals** 230 b.i. and a la carte 210/360

X **Jean-Pierre Frelet,** 25 r. Montgallet (12th) ☎ 01 43 43 76 65 – ▤. GB L 2
closed mid-July-mid-August, Saturday lunch and Sunday – **Meals** 135 and a la cart 160/230.

X **Le Quincy,** 28 av. Ledru-Rollin (12th) ☎ 01 46 28 46 76, bistro – ▤ L 1
closed 10 August-10 September, Saturday, Sunday and Monday – **Meals** a la cart 230/350.

X **Etchégorry,** 41 r. Croulebarbe (13th) ☎ 01 44 08 83 51, Fax 01 44 08 83 69 – ▤. GB JCB N 1
closed Sunday – **Meals** 160/210 b.i. and a la carte 200/280.

X **Chez Jacky,** 109 r. du Dessous-des-Berges (13th) ☎ 01 45 83 71 5 Fax 01 45 86 57 73 – ▤. AE GB P 1
closed August, Saturday and Sunday – **Meals** 188.

X **L'Escapade en Touraine,** 24 r. Traversière (12th) ☎ 01 43 43 14 96 – GB L 1
closed 4 to 30 August, Saturday, Sunday and Bank Holidays – **Meals** 110/140 and a la car 150/280.

X **Anacréon,** 53 bd St-Marcel (13th) ☎ 01 43 31 71 18 – ▤. AE GB. ✗ M 1
closed August, Febuary Holidays, Sunday and Monday – **Meals** 120 (lunch)/180.

X **Le Temps des Cerises,** 216 r. Fg St-Antoine (12th) ☎ 01 43 67 52 0 Fax 01 43 67 60 91 – ▤. AE GB K 2
closed Monday – **Meals** 97/224 and a la carte 210/330 ♨.

X **A la Biche au Bois,** 45 av. Ledru-Rollin (12th) ☎ 01 43 43 34 38 – AE GB
closed mid-July-mid-August, Christmas-New Year, Saturday and Sunday – **Meals** 102/1 and a la carte 130/210 ♨. K 1

X **St-Amarante,** 4 r. Biscornet (12th) ☎ 01 43 43 00 08, bistro – GB K 1
closed 14 July-15 August, Saturday and Sunday – **Meals** (booking essential) a la car approx. 180.

X **Chez Françoise,** 12 r. Butte aux Cailles (13th) ☎ 01 45 80 12 02, Fax 01 45 65 13 6 bistro – AE GB. ✗ P 1
closed 31 July-28 August and Sunday – **Meals** 72 b.i. (lunch), 99/146 and a la carte 160/2 ♨.

X **Sipario,** 69 r. Charenton (12th) ☎ 01 43 45 70 26, Fax 01 43 45 43 48 – AE G JCB K 1
closed 2 to 24 August, 23 December-2 January, Saturday lunch and Sunday – **Meals** - Itali rest. - 100 and a la carte 160/200.

X **Le Rhône,** 40 bd Arago (13th) ☎ 01 47 07 33 57, 🏠 – GB N 1
closed August, Saturday, Sunday and Bank Holidays – **Meals** 75/160 and a la carte 140 230 ♨.

X **Chez Paul,** 22 r. Butte aux Cailles (13th) ☎ 01 45 89 22 11, Fax 01 45 80 26 53, bist – GB. ✗ P 1
Meals a la carte 150/220.

X **Michel,** 20 r. Providence (13th) ☎ 01 45 89 99 27, Fax 01 45 89 99 27 – GB P 1
closed 10 to 25 August and Sunday – **Meals** 120/195 ♨.

X **Les Zygomates,** 7 r. Capri (12th) ☎ 01 40 19 93 04, Fax 01 40 19 93 04, bistro – G ✗ N 2
closed August, Saturday lunch and Sunday – **Meals** 75 (lunch)/130 and a la carte 16 240 ♨.

EUROPE on a single sheet Michelin Map no 970

Vaugirard, Gare Montparnasse, Grenelle, Denfert-Rochereau.

14th and 15th arrondissements.
14th: ✉ 75014
15th: ✉ 75015

Hilton M, 18 av. Suffren (15th) ☎ 01 44 38 56 00, Fax 01 44 38 56 10, 🏖 - |‡| ⇔ rm ▤ TV ☎ ♿ 🚗 - 🎤 25 - 400. AE ⓪ GB JCB J 7
Western *(closed Monday and Tuesday)* **Meals** 139 and a la carte 170/310 - ***La Terrasse :*** **Meals** 140/160 and a la carte 170/290 - ☕ 130 - **444 rm** 1600/2200, 18 suites.

Nikko M, 61 quai Grenelle (15th) ☎ 01 40 58 20 00, Fax 01 40 58 24 44, ≤, 🏋, 🏊 - |‡| ⇔ rm ▤ TV ☎ ♿ 🚗 - 🎤 25 - 600. AE ⓪ GB JCB K 6
see ***Les Célébrités*** below - ***Brasserie Pont Mirabeau :*** **Meals** 160 and a la carte 210/300 - ***Benkay*** Japanese rest. **Meals** 135(lunch), 300/510 and a la carte 260/390 - ☕ 85 - **758 rm** 1690/1980, 6 suites.

Méridien Montparnasse, 19 r. Cdt Mouchotte (14th) ☎ 01 44 36 44 36, Fax 01 44 36 49 00, ≤ - |‡| ⇔ rm ▤ rm TV ☎ ♿ 🚗 - 🎤 25 - 1 000. AE ⓪ GB JCB. ✂ rm M 11
see ***Montparnasse 25*** below - ***Justine*** ☎ 01 44 36 44 00 **Meals** a la carte 200/300 - ☕ 95 - **918 rm** 1350/1550, 36 suites.

Sofitel Porte de Sèvres M, 8 r. L. Armand (15th) ☎ 01 40 60 30 30, Fax 01 45 57 04 22, ≤, panoramic indoor pool, 🏋 - |‡| ⇔ rm ▤ TV ☎ 🚗 - 🎤 25 - 800. AE ⓪ GB JCB. ✂ rest N 5
see ***Le Relais de Sèvres*** below - ***La Tonnelle*** (brasserie) **Meals** 125 and a la carte approx. 200 - ☕ 105 - **524 rm** 1480, 14 suites.

Sofitel Forum Rive Gauche M, 17 bd St-Jacques (15th) ☎ 01 40 78 79 80, Fax 01 45 88 43 93 - |‡| ⇔ rm ▤ TV ☎ ♿ 🚗 - 🎤 25 - 1 200. AE ⓪ GB JCB N 13-14
Le Café Français *(closed Saturday and Sunday in August)* **Meals** 179/209b.i. - ***La Table et la Forme*** (low-calorie menu) *(closed August, Saturday lunch and Sunday)* **Meals** 250 b.i. - ☕ 95 - **783 rm** 1250/1500, 14 suites.

Mercure Porte de Versailles M, 69 bd Victor (15th) ☎ 01 44 19 03 03, Fax 01 48 28 22 11 - |‡| ⇔ rm ▤ TV ☎ ♿ 🚗 - 🎤 25 - 250. AE ⓪ GB N 7
Meals a la carte 150/210 - ☕ 70 - **91 rm** 1129/1200.

Mercure Montparnasse M, 20 r. Gaîté (14th) ☎ 01 43 35 28 28, Fax 01 43 27 98 64 - |‡| ⇔ rm ▤ TV ☎ ♿ 🚗 - 🎤 80. AE ⓪ GB JCB M 11
Bistrot de la Gaîté ☎ 01 43 22 86 46 **Meals** 130/180 - ☕ 70 - **179 rm** 980, 6 suites.

Novotel Porte d'Orléans M, 15-19 bd R. Rolland (14th) ☎ 01 41 17 26 00, Fax 01 41 17 26 26 - |‡| ⇔ rm ▤ TV ☎ ♿ 🚗 - 🎤 130. AE ⓪ GB JCB S 12
Meals 132 - ☕ 62 - **150 rm** 660/710.

L'Aiglon without rest, 232 bd Raspail (14th) ☎ 01 43 20 82 42, Fax 01 43 20 98 72 - |‡| TV ☎ 🚗. AE ⓪ GB JCB M 12
☕ 35 - **38 rm** 550/710, 9 suites.

Novotel Vaugirard M, 257 r. Vaugirard (15th) ☎ 01 40 45 10 00, Fax 01 40 45 10 10, 🏖, 🏋 - |‡| ⇔ rm ▤ rest TV ☎ ♿ 🚗 - 🎤 25 - 200. AE ⓪ GB JCB M 9
Meals *(closed Saturday and Sunday)* 160 and a la carte approx. 200 🍷 - ☕ 75 - **187 rm** 835.

Mercure Tour Eiffel M without rest, 64 bd Grenelle (15th) ☎ 01 45 78 90 90, Fax 01 45 78 95 55 - |‡| ⇔ rm ▤ TV ☎ ♿ 🚗 - 🎤 30. AE ⓪ GB K 7
☕ 68 - **64 rm** 850.

Lenox Montparnasse without rest, 15 r. Delambre (14th) ☎ 01 43 35 34 50, Fax 01 43 20 46 64 - |‡| TV ☎. AE ⓪ GB JCB M 12
☕ 45 - **52 rm** 540/650.

Raspail Montparnasse without rest, 203 bd Raspail (14th) ☎ 01 43 20 62 86, Fax 01 43 20 50 79 - |‡| ▤ TV ☎. AE ⓪ GB JCB. ✂ M 12
☕ 50 - **38 rm** 490/1100.

Alésia Montparnasse without rest, 84 r. R. Losserand (14th) ☎ 01 45 42 16 03, Fax 01 45 42 11 60 - |‡| ⇔ rm TV ☎. AE ⓪ GB JCB N 10
☕ 45 - **45 rm** 490/550.

Mercure Paris XV M without rest, 6 r. St-Lambert (15th) ☎ 01 45 58 61 0
Fax 01 45 54 10 43 – lift rm TV ☎ & – 25. AE ① GB M
55 – **56 rm** 620/720.

Versailles without rest, 213 r. Croix-Nivert (15th) ☎ 01 48 28 48 6
Fax 01 45 30 16 22 – lift TV ☎. AE ① GB N
50 – **41 rm** 495/575.

Alizé Grenelle without rest, 87 av. É. Zola (15th) ☎ 01 45 78 08 22, Fax 01 40 59 03
– lift TV ☎. AE ① GB JCB L
39 – **50 rm** 420/510.

Beaugrenelle St-Charles without rest, 82 r. St-Charles (15th) ☎ 01 45 78 61 6
Fax 01 45 79 04 38 – lift TV ☎. AE ① GB JCB K
39 – **51 rm** 390/500.

Apollinaire without rest, 39 r. Delambre (14th) ☎ 01 43 35 18 40, Fax 01 43 35 30
– lift TV ☎. AE ① GB JCB M
45 – **36 rm** 470/590.

Tour Eiffel Dupleix M without rest, 11 r. Juge (15th) ☎ 01 45 78 29 2
Fax 01 45 78 60 00 – lift TV ☎. AE ① GB JCB K
39 – **40 rm** 450/630.

Arès without rest, 7 r. Gén. de Larminat (15th) ☎ 01 47 34 74 04, Fax 01 47 34 48
– lift TV ☎. AE ① GB K
45 – **42 rm** 530/650.

Delambre M without rest, 35 r. Delambre (14th) ☎ 01 43 20 66 31, Fax 01 45 38 91
– lift TV ☎ &. GB M
45 – **30 rm** 420/460.

Apollon Montparnasse without rest, 91 r. Ouest (14th) ☎ 01 43 95 62 0
Fax 01 43 95 62 10 – lift TV ☎. AE ① GB JCB N 10-
35 – **33 rm** 395/470.

Lilas Blanc M without rest, 5 r. Avre (15th) ☎ 01 45 75 30 07, Fax 01 45 78 66 65
lift rm TV ☎. AE ① GB K
35 – **32 rm** 380/455.

Ariane Montparnasse without rest, 35 r. Sablière (14th) ☎ 01 45 45 67 1
Fax 01 45 45 39 49 – lift TV ☎. AE GB N
35 – **30 rm** 395/460.

Carladez Cambronne without rest, 3 pl. Gén. Beuret (15th) ☎ 01 47 34 07 1
Fax 01 40 65 95 68 – lift TV ☎. AE ① GB M
36 – **27 rm** 400/440.

Modern H. Val Girard without rest, 14 r. Pétel (15th) ☎ 01 48 28 53 9
Fax 01 48 28 69 94 – lift TV ☎. AE ① GB JCB M
35 – **39 rm** 385/450.

Châtillon H. without rest, 11 square Châtillon (14th) ☎ 01 45 42 31 1
Fax 01 45 42 72 09 – lift TV ☎. GB. P
32 – **31 rm** 290/360.

Daguerre without rest, 94 r. Daguerre (14th) ☎ 01 43 22 43 54, Fax 01 43 20 66 8
– lift TV ☎ &. AE ① GB JCB. N
38 – **30 rm** 385/430.

Résidence St-Lambert without rest, 5 r. E. Gibez (15th) ☎ 01 48 28 63 1
Fax 01 45 33 45 50 – lift TV ☎. AE ① GB JCB N
42 – **48 rm** 490/570.

Istria without rest, 29 r. Campagne Première (14th) ☎ 01 43 20 91 8
Fax 01 43 22 48 45 – lift TV ☎. AE ① GB JCB M
40 – **26 rm** 470/580.

Pasteur without rest, 33 r. Dr Roux (15th) ☎ 01 47 83 53 17, Fax 01 45 66 62 39 –
TV ☎. GB M
closed late July-late August – 40 – **19 rm** 315/440.

XXXX ✿ **Les Célébrités** - Hôtel Nikko, 61 quai Grenelle (15th) ☎ 01 40 58 20 0
Fax 01 40 58 24 24, ← – ▤. AE ① GB JCB K
closed August – **Meals** 290/390 and a la carte 340/540
Spec. Ravioli de homard breton aux cèpes. Tronçon de turbot au jus de coques. Volail de Bresse rôtie, pommes de terre farcies.

XXXX ✿ **Montparnasse 25** - Hôtel Méridien Montparnasse, 19 r. Cdt Mouchotte (14t
☎ 01 44 36 44 25, Fax 01 44 36 49 03 – ▤ P. AE ① GB JCB. M
closed 2 August-2 September, Christmas-New Year, Saturday and Sunday – **Meals** 24 (lunch), 300/390 and a la carte 350/440
Spec. Tourte de pomme de terre, pied de porc et foie gras (January-March). Tronçon c turbot en cocotte, fricassée de morilles au vin d'Arbois (April-June). Assiette gourmand du "croqueur" de chocolat.

XXXX ✿ **Relais de Sèvres** - Hôtel Sofitel Porte de Sèvres, 8 r. L. Armand (15th) ✆ 01 40 60 33 66, Fax 01 45 57 04 22 – ▤. AE ⓓ GB JCB. ✂ N 5
closed August, 24 December-4 January, Saturday, Sunday and Bank Holidays – **Meals** 220 (dinner)/350 b.i. and a la carte 280/360
Spec. Cuisses de grenouilles poêlées à la livèche et œuf cassé. Millefeuille de saumon mi-doux aux légumes croquants. Pressé de queue de bœuf en marmite.

XXX **Morot Gaudry,** 6 r. Cavalerie (15th) (8th floor) ✆ 01 45 67 06 85, Fax 01 45 67 55 72, 🏛 – |$| ▤. AE ⓓ GB K 8
closed Sunday – **Meals** 230 (lunch)/390 and a la carte 330/430.

XXX **Mille Colonnes,** 20 bis r. Gaîté (14th) ✆ 01 40 47 08 34, Fax 01 40 64 37 49, 🏛 – ▤. AE ⓓ GB M 11
closed 28 July-24 August, Saturday lunch and Sunday – **Meals** 165.

XXX ✿ **Le Duc,** 243 bd Raspail (14th) ✆ 01 43 20 96 30, Fax 01 43 20 46 73 – ▤. AE GB JCB M 12
closed Saturday in July-August, Sunday and Monday – **Meals** - Seafood - 260 and a la carte 330/520
Spec. Tartare de poissons. Saint-Jacques au naturel (October-May). Médaillons de lotte aux endives caramélisées.

XXX **Pavillon Montsouris,** 20 r. Gazan (14th) ✆ 01 45 88 38 52, Fax 01 45 88 63 40, ≼, 🏛, « 1900 pavilion beside the park » – P. AE GB. ✂ R 14
Meals 175 (lunch)/265.

XXX **Moniage Guillaume,** 88 r. Tombe-Issoire (14th) ✆ 01 43 22 96 15, Fax 01 43 27 11 79 – AE ⓓ GB JCB P 12
closed Sunday – **Meals** 245 and a la carte 280/440.

XXX **Le Dôme,** 108 bd Montparnasse (14th) ✆ 01 43 35 25 81, Fax 01 42 79 01 19, brasserie – ▤. AE ⓓ GB LM 12
closed Monday – **Meals** - Seafood - a la carte 280/470.

XXX **Chen,** 15 r. Théâtre (15th) ✆ 01 45 79 34 34, Fax 01 45 79 07 53 – ▤. AE GB JCB K 6
closed Sunday – **Meals** - Chinese rest. - 170/450 and a la carte 250/340.

XX **Lous Landès,** 157 av. Maine (14th) ✆ 01 45 43 08 04, Fax 01 45 45 91 35 – ▤. AE ⓓ GB N 11
closed August, Saturday lunch and Sunday – **Meals** 195/310 and a la carte 270/420.

XX **Lal Qila,** 88 av. É. Zola (15th) ✆ 01 45 75 68 40, Fax 01 45 79 68 61, « Original decor » – ▤. AE GB L 7
Meals - Indian rest. - 55 (lunch), 125/250.

XX **Philippe Detourbe,** 8 r. Nicolas Charlet (15th) ✆ 01 42 19 08 59, Fax 01 45 67 09 13 – ▤. GB L 10
closed August, 21 to 28 December, Saturday lunch and Sunday – **Meals** 160 (lunch)/180.

XX **Yves Quintard,** 99 r. Blomet (15th) ✆ 01 42 50 22 27, Fax 01 42 50 22 27 – ▤. GB M 8
closed 12 to 30 August, Saturday lunch and Sunday – **Meals** 150 b.i. (lunch)/175 and a la carte 180/310.

XX **La Dînée,** 85 r. Leblanc (15th) ✆ 01 45 54 20 49, Fax 01 40 60 74 88 – AE ⓓ GB
closed 4 to 24 August, Sunday lunch and Saturday – **Meals** 180 (lunch), 290/450 b.i. and a la carte 250/410. M 5

XX **La Coupole,** 102 bd Montparnasse (14th) ✆ 01 43 20 14 20, Fax 01 43 35 46 14, « 1920 Parisian brasserie » – ▤. AE ⓓ GB L 12
Meals a la carte 200/300.

XX **Le Caroubier,** 122 av. Maine (14th) ✆ 01 43 20 41 49 – ▤. ⓓ GB N 11
closed 12 July-18 August and Monday – **Meals** - North African rest. - 140 and a la carte approx. 200 🍷.

XX **Erawan,** 76 r. Fédération (15th) ✆ 01 47 83 55 67, Fax 01 47 34 85 98 – ▤. AE GB. ✂ K 8
closed August and Sunday – **Meals** Thaï rest. a la carte 140/220.

XX **Aux Senteurs de Provence,** 295 r. Lecourbe (15th) ✆ 01 45 57 11 98, Fax 01 45 58 66 84 – AE ⓓ GB JCB M 6
closed 10 to 17 August, Saturday lunch and Sunday – **Meals** - Seafood - 146 and a la carte 200/350.

XX **L'Etape,** 89 r. Convention (15th) ✆ 01 45 54 73 49, Fax 01 45 58 20 91 – ▤. GB
closed 24 December-2 January, Saturday lunch and Sunday – **Meals** 170/190 b.i. and a la carte 160/270. M 6

XX **La Gauloise,** 59 av. La Motte-Picquet (15 th) ✆ 01 47 34 11 64, Fax 01 40 61 09 70, 🏛 – AE ⓓ GB K 8
Meals 144 b.i./350 b.i. and a la carte 210/340.

La Chaumière, 54 av. F. Faure (15th) ✆ 01 45 54 13 91 – AE ⓓ GB M
closed August, February Holidays, Monday dinner and Tuesday – **Meals** 185 b.i. and a carte 200/310.

de la Tour, 6 r. Desaix (15th) ✆ 01 43 06 04 24 – GB J
closed August, Saturday lunch and Sunday – **Meals** 125 (lunch)/185 and a la carte 21(310.

Fontana Rosa, 28 bd Garibaldi (15th) ✆ 01 45 66 97 84 – GB L
Meals - Italian rest. - 120 (lunch)and a la carte 200/290.

L'Épopée, 89 av. É. Zola (15th) ✆ 01 45 77 71 37 – AE GB L
closed 11 to 24 August, Saturday lunch and Sunday – **Meals** 185.

Bistrot du Dôme, 1 r. Delambre (14th) ✆ 01 43 35 32 00, Fax 01 48 04 00 59 – ▤ AE GB M 1
Meals - Seafood - a la carte 190/240.

Le Petit Plat, 49 av. É. Zola (15th) ✆ 01 45 78 24 20, Fax 01 45 78 23 13 – ▤ GB L
closed 4 to 17 August – **Meals** 140 and a la carte 170/240.

Le Gastroquet, 10 r. Desnouettes (15th) ✆ 01 48 28 60 91, Fax 01 45 33 23 70 – ▤ GB N
closed August, Saturday and Sunday – **Meals** 149 and a la carte 200/370.

Les Cévennes, 55 r. Cévennes (15th) ✆ 01 45 54 33 76, Fax 01 44 26 46 95 – AE GB ✱ L
closed 15 to 31 August, Saturday lunch and Sunday – **Meals** 165/350.

Contre-Allée, 83 av. Denfert-Rochereau (14th) ✆ 01 43 54 99 86, Fax 01 43 25 05 2 – AE GB N 1
closed Saturday lunch and Sunday – **Meals** 190.

L'Armoise, 67 r. Entrepreneurs (15th) ✆ 01 45 79 03 31 – ▤. GB L
closed 1 to 20 August, Saturday lunch and Sunday – **Meals** 128 ♁.

Chez Pierre, 117 r. Vaugirard (15th) ✆ 01 47 34 96 12, Fax 01 47 34 96 12, bistro ▤. AE GB L 1
closed 30 April-6 May, 1 to 26 August, Sunday, Monday lunch and Bank Holidays – **Mea** 130/145 and a la carte 180/240.

Le Père Claude, 51 av. La Motte-Picquet (15th) ✆ 01 47 34 03 05, Fax 01 40 56 97 8 – AE GB K
Meals 105/160 and a la carte 260/370.

Château Poivre, 145 r. Château (14th) ✆ 01 43 22 03 68 – AE GB N 1
closed 10 to 20 August, 22 December-2 January and Sunday – **Meals** 89 and a la cart 150/280 ♁.

Les P'tits Bouchons de François Clerc, 32 bd Montparnasse (15th ✆ 01 45 48 52 03, Fax 01 45 48 52 17, bistrot – AE GB L 1
closed Saturday lunch and Sunday – **Meals** 169/199.

La Régalade, 49 av. J. Moulin (14th) ✆ 01 45 45 68 58, Fax 01 45 40 96 74, bistro ▤. GB R 1
closed August, Saturday lunch, Sunday and Monday – **Meals** (booking essential) 170.

L'Os à Moelle, 3 r. Vasco de Gama (15th) ✆ 01 45 57 27 27, bistro – AE GB M
closed 25 July-25 August, Sunday and Monday – **Meals** 145 (lunch)/190.

L'Agape, 281 r. Lecourbe (15th) ✆ 01 45 58 19 29 – GB M
closed August, Saturday lunch and Sunday – **Meals** 120.

Le St-Vincent, 26 r. Croix-Nivert (15th) ✆ 01 47 34 14 94, Fax 01 45 66 02 80, bistr – ▤. AE GB L
closed 11 to 17 August, Saturday lunch and Sunday – **Meals** 165 b.i. and a la carte 150/19 ♁.

Le Petit Mâchon, 123 r. Convention (15th) ✆ 01 45 54 08 62, bistro – GB N
closed 3 to 26 August and Sunday – **Meals** 85 (lunch)/210 and a la carte 160/230.

L'Amuse Bouche, 186 r. Château (14th) ✆ 01 43 35 31 61 – GB N 1
closed 4 to 24 August, Saturday lunch and Sunday – **Meals** (booking essential) 168.

To find your way in the capital, use the MICHELIN street plans of PARIS
10 sheet map, 12 sheet map with street index,
11 atlas with street index and practical information,
14 atlas with street index.

Passy, Auteuil, Bois de Boulogne, Chaillot, Porte Maillot.

16th arrondissement.
16th: ✉ 75016 or 75116

Le Parc M, 55 av. R. Poincaré ✉ 75116 ℘ 01 44 05 66 66, Fax 01 44 05 66 00, « Fine English furniture » – rm TV – 30 - 250. AE GB. rest G 6
see ***Alain Ducasse*** below - ***Le Relais du Parc*** ℘ 01 44 05 66 10 **Meals** a la carte 260/350 – 120 – **117 rm** 1990/2950, 3 duplex.

Raphaël, 17 av. Kléber ✉ 75116 ℘ 01 44 28 00 28, Fax 01 45 01 21 50, « Elegant period decor, fine furniture » – rm TV – 50. AE GB JCB F 7
La Salle à Manger *(closed August, Saturday, Sunday and Bank Holidays)* **Meals** 295 and a la carte 290/430 – 120 – **67 rm** 1850/2950, 23 suites.

St-James Paris, 43 av. Bugeaud ✉ 75116 ℘ 01 44 05 81 81, Fax 01 44 05 81 82, « Attractive 19C mansion », – TV P – 25. AE GB JCB. rest F 5
Meals *(closed weekends and Bank Holidays)* (residents only) 300 (lunch), 350/550 and a la carte 280/400 – 95 – **20 rm** 1600/2000, 20 suites3800, 8 duplex 2400.

Baltimore M, 88bis av. Kléber ✉ 75116 ℘ 01 44 34 54 54, Fax 01 44 34 54 44, « Attractive decor » – rm TV – 30 - 100. AE GB JCB G 7
Bertie's ℘ 01 44 34 54 34 - English rest. *(closed 1 to 15 August)* **Meals** 195 and a la carte 230/380 – 120 – **104 rm** 1990/3500.

K. Palace M without rest, 81 av. Kléber ✉ 75116 ℘ 01 44 05 75 75, Fax 01 44 05 74 74, « Contemporary decor », – rm TV – 40. AE GB JCB. G 7
105 – **83 rm** 1510/2610.

Villa Maillot M without rest, 143 av. Malakoff ✉ 75116 ℘ 01 53 64 52 52, Fax 01 45 00 60 61 – TV – 25. AE GB JCB F 6
110 – **39 rm** 1550/1770, 3 suites.

Pergolèse M without rest, 3 r. Pergolèse ✉ 75116 ℘ 01 40 67 96 77, Fax 01 45 00 12 11, « Contemporary decor » – TV. AE GB JCB E 6
75 – **40 rm** 890/1590.

Majestic without rest, 29 r. Dumont d'Urville ✉ 75116 ℘ 01 45 00 83 70, Fax 01 45 00 29 48 – rm TV. AE GB JCB F 7
60 – **27 rm** 1170/1470, 3 suites.

Élysées Régencia M without rest, 41 av. Marceau ✉ 75016 ℘ 01 47 20 42 65, Fax 01 49 52 03 42, « Attractive decor » – rm TV. AE GB JCB.
80 – **41 rm** 1270/1700.

Garden Élysée M without rest, 12 r. St-Didier ✉ 75116 ℘ 01 47 55 01 11, Fax 01 47 27 79 24 – TV. AE GB JCB. G 7
80 – **48 rm** 800/1600.

Alexander without rest, 102 av. V. Hugo ✉ 75116 ℘ 01 45 53 64 65, Fax 01 45 53 12 51 – TV. AE GB JCB. G 6
78 – **62 rm** 840/1320.

Rond-Point de Longchamp without rest, 86 r. Longchamp ✉ 75116 ℘ 01 45 05 13 63, Fax 01 47 55 12 80 – rm TV – 50. AE GB
65 – **57 rm** 1500. G 6

Élysées Sablons M without rest, 32 r. Greuze ✉ 75116 ℘ 01 47 27 10 00, Fax 01 47 27 47 10 – rm TV. AE GB JCB G 6
75 – **41 rm** 850/1070.

Frémiet without rest, 6 av. Frémiet ✉ 75016 ℘ 01 45 24 52 06, Fax 01 42 88 77 46 – rm TV. AE GB JCB J 6
50 – **34 rm** 650/850.

Élysées Bassano without rest, 24 r. Bassano ✉ 75116 ✆ 01 47 20 49
Fax 01 47 23 06 72 – |‡| ⇔ rm TV ☎. AE ⓓ GB JCB
75 – **40 rm** 850/960.

Union H. Étoile without rest, 44 r. Hamelin ✉ 75116 ✆ 01 45 53 14
Fax 01 47 55 94 79 – |‡| kitchenette TV ☎. AE ⓓ GB JCB
40 – **28 rm** 715/830, 13 suites.

Résidence Impériale M without rest, 155 av. Malakoff ✉ 75116 ✆ 01 45 00 23
Fax 01 45 01 88 82 – |‡| ⇔ rm ≡ TV ☎. AE ⓓ GB
55 – **37 rm** 740/800.

Les Jardins du Trocadéro M without rest, 35 r. Franklin ✉ 751
✆ 01 53 70 17 70, Fax 01 53 70 17 80 – |‡| ⇔ rm ≡ TV ☎. AE ⓓ GB JCB
60 – **18 rm** 850/1950.

Floride Étoile without rest, 14 r. St-Didier ✉ 75116 ✆ 01 47 27 23
Fax 01 47 27 82 87 – |‡| TV ☎ – 40. AE ⓓ GB JCB.
45 – **60 rm** 600/870.

Kléber without rest, 7 r. Belloy ✉ 75116 ✆ 01 47 23 80 22, Fax 01 49 52 07 20 –
TV ☎. AE ⓓ GB JCB
60 – **23 rm** 690/890.

Victor Hugo without rest, 19 r. Copernic ✉ 75116 ✆ 01 45 53 76
Fax 01 45 53 69 93 – |‡| TV ☎. AE ⓓ GB JCB.
65 – **75 rm** 669/828.

Sévigné without rest, 6 r. Belloy ✉ 75116 ✆ 01 47 20 88 90, Fax 01 40 70 98 7
|‡| TV ☎. AE ⓓ GB JCB
48 – **30 rm** 620/750.

Résidence Chambellan Morgane without rest, 6 r. Keppler ✉ 751
✆ 01 47 20 35 72, Fax 01 47 20 95 69 – |‡| TV ☎. AE ⓓ GB JCB.
50 – **20 rm** 650/850.

Holiday Inn Garden Court M without rest, 21 r. Gudin ✉ 75016 ✆ 01 46 51 99
Fax 01 46 51 07 24 – |‡| ⇔ rm ≡ TV ☎. AE ⓓ GB JCB
65 – **47 rm** 710/780.

Étoile Maillot without rest, 10 r. Bois de Boulogne (angle r. Duret) ✉ 751
✆ 01 45 00 42 60, Fax 01 45 00 55 89 – |‡| TV ☎. AE ⓓ GB
40 – **28 rm** 540/780.

Royal Élysées without rest, 6 av. V. Hugo ✉ 75116 ✆ 01 45 00 05
Fax 01 45 00 13 88 – |‡| ≡ TV ☎. AE ⓓ GB JCB
50 – **35 rm** 1100/1200.

Passy Eiffel without rest, 10 r. Passy ✉ 75016 ✆ 01 45 25 55 66, Fax 01 42 88 89
– |‡| ≡ TV ☎. AE ⓓ GB JCB
40 – **48 rm** 580/680.

Massenet without rest, 5bis r. Massenet ✉ 75116 ✆ 01 45 24 43
Fax 01 45 24 41 39 – |‡| TV ☎. AE ⓓ GB JCB.
40 – **41 rm** 500/760.

Régina de Passy without rest, 6 r. Tour ✉ 75116 ✆ 01 45 24 43
Fax 01 40 50 70 62 – |‡| TV ☎. AE ⓓ GB H 6-J
55 – **62 rm** 540/850.

Résidence Foch without rest, 10 r. Marbeau ✉ 75116 ✆ 01 45 00 46
Fax 01 45 01 98 68 – |‡| TV ☎. AE ⓓ GB
45 – **25 rm** 615/650.

Résidence Marceau without rest, 37 av. Marceau ✉ 75116 ✆ 01 47 20 43
Fax 01 47 20 14 76 – |‡| TV ☎. AE ⓓ GB JCB.
35 – **30 rm** 550/650.

Murat without rest, 119 bis bd Murat ✉ 75016 ✆ 01 46 51 12 32, Fax 01 46 51 70
– |‡| TV ☎. AE ⓓ GB.
45 – **28 rm** 650/700.

Hameau de Passy M without rest, 48 r. Passy ✉ 75016 ✆ 01 42 88 47
Fax 01 42 30 83 72 – TV ☎. AE ⓓ GB JCB J 5
30 – **32 rm** 500/550.

Eiffel Kennedy without rest, 12 r. Boulainvilliers ✉ 75016 ✆ 01 45 24 45
Fax 01 42 30 83 32 – |‡| TV ☎. AE ⓓ GB JCB
45 – **30 rm** 480/680.

Nicolo without rest, 3 r. Nicolo ✉ 75116 ✆ 01 42 88 83 40, Fax 01 42 24 45 41 –
TV ☎. AE GB JCB
35 – **28 rm** 380/450.

XXXXX ✿✿✿ **Alain Ducasse,** 59 av. R. Poincaré ✉ 75116 ✆ 01 47 27 12 27, Fax 01 47 27 31 22, « Elegant mansion with Art Nouveau decor » – ▤. AE ⓓ GB. ✂ G 6
closed 4 July-4 August, 24 December-4 January, Saturday and Sunday – **Meals** 480 (lunch), 780/890 and a la carte 750/1 000
Spec. Pâtes mi-séchées crémées et truffées au ris de veau, crêtes et rognons de coq. Turbot aux algues, coquillages et copeaux de beurre demi-sel. Coupe glacée café-chocolat, brioche rôtie.

XXXX ✿✿ **Faugeron,** 52 r. Longchamp ✉ 75116 ✆ 01 47 04 24 53, Fax 01 47 55 62 90, « Attractive decor » – ▤. AE GB JCB. ✂ G 7
closed August, 23 December-3 January, Saturday except dinner from October-April and Sunday – **Meals** 295 (lunch), 470/550 b.i. and a la carte 470/620
Spec. Oeufs coque à la purée de truffes. Truffes (January-March). Gibier (15 October-10 January).

XXXX ✿ **Prunier-Traktir,** 16 av. V. Hugo ✉ 75116 ✆ 01 44 17 35 85, Fax 01 44 17 90 10, « Art Deco decor » – ▤. AE ⓓ GB JCB FG 8
closed 20 July-18 August, Monday lunch and Sunday – **Meals** - Seafood - a la carte 380/600
Spec. Soupe crémeuse de homard aux haricots blancs et chorizo. Grosse sole rôtie. Pieds de mouton Emile Prunier.

XXXX ✿✿ **Vivarois** (Peyrot), 192 av. V. Hugo ✉ 75116 ✆ 01 45 04 04 31, Fax 01 45 03 09 84 – ▤. AE ⓓ GB JCB G 5
closed August, Saturday and Sunday – **Meals** 345 (lunch)and a la carte 430/680
Spec. Terrine de lentilles et queue de bœuf. Croustillant de rouget en tapenade. Trilogie de lièvre aux saveurs d'automne (22 September-3 December).

XXX ✿ **Relais d'Auteuil** (Pignol), 31 bd Murat ✉ 75016 ✆ 01 46 51 09 54, Fax 01 40 71 05 03 – ▤. AE GB L 3
closed 2 to 24 August, Saturday lunch and Sunday – **Meals** 250 (lunch), 420/530 and a la carte 380/520
Spec. Amandine de foie gras de canard. Dos de bar au poivre concassé. Madeleine au miel de bruyère, glace miel et noix.

XXX ✿ **Jamin** (Guichard), 32 r. Longchamp ✉ 75116 ✆ 01 45 53 00 07, Fax 01 45 53 00 15 – AE ⓓ GB G 7
closed 11 July-3 August, Saturday and Sunday – **Meals** 280 (lunch)/375 and a la carte 270/400
Spec. Crème légère aux lentilles et ventrèche juste fumée. Joue et queue de cochon "braisées rôties" à la marjolaine et pommes tapées. Millefeuille au chocolat amer.

XXX **Tsé-Yang,** 25 av. Pierre 1er de Serbie ✉ 75016 ✆ 01 47 20 70 22, Fax 01 49 52 03 68, « Tasteful decor » – ▤. AE ⓓ GB JCB. ✂ G 8
Meals - Chinese rest. - 115 (lunch), 245/285 and a la carte 210/320.

XXX ✿ **Port Alma** (Canal), 10 av. New-York ✉ 75116 ✆ 01 47 23 75 11 – ▤. AE ⓓ GB
closed August and Sunday – **Meals** - Seafood - 200 (lunch)and a la carte 280/410 H 8
Spec. Langoustines rôties aux courgettes, aubergines et tomates épicées. Rouget poêlé au vinaigre, rosace de courgettes. Bar en croûte de sel de Guérande.

XXX **Pavillon Noura,** 21 av. Marceau ✉ 75116 ✆ 01 47 20 33 33, Fax 01 47 20 60 31 – ▤. AE ⓓ GB. ✂ G 8
Meals - Lebanese rest. - 156 (lunch), 220/320 and a la carte 160/200.

XXX ✿ **Le Pergolèse** (Corre), 40 r. Pergolèse ✉ 75116 ✆ 01 45 00 21 40, Fax 01 45 00 81 31 – AE GB F 6
closed August, Saturday and Sunday – **Meals** 230/380 and a la carte 290/420
Spec. Carpaccio de jambon d'agneau de Sologne. Langoustines croustillantes au cresson. Saint-Jacques rôties en robe des champs (October-March).

XXX **Chez Ngo,** 70 r. Longchamp ✉ 75116 ✆ 01 47 04 53 20, Fax 01 47 04 53 20 – ▤. AE ⓓ GB JCB. ✂ G 6
Meals - Chinese and Thai rest. - 98 b.i. (lunch)/168 b.i. and a la carte 130/280.

XX **Zébra Square,** 3 pl. Clément Ader ✉ 75016 ✆ 01 44 14 91 91, Fax 01 45 20 46 41, « Original contemporary decor » – AE ⓓ GB JCB. ✂ K 5
Meals a la carte 210/290.

XX **Al Mounia,** 16 r. Magdebourg ✉ 75116 ✆ 01 47 27 57 28 – ▤. AE GB. ✂ G 7
closed 10 July-31 August and Sunday – **Meals** - Moroccan rest. - (dinner booking essential) a la carte 200/250.

XX ✿ **Conti,** 72 r. Lauriston ✉ 75116 ✆ 01 47 27 74 67, Fax 01 47 27 37 66 – ▤. AE ⓓ GB
closed 4 to 25 August, 25 December-5 January, Saturday, Sunday and Bank Holidays – **Meals** - Italian rest. - 198 and a la carte 310/400 G 7
Spec. Tortellini au crabe (20 April-31 October). Espadon poêlé napolitaine (June-September). Figues rôties farcies aux amaretti (July-October).

XX **Giulio Rebellato,** 136 r. Pompe ✉ 75116 ✆ 01 47 27 50 26 – ▤. AE GB. ✂
closed 27 July-24 August and Sunday – **Meals** - Italian rest. - a la carte 260/390. G 6

XX **Tang,** 125 r. de la Tour ✉ 75116 ✆ 01 45 04 35 35, Fax 01 45 04 58 19 – AE GB.
closed 12 to 15 July, August, Saturday lunch and Monday – **Meals** - Chinese and Thai re
- 200 (lunch)and a la carte 230/320. H

XX **Marius,** 82 bd Murat ✉ 75016 ✆ 01 46 51 67 80, Fax 01 47 43 10 24, – AE G
closed August, Saturday lunch and Sunday – **Meals** a la carte 200/280.# M

XX **Villa Vinci,** 23 r. P. Valéry ✉ 75116 ✆ 01 45 01 68 18 – ▤. AE GB F
closed August, Saturday and Sunday – **Meals** - Italian rest. - 182 and a la carte 240/390.

XX **Paul Chêne,** 123 r. Lauriston ✉ 75116 ✆ 01 47 27 63 17, Fax 01 47 27 53 18 –
AE ◑ GB G
closed 24 December-1 January, Saturday lunch and Sunday – **Meals** 200/250 and a la car
210/370.

XX **Fontaine d'Auteuil,** 35bis r. La Fontaine ✉ 75016 ✆ 01 42 88 04 47 – ▤. AE ◑ GB
closed 4 to 24 August, Saturday lunch and Sunday – **Meals** 175 (lunch), 230/350 and
la carte 270/370. K

XX **Sous l'Olivier,** 15 r. Goethe ✉ 75116 ✆ 01 47 20 84 81, Fax 01 47 20 73 75,
AE GB G
closed August, Saturday, Sunday and Bank Holidays – **Meals** 160.

XX **Chez Géraud,** 31 r. Vital ✉ 75016 ✆ 01 45 20 33 00, Fax 01 45 20 46 60, « Attracti
Longwy porcelain mural » – AE GB H
closed August, Sunday dinner and Saturday – **Meals** 180 and a la carte 220/330.

XX **La Petite Tour,** 11 r. de la Tour ✉ 75116 ✆ 01 45 20 09 31 – AE ◑ GB JCB
closed August and Sunday – **Meals** a la carte 280/420. H

XX **Bellini,** 28 r. Lesueur ✉ 75116 ✆ 01 45 00 54 20, Fax 01 45 00 11 74 – ▤. AE G
closed Saturday lunch, Sunday and Bank Holidays – **Meals** - Italian rest. - 180 and a la car
200/320. F

X **Beaujolais d'Auteuil,** 99 bd Montmorency ✉ 75016 ✆ 01 47 43 03 5
Fax 01 46 51 27 81, bistro – GB K
closed Saturday lunch and Sunday – **Meals** 123/220 b.i. and a la carte 150/220.

X **La Butte Chaillot,** 110 bis av. Kléber ✉ 75116 ✆ 01 47 27 88 88, Fax 01 47 04 85
– ▤. AE GB JCB G
Meals 150/210 and a la carte 210/290.

X **Le Cuisinier François,** 19 r. Le Marois ✉ 75016 ✆ 01 45 27 83 7
Fax 01 45 27 83 74 – AE GB M
closed August, Wednesday dinner, Sunday dinner and Monday – **Meals** 160 and a la car
260/380.

X **Rosimar,** 26 r. Poussin ✉ 75016 ✆ 01 45 27 74 91, Fax 01 45 20 75 05 – ▤. AE G
closed August, Saturday lunch, Sunday and Bank Holidays – **Meals** - Fish and Spanish re
- 120 (lunch)/175 and a la carte 190/270. K

X **Le Driver's,** 6 r. G. Bizet ✉ 75016 ✆ 01 47 23 61 15, Fax 01 47 23 80 17, « Racing c
accessories » – ▤. AE GB G
closed Saturday lunch and Sunday – **Meals** a la carte 120/240.

X **Vin et Marée,** 2 r. Daumier ✉ 75016 ✆ 01 46 47 91 39, Fax 01 46 47 69 07 – ▤.
◑ GB – **Meals** - Seafood - a la carte approx. 170. M

X **Bistrot de l'Étoile,** 19 r. Lauriston ✉ 75016 ✆ 01 40 67 11 16, Fax 01 45 00 99
– ▤. AE GB JCB F
closed Saturday lunch and Sunday – **Meals** a la carte 200/260.

X **Lac Hong,** 67 r. Lauriston ✉ 75116 ✆ 01 47 55 87 17 – GB. G
closed August and Sunday – **Meals** - Vietnamese rest. - 98 (lunch)and a la carte 170/29

X **Le Scheffer,** 22 r. Scheffer ✉ 75016 ✆ 01 47 27 81 11, bistrot – AE GB H
closed Saturday, Sunday and Bank Holidays – **Meals** a la carte 140/190.

in the Bois de Boulogne :

XXXX ✿ **Le Pré Catelan,** rte Suresnes ✉ 75016 ✆ 01 44 14 41 14, Fax 01 45 24 43 25,
– P. AE ◑ GB JCB H
closed 6 to 18 February, Sunday dinner and Monday – **Meals** 290 (lunch), 550/750 a
a la carte 480/760
Spec. Pot de crème prise aux cèpes, mouillettes croustillantes aux noix. Grillons de ris
veau aux choux-fleurs. Cheese-cake aux coings, coulis de potimarron.

XXXX ✿ **La Grande Cascade,** allée de Longchamp (opposite the hippodrome) ✉ 750
✆ 01 45 27 33 51, Fax 01 42 88 99 06, « Second Empire pavilion » – P. AE ◑ G
closed 20 December-10 January – **Meals** 295/600 and a la carte 500/650
Spec. Pâté en croûte "Lucien Tendret". Filet de bœuf grillé sauce béarnaise, pomm
soufflées. Pain perdu aux noix et aux raisins.

Batignolles, Ternes, Wagram.

17th arrondissement.
17th: ✉ 75017

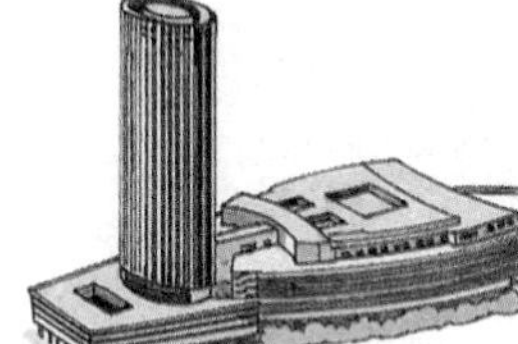

Concorde La Fayette M, 3 pl. Gén. Koenig ✆ 01 40 68 50 68, Fax 01 40 68 50 43, « Panoramic bar on 33th floor with ≤ Paris » – |\$| ⇔ rm ▤ TV ☎ – 🏛 40 - 2 000. AE ⓓ GB JCB. ✗ E 6
see ***L'Étoile d'Or*** below - ***L'Arc-en-Ciel*** ✆ 01 40 68 51 25 *(closed August)* **Meals** 144/225 🍷 - ***Les Saisons*** (coffee shop) ✆ 01 40 68 51 19 **Meals** 149 and a la carte 180/260 🍷 – ☕ 146 – **943 rm** 1650/2050, 27 suites.

Le Meridien M, 81 bd Gouvion St-Cyr ✆ 01 40 68 34 34, Fax 01 40 68 31 31 – |\$| ⇔ rm ▤ TV ☎ ♿ – 🏛 50 - 1 500. AE ⓓ GB JCB E 6
see ***Clos de Longchamp*** below - ***Café Arlequin*** ✆ 01 40 68 30 85 **Meals** 158 – ***Le Yamato*** ✆ 01 40 68 30 41, Japanese rest. *(closed August, 1 to 7 January, Saturday lunch, Sunday, and Monday)* **Meals** 120 (lunch) 160/175 – ☕ 170 – **1 008 rm** 1450/1850, 17 suites.

Splendid Étoile without rest, 1bis av. Carnot ✆ 01 45 72 72 00, Fax 01 45 72 72 01 – |\$| ▤ TV ☎. AE ⓓ GB. ✗ F 7
☕ 85 – **57 rm** 950/1700.

Balmoral without rest, 6 r. Gén. Lanrezac ✆ 01 43 80 30 50, Fax 01 43 80 51 56 – |\$| ⇔ rm ▤ TV ☎. AE ⓓ GB E 7
☕ 40 – **57 rm** 500/800.

Quality Inn Pierre M without rest, 25 r. Th.-de-Banville ✆ 01 47 63 76 69, Fax 01 43 80 63 96 – |\$| ⇔ rm TV ☎ ♿ – 🏛 30. AE ⓓ GB JCB D 8
☕ 70 – **50 rm** 830/970.

Regent's Garden without rest, 6 r. P. Demours ✆ 01 45 74 07 30, Fax 01 40 55 01 42, « Garden » – |\$| TV ☎. AE ⓓ GB JCB. ✗ E 7
☕ 45 – **39 rm** 650/940.

Ternes Arc de Triomphe M without rest, 97 av. Ternes ✆ 01 53 81 94 94, Fax 01 53 81 94 95 – |\$| ⇔ rm ▤ TV ☎ ♿. AE ⓓ GB E 6
☕ 65 – **39 rm** 670/980.

Étoile St-Ferdinand without rest, 36 r. St-Ferdinand ✆ 01 45 72 66 66, Fax 01 45 74 12 92 – |\$| ▤ TV ☎. AE ⓓ GB JCB E 6-7
☕ 50 – **42 rm** 900.

Magellan 🌿 without rest, 17 r. J.B.-Dumas ✆ 01 45 72 44 51, Fax 01 40 68 90 36, 🪑 – |\$| TV ☎. AE ⓓ GB. ✗ D 7
☕ 40 – **75 rm** 590/630.

Champerret-Villiers M without rest, 129 av. Villiers ✆ 01 47 64 44 00, Fax 01 47 63 10 58 – |\$| ⇔ rm ▤ TV ☎. AE ⓓ GB JCB. ✗ D 7
☕ 50 – **45 rm** 585/695.

Banville without rest, 166 bd Berthier ✆ 01 42 67 70 16, Fax 01 44 40 42 77 – |\$| ▤ TV ☎. AE GB D 8
☕ 50 – **39 rm** 635/760.

Mercure Étoile M without rest, 27 av. Ternes ✆ 01 47 66 49 18, Fax 01 47 63 77 91 – |\$| ⇔ rm ▤ TV ☎. AE ⓓ GB E 8
☕ 70 – **56 rm** 860.

de Neuville without rest, 3 r. Verniquet ✆ 01 43 80 26 30, Fax 01 43 80 38 55 – |\$| TV ☎. AE ⓓ GB JCB C 8
☕ 55 – **28 rm** 620/720.

Cheverny without rest, 7 villa Berthier ✆ 01 43 80 46 42, Fax 01 47 63 26 62 – |\$| ⇔ rm ▤ TV ☎ – 🏛 50. AE ⓓ GB JCB D 7
☕ 50 – **48 rm** 520/660.

Neva M without rest, 14 r. Brey ✆ 01 43 80 28 26, Fax 01 47 63 00 22 – |\$| ▤ TV ☎ ♿. AE ⓓ GB. ✗ E 8
☕ 45 – **31 rm** 500/757.

Mercédès without rest, 128 av. Wagram ✆ 01 42 27 77 82, Fax 01 40 53 09 89 – |\$| ▤ TV ☎. AE ⓓ GB D 9
☕ 50 – **37 rm** 590/690.

Étoile Park H. without rest, 10 av. Mac Mahon ☎ 01 42 67 69 63, Fax 01 43 80 18 – |‡| TV ☎. AE ⓓ GB JCB E
closed 24 December-1 January – ☐ 52 – **28 rm** 484/710.

Harvey without rest, 7bis r. Débarcadère ☎ 01 45 74 27 19, Fax 01 40 68 03 56 – ▤ TV ☎. AE ⓓ GB JCB E
☐ 40 – **32 rm** 590/720.

Monceau without rest, 7 r. Rennequin ☎ 01 47 63 07 52, Fax 01 47 66 84 44 – ⇔ rm TV ☎. AE ⓓ GB JCB E
☐ 75 – **25 rm** 600/840.

Tilsitt Étoile without rest, 23 r. Brey ☎ 01 43 80 39 71, Fax 01 47 66 37 63 – |‡| ☎. AE ⓓ GB JCB E
☐ 60 – **39 rm** 586/792.

Monceau Étoile without rest, 64 r. Levis ☎ 01 42 27 33 10, Fax 01 42 27 59 58 – TV ☎. AE ⓓ GB JCB D
☐ 35 – **26 rm** 400/650.

Royal Magda without rest, 7 r. Troyon ☎ 01 47 64 10 19, Fax 01 47 64 02 12 – |‡| ☎. AE ⓓ GB. ✗ E
☐ 45 – **26 rm** 650/730, 11 suites.

Abrial M without rest, 176 r. Cardinet ☎ 01 42 63 50 00, Fax 01 42 63 50 03 – |‡| ☎ ♿ 🚗. AE GB JCB C
☐ 48 – **80 rm** 596/652.

Étoile Péreire ⑧ without rest, 146 bd Péreire ☎ 01 42 67 60 00, Fax 01 42 67 02 – |‡| TV ☎. AE ⓓ GB JCB. ✗ D
☐ 54 – **21 rm** 560/760, 5 duplex.

Monceau Élysées without rest, 108 r. Courcelles ☎ 01 47 63 33 0 Fax 01 46 22 87 39 – |‡| TV ☎. AE ⓓ GB E
☐ 50 – **29 rm** 650/770.

Astrid without rest, 27 av. Carnot ☎ 01 44 09 26 00, Fax 01 44 09 26 01 – |‡| TV AE ⓓ GB JCB E
☐ 50 – **40 rm** 450/715.

Campanile, 4 bd Berthier ☎ 01 46 27 10 00, Fax 01 46 27 00 57, 🏠 – |‡| ⇔ rm TV ☎ ♿ 🚗 – 🏛 40. AE ⓓ GB B
Meals 92 b.i./119 b.i. – ☐ 34 – **247 rm** 416.

Champerret-Héliopolis without rest, 13 r. Héliopolis ☎ 01 47 64 92 5 Fax 01 47 64 50 44 – ⇔ rm TV ☎. AE ⓓ GB JCB D
☐ 38 – **22 rm** 350/495.

XXXX ✿✿ **Guy Savoy,** 18 r. Troyon ☎ 01 43 80 40 61, Fax 01 46 22 43 09 – ▤. AE G JCB
closed Saturday lunch and Sunday – **Meals** 880 and a la carte 570/750 E
Spec. Foie gras de canard au sel gris. Bar en écailles grillées aux épices douces. Côte veau de lait rôtie, purée de pommes de terre aux truffes.

XXXX ✿✿ **Michel Rostang,** 20 r. Rennequin ☎ 01 47 63 40 77, Fax 01 47 63 82 75, « Elega decor » – ▤. AE ⓓ GB JCB D
closed 3 to 17 August, Saturday lunch and Sunday – **Meals** 298 (lunch), 560/740 and la carte 550/780
Spec. Emincé de homard mi-cru, mi-cuit. Truffes (15 December-15 March). Canette Bresse au sang.

XXXX ✿ **L'Étoile d'Or** - Hôtel Concorde La Fayette, 3 pl. Gén. Koenig ☎ 01 40 68 51 2 Fax 01 40 68 50 43 – ▤. AE ⓓ GB JCB. ✗ E
closed August, 22 February-1 March, Saturday and Sunday – **Meals** 270/450 and a la car 290/520
Spec. Piccatas de lotte et tomate confite à la menthe. Canard de Challans rôti au vouvra Soufflé chaud au chocolat.

XXXX ✿ **Le Clos Longchamp** - Hôtel Méridien, 81 bd Gouvion-St-Cyr (Pte Maillo ☎ 01 40 68 00 70, Fax 01 40 68 30 81 – ▤. AE ⓓ GB JCB. ✗ E
closed 2 to 24 August, 20 December-6 January, Saturday, Sunday and Bank Holidays
Meals 250 (lunch), 350/470 and a la carte 400/590
Spec. Crevettes vapeur au vinaigre de champagne. Noix de Saint-Jacques aux parfums Siam (October-April). Volaille de Bresse sautée et sa cuisse en brochette.

XXX **Manoir de Paris,** 6 r. P. Demours ☎ 01 45 72 25 25, Fax 01 45 74 80 98 – ▤. AE GB E
closed Saturday except dinner from September-June and Sunday – **Meals** 295/350 ar a la carte 250/390.

XXXX ✿✿ **Apicius** (Vigato), 122 av. Villiers ✆ 01 43 80 19 66, Fax 01 44 40 09 57 – ▤. AE ⓓ GB JCB D 8
closed August, Saturday and Sunday – **Meals** a la carte 410/680
Spec. Langoustines façon "tempura". Ris de veau à la broche, compote de truffes. Grand dessert au chocolat amer.

XXXX ✿ **Amphyclès** (Groult), 78 av. Ternes ✆ 01 40 68 01 01, Fax 01 40 68 91 88 – ▤. AE ⓓ GB JCB E 7
closed Saturday lunch and Sunday – **Meals** 680 and a la carte 580/700
Spec. Foie gras de canard vapeur, mijotée de cocos. Tronçon de turbot de ligne, risotto aux cèpes. Cochon de lait braisé, lentilles vertes du Puy.

XXXX ✿ **Le Sormani** (Fayet), 4 r. Gén. Lanrezac ✆ 01 43 80 13 91, Fax 01 40 55 07 37 – ▤. GB
closed 1 to 21 August, 24 December-2 January, Saturday and Sunday – **Meals** - Italian rest. - 250 (lunch)and a la carte 320/420 E 7
Spec. Risotto à la truffe blanche (October-mid-December). Carpaccio chaud à la truffe noire. Lasagne de chou vert, petit salé, sauce au jus de truffe.

XXXX ✿ **Faucher,** 123 av. Wagram ✆ 01 42 27 61 50, Fax 01 46 22 25 72 – AE GB D 8
closed Saturday lunch and Sunday – **Meals** a la carte 250/380
Spec. Oeuf au plat, foie gras chaud et coppa grillée. Filets de rouget à l'huile d'olive et rigattoni farcis. Canette rôtie et ses filets laqués.

XXXX **Pétrus,** 12 pl. Mar. Juin ✆ 01 43 80 15 95, Fax 01 43 80 06 96 – ▤. AE ⓓ GB
Meals - Seafood - 250/480 b.i. and a la carte 350/570 D 8

XXXX ✿ **Timgad** (Laasri), 21 r. Brunel ✆ 01 45 74 23 70, Fax 01 40 68 76 46, « Moorish decor » – ▤. AE ⓓ GB. ✂ E 7
Meals - North African rest. - a la carte 240/340
Spec. Couscous princier. Pastilla. Tagine.

XXXX **Augusta,** 98 r. Tocqueville ✆ 01 47 63 39 97, Fax 01 42 27 21 71 – ▤. GB C 9
closed 4 to 25 August, Saturday except dinner from October-April and Sunday – **Meals** - Seafood - a la carte 320/560.

XXXX **Il Ristorante,** 22 r. Fourcroy ✆ 01 47 63 34 00, Fax 01 47 63 72 13 – ▤. AE GB
closed 10 to 24 August, 24 December-1 January, Saturday lunch and Sunday – **Meals** - Italian rest. - 165 (lunch)and a la carte 250/340. D 8

XXX ✿ **Le Petit Colombier** (Fournier), 42 r. Acacias ✆ 01 43 80 28 54, Fax 01 44 40 04 29 – AE GB E 7
closed 1 to 18 August, Sunday lunch and Saturday – **Meals** 200 (lunch)/360 and a la carte 300/410
Spec. Oeufs rôtis à la broche aux truffes fraîches (15 December-15 March). Lièvre à la royale (25 September-30 December). Tournedos rossini.

XXX **La Table de Pierre,** 116 bd Péreire ✆ 01 43 80 88 68, Fax 01 47 66 53 02 – ▤. AE GB
closed Saturday lunch and Sunday – **Meals** 210/300 and a la carte 220/360. D 8

XXX **Graindorge,** 15 r. Arc de Triomphe ✆ 01 47 54 00 28, Fax 01 47 54 00 28 – AE GB E 7
closed 4 au 18 August, Saturday lunch and Sunday – **Meals** 165 (lunch), 188/230 and a la carte 210/300.

XXX **Les Bouchons de François Clerc,** 22 r. Terrasse ✆ 01 42 27 31 51, Fax 01 42 27 45 76, ☂ – ▤. AE GB D 10
closed Saturday lunch and Sunday – **Meals** 117 b.i. (lunch)/219.

XXX **Les Béatilles,** 11 bis r. Villebois-Mareuil ✉ 75017 ✆ 01 45 74 43 80, Fax 01 45 74 43 81 – ▤. AE GB E 7
closed 2 to 24 August, 22 December-4 January, Saturday and Sunday – **Meals** 160/290 and a la carte 210/300.

XXX **La Truite Vagabonde,** 17 r. Batignolles ✆ 01 43 87 77 80, Fax 01 43 87 31 50, ☂ – AE GB JCB D 11
closed 10 to 24 August and Sunday dinner – **Meals** 250 b.i./320 b.i. and a la carte 260/370.

XXX **Billy Gourmand,** 20 r. Tocqueville ✆ 01 42 27 03 71 – AE GB D 10
closed 3 to 24 August, Saturday except dinner from 10 September-15 June, Sunday and Bank Holidays – **Meals** 165 and a la carte 240/370.

XXX **Le Beudant,** 97 r. des Dames ✆ 01 43 87 11 20, Fax 01 43 87 27 35 – ▤. AE ⓓ GB JCB D 11
closed 15 to 30 August, Saturday lunch and Sunday – **Meals** 155/300 and a la carte 220/330.

XXX **Aub. des Dolomites,** 38 r. Poncelet ✆ 01 42 27 94 56, Fax 01 47 66 38 54 – AE GB E 8
closed August, Saturday lunch and Sunday – **Meals** 135/180 and a la carte 210/330.

XXX **Les Marines de Pétrus,** 27 av. Niel ✆ 01 47 63 04 24, Fax 01 44 15 92 20 – ▤. AE ⓓ GB D 8
closed August and Sunday – **Meals** - Seafood - a la carte 210/300.

XX **Dessirier,** 9 pl. Mar. Juin ☎ 01 42 27 82 14, Fax 01 47 63 98 79 – AE ⓓ GB [
closed 1 to 15 August – **Meals** - Seafood - a la carte 220/350.

XX ✿ **La Braisière** (Vaxelaire), 54 r. Cardinet ☎ 01 47 63 40 37, Fax 01 47 63 04 76 – GB
closed August, Saturday and Sunday – **Meals** 175 and a la carte 210/380 [
Spec. Mitonnée de pintadeau à la moutarde. Tarte feuilletée au crabe et tomate. Assie "tout chocolat".

XX **Taïra,** 10 r. Acacias ☎ 01 47 66 74 14, Fax 01 47 66 74 14 – ▤. AE ⓓ GB
closed 15 to 25 August, Saturday lunch and Sunday – **Meals** - Seafood - 160/330 an la carte 260/390.

XX **Baumann Ternes,** 64 av. Ternes ☎ 01 45 74 16 66, Fax 01 45 72 44 32, brasseri ▤. AE ⓓ GB E
Meals 178 and a la carte 190/330 ♁.

XX **La Petite Auberge,** 38 r. Laugier ☎ 01 47 63 85 51, Fax 01 47 63 85 8 GB
closed 25 July-25 August, Monday lunch and Sunday – **Meals** (booking essential) 160 a a la carte 190/320. D

XX **Chez Guyvonne,** 14 r. Thann ☎ 01 42 27 25 43, Fax 01 42 27 25 43 – ▤. AE G
D
closed 4 August-1 September, 23 December-1 January, Saturday, Sunday and Bank H days – **Meals** 150/180 and a la carte 200/280.

XX **La Soupière,** 154 av. Wagram ☎ 01 42 27 00 73 – ▤. AE GB D
closed 9 to 18 August, Saturday lunch and Sunday – **Meals** 138/270 and a la ca 190/260.

XX **Chez Georges,** 273 bd Péreire ☎ 01 45 74 31 00, Fax 01 45 74 02 56, bistro – AE G
E
Meals a la carte 180/310.

XX **Epicure 108,** 108 r. Cardinet ☎ 01 47 63 50 91 – GB D
closed 11 to 23 August, February Holidays, Saturday lunch and Sunday – **Meals** 17 250.

XX **Ballon des Ternes,** 103 av. Ternes ☎ 01 45 74 17 98, Fax 01 45 72 18 84, brasse – AE GB JCB E
closed 1 to 20 August – **Meals** a la carte 180/260.

XX **La Niçoise,** 4 r. P. Demours ☎ 01 45 74 42 41, Fax 01 45 74 80 98 – ▤. AE GB E
closed Saturday except dinner from September-June and Sunday – **Meals** 12 165 ♁.

XX **Chez Léon,** 32 r. Legendre ☎ 01 42 27 06 82, bistro – ⓓ GB D
closed August, Saturday and Sunday – **Meals** 135/185.

XX **Chez Laudrin,** 154 bd Péreire ☎ 01 43 80 87 40 – ▤. AE GB D
closed Saturday and Sunday – **Meals** 155 and a la carte 240/400.

X **La Rôtisserie d'Armaillé,** 6 r. Armaillé ☎ 01 42 27 19 20, Fax 01 40 55 00 93 – AE GB JCB E
closed 10 to 17 August, Saturday lunch and Sunday – **Meals** 198 and a la carte 24 340.

X **L'Impatient,** 14 passage Geffroy Didelot ☎ 01 43 87 28 10 – GB D 10-
closed 11 to 31 August, Febuary Holidays, Monday dinner, Saturday and Sunday – **Me** 102/156 and a la carte 200/310.

X **Caves Petrissans,** 30 bis av. Niel ☎ 01 42 27 52 03, Fax 01 40 54 87 56, 佘, bist – AE GB D
closed 2 to 24 August, 23 December-5 January, Saturday, Sunday and Bank Holidays **Meals** 170 and a la carte 200/350.

X **Le Troyon,** 4 r. Troyon ☎ 01 40 68 99 40, Fax 01 40 68 99 57 – AE GB E
closed Saturday lunch and Sunday – **Meals** (booking essential) a la carte 180/230.

X **Bistro du 17e,** 108 av. Villiers ☎ 01 47 63 32 77, Fax 01 42 27 67 66 – ▤. GB
Meals 169 b.i. D

X **Bistrot d'à Côté Flaubert,** 10 r. G. Flaubert ☎ 01 42 67 05 81, Fax 01 47 63 82 – AE GB D
Meals a la carte 220/330.

X **Bistrot de l'Étoile,** 13 r. Troyon ☎ 01 42 67 25 95, Fax 01 46 22 43 09 – ▤. AE G JCB E
closed Sunday lunch – **Meals** 120 b.i. (lunch), 150 b.i./170 and a la carte 190/250.

Montmartre, La Villette, Belleville.

18th, 19th and 20th arrondissements.
18th: ✉ 75018
19th: ✉ 75019
20th: ✉ 75020

Terrass'H. M, 12 r. J. de Maistre (18th) ✆ 01 46 06 72 85, Fax 01 42 52 29 11, « Rooftop terrace, ≤ Paris » – ⫿ ⇋ rm ▤ TV ☎ – 🏟 160. AE ⓓ GB JCB C 13
La Terrasse ✆ 01 44 92 34 00 **Meals** 125 b.i./165 – ▭ 70 – **88 rm** 820/1300, 13 suites.

Holiday Inn M, 216 av. J. Jaurès (19th) ✆ 01 44 84 18 18, Fax 01 44 84 18 20, – ⫿ ⇋ rm ▤ TV ☎ ♿ – 🏟 180. AE ⓓ GB JCB C 21
Meals 110/160 – ▭ 75 – **174 rm** 890/1050, 8 suites.

Mercure Montmartre without rest, 1 r. Caulaincourt (18th) ✆ 01 44 69 70 70, Fax 01 44 69 70 71 – ⫿ ⇋ rm ▤ TV ☎ ♿ – 🏟 120. AE ⓓ GB D 12
▭ 68 – **308 rm** 860/925.

Roma Sacré Coeur without rest, 101 r. Caulaincourt (18th) ✆ 01 42 62 02 02, Fax 01 42 54 34 92 – ⫿ TV ☎. AE ⓓ GB JCB C 14
▭ 37 – **57 rm** 410/480.

Le Laumière without rest, 4 r. Petit (19th) ✆ 01 42 06 10 77, Fax 01 42 06 72 50 – ⫿ TV ☎. GB D 19
▭ 36 – **54 rm** 270/380.

Regyn's Montmartre without rest, 18 pl. Abbesses (18th) ✆ 01 42 54 45 21, Fax 01 42 23 76 69 – ⫿ TV ☎. AE GB D 13
▭ 40 – **22 rm** 370/445.

Palma without rest, 77 av. Gambetta (20th) ✆ 01 46 36 13 65, Fax 01 46 36 03 27 – ⫿ TV ☎. AE ⓓ GB G 21
▭ 33 – **32 rm** 340/395.

Super H. without rest, 208 r. Pyrénées (20th) ✆ 01 46 36 97 48, Fax 01 46 36 26 10 – ⫿ TV ☎. AE ⓓ GB G 21
closed August – ▭ 32 – **32 rm** 250/500.

Eden H. without rest, 90 r. Ordener (18th) ✆ 01 42 64 61 63, Fax 01 42 64 11 43 – ⫿ TV ☎. AE ⓓ GB B 14
▭ 35 – **35 rm** 375/410.

Damrémont without rest, 110 r. Damrémont (18th) ✆ 01 42 64 25 75, Fax 01 46 06 74 64 – ⫿ ⇋ rm TV ☎. AE ⓓ GB JCB. ✗ B 13
▭ 40 – **35 rm** 350/490.

Crimée without rest, 188 r. Crimée (19th) ✆ 01 40 36 75 29, Fax 01 40 36 29 57 – ⫿ TV ☎. AE GB C 18
▭ 30 – **31 rm** 300/350.

des Arts without rest, 5 r. Tholozé (18th) ✆ 01 46 06 30 52, Fax 01 46 06 10 83 – ⫿ TV ☎. AE GB. ✗ D 13
▭ 30 – **50 rm** 440/470.

Abricotel without rest, 15 r. Lally Tallendal (19th) ✆ 01 42 08 34 49, Fax 01 42 40 83 95 – TV ☎ ♿. AE ⓓ GB D 18
▭ 35 – **39 rm** 290/400.

XXX ✿ **Beauvilliers** (Carlier), 52 r. Lamarck (18th) ✆ 01 42 54 54 42, Fax 01 42 62 70 30, « 1900 decor, terrace » – ▤. AE ⓓ GB JCB C 14
closed Monday lunch and Sunday – **Meals** 185 (lunch)/400 b.i. and a la carte 420/540
Spec. Filets de rougets grillés en fine escabèche. Rognonnade et grenadin de veau aux essences de truffes. Tuilé croustillant praliné, chocolat et pistache.

XXX **Pavillon Puebla,** Parc Buttes-Chaumont, entrance : av. Bolivar, r. Botzaris (19th) ✆ 01 42 08 92 62, Fax 01 42 39 83 16, « Pleasant setting in the park » – P. AE GB
closed Sunday and Monday – **Meals** 180/240 and a la carte 320/450. E 19

XX **Cottage Marcadet,** 151 bis r. Marcadet (18th) ✆ 01 42 57 71 22 – ▤. GB. ✗
closed 13 to 22 April, 3 to 26 August and Sunday – **Meals** 155 (lunch)/215 b.i. and a la carte 240/370. C 13

XX **Les Allobroges,** 71 r. Grands-Champs (20th) ✆ 01 43 73 40 00 – GB K 22
closed August, Sunday and Monday – **Meals** 95/165 and a la carte 220/300.

XX **Relais des Buttes,** 86 r. Compans (19th) ✆ 01 42 08 24 70, Fax 01 42 03 20 44, - GB E 2
closed 9 to 30 August, 24 December-7 January, Saturday lunch and Sunday – **Meals** 16 and a la carte 220/350.

XX **La Chaumière,** 46 av. Secrétan (19th) ✆ 01 42 06 54 69 – AE ⓓ GB E 1
closed 10 to 25 August and Sunday dinner – **Meals** 143/198 b.i. and a la carte 190/36

XX **Au Clair de la Lune,** 9 r. Poulbot (18th) ✆ 01 42 58 97 03 – AE ⓓ GB JCB
closed 25 August-4 September, 3 to 10 Febuary and Sunday – **Meals** 165 and a la cart 220/300. D 1

X **La Verrière d'Eric Frechon,** 10 r. Gén. Brunet (19th) ✆ 01 40 40 03 3(Fax 01 40 40 03 30 – ▤. GB E 2
closed August, Sunday and Monday – **Meals** 190.

X **Le Poulbot Gourmet,** 39 r. Lamarck (18th) ✆ 01 46 06 86 00 – GB C 1
closed Sunday except lunch from October-May – **Meals** 160 and a la carte 210/300.

X **L'Étrier,** 154 r. Lamarck (18th) ✆ 01 42 29 14 01, bistro – ▤. GB. C 1
closed 11 to 31 August, Sunday and Monday – **Meals** (booking essential) 76 (lunch 160/250 and a la carte approx. 250.

X **Bistrot du 19e,** 45 r. Alouettes (19th) ✆ 01 42 00 84 85 – GB E 2
closed Sunday dinner and Monday – **Meals** 165 b.i..

X **Aucune Idée 41** 2 pl. St-Blaise (20th) ✆ 01 40 09 70 67, Fax 01 43 71 38 69 – GB H 2
closed 17 to 23 March, August, Sunday dinner and Monday – **Meals** 155/165 and a la cart 160/310.

X **Marie-Louise,** 52 r. Championnet (18th) ✆ 01 46 06 86 55, bistro – ⓓ GB B 1
closed 28 March-2 April, late July-early September, Sunday and Monday – **Meals** 130 an a la carte 140/260.

ENVIRONS

The outskirts of Paris up to 25Km

11: These reference letters and numbers correspond to the squares on the **Michelin plans of** **risian suburbs** nos 18, 20, 22, 24.

Défense *92 Hauts-de-Seine 101 ⑭, 18 – ✉ 92400 Courbevoie.*
See : *Quarter★★ : perspective★ from the parvis.*
Paris 8,5.

Sofitel CNIT M, 2 pl. Défense ☎ 01 46 92 10 10, Fax 01 46 92 10 50 – rm rm TV ☎ & – 70. AE GB JCB AV-AW 40
see ***Les Communautés*** below – 120 – **141 rm** 1500, 6 suites.

Sofitel La Défense M, 34 cours Michelet by ring road, exit La Défense 4 ✉ 92060 Puteaux ☎ 01 47 76 44 43, Fax 01 47 73 72 10, – rm TV ☎ & – 80. AE GB AW 41
Les 2 Arcs *(closed Sunday lunch and Saturday)* **Meals** 295(lunch)/355(lunch) and a la carte 260/340 – ***Le Botanic*** *(closed dinner except Saturday)* **Meals** 265 – 85 – **150 rm** 1400.

Renaissance M, 60 Jardin de Valmy, by ring road, exit La Défense 7 ✉ 92918 Puteaux ☎ 01 41 97 50 50, Fax 01 41 97 51 51, – rm TV ☎ & – 200. AE GB. rest AW 40
Meals 170 – 95 – **314 rm** 1150/1550, 20 suites.

Novotel La Défense M, 2 bd Neuilly ☎ 01 47 78 16 68, Fax 01 47 78 84 71, ← – rm TV ☎ & – 25 - 150. AE GB JCB AW 42
Meals a la carte approx. 170 – 64 – **280 rm** 790.

Ibis La Défense M, 4 bd Neuilly ☎ 01 41 97 40 40, Fax 01 41 97 40 50, – rm TV ☎ & – 50. AE GB AW 42
Meals 95 – 39 – **284 rm** 495.

XXX **Les Communautés** - Hôtel Sofitel CNIT, 2 pl. Défense, 5th floor ☎ 01 46 92 10 30, Fax 01 46 92 10 50 – . AE GB JCB AV-AW 40
closed Saturday and Sunday – **Meals** 180 (dinner)/310 and a la carte approx. 280.

arne-la-Vallée *77206 S.-et-M. 101 ⑲.*
18 of Bussy-St-Georges (private) ☎ 01 64 66 00 00 ; 9 18 of Disneyland Paris ☎ 01 60 45 69 14.
Paris 28.

t Collégien – *pop. 2 331 alt. 105 – ✉ 77080 :*

Novotel M, at Motorway junction Lagny A 4 ☎ 01 64 80 53 53, Fax 01 64 80 48 37, , , – rm TV ☎ & P – 300. AE GB
Meals 120 – 55 – **197 rm** 500/550.

t Disneyland Paris *access by Highway A 4 and Disneyland exit.*
See : *Disneyland Paris Park★★★*

Disneyland Hôtel M, ☎ 01 60 45 65 00, Fax 01 60 45 65 33, ←, « Victorian style architecture, at the entrance to the Disneyland Resort », , , – rm TV ☎ & P – 50. AE GB JCB.
California Grill (dinner only) **Meals** 195/260 – ***Inventions*** : **Meals** 180 (lunch)/250 – 160 – **478 rm** 2050/3300, 18 suites.

New-York M, ☎ 01 60 45 73 00, Fax 01 60 45 73 33, ←, , « Evokes the architecture of Manhattan », , , , – rm TV ☎ & P – 1 500. AE GB JCB.
Manhattan Restaurant (dinner only) **Meals** 195/260 – ***Parkside Diner*** : **Meals** a la carte approx. 150 – 80 – **532 rm** 1200/1400, 31 suites.

Newport Bay Club M, ☎ 01 60 45 55 00, Fax 01 60 45 55 33, ←, « In the style of a New England seaside resort », , , – rm TV ☎ & P – 50. AE GB JCB.
Cape Cod : **Meals** 145 – ***Yacht Club*** (dinner only) **Meals** 195/260 – 65 – **1 077 rm** 950/1150, 15 suites.

Séquoia Lodge M, ☎ 01 60 45 51 00, Fax 01 60 45 51 33, ←, « The atmosphere of an American mountain lodge », , , – rm TV ☎ & P – 120. AE GB JCB.
Hunter's Grill (dinner only) **Meals** 150/175 – ***Beaver Creek Tavern*** (dinner only out of season) **Meals** a la carte 130/190 – 65 – **997 rm** 835/1035, 14 suites.

Cheyenne, ✆ 01 60 45 62 00, Fax 01 60 45 62 33, « Resembles a frontier town of the American Wild West » – rm rest AE GB JCB.
Chuck Wagon Café : **Meals** a la carte approx. 120 – 45 – **1 000 rm** 750.

Santa Fé M, ✆ 01 60 45 78 00, Fax 01 60 45 78 33, « Evokes a New Mexican pueblo » – rm rest AE GB JCB.
La Cantina : **Meals** a la carte approx. 120 – 45 – **1 000 rm** 615.

Orly (Paris Airports) *94396 Val-de-Marne 101 ㉖, 24 – pop. 21 646.*

✆ 01 49 75 15 15.

Paris 15.

Hilton Orly M, near airport station ✉ 94544 ✆ 01 45 12 45 12, Fax 01 45 12 45 00 – rm – 300. AE GB JCB BR 5
Meals 160 (lunch), 170/250 and a la carte 170/300 – 90 – **357 rm** 870/1270.

Mercure M, N 7, Z.I. Nord, Orly tech ✉ 94547 ✆ 01 46 87 23 37, Fax 01 46 87 71 9 – rm – 80. AE GB
Meals a la carte 160/230 – 65 – **194 rm** 590/690.

Orly Airport West :

Maxim's, 2nd floor ✉ 94546 ✆ 01 49 75 16 78, Fax 01 46 87 05 39 – AE GB
✿ *closed August, 24 December-5 January, Saturday, Sunday and Bank Holidays* – **Meals** 230/480 b.i. and a la carte 270/370
Spec. Terrine de canard. Sole de ligne braisée au vermouth. Volaille de Loué étuvée au vin jaune, pâtes fines au beurre de truffe.

See also *Rungis*

Roissy-en-France (Paris Airports) *95700 Val-d'Oise 101 ⑧ – pop. 2 054 alt. 85.*

✆ 01 48 62 22 80.

Paris 26.

at Roissy-Town :

Copthorne M, allée Verger ✆ 01 34 29 33 33, Fax 01 34 29 03 05, – rm – 150. AE GB JCB
Brasserie l'Europe *(closed Sunday dinner and Saturday)* **Meals** 260 and a la carte 190/37 – 70 – **237 rm** 1150/1450.

Holiday Inn, allée Verger ✆ 01 34 29 30 00, Fax 01 34 29 90 52, – rm – 120. AE GB JCB
Meals a la carte 180/280 – 90 – **243 rm** 850/1150.

Mercure, allée Verger ✆ 01 34 29 40 00, Fax 01 34 29 00 18, – rm – 200. AE GB
Meals 142 b.i. – 67 – **202 rm** 660/760.

Bleu Marine M, Z.A. parc de Roissy ✆ 01 34 29 00 00, Fax 01 34 29 00 11, – rm – 80. AE GB
Meals 145 – 60 – **153 rm** 610.

Ibis M, av. Raperie ✆ 01 34 29 34 34, Fax 01 34 29 34 19 – rm – 150. AE GB
Meals 130 b.i./215 b.i. – 42 – **315 rm** 490.

in the airport area :

Hilton M, Roissypole ✆ 01 49 19 77 77, Fax 01 49 19 77 78, – rm – 1 000. AE GB. rest
Le Gourmet *(closed 19 July-18 August, Saturday and Sunday)* **Meals** 230 – ***Les Aviateurs :*** **Meals** 179 b.i. – 115 – **378 rm** 1200/1700, 4 suites.

Sheraton M, Aérogare nº 2 ✆ 01 49 19 70 70, Fax 01 49 19 70 71, ←, – rm – 80. AE GB JCB
Les Étoiles *(closed August, Saturday and Sunday)* **Meals** 170 (lunch), 190/300 ***Les Saisons :*** **Meals** 120 (lunch), 140/220 – 120 – **244 rm** 1400/1850, 12 suites.

Sofitel M, ✆ 01 49 19 29 29, Fax 01 49 19 29 00, – rm – 150. AE GB JCB
Meals 145 – 100 – **352 rm** 950/1450.

Novotel M, ✆ 01 48 62 00 53, Fax 01 48 62 00 11 – rm – 2 - 100. AE GB JCB
Meals a la carte approx. 170 – 60 – **201 rm** 660.

.I. Paris Nord II – ✉ 95912 :

Hyatt Regency M, 351 av. Bois de la Pie ☏ 01 48 17 12 34, Fax 01 48 17 17 17, « Original contemporary decor », – rm – 250. AE GB JCB
Apollo : **Meals** 185 (lunch) 205 and a la carte 200/340 – 95 – **383 rm** 1200/1500, 5 suites.

Rungis 94150 Val-de-Marne 101 ㉖, 24 – pop. 2 939 alt. 80.
Paris 14.

at Pondorly : Access : from Paris, Highway A 6 and take Orly Airport exit ; from outside of Paris, A 6 and Rungis exit :

Gd Hôtel Mercure Orly M, 20 av. Ch. Lindbergh ✉ 94656 ☏ 01 46 87 36 36, Fax 01 46 87 08 48, – rm – 180. AE GB BM 50
La Rungisserie : **Meals** 180 – 63 – **190 rm** 860.

Holiday Inn M, 4 av. Ch. Lindbergh ✉ 94656 ☏ 01 46 87 26 66, Fax 01 45 60 91 25 – rm – 150. AE GB JCB BM 50
Meals 95/140 and a la carte 150/250 – 70 – **168 rm** 825/1025.

Novotel M, Zone du Delta, 1 r. Pont des Halles ☏ 01 45 12 44 12, Fax 01 45 12 44 13, – rm – 150. AE GB BM 50
Meals a la carte approx. 180 – 60 – **181 rm** 650.

Ibis, 1 r. Mondétour ✉ 94656 ☏ 01 46 87 22 45, Fax 01 46 87 84 72, – rm – 100. AE GB BM 50
Meals 95 – 39 – **119 rm** 330.

Versailles 78000 Yvelines 101 ㉒, 22 – pop. 87 789 alt. 130.
See : Palace★★★ Y – Gardens★★★ (fountain display★★★ (grandes eaux) and illuminated night performances★★★ (fêtes de nuit) in summer) – Ecuries Royales★ Y – The Trianons★★ – Lambinet Museum★ Y **M**.
9 18 18 of la Boulie (private) ☏ 01 39 50 59 41 by ③ : 2,5 km.
Tourist Office 7 r. Réservoirs ☏ 01 39 50 36 22, Fax 01 39 50 68 07.
Paris 20 ①.

Plan on next page

Trianon Palace M, 1 bd Reine ☏ 01 30 84 38 00, Fax 01 39 49 00 77, ←, park, « Tasteful early 20C decor », – rm – 30. AE GB JCB X r
see *Les Trois Marches* below - *Grill* ☏ 01 30 84 38 80 **Meals** 270 – 110 – **67 rm** 1800, 27 suites.

Sofitel Château de Versailles M, 2 av. Paris ☏ 01 39 53 30 31, Fax 01 39 53 87 20, – rm – 150. AE GB JCB Y a
Meals 170 and a la carte 170/330 – 85 – **146 rm** 990, 6 suites.

Le Pavillon Trianon M, 1 bd Reine ☏ 01 30 84 38 00, Fax 01 39 51 57 79, – 300. AE GB JCB X r
closed August – *Brasserie La Fontaine* ☏ 01 30 84 38 47 **Meals** 165 and a la carte 170/260 – 75 – **98 rm** 900.

Le Versailles M without rest, 7 r. Ste-Anne (Petite place) ☏ 01 39 50 64 65, Fax 01 39 02 37 85 – rm. AE GB JCB Y p
55 – **45 rm** 450/520.

Relais Mercure M without rest, 19 r. Ph. de Dangeau ☏ 01 39 50 44 10, Fax 01 39 50 65 11 – – 35. AE GB JCB Y n
40 – **60 rm** 375/395.

Ibis M without rest, 4 av. Gén. de Gaulle ☏ 01 39 53 03 30, Fax 01 39 50 06 31 – rm. AE GB Y u
39 – **82 rm** 380.

Les Trois Marches (Vié), 1 bd Reine ☏ 01 39 50 13 21, Fax 01 30 21 01 25, ←, – AE GB JCB X r
closed August, Sunday and Monday – **Meals** 270 (lunch), 510/610 and a la carte 460/710
Spec. Céleri rave à la manière des ravioli. Côte de veau de lait, croustillant de foie gras. Abricots secs au sauternes.

Rescatore, 27 av. St-Cloud ☏ 01 39 25 06 34, Fax 01 30 24 15 39 – AE GB
closed August, Saturday lunch and Sunday – **Meals** - Seafood - 180/210 and a la carte 240/360. Y s

Le Potager du Roy, 1 r. Mar.-Joffre ☏ 01 39 50 35 34, Fax 01 30 21 69 30 – AE GB Z r
closed Sunday dinner and Monday – **Meals** 169.

VERSAILLES

Carnot (R.) . . . . Y
Clemenceau (R. Georges) . . . . Y 7
États-Généraux (R. des) . . Z
Foch (R. du Mar.) . . . . . XY
Hoche (R.) . . . . Y

Leclerc (R. du Gén.) . . . Z 24
Marché N.D. (Pl. du) . . . Y 25
Orangerie (R. de l') . . . . YZ
Paroisse (R. de la) . . . . . Y
Royale (R.) . . . . Z
Satory (R. de) . . . . YZ 42
Vieux-Versailles (R. du) . YZ 47

Chancellerie (R. de la) . . Y 3

Cotte (R. Robert-de) . . . Y 10
Europe (Av. de l') . . . . . Y 14
Gambetta (Pl.) . . . . Y 17
Gaulle (Av. Gén.-de) . . . YZ 19
Indép. Américaine (R.) . Y 20
Mermoz (R. Jean) . . . . . Z 27
Nolhac (R. Pierre-de) . . . Y 30
Porte de Buc (R. de la) . Z 34
Rockefeller (Av.) . . . . . . Y 37

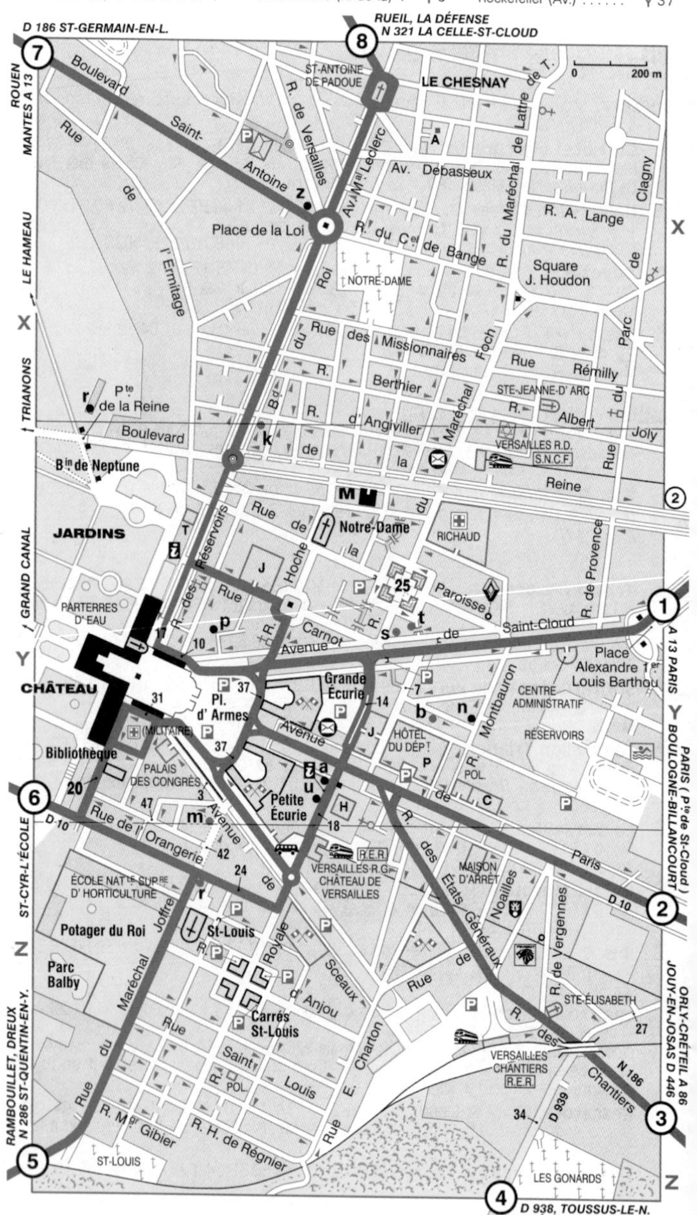

XX **La Marée de Versailles,** 22 r. au Pain ☎ 01 30 21 73 73, Fax 01 39 50 55 87 – ▤. AE GB Y t
closed 3 to 19 August, February Holidays, Monday dinner and Sunday – **Meals** - Seafood - 260 and a la carte 200/270 ♁.

XX **Pascal Le Falher,** 22 r. Satory ☎ 01 39 50 57 43, Fax 01 39 49 04 66 – AE GB. ✻ Y m
closed Saturday lunch and Sunday – **Meals** 128/180 and a la carte 230/310.

X **La Cuisine Bourgeoise,** 10 bd Roi ☎ 01 39 53 11 38, Fax 01 39 53 25 26 – AE GB XY k
closed 9 to 25 August, February Holidays, Saturday lunch and Sunday – **Meals** 168/250 and a la carte 250/300.

X **Le Chevalet,** 6 r. Ph. de Dangeau ☎ 01 39 02 03 13 – GB Y b
closed August, Monday dinner and Sunday – **Meals** 138/180.

Le Chesnay – *pop. 29 542. alt. 120* – ✉ *78150 :*

Novotel M, 4 bd St-Antoine ☎ 01 39 54 96 96, Fax 01 39 54 94 40 – ⎈ ⇔ rm ▤ TV ☎ ♿ ⇔ – 🔏 25 - 150. AE ⓓ GB X z
Meals a la carte approx. 180 – ☕ 60 – **105 rm** 540.

Mercure M without rest, r. Marly-le-Roi, in front of Commercial Centre Parly II ☎ 01 39 55 11 41, Fax 01 39 55 06 22 – ⎈ ⇔ rm ▤ rm TV ☎ ♿ P – 🔏 70. AE ⓓ GB JCB
☕ 52 – **80 rm** 580.

Ibis M without rest, av. Dutartre, Commercial Centre Parly II ☎ 01 39 63 37 93, Fax 01 39 55 18 66 – ⎈ ⇔ rm TV ☎ ♿. AE ⓓ GB
☕ 39 – **72 rm** 380.

XX **Le Chesnoy,** 24 r. Pottier ☎ 01 39 54 01 01 – ▤. AE ⓓ GB
closed 4 to 24 August, Sunday dinner and Monday – **Meals** 178.

XX **Le Connemara,** 41 rte Rueil ☎ 01 39 55 63 07, Fax 01 39 55 15 97 – AE GB
closed 15 July-7 August, February Holidays, Sunday dinner and Monday – **Meals** 135 (lunch), 165/280.

AND BEYOND...

Joigny *89300 Yonne* 65 ④ *– pop. 9 697 alt. 79.*
See : *Vierge au Sourire★ in St-Thibault's Church – Côte St-Jacques ≤★ 1,5 km by D*
of Roncemay ☎ 03 86 73 68 87.
Tourist Office 4 quai H.-Ragobert ☎ 03 86 62 11 05, Fax 03 86 91 76 38.
Paris 147 – Auxerre 27 – Gien 75 – Montargis 59 – Sens 30 – Troyes 76.

✿✿✿ **La Côte St-Jacques** (Lorain) M, 14 fg Paris ☎ 03 86 62 09 70, Fax 03 86 91 49
≤, « Tasteful decor », – – 30. AE GB
Meals (Sunday booking essential) 320 b.i. (lunch), 510/720 and a la carte 580/810 –
110 – **25 rm** 740/1780, 4 suites
Spec. Huîtres bretonnes en petite terrine océane. Noix de Saint-Jacques, endives et ch
terelles. Poularde de Bresse à la vapeur de champagne. **Wines** Chardonnay, Irancy.

Pontoise *95300 Val d'Oise* 106 ⑤ *– pop. 27 150 alt. 48.*
Paris 36 – Beauvais 50 – Dieppe 135 – Mantes-la-Jolie 39 – Rouen 91.

at Cormeilles-en-Vexin *NW – alt. 111 – ✉ 95830 :*

✿✿ **Gérard Cagna,** on D 915 ☎ 01 34 66 61 56, Fax 01 34 66 40 31, « Garden » – P. AE
closed August, 23 to 28 December, Sunday dinner, Tuesday dinner and Monday – **Me**
200/550 b.i. and a la carte 470/610
Spec. Huîtres chaudes au curry léger. Saint-Jacques au lard et artichaut (October-Mar
Pigeon rôti, jus à l'estragon, poêlée de légumes confits.

Rheims *51100 Marne* 56 ⑥ ⑯ *– pop. 180 620 alt. 85.*
See : *Cathedral★★★ – St-Remi Basilica★★ : interior★★★ – Palais du Tau★★ – Champa cellars★ – Place Royale★ – Porte Mars★ – Hôtel de la Salle★ – Foujita Chapel★ – Librar of Ancien Collège des Jésuites – St-Remi Museum★★ – Hôtel le Vergeur Museum★ – F Arts Museum★ – French Automobile Heritage Centre★.*
Envir. : *Fort de la Pompelle : German helmets★ 9 km to the SE by N 44.*
Rheims-Champagne ☎ 03 26 03 60 14 at Gueux ; to the NW by N 31-E 46 : 9,5 k
Rheims-Champagne ☎ 03 26 07 15 15 : 6 km.
☎ 08 36 35 35 35.
Tourist Office 2 r. Guillaume-de-Machault ☎ 03 26 77 45 25, Fax 03 26 77 45 2
A.C. de Champagne 7 bd Lundy ☎ 03 26 47 34 76, Fax 03 26 88 52 24.
Paris 144 – Brussels 214 – Châlons-sur-Marne 48 – Lille 199 – Luxembourg 232.

✿✿✿ **Boyer "Les Crayères"** M, 64 bd Vasnier ☎ 03 26 82 80 80, Fax 03 26 82 65
≤, « Elegant mansion in park », – P. AE GB
closed 22 December-12 January – **Meals** *(closed Tuesday lunch and Monday)* (book
essential) a la carte 460/640 – 104 – **16 rm** 990/1950, 3 suites
Spec. Escargots "petits-gris" en barigoule d'artichauts. Filets de rouget de roche gril
sauce au thym. Pigeonneau au foie gras en habit vert, fumet de truffe. **Wines** Champag

Saulieu *21210 Côte-d'Or* 65 ⑰ *– pop. 2 917 alt. 535.*
Tourist Office r. d'Argentine ☎ 03 80 64 00 21, Fax 03 80 64 21 96.
Paris 249 – Autun 41 – Avallon 38 – Beaune 64 – Clamecy 76 – Dijon 73.

✿✿✿ **La Côte d'Or** (Loiseau) M, 2 r. Argentine ☎ 03 80 90 53 53, Fax 03 80 64 08
« Tasteful inn with flowered garden » – – 30. AE GB JCB
Meals 420 (lunch), 680/890 and a la carte 600/980 – 120 – **24 rm** 340/2100, 3 dup
Spec. Jambonnettes de grenouilles à la purée d'ail et au jus de persil. Sandre à la fonc
d'échalote, sauce au vin rouge. Blanc de volaille au foie gras chaud et purée truffée. **Wir**
Sauvignon de Saint-Bris, Côte de Nuits-Village.

Vézelay *89450 Yonne* 65 ⑮ *– pop. 571 alt. 285.*
See : *Ste-Madeleine Basilica★★★ : tower ★.*
Envir. : *Site★ of Pierre-Perthuis SE : 6 km.*
Tourist Office r. St-Pierre ☎ 03 86 33 23 69, Fax 03 86 33 34 00.
Paris 223 – Auxerre 51 – Avallon 15 – Château-Chinon 60 – Clamecy 22.

at St-Père : *SE : 3 km by D 957 – alt. 148 – ✉ 89450.*
See : *Church of N.-Dame★*

✿✿✿ **L'Espérance** (Meneau), ☎ 03 86 33 39 10, Fax 03 86 33 26 15, ≤, « Conservato
restaurant opening onto the garden », – rest P – 50. AE
Meals *(closed February, Wednesday lunch and Tuesday)* (booking essential) 360 (lunc
500/860 and a la carte 670/860 – 130 – **34 rm** 500/1400, 6 suites
Spec. Terrine d'écrevisses aux truffes. Rougets aux échalotes et betteraves roug
"Oeuvre d'agneau" en trois services. **Wines** Vézelay, Chablis.

ORDEAUX *33000 Gironde* **71** ⑨ – *pop. 210 336 alt. 4 Greater Bordeaux 696 364 h.*

See : *18C Bordeaux : façades along the quayside★★* EX, *Esplanade des Quinconces* DX, *Grand Théâtre★★* DX, *Notre-Dame Church★* DX, *Allées de Tourny* DX, – *Cours Clemenceau* DX, *Place Gambetta* DX, *Cours de l'Intendance* DX – *Old Bordeaux★★ : Place de la Bourse★★* EX, *Place du Parlement★* EX **109**, *St-Michel Basilica★* EY, *Great Bell★ (Grosse Cloche)* EY **D** – *Pey-Berland district : St-André Cathedral★* DY *(Pey-Berland Tower★* **E**) – *Mériadeck district* CY – *Battle-Cruiser Colbert★* – *World Wine Centre (Centre mondial du vin)* – *Museums : Fine Arts★★ (Beaux-Arts)* CDY **M**³, *Decorative Arts★* DY **M**², *Aquitaine★★* DY **M**⁴ – *Entrepôt Lainé★★ : museum of contemporary art★.*

18 Golf Bordelais ✆ 05 56 28 56 04 by av. d'Eysines : 4 km ; 18 18 de Bordeaux Lac ✆ 05 56 50 92 72, to the N by D 209 : 10 km ; 18 18 of Medoc at Louens ✆ 05 56 70 21 10 to the NW by D 6 : 6 km ; 9 9 9 9 Internat. of Bordeaux-Pessac ✆ 05 56 36 03 33 by N 250 ; 18 Bordeaux-Cameyrac ✆ 05 56 72 96 79 by N 89 : 18 km.

✈ *of Bordeaux-Mérignac : ✆ 05 56 34 50 00 to the W : 11 km.*

🚗 *✆ 08 36 35 35 35.*

Tourist Office 12 cours 30-Juillet ✆ 05 56 44 28 41, Fax 05 56 81 89 21, at the Gare St-Jean ✆ 05 56 91 64 70 and the airport ✆ 05 52 34 39 39 – Automobile-Club du Sud-Ouest 8 pl. Quiconces ✆ 05 56 44 22 92 – Bordeaux wine Exhibition (Maison du vin de Bordeaux) 3 cours 30-juil. (closed weekend from mid Oct.-mid May) ✆ 05 56 00 22 66 DX.

Paris 579 – Lyons 531 – Nantes 324 – Strasbourg 919 – Toulouse 245.

Plans on following pages

Burdigala M, 115 r. G. Bonnac ✆ 05 56 90 16 16, Fax 05 56 93 15 06 – – 100. AE GB JCB CX r
Meals 190/290 – ☕ 80 – **68 rm** 860/1500, 8 suites, 7 duplex.

Mercure Château Chartrons M, 81 cours St-Louis ✉ 33300 ✆ 05 56 43 15 00, Fax 05 56 69 15 21, – rm rest – 150. AE GB
Meals 110/250 – ☕ 56 – **144 rm** 495/690.

Holiday Inn Garden Court, 30 r. de Tauzia ✉ 33800 ✆ 05 56 92 21 21, Fax 05 56 91 08 06, – rm – 70. AE GB FZ v
Meals *(closed Sunday lunch)* 65 (lunch), 95 b.i./130 b.i. – ☕ 60 – **89 rm** 420.

Novotel Bordeaux-Centre M, 45 cours Mar. Juin ✆ 05 56 51 46 46, Fax 05 56 98 25 56, – rm P – 80. AE GB CY m
Meals a la carte approx. 170 – ☕ 52 – **138 rm** 470/510.

Claret M, Cité Mondiale du Vin, 18 parvis des Chartrons ✆ 05 56 01 79 79, Fax 05 56 01 79 00, – – 800. AE GB
Meals 140 – ☕ 60 – **97 rm** 505/570.

Ste-Catherine without rest, 27 r. Parlement Ste-Catherine ✆ 05 56 81 95 12, Fax 05 56 44 50 51 – rm – 40. AE GB JCB DX m
☕ 70 – **84 rm** 530/1200.

Normandie without rest, 7 cours 30-Juillet ✆ 05 56 52 16 80, Fax 05 56 51 68 91 – – 30. AE GB JCB DX z
☕ 50 – **100 rm** 310/680.

Gd H. Français without rest, 12 r. Temple ✆ 05 56 48 10 35, Fax 05 56 81 76 18 – . AE GB DX v
☕ 60 – **35 rm** 370/640.

Majestic without rest, 2 r. Condé ✆ 05 56 52 60 44, Fax 05 56 79 26 70 – . AE GB JCB DX a
☕ 55 – **50 rm** 400/600.

Le Bayonne M without rest, 4 r. Martignac ✆ 05 56 48 00 88, Fax 05 56 52 03 79 – . AE GB DX f
closed 24 December-5 January – ☕ 60 – **36 rm** 390/595.

Presse M without rest, 6 r. Porte Dijeaux ✆ 05 56 48 53 88, Fax 05 56 01 05 82 – . AE GB. DX k
☕ 38 – **29 rm** 280/450.

Continental without rest, 10 r. Montesquieu ✆ 05 56 52 66 00, Fax 05 56 52 77 97 – . AE GB DX b
☕ 35 – **50 rm** 300/430.

Royal St-Jean without rest, 15 r. Ch. Domercq ✉ 33800 ✆ 05 56 91 72 16, Fax 05 56 94 08 32 – . AE GB JCB FZ u
☕ 45 – **37 rm** 330/440.

Opéra without rest, 35 r. Esprit des Lois ✆ 05 56 81 41 27, Fax 05 56 51 78 80 – . GB DX n
☕ 35 – **27 rm** 200/300.

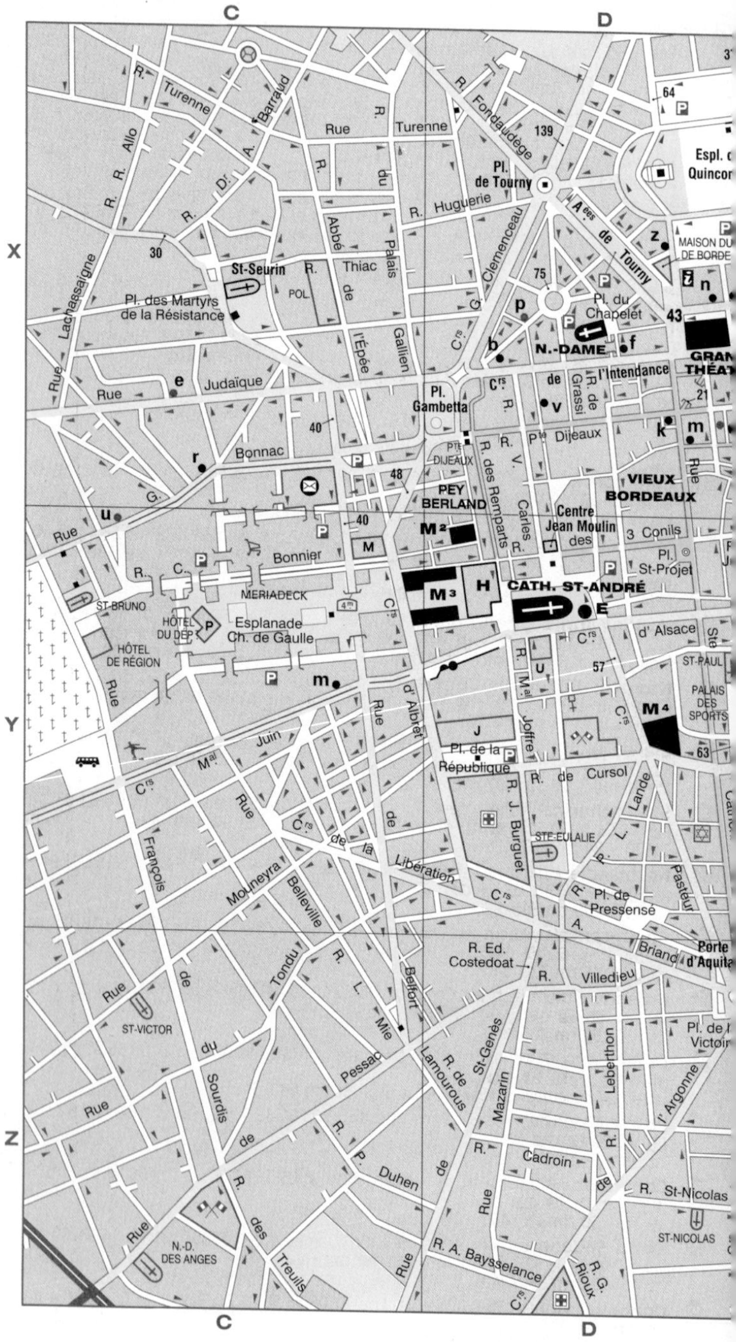
C
D
R. Turenne
R. A. Barraud
R. R. Allo
R. Dr.
Rue Turenne
R. du Palais Gallien
R. Fondaudège
139
64
Espl. d
Quincon
Pl. de Tourny
R. Huguerie
Abbé de l'Épée
R. Thiac
Crs G. Clemenceau
Allées de Tourny
z
MAISON DU DE BORDE
X
30
St-Seurin
POL.
Pl. des Martyrs de la Résistance
Rue Lachassaigne
75
p
Pl. du Chapelet
43
n
b
N.-DAME
f
GRAN THÉAT
e
Rue Judaïque
Crs de l'Intendance
Pl. Gambetta
R. de Grassi
v
21
40
R. V.
Pte Dijeaux
k
m
r
Bonnac
PTE DIJEAUX
R. des Remparts
Rue
48
PEY BERLAND
VIEUX BORDEAUX
G.
u
Rue
40
M2
Carles
Centre Jean Moulin
des 3 Conils
R. C.
Bonnier
M
Pl. St-Projet
MERIADECK
M3
H
CATH. ST-ANDRÉ
E
ST-BRUNO
HÔTEL DU DÉP.
Esplanade Ch. de Gaulle
Crs
Crs d'Alsace
HÔTEL DE RÉGION
R. Mal Joffre
U
57
ST-PAUL
Rue
m
d'Albret
Rue
PALAIS DES SPORTS
M4
Y
Juin
Mal
J
Pl. de la République
63
Crs
R. de Cursol
Lande
Rue
R. J. Burguet
STE-EULALIE
R. L.
François
Crs de la Libération
Moneyra
Belleville
Crs
Pl. de Pressensé
Pasteur
A. Briand
Porte d'Aquita
R. Ed. Costedoat
R. Villedieu
Tondu
R. L. Mie
Belfort
Rue
ST-VICTOR
du Sourdis
Pessac
R. de Lamourous
St-Genès
Mazarin
Leberthon
Pl. de la Victoir
l'Argonne
Rue
Z
R. P. Duhen
de
R. Cadroin
R.
R. St-Nicolas
de
Rue
ST-NICOLAS
R. des Treuils
N.-D. DES ANGES
Rue
R. A. Bayssélance
R. G. Rioux
Crs
Rue
C
D

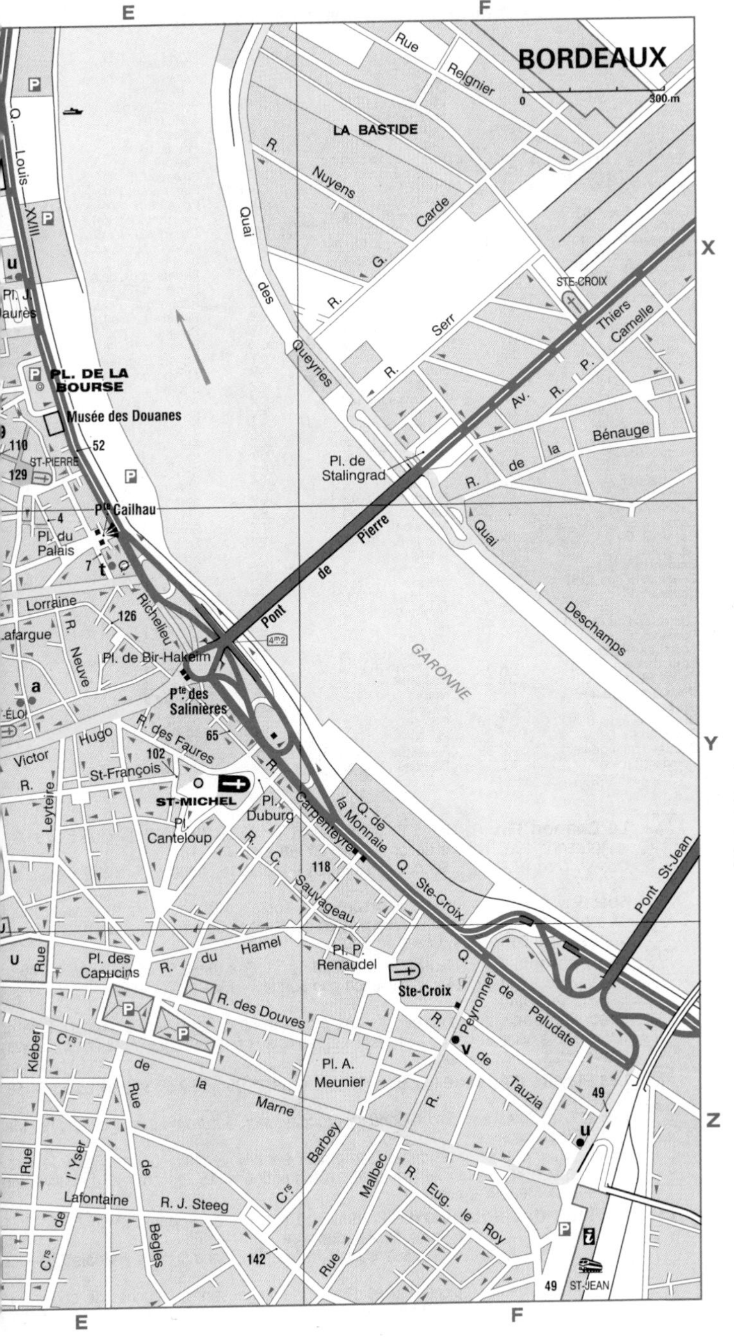
BORDEAUX
0
300 m
E
F
X
Y
Z
LA BASTIDE
PL. DE LA BOURSE
Musée des Douanes
ST-PIERRE
Pte Cailhau
Pl. du Palais
Pl. de Bir-Hakeim
Pte des Salinières
ST-MICHEL
Pl. Duburg
Pl. Canteloup
Pl. des Capucins
Pl. P. Renaudel
Ste-Croix
Pl. A. Meunier
Pl. de Stalingrad
Pont de Pierre
GARONNE
Pont St-Jean
ST-JEAN
STE-CROIX
Quai des Queyries
Quai Deschamps
Q. Louis XVIII
Q. Richelieu
Q. de la Monnaie
Q. Ste-Croix
Q. de Paludate
R. Nuyens
R. G. Carde
R. Serr
Av. Thiers
R. P. Camelle
R. de la Bénauge
Rue Reignier
R. des Faures
R. Carpenteyre
R. C. Sauvageau
R. du Hamel
R. des Douves
Crs de la Marne
R. de Tauzia
R. Peyronnet
R. Eug. le Roy
Rue Malbec
Rue Barbey
Crs Victor Hugo
R. Leyteire
R. St-François
R. Neuve
Lorraine
Lafargue
Rue Kléber
Rue de l'Yser
Rue de Bègles
R. J. Steeg
Lafontaine
Crs de la Marne
Pl. J. Jaurès
110
129
52
4
7
126
65
102
118
142
49
4m2

STREET INDEX TO BORDEAUX TOWN PLAN

Albret (Crs d') .... CY
Alsace-Lorraine
 (Crs d') .... DEZ
Clemenceau (Crs G.) ..... DX
Intendance (Crs de l') .... DX
Jaurès (Pl. J.) .... EX
Porte-Dijeaux (R. de la) ... DX
Ste-Catherine (R.) .... DXY
Tourny (Allées de) .... DX
Victor-Hugo (Crs) .... EY

Abbé de l'Epée (R.) CX
Allo (R. R.) CX
Argentiers (R. des) ...... EY 4
Argonne (Crs de l') ...... DZ
Ausone (R.) .... EY 7
Barbey (Crs) .... EFZ
Bayssélance (R. A.) ...... DZ
Bègles (R. de) .... EZ
Belfort (R. de) .... CYZ
Belleville (R.) .... CY
Bénauge (R. de la) ...... FX
Bir-Hakeim (Pl. de) .... EY
Bonnac (R. G.) .... CXY
Bonnier (R. C.) .... CY
Bordelaises (Galeries) .... DX 21
Bourse (Pl. de la) .... EX
Briand (Crs A.) .... DYZ
Burguet (R. J.) .... DY
Cadroin (R.) .... DZ
Camelle (R.P.) .... FX
Canteloup (Pl.) .... EY
Capdeville (R.) .... CX 30
Carde .... EZ
Garde (R. G.) .... FX
Carles (R. V.) .... DXY
Carpenteyre (R.) .... EFY
Chapeau-Rouge (Crs) .... EX 36
Chapelet (Pl. du) .... DX
Chartres (Allées de) ...... DX 37
Château-d'Eau (R. du) .... CXY 40
Comédie (Pl. de la) ...... DX 43
Costedoat (R. Ed.) .... DZ
Croix de Seguey (R.) ..... CX 45
Cursol (R. de) .... DY
Deschamps (Quai) .... FY
Dr. Barraud (R. A.) CX
Dr. Nancel-Pénard (R.) .... CX 48
Domercq (R. C.) .... FZ 49
Douane (Quai de la) ..... EX 52
Douves (R. des) .... EZ
Duburg (Pl.) .... EY
Duffour-Dubergier (R.) .... DY 57
Duhen (R.P.) .... CDZ
Duplessy (R.) .... DX 58
Esprit des Lois
 (R. de l') .... EX 62
Faures (R. des) .... EY
Ferme de Richemont
 (Pl. de la) .... DY 63
Foch (R. Mar.) .... DX 64
Fondaudège (R.) .... DX
Fusterie (R. de la) .... EY 65
Gambetta (Pl.) .... DX
Gaulle (Espl. Ch. de) ..... CY
Grands Hommes
 (Pl. des) .... DX 75
Grassi (R. de) .... DX
Hamel (R. du) .... EZ
Huguerie (R.) .... DX
Joffre (Crs Mar.) .... DY
Judaïque (R.) CX
Juin (Crs Mar.) .... CY
Jullian (Pl. C.) .... DY
Kléber (R.) .... EZ
Lachassaigne (R.) CX
Lafargue (Pl.) .... EY
Lafontaine (R.) .... EZ
Lamourous (R. de) ...... CDZ
Lande (R. P. L.) .... DY
Leberthon (R.) .... DZ
Leyteire (R.) .... EYZ
Libération (Crs de la) .... CDY
Louis XVIII (Quai) .... EX
Malbec (R.) .... FZ
Marne (Crs de la) .... EZ
Martyrs de la Résistance
 (Pl. des) CX
Mazarin (R.) .... DZ
Meuniers (Pl. A.) .... FZ
Meynard (Pl.) .... EY 102
Mie (R. L.) .... CZ
Mirail (R. du) .... EY
Monnaie (Quai de la) .... FY
Mouneyra (R.) .... CYZ
Neuve (R.) .... EY
Notre-Dame (R.) .... EX 105
Nuyens (R.) .... FX
Orléans (Allées d') .... EX 106
Palais (Pl. du) .... EY
Palais Gallien (R. du) CX
Paludate (Quai de) ...... FZ
Parlement (Pl. du) ...... EX
Parlement St-Pierre
 (R. du) .... EX
Pas-St-Georges
 (R. du) .... EXY
Pasteur (R. de) .... DY
Pessac (R. de) .... CZ
Peyronnet (R.) .... FZ
Philippart (R. F.) .... EX
Pierre (Pont de) .... EFY
Porte de la Monnaie (R.). FY
Pressensé (Pl. de) .... DZ
Queyries (Quai des) ..... EFX
Quinconces (Espl. des) .. DX
Reignier (R.) .... FX
Remparts (R. des) ...... DXY
Renaudel (Pl. P.) .... FZ
République (Pl. de la) ... DY
Richelieu (Quai) .... EY
Rioux (R. G.) .... DZ
Rousselle (R. de la) ...... EY
Roy (R. Eug. le) .... FZ
St-François (R.) .... EY
St-Genès (R. de) .... DZ
St-James (R.) .... EY
St-Jean (Pont) .... FY
St-Nicolas (R.) .... DZ
St-Pierre (Pl.) .... EX
St-Projet (Pl.) .... DY
St-Rémi (R.) .... EX
Ste-Croix (Quai) .... FY
Sauvageau (R. C.) ...... EFY
Serr (R.) .... FX
Somme (Crs de la) ...... DZ
Sourdis (R. F. de) ...... CYZ
Stalingrad (Pl. de) ...... FX
Steeg (R. J.) .... EZ
Tauzia (R. des) .... FZ
Thiac (R.) CX
Thiers (Av.) .... EX
Tondu (R. du) .... CZ
Tourny (Pl. de) .... DX
Treuils (R. des) .... CZ
Turenne (R.) .... CDX
Verdun (Crs de) .... DX
Victoire (Pl. de la) ...... DZ
Vilaris (R.) .... EZ
Villedieu (R.) .... DZ
Yser (Crs de l') .... EZ
Zola (R. E.) CX
3 Conils (R. des) .... DY

XXXX ✿ **Le Chapon Fin** (Garcia), 5 r. Montesquieu ✆ 05 56 79 10 10, Fax 05 56 79 09 « Authentic 1900 rocaille decor » – ▤. AE ⓓ GB JCB DX
closed 10 to 18 August, Sunday and Monday – **Meals** 160 (lunch), 260/400 and a la ca 360/560
Spec. Ravioles de langoustines au citron vert. Risotto aux langoustines, ris de veau, mori et asperges (September-April). Aiguillettes de caneton au foie gras aux fruits de sais **Wines** Entre-Deux-Mers, Côtes de Bourg.

XXX ✿ **Jean Ramet,** 7 pl. J. Jaurès ✆ 05 56 44 12 51, Fax 05 56 52 19 80 – ▤. AE GB
closed 3 to 24 August, Saturday lunch and Sunday – **Meals** 160 (lunch), 250/300 an la carte 260/440 EX
Spec. Petite marmite d'écrevisses aux mousserons (September-December). Foie g poêlé, fumé, vinaigrette de lentilles. Trois sablés aux fruits rouges (April-October). **Wi** Graves blanc, Pessac-Léognan.

XXX ✿ **Les Plaisirs d'Ausone** (Gauffre), 10 r. Ausone ✆ 05 56 79 30 30, Fax 05 56 51 38 – AE GB EY
closed 12 to 24 August, 3 to 10 January, Monday lunch, Saturday lunch and Sunday – **Me** 160/300 and a la carte 270/350
Spec. Soupe crèmeuse de cèpes (September-early November). Gourmandise de foie canard aux trois façons. Canard colvert rôti aux figues (15 September-February). **Wi** Entre-Deux-Mers, Margaux.

XXX ✿ **Pavillon des Boulevards** (Franc), 120 r. Croix de Seguey ✆ 05 56 81 51 C Fax 05 56 51 14 58, 帘 – ▤. AE ⓓ GB JCB
closed 9 to 25 August, 6 to 13 January, Saturday lunch and Sunday – **Meals** 220 (lunc 270/420
Spec. Foie gras aux épices douces. Poêlée de langoustines, tranches de boudin gri Côte de veau, hachis d'échalotes aux herbes. **Wines** Bordeaux blanc, Côtes Bourg.

XXX **Le Vieux Bordeaux** (Bordage), 27 r. Buhan ☎ 05 56 52 94 36, Fax 05 56 44 25 11, 余 - ▤. AE ① GB EY a
✿ *closed Saturday lunch, Sunday and Bank Holidays* – **Meals** 100 b.i. (lunch), 160/270 and a la carte 250/320
Spec. Marbré de cèpes frais (season). Turbot au beurre de piments d'Espelette et au jambon. Crème tendre au chocolat guayaquil, glace à l'Izarra verte. **Wines** Côtes de Bourg, Côtes de Blaye.

XXX **L'Alhambra,** 111 bis r. Judaïque ☎ 05 56 96 06 91, Fax 05 56 98 00 52 – ▤. GB
closed 1 to 15 August, Saturday lunch and Sunday – **Meals** 110 (lunch), 150/210 and a la carte 240/340. CX e

XXX **La Chamade,** 20 r. Piliers de Tutelle ☎ 05 56 48 13 74, Fax 05 56 79 29 67 – ▤. AE GB JCB DX d
closed 26 July-3 August and Saturday lunch – **Meals** 120/290 and a la carte 220/310.

XX **Didier Gélineau,** 26 r. Pas St Georges ☎ 05 56 52 84 25, Fax 05 56 51 93 25 – ▤. AE ① GB JCB EX n
closed Saturday lunch and Sunday – **Meals** (booking essential) 120/260.

XX **Le Buhan,** 28 r. Buhan ☎ 05 56 52 80 86, Fax 05 56 52 80 86 – AE GB EY a
closed 24 August-1 September, February Holidays, Sunday except lunch from September-June and Monday – **Meals** 135/285.

X **L'Oiseau Bleu,** 65 cours Verdun ☎ 05 56 81 09 39, Fax 05 56 81 09 39 – ▤. AE GB
closed 3 to 25 August, Saturday lunch and Sunday – **Meals** 105 (lunch)/155.

X **Bistro du Sommelier,** 163 r. G. Bonnac ☎ 05 56 96 71 78, Fax 05 56 24 52 36, 余 – AE GB CY u
closed 11-17 August, Saturday lunch and Sunday – **Meals** 121.

t Parc des Expositions *: North of the town – ✉ 33300 Bordeaux :*

Sofitel Aquitania M, ☎ 05 56 50 83 80, Fax 05 56 39 73 75, ←, ⛱ – |‡| ⇔ rm ▤ TV ☎ P – 🏛 25 - 400. AE ① GB
closed 27 July-18 August and 20 December-12 January – ***Le Flore :*** **Meals** 145/200 – ☕ 75 – **185 rm** 750.

Novotel-Bordeaux Lac M, ☎ 05 56 50 99 70, Fax 05 56 43 00 66, ←, 余, ⛱, 🌳 – |‡| ⇔ rm ▤ TV ☎ ♿ P – 🏛 200. AE ① GB
Meals 95/150 – ☕ 50 – **176 rm** 430/470.

Mercure Pont d'Aquitaine, ☎ 05 56 43 36 72, Fax 05 56 50 23 95, 余, ⛱, 🌳 – |‡| ⇔ rm ▤ TV ☎ ♿ P – 🏛 80. AE ① GB
Meals *(closed Saturday lunch and Sunday lunch)* 80/100 ♨ – ☕ 55 – **100 rm** 430/900.

t Bouliac *SE : 8 km – alt. 74 – ✉ 33270 :*

Le St-James M 🐦, pl. C. Hostein, near church ☎ 05 57 97 06 00, Fax 05 56 20 92 58, ← Bordeaux, 余, « Original contemporary decor », ⛱, 🌳 – |‡| ▤ rm TV ☎ P. AE ① GB. ✗
✿ **Meals** 185 b.i. (lunch), 255/360 and a la carte 270/390 - ***Le Bistroy*** ☎ 05 57 97 06 06 **Meals** a la carte 130 to 180 – ☕ 75 – **17 rm** 650/1350
Spec. Salade d'huîtres au caviar, crépinette grillée (September-June). Filets d'anguilles sautés aux lardes. Civet de canard désossé et compoté aux cèpes. **Wines** Premières Côtes de Bordeaux, Pessac-Léognan.

to the W :

t the airport *11 km by A 630 : from the North, exit nr 11b, from the South, exit nr 11 – ✉ 33700 Mérignac :*

Mercure Aéroport M, 1 av. Ch. Lindbergh ☎ 05 56 34 74 74, Fax 05 56 34 30 84, 余, ⛱ – |‡| ⇔ rm ▤ TV ☎ ♿ P – 🏛 110. AE ① GB
Meals 120 ♨ – ☕ 55 – **105 rm** 650/680.

Novotel Aéroport, av. J. F. Kennedy ☎ 05 56 34 10 25, Fax 05 56 55 99 64, 余, ⛱, 🌳 – |‡| ⇔ rm ▤ TV ☎ ♿ P – 🏛 50. AE ① GB JCB
Meals 88 – ☕ 51 – **137 rm** 480/520.

Soretel, 97 av. J.-F. Kennedy ☎ 05 56 34 33 08, Fax 05 56 34 01 90, 余, ⛱ – |‡| TV ☎ ♿ P – 🏛 25. AE ① GB
Meals 80/110 ♨ – ☕ 38 – **60 rm** 295/315.

Do not use yesterday's maps for today's journey.

Eugénie-les-Bains *40320 Landes 82 ① – pop. 467 alt. 65 – Spa Spa (Feb.-Nov.).*
Tourist Office (Feb.-Dec.) 05 58 51 13 16.
Bordeaux 151.

Les Prés d'Eugénie (Guérard) M, 05 58 05 06 07, Fax 05 58 51 10 10, «Elegantly decorated 19C mansion, park », – 60. AE GB.
closed 1 to 20 December and 5 January-27 February – (low-calorie menu for resider only) - ***rest. Michel Guérard*** (booking essential) *(closed Thursday lunch and Wednesd from 9 September-6 July except Bank Holidays)* **Meals** 590/750 and a la carte 480/6 – 110 – **28 rm** 1450, 7 suites
Spec. Salade baroque aux crevettes grillées. Turbot au lard et au chou cuit en cocot de fonte. Caneton à la broche arrosé de jus d'orange. **Wines** Tursan blanc.

Le Couvent des Herbes M, park, « 18C convent » – AE rest
closed 1 to 20 December and 5 January-27 February – **Meals** see ***Les Prés d'Eugén*** and ***Michel Guérard*** – 110 – **5 rm** 1450/1650, 3 suites.

La Maison Rose M (see also rest. Michel Guérard), 05 58 05 06 0 Fax 05 58 51 10 10, « Guesthouse ambience », – kitchenette AE GB. rest
closed 1 to 20 December and 5 January-9 February – **Meals** (residents only) – 60 **32 rm** 460/820.

La Ferme aux Grives, 05 58 51 19 08, Fax 05 58 51 10 10, « Old country inn – GB
closed 5 January-7 February, Monday dinner and Tuesday from 9 September-6 July exce Bank Holidays – **Meals** 175.

Typical little Greek restaurants, generally very modest, where it is pleasant to spend the evening, surrounded with noisy but friendly locals, sometimes with guitar or bouzouki entertainment. These particular restaurants are usually open for dinner only.

CANNES *06400 Alpes-Mar. 84 ⑨, 115 ㉟ ㊳ – pop. 68 676 alt. 2 – Casinos Carlton Casino BY Palm Beach (temp. closed) X, Croisette BZ.*

See *: Site★★ – Seafront★★ : Boulevard★★ BCDZ and Pointe de la Croisette★ X – ★ fro the Mont Chevalier Tower AZ* **V** *– The Castre Museum★ (Musée de la Castre) AZ – To into the Hills★ (Chemin des Collines) NE : 4 km V – The Croix des Gardes X* **E** *★ W 5 km then 15 mn.*

Country-Club of Cannes-Mougins 04 93 75 79 13 by ⑤ : 9 km ; Golf-Club Cannes-Mandelieu 04 93 49 55 39 by ② : 6,5 km ; Royal Mougins Golf Club at Mougi 04 92 92 49 69 by ④ : 10 km ; Riviera Golf Club at Mandelieu 04 93 97 67 67 ② : 8 km.

Tourist Office "SEMEC", Palais des Festivals 04 93 39 24 53, Fax 04 93 39 37 06 ar railway station 04 93 99 19 77, Fax 04 93 39 40 19 – A.C. 12bis r. L. Blar 04 93 39 38 94.

Paris 903 ⑤ – Aix-en-Provence 146 ⑤ – Grenoble 312 ⑤ – Marseilles 159 ⑤ – Nice 3 ⑤ – Toulon 121 ⑤.

Plans on following pages

Carlton Inter-Continental, 58 bd Croisette 04 93 06 40 06, Fax 04 93 06 40 2 – rm – 25 - 250. AE GB JCB.
see ***La Belle Otéro*** below - ***La Côte*** 04 93 06 40 23 *(closed Tuesday and Wednesda* **Meals** 275 (lunch), 350/460 – ***Brasserie Carlton*** : **Meals** 235 – 135 – **310 r** 1990/3690, 28 suites. CZ

Martinez, 73 bd Croisette 04 92 98 73 00, Fax 04 93 39 67 82, – – 600. AE GB JCB DZ
see ***La Palme d'Or*** below - ***Le Relais*** 04 92 98 74 12 *(closed 15 February-15 Marc and lunch from Easter-September)* **Meals** 180 – 115 – **382 rm** 1900/3460, 12 suite

Majestic, 14 bd Croisette 04 92 98 77 00, Fax 04 93 38 97 90, – – 400. AE GB JCB BZ
see ***Villa des Lys*** below – 120 – **239 rm** 1950/4100, 23 suites.

Noga Hilton M, 50 bd Croisette 04 92 99 70 00, Fax 04 92 99 70 11, « Roofto swimming pool and terraces Cannes », – rm – 80 AE GB JCB CZ
La Scala *: Italian rest. 04 92 99 70 93* **Meals** 168 (lunch)/295 – ***Le Grand Bleu*** brasser 04 92 99 70 92 **Meals** 138(lunch)/170 – 135 – **196 rm** 1490/499 33 suites.

Gray d'Albion M, 38 r. Serbes ☎ 04 92 99 79 79, Fax 04 92 99 26 10, – rm – 30 - 200. AE GB JCB BZ d
Royal Gray : **Meals** 190/265 and a la carte 290/390 – 97 – **172 rm** 1050/1700, 14 suites.

L'Horset-Savoy M, 5 r. F. Einessy ☎ 04 92 99 72 00, Fax 04 93 68 25 59, – rm – 90. AE GB CZ u
Meals 160 – 98 – **101 rm** 970/1430, 5 suites.

Sofitel Méditerranée, 2 bd J. Hibert ☎ 04 92 99 73 00, Fax 04 92 99 73 29, « Rooftop swimming pool and restaurant ≤ bay of Cannes » – rm – 100. AE GB JCB AZ n
closed 23 November-22 December – ***Le Méditerranée*** ☎ 04 92 99 73 02 **Meals** 180(lunch)/230 – ***Le Palmyre*** ☎ 04 92 99 73 10 **Meals** 150/250 – 50 – **141 rm** 1050/1780, 8 suites.

Belle Plage M without rest, 6 r. J. Dollfus ☎ 04 93 06 25 50, Fax 04 93 99 61 06 – – 50. AE GB JCB AZ u
80 – **48 rm** 960/1460.

Croisette Beach H. M without rest, 13 r. Canada ☎ 04 93 94 50 50, Fax 04 93 68 35 38, – rm . AE GB JCB DZ y
closed 19 November-25 December – 90 – **93 rm** 800/1300.

Splendid without rest, 4 r. F. Faure ☎ 04 93 99 53 11, Fax 04 93 99 55 02, ≤ – kitchenette . AE GB BZ a
50 – **64 rm** 590/890.

Amarante M, 78 bd Carnot ☎ 04 93 39 22 23, Fax 04 93 39 40 22, – rm – 25. AE GB JCB V e
Meals 135/170 b.i. – 60 – **70 rm** 950.

Sun Riviera M without rest, 138 r. d'Antibes ☎ 04 93 06 77 77, Fax 04 93 38 31 10, – rm . AE GB JCB CZ h
85 – **42 rm** 810/1800.

Cristal M, 15 rd-pt Duboys d'Angers ☎ 04 93 39 45 45, Fax 04 93 38 64 66, – rm . AE GB CZ s
closed 18 November-23 December ; rest. : closed 18 November-27 December, Sunday dinner and Monday – **Meals** 140/350 – 82 – **51 rm** 870/1900.

Victoria without rest, rd-pt Duboys d'Angers ☎ 04 93 99 36 36, Fax 04 93 38 03 91, – . AE GB JCB CZ x
closed 20 November-28 December – 70 – **25 rm** 750/1250.

Fouquet's without rest, 2 rd-pt Duboys d'Angers ☎ 04 93 38 75 81, Fax 04 92 98 03 39 – . AE GB JCB CZ y
1 April-30 October – 60 – **10 rm** 1100/1300.

Paris without rest, 34 bd Alsace ☎ 04 93 38 30 89, Fax 04 93 39 04 61, – – 25. AE GB JCB. CY a
closed 20 November to 29 December – 47 – **50 rm** 650/720, 3 suites.

Embassy, 6 r. Bône ☎ 04 93 38 79 02, Fax 04 93 99 07 98, – – 50. AE GB JCB DY j
Meals 120/250 – 40 – **60 rm** 600/950.

Mondial without rest, 1 r. Tesseire ☎ 04 93 68 70 00, Fax 04 93 99 39 11 – rm . AE GB CY e
60 – **56 rm** 620/770.

America M without rest, 13 r. St-Honoré ☎ 04 93 06 75 75, Fax 04 93 68 04 58 – . AE GB JCB. BZ r
closed 27 November-27 December – 60 – **28 rm** 550/730.

Villa de l'Olivier without rest, 5 r. Tambourinaires ☎ 04 93 39 53 28, Fax 04 93 39 55 85, – . AE GB. AZ e
52 – **24 rm** 525/715.

Château de la Tour , 10 av. Font-de-Veyre by ③ ✉ 06150 Cannes-La-Bocca ☎ 04 93 47 34 64, Fax 04 93 47 86 61, – . AE GB JCB
Meals *(closed 15 November-25 December)* 95/120 – 40 – **42 rm** 550/615.

Beau Séjour, 5 r. Fauvettes ☎ 04 93 39 63 00, Fax 04 92 98 64 66, – rm . AE GB JCB. rest AZ d
closed 23 November-23 December – **Meals** 80/125 – 60 – **45 rm** 650/750.

Ligure without rest, 5 pl. Gare ☎ 04 93 39 03 11, Fax 04 93 39 19 48 – . AE GB BY n
35 – **36 rm** 300/750.

CANNES

André (R. du Cdt) CZ
Antibes (R. d') BCY
Belges (R. des) BZ 12
Chabaud (R.) CY 22
Croisette (Bd de la) BDZ
Félix-Faure (R.) ABZ
Foch (R. du Mar.) BY 44
Joffre (R. du Mar.) BY 60
Riouffe (R. Jean de) BY 98

Albert-Édouard (Jetée) BZ
Alexandre-III (Bd) X 2
Alsace (Bd) BDY
Anc. Combattants d'Afrique du Nord (Av.) AYZ 4
Bachaga Saïd Boualam (Av.) AY 5
Beauséjour (Av.) DYZ
Beau-Soleil (Bd) X 10
Blanc (R. Louis) AYZ
Broussailles (Av. des) V 16
Buttura (R.) BZ 17
Canada (R. du) DZ
Carnot (Bd) X
Carnot (Square) V 20
Castre (Pl. de la) AZ 21
Clemenceau (R. G.) AZ
Coteaux (Av. des) V
Croix-des-Gardes (Bd) VX 29
Delaup (Bd) AY 30
Dr-Pierre Gazagnaire (R.) AZ 32
Dr-R. Picaud (Av.) X
Dollfus (R. Jean) AZ 33
Faure (R. Félix) ABZ
Favorite (Av. de la) X 38
Ferrage (Bd de la) ABY 40
Fiesole (Av.) X 43
Gallieni (R. du Mar.) BY 48
Gaulle (Pl. Gén.-de) BZ 51
Gazagnaire (Bd Eugène) X
Grasse (Av. de) VX 53
Guynemer (Bd) AY
Haddad-Simon (R. Jean) CY 54
Hespérides (Av. des) X 55
Hibert (Bd Jean) AZ
Hibert (R.) AZ
Isola-Bella (Av. d') X
Jaurès (R. Jean) BCY
Juin (Av. Mar.) DZ
Koenig (Av. Gén.) DY
Lacour (Bd Alexandre) X 62
Latour-Maubourg (R.) DZ
Lattre-de-T. (Av. de) AY 63
Laubeuf (Quai Max) AZ
Leader (Bd) VX 64
Lérins (Av. de) X 65
Lorraine (Bd. de) CDY
Macé (R.) CZ 66
Madrid (Av. de) DZ
Meynadier (R.) ABY
Midi (Bd du) X
Mimont (R. de) BY
Mont-Chevalier (R. du) AZ 72
Montfleury (Bd) CDY 74
Monti (R. Marius) AY 75
Moulin (Bd du) AY 76
Noailles (Av. J.-de) X
Observatoire (Bd de l') X 84
Oxford (Bd d') V 87
Pantiero (la) ABZ
Paradis-Terrestre (Corniches du) V 88
Pasteur (R.) DZ
Pastour (R. Louis) AY 90
Perier (Bd du) V 92
Perrissol (R. Louis) AZ 93
Petit-Juas (Av. du) VX
Pins (Bd des) X 95
Pompidou (Espl. G.) BZ
Prince-de-Galles (Av. du) X 97
République (Bd de la) X
Riou (Bd du) VX
Roi-Albert 1er (Av.) X
Rouguière (R.) BY 100
St-Nicolas (Av.) BY 105
St-Pierre (Quai) AZ
Sardou (R. Léandre) X 108
Serbes (R. des) BZ 110
Source (Bd de la) X 112
Stanislas (Pl.) AY
Strasbourg (Bd de) CDY
Teisseire (R.) CY 114
Tuby (Bd Victor) AYZ 1
Vallauris (Av. de) VX 1
Vallombrosa (Bd) AY 1
Vautrin (Bd Gén.) DZ
Vidal (R. du Cdt) CY 1
Wemyss (Av. Amiral Wester) X 1

LE CANNET

Aubarède (Ch. de l') V 8
Bellevue (Pl.) V 1
Bréguières (Ch. de) V 1
Cannes (R. des) V 1
Carnot (Bd de) V
Cheval (Av. Maurice) V 2
Collines (Ch. des) V
Doumer (Bd Paul) V
Écoles (R. des) V 3
Four-à-Chaux (Bd du) V 4
Gambetta (Bd) V 5
Gaulle (Av. Gén.-de) V
Jeanpierre (Av. Maurice) V 5
Mermoz (Av. Jean) V 6
Monod (Bd Jacques) V 6
Mont-Joli (Av. du) V 7
N.-D.-des-Anges (Av.) V 7
Olivet (Ch. de l') V 8
Olivetum (Av. d') V 8
Paris (R. de) V 8
Pinède (Av. de la) V 9
Pompidou (Av. Georges) V 9
République (Bd de la) V
Roosevelt (Av. Franklin) V
St-Sauveur (R.) V 1
Victor-Hugo (R.) V 1
Victoria (Av.) V

VALLAURIS

Cannes (Av. de) V 1
Clemenceau (Av. G.) V 2
Fournas (Av. du) V 4
Golfe (Av. du) V 5
Isnard (Pl. Paul) V 5
Rouvier (Bd Maurice) V 1
Tapis-Vert (Av. du) V 1

CANNES

0 200 m

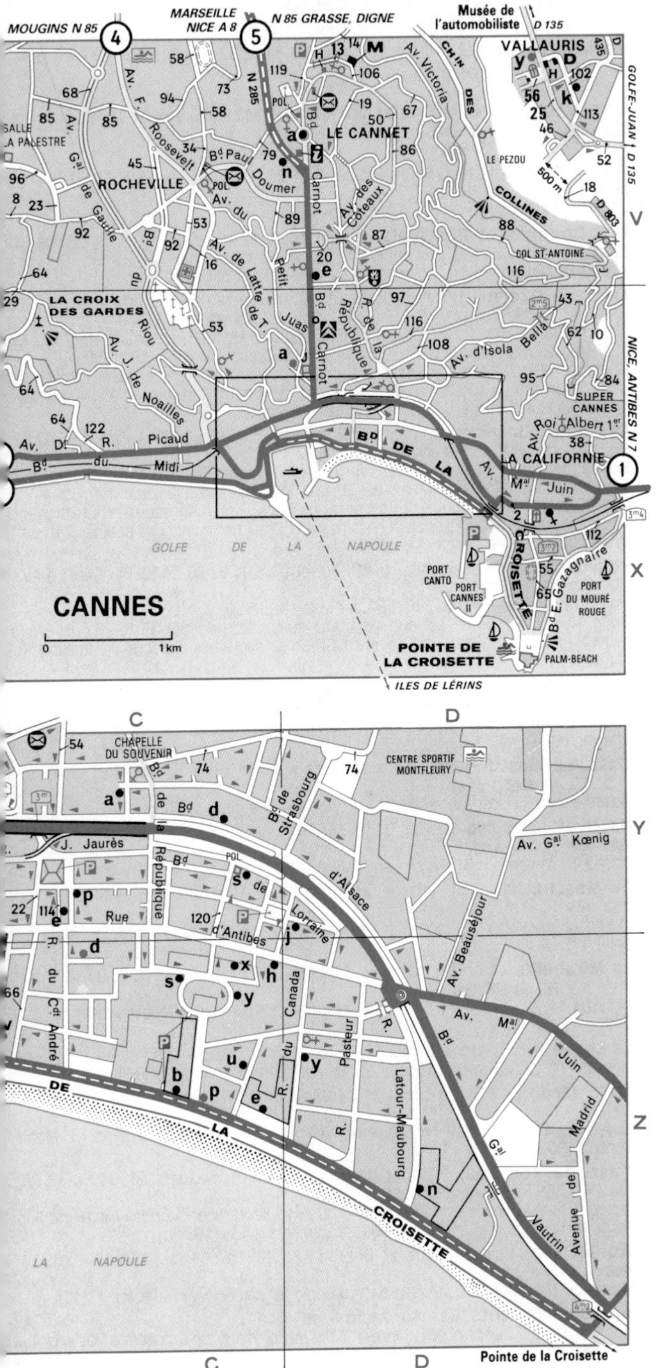
CANNES
MOUGINS N 85
MARSEILLE NICE A 8
N 85 GRASSE, DIGNE
Musée de l'automobiliste
D 135
VALLAURIS
GOLFE-JUAN D 135
LE CANNET
ROCHEVILLE
LA CROIX DES GARDES
LE PEZOU
COL ST-ANTOINE
SUPER CANNES
LA CALIFORNIE
NICE, ANTIBES N 7
GOLFE DE LA NAPOULE
PORT CANTO
PORT CANNES II
PORT DU MOURÉ ROUGE
POINTE DE LA CROISETTE
PALM-BEACH
ILES DE LÉRINS
SALLE LA PALESTRE
CHAPELLE DU SOUVENIR
CENTRE SPORTIF MONTFLEURY
Bd de la République
Bd de Strasbourg
Bd d'Alsace
Bd de Lorraine
Rue d'Antibes
R. du Canada
R. Pasteur
R. Latour-Maubourg
Av. Beauséjour
Av. Gal Kœnig
Av. Mal Juin
Bd Gal Vautrin
Avenue de Madrid
Bd DE LA CROISETTE
Pointe de la Croisette
LA NAPOULE
1 km

Abrial without rest, 24 bd Lorraine ✆ 04 93 38 78 82, Fax 04 92 98 67 41 – CY
50 – **50 rm** 700.

Alsace H. without rest, 40 bd Alsace ✆ 04 93 38 50 70, Fax 04 93 38 20 44 – CY
45 – **30 rm** 585/630.

Albert 1er without rest, 68 av. Grasse ✆ 04 93 39 24 04, Fax 04 93 38 83 75 – AY
30 – **11 rm** 340.

Des Congrès et Festivals without rest, 12 r. Teisseire ✆ 04 93 39 13 Fax 04 93 39 56 28 – rm rm CY
closed 20 November-27 December – 40 – **20 rm** 350/550.

La Belle Otéro - Hôtel Carlton Inter-Continental, 58 bd Croisette, 7th fl ✆ 04 93 68 00 33, Fax 04 93 39 09 06, – CZ
closed 8 June-7 July, 2 to 17 November, Sunday and Monday except July-August – **Me** (dinner only July-August) 290 b.i. (lunch), 390/620 and a la carte 480/650
Spec. Saint-Pierre poêlé aux artichauts, gnocchi de ricotta (December-May). Carré d'agne de Sisteron rôti en confit d'ail persillé. Figues fraîches en gratiné d'amandes aux save orientales (July-October). **Wines** Côtes de Provence.

La Palme d'Or - Hôtel Martinez, 73 bd Croisette ✆ 04 92 98 74 14, Fax 04 93 39 67 – DZ
closed mid-November-mid-December, Tuesday except dinner from mid-June to m September and Monday – **Meals** 295 (lunch), 350/580 and a la carte 430/600
Spec. Symphonie de légumes de Provence aux fruits de mer. Agneau en croûte provença flan et gousses d'ail confites au miel de romarin. Croustillant chocolat praliné "Palme d'C **Wines** Côtes de Provence.

Villa des Lys - Hôtel Majestic, 14 bd Croisette ✆ 04 92 98 77 00, Fax 04 93 38 97 –
closed December – **Meals** 240/560 and a la carte 350/500
Spec. Ravioli de queue et joue de bœuf au bouillon de pot-au-feu. Loup étuvé risotto au jus de légumes de Provence. Gratin de suprêmes d'orange caramélisés au d'agrumes.

Poêle d'Or, 23 r. États-Unis ✆ 04 93 39 77 65, Fax 04 93 40 45 59 – CZ
closed 1 to 7 July, 24 to 30 November, February Holidays, Tuesday lunch in summ Sunday dinner in winter and Monday – **Meals** (weekends : booking essential) 125/350 a la carte 270/440.

Gaston et Gastounette, 7 quai St-Pierre ✆ 04 93 39 47 92, Fax 04 93 99 45 34, – AZ
closed 1 to 20 December – **Meals** 130/200 and a la carte 270/390.

Festival, 52 bd Croisette ✆ 04 93 38 04 81, Fax 04 93 38 13 82, – CZ
closed 19 November-27 December – **Meals** 190 (lunch)/220.

Le Mesclun, 16 r. St-Antoine ✆ 04 93 99 45 19, Fax 04 93 47 68 29 – AZ
closed 15 November-15 December and Wednesday except in July-August – **Meals** (dinr only) 175.

La Mirabelle, 24 r. St-Antoine ✆ 04 93 38 72 75, Fax 04 93 90 66 95, « Proven style » – AZ
closed 1 to 20 December, 10 to 28 February and Tuesday – **Meals** (dinner only) 18 240.

La Cigale, 1 r. Florian ✆ 04 93 39 65 79, – CZ
closed 1 to 15 November, Sunday dinner and Monday – **Meals** 130/170.

Côté Jardin, 12 av. St-Louis ✆ 04 93 38 60 28, Fax 04 93 38 60 28, – X
closed February, Monday except dinner from May-September and Sunday – **Meals** (lunch)/180.

Taverna Romana, 10 r. St-Dizier (quartier du Suquet) ✆ 04 93 39 96 C Fax 04 93 68 54 38 – AZ
closed 1 to 14 December, lunch from 1 June-15 September, Monday lunch and Sund from 16 September-31 May – **Meals** - Italian rest. - 135/185.

Au Bec Fin, 12 r. 24 Août ✆ 04 93 38 35 86, Fax 04 93 38 43 47 – BY
closed 20 December-20 January, Saturday dinner and Sunday – **Meals** 90/115.

Aux Bons Enfants, 80 r. Meynadier – AZ
closed August, 23 December-3 January, Saturday dinner from October to May and Sund – **Meals** 92.

Grasse *06130 Alpes-Mar.* 84 ⑧, 114 ⑬, 115 ㉔ *– pop. 41 388 alt. 250.*
Victoria Golf Club ☏ 04 93 12 23 26 by D 4, D 3 and D 103 : 13 km ; Grande Bastide at Opio ☏ 04 93 77 70 08, E : 6 km by D 7 ; of St-Donat ☏ 04 93 09 76 60 : 5,5 km ; Opio-Valbonne ☏ 04 93 42 00 08 by D 4 : 11 km.
Tourist Office, 22 cours H. Cresp ☏ 04 93 36 66 66, Fax 04 93 36 86 36.
Cannes 17.

XXXX ✿✿ **La Bastide St-Antoine** (Chibois) (rooms planned), 48 av. H. Dunant (by bd Mar. Leclerc) : 1,5 km ☏ 04 93 09 16 48, Fax 04 92 42 03 42, ≤, « 18C country farm in an olive-grove », – P. AE GB
Meals 210 (lunch), 380/550 and a la carte 400/540
Spec. Douceur de fèves à la brunoise de crustacés et aux morilles. Petit pageot à l'huile d'olive, jus de fenouil à l'oignon nouveau. Mirliton épicé tiède à la glace vanille, jus d'agrumes.

Juan-les-Pins *06160 Alpes-Mar.* 84 ⑨, 115 ㉟ ㊴
Tourist Office 51 bd Ch.-Guillaumont ☏ 04 92 90 53 05.
Cannes 8,5.

✿✿ **Juana and rest. La Terrasse**, la Pinède, av. G. Gallice ☏ 04 93 61 08 70, Fax 04 93 61 76 60, ≤, – rm TV P – 25. AE GB
Easter-late October – **Meals** *(closed Wednesday except July-August and Bank Holidays)* 270 (lunch), 410/630 and a la carte 530/660 – 95 – **45 rm** 950/2050, 5 suites
Spec. Ravioles de scampis frais, fumet de crustacés au parfum d'olives. Selle d'agneau de Pauillac cuite en terre d'argile. Chaud "Juanais" au cœur tendre de guanaja, sorbet chocolat en plissé de noisette. **Wines** Palette, Bandol.

La Napoule *06210 Alpes-Mar.* 84 ⑧, 115 ㉞
of Mandelieu ☏ 04 93 49 55 39 ; Riviera Golf Club ☏ 04 92 97 67 67.
Cannes 9,5.

XXXX ✿✿ **L'Oasis,** r. J. H. Carle ☏ 04 93 49 95 52, Fax 04 93 49 64 13, « Shaded and flowered patio » – AE GB JCB
closed Sunday dinner and Monday from November-March – **Meals** 275 b.i. (lunch), 390/650 and a la carte 500/640
Spec. Asperges violettes du pays et morilles à l'oseille (spring). Risotto de daurade royale aux palourdes et thym citron (summer). Selle de chevreuil en noisettes aux myrtilles, poires rôties à la cannelle (autumn and winter). **Wines** Côtes de Provence.

LILLE *59000 Nord* 51 ⑯, 111 ㉒ *– pop. 172 142 alt. 10.*
See : *Old Lille★★ : Old Stock Exchange★★ (Vieille Bourse)* EY, *Place du Général-de-Gaulle* EY **66**, *Hospice Comtesse★ (panelled timber vault★★)* EY, *– Rue de la Monnaie★* EY **120** – *Vauban's Citadel★* BV – *St-Sauveur district : Paris Gate★* EFZ, *≤★ from the top of the belfry of the Hôtel de Ville* FZ – *Fine Arts Museum★★★ (Musée des Beaux-Arts)* EZ – *Général de Gaulle's Birthplace (Maison natale)* EY. – *of Flandres (private) ☏ 03 20 72 20 74 : 4,5 km ; of Sart (private) ☏ 03 20 72 02 51 : 7 km ; of Brigode at Villeneuve d'Ascq ☏ 03 20 91 17 86 : 9 km ; of Bondues ☏ 03 20 23 20 62 : 9,5 km.*
of Lille-Lesquin : ☏ 03 20 49 68 68 : 8 km.
☏ 08 36 35 35 35.
Tourist Office Palais Rihour ☏ 03 20 21 94 21, Fax 03 20 21 94 20 – Automobile Club du Nord, 8 r. Quennette ☏ 03 20 56 21 41.
Paris 221 ④ – Brussels 116 ② – Ghent 71 ② – Luxembourg 312 ④ – Strasbourg 525 ④.

Plans on following pages

Alliance M, 17 quai du Wault ✉ 59800 ☏ 03 20 30 62 62, Fax 03 20 42 94 25, « Former 17C convent » – rm TV P – 120. AE GB JCB. rest BV d
Meals 110/195 – 70 – **75 rm** 640/900, 8 suites.

Carlton, 3 r. Paris ✉ 59800 ☏ 03 20 13 33 13, Fax 03 20 51 48 17 – rm TV P – 25 - 100. AE GB JCB EY u
Le Clos Opéra (1st floor) *(closed Sunday dinner and Monday)* **Meals** 135/195 – ***Brasserie Jean*** *(closed August and Sunday lunch)* **Meals** 130/140 b.i. – 75 – **57 rm** 820/1050, 3 suites.

Novotel Lille Centre M, 116 r. Hôpital Militaire ✉ 59800 ☏ 03 20 30 65 26, Fax 03 20 30 04 04 – rm TV – 30. AE GB EY s
Meals a la carte approx. 170 – 55 – **102 rm** 540/620.

Gd H. Bellevue without rest, 5 r. J. Roisin ✉ 59800 ☏ 03 20 57 45 64, Fax 03 20 40 07 93 – rm TV – 50. AE GB EY z
62 – **61 rm** 460/760.

Mercure Royal M without rest, 2 bd Carnot ✉ 59800 ☏ 03 20 14 71 47, Fax 03 20 14 71 48 – rm TV – 25. AE GB JCB EY h
55 – **102 rm** 440/510.

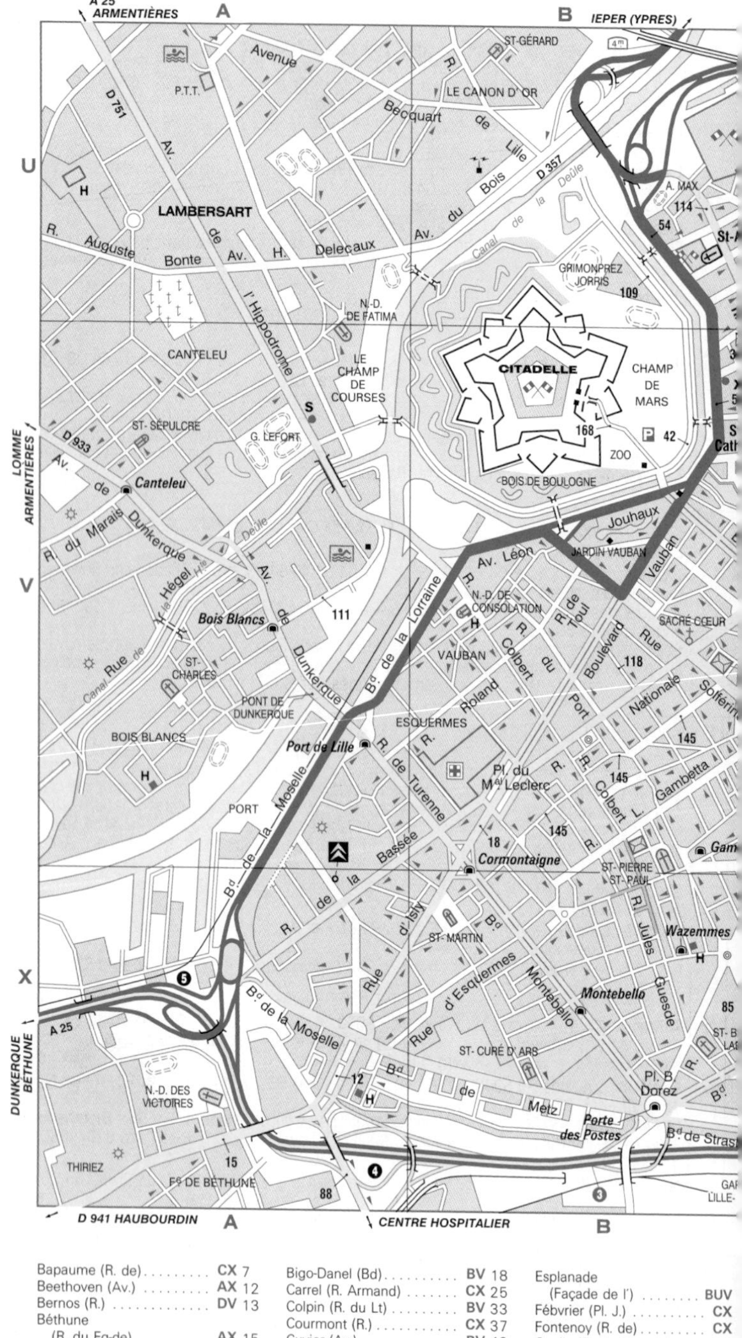

Bapaume (R. de) .... CX 7
Beethoven (Av.) .... AX 12
Bernos (R.) .... DV 13
Béthune
(R. du Fg-de) .... AX 15

Bigo-Danel (Bd) .... BV 18
Carrel (R. Armand) .... CX 25
Colpin (R. du Lt) .... BV 33
Courmont (R.) .... CX 37
Cuvier (Av.) .... BV 42

Esplanade
(Façade de l') .... BUV
Fébvrier (Pl. J.) CX
Fontenoy (R. de) CX
Gaulle (R. du Gén.-de) .... CU

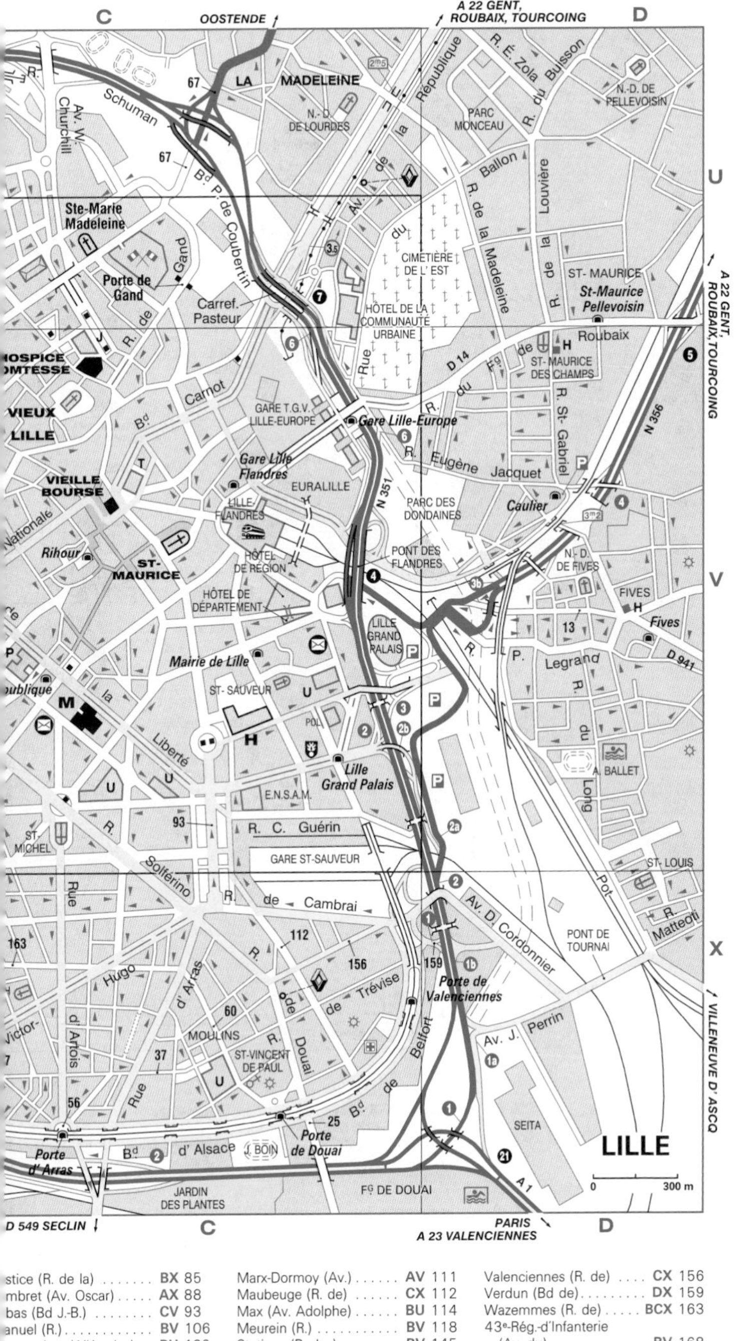

stice (R. de la) . . . . BX 85
mbret (Av. Oscar) . . . . . AX 88
bas (Bd J.-B.) . . . . CV 93
anuel (R.) . . . . BV 106
arronniers (Allée des) . . BU 109

Marx-Dormoy (Av.) . . . . . . AV 111
Maubeuge (R. de) . . . . . . CX 112
Max (Av. Adolphe) . . . . . . BU 114
Meurein (R.) . . . . BV 118
Stations (R. des) . . . . BV 145

Valenciennes (R. de) . . . . CX 156
Verdun (Bd de) . . . . DX 159
Wazemmes (R. de) . . . . . BCX 163
43e-Rég.-d'Infanterie (Av. du) . . . . BV 168

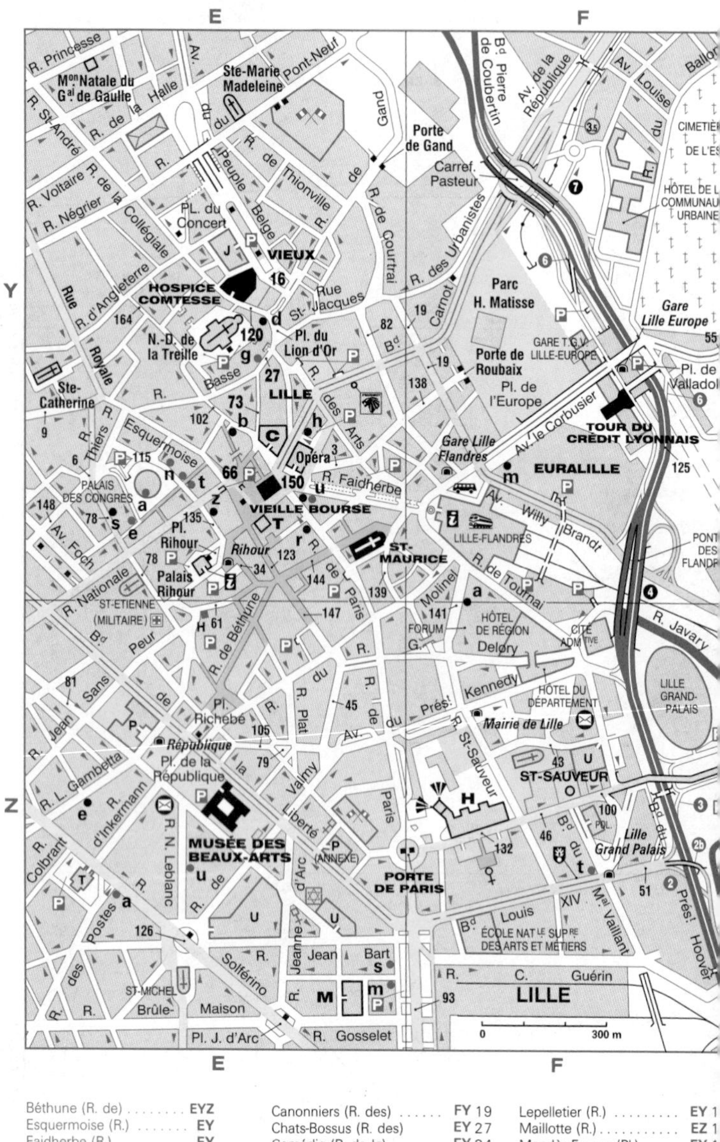

Béthune (R. de) . . . . EYZ
Esquermoise (R.) . . . . EY
Faidherbe (R.) . . . . EY
Gambetta (R. Léon) . . . . . EZ
Gaulle (Pl. Gén.-de)
(Grand Place) . . . . EY 66
Grande Chaussée (R. de la) EY 73
Monnaie (R. de la) . . . . . . EY 120
Nationale (R.) . . . . EYZ
Neuve (R.) . . . . EY 123

Anatole-France (R.) . . . . . . EY 3
Arsenal (Pl. de l') . . . . EY 6
Barre (R. de la) . . . . EY 9
Bettignies (Pl. L. de) . . . . . EY 16

Canonniers (R. des) . . . . . . FY 19
Chats-Bossus (R. des) . . . . . EY 27
Comédie (R. de la) . . . . EY 34
Debierre (R. Ch.) . . . . FZ 43
Delesalle (R. E.) . . . . EZ 45
Déportés (R. des) . . . . FY 46
Dr.-Calmette (Bd) . . . . FY 51
Faubourg de Roubaix . . . . . FY 55
Fosses (R. des) . . . . EYZ 61
Hôpital-Militaire (R.) . . . . . . EY 78
Jacquart (Pl.) . . . . EZ 79
Jacquemars-Giélée (R.) . . . . EZ 81
Jardins (R. des) . . . . EY 82
Lebas (Bd J.-B.) . . . . FZ 93
Lefèvre (R. G.) . . . . FZ 100

Lepelletier (R.) . . . . EY 1
Maillotte (R.) . . . . EZ 1
Mendès-France (Pl.) . . . . . . EY 1
Pasteur (Bd. L.) . . . . FY 1
Philippe-le-Bon (Pl.) . . . . . . EZ 1
Réduit (R. du) . . . . FZ 1
Roisin (R. Jean) . . . . EY 1
Roubaix (R. de) . . . . EFY 1
St-Génois (R.) . . . . EY 1
St-Venant (Av. Ch.) . . . . . . FYZ 1
Sec-Arembault (R. du) . . . . EY 1
Tanneurs (R. des) . . . . EYZ 1
Tenremonde (R.) . . . . EY 1
Théâtre (Pl. du) . . . . EY 1
Trois-Mollettes (R. des) . . . EY 1

Fimotel M, 75 bis r. Gambetta 03 20 42 90 90, Fax 03 20 57 14 24 – rm TV – 80. AE GB EZ e
Meals *(closed Friday dinner, Sunday lunch and Saturday)* 91 – 45 – **98 rm** 370.

Paix without rest, 46 bis r. Paris 59800 03 20 54 63 93, Fax 03 20 63 98 97 – TV. AE GB EY r
38 – **35 rm** 300/430.

Treille M without rest, 7 pl. L. de Bettignies 59800 03 20 55 45 46, Fax 03 20 51 51 69 – rm TV – 40. AE GB EY d
45 – **40 rm** 360/390.

Ibis Centre M, av. Ch. St-Venant 59800 03 20 55 44 44, Fax 03 20 31 06 25, – rm TV – 25 - 70. AE GB FYZ a
Meals 95 – 35 – **151 rm** 350.

Lille Europe M without rest, allée de Liège, av. Le Corbusier 03 20 21 41 51, Fax 03 20 21 41 59 – TV P. AE GB FY m
40 – **97 rm** 350.

Ibis Opéra M without rest, 21 r. Lepelletier 59800 03 20 06 21 95, Fax 03 20 74 91 30 – rm TV. AE GB EY b
35 – **60 rm** 340.

Clarine, 46 r. Fg d'Arras 03 20 53 53 40, Fax 03 20 53 20 95 – rm TV P – 40. AE GB
Meals 80/100 – 32 – **80 rm** 230/280.

A L'Huîtrière, 3 r. Chats Bossus 59800 03 20 55 43 41, Fax 03 20 55 23 10, « Original decoration with ceramics in the fish shop » – . AE GB EY g
closed 22 July-25 August, and dinner Sunday and Bank Holidays – **Meals** 260 (lunch)/480 and a la carte 350/490
Spec. Huîtres et produits de la mer. Homard poêlé aux pommes de terre et à l'estragon. Foie gras de canard en hochepot.

Le Sébastopol, 1 pl. Sébastopol 03 20 57 05 05, Fax 03 20 40 11 31 – AE GB EZ a
closed Sunday in July-August and Saturday lunch – **Meals** 160/265 and a la carte 280/390.

La Laiterie, 138 av. Hippodrome at Lambersart NW : 2 km 59130 Lambersart 03 20 92 79 73, Fax 03 20 22 16 19, , – P. AE GB AV s
closed mid-August-early September, February Holidays, Sunday dinner and Monday – **Meals** 155/370 b.i. and a la carte 290/410.

Baan Thaï, 22 bd J.-B. Lebas 03 20 86 06 01, Fax 03 20 86 03 23 – AE GB. EZ s
closed 20 July-18 August, Saturday lunch and Sunday – **Meals** - Thai rest. - 220.

Clément Marot, 16 r. Pas 59800 03 20 57 01 10, Fax 03 20 57 39 69 – AE GB
closed 3 to 25 August, 25 December-5 January, Monday dinner and Sunday – **Meals** 138/218. EY n

Le Champlain, 13 r. N. Leblanc 03 20 54 01 38, Fax 03 20 40 07 28, – AE GB. EZ u
closed 4 to 24 August, Saturday lunch and Sunday dinner – **Meals** 145 b.i. (lunch), 165/360 b.i.

Le Cardinal, 84 façade Esplanade 59800 03 20 06 58 58, Fax 03 20 51 42 59 – AE GB BV x
closed 11 to 17 August and Sunday – **Meals** 270 b.i..

Le Varbet, 2 r. Pas 59800 03 20 54 81 40, Fax 03 20 57 55 18 – AE GB
closed 12 July-18 August, Christmas-New Year, Sunday, Monday and Bank Holidays – **Meals** 165/400. EY t

Le Bistrot Tourangeau, 61 bd Louis XIV 59800 03 20 52 74 64, Fax 03 20 85 06 39 – AE GB JCB CV t
closed Sunday – **Meals** (booking essential) 149.

Le Queen, l'Écume des Mers, 10 r. Pas 59800 03 20 54 95 40, Fax 03 20 54 96 66 – . AE GB EY n
closed 27 July-19 August, and dinner Sunday and Bank Holidays – **Meals** a la carte 180/270 .

Lutterbach, 10 r. Faidherbe 59800 03 20 55 13 74 – AE GB EY u
closed 28 July-12 August and dinner Friday and Sunday – **Meals** 137 .

La Coquille, 60 r. St-Étienne 59800 03 20 54 29 82, Fax 03 20 54 29 82, 17C house – AE GB EY e
closed 1 to 19 August, February Holidays, Saturday lunch and Sunday – **Meals** 128 (lunch), 156/225 .

Charlot II, 26 bd J.-B. Lebas 03 20 52 53 38 – AE GB EZ m
closed Saturday lunch and Sunday – **Meals** - Seafood - 110/160.

Le Hochepot, 6 r. Nouveau Siècle 03 20 54 17 59, Fax 03 20 57 91 68, – GB
closed Saturday lunch and Sunday – **Meals** 99/140. EY a

at Marcq-en-Baroeul - *pop. 36 601 alt. 15 - ✉ 59700 :*

Sofitel M, av. Marne, by N 350 : 5 km ☎ 03 20 72 17 30, Fax 03 20 89 92 34 - |≡| ⇔ r
▤ TV ☎ ♿ P - 🎓 200. AE ⓓ GB JCB
L'Europe : Meals 95 ♨ - ☕ 85 - **125 rm** 640/820.

Septentrion, parc du Château Vert Bois, by N 17 : 9 km ☎ 03 20 46 26 9
Fax 03 20 46 38 33, ☂, « In a park with a lake » - P. AE ⓓ GB
closed 3 to 25 August, February Holidays, Thursday dinner, Sunday dinner and Monda
- **Meals** 150/290 and a la carte 220/310.

L'Épicurien, 18 av. Flandre by N 350 : 4 km ☎ 03 20 45 82 15, Fax 03 20 72 21 45,
- P. AE GB
closed Sunday dinner - **Meals** 135/290 and a la carte 170/280.

at Lille-Lesquin Airport *by A 1 : 8 km - ✉ 59810 Lesquin :*

Mercure Lille Aéroport M ⛷, ☎ 03 20 87 46 46, Fax 03 20 87 46 47 - |≡| ⇔ r
▤ TV ☎ ♿ P - 🎓 25 - 800. AE ⓓ GB JCB
Grill La Flamme : Meals a la carte approx. 160 - ***Le Poêlon*** *(closed dinner and weekend*
Meals a la carte approx. 140 - ☕ 56 - **212 rm** 490/520.

Novotel Lille Aéroport, ☎ 03 20 62 53 53, Fax 03 20 97 36 12, ☂, ⛱, ⛲ - ⇔ r
▤ rest TV ☎ P - 🎓 25 - 200. AE ⓓ GB
Meals a la carte approx. 180 - ☕ 51 - **92 rm** 470/490.

Agena without rest, ✉ 59155 Faches-Thumesnil ☎ 03 20 60 13 14, Fax 03 20 97 31 7
- TV ☎ ♿ P. AE GB JCB
☕ 50 - **40 rm** 350/380.

at Englos *by A 25 : 10 km (exit Lomme) - alt. 46 - ✉ 59320 :*

Novotel Lille Englos M, ☎ 03 20 10 58 58, Fax 03 20 10 58 59, ☂, ⛱, ⛲ - ⇔ r
TV ☎ ♿ P - 🎓 60. AE ⓓ GB
Meals a la carte approx. 170 ♨ - ☕ 51 - **124 rm** 415/440.

at Verlinghem *by D 257 : 8 km - pop. 2 182 alt. 27 - ✉ 59237 :*

Château Blanc, 20 rte Lambersart ☎ 03 20 21 81 41, Fax 03 20 21 81 40, ☂, pa
- P. AE GB
closed 11 to 24 August, Saturday lunch, Sunday dinner, Monday and dinner Bank Holida
- **Meals** 250/300 and a la carte 280/450
Spec. Foie gras de canard en terrine. Blanc de turbot rôti, pommes acidulées, palets
légumes. Caneton de Challans rôti aux cinq épices, caramel d'orange et glace de vianc

If you would like a more complete selection of hotels and restaurants, consult the MICHELIN Red Guides for the following countries :

Benelux, Deutschland, España Portugal, France, Great Britain and Ireland, Italia, Suisse

all in annual editions.

LYONS *69000 Rhône* 74 ⑪ ⑫ - *pop. 415 487 alt. 175.*

*See : Site★★★ (panorama★★ from Fourvière) - Fourvière hill : Notre-Dame Basilica E Museum of Gallo-Roman Civilization★★ (Claudian tablet★★★) EY **M**³, Roman ruins EY - C Lyons★★ : Rue St-Jean★ FX, St-Jean Cathedral★ FY, Hôtel de Gadagne★ (Lyons Histori Museum★ and International Marionette Museum★) EX **M**¹ - Guignol de Lyon FX **N** - Cent Lyons (Peninsula) : to the North, Place Bellecour FY, Hospital Museum (pharmacy★) FY Museum of Printing and Banking★★ FX **M**⁶, - Place des Terreaux FX, Hôtel de Ville FX, Pal St-Pierre, Fine Arts Museum (Beaux-Arts)★★ FX **M**⁴ - to the South, St-Martin-d'Ain Basilica (capitals★) FY, Weaving and Textile Museum★★★ FY **M**², Decorative A Museum★★ FY **M**⁵ - La Croix-Rousse : Silkweavers' House FV **M**¹¹, Trois Gaules Amp theatre FV **E** - Tête d'Or Park★ GHV - Guimet Museum of Natural History★★ GV M Historical Information Centre on the Resistance and the Deportation★ FZ **M**⁹.*

Envir. : Rochetaillée : Henri Malartre Car Museum★★, 12 km to the North.

18 Verger-Lyon at St-Symphorien-d'Ozon ☎ 04 78 02 84 20, S : 14 km ; 9 18 Lyon-Chass at Chassieu ☎ 04 78 90 84 77, E : 12 km by D 29 ; 18 Salvagny (private) at the Tour Salvagny ☎ 04 78 48 83 60 ; junction Lyon-Ouest : 8 km ; 18 18 Golf Club of Lyon at Villet d'Anthon ☎ 04 78 31 11 33.

✈ of Lyon-Satolas ☎ 04 72 22 72 21 to the E : 27 km.

🚗 ☎ 08 36 35 35 35.

ℹ Tourist Office pl. Bellecour ☎ 04 72 77 69 69, Fax 04 78 42 04 32 - A.C. du Rhône Grolée ☎ 04 78 42 51 01, Fax 04 78 37 73 74.

Paris 462 - Geneva 151 - Grenoble 105 - Marseilles 313 - St-Étienne 60 - Turin 3C

STREET INDEX TO LYON TOWN PLAN

llotière
Grande R. de la) . . . . . . GYZ
rès (Av. J.) . . . . GY
Part Dieu . . . . HXY
publique (R. de la) . . . . . FXY 73
me (Rue) . . . . FV 94
tor-Hugo (Rue) . . . . FY 99
on (Cours) . . . . HV

nonciade (R. de l') . . . . . FV 4
tiquaille (R. de l') . . . . . . EY 5
oigny (R. d') . . . . HX
ret (R. Croix) . . . . GZ
sses-Vercheres (R. des) . EY 6
chevelin (R.) . . . . GY
fort (R. de) . . . . FV
ges (Bd des) . . . . GHV
lecour (Place) . . . . FY
liet (R. M.) . . . . HZ
nard (Quai Cl.) . . . . FY
t (R. P.) . . . . GHY
thelot (Av.) . . . . GHZ
ch (R. M.) . . . . GZ
naparte (Pont) . . . . FY 7
nnel (R. de) . . . . GX
ny (R.) . . . . EV
ucle (Montée de la) . . . . FU
tteaux (Bd des) . . . . . . HVX
geaud (R.) . . . . HX
deau (Rue) . . . . FV 9
nuts (Bd des) . . . . FUV
mélites
Montée des) . . . . FV 12
not (Pl.) . . . . FY
arlemagne (Cours) . . . . . EZ
armettes (R. des) . . . . . HVX
artreux (Pl. des) . . . . EV
artreux (R. des) . . . . EV
azière (Rue) . . . . EV
evreul (Rue) . . . . GYZ
oulans (Chin de) . . . . EY
urchill (Pt W.) . . . . GV 18
ndé (R. de) . . . . FY
urmont (Quai J.) . . . . FX 19
pet (Rue) . . . . FZ
qui (R. de) . . . . GVY
ix-Rousse (Bd de) . . . . . EFV
ix-Rousse
Grande R. de la) . . . . . . FV 21
brousse (Av.) . . . . EY

Deleuvre (R.) . . . . EUV
Dr-Gailleton (Quai) . . . . FY
Duguesclin (Rue) . . . . GVY
Duquesne (Rue) . . . . GV
Epargne (R. de l') . . . . HZ 25
Etroits (Quai des) . . . . EY
Europe (Av. de l') . . . . HZ
Farge (Bd Y.) . . . . FZ
Farges (R. des) . . . . EY 28
Faure (Av. F.) . . . . GHY
Favre (Bd J.) . . . . HX 30
Ferry (Pl. J.) . . . . HX 31
Flandin (R. M.) . . . . HXY
France (Bd A.) . . . . HV 34
Frères Lumière (Av. des) . . HZ
Fulchiron (Quai) . . . . EY
Gallieni (Pont) . . . . FY 37
Gambetta (Cours) . . . . GHY
Garibaldi (Rue) . . . . GVZ
Garillan (Montée de) . . . . . EFX
Gaulle (Q. Ch. de) . . . . GHU
Gerland (R. de) . . . . GZ
Gerlier (R. Cardinal) . . . . . . EY 39
Gillet (Quai J.) . . . . EUV
Giraud (Cours Gén.) . . . . . . EV
Grande-Bretagne
(Av. de) . . . . GV
Grenette (Rue) . . . . FX 40
Guillotière (Pt de la) . . . . . . FY 41
Hénon (Rue) . . . . EFV
Herbouville (Cours d') . . . . . FV 42
Joffre (Quai Mar.) . . . . EY 46
Juin (Pt Alphonse) . . . . FX 48
Jutard (Pl. A.) . . . . GY
Koening (Pt Gén.) . . . . EV 49
La Fayette (Cours) . . . . GHX
La Fayette (Pont) . . . . GX 51
Lassagne (Quai A.) . . . . FV 54
Lassalle (R. Ph. de) . . . . . . EUV
Leclerc (Av.) . . . . EFZ
Leclerc (Pl. Gén.) . . . . GV
Liberté (Cours de la) . . . . . GXY
Lortet (Rue) . . . . FZ
Lyautey (Pl. Mar.) . . . . GVX
Marchand (Pt Kitchener) . . EY 55
Marius Vivier Merle (Bd) . . HY 57
Marseille (R. de) . . . . GY
Montrochet (R. P.) . . . . EZ 59
Morand (Pont) . . . . FVX 60
Moulin (Quai J.) . . . . FX 61

Nadaud (R. G.) . . . . FZ
Peissel (R. F.) . . . . FU 64
Perrache (Quai) . . . . EZ
Pompidou (Av. G.) . . . . . . HY
Pradel (Pl. L.) . . . . FX 67
Pré Gaudry (Rue) . . . . FZ 69
Prés. Herriot (R. du) . . . . . FX 70
Radisson (R. R.) . . . . EY
Rambaud (Quai) . . . . EYZ
Repos (R. du) . . . . GZ 71
Rolland (Quai R.) . . . . FX 76
Roosevelt (Cours F.) . . . . GVX
St-Antoine (Quai) . . . . FX 82
St-Barthélemy
(Montée) . . . . EX 84
St-Jean (Rue) . . . . FX
St-Vincent (Quai) . . . . EFX
Sarrail (Quai Gén.) . . . . . . GX 85
Saxe (Av. Mar. de) . . . . . . GXY
Scize (Quai P.) . . . . EX
Sedallian (Quai P.) . . . . . . EU
Serbie (Quai de) . . . . GV
Servient (R.) . . . . GY
Stalingrad (Bd de) . . . . . . GHU
Stalingrad (Pl. de) . . . . . . GHY
Suchet (Cours) . . . . EFZ
Sully (Rue) . . . . GV
Tassigny
(Pt de Lattre de) . . . . . . FV 93
Tchécoslovaques
(Bd des) . . . . HZ
Terreaux (Pl. des) . . . . FX
Tête d'Or (Rue) . . . . GVX
Thiers (Av.) . . . . HVX
Tilsitt (Quai) . . . . FY
Trion (Pl. de) . . . . EY
Trion (R. de) . . . . EY
Université (Pont de l') . . . FY 96
Université (R. de l') . . . . . GY 97
Vauban (Rue) . . . . GHX
Verguin (Av.) . . . . HV
Viabert (R. de la) . . . . HX
Vienne (Rte de) . . . . GZ
Villette (R. de la) . . . . HY 100
Villon (Rue) . . . . HZ
Vitton (Cours) . . . . HV
Vivier (R. du) . . . . GZ 102
Wilson (Pont) . . . . FY 103
1re Div. Fr. Libre
(Av.) . . . . EY 104

Hotels

wn Centre (Bellecour-Terreaux) :

Sofitel M, 20 quai Gailleton ✉ 69002 ✆ 04 72 41 20 20, Fax 04 72 40 05 50, ← – |♦| ⇆ rm ▤ TV ☎ ♿ – 🏛 200. AE ⓓ GB JCB FY p
Les Trois Dômes (8th floor) ✆ 04 72 41 20 97 *(closed August)* **Meals** 180/330 – ***Sofi Shop*** (ground floor) ✆ *04 72 41 20 80* **Meals** 98(lunch)/130 🍷 – ☕ 90 – **138 rm** 980/1050, 29 suites.

Gd Hôtel Concorde, 11 r. Grolée ✉ 69002 ✆ 04 72 40 45 45, Fax 04 78 37 52 55 – |♦| ⇆ rm ▤ TV ☎ – 🏛 80. AE ⓓ GB JCB. ✂ rest FX y
Le Fiorelle : ✆ 04 78 42 99 84 *(closed 3 to 18 August, Saturday lunch and Sunday lunch)* **Meals** 98/168 – ☕ 69 – **143 rm** 650/980.

Royal, 20 pl. Bellecour ✉ 69002 ✆ 04 78 37 57 31, Fax 04 78 37 01 36 – |♦| ⇆ rm ▤ rm TV ☎. AE ⓓ GB JCB FY g
Meals *(closed 2 to 24 August and Saturday)* 98/148 🍷 – ☕ 69 – **80 rm** 630/950.

Carlton without rest, 4 r. Jussieu ✉ 69002 ✆ 04 78 42 56 51, Fax 04 78 42 10 71 – |♦| ▤ TV ☎. AE ⓓ GB JCB – ☕ 58 – **83 rm** 430/750. FX b

Plaza République M without rest, 5 r. Stella ✉ 69002 ✆ 04 78 37 50 50, Fax 04 78 42 33 34 – |♦| ⇆ rm ▤ TV ☎ ♿ – 🏛 35. AE ⓓ GB JCB FY k
☕ 60 – **78 rm** 500/820.

Gd H. des Beaux-Arts without rest, 75 r. Prés. E. Herriot ✉ 69002 ✆ 04 78 38 09 50, Fax 04 78 42 19 19 – |♦| ⇆ rm ▤ TV ☎ – 🏛 25. AE ⓓ GB JCB FX t
☕ 58 – **75 rm** 430/625.

Globe et Cécil without rest, 21 r. Gasparin ✉ 69002 ✆ 04 78 42 58 95, Fax 04 72 41 99 06 – |♦| TV ☎. AE ⓓ GB JCB FY b
☕ 50 – **65 rm** 399/550.

La Résidence without rest, 18 r. V. Hugo ✉ 69002 ✆ 04 78 42 63 28, Fax 04 78 42 85 76 – |♦| TV ☎. AE ⓓ GB FY s
☕ 35 – **64 rm** 300/330.

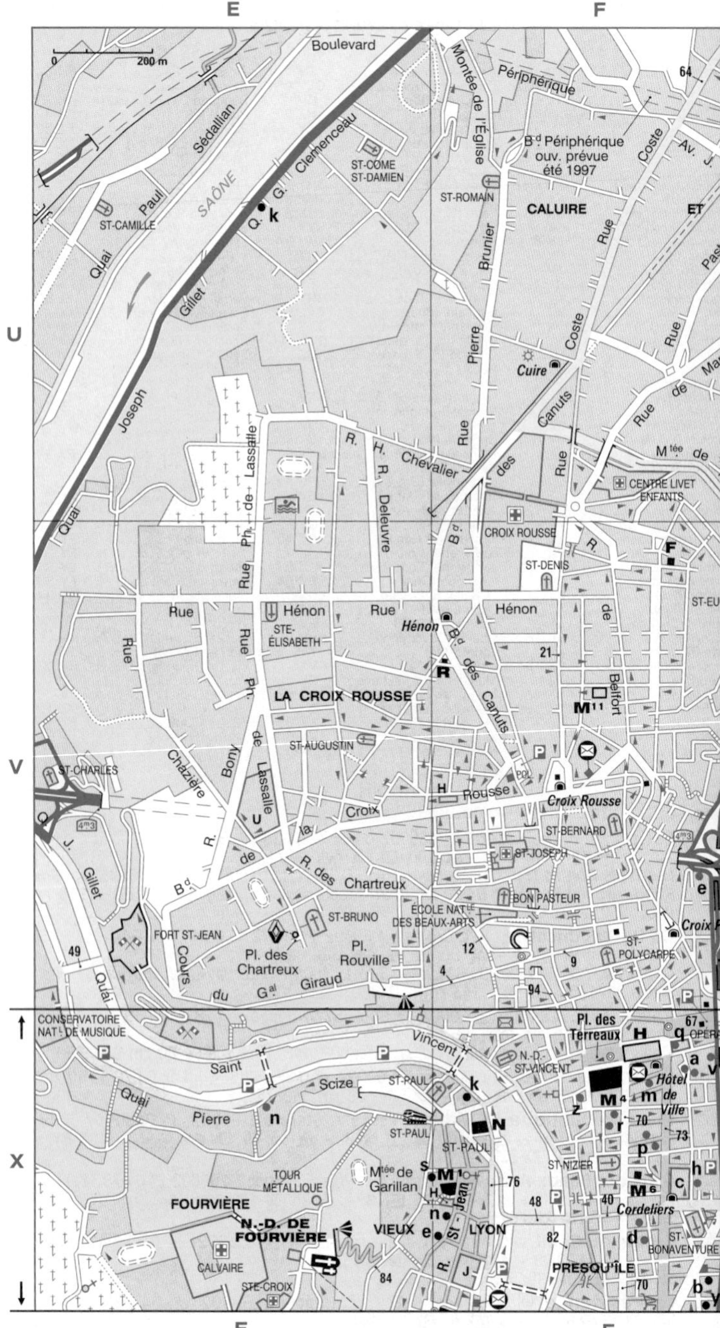
E
F
U
V
X
0
200 m
Boulevard
Périphérique
Montée de l'Église
Bd Périphérique ouv. prévue été 1997
Coste
Av. J.
64
Sédallian
Clemenceau
ST-COME ST-DAMIEN
SAÔNE
Paul
Quai
ST-CAMILLE
Q. G.
k
ST-ROMAIN
CALUIRE
ET
Rue
Brunier
Pierre
Gillet
Joseph
Coste
Rue
Cuire
Canuts
de
Rue
Quai
R. H. Chevalier
R. Deleuvre
Rue
des
Rue
Mtée de
CENTRE LIVET ENFANTS
Rue Ph. de Lassalle
Bd
CROIX ROUSSE
ST-DENIS
R.
F
ST-EU
Rue
Hénon
Rue
Hénon
Hénon
STE-ÉLISABETH
Bd des Canuts
21
de
Belfort
R
LA CROIX ROUSSE
M11
Rue
Rue Ph.
ST-AUGUSTIN
ST-CHARLES
Chazière
Bony
de Lassalle
P
H
Rousse
POL
Croix Rousse
Croix
la
ST-BERNARD
U
R.
de
ST-JOSEPH
Q. J. Gillet
4m3
Bd
R. des Chartreux
BON PASTEUR
ST-BRUNO
ÉCOLE NATLE DES BEAUX-ARTS
Croix P
FORT ST-JEAN
Pl. des Chartreux
Pl. Rouville
12
9
ST-POLYCARPE
49
Quai
Cours
du Gal Giraud
4
94
CONSERVATOIRE NATL DE MUSIQUE
Pl. des Terreaux
H
q
67
OPÉRA
Vincent
N.-D.-ST-VINCENT
a
Saint
Scize
ST-PAUL
k
Hôtel de Ville
Quai
Pierre
n
M4
m
z
N
70
r
73
ST-PAUL
ST-PAUL
ST-NIZIER
p
TOUR MÉTALLIQUE
Mtée de Garillan
s
M1
76
h
M6
c
FOURVIÈRE
H
48
40
Cordeliers
N.-D. DE FOURVIÈRE
n
St-Jean
VIEUX
e
LYON
d
82
ST-BONAVENTURE
CALVAIRE
R.
J
PRESQU'ÎLE
84
STE-CROIX
70
b

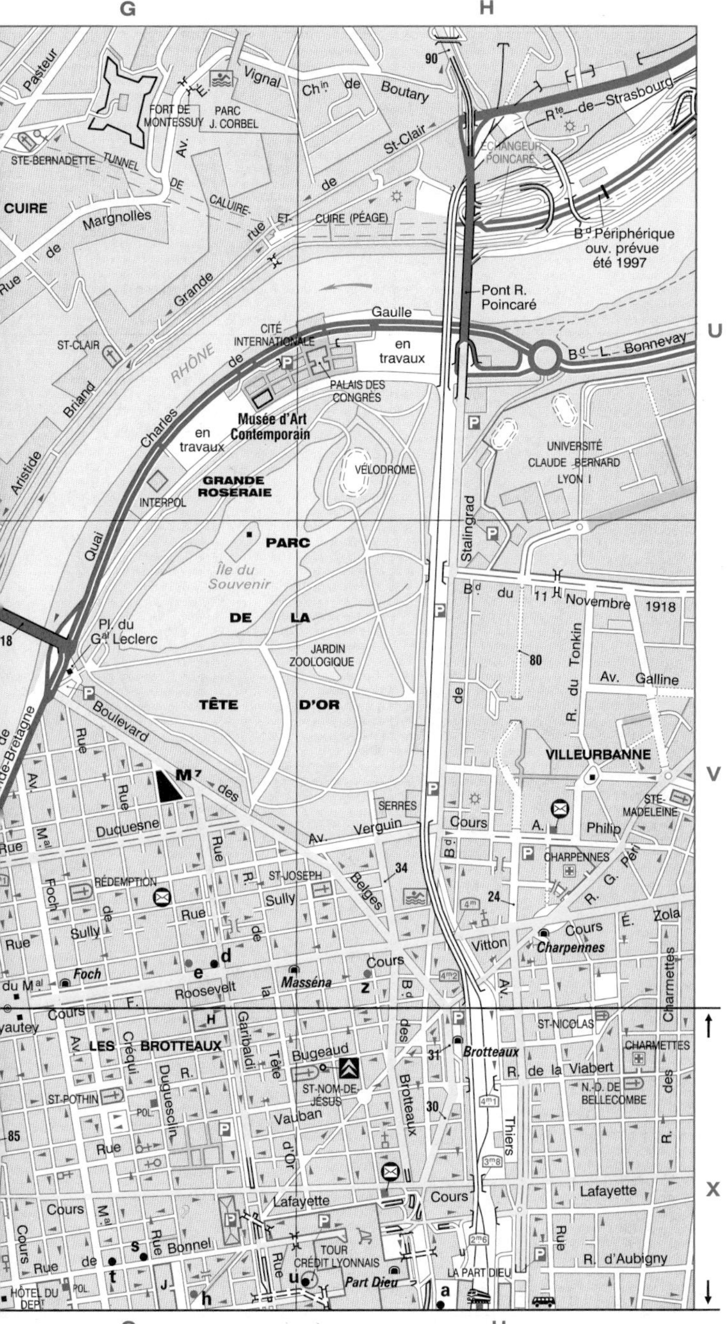
G
H
FORT DE MONTESSUY
PARC J. CORBEL
Vignal
Chin de Boutary
Rte de Strasbourg
ÉCHANGEUR POINCARÉ
STE-BERNADETTE
TUNNEL DE CALUIRE-ET-CUIRE (PÉAGE)
CUIRE
Rue de Margnolles
Grande rue de St-Clair
Bd Périphérique ouv. prévue été 1997
Pont R. Poincaré
RHÔNE
ST-CLAIR
CITÉ INTERNATIONALE
Gaulle
en travaux
Bd L. Bonnevay
U
PALAIS DES CONGRÈS
Musée d'Art Contemporain
Quai Charles de Gaulle
Aristide Briand
VÉLODROME
UNIVERSITÉ CLAUDE BERNARD LYON I
GRANDE ROSERAIE
INTERPOL
PARC DE LA TÊTE D'OR
Île du Souvenir
Stalingrad
Bd du 11 Novembre 1918
Pl. du Gal Leclerc
JARDIN ZOOLOGIQUE
R. du Tonkin
Av. Galline
Boulevard des Belges
VILLEURBANNE
V
SERRES
Cours A. Philip
STE-MADELEINE
Rue Duquesne
Av. Verguin
CHARPENNES
R. G. Péri
RÉDEMPTION
ST-JOSEPH
Rue de Sully
Cours É. Zola
Cours Vitton
Charpennes
Foch
Masséna
Cours Roosevelt
Cours F.
LES BROTTEAUX
Bugeaud
ST-NOM-DE-JÉSUS
Brotteaux
R. de la Viabert
ST-NICOLAS
CHARMETTES
N.-D. DE BELLECOMBE
ST-POTHIN
Duguesclin
Vauban
Garibaldi
Tête d'Or
Bd des Brotteaux
Thiers
R. des Charmettes
Cours Lafayette
X
Rue Bonnel
TOUR CRÉDIT LYONNAIS
Part Dieu
LA PART DIEU
R. d'Aubigny
HÔTEL DU DEPT
G
H

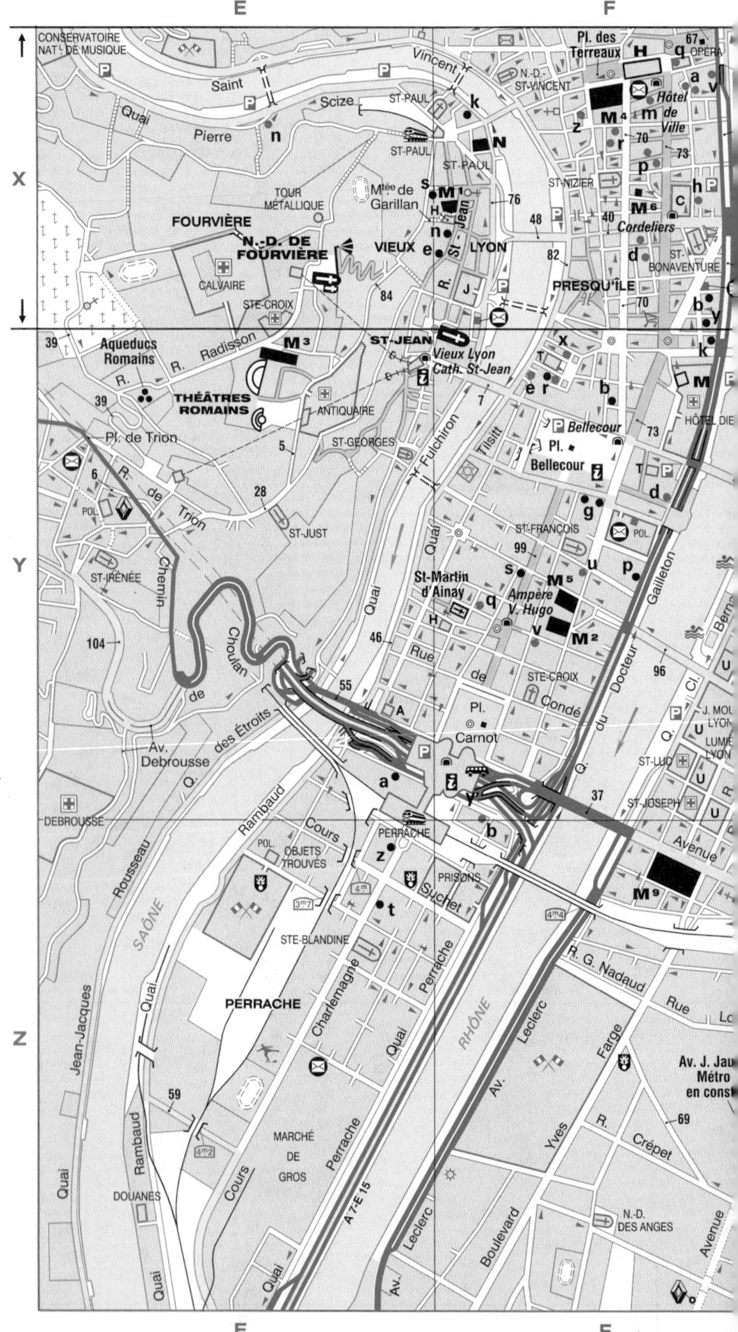
E
F
X
Y
Z
CONSERVATOIRE NAT^L DE MUSIQUE
Quai
Saint
Pierre
Scize
Vincent
ST-PAUL
N.-D.-ST-VINCENT
Pl. des Terreaux
OPÉRA
Hôtel de Ville
ST-NIZIER
Cordeliers
ST-BONAVENTURE
PRESQU'ÎLE
TOUR MÉTALLIQUE
M^tée de Garillan
FOURVIÈRE
N.-D. DE FOURVIÈRE
VIEUX
LYON
R. St-Jean
CALVAIRE
STE-CROIX
Aqueducs Romains
R. Radisson
THÉÂTRES ROMAINS
ST-JEAN
Vieux Lyon Cath. St-Jean
ANTIQUAIRE
ST-GEORGES
Pl. de Trion
R. de Trion
ST-JUST
Fulchiron
Tilsitt
Bellecour
Pl. Bellecour
ST-FRANÇOIS
POL.
ST-IRÉNÉE
Chemin de Choulan
St-Martin d'Ainay
Ampère V. Hugo
Gailleton
Rue de Condé
STE-CROIX
Q. du Docteur
Pl. Carnot
Av. Debrousse
Q. des Étroits
DEBROUSSE
Rambaud
Cours
PERRACHE
POL. OBJETS TROUVÉS
PRISONS
Suchet
STE-BLANDINE
SAÔNE
Rousseau
Quai Jean-Jacques
Charlemagne
Quai Perrache
RHÔNE
Av. Leclerc
R. G. Nadaud
Rue
Farge
Yves
R. Crépet
Boulevard
Av. J. Jaurès Métro en const.
MARCHÉ DE GROS
A7-E 15
Quai Rambaud
DOUANES
N.-D. DES ANGES
Avenue
ST-LUC
ST-JOSEPH
J. MOULIN LYON
LUMIÈRE LYON
HÔTEL DIEU
Avenue
Berne
Q. Cl.

G H

Cours
yautey
Av.
LES BROTTEAUX
Créqui
Garibaldi
Tête
Bugeaud
des
Brotteaux
31
ST-NICOLAS
CHARMETTES
R. de la Viabert
R.
ST-NOM-DE-JÉSUS
N.-D. DE BELLECOMBE
des
ST-POTHIN
POL.
Duguesclin
Vauban
30
Thiers
R.
85
Rue
d'Or
Lafayette
Cours
Lafayette
X
Cours
Mal
Rue
Bonnel
Rue
TOUR CRÉDIT LYONNAIS
Part Dieu
LA PART DIEU
R. d'Aubigny
Cours
Rue de
s
t
u
a
HÔTEL DU DÉPT
POL.
h
de
IMMACULÉE CONCEPTION
Servient
CITÉ ADMVE D'ÉTAT
POL.
M.
R.
n
R.
100
Pompidou
G.
Av.
la
Pl. Guichard
PART DIEU
de
de
57
ST-SACREMENT
Bert
Paul
Flandin
Av. Lacassagne
A.
ard
Liberté
Rue
Duguesclin
Garibaldi
Y
Cours
illotière
Saxe
Créqui
ST-JACQUES
Av. F. Faure
Secteur en travaux
Grande
Saxe Gambetta
Faure
57
ST-ANDRÉ
Félix
Garibaldi
Av.
Jaurès
Gambetta
Rue
ST-LOUIS
de
PRISON MONTLUC
e
97
Jean
la
Pl. de Stalingrad
M
u
LA GUILLOTIÈRE
STE-MARIE
Cours
U
J. MOULIN LYON III
Sans Souci
R.
A.
Thomas
L'ANNONCIATION
Guillotière
M.
Av.
Chevreul
Bloch
Garibaldi
Tchécoslovaques
Av. des Frères Lumière
Villon
Pl. J. Macé
J. Macé
71
Berthelot
Rue
Route
des
Rue
Rue
25
POL.
Z
Bd
25
Avenue
Av. de l'Europe
M.
102
de
Berliet
Gerland
CIMETIÈRE ISRAÉLITE
Villon
Berthelot
Bd des États-Unis
Vienne
Barret
Croix
Rue
Rue
ST-VINCENT DE PAUL

G H

Perrache :

Château Perrache, 12 cours Verdun ✉ 69002 ☎ 04 72 77 15 0
Fax 04 78 37 06 56, « Art Nouveau decor » – rm – 250.
GB EY
Les Belles Saisons : **Meals** 137/177 – 69 – **123 rm** 505/865.

Charlemagne M, 23 cours Charlemagne ✉ 69002 ☎ 04 72 77 70 0
Fax 04 78 42 94 84, – rm – 120. AE GB. rest
Meals 130 b.i./180 – 52 – **116 rm** 395/435. EZ

Berlioz M without rest, 12 cours Charlemagne ✉ 69002 ☎ 04 78 42 30 3
Fax 04 72 40 97 58 – . AE GB JCB EZ
40 – **38 rm** 233/396.

at Vaise :

Saphir M, 18 r. L. Loucheur ✉ 69009 ☎ 04 78 83 48 75, Fax 04 78 83 30 81 –
– 50. AE GB
Meals 60 (lunch), 95/165 – 50 – **110 rm** 450/470.

Vieux-Lyon :

Villa Florentine M, 25 montée St-Barthélémy ✉ 69005 ☎ 04 72 56 56 5
Fax 04 72 40 90 56, ≤ Lyon, , – . AE GB JCB
Les Terrasses de Lyon : **Meals** 170 (lunch), 290/400 and a la carte 420/580 –
– **16 rm** 1300/1900, 3 suites EFX
Spec. Rouget en filets grillés, envolée de cannelloni aux poivrons. Couronne d'agneau lait des Pyrénées cloutée aux anchois de Collioure. Cristalline de laitue, gelée de faise aux noix de pécan. **Wines** Condrieu, Côte-Rôtie.

Cour des Loges M, 6 r. Bœuf ✉ 69005 ☎ 04 72 77 44 44, Fax 04 72 40 93 6
« Contemporary decor in houses of Old Lyons » – rm –
AE GB JCB FX
Les Loges : **Meals** à la carte 190/350 – 110 – **53 rm** 1150/1800, 10 suites.

Tour Rose (Chavent) M, 22 r. Bœuf ✉ 69005 ☎ 04 78 37 25 9
Fax 04 78 42 26 02, « 17C house, tasteful silk themed decor », –
AE GB JCB EFX
Meals *(closed Sunday)* 295/595 and a la carte 420/600 – 95 – **8 rm** 950/1650, 6 suit
Spec. Saumon mi-cuit au fumoir. Crème d'artichaut au foie de canard et à la truffe. Cro tillant d'agneau aux abricots secs, jus au citron confit et à la coriandre. **Wines** Vin du Bug

Phénix H. M without rest, 7 quai Bondy ✉ 69005 ☎ 04 78 28 24 2
Fax 04 78 28 62 86 – – 35. AE GB JCB FX
60 – **36 rm** 620/1080.

La Croix-Rousse (bank of the River Saône) :

Lyon Métropole M, 85 quai J. Gillet ✉ 69004 ☎ 04 72 10 44 44, Fax 04 78 39 99 2
, , – – 350. AE GB EU
Les Eaux Vives ☎ 04 72 10 44 30 *(closed Sunday dinner and Monday)* **Meals** 180/4
– ***Grill*** ☎ 04 72 10 44 30 **Meals** 130 b.i./160 b.i. – 80 – **119 rm** 620/850.

Les Brotteaux :

Olympique without rest, 62 r. Garibaldi ✉ 69006 ☎ 04 78 89 48 0
Fax 04 78 89 49 97 – rm . AE GB GV
35 – **23 rm** 255/290.

La Part-Dieu :

Holiday Inn Crowne Plaza M, 29 r. Bonnel ✉ 69003 ☎ 04 72 61 90 9
Fax 04 72 61 17 54, – rm – 300. AE GB JCB
Meals 105/200 – 80 – **156 rm** 915/1600. GX

Méridien M, 129 r. Servient (32nd floor) ✉ 69003 ☎ 04 78 63 55 0
Fax 04 78 63 55 20, ≤ Lyons and Rhône Valley – rm – 170.
GB JCB. rest GX
L'Arc-en-Ciel *(closed 15 July-24 August)* **Meals** 195/295 – ***Le Bistrot de la Tour*** (grou floor) *(closed Sunday, dinner Friday and Saturday)* **Meals** 110 – 70 – **245 rm** 630/7

Mercure La Part-Dieu M, 47 bd Vivier-Merle ✉ 69003 ☎ 04 72 13 51 5
Fax 04 72 13 51 99 – rm – 80. AE GB JCB HX
closed Sunday dinner and Saturday from 12 July-24 August – **Meals** 109/200 –
– **124 rm** 595.

de Créqui M, 158 r. Créqui ✉ 69003 ☎ 04 78 60 20 47, Fax 04 78 62 21 12,
rm . AE GB. rest GX
Meals *(closed August, Saturday and Sunday)* 98 – 42 – **28 rm** 360/390.

a Guillotière :

Libertel Wilson without rest, 6 r. Mazenod ✉ 69003 ☎ 04 78 60 94 94, Fax 04 78 62 72 01 – rm . AE GB JCB
60 – **54 rm** 435/550.

Ibis Université without rest, 51 r. Université ✉ 69007 ☎ 04 78 72 78 42, Fax 04 78 69 24 36 – rm . AE GB GY u
36 – **53 rm** 345.

Gerland :

Mercure Gerland, 70 av. Leclerc ✉ 69007 ☎ 04 72 71 11 11, Fax 04 72 71 11 00, – rm – 200. AE GB JCB
Meals 85/100 – 58 – **194 rm** 525/750.

Montchat-Monplaisir :

Relais Mercure Park H., 4 r. Prof. Calmette ✉ 69008 ☎ 04 78 74 11 20, Fax 04 78 01 43 38, – rm . AE GB
Meals *(closed 8 to 25 August and 24 December-2 January)* 105/150 – 48 – **72 rm** 390/435.

at Bron – *pop. 39 683 alt. 204 – ✉ 69500 :*

Novotel Bron, av. J. Monnet ☎ 04 78 26 97 48, Fax 04 78 26 45 12, – rm – 25 - 800. AE GB
Meals 125/150 – 52 – **189 rm** 510.

Restaurants

XXXXX ✿✿✿ **Paul Bocuse**, bridge of Collonges N : 12 km by the banks of River Saône (D 433, D 51 ✉ 69660 Collonges-au-Mont-d'Or ☎ 04 72 42 90 90, Fax 04 72 27 85 87, « Fresco representing great chefs » – . AE GB JCB
Meals 410 (lunch), 510/740 and a la carte 490/630
Spec. Soupe aux truffes. Rouget barbet en écailles de pommes de terre. Volaille de Bresse en vessie. **Wines** Saint-Véran, Brouilly.

XXXX ✿✿ **Léon de Lyon** (Lacombe), 1 r. Pleney ✉ 69001 ☎ 04 78 28 11 33, Fax 04 78 39 89 05 – . AE GB JCB FX r
closed 10 to 18 August and Sunday – **Meals** 290 (lunch), 490/650 and a la carte 430/590
Spec. Cochon de lait, foie gras et oignons confits en terrine. Brochet de la Dombes en quenelle et meunière, étuvée de grenouilles et champignons. Six desserts sur le thème de la praline. **Wines** Saint-Véran, Chiroubles.

XXXX ✿ **Orsi**, 3 pl. Kléber ✉ 69006 ☎ 04 78 89 57 68, Fax 04 72 44 93 34, « Elegant decor » – . AE GB JCB GV e
closed Sunday except lunch in winter – **Meals** 240 (lunch), 320/550 and a la carte 400/600
Spec. Ravioles de foie gras au jus de porto et truffes. Homard et rouget en barigoule d'artichaut. Pigeonneau rôti aux gousses d'ail confites. **Wines** Mâcon-Clessé, Saint-Amour.

XXX **Christian Têtedoie**, 54 quai Pierre Scize ✉ 69005 ☎ 04 78 29 40 10, Fax 04 72 07 05 65 – . AE GB EX n
closed 1 to 25 August, Saturday lunch and Sunday – **Meals** 160/280 and a la carte 240/330.

XXX ✿ **Mère Brazier**, 12 r. Royale ✉ 69001 ☎ 04 78 28 15 49, Fax 04 78 28 63 63, « Lyonnaise atmosphere » – AE GB FV e
closed 1 August-1 September, Saturday except dinner from August-mid-June and Sunday – **Meals** 170 (lunch), 290/370 and a la carte 200/360
Spec. Fond d'artichaut au foie gras. Quenelle au gratin. Volaille de Bresse demi-deuil. **Wines** Chiroubles, Côtes du Rhône.

XXX **Le Saint Alban**, 2 quai J. Moulin ✉ 69001 ☎ 04 78 30 14 89, Fax 04 72 00 88 82 – . AE GB FX v
closed 20 July- 20 August, February Holidays, Saturday lunch, Sunday and Bank Holidays – **Meals** 150/300 and a la carte 230/350.

XX **Le Passage**, 8 r. Plâtre ✉ 69001 ☎ 04 78 28 11 16, Fax 04 72 00 84 34 – . AE GB JCB FX r
closed Saturday lunch, Sunday and Bank Holidays – **Meals** 95 (lunch), 120/185.

XX ✿ **Aub. de l'Ile** (Ansanay-Alex), sur l'Ile Barbe ✉ 69009 ☎ 04 78 83 99 49, Fax 04 78 47 80 46 – . AE GB.
closed 5 to 26 January, Sunday dinner and Monday – **Meals** 180/365 and a la carte 320/470
Spec. Foie gras de canard en croque au sel. Bar en écailles de cèpes (October-January). Glace réglisse, lait d'amande et pain d'épice. **Wines** Morgon, Condrieu.

XX **Gourmet de Sèze**, 129 r. Sèze ✉ 69006 ☎ 04 78 24 23 42, Fax 04 78 24 66 81 – . AE GB HV z
closed 1 to 11 May, 26 July-20 August, Saturday lunch and Sunday – **Meals** (booking essential) 130 (lunch), 170/300 b.i..

XX **Fleur de Sel,** 7 r. A. Perrin ✉ 69002 ☎ 04 78 37 40 37, Fax 04 78 37 26 37 GB FY
closed 20 July-18 August, Saturday and Sunday – **Meals** 128 (lunch), 220/280.

XX **Thierry Gache,** 37 r. Thibaudière ✉ 69007 ☎ 04 78 72 81 77, Fax 04 78 72 01 75 ▤. AE GB GY
closed Sunday – **Meals** 99 b.i. (lunch)/398.

XX **L'Alexandrin,** 83 r. Moncey ✉ 69003 ☎ 04 72 61 15 69, Fax 04 78 62 75 57 – ▤. GB GX
closed 1 to 12 May, 3 to 25 August, 21 December-5 January, Sunday and Monday – **Mea** 160/210.

XX **Le Nord,** 18 r. Neuve ✉ 69002 ☎ 04 72 10 69 69, Fax 04 72 10 69 68, – ▤. GB JCB FX
Meals brasserie 120 b.i./158.

XX **La Tassée,** 20 r. Charité ✉ 69002 ☎ 04 78 37 02 35, Fax 04 72 40 05 91 – ▤. AE GB JCB FY
closed Sunday – **Meals** 110 (lunch), 130/260 ♁.

XX **Brasserie Georges,** 30 cours Verdun ✉ 69002 ☎ 04 72 56 54 5 Fax 04 78 42 51 65, brasserie 1925 – AE ⓓ GB JCB FZ
Meals 87/170 ♁.

XX **Tante Alice,** 22 r. Remparts d'Ainay ✉ 69002 ☎ 04 78 37 49 83, Fax 04 78 37 49 – ▤. AE GB FY
closed August, Friday dinner and Saturday – **Meals** 75 (lunch), 94/194 ♁.

XX **Chez Jean-François,** 2 pl. Célestins ✉ 69002 ☎ 04 78 42 08 26, Fax 04 72 40 04 – ▤. AE GB JCB FY
closed 19 July-19 August, Sunday and Bank Holidays – **Meals** (booking essential) 9 160 ♁.

XX **La Voûte - Chez Léa,** 11 pl. A. Gourju ✉ 69002 ☎ 04 78 42 01 33, Fax 04 78 37 36 – ▤. AE ⓓ GB FY
closed Sunday – **Meals** 125/169.

X **Assiette et Marée,** 49 r. Bourse ✉ 69002 ☎ 04 78 37 36 58, Fax 04 78 37 98 – ▤. AE GB FX
closed Sunday – **Meals** - Seafood - 100 (lunch)and a la carte 150/220.

X **Assiette et Marée,** 26 r. Servient ✉ 69002 ☎ 04 78 62 89 94, Fax 04 78 60 39 – ▤. AE GB GY
closed Saturday lunch and Sunday – **Meals** - Seafood - a la carte 150/220.

X **Francotte,** 8 pl. Célestins ✉ 69002 ☎ 04 78 37 38 64, Fax 04 78 38 20 35 – ▤. GB FY
closed Sunday – **Meals** 84/140.

X **Le Sud,** 11 pl. Antonin Poncet ✉ 69002 ☎ 04 72 77 80 00, Fax 04 72 77 80 01, – ▤. AE GB FY
Meals (booking essential) 120 b.i./158.

X **Les Muses de l'Opéra,** pl. Comédie, 7th floor of the Opera ✉ 690 ☎ 04 72 00 45 58, Fax 04 78 29 34 01, ≤ Fourvière, , « Contemporary decor » – AE GB FX
closed Sunday – **Meals** 119 (lunch)/149.

BOUCHONS : *Regional specialities and wine tasting in a Lyonnaise atmosphere*

X **Le Garet,** 7 r. Garet ✉ 69001 ☎ 04 78 28 16 94, Fax 04 72 00 06 84 – ▤. AE G
closed 15 July-15 August, Saturday, Sunday and Bank Holidays – **Meals** (booking essenti 88 (lunch)/115 ♁. FX

X **La Meunière,** 11 r. Neuve ✉ 69001 ☎ 04 78 28 62 91 – AE ⓓ GB FX
closed 14 July-15 August, Sunday and Monday – **Meals** (booking essential) 95 (lunc 120/145.

X **Café des Fédérations,** 8 r. Major Martin ✉ 69001 ☎ 04 78 28 26 00 – ▤. GB FX
closed August, Saturday and Sunday – **Meals** (booking essential) 116 (lunch)/150.

X **Le Jura,** 25 r. Tupin ✉ 69002 ☎ 04 78 42 20 57 – GB FX
closed August, Saturday from May-October, Monday lunch from November-April and Su day – **Meals** (booking essential) 98 ♁.

X **Au Petit Bouchon "chez Georges",** 8 r. Garet ✉ 69001 ☎ 04 78 28 30 46 – G
closed 2 to 24 August, 22 February-2 March, Saturday and Sunday – **Meals** 84/115 dinn a la carte approx 180. FX

X **Chez Hugon,** 12 rue Pizay ✉ 69001 ☎ 04 78 28 10 94 – GB FX
closed August, Saturday and Sunday – **Meals** (booking essential) 120 (lunch), 125/145

Environs

to the NE :

Rillieux-la-Pape : *7 km by N 83 and N 84 – pop. 30 791 alt. 269 – ✉ 69140 :*

XXX ✿ **Larivoire** (Constantin), chemin des Iles ✆ 04 78 88 50 92, Fax 04 78 88 35 22, ☂ – P. GB
closed 18 to 22 August, Monday lunch and Tuesday – **Meals** 160 (lunch), 200/400 and a la carte 320/400
Spec. Papillotes d'escargots et quenelle de volaille au gaspacho de tomate. Viennoise de féra à la crème de pois frais et jeunes carottes (June-October). Volaille de Bresse au vinaigre de vieux vin. **Wines** Mondeuse du Bugey, Mâcon.

to the E :

the Satolas airport : *27 km by A 43 – ✉ 69125 Lyon Satolas Airport :*

Sofitel Lyon Aéroport M without rest, 3rd floor ✆ 04 72 23 38 00, Fax 04 72 23 98 00, ← – |♦| ⇔ rm ▤ TV ☎ ♿. AE ⓓ GB JCB
☕ 85 – **120 rm** 790.

XXX **La Grande Corbeille,** 1st floor ✆ 04 72 22 71 76, Fax 04 72 22 71 72, ← – ▤. AE ⓓ GB
closed August, Saturday and Sunday – **Meals** 150/250.

X **Le Bouchon,** 1st floor ✆ 04 72 22 71 86, Fax 04 72 22 71 72 – ▤. AE ⓓ GB
Meals brasserie 120 b.i./180 b.i.

to the NW :

Porte de Lyon *- motorway junction A 6 N 6 Exit road signposted Limonest N : 10 km – ✉ 69570 Dardilly :*

Novotel Lyon Nord M, ✆ 04 72 17 29 29, Fax 04 78 35 08 45, ☂, ⛱, 🌳 – |♦| ⇔ rm ▤ TV ☎ P – 🏛 80. AE ⓓ GB
Meals a la carte approx. 170 🍷 – ☕ 52 – **107 rm** 440/480.

Relais Mercure Lyon Nord M, ✆ 04 78 35 28 05, Fax 04 78 47 47 15, ☂, ⛱, 🎾 – |♦| ⇔ rm ▤ rest TV ☎ P – 🏛 30 - 80. AE ⓓ GB JCB
Meals 90/150 – ☕ 48 – **172 rm** 330/440.

Ibis Lyon Nord, ✆ 04 78 66 02 20, Fax 04 78 47 47 93, ☂, ⛱, 🌳 – ⇔ rm TV ☎ ♿ P – 🏛 30. AE ⓓ GB
Meals 82/130 🍷 – ☕ 36 – **64 rm** 320/375.

Annecy *74000 H.-Savoie 74 ⑥ – pop. 49 644 alt. 448.*

See : *Old Annecy★★ : Descent from the Cross★ in church of St-Maurice, Palais de l'Isle★, rue Ste-Claire★, bridge over the Thiou ←★ – Château★ – Jardins de l'Europe★ – Crêt du Maure forest★ : ←★★ 3 km on the D 41.*

Envir. : *Tour of the lake★★★ 39 km (or 1 hour 30 min by boat).*

18 of the lac d'Annecy ✆ 04 50 60 12 89 : 10 km ; 9 18 of Giez ✆ 04 50 44 48 41.

✈ of Annecy-Haute Savoie : T.A.T. ✆ 04 50 27 30 30 by N 508 andD 14 : 4 km.

ℹ Tourist Office Clos Bonlieu 1 r. J. Jaurès ✆ 04 50 45 00 33, Fax 04 50 51 87 20 – A.C. 15 r. Préfecture ✆ 04 50 45 09 12, Fax 04 50 23 61 31.

Veyrier-du-Lac *E : 5,5 km – pop. 1 967 alt. 504 – ✉ 74290*

XXXX ✿✿✿ **Aub. de l'Éridan** (Veyrat) M ⛰ with rm, 13 Vieille rte des Pensières ✆ 04 50 60 24 00, Fax 04 50 60 23 63, ← lake, ☂, 🌳 – |♦| ▤ TV ☎ ♿ 🚗 P. AE ⓓ GB JCB
Meals *(closed Monday)* 385 (lunch), 595/995 and a la carte 680/900 – ☕ 195 – **11 rm** 1500/4850
Spec. Ravioles aux plantes des Alpes. Omble chevalier aux coquelicots. Coquelet en pot-au-feu de génépi. **Wines** Chignin, Mondeuse.

Chagny *71150 S.-et-L. 69 ⑨ – pop. 5 346 alt. 215.*

ℹ Tourist Office 2 r. des Halles ✆ 03 85 87 25 95, Fax 03 85 87 24 19.

Lyons 145.

✿✿✿ **Lameloise** M, pl. d'Armes ✆ 03 85 87 08 85, Fax 03 85 87 03 57, « Old Burgundian house, tasteful decor » – |♦| ▤ TV ☎ 🚗. AE GB JCB
closed 17 December-22 January, Wednesday except 1 July-30 September and Thursday lunch – **Meals** (booking essential) 370/600 and a la carte 420/580 – ☕ 90 – **17 rm** 750/1500
Spec. Ravioli d'escargots de Bourgogne dans leur bouillon d'ail doux. Pigeonneau rôti à l'émietté de truffes. Griottines au chocolat noir. **Wines** Rully, Chassagne-Montrachet.

Fleurie *69820 Rhône 74 ① – pop. 1 105 alt. 320.*
Lyons 59.

XXX **Aub. du Cep,** pl. Église ☎ 04 74 04 10 77, Fax 04 74 04 10 28 – ▤. AE GB
✿✿ *closed 27 July-7 August, 15 December-15 January, Sunday dinner and Monday* – **Me**
(booking essential) 200/400 and a la carte 300/460
Spec. Cuisses de grenouilles rôties. Queues d'écrevisses en petit ragoût. Volaille mijot
au vin de Fleurie. **Wines** Beaujolais blanc, Fleurie.

Mionnay *01390 Ain 74 ② – pop. 1 103 alt. 276.*
Lyons 23.

XXXX **Alain Chapel** with rm, ☎ 04 78 91 82 02, Fax 04 78 91 82 37, « Flower
✿✿ garden » – TV ☎ P. AE GB
closed January, Tuesday lunch and Monday except Bank Holidays – **Meals** 330 (lunc
600/800 and a la carte 510/660 – 87 – **13 rm** 600/800
Spec. Moelleux de pommes de terre et langoustines. Lapin de quatre heures (Ap
September). Poulette en vessie (July-September). **Wines** Mâcon-Clessé.

Montrond-les-Bains *42210 Loire 73 ⑱ – pop. 3 627 alt. 356 – Spa Spa (March-Novemb*
– Casino. – 18 Forez ☎ 04 77 30 86 85 at Craintilleux, S : 12 km by N 82 and D 16.
Syndicat d'Initiative 1 r. des Ecoles ☎ 04 77 94 64 74, Fax 04 77 54 51 96.
Lyons 62.

Host. La Poularde (Etéocle), ☎ 04 77 54 40 06, Fax 04 77 54 53 14 – ▤ TV ☎
✿✿ – 30. AE GB JCB
closed 2 to 16 January, Tuesday lunch and Monday except Bank Holidays – **Meals** (Sunda
booking essential) 220/580 and a la carte 450/700 – 80 – **11 rm** 340/560, 3 dup
Spec. Ecrevisses et huîtres sautées, fleurette ambrée au corail d'oursins. Pigeonneau
Forez en vessie. Surprise aztèque au chocolat. **Wines** Condrieu, Saint-Joseph.

Roanne *42300 Loire 73 ⑦ – pop. 41 756 alt. 265.*
9 of Champlong at Villerest ☎ 04 77 69 70 60.
Roanne-Renaison ☎ 04 77 66 83 55 by D 9.
Tourist Office cours République ☎ 04 77 71 51 77, Fax 04 77 70 96 62 – A.C. 24 r. Rabe
☎ 04 77 71 31 67.
Lyons 87.

Troisgros M, pl. Gare ☎ 04 77 71 66 97, Fax 04 77 70 39 77, « Tasteful contempor
✿✿✿ decor », – ▤ TV ☎. AE GB JCB
closed 29 July-13 August, February Holidays, Tuesday dinner and Wednesday – **Me**
(booking essential) 300 (lunch), 600/730 and a la carte 530/850 – 110 – **16 r**
700/1400, 3 suites
Spec. Cassolette de queues d'écrevisses à la nage (July-December). Lièvre à la royale (Oc
ber). Jarret de veau confit. **Wines** Bourgogne blanc, Saint-Joseph.

St-Bonnet-le-Froid *43290 H.-Loire 76 ⑨ – pop. 180 alt. 1 126.*
Lyons 101.

XXX **Aub. des Cimes** (Marcon) M with rm, ☎ 04 71 59 93 72, Fax 04 71 59 93 40,
✿✿ rm ▤ rest TV ☎ P. AE GB
Easter-15 November and closed Sunday dinner and Monday except in July-August – **Me**
150/550 and a la carte 300/450 – 80 – **18 rm** 380/750
Spec. Ragoût de lentilles vertes du Puy. Omble chevalier à l'oseille sauvage, purée aux cèp
Menu champignons (spring-autumn). **Wines** Crozes-Hermitage blanc et rouge.

Valence *26000 Drôme 77 ⑫ – pop. 63 437 alt. 126.*
See : *House of the Heads (Maison des Têtes)★ – Interior★ of the cathedral – Champ*
Mars ★ – Red chalk sketches by Hubert Robert★★ in the museum.
9 of Chanalets ☎ 04 75 55 16 23 ; 18 of St-Didier ☎ 04 75 59 67 01, E : 14 km by D 11
18 of Bourget ☎ 04 75 59 41 71 at Montmeyran.
of Valence-Chabeuil ☎ 04 75 85 26 26.
Tourist Office Parvis de la Gare ☎ 04 75 44 90 44, Fax 04 75 44 90 41 – A.C. 33
av. F. Faure ☎ 04 75 43 61 07, Fax 04 75 55 62 04.
Lyons 101.

XXXX **Pic** with rm, 285 av. V. Hugo, Motorway exit signposted Valence-Sud ☎ 04 75 44 15 3
✿✿ Fax 04 75 40 96 03, « Shaded garden », – ▤ rest ☎ P. AE GB JC
rm
closed 4 to 27 August – **Meals** *(closed Sunday dinner)* (Sunday : booking essential) 2
(lunch), 560/660 and a la carte 530/830 – 100 – **14 rm** 750/1200
Spec. Fricassée d'asperges vertes aux écrevisses, beurre d'oranges sanguines (Febua
July). Filet de loup au caviar. Millefeuille de cerf aux chataignes (October-Febuary). **Win**
Condrieu, Hermitage.

t Pont-de-l'Isère *to the N by N 7 : 9 km – alt. 120 – ✉ 26600 :*

XXXX **Michel Chabran** with rm, N 7 ☎ 04 75 84 60 09, Fax 04 75 84 59 65, – AE GB
✿✿ **Meals** 215 b.i. (lunch), 290/795 and a la carte 440/680 – ☐ 80 – **12 rm** 400/690
Spec. Millefeuille de foie gras de canard aux artichauts et courgettes. Filets de rougets poêlés, purée de pommes de terre à l'huile d'olive. Dos d'agneau de Rémuzat cuit à l'os aux gousses d'ail. **Wines** Crozes-Hermitage, Saint-Joseph.

ienne *38200 Isère 74 ⑪ ⑫ – pop. 29 449 alt. 160.*

See : Site★ – St-Maurice cathedral★★ – Temple of Augustus and Livia★★ – Roman Theatre★ – Church★ and cloisters★ of St-André-le-Bas – Mont Pipet Esplanade ≤★ – Old church of St-Pierre★ : lapidary museum★ – Sculpture group★ in the church of Ste-Colombe.

Tourist Office 3 cours Brillier ☎ 04 74 85 12 62, Fax 04 74 31 75 98.

Lyons 31.

La Pyramide (Henriroux), 14 bd F. Point ☎ 04 74 53 01 96, Fax 04 74 85 69 73, – rm – 25. AE GB
✿✿ **Meals** *(closed Thursday lunch and Wednesday from 15 September-15 June)* 275 b.i. (lunch), 430/630 and a la carte 480/660 – ☐ 105 – **20 rm** 650/970, 4 suites
Spec. Foie gras poêlé et foie gras poché, magret fumé et magret poêlé en marbré. Homard à la cornouaillaise. Piano au chocolat en "ut" praliné. **Wines** Condrieu, Côtes-du-Rhône.

onnas *01540 Ain 74 ② – pop. 2 381 alt. 200.*

Lyons 63.

Georges Blanc ☎ 04 74 50 90 90, Fax 04 74 50 08 80, « Elegant inn on the banks of the Veyle, flowered garden », – – 80. AE GB
✿✿✿ *closed 2 January-9 February* – **Meals** *(closed Tuesday except dinner from 15 June-15 September and Monday except Bank Holidays)* (booking essential) 470/850 and a la carte 480/700 – ☐ 105 – **32 rm** 900/1800, 6 suites
Spec. Crêpe parmentière au saumon et caviar. Poularde de Bresse aux gousses d'aïl et foie gras. "Panouille" bressane glacée à la confiture de lait. **Wines** Mâcon-Azé, Chiroubles.

IARSEILLES *13000 B.-du-R. 84 ⑬ – pop. 800 550.*

See : N.-D.-de-la-Garde Basilica ✱★★★ – Old Port★★ – Palais Longchamp★ GS : Fine Arts Museum★, Natural History Museum★ – St-Victor Basilica★ : crypt★★ DU – Old Major Cathedral★ DS **N** *– Pharo Park ≤★ DU – Hôtel du département et Dôme-Nouvel Alcazar★ – Vieille Charité★★ (Mediterranean archaeology) DS* **R** *– Museums : Grobet-Labadié★★ GS* **M⁷**, *Cantini★ FU* **M⁵**, *Vieux Marseille★ DT* **M²**, *History of Marseilles★ ET* **M¹** *– Fish market (quai des Belges ET 5).*

Envir. : Corniche road★★ of Callelongue S : 13 km along the sea front.

Exc. : – Château d'If★★ (✱★★★) 1 h 30.

18 of Marseilles-Aix ☎ 04 42 24 20 41 to the N : 22 km ; 18 of Allauch-Fonvieille (private) ☎ 04 91 07 28 22 ; junction Marseilles-East : 15 km, by D 2 and D 4 A ; 9 18 Country Club of la Salette ☎ 04 91 27 12 16 by A 50.

Marseilles-Provence : ☎ 04 42 78 21 00 to the N : 28 km.

☎ 08 36 35 35 35.

Tourist Office 4 Canebière, 13001 ☎ 04 91 13 89 00, Fax 04 91 13 89 20 and St-Charles railway station ☎ 04 91 50 59 18 – A.C. of Provence 149 bd Rabatau, 13010 ☎ 04 91 78 83 00.

Paris 772 – Lyons 312 – Nice 188 – Turin 407 – Toulon 64 – Toulouse 401.

Plans on following pages

Sofitel Vieux Port, 36 bd Ch. Livon ✉ 13007 ☎ 04 91 15 59 00, Fax 04 91 15 59 50, ≤, « Panoramic restaurant ≤ old port », – rm – 130. AE GB DU n
Les Trois Forts : **Meals** 210 – ☐ 75 – **127 rm** 680/990, 3 suites.

Le Petit Nice (Passédat), anse de Maldormé (turn off when level with no 160 Corniche Kennedy) ✉ 13007 ☎ 04 91 59 25 92, Fax 04 91 59 28 08, « Villas overlooking the sea, elegant decor, ≤ », – AE GB
✿✿ **Meals** *(closed Saturday lunch and Sunday from November-March)* 310 b.i. (lunch), 590/750 and a la carte 480/720 – ☐ 115 – **13 rm** 1200/2200
Spec. Beignets d'anémones de mer et tempura (summer). Loup "Lucie Passédat". Escalope de foie de canard des landes poêlée aux figues (season). **Wines** Palette, Bandol.

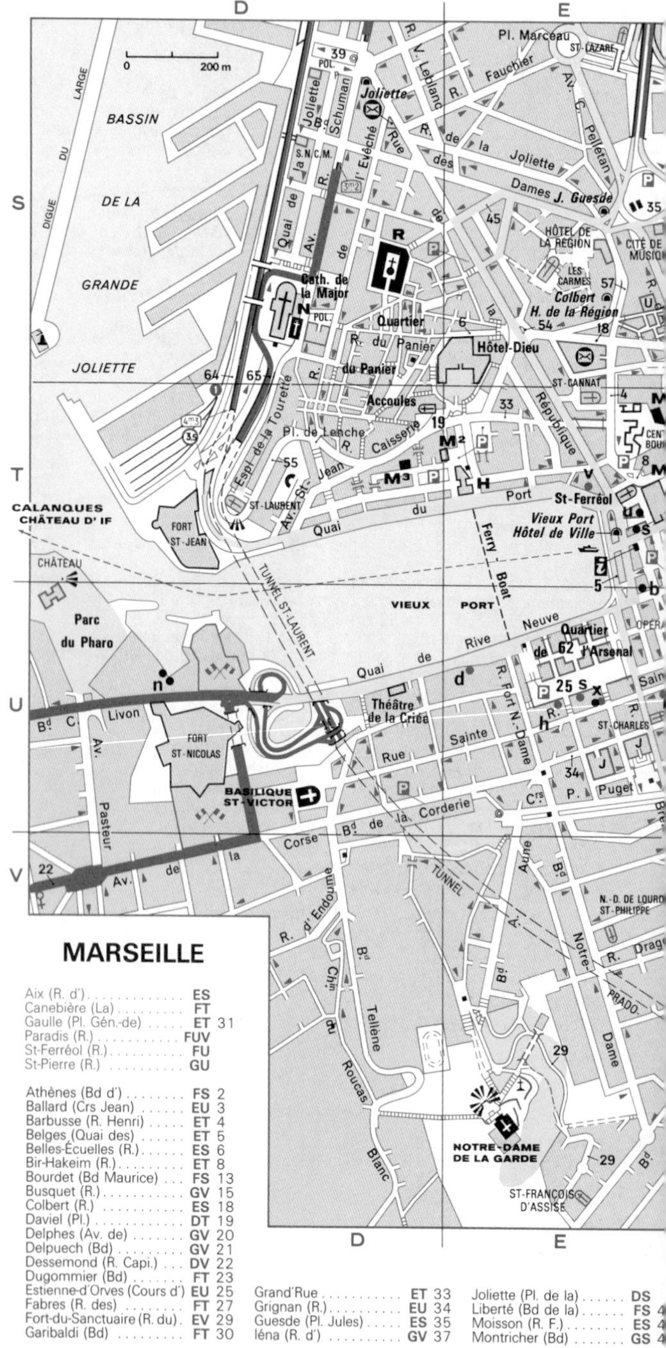

MARSEILLE

Aix (R. d') . . . . **ES**
Canebière (La) . . . . **FT**
Gaulle (Pl. Gén.-de) . . . . . **ET** 31
Paradis (R.) . . . . **FUV**
St-Ferréol (R.) . . . . **FU**
St-Pierre (R.) . . . . **GU**

Athènes (Bd d') . . . . **FS** 2
Ballard (Crs Jean) . . . . . . **EU** 3
Barbusse (R. Henri) . . . . . **ET** 4
Belges (Quai des) . . . . . . **ET** 5
Belles-Écuelles (R.) . . . . . . **ES** 6
Bir-Hakeim (R.) . . . . **ET** 8
Bourdet (Bd Maurice) . . . **FS** 13
Busquet (R.) . . . . **GV** 15
Colbert (R.) . . . . **ES** 18
Daviel (Pl.) . . . . **DT** 19
Delphes (Av. de) . . . . **GV** 20
Delpuech (Bd) . . . . **GV** 21
Dessemond (R. Capi.) . . . **DV** 22
Dugommier (Bd) . . . . **FT** 23
Estienne-d'Orves (Cours d') **EU** 25
Fabres (R. des) . . . . **FT** 27
Fort-du-Sanctuaire (R. du) . **EV** 29
Garibaldi (Bd) . . . . **FT** 30

Grand'Rue . . . . **ET** 33
Grignan (R.) . . . . **EU** 34
Guesde (Pl. Jules) . . . . . . **ES** 35
Iéna (R. d') . . . . **GV** 37

Joliette (Pl. de la) . . . . . . **DS**
Liberté (Bd de la) . . . . . . **FS** 4
Moisson (R. F.) . . . . **ES** 4
Montricher (Bd) . . . . **GS** 4

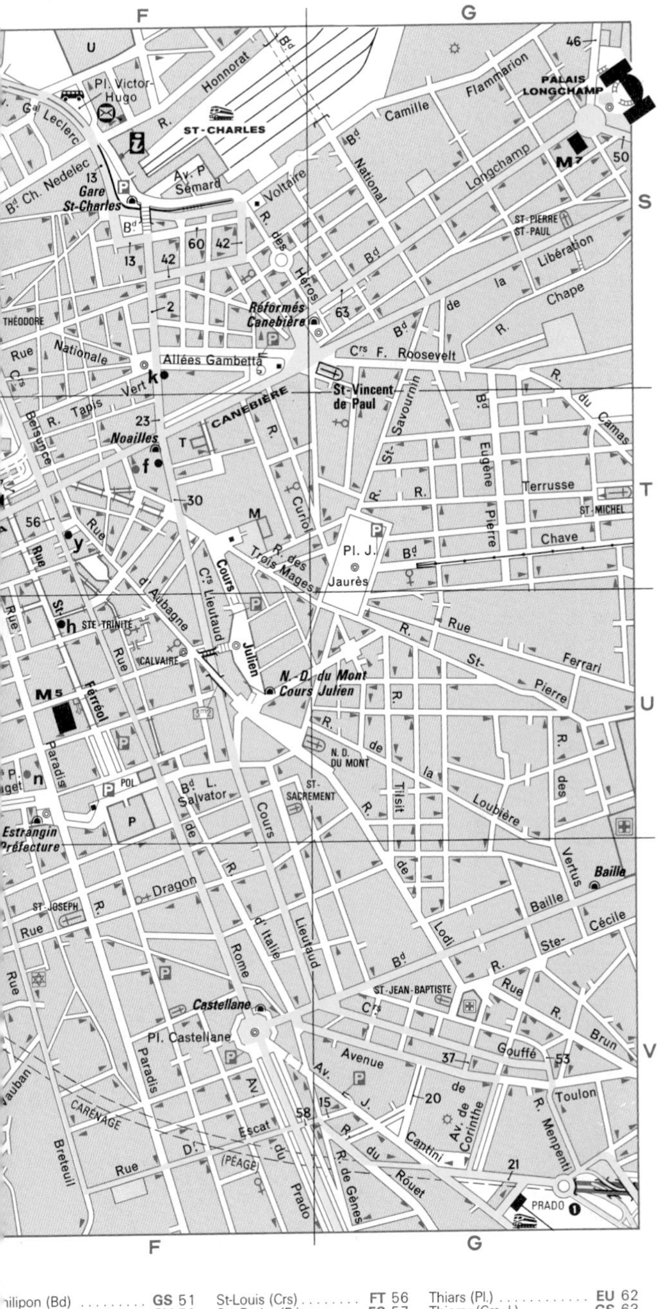

hilipon (Bd) . . . . GS 51
aynouard (Traverse) . . . GV 53
adi-Carnot (Pl.) . . . . ES 54
-Laurent (R.) . . . . DT 55
St-Louis (Crs) . . . . FT 56
Ste-Barbe (R.) . . . . ES 57
Ste-Philomène (R.) . . . . FV 58
Sembat (R. Marcel) . . . FS 60
Thiars (Pl.) . . . . EU 62
Thierry (Crs J.) . . . . GS 63
Tourette (Quai) . . . . DS 64
Vaudoyer (Av.) . . . . DS 65

Holiday Inn M, 103 av. Prado ✉ 13008 ℘ 04 91 83 10 10, Fax 04 91 79 84 12 – rm – 170. AE GB
Meals *(closed Saturday and Sunday)* 130 – 55 – **119 rm** 510, 4 suites.

Mercure Euro-Centre M, r. Neuve St-Martin ✉ 13001 ℘ 04 91 39 20 0 Fax 04 91 56 24 57, ←, – rm – 200. AE JCB EST
Oursinade : ℘ 04 91 39 20 14 *(closed 14 July-2 September, 22 December-2 Janua Saturday lunch, Sunday and Bank Holidays)* **Meals** 150/230 – ***Oliveraie*** grill **Meals** (lun only) 95/110 – 63 – **199 rm** 525/600.

Novotel Vieux Port M, 36 bd Ch. Livon ✉ 13007 ℘ 04 91 59 22 2 Fax 04 91 31 15 48, ←, – rm – 200. AE GB
Meals 128/160 b.i. – 55 – **93 rm** 510/590. DU

New H. Bompard without rest, 2 r. Flots Bleus ✉ 13007 ℘ 04 91 52 10 Fax 04 91 31 02 14, – kitchenette – 25. AE JCB
50 – **46 rm** 400/440.

St-Ferréol's M without rest, 19 r. Pisançon ✉ 13001 ℘ 04 91 33 12 2 Fax 04 91 54 29 97 – AE GB JCB FU
closed 1 to 15 August – 39 – **19 rm** 300/480.

Mascotte M without rest, 5 La Canebière ✉ 13001 ℘ 04 91 90 61 6 Fax 04 91 90 95 61 – rm – 30. AE GB ET
42 – **45 rm** 450/490.

New H. Vieux Port without rest, 3 bis r. Reine Élisabeth ✉ 13001 ℘ 04 91 90 51 4 Fax 04 91 90 76 24 – – 25. AE GB JCB ET
45 – **48 rm** 370.

New H. Astoria without rest, 10 bd Garibaldi ✉ 13001 ℘ 04 91 33 33 5 Fax 04 91 54 80 75 – AE GB JCB FT
42 – **58 rm** 325.

New H. Sélect without rest, 4 allées Gambetta ✉ 13001 ℘ 04 91 50 65 5 Fax 04 91 50 45 56 – – 25. AE GB JCB FS
42 – **60 rm** 310.

Alizé M without rest, 35 quai Belges ✉ 13001 ℘ 04 91 33 66 97, Fax 04 91 54 80 0 ← – AE GB ETU
35 – **37 rm** 285/365.

Miramar (Minguella), 12 quai Port ✉ 13002 ℘ 04 91 91 10 40, Fax 04 91 56 64 31, – AE GB JCB ET
closed 3 to 24 August, 4 to 18 January and Sunday – **Meals** a la carte 30 420
Spec. Bouillabaisse. Flan d'orties de mer au beurre rouge. Croustillant de Saint-Pierre beurre de miel et crèpe de maïs. **Wines** Cassis, Côtes de Provence.

La Ferme, 23 r. Sainte ✉ 13001 ℘ 04 91 33 21 12, Fax 04 91 33 81 21 – AE GB EU
closed August, Saturday lunch and Sunday – **Meals** 215/350 and a la carte 27 330.

Michel-Brasserie des Catalans, 6 r. Catalans ✉ 13007 ℘ 04 91 52 30 6 Fax 04 91 59 23 05 – AE GB
Meals - Seafood - a la carte 250/450.

Les Échevins, 44 r. Sainte ✉ 13001 ℘ 04 91 33 08 08, Fax 04 91 54 08 21 – GB JCB EU
closed 13 July-17 August, Saturday lunch and Sunday – **Meals** 160/330.

Les Arcenaulx, 25 cours d'Estienne d'Orves ✉ 13001 ℘ 04 91 54 77 0 Fax 04 91 54 76 33, « Bookshop and restaurant in original decor » – AE JCB EU
closed 11 to 17 August and Sunday – **Meals** 135/280.

Les Mets de Provence "Chez Maurice Brun", 18 quai de Rive Neuve (2nd floo ✉ 13007 ℘ 04 91 33 35 38, Fax 04 91 33 05 69 – AE GB EU
closed Monday lunch and Sunday – **Meals** 200 b.i. (lunch)/270.

L'Ambassade des Vignobles, 42 pl. aux Huiles ✉ 13001 ℘ 04 91 33 00 2 Fax 04 91 54 25 60 – AE GB EU
closed August, Saturday lunch and Sunday – **Meals** 200 b.i./300 b.i..

René Alloin, 9 pl. Amiral Muselier (by prom. G. Pompidou) ✉ 13008 ℘ 04 91 77 88 2 Fax 04 91 77 76 84, – GB
closed Sunday dinner from September-July, Sunday lunch in August and Saturday lunc – **Meals** 135 (lunch), 195/270.

.es Baux-de-Provence *13520 B.-du-R. 84 ① – pop. 457 alt. 185.*

See : Site★★★ – Château – Charloun Rieu monument ≤★★ – Place St-Vincent★ – Rue du Trencat★ – Paravelle Tower ≤★ – Yves-Brayer museum★ (in Hôtel des Porcelet) – Shepherds' Festival (Christmas midnight mass) – Cathédrale d'Images★ N : 1 km on the D 27 – ☀★★★ of the village N : 2,5 km on the D 27.

9 ✆ 04 90 54 40 20, S : 2 km.

Tourist Office Ilôt "Post Tenebras Lux" ✆ 04 90 54 34 39, Fax 04 90 54 51 15.

Marseilles 83.

n the Vallon :

XXXXX ✿✿ **Oustaù de Baumanière** (Charial) with rm, ✆ 04 90 54 33 07, Fax 04 90 54 40 46, ≤, « 16C period house tastefully decorated », – TV ☎ P. AE ① GB JCB
closed 15 January-1 March, Thursday lunch and Wednesday from November-March – **Meals** 480/740 – 115 – **7 rm** 1300, 4 suites
Spec. Ravioli de truffes. Filets de rougets au basilic. Gigot d'agneau en croûte. **Wines** Coteaux d'Aix-en-Provence.

Le Manoir without rest, ≤, – TV ☎ P. AE ① GB JCB
closed 15 January-1 March – 115 – **5 rm** 1300, 4 suites2000.

XXX ✿ **La Riboto de Taven** (Novi et Theme) with rm, ✆ 04 90 54 34 23, Fax 04 90 54 38 88, ≤, « Terrace and flowered garden near the rocks » – TV ☎ P. AE ① GB JCB
closed 7 January-15 March, Tuesday dinner out of season and Wednesday – **Meals** 200 (lunch), 300/450 and a la carte 330/470 – 80 – **3 rm** 990
Spec. Gratinée d'escargots "petits gris" de Provence. Tagliatelli de légumes aux langoustines rôties. Tarte au fenouil caramélisé et glace à la vanille. **Wines** Coteaux d'Aix-en-Provence, Châteauneuf-du-Pape.

road of Arles *to the SW by D 78F road :*

La Cabro d'Or , à 1 km ✆ 04 90 54 33 21, Fax 04 90 54 45 98, ≤, « Flowered gardens », – rm TV ☎ P – 60. AE ① GB JCB
closed 11 November-20 December, Tuesday lunch and Monday from November-March – **Meals** 180 (lunch), 270/395 – 75 – **23 rm** 750/1100, 8 suites.

Carry-le-Rouet *13620 B.-du-R. 84 ⑫ – pop. 5 224 alt. 5.*

Tourist Office av. A. Briand ✆ 04 42 13 20 36, Fax 04 42 44 52 03.

Marseilles 27.

XXX ✿✿ **L'Escale** (Clor), prom. du Port ✆ 04 42 45 00 47, Fax 04 42 44 72 69, « Terrace overlooking the harbour, pleasant view », – AE GB
1 February-31 October and closed Sunday dinner from September-June and Monday except dinner in July-August – **Meals** (Sunday : booking essential) 320 and a la carte 420/520
Spec. Terrine de baudroie en gelée d'oignons et basilic. Rougets, étuvée de fenouil à la réglisse. Ragoût de la marée aux lasagnes maison. **Wines** Cassis, Bandol.

MONACO (Principality of) *84 ⑩, 115 ㉗ ㉘ – pop. 29 972 alt. 65 – Casino – 00377.*

Monaco *Capital of the Principality – 98000.*

See : Tropical Garden★★ (Jardin exotique) : ≤★ – Observatory Caves★ (Grotte de l'Observatoire) – St-Martin Gardens★ – Early paintings of the Nice School★★ in Cathedral – Recumbent Christ★ in the Misericord Chapel – Place du Palais★ – Prince's Palace★ – Museums : oceanographic★★ (aquarium★★, ≤★★ from the terrace), Prehistoric Anthropology★, Napoleon and Monaco History★, Royal collection of vintage cars★.

Urban racing circuit – A.C.M. 23 bd Albert-1er ✆ 93 15 26 00, Fax 93 25 80 08.

Paris 956 – Nice 21 – San Remo 44.

Monte-Carlo *Fashionable resort of the Principality – Casinos Grand Casino, Monte-Carlo Sporting Club, Sun Casino.*

See : Terrace★★ of the Grand Casino – Museum of Dolls and Automata★.

18 Monte-Carlo ✆ 04 93 41 09 11 to the S by N 7 : 11 km.

Tourist Office 2A bd Moulins ✆ 92 16 61 66, Fax 92 16 60 00.

Paris, pl. Casino ✆ 92 16 30 00, Fax 92 16 38 50, ≤, health center, – rm TV ☎ – 70. AE ① GB JCB. rest
see ***Le Louis XV*** *and* ***Grill*** *below -* ***Côté Jardin*** ✆ 92 16 68 44 (lunch only) *(closed 11 July-31 August)* **Meals** 290 and a la carte 320/410 – ***Salle Empire*** ✆ *92 16 29 52 (11 July-7 September)* **Meals** a la carte 510/720 – 150 – **160 rm** 2300/3100, 40 suites.

Hermitage, square Beaumarchais ✆ 92 16 40 00, Fax 92 16 38 52, ←, terrace, health centre, « Dining room in baroque style », gym, pool – lift ▤ TV ☎ garage – 80. AE ① GB JCB. rest
Meals 320/430 – ☕ 150 – **215 rm** 1850/2750, 16 suites.

Loews M, 12 av. Spélugues ✆ 93 50 65 00, Fax 93 30 01 57, ←, terrace, Casino and cabaret, gym, pool – lift ▤ TV ☎ ♿ garage – 1 100. AE ① GB JCB. rest
L'Argentin (dinner only) **Meals** 325 – ***Le Pistou :*** (dinner only) *(15 June-30 September)* **Meals** à la carte 240/320 – ***Café de la Mer :*** **Meals** a la carte 210/310 – ☕ 110 – **581 rm** 1450/1850, 38 suites.

Métropole Palace M, 4 av. Madone ✆ 93 15 15 15, Fax 93 25 24 44, « "Belle Epoque" decor », pool – lift ▤ TV ☎ ♿ garage – 220. AE ① GB JCB
Le Jardin : **Meals** 190(lunch), 225/250 – ☕ 110 – **138 rm** 1300/1800, 23 suites.

Beach Plaza M, av. Princesse Grace, à la Plage du Larvotto ✆ 93 30 98 80, Fax 93 50 23 14, ←, terrace, « Attractive resort with pool, beach », gym, pool – lift rm ▤ TV ☎ ♿ garage – 500. AE ① GB. rest
La Pergola -Italian rest. *(closed December, Sunday and Monday)* **Meals** (dinner only) a la carte 300/340 – ***La Terrasse :*** **Meals** 175/220 – ☕ 125 – **295 rm** 1700/3450, 9 suites.

Mirabeau M, 1 av. Princesse Grace ✆ 92 16 65 65, Fax 93 50 84 85, ←, pool – lift rm ▤ TV ☎ garage – 80. AE ① GB JCB. rest
see ***La Coupole*** below - ***Le Café Mirabeau*** at the swimming pool *(May-September)* **Meals** (lunch only) à la carte 260/320 – ☕ 140 – **99 rm** 1400/2400, 4 suites.

Alexandra without rest, 35 bd Princesse Charlotte ✆ 93 50 63 13, Fax 92 16 06 48 – lift ▤ TV ☎. AE ① GB JCB.
☕ 62 – **56 rm** 570/850.

Balmoral, 12 av. Costa ✆ 93 50 62 37, Fax 93 15 08 69, ← – lift ▤ rm TV ☎. AE ① GB JCB.
Meals coffee shop *(closed November, Sunday dinner and Monday)* 130 – ☕ 78 – **67 rm** 600/900, 5 suites.

Le Louis XV - Hôtel de Paris, pl. Casino ✆ 92 16 30 01, Fax 92 16 69 21 – ▤ P. AE ① GB JCB.
closed 1 to 30 December, 17 February-4 March, Wednesday except dinner from 18 June-20 August and Tuesday – **Meals** 780/890 and a la carte 630/870
Spec. Légumes des jardins de Provence mijotés à la truffe noire écrasée. Poitrine de pigeonneau et foie gras de canard sur la braise. "Louis XV" au croustillant de praliné.
Wines Bellet, Côtes de Provence.

Grill de l'Hôtel de Paris, pl. Casino ✆ 92 16 29 66, Fax 92 16 38 40, « Rooftop restaurant with sliding roof and ← the Principality » – lift ▤ P. AE ① GB JCB.
closed 5 January-5 February – **Meals** a la carte 560/770
Spec. Salade de homard à l'emincé de truffes noires. Poissons grillés sur la braise. Soufflés.
Wines Côtes de Provence.

La Coupole - Hôtel Mirabeau, 1 av. Princesse Grace ✆ 92 16 66 99, Fax 93 50 84 85 – ▤ garage. AE ① GB JCB.
closed lunch in July-August – **Meals** 300/450 and a la carte 390/540
Spec. Dos de thon en paysanne de légumes d'été (season). Râble de lapereau au genièvre (autumn). Tarte fine de fraises des bois en gratin de cassonade.

L'Hirondelle (Thermes Marins), 2 av. Monte-Carlo ✆ 92 16 49 47, Fax 92 16 49 49, ← port and the Rock, terrace – lift ▤. AE ① GB JCB.
closed Sunday dinner – **Meals** (booking essential) 270 and a la carte 310/370.

Le Saint Benoit, 10 ter av. Costa ✆ 93 25 02 34, Fax 93 30 52 64, ← port and Monaco, terrace – ▤. AE ① GB JCB
closed 22 December-5 January and Monday except dinner in July and August – **Meals** 164/230 and a la carte 270/390.

Café de Paris, pl. Casino ✆ 92 16 20 20, Fax 92 16 38 58, terrace, « 1900 brasserie decor » – ▤. AE ① GB JCB
Meals 180/450 and a la carte 240/410.

Polpetta, 2 r. Paradis ✆ 93 50 67 84 – ▤. AE GB
closed February, Saturday lunch and Tuesday – **Meals** - Italian rest. - 150.

at Monte-Carlo-Beach *(06 Alpes-Mar.) at 2,5 km* – ✉ *06190 Roquebrune-Cap-Martin :*

Monte-Carlo Beach H. M, av. Princesse Grace ✆ 04 93 28 66 66, Fax 04 93 78 14 18, ← sea and Monaco, terrace, « Extensive swimming complex », pool, beach – lift ▤ rm TV ☎ ♿ P – 40. AE ① GB JCB. rest
4 April-6 October – ***La Salle à Manger*** (dinner only) (residents only) **Meals** a la carte 300/470 – ***La Potinière*** (lunch only) *(5 June-15 September)* **Meals** a la carte 310/440 – ***Le Rivage*** (lunch only) **Meals** a la carte 190/280 – ***La Vigie*** -buffet- *(27 June-1 September)* **Meals** (lunch only) 280 – ☕ 150 – **44 rm** 2350/2550.

ICE *06000 Alpes-Mar.* 84 ⑨ ⑩, 115 ㉖ ㉗ – *pop. 342 439 alt. 6 – Casino Ruhl* FZ.

See : *Site*★★ – *Promenade des Anglais*★★ EFZ – *Old Nice*★ : *Château* ≤★★ JZ, *Interior*★ *of church of St-Martin-St-Augustin* HY **D** – *Balustraded staircase*★ *of the Palais Lascaris* HZ **K**, *Interior*★ *of Ste-Réparate Cathedral* – HZ **L**, *St-Jacques Church*★ HZ **N**, *Decoration*★ *of St-Giaume's Chapel* HZ **R** – *Mosaic*★ *by Chagall in Law Faculty* DZ **U** – *Palais des Arts*★ HJY – *Miséricorde Chapel*★ HZ **S** – *Cimiez : Monastery*★ *(Masterpieces*★★ *of the early Nice School in the church)* HV **Q**, *Roman Ruins*★ HV – *Museums : Marc Chagall*★★ GX, *Matisse*★ HV **M2**, *Fine Arts Museum*★★ DZ **M**, *Masséna*★ FZ **M1** – *Modern and Contemporary Art*★★ HY – *Parc Phoenix*★ – *Carnival*★★★ *(before Shrove Tuesday).*

Envir. : *St-Michel Plateau* ≤★★ *9,5 km.*

✈ *of Nice-Côte d'Azur* ☎ *04 93 21 30 12 : 7 km.*

🚗 ☎ *08 36 35 35 35.*

ℹ *Tourist Office av. Thiers* ☎ *04 93 87 07 07, Fax 04 93 16 85 16 - 5 promenade des Anglais* ☎ *04 93 87 60 60, Fax 04 93 82 07 99, and Nice-Ferber near the Airport, Terminal 1* ☎ *04 93 21 41 11, Fax 04 93 21 44 50 – Automobile-Club, 9 r. Massenet* ☎ *04 93 87 18 17, Fax 04 93 88 90 00.*

Paris 932 – Cannes 32 – Genova 194 – Lyons 472 – Marseilles 188 – Turin 220.

Plans on following pages

Négresco, 37 promenade des Anglais ☎ 04 93 16 64 00, Fax 04 93 88 35 68, ≤, « 17C, 18C, Empire and Napoléon III furnishings » – |♦| ▤ TV ☎ ♿ 🚗 – 🏛 50 - 200. AE ⓓ GB JCB FZ k
see ***Chantecler*** below - ***La Rotonde :*** **Meals** 155, Sunday a la carte – ☕ 120 – **122 rm** 1630/2350, 18 suites.

Palais Maeterlinck M 🐚, 6 km by Inferior Corniche ✉ 06300 ☎ 04 92 00 72 00, Fax 04 92 04 18 10, ≤, 🍽, « Swimming pool, garden and terraces overlooking sea », 🏋, 🏖 – |♦| kitchenette ⊬ rm ▤ TV ☎ ♿ 🚗 P – 🏛 25. AE ⓓ GB
closed 5 January-15 March – ***Le Mélisande :*** **Meals** 200(lunch)/240 – ☕ 160 – **9 rm** 1800/2000, 10 suites 2500/10000, 9 duplex.

Méridien M, 1 promenade des Anglais ☎ 04 93 82 25 25, Fax 04 93 16 08 90, 🍽, « Rooftop swimming pool, ≤ bay » – |♦| ⊬ rm ▤ TV ☎ – 🏛 25 - 200. AE ⓓ GB JCB FZ d
L'Habit Blanc *(October-April)* **Meals** 130/200 – ***La Terrasse*** *(May-September)* **Meals** 145/190, 🍷 – ☕ 95 – **306 rm** 1250/2850, 8 suites.

Abela Regency M, 223 promenade des Anglais ✉ 06200 ☎ 04 93 37 17 17, Fax 04 93 71 21 71, 🍽, « Rooftop swimming pool ≤ bay », 🏋 – |♦| ⊬ rm ▤ TV ☎ 🚗 – 🏛 30 - 180. AE ⓓ GB
Les Mosaïques *(closed July-August)* **Meals** 155 – ***La Terrasse-Les Jardins*** grill *(21 June-15 September)* **Meals** 95(lunch), 165/195 – ☕ 90 – **321 rm** 980/1280, 12 suites.

Élysée Palace M, r. Sauvan ☎ 04 93 86 06 06, Fax 04 93 44 50 40, 🍽, « Rooftop swimming pool ≤ Nice » – |♦| ⊬ rm ▤ TV ☎ ♿ 🚗 – 🏛 45. AE ⓓ GB JCB EZ d
Meals *(closed Sunday from 1 November-1 March)* 150/190 – ☕ 95 – **143 rm** 1000/1300.

Plaza Concorde, 12 av. Verdun ☎ 04 93 16 75 75, Fax 04 93 82 50 70, ≤, 🍽, « Rooftop terrace » – |♦| ▤ TV ☎ – 🏛 260. AE ⓓ GB JCB GZ f
Meals a la carte 170/250 🍷 – ☕ 80 – **173 rm** 900/1500, 10 suites.

Sofitel M, 2-4 parvis de l'Europe ✉ 06300 ☎ 04 92 00 80 00, Fax 04 93 26 27 00, 🍽, « Panoramic rooftop swimming pool », 🏋 – |♦| ⊬ rm ▤ TV ☎ 🚗 – 🏛 50. AE ⓓ GB JCB JX t
Meals 92/260 b.i. – ☕ 90 – **152 rm** 1160/1300.

Beau Rivage M, 24 r. St-François-de-Paule ✉ 06300 ☎ 04 93 80 80 70, Fax 04 93 80 55 77, 🏖 – |♦| ⊬ rm ▤ TV ☎ ♿ – 🏛 35. AE ⓓ GB GZ y
Bistrot du Rivage *(closed Sunday dinner and Saturday)* **Meals** a la carte 170/280 – ***Brasserie de la Plage*** *(open May-September)* **Meals** (lunch only) a la carte 190/270 – ☕ 95 – **118 rm** 700/1800.

Splendid, 50 bd V. Hugo ☎ 04 93 16 41 00, Fax 04 93 87 02 46, 🍽, « Rooftop swimming pool ≤ Nice » – |♦| ⊬ rm ▤ TV ☎ 🚗 – 🏛 30 - 100. AE ⓓ GB JCB. ⛔ rest FYZ g
Meals 145 🍷 – ☕ 80 – **115 rm** 890/1190, 14 suites.

West End, 31 promenade des Anglais ☎ 04 92 14 44 00, Fax 04 93 88 85 07, ≤, 🍽 – |♦| ⊬ rm ▤ TV ☎ – 🏛 120. AE ⓓ GB JCB FZ p
Meals 120/185 🍷 – ☕ 60 – **123 rm** 600/1350, 6 suites.

Westminster Concorde, 27 promenade des Anglais ☎ 04 93 88 29 44, Fax 04 93 82 45 35, 🍽 – |♦| ▤ rm TV ☎ – 🏛 150. AE ⓓ GB JCB. ⛔ rest FZ m
Le Farniente *(closed November and Sunday from 15 October-15 April)* **Meals** (dinner only in July-August) 170/200 – ☕ 85 – **102 rm** 900/1200.

NICE

Félix-Faure (Av.) . . . . . GZ 21
France (R. de) . . . . . . DFZ
Gambetta (Bd) . . . . . . EXZ
Gioffredo (R.) . . . . HY
Hôtel-des-Postes (R.) . . HY 30
Liberté (R. de la) . . . . . GZ 35
Masséna (Espace, Pl.) . . . . . . GZ
Masséna (R.) . . . . FGZ 43
Médecin (Av. J.) . . . . FGY 44
Paradis (R.) . . . . GZ 55
Pastorelli (R.) . . . . GY 58
République (Av. de la) . JXY 64

Alberti (R.) . . . . GHY 2
Alsace-Lorraine (Jardin) EZ 3
Armée-du-Rhin (Pl.) . . . JX 5
Auriol (Pont V.) . . . . . . JV 7
Bellanda (Av.) . . . . HV 10
Berlioz (R.) . . . . FY 12
Bonaparte (R.) . . . . JY 13
Carnot (Bd) . . . . JZ 15
Desambrois (Av.) . . . GHX 18
Diables-Bleus (Av. des) . . . . JX 19
Gallieni (Av.) . . . . HJX 23
Gautier (Pl. P.) . . . . HZ 25
Ile-de-Beauté (Pl. de l') . . . . JZ 32
J.-Jaurès (Bd) . . . . HYZ 33

Lunel (Quai) . . . . JZ 37
Meyerbeer (R.) . . . . FZ 45
Monastère (Av. et Pl. du) . . . . HV 46

Moulin (Pl. J.) . . . . HY 4
Parvis (de l'Europe) . . . . JX 5
Passy (R. F.) . . . . EY 5

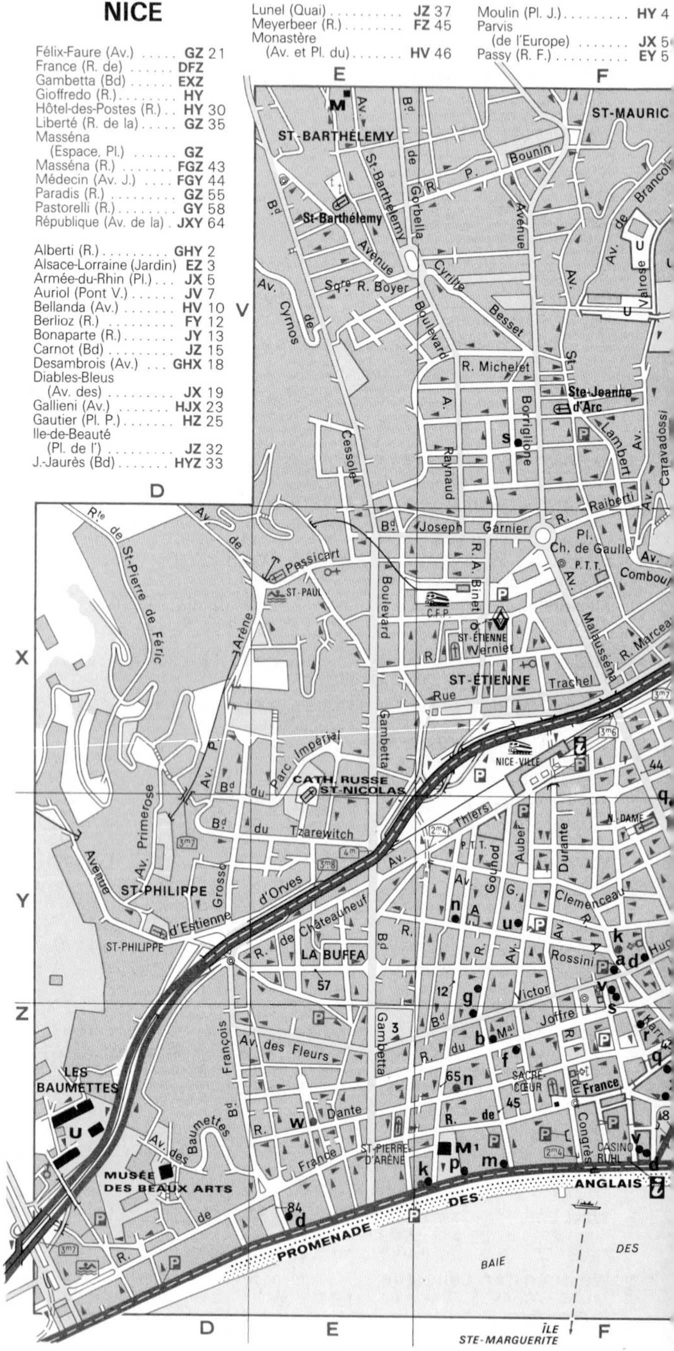

ıocéens (Av. des) . . . . **GZ** 59
voli (R. de) . . . . **FZ** 65
-François
de Paule (R.) . . . . . . **GHZ** 72

St-Jean
Baptiste (Av.) . . . . **HY** 73
Saleya (Cours) . . . . **HZ** 82
Sauvan (R. H.) . . . . **EZ** 84

Verdun (Av. de) . . . . **FGZ** 89
Walesa
(Bd Lech) . . . . **JYZ** 91
Wilson (Pl.) . . . . **HY** 92

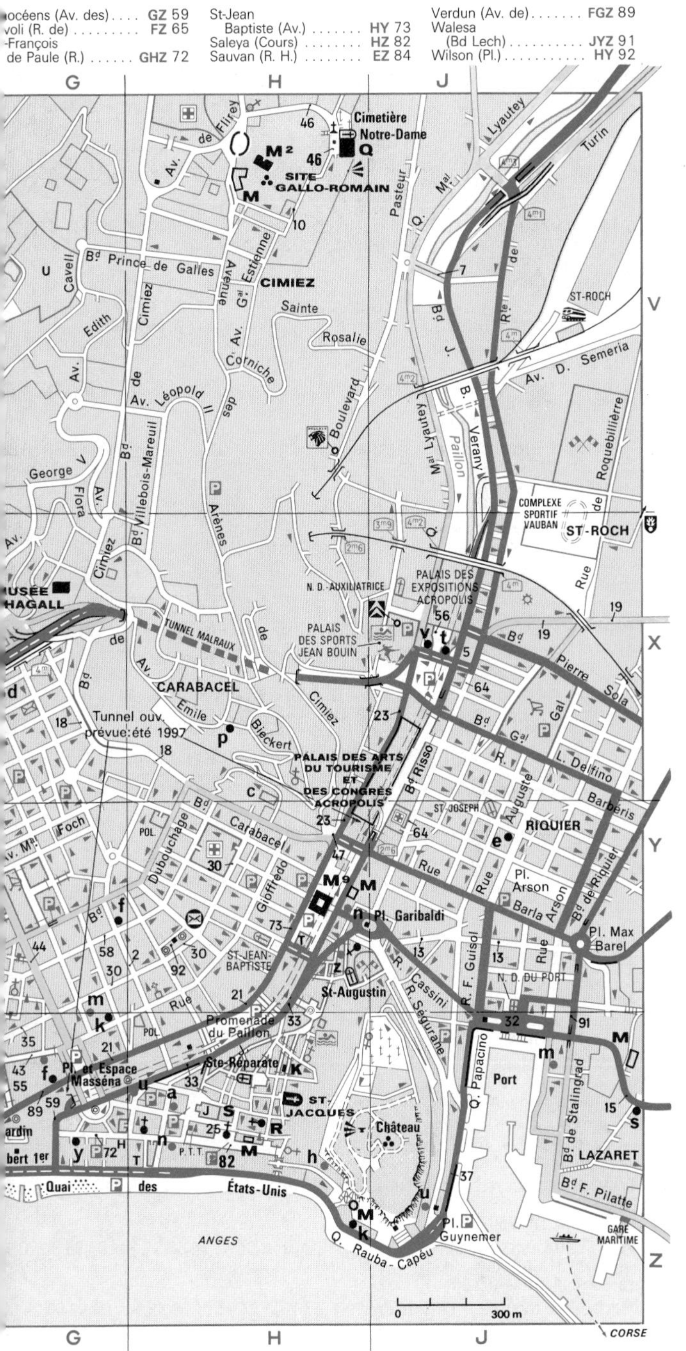

La Pérouse, 11 quai Rauba-Capéu ✉ 06300 ☎ 04 93 62 34 63, Fax 04 93 62 59 4
, « ≤ Nice and Baie des Anges », – rm . AE GB JCB. rest HZ
Meals grill *(14 May-16 September)* a la carte approx. 230 – 85 – **64 rm** 890/132

Atlantic, 12 bd V. Hugo ☎ 04 93 88 40 15, Fax 04 93 88 68 60, –
50. AE GB JCB FY
Meals 130/150 – 80 – **125 rm** 650/900.

Holiday Inn M, 20 bd V. Hugo ☎ 04 93 16 55 00, Fax 04 93 16 55 55, – rm
 – 90. AE GB JCB FY
Meals 108/152 – 85 – **131 rm** 700/1150.

Gd H. Mercure Centre without rest, 28 av. Notre-Dame ☎ 04 93 13 36 36
Fax 04 93 62 61 69, « Hanging garden on 2nd floor, on 8th floor, ≤ » – rm
 – 25 - 120. AE GB JCB FXY
 75 – **201 rm** 625/695.

Novotel M, 8-10 Parvis de l'Europe ✉ 06300 ☎ 04 93 13 30 93, Fax 04 93 13 09 0
, « Panoramic rooftop swimming pool » – rm – 80. AE
 GB JCB JX
Meals a la carte approx. 170 – 55 – **173 rm** 510/750.

Napoléon without rest, 6 r. Grimaldi ☎ 04 93 87 70 07, Fax 04 93 16 17 80 –
. AE GB JCB FZ
 60 – **83 rm** 655/820.

Mercure Promenade des Anglais M without rest, 2 r. Halévy ☎ 04 93 82 30 8
Fax 04 93 82 18 20 – rm – 25. AE GB FZ
 75 – **122 rm** 590/890.

Ambassador without rest, 8 av. de Suède ☎ 04 93 87 90 19, Fax 04 93 82 14 90 –
. AE GB JCB FZ
15 February-15 November – 50 – **45 rm** 520/850.

Petit Palais without rest, 10 av. E. Bieckert ☎ 04 93 62 19 11, Fax 04 93 62 53 6
≤ Nice and sea – . AE GB HX
 50 – **25 rm** 530/780.

Mercure Masséna M without rest, 58 r. Gioffredo ☎ 04 93 85 49 25
Fax 04 93 62 43 27 – rm . AE GB JCB GZ
 70 – **116 rm** 590/795.

Apogia M without rest, 26 r. Smolett ✉ 06300 ☎ 04 93 89 18 88, Fax 04 93 89 16 0
– rm . AE GB JCB JY
 51 – **101 rm** 480/560.

Grimaldi without rest, 15 r. Grimaldi ☎ 04 93 87 73 61, Fax 04 93 88 30 05 –
. AE GB JCB FY
 50 – **24 rm** 600/800.

Windsor, 11 r. Dalpozzo ☎ 04 93 88 59 35, Fax 04 93 88 94 57, , , , –
 rm . AE GB. rest FZ
Meals (coffee shop) *(closed Sunday)* a la carte approx. 150 – 40 – **57 rm** 415/67

Gounod without rest, 3 r. Gounod ☎ 04 93 88 26 20, Fax 04 93 88 23 84 –
 P. AE GB JCB FYZ
 60 – **41 rm** 515/590, 6 suites.

Vendôme without rest, 26 r. Pastorelli ☎ 04 93 62 00 77, Fax 04 93 13 40 78 –
 P. AE GB JCB GY
 40 – **51 rm** 390/560, 5 duplex.

Agata without rest, 46 bd Carnot ✉ 06300 ☎ 04 93 55 97 13, Fax 04 93 55 67 38
 . AE GB JCB JZ
 40 – **45 rm** 400/550.

Lausanne without rest, 36 r. Rossini ☎ 04 93 88 85 94, Fax 04 93 88 15 88 – r
 . AE GB FY
closed 21 to 28 December – 50 – **36 rm** 415.

Régence without rest, 21 r. Masséna ☎ 04 93 87 75 08, Fax 04 93 82 41 31 –
. AE GB JCB FZ
 35 – **37 rm** 335/380.

Trianon without rest, 15 av. Auber ☎ 04 93 88 30 69, Fax 04 93 88 11 35 –
AE GB FY
 35 – **32 rm** 230/320.

Villa St-Hubert without rest, 26 r. Michel-Ange ☎ 04 93 84 66 51, Fax 04 93 84 70 9
– kitchenette . GB. FV
 30 – **11 rm** 230/330.

Marbella without rest, 120 bd Carnot ✉ 06300 ☎ 04 93 89 39 35, Fax 04 92 04 22 5
≤ coastline – rm . AE GB.
 30 – **17 rm** 230/430.

XXXX **Chantecler** - Hôtel Négresco, 37 promenade des Anglais ✆ 04 93 16 64 00, Fax 04 93 88 35 68 – ▤. AE ⓪ GB JCB FZ k
✿✿ *closed 18 November-16 December* – **Meals** 255 b.i. (lunch), 395/560 and a la carte 500/700
Spec. Légumes mijotés en casserole, grosses langoustines rôties. Filets de rougets poêlés, panisses "façon socca". Selle d'agneau de Sisteron rôtie, ragoût d'artichauts violets. **Wines** Côtes de Provence.

XXX **L'Ane Rouge,** 7 quai Deux-Emmanuel ✉ 06300 ✆ 04 93 89 49 63, Fax 04 93 89 49 63 – ▤. AE ⓪ GB JZ m
closed 7 to 21 February and Wednesday – **Meals** 148/198 and a la carte 240/330.

XX **Le Florian,** 22 r. A. Karr ✆ 04 93 88 86 60, Fax 04 93 87 31 98 – ▤. AE GB FY k
closed Saturday lunch and Sunday – **Meals** 149 b.i./250 ♨.

XX **Boccaccio,** 7 r. Masséna ✆ 04 93 87 71 76, Fax 04 93 82 09 06, 🏖, « Carvel decor » – ▤. AE ⓪ GB JCB GZ f
Meals - Seafood - 140 (lunch)and a la carte 290/410.

XX **Les Dents de la Mer,** 2 r. St-François-de-Paule ✉ 06300 ✆ 04 93 80 99 16, Fax 04 93 85 05 78, 🏖, « Unusual decor depicting a submerged galleon » – ▤. AE ⓪ GB HZ n
Meals - Seafood - 148/199.

XX **Flo,** 4 r. S. Guitry ✆ 04 93 13 38 38, Fax 04 93 13 38 39, brasserie, « Former theatre » – ▤. AE ⓪ GB GYZ m
Meals 109 b.i./149 b.i..

XX **Don Camillo,** 5 r. Ponchettes ✉ 06300 ✆ 04 93 85 67 95, Fax 04 93 13 97 43 – ▤. AE GB HZ h
closed Monday lunch and Sunday – **Meals** - Niçoise and Italian specialities - 200/320.

XX **L'Univers,** 54 bd J. Jaurès ✉ 06300 ✆ 04 93 62 32 22, Fax 04 93 62 55 69 – ▤. AE ⓪ GB JCB HZ u
closed 7 to 21 July and Sunday in summer – **Meals** 160 b.i. (lunch)/170.

XX **La Toque Blanche,** 40 r. Buffa ✆ 04 93 88 38 18, Fax 04 93 88 38 18 – ▤. GB
closed Sunday except lunch September-June and Monday – **Meals** 145/160. FZ n

X **Mireille,** 19 bd Raimbaldi ✆ 04 93 85 27 23 – ▤. GB GX d
closed 2 to 24 June, 22 to 30 September, Monday and Tuesday – **Meals** - One dish only : paella - 110/150.

X **La Merenda,** 4 r. Terrasse ✉ 06300 HZ a
closed 4 to 18 August, 24 December-4 January, 16 to 22 February, Saturday and Sunday – **Meals** - Niçoise specialities - a la carte 150/210.

t the airport : *7 km – ✉ 06200 Nice :*

🏠 **Campanile,** 459 promenade des Anglais ✆ 04 93 21 20 20, Fax 04 93 83 83 96 – 🛗 ⇆ rm ▤ 📺 ☎ ♿ 🚗 – 🏛 25 - 80. AE ⓪ GB
Meals 84 b.i./107 b.i. – ☕ 34 – **170 rm** 370.

XXX **Ciel d'Azur,** aérogare 1, 2e étage ✆ 04 93 21 36 36, Fax 04 93 21 35 31 – ▤. AE ⓪ GB JCB
Meals (lunch only) 240/300.

t-Martin-du-Var *06670 Alpes-Mar. 84 ⑨, 115 ⑯ – pop. 1 869 alt. 110.*

Nice 26.

XXXX **Jean-François Issautier,** on Nice road (N 202) 3 km ✆ 04 93 08 10 65, Fax 04 93 29 19 73 – ▤ 🅿. AE ⓪ GB
✿✿ *closed 13 to 21 October, late February-late March, Sunday except lunch from 8 September-24 June and Monday* – **Meals** 250 b.i. (lunch), 320/515 and a la carte 390/600
Spec. Grosses crevettes en robe de pomme de terre. Poisson de Méditerranée rôti au jus de tomate, sauce pistou. "Cul" d'agneau de Sisteron à la menthe fraiche. **Wines** Côtes de Provence, Bellet.

ence *06140 Alpes-Mar. 84 ⑨, 115 ㉕ – pop. 15 330 alt. 325.*

Tourist Office, pl. Grand-Jardin ✆ 04 93 58 06 38, Fax 04 93 58 91 81.

Nice 23.

XXX **Jacques Maximin,** 689 chemin de La Gaude, by road of Cagnes : 3 km ✆ 04 93 58 90 75, Fax 04 93 58 22 86, 🏖, 🌳 – 🅿. GB
✿✿ *closed 12 January-9 February, Sunday dinner and Monday* – **Meals** (booking essential) 240 and a la carte 340/450
Spec. Gâteau d'aubergines confites à la niçoise. Ratatouille de crustacés, beurre de basilic. Pigeonneau du Lauragais.

Don't get lost, use Michelin Maps which are updated annually.

STRASBOURG *67000 B.-Rhin* 62 ⑩ *– pop. 252 338 alt. 143.*

See : *Cathedral★★★ : Astronomical clock★ – La Petite France★★ : rue d[...] Bains-aux-Plantes★★* HJZ *– Barrage Vauban ※★★ – Ponts couverts★ – Place de [...] Cathédrale★* KZ **26** *: Maison Kammerzell★* KZ **e** *– Mausoleum★★ in St-Thomas Church [...] – Place Kléber★ – Hôtel de Ville★* KY **H** *– Orangery★ – Palais de l'Europe★ – Museum [...] Oeuvre N.-Dame★★* KZ **M¹** *– Boat trips on the Ill river and the canals★* KZ *– Museums★ (decorative Arts, Fine Arts, Archaeology) in the Palais Rohan★* KZ *– Alsatia[...] Museum★★* KZ **M²** *– Historical Museum★* KZ **M³** *– Guided tours of the Port★ by boa[...]*

at Illkirch-Graffenstaden (private) ✆ 03 88 66 17 22 ; of the Wantzenau [...] Wantzenau (private) ✆ 03 88 96 37 73 ; N by D 468 : 12 km ; of Kempferhof [...] Plobsheim ✆ 03 88 98 72 72, S by D 468 : 15 km.

of Strasbourg International : ✆ 03 88 64 67 67 by D 392 : 12 km FR.

✆ 08 36 35 35 35.

Tourist Office 17 pl. de la Cathédrale ✆ 03 88 52 28 28, Fax 03 88 52 28 29, pl. ga[...] ✆ 03 88 32 51 49, Pont de l'Europe ✆ 03 88 61 39 23 – Automobile Club, 5 av. Pa[...] ✆ 03 88 36 04 34, Fax 03 88 36 00 63.

Paris 490 – Basle 145 – Bonn 360 – Bordeaux 915 – Frankfurt 218 – Karlsruhe 81 – Lille 54[...] – Luxembourg 223 – Lyons 485 – Stuttgart 157.

Plans on following pages

Régent Petite France M, 5 r. Moulins ✆ 03 88 76 43 43, Fax 03 88 76 43 7[...] ≤, , « Former ice factory on the banks of River Ill - contemporary decor », [...] – rm ▤ rm TV ☎ & – 25 - 60. AE ① GB JCB JZ
closed 23 December-3 January – **Meals** *(closed Monday in summer, Saturday and Sunda[...] in winter)* 175 b.i. – ☕ 87 – **63 rm** 1050/1460, 5 suites, 4 duplex.

Hilton, av. Herrenschmidt ✆ 03 88 37 10 10, Fax 03 88 36 83 27, – rm [...] TV ☎ & P – 25 - 300. AE ① GB JCB
La Maison du Bœuf ✆ 03 88 35 72 31 *(closed 12 July-2 September, Saturday lunch ar[...] Sunday)* **Meals** 195(lunch)/290 – ***Le Jardin*** ✆ 03 88 35 72 61 **Meals** 105(lunch), 15[...] 182 – ☕ 98 – **241 rm** 1060/1300, 5 suites.

Sofitel M, pl. St-Pierre-le-Jeune ✆ 03 88 15 49 00, Fax 03 88 15 49 99, , patio – [...] rm ▤ TV ☎ – 25 - 150. AE ① GB JY
L'Alsace Gourmande : **Meals** 150 – ☕ 98 – **158 rm** 1100/1200.

Beaucour M without rest, 5 r. Bouchers ✆ 03 88 76 72 00, Fax 03 88 76 72 6[...] « Old Alsatian houses elegantly decorated » – ▤ TV ☎ & – 30. AE ① GB
☕ 65 – **49 rm** 550/950. KZ

Régent Contades M without rest, 8 av. Liberté ✆ 03 88 15 05 05, Fax 03 88 15 05 1[...] « 19C mansion », – rm ▤ TV ☎. AE ① GB JCB LY
☕ 87 – **45 rm** 790/1300.

Maison Rouge without rest, 4 r. Francs-Bourgeois ✆ 03 88 32 08 6[...] Fax 03 88 22 43 73, « Tasteful decor » – TV ☎ & – 40. AE ① GB JZ
☕ 65 – **140 rm** 540/590.

Monopole-Métropole without rest, 16 r. Kuhn ✆ 03 88 14 39 1[...] Fax 03 88 32 82 55, « Alsatian and contemporary decor » – rm TV ☎ . AE [...] GB JCB HY
closed 23 December-4 January – ☕ 65 – **90 rm** 420/730.

Holiday Inn, 20 pl. Bordeaux ✆ 03 88 37 80 00, Fax 03 88 37 07 04, , – r[...] ▤ TV ☎ & P – 50 - 500. AE ① GB JCB
Meals 150 – ☕ 85 – **170 rm** 950/1120.

Europe without rest, 38 r. Fossé des Tanneurs ✆ 03 88 32 17 88, Fax 03 88 75 65 4[...] « Half timbered Alsatian house, beautiful 1/50th copy of the Cathedral » – TV ☎ [...] – 40. AE GB JCB JZ
closed 22 to 29 December – ☕ 46 – **55 rm** 370/600, 5 suites.

France without rest, 20 r. Jeu des Enfants ✆ 03 88 32 37 12, Fax 03 88 22 48 08 – [...] rm TV ☎ – 30. AE GB JCB JY
☕ 65 – **66 rm** 470/700.

Mercure Centre M without rest, 25 r. Thomann ✆ 03 88 75 77 88 Fax 03 88 32 08 66 – rm ▤ TV ☎ & . AE ① GB JY
☕ 57 – **98 rm** 650.

Novotel Centre Halles M, 4 quai Kléber ✆ 03 88 21 50 50, Fax 03 88 21 50 51 – [...] rm ▤ TV ☎ & – 25 - 100. AE ① GB JY
Meals a la carte approx. 170 – ☕ 57 – **97 rm** 560/670.

Grand Hôtel without rest, 12 pl. Gare ✆ 03 88 52 84 84, Fax 03 88 52 84 00 – r[...] TV ☎. AE ① GB HY
☕ 65 – **83 rm** 380/610.

Plaza, 10 pl. Gare ✆ 03 88 15 17 17, Fax 03 88 15 17 15, – rm. AE GB JCB HY m
La Brasserie : Meals 95 – 58 – **72 rm** 480/560, 6 suites.

Cathédrale M without rest, 12 pl. Cathédrale ✆ 03 88 22 12 12, Fax 03 88 23 28 00 – rm. AE GB KZ n
48 – **32 rm** 350/790, 3 duplex.

des Rohan without rest, 17 r. Maroquin ✆ 03 88 32 85 11, Fax 03 88 75 65 37 – rm. AE GB JCB KZ u
50 – **36 rm** 410/695.

La Dauphine without rest, 30 r. 1e Armée ✆ 03 88 36 26 61, Fax 03 88 35 50 07 – . AE GB
closed 23 December-2 January – 60 – **45 rm** 475/560.

Dragon M without rest, 2 r. Ecarlate ✆ 03 88 35 79 80, Fax 03 88 25 78 95 – rm. AE GB. JZ d
closed 23 to 27 December – 58 – **32 rm** 430/655.

Relais Mercure without rest, 3 r. Maire Kuss ✆ 03 88 32 80 80, Fax 03 88 23 05 39, – rm – 30. AE GB HY e
49 – **52 rm** 370/420.

Princes without rest, 33 r. Geiler ✆ 03 88 61 55 19, Fax 03 88 41 10 92 – . AE GB
closed 1 to 21 August – 45 – **43 rm** 395/480.

Pax, 24 r. Fg National ✆ 03 88 32 14 54, Fax 03 88 32 01 16, – rm – 25 - 70. AE GB JCB HYZ u
closed 24 December-2 January – **Meals** *(closed Sunday from November-1 March)* 90/115 – 38 – **106 rm** 345/385.

Couvent du Franciscain without rest, 18 r. Fg de Pierre ✆ 03 88 32 93 93, Fax 03 88 75 68 46 – . AE GB JY e
closed 23 December-4 January – 44 – **43 rm** 290/315.

Continental without rest, 14 r. Maire Kuss ✆ 03 88 22 28 07, Fax 03 88 32 22 25 – . AE GB. HY s
closed 24 to 30 December – 36 – **48 rm** 297/340.

Au Crocodile (Jung), 10 r. Outre ✆ 03 88 32 13 02, Fax 03 88 75 72 01, « Elegant decor » – . AE GB. KY x
closed 13 July-4 August, 21 December-1 January, Sunday and Monday – **Meals** 295 (lunch), 395/640 and a la carte 470/700
Spec. Foie d'oie poêlé et pommes reinette au gingembre (season). Timbale de grenouilles et flan de cresson. "Délice ébène" au Grand Marnier. **Wines** Sylvaner, Pinot blanc.

Buerehiesel (Westermann), set in the Orangery Park ✆ 03 88 45 56 65, Fax 03 88 61 32 00, ←, park, « Reconstructed authentic Alsatian farmhouse with conservatory » – . AE GB
closed 7 to 20 August, 24 December-7 January, 24 February-4 March, Tuesday and Wednesday – **Meals** 290 (lunch), 360/690 and a la carte 500/650
Spec. Gelée légère aux queue d'écrevisses et fondant au foie gras de canard. Schniederspaetle et cuisses de grenouilles poêlées au cerfeuil. Poulette de Bresse aux truffes cuite comme un baeckeoffe. **Wines** Riesling, Tokay-Pinot gris.

Maison Kammerzell and H. Baumann M with rm, 16 pl. Cathédrale ✆ 03 88 32 42 14, Fax 03 88 23 03 92, « Attractive 16C Alsatian house » – rm – 120. AE GB KZ e
Meals 195/295 and a la carte 190/310 – 55 – **9 rm** 420/630.

Zimmer, 8 r. Temple Neuf ✆ 03 88 32 35 01, Fax 03 88 32 42 28 – AE GB KY y
closed 3 to 17 August, 24 December-4 January and Sunday – **Meals** 170/270.

Maison des Tanneurs dite "Gerwerstub", 42 r. Bain aux Plantes ✆ 03 88 32 79 70, Fax 03 88 22 17 26, « Old Alsatian house on the banks of the River Ill » – AE GB JZ t
closed 21 July-11 August, 30 December-20 January, Sunday and Monday – **Meals** a la carte 270/350.

Estaminet Schloegel, 19 r. Krütenau ✆ 03 88 36 21 98, Fax 03 88 36 21 98 – . AE GB LZ q
closed 9 to 24 August, Saturday lunch and Sunday – **Meals** 110 (lunch), 180/300 and a la carte 240/300.

Julien, 22 quai Bateliers ✆ 03 88 36 01 54, Fax 03 88 35 40 14 – . AE GB KZ x
closed 3 to 24 August, 1 to 10 January, Sunday and Monday – **Meals** 195 (lunch), 295/385 and a la carte 290/410
Spec. Foie gras de canard poêlé à la rhubarbe (season). Langoustines à l'infusion de gewurztraminer. Croustillant de lapereau aux champignons. **Wines** Klevener, Riesling.

STRASBOURG

Division-Leclerc (R.) . . . . . **JKZ**
Gdes-Arcades (R. des) . . . **JKY**
Kléber (Place) . . . . **JY**
Maire Kuss (R. du) . . . . . **HY** 120
Mésange (R. de la) . . . . . **JKY** 136
Nuée-Bleue (R. de la) . . . **KY**
Vieux-Marché-aux-
Poissons (R. du) . . . . . . **KZ** 229
22-Novembre (R. du) . . . **HJY**

Abreuvoir (R. de l') . . . . . **LZ** 3
Arc-en-Ciel (R. de l') . . . . **KLY** 7
Austerlitz (R. d') . . . . **KZ** 10
Auvergne (Pont d') . . . . . . **LY** 12
Bateliers (R. des) . . . . **LZ** 14
Bonnes-Gens (R. des) . . . . **JY** 19
Boudier (R. du) . . . . **JZ** 20
Castelnau (R. Gén. de) . . . **KY** 25
Cathédrale (Pl. de la) . . . . . **KZ** 26
Chaudron (R. du) . . . . **KY** 28
Cheveux (R. des) . . . . **JZ** 29
Corbeau (Pl. du) . . . . **KZ** 31
Cordiers (R. des) . . . . **KZ** 32
Courtine (R. de la) . . . . **LY** 34
Dentelles (R. des) . . . . **JZ** 36
Écarlate (R. de l') . . . . **JZ** 43
Escarpée (R.) . . . . **JZ** 45
Étudiants (R. et Pl. des) . . **KY** 46
Faisan (Pont du) . . . . **JZ** 4
Fossé-des-Tanneurs
(Rue du) . . . . **JZ** 5
Fossé-des-Treize (R. du) . **KY** 5
Francs-Bourgeois (R. des) **JZ** 6
Frey (Q. Charles) . . . . **JZ** 6
Grande-Boucherie
(Pl. de la) . . . . **KZ** 7
Gutenberg (R.) . . . . **JKZ** 7
Haute-Montée (R.) . . . . . **JY** 8
Homme-de-Fer (Pl. de l') . **JY** 9
Hôpital-Militaire (R. de l') . **LZ** 9
Humann (R.) . . . . **HZ** 9
Ill (Quai de l') . . . . **HZ** 9

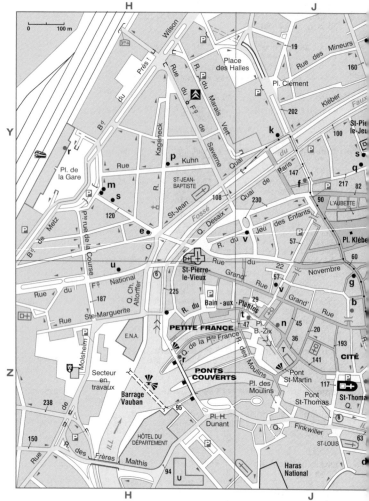

Town plans : the names of main shopping streets are indicated in red at th beginning of the list of streets.

ıllermann (Quai)	JY	100
utenau (Rue de la)	LZ	106
ıss (Pont)	HY	108
mey (R. Auguste)	LY	109
zay-Marnésia (Quai)	LY	114
ıther (R. Martin)	JZ	117
arché-aux-Cochons-de-Lait (Pl. du)	KZ	124
arché-aux-Poissons (Pl. du)	KZ	125
arché-Gayot (Pl. du)	KYZ	126
arché-Neuf (Pl. du)	KYZ	127
aroquin (R. du)	KZ	129
ercière (R.)	KZ	135
onnaie (R. de la)	JZ	141

Munch (R.)	LZ	142
Noyer (R. du)	JY	147
Obernai (R. d')	HZ	150
Outre (R. de l')	KY	153
Paix (Av. de la)	KLY	154
Parchemin (R. du)	KY	156
Pierre (R. du Fg-de)	JY	160
Pontonniers (R. des)	LY	167
Récollets (R. des)	KLY	172
St-Étienne (Quai)	LY	183
St-Michel (R.)	HZ	187
St-Nicolas (Pont)	KZ	189
St-Pierre-le-Jeune (Pl.)	JKY	190
Ste-Madeleine (Pont et R.)	KLZ	192
Salzmann (R.)	JZ	193

Sanglier (R. du)	KY	194
Saverne (Pont de)	HY	195
Sébastopol (R. de)	JY	202
Serruriers (R. des)	JKZ	205
Temple-Neuf (Pl. du)	KY	213
Temple-Neuf (R. du)	KY	214
Théâtre (Pont du)	KY	216
Thomann (R.)	JY	217
Tonneliers (R. des)	KZ	220
Turckheim (Quai)	HZ	225
Vieil-Hôpital (R. du)	KZ	228
Vieux-Marché-aux-Vins (R. et Pl. du)	JY	230
Vieux-Seigle (R. du)	JZ	231
Wasselonne (R. de)	HZ	238

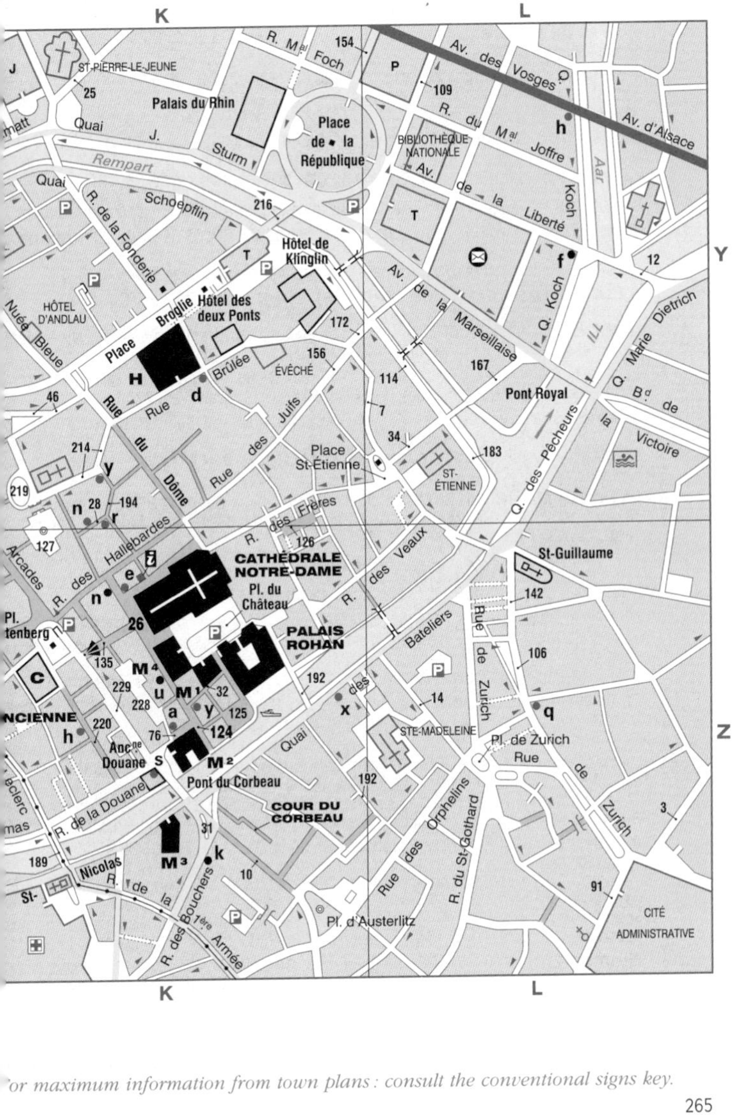

K L Y Z

ST-PIERRE-LE-JEUNE
Palais du Rhin
Place de la République
BIBLIOTHÈQUE NATIONALE
R. Mal Foch
Av. des Vosges
R. du Mal Joffre
Av. d'Alsace
Av. de la Liberté
Quai Sturm
Rempart
Quai Schoepflin
R. de la Fonderie
Hôtel de Klinglin
Hôtel des deux Ponts
HÔTEL D'ANDLAU
Place Broglie
Nuée Bleue
Rue Brûlée
ÉVÊCHÉ
Av. de la Marseillaise
Q. Koch
ILL
Q. Marie Dietrich
Pont Royal
Bd de la Victoire
Rue du Dôme
Rue des Juifs
Place St-Étienne
ST-ÉTIENNE
Q. des Pêcheurs
R. des Frères
R. des Hallebardes
R. des Arcades
CATHÉDRALE NOTRE-DAME
Pl. du Château
R. des Veaux
St-Guillaume
PALAIS ROHAN
R. des Bateliers
Rue de Zurich
Pl. de Zurich
Pl. Gutenberg
ANCIENNE DOUANE
Anc.ne Douane
Pont du Corbeau
COUR DU CORBEAU
Quai des Bateliers
STE-MADELEINE
Rue des Orphelins
R. du St-Gothard
R. de la Douane
St-Nicolas
R. de la 1ère Armée
R. des Bouchers
Pl. d'Austerlitz
CITÉ ADMINISTRATIVE

For maximum information from town plans: consult the conventional signs key.

XX **Au Gourmet Sans Chiqué,** 15 r. Ste-Barbe ✆ 03 88 32 04 07, Fax 03 88 22 42 4 – ▤. AE ⓓ GB. ✻ JZ
closed 14 to 23 April, 11 to 26 August, Monday lunch and Sunday – **Meals** 148/385.

XX **Pont des Vosges,** 15 quai Koch ✆ 03 88 36 47 75, Fax 03 88 25 16 85, 🍴 – AE GB
closed Saturday lunch, Sunday and Bank Holidays – **Meals** a la carte 200/270 ♁. LY

XX **Zuem Sternstebele,** 17 r. Tonneliers ✆ 03 88 21 01 01, Fax 03 88 21 01 02, 🍴 ▤. AE GB KZ
closed Monday lunch and Sunday – **Meals** (booking essential) 75/200 ♁.

XX **Au Bœuf Mode,** 2 pl. St-Thomas ✆ 03 88 32 39 03, Fax 03 88 21 90 80 – AE GB
closed Sunday – **Meals** 95/155 ♁. JZ

XX **Le Benjamin,** 3 r. Dentelles ✆ 03 88 75 16 67, Fax 03 88 75 16 67 – AE GB JZ
closed 5 to 11 January, Monday lunch and Sunday – **Meals** 60 (lunch), 140/200 ♁.

XX **Buffet de la Gare,** pl. Gare ✆ 03 88 32 68 28, Fax 03 88 32 88 34 – GB HY
Meals 64/150 ♁.

X **Ami Schutz,** 1 r. Ponts Couverts ✆ 03 88 32 76 98, Fax 03 88 32 38 40, 🍴 – AE ⓓ GB HZ
Meals 120 (lunch), 150/250 ♁.

X **Au Rocher du Sapin,** 6 r. Noyer ✆ 03 88 32 39 65, Fax 03 88 75 60 99, 🍴 GB JY
closed 7 to 21 July, Sunday and Monday – **Meals** - Alsatian rest. - 88/125 ♁.

WINSTUBS : *Regional specialities and wine tasting in a typical Alsatian atmosphere :*

X **Zum Strissel,** 5 pl. Gde Boucherie ✆ 03 88 32 14 73, Fax 03 88 32 70 24, rustic deco – ▤. GB KZ
closed 4 to 31 July, February Holidays, Sunday and Monday – **Meals** 62/133 ♁.

X **S'Burjerstuewel (Chez Yvonne),** 10 r. Sanglier ✆ 03 88 32 84 15 Fax 03 88 23 00 18 – GB KYZ
closed 13 July-10 August, 23 December-2 January, Monday lunch and Sunday – **Meals** (booking essential) a la carte 140/240 ♁.

X **Le Clou,** 3 r. Chaudron ✆ 03 88 32 11 67, Fax 03 88 75 72 83 – AE GB KY
closed Wednesday lunch, Sunday and Bank Holidays – **Meals** 125/220 b.i.

X **S'Munsterstuewel,** 8 pl. Marché aux Cochons de Lait ✆ 03 88 32 17 63 Fax 03 88 21 96 02, 🍴 – AE GB KZ
closed 28 July-15 August, February Holidays, Sunday and Monday – **Meals** 128 b.i./196 b.i.

X **La Petite Mairie,** 8 r. Brûlée ✆ 03 88 32 83 06, Fax 03 88 32 83 06 – GB KY
closed 1 to 26 August, 23 February-2 March, Saturday dinner and Sunday – **Meals** a la carte 155/200 ♁.

Environs

at La Wantzenau *NE by D 468 : 12 km – pop. 4 394 alt. 130 – ✉ 67610 :*

Hôtel Au Moulin without rest, S : 1,5 km by D 468 ✆ 03 88 59 22 22 Fax 03 88 59 22 00, ←, « Old watermill on a branch of the River Ill », – |‡| TV ☎ P AE GB
closed 24 December-2 January see ***Rest. Au Moulin*** below – ☕ 58 – **19 rm** 460.

La Roseraie without rest, 32 r. Gare ✆ 03 88 96 63 44, Fax 03 88 96 64 95 – TV ☎ P. GB. ✻
☕ 35 – **15 rm** 250/300.

XXX **Relais de la Poste** M with rm, 21 r. Gén. de Gaulle ✆ 03 88 59 24 80 Fax 03 88 59 24 89, 🍴, – |‡| ▤ rest TV ☎ ♿ P. AE ⓓ GB
closed 21 July-3 August and 2 to 22 January – **Meals** *(closed Saturday lunch, Sunday dinner and Monday)* 175 (lunch), 225/395 and a la carte 290/410 ♁ – ☕ 50 – **19 rm** 300/550

XXX **A la Barrière** (Sutter), 3 rte Strasbourg ✆ 03 88 96 20 23, Fax 03 88 96 25 59, 🍴 – P. AE ⓓ GB JCB
✿ *closed 11 to 31 August, February Holidays, Tuesday dinner and Wednesday* – **Meals** (Sunday : booking essential) 150 (lunch)/250 and a la carte 280/360 ♁
Spec. Bouillon de chou-fleur et huîtres au caviar (September-March). Salade de choucroute "terre et mer". Lièvre à la royale (season). **Wines** Muscat d'Alsace, Riesling.

XXX **Zimmer,** 23 r. Héros ✆ 03 88 96 62 08, Fax 03 88 96 37 40, 🍴 – AE ⓓ GB
closed 15 July-5 August, 18 January-4 February, Sunday dinner and Monday – **Meals** 135/245 and a la carte 210/350 ♁.

XX **Rest. Au Moulin** - Hôtel Au Moulin, S : 1,5 km by D 468 ✆ 03 88 96 20 01 Fax 03 88 59 22 00, 🍴, « Floral garden » – ▤ P. AE ⓓ GB
closed 7 to 27 July, 31 December-15 January, and dinner Sunday and Bank Holidays – **Meals** 140/395 ♁.

XX **Les Semailles,** 10 r. Petit-Magmod ✆ 03 88 96 38 38, 🍽 – GB. ✗
closed 15 August-6 September, Saturday lunch, Sunday dinner and Monday – **Meals** 185.

XX **Au Soleil,** 1 quai Bateliers ✆ 03 88 96 20 29, Fax 03 88 68 08 58, 🍽 – P. AE GB
closed February Holidays and Thursday dinner except July-August – **Meals** 52 (lunch), 125/199 ♂.

Illhaeusern *68970 H.-Rhin* 62 ⑲ – *pop. 578 alt. 173.*
Strasbourg 60.

La Clairière M ⛰ without rest, rte Guémar ✆ 03 89 71 80 80, Fax 03 89 71 86 22, ⛱, ✂ – |‡| TV ☎ P. GB
closed January and February – ☕ 75 – **26 rm** 440/1000.

XXXX ✿✿ **Auberge de l'Ill** (Haeberlin), ✆ 03 89 71 89 00, Fax 03 89 71 82 83, « Elegant installation, on the banks of the River Ill, ⇐ floral gardens » – ▤ P. AE ⓓ GB
closed 1 February-9 March, Monday except lunch from 25 March-17 November and Tuesday – **Meals** (booking essential) 510 (lunch), 610/720 and a la carte 490/650
Spec. Salade de tripes aux fèves et au foie gras d'oie. Filets de bar à la mousseline de céleri et truffes de la Saint-Jean (June-August). Croustillant aux poires, glace à la chicorée confite. **Wines** Pinot blanc, Riesling.

H. des Berges M ⛰, ✆ 03 89 71 87 87, Fax 03 89 71 87 88, ⇐, « Resembling a tobacco shed in the Ried country », 🍽 – |‡| ▤ rm TV ☎ ♿ 🚗. AE ⓓ GB
closed February, Monday and Tuesday – **Meals** see ***Aub. de l'Ill*** – ☕ 130 – **7 rm** 1500/1750.

Lembach *67510 B.-Rhin* 57 ⑲ – *pop. 1 710 alt. 190.*
ℹ *Tourist Office rte Bitche ✆ 03 88 94 43 16, Fax 03 88 94 20 04.*
Strasbourg 55.

XXXX ✿✿ **Aub. Cheval Blanc** (Mischler), 4 rte Wissembourg ✆ 03 88 94 41 86, Fax 03 88 94 20 74, « Old coaching inn », 🍽 – ▤ P. AE GB
closed 7 to 25 July, 2 to 27 February, Monday and Tuesday – **Meals** 175/410 and a la carte 300/400
Spec. Farandole de quatre foies d'oie chauds. Lasagne de langoustines et crevettes, sabayon au traminer. Médaillons de dos de chevreuil à la moutarde de fruits rouges (25 May- 10 February). **Wines** Pinot blanc, Muscat d'Alsace.

Marlenheim *67520 B.-Rhin* 62 ⑨ – *pop. 2 956 alt. 195.*
Strasbourg 20.

XXXX ✿✿ **Le Cerf** (Husser) with rm, ✆ 03 88 87 73 73, Fax 03 88 87 68 08, 🍽 – TV ☎ P. AE ⓓ GB
closed Tuesday and Wednesday – **Meals** 250 b.i. (lunch), 295/500 and a la carte 260/370 – ☕ 65 – **15 rm** 300/650
Spec. Marbré de saumon fumé et anguille à l'aneth. Choucroute au cochon de lait rôti et foie gras fumé. Suprême de sandre au pinot noir. **Wines** Pinot noir, Riesling.

VALLEY OF THE LOIRE

Tours *37000 I.-et-L.* 64 ⑮ – *pop. 129 509 alt. 60.*
See : *Cathedral quarter★★ : Cathedral★★* CDY, *Fine Arts Museum★★* CDY, *Historial de Touraine★ (Château)* CY **M**[3], *The Psalette★* CY, – *Place Grégoire de Tours★* DY 46 – *Old Tours★★ : Place Plumereau★* ABY, *Hôtel Gouin★* BY, *rue Briçonnet★* AY **12** – *St-Julien quarter★ : Craft Guilds Museum★★ (Musée du Compagnonnage)* BY, *Beaune-Semblançay Garden★* BY **B** – *St-Cosme Priory★ W : 3 km* V – *Museum of military transport and trains★* V **M**[6] – *Meslay Tithe Barn★ (Grange de Meslay) NE : 10 km par ②.*
⛳18 *of Touraine ✆ 02 47 53 20 28 ; domaine de la Touche at Ballan-Miré : 14 km ;* ⛳18 *of Ardrée ✆ 02 47 56 77 38 : 14 km.*
✈ *of Tours-St-Symphorien : T.A.T ✆ 02 47 54 19 46, NE : 7 km.*
ℹ *Tourist Office 78 r. Bernard Palissy ✆ 02 47 70 37 37, Fax 02 47 61 14 22 – A.C. 4 pl. J. Jaurès ✆ 02 47 05 50 19.*
Paris 234 – Angers 109 – Bordeaux 346 – Chartres 140 – Clermont-Ferrand 335 – Limoges 220 – Le Mans 80 – Orléans 115 – Rennes 219 – St-Étienne 474.

Plans on following pages

✿✿ **Jean Bardet** M ⛰, 57 r. Groison ✉ 37100 ✆ 02 47 41 41 11, Fax 02 47 51 68 72, ⇐, « Flowered park, attractive kitchen garden », ⛱ – ▤ TV ☎ P – 🏛 30. AE ⓓ GB JCB
Meals *(closed Sunday dinner from 1 November-31 March and Monday except dinner from 1 April-31 October)* 250/750 and a la carte 550/650 – ☕ 120 – **16 rm** 750/1050, 5 suites
Spec. Terrine de foie gras de canard au poivre. Pintadeau fermier truffé. Vaporeux glacé au café. **Wines** Vouvray, Bourgueil.

TOURS

Bordeaux (R. de) .... CZ
Commerce (R. du) .... BY 22
Grammont (Av. de) .... CZ
Grand Passage .... CZ 50
Halles (Pl. des) .... AZ
Halles (R. des) .... BY

Marceau (R.) .... BYZ
Nationale (R.) .... BYZ
Scellerie (R. de la) .... BCY

Amandiers (R. des) ...... CY 4
Berthelot (R.) .... BCY 7
Bons Enfants (R. des) .... BY 8
Boyer (R. Léon) .... AZ 10
Briçonnet (R.) .... AY 13

Carmes (Pl. des) .... BY 1
Châteauneuf (Pl. de) ...... BY 1
Châteauneuf (R. de) ...... AY 1
Cœur-Navré
(Passage du) .... CY 2
Constantine (R. de) .... BY 2
Corneille (R.) .... CY 2
Courier (Rue Paul-Louis) ... BY 2
Courteline (R. G.) .... AY 2

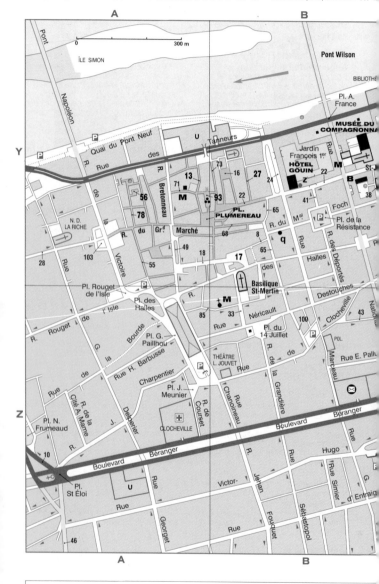

EUROPE on a single sheet Michelin Map no 970

gne (R. du) . . . . CY 29
scartes (R.) . . . . BZ 33
ve (R. de la) . . . . BZ 35
re (R. Jules) . . . . BY 38
illés (R. des) . . . . BY 41
nbetta (R.) . . . . BZ 43
audeau (R.) . . . . AZ 46
nd-Marché (Pl. du) . . . . AY 49
goire-de-Tours (Pl.) . . . . DY 52

Grosse-Tour (R. de la) . . . . . AY 55
Herbes (Carroi aux) . . . . . . AY 56
Lavoisier (R.) . . . . CY 60
Marceau (R.) . . . . DY 61
Merville (R. du Prés.) . . . . . BY 65
Meusnier (R. Gén.) . . . . DY 66
Monnaie (R. de la) . . . . BY 68
Mûrier (R. du) . . . . AY 71
Paix (R. de la) . . . . BY 73

Petit-Cupidon (R. du) . . . . DY 77
Petit-St-Martin (R. du) . . . . AY 78
Petites-Boucheries
(Pl. des) . . . . DY 80
Racine (R.) . . . . DY 84
Rapin (R.) . . . . AZ 85
St-Pierre-le-Puellier (Pl.) . . ABY 93
Sully (R. de) . . . . BZ 100
Victoire (Pl. de la) . . . . AY 103

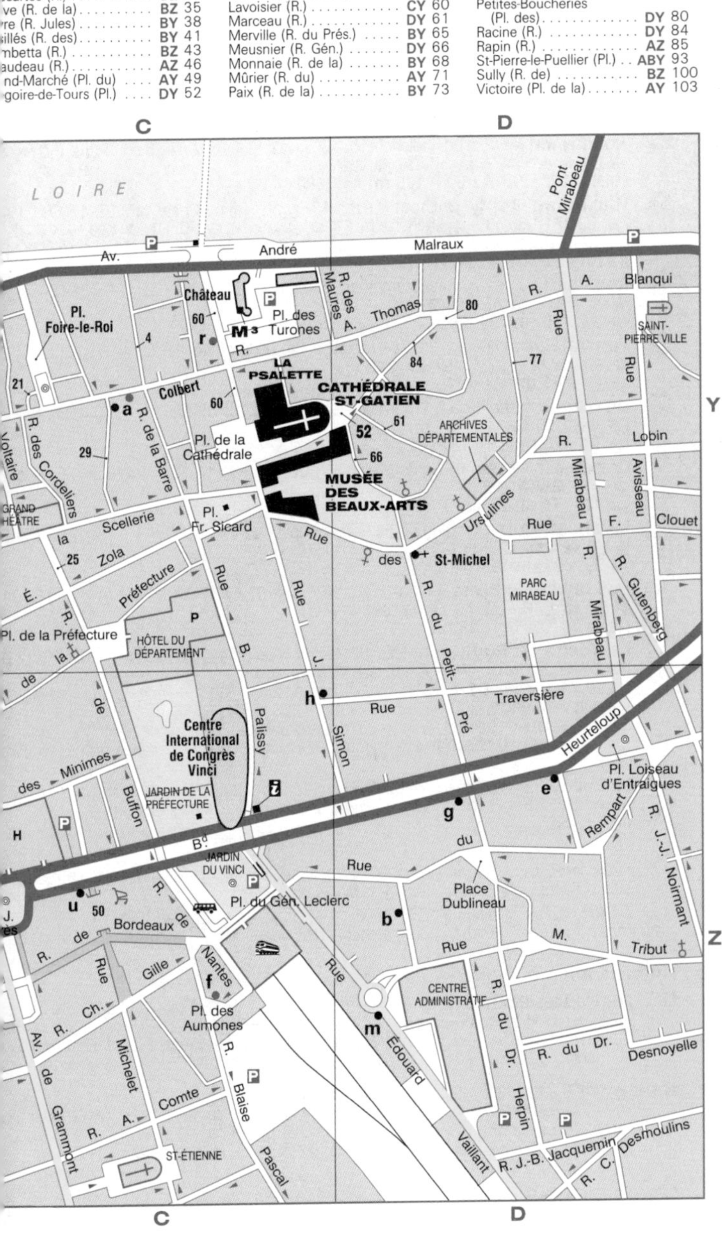

Don't get lost, use Michelin Maps which are updated annually.

Univers and rest. La Touraine M, 5 bd Heurteloup 02 47 05 37 Fax 02 47 61 51 80, « Murals depicting famous past visitors » – rm – 120. AE GB CZ
Meals 130/170 – 65 – **77 rm** 650/780, 8 suites.

Mercure M, 4 pl. Thiers 02 47 05 50 05, Fax 02 47 20 22 07 – rm – 70. AE GB
Meals 125/245 b.i. – 55 – **120 rm** 395/490.

Holiday Inn M, 15 r. Ed. Vaillant 02 47 31 12 12, Fax 02 47 38 53 35, – – 50. AE GB DZ
Meals 120/250 – 60 – **105 rm** 440/680.

Harmonie M without rest, 15 r. F. Joliot-Curie 02 47 66 01 Fax 02 47 61 66 38 – kitchenette – 40. AE GB JCB DZ
closed 20 December-5 January and weekends from 1 November to 31 March – 5
48 rm 450/500, 6 suites.

Royal without rest, 65 av. Grammont 02 47 64 71 78, Fax 02 47 05 84 62 – – 35. AE GB
37 – **50 rm** 295/350.

Central H. without rest, 21 r. Berthelot 02 47 05 46 44, Fax 02 47 66 10 26 – – 40. AE GB JCB CY
45 – **41 rm** 400/650.

du Manoir without rest, 2 r. Traversière 02 47 05 37 37, Fax 02 47 05 16 00 – . AE GB CZ
30 – **20 rm** 240/320.

Criden without rest, 65 bd Heurteloup 02 47 20 81 14, Fax 02 47 05 61 65 – . AE GB DZ
40 – **33 rm** 265/315.

Mirabeau without rest, 89 bis bd Heurteloup 02 47 05 24 60, Fax 02 47 05 31 0 . AE GB JCB DZ
39 – **25 rm** 198/310.

Holiday Inn Express M, 247 r. Giraudeau 02 47 37 00 36, Fax 02 47 38 50 9 – 40. AE GB JCB
Meals 75/100 b.i. – **48 rm** 370/390.

La Roche Le Roy (Couturier), 55 rte St-Avertin 37200 02 47 27 22 Fax 02 47 28 08 39, – . AE GB
closed 26 July-19 August, February Holidays, Saturday lunch, Sunday dinner and Mon – **Meals** 160 (lunch), 200/350 and a la carte 260/420
Spec. Matelote d'anguilles au vieux chinon et pruneaux. Fricassée de géline aux écreviss (season). Tarte au chocolat aux framboises et glace au lait d'amande. **Wines** Vouvr Chinon.

La Ruche, 105 r. Colbert 02 47 66 69 83, Fax 02 47 20 41 76 – . GB CY
closed Christmas Holidays, Sunday dinner and Monday – **Meals** 90/160 .

Les Tuffeaux, 21 r. Lavoisier 02 47 47 19 89 – . GB CY
closed Monday lunch and Sunday – **Meals** 110/200.

L'Arc-en-Ciel, 2 pl. Aumônes 02 47 05 48 88, Fax 02 47 66 94 05 – AE GB CZ
closed Sunday dinner and Monday – **Meals** 88/290 b.i..

Le Rif, 12 av. Maginot 37100 02 47 51 12 44 – AE GB
closed 25 July-25 August, Sunday dinner and Monday – **Meals** North-African rest. a la car 120/170.

at Rochecorbon *NE : 6 km by N 152 – alt. 58 – 37210 :*

Les Hautes Roches M, 86 quai Loire 02 47 52 88 88, Fax 02 47 52 81 30, <, « Former troglodyte dwelling », , – . AE GB
closed mid January-mid March – **Meals** *(closed Monday lunch except Bank Holida* 150 (lunch), 270/355 – 85 – **12 rm** 995/1200, 3 suites.

Amboise *37400 I.-et-L. 64 ⑯ – pop. 10982 alt. 60.*

See : *Château★★ (son et lumière show) : <★★ from the terrace, <★★ from the Minim tower – Clos-Lucé★ – Chanteloup Pagoda★ SW : 3 km par ④ by D431.*

Tourist Office quai Gén.-de-Gaulle 02 47 57 09 28, Fax 02 47 57 14 35.

Tours 26.

Le Choiseul, 36 quai Ch. Guinot 02 47 30 45 45, Fax 02 47 30 46 10, <, « Elegant installation, and flowered garden » – – 80. AE JCB
closed 30 November-20 January – **Meals** 220 b.i. (lunch), 270/440 and a la carte 290/4 – 130 – **28 rm** 600/1300
Spec. Vichyssoise d'asperges vertes et huîtres de Marennes. Blanc de géline farci de giroll et moules bouchot. Crumble de framboises acidulées à la fleur d'hibiscus. **Wines** Tourai

acieux *41250 L.-et-Ch. 64 ⑱ – pop. 1 157 alt. 70.*
Tours 82.

XXX ✿✿ **Bernard Robin,** ✆ 02 54 46 41 22, Fax 02 54 46 03 69, ≤, « Garden » – AE GB
closed 20 December-20 January, Tuesday dinner and Wednesday except July-August –
Meals (booking essential) 160/545 and a la carte 350/450
Spec. Salade de pigeon et homard, vinaigrette de légumes confits. Queue de bœuf en hachis parmentier. Gibier (October-December). **Wines** Cour-Cheverny, Bourgueil.

zain *41150 L.-et-Ch. 64 ⑯ – pop. 3 080 alt. 69.*
Tours 47.

✿✿ **Domaine des Hauts de Loire** M ⛰, NW : 3 km by D 1 and private lane ✆ 02 54 20 72 57, Fax 02 54 20 77 32, ≤, « Elegant hunting lodge in a park », ⛱, ✂ – TV ☎ ♿ P – 🏛 70. AE ⓓ GB. ⚘
closed 1 December-5 February – **Meals** *(closed Tuesday lunch and Monday in February and March)* 290/375 and a la carte 360/560 – ☕ 85 – **25 rm** 650/1400, 10 suites
Spec. Salade d'anguille croustillante à la vinaigrette d'échalotes. Filet de bœuf poché au vin de Montlouis. Pigeonneau du Vendômois au jus de presse. **Wines** Sauvignon, Touraine-Mesland.

morantin-Lanthenay *41200 L.-et-Ch. 64 ⑱ – pop. 17 865 alt. 93.*
ℹ Tourist Office pl. Paix ✆ 02 54 76 43 89, Fax 02 54 76 96 24.
Tours 91.

✿✿ **Gd H. Lion d'Or** M, 69 r. Clemenceau ✆ 02 54 94 15 15, Fax 02 54 88 24 87, ≤, « Tasteful decor, floral patio » – ▮ ▤ rest TV ☎ ♿ P – 🏛 50. AE ⓓ GB
closed mid February-late March – **Meals** (booking essential) 420/620 and a la carte 490/610 – ☕ 110 – **13 rm** 600/2000, 3 suites
Spec. Cuisses de grenouilles à la rocambole. Langoustines bretonnes rôties à la poudre d'épices douces. Brioche caramélisée au sorbet d'angélique (May-October). **Wines** Pouilly Fumé, Bourgueil. bet d'angélique (May-October). **Wines** Pouilly Fumé, Bourgueil.

Germany

Deutschland

BERLIN – COLOGNE – DRESDEN
DÜSSELDORF – FRANKFURT ON MAIN
HAMBURG – HANOVER – LEIPZIG
MUNICH – STUTTGART

PRACTICAL INFORMATION

LOCAL CURRENCY

Deutsche Mark: *100 DEM = 64.37 USD ($) (Jan. 97)*

TOURIST INFORMATION

Deutsche Zentrale für Tourismus (DZT):
Beethovenstr. 69, 60325 Frankfurt, ✆ 069/7 57 20, Fax 069/75 19 03

Hotel booking service:
Allgemeine Deutsche Zimmerreservierung (ADZ)
Corneliusstr. 34, 60325 Frankfurt, ✆ 069/74 07 67
Fax 069/75 10 56

National Holiday in Germany: *3 Octobre.*

AIRLINES

DEUTSCHE LUFTHANSA AG: *Wilhelmshöher Allee 254, 34119 Kassel, ✆ 01803/803803, Fax 0561/9933115*

AIR CANADA: *60311 Frankfurt, Friedensstr. 7, ✆ 069/27 11 51 11, Fax 27 11 51 12*

AIR FRANCE: *60311 Frankfurt, Friedensstr. 11, ✆ 0180/5 36 03 70, Fax 069/23 05 81*

AMERICAN AIRLINES: *60329 Frankfurt, Wiesenhüttenplatz 26, ✆ 01803/242324, Fax 069/66 58 30 95*

BRITISH AIRWAYS: *28320 Bremen, Sonneberger Str. 20, ✆ 0180/340 340, Fax 0421/55 75189*

JAPAN AIRLINES: *60311 Frankfurt, Roßmarkt 15, ✆ 0130/6878, Fax 069/29 57 84*

SABENA: *60329 Frankfurt, Am Hauptbahnhof 6, ✆ 0180/52 58 520, Fax 0180/52 21 591*

SAS: *60528 Frankfurt, Saonestr. 3, ✆ 069/66 55 81 11, Fax 66 55 81 23*

TWA: *60486 Frankfurt, Hamburger Allee 2, ✆ 069/79 50 42 00, Fax 77 41 23*

FOREIGN EXCHANGE

Is possible in banks, savings banks and at exchange offices.
Hours of opening from Monday to Friday 8.30am to 12.30pm and 2.30pm to 4pm except Thursday 2.30pm to 6pm.

SHOPPING

In the index of street names, those printed in red are where the principal shops are found.

BREAKDOWN SERVICE

ADAC: *for the addresses see text of the towns mentioned*

AvD: *Lyoner Str. 16, 60528 Frankfurt-Niederrad, ✆ 069/6 60 60, Fax 069/660 62 10*
In Germany the ADAC (emergency number 01802/22 22 22), and the AvD (emergency number 0130/99 09), make a special point of assisting foreign motorists. They have motor patrols covering main roads.

TIPPING

In Germany, prices include service and taxes. You may choose to leave a tip if you wish but there is no obligation to do so.

SPEED LIMITS

The speed limit, generally, in built up areas is 50 km/h - 31 mph and on all other roads it is 100 km/h - 62mph. On motorways and dual carriageways, the recommended speed limit is 130 km/h - 80 mph.

SEAT BELTS

The wearing of seat belts is compulsory for drivers and passengers.

BERLIN

L Berlin 987 ⑱ ⑲, 984 ⑮ ⑯, 416, 418 J 23 – *Pop. 3 500 000 – alt. 40 m. – ✪ 30.*

Frankfurt/Oder 105 – Hamburg 289 – Hannover 288 – Leipzig 183 – Rostock 222.

Berlin Tourist-Information, Europa-Center (Budapester Straße), ✉ 10787 ✆ 25 00 25, Fax 25 00 24 24.
ADAC, Berlin-Wilmersdorf, Bundesallee 29 ✉ 10717, ✆ 8 68 60, Fax 86 16 025.

18 Berlin-Wannsee, Am Stölpchenweg, ✆ 8 05 50 75 – 9 Kladower Damm 182, ✆ 365 76 60.
Tegel, ✆ 4 10 11 – Schönefeld (S: 25 km), 6 09 10.
Berlin – Wannsee, Nibelnngenstraße.
Exhibition Grounds (Messegelände), ✆ 3 03 80, Fax 30 38 23 25.

MUSEUMS, GALLERIES

Pergamon Museum★★★ PY – *Old National Gallery★ (Alte Nationalgalerie)* PY **M¹** – *Bode-Museum★★* PY **M²** – *Altes Museum★* PY **M³** – *Museum of Decorative Arts★ (Kunstgewerbemuseum)* NZ **M⁴** – *New National Gallery★ (Neue Nationalgalerie)* NZ **M⁵** – *Schloß Charlottenburg★★ (Equestrian Statue of the Great Elector★★, Historical Rooms★, Porcelain Room★★) – National Gallery★★ White Hall★ (Nationalgalerie, Weißer Saal) – Golden Gallery★★ (Goldene Galerie)* EY – *Antique Museum★ (Antikenmuseum) (Ancient Treasure★★★)* EY **M⁶** – *Egyptian Museum★ (Ägyptisches Museum) (Bust of Queen Nefrititi★★)* EY **M⁶** – *Dahlem Museums★★★ (Museum Dahlem) (Painting Gallery★★, Sculpture Department★★, Drawing and Prints Department★, Ethnographic Museum★★) by Rheinbabenallee* EZ – *Museum of Transport and Technology★ (Museum für Verkehr und Technik)* GZ **M⁸** – *Käthe-Kollwitz-Museum★* LXY **M⁹** – *Berlin Museum★* GY – *Museum of Decorative Arts★ (at Schloß Köpenick) (Kunstgewerbemuseum) by Stralauer Allee* HY.

HISTORIC BUILDINGS AND MONUMENTS, STREETS, SQUARES

Brandenburg Gate★★ (Brandenburger Tor) NZ – *Unter den Linden★* NPZ – *Gendarmenmarkt★* PZ – *State Opera House★ (Deutsche Staatsoper)* PZ – *Neue Wache★* PY – *Arsenal★★ (Zeughaus)* PY – *Nikolaiviertel★* RZ – *Philharmonie★★★* NZ – *Kurfürstendamm★* JLY – *Martin-Gropius-Building★* NZ – *Olympic Stadium★ (Olympia Stadion) by Kaiserdamm* EY – *Nikolai Church★ (Nikolaikirche)* RZ.

PARKS, GARDENS, LAKES

Zoological Park★★ (Zoologischer Garten) MX – *Castle Park of Charlottenburg★ (Schloßpark Charlottenburg) (at Belvedere Historical Porcelain Exhibition★)* EY – *Botanical Gardens★★ (Botanischer Garten) by Rheinbabenallee* EZ – *Grunewald Forest★ (at Grunewald Lake : Hunting Lodge★) by Rheinbabenallee* EZ – *Havel★ and Peacook Island★ by Clay-Allee* EZ – *Wannsee★★ by Clay-Allee* EZ.

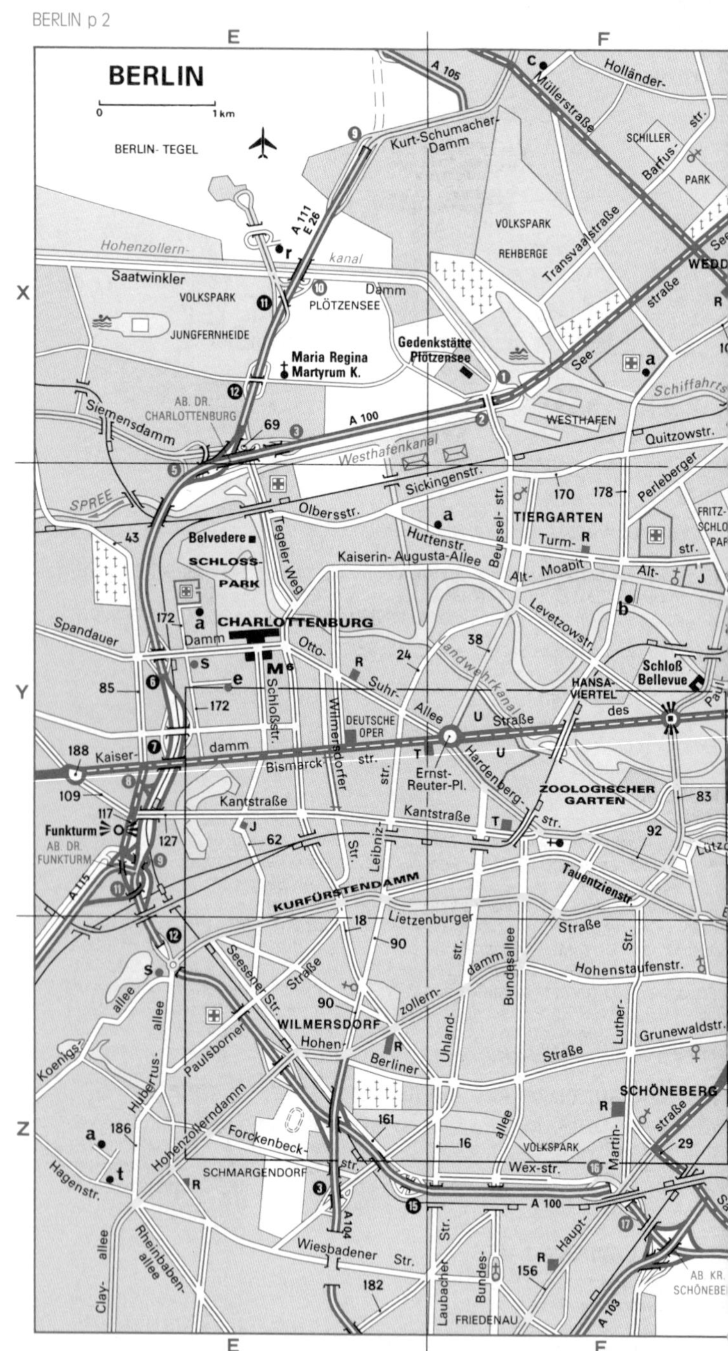

BERLIN
0
1 km
BERLIN- TEGEL
E
F
X
Y
Z
Hohenzollern-
kanal
Saatwinkler
Damm
VOLKSPARK
JUNGFERNHEIDE
PLÖTZENSEE
Maria Regina
Martyrum K.
Gedenkstätte
Plötzensee
Kurt-Schumacher-
Damm
Müllerstraße
Holländer-
SCHILLER
PARK
Barfus-
str.
VOLKSPARK
REHBERGE
Transvaalstraße
See-
straße
WEDD
Schiffahrts
WESTHAFEN
Quitzowstr.
Westhafenkanal
A 100
A 105
A 111
E 26
Siemensdamm
AB. DR.
CHARLOTTENBURG
SPREE
Sickingenstr.
Olbersstr.
Perleberger
TIERGARTEN
Beussel-
str.
Turm-
str.
Huttenstr.
Kaiserin-Augusta-Allee
Alt-
Moabit
Belvedere
SCHLOSS-
PARK
Tegeler Weg
Levetzowstr.
CHARLOTTENBURG
Spandauer
Damm
Otto-
Suhr-
Allee
Landwehrkanal
Schloß
Bellevue
HANSA-
VIERTEL
des
Straße
Schloßstr.
DEUTSCHE
OPER
Wilmersdorfer
str.
Kaiser-
damm
Bismarck-
Ernst-
Reuter-Pl.
Hardenberg-
str.
ZOOLOGISCHER
GARTEN
Kantstraße
Funkturm
AB. DR.
FUNKTURM
Leibniz-
Str.
Tauentzienstr.
KURFÜRSTENDAMM
Lietzenburger
Straße
Seesener
Str.
Hohenstaufenstr.
Uhland-
Bundesallee
WILMERSDORF
Hohen-
zollern-
damm
Berliner
Grunewaldstr.
Luther-
Str.
SCHÖNEBERG
Martin-
Luther-
straße
VOLKSPARK
Wex-str.
Koenigs-
allee
Hubertus-
allee
Paulsborner
Hohenzollerndamm
Forckenbeck-
str.
SCHMARGENDORF
Hagenstr.
A 104
A 115
A 103
Wiesbadener
Str.
Clay-
allee
Rheinbaben-
allee
Laubacher
Str.
Bundes-
allee
FRIEDENAU
Haupt-
str.
AB. KR.
SCHÖNEBE
FRITZ-
SCHLO
PAR

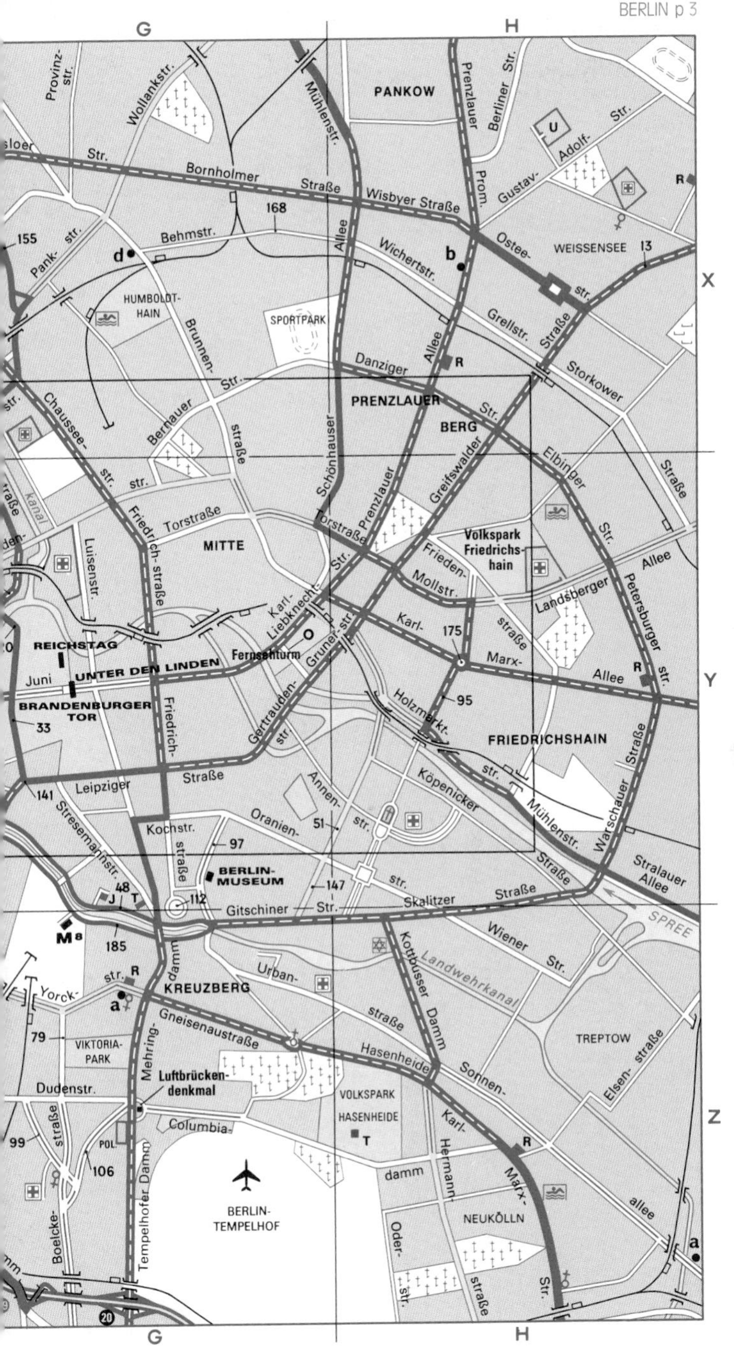
G
H
X
Y
Z
PANKOW
Provinz-str.
Wollankstr.
Mühlenstr.
Prenzlauer Prom.
Berliner Str.
Gustav-Adolf-Str.
Bornholmer Straße
Wisbyer Straße
Behmstr.
Pankstr.
168
155
Schönhauser Allee
Wichertstr.
Ostee-str.
WEISSENSEE
13
HUMBOLDT-HAIN
SPORTPARK
Brunnen-straße
Grellstr.
Storkower Straße
Danziger Str.
PRENZLAUER BERG
Bernauer Str.
Chaussee-str.
Greifswalder Straße
Elbinger Str.
Prenzlauer Allee
Torstraße
MITTE
Luisenstr.
Friedrich-straße
Volkspark Friedrichshain
Landsberger Allee
Petersburger str.
Mollstr.
Friedenstraße
Karl-Liebknecht-Str.
Karl-Marx-Allee
175
REICHSTAG
Fernsehturm
Gruner-str.
UNTER DEN LINDEN
Juni
BRANDENBURGER TOR
33
Gertrauden-str.
Holzmarkt-str.
95
FRIEDRICHSHAIN
Warschauer Straße
Leipziger Straße
141
Stresemannstr.
Köpenicker Straße
Mühlenstr.
Kochstr.
Oranien-str.
Annen-str.
51
97
BERLIN-MUSEUM
147
Stralauer Allee
48
112
Gitschiner Str.
Skalitzer Straße
SPREE
M8
185
Wiener Str.
Kottbusser Damm
Landwehrkanal
Mehringdamm
Yorck-str.
KREUZBERG
Urban-straße
Gneisenaustraße
79
VIKTORIA-PARK
Hasenheide
Sonnen-allee
TREPTOW
Elsen-straße
Dudenstr.
Luftbrücken-denkmal
VOLKSPARK HASENHEIDE
Columbia-damm
99
106
Karl-Marx-Str.
Hermann-straße
BERLIN-TEMPELHOF
NEUKÖLLN
Tempelhofer Damm
Boelcke-straße
Oder-str.
20

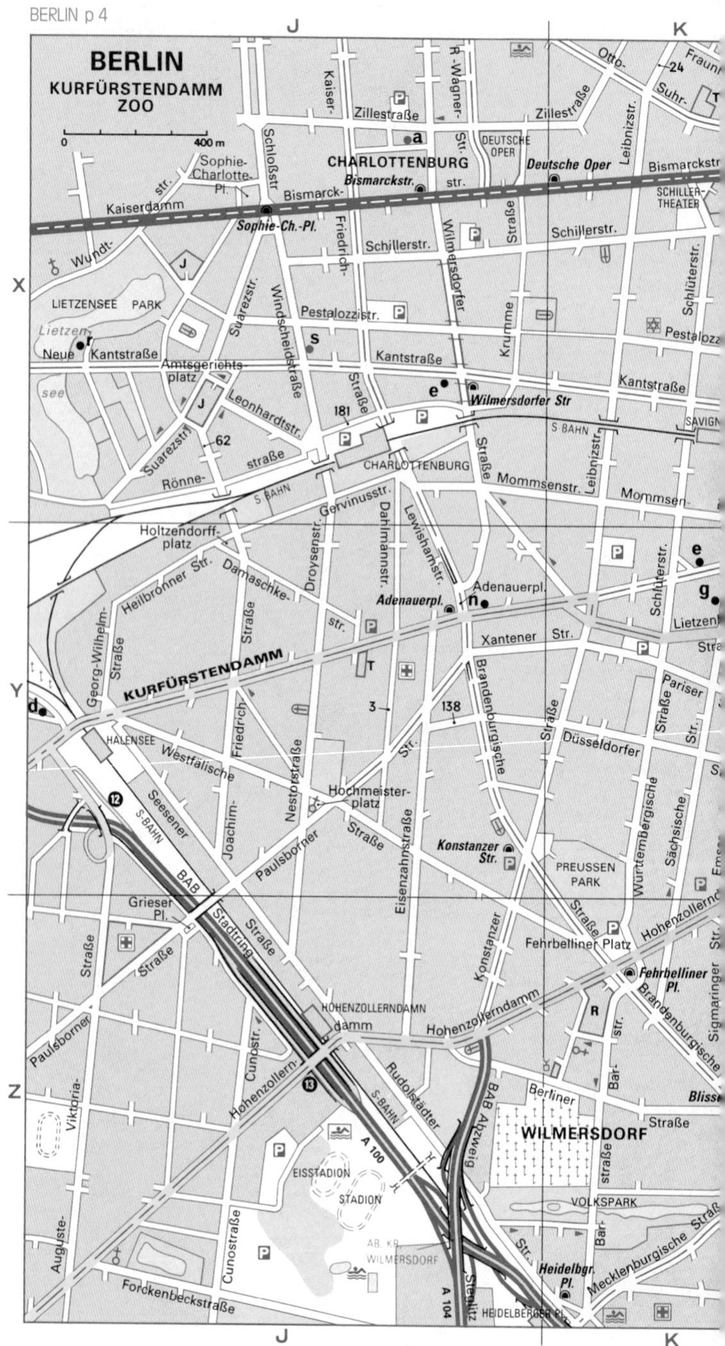
BERLIN
KURFÜRSTENDAMM
ZOO
0
400 m
J
K
X
Y
Z
CHARLOTTENBURG
Bismarckstr.
Deutsche Oper
DEUTSCHE OPER
SCHILLER-THEATER
Sophie-Ch.-Pl.
Sophie-Charlotte-Pl.
Kaiserdamm
Zillestraße
Schillerstr.
Pestalozzistr.
Kantstraße
Wilmersdorfer Str
S. BAHN
CHARLOTTENBURG
Mommsenstr.
LIETZENSEE PARK
Amtsgerichtsplatz
Leonhardtstr.
Rönne-straße
Holtzendorffplatz
Heilbronner Str.
Damaschke-str.
Gervinusstr.
Dahlmannstr.
Lewishamstr.
Adenauerpl.
Xantener Str.
KURFÜRSTENDAMM
HALENSEE
Westfälische
Hochmeister-platz
Düsseldorfer
Paulsborner
Konstanzer Str.
PREUSSEN PARK
Fehrbelliner Platz
Fehrbelliner Pl.
Hohenzollerndamm
HOHENZOLLERNDAMM
BAB Stadtring
Grieser Pl.
Rudolstädter
BAB Abzweig
WILMERSDORF
Berliner Straße
VOLKSPARK
EISSTADION
STADION
A 100
A 104
AB. KR. WILMERSDORF
Heidelbgr. Pl.
HEIDELBERGER PL.
Mecklenburgische Straße
Forckenbeckstraße
Cunostraße
Viktoria-
Auguste-
Paulsborner
Brandenburgische
Württembergische
Sächsische
Schlüterstr.
Leibnizstr.
Blissestr.

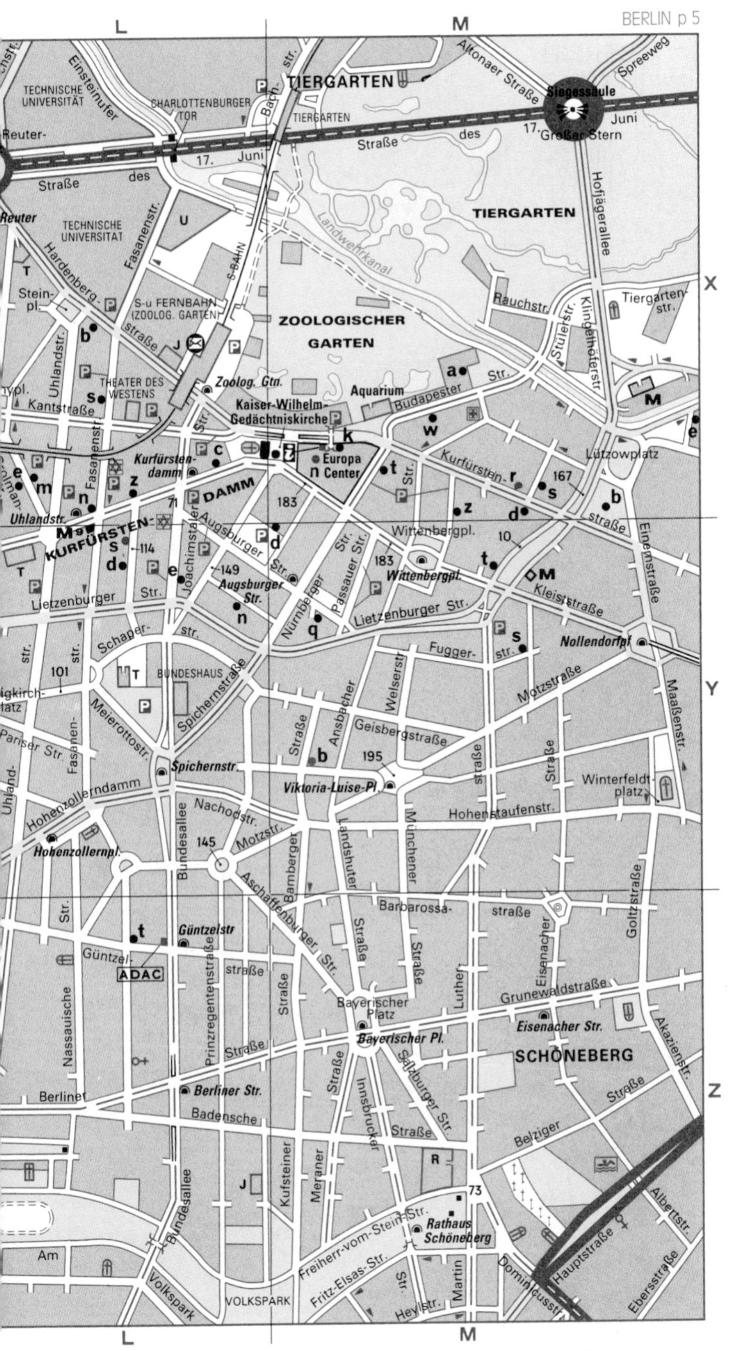
TIERGARTEN
Siegessäule
Großer Stern
TECHNISCHE UNIVERSITÄT
CHARLOTTENBURGER TOR
ZOOLOGISCHER GARTEN
Aquarium
Kaiser-Wilhelm-Gedächtniskirche
Europa Center
KURFÜRSTENDAMM
Zoolog. Gtn.
Kurfürstendamm
Uhlandstr.
Wittenbergpl.
Augsburger Str.
Nollendorfpl.
Spichernstr.
Viktoria-Luise-Pl.
Hohenzollernpl.
Güntzelstr
ADAC
Bayerischer Platz
Bayerischer Pl.
Eisenacher Str.
SCHÖNEBERG
Berliner Str.
Rathaus Schöneberg
VOLKSPARK
BUNDESHAUS
THEATER DES WESTENS
Lützowplatz
Winterfeldtplatz
Straße des 17. Juni
Hardenbergstraße
Kantstraße
Budapester Str.
Kurfürstenstraße
Lietzenburger Str.
Motzstraße
Hohenstaufenstr.
Grunewaldstraße
Barbarossastraße
Bundesallee
Hauptstraße
Landwehrkanal
L
M
X
Y
Z

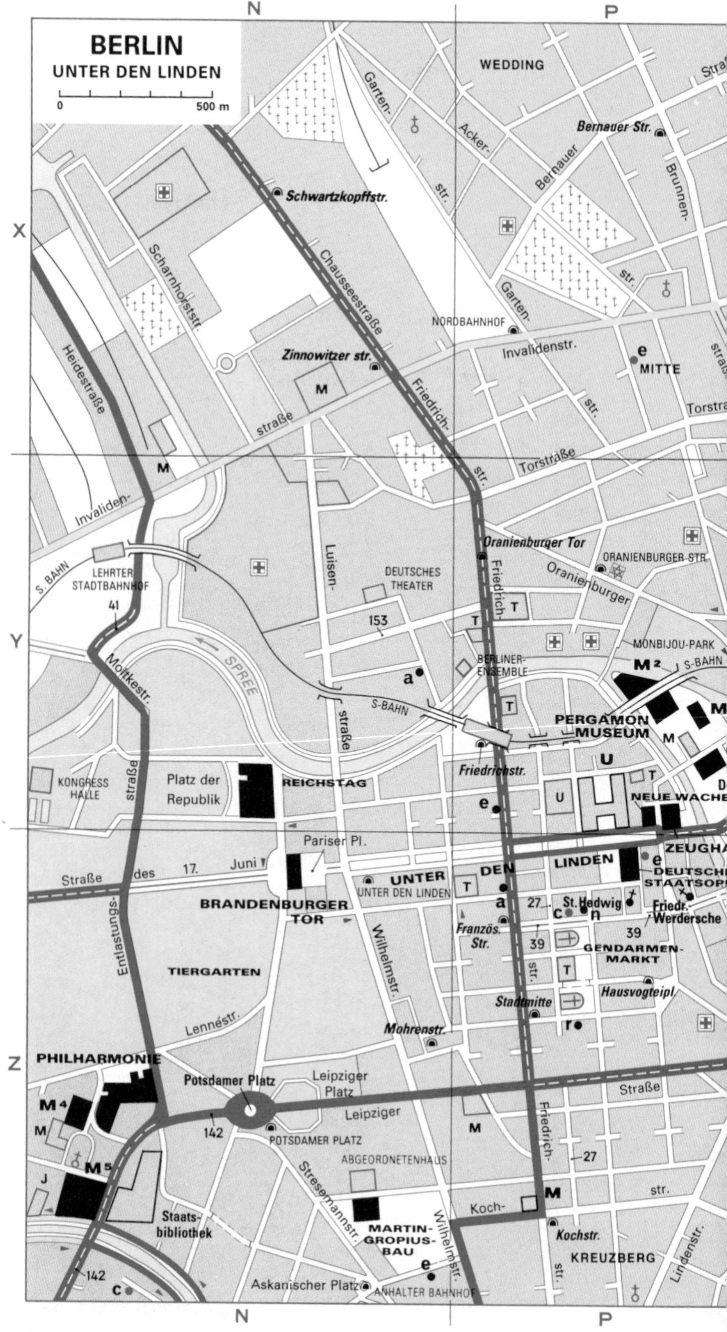

BERLIN
UNTER DEN LINDEN
0
500 m
N
P
X
Y
Z
WEDDING
Bernauer Str.
Brunnen-
Acker-
str.
Garten-
Bernauer
Schwartzkopffstr.
Chausseestraße
Scharnhorststr.
Heidestraße
NORDBAHNHOF
Garten-
Invalidenstr.
MITTE
Torstraße
Zinnowitzer str.
Friedrich-
straße
Invaliden-
LEHRTER STADTBAHNHOF
S. BAHN
41
Moltkestr.
SPREE
Luisen-
straße
DEUTSCHES THEATER
153
Oranienburger Tor
Friedrich-
ORANIENBURGER STR.
Oranienburger
MONBIJOU-PARK
S-BAHN
BERLINER-ENSEMBLE
S-BAHN
PERGAMON MUSEUM
Friedrichstr.
KONGRESS HALLE
Platz der Republik
REICHSTAG
NEUE WACHE
ZEUGHA
Pariser Pl.
Straße des 17. Juni
UNTER DEN LINDEN
UNTER DEN LINDEN
BRANDENBURGER TOR
DEUTSCHE STAATSOP
St. Hedwig
Friedr.-Werdersche
27
39
39
Französ. Str.
GENDARMEN-MARKT
Hausvogteipl.
Stadtmitte
Entlastungs-
straße
TIERGARTEN
Wilhelmstr.
Lennéstr.
Mohrenstr.
PHILHARMONIE
Potsdamer Platz
Leipziger Platz
Leipziger
Straße
M4
M5
142
POTSDAMER PLATZ
ABGEORDNETENHAUS
Stresemannstr.
Friedrich-
27
str.
Koch-
Kochstr.
Staats-bibliothek
MARTIN-GROPIUS-BAU
Wilhelmstr.
KREUZBERG
Lindenstr.
142
Askanischer Platz
ANHALTER BAHNHOF

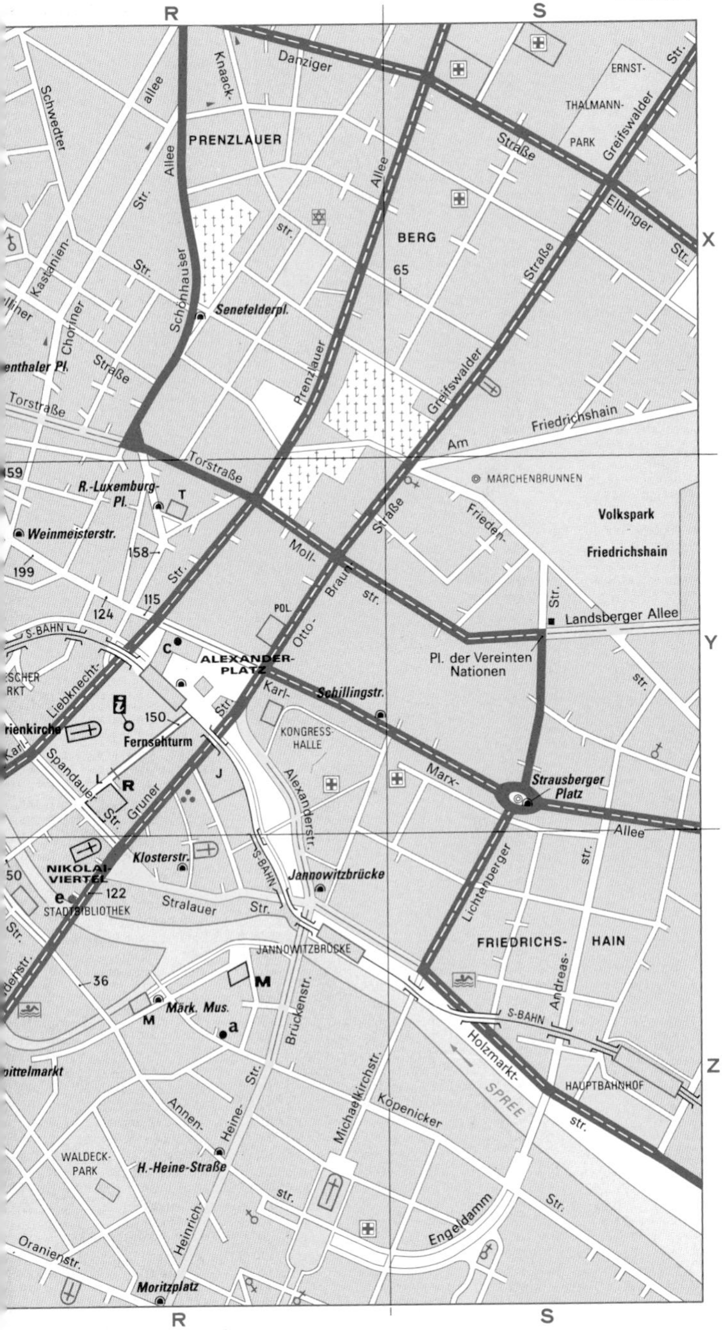

R S

PRENZLAUER
BERG
Danziger
Knaack-
Schwedter
allee
Schönhauser
Allee
Str.
Kastanien-
Choriner
Straße
Senefelderpl.
Prenzlauer
Allee
str.
65
ERNST-
THÄLMANN-
PARK
Greifswalder
Straße
Elbinger
Str.
X
Greifswalder
Straße
Am Friedrichshain
Torstraße
R.-Luxemburg-
Pl.
T
Weinmeisterstr.
158
199
115
124
Str.
Torstraße
Moll-
Otto-
Braun-
str.
Straße
MÄRCHENBRUNNEN
Frieden-
Volkspark
Friedrichshain
Str.
Landsberger Allee
Pl. der Vereinten
Nationen
Y
POL.
S-BAHN
C
ALEXANDER-
PLATZ
Liebknecht-
Karl-
Schillingstr.
str.
150
Fernsehturm
KONGRESS-
HALLE
Alexanderstr.
Marx-
Strausberger
Platz
Allee
Spandauer
Str.
Gruner
Str.
L
R
J
NIKOLAI-
VIERTEL
Klosterstr.
S-BAHN
Jannowitzbrücke
Lichtenberger
str.
50
122
STADTBIBLIOTHEK
Stralauer
Str.
JANNOWITZBRÜCKE
FRIEDRICHS-
HAIN
Andreas-
36
M
Märk. Mus.
M
a
Brückenstr.
S-BAHN
Holzmarkt-
str.
SPREE
HAUPTBAHNHOF
Z
Str.
Annen-
Heine-
Michaelkirchstr.
Köpenicker
WALDECK-
PARK
H.-Heine-Straße
str.
Heinrich
Engeldamm
Str.
Oranienstr.
Moritzplatz

R S

Karl-Marx-Straße . . . . . p 3 **HZ**
Kurfürstendamm . . . . p 4 **JY**
Rheinstraße . . . . p 2 **FZ** 156
Tauentzienstraße . . . . p 5 **MX** 183
Wilmersdorfer Str. . . . p 4 **JX**

Ackerstraße . . . . p 6 **PX**
Adenauerplatz . . . . . . p 4 **JY**
Akazienstraße . . . . p 5 **MZ**
Albertstraße . . . . p 5 **MZ**
Albrecht-Achilles-Straße . . . . p 4 **JY** 3
Alexanderplatz . . . . . . p 7 **RY**
Alexanderstraße . . . . . p 7 **SY**
Alt-Moabit . . . . p 2 **FY**
Altonaer Straße . . . . . p 5 **MX**
Am Friedrichshain . . . p 7 **SX**
Am Volkspark . . . . p 5 **LZ**
Amtsgerichtsplatz . . . . p 4 **JX**
An der Urania . . . . . . p 5 **MY** 10
Andreasstraße . . . . . . p 7 **SZ**
Annenstraße . . . . p 7 **RZ**
Ansbacher Straße . . . p 5 **MY**
Aschaffenburger Straße . . . . p 5 **MZ**
Askanischer Platz . . . . p 6 **NZ**
Augsburger Straße . . . p 5 **LY**
Auguste-Viktoria-Straße . . . . p 4 **JZ**
Bachstraße . . . . p 5 **MX**
Badensche Straße . . . p 5 **LZ**
Bamberger Straße . . . p 5 **MY**
Barbarossastraße . . . . p 5 **MZ**
Barfußstraße . . . . p 2 **FX**
Barstraße . . . . p 4 **KZ**
Bayerischer Platz . . . . p 5 **MZ**
Behmstraße . . . . p 3 **GX**
Belziger Straße . . . . . . p 5 **MZ**
Berliner Allee . . . . p 3 **HX** 13
Berliner Straße . . . . . . p 5 **LZ**
Berliner Straße (PANKOW) . . . . p 3 **HX**
Bernauer Straße (WEDDING) . . . . . . p 6 **PX**
Beusselstraße . . . . p 2 **FY**
Bismarckstraße . . . . . . p 4 **JX**
Bleibtreustraße . . . . . . p 4 **KX**
Blissestraße . . . . p 2 **FZ** 16
Boelckestraße . . . . p 3 **GZ**
Bornholmer Straße . . . p 3 **GX**
Brandenburgische Straße . . . . p 2 **EZ** 18
Breite Straße . . . . p 7 **RZ**
Breitscheidstr. . . . . p 7 **SX**
Brückenstraße . . . . . . p 7 **RZ**
Brunnenstraße . . . . . . p 6 **PX**
Budapester Straße . . . p 5 **MX**
Bülowstraße . . . . p 2 **FZ**
Bundesallee . . . . p 5 **LY**
Cauerstraße . . . . p 4 **KX** 24
Charlottenstraße . . . . . p 6 **PZ** 27
Chausseestraße . . . . . p 6 **NX**
Choriner Str. . . . . p 7 **RX**
Clayallee . . . . p 2 **EZ**
Columbiadamm . . . . . p 3 **GZ**
Cunostraße . . . . p 4 **JZ**
Dahlmannstraße . . . . . p 4 **JY**
Damaschkestraße . . . . p 4 **JY**
Danziger Str. . . . . p 7 **RSX**
Dominicusstraße . . . . p 2 **FZ** 29
Droysenstraße . . . . . . p 4 **JY**
Dudenstraße . . . . p 3 **GZ**
Düsseldorfer Str. . . . . p 4 **KY**
Einemstraße . . . . p 5 **MY**
Einsteinufer . . . . p 5 **LX**
Eisenacher Straße . . . p 5 **MZ**
Eisenzahnstraße . . . . . p 4 **JY**

Elbinger Str. . . . . p 3 **HY**
Elsenstraße . . . . p 3 **HZ**
Emser Platz . . . . p 4 **KZ**
Emser Straße . . . . p 4 **KY**
Engeldamm . . . . p 7 **SZ**
Entlastungsstraße . . . . . p 3 **GY** 33
Ernst-Reuter-Platz . . . . . p 5 **LX**
Fasanenstraße . . . . p 5 **LX**
Fehrbelliner Platz . . . . . p 4 **KZ**
Fehrbelliner Straße . . . p 7 **RX**
Fischerinsel . . . . p 7 **RZ** 36
Forckenbecktraße . . . . p 4 **JZ**
Franklinstraße . . . . p 2 **FY** 38
Französische Straße . . p 6 **PZ** 39
Fraunhoferstraße . . . . . p 4 **KX**
Freiherr-vom-Stein-Straße . . . . p 5 **MZ**
Friedenstraße . . . . p 7 **SY**
Friedrich-List-Ufer . . . . . p 3 **GY** 41
Friedrichstraße . . . . p 6 **PY**
Fritz-Elsas-Straße . . . . . p 5 **MZ**
Fürstenbrunner Weg . . . . p 2 **EY** 43
Fuggerstraße . . . . p 5 **MY**
Gartenstraße . . . . p 6 **NX**
Geisbergstraße . . . . p 5 **MY**
Gendarmenmarkt . . . . . p 6 **PZ**
Georg-Wilhelm-Straße . . . . . p 4 **JY**
Gertraudenstraße . . . . . p 7 **RZ**
Gervinusstraße . . . . p 4 **JX**
Gitschiner Straße . . . . . p 3 **GZ**
Gneisenaustraße . . . . . p 3 **GZ**
Goltzstraße . . . . p 5 **MZ**
Greifswalder Straße . . . p 7 **SX**
Grellstraße . . . . p 3 **HX**
Grieser Platz . . . . p 4 **JZ**
Grolmanstraße . . . . p 5 **LX**
Großer Stern . . . . p 5 **MX**
Grunerstraße . . . . p 7 **RY**
Grunewaldstraße . . . . . p 5 **MZ**
Güntzelstraße . . . . p 5 **LZ**
Gustav-Adolf-Str. . . . . . p 3 **HX**
Hallesches Ufer . . . . . . p 3 **GY** 48
Hagenstraße . . . . p 2 **EZ**
Hardenbergstraße . . . . p 5 **LX**
Hasen Heide . . . . p 3 **HZ**
Hauptstraße (SCHÖNEBERG) . . . . p 5 **MZ**
Heidestraße . . . . p 6 **NX**
Heilbronner Straße . . . p 4 **JY**
Heinrich-Heine-Straße . . . . . . p 3 **HY** 51
Hermannstraße . . . . . . p 3 **HZ**
Heylstraße . . . . p 5 **MZ**
Hochmeisterplatz . . . . . p 4 **JY**
Hofjägerallee . . . . p 5 **MX**
Hohenstaufenstraße . . . p 5 **MY**
Hohenzollerndamm . . . p 4 **KZ**
Holländerstraße . . . . . . p 2 **FX**
Holtzendorffplatz . . . . . p 4 **JY**
Holtzendorffstraße . . . . p 2 **EY** 62
Holzmarktstraße . . . . . . p 7 **SZ**
Hubertusallee . . . . p 2 **EZ**
Huttenstraße . . . . p 2 **FY**
Immanuelkirchstr. . . . . p 7 **SX** 65
Innsbrucker Straße . . . p 5 **MZ**
Invalidenstraße . . . . p 6 **NY**
Jakob-Kaiser-Platz . . . . . p 2 **EX** 69
Joachim-Friedrich-Straße . . . . p 4 **JY**
Joachimstaler Platz . . . p 5 **LX** 71
Joachimstaler Str. . . . . p 5 **LY**
J.-F.-Kennedy-Pl. . . . . . . p 5 **MZ** 73
Kaiserdamm . . . . p 4 **JX**
Kaiser-Friedrich-Straße . . . . p 4 **JX**

Kaiserin-Augusta-Allee . . . . . p 2 **EY**
Kantstraße . . . . p 4 **JX**
Karl-Liebknecht-Straße . . . . p 7 **RY**
Karl-Marx-Allee . . . . . . p 7 **RY**
Kastanienallee . . . . . . p 7 **RX**
Katzbachstraße . . . . . . p 3 **GZ** 7
Kleiststraße . . . . p 5 **MY**
Klingelhöferstraße . . . p 2 **FX** 8
Knaackstraße . . . . p 7 **RX**
Knesebeckstraße . . . . p 5 **LX**
Kochstraße . . . . p 6 **PZ**
Königin-Elisabeth-Straße . . . p 2 **EY** 8
Koenigsallee . . . . p 2 **EZ**
Köpenicker Straße (FRIEDRICHSHAIN) . p 7 **SZ**
Kolonnenstraße . . . . . p 2 **FZ** 8
Konstanzer Straße . . . p 2 **EZ** 9
Kottbusser Damm . . . p 3 **HZ**
Krumme Straße . . . . . p 4 **JX**
Kufsteiner Straße . . . . p 5 **MZ**
Kurfürstenstraße . . . . . p 2 **FY** 9
Kurt-Schumacher-Damm . . . . p 2 **FX**
Landsberger Allee . . . p 7 **SY**
Landshuter Straße . . . p 5 **MY**
Laubacher Straße . . . p 2 **FZ**
Leibnizstraße . . . . p 4
Leipziger Straße . . . . . p 6 **NZ**
Lennestr. . . . . p 6 **NZ**
Leonhardtstraße . . . . . p 4 **JX**
Levetzowstraße . . . . . p 2 **FY**
Lewishamstraße . . . . . p 4 **JY**
Lichtenberger Straße . p 3 **HY** 9
Lietzenburger Straße . p 5 **LY**
Lindenstraße (KREUZBERG) . . . . . p 3 **GY** 9
Loewenhardtdamm . . p 3 **GZ** 9
Ludwigkirchplatz . . . . p 5 **LY**
Ludwigkirchstraße . . . p 5 **LY** 1
Luisenstraße . . . . p 6 **NY**
Lustgarten . . . . p 6 **PZ** 1
Lützowplatz . . . . p 5 **MX**
Lützowufer . . . . p 2 **FX**
Luxemburger Straße . p 2 **FX** 1
Maaßenstraße . . . . . . p 5 **MY**
Manfred-von-Richthofen-Str. . p 3 **GZ** 1
Marchstraße . . . . p 5 **LX**
Markstraße . . . . p 3 **GX**
Martin-Luther-Straße . p 5 **MZ**
Masurenallee . . . . p 2 **EY** 1
Mecklenburgische Straße . . . . p 4 **KZ**
Mehringdamm . . . . . . p 3 **GZ**
Mehringplatz . . . . p 3 **GY** 1
Meierottostraße . . . . . p 5 **LY**
Meinekestraße . . . . . . p 5 **LY** 1
Memhardstraße . . . . . p 7 **RY** 1
Meraner Straße . . . . . p 5 **MZ**
Messedamm . . . . p 2 **EY** 1
Michaelkirchstraße . . . p 7 **RZ**
Mollstraße . . . . p 7 **RY**
Moltkestraße . . . . p 3 **GY** 1
Mommsenstraße . . . . p 4 **JX**
Motzstraße . . . . p 5 **LY**
Mühlendamm . . . . p 7 **RZ** 1
Mühlenstraße (FRIEDRICHSHAIN) p 3 **HY**
Mühlenstraße (PANKOW) . . . . p 3 **GX**
Müllerstraße . . . . p 2 **FX**
Münchener Straße . . . p 5 **MY**

Continued p 9

TREET INDEX TO BERLIN TOWN PLANS (Concluded)

inzstraße . . . . p 7 RY 124
chodstr. . . . . p 5 LY
ssauische Straße . . p 5 LZ
storstraße . . . . p 4 JY
ue Kantstraße . . . . p 4 EY 127
ue Königstr. . . . . . . p 7 RY
rnberger Str. . . . . . p 5 MY
erstraße . . . . p 3 HZ
persstraße . . . . p 2 EY
anienburger Str. . . . p 6 PY
anienstraße . . . . p 7 RZ
loer Straße . . . . p 3 GX
teestraße . . . . p 3 HX
to-Braun-Str. . . . . . RY
to-Suhr-Allee . . . . . . p 4 KX
derborner Str. . . . . . p 4 JY 138
nkstraße . . . . p 3 GX
riser Platz . . . . p 6 NZ
riser Straße . . . . p 4 KY
ssauer Straße . . . . . p 5 MY
ulsborner Straße . . p 4 JZ
ulstraße . . . . p 2 FY
rleberger Straße . . . p 2 FY
stalozzistraße . . . . . p 4 JX
tersburger Str. . . . . p 3 HY
atz der Republik . . . p 6 NY
atz der vereinten Nationen . . . . p 7 SY
tsdamer Platz . . . . . p 3 GY 141
tsdamer Straße . . . p 6 NZ 142
ager Platz . . . . p 5 LY 145
enzlauer Allee . . . . . p 7 RX
enzlauer Prom . . . . . p 3 HX
inzenstraße . . . . p 3 GY 147
inzregentenstr. . . . . p 5 LZ
ovinzstraße . . . . p 3 GX
iitzowstraße . . . . . . p 2 FX
inkestraße . . . . p 5 LY 149
thausstraße . . . . . . p 7 RY 150
uchstraße . . . . p 5 MX
ichpietschufer . . . . . p 2 FY 152
inhardtstraße . . . . . p 6 NY 153
inickendorfer Str. . . p 3 GX 155
Rheinbabenallee . . . . . p 2 EZ
Richard-Wagner-Str. . . . p 4 JX
Rönnestraße . . . . p 4 JX
Rosa-Luxemburg-Str. . . p 7 RY 158
Rosenthaler Straße . . . p 7 RY 159
Rudolstädter Str. . . . . p 2 EZ 161
Saatwinkler Damm . . . p 2 EX
Sachsendamm . . . . p 2 FZ
Sächsische Straße . . . . p 4 KY
Salzburger Straße . . . . p 5 MZ
Savignyplatz . . . . p 5 LX
Schaperstraße . . . . p 5 LY
Scharnhorststr. . . . . p 6 NX
Schillerstraße . . . . p 4 JX
Schillstraße . . . . p 5 MX 167
Schivelbeiner Str. . . . . . p 3 GX 168
Schloßstraße . . . . p 4 JX
Schlüterstraße . . . . p 4 KX
Schönhauser Allee . . . . p 7 RX
Schwedter Str. . . . . p 7 RX
Seesener Straße . . . . . p 4 JY
Seestraße . . . . p 2 FX
Sellerstraße . . . . p 3 GX
Sickingenstraße . . . . . . p 2 FY
Siemensdamm . . . . p 2 EX
Siemensstraße . . . . p 2 FY 170
Sigmaringer Straße . . . p 4 KZ
Skalitzer Straße . . . . . . p 3 HY
Sonnenallee . . . . p 3 HZ
Sophie-Charlotten-Platz . . . . p 4 JX
Sophie-Charlotten-Str. . p 2 EY 172
Spandauer Damm . . . . p 2 EY
Spandauer Str. . . . . p 7 RY
Spichernstraße . . . . p 5 LY
Spreeweg . . . . p 5 MX
Steinplatz . . . . p 5 LX
Storkower Straße . . . . . p 3 HX
Stralauer Allee . . . . p 3 HY
Stralauer Straße . . . . . . p 7 RZ
Straße des 17 Juni . . . p 5 MX
Strausberger Platz . . . . p 3 HY 175
Stresemannstraße . . . . p 6 NZ
Stromstraße . . . . p 2 FY 178
Stülerstraße . . . . p 5 MX
Stuttgarter Platz . . . . . p 4 JX 181
Suarezstr. . . . . p 4 JX
Südwestkorso . . . . p 2 EZ 182
Tegeler Weg . . . . p 2
Tempelhofer Damm . . . . p 3 GZ
Tempelhofer Ufer . . . . p 3 GZ 185
Teplitzer Straße . . . . . p 2 EZ 186
Theodor-Heuss-Platz . . . . p 2 EY 188
Tiergartenstraße . . . . . p 5 MX
Torstraße . . . . p 6 PX
Transvallstraße . . . . . . p 2 FX
Turmstraße . . . . p 2 FY
Uhlandstraße . . . . p 5 LZ
Unter den Linden . . . . p 6 NZ
Urbanstraße . . . . p 3 GZ
Veteranenstraße . . . . . p 6 PX 194
Viktoria-Luise-Platz . . . p 5 MY 195
Warschauer Straße . . . p 3 HY
Weinmeisterstraße . . . p 7 RY 199
Welserstraße . . . . p 5 MY
Werderstraße . . . . p 6 PZ 203
Westfälische Str. . . . . . p 4 JY
Wexstraße . . . . p 2 FZ
Wichertstraße . . . . p 3 HX
Wiener Straße . . . . p 3 HZ
Wiesbadener Str. . . . . p 2 EZ
Wilhelmstraße . . . . p 6 NZ
Wilmersdorfer Str. . . . p 2 EY
Windscheidstraße . . . . p 4 JX
Winterfeldplatz . . . . . . p 5 MY
Wisbyer Straße . . . . . . p 3 HX
Wittenbergplatz . . . . . p 5 MY
Wollankstraße . . . . p 3 GX
Württembergische Straße . . . . p 4 KY
Wundtstraße . . . . p 4 JX
Xantener Straße . . . . . p 4 JY
Yorckstraße . . . . p 3 GZ
Zillestraße . . . . p 4 JX

own Centre (Berlin - City, -Charlottenburg, -Schöneberg and -Wilmersdorf

Kempinski Hotel Bristol Berlin, Kurfürstendamm 27, ⊠ 10719, ☎ 88 43 40, Fax 8836075, Massage, – rm – 250. AE E VISA JCB. rest LX n
Kempinski-Restaurant *: (closed Monday)* **Meals** à la carte 57/93 – ***Kempinski-Eck*** **:** **Meals** à la carte 47/80 – **301 rm** 372/594 – 29 suites.

Grand Hotel Esplanade, Lützowufer 15, ⊠ 10785, ☎ 25 47 80, Telex 185986, Fax 2651171, (conference boat with own landing stage), « Modern hotel featuring contemporary art », Massage, – rm – 300. AE E VISA JCB. rest MX e
Meals see also ***Harlekin*** below – ***Eckkneipe*** : **Meals** à la carte 34/51 – **402 rm** 409/708 – 33 suites.

Four Seasons, Charlottenstr. 49/at Gendarmenplatz, ⊠ 10177, ☎ 2 03 38, Fax 20336166, Massage, – rm – 75. AE E VISA JCB. rest
Seasons **:** **Meals** à la carte 55/78 – **204 rm** 427/759 – 42 suites. PZ n

Grand Hotel, Friedrichstr. 158, ⊠ 10117, ☎ 2 02 70, Fax 20273362, Massage, – rm – 100. AE E VISA JCB PZ a
Coelln (outstanding wine list) **Meals** 39 (buffet lunch) and à la carte 51/96 – ***Goldene Gans*** *(dinner only)* **Meals** à la carte 41/70 – **358 rm** 354/588 – 20 suites.

Inter-Continental, Budapester Str. 2, ⊠ 10787, ☎ 2 60 20, Telex 184380, Fax 260280760, Massage, – rm – 800. AE E VISA
Meals see also ***Zum Hugenotten*** below – ***L.A. Café*** **:** **Meals** à la carte 38/68 – **511 rm** 377/609 – 40 suites. MX a

Palace, Budapester Str. 42 (Europa-Centre), ⊠ 10789, ☎ 2 50 20, Telex 184825, Fax 2626577, free entrance to the thermal recreation centre – rm – 260. AE E VISA JCB. rest MX k
Meals see also ***First Floor*** below – ***Alt Nürnberg*** : **Meals** à la carte 37/53 – **321 rm** 279/588 – 18 suites.

Berlin, Lützowplatz 17, ✉ 10785, ☎ 2 60 50, Fax 26052715, Massage, – rm rest – 🏋 500. AE ① E VISA JCB. ✻ rest MX
Meals 39 (buffet lunch) and à la carte 49/80 – **701 rm** ☕ 290/450 – 7 suites.

Radisson SAS-Hotel Berlin, Karl-Liebknecht-Str. 5, ✉ 10178, ☎ 2 38 2 Fax 23827590, Massage, – rm – 360. AE ① VISA JCB. ✻ RY
Meals à la carte 43/87 – **540 rm** ☕ 290/550 – 17 suites.

Berlin Hilton (with Kroneflügel), Mohrenstr. 30, ✉ 10117, ☎ 2 02 3 Fax 20342699, – rm – 300. AE ① E VISA JC
La Cupole (dinner only, closed Sunday - Monday) **Meals** à la carte 60/115 – ***Fellini*** (Itali rest.) *(dinner only, closed Sunday - Monday)* **Meals** à la carte 45/87 – ***Mark Brandenbur*** **Meals** à la carte 43/85 – **502 rm** ☕ 367/539 – 12 suites. PZ

Steigenberger Berlin, Los-Angeles-Platz 1, ✉ 10789, ☎ 2 12 70, Telex 18144 Fax 212117, Massage, – rm – 300. AE ① VISA JCB. ✻ rest MY
Park-Restaurant *(dinner only, closed Sunday - Monday)* **Meals** à la carte 54/80 – ***Berlin Stube :*** **Meals** à la carte 39/64 – **397 rm** ☕ 319/563 – 11 suites.

Holiday Inn Crown Plaza, Nürnberger Str. 65, ✉ 10787, ☎ 21 00 7 Telex 182877, Fax 2132009, Massage, – rm – 12 AE ① E VISA JCB. ✻ rest MX
Meals à la carte 50/76 – **425 rm** ☕ 346/562 – 10 suites.

Schweizerhof, Budapester Str. 21, ✉ 10787, ☎ 2 69 60, Telex 185501, Fax 26969C Massage, – rm – 340. AE ① E VISA JCB
Meals *(closed Sunday - Monday)* (dinner only) à la carte 47/70 – **424 rm** ☕ 325/503 10 suites. MX

Savoy, Fasanenstr. 9, ✉ 10623, ☎ 31 10 30, Fax 31103333, – rm 50. AE ① E VISA JCB. ✻ rest LX
Meals à la carte 48/80 – **125 rm** ☕ 262/450 – 6 suites.

Brandenburger Hof, Eislebener Str. 14, ✉ 10789, ☎ 21 40 50, Fax 2140510 « Modernized Wilhelminian mansion with Bauhaus furniture » – – 2 AE ① E VISA JCB. ✻ rest LY
Die Quadriga (dinner only) *(closed Saturday - Sunday, 1 - 12 January and 19 July 17 August)* **Meals** à la carte 76/114 – ***Der Wintergarten :*** **Meals** à la carte 52/79 – **87 r** ☕ 290/445.

Mondial, Kurfürstendamm 47, ✉ 10707, ☎ 88 41 10, Telex 182839, Fax 8841115 – – 50. AE ① E VISA. ✻ rest KY
Meals à la carte 47/77 – **75 rm** ☕ 220/480.

Maritim Pro Arte, Friedrichstr. 150, ✉ 10117, ☎ 2 03 35, Fax 20334209, – rm – 1050. AE ① E VISA JCB PY
Meals à la carte 51/80 – **403 rm** ☕ 245/558 – 29 suites.

President, An der Urania 16, ✉ 10787, ☎ 21 90 30, Fax 2141200, – r – 40. AE ① E VISA. ✻ rest MY
Meals *(closed Sunday)* à la carte 46/67 – **188 rm** ☕ 235/357.

Seehof, Lietzensee-Ufer 11, ✉ 14057, ☎ 32 00 20, Fax 32002251, ≤, « Gard terrace », – rest – 40. AE E VISA. ✻ rest JX
Meals à la carte 59/76 – **77 rm** ☕ 245/444.

Luisenhof without rest, Kopenicker Str. 92, ✉ 10179, ☎ 2 70 05 43, Fax 279798 « Elegant installation » – – 25. AE ① E VISA JCB RZ
28 rm ☕ 175/360.

Forum-Hotel Berlin, Alexanderplatz, ✉ 10178, ☎ 2 38 90, Telex 30768 Fax 23894305, – rm – 300. AE ① E VISA. ✻ rest RY
Meals à la carte 35/70 – **1006 rm** ☕ 250/367.

Ambassador, Bayreuther Str. 42, ✉ 10787, ☎ 21 90 20, Telex 184259, Fax 2190238 Massage, – rm rest – 70. AE ① E VISA JCB MX
Meals à la carte 34/65 – **199 rm** ☕ 230/310.

Alsterhof, Augsburger Str. 5, ✉ 10789, ☎ 21 24 20, Fax 2183949, Massage, – rm – 20. AE ① E VISA JCB MY
Meals à la carte 42/58 – **200 rm** ☕ 225/390.

Berlin Excelsior Hotel, Hardenbergstr. 14, ✉ 10623, ☎ 3 15 50, Fax 31551002, – rm rest – 60. AE ① E VISA JCB. ✻ rest LX
Meals à la carte 37/65 – **320 rm** ☕ 325/400.

Residenz, Meinekestr. 9, ✉ 10719, ☎ 88 44 30, Fax 8824726 – . AE ① VISA. ✻ rest LY
Meals à la carte 53/88 – **88 rm** ☕ 220/310.

Bleibtreu-Hotel, Bleibtreustr. 31, ✉ 10707, ☎ 88 47 40, Fax 88474444, « Modern interior », - rm. AE VISA JCB KY s
Meals à la carte 46/71 - **60 rm** 259/364.

Am Zoo without rest, Kurfürstendamm 25, ✉ 10719, ☎ 88 43 70, Fax 88437714 - 30. AE VISA JCB LX z
136 rm 245/395.

Hamburg, Landgrafenstr. 4, ✉ 10787, ☎ 26 47 70, Fax 2629394 - rm - 80. AE VISA JCB. rest MX s
Meals à la carte 40/71 - **240 rm** 225/320.

Sorat Art'otel without rest, Joachimstalerstr. 28, ✉ 10719, ☎ 88 44 70, Fax 88447700, « Modern hotel with exhibition of contemporary art » - . AE VISA JCB LY e
75 rm 260/375.

Hecker's Hotel without rest, Grolmanstr. 35, ✉ 10623, ☎ 8 89 00, Fax 8890260 - rest . AE VISA JCB LX e
72 rm 250/400.

Queens Hotel without rest, Güntzelstr. 14, ✉ 10717, ☎ 87 02 41, Telex 182948, Fax 8619326 - . AE VISA LZ t
109 rm 199/252.

Sylter Hof, Kurfürstenstr. 116, ✉ 10787, ☎ 2 12 00, Fax 2142826 - - 80. AE VISA. rest MX d
Meals *(closed Sunday dinner)* à la carte 26/41 - **160 rm** 192/376 - 18 suites.

Concept Hotel, Grolmanstr. 41, ✉ 10623, ☎ 88 42 60, Fax 88426820, - - 45. AE VISA JCB. LX m
Meals à la carte 34/59 - **100 rm** 240/350 - 3 suites.

Kanthotel without rest, Kantstr. 111, ✉ 10627, ☎ 32 30 20, Fax 3240952 - . AE VISA JCB. JX e
55 rm 249/269.

Schloßparkhotel, Heubnerweg 2a, ✉ 14059, ☎ 3 22 40 61, Fax 3258861, - - 50. AE VISA JCB EY a
Meals à la carte 36/60 - **39 rm** 189/285.

Albrechtshof, Albrechtstr. 8, ✉ 10117, ☎ 30 88 60, Fax 30886100, - - 70. AE VISA JCB. rest NY a
Meals à la carte 35/56 - **99 rm** 195/365 - 11 suites.

Holiday Inn Garden Court without rest, Bleibtreustr. 25, ✉ 10707, ☎ 88 09 30, Fax 88093939 - - 15. AE VISA JCB KY g
73 rm 245/350.

Boulevard without rest, Kurfürstendamm 12, ✉ 10719, ☎ 88 42 50, Fax 88425450 - - 30. AE VISA LX c
57 rm 198/320.

Kronprinz without rest (restored 1894 house), Kronprinzendamm 1, ✉ 10711, ☎ 89 60 30, Fax 8931215 - - 25. AE VISA JCB JY d
65 rm 125/295.

Kurfürstendamm am Adenauerplatz without rest, Kurfürstendamm 68, ✉ 10707, ☎ 88 46 30, Telex 184630, Fax 8825528 - - 35. AE VISA
34 rm 180/270 - 4 suites. JY n

Scandotel Castor without rest, Fuggerstr. 8, ✉ 10777, ☎ 21 30 30, Fax 21303160 - . AE VISA. MY s
78 rm 210/265.

Delta without rest, Pohlstr. 58, ✉ 10785, ☎ 26 00 20, Fax 26002111 - . AE VISA FY c
47 rm 150/300.

Harlekin - Grand Hotel Esplanade, Lützowufer 15, ✉ 10785, ☎ 25 47 88 58, Fax 2651171 - . AE VISA JCB. MX e
closed Sunday - Monday - **Meals** (dinner only) 95/130 and à la carte 70/94
Spec. Marinierte Jakobsmuschel mit Paprikabrioche, Täubchen und Kalbsbries auf glaciertem Artischockengemüse, Mille feuille von Nougatparfait mit Variation von Beeren.

First Floor - Hotel Palace, Budapester Str. 42, ✉ 10789, ☎ 25 02 10 20, Fax 25021160 - AE VISA JCB. MX k
closed Saturday lunch, Sunday and 23 June - 3 August - **Meals** à la carte 85/112
Spec. Steinbutt auf Stielmus mit Madeira-Ochsenschwanzsauce, Salzlammrücken mit jungen Gemüsen, Eis-Soufflé Grand Marnier mit Orangenragout.

Hugenotten - Hotel Inter-Continental, Budapester Str. 2, ✉ 10787, ☎ 26 02 12 63, Fax 260280760 - AE VISA JCB. MX a
closed Sunday - **Meals** (dinner only) (outstanding wine list) 109/152 and à la carte 83/100.

XXX **Opernpalais-Königin Luise**, Unter den Linden 5, ✉ 10117, ☎ 20 26 84, Fax 20044438 – 🏛 50. AE ⓓ E VISA. ✻ PZ
closed Sunday - Monday, January and 6 weeks June - July – **Meals** (dinner only, book essential) à la carte 59/83.

XXX ✿ **Bamberger Reiter**, Regensburger Str. 7, ✉ 10777, ☎ 2 18 42 82, Fax 2142348, – AE ⓓ VISA. ✻ MY
closed Sunday - Monday, 1 to 15 January and 1 to 15 August – **Meals** (dinner only, book essential) 145/185 and à la carte 99/123 – ***Bistro :*** **Meals** à la carte 66/76
Spec. Terrine von Lachs und Stör mit Imperial Kaviar, Langustinen und Jakobsmusch mit Seebohnensalat, Karamelisierter Haselnußschmarrn mit Mandelschaum und Pralinen

XX ✿ **Alt Luxemburg**, Windscheidtstr. 31, ✉ 10627, ☎ 3 23 87 30, Fax 3274003 – AE VISA JX
closed Sunday – **Meals** (dinner only, booking essential) à la carte 95/135
Spec. Gebratene Gänsestopfleber mit Honigkarotten und Paprika, Hummercrémesup Spieß von Entenbrust.

XX **Ephraim - Palais**, Spreeufer 1, ✉ 10178, ☎ 2 42 51 08, Fax 3219292, « Elega restaurant » – AE ⓓ E VISA RZ
Monday to Friday dinner only – **Meals** à la carte 44/73.

XX **Ponte Vecchio** (Tuscan rest.), Spielhagenstr. 3, ✉ 10585, ☎ 3 42 19 99 – ⓓ
closed Tuesday and 4 weeks July - August – **Meals** (dinner only, booking essential) à la ca 60/93. JX

XX **Ana e Bruno** (Italian rest.), Sophie-Charlotten-Str. 101, ✉ 14059, ☎ 3 25 71 Fax 3226895 – AE. ✻ EY
closed Sunday and Monday, 1 week January and 3 weeks June - July – **Meals** (dinner or outstanding Italian wine list) à la carte 80/100.

XX **Borchardt**, Französische Str. 47, ✉ 10117, ☎ 20 39 71 17, Fax 20397150, « Co yard-terrace » – AE VISA PZ
Meals à la carte 43/82.

XX **Il Sorriso** (Italian rest.), Kurfürstenstr. 76, ✉ 10787, ☎ 2 62 13 13, Fax 2650277, – AE ⓓ E VISA. ✻ MX
closed Sunday and 22 December - 5 January – **Meals** (booking essential for dinner) à carte 50/75.

XX **Peppino** (Italian rest.), Fasanenstr. 65, ✉ 10719, ☎ 8 83 67 22 – AE LY
closed Sunday and 4 weeks July - August – **Meals** à la carte 63/77.

XX **Trio**, Klausenerplatz 14, ✉ 14059, ☎ 3 21 77 82 EY
closed Wednesday and Thursday – **Meals** (dinner only, booking essential) à la carte 47/

X **Maxwell**, Bergstr. 3 (Entrance in courtyard), ✉ 10115, ☎ 2 80 71 21, « Art nouve facade ; courtyard-terrace » – AE ⓓ E VISA PX
Meals (booking essential) 29 (lunch) and à la carte 49/67.

X ☺ **Am Karlsbad** (modern restaurant in bistro style), Am Karlsbad 11, ✉ 107 ☎ 2 64 53 49, Fax 2644240, ☂ NZ
closed Saturday lunch and Sunday – **Meals** à la carte 43/76.

X **Daitokai** (Japanese rest.), Tauentzienstr. 9 (Europa Centre, 1st floor), ✉ 107 ☎ 2 61 80 99, Fax 2616036 – AE ⓓ E VISA JCB. ✻ MX
closed Monday – **Meals** 48/98 and à la carte.

at Berlin-Britz *by Karl-Marx-Straße* HZ :

🏨 Park Hotel Blub without rest, Buschkrugallee 60, ✉ 12359, ☎ 60 00 36 00, Fax 600037 – 🛗 ⇔ 📺 ☎ 📞 ♿ 🚗 Ⓟ – 🏛 60
123 rm.

🏨 **Britzer Hof** without rest, Jahnstr. 13, ✉ 12347, ☎ 6 85 00 80, Fax 68500868 – ⇔ 📺 ☎ 📞 🚗. AE ⓓ E VISA JCB
57 rm ☕ 155/286.

🏨 **Buschkrugpark** without rest, Buschkrugallee 107, ✉ 12359, ☎ 6 00 99 (Fax 60099020 – 🛗 📺 ☎. AE ⓓ E VISA
closed 23 December - 1 January – **25 rm** ☕ 195/265.

at Berlin-Dahlem *by Clayallee* EZ :

🏨 **Forsthaus Paulsborn** 🌲, Am Grunewaldsee, ✉ 14193, ☎ 8 13 80 10, Fax 81411 ☂ – 📺 ☎ Ⓟ – 🏛 70. AE ⓓ E VISA
Meals *(closed Monday)* à la carte 42/81 – **10 rm** ☕ 160/245.

XX **Alter Krug**, Königin-Luise-Str. 52, ✉ 14195, ☎ 8 32 50 89, Fax 8327749, « Gard terrace » – Ⓟ. AE ⓓ E VISA
closed Sunday dinner and Monday – **Meals** à la carte 47/79.

at Berlin-Grunewald :

Schloßhotel Vier Jahreszeiten, Brahmsstr. 6, ✉ 14193, ✆ 89 58 40, Fax 89584800, « Former Wilhelminian mansion », ₣₺, ≘s, ⊡ – |‡| ⇹ rm ▤ TV ☎ ✆ ⟹ ⓟ – ₰ 40. AE ⓓ E VISA JCB. ✗ rest EZ a
Vivaldi *(dinner only)* **Meals** 104/168 – ***Le Jardin*** **: Meals** à la carte 56/83 – **52 rm** 571/777 – 10 suites.

Grand Slam, Gottfried-von-Cramm-Weg 47, ✉ 14193, ✆ 8 25 38 10, Fax 8266300, ☂ – AE ⓓ E VISA. ✗ by Königsallee EZ
closed Sunday, Monday, 2 weeks January and 3 weeks July - August – **Meals** (dinner only, booking essential) 135/175 à la carte 88/111
Spec. Carpaccio und Tatar vom Schwertfisch provençalisch gewürzt, Hummer-Eintopf im Strudelteig, Geeister Knusper-Apfel.

Rockendorf im Grunewald, Hagenstr. 18, ✉ 14193, ✆ 8 25 45 71, Fax 8252213, ☂ – AE ⓓ E VISA EZ t
closed Tuesday **Meals** (dinner only, booking essential) à la carte 70/94.

at Berlin-Kreuzberg :

Stuttgarter Hof, Anhalter Str. 9, ✉ 10963, ✆ 26 48 30, Fax 26483900, ≘s – |‡| ⇹ rm TV ☎ ⟹ – ₰ 25. AE ⓓ E VISA JCB NZ e
Meals à la carte 41/76 – **110 rm** ☐ 235/370.

Riehmers Hofgarten without rest, Yorckstr. 83, ✉ 10965, ✆ 78 10 11, Fax 7866059 – |‡| TV ☎ – ₰ 25. AE ⓓ E VISA GZ a
21 rm ☐ 200/290.

at Berlin-Lichtenberg *by Karl-Marx-Allee* HY :

Ramada without rest, Frankfurter Allee 73a/corner Voigtstraße, ✉ 10247, ✆ 42 83 10, Fax 43831831 – |‡| ⇹ ▤ TV ☎ ✆ ⟹ – ₰ 25. AE ⓓ E VISA JCB
120 rm ☐ 179/223 – 4 suites.

Abacus Tierpark Hotel, Franz-Mett-Str. 7, ✉ 10319, ✆ 5 16 20, Fax 5162400, ≘s – |‡| ⇹ rm TV ☎ ✆ ♿ ⓟ – ₰ 90. AE ⓓ E VISA
Meals (buffet only) 25/32 – **278 rm** ☐ 190/310.

at Berlin-Lichterfelde *by Boelcke Straße* GZ :

Villa Toscana without rest, Bahnhofstr. 19, ✉ 12207, ✆ 7 68 92 70, Fax 7734488, « Villa with elegant installation » – |‡| TV ☎. AE ⓓ E VISA JCB. ✗
16 rm ☐ 160/240.

at Berlin-Mariendorf *by Tempelhofer Damm* GZ :

Landhaus Alpinia, Säntisstr. 32, ✉ 12107, ✆ 76 17 70 (Hotel) 7 41 99 98 (Rest.), Fax 7419835, « Garden-terrace », ≘s – |‡| ⇹ rm TV ⟹ – ₰ 20. AE E VISA
Säntisstuben **: Meals** à la carte 64/86 – **58 rm** ☐ 168/380.

at Berlin-Neukölln :

Estrel Residence, Sonnenallee 225, ✉ 12057, ✆ 6 83 10, Fax 68312345, ₣₺, ≘s – |‡| ⇹ rm TV ✆ ♿ ⟹ – ₰ 675. AE ⓓ E VISA. ✗ rest HZ a
Portofino (Italian rest.) **Meals** à la carte 34/63 – ***Sans Souci*** **: Meals** à la carte 37/63 – ***Sun Thai*** (Thai rest.) **Meals** à la carte 34/63 – **1125 rm** ☐ 196/318 – 80 suites.

at Berlin-Prenzlauerberg :

Sorat Hotel Gustavo without rest, Prenzlauer Allee 169, ✉ 10409, ✆ 44 66 10, Fax 44661661 – |‡| ⇹ TV ☎ ✆ ⟹ – ₰ 50. AE ⓓ E VISA JCB HX b
123 rm ☐ 190/310.

at Berlin-Reinickendorf *by Sellerstr.* GX :

Rheinsberg am See, Finsterwalder Str. 64, ✉ 13435, ✆ 4 02 10 02, Fax 4035057, « Lakeside garden terrace », ₣₺, ≘s, ⊥, ⊡, ☂ – |‡| ⇹ rm TV ☎ ⓟ – ₰ 60. E VISA
Meals à la carte 34/78 – **81 rm** ☐ 179/230.

Econtel Tegel Airport, Gotthardstr.96, ✉ 13043, ✆ 49 88 40, Fax 49884555 – |‡| ⇹ TV ☎ ✆ ♿ ⓟ – ₰ 60. AE E VISA JCB FX c
Meals à la carte 32/53 – **304 rm** ☐ 165/265.

at Berlin-Rudow :

Sorat Hotel u. Office without rest, Rudower Str. 90, ✉ 12351, ✆ 60 00 80, Fax 60008666, ≘s – |‡| ⇹ ▤ TV ☎ ✆ ⟹ – ₰ 35. AE ⓓ E VISA JCB
96 rm ☐ 185/290. by Karl-Marx-Straße HZ

at Berlin-Siemensstadt *by Siemensdamm* EX :

Holiday Inn Berlin Esplanade, Rohrdamm 80, ✉ 13629, ✆ 38 38 9[...] Fax 38389900, ⛱, Fō, ≦s, ⛆ - |$| ⇔ rm ▤ TV ♿ 🚗 P - 🏫 190. AE ⦿ E VISA JCB. ⚘ rest
Meals *(closed Saturday and Sunday dinner)* à la carte 46/70 - **336 rm** ☕ 255/410 - 4 suite[...]

Novotel, Ohmstr. 4, ✉ 13629, ✆ 3 80 30, Fax 3819403, ⛆ - |$| ⇔ rm TV ☎ ♿ [...] - 🏫 200. AE ⦿ E VISA JCB
Meals à la carte 34/58 - **119 rm** ☕ 207/272.

at Berlin-Steglitz *by Hauptstr.* FZ :

Steglitz International, Albrechtstr. 2 (corner of Schloßstraße), ✉ 1212[...] ✆ 79 00 50, Telex 183545, Fax 79005530 - |$| ⇔ rm TV ♿ - 🏫 260. AE ⦿ E V[...]
Meals à la carte 39/82 - **211 rm** ☕ 210/320 - 3 suites.

at Berlin-Tegel :

Sorat-Hotel Humboldt-Mühle, An der Mühle 5, ✉ 13507, ✆ 43 90 4[...] Fax 43904444, ⛱, Fō, ≦s - |$| ⇔ rm ▤ TV ☎ 🚗 - 🏫 50. AE ⦿ E VISA JC[...]
Meals à la carte 40/61 - **120 rm** ☕ 203/366. by Müllerstraße FX

Novotel Berlin Airport, Kurt-Schumacher-Damm 202 (by airport approac[...] ✉ 13405, ✆ 4 10 60, Telex 181605, Fax 4106700, ⛱, ≦s, ⛆ (heated) - |$| ⇔ [...] TV ☎ ♿ P - 🏫 150. AE ⦿ E VISA EX
Meals à la carte 35/65 - **181 rm** ☕ 207/299.

at Berlin-Tiergarten :

Sorat Hotel Am Spreebogen ⛴, Alt Moabit 99, ✉ 10559, ✆ 39 92 0[...] Fax 39920999, ⛱, Fō, ≦s - |$| ⇔ rm ▤ TV ✆ ♿ 🚗 - 🏫 150. AE ⦿ E VISA JC[...] ⚘ rest FY
Meals à la carte 42/58 - **221 rm** ☕ 250/420.

at Berlin-Waidmannslust *by Sellerstr.* GX :

Rockendorf's Restaurant, Düsterhauptstr. 1, ✉ 13469, ✆ 4 02 30 9[...] Fax 4022742, « Elegant installation » - P. AE ⦿ E VISA
✿ *closed Sunday - Monday, 22 December - 6 January and July* - **Meals** *(booking essent[...]* 110/175 (lunch) 130/225 (dinner)
Spec. Gänsemastleber mit Sauternegelee, Bresse Poularde mit Rosinensauce, Warr[...] Schockoladentaler mit Apfelkugeln und Minz-Sorbet.

COLOGNE (KÖLN) *Nordrhein-Westfalen* 417 N 4, 987 ㉕ ㉖ - *pop.* - *alt.* 65 *m* - ☎ 022[...]

See : Cathedral (Dom)★★ (Magi's Shrine★★★, Gothic stained glass windows★ Cross of Ge[...] (Gerokreuz)★, South chapel (Marienkapelle) : altarpiece★★★, stalls★, treasury★ GY *Roman-Germanic Museum (Römisch-Germanisches Museum)★★★ (Dionysos Mosaic)* GY **M**[...] *- Wallraf-Richartz-Museum and Museum Ludwig★★★ (Photo-Historama Agfa★)* Gy **M2** *Diocesan Museum (Diözesean Museum)★* GY **M3** *- Schnütgen-Museum★★* GZ **M4** *Museum of East-Asian Art (Museum für Ostasiatische Kunst)★★ by Hahnenstraßea[...] Richard Wagner Straße* EV *- Museum for Applied Art (Museum für Angewandte Kunst[...]* GYZ **M6** *- St. Maria Lyskirchen (frescoes★★)* FX *- St. Pantaleon (rood screen★)* EV *- [...] Ursula : treasure★ (Goldene Kammer)* FX *- St. Kunibert (chancel : stained glass windows[...]* FU *- St. Mary the Queen (St. Maria Königin) : wall of glass★ by Bonnerstraße* FX *- Old To[...] Hall (Altes Rathaus)★* GZ *- Botanical garden Flora★ by Konrad-Adenauer-Ufer* FU.

⛳9 Köln-Marienburg, Schillingsrotter Weg, ✆ 38 40 53 ; ⛳18 Bergisch Gladbach-Refra[...] (E : 17km), (02204) 6 31.

✈ Köln-Bonn at Wahn (SE : 17 km) ✆ (02203) 4 01.

🚘 Köln-Deutz, Barmer Straße by Deutzer Brücke FV.

Exhibition Centre (Messegelände) by Deutzer Brücke (FV), *✆ 82 11, Telex 8873426.*

🅸 Tourist office (Verkehrsamt), Am Dom ✉ 50667, ✆ 2 21 33 45, Telex 88834[...] Fax 2213320.

ADAC, *Luxemburger Str. 169, ✉50963, ✆ 472747, Fax 4727452.*

Düsseldorf 40 - Aachen 69 - Bonn 28 - Essen 68.

Plans on following pages

Excelsior Hotel Ernst, Domplatz, ✉ 50667, ✆ 27 01, Fax 135150, Massage, ≦[...] |$| ⇔ rm ▤ TV ☎ - 🏫 80. AE ⦿ E VISA. ⚘ rest GY
Meals à la carte 78/112 - **160 rm** ☕ 310/630 - 8 suites.

Maritim, Heumarkt 20, ✉ 50667, ✆ 2 02 70, Fax 2027826, Massage Fō, ≦s, ⛆ |$| ⇔ rm ▤ TV ✆ ♿ - 🏫 1300. AE ⦿ E VISA JCB. ⚘ rest GZ
Bellevue « Terrace with ≤ Cologne » **Meals** à la carte 72/96 - ***La Gallerie*** *(dinner o[...] closed Sunday - Monday and July to August)* **Meals** à la carte 49/77 - ***Rôtisserie*** **: Me**[...] 49 (buffet lunch only) - **454 rm** ☕ 280/540 - 28 suites.

Hotel im Wasserturm (former 19C water tower, elegant modern installation), Kaygasse 2, 50676, 2 00 80, Telex 8881109, Fax 2008888, , roof garden terrace with < Cologne, – rm rest – 20. rest FX c
Meals à la carte 68/93 – **90 rm** 419/548 – 42 suites.

Dom-Hotel , Domkloster 2a, 50667, 2 02 40, Telex 8882919, Fax 2024444, « Terrace with < » – rm – 60. GY d
Meals à la carte 65/98 – **125 rm** 370/770.

Renaissance Köln Hotel, Magnusstr. 20, 50672, 2 03 40, Fax 2034777, , Massage, , – rm – 200. rest EV b
Meals à la carte 62/88 – **236 rm** 298/696.

Holiday Inn Crowne Plaza, Habsburger Ring 9, 50674, 2 09 50, Fax 251206, Massage, , – rm – 230. by Hahnenstraße EV
Meals à la carte 45/67 – **299 rm** 323/656.

Dorint Kongress-Hotel, Helenenstr. 14, 50667, 22 80, Fax 2281301, Massage, , – rm – 500. rest EV p
Meals à la carte 48/92 – **285 rm** 323/606 – 10 suites.

Consul, Belfortstr. 9, 50668, 7 72 10, Fax 7721259, Massage, , – rm – 120. rest FU v
Meals à la carte 46/78 – **120 rm** 230/395.

Sofitel Mondial am Dom, Kurt-Hackenberg-Platz 1, 50667, 2 06 30, Telex 8881932, Fax 2063522, – rm – 180. rest GY f
Meals à la carte 55/75 – **205 rm** 241/420.

Savoy without rest, Turiner Str. 9, 50668, 1 62 30, Fax 1623200, – – 70. FU s
closed 24 December - 2 January – **100 rm** 175/575.

Haus Lyskirchen, Filzengraben 28, 50676, 2 09 70, Fax 2097718, , – rm rest – 60. FX u
Meals *(closed Saturday lunch, Sunday and Bank Holidays)* à la carte 35/67 – **94 rm** 180/350.

Euro Plaza Cologne, Breslauer Platz 2, 50668, 1 65 10, Telex 8885123, Fax 1651333 – rm – 20. GY c
Meals à la carte 53/71 – **110 rm** 205/290 – 6 suites.

Ascot-Hotel without rest, Hohenzollernring 95, 50672, 52 10 76, Fax 521070, , – . EV a
closed 23 December - 2 January – **46 rm** 171/411.

Flandrischer Hof without rest, Flandrische Str. 3, 50674, 25 20 95, Fax 251052 – – 20. by HahnenStraße EV
143 rm 120/380.

Senats Hotel without rest, Unter Goldschmied 9, 50667, 2 06 20, Fax 2062200 – – 200. GZ b
closed 21 December - 1 January – **59 rm** 155/205.

Dorint Hotel, Friesenstr. 44, 50670, 1 61 40, Fax 1614100, – rm – 100. EV n
Meals à la carte 35/57 – **103 rm** 215/630.

Viktoria without rest, Worringer Str. 23, 50668, 72 04 76, Fax 727067 – . FU t
closed 24 December - 1 January – **47 rm** 175/460.

Mercure Severinshof, Severinstr. 199, 50676, 2 01 30, Telex 8881852, Fax 2013666, , – rm – 140. rest FX a
Meals à la carte 36/80 – **252 rm** 220/396 – 11 suites.

Coellner Hof, Hansaring 100, 50670, 12 20 75, Fax 135235 – rm – 30. FU k
Meals *(closed Friday - Saturday)* à la carte 40/73 – **71 rm** 140/330.

CM Cityclass-Hotel Europa am Dom without rest, Am Hof 38, 50667, 2 05 80, Fax 2582032 – . GYZ z
92 rm 290/390.

Cristall without rest, Ursulaplatz 9, 50668, 1 63 00, Fax 1630333, « Modern interior » – . FU r
85 rm.

Euro Garden Cologne without rest, Domstr. 10, 50668, 1 64 90, Fax 1649333, – – 30. FU a
85 rm 205/545.

Königshof without rest, Richartzstr. 14, 50667, 2 57 87 71, Fax 2578762 – . GY n
85 rm 155/395.

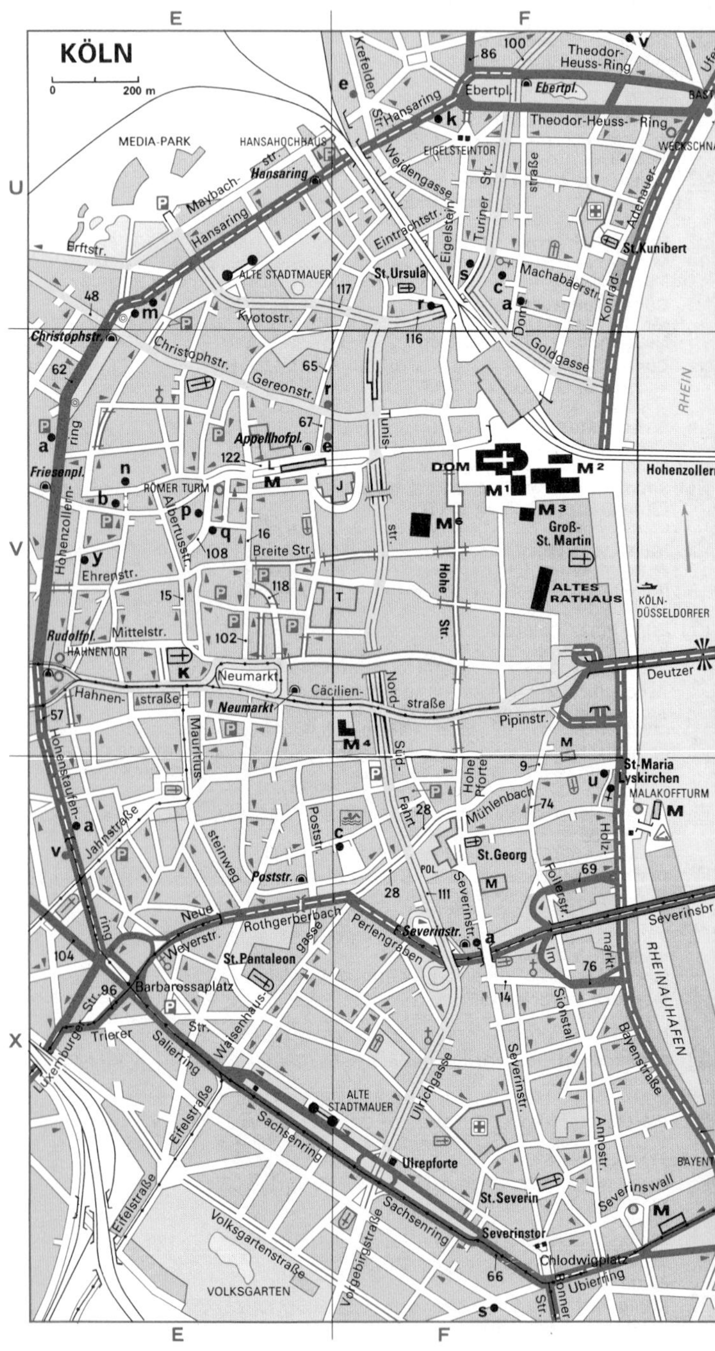
KÖLN
0
200 m
E
F
U
V
X
MEDIA-PARK
HANSAHOCHHAUS
Hansaring
ALTE STADTMAUER
Christophstr.
Friesenpl.
RÖMER TURM
Appellhofpl.
DOM
Groß-St. Martin
ALTES RATHAUS
Rudolfpl.
HAHNENTOR
Neumarkt
Poststr.
St. Pantaleon
Barbarossaplatz
St. Ursula
St. Kunibert
Ebertpl.
EIGELSTEINTOR
Theodor-Heuss-Ring
St-Maria Lyskirchen
MALAKOFFTURM
St. Georg
Severinstr.
Ulrepforte
St. Severin
Severinstor
Chlodwigplatz
VOLKSGARTEN
RHEIN
RHEINAUHAFEN
KÖLN-DÜSSELDORFER
Hohenzollern
Deutzer
Severinsbr.

eite Straße . . . . GZ
renstraße . . . . EV
gelstein . . . . FU
ürzenichstraße . . . . GZ 55
absburgerring . . . . EV 57
ahnenstraße . . . . EV
ohenstaufenring . . . . . . EX
ohenzollernring . . . . . . EV
ohe Straße . . . . GYZ
ttelstraße . . . . EV
eumarkt . . . . EV
chmodstraße . . . . EV 102
childergasse . . . . GZ
everinstraße . . . . FX
eppelinstraße . . . . EV 118

n Bayenturm . . . . FX 3
n Leystapel . . . . GZ 4
n Malzbüchel . . . . GZ 5
n den Dominikanern . . GY 8
n der Malzmühle . . . . . FX 9
n St-Katharinen . . . . . . FX 14
postelnstraße . . . . EV 15
uf dem Berlich . . . . . . EV 16
ugustinerstraße . . . . . GZ 19
echergasse . . . . GZ 22
ischofsgarten-Straße . . GY 26
laubach . . . . FX 28
rückenstraße . . . . GZ 32
ompropst-
Ketzer-Straße . . . . GY 38
ususgasse . . . . GY 39
adbacher Straße . . . . . EU 48
ockengasse . . . . GZ 50
oße Budengasse . . . . . GZ 52
oße Neugasse . . . . GY 54
einrich-Böll-Platz . . . . . GY 58
iser-Wilhelm-Ring . . . . EV 62
rdinal-Frings-
Straße . . . . EV 65
rolingerring . . . . FX 66
ttenbug . . . . EV 67
eine Budengasse . . . . . GZ 68
eine Witschgasse . . . . FX 69
mödienstraße . . . . GY 71
rt-Hackenberg-Platz . . GY 72
athiasstraße . . . . FX 74
echtildisstraße . . . . . . FX 76
noritenstraße . . . . GZ 79
usser Straße . . . . FU 86
fenbachplatz . . . . GZ 90
älzer Straße . . . . EX 96
atermarkt . . . . GZ 99

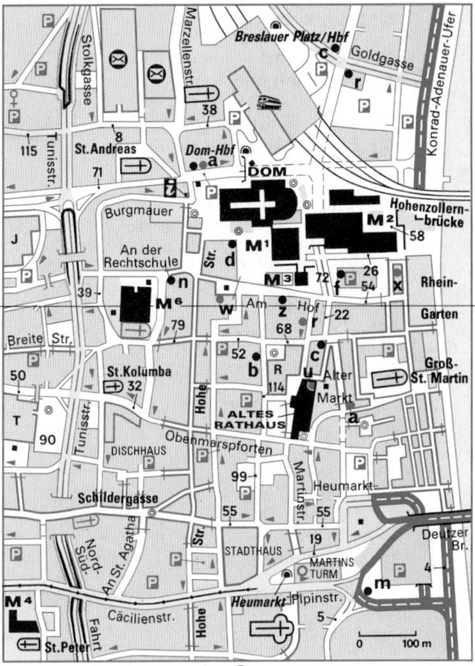

Riehler Straße . . . . FU 100
Roonstraße . . . . EX 104
Sankt-Apern-
Straße . . . . EV 108
Tel-Aviv-Straße . . . . FX 111

Unter Goldschmied . . . . . . GZ 114
Unter Sachsenhausen . . . . GY 115
Ursulaße . . . . FU 116
Victoriastraße . . . . FU 117
Zeughausstraße . . . . EV 122

Kommerzhotel without rest, Breslauer Platz, ✉ 50668, ☎ 1 61 00, Fax 1610122, – TV ☎. AE ① E VISA JCB GY r
77 rm ☐ 240/380.

Antik Hotel Bristol without rest (antique furniture), Kaiser-Wilhelm-Ring 48, ✉ 50672, ☎ 12 01 95, Fax 131495 – TV ☎. AE ① E VISA JCB EU m
closed 22 December - 2 January – **44 rm** ☐ 165/330.

Esplanade without rest, Hohenstaufenring 56, ✉ 50674, ☎ 21 03 11, Fax 216822 – TV ☎. AE ① E VISA EX a
closed 24 December - 2 January – **33 rm** ☐ 165/315.

CM Classica Hotel Residence without rest, Alter Markt 55, ✉ 50667, ☎ 2 57 69 91, Fax 2577659 – TV ☎ – 15. AE ① E VISA JCB GZ c
56 rm ☐ 230/340.

Astor without rest, Friesenwall 68, ✉ 50672, ☎ 25 31 01, Fax 253106 – TV ☎ P. AE ① E VISA. EV y
51 rm ☐ 174/340.

Conti without rest, Brüsseler Str. 40, ✉ 50674, ☎ 25 20 62, Fax 252107 – ☎. AE E VISA by Hahnenstraße EV
closed 22 December - 5 January – **44 rm** ☐ 130/305.

Merian-Hotel without rest, Allerheiligenstr. 1, ✉ 50668, ☎ 1 66 50, Fax 1665200 – TV ☎ FU c
32 rm ☐ 120/370.

Metropol without rest, Hansaring 14, ✉ 50670, ☎ 13 33 77, Fax 138307 – TV ☎ – 25. AE ① E VISA JCB EU m
closed 22 December - 2 January – **26 rm** ☐ 145/320.

Altstadt Hotel without rest, Salzgasse 7, ✉ 50667, ☎ 2 57 78 51, Fax 2577853,
– |‡| 📺 ☎. AE ⓓ E VISA GZ
closed 20 December - 2 January – **28 rm** ☕ 110/180.

Ambiance am Dom (in Excelsior Hotel Ernst), Trankgasse 1, ✉ 50667, ☎ 1 39 19
– AE ⓓ E VISA. ✻ GY
closed Saturday - Sunday, Bank Holidays and 3 weeks August – **Meals** à la carte 81/1

Die Bastei, Konrad-Adenauer-Ufer 80, ✉ 50668, ☎ 12 28 25, Fax 1390187, ≤ Rh
– AE ⓓ E VISA. ✻ FU
closed Saturday lunch – **Meals** à la carte 54/99.

Börsen-Restaurant Maître, Unter Sachsenhausen 10, ✉ 50667, ☎ 13 30 2
Fax 133040 – ▤. AE ⓓ E VISA. ✻ EV
closed Saturday lunch, Sunday, Bank Holidays and 4 weeks July - August – **Meals** à la ca
67/98 – ***Börsenstube :*** **Meals** à la carte 50/82.

Grande Milano (Italian rest.), Hohenstaufenring 37, ✉ 50674, ☎ 24 21 21, Fax 2448
– AE ⓓ E VISA EX
closed Saturday lunch, Sunday and 3 weeks July - August – **Meals** à la carte 63/96 – ***Pin***
di Pinot : **Meals** à la carte 38/54.

Em Krützche, Am Frankenturm 1, ✉ 50667, ☎ 2 58 08 39, Fax 253417, 🏠 – AE
E VISA GY
closed Monday – **Meals** *(booking essential)* à la carte 56/85.

Ratskeller, Rathausplatz 1 (entrance Alter Markt), ✉ 50667, ☎ 2 57 69 2
Fax 2576946, « Courtyard » – ▤ ♿ – 🏛 80. AE ⓓ E VISA GZ
Meals à la carte 38/75.

Daitokai (Japanese rest.), Kattenbug 2, ✉ 50667, ☎ 12 00 48, Fax 137503 – ▤.
ⓓ E VISA JCB. ✻ EV
closed Sunday – **Meals** à la carte 48/78.

Le Moissonnier (Typical French bistro), Krefelder Str. 25, ✉ 50670, ☎ 72 94 7
✿ Fax 7325461 FU
closed Sunday - Monday, Bank Holidays dinner only – **Meals** (booking essential) à la ca
55/79
Spec. Foie gras maison, Pigeon farci en porchetta gratiné, Craquelin de fraises et de fra
boises à la canelle et au chocolat.

Cologne brewery inns :

Alt Köln am Dom, Trankgasse 7, ✉ 50667, ☎ 13 74 71, Fax 136885. AE ⓓ E
Meals à la carte 24/41. GY

Früh am Dom, Am Hof 12, ✉ 50667, ☎ 2 58 03 97, Fax 256326, beer garden GY
Meals à la carte 27/53.

Gaffel-Haus, Alter Markt 20, ✉ 50667, ☎ 2 57 76 92, Fax 253879, 🏠. AE ⓓ E
Meals à la carte 34/57. GZ

Brauhaus Sion, Unter Taschenmacher 5, ✉ 50667, ☎ 2 57 85 40, Fax 2582081,
Meals à la carte 27/48. GZ

at Cologne-Braunsfeld *by Rudolfplatz* EV *and Aachener Str.* :

Regent without rest, Melatengürtel 15, ✉ 50933, ☎ 5 49 90, Fax 5499998, ≘s –
⚭ 📺 Ⓟ – 🏛 80. AE ⓓ E VISA
171 rm ☕ 225/411 – 5 suites.

at Cologne-Deutz *by Deutzer Brücke* FV :

Hyatt Regency, Kennedy-Ufer 2a, ✉ 50679, ☎ 8 28 12 34, Fax 8281370, ≤, be
garden, Massage, 🏋, ≘s, 🏊 – |‡| ⚭ rm ▤ 📺 ☎ ♿ 🚗 Ⓟ – 🏛 350. AE ⓓ E
JCB. ✻ rest
Graugans *(Saturday and Sunday dinner only)* **Meals** à la carte 74/96 – ***Glashaus :*** **Me**
à la carte 55/74 – **307 rm** ☕ 333/691 – 18 suites.

Der Messeturm, Kennedy-Ufer (18th floor, |‡|), ✉ 50679, ☎ 88 10 08, Fax 8185
≤ Cologne – ▤ – 🏛 30. AE ⓓ E VISA. ✻
closed Saturday lunch – **Meals** à la carte 50/84.

at Cologne-Ehrenfeld *by Rudolfplatz* EV *and Aachener Str.* :

Imperial, Barthelstr. 93, ✉ 50823, ☎ 51 70 57, Fax 520993, ≘s – |‡| ⚭ rm ▤ r
📺 ☎ ♿ 🚗. AE ⓓ E VISA. ✻ rest
Meals *(closed Saturday - Sunday)* (dinner only) à la carte 39/63 – **35 rm** ☕ 198/34

Zum offenen Kamin, Eichendorffstr. 25, ✉ 50823, ☎ 55 68 78, Fax 5502425 –
ⓓ E VISA by Erftstraße EU
closed Sunday, Monday and Bank Holidays except exhibitions – **Meals** à la carte 70/

Cologne-Junkersdorf *by Rudolfplatz* EV *and Aachener Str.* :

Brenner'scher Hof, Wilhelm-von-Capitaine-Str. 15, ✉ 50858, ☎ 9 48 60 00, Fax 94860010, « Installation in country house style » – 50. AE E VISA
Meals *(closed Monday)* à la carte 58/79 – **40 rm** 225/410 – 7 suites.

Cologne-Lindenthal *by Rudolfplatz* EV *and B 264* :

Queens Hotel, Dürener Str. 287, ✉ 50935, ☎ 4 67 60, Fax 433765, « Garden terrace » – rm rest – 350. AE E VISA. rest
Meals à la carte 44/78 – **147 rm** 260/554.

Cologne-Marienburg *by Bonner Straße* FX :

Marienburger Bonotel, Bonner Str. 478, ✉ 50968, ☎ 3 70 20, Fax 3702132, – rm – 40. AE E VISA
Meals à la carte 46/64 – **93 rm** 180/415 – 4 suites.

Cologne-Marsdorf *by Rudolfplatz* EV *and B 264* :

Novotel Köln-West, Horbeller Str. 1, ✉ 50858, ☎ (02234) 51 40, Fax 514106, beer garden, (heated), – rm rest – 100. AE E VISA
Meals à la carte 34/62 – **199 rm** 185/310.

Cologne-Merheim *by Deutzer Brücke* FV :

Goldener Pflug, Olpener Str. 421, ✉ 51109, ☎ 89 61 24, Fax 8908176 – AE E VISA
closed Saturday lunch, Sunday and Bank Holidays – **Meals** 65 lunch and à la carte 104/148.

Cologne-Müngersdorf *by Rudolfplatz* EV *and B 55* :

Landhaus Kuckuck, Olympiaweg 2, ✉ 50933, ☎ 4 91 23 23, Fax 4972847, – 120. AE E VISA
closed Monday and 3 - 13 February – **Meals** (booking essential) à la carte 65/85.

Cologne-Porz-Grengel *SE : 15 km by A 59* :

Holiday Inn, Waldstr. 255, ✉ 51147, ☎ (02203) 56 10, Fax 5619, – rm – 90. AE E VISA JCB
Meals à la carte 53/89 *(also vegetarian dishes)* – **177 rm** 330/560.

Cologne-Porz-Wahnheide *SE : 17 km by A 59* :

Quelle without rest, Heidestr. 246, ✉ 51147, ☎ (02203) 9 64 70, Fax 9647317 – – 30. VISA
120 rm 90/210.

Cologne - Rodenkirchen *by Bayen Straße* FX :

Atrium Rheinhotel without rest, Karlstr. 2, ✉ 50996, ☎ 93 57 20, Fax 93572222, – AE E VISA
68 rm 153/378.

by Am Bayenturm FX

ergisch Gladbach *Nordrhein-Westfalen* 417 N 5, 987 ㉖ – *pop. 104 000 – alt. 86 m* ☎ *02202.*
Köln 17.

Restaurant Dieter Müller – at Schloßhotel Lerbach, Lerbacher Weg, ✉ 51465, ☎ 20 40, Fax 204940 – AE E VISA JCB.
closed Sunday - Monday, 1-15 January and 3 weeks July – August – **Meals** (booking essential) 148/198 and à la carte 112/146
Spec. Gratin von Flußkrebsen auf Koriander-Karotten, Crépinette von der Taube mit gebackener Blutwurst auf Kartoffelpüree, Crème brûlée mit marinierten Beere und Tonkabohneneis.

aasphe, Bad *Nordrhein-Westfalen* 417 N 9, 987 ㉖ – *pop. 16 000 – alt. 335 m* – ☎ *02752.*
Köln 144.

Bad Laasphe-Hesselbach *SW : 10 km* :

L'ecole, Hesselbacher Str. 23, ✉ 57334, ☎ 53 42, « Elegant installation » – AE E
closed Monday - Tuesday and January – **Meals** (weekdays dinner only)(booking essential) 140 and à la carte 72/100
Spec. Gebratene Gänseleber mit glacierten Apfelspalten, Das Beste vom Reh auf Spitzkohl mit Preiselbeerapfel, Moccacharlotte mit Mascarponesauce.

Wittlich *Rheinland - Pfalz* 417 Q 4, 987 ㉕ ㉖ – *pop. 17 300 – alt. 155 m – ☎ 06571.*
Köln 130.

at Dreis *SW : 8 km :*

XXXX **Waldhotel Sonnora** with rm, Auf dem Eichelfeld, ✉ 54518, ☎ (06578) 4
✿✿ Fax 1402, ≤, « Garden » – TV ☎ P. AE E VISA.
closed January – **Meals** *(closed Monday and Tuesday)* (booking essential) 139/169
à la carte 97/125 – **20 rm** 100/300
Spec. Chartreuse von Gänsestopfleber auf Gewürztraminergelee, Kroß gebrate
St. Pierre in Curry-Ingwer-Würze, Taubenbrust mit Trüffel im Sellerie-Schiffchen.

DRESDEN L *Sachsen* 418 M 25, 987 ⑲, 984 ㉔ – *pop. 480 000 – alt. 105 m*
☎ 0351.

See : *Zwinger★★★ (Wall Pavilion★★, Nymphs' Bath★★, Porcelain Collection★★, Mathematical-Physical Salon★★, Armoury★★)* AY – *Semper Opera★★* AY – *Former court church (Hofkirche)* BY – *Palace (Schloß) : royal houses★ (Fürstenzug-Mosaik), Long Passage★ (Langer Gang)* BY – *Albertinum : Picture Gallery Old Masters★★★ (Gemäldegalerie Alte Meister), Picture Gallery New Masters★★★ (Gemäldegalerie Neue Meister), Green Vault★★★ (Grünes Gewölbe)* BY – *Prager Straße★* ABZ – *Museum of History of Dresden★ (Museum für Geschichte der Stadt Dresden)* BY **L** – *Church of the Cross★ (Kreuzkirche)* BY – *Japanese Palace★ (Japanisches Palais)(garden ≤★)* ABX – *Museum of Folk Art★ (Museum für Volkskunst)* BX **M 2** – *Great Garden★ (Großer Garten)* CDZ – *Russian-Orthodox Church (Russisch-orthodoxe Kirche) (by Leningrader Str.* BZ *)* – *Brühl's Terrace ≤★ (Brühlsche Terrasse)* BY – *Equestrian statue of Augustus the Strong ★ (Reiterstandbild August des Starken)* BX **E.**

Envir. : *Schloß (palace) Moritzburg★ (NW : 14 km by Hansastr.* BX *)* – *Schloß (palace) Pillnitz★ (SE : 15 km by Bautzener Str.* CX *)* – *Saxon Swiss★★★ (Sächsische Schweiz), Bastei★★★, Festung (fortress) Königstein★★ ≤★★, Großsedlitz : Baroque Garden★.*

18 Possendorf (S : 13 km) ☎ (035206) 33 76 51 11 ; 18 Herzogswaldeb (SW : 19 km) ☎ (0172) 3 57 68 88.

✈ Dresden-Klotzsche (N : 13 km), ☎ 58 31 41. City Office, Rampische Str. ☎ 4 95 60 13.

ℹ Dresden-Information, Prager Str. 10, ✉ 01069, ☎ 4 95 50 25, Fax 4951276.
ℹ Tourist-Information, Neustädter Narkt, ✉ 01097, ☎ 5 35 39.
ADAC, *Schandauer Str. 46, ✉ 01277, ☎ 3 45 80, Fax 30214.*
Berlin 198 – Chemnitz 70 – Görlitz 98 – Leipzig 111 – Praha 152.

Plans on following pages

Kempinski Hotel Taschenbergpalais, Am Taschenberg 3, ✉ 01067, ☎ 4 91
Fax 4912812, « Modern hotel in 18C baroque palace », Massage, ≘s, –
rm TV & – 320. AE ⓓ E VISA JCB BY
Meals à la carte 59/84 – **213 rm** 424/603 – 25 suites.

Bellevue, Große Meißner Str. 15, ✉ 01097, ☎ 8 12 00, Telex 329330, Fax 81206
≤, « Courtyard terraces », ≘s, – rm TV & P – 260. AE
E VISA JCB BX
Meals *(closed Monday)* à la carte 45/91 – **340 rm** 253/490 – 16 suites.

Dresden Hilton, An der Frauenkirche 5, ✉ 01067, ☎ 8 64 20, Fax 8642725,
– rm TV & – 350. AE ⓓ E VISA JCB BY
Rossini (Italian rest.) *(closed 1 July - 12 August)* **Meals** à la carte 45/74 – ***Grüner Bau***
Meals (buffet only) 45/49 – **333 rm** 341/527 – 4 suites.

Dorint Hotel, Grunauer Str. 14, ✉ 01069, ☎ 4 91 50, Fax 4915100, ≘s, –
TV & – 160. AE ⓓ E VISA JCB. rest CYZ
Meals à la carte 40/63 – **244 rm** 225/290.

Bülow Residenz, Rähnitzgasse 19, ✉ 01097, ☎ 89 00 30, Fax 8003100,
« Courtyard terrace » – TV & P – 25. AE ⓓ E VISA. rest BX
Meals (dinner only) (booking essential) à la carte 60/84 – **31 rm** 315/470.

Bayerischer Hof, Antonstr. 35, ✉ 01097, ☎ 82 93 70, Fax 8014860, – TV
– 25. AE ⓓ E VISA. rest BX
closed 19 December - 6 January – **Meals** *(closed Saturday - Sunday)* (dinner only) à la ca
26/51 – **23 rm** 165/260 – 3 suites.

art'otel, Ostra-Allee 33, ✉ 01067, ☎ 4 92 20, Fax 4922777, « Modern interior »,
≘s – rm TV ☎ & – 350. AE ⓓ E VISA. rest AY
Meals à la carte 45/55 – **174 rm** 195/450.

Alba Residenz, Stauffenbergsallee 25, ✉ 01099, ☎ 8 15 10, Fax 8151333, ≘s –
rm rest TV ☎ & P – 120. ⓓ E VISA.
Meals à la carte 50/78 – **121 rm** 228/298. by Königsbrücker Straße BX

Elbflorenz without rest, Rosenstr. 36, 01067, 8 64 00, Fax 8640100 – 150. BZ v
209 rm 180/240 – 13 suites.

Terrassenufer, Terrassenufer 12, 01069, 4 40 95 00, Fax 4409600, – rm 20. rest CY a
Meals à la carte 27/49 – **196 rm** 195/440 – 6 suites.

Windsor, Roßmäßlerstr. 13, 01139, 8 49 01 41, Fax 8490144 – rest by Leipziger Straße AX
Meals à la carte 27/40 – **25 rm** 175/280.

Astron, Hansastr. 37, 01097, 4 77 20, Fax 4772200, – rm – 250. by Hansastraße BX
Meals à la carte 36/55 – **269 rm** 230/370.

Verde, Buchenstr. 10, 01097, 8 11 10, Fax 8111333, – rm – 25. by Königsbrücker Str. BX
Meals à la carte 27/46 – **77 rm** 170/230.

Mercure Newa, St Petersburger Str. 34, 01069, 4 81 41 09, Fax 4955137, – rm – 180. BZ n
Meals à la carte 33/61 – **315 rm** 200/440.

Martha Hospiz without rest, Nieritzstr. 11, 01097, 8 17 60, Fax 8176222 – BX s
closed 23 to 27 December – **36 rm** 155/260.

Tulip Inn, Fritz-Reuter-Str. 21, 01097, 8 04 69 02, Fax 8046901, – rest by Hansastr. BX
Meals *(closed Sunday)* (dinner only) à la carte 33/53 – **76 rm** 180/230.

Novalis without rest, Bärnsdorfer Str. 185, 01127, 8 21 30, Fax 8213180, – – 40. by Hansastraße BX
85 rm 160/195.

Wenotel without rest, Schlachthofring 24, 01067, 4 97 60, Fax 4976100 – – 20. by Pieschener Allee AX
82 rm 114/140.

Italienisches Dörfchen, Theaterplatz 3, 01067, 49 81 60, Fax 4981688, « Terrace with » – BY n
Erlwein : (dinner only) *(closed Sunday - Monday, 2 weeks January and 3 weeks July - August)* Meals à la carte 77/118 – ***Weinzimmer :*** Meals à la carte 43/60 – ***Kurfürstenzimmer :*** Meals à la carte 35/50.

Opernrestaurant, Theatherplatz 2 (1st floor), 01067, 4 91 15 21, Fax 4956097, – AY r
closed Monday and July – Meals à la carte 40/70.

Fischgalerie, Maxstr. 2, 01067, 4 90 35 06, Fax 4903508, – AY s
closed Sunday - Monday – Meals (only fish-dishes), (booking essential) à la carte 45/74.

König Albert (bistro style restaurant), Königstr. 28, 01097, 5 48 83, Fax 54883, – BX e
closed Saturday lunch and Sunday – Meals à la carte 46/75.

Dresden-Blasewitz :

Am Blauen Wunder, Loschwitzer Str. 48, 01309, 3 36 60, Fax 3366299, – rm – 35. by Blasewitzer Straße DY
closed 23 to 28 December – Meals *(closed Sunday - Monday and 23 to 30 December)* (Italian rest.) à la carte 37/72 – **38 rm** 155/260.

Dresden-Cotta *by Schweriner Str.* AY :

Cotta-Hotel, Mobschatzer Str. 17, 01157, 4 28 60, Fax 4286333 – rm – 45. rest
Meals à la carte 27/47 – **44 rm** 170/255.

Residenz Alt Dresden, Mobschatzerstr. 29, 01157, 4 28 10, Fax 4281988, – rm – 100. rm
Meals à la carte 44/61 – **124 rm** 170/210.

Dresden-Klotzsche :

Airport Hotel, Karl-Marx-Str. 25, 01109, 8 83 30, Fax 8833333, – rm rest – 45.
Meals à la carte 31/60 – **100 rm** 240/310 – 6 suites. by Königsbrücker Straße BX

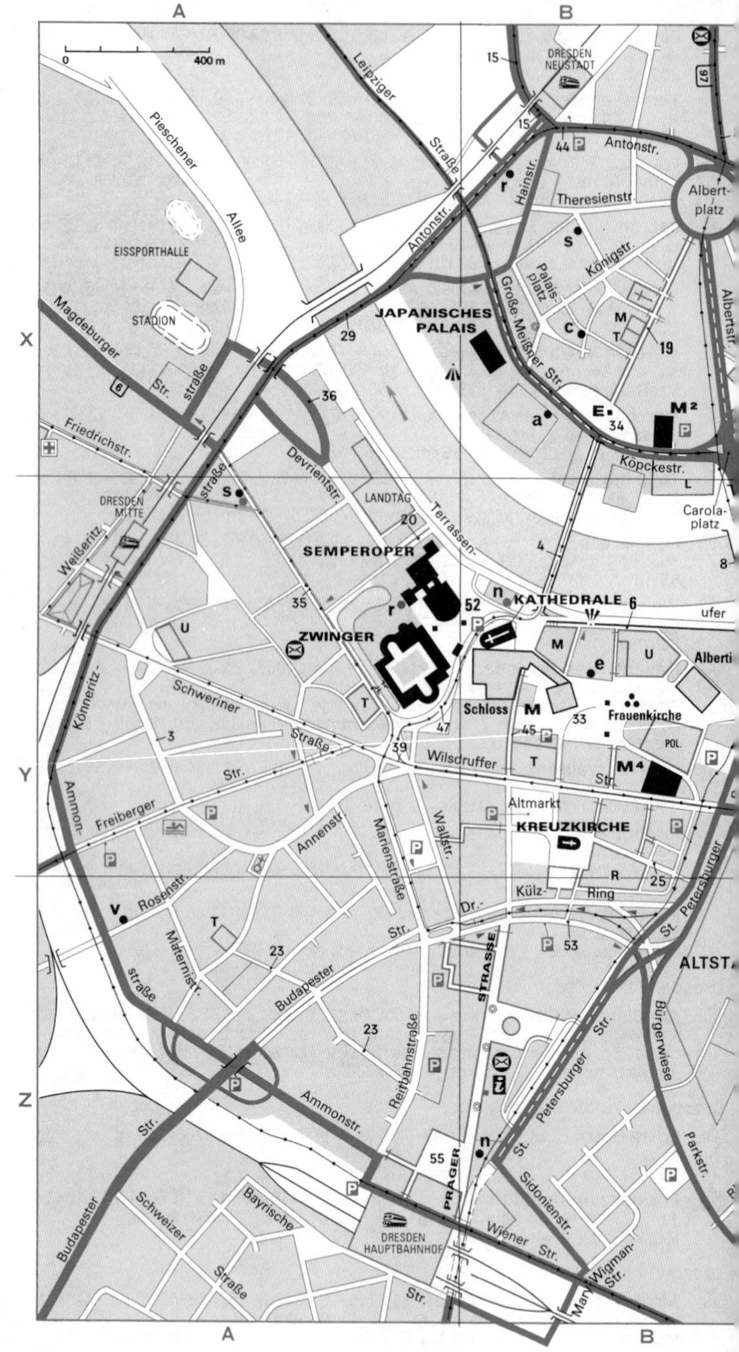
A
B
400 m
DRESDEN NEUSTADT
Leipziger Straße
Pieschener Allee
EISSPORTHALLE
STADION
Magdeburger Str.
straße
Antonstr.
Hainstr.
Theresienstr.
Albertplatz
Königstr.
Palaisplatz
Große-Meißner Str.
JAPANISCHES PALAIS
Albertstr.
X
Friedrichstr.
Devrientstr.
LANDTAG
Terrassen-ufer
Köpckestr.
Carolaplatz
DRESDEN MITTE
Weißeritz-
SEMPEROPER
KATHEDRALE
ZWINGER
Schloss
Frauenkirche
Albertinum
POL.
Schweriner Straße
Wilsdruffer Str.
Könneritz-
Ammon-straße
Y
Freiberger Str.
Altmarkt
KREUZKIRCHE
Annenstr.
Marienstraße
Wallstr.
Dr.-Külz-Ring
St. Petersburger
Rosenstr.
Maternistr.
Budapester Str.
ALTST.
PRAGER STRASSE
Bürgerwiese
Reitbahnstraße
Petersburger Str.
Z
Ammonstr.
Parkstr.
Sidonienstr.
Schweizer Straße
Bayrische Str.
Budapester Str.
DRESDEN HAUPTBAHNHOF
Wiener Str.
Mary-Wigman-Str.

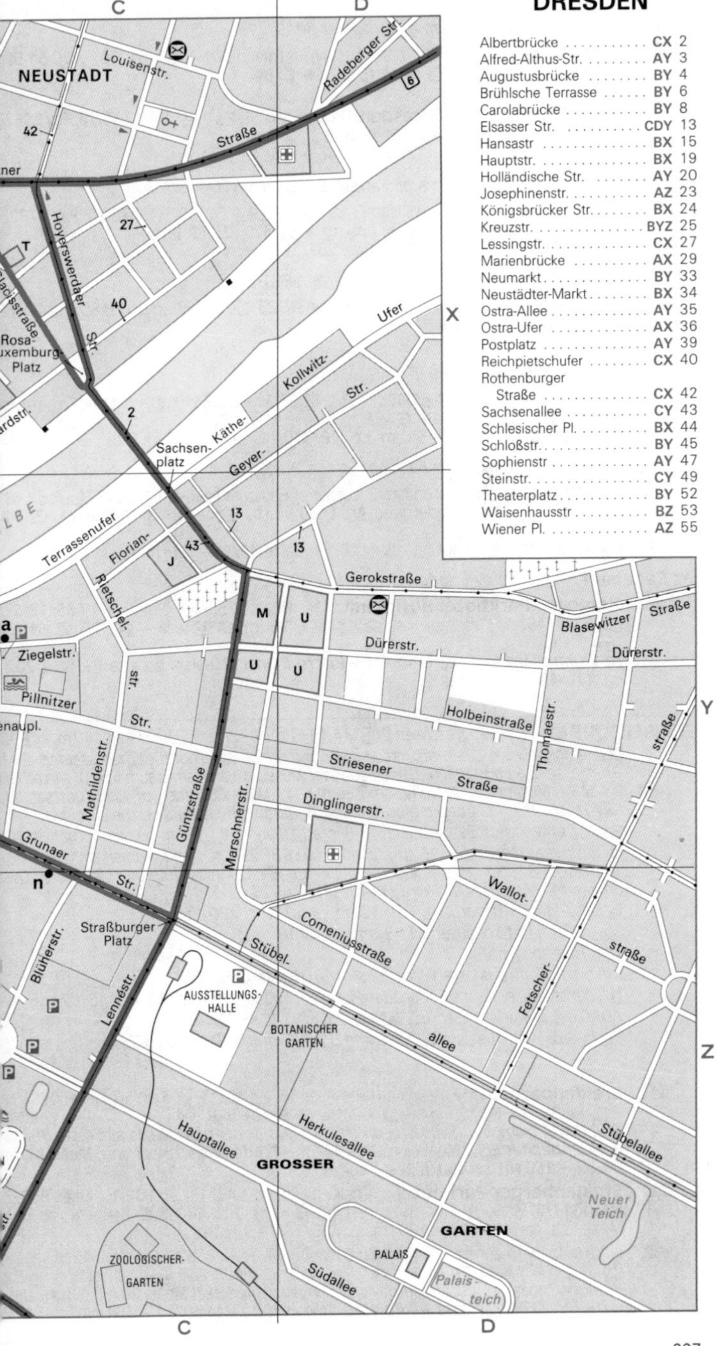
DRESDEN
Albertbrücke . . . . CX 2
Alfred-Althus-Str. . . . . AY 3
Augustusbrücke . . . . BY 4
Brühlsche Terrasse . . . . . . BY 6
Carolabrücke . . . . BY 8
Elsasser Str. . . . . CDY 13
Hansastr . . . . BX 15
Hauptstr. . . . . BX 19
Holländische Str. . . . . AY 20
Josephinenstr. . . . . AZ 23
Königsbrücker Str. . . . . . . BX 24
Kreuzstr. . . . . BYZ 25
Lessingstr. . . . . CX 27
Marienbrücke . . . . AX 29
Neumarkt . . . . BY 33
Neustädter-Markt . . . . BX 34
Ostra-Allee . . . . AY 35
Ostra-Ufer . . . . AX 36
Postplatz . . . . AY 39
Reichpietschufer . . . . CX 40
Rothenburger
Straße . . . . CX 42
Sachsenallee . . . . CY 43
Schlesischer Pl. . . . . BX 44
Schloßstr. . . . . BY 45
Sophienstr . . . . AY 47
Steinstr. . . . . CY 49
Theaterplatz . . . . BY 52
Waisenhausstr . . . . BZ 53
Wiener Pl. . . . . AZ 55
C
D
X
Y
Z
NEUSTADT
Louisenstr.
Radeberger Str.
Straße
Hoyerswerdaer Str.
Rosa-Luxemburg-Platz
Kollwitz-
Käthe-
Ufer
Str.
Sachsen-platz
Geyer-
Terrassenufer
Florian-
Rietschel-str.
Ziegelstr.
Pillnitzer Str.
Gerokstraße
Dürerstr.
Blasewitzer Straße
Holbeinstraße
Thomaestr.
Striesener Straße
Dinglingerstr.
Mathildenstr.
Güntzstraße
Marschnerstr.
Grunaer Str.
Straßburger Platz
Wallot-straße
Comeniusstraße
Stübel-allee
Fetscher-straße
Blüherstr.
Lennéstr.
AUSSTELLUNGS-HALLE
BOTANISCHER GARTEN
Hauptallee
Herkulesallee
Stübelallee
GROSSER GARTEN
Neuer Teich
PALAIS
Palais-teich
Südallee
ZOOLOGISCHER-GARTEN

at Dresden-Laubegast *E : 9 km by Striesener Straße* DY :

Prinz Eugen without rest, Gustav-Hartmann-Str. 4, 01279, 2 51 59
Fax 2515986 – rm. AE E VISA
47 rm 190/240.

Treff Resident Hotel Dresden, Brünner Str. 11, 01279, 2 56 20, Fax 25628
– rm. AE E VISA. rest
Meals à la carte 37/63 – **125 rm** 135/235.

at Dresden-Leubnitz-Neuostra *by Parkstr.* BCZ *and Teplitzer Str.*

Treff Hotel Dresden, Wilhelm-Franke-Str. 90, 01219, 4 78 20, Fax 47825
– rm – 370. AE E VISA
Meals à la carte 37/63 – **262 rm** 209/273.

at Dresden-Niedersedlitz *SE : 10 km by Parkstraße* BZ :

Ambiente without rest, Meusegaster Str. 23, 01259, 20 78 80, Fax 20788
–. E VISA
20 rm 158/265.

at Dresden-Reick *by Parkstraße (B 172)* BCZ :

Coventry, Hüßestr. 1, 01237, 2 82 60, Fax 2816310, – rm
– 25. AE E VISA
Meals à la carte 33/56 – **54 rm** 220/330 – 3 suites.

at Dresden-Weißer Hirsch *by Bautzner Straße* CDX :

Villa Emma, Stechgrundstr. 2 (corner of Bautzner Landstr.), 01324, 37 48
Fax 3748118, « Modernized Art Deco villa », – rm. AE
VISA
Meals (dinner only) (booking essential) à la carte 49/68 – **21 rm** 210/450.

at Radebeul *NW : 7 km by Leipziger Straße* AX :

Flamberg Parkhotel Hoflössnitz, Nizzastr. 55, 01445, (0351) 8 32
Fax 8321445, Massage – rm – 170. AE E
JCB
La Vigna : Meals à la carte 48/74 – ***Bistro Rienzi :*** Meals à la carte 39/56 – **202**
245/400 – 13 suites.

DÜSSELDORF *Nordrhein-Westfalen* 417 M 4, 987 ㉕ ㉖ – *pop. 570 000 – alt. 40 m –* 02

See : *Königsallee★* EZ – *Hofgarten★* DEY *und Schloß Jägerhof (Goethemuseum★* EY M
– Hetjensmuseum★ DZ **M4** *– Land Economic Museum (Landesmuseum Volk u. Wirtschaf*
DY **M5** – *Museum of Art (Kunstmuseum)★* DY **M2** – *Collection of Art (Kunstsammlu*
NRW)★ DY **M3** – *Löbbecke-Museum und Aquazoo★ by Kaiserswerther Str.* AU.

Envir. : *Chateau of Benrath (Schloß Benrath) (Park★) S : 10 km by Siegburger Str.* C
Ratingen-Hösel, NE : 16 km, (02102) 6 86 29 ; Gut Rommeljans, NE : 12 k
(02102) 8 10 92 ; Düsseldorf-Hubbelrath, E : 12 km, (02104) 7 21 78 ; Düss
dorf-Hafen, Auf der Lausward, (0211) 39 65 98
Düsseldorf-Schmidtberg, NE : 12 km, (02104) 7 70 60.
Düsseldorf-Lohausen (N : 8 km), 42 10.
Hauptbahnhof.
Exhibition Centre (Messegelände), 4 56 01, Telex 8584853.
Tourist office, Konrad-Adenauer-Platz, 40210, 17 20 20, Fax 161071.
ADAC, *Himmelgeister Str. 63, 40225, 3 10 93 33.*
Berlin 552 – Amsterdam 225 – Essen 31 – Köln 40 – Rotterdam 237.

Plans on following pages

Breidenbacher Hof, Heinrich-Heine-Allee 36, 40213, 1 30 30, Fax 1303830,
– rm – 60. AE E VISA JCB. EY
Grill Royal *(Saturday, Sunday and Bank Holidays dinner only)* Meals à la carte 76/12
Breidenbacher Eck : Meals à la carte 44/89 – ***Trader Vic's*** *(dinner only)* Meals à la ca
56/92 – **130 rm** 480/850 – 7 suites.

Steigenberger Parkhotel, Corneliusplatz 1, 40213, 1 38 10, Telex 85823
Fax 131679, – rm rest – 200. AE E VISA JCB. rest
Meals à la carte 65/97 – **160 rm** 335/590 – 9 suites. EY

Nikko, Immermannstr. 41, 40210, 83 40, Telex 8582080, Fax 161216,
– rm – 450. AE E VISA JCB. rest BV
Benkay (Japanese rest.) *(Saturday and Sunday dinner only)* Meals 28/65 (lunch) and
carte 65/90 – ***Brasserie Nikkolette :*** Meals à la carte 39/71 – **301 rm** 340/5
– 5 suites.

DÜSSELDORF

Street	Square	No.
Wehrhahn	EY	3
rliner Allee	EZ	
nger Str.	DY	28
f-Adolf-Str.	EZ	
nigsallee	EZ	
hadowstraße	EY	91
menstraße	EZ	7
kerstraße	DY	8
adellstraße	DZ	13
Corneliusstraße	EZ	15
Elberfelder Str.	EY	21
Ernst-Reuter-Platz	EZ	23
Fischerstraße	EY	27
Friedrich-Ebert-Straße	EZ	29
Grabbeplatz	DY	32
Graf-Adolf-Platz	EZ	33
Heinrich-Heine-Allee	EY	42
Hofgartenrampe	DY	45
Jan-Wellem-Platz	EY	51
Marktplatz	DY	68
Martin-Luther-Platz	EZ	69
Maximilian-Weyhe-Allee	EY	70
Mühlenstraße	DY	73
Ratinger Str.	DY	88
Schadowplatz	EY	90
Schneider-Wibbel-Gasse	DY	95
Schwanenmarkt	DZ	96
Tonhallenstraße	EY	101
Vagedesstraße	EY	104
Venloer Str.	EY	105

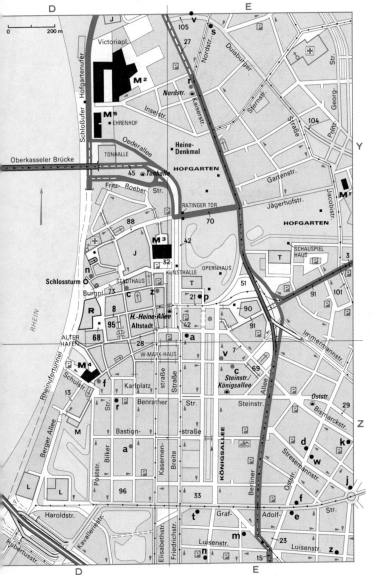

ADAC
GOLZHEIM
DERENDORF
Reeser Pl.
Th.-Heuss-Brücke
THEODOR-HEUSS-BRÜCKE
Golzheimer Platz
RHEIN-PARK
KÖLN-DÜSSELDORFER
Kennedydamm
Klever Straße
Klever Str.
Münsterstr.
OBERKASSEL
Luegplatz
OBERKASSELER BRÜCKE
RHEIN
TONHALLE
HOF-GARTEN
Jägerhofstr.
Schlossturm
ALTSTADT
Königsallee
Berliner Allee
Rheinufertunnel
RHEINKNIEBRÜCKE
LANDTAG RHEINTURM
HAFEN
Hauptbahnhof
Handelszentrum
Stahlwerkstr.
Graf-Adolf-Str.
Fürstenwall
Bilker Allee
D.-FRIEDRICHSTADT
D.-VOLKSGARTEN
D.-BILK
D.-VÖLKLINGER STR.
S.-BAHN
VOLKSGARTEN
Lessingplatz
Oberbilker Markt
Südring
Völklinger
Aachener Straße
Merowingerstr.
D.-WEHRHAHN
D.-ZOO
Grafenberger Allee
Stoffeler Kapellenweg

STREET INDEX

DÜSSELDORF

Am Wehrhahn .... EY 3
Berliner Allee .... EZ
Flinger Straße .... DY 28
Graf-Adolf-Straße ..... EZ
Königsallee .... EZ
Schadowstraße .... EY 91

Aachener Straße ..... AX
Achenbachstraße .... BV 2
Ackerstraße .... BV
Adlerstraße .... BV
Auf'm Hennekamp ... BX
Bachstraße .... AX
Bagelstraße .... BV
Bastionstraße .... DZ
Benrather Straße ..... DZ
Benzenbergstraße .... AX 5
Berger Allee .... DZ
Bilker Allee .... AX
Bilker Straße .... DZ
Birkenstraße CV
Bismarckstraße .... EZ
Blumenstraße .... EZ 7
Bolkerstraße .... DY 8
Brehmplatz .... BU 9
Brehmstraße .... BU
Breite Straße .... EZ
Brunnenstraße .... BX 12
Burgplatz .... DY
Cecilienallee .... AU
Citadellstraße .... DZ 13
Collenbachstraße .... BU
Corneliusstraße .... EZ 15
Cranachstraße CV
Danziger Straße ..... AU 16
Dorotheenstraße CV
Duisburger Straße .... EY
Eisenstraße .... BV
Elberfelder Straße .... EY 21
Elisabethstraße .... DZ
Ellerstraße .... BX
Erasmusstraße .... BX 22
Erkrather Straße CV
Ernst-Reuter-Pl. .... EZ 23
Eulerstraße .... BU 24
Fischerstraße .... EY 27
Friedrich-Ebert-Straße .... EZ 29
Friedrichstraße .... EZ
Fritz-Roeber-Straße .... DY
Fürstenplatz .... BX 30
Fürstenwall .... AX
Gartenstraße .... EY
Gladbacher Straße .... AX 31
Grabbeplatz .... DY 32
Graf-Adolf-Platz ...... EZ 33
Grafenberger Allee .... BV
Graf-Recke-Str. .... CU
Grashofstraße .... BU
Grunerstraße .... BU
Hans-Sachs-Straße .... CV 39
Harkortstraße .... BV 40
Haroldstraße .... DZ
Heinr.-Ehrhardt-Straße .... BU
Heinr.-Heine-Allee .... EY 42
Heinrichstraße .... CU
Hellweg CV
Heresbachstraße ..... BX 43
Herzogstraße .... BX 44
Höherweg CV
Hofgartenrampe ...... DY 45
Hofgartenufer .... DY
Homberger Straße .... AU 46
Hubertusstraße .... DZ
Hüttenstraße .... BX
Immermannstraße .... EY
Inselstraße .... DY
Jacobistraße .... EY
Jägerhofstraße .... EY
Jan-Wellem-Platz ..... EY 51
Johannstraße .... AU
Jülicher Straße ...... BU 52
Jürgensplatz .... AX 54
Kaiser-Friedrich-Ring .... AU
Kaiserstraße .... EY
Kaiserwerther Straße .... AU
Kaiser-Wilhelm-Ring .... AV
Karl-Geusen-Straße CX
Karlplatz .... DZ
Karlstraße .... BV
Kasernenstraße ..... DZ
Kavalleriestraße .... DZ
Kennedydamm .... AU
Kettwiger Straße ... CV
Klever Straße ...... AU
Klosterstraße ...... BV 56
Kölner Straße ..... BV
Königsberger Straße .... CV 58
K.-Adenauer-Pl. ..... BV 59
Kopernikusstr. ...... AX 60
Kronprinzenstr. .... AX
Kruppstraße .... BX
Lenaustraße .... CU
Lessingplatz .... BX
Lichtstraße .... CV 62
Lindemannstr. CV
Lorettostraße .... AX 64
Luegallee .... AV
Luisenstraße ...... EZ
Marktplatz .... DY 68
Martin-Luther-Platz .... EZ 69
Max.-Weyhe-Allee .. EY 70
Mecumstraße ...... BX
Merowingerstr. ..... AX
Mintropstraße ..... BV 71
Mörsenbroicher Weg .... CU
Moltkestraße ...... BU
Mühlenstraße ..... DY 73
Münsterstraße ..... BU
Nördl.Zubringer .... BU 77
Nordstraße .... EY
Oberbilker Allee .... BX
Oberbilker Markt ... BX 80
Oberkasseler Br. ... DY
Oststraße .... EZ
Pempelforter Str. ... BV 84
Plockstraße .... AX 86
Poststraße .... DZ
Prinz-Georg-Str. .... EY
Rather Straße ..... BU
Ratinger Straße .... DY 88
Reichsstraße ...... AX
Rethelstraße ...... BV
Ronsdorfer Str. CX
Roßstraße .... BU
Schadowplatz ..... EY 90
Scheurenstraße .... BV 92
Schillerplatz .... BV 93
Schinkelstraße ..... BV
Schirmestraße ..... BV 94
Schloßufer .... DY
Schneider-Wibbel-Gasse .... DY 95
Schulstraße .... DZ
Schumannstr. ..... BV
Schwanenmarkt ... DZ 96
Siegburger Straße CX
Simrockstraße ..... CU 97
Sonnenstraße ..... BX 98
Steinstraße .... EZ
Sternstraße .... EY
Stoffeler Kapellenweg .... BX
Stoffeler Straße .... CX 100
Stresemannstr. .... EZ
Stromstraße .... AV
Südring .... AX
Th.-Heuss-Br. ...... AU
Tiergartenstraße ... CU
Tonhallenstraße .... EY 101
Uerdinger Str. ..... AU
Ulmenstraße ...... BU
Vagedesstraße ..... EY 104
Vautierstraße ..... CU
Venloer Straße .... EY 105
Victoriaplatz .... DY
Völklinger Str. ...... AX
Volmerswerther Straße .... AX
Werdener Straße ... CV
Witzelstraße .... BX 114
Worringer Platz .... BV 115
Worringer Straße .... BV

Queens Hotel, Ludwig-Erhard-Allee 3, ✉ 40227, ✆ 7 77 10, Fax 7771777, – rm TV – 55. AE VISA. rest BV
Meals à la carte 34/50 – **120 rm** 297/624 – 5 suites.

Holiday Inn, Graf-Adolf-Platz 10, ✉ 40213, ✆ 3 84 80, Fax 3848390, – rm TV – 80. AE VISA JCB. rest EZ
Meals à la carte 51/83 – **177 rm** 375/615.

Majestic, Cantadorstr. 4, ✉ 40211, ✆ 36 70 30 (hotel) 35 72 92 (rest.), Fax 36703 – rm TV – 30. AE VISA JCB. BV
closed 21 December - 5 January – ***La Grappa*** (Italian rest.) *(closed Sunday and Bank Holidays except exhibitions)* **Meals** à la carte 60/82 – **52 rm** 245/460.

Esplanade, Fürstenplatz 17, ✉ 40215, ✆ 38 68 50, Fax 374032, – TV – 60. AE VISA JCB. BX
Meals à la carte 42/70 – **81 rm** 169/450.

Madison I without rest, Graf-Adolf-Str. 94, ✉ 40210, ✆ 1 68 50, Fax 1685328, – TV – 50. AE VISA JCB BV
95 rm 170/280.

Eden, Adersstr. 29, ✉ 40215, ✆ 3 89 70, Fax 3897777 – TV – AE VISA JCB EZ
closed 22 December - 6 January **Meals** *(closed Sunday)* à la carte 43/58 – **121 r** 175/472.

Dorint Hotel, Stresemannplatz 1, ✉ 40210, ✆ 3 55 40, Fax 354120 – rm – 50. AE VISA JCB EZ
Meals (dinner only) à la carte 42/60 – **152 rm** 227/459 – 3 suites.

Madison II without rest, Graf-Adolf-Str. 47, ✉ 40210, ✆ 38 80 30, Fax 3880388 – TV. AE VISA JCB EZ
closed July and 20 December - 8 January – **24 rm** 145/255.

Hotel An der Kö without rest, Talstr. 9, ✉ 40217, ✆ 37 10 48, Fax 370835 – P. AE VISA JCB EZ
45 rm 158/410.

Astoria without rest, Jahnstr. 72, ✉ 40215, ✆ 38 51 30, Fax 372089 – TV P. AE VISA JCB. BX
closed 22 December - 8 January – **26 rm** 149/380 – 4 suites.

Rema Hotel Savoy without rest, Oststr. 128, ✉ 40210, ✆ 36 03 36, Fax 3566 – TV – 90. AE VISA JCB EZ
123 rm 290/390.

Rema-Hotel Concorde without rest, Graf-Adolf-Str. 60, ✉ 40210, ✆ 36 98 2 Fax 354604 – TV. AE VISA JCB EZ
82 rm 170/340.

Carat Hotel without rest, Benrather Str. 7a, ✉ 40213, ✆ 1 30 50, Fax 322214, – TV – 20. AE VISA DZ
73 rm 220/395.

Rema-Hotel Monopol without rest, Oststr. 135, ✉ 40210, ✆ 8 42 08, Fax 3288 – TV. AE VISA JCB EZ
50 rm 170/340.

Uebachs without rest, Leopoldstr. 5, ✉ 40211, ✆ 17 37 10, Fax 358064 – – 30. AE VISA BV
82 rm 179/380.

Bellevue without rest, Luisenstr. 98, ✉ 40215, ✆ 38 41 40, Fax 3841413 – P. AE VISA. EZ
closed 23 December - 1 January – **55 rm** 165/395.

Cornelius without rest, Corneliusstr. 82, ✉ 40215, ✆ 38 20 55, Fax 382050, – TV P – 25. AE VISA BX
closed 20 December - 7 January – **48 rm** 130/250.

City without rest, Bismarckstr. 73, ✉ 40210, ✆ 36 50 23, Fax 365343 – TV. VISA JCB EZ
closed 23 December - 2 January – **54 rm** 148/320.

Terminus without rest, Am Wehrhahn 81, ✉ 40211, ✆ 35 05 91, Fax 358350, – TV. AE VISA BV
closed 23 December - 4 January – **45 rm** 170/480.

Prinz Anton without rest, Karl-Anton-Str. 11, ✉ 40211, ✆ 35 20 00, Fax 362010 TV. AE VISA JCB BV
40 rm 160/398.

Residenz without rest, Worringer Str. 88, ✉ 40211, ✆ 36 08 54, Fax 364676 – TV. AE VISA BV
34 rm 148/390.

Ibis Hauptbahnhof without rest, Konrad-Adenauer-Platz 14, ✉ 40210, ☎ 1 67 20, Fax 1672101 – AE VISA JCB BV u
166 rm 165/247.

Schumacher without rest, Worringer Str. 55, ✉ 40211, ☎ 36 78 50, Fax 3678570, – AE VISA JCB – **29 rm** 150/380. BV d

Victorian, Königstr. 3a (1st floor), ✉ 40212, ☎ 8 65 50 22, Fax 8655013 – AE E VISA. EZ c
closed Sunday and Bank Holidays – **Meals** (booking essential) 55 (lunch) and à la carte 84/125 – ***Bistro im Victorian*** *(closed Sunday July and August)* **Meals** à la carte 37/78
Spec. Terrine von Wachtel und Gänseleber im Baumkuchen, Steinbutt auf Salat gedämpft, Geräuchertes Lammfilet mit Wacholderglace.

Weinhaus Tante Anna (former 16C house-chapel), Andreasstr. 2, ✉ 40213, ☎ 13 11 63, Fax 132974, « Antique pictures and furniture » – AE E VISA JCB.
closed Sunday except exhibitions – **Meals** (dinner only, booking essential, outstanding wine list) à la carte 55/88. DY c

La Terrazza (Italian rest.), Königsallee 30 (Kö-Centre, 2nd floor,), ✉ 40212, ☎ 32 75 40, Fax 320975 – AE E VISA JCB EZ v
closed Sunday and Bank Holidays except exhibitions – **Meals** (booking essential) à la carte 63/86.

Calvados, Hohe Str. 33, ✉ 40213, ☎ 32 84 96, Fax 327877, – AE E VISA DZ a
closed Sunday – **Meals** à la carte 48/78.

Nippon Kan (Japanese rest.), Immermannstr. 35, ✉ 40210, ☎ 35 31 35, Fax 3613625 – AE E VISA JCB. BV g
closed Easter and Christmas – **Meals** (booking essential) à la carte 55/150.

Daitokai (Japanese rest.), Mutter-Ey-Str. 1, ✉ 40213, ☎ 32 50 54, Fax 325056 – AE E VISA JCB. DY z
Meals 64/98 and à la carte.

rewery-inns :

Zum Schiffchen, Hafenstr. 5, ✉ 40213, ☎ 13 24 21, Fax 134596, – AE E VISA JCB DZ f
closed Christmas - New Year, Sunday and Bank Holidays – **Meals** à la carte 36/72.

Im Goldenen Ring, Burgplatz 21, ✉ 40213, ☎ 13 31 61, Fax 324780, beer garden – AE E VISA DY n
closed Christmas – **Meals** à la carte 31/60.

t Düsseldorf-Angermund *N : 15 km by Danziger Straße* AU :

Haus Litzbrück, Bahnhofstr. 33, ✉ 40489, ☎ (0203) 99 79 60, Fax 9979653, « Garden terrace », – – 30. AE E VISA.
Meals à la carte 54/77 – **21 rm** 175/285.

t Düsseldorf-Bilk :

Grand Hotel without rest, Varnhagenstr. 37, ✉ 40225, ☎ 31 08 00, Fax 316667, – – 30. AE E VISA JCB BX a
70 rm 175/295.

Aida without rest, Ubierstr. 36, ✉ 40223, ☎ 1 59 90, Fax 1599103, – – 30. AE E VISA – **93 rm** 158/298. by Aachener Str. AX

t Düsseldorf-Derendorf *by Prinz-Georg-Str.* BU :

Villa Viktoria without rest, Blumenthalstr. 12, ✉ 40476, ☎ 46 90 00, Fax 46900601, « Elegant modern installation », – AE E VISA JCB
closed 24 December - 1 January – **40 suites** 415/1145.

Lindner Hotel Rhein Residence, Kaiserswerther Str. 20, ✉ 40477, ☎ 4 99 90, Fax 4999499, , Massage – rm – 18. AE E VISA JCB. rest
Meals à la carte 42/74 – **126 rm** 252/449. ABU f

Gildors Hotel without rest (with guest house), Collenbachstr. 51, ✉ 40476, ☎ 48 80 05, Fax 444844 – AE E VISA BU n
50 rm 170/350.

Cascade without rest, Kaiserswerther Str. 59, ✉ 40477, ☎ 49 22 00, Fax 4922022 – AE E VISA – **29 rm** 155/320. AU c

Amalfi (Italian rest.), Ulmenstr. 122, ✉ 40476, ☎ 43 38 09, Fax 4708112 – AE E VISA
closed Saturday lunch and Sunday except exhibitions – **Meals** à la carte 46/76. BU r

t Düsseldorf-Düsseltal :

Haus am Zoo without rest, Sybelstr. 21, ✉ 40239, ☎ 62 63 33, Fax 626536, « Garden », (heated) – AE E VISA BU h
23 rm 180/350.

at Düsseldorf-Golzheim *by Fischerstr.* BV :

Radisson SAS Hotel, Karl-Arnold-Platz 5, ✉ 40474, ☎ 4 55 30, Fax 4553110, ... – rm ... – 400. AE ① E VISA JCB. ✻ res
Meals à la carte 46/80 – **309 rm** ☕ 345/752 – 15 suites. AU

Düsseldorf Hilton, Georg-Glock-Str. 20, ✉ 40474, ☎ 4 37 70, Telex 858437 Fax 4377650, ..., Massage ... – rm ... – 10(AE ① E VISA JCB. ✻ rest AU
Meals à la carte 49/89 – **372 rm** ☕ 367/679 – 8 suites.

Ashley's Garden ..., Karl-Kleppe-Str. 20, ✉ 40474, ☎ 43 44 53(hotel) 4 70 83 05(res Fax 453299, ... – rm ... – 30. AE ① E VISA JCB AU
Golzheimer Krug *(Saturday dinner only)* **Meals** à la carte 48/80 – **35 rm** ☕ 19 380.

Rosati (Italian rest.), Felix-Klein-Str. 1, ✉ 40474, ☎ 4 36 05 03, Fax 452963, ... – AE ① E VISA JCB. ✻ AU
closed Saturday lunch and Sunday – **Meals** (booking essential) à la carte 55/85.

An'ne Bell, Rotterdamer Str. 11, ✉ 40474, ☎ 4 37 08 88, Fax 4380369, ... – E
closed Saturday lunch, Thursday October to April, early January, 24 to 31 March ar 2 weeks October – **Meals** 68/82 and à la carte 67/100 AU
Spec. Parmentier mit gebratener Gänsestopfleber und Trüffelmarinade, Pochier Bressepoularde im Trüffelduft, Crème brulée mit Lavendelduft.

at Düsseldorf-Kaiserswerth *by Kaiserswerther Str.* AU :

Im Schiffchen, Kaiserswerther Markt 9 (1st floor), ✉ 40489, ☎ 40 10 50, Fax 4036 – AE ① E VISA. ✻
closed Sunday - Monday – **Meals** (dinner only, booking essential) 179/196 and à la car 117/147
Spec. Sainte-Maure-Frischkäse mit Kaviar und Bonnette von Noirmoutier, Gebrate Bresse-Perlhuhn in Mokka-Duft, Dèpêche aus Ceylon.

Aalschokker, Kaiserswerther Markt 9 (ground floor), ✉ 40489, ☎ 40 39 4 Fax 403667 – AE ① E VISA. ✻
closed Sunday - Monday – **Meals** (dinner only, booking essential) à la carte 68/97
Spec. Kartoffel mit Sylter Royal gefüllt in Kaviar-Sud, "Himmel und Erde" mit gebraten Gänseleber, Schwarzwälder Kirschtorte "neue Art".

at Düsseldorf-Lörick *by Luegallee* AV :

Fischerhaus ..., Bonifatiusstr. 35, ✉ 40547, ☎ 59 79 79, Telex 858444 Fax 5979759 – ... AE ① E VISA
Meals (see ***Hummerstübchen)*** – **35 rm** ☕ 139/368.

Hummerstübchen - Hotel Fischerhaus, Bonifatiusstr. 35 ✉ 40547, ☎ 59 44 0 Fax 5979759 – ... AE ① E VISA
closed Sunday, Monday and 1 to 10 January – **Meals** (dinner only, booking essenti 135/169 and à la carte 110/135
Spec. Hummer-Menu, Hummersuppe mit Champagner, Crépinette von der Bresse Taub

at Düsseldorf-Lohausen *by Danziger Str.* AU :

Arabella Airport Hotel ..., at airport, ✉ 40474, ☎ 4 17 30, Telex 858461 Fax 4173707 – ... rm ... – 180. AE ① E VISA JCB. ✻ rest
Meals à la carte 47/75 – **184 rm** ☕ 304/368.

at Düsseldorf-Mörsenbroich *by Rethelstr.* DV :

Düsseldorf-Renaissance-Hotel, Nördlicher Zubringer 6, ✉ 40470, ☎ 6 21 6 Fax 6216666, ..., Massage, ... – rm ... – 260. AE ① VISA JCB BU
Meals à la carte 62/76 – **245 rm** ☕ 309/538 – 3 suites.

at Düsseldorf-Oberkassel *by Luegallee* AV :

Lindner-Hotel-Rheinstern, Emanuel-Leutze-Str. 17, ✉ 40547, ☎ 5 99 7 Telex 8584242, Fax 5997339, ... – rm ... – 320. AE ① E VISA JCB
Meals 39 buffet lunch and à la carte 50/78 – **254 rm** ☕ 212/648.

Ramada, Am Seestern 16, ✉ 40547, ☎ 59 59 59, Fax 593569, ... – r ... – 120. AE ① E VISA JCB
Meals à la carte 39/72 – **222 rm** ☕ 246/512.

Hanseat without rest, Belsenstr. 6, ✉ 40545, ☎ 57 50 69, Fax 589662, « Elegar installation » – ... AE ① E VISA
closed Christmas - New Year – **37 rm** ☕ 180/300.

XXX **De' Medici** (Italian rest.), Amboßstr. 3, ✉ 40547, ✆ 59 41 51, Fax 592612 – AE ⓓ E VISA JCB
closed Saturday lunch, Sunday and Bank Holidays except exhibitions – **Meals** (booking essential) à la carte 48/82.

XX **Edo** (Japanese restaurants : Teppan, Robata and Tatami), Am Seestern 3, ✉ 40547, ✆ 59 10 82, Fax 591394, « Japanese garden » – ▤ P. AE ⓓ E VISA JCB. ✂
closed Saturday lunch, Sunday and Bank Holidays except exhibitions – **Meals** à la carte 57/107.

at Düsseldorf-Unterbach *SE : 11 km by Grafenberger Allee* BV :

Landhotel Am Zault - Residenz, Gerresheimer Landstr. 40, ✉ 40627, ✆ 25 10 81, Fax 254718, ☂, ≘s – TV ☎ P – 🏛 100. AE ⓓ E VISA. ✂ rest
Meals à la carte 52/83 – **59 rm** ☐ 190/380.

at Düsseldorf-Unterbilk :

Sorat (elegant modern installation), Volmerswerther Str. 35, ✉ 40221, ✆ 3 02 20, Fax 3022555 – |♦| ⇔ rm ▤ TV ☎ ✆ ⇔ – 🏛 160. AE ⓓ E VISA JCB AX c
Meals à la carte 46/68 – **160 rm** ☐ 198/461.

XX **Savini**, Stromstr. 47, ✉ 40221, ✆ 39 39 31, Fax 391719, ☂ – AE ⓓ E VISA
closed Saturday lunch, Sunday and Monday except exhibitions – **Meals** (booking essential) à la carte 62/88. AX e

XX **Rheinturm Top 180** (revolving restaurant at 172 m), Stromstr. 20, ✉ 40221, ✆ 8 48 58, Fax 325619, ✻ Düsseldorf and Rhein (|♦|, charge) – ▤ ♿ – 🏛 60. AE ⓓ E VISA JCB. ✂ AV a
Meals à la carte 53/82.

at Düsseldorf-Unterrath *by Ulmenstraße* BU :

Lindner Hotel Airport, Unterrather Str. 108, ✉ 40468, ✆ 9 51 60, Fax 9516516, ⅎ6, ≘s – |♦| ⇔ rm TV ✆ ⇔ P – 🏛 140. AE ⓓ E VISA JCB. ✂ rest
Meals à la carte 47/70 – **202 rm** ☐ 287/520.

at Meerbusch-Büderich *by Luegallee* AV – ☎ *02132* :

XXX **Landsknecht** with rm, Poststr. 70, ✉ 40667, ✆ 59 47, Fax 10978, ☂ – TV ☎ P. AE ⓓ E VISA. ✂
closed Saturday lunch and Monday – **Meals** (outstanding wine list) à la carte 61/90 – **9 rm** ☐ 160/280.

XXX **Landhaus Mönchenwerth**, Niederlöricker Str. 56 (at the boat landing stage), ✉ 40667, ✆ 7 79 31, Fax 71899, ≤, « Garden terrace » – P. AE ⓓ E VISA JCB. ✂
closed Monday – **Meals** à la carte 51/80.

X **Lindenhof**, Dorfstr. 48, ✉ 40667, ✆ 26 64, ☂ – AE
closed Monday – **Meals** (booking essential) à la carte 42/67.

at Meerbusch - Langst-Kirst *NW : 14 km by Luegallee AV and Neusser Straße*

Rheinhotel Vier Jahreszeiten ⛵, Zur Rheinfähre 14, ✉ 40668, ✆ (02150) 91 40, Fax 919400, ☂, beer garden, ≘s, ⛵ – |♦| ⇔ rm ▤ TV ✆ P – 🏛 250. AE ⓓ E VISA
***Bellevue* :** **Meals** à la carte 51/84 – **78 rm** ☐ 190/350.

Essen *Nordrhein-Westfalen* 417 L 5, 987 ⑭ – *pop. 670 000 – alt. 120 m* – ☎ *0201.*
Düsseldorf 31.

at Essen-Kettwig *S : 11 km* :

XXXX **Résidence** ⛵ with rm, Auf der Forst 1, ✉ 45219, ✆ (02054) 89 11, Fax 82501, ☂ – ⇔ rest TV ☎ P. AE ⓓ VISA
✿✿ *closed 1 to 8 January and 3 weeks July - August* – **Meals** *(closed Sunday - Monday)* (dinner only, booking essential, outstanding wine list) 112/168 and à la carte 92/128 – **18 rm** ☐ 188/373
Spec. Hummer mit Dicken Bohnen in Thymianrahm, Roulade vom Entrecôte mit Gänseleberkartoffel, Quarksoufflé mit Beerenkompott und Zitronengrassorbet.

Grevenbroich *Nordrhein-Westfalen* 417 C 13, 987 ㉓ – *pop. 62 000 – alt. 60 m* – ☎ *02181.*
Düsseldorf 28.

XXXX **Zur Traube** with rm, Bahnstr. 47, ✉ 41515, ✆ 6 87 67, Fax 61122 – TV P. ⓓ E VISA. ✂ rm
✿✿ *closed 29 March - 4 April, 19 July - 1 August and 24 December - 24 January* – **Meals** *(closed Sunday and Monday)* (booking essential, outstanding wine list) 78 (lunch) and à la carte 96/139 – **6 rm** ☐ 220/490
Spec. Parfait vom Stör mit Kaviar, Täubchen im Spitzkohlblatt mit Trüffelbutter, Variation von Bitterschockolade.

FRANKFURT ON MAIN *Hessen* 417 P 10, 987 ㉗ – *pop. 660 000 – alt. 91 m* – ☎ 069
See : *Zoo*★★★ FX – *Goethe's House (Goethehaus)*★ GZ – *Cathedral (Dom)*★ *(Gothic Tower*★★, *Choir-stalls*★, *Museum*★*)* HZ – *Tropical Garden (Palmengarten)*★ CV – *Senckenberg-Museum*★ *(Palaeontology department*★★*)* CV **M9** – *Städel Museum (Städelsches Museum and Städtische Galerie)* ★★ GZ – *Museum of Applied Arts (Museum für Kunsthandwerk)*★ HZ – *German Cinema Museum*★ GZ **M7** – *Henninger Turm* ✻★ FX

Frankfurt-Niederrad, by Kennedy-Allee CDX, ☎ *6 66 23 17.*
Rhein-Main (SW : 12 km), ☎ *6 90 25 95.*
at Neu-Isenburg (S : 7 km).
Exhibition Centre (Messegelände) (CX), ☎ *7 57 50, Fax 75756433.*
Tourist Information, Main Station (Hauptbahnhof), ✉ *60329,* ☎ *21 23 88 4… Fax 21240512.*
Tourist Information, im Römer, ✉ *60311,* ☎ *21 23 87 08.*
ADAC, *Schumannstr. 4,* ✉ *60325,* ☎ *74 38 00, Fax 749254.*
ADAC, *Schillerstr. 12,* ✉ *60313,* ☎ *74 38 03 35, Fax 283597.*
Berlin 537 – Wiesbaden 41 – Bonn 178 – Nürnberg 226 – Stuttgart 204.

Plans on following pages

Steigenberger Frankfurter Hof, Bethmannstr. 33, ✉ 60311, ☎ 2 15 0… Telex 411806, Fax 215900, Massage – rm TV – 120. AE E VISA JCB. rest GZ
Meals see ***Restaurant Francais*** *below* – ***Hofgarten*** *(closed Friday - Saturday)* **Meals** à la carte 62/85 – ***Frankfurter Stubb*** (booking essential) *(closed Saturday, Sunday, Bank Holidays and 4 weeks July - August)* **Meals** à la carte 39/63 – ***Kaiserbrunnen*** *(closed Sunday - Monday)* **Meals** à la carte 38/56 – **332 rm** 386/652 – 20 suites.

Hessischer Hof, Friedrich-Ebert-Anlage 40, ✉ 60325, ☎ 7 54 00, Telex 41177… Fax 7540924, « Rest. with collection of Sèvres porcelain » – rm TV – 120. AE E VISA JCB. rest CX
Meals 40 lunch and à la carte 55/88 – **117 rm** 390/660 – 11 suites.

Arabella Grand Hotel, Konrad-Adenauer-Str. 7, ✉ 60313, ☎ 2 98 10, Fax 29818… Massage, – rm TV – 300. AE E VISA JCB. rest HY
– ***Premiere*** *(dinner only, closed 4 weeks July - August)* **Meals** 90/136 and à la carte 76/107 – ***Brasserie*** *: (lunch only)* **Meals** à la carte 46/89 – ***Dynasty*** (Chinese rest.) **Meals** à la carte 47/84 – **378 rm** 406/697 – 11 suites.

Martim Hotel Frankfurt, Theodor-Heuss-Allee 3, ✉ 60486, ☎ 7 57 8… Fax 75781000, – rm TV – 2300. AE E VISA JCB rest CVX
Classico *(closed Sunday lunch and Saturday)* **Meals** à la carte 55/80 – ***Ambiente*** *(closed Sunday dinner and Saturday)* **Meals** à la carte 45/68 – **543 rm** 322/704 – 24 suites.

Intercontinental Frankfurt, Wilhelm-Leuschner-Str. 43, ✉ 60329, ☎ 2 60 5… Telex 413639, Fax 252467, – rm TV – 500. AE VISA JCB GZ
Meals à la carte 56/78 – ***Kyoto*** (Japanese rest.) *(closed Saturday lunch and Sunday)* **Meals** à la carte 36/72 – **465 rm** 387/659 – 49 suites.

Frankfurt Marriott Hotel, Hamburger Allee 2, ✉ 60486, ☎ 7 95 50, Telex 41674… Fax 79552432, ≤ Frankfurt, Massage, – rm TV – 600. E VISA JCB. rest CV
Meals à la carte 38/79 – **588 rm** 316/542 – 17 suites.

Le Meridien Parkhotel, Wiesenhüttenplatz 28, ✉ 60329, ☎ 2 69 70, Telex 4128… Fax 2697884, – rm TV – 160. AE E VISA JCB CX
Meals à la carte 50/75 – **296 rm** 323/756 – 11 suites.

Alexander am Zoo without rest, Waldschmidtstr. 59, ✉ 60316, ☎ 94 96 0… Fax 94960720, – TV – 30. AE E VISA. FV
59 rm 210/260 – 9 suites.

Palmenhof, Bockenheimer Landstr. 89, ✉ 60325, ☎ 7 53 00 60, Fax 75300666 – TV. AE E VISA JCB CV
closed 23 December - 2 January – **Meals** *(closed Saturday, Sunday and Bank Hollida… except exhibitions)* à la carte 60/85 – **47 rm** 195/395.

An der Messe without rest, Westendstr. 104, ✉ 60325, ☎ 74 79 79, Fax 748349 TV. AE E VISA CV
46 rm 210/460.

Forum Hotel without rest, Wilhelm-Leuschner-Str. 34, ✉ 60329, ☎ 2 60 60, Fax 252… – rm TV. AE E VISA JCB CZ
301 rm 327/559.

Sofitel, Savignystr. 14, ✉ 60325, ☎ 7 53 30, Fax 7533175 – rm TV – 8… AE E VISA CX
Meals à la carte 42/87 – **155 rm** 530/614.

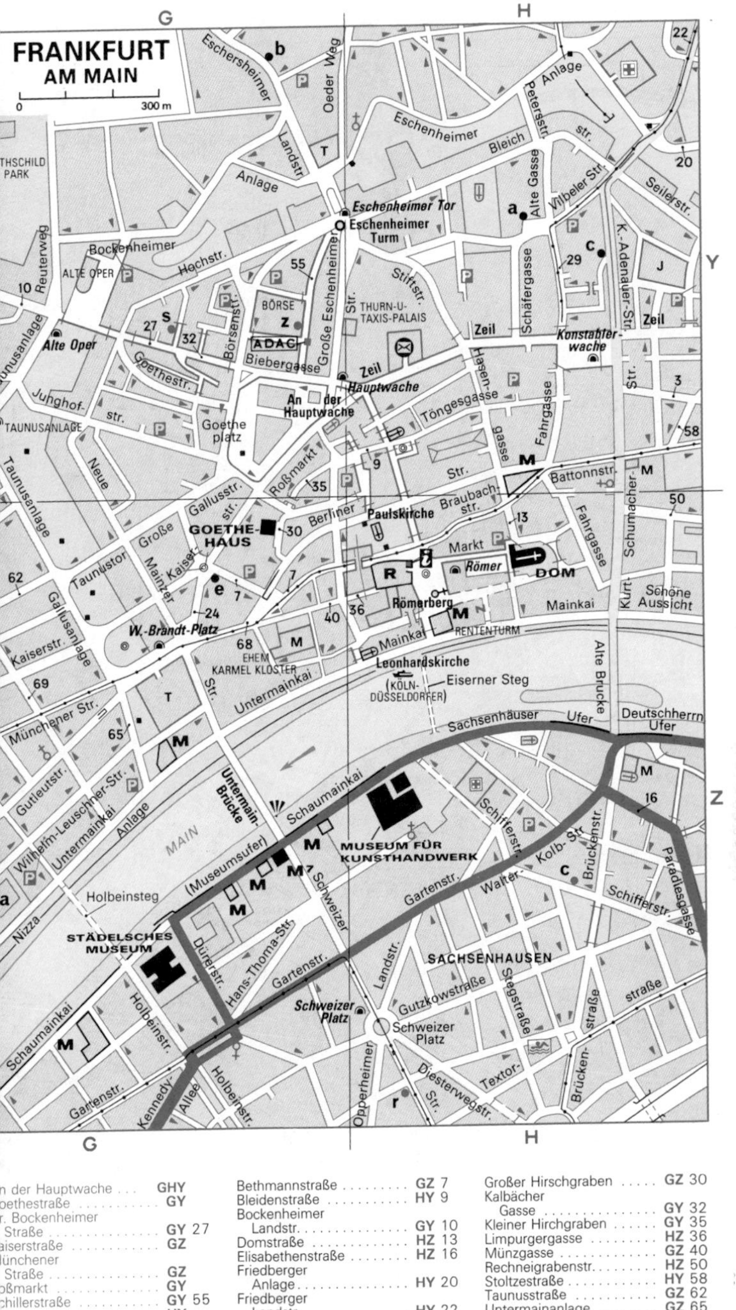

n der Hauptwache . . . GHY
oethestraße . . . . GY
r. Bockenheimer
Straße . . . . GY 27
aiserstraße . . . . GZ
ünchener
Straße . . . . GZ
oßmarkt . . . . GY
chillerstraße . . . . GY 55
eil . . . . HY
llerheiligenstraße . . . . . . HY 3

Bethmannstraße . . . . GZ 7
Bleidenstraße . . . . HY 9
Bockenheimer
Landstr. . . . . GY 10
Domstraße . . . . HZ 13
Elisabethenstraße . . . . HZ 16
Friedberger
Anlage . . . . HY 20
Friedberger
Landstr. . . . . HY 22
Friedensstraße . . . . GZ 24
Große Friedberger Str. . . . . HY 29

Großer Hirschgraben . . . . . GZ 30
Kalbächer
Gasse . . . . GY 32
Kleiner Hirchgraben . . . . . . GY 35
Limpurgergasse . . . . HZ 36
Münzgasse . . . . GZ 40
Rechneigrabenstr. . . . . HZ 50
Stoltzestraße . . . . HY 58
Taunusstraße . . . . GZ 62
Untermainanlage . . . . GZ 65
Weißfrauenstraße . . . . GZ 68
Weserstraße . . . . GZ 69

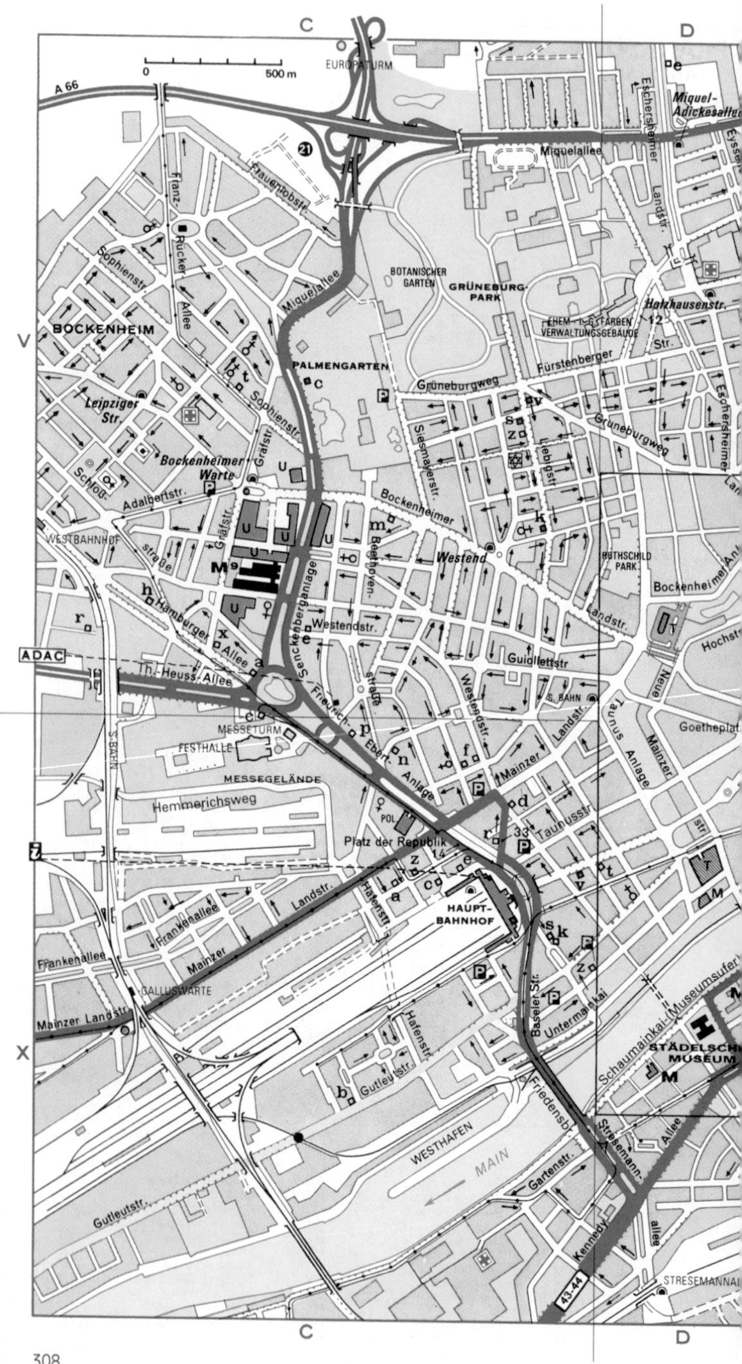

FRANKFURT AM MAIN

Alfred-Brehm-Platz .... FV 2
Arnsburger Straße .... FV 4
Bärenstraße .... FV 6
Bremer Straße .... DV 12
Düsseldorfer Straße .... CX 14
Flößerbrücke .... FX 17
Karlstraße .... CX 33
Neebstraße .... FV 42
Obermainbrücke ...... FX 45
Pfingstweidstraße .... FV 47
Seehofstraße .... FX 54
Siemensstraße .... FX 56
Wasserweg .... FX 67
Windeckstraße ...... FX 74

Mercure, Voltastr. 29, ✉ 60486, ℘ 7 92 60, Telex 413791, Fax 79261606, – rm – 20. AE VISA JCB by Th.-Heuss-Allee CV
Meals à la carte 38/75 – **346 rm** 295/430 – 12 suites.

Holiday Inn, Wiesenhüttenstr. 42, ✉ 60329, ℘ 27 39 60, Telex 4163
Fax 27396795, Massage, – rm rest – 100. AE VISA CX
Meals à la carte 44/67 – **144 rm** 260/440.

Imperial, Sophienstr. 40, ✉ 60487, ℘ 7 93 00 30, Telex 4189636, Fax 79300388 – AE VISA JCB. rest CV
Meals *(closed Sunday)* (dinner only) à la carte 40/66 – **60 rm** 190/480.

Novotel Frankfurt City West, Lise-Meitner-Str. 2, ✉ 60486, ℘ 79 30
Telex 412054, Fax 79303930, – rm – 140. VISA CV
Meals à la carte 36/63 – **235 rm** 271/292.

Victoria Hotel without rest, Elbestr. 24, ✉ 60329, ℘ 27 30 60, Fax 27306100 – AE VISA JCB CDX
75 rm 160/365.

Bauer Hotel Domicil without rest, Karlstr. 14, ✉ 60329, ℘ 27 11 10, Fax 2532 – AE VISA JCB CX
closed Christmas - New Year – **70 rm** 166/289.

Rema-Hotel Bristol without rest, Ludwigstr. 13, ✉ 60327, ℘ 24 23 90, Fax 2515 – – 25. AE VISA JCB CX
145 rm 170/360.

Turm-Hotel without rest, Eschersheimer Landstr. 20, ✉ 60322, ℘ 15 40 5
Fax 553578 – AE VISA JCB GY
closed 24 December - 2 January – **75 rm** 140/250.

Die Villa without rest, Emil-Sulzbach-Str. 14, ✉ 60486, ℘ 9 79 90 70, Fax 979907 – AE VISA JCB CV
closed 20 December - 2 January – **22 rm** 250/450.

InterCityHotel, Poststr. 8, ✉ 60329, ℘ 27 39 10, Fax 27391999 – rm – 35. AE VISA JCB. rest CX
Meals *(closed Saturday - Sunday)* à la carte 40/69 – **224 rm** 228/395.

Rhein-Main without rest, Heidelberger Str. 3, ✉ 60327, ℘ 25 00 35, Fax 252518 – AE VISA JCB. CX
50 rm 195/380.

Concorde without rest, Karlstr. 9, ✉ 60329, ℘ 23 32 30, Fax 237828 – AE VISA. CX
closed 20 December - 2 January – **45 rm** 140/300.

Topas without rest, Niddastr. 88, ✉ 60329, ℘ 23 08 52, Fax 237228 – VISA JCB. CX
31 rm 110/310.

Cristall without rest, Ottostr. 3, ✉ 60329, ℘ 23 03 51, Telex 4170654, Fax 2533 – AE VISA JCB. CX
30 rm 110/310.

Restaurant Français - Hotel Steigenberger Frankfurter Hof, Bethmannstr. 3
✉ 60311, ℘ 2 15 02 – AE VISA JCB. GZ
closed Saturday lunch, Sunday - Monday and Bank Holidays except exhibitions and end Ju - early September – **Meals** (booking essential) à la carte 79/110
Spec. Warme Gänseleberterrine mit Granatapfeljus, Jakobsmuscheln mit luftgetocknete Speck auf Spitzkohl (January-March), Geschmortes Rindfleisch en Daube mit schwarze Trüffel.

Humperdinck, Grüneburgweg 95, ✉ 60323, ℘ 72 21 22, Fax 97203155, – AE VISA CV
closed Saturday lunch, Sunday and Bank Holidays, 3 weeks July - August and Christm - early January **Meals** à la carte 86/125
Spec. Steinbutt und Kalbskopf mit Balsamico-Senfsauce, Sauté vom Kaninchen mit Majoran, Warmer Schockoladenbisquit mit Karameleis.

Villa Leonhardi, Zeppelinallee 18, ✉ 60325, ℘ 74 25 35, Fax 740476, « Terrace park » – AE VISA JCB. CV
closed Saturday, Sunday, Bank Holidays and 23 December - early January – **Meals** à la car 68/88.

Tse-Yang (Chinese rest.), Kaiserstr. 67, ✉ 60329, ℘ 23 25 41, Fax 237825 – AE VISA JCB. CX
Meals à la carte 44/80.

Gallo Nero (Italian rest.), Kaiserhofstr. 7, ✉ 60313, ℘ 28 48 40, Fax 291645, – VISA JCB GY
closed Sunday except exhibitions – **Meals** à la carte 57/93.

Gargantua (Bistro style rest.), Liebigstr. 47, ✉ 60323, ☎ 72 07 18, Fax 720717, – AE E VISA CV s
closed Saturday lunch, Sunday and late December - early January – **Meals** (booking essential) 49 (lunch) and à la carte 78/104.

Ernos Bistro (French rest.), Liebigstr. 15, ✉ 60323, ☎ 72 19 97, Fax 173838, – AE E VISA
closed Saturday and Sunday except exhibitions, 21 June - 13 July and 20 December - 4 January – **Meals** (booking essential) 50 (lunch) à la carte 90/117. CV k

Frankfurt-Bergen-Enkheim *by Wittelsbacherallee* FV ✆ *06109* :

Amadeus, Röntgenstr. 5, ✉ 60338, ☎ 37 00, Fax 370720 – rm – 80. AE E VISA JCB
Meals *(closed Friday dinner - Saturday lunch)* à la carte 39/60 – **160 rm** 195/295.

Frankfurt-Griesheim *by Th.-Heuss-Allee* CV :

Ramada, Oeserstr. 180, ✉ 65933, ☎ 3 90 50, Telex 416812, Fax 3808218, – rm rest – 220. AE E VISA JCB. rm
Meals à la carte 50/69 – **236 rm** 220/425.

Frankfurt-Höchst *W : 10 km by Mainzer Landstraße CX* :

Lindner Congress Hotel, Alt Erlenbach 44, ✉ 60437, ☎ 3 30 02 00, Fax 33002999, – rm – 200. AE E VISA JCB. rest
Meals à la carte 46/64 – **285 rm** 281/600.

Frankfurt-Nieder-Erlenbach *by Friedberger Landstr.* FV *and Homburger Landstr. N : 14 km* :

Erlenbach 33, Alt Erlenbach 33, ✉ 60437, ☎ (06101) 4 80 98, Fax 48783 – AE E VISA
closed Thursday and 3 weeks July - August – **Meals** (weekdays dinner only) à la carte 48/72.

Frankfurt-Niederrad *by Kennedy-Allee* CDX :

Queens Hotel, Isenburger Schneise 40, ✉ 60528, ☎ 6 78 40, Fax 6784190, – rm – 420. AE E VISA JCB
Meals à la carte 42/74 – **277 rm** 316/592.

Arabella Congress Hotel, Lyoner Str. 44, ✉ 60528, ☎ 6 63 30, Fax 6633666, – rm – 330. AE E VISA
Meals à la carte 42/72 – **396 rm** 439/502 – 8 suites.

Dorint, Hahnstr. 9, ✉ 60528, ☎ 66 30 60, Fax 66306600, – rm – 180. AE E VISA JCB. rest
Meals à la carte 42/66 – **191 rm** 270/460.

Weidemann, Kelsterbacher Str. 66, ✉ 60528, ☎ 67 59 96, Fax 673928, – . AE E VISA by Gartenstraße CX
closed Saturday lunch, Sunday and Bank Holidays – **Meals** (booking essential) 51 (lunch) and à la carte 77/107.

Frankfurt-Nordweststadt *by Miquelallee (CV)* :

Ramada Hotel Nordwest Zentrum without rest, Walter-Möller-Platz, ✉ 60439, ☎ 58 09 30, Fax 582447 – – 20. AE E VISA JCB
93 rm 175/218.

Frankfurt-Rödelheim *NW : 6 km by Theodor-Heuss-Allee* CV *and Ludwig-Landmann-Str* :

Osteria Enoteca (Italian rest.), Arnoldshainer Str. 2 (corner Lorcher Str.), ✉ 60489, ☎ 7 89 22 16, – AE E VISA.
closed Saturday lunch, Sunday and late December - early January – **Meals** (booking essential) 95 and à la carte 77/94
Spec. Kleiner Salat von Seezunge und Gamberoni auf gebackenem Endivien, Testaroli mit Pesto, Kartoffeln, grüne Bohnen und Salmone, Kaninchen aus dem Ofen.

Frankfurt-Sachsenhausen :

Holiday Inn Crowne Plaza, Mailänder Str. 1, ✉ 60598, ☎ 6 80 20, Telex 411805, Fax 6802333, – rm – 400. AE E VISA JCB. rest by Darmstädter Landstr. (B 3) FX
Meals 45 and à la carte 53/99 – **404 rm** 325/589.

Bistrot 77, Ziegelhüttenweg 1, ✉ 60598, ☎ 61 40 40, Fax 615998, – AE E VISA EX a
closed Saturday lunch, Sunday, 3 weeks July - August and Christmas - early January – **Meals** (outstanding wine list) 48 (lunch) and à la carte 75/103.

at Eschborn *NW : 12 km by A66 :*

Novotel, Philipp-Helfmann-Str. 10, ✉ 65760, ℘ (06196) 90 10, Telex 40728‹ Fax 482114, ⛱, ⛱ (heated), – |‡| ⇸ rm ▤ 📺 ☎ ♿ 🅿 – 🏛 200. AE ⓓ E V Meals à la carte 37/65 – **227 rm** ☕ 200/260. by A 66 CV

at Neu-Isenburg - Gravenbruch *SE : 11 km by Darmstädter Landstr. FX and B 459 :*

Gravenbruch-Kempinski-Frankfurt, ✉ 63263, ℘ (06102) 50 50, Fax 5059(⛱, « Park », ⇒, ⛱ (heated), ⛱, , 🎾 – |‡| ⇸ rm ▤ 📺 🚗 🅿 – 🏛 350. ⓓ E VISA JCB
Meals 49 (lunch) and à la carte 58/86 – **285 rm** ☕ 337/586 – 21 suites.

near Rhein-Main airport *SW : 12 km by Kennedy-Allee CX – ☎ 069 :*

Sheraton, at the airport (Terminal1), ✉ 60549, ℘ 6 97 70, Telex 41892(Fax 69772209, ⇒, ⛱ – |‡| ⇸ rm ▤ 📺 ☎ ♿ 🅿 – 🏛 900. AE ⓓ E VISA JCB. ⚒ re ***Papillon*** (outstanding wine list) *(closed Saturday lunch, Sunday and Bank Holidays)* **Me** 65 (lunch) and à la carte 98/135 – ***Maxwell's Bistro :*** **Meals** à la carte 60/86 – ***Taver*** *(closed Saturday - Sunday lunch)* **Meals** à la carte 54/82 – **1050 rm** ☕ 465/745 28 suites.

Steigenberger Avance Frankfurt Airport, Unterschweinstiege 1 ✉ 60549 Frankfurt, ℘ 6 97 50, Telex 413112, Fax 69752505, Massage, ⇒, ⛱ – ⇸ rm ▤ 📺 🚗 🅿 – 🏛 300. AE ⓓ E VISA JCB
Meals 49 (only buffet lunch) – **420 rm** ☕ 295/620 – 10 suites.

Waldrestaurant Unterschweinstiege, Unterschweinstiege 16, ✉ 6054 ℘ 69 75 25 00, « Country house atmosphere, terrace » – ▤ 🅿. AE ⓓ E VISA JCB
Meals (booking essential) 49 (buffet) and à la carte 49/86.

Eltville *Hessen* 417 P 8 – *pop. 16 500 – alt. 90 m – ☎ 06123.*
Frankfurt am Main 55.

at Eltville-Hattenheim *W : 4 km :*

✿✿ **Marcobrunn**, Hauptstr. 43 (at Hotel Schloss Reinhartshausen), ✉ 65346, ℘ 67 64 3 Fax 676400, « Terrace in park » – ▤ 🅿. AE ⓓ E VISA. ⚒
closed Monday - Tuesday and 1 to 28 January – **Meals** (weekdays dinner only, Sunday lun only) (booking essential) 95/170 and à la carte 88/126
Spec. Törtchen von mild geräucherter Taube und Gänseleber im Baumkuchenmantel, La gustinentempura mit exotischem Ratatouille und Limonen-Ingwerschaum, Pfannkuche charlotte mit Steinpilzen und Gänseleber (September-October).

Maintal *Hessen* 417 P 10 – *pop. 40 000 – alt. 95 m – ☎ 06181.*
Frankfurt am Main 13.

at Maintal-Dörnigheim :

✿ **Hessler** with rm, Am Bootshafen 4, ✉ 63477, ℘ (06181) 4 30 30, Fax 430333 – ☎ 🅿. AE E VISA. ⚒ rest
closed 3 weeks July – **Meals** *(closed Sunday - Monday)* (booking essential, outstanding wi list) 48 (lunch) and à la carte 84/110 – **7 rm** ☕ 180/290
Spec. Marinierter Seeteufel auf Kokosreis, Lammrücken in orientalischer Würze auf Cou cous, Taube im Strudelteig mit Wacholderjus.

Mannheim *Baden-Württemberg* 417 419 R 9, 987 ㉗ – *pop. 324 000 – alt. 95 m – ☎ 062*
Frankfurt am Main 79.

✿✿ **Da Gianni** (elegant Italian rest.), R 7, 34 (Friedrichsring), ✉ 68161, ℘ 2 03 26 – ▤. E
closed Monday, Bank Holidays and 3 weeks July - August – **Meals** (booking essential) à carte 97/119
Spec. Variation von Antipasti, Steinbut auf Borlotti Bohnen in Olivenmarinade, Ente Barolosauce.

Stromberg Kreis Kreuznach *Rheinland-Pfalz* 417 Q 7, 987 ㉖ – *pop. 3 000 – alt. 235* – *☎ 06724.*
Frankfurt am Main 82.

✿✿ **Le Val d'Or in Lafer's Stromburg** with rm, Schloßberg (E : 1,5km), ✉ 5544 ℘ 9 31 00, Fax 931090, ←, ⛱, beergarden – 📺 ☎ 🅿 – 🏛 100. AE ⓓ E VISA
Meals *(Tuesday - Friday dinner only, closed Monday)* 155/189 and à la carte 103/134
Turmstube : **Meals** à la carte 52/76 – **13 rm** ☕ 180/370
Spec. Asiatischer Vorspeisenteller von Fischen und Meeresfrüchten, Rehrücken in d Haselnußkruste mit Petersilienwurzelpüree, Dessertimpressionen.

Wertheim *Baden-Württemberg* 417 419 Q 12, 987 ㉗ – *pop. 21 700 – alt. 142 m* – ☎ *09342.*
Frankfurt am Main 87.

At Wertheim-Bettingen *E : 10 km :*

Schweizer Stuben ⑤, Geiselbrunnweg 11, ✉ 97877, ☎ 30 70, Fax 307155, ☂, « Hotel in a park », Massage, ≘s, ⛱ (heated), ☒, ⛟, ✂ (indoor) – TV P – 🏛 30. AE ① E VISA
Meals *(closed Tuesday and January)* (Monday - Saturday dinner only, booking essential) 140/210 and à la carte 85/165 – **33 rm** ☐ 225/496 – 3 suites
Spec. Terrine von der Entenstopfleber mit Gelee von Muscat, Brandade vom Stockfisch, Sisteron-Lamm mit Artischocken à la barigoule.

HAMBURG L *Stadtstaat Hamburg* 415 416 F 14, 987 ⑤ – *pop. 1 650 000 – alt. 10 m* – ☎ *040.*

See : *Jungfernstieg★* GY – *Außenalster★★★ (trip by boat★★★)* GHXY – *Hagenbeck Zoo (Tierpark Hagenbeck)★★ by Schröderstiftstr.* EX – *Television Tower (Fernsehturm)★ (✻★★)* EX – *Fine Arts Museum (Kunsthalle)★★* HY **M1** – *St. Michael's church (St. Michaelis)★ (tower ✻★)* EFZ – *Stintfang (≤★)* EZ – *Port (Hafen)★★* EZ – *Decorative Arts and Crafts Museum (Museum für Kunst und Gewerbe)★* HY **M2** – *Historical Museum (Museum für Hamburgische Geschichte)★* EYZ **M3** – *Post-Museum★* FY **M4** – *Planten un Blomen Park★* EFX – *Museum of Ethnography (Hamburgisches Museum für Völkerkunde)★ by Rothenbaumchaussee* FX.

Envir. : *Altona and Northern Germany Museum (Norddeutsches Landesmuseum)★★ by Reeperbahn* EZ – *Altona Balcony (Altonaer Balkon) ≤★ by Reeperbahn* EZ – *Elbchaussee★ by Reeperbahn* EZ.

18 Hamburg-Blankenese, In de Bargen 59 (W : 17 km), ☎ 81 21 77 ; 18 Ammersbek (NE : 15 km), ☎ (040) 6 05 13 37 ; 18 Hamburg-Wendlohe (N : 14 km), ☎ 5 50 50 14 ; 18 Wentorf, Golfstr. 2 (SE : 21 km), ☎ (040) 7 20 21 41.

✈ Hamburg-Fuhlsbüttel (N : 15 km), ☎ 50 80.

🚗 Hamburg-Altona, Sternschanze.

Exhibition Centre (Messegelände) (EFX), ☎ 3 56 91, Telex 212609.

ℹ Tourismus-Zentrale Hamburg, Burchardstr. 14, ✉ 20095, ☎ 30 05 10, Fax 30051220.

ℹ Tourist-Information, Harbour, Landungsbrücke 4-5, ✉ 20459, ☎ 30 05 12 00.

ADAC, *Amsinckstr. 39, ✉ 20097, ☎ 23 91 90, Fax 23919271.*

Berlin 289 – Bremen 120 – Hannover 151.

Plans on following pages

Near Hauptbahnhof, at St. Georg, east of the Außenalster :

Kempinski Hotel Atlantic Hamburg ⑤, An der Alster 72, ✉ 20099, ☎ 2 88 80, Fax 247129, ≤ Außenalster, ☂, Massage, ≘s, ☒ – 🛗 ⇔ rm TV ☏ 🚗 – 🏛 300. AE ① E VISA JCB. ✂ rest HY a
Meals *(closed Sunday lunch)* à la carte 65/104 – ***Atlantic-Mühle*** *(closed Sunday, dinner only)* **Meals** à la carte 36/70 – **254 rm** ☐ 399/598 – 13 suites.

Holiday Inn Crowne Plaza, Graumannsweg 10, ✉ 22087, ☎ 22 80 60, Fax 2208704, Massage, ≘s, ☒ – 🛗 ⇔ rm ▤ TV ☎ ♿ 🚗 – 🏛 120. AE ① E VISA JCB. ✂ rest by Lange Reihe HX
Lord Nelson *(Sunday and Monday lunch only)* **Meals** à la carte 42/81 – ***King George Pub :*** **Meals** à la carte 34/51 – **286 rm** ☐ 308/416.

Europäischer Hof, Kirchenallee 45, ✉ 20099, ☎ 24 82 48, Telex 2162493, Fax 24824799, ☂, Massage, Fitness, ≘s, ☒ Squash – 🛗 ⇔ rm ▤ rest TV 🚗 – 🏛 150. AE ① E VISA HY e
Meals à la carte 43/70 – **320 rm** ☐ 180/420.

Maritim Hotel Reichshof, Kirchenallee 34, ✉ 20099, ☎ 24 83 30, Fax 24833588, ≘s, ☒ – 🛗 ⇔ rm TV 🚗 – 🏛 200. AE ① E VISA JCB. ✂ rest HY d
Meals à la carte 64/87 – **303 rm** ☐ 239/448 – 6 suites.

Prem, An der Alster 9, ✉ 20099, ☎ 24 17 26, Fax 2803851, « Antique furnishings, garden », ≘s – 🛗 TV P. AE ① E VISA JCB HX c
La mer *(closed Saturday lunch and Sunday lunch)* **Meals** à la carte 61/104 – **53 rm** ☐ 220/454 – 3 suites.

Senator, Lange Reihe 18, ✉ 20099, ☎ 24 12 03, Fax 2803717 – 🛗 ⇔ rm TV ☎ 🚗. AE ① E VISA JCB. ✂ rest HY u
Meals (residents only) (dinner only) – **56 rm** ☐ 185/285.

Berlin, Borgfelder Str. 1, ✉ 20537, ☎ 25 16 40, Telex 213939, Fax 25164413, ☂ – 🛗 ⇔ rm ▤ rest TV ☎ 🚗 P – 🏛 30. AE ① E VISA JCB
Meals à la carte 45/60 – **93 rm** ☐ 198/271. by Kurt-Schumacher-Allee HY

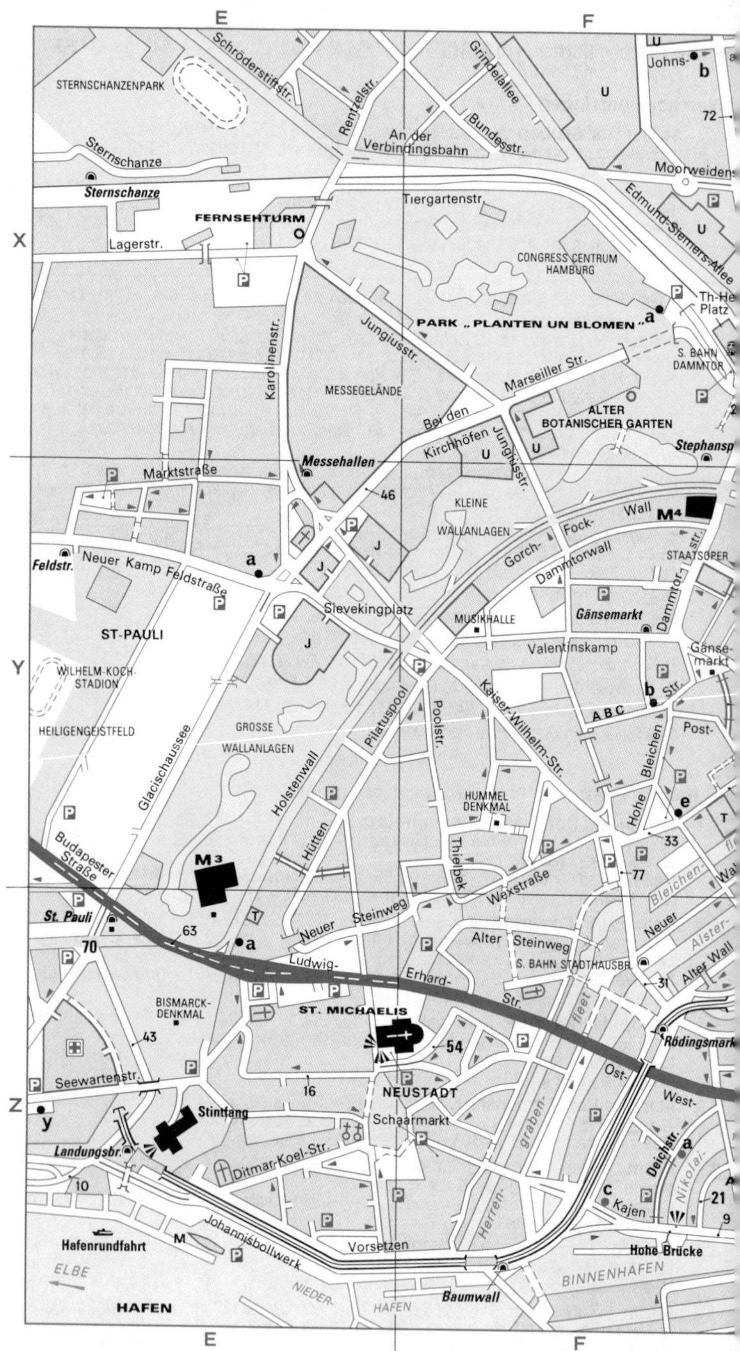
E
F
X
Y
Z
STERNSCHANZENPARK
Schröderstiftstr.
Rentzelstr.
Grindelallee
Bundesstr.
An der Verbindingsbahn
Johns-
Moorweidens
Edmund-Siemers-Allee
Sternschanze
Tiergartenstr.
FERNSEHTURM
Lagerstr.
CONGRESS CENTRUM HAMBURG
Th-He Platz
PARK „PLANTEN UN BLOMEN"
Jungiusstr.
Karolinenstr.
MESSEGELÄNDE
Marseiller Str.
S. BAHN DAMMTOR
Bei den Kirchhöfen
ALTER BOTANISCHER GARTEN
Stephansp
Messehallen
Marktstraße
KLEINE WALLANLAGEN
Wall
Fock-
Gorch-
M4
Feldstr.
Neuer Kamp
Feldstraße
Dammtorwall
Dammtorstr.
STAATSOPER
Sievekingplatz
MUSIKHALLE
Gänsemarkt
ST-PAULI
Valentinskamp
Gänse-markt
WILHELM-KOCH-STADION
Pilatuspool
Poolstr.
Kaiser-Wilhelm-Str.
ABC Str.
Post-
HEILIGENGEISTFELD
GROSSE WALLANLAGEN
Glacischaussee
Holstenwall
HUMMEL DENKMAL
Bleichen
Hohe
Hütten
Thielbek
Budapester Straße
M3
Wexstraße
Bleichen-
St. Pauli
Neuer Steinweg
Alter Steinweg
Neuer
Alster-
Alter Wall
S. BAHN STADTHAUSBR.
Ludwig-
Erhard-Str.
fleet
BISMARCK-DENKMAL
ST. MICHAELIS
Rödingsmark
Ost-West-
Seewartenstr.
NEUSTADT
Stintfang
Schaarmarkt
Herrengraben-
Deichstr.
Landungsbr.
Ditmar-Koel-Str.
Nikolai-
Kajen
Johannisbollwerk
Vorsetzen
Hohe Brücke
Hafenrundfahrt
ELBE
NIEDER-
HAFEN
BINNENHAFEN
Baumwall
HAFEN

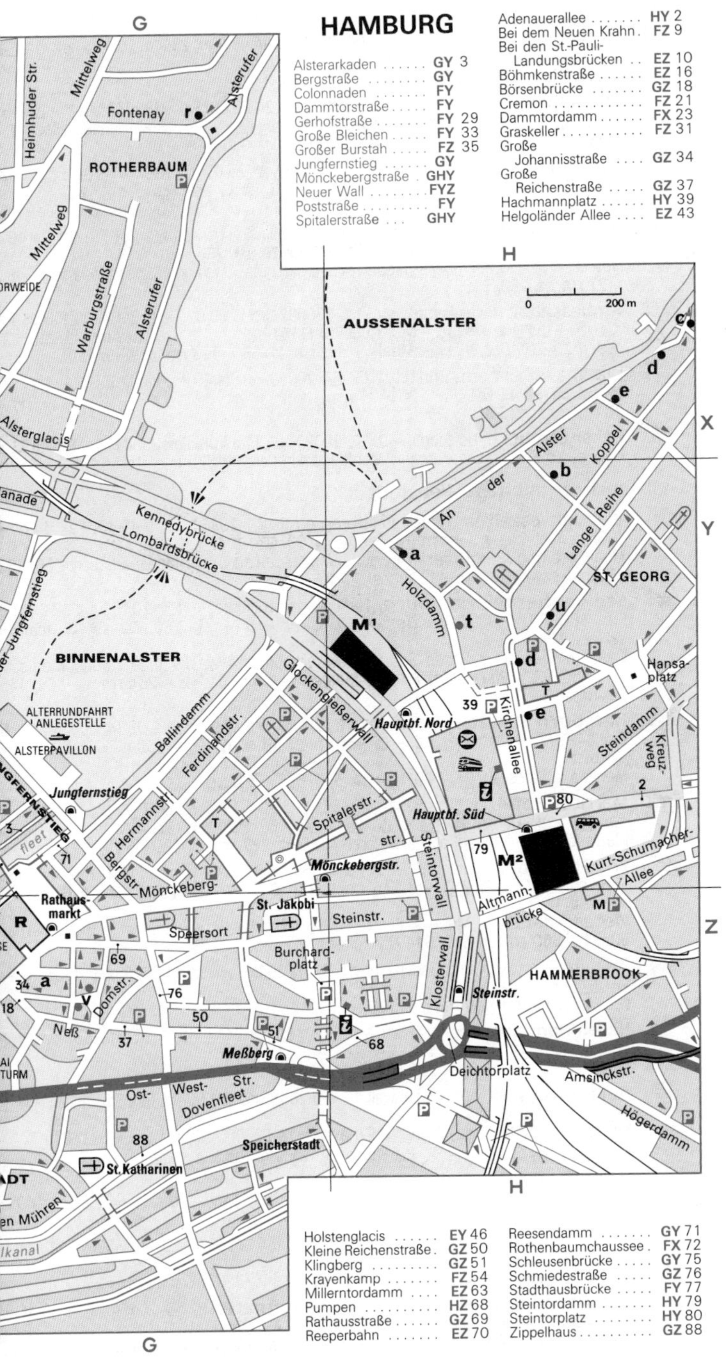
HAMBURG
Alsterarkaden . . . . . . GY 3
Bergstraße . . . . GY
Colonnaden . . . . FY
Dammtorstraße . . . . . FY
Gerhofstraße . . . . FY 29
Große Bleichen . . . . . FY 33
Großer Burstah . . . . . FZ 35
Jungfernstieg . . . . . . GY
Mönckebergstraße . GHY
Neuer Wall . . . . FYZ
Poststraße . . . . FY
Spitalerstraße . . . GHY
Adenauerallee . . . . HY 2
Bei dem Neuen Krahn . FZ 9
Bei den St.-Pauli-Landungsbrücken . . EZ 10
Böhmkenstraße . . . . . . EZ 16
Börsenbrücke . . . . GZ 18
Cremon . . . . FZ 21
Dammtordamm . . . . . . FX 23
Graskeller . . . . FZ 31
Große Johannisstraße . . . . GZ 34
Große Reichenstraße . . . . . GZ 37
Hachmannplatz . . . . . . HY 39
Helgoländer Allee . . . . EZ 43
Holstenglacis . . . . . . EY 46
Kleine Reichenstraße . GZ 50
Klingberg . . . . GZ 51
Krayenkamp . . . . FZ 54
Millerntordamm . . . . EZ 63
Pumpen . . . . HZ 68
Rathausstraße . . . . . . GZ 69
Reeperbahn . . . . EZ 70
Reesendamm . . . . GY 71
Rothenbaumchaussee . FX 72
Schleusenbrücke . . . . . GY 75
Schmiedestraße . . . . . GZ 76
Stadthausbrücke . . . . . FY 77
Steintordamm . . . . . . HY 79
Steintorplatz . . . . HY 80
Zippelhaus . . . . GZ 88
G
H
X
Y
Z
0
200 m
ROTHERBAUM
AUSSENALSTER
BINNENALSTER
ST. GEORG
HAMMERBROOK
Fontenay
Heimhuder Str.
Mittelweg
Alsterufer
Warburgstraße
Alsterglacis
Kennedybrücke
Lombardsbrücke
An der Alster
Koppel
Lange Reihe
Holzdamm
Glockengießerwall
Ballindamm
Ferdinandstr.
Hermannstr.
Spitalerstr.
Mönckeberg-str.
Steintorwall
Kirchenallee
Steindamm
Kreuzweg
Hauptbf. Nord
Hauptbf. Süd
Hansaplatz
Kurt-Schumacher-Allee
Altmannbrücke
Mönckebergstr.
Jungfernstieg
ALSTERRUNDFAHRT ANLEGESTELLE
ALSTERPAVILLON
Rathausmarkt
St. Jakobi
Steinstr.
Speersort
Burchardplatz
Klosterwall
Steinstr.
Domstr.
Neß
Meßberg
Deichtorplatz
Amsinckstr.
Högerdamm
Ost-West-Str.
Dovenfleet
Speicherstadt
St. Katharinen
Bergstr.
M1
M2

Bellevue, An der Alster 14, ✉ 20099, ☎ 28 44 40, Fax 28444222 – |$| ✻ rm TV
P – 40. AE ⓓ E VISA JCB HX
Meals à la carte 48/63 – **78 rm** 190/330.

St. Raphael, Adenauerallee 41, ✉ 20097, ☎ 24 82 00, Fax 24820333, – |$| ✻
TV ☎ P – 40. AE ⓓ E VISA JCB. ✻ rest by Adenauerallee HY
Meals à la carte 36/60 – **130 rm** 190/300.

Novotel City Süd, Amsinckstr. 53, ✉ 20097, ☎ 23 63 80, Telex 211001, Fax 2342
– |$| ✻ rm TV ☎ P – 50. AE ⓓ E VISA JCB
Meals à la carte 40/60 – **185 rm** 199/298. by Amsinckstraße HZ

Aussen-Alster-Hotel (Italian rest.), Schmilinskystr. 11, ✉ 20099, ☎ 24 15
Fax 2803231, – |$| ✻ rm TV ☎. AE ⓓ E VISA JCB HX
closed 24 to 27 December – **Meals** *(closed Saturday lunch and Sunday)* à la carte 48/
– **27 rm** 180/310.

Ambassador, Heidenkampsweg 34, ✉ 20097, ☎ 23 00 02, Telex 2166100, Fax 2300
, – |$| TV ☎ P – 120. AE ⓓ E VISA. ✻ by Amsinckstr. HZ
closed 20 - 29 December – **Meals** à la carte 41/68 – **123 rm** 135/330.

Wedina without rest, Gurlittstr. 23, ✉ 20099, ☎ 24 30 11, Fax 2803894, ,
TV ☎. AE ⓓ E VISA HY
28 rm 145/240.

Peter Lembcke, Holzdamm 49, ✉ 20099, ☎ 24 32 90, Fax 2804123 – AE ⓓ E
Monday to Friday dinner only – **Meals** (booking essential) à la carte 56/111. HY

at Binnenalster, Altstadt, Neustadt :

Vier Jahreszeiten, Neuer Jungfernstieg 9, ✉ 20354, ☎ 3 49 40, Fax 349460
Binnenalster – |$| ✻ rm TV – 70. AE ⓓ E VISA JCB. ✻ GY
Meals see also ***Rest. Haerlin*** below – ***Jahreszeiten Grill :*** **Meals** à la carte 56/103
158 rm 413/1000 – 12 suites.

Steigenberger Hamburg, Heiligengeistbrücke 4, ✉ 20459, ☎ 36 80 6
Fax 36806777 – |$| ✻ rm TV – 180. AE ⓓ E VISA JC
✻ rest FZ
Calla *(dinner only, closed Sunday - Monday and 4 weeks June - July)* **Meals** à
carte 50/88 – ***Bistro am Fleet :*** **Meals** à la carte 41/62 – **234 rm** 304/443
6 suites.

Hamburg Renaissance Hotel, Große Bleichen, ✉ 20354, ☎ 34 91 8
Fax 34918431, Massage, – |$| ✻ rm TV P – 130. AE ⓓ E VISA JC
✻ rest FY
Meals à la carte 50/85 – **207 rm** 313/635 – 3 suites.

Marriott Hotel, ABC-Str. 52, ✉ 20354, ☎ 3 50 50, Fax 35051777, , Massage,
, – |$| ✻ rm TV – 160. AE ⓓ E VISA JCB FY
Meals 25 (buffet lunch) and à la carte 45/69 – **277 rm** 380/554 – 4 suites.

SAS Plaza Hotel, Marseiller Str. 2, ✉ 20355, ☎ 3 50 20, Telex 214400, Fax 350235
Hamburg, , , – |$| ✻ rm TV – 320. AE ⓓ E VISA JC
✻ rest FX
Vierländer Stuben : **Meals** à la carte 36/56 – ***Trader Vic's*** *(dinner only)* **Meals** à la car
50/84 – **560 rm** 312/514 – 7 suites.

Residenz Hafen Hamburg, Seewartenstr. 7, ✉ 20459, ☎ 31 11 90, Fax 314505, –
✻ TV – 60 EZ
see ***Hotel Hafen Hamburg*** – **125 rm.**

Hafen Hamburg, Seewartenstr. 9, ✉ 20459, ☎ 31 11 30, Fax 3192736, – |$|
☎ P – 80. AE ⓓ E VISA. ✻ rest EZ
Meals à la carte 46/80 – **239 rm** 175/220.

Am Holstenwall, Am Holstenwall 19, ✉ 20355, ☎ 31 80 80, Fax 31808222 – |$|
☎ . AE ⓓ E VISA EZ
Meals (Monday to Friday dinner only) à la carte 58/90 – **50 rm** 196/340.

Baseler Hof, Esplanade 11, ✉ 20354, ☎ 35 90 60, Fax 35906918 – |$| TV ☎ – 3
AE ⓓ E. ✻ GY
closed 23 to 29 December – **Meals** *(Sunday lunch only)* à la carte 47/65 – **149 r**
140/210.

Alster-Hof without rest, Esplanade 12, ✉ 20354, ☎ 35 00 70, Fax 35007514 – |$|
☎. AE ⓓ E VISA GY
closed 22 December - 2 January – **118 rm** 145/320 – 3 suites.

Haerlin - Hotel Vier Jahreszeiten, Neuer Jungfernstieg 9, ✉ 20354, ☎ 3 49 46 4
Fax 3494602, Binnenalster – AE ⓓ E VISA JCB. ✻ GY
closed Sunday - Monday and Saturday lunch **Meals** 62 (lunch) and à la carte 87/136.

XXX Cölln's Austernstuben (private dining rooms), Brodschrangen 1, ✉ 20457, ☎ 32 60 59, Fax 326059 – AE ⓓ E GZ v
✿ closed Saturday to Sunday January - August, September - December Saturday lunch, Sunday and Bank Holidays – Meals (booking essential) (mainly seafood) à la carte 74/112
Spec. Hummer in Rösti, "Feines vom Fischmarkt", Karamelisierter Apfelpfannkuchen.

XX Deichgraf, Deichstr. 23, ✉ 20459, ☎ 36 42 08, Fax 364268 – AE ⓓ E VISA JCB FZ a
closed Saturday lunch and Sunday – Meals (booking essential) à la carte 56/94.

XX il Ristorante (Italian rest.), Große Bleichen 16 (1st floor), ✉ 20354, ☎ 34 33 35, Fax 345748 – AE ⓓ E FY c
Meals à la carte 61/94.

XX Ratsweinkeller, Große Johannisstr. 2, ✉ 20457, ☎ 36 41 53, Fax 372201, « 1896 Hanseatic rest. » – 280. AE ⓓ E VISA JCB GZ R
closed Sunday dinner – Meals à la carte 36/69.

X al Pincio (Italian rest.), Schauenburger Str. 59 (1st floor, |♦|), ✉ 20095, ☎ 36 52 55, Fax 362244 – AE ⓓ E VISA. GZ a
closed Saturday, Sunday and Bank Holidays – Meals (booking essential) à la carte 53/86.

Hamburg-Alsterdorf *by Grindelallee* FX :

Alsterkrug-Hotel, Alsterkrugchaussee 277, ✉ 22297, ☎ 51 30 30, Fax 51303403, , – |♦| rm ⓟ – 50. AE ⓓ E VISA JCB.
Meals (closed Sunday lunch) à la carte 51/64 – 105 rm ☐ 210/290.

Hamburg-Altona *by Reeperbahn* EZ :

Rema-Hotel Domicil without rest, Stresemannstr. 62, ✉ 22769, ☎ 4 31 60 26, Fax 4397579 – |♦| . AE ⓓ E VISA JCB by Budapester Straße EY
75 rm ☐ 200/360.

InterCityHotel, Paul-Nevermann-Platz 17, ✉ 22765, ☎ 38 03 40, Fax 38034999 – |♦| rm rest – 100. AE ⓓ E VISA JCB
Meals (closed Sunday) à la carte 31/56 – 133 rm ☐ 190/270.

XXXX Landhaus Scherrer, Elbchaussee 130, ✉ 22763, ☎ 8 80 13 25, Fax 8806260 – ⓟ. AE ⓓ E
✿ closed Sunday and Bank Holidays – Meals (outstanding wine list) 159/189 and à la carte 78/126 – *Bistro-Restaurant* (lunch only) Meals à la carte 68/83
Spec. Gebratener Hummer auf geschmortem Weißkohl, Seeteufel in der Kartoffelkruste, Gratiniertes Caiprinhiaparfait.

XXX Le canard, Elbchaussee 139, ✉ 22763, ☎ 8 80 50 57, Fax 472413, <, – ⓟ. AE ⓓ E VISA.
✿ closed Sunday – Meals (booking essential) (outstanding wine list) 149/189 and à la carte 96/149
Spec. Hummer mit Artischocken, Seesaibling mit weißem Bohnenpüree und Ingwersauce, Variation von der Schockolade.

XXX Fischereihafen-Restaurant Hamburg (only seafood), Große Elbstr. 143, ✉ 22767, ☎ 38 18 16, Fax 3893021, < – ⓟ. AE ⓓ E VISA
Meals (booking essential) à la carte 53/111.

X Rive Bistro, Van-der Smissen-Str. 1 (Kreuzfahrt-Center), ✉ 22767, ☎ 3 80 59 19, Fax 3894775, <, – AE
Meals (booking essential) à la carte 47/79.

Hamburg-Bahrenfeld *by Budapester Str.* EY :

Novotel Hamburg West, Albert-Einstein-Ring 2, ✉ 22761, ☎ 89 95 20, Fax 89952333, , – |♦| rm ⓟ – 50. AE ⓓ E VISA
Meals à la carte 35/64 – 137 rm ☐ 191/229 – 4 suites.

X Tafelhaus, Holstenkamp 71, ✉ 22525, ☎ 89 27 60, Fax 8993324, – ⓟ
✿ closed Saturday lunch, Sunday, Monday, 2 weeks January, 3 weeks July and 1 week over Easter – Meals (booking essential) 58 (lunch) and à la carte 74/83
Spec. Seeteufel in Brickteig mit Curry, Steinbutt auf Kartoffelpüree mit Trüffel, Maispoularde mit geschmortem Gemüse.

Hamburg-Barmbek *by An der Alster* HX :

Rema-Hotel Meridian without rest, Holsteinischer Kamp 59, ✉ 22081, ☎ 2 91 80 40, Fax 2983336, , – |♦| ⓟ – 30. AE ⓓ E VISA JCB
68 rm ☐ 200/360.

Hamburg-Billbrook *by Amsinckstr.* HZ *and Billstr.* :

Böttcherhof, Wöhlerstr. 2, ✉ 22113, ☎ 73 18 70, Fax 73187899, , – |♦| rm ⓟ – 140. AE E VISA. rest
Meals à la carte 42/73 – 155 rm ☐ 210/370 – 6 suites.

at Hamburg-Billstedt *by Kurt Schumacher-Allee and B 5* HY :

Panorama without rest, Billstedter Hauptstr. 44, 22111, 73 35 90, Fax 7335995 – – 150. AE E VISA JCB
closed 23 to 28 December – **111 rm** 180/275 – 7 suites.

at Hamburg-Blankenese *W : 16 km by Reeperbahn* EZ :

Strandhotel, Strandweg 13, 22587, 86 13 44, Fax 864936, « Vi with elegant installation », – . AE
Meals *(closed Saturday - Sunday)* (dinner only) (outstanding wine list) à la carte 54/87
16 rm 228/436.

at Hamburg-City Nord *by Grindelallee* FX :

Queens Hotel, Mexicoring 1, 22297, 63 29 40, Fax 6322472, – r – 120. AE E VISA. rest
Meals à la carte 47/65 – **181 rm** 259/328.

at Hamburg-Duvenstedt *by Grindelallee* FX :

Le Relais de France, Poppenbütteler Chaussee 3, 22397, 6 07 07 5 Fax 6072673 – .
closed Sunday and Monday – **Meals** (dinner only, booking essential) à la carte 67/84
Bistro *(also lunch)* **Meals** à la carte 57/68.

at Hamburg-Eimsbüttel *by Schröderstiftstraße* EX :

Norge, Schäferkampsallee 49, 20357, 44 11 50, Fax 44115577 – rm res – 80. AE E VISA JCB. rest
Meals *(closed Sunday dinner)* à la carte 40/89 – **130 rm** 199/328.

at Hamburg-Eppendorf *by Grindelallee* FX :

Anna e Sebastiano (Italian rest.), Lehmweg 30, 20251, 4 22 25 95, Fax 420800 – AE E VISA.
closed Sunday and Monday, 23 December - 16 January and 3 weeks June - July – **Mea** (dinner only, booking essential) 100/120 and à la carte 80/88
Spec. Gegrillte Moscardini in warmer Vinaigrette, Maccheroni alla chitarra mit Entenragou Kleine Charlotte von Passionsfrucht und Schockolade.

Il Gabbiano (Italian rest.), Eppendorfer Landstr. 145, 20251, 4 80 21 5 Fax 4807921, – AE E VISA
closed Saturday lunch, Sunday and 3 weeks July – **Meals** (booking essential) à la cart 54/69.

Sellmer (mainly seafood), Ludolfstr. 50, 20249, 47 30 57, Fax 4601569 – . E VISA
Meals à la carte 51/104.

Österreich, Martinistr. 11, 20251, 4 60 48 30, Fax 472413, – AE
closed Sunday and Monday – **Meals** à la carte 50/73.

at Hamburg-Fuhlsbüttel *by Grindelallee* FX :

Airport Hotel, Flughafenstr. 47, 22415, 53 10 20, Telex 216639 Fax 53102222, – rm rest – 140. AE E VISA
Meals à la carte 49/74 – **159 rm** 262/399 – 10 suites.

at Hamburg-Hamm *by Kurt-Schumacher-Allee* HY :

Hamburg International, Hammer Landstr. 200, 20537, 21 14 01, Fax 21140 – – 25. AE E VISA. rest
Meals *(closed Sunday)* à la carte 62/98 – **112 rm** 130/290.

at Hamburg-Harburg 2100 *S : 15 km by Amsinckstr.* HZ :

Lindtner, Heimfelder Str. 123, 21075, 79 00 90, Fax 79009482, « Elegan modern installation », – rm – 450. AE E VISA. res
Lilium : **Meals** 35 (lunch) and à la carte 60/84 – ***Hofgarten :*** **Meals** à la carte 49/82
115 rm 245/355 – 6 suites.

Panorama, Harburger Ring 8, 21073, 76 69 50, Fax 76695183 – rm – 110. AE E VISA
Meals *(closed Sunday dinner)* à la carte 38/65 – **98 rm** 180/250.

Marinas, Schellerdamm 26, 21079, 7 65 38 28, Fax 7651491, – AE E VIS
closed Saturday lunch and Sunday – **Meals** (booking essential for dinner) 44 (lunch) an à la carte 59/81
Spec. Riesengarnelen vom Grill mit Petersilienmarinade, Gebratener Zander auf Weinkrau mit Kürbis, Gekochter Nordsee-Steinbutt mit Sahnemeerrettich.

at **Hamburg-Harvestehude** :

Inter-Continental, Fontenay 10, ✉ 20354, ☎ 41 41 50, Telex 211099, Fax 41415186, ≤ Hamburg and Alster, Massage, – rm – 350. AE VISA JCB. rest GX r
Fontenay-Grill *(dinner only)* **Meals** à la carte 65/117 – ***Orangerie :*** **Meals** à la carte 49/69 – **286 rm** 314/518 – 12 suites.

Garden Hotels Pöseldorf without rest, Magdalenenstr. 60, ✉ 20148, ☎ 41 40 40, Fax 4140420, « Elegant modern installation » – . AE E VISA
60 rm 200/450. by Mittelweg GX

Abtei, Abteistr. 14, ✉ 20149, ☎ 44 29 05, Fax 449820, – . AE E VISA. rest by Rothenbaumchaussee FX
closed 1 week January and July – **Meals** *(closed Sunday and Monday)* (dinner only, booking essential) à la carte 75/105 – **11 rm** 260/500
Spec. Törtchen von Steinpilzen und Gänsestopfleber mit Trüffeljus, Steinbutt auf Gemüse, Pesto und Gnocchi, Deichlammrückenfilet im Strudelblatt.

Smolka, Isestr. 98, ✉ 20149, ☎ 48 09 80, Fax 4809811 – . AE E VISA JCB. rest by Rothenbaumchaussee FX
Meals *(closed Sunday and Bank Holidays)* (dinner only) à la carte 45/70 – **40 rm** 170/320.

at **Hamburg-Langenhorn** *N : 8 km by B 433 :*

Dorint-Hotel-Airport, Langenhorner Chaussee 183, ✉ 22415, ☎ 53 20 90, Fax 53209600, – rm – 80. AE E VISA. rest
Meals à la carte 41/72 – **147 rm** 243/408.

Zum Wattkorn, Tangstedter Landstr. 230, ✉ 22417, ☎ 5 20 37 97, Fax 4209044, –
closed Monday – **Meals** à la carte 59/67.

at **Hamburg-Lemsahl-Mellingstedt** *by An der Alster NE : 16 km :*

Mariot Hotel Treudelberg, Lemsahler Landstr. 45, ✉ 22397, ☎ 60 82 20, Fax 60822444, ≤, – rm – 125. AE E VISA JCB. rest
Meals à la carte 54/77 – **135 rm** 285/330.

Ristorante Dante (Italian rest.), An der Alsterschleife 3, ✉ 22399, ☎ 6 02 00 43, Fax 6022826, – . AE E VISA
closed Monday, Tuesday to Friday dinner only – **Meals** (booking essential) à la carte 53/75.

at **Hamburg-Nienstedten** *W : 13 km by Reeperbahn* EZ *:*

Louis C. Jacob, Elbchaussee 401, ✉ 22609, ☎ 82 25 50, Fax 82255444, ≤ Hafen and Elbe, « Elbe side setting ; lime-tree-terrace », – rm – 200. AE E VISA JCB.
Meals à la carte 69/104 – ***Kleines Jacob*** *(dinner only)* **Meals** à la carte 48/63 – **86 rm** 322/764 – 8 suites.

at **Hamburg-Rothenburgsort** *by Amsinkstr.* HZ *:*

Forum Hotel, Billwerder Neuer Deich 14, ✉ 20539, ☎ 78 84 00, Fax 78841000, ≤, – – 90. AE E VISA JCB. rest
Meals à la carte 43/57 – **385 rm** 198/310 – 12 suites.

at **Hamburg-Rotherbaum** :

Elysee, Rothenbaumchaussee 10, ✉ 20148, ☎ 41 41 20, Fax 41412733, Massage, – rm – 350. AE E VISA JCB FX m
Piazza Romana : **Meals** à la carte 53/84 – ***Brasserie :*** **Meals** à la carte 41/60 – **305 rm** 269/488 – 4 suites.

Vorbach without rest, Johnsallee 63, ✉ 20146, ☎ 44 18 20, Fax 44182888 – – 20. AE E VISA FX b
115 rm 170/280.

L'auberge française (French rest.), Rutschbahn 34, ✉ 20146, ☎ 4 10 25 32, Fax 4105857 – AE E VISA. by Grindelallee FX
closed Saturday lunch and Sunday, June - August Saturday to Sunday – **Meals** (booking essential) à la carte 60/90
Spec. Gebratene Gänsestopfleber in Trüffelsauce, Kalbsleber in Senfsauce, Crêpe Normande mit Vanilleeis.

at **Hamburg-St. Pauli** :

Astron Suite-Hotel without rest, Feldstr. 54, ✉ 20357, ☎ 43 23 20, Fax 43232300, – – 15. AE E VISA JCB EY a
119 rm 230/280.

at Hamburg-Stellingen *by Grindelallee* FX :

Holiday Inn, Kieler Str. 333, ✉ 22525, ℘ 54 74 00, Fax 54740100, – rm – 🅿 – 25. AE VISA JCB
Meals à la carte 37/53 – **105 rm** 218/310.

Helgoland, Kieler Str. 177, ✉ 22525, ℘ 85 70 01, Fax 8511445 – rm – 🅿 – 25. AE VISA.
Meals (dinner only) à la carte 38/53 – **110 rm** 160/230.

at Hamburg-Stillhorn *by Amsinckstr.* HZ :

Forte Hotel Hamburg, Stillhorner Weg 40, ✉ 21109, ℘ 7 52 50, Fax 7525444, – rm rest 🅿 – 160. AE VISA. rest
Meals à la carte 42/76 – **148 rm** 238/356.

at Hamburg-Uhlenhorst *by An der Alster* HX :

Parkhotel Alster-Ruh without rest, Am Langenzug 6, ✉ 22085, ℘ 22 45 7
Fax 2278966 – . AE VISA
23 rm 159/392.

Nippon (Japanese installation and rest.), Hofweg 75, ✉ 22085, ℘ 2 27 11 4
Telex 211081, Fax 22711490 – – 20. AE VISA.
Meals *(closed Monday)* (dinner only) à la carte 45/68 – **41 rm** 194/303.

HANOVER (HANNOVER) L *Niedersachsen* 415 416 417 418 I 13, 987 ⑯ – *pop. 51000 – alt. 55 m* – ☎ *0511.*

See : *Herrenhausen Gardens (Herrenhäuser Gärten)★★ (Großer Garten★★, Berggarten★)* CV – *Kestner-Museum★* DY **M1** – *Market Church (Marktkirche) (Altarpiece★★)* DY – *Museum of Lower Saxony (Niedersächsisches Landesmuseum) (Prehistorical department★)* EZ **M2** – *Museum of Arts (Kunstmuseum) (Collection Sprengel★)* EZ.

Garbsen, Am Blauen See (W : 14 km), ℘ (05137) 7 30 68 ; Isernhagen, Gut Lohne, ℘ (05139) 29 98 ; Langenhagen, Hainhaus 22 (N : 12 km), ℘ (0511) 73 93 00.

Hanover-Langenhagen (N : 11 km), ℘ 9 77 12 23.

Raschplatz (EX).

Exhibition Centre (Messegelände) (by Bischofsholer Damm FY *and Messe Schnellweg) ℘ 8 90, Telex 922728.*

Tourist office, Ernst-August-Platz 2, ✉ 30159, ℘ 30 14 22, Fax 301414.

ADAC, *Hindenburgstr. 37, ✉ 30175, ℘ 8 50 00, Fax 8500333.*

Berlin 288 – Bremen 123 – Hamburg 151.

Plans on following pages

Kastens Hotel Luisenhof, Luisenstr. 1, ✉ 30159, ℘ 3 04 40, Telex 922325
Fax 3044807 – rm rest – 🅿 – 160. AE VISA JCB
rest EX
Meals *(closed Sunday July - August)* 35 lunch and à la carte 55/82 – **160 rm** 209/59
– 5 suites.

Maritim Grand Hotel, Friedrichswall 11, ✉ 30159, ℘ 3 67 70, Fax 325195 – rm
rest – 250. AE VISA JCB DY
L'Adresse - Brasserie : Meals à la carte 50/96 – ***Wilhelm-Busch-Stube :*** *(dinner only, closed Sunday and Bank Holidays)* **Meals** à la carte 30/48 – **285 rm** 255/588 – 14 suites.

Maritim Stadthotel, Hildesheimer Str. 34, ✉ 30169, ℘ 9 89 40, Fax 9894900,
– rm – 🅿 – 380. AE VISA JCB. rest EZ
Meals à la carte 63/108 – **293 rm** 255/598.

Forum Hotel Schweizerhof, Hinüberstr. 6, ✉ 30175, ℘ 3 49 50, Fax 3495123
rm – 250. AE VISA JCB EX
Meals *(closed Sunday)* (dinner only) à la carte 41/72 – ***Gourmet's Buffet :*** **Meals** à la carte 43/71 – **200 rm** 289/393 – 3 suites.

Congress-Hotel am Stadtpark, Clausewitzstr. 6, ✉ 30175, ℘ 2 80 50
Fax 814652, , Massage, – rm 🅿 – 1550. AE
VISA by Hans-Böckler Allee FY
Meals à la carte 44/69 *(also diet menu)* – **252 rm** 180/480 – 4 suites.

Grand Hotel Mussmann without rest, Ernst-August-Platz 7, ✉ 30159, ℘ 3 65 60
Fax 3656145, – – 50. AE VISA EX
137 rm 178/598.

Königshof without rest, Königstr. 12, ✉ 30175, ℘ 31 20 71, Fax 312079 –
– 30. AE VISA. EX
79 rm 158/390.

Plaza, Fernroder Str. 9, ✉ 30161, ℘ 3 38 80, Fax 3388488, – rm – 100. AE VISA EX e
Meals à la carte 42/73 – **102 rm** 168/466.

Mercure, Willy-Brandt-Allee 3, ✉ 30169, ℘ 8 00 80, Fax 8093704, – rm rest – 130. AE VISA EZ n
Meals à la carte 35/60 – **145 rm** 215/475.

Am Funkturm, Hallerstr. 34, ✉ 30161, ℘ 3 39 80 (hotel) 33 23 09 (rest.), Fax 3398111 – rm . AE VISA EV s
Ristorante Milano : Meals à la carte 40/64 – **51 rm** 88/296.

Loccumer Hof, Kurt-Schumacher-Str. 16, ✉ 30159, ℘ 1 26 40, Fax 131192 – – 40. AE VISA DX s
Meals à la carte 44/74 *(vegetarian menu available)* – **78 rm** 135/380.

Körner, Körnerstr. 24, ✉ 30159, ℘ 1 63 60, Fax 18048, – rm – 50. AE VISA DX e
closed Christmas - New Year – **Meals** *(closed Sunday)* 22 lunch and à la carte 33/67 – **75 rm** 140/240.

Am Rathaus, Friedrichswall 21, ✉ 30159, ℘ 32 62 68, Fax 328868, – EY y
47 rm.

Am Leineschloß without rest, Am Markte 12, ✉ 30159, ℘ 32 71 45, Fax 325502 – . AE VISA DY z
Meals **81 rm** 196/265.

InterCityHotel, Ernst-August-Platz 1, ✉ 30159, ℘ 3 02 60, Fax 3026499 – rest – 100. AE VISA EX r
Meals à la carte 29/55 – **57 rm** 125/380.

Landhaus Ammann with rm, Hildesheimer Str. 185, ✉ 30173, ℘ 83 08 18, Fax 8437749, « Elegant installation, patio with terrace », – rest – 50. AE VISA. rest by Hildesheimer Str. EFZ
Meals (outstanding wine list) 128/168 and à la carte 75/112 – **15 rm** 265/398
Spec. Hummer mit Kaviarcrème und grünem Spargel, Gebackene Langustinen mit Zitronennudeln, Taubenbrüstchen mit Gänseleber in Pomerol.

Bakkarat im Casino am Maschsee, Arthur-Menge-Ufer 3 (1st floor), ✉ 30169, ℘ 88 40 57, Fax 885733, ←, – AE VISA. DZ a
closed Sunday - Monday, Saturday lunch and 3 weeks January - February – **Meals** 49 (lunch) and à la carte 78/99
Spec. Baby-Steinbutt in roter Zwiebelkruste, Charlotte vom Bauerntäubchen mit Wirsing in Trüffelbutter, Cappucinosoufflé mit weißem Schockoladeneis.

Feuchter's Lila Kranz with rm, Berliner Str. 33, ✉ 30175, ℘ 85 89 21, Fax 854383, – . AE VISA. rm FX b
closed Saturday lunch – **Meals** 42 (lunch) and à la carte 62/90 – **5 rm** 180/340.

Romantik Hotel Georgenhof - Stern's Restaurant with rm, Herrenhäuser Kirchweg 20, ✉ 30167, ℘ 70 22 44, Fax 708559, « Lower Saxony country house in a park, terrace » – . AE VISA by Engelbosteler Damm CV
Meals (outstanding wine list) 36 (lunch) and à la carte 97/139 – **14 rm** 170/450
Spec. Nudeln mit schwarzen und weißen Trüffeln (November - February), Heidschnukkenrücken in Schwarzbrotkruste (October - November), Hummer auf zwei Saucen.

Clichy, Weißekreuzstr. 31, ✉ 30161, ℘ 31 24 47, Fax 318283 – AE VISA EV d
closed Saturday lunch and Sunday – **Meals** à la carte 74/89.

Maritim Seeterrassen, Arthur-Menge-Ufer 3, ✉ 30169, ℘ 88 40 57, Fax 887533, ←, – AE VISA DZ a
Meals à la carte 38/69.

Gattopardo (Italian rest.), Hainhölzer Str. 1 (Am Klagesmarkt), ✉ 30159, ℘ 1 43 75, Fax 318283, – AE DV f
Meals (dinner only) à la carte 46/58.

at Hannover-Bemerode *by Bischofsholer Damm* FY :

Treff Hotel Europa, Bergstr. 2, ✉ 30539, ℘ 9 52 80, Fax 9528488, – rm – 300. AE VISA. rest
Meals à la carte 41/75 – **183 rm** 165/595.

at Hanover-Buchholz *by Bödekerstr.* FV :

Pannonia Atrium Hotel, Karl-Wiechert-Allee 68, ✉ 30625, ℘ 5 40 70, Fax 572878, , Massage, – rm – 180. AE VISA. rest
Meals à la carte 42/80 – **222rm** 220/290 – 6 suites.

Gallo Nero, Groß Buchholzer Kirchweg 72 b, ✉ 30655, ℘ 5 46 34 34, Fax 548283, , « 18C farmhouse with contemporary interior design » – . VISA
closed Sunday, 1 week January and 3 weeks July - August – **Meals** à la carte 58/89.

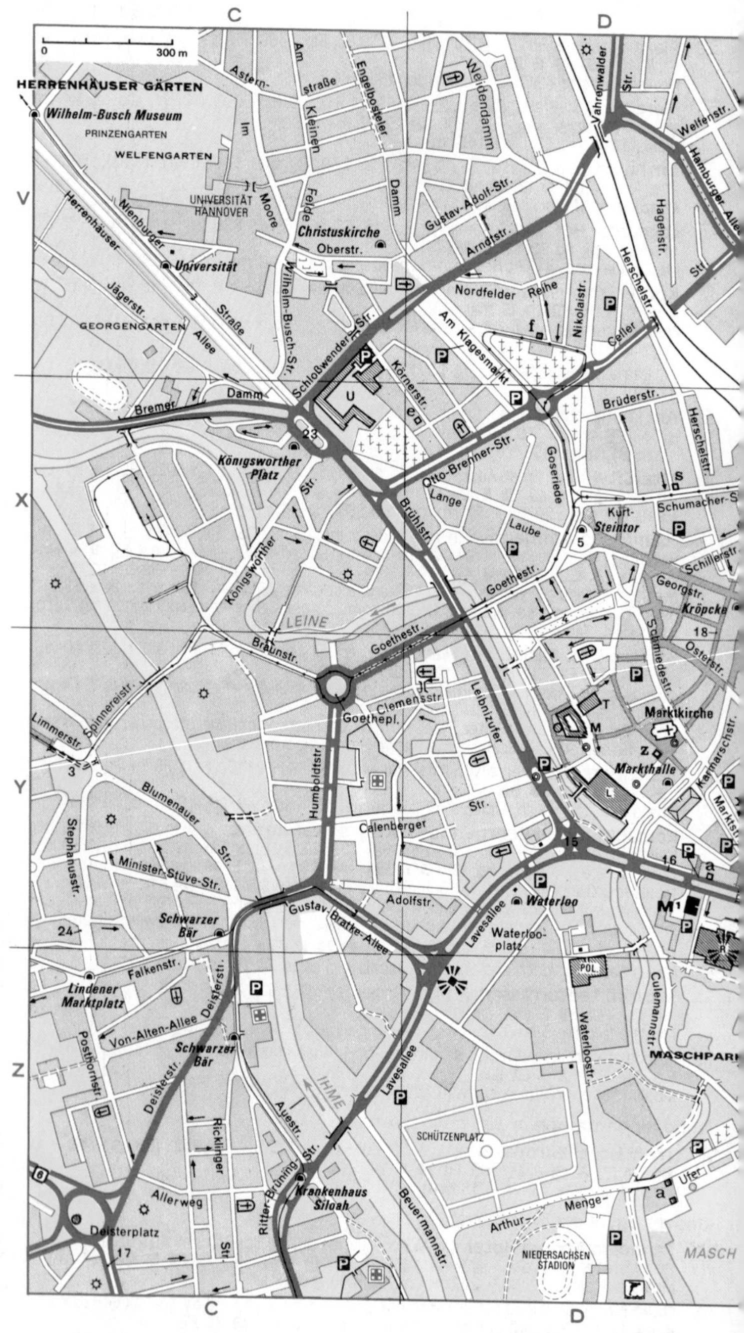
C
D
0
300 m
HERRENHÄUSER GÄRTEN
Wilhelm-Busch Museum
PRINZENGARTEN
WELFENGARTEN
UNIVERSITÄT HANNOVER
Universität
GEORGENGARTEN
Christuskirche
Königsworther Platz
Kurt-Steintor
Kröpcke
Marktkirche
Markthalle
Waterloo
Schwarzer Bär
Lindener Marktplatz
Krankenhaus Siloah
Deisterplatz
SCHÜTZENPLATZ
NIEDERSACHSEN STADION
MASCHPARK
MASCH
LEINE
IHME
V
X
Y
Z

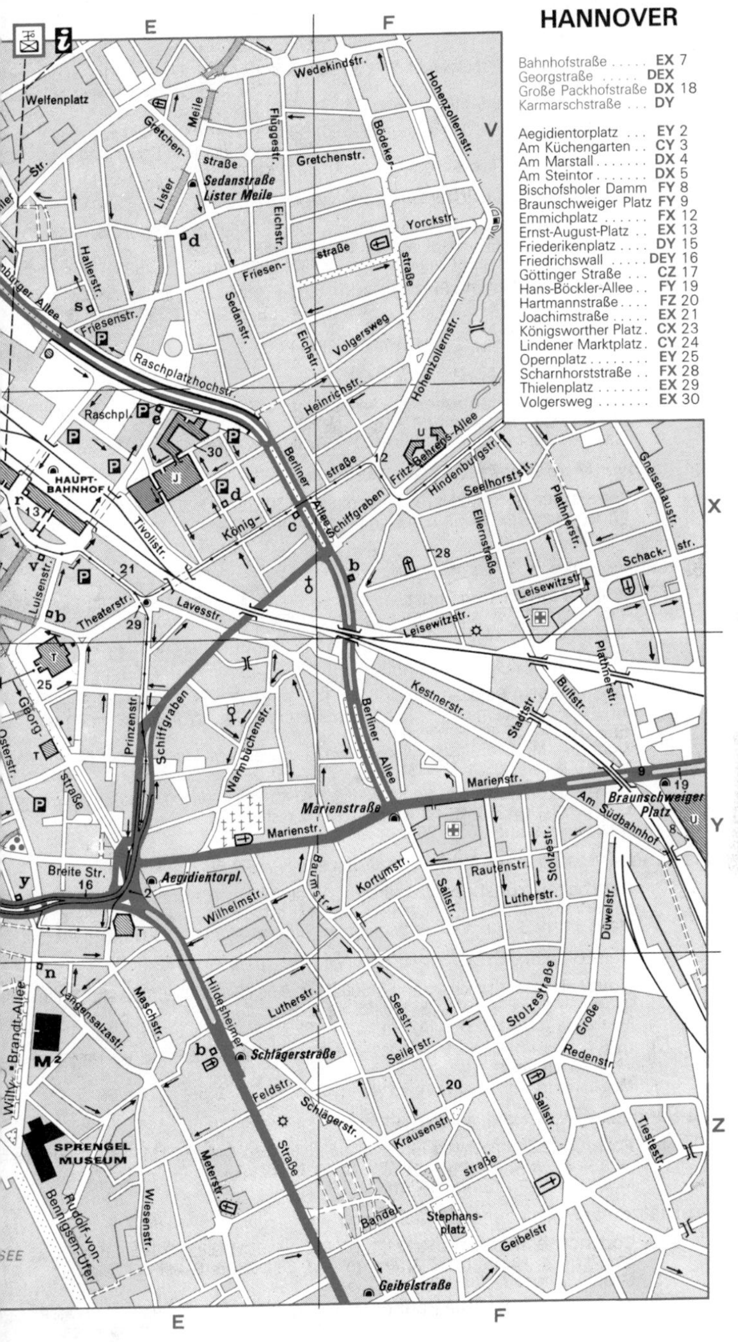

HANNOVER
Bahnhofstraße . . . . . EX 7
Georgstraße . . . . . DEX
Große Packhofstraße DX 18
Karmarschstraße . . . DY
Aegidientorplatz . . . EY 2
Am Küchengarten . . CY 3
Am Marstall . . . . . . DX 4
Am Steintor . . . . . . DX 5
Bischofsholer Damm FY 8
Braunschweiger Platz FY 9
Emmichplatz . . . . . . FX 12
Ernst-August-Platz . . EX 13
Friederikenplatz . . . . DY 15
Friedrichswall . . . . . DEY 16
Göttinger Straße . . . CZ 17
Hans-Böckler-Allee . . FY 19
Hartmannstraße . . . . FZ 20
Joachimstraße . . . . . EX 21
Königsworther Platz . CX 23
Lindener Marktplatz . CY 24
Opernplatz . . . . EY 25
Scharnhorststraße . . FX 28
Thielenplatz . . . . EX 29
Volgersweg . . . . EX 30
E
F
V
X
Y
Z
Welfenplatz
Wedekindstr.
Hohenzollernstr.
Gretchenstraße
Meile
Flüggestr.
Bödeker-
Gretchenstr.
Lister
Sedanstraße
Lister Meile
Eichstr.
Yorckstr.
Friesen-
straße
Hallerstr.
Sedanstr.
Volgersweg
Friesenstr.
Raschplatzhochstr.
Heinrichstr.
Raschpl.
Berliner Allee
Fritz-Behrens-Allee
Hindenburgstr.
Seelhorststr.
Plathnerstr.
Gneisenaustr.
HAUPT-BAHNHOF
Schiffgraben
König-
Tivolistr.
Ellernstraße
Schack-str.
Leisewitzstr.
Luisenstr.
Theaterstr.
Lavesstr.
Kestnerstr.
Bultstr.
Stadtstr.
Georg-
straße
Prinzenstr.
Warmbüchenstr.
Osterstr.
Marienstr.
Braunschweiger Platz
Am Südbahnhof
Marienstraße
Breite Str.
Aegidientorpl.
Baumstr.
Kortumstr.
Rautenstr.
Stolzestr.
Lutherstr.
Sallstr.
Wilhelmstr.
Düwelstr.
Langensalzastr.
Maschstr.
Hildesheimer Straße
Lutherstr.
Seestr.
Stolzestraße
Große Redenstr.
Schlägerstraße
Seilerstr.
Willy-Brandt-Allee
M²
Feldstr.
Schlägerstr.
Krausenstr.
Tiestestr.
SPRENGEL MUSEUM
Meterstr.
Bandel-
Stephans-platz
Rudolf-von-Bennigsen-Ufer
Wiesenstr.
Geibelstr.
Geibelstraße

at Hanover-Döhren :

Wichmann, Hildesheimer Str. 230, ✉ 30519, ✆ 83 16 71, Fax 8379811, « Courtyard » – AE E VISA. by Hildesheimer Str. EFZ
Meals à la carte 62/110.

Die Insel, Rudolf-von-Bennigsen-Ufer 81, ✉ 30519, ✆ 83 12 14, Fax 831322, ←, – P by Rudolf-von Benningsen-Ufer EZ
closed Monday – **Meals** (booking essential) à la carte 49/71.

at Hanover-Flughafen (Airport) *by Vahrenwalder Str* DV *: 11 km :*

Maritim Airport Hotel, Flughafenstr. 5, ✉ 30669, ✆ 9 73 70, Fax 9737590, – rm TV – 800. AE E VISA JCB. rest
Meals 45 (buffet lunch) and à la carte 46/80 – **528 rm** 255/588 – 31 suites.

Holiday Inn Crowne Plaza, Petzelstr. 60, ✉ 30855 *Langenhagen*, ✆ (0511) 7 70 7 Telex 924030, Fax 737781, Massage, – rm TV P – 10 AE E VISA JCB
Meals à la carte 54/77 – **210 rm** 215/545.

at Hanover-Kirchrode *by Hans-Böckler Allee* FY *:*

Queens Hotel Hannover, Tiergartenstr. 117, ✉ 30559, ✆ 5 10 30, Fax 52692 – rm TV P – 300. AE E VISA
Meals à la carte 47/74 – **176 rm** 236/510 – 3 suites.

at Hanover-Kleefeld *by Hans-Böckler Allee* FY *:*

Kleefelder Hof without rest, Kleestr. 3a, ✉ 30625, ✆ 5 30 80, Fax 5308333 – TV P. AE E VISA JCB
86 rm 165/475.

at Hanover-Lahe *by Hohenzollernstraße* FV *:*

Holiday Inn Garden Court, Oldenburger Allee 1, ✉ 30659, ✆ 6 15 50, Fax 61555 – rm TV P – 280. AE E VISA
Meals à la carte 36/64 – **150 rm** 185/267.

at Hannover-List *by Hohenzollernstr.* FV *:*

Seidler Hotel Pelikan, Podbielskistr. 145, ✉ 30177, ✆ 9 09 30, Fax 9093555, « Hotel with modern interior in a former factory », – rm TV P – 140. AE E VISA JCB
Signatur : **Meals** à la carte 41/63 – ***Edo :*** (Japanese rest.) *(dinner only, closed Sunda*
Meals à la carte 65/130 – **138 rm** 250/490.

Dorint, Podbielskistr. 21, ✉ 30163, ✆ 3 90 40, Fax 3904100, – rm TV – 250. AE E VISA JCB. rest
Meals à la carte 39/63 – **206 rm** 199/495.

at Hanover-Messe (near Exhibition Centre) *by Hans-Böckler Allee* FY *:*

Parkhotel Kronsberg, Laatzener Str. 18 (at Exhibition Centre), ✉ 30539, ✆ 8 74 0 Fax 867112, – rm rest TV P – 200. AE E VISA JC
Meals *(closed 27 December - 2 January)* à la carte 40/71 – **169 rm** 190/330.

at Hanover-Roderbruch *by Hans-Böckler Allee* FY *E : 7 km :*

Novotel, Feodor-Lynen-Str. 1, ✉ 30625, ✆ 9 56 60, Fax 9566333, (heated) rm TV P – 110. AE E VISA
Meals à la carte 39/63 – **112 rm** 175/225.

Ibis, Feodor-Lynen-Str. 1, ✉ 30625, ✆ 9 56 70, Fax 576128 – rm TV – 30. AE E VISA
Meals (dinner only) à la carte 28/46 – **96 rm** 130/205.

at Hanover-Vahrenwald *by Vahrenwalder Str.* DV *N : 4km :*

Fora, Großer Kolonnenweg 19, ✉ 30163, ✆ 6 70 60, Fax 7606111, – r rest TV – 100. AE E VISA JCB
Meals à la carte 41/74 – **142 rm** 235/288.

at Laatzen *by Hildesheimer Str.* EFZ *S : 9 km :*

Copthorne, Würzburger Str. 21, ✉ 30880, ✆ (0511) 9 83 60, Fax 9836666, – rm TV P – 280. AE E VISA JCB. rest
Meals à la carte 44/63 – **222 rm** 225/490.

Treff-Hotel Britannia Hannover, Karlsruher Str. 26, ✉ 30880, ✆ (0511) 8 78 2 Fax 863466, indoor – rm TV P – 180. AE E VISA. res
Meals à la carte 44/80 – **100 rm** 180/595.

t Ronnenberg-Benthe *by Bornumer Str. CZ and B 65, SW : 10 km :*

Benther Berg ⛰, Vogelsangstr. 18, ✉ 30952, ☎ (05108) 6 40 60, Fax 640650, ☂, ≘s, ⬚, ⛱ – ☰ ▤ rest TV P – 🏆 60. AE ① E VISA JCB. ✗ rm
Meals à la carte 60/95 – **70 rm** ☐ 145/280.

EIPZIG *Sachsen* 418 L 21, 987 ⑰, 984 ⑱ – *pop. 480 000 – alt. 113 m –* ☎ *0341.*
See : *Old Town Hall*★ *(Altes Rathaus)* BY – *Old Stock Exchange*★ *(Naschmarkt)* BY – *Museum of Fine Arts*★ *(Museum der Bildenden Künste)* BZ.
✈ *Leipzig-Halle (NW : 13 km by Gerberstr. und Eutritzscher Str.*BY*),* ☎ *22 40.*
Exhibition Grounds (Messegelände), Prager Str. 200 (by Windmühlenstr CZ), ✉ *04103,* ☎ *22 30, Telex 312055, Fax 2232198.*
ℹ *Tourist-Information, Sachsenplatz 1,* ✉ *04109,* ☎ *71 0 40, Fax 281854.*
ADAC, *Augustusplatz 6,* ✉ *04109,* ☎ *(0351) 44 78 80, Fax (0341) 2110540.*
Berlin 180 – Dresden 109 – Erfurt 126.

Plans on following pages

Kempinski Hotel Fürstenhof, Tröndlinring 8, ✉ 04105, ☎ 14 00, Fax 1403700, ☂, « 1770 Patrician palace », Fō, ≘s, ⬚ – ☰ ⇆ ▤ TV ☎ ♿ ⛟ – 🏆 60. AE ① E VISA JCB — BY c
Meals à la carte 58/78 – **92 rm** ☐ 349/668 – 4 suites.

Inter-Continental, Gerberstr. 15, ✉ 04105, ☎ 98 80, Telex 311245, Fax 9881229, beer garden, Massage, Fō, ≘s, ⬚ – ☰ ⇆ rm ▤ TV ☎ ♿ – 🏆 450. AE ① E VISA JCB. ✗ rest — BY a
Meals à la carte 48/79 – **447 rm** ☐ 319/509 – 18 suites.

Renaissance, Querstr. 12, ✉ 04103, ☎ 1 29 20, Fax 1292800, Fō, ≘s, ⬚ – ☰ ⇆ rm ▤ TV ☎ ♿ ⛟ – 🏆 350. AE ① E VISA JCB — DY a
Meals à la carte 42/72 – **365 rm** ☐ 301/457.

Dorint Hotel Leipzig, Stephanstr. 6, ✉ 04103, ☎ 9 77 90, Fax 9779100, beer garden, ≘s – ☰ ⇆ rm TV ♿ ⛟ – 🏆 150. AE ① E VISA JCB — DZ n
Meals à la carte 39/68 – **179 rm** ☐ 220/300.

Parkhotel-SeaSide, Richard-Wagner-Str. 7, ✉ 04109, ☎ 9 85 20, Fax 9852750 – ☰ ⇆ rm TV ☎ ♿ P – 🏆 80. AE ① E VISA. ✗ rest — CY s
Meals à la carte 37/65 – **288 rm** ☐ 230/295 – 9 suites.

Ramada without rest, Gutenbergplatz 1, ✉ 04103, ☎ 1 29 30, Fax 1293444 – ☰ ⇆ ▤ TV ☎ ☎ ♿ – 🏆 20. AE ① E VISA JCB — DZ s
122 rm ☐ 138/206.

Markgraf without rest, Körnerstr.36, ✉ 04107, ☎ 30 30 30, Fax 3030399 – ☰ ⇆ TV ☎ ☎ ⛟. AE ① E VISA — by Peterssteinweg BZ
54 rm ☐ 145/275.

Novotel, Goethestr. 11, ✉ 04109, ☎ 9 95 80, Fax 9958200, ☂, ≘s – ☰ ⇆ rm ▤ TV ☎ ☎ ♿ ⛟ – 🏆 120. AE ① E VISA — CY n
Meals à la carte 39/57 – **200 rm** ☐ 189/249.

Mercure Leipzig, Augustusplatz 5, ✉ 04109, ☎ 2 14 60, Fax 9604916 – ☰ ⇆ rm TV ☎ – 🏆 120. AE ① E VISA JCB — CZ f
Meals à la carte 35/64 – **283 rm** ☐ 190/335 – 10 suites.

Holiday Inn Garden Court, Rudolf-Breitscheid-Str. 3, ✉ 04105, ☎ 1 25 10, Fax 1251100, ≘s – ☰ ⇆ rm ▤ TV ☎. AE ① E VISA JCB — CY g
Meals à la carte 28/51 – **121 rm** ☐ 190/270 – 6 suites.

Rema Hotel Vier Jahreszeiten without rest, Rudolf Breitscheidstr. 23, ✉ 04105, ☎ 985 10, Fax 985122 – ☰ ⇆ TV ☎ ♿. AE ① E VISA JCB — CY b
67 rm ☐ 170/330.

Leipziger Hof, Hedwigstr. 3, ✉ 04315, ☎ 6 97 40, Fax 6974150, « Permanent exhibition of paintings », ≘s – ☰ ⇆ rm TV ☎ ☎. AE ① E VISA. ✗ rest
Meals *(closed Saturday - Sunday)* (dinner only) à la carte 35/52 – **73 rm** ☐ 155/240. — by Eisenbahnstraße DY

Deutscher Hof, Waldstr. 31, ✉ 04105, ☎ 7 11 00, Fax 7110222 – ☰ TV ☎. AE ① E VISA JCB — by Gustav-Adolf-Str. AY
Meals *(closed Sunday except exhibitions)* (dinner only) à la carte 29/65 – **39 rm** ☐ 170/215.

Ibis without rest, Brühl 69, ✉ 04109, ☎ 2 18 60, Fax 2186222 – ☰ ⇆ TV ☎ ♿ ⛟. AE ① E VISA — CY a
126 rm ☐ 139/154.

Stadtpfeiffer, Augustusplatz 8 (Neues Gewandhaus), ✉ 04109, ☎ 9 60 51 86, Fax 2113594, ☂ – AE E VISA — CZ
closed Sunday – **Meals** (outstanding winelist) à la carte 44/67.

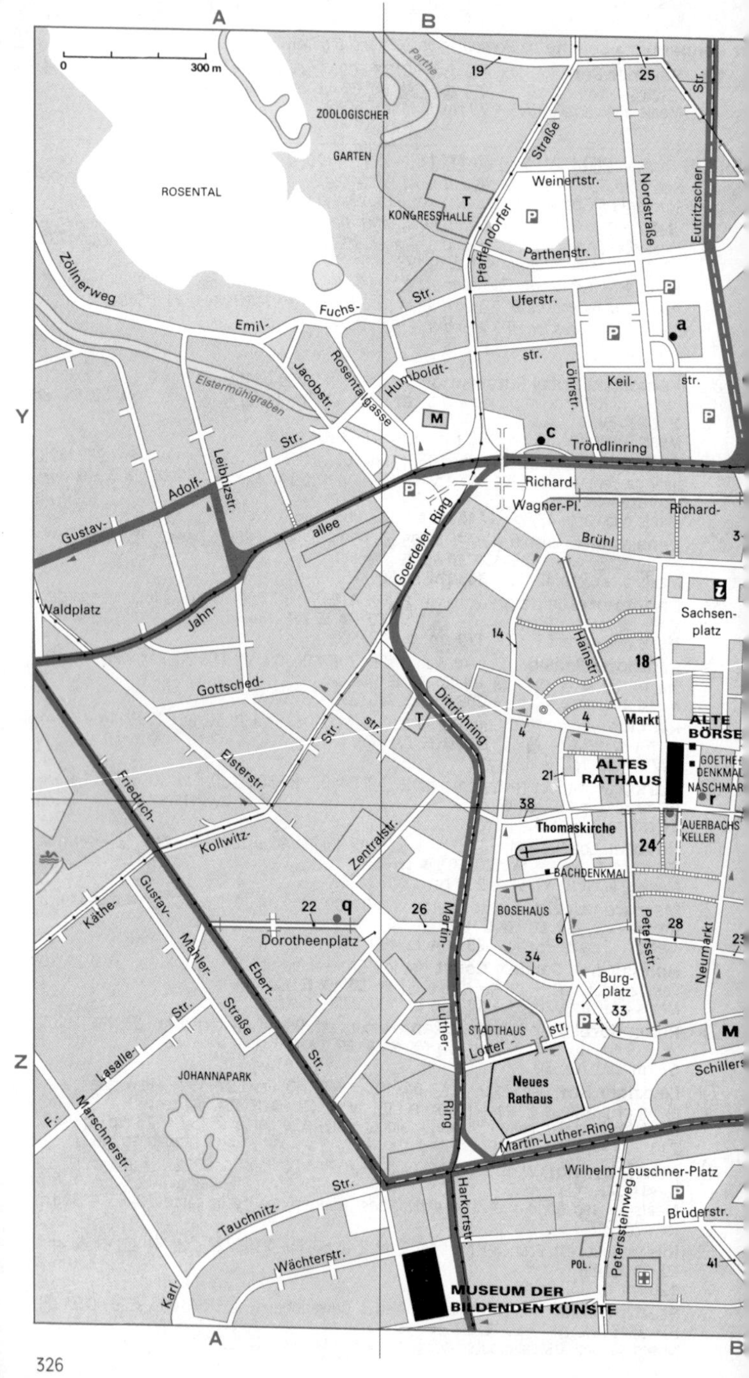
A
B
300 m
ZOOLOGISCHER GARTEN
ROSENTAL
KONGRESSHALLE
Zöllnerweg
Emil-Fuchs-Str.
Pfaffendorfer Straße
Weinertstr.
Parthenstr.
Uferstr.
Nordstraße
Eutritzscher Str.
Löhrstr.
Keil-str.
Humboldt-str.
Rosentalgasse
Jacobstr.
Elstermühlgraben
Tröndlinring
Richard-Wagner-Pl.
Richard-
Gustav-Adolf-Str.
Leibnizstr.
allee
Goerdeler Ring
Brühl
Sachsenplatz
Waldplatz
Jahn-allee
Hainstr.
Gottsched-str.
Dittrichring
Markt
ALTE BÖRSE
GOETHE-DENKMAL
NASCHMARKT
ALTES RATHAUS
Elsterstr.
Friedrich-Ebert-Str.
Kollwitz-str.
Zentralstr.
Thomaskirche
AUERBACHS KELLER
BACHDENKMAL
BOSEHAUS
Käthe-Kollwitz-Str.
Gustav-Mahler-Straße
Dorotheenplatz
Martin-Luther-Ring
Petersstr.
Neumarkt
Burgplatz
STADTHAUS
Lotterstr.
Neues Rathaus
Schillerstr.
Lasalle-Str.
JOHANNAPARK
Marschnerstr.
F.-
Martin-Luther-Ring
Wilhelm-Leuschner-Platz
Harkortstr.
Peterssteinweg
Brüderstr.
Tauchnitz-Str.
Wächterstr.
Karl-
POL.
MUSEUM DER BILDENDEN KÜNSTE
Y
Z

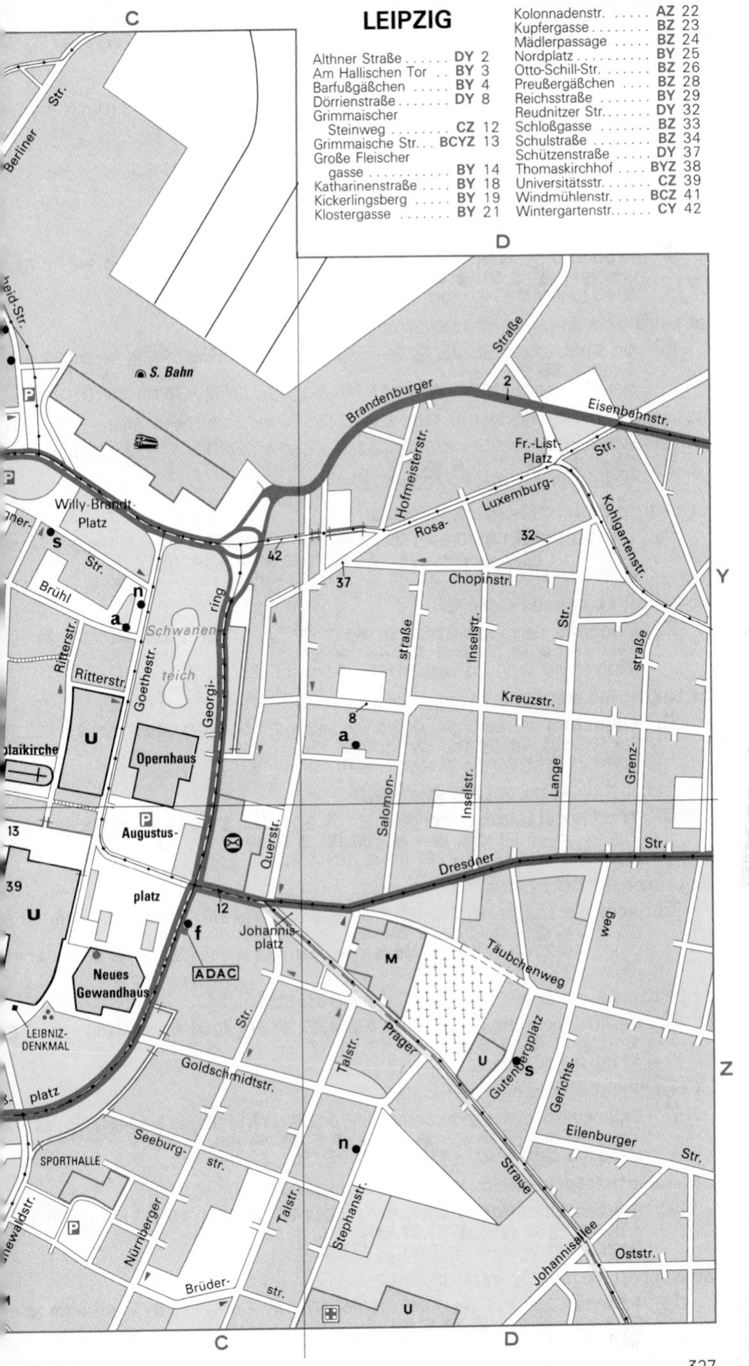
LEIPZIG
Althner Straße . . . . . . DY 2
Am Hallischen Tor . . BY 3
Barfußgäßchen . . . . . BY 4
Dörrienstraße . . . . DY 8
Grimmaischer Steinweg . . . . CZ 12
Grimmaische Str. . . BCYZ 13
Große Fleischer gasse . . . . BY 14
Katharinenstraße . . . . BY 18
Kickerlingsberg . . . . . BY 19
Klostergasse . . . . BY 21
Kolonnadenstr. . . . . . AZ 22
Kupfergasse . . . . BZ 23
Mädlerpassage . . . . . BZ 24
Nordplatz . . . . BY 25
Otto-Schill-Str. . . . . . . BZ 26
Preußergäßchen . . . . BZ 28
Reichsstraße . . . . BY 29
Reudnitzer Str. . . . . . . DY 32
Schloßgasse . . . . BZ 33
Schulstraße . . . . BZ 34
Schützenstraße . . . . . DY 37
Thomaskirchhof . . . . BYZ 38
Universitätsstr. . . . . . . CZ 39
Windmühlenstr. . . . . . BCZ 41
Wintergartenstr. . . . . . CY 42
C
D
Y
Z
Berliner Str.
S. Bahn
Brandenburger Straße
Eisenbahnstr.
Fr.-List-Platz
Hofmeisterstr.
Rosa-Luxemburg-Str.
Kohlgartenstr.
Willy-Brandt-Platz
Brühl
Ritterstr.
Goethestr.
Schwanenteich
Georgiring
Chopinstr.
Inselstr.
Kreuzstr.
Lange Str.
Grenzstraße
Salomonstraße
Opernhaus
Augustusplatz
Querstr.
Dresdner Str.
Johannisplatz
ADAC
Neues Gewandhaus
LEIBNIZ-DENKMAL
Täubchenweg
Prager Straße
Gutenbergplatz
Gerichtsweg
Talstr.
Goldschmidtstr.
Eilenburger Str.
Seeburgstr.
SPORTHALLE
Nürnberger Str.
Stephanstr.
Brüderstr.
Johannisallee
Oststr.

Apels Garten Kolonnadenstr. 2, ✉ 04109, ☎ 9 60 77 77, Fax 9607777, – ♿. E VISA AZ
closed dinner Sunday and Bank Holidays – **Meals** à la carte 24/53.

Auerbachs Keller (16C historical wine tavern), Grimmaische Str. 2 (Mädler-Passage ✉ 04109, ☎ 21 61 00, Fax 2161011 – AE E VISA BYZ
Meals à la carte 36/63.

Mövenpick, Naschmarkt 1, ✉ 04109, ☎ 2 11 77 22, Fax 2114810, – AE E VISA BY
Meals à la carte 31/60.

at Leipzig-Eutritzsch *by Eutritzscher Str.* BY :

Prodomo, Gräfestr. 15a, ✉ 04129, ☎ 5 96 30, Fax 5963113 – rm – 40. AE E VISA
Meals (dinner only) à la carte 32/53 – **83 rm** 145/235.

at Leipzig-Gohlis *by Pfaffendorfer Str.* BY :

De Saxe, Gohliser Str. 25, ✉ 01455, ☎ 5 93 80, Fax 5938299 – rm AE E VISA
Meals à la carte 31/49 – ***Bistro :*** **Meals** à la carte 29/39 – **33 rm** 150/230.

at Leipzig-Grosszschocher *by Käthe-Kollwitz-Str.* AZ *and Erich-Zeigner-Allee :*

Windorf, Gerhard-Ellrodt-Str. 21, ✉ 04249, ☎ 4 27 70, Fax 4277222, – r – 30. AE E VISA
Meals à la carte 26/46 – **100 rm** 145/185.

at Leipzig-Leutzsch *by Friedrich-Ebert-Str.* AY :

Lindner Hotel, Hans-Driesch-Str. 27, ✉ 04179, ☎ 4 47 80, Fax 4478478, – rm ♿ – 120. AE E VISA JCB. rest
Meals à la carte 50/72 – **200 rm** 241/500 – 15 suites.

at Leipzig-Lindenau *by Jahn-Allee* AY :

Lindenau, Georg-Schwarz-Str. 33, ✉ 04177, ☎ 4 48 03 10, Fax 4480300, – rm . AE E VISA JCB. rest
Meals (dinner only) à la carte 31/50 – **52 rm** 135/190.

at Leipzig-Möckern *by Eutritzscher Str.* BY :

Silencium without rest, Georg-Schumann-Str. 268, ✉ 04159, ☎ 9 01 29 9(Fax 9012991 – – 15. AE E VISA
closed 24 December - 6 January – **34 rm** 97/180.

at Leipzig-Paunsdorf *by Eisenbahnstraße* DY :

Treff Hotel Leipzig, Schongauer Str. 39, ✉ 04329, ☎ 25 40, Fax 2541550, – rm ♿ – 600. AE E VISA
Meals à la carte 37/65 – **291 rm** 189/339.

at Leipzig-Portitz *by Berliner Str.* CY :

Accento, Tauchaer Str. 260, ✉ 04349, ☎ 9 26 20, Fax 9262100, – rm res – 60. AE E VISA JCB. rest
closed Christmas - 6 January – **Meals** *(closed Saturday and Sunday)* (dinner only) à la cart 24/42 – **115 rm** 179/269.

at Leipzig-Reudnitz *by Dresdner Str.* DZ *and Breite Str.* :

Berlin without rest, Riebeckstr. 30, ✉ 04317, ☎ 2 67 30 00, Fax 2673280 – – 10. AE E VISA JCB
51 rm 150/199.

at Leipzig-Stötteritz *by Prager Str.* DZ :

Balance Hotel, Wasserturmstr. 33, ✉ 04299, ☎ 8 67 90, Fax 8679444, – rm rest ♿ – 35. AE E VISA. rest
Meals à la carte 40/60 – **134 rm** 195/255 – 3 suites.

at Lindenthal-Breitenfeld *NW : 8 km, by Euritzscher Str.* BX :

Breitenfelder Hof, Lindenallee 8, ✉ 04466, ☎ (0341) 4 65 10, Fax 4651133, – rm – 20. AE E VISA. rest
Meals à la carte 30/46 – **73 rm** 175/225.

at Wachau *SO : 8 km, by Prager Straße* DZ :

Atlanta, Südring 21, ✉ 04445, ☎ (034297) 8 40, Fax 84999, – rm rn ♿ – 220. AE E VISA
Meals à la carte 39/57 – **197 rm** 195/245 – 6 suites.

UNICH (MÜNCHEN) L *Bayern* 419 420 V 18, 987 ⑩, 426 G 4 – *pop.* 1 300 000 – *alt.* 520 m – ✆ 089.

See : *Marienplatz*★ KZ – *Church of Our Lady (Frauenkirche)*★ *(tower* ❋★*)* KZ – *Old Pinakothek (Alte Pinakothek)*★★★ KY – *German Museum (Deutsches Museum)*★★★ LZ – *The Palace (Residenz)*★ *(Treasury*★★ *Palace Theatre*★*)* KY – *Church of Asam Brothers (Asamkirche)*★ KZ – *Nymphenburg*★★ *(Castle*★, *Park*★, *Amalienburg*★★, *Botanical Garden (Botanischer Garten)*★★, *Carriage Museum (Marstallmuseum) and China-Collection (Porzellansammlung*★*) by Arnulfstr.* EV – *New Pinakothek (Neue Pinakothek)*★ KY – *City Historical Museum (Münchener Stadtmuseum)*★ *(Moorish Dancers*★★*)* KZ **M7** – *Villa Lenbach Collections (Städt. Galerie im Lenbachhaus) (Portraits by Lenbach*★*)* JY **M4** – *Antique Collections (Staatliche Antikensammlungen)*★ JY **M3** – *Glyptothek*★ JY **M2** – *German Hunting Museum (Deutsches Jagdmuseum)*★ KZ **M1** – *Olympic Park (Olympia-Park) (Olympic Tower* ❋★★★*) by Schleißheimer Str.* FU – *Hellabrunn Zoo (Tierpark Hellabrunn)*★ *by Lindwurmstr. (B 11)* EX – *English garden (Englischer Garten)*★ *(view from Monopteros Temple* ★*)* LY.

18 *Straßlach, Tölzer Straße (S : 17 km),* ✆ *(08170) 4 50 ;* 9 *München-Thalkirchen, Zentralländstr. 40,* ✆ *(089) 7 23 13 04 ;* 18 *Eichenried (NE : 24 km), Münchener Str. 55,* ✆ *(08123) 10 05.*

München (NE : 29 km) by Ungererstraße HU, *City Air Terminal, Arnulfstraße (Main Station),* ✆ *9 75 00, Fax 97557906.*

Ostbahnhof, Friedenstraße(HX).

Exhibition Centre (Messegelände) (EX), ✆ *5 10 70, Telex 5212086, Fax 5107506.*

Tourist office in the Main Station, (opposite platform 11), ✉ *80335,* ✆ *2 33 03 00, Fax 23330233.*

Tourist-office, airport "Franz-Josef-Strauß", ✆ *97 59 28 15, Fax 975292813*.

ADAC, *Sendlinger-Tor-Platz 9,* ✉ *80336,* ✆ *5 40 19 44 56, Fax 5504449.*

Berlin 586 – Innsbruck 162 – Nürnberg 165 – Salzburg 140 – Stuttgart 222.

Plans on following pages

Rafael, Neuturmstr. 1, ✉ 80331, ✆ 29 09 80, Fax 222539, « Roof garden with terrace and » – rm – 50. AE E VISA JCB. rest KZ s
Meals 52 (lunch) and à la carte 74/102 – **73 rm** 485/980 – 7 suites.

Kempinski Hotel Vier Jahreszeiten, Maximilianstr. 17, ✉ 80539, ✆ 2 12 50, Fax 21252000, Massage, – rm – 350. AE E VISA JCB. rest LZ a
Meals *(closed August)* à la carte 65/106 – ***Bistro-Eck*** (also vegetarian dishes) **Meals** à la carte 44/71 – **316 rm** 441/742 – 48 suites.

Bayerischer Hof, Promenadeplatz 6, ✉ 80333, ✆ 2 12 00, Telex 523409, Fax 2120906, , Massage, – rm – 600. AE E VISA JCB KY y
Garden-Restaurant *(booking essential)* **Meals** à la carte 72/116 – ***Trader Vic's*** *(dinner only)* **Meals** à la carte 67/87 – ***Palais Keller :*** **Meals** à la carte 37/57 – **428 rm** 322/583 – 45 suites.

Königshof, Karlsplatz 25, ✉ 80335, ✆ 55 13 60, Fax 55136113 – – 100. AE E VISA JCB. rest JY s
Meals (booking essential) (outstanding wine list) à la carte 76/106 – **90 rm** 325/510 – 9 suites.

Park Hilton, Am Tucherpark 7, ✉ 80538, ✆ 3 84 50, Telex 5215740, Fax 38451845, , beer garden, Massage, – rm – 780. AE E VISA JCB HU n
Meals see also ***Hilton Grill*** *below* ***Tse Yang*** (Chinese rest.) *(closed Monday)* **Meals** à la carte 47/88 – ***Isar Terrassen :*** **Meals** à la carte 51/79 – **477 rm** 329/560 – 21 suites.

Excelsior, Schützenstr. 11, ✉ 80335, ✆ 55 13 70, Fax 55137121 – rm . AE E VISA JCB JY z
– ***Vinothek*** *(closed Sunday and Bank Holidays)* **Meals** à la carte 44/57 – **113 rm** 245/420 – 4 suites.

Maritim, Goethestr. 7, ✉ 80336, ✆ 55 23 50, Fax 55235900, , , – rm – 280. AE E VISA JCB. rest JZ j
Meals à la carte 53/86 – **339 rm** 288/548 – 5 suites.

Arabella Westpark Hotel, Garmischer Str. 2, ✉ 80339, ✆ 5 19 60, Telex 523680, Fax 5196649, , , – rm rest – 80. AE E VISA JCB by Leopoldstr. GU
closed 20 December - 6 January – **Meals** 43 (buffet lunch) and à la carte 44/72 – **258 rm** 220/450 – 6 suites.

Eden-Hotel-Wolff, Arnulfstr. 4, ✉ 80335, ✆ 55 11 50, Fax 55115555 – rm – 140. AE E VISA JCB JY p
Meals à la carte 35/65 – **211 rm** 210/450 – 4 suites.

STREET INDEX

Brienner Straße . . . . JKY
Dienerstraße . . . . KZ 36
Karlsplatz (Stachus) . . . . . . JY 91
Kaufingerstraße . . . . KZ
Marienplatz . . . . KZ
Maximilianstraße . . . . KYZ
Neuhauser Straße . . . . JZ 147
Residenzstraße . . . . KY 177
Sendlinger Straße . . . . KZ
Sonnenstraße . . . . JZ
Theatinerstraße . . . . KY 206
Weinstraße . . . . KZ 228

Ackermannstraße . . . . FU
Adalbertstraße . . . . GU
Albrechtstraße . . . . EU
Amalienstraße . . . . KY
Am Gasteig . . . . LZ 4
Amiraplatz . . . . KY 6
An der Hauptfeuerwache . JZ 7
Arcisstraße . . . . JY
Arnulfstraße . . . . EV
Asamstraße . . . . GX
Auenstraße . . . . GX
Auerfeldstraße . . . . GX
Augustenstraße . . . . JY
Aventinstraße . . . . KZ
Baaderstraße . . . . KLZ
Bahnhofplatz . . . . JY
Baldeplatz . . . . GX 14
Barer Straße . . . . JKY
Baumgartnerstraße . . . . . . EX 17
Bavariaring . . . . EFX
Bayerstraße . . . . JY
Beethovenplatz . . . . JZ
Beethovenstraße . . . . JZ 20
Belgradstraße . . . . GU
Biedersteiner Straße . . . . . HU 25
Blumenstraße . . . . KZ
Blutenburgstraße . . . . EV
Bonner Platz . . . . GU
Bonner Straße . . . . GU 26
Burgstraße . . . . KZ 30
Clemensstraße . . . . GU
Corneliusbrücke . . . . KZ
Corneliusstraße . . . . KZ
Dachauer Straße . . . . JY
Damenstiftstraße . . . . JZ 32
Denninger Straße . . . . HV 34
Dietlindenstraße . . . . GHU
Dom-Pedro-Straße . . . . EU
Eduard-Schmid-Str. . . . . KLZ
Ehrengutstraße . . . . FX
Einsteinstraße . . . . HX
Eisenmannstraße . . . . KZ 39
Elisabethstraße . . . . FGU
Elisenstraße . . . . JY
Elsässer Straße . . . . HX 42
Emil-Riedel-Straße . . . . HV 45
Erhardtstraße . . . . KLZ
Feilitzschstraße . . . . GU
Flurstraße . . . . HX 49
Franziskanerstraße . . . . GX
Franz-Joseph-Straße . . . . . . GU
Franz-Joseph-Strauß-Ring . . LY 50
Frauenstraße . . . . KZ
Fraunhoferstraße . . . . KZ
Friedenstraße . . . . HX
Friedrichstraße . . . . GU 52
Gabelsbergerstraße . . . . . . JKY
Gärtnerplatz . . . . KZ
Galileiplatz . . . . HV 53
Ganghoferstraße . . . . EX
Gebsattelstraße . . . . GX 55

Continued on following pages

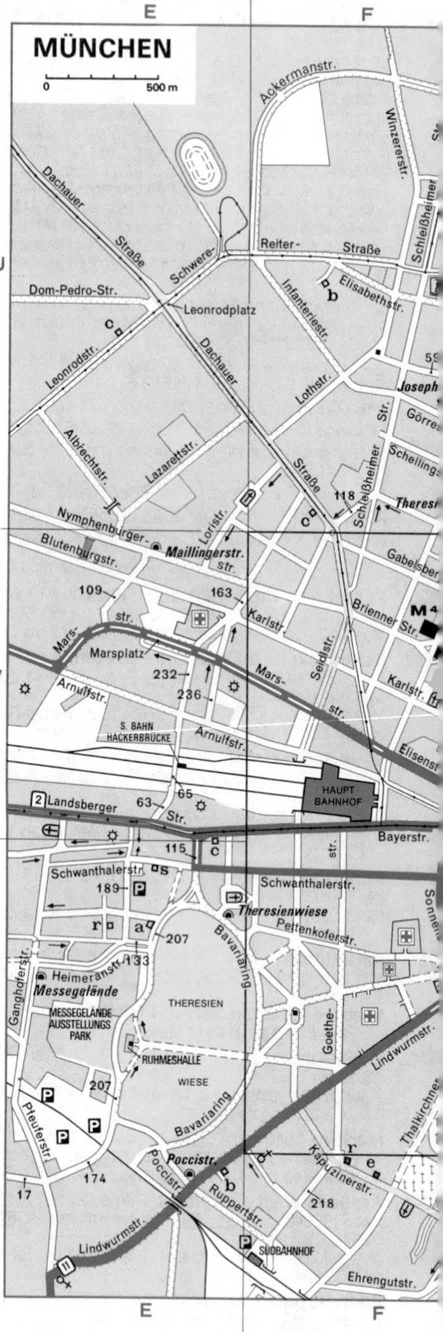

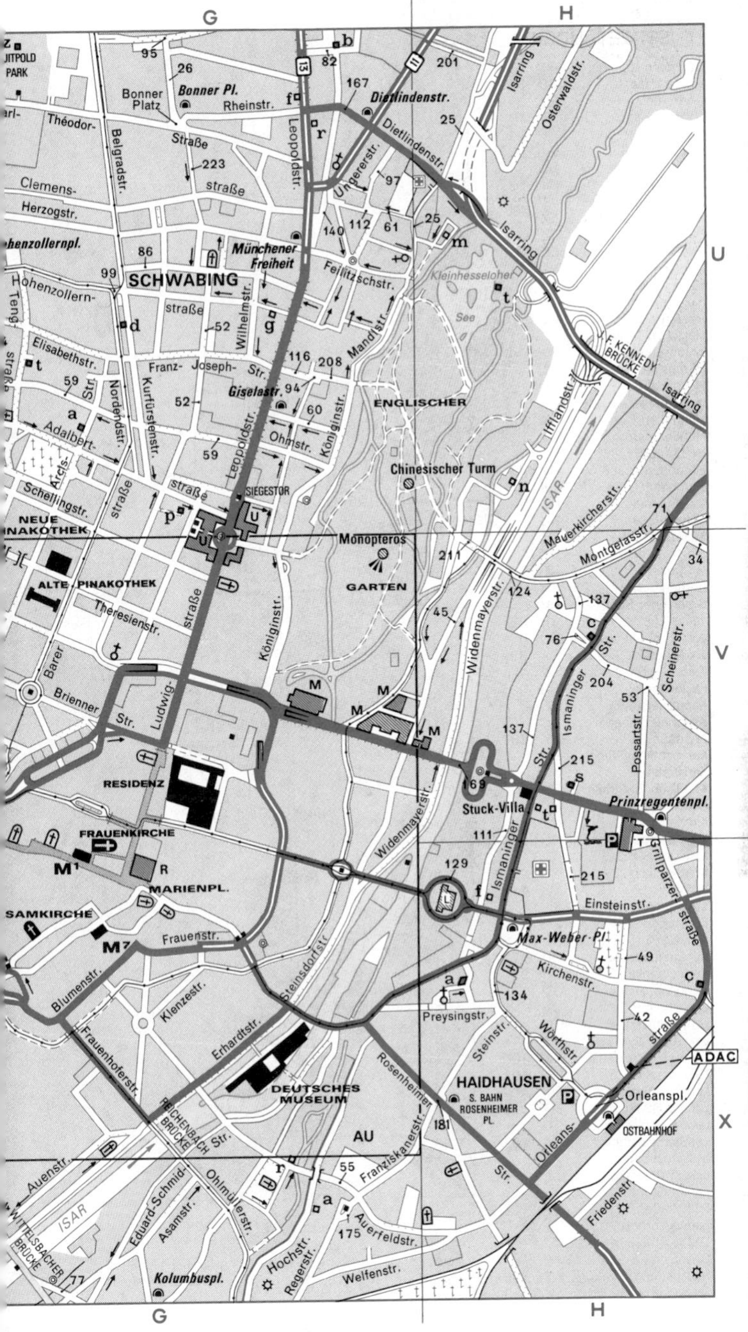

G
H
U
V
X
SCHWABING
ENGLISCHER
GARTEN
Chinesischer Turm
Monopteros
NEUE PINAKOTHEK
ALTE PINAKOTHEK
RESIDENZ
FRAUENKIRCHE
MARIENPL.
DEUTSCHES MUSEUM
HAIDHAUSEN
AU
OSTBAHNHOF
ADAC
Stuck-Villa
Prinzregentenpl.
Max-Weber-Pl.
Orleanspl.
Bonner Pl.
Dietlindenstr.
Münchener Freiheit
Giselastr.
Kolumbuspl.
Leopoldstr.
Ludwig-straße
Isarring
F. KENNEDY BRÜCKE
REICHENBACH BRÜCKE
WITTELSBACHER BRÜCKE
ISAR

STREET INDEX

Georgenstraße . . . . . . FGU 59
Giselastraße . . . . GU 60
Görresstraße . . . . FU
Goethestraße . . . . JZ
Gohrenstraße . . . . GU 61
Grasserstraße . . . . EV 63
Grillparzerstraße . . . . . HX
Hackerbrücke . . . . EV 65
Häberlstraße . . . . JZ
Hans-Sachs-Straße . . . KZ
Haydnstraße . . . . JZ
Heimeranstraße . . . . . EX
Herkomerplatz . . . . . . HU 71
Herrnstraße . . . . LZ
Herzog-Heinrich-Str. . . JZ
Herzogstraße . . . . GU
Herzog-Wilhelm-Str. . . JZ
Hiltenspergerstraße . . FGU 74
Hirtenstraße . . . . JY
Hochstraße . . . . LZ
Hofgartenstraße . . . . . KY
Hofgraben . . . . KZ 75
Hohenzollernstraße . . GU
Holzstraße . . . . JZ
Hompeschstraße . . . . HV 76
Humboldtstraße . . . . . GX 77
Ickstattstraße . . . . . . KZ
Ifflandstraße . . . . HU
Infanteriestraße . . . . . FU
Innere Wiener Straße . . . . LZ 79
Isarring . . . . HU
Ismaninger Straße . . . HVX
Johann-Fichte-Str. . . . . GU 82
John-F.-Kennedy-Br. . . HU
Josephsplatz . . . . FU 83
Kaiser-Ludwigs-Platz . . JZ
Kaiserstraße . . . . GU 86
Kapuzinerstraße . . . . . JZ
Kardinal-Faulhaber-Straße . . . . KY 88
Karl-Scharnagl-Ring . . LY
Karlstraße . . . . JY
Karl-Theodor-Straße . . GU
Karolinenplatz . . . . KY
Kirchenstraße . . . . HX
Kißkaltplatz . . . . GU 94
Klenzestraße . . . . KZ
Kölner Platz . . . . GU 95
Königinstraße . . . . LY
Königsplatz . . . . JY
Kohlstraße . . . . KLZ
Kreuzstraße . . . . JZ
Kunigundenstraße . . . GU 97
Kurfüstenplatz . . . . . . GU 99
Kurfürstenstraße . . . . . GU
Landsberger Straße . . EV
Landwehrstraße . . . . . JZ
Lazarettstraße . . . . EU
Ledererstraße . . . . KZ 100
Lenbachplatz . . . . KY 101
Leonrodplatz . . . . EU
Leonrodstraße . . . . . . EU
Leopoldstraße . . . . GU
Lerchenfeldstraße . . . . LY 102
Lessingstraße . . . . JZ
Lindwurmstraße . . . . . JZ
Loristraße . . . . EUV
Lothstraße . . . . FU
Ludwigsbrücke . . . . . . LZ
Ludwigstraße . . . . KY
Luisenstraße . . . . JY
Maffeistraße . . . . KY 106
Maillingerstraße . . . . . EV 109
Maistraße . . . . JZ
Mandlstraße . . . . GU
Maria-Theresia-Str. . . . HV 111
Marschallstraße . . . . GU 112
Marsplatz . . . . EV
Marsstraße . . . . JY
Marstallplatz . . . . KLY
Martin-Greif-Straße . . . . . . EX 115
Martiusstraße . . . . GU 116
Maßmannstraße . . . . FU 1
Mauerkircherstraße . . . . . HUV
Maxburgstraße . . . . KY
Maximiliansbrücke . . . . . . LZ 1
Maximiliansplatz . . . . KY 12
Max-Josephs-Br. . . . . HV 12

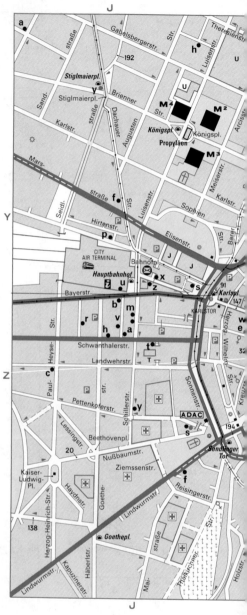

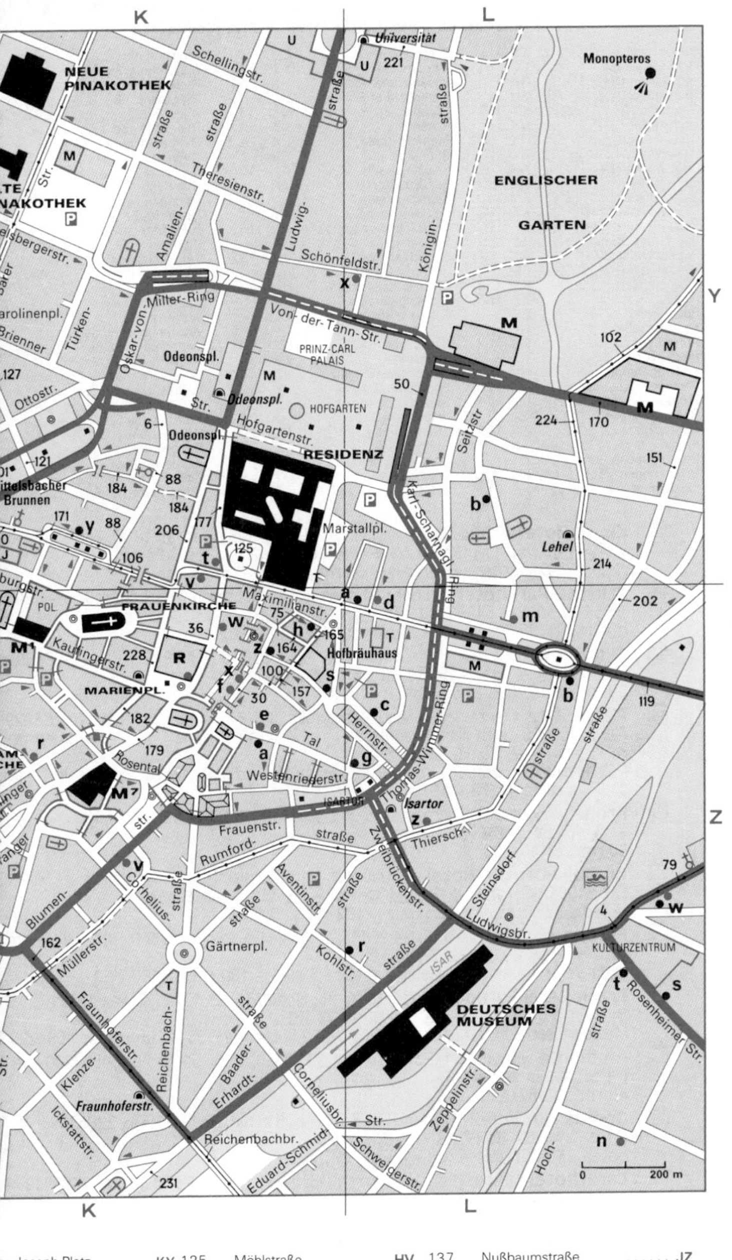

ax-Joseph-Platz . . . . KY 125
ax-Joseph-Straße . . . . . . KY 127
ax-Planck-Straße . . . . . . HX 129
eiserstraße . . . . JY
esseplatz . . . . EX 133
etzgerstraße . . . . HX 134

Möhlstraße . . . . HV 137
Montgelasstraße . . . . HUV
Mozartstraße . . . . JZ 138
Müllerstraße . . . . KZ
Münchener Freiheit . . . . GU 140
Nordendstraße . . . . GU

Nußbaumstraße . . . . JZ
Nymphenburger
Straße . . . . EUV
Oberanger . . . . KZ

Continued on following page

STREET INDEX TO MÜNCHEN TOWN PLANS (Concluded)

Street	Plan	No.
Odeonsplatz	KY	
Oettingenstraße	LY	151
Ohlmüllerstraße	GX	
Ohmstraße	GU	
Orlandostraße	KZ	157
Orleansplatz	HX	
Orleansstraße	HX	
Oskar-von-Miller-Ring	KY	
Osterwaldstraße	HU	
Ottostraße	KY	
Pacellistraße	KY	160
Papa-Schmid-Straße	KZ	162
Pappenheimstraße	EV	163
Paul-Heyse-Straße	JZ	
Pettenkoferstraße	JZ	
Pfeuferstraße	EX	
Pfisterstraße	KZ	164
Platzl	KZ	165
Poccistraße	EX	
Possartstraße	HV	
Potsdamer Straße	GU	167
Preysingstraße	HX	
Prinzregentenbrücke	HV	169
Prinzregentenstraße	LY	170
Promenadeplatz	KY	171
Radlkoferstraße	EX	174
Regerplatz	GX	175
Regerstraße	GX	
Reichenbachbrücke	KZ	
Reichenbachstraße	KZ	
Reisingerstraße	JZ	
Rheinstraße	GU	
Rindermarkt	KZ	179
Rosenheimer Platz	HX	181
Rosenheimer Straße	LZ	
Rosenstraße	KZ	182
Rosental	KZ	
Rumfordstraße	KZ	
Ruppertstraße	EFX	
Salvatorstraße	KY	184
Sandstraße	JY	
Scheinerstraße	HV	
Schellingstraße	KY	
Schießstättstraße	EX	189
Schillerstraße	JZ	
Schleißheimer Str.	JY	192
Schönfeldstraße	KLY	
Schwanthalerstraße	JZ	
Schweigerstraße	LZ	
Schwere-Reiter-Straße	EFU	
Seidlstraße	JY	
Seitzstraße	LY	
Sendlinger-Tor-Platz	JZ	194
Sophienstraße	JY	
Steinsdorfstraße	LZ	
Steinstraße	HX	
Stengelstraße	HU	201
Sternstraße	LZ	202
Sternwartstraße	HV	204
Stiglmaierplatz	JY	
Tal	KZ	
Tengstraße	GU	
Thalkirchner Straße	JZ	
Theresienhöhe	EX	20
Theresienstraße	JK	
Thiemestraße	GU	20
Thierschstraße	LZ	
Thomas-Wimmer-Ring	LZ	
Tivolistraße	HV	21
Triftstraße	LY	21
Trogerstraße	HVX	21
Türkenstraße	KY	
Tumblingerstraße	FX	21
Ungererstraße	GU	
Veterinärstraße	LY	22
Viktoriastraße	GU	22
Von-der-Tann-Straße	KLY	
Wagmüllerstraße	LY	22
Welfenstraße	GX	
Westenriederstraße	KZ	
Widenmayerstraße	GHV	
Wilhelmstraße	GU	
Winzererstraße	FU	
Wittelsbacherbrücke	GX	
Wittelsbacherstraße	KZ	23
Wörthstraße	HX	
Wredestraße	EV	23
Zeppelinstraße	LZ	
Ziemssenstraße	JZ	
Zirkus-Krone-Straße	EV	23
Zweibrückenstraße	LZ	

King's Hotel without rest, Dachauer Str. 13, ✉ 80335, ☎ 55 18 70, Fax 55187300 – 30. AE ⓓ E VISA JCB JY
closed 23 December - 6 January – **96 rm** 205/285.

Trustee Parkhotel without rest, Parkstr. 31 (approach in Gollierstraße), ✉ 8033 ☎ 51 99 50, Fax 51995420 – – 25. AE ⓓ E VISA JCB EX
closed 23 - 28 December – **35 rm** 245/476 – 6 suites.

Exquisit without rest, Pettenkoferstr. 3, ✉ 80336, ☎ 5 51 99 00, Fax 55199499, – – 30. AE ⓓ E VISA JZ
50 rm 195/280 – 5 suites.

Platzl, Platzl 1 (entrance in Sparkassenstraße), ✉ 80331, ☎ 23 70 30, Telex 52291 Fax 23703800, (with dinner-variete theatre "Platzl's Theaterie"), – rm – 70. AE ⓓ E VISA KZ
Pfistermühle *(closed Saturday lunch, Sunday and mid July - mid August)* **Meals** 37 (lunc and à la carte 42/78 – **167 rm** 220/410.

Krone without rest, Theresienhöhe 8, ✉ 80339, ☎ 50 40 52, Fax 506706 – – 15. ⓓ E VISA EX
30 rm 110/300.

Arabella-Central-Hotel without rest, Schwanthalerstr. 111, ✉ 80339, ☎ 51 08 3 Fax 51083249, – – 30. AE ⓓ E VISA EX
closed 22 December - 6 January – **102 rm** 216/412.

Europa, Dachauer Str. 115, ✉ 80335, ☎ 54 24 20, Fax 54242500, – rm – 60. AE ⓓ E VISA FU
Isola Bella (Italian rest.) **Meals** à la carte 30/56 – **180 rm** 180/350.

Erzgießerei-Europe, Erzgießereistr. 15, ✉ 80335, ☎ 12 68 20, Fax 1236198, rm – 50. AE ⓓ E VISA JY
Meals *(closed Sunday lunch and Saturday)* à la carte 33/58 – **106 rm** 165/290.

Ambiente without rest, Schillerstr. 12, ✉ 80336, ☎ 54 51 70, Fax 54517200 – . AE ⓓ E VISA JCB JZ
46 rm 182/250.

Domus without rest, St.-Anna-Str. 31, ✉ 80538, ☎ 22 17 04, Fax 2285359 – . AE ⓓ E VISA LY
closed 23 to 28 December – **45 rm** 190/290.

Carathotel without rest, Lindwurmstr. 13, ✉ 80337, ☎ 23 03 80, Fax 23038199 – . AE ⓓ E VISA JZ
70 rm 205/320.

Deutsches Theater (Italian rest.), Schwanthaler Str. 15, ✉ 80336, ☎ 5 52 24 9 Fax 552249614, – – 15. AE ⓓ E VISA JCB JZ
Meals *(closed Monday)* à la carte 37/62 – **25 rm** 160/290.

Drei Löwen, Schillerstr. 8, ✉ 80336, ☎ 55 10 40, Telex 523867, Fax 55104905 – – 15. AE ⓓ E VISA JCB JZ
Meals à la carte 33/54 – **82 rm** 182/280.

InterCityHotel, Bayerstr. 10, 80335, 54 55 60, Fax 54556610 – rm – 100. AE E VISA JCB JY u
Meals *(closed Sunday)* à la carte 36/57 – **193 rm** 198/398 – 4 suites.

Admiral without rest, Kohlstr. 9, 80469, 22 66 41, Fax 293674 – . AE E VISA LZ r
33 rm 230/330.

Torbräu without rest, Tal 41, 80331, 22 50 16, Fax 225019 – – 15. AE E VISA JCB LZ g
86 rm 225/370 – 3 suites.

Mercure City without rest, Senefelder Str. 9, 80336, 55 13 20, Fax 596444 – – 50. AE E VISA JCB JZ v
167 rm 188/340.

Kraft without rest, Schillerstr. 49, 80336, 59 48 23, Fax 5503856 – . AE E VISA JZ y
closed 23 to 26 December – **35 rm** 140/240.

Sol Inn Hotel, Paul-Heyse-Str. 24, 80336, 51 49 00, Fax 51490701, – rm – 35. AE E VISA JCB. rest JZ c
Meals *(closed Sunday lunch)* à la carte 35/50 – **182 rm** 175/410.

Concorde without rest, Herrnstr. 38, 80539, 22 45 15, Fax 2283282 – . AE E VISA LZ c
closed Christmas - early January – **71 rm** 175/285.

Cristal without rest, Schwanthalerstr. 5, 80336, 55 11 10, Fax 55111992 – rm rest – 80. AE E VISA JZ h
100 rm 209/355.

Splendid without rest, Maximilianstr. 54, 80538, 29 66 06, Fax 2913176 – . AE E VISA JCB LZ b
40 rm 175/340.

Germania without rest, Schwanthaler Str. 28, 80336, 59 04 60, Fax 591171, – . AE E VISA JZ a
96 rm 160/280.

Schlicker without rest, Tal 8, 80331, 22 79 41, Fax 296059 – . AE E VISA KZ a
closed 20 December - 7 January – **69 rm** 130/360.

Königswache without rest, Steinheilstr. 7, 80333, 5 42 75 70, Fax 5232114 – . AE E VISA JY h
40 rm 140/290.

Brack without rest, Lindwurmstr. 153, 80337, 7 47 25 50, Fax 74725599 – . AE E VISA JCB EX b
50 rm 150/270.

Europäischer Hof without rest, Bayerstr. 31, 80335, 55 15 10, Fax 55151222 – – 20. AE E VISA JCB JZ b
150 rm 178/360.

Olympic without rest, Hans-Sachs-Str. 4, 80469, 23 18 90, Fax 23189199 – . AE E VISA KZ c
32 rm 155/280.

Acanthus without rest, An der Hauptfeuerwache 14, 80331, 23 18 80, Fax 2607364 – . AE E VISA JZ n
36 rm 155/260.

Hilton Grill - Hotel Park Hilton, Am Tucherpark 7, 80538, 3 84 52 61, Fax 38451845 – . AE E VISA JCB. HU n
closed Saturday lunch, Monday, 2 to 14 January, 24 to 31 March and late July - mid August – **Meals** 53 (lunch) and à la carte 74/100
Spec. Lachstranche mit Kaviar in Gemüsegelee, Rehrücken im Wirsingcrêpe mit Pfeffersauce, Himbeermousse und Himbeeren im Haselnußbaiser.

El Toula, Sparkassenstr. 5, 80331, 29 28 69, Fax 298043 – . AE E VISA JCB KZ f
closed Sunday - Monday lunch and 1 to 21 August – **Meals** (booking essential for dinner) à la carte 68/84.

Gasthaus Glockenbach (former old Bavarian pub), Kapuzinerstr. 29, 80337, 53 40 43, Fax 534043 – E VISA FX e
closed Saturday lunch, Sunday - Monday, Bank Holidays and 2 weeks August – **Meals** (booking essential) 35/45 lunch and à la carte 61/105
Spec. Blutwurstravioli mit Gänseleber, Tranche vom Steinbutt mit Octopus und Tomatenconfit, Schokoladenpastete mit Früchten.

XX **Böswirth an der Oper**, Falkenturmstr. 10, ✉ 80331, ☎ 29 79 09, Fax 297909 – E VISA KZ
closed Sunday - Monday lunch, Bank Holidays and 3 weeks August **Meals** à la carte 49/8

XX **Zum Bürgerhaus**, Pettenkoferstr. 1, ✉ 80336, ☎ 59 79 09, Fax 595657, « Bavaria farmhouse furniture ; courtyard terrace » – AE E VISA JZ
closed Saturday lunch, Sunday and Bank Holidays – **Meals** (booking essential) à la car 44/64.

XX **Halali**, Schönfeldstr. 22, ✉ 80539, ☎ 28 59 09, Fax 282786 – AE E VISA LY
closed Saturday lunch, Sunday and Bank Holidays – **Meals** (booking essential) 35 lunch ar à la carte 51/73.

XX **Chesa**, Wurzerstr. 18, ✉ 80539, ☎ 29 71 14, Fax 2285698, 🏡 – AE ⓓ VISA LZ
closed Sunday – **Meals** (booking essential) 26 lunch and à la carte 43/72.

XX **Galleria** (Italian rest.), Ledererstr. 2 (corner of Sparkassenstr.), ✉ 80331, ☎ 29 79 9 Fax 2913653 – AE ⓓ E VISA KZ
closed Sunday and 1 to 7 January – **Meals** (booking essential) à la carte 60/76.

X **Straubinger Hof** (Bavarian pub), Blumenstr. 5, ✉ 80331, ☎ 2 60 84 44, Fax 260891 beer garden – AE E VISA. ✻ KZ
closed Sunday and Bank Holidays – **Meals** à la carte 24/52.

Brewery - inns :

X **Spatenhaus-Bräustuben**, Residenzstr. 12, ✉ 80333, ☎ 2 90 70 60, Fax 291305 🏡, « Furnished in traditional Alpine style » – AE ⓓ E VISA KY
Meals à la carte 42/74.

X **Weisses Bräuhaus**, Tal 7, ✉ 80331, ☎ 29 98 75, Fax 29013875, 🏡 – 🏛 30. KZ
Meals à la carte 26/48.

X **Augustiner Gaststätten**, Neuhauser Str. 27, ✉ 80331, ☎ 23 18 32 5 Fax 2605379, « Beer garden » – AE ⓓ E VISA JZ
Meals à la carte 30/59.

X **Altes Hackerhaus**, Sendlinger Str. 14, ✉ 80331, ☎ 2 60 50 26, Fax 2605027, 🏡 AE ⓓ E VISA JCB KZ
Meals à la carte 30/67.

X **Franziskaner Fuchsenstuben**, Perusastr. 5, ✉ 80333, ☎ 2 31 81 2 Fax 23181244, 🏡 – AE ⓓ E VISA JCB KY
Meals à la carte 33/66.

X **Paulaner Bräuhaus**, Kapuzinerplatz 5, ✉ 80337, ☎ 5 44 61 10, Fax 54461118, bee garden – E VISA FX
Meals à la carte 32/62.

at Munich-Allach *by Arnulfstr.* EV :

Lutter without rest, Eversbuschstr. 109, ✉ 80999, ☎ 8 12 70 04, Fax 8129584 – ☎ P. AE E VISA
closed 24 December - 4 January – **26 rm** ☕ 110/180.

at Munich-Bogenhausen :

Palace, Trogerstr. 21, ✉ 81675, ☎ 41 97 10, Fax 41971819, « Elegant installation wi period furniture », ≘s, 🌳 – |♦| ⇔ rm TV ☎ 🚗 – 🏛 40. AE ⓓ E VISA JCB
Meals (residents only) – **71 rm** ☕ 276/568 – 6 suites. HV

Arabella-Hotel, Arabellastr. 5, ✉ 81925, ☎ 9 23 20, Fax 92324449, ≤ Munich, 🏡 Massage, 🏋, ≘s, 🏊 – |♦| ⇔ rm ▤ rest TV ☎ ♿ 🚗 P – 🏛 350. AE ⓓ E VIS ✻ rest by Isarring HU
Meals à la carte 40/65 – **467 rm** ☕ 250/450 – 39 suites.

Prinzregent without rest, Ismaninger Str. 42, ✉ 81675, ☎ 41 60 50, Fax 4160546 ≘s – |♦| ⇔ TV 🚗 – 🏛 35. AE ⓓ E VISA HV
closed Christmas - early January – **66 rm** ☕ 270/370.

Rothof without rest, Denniger Str. 114, ✉ 81925, ☎ 91 50 61, Fax 915066, 🌳 – ⇔ TV 🚗. AE ⓓ E VISA by Einsteinstr. HX
closed 24 December - 6 January – **37 rm** ☕ 198/360.

Queens Hotel München, Effnerstr. 99, ✉ 81925, ☎ 92 79 80, Telex 52475 Fax 983813 – |♦| ⇔ rm ▤ rest TV ☎ 🚗 P – 🏛 200. AE ⓓ E VISA. ✻ rest
Meals à la carte 33/76 – **152 rm** ☕ 262/468. by Ismaninger Str. HV

XXX **Bogenhauser Hof** (1825 former hunting lodge), Ismaninger Str. 85, ✉ 8167 ☎ 98 55 86, Fax 9810221, « Garden terrace » – AE ⓓ VISA HV
closed Sunday, Bank Holidays and Christmas - 6 January – **Meals** (booking essential) à carte 64/94.

XX **Acquarello** (Italian rest.), Mühlbaurstr. 36, ✉ 81677, ☎ 4 70 48 48, Fax 476464, – AE E. by Mühlbaurstr HV
closed Saturday and Sunday lunch – **Meals** à la carte 59/75.

XX **Käfer Schänke**, Schumannstr. 1, ✉ 81675, ☎ 4 16 82 47, Fax 4168623, « Several rooms with elegant rustic installation » – AE E VISA HV s
closed Sunday and Bank Holidays – **Meals** (booking essential) 43 lunch and à la carte 55/103.

XX **Prielhof**, Oberföhringer Str. 44, ✉ 81925, ☎ 98 53 53, Fax 9827289, – E VISA.
closed Saturday lunch, Sunday, Bank Holidays and 23 December - 6 January – **Meals** (booking essential) à la carte 51/74. by Ismaninger Str. HV

t Munich-Denning *by Denninger Str.* HV :

XXX **Casale** (Italian rest.), Ostpreußenstr. 42, ✉ 81927, ☎ 93 62 68, Fax 9306722, – P. AE E VISA
Meals à la carte 45/75.

t Munich-Englschalking *by Ismaninger Str.* HU *and Englschalkinger Str.* :

XX **La Vigna** (Italian rest.), Wilhelm-Dieß-Weg 2, ✉ 81927, ☎ 93 14 16, Fax 92401649, – AE E VISA
closed Saturday, 23 December to 5 January and 1 week May – **Meals** (booking essential) à la carte 60/80
Spec. Rochenflügel mit Kapern, Oliven und Thymian, Geschmorte Rindsbäckchen mit Polenta und Steinpilzen, Lauwarmer Brot-Apfelkuchen mit Vanillesauce.

t Munich-Haidhausen :

City Hilton, Rosenheimer Str. 15, ✉ 81667, ☎ 4 80 40, Telex 529437, Fax 48044804, – rm – 180. AE E VISA. rest LZ s
Meals 53 (buffet) and à la carte 54/76 – **479 rm** 372/616 – 4 suites.

Preysing, Preysingstr. 1, ✉ 81667, ☎ 45 84 50, Fax 45845444, – – 50. AE E VISA LZ w
closed 23 December - 6 January – **Meals** see ***Preysing-Keller*** *below* – **76 rm** 160/298 – 5 suites.

Forum Hotel München, Hochstr. 3, ✉ 81669, ☎ 4 80 30, Telex 529046, Fax 4488277, Massage, – rm – 350. AE E VISA JCB
Meals à la carte 51/83 – **582 rm** 300/410 – 12 suites. LZ t

XXX **Preysing-Keller** - Hotel Preysing, Innere-Wiener-Str. 6, ✉ 81667, ☎ 45 84 52 60, Fax 45845444, « Vaulted cellar, country house furniture » – . AE E VISA LZ w
closed Sunday, Bank Holidays and 23 December - 6 January – **Meals** (dinner only) (outstanding wine list) 89/125 and à la carte 65/101
Spec. Steinbutt mit Räucherlachskruste, Lammfilet mit Ziegentopfen gratiniert, Aprikosenterrine und weißes Schockoladeneis auf Amarettosauce.

XX **Massimiliano**, Rablstr. 10, ✉ 81699, ☎ 4 48 44 77, Fax 4484405, – P. E VISA
closed Saturday lunch – **Meals** 37 lunch and à la carte 58/99. LZ n
Spec. St. Petersfisch auf Petersilienpüree mit Champagner-Rotweinsauce, Sauté von der Bresse Taube mit Truffelsauce, Marmoriertes Grießsoufflé (2 Pers.).

XX **Gallo Nero** (Italian rest.), Grillparzerstr. 1, ✉ 81675, ☎ 4 70 54 72, Fax 4701321, – AE E HX c
closed Saturday lunch, Bank Holidays lunch and Sunday – **Meals** à la carte 51/73.

X **Rue Des Halles** (Bistro), Steinstr. 18, ✉ 81667, ☎ 48 56 75 – E VISA HX a
Meals (dinner only, booking essential) à la carte 54/76.

t Munich-Laim *by Landsberger Str. (B 2)* EV :

Transmar-Park-Hotel without rest, Zschokkestr. 55, ✉ 80686, ☎ 57 93 60, Fax 57936100, – – 30. AE E VISA JCB
68 rm 180/270.

t Munich-Neu Perlach *by Rosenheimer Str.* HX :

Mercure, Karl-Marx-Ring 87, ✉ 81735, ☎ 6 32 70, Telex 5213357, Fax 6327407, – rm rest P – 100. AE E VISA
Meals 37 (buffet lunch) and à la carte 38/62 – **184 rm** 195/315 – 4 suites.

Villa Waldperlach without rest, Putzbrunner Str. 250(Waldperlach), ✉ 81739, ☎ 6 60 03 00, Fax 66003066 – . AE E VISA
21 rm 150/250.

t Munich-Pasing *by Landsberger Straße* EV :

XX **Zur Goldenen Gans**, Planegger Str.31, ✉ 81241, ☎ 83 70 33, Fax 8204680, « Baverian Inn with cosy atmosphere » – P. E VISA
closed Sunday and Bank Holidays – **Meals** 25 lunch and à la carte 45/71.

at Munich-Schwabing :

Marriott-Hotel, Berliner Str. 93, ✉ 80805, ℘ 36 00 20, Telex 521664
Fax 36002200, Massage, ≘s, 🅂 – |‡| ⇹ rm ▤ TV ♿ – 🅰 320. AE ⓓ E VISA
JCB. ⇹ rest by Ungererstr. (B 11) HU
Meals 38 buffet lunch and à la carte 39/73 – **348 rm** ☐ 239/556 – 16 suites.

Holiday Inn Crowne Plaza, Leopoldstr. 194, ✉ 80804, ℘ 38 17 90, Telex 521543
Fax 38179888, ⛱, Massage, ≘s, 🅂 – |‡| ⇹ rm TV ℡ – 🅰 320. AE ⓓ E VISA
JCB by Leopoldstr. GU
Meals à la carte 51/87 – **365 rm** ☐ 324/569.

Ramada Parkhotel, Theodor-Dombart-Str. 4 (corner of Berliner Straße), ✉ 8080
℘ 36 09 90, Telex 5218720, Fax 36099684, ⛱, Massage, ≘s – |‡| ⇹ rm TV
🅰 40. AE ⓓ E VISA JCB by Ungererstr. (B 11) HU
Meals à la carte 43/70 – **260 rm** ☐ 243/441 – 80 suites.

Arabella - Olympiapark-Hotel, Helene-Mayer-Ring 12, ✉ 80809, ℘ 35 75 1
Fax 3543730, ⛱ – |‡| ⇹ rm TV ☎ Ⓟ – 🅰 30. AE ⓓ E VISA by Schleißheimer Str. FU
closed 23 December - 6 January – **Meals** à la carte 38/62 – **105 rm** ☐ 216/412.

Vitalis, Kathi-Kobus-Str. 24, ✉ 80797, ℘ 12 00 80, Fax 1298382, 🅂 – |‡| ⇹ rm
☎ Ⓟ – 🅰 60. AE ⓓ E VISA FU
Meals à la carte 28/51 – **101 rm** ☐ 255/375.

Cosmopolitan without rest, Hohenzollernstr. 5, ✉ 80801, ℘ 38 38 10, Fax 383811
– |‡| ⇹ TV ☎ ℡. AE ⓓ E VISA JCB GU
71 rm ☐ 155/220.

Mercure without rest, Leopoldstr. 120, ✉ 80802, ℘ 39 05 50, Fax 349344 – |‡|
TV ☎. AE ⓓ E VISA GU
65 rm ☐ 170/305.

Leopold, Leopoldstr. 119, ✉ 80804, ℘ 36 70 61, Fax 36043150, ⛱ – |‡| TV ☎
Ⓟ. AE ⓓ E VISA GU
closed 23 December - 1 January – **Meals** à la carte 27/63 – **75 rm** ☐ 160/265.

Tantris, Johann-Fichte-Str. 7, ✉ 80805, ℘ 36 20 61, Fax 3618469, ⛱ – ▤ Ⓟ. AE
E VISA. ⇹ GU
closed Sunday, Monday, Bank Holidays and 1 week January – **Meals** (booking essential) 2
and à la carte 88/134
Spec. Langustinen im Kartoffelmantel auf mariniertem Gemüse, Milchkalbskotelette m
geschmorten Tomaten und Artischocken, Karamelisiertes Hippenblatt mit Weinbergpf
sich und Walderdbeeren.

Savoy (Italian rest.), Tengstr. 20, ✉ 80798, ℘ 2 71 14 45 – AE ⓓ E VISA GU
closed Sunday – **Meals** (booking essential for dinner) à la carte 43/75.

Spago (Italian rest.), Neureutherstr. 15, ✉ 80799, ℘ 2 71 24 06, Fax 2780442, ⛱
AE E GU
dinner only Saturday, Sunday and Bank Holidays – **Meals** à la carte 49/72.

Bistro Terrine, Amalienstr. 89 (Amalien-Passage), ✉ 80799, ℘ 28 17 8
Fax 2809316, ⛱ – AE E VISA GU
closed Saturday and Monday lunch, Sunday and Bank Holidays – **Meals** (booking essent
for dinner) 43 (lunch) and à la carte 47/65.

Seehaus, Kleinhesselohe 3, ✉ 80802, ℘ 3 81 61 30, Fax 341803, ≤, « Lakeside setti
terrace » – Ⓟ. AE ⓓ E VISA HU
Meals à la carte 44/69.

Bamberger Haus, Brunnenstr. 2 (at Luitpoldpark), ✉ 80804, ℘ 3 08 89 6
Fax 3003304, « 18C palace ; terrace » – Ⓟ. AE E VISA GU
closed Monday lunch – **Meals** à la carte 39/65 – ***Bräukeller*** *(dinner only)* **Meals** à la car
28/60.

at Munich-Sendling *by Lindwurmstr. (B 11)* EX :

Holiday Inn München - Süd, Kistlerhofstr. 142, ✉ 81379, ℘ 78 00 2
Fax 78002672, beer garden, Massage, ≘s, 🅂 – |‡| ⇹ rm ▤ TV ♿ – 🅰 90.
ⓓ E VISA JCB
closed 23 December - 6 January – **Meals** à la carte 40/69 – **320 rm** ☐ 287/444 – 7 suit

Ambassador Parkhotel (Italian rest.), Plinganserstr. 102, ✉ 81369, ℘ 72 48
Fax 72489100, beer garden – |‡| TV ☎. AE ⓓ E VISA
closed 23 December - 7 January – **Meals** *(closed Saturday lunch)* à la carte 38/66 – **42**
☐ 175/275.

K u. K Hotel am Harras, Albert-Rosshaupter-Str. 4, ✉ 81369, ℘ 77 00
Fax 7212820 – |‡| ⇹ rm TV ☎ ℡. AE ⓓ E VISA
Meals (residents only) (dinner only) – **120 rm** ☐ 199/335.

at Munich-Untermenzing *by Arnulfstr.* EV :

Romantik-Hotel Insel Mühle, von-Kahr-Str. 87, ✉ 80999, ☎ 8 10 10, Fax 8120571, beer garden, « Converted 16C riverside mill », – TV ♿ – 🅟 – 40. AE E VISA
Meals *(closed Sunday and Bank Holidays)* à la carte 49/72 – **37 rm** 185/350.

at Unterhaching *by Kapuzinerstr.* GX :

Schrenkhof without rest, Leonhardsweg 6, ✉ 82008, ☎ 6 10 09 10, Fax 61009150, « Bavarian farmhouse furniture », – TV – 🅟 – 40. AE E VISA
closed 20 December - 8 January – **25 rm** 185/300.

Holiday Inn Garden Court, Inselkamer Str. 7, ✉ 82008, ☎ 66 69 10, Fax 66691600, beer garden, – rm TV ♿ – 🅟 – 230. AE E VISA JCB
Meals à la carte 36/77 – **282 rm** 220/350 – 6 suites.

at Aschheim *NE : 13 km by Riem* :

Schreiberhof, Erdinger Str. 2, ✉ 85609, ☎ (089) 90 00 60, Fax 90006459, Massage, – rm TV ♿ – 🅟 – 90. AE E VISA JCB
closed Christmas - early January – ***Alte Gaststube*** : **Menu** à la carte 48/78 – **87 rm** 205/325.

at Grünwald *S : 13 km by Wittelsbacher Brücke* GX – *089* :

Tannenhof without rest, Marktplatz 3, ✉ 82031, ☎ 6 41 89 60, Fax 6415608, « Period house with elegant interior » – TV 🅟. AE E VISA.
closed 20 December - 6 January – **21 rm** 150/240 – 3 suites.

at airport Franz-Josef-Strauß *NE : 37km by A 9 and A 92* :

Kempinski Airport München, Terminalstraße/Mitte 20, ✉ 85356 *München*, ☎ (089) 9 78 20, Fax 97822610, – rm TV ♿ – 280. AE E VISA JCB. rest
Meals à la carte 58/90 – **389 rm** 309/438 – 17 suites.

Il Mondo (Italian rest.), Bereich B - Ebene 07, ✉ 85356 *München*, ☎ (089) 97 59 32 22, Fax 97593106 – 🅟. AE E VISA
Meals à la carte 45/76.

Zirbelstube, Zentralgebäude - Ebene 04, ✉ 85356 *Munich*, ☎ (089) 97 59 31 11, Fax 97593106, « Original pine interior » – 🅟. AE E VISA
Meals à la carte 36/55.

Aschau im Chiemgau *Bayern* 420 W 20, 987 ⑳, 426 I 5 – *pop. 5 200 – alt. 615 m* – *08052.*
München 82.

Residenz Heinz Winkler , Kirchplatz 1, ✉ 83229, ☎ 1 79 90, Fax 179966, ≤ Kampenwand, , « Elegant hotel and renovated 17C inn », Massage, – rm TV – 🅟 – 25. E VISA JCB. rest
Meals *(closed Monday lunch)* 165/215 and à la carte 87/120 – **32 rm** 220/460
Spec. Hummer in Safran mit schwarzen Nudeln, Rehrücken im Salzteig mit Selleriemousseline, Dôme chocolaté mit Kirschen.

STUTTGART L *Baden-Württemberg* 419 T 11, 987 ㊳ – *pop. 559 000 – alt. 245 m* – *0711.*

See : *Linden Museum* ★★ KY **M1** – *Park Wilhelma*★ HT *and Killesberg-Park*★ GT – *Television Tower (Fernsehturm)* ★ HX – *Stuttgart Gallery (Otto-Dix-Collection*★*)* LY **M4** – *Swabian Brewery Museum (Schwäb. Brauereimuseum)*★ *by Böblinger Straße* FX – *Old Castle (Altes Schloß) (Renaissance courtyard*★*)* – *Württemberg Regional Museum*★ *(Sacred Statuary*★★*)* LY **M3** – *State Gallery*★ *(Old Masters Collection*★★*)* LY **M2** – *Collegiate church (Stiftskirche) (Commemorative monuments of dukes*★*)* KY **A** – *State Musem of Natural History (Staatl. Museum für Naturkunde)*★ HT **M5** – *Daimler-Benz Museum*★ JV **M6** – *Porsche Museum*★ *by Heilbronner Straße* GT – *Schloß Solitude*★ *by Rotenwaldstraße* FX.

Envir. : *Bad Cannstatt Spa Park (Kurpark)*★ *E : 4 km* JT.

Kornwestheim, Aldinger Str. (N : 11 km), ☎ *(07141) 87 13 19 ;* *Mönsheim (NW : 30 km by A 8),* ☎ *(07044) 69 09.*

Stuttgart-Echterdingen, by Obere Weinsteige (B 27) GX, ☎ *94 80, City Air Terminal, Stuttgart, Lautenschlagerstr. 14(LY),* ☎ *20 12 68.*

Exhibition Centre (Messegelände Killesberg) (GT), ☎ *2 58 90, Fax 2589440.*

Tourist-Info, Königstr. 1a, ✉ *70173,* ☎ *2 22 82 40, Fax 2228253.*

ADAC, *Am Neckartor 2,* ✉ *70190,* ☎ *2 80 00, Fax 2800167.*

Berlin 630 – Frankfurt am Main 204 – Karlsruhe 88 – München 222 – Strasbourg 156.

STUTTGART

Alexanderstraße . HV 2
Am Neckartor . . HU 4
Augustenstraße . FV 7
Berliner Platz . . . . GV 8
Bismarckstraße . . FV 9
Blumenstraße . . . GV 10
Bolzstraße . . . . . GV 15
Botnanger Straße . . . . . . FV 16
Brückenstraße . . HT 17
Charlottenplatz . . GV 20
Charlottenstraße . GV 21
Dillmannstraße . . FV 22
Dobelstraße . . . . GV 23
Eberhardstraße . . GV 25

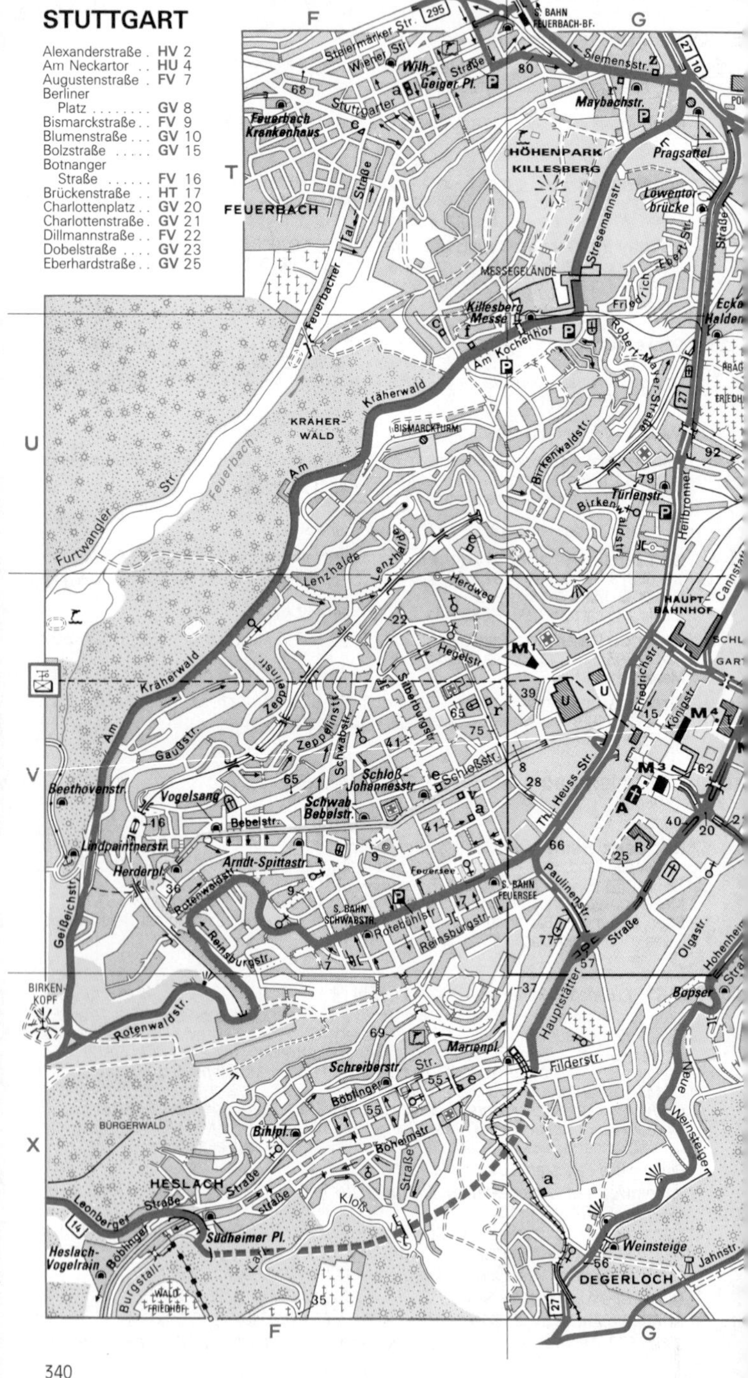

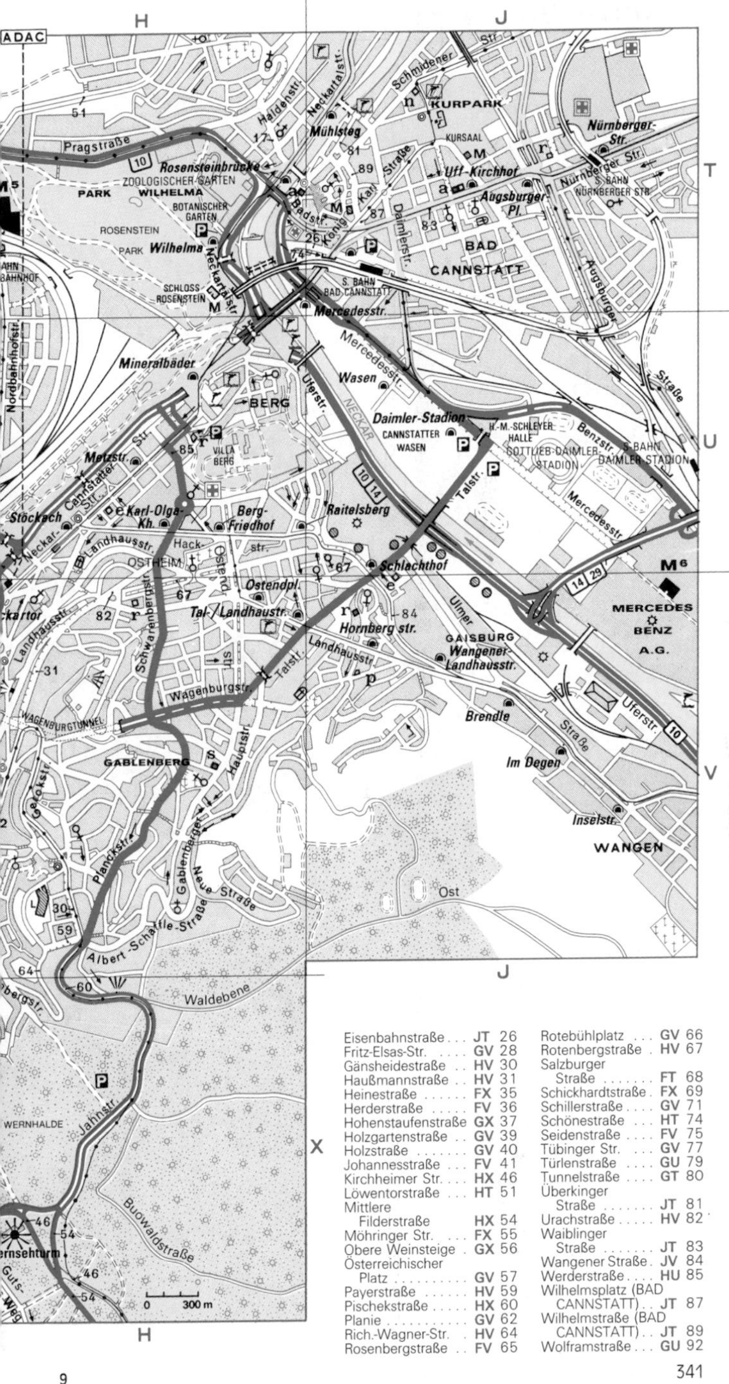

Eisenbahnstraße . . . JT 26
Fritz-Elsas-Str. . . . . GV 28
Gänsheidestraße . . HV 30
Haußmannstraße . . HV 31
Heinestraße . . . . . FX 35
Herderstraße . . . . . FV 36
Hohenstaufenstraße GX 37
Holzgartenstraße . . GV 39
Holzstraße . . . . . . GV 40
Johannesstraße . . . FV 41
Kirchheimer Str. . . . HX 46
Löwentorstraße . . . HT 51
Mittlere Filderstraße HX 54
Möhringer Str. . . . FX 55
Obere Weinsteige . GX 56
Österreichischer Platz . . . . GV 57
Payerstraße . . . . . HV 59
Pischekstraße . . . . HX 60
Planie . . . . GV 62
Rich.-Wagner-Str. . HV 64
Rosenbergstraße . . FV 65
Rotebühlplatz . . . GV 66
Rotenbergstraße . HV 67
Salzburger Straße . . . . FT 68
Schickhardtstraße . FX 69
Schillerstraße . . . . GV 71
Schönestraße . . . HT 74
Seidenstraße . . . . FV 75
Tübinger Str. . . . GV 77
Türlenstraße . . . . GU 79
Tunnelstraße . . . . GT 80
Überkinger Straße . . . . JT 81
Urachstraße . . . . . HV 82
Waiblinger Straße . . . . JT 83
Wangener Straße . JV 84
Werderstraße . . . . HU 85
Wilhelmsplatz (BAD CANNSTATT) . . JT 87
Wilhelmstraße (BAD CANNSTATT) . . JT 89
Wolframstraße . . . GU 92

STUTTGART

Charlottenplatz . . . . LZ 20
Eberhardstraße . . . . KLZ 25
Königstraße . . . . KLYZ
Schulstraße . . . . KZ 75
Theodor- Heuss- Str. . . . . . KYZ 80

Arnulf-Klett-Platz . . . . LY 6
Augustenstraße . . . . KZ 7
Blumenstraße . . . . LZ 10
Bolzstraße . . . . LY 15
Calwer Str. . . . . KYZ 18
Dorotheenstraße . . . . LZ 24
Friedrichsplatz . . . . KY 27
Hauptstätter Str. . . . . KZ 30
Hegelplatz . . . . KY 32
Heilbronner Str. . . . . LY 34
Holzstraße . . . . LZ 40
Karlsplatz . . . . LY 43
Karlstraße . . . . LZ 44
Katharinenplatz . . . . LZ 45
Kirchstraße . . . . LZ 46
Konrad- Adenauer- Str. . . . LY 47
Kronenstraße . . . . KLY 48
Kronprinzstraße . . . . KYZ 49
Leonhardsplatz . . . . LZ 50
Marktplatz . . . . KLZ
Marktstraße . . . . LZ
Österreichischer Platz . . . . KZ
Pfarrstraße . . . . LZ
Rotebühlplatz . . . . KZ
Rotebühlstraße . . . . KZ
Schloßplatz . . . . LY
Silberburgstraße . . . . KZ
Sophienstraße . . . . KZ
Torstraße . . . . KZ
Wilhelmsplatz . . . . LZ
Wilhelmstraße . . . . LZ
Willi- Bleicher- Str. . . . . . KY

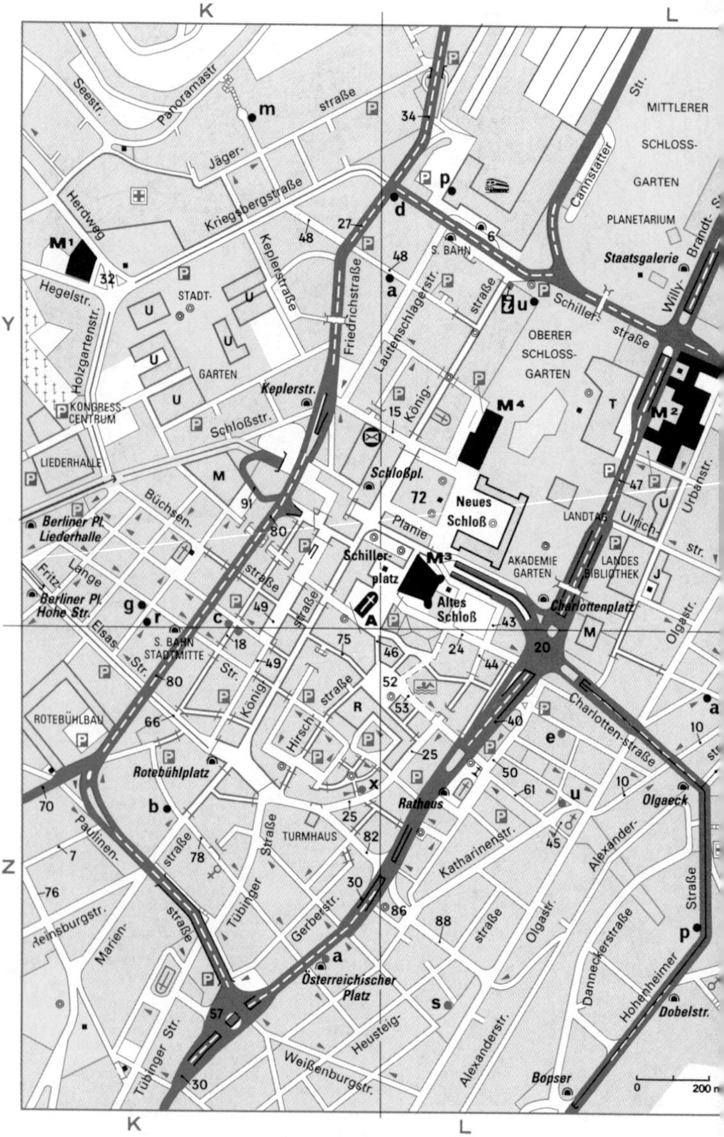

Maritim, Forststr. 2, ✉ 70174, ℘ 94 20, Fax 9421000, Massage, – rm – 800. AE E VISA JCB. rest FV r
Meals à la carte 58/88 – **555 rm** 257/450 – 50 suites.

Inter-Continental, Willy-Brandt-Str. 30, ✉ 70173, ℘ 2 02 00, Fax 202012, Massage, – rm – 350. AE E VISA JCB HV t
Meals à la carte 48/70 – **277 rm** 359/498 – 24 suites.

Am Schloßgarten, Schillerstr. 23, ✉ 70173, ℘ 2 02 60, Fax 2026888, « Terrace with » – rm – 100. AE E VISA. rest LY u
Meals à la carte 64/96 – **116 rm** 255/425.

Royal, Sophienstr. 35, ✉ 70178, ℘ 62 50 50, Fax 628809 – rm rest – 70. AE E VISA JCB KZ b
Meals *(closed Sunday and Bank Holidays)* à la carte 43/86 – **100 rm** 185/490 – 3 suites.

Parkhotel, Villastr. 21, ✉ 70190, ℘ 2 80 10, Fax 2864353, – rm – 80. AE E VISA. HU r
Meals *(closed Saturday and Sunday)* à la carte 53/75 – **72 rm** 195/260.

Rema-Hotel-Ruff without rest, Friedhofstr. 21, ✉ 70191, ℘ 2 58 70, Fax 2587404, – – 15. AE E VISA JCB GU a
81 rm 170/230.

Rega Hotel, Ludwigstr. 18, ✉ 70176, ℘ 61 93 40, Fax 6193477 – – 25. AE E VISA FV a
Meals *(Sunday lunch only)* à la carte 29/55 – **60 rm** 175/235.

InterCityHotel without rest, Arnulf-Klett-Platz 2, ✉ 70173, ℘ 2 25 00, Fax 2250499 – – 25. AE E VISA LY p
112 rm 200/250.

Unger without rest, Kronenstr. 17, ✉ 70173, ℘ 2 09 90, Fax 2099100 – – 20. AE E VISA LY a
97 rm 189/349.

Bergmeister without rest, Rotenbergstr. 16, ✉ 70190, ℘ 28 33 63, Fax 283719, – . AE E VISA JCB HV r
47 rm 129/210.

Kronen-Hotel without rest, Kronenstr. 48, ✉ 70174, ℘ 2 25 10, Fax 2251404, – – 20. AE E VISA JCB KY m
closed 22 December - 7 January – **83 rm** 160/320.

Wörtz zur Weinsteige, Hohenheimer Str. 30, ✉ 70184, ℘ 2 36 70 00, Fax 2367007, « Garden terrace » – rm . AE E VISA JCB LZ p
closed 20 December - 7 January – Meals *(closed Sunday, Monday and Bank Holidays)* à la carte 45/89 – **25 rm** 140/280.

Azenberg, Seestr. 114, ✉ 70174, ℘ 22 10 51, Fax 297426, – rm . AE E VISA. rest FU e
Meals (dinner only) (residents only) – **56 rm** 120/250.

Wartburg, Lange Str. 49, ✉ 70174, ℘ 2 04 50, Fax 2045450 – rm rest – 60. AE E VISA JCB KY g
closed Easter and 21 December - 2 January – **Meals** *(closed Saturday, Sunday and Bank Holidays)* (lunch only) à la carte 36/55 – **81 rm** 155/265.

Rema-Hotel Astoria without rest, Hospitalstr. 29, ✉ 70174, ℘ 29 93 01, Fax 299307 – – 20. AE E VISA JCB KY r
57 rm 170/330.

Rieker without rest, Friedrichstr. 3, ✉ 70174, ℘ 22 13 11, Fax 293894 – . AE E VISA LY d
66 rm 178/228.

City-Hotel without rest, Uhlandstr. 18, ✉ 70182, ℘ 21 08 10, Fax 2369772 – . AE E VISA JCB. LZ a
31 rm 150/210.

Bellevue, Schurwaldstr. 45, ✉ 70186, ℘ 48 10 10, Fax 481010 – . AE E VISA JV p
Meals *(closed Tuesday - Wednesday)* à la carte 37/53 – **12 rm** 90/150.

Delice, Hauptstätter Str. 61, ✉ 70178, ℘ 6 40 32 22, « Vaulted cellar with contemporary art » – KZ a
closed Saturday, Sunday and Bank Holidays – **Meals** (dinner only, booking essential, outstanding wine list) 125 and à la carte 73/104
Spec. Gänseleberterrine mit Brioche, Etouffé-Taube aus dem Backofen, Kaninchenrücken mit Rotweinbutter.

Da Franco (Italian rest.), Calwer Str. 23, ✉ 70173, ℘ 29 15 81, Fax 294549 – . AE E VISA KYZ c
closed Monday and August – **Meals** à la carte 47/76.

XX **La nuova Trattoria da Franco** (Italian rest.), Calwer Str. 32 (1st floor), ✉ 7017 ✆ 29 47 44, Fax 294549 – AE ⓓ E VISA KYZ
Meals à la carte 43/67.

XX **Gaisburger Pastetchen**, Hornbergstr. 24, ✉ 70188, ✆ 48 48 55, Fax 487565 JV
closed Sunday, Bank Holidays and end July - mid August – **Meals** (dinner only) à la car 66/92.

XX **Alter Fritz am Killesberg**, Feuerbacher Weg 101, ✉ 70192, ✆ 13 56 5 Fax 1356565, – TV ☎. FU
closed 2 weeks December - January and August – **Meals** *(closed Monday and Bank Holiday* (dinner only) à la carte 56/78 – **10 rm** 130/215.

XX **Goldener Adler**, Böheimstr. 38, ✉ 70178, ✆ 6 40 17 62, Fax 6492405 – P. E V
closed Tuesday and Saturday lunch, Monday and 4 weeks August - September – **Mea** à la carte 41/82. FX

XX **La Scala** (Italian rest.), Friedrichstr. 41 (1st floor,), ✉ 70174, ✆ 29 06 07, Fax 29916 – . AE ⓓ E VISA KY
closed Sunday and 3 weeks August - September – Meals à la carte 39/61.

Swabian wine taverns (Weinstuben) *(mainly light meals only)* :

X **Kachelofen**, Eberhardstr. 10 (entrance in Töpferstraße), ✉ 70173, ✆ 24 23 7 KZ
closed Sunday and 22 December - 2 January – **Meals** (dinner only) à la carte 41/45.

X **Weinstube Schellenturm**, Weberstr. 72, ✉ 70182, ✆ 2 36 48 88, Fax 2262699, – AE. LZ
closed Sunday and Bank Holidays – **Meals** (dinner only) à la carte 34/59.

X **Weinstube Träuble**, Gablenberger Hauptstr. 66, ✉ 70186, ✆ 46 54 28, –
closed Sunday, Bank Holidays and late August - mid September – **Meals** *(open from 4pm* only cold and warm light meals. HV

X **Weinstube Klösterle** (part of former monastery), Marktstr. 71 (Bad Cannstatt ✉ 70372, ✆ 56 89 62, , « Former monastery, rustic interior » – E HT
closed Sunday and Bank Holidays – **Meals** *(open from 5pm)* à la carte 35/61.

X **Weinstube Vetter**, Bopserstr. 18, ✉ 70180, ✆ 24 19 16, LZ
closed Sunday and Bank Holidays – **Meals** *(open from 5pm)* à la carte 31/53.

X **Weinhaus Stetter**, Rosenstr. 32, ✉ 70182, ✆ 24 01 63, LZ
open Monday to Friday from 3 p.m., closed Saturday 2pm, Sunday, Bank Holidays a 24 December - 8 January – **Meals** (only cold dishes, outstanding wine list) 15/25.

at Stuttgart-Botnang *by Botnanger Str.* FV :

Hirsch, Eltinger Str. 2, ✉ 70195, ✆ 69 29 17, Fax 6990788, beer garden – TV P – 140. AE ⓓ E VISA
Meals *(closed Sunday dinner and Monday)* à la carte 32/67 – **44 rm** 96/150.

XX **La Fenice**, Beethovenstr. 9, ✉ 70195, ✆ 6 99 07 03, Fax 6990703, – AE. re
closed Monday – **Meals** (booking essential for dinner) à la carte 64/85.

at Stuttgart-Büsnau *by Rotenwaldstraße* FX :

Relexa Waldhotel Schatten, Magstadter Straße (Solitudering), ✉ 7056 ✆ 6 86 70, Fax 6867999, , – rm TV P – 80. AE ⓓ E VISA. res
Meals à la carte 43/87 – **136 rm** 195/690 – 7 suites.

at Stuttgart-Bad Cannstatt :

Pannonia Hotel Stuttgart, Teinacher Str. 20, ✉ 70372, ✆ 9 54 00, Fax 954063 , – rm rest TV ☎ – 120. AE ⓓ E VISA JT
Meals à la carte 43/76 – **156 rm** 175/295 – 5 suites.

Krehl's Linde, Obere Waiblinger Str. 113, ✉ 70374, ✆ 52 75 67, Fax 5286370, – TV ☎ JT
closed 3 weeks July - August – Meals *(closed Sunday - Monday)* à la carte 43/88 – **18 r** 100/220.

at Stuttgart-Degerloch :

Waldhotel Degerloch, Guts-Muths-Weg 18, ✉ 70597, ✆ 76 50 17, Fax 765376 , , – TV ☎ P – 100. AE ⓓ E VISA by Guts-Muths-Weg HX
Meals à la carte 42/73 – **50 rm** 175/260.

XXXX **Wielandshöhe**, Alte Weinsteige 71, ✉ 70597, ✆ 6 40 88 48, Fax 6409408, « Beautiful situation ≤ Stuttgart » – AE ⓓ E VISA GX
closed Sunday, Monday and Bank Holidays – **Meals** (booking essential) 118/178 and à carte 86/139
Spec. Salat von Kalbskopf mit Bohnen, Hummer mit Basilikum-Kartoffelsalat, Gänselber cocotte.

XXX **Skyline-Restaurant** (in TV-tower at 144 m,), Jahnstr. 120, ✉ 70597, ✆ 24 61 04, Fax 2360633, ✳ Stuttgart and surroundings – AE ⓓ E VISA
closed Monday – **Meals** (booking essential for dinner) à la carte 65/97.

XX **Das Fässle**, Löwenstr. 51, ✉ 70597, ✆ 76 01 00, Fax 764432, – AE ⓓ E VISA
by Jahnstraße GX
closed Sunday – **Meals** à la carte 48/74.

at Stuttgart-Fasanenhof *by Obere Weinsteige (B 27)* GX :

Mercure, Eichwiesenring 1, ✉ 70567, ✆ 7 26 60, Fax 7266444, – rm 120. AE ⓓ E VISA
Meals à la carte 45/77 – **148 rm** 207/294.

Fora Hotel, Vor dem Lauch 20 (Businesspark), ✉ 70567, ✆ 7 25 50, Fax 7255666, – rm rest – 80. AE ⓓ E VISA JCB
Meals à la carte 38/60 – **101 rm** 190/228.

at Stuttgart-Feuerbach :

Messehotel Europe without rest, Siemensstr. 33, ✉ 70469, ✆ 81 48 30, Fax 8148348 – . AE ⓓ E VISA GT r
114 rm 165/310.

Kongresshotel Europe, Siemensstr. 26, ✉ 70469, ✆ 81 00 40, Fax 854082, – rm – 130. AE ⓓ E VISA GT z
Meals *(closed Saturday and Sunday lunch)* à la carte 45/90 – **146 rm** 130/275.

Weinsberg (Rest. Bistro style), Grazer Str. 32, ✉ 70469, ✆ 13 54 60, Fax 1354666, – rm – 30. AE ⓓ E VISA FT a
Meals *(closed Saturday dinner and Sunday)* à la carte 30/75 – **37 rm** 175/215.

at Stuttgart-Flughafen (Airport) *S : 15 km by Obere Weinsteige (B 27)* GX :

Airport Mövenpick-Hotel, Randstr. 7, ✉ 70629, ✆ 7 90 70, Telex 7245677, Fax 793585, – rm – 45. AE ⓓ E VISA JCB
Meals à la carte 46/80 – **230 rm** 289/534.

XXX **top air**, Randstraße (in the airport) Terminal 1, ✉ 70621, ✆ 9 48 21 37, Fax 7979210 – – 170. AE ⓓ E VISA
closed Saturday lunch and late July - mid August – **Meals** 125/150 and à la carte 80/126
Spec. Lachs-Seeteufel-Carpaccio, Frikasse vom Perlhuhn mit kleinen Gemüsen, Seeteufel im ganzen gebraten mit Artischocken.

at Stuttgart-Hoheheim *by Mittlere Filderstraße* HX :

XXXX **Speisemeisterei**, Am Schloß Hohenheim, ✉ 70599, ✆ 4 56 00 37, Fax 4560038, –
closed Sunday dinner, Monday and 1 to 15 January – **Meals** (weekdays dinner only, booking essential) à la carte 75/115
Spec. Seeteufel mit Nudeln und Tomaten-Zucchinigemüse, Taubenbrust mit Gänseleber in Blätterteig, Rhabarberkompott mit Topfenknödel.

at Stuttgart-Möhringen *SW : 7 km by Obere Weinsteige* GX :

Copthorne Hotel (with Stuttgart International), Plienienger Str. 100, ✉ 70567, ✆ 7 21 10 50, Fax 7212931, , (direct entrance to the recreation centre Schwaben Quelle) – rm – 80. AE ⓓ E VISA JCB
Meals à la carte 40/78 – **454 rm** 276/528.

Möhringen without rest, Filderbahnstr. 43, ✉ 70567, ✆ 71 60 80, Fax 7160850 – . AE ⓓ E VISA JCB
closed end December - early January – **41 rm** 160/198.

XX **Landgasthof Riedsee** with rm, Elfenstr. 120, ✉ 70567, ✆ 71 24 84, Fax 7189764, « Lakeside garden terrace » – . AE ⓓ E VISA
closed Monday – **Meals** à la carte 41/71 – **12 rm** 85/130.

at Stuttgart-Obertürkheim *by Augsburger Straße* JU :

Brita Hotel, Augsburger Str. 671, ✉ 70329, ✆ 32 02 30, Fax 324440 – rm rest – 80. AE ⓓ E VISA
closed 24 December - 1 January – ***Post*** *(closed Saturday, Sunday, Bank Holidays and 5 to 25 August,* **Meals** à la carte 32/46 – **70 rm** 143/268.

at Stuttgart-Plieningen *S : 14 km by Mittlere Filderstraße* HX :

Fissler-Post, Schoellstr. 4, ✉ 70599, ✆ 4 58 40, Fax 4584333, – rm – 80. AE ⓓ E VISA JCB.
Meals (booking essential) à la carte 42/68 *(vegetarian menu available)* – **60 rm** 88/190.

Romantik Hotel Traube, Brabandtgasse 2, ✉ 70599, ☎ 45 89 20, Fax 458922 – ☎ ℗. AE ⓓ E VISA
closed 23 December - 3 January – **Meals** *(closed Sunday)* (booking essential) à la carte 58/95 – **20 rm** ☐ 140/280.

at Stuttgart-Stammheim *by Heilbronner Straße* GT :

Novotel-Nord, Korntaler Str. 207, ✉ 70439, ☎ 98 06 20, Fax 803673, (heated) – rm ☎ ℗ – 200. AE ⓓ E VISA
Meals à la carte 31/61 – **117 rm** ☐ 165/205.

at Stuttgart-Vaihingen *by Böblinger Str.* FX :

Dorint-Hotel Fontana, Vollmöllerstr. 5, ✉ 70563, ☎ 73 00, Telex 7255763, Fax 7302525, Massage, – rm ☎ – 250. ⓓ E VISA. rest
Meals à la carte 39/82 – **250 rm** ☐ 255/395 – 5 suites.

at Stuttgart-Weilimdorf *by B 295* FT :

Holiday Inn Garden Court, Mittlerer Pfad 27, ✉ 70499, ☎ 98 88 80, Fax 9888, beer garden, – rm ☎ – 200. AE ⓓ E VISA JCB
Meals 28/36 buffet and à la carte 39/65 – **325 rm** ☐ 232/314 – 7 suites.

at Stuttgart-Zuffenhausen *by Heilbronner Straße* GT :

Fora Hotel Residence, Schützenbühlstr. 16, ✉ 70435, ☎ 8 20 01 00, Fax 820010 – rm rest ☎ – 60. AE ⓓ E VISA
Meals *(closed Saturday)* (dinner only) à la carte 34/57 – **120 rm** ☐ 175/210.

at Fellbach *NE : 8 km by Nürnberger Straße (B 14)* JT – ☎ *0711* :

Classic Congress Hotel, Tainer Str. 7, ✉ 70734, ☎ 5 85 90, Fax 5859304, – rm ☎ ℗ – 60. AE ⓓ E VISA JCB
closed 23 December - 6 January – **Meals** see ***Alt Württemberg*** *below* – **148 rm** ☐ 195/350.

Alt Württemberg, Tainer Str. 7 (Schwabenlandhalle), ✉ 70734, ☎ 58 00 8, Fax 581927, – ℗. AE ⓓ E VISA JCB
Meals à la carte 52/87.

Aldinger's Weinstube Germania with rm, Schmerstr. 6, ✉ 70734, ☎ 58 20 3, Fax 582077, – ☎.
closed 2 weeks February - March and 3 weeks July - August – **Meals** *(closed Sunday, Monday and Bank Holidays)* (booking essential) à la carte 40/70 – **7 rm** ☐ 75/140.

at Fellbach-Schmiden *NE : 8,5 km by Nürnberger Straße (B 14)* JT :

Hirsch, Fellbacher Str. 2, ✉ 70736, ☎ (0711) 9 51 30, Fax 5181065, – rm ☎ ℗ – 25. AE ⓓ E VISA
Meals *(closed Friday, Sunday and Christmas - early January)* à la carte 40/65 – **116 rm** ☐ 90/130.

at Gerlingen *W : 10 km by Rotenwaldstraße* FX – ☎ *07156* :

Krone, Hauptstr. 28, ✉ 70839, ☎ 4 31 10, Fax 4311100, – rm ☎ ℗ – 120. AE ⓓ E VISA
Meals *(closed Sunday, Monday, Bank Holidays, Easter and Christmas)* (booking essential) à la carte 38/83 *(vegetarian menu available)* – **56 rm** ☐ 141/249.

at Korntal-Münchingen *NW : 9 km, by Heilbronner Str.* GT :

Mercure, Siemensstr. 50, ✉ 70825, ☎ (07150) 1 30, Fax 13266, beer garden, – rm ☎ ℗ – 160. AE ⓓ E VISA
Meals à la carte 53/75 – **200 rm** ☐ 165/220.

at Leinfelden-Echterdingen *S : 11 km by Obere Weinsteige (B 27)* GX :

Filderland without rest, Tübinger Str. 16 (Echterdingen), ✉ 70771, ☎ (0711) 9 49 4, Fax 9494888 – ☎ – 20. AE ⓓ E VISA.
closed 24 December - 2 January – **48 rm** ☐ 135/190.

Baiersbronn *Baden-Württemberg* 419 U 9, 987 ㊳ – *pop. 16 000 – alt. 550 m* – ☎ *0744*
Stuttgart 100.

Schwarzwaldstube (French rest.), Tonbachstr. 237 (at Kur- and Sporthotel Traube Tonbach), ✉ 72270, ☎ 49 26 65, Fax 492692, ≤ – ℗. AE ⓓ E VISA
closed Monday, Tuesday, 13 January - 4 February and 4 to 26 August – **Meals** (booking essential) 160/205 and à la carte 98/140
Spec. Stubenkücken mit Gemüse und Trüffeln in Gänselebersauce, Hummer auf gedämpftem Lauch in Zitronengrassud, Soufflé von weißer Schockolade mit Walderdbeeren und Champagnereis.

XXXX ✿✿ **Restaurant Bareiss**, Gärtenbühlweg 14 (at Hotel Bareiss), ✉ 72270, ✆ 4 70, Fax 47320, ← – ▤ Ⓟ. AE ⓓ E VISA
closed Monday, Tuesday, 22 June - 18 July and 23 November - 24 December – **Meals** (booking essential, outstanding wine list) 148/189 and à la carte 98/118
Spec. Warm geräucherter Wildlachs mit Blinis und Imperialkaviar, Rascasse in Knoblauchbutter gebraten auf toskanischem Gemüse, Schwarzfederhuhn mit Rosmarin gespickt.

hringen *Baden-Württemberg* 419 S 12, 987 ㉗ – *pop. 20 000 – alt. 230 m* – ☎ *07941.*
Stuttgart 68.

: Friedrichsruhe *N : 6 km :*

✿✿ **Wald- und Schloßhotel Friedrichsruhe** ⌂, ✉ 74639 *Zweiflingen*, ✆ (07941) 6 08 70, Telex 74498, Fax 61468, « Garden, park », ≘s, ⛱, ▢, ✂, ⛳ – ⏚ ⇔ Ⓟ – 🏛 60. AE ⓓ E VISA
Meals *(closed Monday - Tuesday)* (outstanding wine list) 145/198 and à la carte 86/132 – ***Jägerstube :*** **Meals** à la carte 53/74 – **45 rm** ▭ 195/395 – 12 suites
Spec. Sauté von bretonischem Hummer, Loup de mer kroß gebraten mit Artischockenragout, Variation vom Milchferkel.

Greece

Elláda

PRACTICAL INFORMATION

LOCAL CURRENCY

Greek Drachma: *100 GRD = 0.40 USD ($) (Jan. 97)*

TOURIST INFORMATION

National Tourist Organisation (EOT): *2 Karageorgi Servias (Sindagma), ☎ 322 25 45 (information). Hotel reservation: Hellenic Chamber of Hotels, 24 Stadiou, ☎ 323 71 93, Telex: 214 269. Fax 322 54 49, also at East Airport ☎ 961 27 22 - Tourist Police: 4 Stadiou ☎ 171.*

National Holidays in Greece: *25 March and 28 October.*

FOREIGN EXCHANGE

Banks are usually open on weekdays from 8am to 2pm. A branch of the National Bank of Greece is open daily from 8am to 2pm (from 9am to 1pm at weekends) at 2 Karageorgi Servias (Sindagma). East Airport offices operate a 24-hour service.

AIRLINES

OLYMPIC AIRWAYS: *96 Singrou 117 41 Athens, ☎ 926 73 33/926 91 11-3, 2 Kotopouli (Omonia), ☎ 926 72 16-9, reservations only ☎ 966 66 66.*
All following Companies are located in Sindagma area:
AIR FRANCE: *18 Vouliagmenis 166 75 Athens, ☎ 960 11 00.*
BRITISH AIRWAYS: *10 Othonos (Sindagma) 105 57 Athens, ☎ 325 06 01.*
JAPAN AIRLINES: *22 Voulis 105 57 Athens, ☎ 325 20 75.*
LUFTHANSA: *11 Vas. Sofias 106 71 Athens, ☎ 771 60 02.*
SABENA: *41 c, Vouliagmenis, ☎ 960 00 21-4.*
SWISSAIR: *4 Othonos (Sindagma) 105 57 Athens, ☎ 323 75 81.*
TWA: *8 Xenofondos 105 57 Athens, ☎ 322 64 51.*

TRANSPORT IN ATHENS

Taxis: *may be hailed in the street even when already engaged: it is advised to always pay by the meter.*
Bus: *good for sightseeing and practical for short distances: 75 GRD.*
Metro: *one single line crossing the city from North (Kifissia) to South (Pireas) : 100 GRD.*

POSTAL SERVICES

General Post Office: *100 Eolou (Omonia) with poste restante, and also at Sindagma.*
Telephone (OTE): *15 Stadiou and 85 Patission (all services).*

SHOPPING IN ATHENS

In summer, shops are usually open from 8am to 1.30pm, and 5.30 to 8.30pm. They close on Sunday, and at 2.30pm on Monday, Wednesday and Saturday. In winter they open from 9am to 5pm on Monday and Wednesday, from 10am to 7pm on Tuesday, Thursday and Friday, from 8.30am to 3.30pm on Saturday. Department Stores in Patission and Eolou are open fron 8.30 am to 8 pm on weekdays and 3 pm on Saturdays. The main shopping streets are to be found in Sindagma, Kolonaki, Monastiraki and Omonia areas. Flea Market (generally open on Sunday) and Greek Handicraft in Plaka and Monastiraki.

TIPPING

Service is generally included in the bills but it is usual to tip employees.

SPEED LIMITS

The speed limit in built up areas is 50 km/h (31 mph); on motorways the maximum permitted speed is 100 km/h (62 mph) and 80 km/h (50 mph) on others roads.

SEAT BELTS

The wearing of seat belts is compulsory for drivers and front seat passengers.

BREAKDOWN SERVICE

The ELPA (Automobile and Touring Club of Greece, ☎ 74 88 800) operate a 24 hour breakdown service: phone 174.

ATHENS

(ATHÍNA) *Atikí* 980 ㉚ – *Pop. 3 076 786 (Athens and Piraeus area)* – ✪ *1.*

Igoumenítsa 581 – Pátra 215 – Thessaloníki 479.

Tourist Information (EOT), 2 Amerikis ☎ 322 31 11, Information center, 2 Karageorgi Servias (Sindagma) ☎ 322 25 45 and East Airport ☎ 961 27 22.
ELPA (Automobile and Touring Club of Greece), 2 Messogion ☎ 748 88 00.

Glifáda (near airport) ☎ 894 68 20, Fax 894 37 21.
S : 15 km, East Airport ☎ 969 41 11 (International Airport – All companies except Olympic Airways), West Airport ☎ 966 66 66 (Elinikó Airport – Olympic Airways only).
1 Karolou ☎ 524 06 01.

SIGHTS

Views of Athens: Lycabettos (Likavitós) ☀★★★ DX – *Philopappos Hill (Lófos Filopápou)* ←★★★ AY.

ANCIENT ATHENS

Acropolis★★★ (Akrópoli) ABY – *Theseion★★ (Thissío)* AY *and Agora★ (Arhéa Agorá)* AY – *Theatre of Dionysos★★ (Théatro Dionissou)* BY *and Odeon of Herod Atticus★ (Odío Iródou Atikoú)* AY – *Olympieion★★ (Naós Olimbíou Diós)* BY *and Hadrian's Arch★ (Píli Adrianoú)* BY – *Tower of the Winds★* BY **G** *in the Roman Forum (Romaïkí Agorá).*

OLD ATHENS AND THE TURKISH PERIOD

Pláka★★ : Old Metropolitan★★ BY **A2** – *Monastiráki★ (Old Bazaar) : Kapnikaréa (Church)* BY **A6**, *Odós Pandróssou★* BY **29**, *Monastiráki Square★* BY.

MODERN ATHENS

Sindagma Square★ CY : *Greek guard on sentry duty – Academy, University and Library Buildings★ (Akadimía* CX, *Panepistímio* CX, *Ethnikí Vivliothíki* BX) – *National Garden★ (Ethnikós Kípos)* CY.

MUSEUMS

National Archaelogical Museum★★★ (Ethnikó Arheologikó Moussío) BX – *Acropolis Museum★★★* BY **M¹** – *Museum of Cycladic and Ancient Greek Art★★* DY **M¹⁵** – *Byzantine Museum★★ (Vizandinó Moussío)* DY – *Benaki Museum★★ (Moussío Benáki, private collection of antiquities and traditional art)* CDY – *Museum of Traditional Greek Art★* BY **M²** – *National Historical Museum★* BY **M⁷** – *Jewish Museum of Greece★* BY **M¹⁶** – *National Gallery and Soutzos Museum★ (painting and sculpture)* DY **M⁸**.

EXCURSIONS

Cape Sounion★★★ (Soúnio) SE : 71 km BY – *Kessariani Monastery★★, E : 9 km* DY – *Daphne Monastery★★ (Dafní) NW : 10 km* AX – *Aigina Island★ (Égina) : Temple of Aphaia★★, 3 hours Return.*

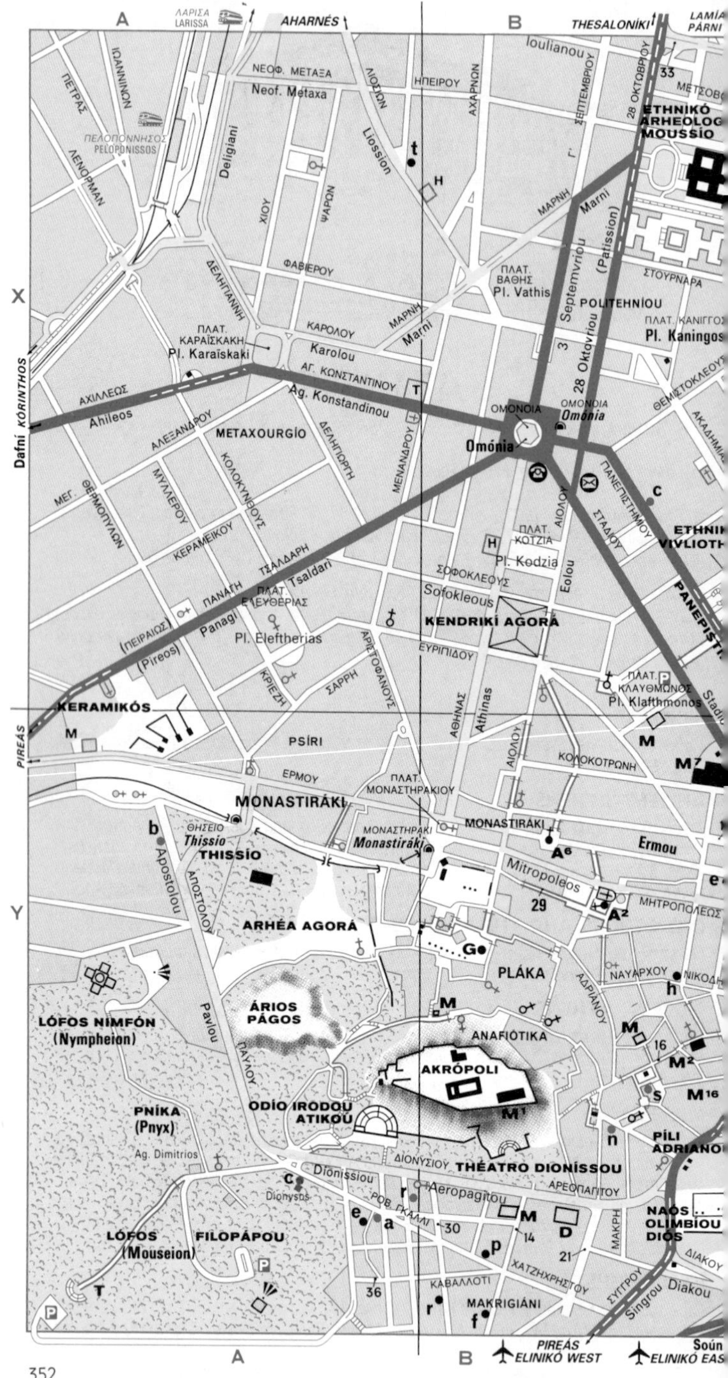

AHARNÉS
THESALONÍKI
LAMÍA
PÁRNI
LARISSA
PELOPONISSOS
Deligiani
Neof. Metaxa
Liossion
Marni
Septemvriou
28 Oktovriou
(Patission)
ETHNIKÓ ARHEOLOG MOUSSÍO
POLITEHNÍOU
Pl. Vathis
Pl. Kaningos
Pl. Karaïskaki
Karolou
Ag. Konstandinou
Ahileos
METAXOURGÍO
Omónia
Dafní KÓRINTHOS
Pl. Kodzia
Eolou
Sofokleous
KENDRIKÍ AGORÁ
Tsaldari
Panagi
Pl. Eleftherias
(Pireos)
Athinas
Pl. Klafthmonos
KERAMIKÓS
PIREÁS
PSÍRI
MONASTIRÁKI
Thissio
THISSÍO
Monastiráki
Ermou
Mitropoleos
Apostolou
ARHÉA AGORÁ
PLÁKA
ÁRIOS PÁGOS
LÓFOS NIMFÓN (Nympheion)
Pavlou
ANAFIÓTIKA
AKRÓPOLI
PNÍKA (Pnyx)
ODÍO IRODOU ATIKOÚ
PÍLI ADRIANO
Ag. Dimitrios
Dionissiou
THÉATRO DIONÍSSOU
Aeropagitou
Dionysos
NAÓS OLIMBÍOU DIÓS
LÓFOS (Mouseion)
FILOPÁPOU
MAKRIGIÁNI
Singrou
Diakou
PIREÁS
ELINIKÓ WEST
ELINIKÓ EAS
Soún

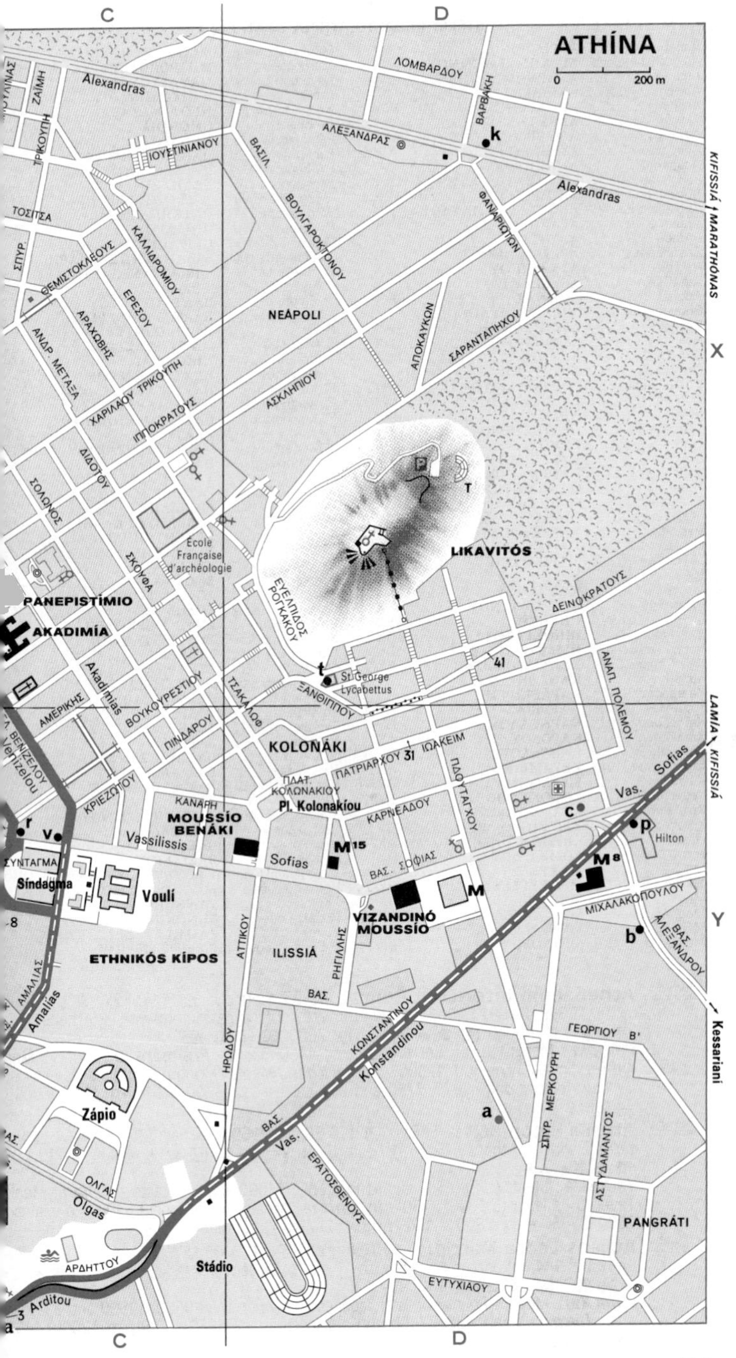

ATHÍNA
0
200 m
C
D
X
Y
Alexandras
ΛΟΜΒΑΡΔΟΥ
ΑΛΕΞΑΝΔΡΑΣ
ΙΟΥΣΤΙΝΙΑΝΟΥ
ΒΑΡΒΑΚΗ
ΦΑΝΑΡΙΩΤΩΝ
ΒΟΥΛΓΑΡΟΚΤΟΝΟΥ
ΚΑΛΛΙΔΡΟΜΙΟΥ
ΘΕΜΙΣΤΟΚΛΕΟΥΣ
ΕΡΕΣΟΥ
ΑΡΑΧΩΒΗΣ
ΝΕÁΠΟLI
ΑΠΟΚΑΥΚΩΝ
ΣΑΡΑΝΤΑΠΗΧΟΥ
ΑΣΚΛΗΠΙΟΥ
ΧΑΡΙΛΑΟΥ ΤΡΙΚΟΥΠΗ
ΙΠΠΟΚΡΑΤΟΥΣ
ΣΟΛΩΝΟΣ
ΔΙΔΟΤΟΥ
ΣΚΟΥΦΑ
École Française d'archéologie
LIKAVITÓS
ΕΥΕΛΠΙΔΟΣ ΡΟΓΚΑΚΟΥ
ΔΕΙΝΟΚΡΑΤΟΥΣ
PANEPISTÍMIO
AKADIMÍA
Akadimias
ΑΜΕΡΙΚΗΣ
ΒΟΥΚΟΥΡΕΣΤΙΟΥ
ΤΣΑΚΑΛΩΦ
ΠΙΝΔΑΡΟΥ
St George Lycabettus
ΞΑΝΘΙΠΠΟΥ
ΑΝΑΠ. ΠΟΛΕΜΟΥ
KOLONÁKI
ΠΑΤΡΙΑΡΧΟΥ
ΙΩΑΚΕΙΜ
ΠΛΑΤ. ΚΟΛΩΝΑΚΙΟΥ
Pl. Kolonakíou
ΚΑΡΝΕΑΔΟΥ
ΠΛΟΥΤΑΡΧΟΥ
ΚΡΙΕΖΩΤΟΥ
ΚΑΝΑΡΗ
MOUSSÍO BENÁKI
Vassilissis
Sofias
ΒΑΣ. ΣΟΦΙΑΣ
Vas. Sofias
Hilton
ΣΥΝΤΑΓΜΑ
Síndagma
Vouli
VIZANDINÓ MOUSSÍO
ΜΙΧΑΛΑΚΟΠΟΥΛΟΥ
ΒΑΣ. ΑΛΕΞΑΝΔΡΟΥ
ETHNIKÓS KÍPOS
ΑΤΤΙΚΟΥ
ILISSIÁ
ΡΗΓΙΛΛΗΣ
ΑΜΑΛΙΑΣ
Amalias
ΚΩΝΣΤΑΝΤΙΝΟΥ
Konstandinou
ΓΕΩΡΓΙΟΥ Β'
ΗΡΩΔΟΥ
Zápio
ΣΠΥΡ. ΜΕΡΚΟΥΡΗ
ΑΣΤΥΔΑΜΑΝΤΟΣ
ΕΡΑΤΟΣΘΕΝΟΥΣ
ΟΛΓΑΣ
Olgas
PANGRÁTI
Stádio
ΑΡΔΗΤΤΟΥ
Arditou
ΕΥΤΥΧΙΑΟΥ
KIFISSIÁ
MARATHÓNAS
LAMÍA
KIFISSIÁ
Kessariani

STREET INDEX TO ATHÍNA TOWN PLAN

Street		Grid	
Adrianou	ΑΔΡΙΑΝΟΥ	BY	
Ag. Konstandinou	ΑΓ. ΚΩΝΣΤΑΝΤΙΝΟΥ	AX	
Aharnon	ΑΧΑΡΝΩΝ	BX	
Ahilleos	ΑΧΙΛΛΕΩΣ	AX	
Akadimias	ΑΚΑΔΗΜΙΑΣ	BCX	
Alexandras	ΑΛΕΞΑΝΔΡΑΣ	CDX	
Amerikis	ΑΜΕΡΙΚΗΣ	CXY	
Anapavseos	ΑΝΑΠΑΥΣΕΩΣ	CY	3
Anapiron Polemou	ΑΝΑΠΗΡΩΝ ΠΟΛΕΜΟΥ	DXY	
Apokafkon	ΑΠΟΚΑΥΚΩΝ	DX	
Apostolou Pavlou	ΑΠΟΣΤΟΛΟΥ ΠΑΥΛΟΥ	AY	
Arahovis	ΑΡΑΧΩΒΗΣ	CX	
Arditou	ΑΡΔΗΤΤΟΥ	CY	
Aristofanous	ΑΡΙΣΤΟΦΑΝΟΥΣ	AX	
Asklipiou	ΑΣΚΛΗΠΙΟΥ	DX	
Ath. Diakou	ΑΘ. ΔΙΑΚΟΥ	BY	
Athinas	ΑΘΗΝΑΣ	BXY	
Bouboulinas	ΜΠΟΥΜΠΟΥΛΙΝΑΣ	CX	
Deligiani	ΔΕΛΗΓΙΑΝΝΗ	AX	
Deligiorgi	ΔΕΛΗΓΙΩΡΓΗ	AX	
Didotou	ΔΙΔΟΤΟΥ	CX	
Dionissiou Areopagitou	ΔΙΟΝΥΣΙΟΥ ΑΡΕΟΠΑΓΙΤΟΥ	ABY	
El. Venizelou	ΕΛ ΒΕΝΙΖΕΛΟΥ	CXY	
Eolou	ΑΙΟΛΟΥ	BXY	
Eratosthenous	ΕΡΑΤΟΣΘΕΝΟΥΣ	DY	
Ermou	ΕΡΜΟΥ	ABY	
Evelpidos Rongakou	ΕΥΕΛΠΙΔΟΣ ΡΟΓΚΑΚΟΥ	DX	
Fanarioton	ΦΑΝΑΡΙΩΤΩΝ	DX	
Favierou	ΦΑΒΙΕΡΟΥ	AX	
Filelinon	ΦΙΛΕΛΛΗΝΩΝ	BCY	8
Hadzihristou	ΧΑΤΖΗΧΡΗΣΤΟΥ	BY	
Harilaou Trikoupi	ΧΑΡΙΛΑΟΥ ΤΡΙΚΟΥΠΗ	CX	
Hiou	ΧΙΟΥ	AX	
Ioulianou	ΙΟΥΛΙΑΝΟΥ	AX	
Ioustinianou	ΙΟΥΣΤΙΝΙΑΝΟΥ	CX	
Ipirou	ΗΠΕΙΡΟΥ	ABX	
Ipokratous	ΙΠΠΟΚΡΑΤΟΥΣ	CX	
Irodou Atikou	ΗΡΩΔΟΥ ΑΤΤΙΚΟΥ	DY	
Kalidromiou	ΚΑΛΛΙΔΡΟΜΙΟΥ	CX	
Kanari	ΚΑΝΑΡΗ	CY	
Karageorgi Servias	ΚΑΡΑΓΙΩΡΓΗ ΣΕΡΒΙΑΣ	BY	13
Karneadou	ΚΑΡΝΕΑΔΟΥ	DY	
Karolou	ΚΑΡΟΛΟΥ	AX	
Kavaloti	ΚΑΒΑΛΛΟΤΙ	BY	
Keramikou	ΚΕΡΑΜΕΙΚΟΥ	AX	
Kidathineon	ΚΥΔΑΘΗΝΑΙΩΝ	BY	16
Kolokinthous	ΚΟΛΟΚΥΝΘΟΥΣ	AX	
Kolokotroni	ΚΟΛΟΚΟΤΡΩΝΗ	BY	
Kriezotou	ΚΡΙΕΖΩΤΟΥ	CY	
Liossion	ΛΙΟΣΙΩΝ	AX	
Lomvardou	ΛΟΜΒΑΡΔΟΥ	DX	
Makri	ΜΑΚΡΗ	BY	
Makrigiani	ΜΑΚΡΥΓΙΑΝΝΗ	BY	21
Marni	ΜΑΡΝΗ	ABX	
Meg. Alexandrou	ΜΕΓ. ΑΛΕΞΑΝΔΡΟΥ	AX	
Menandrou	ΜΕΝΑΝΔΡΟΥ	AX	
Metsovou	ΜΕΤΣΟΒΟΥ	BX	
Mihalakopoulou	ΜΙΧΑΛΑΚΟΠΟΥΛΟΥ	DY	
Mitropoleos	ΜΗΤΡΟΠΟΛΕΩΣ	BY	
Navarhou Nikodimou	ΝΑΥΑΡΧΟΥ ΝΙΚΟΔΗΜΟΥ	BY	
Neof. Metaxa	ΝΕΟΦ. ΜΕΤΑΞΑ	AX	
Omonia	ΟΜΟΝΟΙΑ	BX	
Pandrossou	ΠΑΝΔΡΟΣΟΥ	BY	
Panepistimiou	ΠΑΝΕΜΙΣΤΗΜΙΟΥ	BX	
Parthenonos	ΠΑΡΘΕΝΩΝΟΣ	BY	
Patission (28 Oktovriou)	ΠΑΤΗΣΙΩΝ (28 ΟΚΤΩΒΡΙΟΥ)	BX	
Patr. Ioakim	ΠΑΤΡ. ΙΩΑΚΕΙΜ	DY	
Pindarou	ΠΙΝΔΑΡΟΥ	CY	
Pireos (Panagi Tsaldari)	ΠΕΙΡΑΙΩΣ (ΠΑΝΑΓΗ ΤΣΑΛΔΑΡΗ)	AX	
Pl. Anexartissias (Vathis)	ΠΛΑΤ. ΑΝΕΞΑΡΤΗΣΙΑΣ (ΒΑΘΗΣ)	BX	
Pl. Egiptou	ΠΛΑΤ. ΑΙΓΥΠΤΟΥ	BX	
Pl. Eleftherias	ΠΛΑΤ. ΕΛΕΥΘΕΡΙΑΣ	AX	
Pl. Eth. Andistasseos (Kodzia)	ΠΛΑΤ. ΕΘΝ. ΑΝΤΙΣΤΑΣΕΩΣ (ΚΟΤΖΙΑ)	BX	
Pl. Kaningos	ΠΛΑΤ. ΚΑΝΙΓΓΟΣ	BX	
Pl. Karaïskaki	ΠΛΑΤ. ΚΑΡΑΙΣΚΑΚΗ	AX	
Pl. Klafthmonos	ΠΛΑΤ. ΛΑΥΘΕΡΙΑΖ	BX	
Pl. Kolonakiou	ΠΛΑΤ. ΚΟΛΩΝΑΚΙΟΥ	DY	
Pl. Monastirakiou	ΠΛΑΤ. ΜΟΝΑΣΤΗΡΑΚΙΟΥ	ABY	
Ploutarhou	ΠΛΟΥΤΑΡΧΟΥ	DX	
Psaron	ΨΑΡΩΝ	AX	
Radzieri	ΡΑΤΖΙΕΡΗ	AY	
Rigilis	ΡΗΓΙΛΛΗΣ	DY	
Rovertou Galli	ΡΟΒΕΡΤΟΥ ΓΚΑΛΛΙ	AY	
Sarandapihou	ΣΑΡΑΝΤΑΠΗΧΟΥ	DX	
Sindagma	ΣΥΝΤΑΓΜΑ	CY	
Singrou	ΣΥΓΓΡΟΥ	BY	
Skoufa	ΣΚΟΥΦΑ	CX	
Sofokleous	ΣΟΦΟΚΛΕΟΥΣ	ABX	
Solonos	ΣΟΛΩΝΟΣ	CX	
Spir. Merkouri	ΣΗΥΡ. ΜΕΡΚΟΥΡΗ	DY	
Spir. Trikoupi	ΣΗΥΡ. ΤΡΙΚΟΥΠΗ	CX	
Stadiou	ΣΤΑΔΙΟΥ	BXY	
Stournara	ΣΤΟΥΡΝΑΡΑ	BX	
Themistokleous	ΘΕΜΙΣΤΟΚΛΕΟΥΣ	BCX	
Thermopilon	ΘΕΡΜΟΠΥΛΩΝ	AX	
Tossitsa	ΤΟΣΙΤΖΑ	CX	
Tsakalof	ΤΣΑΚΑΛΩΦ	DXY	
Varvaki	ΒΑΡΒΑΚΗ	DX	
Vas. Alexandrou	ΒΑΣ. ΑΛΕΞΑΝΔΡΟΥ	DY	
Vas. Amalias	ΒΑΣ. ΑΜΑΛΙΑΣ	CY	
Vas. Georgiou B'	ΒΑΣ. ΓΕΩΡΓΙΟΥ Β	DY	
Vas. Konstandinou	ΒΑΣ. ΚΩΝΣΤΑΝΤΙΝΟΥ	DY	
Vas. Olgas	ΒΑΣ. ΟΛΓΑΣ	CY	
Vas. Sofias	ΒΑΣ. ΣΟΦΙΑΣ	CDY	
Vassiliou Voulgaroktonou	ΒΑΣΙΛΕΙΟΥ ΒΟΥΛΓΑΡΟΚΤΟΝΟΥ	DX	
Voukourestiou	ΒΟΥΚΟΥΡΕΣΤΙΟΥ	CXY	
Xanthipou	ΞΑΝΘΙΠΠΟΥ	DXY	
Xenokratous	ΞΕΝΟΚΠΑΤΟΥΣ	DX	
Zaïmi	ΖΑΙΜΗ	CX	
3 Septemvriou	Γ'ΣΕΠΤΕΜΒΡΙΟΥ	BX	

Athenaeum Inter-Continental, 89-93 Singrou, ✉ 117 45, SW : 2 ¾ k
℘ 9023 666, Fax 9243 000, « Première rooftop restaurant with ≤ Athens »,
– |‡| ⇹ ▤ TV ☎ ♿ – 🅰 2000. AE ⓓ E VISA.
Pergola : Meals (buffet lunch) a la carte 4450/8250 – *Première* (9th floor) *:* Mea
(buffet dinner only) 9500/12500 – *Kublai Khan :* Meals - Mongolian and Chinese - *(close
Sunday)* (dinner only) 6950/7750 and a la carte – ☐ 3600 – **515 rm** 58000/9600
44 suites.

Athens Hilton, 46 Vas. Sofias, ✉ 115 28, ℘ 7250 201, Fax 7253 110, « Ro
terrace with ≤ Athens », heated – |‡| ⇹ rm ▤ TV ☎ ♿ – 🅰 1000.
ⓓ E VISA JCB
DY
Ta Nissia : Meals *(closed Sunday)* (dinner only) 11000 and a la carte – *Kellari :* Meals
Taverna - a la carte 3000/5750 – *Byzantine :* Meals (buffet lunch) 6300 and a la car
7500/12550 – ☐ 3800 – **434 rm** 55152/77447, 19 suites.

Athens Ledra Marriott, 115 Singrou, ✉ 117 45, SW : 3 km ℘ 9347 71
Fax 9318 144, « Rooftop terrace with and ✻ Athens » – |‡| ⇹ rm ▤ TV ☎ ♿
– 🅰 400. AE ⓓ E VISA JCB.
Kona Kai : Meals - Polynesian and Japanese - (dinner only) 9500/12500 and a la car
– *Zephyros :* Meals 4250/7400 and a la carte – ☐ 3850 – **244 rm** 32000/4460
15 suites.

Grande Bretagne, 1 Vas. Georgiou A, Sindagma Sq., ✉ 105 63, ☎ 3330 000, Fax 3328 034 – |‡| ▤ TV ☎ – 🏛 500. AE ⓓ E VISA JCB. ✱ rest CY v
G B Corner : **Meals** (buffet lunch) 4459/9857 and a la carte – ☐ 3990 – **341 rm** 80967/89182, 23 suites.

Divani Palace Acropolis, 19-25 Parthenonos, ✉ 117 42, ☎ 9222 945, Fax 9214 993, « Ancient ruins of Themistocles wall in basement », 🏊 – |‡| ▤ TV ☎ – 🏛 300. AE ⓓ E VISA JCB. ✱ BY r
Aspassia : **Meals** 5800 and a la carte – ***Roof Garden :*** **Meals** *(closed Tuesday and November-April)* (live music) (buffet dinner only) 8200 – **246 rm** ☐ 39000/60000, 7 suites.

Divani Caravel, 2 Vas. Alexandrou, ✉ 116 10, ☎ 7253 725, Fax 7253 770, « Rooftop 🏊 with ≤ Athens », 🏊 – |‡| ⊭ rm ▤ TV ☎ 🚗 – 🏛 1300. AE ⓓ E VISA JCB. ✱ DY b
Amalia : **Meals** 4000/7000 and a la carte – ☐ 3800 – **423 rm** 36000/55000, 48 suites.

Le NJV Meridien, 2 Vas. Georgiou A, Sindagma Sq., ✉ 105 64, ☎ 325 5301, Fax 323 5856 – |‡| ⊭ rm ▤ TV ☎ – 🏛 300. AE ⓓ E VISA JCB. ✱ CY r
closed 30 July-15 August – ***Marco Polo :*** **Meals** 5000/10000 and a la carte – ☐ 4900 – **152 rm** 49284, 25 suites.

Novotel Athens, 4-6 Mihail Voda, ✉ 104 39, ☎ 8250 422, Fax 8837 816, « Roof garden with 🏊 and ✳ Athens » – |‡| ▤ TV ☎ 🚗 – 🏛 600. AE ⓓ E VISA JCB AX t
Meals 4000/6500 and a la carte – ☐ 3300 – **190 rm** 32000/36000, 5 suites.

St. George Lycabettus, 2 Kleomenous, ✉ 106 75, ☎ 7290 711, Fax 7290 439, 🍽, « ≤ Athens from rooftop restaurant », 🏊 – |‡| ▤ TV ☎ 🚗 – 🏛 280. AE ⓓ E VISA JCB. ✱ rest DX t
Grand Balcon : **Meals** *(closed Sunday and Monday)* (dinner only) 17000 and a la carte – ***Mediterraneo :*** **Meals** a la carte approx. 6000 – **155 rm** ☐ 39900/51000, 7 suites.

Holiday Inn, 50 Mihalakopoulou, ✉ 115 28, ☎ 7248 322, Fax 7248 187, 🏊 – |‡| ⊭ rm ▤ TV ☎ 🚗 – 🏛 600. AE ⓓ E VISA JCB. ✱ DY
Meals 5000/5500 and a la carte – ☐ 3800 – **188 rm** 50000/63000, 3 suites.

Zafolia, 87-89 Alexandras, ✉ 114 74, ☎ 6449 002, Fax 6442 042, « Rooftop terrace with 🏊 and ≤ Athens » – |‡| ▤ TV ☎ 🚗 – 🏛 200. AE ⓓ E VISA JCB. ✱ DX k
Meals 4700 and a la carte – **183 rm** ☐ 20900/25700, 8 suites.

Electra, 5 Ermou, ✉ 105 63, ☎ 3223 223, Fax 3220 310 – |‡| ⊭ rm ▤ TV ☎. AE ⓓ E VISA. ✱ BY e
Meals 4800 and a la carte – **110 rm** ☐ 30800/37800.

Herodion, 4 Rovertou Galli, ✉ 117 42, ☎ 9236 832, Fax 9235 851, « Roof garden with ≤ Acropolis » – |‡| ▤ TV ☎ – 🏛 50. AE ⓓ E VISA JCB. ✱ BY p
Meals 4800 and a la carte – **90 rm** ☐ 29000/38000.

Electra Palace, 18 Nikodimou, ✉ 105 57, ☎ 3241 401, Fax 3241 875, « Terrace with 🏊 and ≤ Athens » – |‡| ⊭ rm ▤ TV ☎ – 🏛 200. AE ⓓ E VISA. ✱ BY h
Meals 4800 and a la carte – **101 rm** ☐ 30800/37800, 5 suites.

Philippos without rest., 3 Mitseon, ✉ 117 42, ☎ 9223 611, Fax 9223 615 – |‡| ▤ TV ☎. AE ⓓ E VISA JCB. ✱ BY f
48 rm ☐ 19500/26000.

Acropolis View without rest., 10 Wemster, off Rovertou Galli, ✉ 117 42, ☎ 9217 303, Fax 9230 705, « Roof terrace with ≤ Acropolis » – |‡| ▤ ☎. AE E VISA AY e
32 rm ☐ 16000/21000.

Boschetto, Evangelismou, off Vas. Sofias, ✉ 106 75, ☎ 7210 893, Fax 7223 598, 🍽, « Summerhouse in small park » – ▤. AE VISA DY c
closed Saturday lunch, Sunday, 1 week Easter, 10 to 20 August and 1-2 January – **Meals** - Italian - *(closed lunch 15 October-15 April)* a la carte 6000/14000.

Bajazzo, 1 Tyrteou & corner of Anapavseos, ✉ 116 36, ☎ 9213 012, Fax 9213 013, 🍽 – ▤. AE ⓓ VISA CY a
closed lunch Sunday and Monday – **Meals** (booking essential) a la carte 13200/19900
Spec. Lentil broth with fried shrimps, Suprême of partridge with ceps and apple gratin, Cinnamon parfait with Mavrodaphne cherries.

Symbosio, 46 Erehthiou, ✉ 117 42, ☎ 9225 321, Fax 9232 780, « Attractive conservatory, 🍽 » – AE ⓓ E VISA JCB AY r
closed Sunday, 1 week Easter and 10 to 20 August – **Meals** (booking essential) (dinner only) 10000/14000 and a la carte.

Pil-Poul, 51 Apostolou Pavlou, ✉ 118 51, ☎ 3423 665, Fax 3413 046, 🍽, « Former mansion with ≤ Acropolis and Athens from the rooftop terrace » – AE ⓓ E VISA JCB
closed Sunday – **Meals** (dinner only) 12500/16000 and a la carte. AY b

Dionysos, 43 Rovertou Galli, Lofos Filopapou, ✉ 117 42, ☎ 9233 182, Fax 9221 998, 🍽, « ≤ Acropolis » – ▤. AE ⓓ E VISA JCB AY c
Meals 5500/10500 and a la carte.

XX **Daphne's,** 4 Lysikratous, Plaka, ✉ 105 58, ☎ 3227 971, Fax 3227 971, 🏠, « Fresco depicting ancient Greek myths ; attractive inner courtyard » – ▤. AE ⓓ VISA BY
Meals (booking essential) (dinner only) a la carte 9000/13000.

XX **Ideal,** 46 Panepistimiou, (El. Venizelou), ✉ 106 78, ☎ 330 3000, Fax 330 3003 – ▤. ⓓ E VISA JCB BX
closed Sunday and 25 December – **Meals** a la carte 4790/9400.

XX **Dioscuri,** 16 Dimitriou Vassiliou, N. Psihiko, ✉ 154 51, NE : 7 km by Kifissia Rd turni at A.B. supermarket ☎ 6713 997, Fax 6746 546, 🏠 – ▤. AE ⓓ E VISA
closed Sunday and Bank Holidays – **Meals** a la carte 6800/7500.

X **Kidathineon,** 1 Filomoussou Pl., Eterias, ✉ 105 58, ☎ 3234 281, 🏠 – AE ⓓ E V JCB BY
Meals (buffet lunch) 2400/4000 and a la carte.

X **Strofi,** 25 Rovertou Galli, ✉ 117 42, ☎ 9214 130, 🏠, « ≤ Acropolis from roofto terrace » – ▤. ⓓ E VISA AY
closed Sunday, 4 days Easter, 2 days Christmas and 2 days New Year – **Meals** (dinner on a la carte 5000/6500.

"The Tavernas"

Typical Greek restaurants, generally very modest, where it is pleasant to spend the evening, surrounded by noisy but friendly locals, sometimes with guitar or bouzouki ente tainment. These restaurants are usually open for dinner only.

XX **Myrtia,** 32 Trivonianou, ✉ 116 36, ☎ 7012 276, Fax 9247 181 – ▤. AE ⓓ VISA by Anapavseos Rd CY
closed Sunday and 15 July-30 August – **Meals** (music) (booking essential) (dinner on 8000/10000.

X **O Anthropos,** 13 Arhelaou, Pangrati, ✉ 116 35, ☎ 7235 914 – AE ⓓ E VISA
closed in summer – **Meals** - Seafood - (dinner only) a la carte approx. 10000. DY

Environs

at Kifissia *NE : 15 km by Vas. Sofias* DY :

🏨 **Pentelikon** ⛱, 66 Diligianni, Kefalari, ✉ 145 62, off Harilaou Trikoupi, follow signs Politia ☎ 8080 311, Fax 8019 223, 🏠, ⛱, 🌳 – 🛗 ▤ TV ☎ P – 🎤 150. AE ⓓ VISA. ✈
Vardis : **Meals** - French - *(closed Sunday and August)* (dinner only) 9500/14000 and a carte 9850/12750 – ***La Terrasse :*** **Meals** 6000/9000 and a la carte 6650/8500 – ☕ 35(– **33 rm** 48000/80000, 6 suites.

XXX **Varoulko,** 14 Deligiorgi, off Omiridou Skilitsi, ✉ 185 33, ☎ 4112 043, Fax 4221 28 – ▤. AE VISA JCB
closed Sunday, 5 days Easter, August and 5 days Christmas – **Meals** - Seafood - (bookir essential) (dinner only) 8000/11000 and a la carte 8000/11000.

at Pireas *SW : 10 km by Singrou* BY :

XX **Aglamer,** 54-56 Akti Koumoundourou, Mikrolimano, ✉ 185 33, ☎ 4115 51 Fax 4530 335, ≤ Harbour, 🏠 – ▤. AE ⓓ E VISA
closed Easter Sunday and 1 December – **Meals** - Seafood - a la carte 5000/10000.

X **Dourambeis,** 29 Akti Athinas Dilaveri, ✉ 185 33, ☎ 4122 092, 🏠 – AE VISA
closed Easter – **Meals** - Seafood - a la carte 8000/10000.

Hungary

Magyarország

BUDAPEST

PRACTICAL INFORMATION

LOCAL CURRENCY

Forint: *100 UF = 0.61 US $ (Jan. 97)*

National Holiday in Hungary: *20 August.*

PRICES

Prices may change if goods and service costs in Hungary are revised and it is therefore always advisable to confirm rates with the hotelier when making a reservation.

FOREIGN EXCHANGE

It is strongly advised against changing money other than in banks, exchange offices or authorised offices such as large hotels, tourist offices, etc... Banks are usually open on weekdays from 8.30am to 4pm.

HOTEL RESERVATIONS

In case of difficulties in finding a room through our hotel selection, it is always possible to apply to IBUSZ Hotel Service, Apáczai ut. 1, Budapest 5th ☎ (1) 118 57 76, Fax 117 90 99. This office offers a 24-hour assistance to the visitor.

POSTAL SERVICES

Main Post offices are open from 8am to 7pm on weekdays and 8am to 3pm on Saturdays.

General Post Office: *Városház ut. 18, Budapest 5th, ☎ (1) 118 48 11.*

SHOPPING IN BUDAPEST

In the index of street names, those printed in red are where the principal shops are found. Typical goods to be bought include embroidery, lace, china, leather goods, paprika, salami, Tokay, palinka, foie-gras... Shops are generally open from 10am to 6pm on weekdays (7pm on Thursday) and 9am to 1pm on Saturday.

TIPPING

Hotel, restaurant and café bills include service in the total charge but it is usual to leave the staff a gratuity which will vary depending upon the service given.

CAR HIRE

The international car hire companies have branches in Budapest. Your hotel porter should be able to give details and help you with your arrangements.

BREAKDOWN SERVICE

A breakdown service is operated by SARGA ANGYAL (Yellow Angel), ☎ 252 80 00.

SPEED LIMIT

On motorways, the maximum permitted speed is 120 km/h – 74 mph, 100 km/h – 62 mph on main roads, 80 km/h – 50 mph on others roads and 50 km/h – 31 mph in built up areas.

SEAT BELTS

In Hungary, the wearing of seat belts is compulsory for drivers and front seat passengers.

BUDAPEST

Hungary 970 N 6 - *Pop. 1 909 000* - ✪ *1.*

Munich 678 - Prague 533 - Venice 740 - Vienna 243 - Zagreb 350

Tourinform, Sütő u. 2, ✉ *H 1052* ☎ *117 98 00 - IBUSZ Head Office, Ferenciek tér 5, Budapest 5th* ☎ *118 68 66.*

✈ *Ferihegy SE : 16 km by Üllői* FX, ☎ *296 96 96 (information), Bus to airport : from International Bus station, Elisabeth tér, Station 6 Budapest 5th and Airport Bus Service CRI - MALEV, Roosevelt tér 2, Budapest 5th* ☎ *267 29 11*

Views of Budapest

St. Gellert Monument and Citadel (Szt. Gellért-szobor, Citadella) ⩽★★★ EX - *Fishermen's Bastion (Halászbástya)* ⩽★★ DU.

BUDA

Matthias Church★★ *(Mátyás-templom)* DU - *Attractive Streets*★★ *(Tancsics Mihaly utca - Fortuna utca - Uri utca)* CDU - *Royal Palace*★★ *(Budavári palota)* DV - *Hungarian National Gallery*★★ *(Magyar Nemzeti Galéria)* DV **M¹** - *Budapest Historical Museum*★ *(Budapesti Történeti Múzeum)* DV **M¹** - *Vienna Gate*★ *(Bécsi kapu)* CU - *War History Museum*★ *(Hadtörténety Múzeum)* CU.

PEST

Parliament Building★★★ *(Országház)* EU - *Museum of Fine Arts*★★★ *(Szepmüveszeti Múzeum)* BY **M³** - *Hungarian National Museum*★★ *(Magyar Nemzeti Múzeum)* FVX - *Museum of Applied Arts*★★ *(Iparmüvészeti Múzeum)* BZ **M⁵** - *Szechenyi Thermal Baths*★★ *(Széchenyi Gyógyés Strandfürdö)* BY **F²** - *Hungarian State Opera House*★ *(Magyar Állami Operaház)* FU - *Liszt Conservatory : foyer*★ *(Liszt Ferenc Zenemüvészeti Föiskola)* FU **D** - *Chinese Art Museum*★ *(Kína Muzéum)* BYZ **M⁶** - *St. Stephen's Basilica*★ *(Szt. István-bazilika)* EU - *City Parish Church*★ *(Belvárosi plébániatemplom)* EV - *University Church*★ *(Egyetemi Templom)* FX - *Franciscan Church*★ *(Ferences templom)* FV - *Municipal Concert Hall*★ *(Vigadó)* EV - *Town Hall*★ *(Fövárosi Tanács)* EFV - *Paris Arcade*★ *(Párizsi udvar)* EV - *Vaci Street*★ *(Váci utca)* EV - *Hungaria Restaurant*★ *(Hungaria Ettermek)* BZ **N** - *Budapest West Station*★ *(Nyugati pályaudvar)* AY - *Millenary Monument*★ *(Millenniumi emlékmu)* BY - *City Park*★ *(Városliget)* BYZ - *Vajdahunyad Castle*★ *(Vajdahunyad vára)* BY **B** - *Hungarian Transport Museum*★ *(Magyar Közlekedesi Múzeum)* BY **M⁷**.

ADDITIONAL SIGHTS

Chain Bridge★★ *(Széchenyi Lánchíd)* DEV - *Margaret Island*★ *(Margitsziget)* AY - *Aquincum Museum*★ *(Aquincumi Muzéum)* N : *12 km by Szentendrei út* AY - *Gellert Thermal Baths*★ *(Gellért gyógyfürdö)* EX - *St. Ann's Church*★ *(Szent Anna templom)* DU.

Envir.: *Szentendre*★ *N : 20 km - Visegrad N : 42 km : Citadel, view*★★

Kempinski H. Corvinus Budapest M, Erzsébet Tér 7-8, ✉ 1051, ✆ 266 10 Fax 266 2000, – rm – 450. AE E VISA EV
Corvinus : Meals *(closed Saturday lunch and Sunday)* 7403/12832 and a la carte – ***Bist Jardin :*** Meals (buffet lunch) 2566/4442 and a la carte – 2863 – **345 rm** 326 22 suites.

Budapest Hilton, Hess András Tér 1-3, ✉ 1014, ✆ 214 3000, Fax 156 02 < Danube and Buda, « Remains of a 13C Dominican church » – rm – 500. AE E VISA JCB. rest DU
Dominican : Meals 4442 and a la carte – ***Kalocsa :*** Meals *(closed Sunday)* 3455 a a la carte – 2863 – **294 rm** 24678/33068, 28 suites.

Budapest Marriott M, Apáczai Csere János Utca 4, ✉ 1364, ✆ 266 70 Fax 266 5000, < Danube and Buda, – rm – 5 AE E VISA JCB. EV
Csarda : Meals *(closed Sunday)* (dinner only) a la carte 1600/3550 – ***Duna Grill :*** Me (buffet lunch) 1895 and a la carte 1400/3600 – 2100 – **342 rm** 29514/324 20 suites.

Forum H. Budapest, Apáczai Csere János Utca 12-14, ✉ 1368, ✆ 117 91 Fax 117 9808, < Danube and Buda, – rm – 2 AE E VISA JCB. rest EV
Silhouette : Meals 4000/9000 and a la carte – ***Grill :*** Meals 1900/4400 and a la ca – 1481 – **385 rm** 31587/41458, 15 suites.

Atrium Hyatt Budapest M, Roosevelt Tér 2, ✉ 1051, ✆ 266 1234, Fax 266 91 <, – rm – 350. AE E VISA JCB. rest
Old Timer : Meals (dinner only Saturday and Sunday) 3455 and a la carte – ***Atriu Terrace :*** Meals (buffet lunch) 2961 and a la carte – ***Clark Brasserie :*** Meals 2961 a a la carte – 2566 – **319 rm** 27639/46394, 26 suites. EV

Radisson SAS Béke, Teréz Körut 43, ✉ 1067, ✆ 301 1600, Fax 301 1615, – rm – 150. AE E VISA JCB. rest FU
Shakespeare : Meals (lunch only) 3948/4936 and a la carte – ***Szondi :*** Meals (dinner on 3948/4936 and a la carte – 1974 – **238 rm** 33601, 8 suites.

Aquincum M, Árpád Fejedelem Utja 94, ✉ 1036, ✆ 250 3360, Fax 250 4672, Therapy centre, – – 280. AE E VISA JCB. re
Ambrosia : Meals (dinner only) a la carte 1460/5040 – ***Apicius :*** Meals 4442 and a carte – **304 rm** 28626/33561, 8 suites. AY

Gellért, Gellért Tér 1, ✉ 1111, ✆ 185 2200, Fax 166 6631, « Art Nouveau decor Direct entrance to the Therapeutic bath, heated, – 320. AE E VISA JCB EX
Meals 1500/6000 and a la carte – **226 rm** 15596/37312, 13 suites.

Ramada Grand H., Margitsziget, ✉ 1138, ✆ 311 1000, Fax 153 3029, <, Direct entrance to Thermal Hotel, – rm – 85. AE E VISA JCB AY
Meals a la carte 2800/4000 – **154 rm** 22000/31000, 10 suites.

Danubius Thermal H. Helia, Kárpát Utca 62-64, ✉ 1133, ✆ 270 327 Fax 270 2262, <, Therapy centre, – rm – 34 AE E VISA JCB AY
Meals (buffet lunch) 1579/2961 and a la carte – **254 rm** 27639/31587, 8 suites

K + K Hotel Opera M without rest., Révay Utca 24, ✉ 1065, ✆ 269 022 Fax 269 0230 – rm – 50. AE E VISA. rest FU
113 rm 19248/31587, 2 suites.

Mercure Korona M, Kecskeméti Utca 14, ✉ 1053, ✆ 117 4111, Fax 118 3867, – rm – 80. AE E VISA JCB. rest FX
Meals (buffet lunch) 1974/3948 and a la carte – **422 rm** 18755/25665, 10 suite

Astoria, Kossuth Lajos Utca 19, ✉ 1053, ✆ 117 3411, Fax 118 6798, « Art Nouve decor » – – 30. AE E VISA JCB. rest FV
Meals 1777/2468 and a la carte – **124 rm** 16484/23888, 5 suites.

Grand H. Hungaria, Rákóczi Utca 90, ✉ 1074, ✆ 322 9050, Fax 351 0675, – – 350. AE E VISA JCB BZ
Meals 2400/4700 and a la carte – **503 rm** 16287/21716, 8 suites.

Flamenco, Tas Vezér Utca 7, ✉ 1113, ✆ 372 2000, Fax 165 8007, – rm – 200. AE E VISA JCB. rest AZ
Meals 1500/5000 and a la carte – **338 rm** 19742/24678.

Novotel Budapest Centrum, Alkotás Utca 63-67, ✉ 1444, ✆ 186 958 Fax 166 5636, – . AE E VISA JCB. CX
Meals 1777 and a la carte – **321 rm** 16189/21716, 3 suites.

BUDAPEST

Street	Grid	No.
si u.	EV	
k Ferenc u.	EV	8
is Köz	EV	21
zsi u.	EV	53
ófi		
ándor u.	EV	55
i posta u.	EV	58
i u.	EFV	
ösmarty Tér	EV	
áczai Csere		
ános u.	EV	2
ád Fejedelem		
tja	AY	3
czy István u.	EV	4
thyány u.	CDU	5
sébet Krt	BZ	10
érvári út	AZ	11
Ferenciek Tér	EFV	12
Ferenc Krt.	BZ	14
Fortuna u.	CDU	15
Fö u.	DUV	17
Gerlóczy u.	FV	19
Groza Péter		
Rakpart	EVX	20
Hattyú u.	CU	22
Hunfalvy u.	CDU	24
Irányi u.	EX	26
Irinyi József u.	AZ	27
Istenhegyi út	CV	28
Kálmán Imre u.	EU	29
Karinthy Frigyes út.	AZ	31
Karolina út.	AZ	32
Károlyi Mihály u.	FVX	33
Kecskeméti u.	FX	35
Kosciuszko		
Tádé u.	CV	37
Kuny Domokos u.	CV	39
Lajos u.	AY	40
Logodi u.	CU	42
Magyar u.	FVX	44
Nagyenyed u.	CV	46
Nagyszölös u.	AZ	47
Naphegy u.	CDV	48
Országház u.	CDU	50
Pacsirtamezö u.	AY	52
Reáltanoda u.	FV	57
Rumbach		
Sebestyén u.	FV	60
Schönherz		
Zoltán u.	AZ	61
Szabó Ilonka u.	CDU	63
Szentendrei út.	AY	65
Szerb u.	FX	66
Szt. István Krt.	AY	67
Szilágyi Erzsébetfasor	CU	69
Tábor u.	CDV	70
Táncsics Mihály u.	CDU	71
Városház u.	EFV	73
Vörösvári út.	AY	75

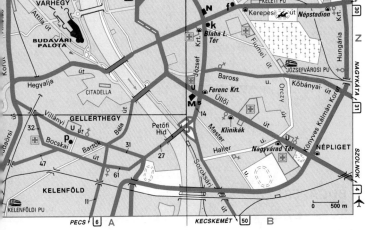

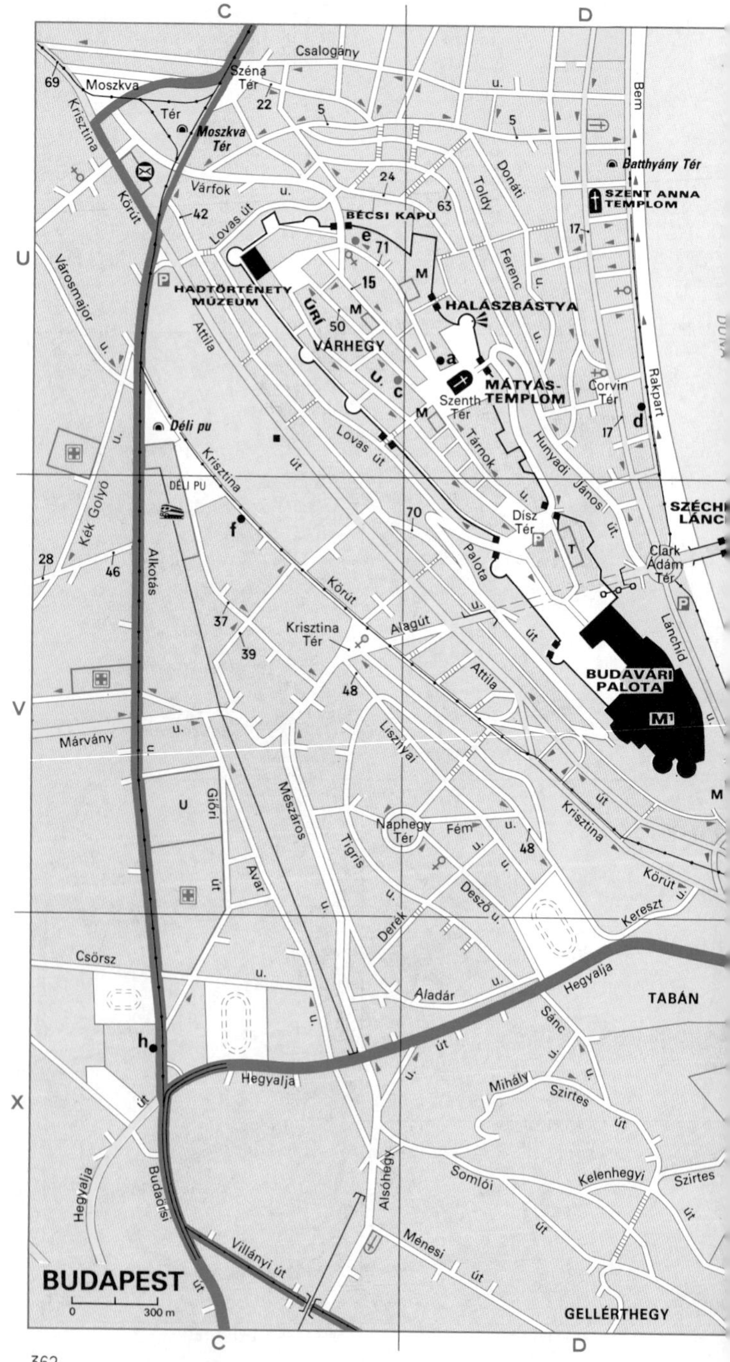
BUDAPEST
0
300 m
C
D
U
V
X
Csalogány
Széna Tér
Moszkva Tér
Moszkva Tér
Várfok u.
Lovas út
BÉCSI KAPU
HADTÖRTÉNETI MÚZEUM
ÚRI u.
VÁRHEGY
HALÁSZBÁSTYA
MÁTYÁS-TEMPLOM
Szenth Tér
Tárnok
Batthyány Tér
SZENT ANNA TEMPLOM
Bem Rakpart
Corvin Tér
Donáti
Toldy
Ferenc u.
Hunyadi János út
Dísz Tér
Palota út
Clark Ádám Tér
Lánchíd
BUDAVÁRI PALOTA
Déli pu
DÉLI PU
Krisztina Körút
Városmajor u.
Kék Golyó
Alkotás
Attila
Krisztina Tér
Alagút
Márvány u.
Győri út
Mészáros u.
Lisznyai
Naphegy Tér
Fém u.
Tigris u.
Avar
Derék
Dessző u.
Kereszt
Csörsz u.
Aladár u.
Hegyalja
Sánc u.
Mihály u.
Szirtes út
Kelenhegyi út
Somlói út
Alsóhegy
Ménesi út
Villányi út
Budaörsi út
TABÁN
GELLÉRTHEGY

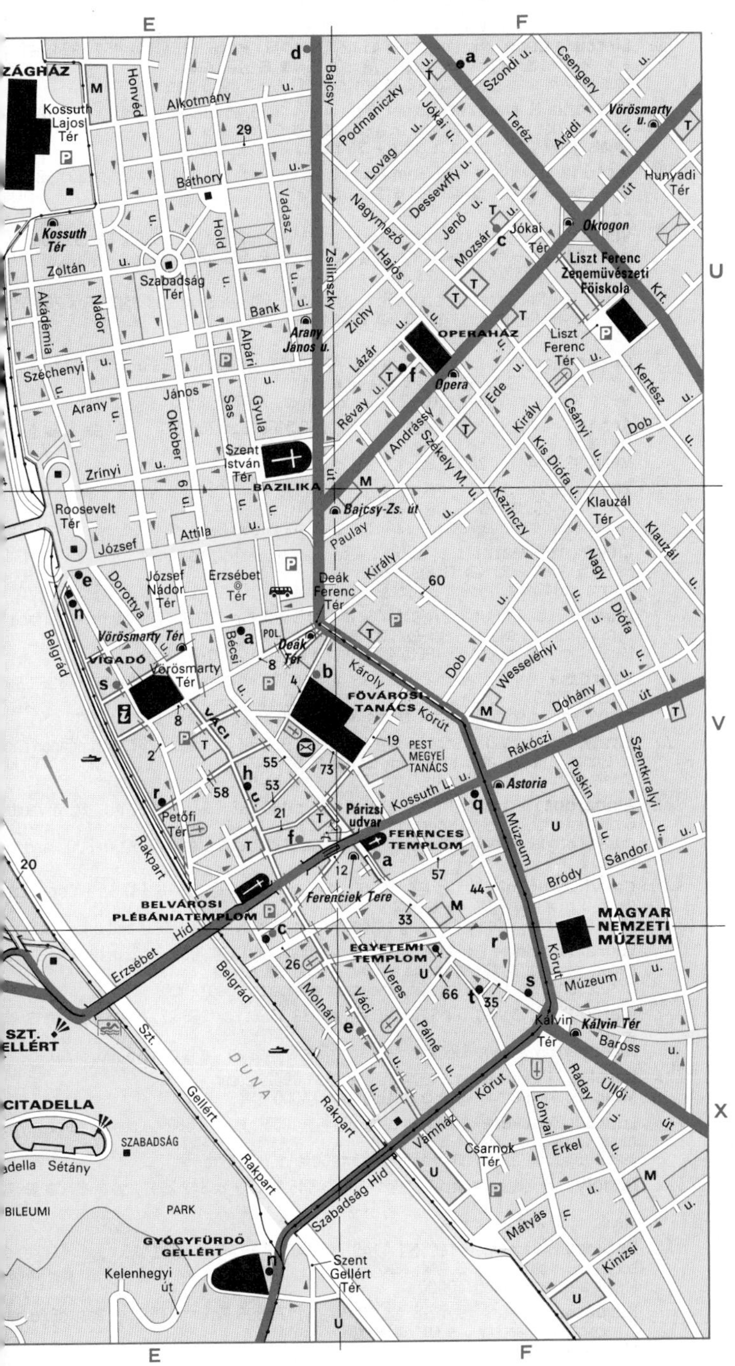
Kossuth Lajos Tér
Kossuth Tér
Szabadság Tér
Roosevelt Tér
József Nádor Tér
Erzsébet Tér
Deák Ferenc Tér
Vörösmarty Tér
VIGADÓ
BAZILIKA
Szent István Tér
OPERAHÁZ
Opera
Oktogon
Liszt Ferenc Zeneművészeti Főiskola
Liszt Ferenc Tér
Jókai Tér
Hunyadi Tér
Klauzál Tér
FŐVÁROSI TANÁCS
PEST MEGYEI TANÁCS
Párizsi udvar
FERENCES TEMPLOM
Ferenciek Tere
Astoria
BELVÁROSI PLÉBÁNIATEMPLOM
EGYETEMI TEMPLOM
MAGYAR NEMZETI MÚZEUM
Kálvin Tér
Petőfi Tér
Erzsébet Híd
Szabadság Híd
DUNA
SZT. GELLÉRT
CITADELLA
SZABADSÁG
GYÓGYFÜRDŐ GELLÉRT
Szent Gellért Tér
Csarnok Tér
Kelenhegyi út
PARK

Mercure Buda, Krisztina Körut 41-43, 1013, 156 6333, Fax 155 6964, – rm TV – 80. AE E VISA JCB CV
Meals 3718 and a la carte – **388 rm** 14807/34549, 6 suites.

Pannonia H. Nemzeti, József Körut 4, 1088, 269 9310, Fax 314 0019, « Nouveau decor » – TV – 25. AE E VISA JCB BZ
Meals 1500/2000 and a la carte – **76 rm** 13819/19742.

Victoria M without rest., Bem Rakpart 11, 1011, 201 8644, Fax 201 5816, – TV . AE E VISA JCB. rest DU
26 rm 18261/19248, 1 suite.

Villa Korda without rest., Szikla Utca 9, 1025, 325 9123, Fax 325 9127, Budapest, – TV – 40. AE E VISA JCB by Szépvölgyi Utca AY
18 rm 12832/14807, 3 suites.

Liget M without rest., Dózsa György Utca 106, 1068, 269 5300, Fax 269 532 – TV . AE E VISA JCB BY
139 rm 18755/20137.

Queen Mary, Béla Király Utca 47, 1121, 274 4000, Fax 156 8377, – rest TV . AE VISA JCB.
Meals (dinner only) a la carte 2172 – **22 rm** 7107/11845.

Art M, Királyi Pál Utca 12, 1053, 266 2166, Fax 266 2170, – TV AE E VISA JCB. FX
Meals 987/4442 – **29 rm** 12832/16781, 3 suites.

Taverna, Váci Utca 20, 1052, 138 4999, Fax 118 7188, – rest TV – 50. AE E VISA JCB EV
Meals 3200 and a la carte – **224 rm** 23400/30000.

City Panzio Mathias M without rest., Március 15 Tér, No. 8, 1056, 138 471 Fax 117 9086 – AE E VISA JCB EX
23 rm 12141/15399, 2 suites.

Gundel, Állatkerti Utca 2, 1146, 321 3550, Fax 342 2917, « Summer terrace Gypsy music at dinner – . AE E VISA JCB BY
Meals (booking essential) 1900/4000 and a la carte 2600/6000.

Vadrózsa, Pentelei Molnár Utca 15, 1025, by Rómer Flóris Utca 326 581 Fax 326 5809, « Summer terrace » – AE E VISA JCB AY
closed mid July-mid August – **Meals** 4500/8000 and a la carte 3280/10560.

Király, Táncsics Mihály Utca 25, 1014, 156 8565, Fax 201 3767, « Hungarian shc at dinner », Music at dinner – . AE E VISA JCB CU
Meals (booking essential) 1600/10000 and a la carte.

Alabárdos, Országház Utca 2, 1014, 156 0851, Fax 214 3814, , « Vault Gothic interior, covered courtyard » – . AE E VISA JCB CU
closed October-April lunch and Sunday – **Meals** (booking essential) 3000/8000 and a carte.

Garvics, Urömí Köz 2, 1023, 326 3878, Fax 326 3876, « Converte vaulted chapel » – AE E VISA AY
closed Sunday – **Meals** (booking essential) (dinner only) 3500/6000 and a la carte.

Légrádi Antique, Bárczy István Utca 3-5 (first floor), 1052, 266 4993, « Elega decor, antiques », Gypsy music at dinner – AE E VISA EV
closed Sunday – **Meals** (booking essential) a la carte 4000/8000.

Marco Polo, Vigadó Tér 3, 1051, 138 3354, Fax 266 2727 – . AE E VI JCB EV
closed Sunday except July and August – **Meals** - Italian - a la carte 3000/5000.

Barokk, Mozsár Utca 12, 1066, 131 8942, Cellar – FU
Meals (booking essential) a la carte approx. 4000.

Légrádi Testvérek, Magyar Utca 23, 1053, 118 6804, Vaulted cellar, Gyp music at dinner – AE FX
Meals (booking essential) (dinner only) 1900 and a la carte.

Bagolyvár, Állatkerti Utca 2, 1146, 343 0217, Fax 342 2917, – AE E VI JCB BY
Meals 1100 and a la carte.

Robinson, Városligeti Tér, 1146, 343 09 55, Fax 343 37 76, , « Lakesic setting » – . AE E VISA JCB BY
Meals a la carte 3000/10000.

Kárpátia, Ferenciek Tere 7-8, 1053, 117 3596, Fax 118 0591, « Part of form Franciscan monastery » – AE E VISA FV
Meals a la carte 2500/7000.

XX **Belcanto,** Dalszínház Utca 8, ✉ 1067, ✆ 269 2786, Fax 111 2091, « Classical and operatic recitals » – AE ⓓ E VISA JCB FU f
Meals (booking essential) (dinner only) a la carte 3000/5000.

XX **Mátyás Pince,** Március 15 Tér, No. 7, ✉ 1056, ✆ 118 1693, Fax 118 1650, « Vaulted cellar, murals », Gypsy music at dinner – ▤. AE ⓓ E VISA JCB EX c
Meals 2000/15000 and a la carte.

XX **Lugas,** Szilágyi Erzsbetfasor 77, ✉ 1026, ✆ 212 3734, 🏠 – AE ⓓ E VISA
Meals a la carte approx. 2800. by Moszkva Tér AZ

LOCAL ATMOSPHERE

X **Kisbuda Gyöngye,** Kenyeres Utca 34, ✉ 1034, ✆ 168 6402, Fax 168 9227 – ▤. AE VISA AY f
closed Sunday – **Meals** (booking essential) a la carte 2600/5000.

X **Apostolok,** Kigyó Utca 4, ✉ 1052, ✆ 267 0290, Fax 118 3658, « Old chapel decor, wood carving » – AE ⓓ E VISA EV f
Meals a la carte 1300/2000.

X **Aranymókus,** Istenhegyi Utca 25, ✉ 1126, ✆ 155 6728, Fax 155 6728, 🏠 – AE ⓓ E VISA by Nagyenyed Utca CV
Meals a la carte 2500/3600.

X **Fatâl,** Váci Utca 67, ✉ 1056, entrance on Pintér Utca ✆ 266 2607, Vaulted basement
Meals a la carte 1400/1900. FX e

the Motorway *M 1/M 7, South 12 km* – BZ – ✉ *Budapest* – ✆ *06 Budaörs :*

Forte Agip H. Budapest M, Agip Utca 2, ✉ 2040, ✆ 23 415 500, Fax 23 415 505, 🏠, ≘s – |$| ⇔ rm ▤ TV ☎ 🚗 P – 🔬 300. AE ⓓ E VISA JCB. ✻ rest
Meals (buffet lunch) 1777/2961 and a la carte – **158 rm** ☐ 10167/18656, 3 suites.

Republic of
Ireland
Eire

DUBLIN

The town plans in the Republic of Ireland Section of this Guide are based upon the Ordnance Survey of Ireland by permission of the Government of the Republic, Permit number 6326.

PRACTICAL INFORMATION

LOCAL CURRENCY

Punt (Irish Pound): *1 IEP = 1.68 USD ($) (Jan. 97)*

TOURIST INFORMATION

The telephone number and address of the Tourist Information office is given in the text under ℹ.

National Holiday in the Republic of Ireland: *17 March.*

FOREIGN EXCHANGE

Banks are open between 10am and 4pm on weekdays only.

Banks in Dublin stay open to 5pm on Thursdays and banks at Dublin and Shannon airports are open on Saturdays and Sundays.

SHOPPING IN DUBLIN

In the index of street names those printed in red are where the principal shops are found.

CAR HIRE

The international car hire companies have branches in each major city. Your hotel porter should be able to give details and help you with your arrangements.

TIPPING

Many hotels and restaurants include a service charge but where this is not the case an amount equivalent to between 10 and 15 per cent of the bill is customary. Additionally doormen, baggage porters and cloakroom attendants are generally given a gratuity.

Taxi drivers are tipped between 10 and 15 per cent of the amount shown on the meter in addition to the fare.

SPEED LIMITS

The maximum permitted speed in the Republic is 60 mph (97 km/h) except where a lower speed limit is indicated.

SEAT BELTS

The wearing of seat belts is compulsory if fitted for drivers and front seat passengers. Additionaly, children under 12 are not allowed in front seats unless in a suitable safety restraint.

ANIMALS

It is forbildden to bring domestic animals (dogs, cats...) into the Republic of Ireland.

DUBLIN

(Baile Átha Cliath) *Dublin* 405 N 7 – *pop. 859 976* – ✪ *1.*

Belfast 103 – Cork 154 – Londonderry 146.

🅸 *Suffolk St. D 2 ☏ 605 7797/605 7777 – Baggot Street Bridge, D 2 – Arrivals Hall, Dublin Airport – Tallaght, D 24.*

⛳18 *Edmondstown, Rathfarnham ☏ 493 2461, S : 3 m by N 81* – ⛳18 *Elm Park, G & S.C., Nutley House, Donnybrook ☏ 269 3438* – ⛳18 *Milltown, Lower Churchtown Rd, ☏ 977060, S : by R 117* – ⛳18 *Royal Dublin, North Bull Island, Dollymont, ☏ 833 6346 NE : by R 105* – ⛳18 *Forrest Little, Cloghran ☏ 840 1183* – ⛳18 *Lucan, Celbridge Rd, Lucan ☏ 628 0246.*

✈ *Dublin Airport ☏ 8444900, N : 5 ½ m. by N 1 – Terminal : Busaras (Central Bus Station) Store St.*

⛴ *to Holyhead (Irish Ferries) 2 daily (3 h 30 mn) – to the Isle of Man (Douglas) (Isle of Man Steam Packet Co Ltd.) (4 h 30 mn).*

See: *City★★★ – Trinity College★★★ (Library★★★)* JY – *Chester Beatty Library★★★ – Phoenix Park★★★ – Dublin Castle★★* HY – *Christ Church Cathedral★★* HY – *St. Patrick's Cathedral★★* HZ – *Marsh's Library★★* HZ – *National Museum★★ (Treasury★★),* KZ – *National Gallery★★* KZ – *Merrion Square★★* KZ – *Rotunda Hospital Chapel★★* JX – *Kilmainham Hospital★★ – Kilmainham Gaol Museum★★ – National Botanic Gardens★★ – N° 29★* KZ **D** – *Liffey Bridge★* JY – *Taylors' Hall★* HY – *City Hall★* HY – *St. Audoen's Gate★* HY **B** – *St. Stephen's Green★* JZ – *Grafton Street★* JZ – *Powerscourt Centre★* JYY – *Civic Museum★* JY **M1** – *Bank of Ireland★* JY – *O'Connell Street★ (Anna Livia Fountain★),* JX – *St. Michan's Church★* HY **E** – *Hush Lane Municipal Gallery of Modern Art★* JX **M4** – *Pro-Cathedral★* JX – *Garden of Remembrance★* JX – *Custom House★* KX – *Bluecoat School★ – Guiness Museum★ – Marino Casino★ – Zoological Gardens★ – Newman House* JZ.

Envir.: *Powerscourt★★ (Waterfall★★★), S : 14 m by N 11 and R 117 – Russborough House★★★, SW : 22 m by N 81 – Rathfarnham Castle★, S : 3 m by N 81 and R 115 8 T.*

DUBLIN

SOUTH EAST BUILT UP AREA

Street	Ref
Ailesbury Road	FV 4
Baggot Street Upper	EU 7
Beech Hill Avenue	FV 10
Beechwood Road	EV 12
Belgrave Road	DV 13
Bloomfield Avenue	DU 18
Brighton Road	DV 22
Camder Street	DU 28
Castlewood Avenue	DV 31
Charlemont Street	DU 34
Charlotte Street	DU 36
Chelmsford Road	EV 37
Church Avenue	FU 39
Clyde Road	EFU 43
Eastmoreland Place	EU 61
Elgin Road	EFU
Harrington Street	DU
Herbert Place	EU
Irishtown Road	FU
Lansdowne Road	FU
Lea Road	GU
Leeson Street Lower	EU
Leinster Road West	DV
Londonbridge Road	FU
Maxwell Road	DV

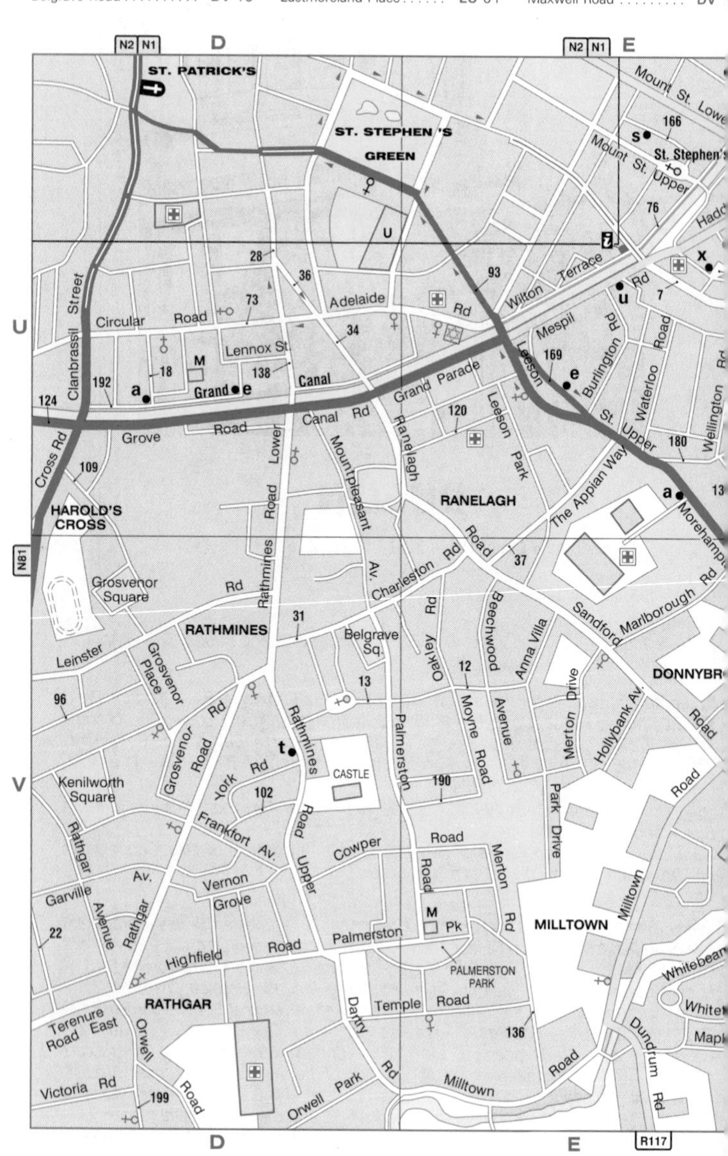

Your recommendation is self-evident if you always walk into a hotel Guide in hand.

rlyn Park . . . . GV 105
unt Drummond
Avenue . . . . DU 109
wbridge Avenue . . . . . FU 115
wgrove Avenue . . . . . . GU 117
rthbrook Road . . . . EU 120
tgrove Park . . . . FV 121
nell Road . . . . DU 124
mbroke Park . . . . EU 130
glan Road . . . . FU 133
Richmond Avenue
South . . . . EV 136
Richmond Street South . . DU 138
St Alban's Park . . . . GV 142
St John's Road East . . . . . GV 145
Seafort Avenue . . . . GU 153
Sean Moore Road . . . . . . GU 154
Serpentine Avenue . . . . . . FU 156
Simmonscourt Road . . . . . FU 160
South Lotts Road . . . . FU 163
Stephen's Lane . . . . EU 166
Sussex Road . . . . EU 169
Trimbleston
Avenue . . . . GV 175
Victoria Avenue . . . . FV 177
Wellington Place . . . . EU 180
Windsor Road . . . . EV 190
Windsor Terrace . . . . DU 192
Wynnsward Drive . . . . . . FV 198
Zion Road . . . . DV 199

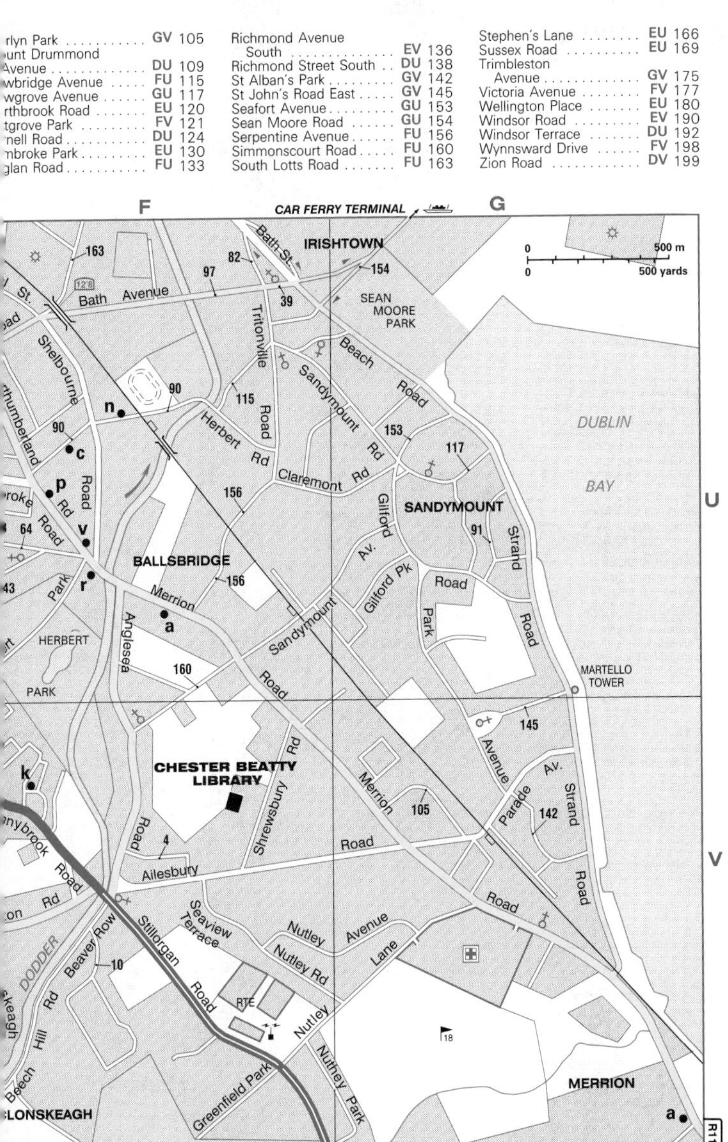

If you find you cannot take up a hotel booking you have made, please let the hotel know immediately.

DUBLIN
CENTRE

Street	Grid	No.
Anne Street South	JYZ	6
Dawson Street	JYZ	
Duke Street	JY	58
Grafton Street	JYZ	
Henry Street	JX	
Ilac Centre	HJX	
Irish Life Mall Centre	JKX	
O'Connell Street	JX	
Brunswick Street North	HX	24
Buckingham Street		25
Bull Alley		27
Chancery Street		33
Clanbrassil Street	HZ	40
College Green		45
College Street		46
Cornmarket	HY	49
D'Olier Street	JY	51
Earlsfort Terrace	JZ	60
Essex Quay	HY	66
Fishamble Street	HY	67
George's Quay	KY	69
Golden Lane	HZ	70
Henrietta Street	HX	75
High Street	HY	78
Kevin Street Upper	HZ	85
Kildare Street	JKZ	87
King Street South	JZ	88
Marlborough Street	JX	100
Merchants Quay	HY	103
Montague Street	JZ	106
Mount Street Upper	KZ	112
Nicholas Street	HY	118
Parnell Square East	JX	126
Parnell Square North	JX	127
Parnell Square West	HJX	129
St Mary's Abbey Street	HY	148
St Patrick Close	HZ	150
Stephen Street	HJY	165
Tara Street	KY	171
Wellington Quay	HJY	181
Werburgh Street	HY	183
Westland Row	KY	186
Westmoreland Street	JY	187
Wexford Street	HZ	189
Winetavern Street	HY	193
Wood Quay	HY	196

Town plans: roads most used by traffic and those on which guide-listed hotels and restaurants stand are fully drawn; only the beginning of lesser roads is indicated.

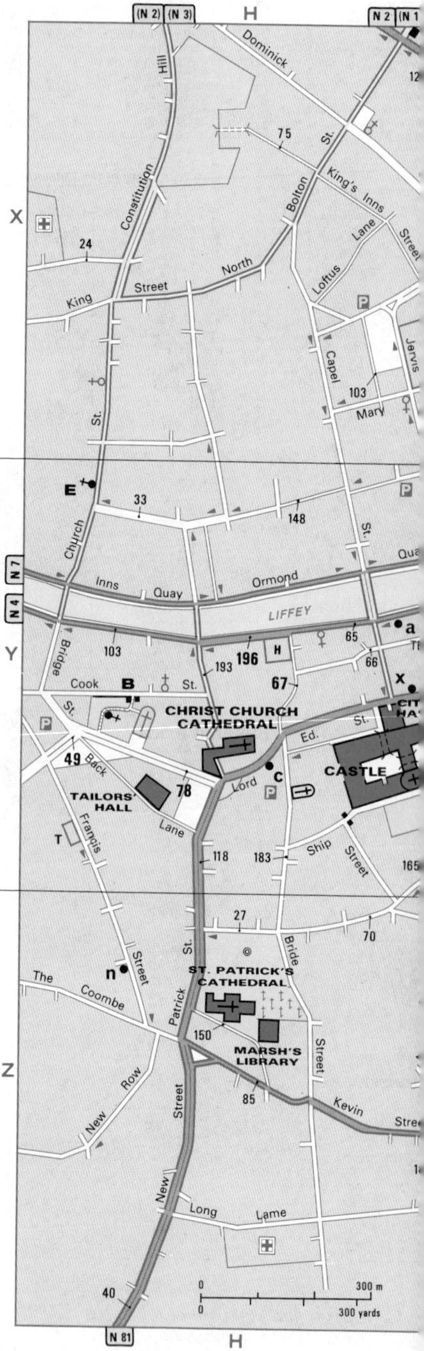

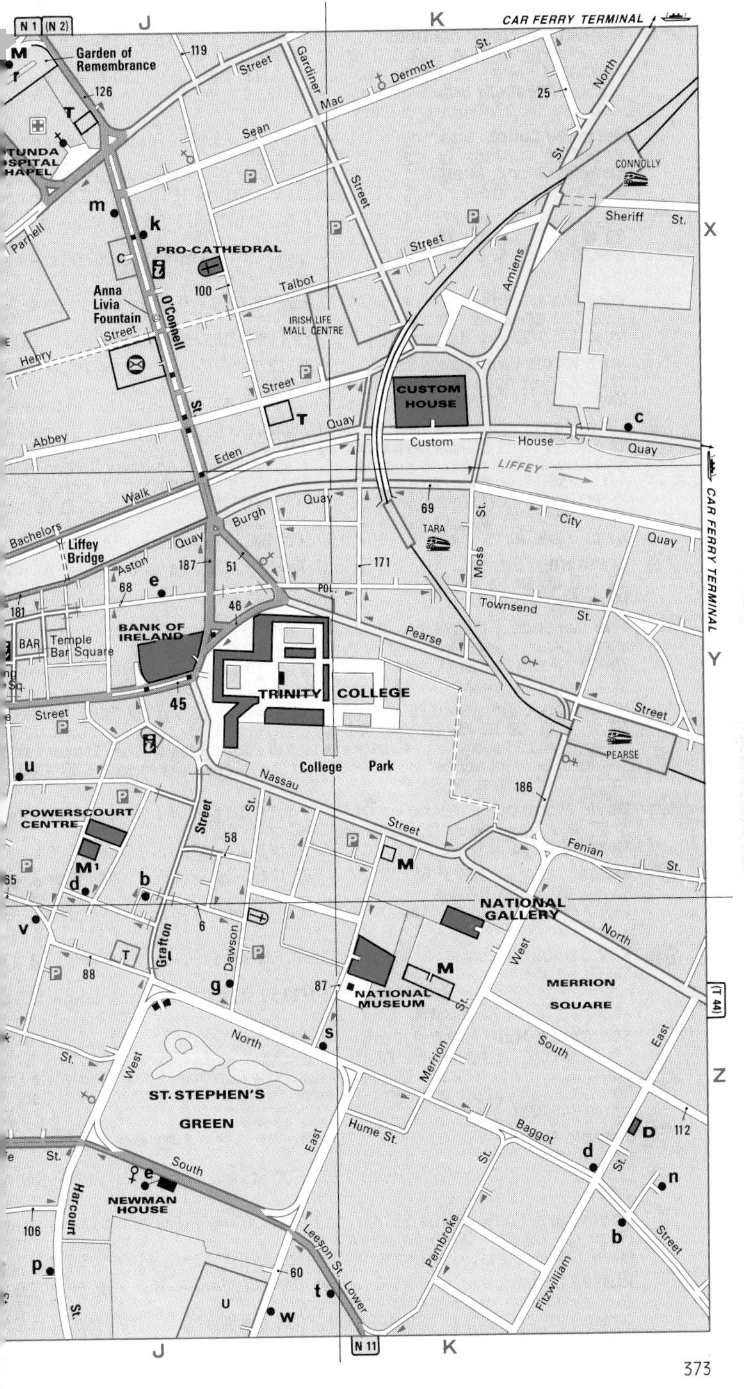

CAR FERRY TERMINAL
Garden of Remembrance
PRO-CATHEDRAL
Anna Livia Fountain
IRISH LIFE MALL CENTRE
CUSTOM HOUSE
CONNOLLY
LIFFEY
Liffey Bridge
TARA
BANK OF IRELAND
Temple Bar Square
TRINITY COLLEGE
College Park
PEARSE
POWERSCOURT CENTRE
NATIONAL GALLERY
MERRION SQUARE
NATIONAL MUSEUM
ST. STEPHEN'S GREEN
NEWMAN HOUSE
O'Connell St.
Talbot Street
Sean Mac Dermott St.
Gardiner Street
Amiens St.
Sheriff St.
Abbey Street
Henry Street
Custom House Quay
Eden Quay
Burgh Quay
Aston Quay
Bachelors Walk
City Quay
Townsend St.
Pearse Street
Moss St.
Nassau Street
Grafton Street
Dawson St.
Fenian St.
Merrion Square North
Merrion St.
Baggot Street
Hume St.
Leeson St. Lower
Harcourt St.
Pembroke St.
Fitzwilliam St.

Conrad International Dublin, Earlsfort Terr., D2, ✆ 676 5555, Fax 676 5424 – ⇔ rm ▤ TV ☎ ♿ P – 300. AE VISA JCB. JZ
Alexandra : Meals *(closed Saturday lunch and Sunday)* 17.00/29.50 **t.** and a la carte 6.50 – ***Plurabelle Brasserie*** : Meals 14.00/16.50 **t.** and a la carte 6.50 – ☕ 12.5 – **182 rm** 165.00/190.00 **t.**, 9 suites.

Berkeley Court, Lansdowne Rd, Ballsbridge, D4, ✆ 660 1711, Fax 661 7238 – ⇔ r ▤ rest TV ☎ ♿ P – 440. AE VISA. FU
Berkeley Room : Meals 16.75/26.50 **t.** and a la carte – ***Conservatory Grill*** : Mea 9.75/15.00 **t.** and a la carte 6.80 – ☕ 10.75 – **181 rm** 165.00/185.00 **t.**, 5 suites

Shelbourne (Forte), 27 St. Stephen's Green, D2, ✆ 676 6471, Fax 661 6006 – ⇔ r TV ☎ – 400. AE VISA JZ
Meals 18.00/25.50 **t.** and a la carte 7.50 – ☕ 12.50 – **155 rm** 138.00/207.00 **t.**, 9 suite – SB.

Westbury, Grafton St., D2, ✆ 679 1122, Fax 679 7078 – ⇔ rm ▤ rest TV ☎ – 150. AE VISA JCB. JY
Meals 17.50/27.50 **t.** and a la carte 7.50 – ☕ 11.00 – **195 rm** 175.00/195.00 **t.**, 8 suite

Burlington, Upper Leeson St., D4, ✆ 660 5222, Fax 660 3172 – ⇔ rm ▤ rest ☎ ♿ P – 1000. AE VISA JCB. EU
Meals 12.50/17.50 **t.** and a la carte 6.00 – ☕ 9.65 – **447 rm** 115.00/135.00 **t.**, 4 suite

Jurys, Pembroke Rd, Ballsbridge, D4, ✆ 660 5000, Fax 660 5540, heated – ⇔ r ▤ rest TV ☎ ♿ P – 850. AE VISA. FU
Kish : Meals - Seafood - (dinner only) 27.50 **t.** and a la carte – ***Embassy Garden*** : Mea 17.00/23.50 **t.** and a la carte – ☕ 9.50 – **274 rm** 129.00/149.00 **t.**, 2 suites – SB.

The Towers, Lansdowne Rd, D4, ✆ 667 0033, Fax 660 5324, , heated ⇔ rm ▤ TV ☎ ♿ P
Meals – (see ***Jurys H.*** above) – **96 rm** 176.00/196.00 **t.**, 4 suites – SB.

Gresham, O'Connell St., D1, ✆ 874 6881, Fax 878 7175 – ▤ rest TV ☎ ♿ 250. AE VISA. JX
Meals 15.00/22.00 **t.** and a la carte 7.00 – ☕ 15.00 – **194 rm** 160.00 **t.**, 6 suites

The Clarence, 6-8 Wellington Quay, D2, ✆ 670 9000, Fax 670 7800, « Contemporar interior design » – ⇔ rm TV ☎ ♿ P – 40. AE VISA HY
The Tea Room : Meals *(closed lunch Saturday and Sunday)* 17.50 **st.** (lunch) and a la cart 19.85/34.45 **st.** 8.00 – ☕ 13.00 – **49 rm** 165.00 **st.**, 4 suites.

Hibernian, Eastmoreland Pl., Ballsbridge, D4, ✆ 668 7666, Fax 660 2655 – ⇔ r TV ☎ ♿ P. AE VISA JCB. EU
closed 25 and 26 December – ***Patrick Kavanagh Room*** : Meals *(closed Saturday lunc* (residents only Sunday dinner) 13.95/23.50 **t.** and dinner a la carte 6.50 – **40 r** ☕ 110.00/180.00 **st.** – SB.

Doyle Montrose, Stillorgan Rd, D4, SE : 4 m. by N 11 ✆ 269 3311, Fax 269 1164 TV ☎ ♿ P – 80. AE VISA JCB. GV
Meals 10.30/18.20 **t.** and a la carte 5.00 – ☕ 7.40 – **179 rm** 83.00/173.00 **t.**

Mespil, Mespil Rd, D4, ✆ 667 1222, Fax 667 1244 – ⇔ rm ▤ rest TV ☎ ♿ P 40. AE VISA. EU
closed 24 to 26 December – **Meals** (buffet lunch)/dinner 15.95 **st.** and a la carte 5.7 – ☕ 7.00 – **153 rm** 72.00 **st.**

Royal Dublin, O'Connell St., D1, ✆ 873 3666, Fax 873 3120 – TV ☎ – 22 AE VISA. JX
closed 24 and 25 December – **Meals** 12.50/18.50 **st.** and a la carte 6.50 – **117 r** ☕ 95.00/120.00 **st.**, 3 suites.

Stephen's Hall, Earlsfort Centre, 14-17 Lower Leeson St., D2, ✆ 661 058 Fax 661 0606 – TV ☎ . AE VISA. JZ
closed 25 to 27 December – ***Morels*** : Meals *(closed Saturday lunch, Sunday and Bar Holidays)* 12.50/25.00 **t.** and dinner a la carte – ☕ 8.00 – **3 rm** 105.00/145.00 **st.**, 3 suites 145.00 **st.**

Temple Bar, Fleet St., D2, ✆ 677 3333, Fax 677 3088 – TV ☎ ♿ – 30. VISA. JY
closed 24 to 27 December – **Meals** 9.25/15.00 **st.** and a la carte 6.50 – **108 r** ☕ 95.00/120.00 **st.**

Doyle Tara, Merrion Rd, D4, SE : 4 m. on T 44 ✆ 269 4666, Fax 269 1027 – ▤ res TV ☎ P – 300. AE VISA JCB GV
Meals 8.40/13.50 **t.** and a la carte 4.90 – ☕ 7.35 – **113 rm** 85.00/105.00 **t.**

Russell Court, 21-25 Harcourt St., D2, ✆ 478 4066, Fax 478 1576 – ⇔ rm TV P – 150. AE VISA. JZ
closed 24 to 28 December – **Meals** 9.95/17.00 **st.** and dinner a la carte 6.00 – ☕ 6.5 – **42 rm** 65.00/140.00 **t.**, 6 suites – SB.

Doyle Skylon, Upper Drumcondra Rd, N : 2 ½ m. on N 1 ✆ 837 9121, Fax 837 2778 – |‡| ▤ rest TV ☎ P. MC AE ◑ VISA JCB. ✻
Meals 11.00/14.00 **t.** and a la carte 🍷 4.90 – ☕ 7.35 – **92 rm** 85.00/105.00 **t.**

Grafton Plaza, Johnsons Pl., D2, ✆ 475 0888, Fax 475 0908 – |‡| TV ☎ ♿. MC AE ◑ VISA. ✻ JZ v
closed 24 to 26 December – **Meals** *(closed Sunday)* a la carte 10.50/23.00 **st.** 🍷 8.50 – ☕ 7.50 – **75 rm** 90.00/115.00 **st.**

Bewley's, 19-20 Fleet St., D2, ✆ 670 8122, Fax 670 8103 – |‡| ⇆ rm TV ☎. MC AE ◑ VISA. ✻ JY d
closed 24 to 26 December – **Meals** a la carte 13.00/16.00 **st.** 🍷 7.00 – ☕ 6.00 – **70 rm** 74.00/94.00 **st.**

Jurys Custom House Inn, Custom House Quay, D1, ✆ 607 5000, Fax 829 0400, 🏋 – |‡| ⇆ rm TV ☎ ♿ – 🏛 100. MC AE ◑ VISA. ✻ KX c
closed 24 to 26 December – **Meals** *(closed lunch Saturday and Sunday)* (buffet lunch)/dinner 14.50 **t.** and a la carte 🍷 5.25 – ☕ 6.00 – **234 rm** 55.00 **t.**

Jurys Christchurch Inn, Christchurch Pl., D8, ✆ 454 0000, Fax 454 0012 – |‡| ⇆ rm ▤ rest TV ☎ ♿ P. MC AE ◑ VISA. ✻ HY c
closed 24 to 26 December – **Meals** (bar lunch)/dinner 14.50 **st.** and a la carte – ☕ 6.00 – **182 rm** 55.00 **t.**

Sachs, 12-29 Morehampton Rd, Donnybrook, D4, ✆ 668 0995, Fax 668 6147 – |‡| TV ☎ P – 🏛 120. MC AE ◑ VISA. ✻ EU a
Meals 14.50/23.50 **st.** and a la carte 🍷 5.50 – **20 rm** ☕ 64.60/95.50 **st.** – SB.

Ariel House without rest., 52 Lansdowne Rd, Ballsbridge, D4, ✆ 668 5512, Fax 668 5845, 🚗 – TV ☎ P. MC VISA. ✻ FU n
closed 23 December-13 January except 31 December – ☕ 7.50 – **28 rm** 60.00/150.00 **t.**

Central, 1-5 Exchequer St., D2, ✆ 679 7302, Fax 679 7303 – |‡| TV ☎ – 🏛 80. MC AE ◑ VISA. ✻ JY u
closed 24 to 26 December – **Meals** (bar lunch Monday to Friday)/dinner a la carte 8.25/13.50 **t.** 🍷 5.25 – ☕ 7.50 – **69 rm** 75.00/110.00 **t.**, 1 suite – SB.

XXX ✿✿ **Patrick Guilbaud,** 46 James' Pl., James' St., off Lower Baggot St., D2, ✆ 676 4192, Fax 661 0052 – ▤. MC AE ◑ VISA KZ n
closed Sunday, Monday and first week Janaury – **Meals** - French - 22.00/35.00 **st.** and a la carte 34.00/51.00 **st.** 🍷 15.00
Spec. Pan seared Bantry Bay king scallops, watercress and deep fried leeks, Roast squab pigeon, almond and Bunratty mead sauce, Hot rhubarb soufflé.

XXX ✿ **The Commons,** Newman House, 85-86 St. Stephen's Green, D2, ✆ 475 2597, Fax 478 0551, « Contemporary collection of James Joyce inspired Irish Art » – MC AE ◑ VISA JZ e
closed Saturday lunch, Sunday, 2 weeks Christmas and Bank Holidays – **Meals** 18.00/32.00-42.00 **t.** 🍷 7.00
Spec. Galantine of foie gras and black pudding, Roast squab, vegetables à la grecque, tarragon oil, Pistachio and chocolate ravioli, ruby orange sauce.

XXX ☺ **Ernie's,** Mulberry Gdns., off Morehampton Rd, Donnybrook, D4, ✆ 269 3300, Fax 269 3260, « Contemporary Irish Art collection » – ▤. MC AE ◑ VISA FV k
closed Saturday lunch, Sunday, Monday and 24 December-1 January – **Meals** 13.95/25.00 **t.** and a la carte 26.90/36.35 **t.** 🍷 7.50.

XXX **Viking at Clontarf Castle,** Castle Av., Clontarf, D3, NE : 3 ½ m. ✆ 833 2271, Fax 833 4549 – ▤ P. MC AE VISA KX
closed Sunday dinner, Monday, Good Friday and 24 to 26 December – **Meals** (dinner only and Sunday lunch)/dinner a la carte 12.95/19.40 🍷 5.50.

XXX **Le Coq Hardi,** 35 Pembroke Rd, D4, ✆ 668 9070, Fax 668 9887 – P. MC AE ◑ VISA JCB
closed Saturday lunch, Sunday, 2 weeks August, 1 week Christmas and Bank Holidays – **Meals** 18.00/33.00 **t.** and a la carte 🍷 8.00. EU m

XX ☺ **Chapter One,** The Dublin Writers Museum, 18-19 Parnell Sq., D1, ✆ 873 2266, Fax 873 2330 – ▤ P. MC AE ◑ VISA JX r
closed Monday dinner, Sunday, 25 December-8 January and Bank Holidays – **Meals** 13.50/17.50 and dinner a la carte 19.25/24.75 **t.** 🍷 6.50.

XX ✿ **Thornton's** (Thornton), 1 Portobello Rd, D8, ✆ 454 9067, Fax 454 9067 – ▤. MC AE ◑ VISA DU e
closed Sunday, Monday, 1 to 14 January and 5 to 12 August – **Meals** (booking essential) (dinner only) a la carte 31.85/40.85 **t.** 🍷 8.50
Spec. Marinated wild Irish salmon with cucumber and Beluga caviar, Magret of duck with gizzards and a girolle sauce, Nougat pyramid with glazed fruit and orange sauce.

XX **Locks,** 1 Windsor Terr., Portobello, ✆ 4543391, Fax 4538352 – MC AE ◑ VISA
closed Saturday lunch, Sunday, last week July-first week August and 1 week Christmas – **Meals** 13.95/23.50 **t.** and a la carte 🍷 6.50. DU a

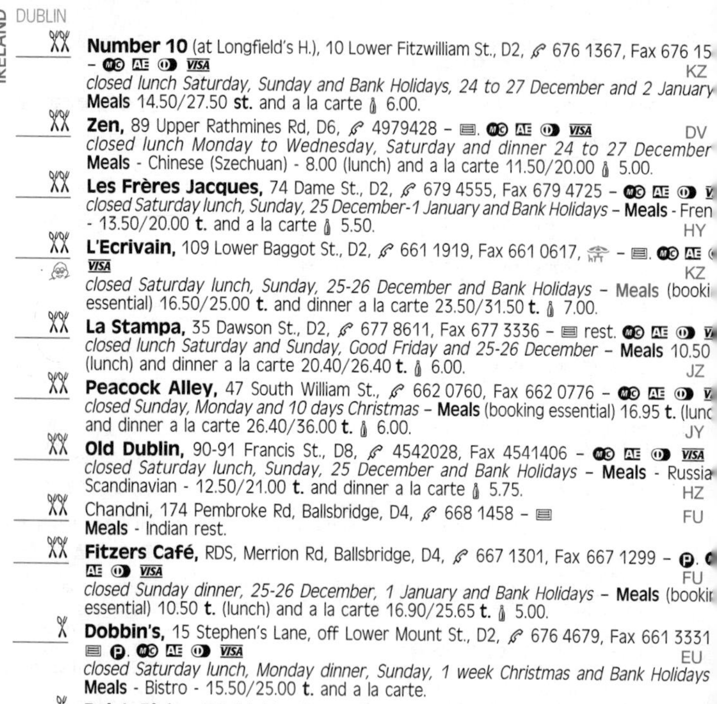

XX **Number 10** (at Longfield's H.), 10 Lower Fitzwilliam St., D2, ✆ 676 1367, Fax 676 15 – MC AE ⓓ VISA KZ
closed lunch Saturday, Sunday and Bank Holidays, 24 to 27 December and 2 January
Meals 14.50/27.50 **st.** and a la carte ₰ 6.00.

XX **Zen,** 89 Upper Rathmines Rd, D6, ✆ 4979428 – ▤. MC AE ⓓ VISA DV
closed lunch Monday to Wednesday, Saturday and dinner 24 to 27 December
Meals - Chinese (Szechuan) - 8.00 (lunch) and a la carte 11.50/20.00 ₰ 5.00.

XX **Les Frères Jacques,** 74 Dame St., D2, ✆ 679 4555, Fax 679 4725 – MC AE ⓓ V
closed Saturday lunch, Sunday, 25 December-1 January and Bank Holidays – **Meals** - Fren - 13.50/20.00 **t.** and a la carte ₰ 5.50. HY

XX **L'Ecrivain,** 109 Lower Baggot St., D2, ✆ 661 1919, Fax 661 0617, 🏠 – ▤. MC AE (VISA KZ
closed Saturday lunch, Sunday, 25-26 December and Bank Holidays – **Meals** (booki essential) 16.50/25.00 **t.** and dinner a la carte 23.50/31.50 **t.** ₰ 7.00.

XX **La Stampa,** 35 Dawson St., D2, ✆ 677 8611, Fax 677 3336 – ▤ rest. MC AE ⓓ V
closed lunch Saturday and Sunday, Good Friday and 25-26 December – **Meals** 10.50 (lunch) and dinner a la carte 20.40/26.40 **t.** ₰ 6.00. JZ

XX **Peacock Alley,** 47 South William St., ✆ 662 0760, Fax 662 0776 – MC AE ⓓ V
closed Sunday, Monday and 10 days Christmas – **Meals** (booking essential) 16.95 **t.** (lunc and dinner a la carte 26.40/36.00 **t.** ₰ 6.00. JY

XX **Old Dublin,** 90-91 Francis St., D8, ✆ 4542028, Fax 4541406 – MC AE ⓓ VISA
closed Saturday lunch, Sunday, 25 December and Bank Holidays – **Meals** - Russia Scandinavian - 12.50/21.00 **t.** and dinner a la carte ₰ 5.75. HZ

XX Chandni, 174 Pembroke Rd, Ballsbridge, D4, ✆ 668 1458 – ▤ FU
Meals - Indian rest.

XX **Fitzers Café,** RDS, Merrion Rd, Ballsbridge, D4, ✆ 667 1301, Fax 667 1299 – Ⓟ. (AE ⓓ VISA FU
closed Sunday dinner, 25-26 December, 1 January and Bank Holidays – **Meals** (bookir essential) 10.50 **t.** (lunch) and a la carte 16.90/25.65 **t.** ₰ 5.00.

X **Dobbin's,** 15 Stephen's Lane, off Lower Mount St., D2, ✆ 676 4679, Fax 661 3331 ▤ Ⓟ. MC AE ⓓ VISA EU
closed Saturday lunch, Monday dinner, Sunday, 1 week Christmas and Bank Holidays
Meals - Bistro - 15.50/25.00 **t.** and a la carte.

X **Roly's Bistro,** 7 Ballsbridge Terr., Ballsbridge, D4, ✆ 668 2611, Fax 660 8535 – ▤. (AE ⓓ VISA FU
Meals 10.50 **t.** (lunch) and a la carte 16.75/20.75 **t.** ₰ 4.75.

Italy

Italia

ROME – FLORENCE – MILAN – NAPLES
PALERMO – TAORMINA – TURIN – VENICE

PRACTICAL INFORMATION

LOCAL CURRENCY

Italian Lire: *1000 ITL = 0.65 USD ($) (Jan. 97)*

TOURIST INFORMATION

Welcome Office *(Ente Provinciale per il Turismo):*
– *Via Parigi 11 - 00185 ROMA (closed Sunday), ☏ 06/488991, Fax 488 99 250*
– *Via Marconi 1 - 20123 MILANO, ☏ 02/72 52 43 00, Fax 72 52 42 50*
See also telephone number and address of other Tourist Information offices in the text of the towns under **i**.
American Express:
– *Piazza di Spagna 38 - 00187 ROMA, ☏ 06/67641, Fax 678 76 69*
– *Via Brera 3 - 20121 MILANO, ☏ 02/72 00 36 91, Fax 86 10 28*

National Holiday in Italy: *25 April.*

AIRLINES

ALITALIA: *Via Bissolati 20 - 00187 ROMA, ☏ 06/65621, Fax 656 28 310*
Via Albricci 5 - 20122 MILANO, ☏ 02/62811, Fax 805 67 57

AIR FRANCE: *Via Sardegna 40 - 00187 ROMA, ☏ 06/48187911, Fax 488 45 03*
Piazza Cavour 2 - 20121 MILANO, ☏ 02/760731, Fax 760 73 333

DELTA AIRLINES: *Via Melchiorre Gioia 66 - 20124 MILANO, ☏ 02/67 07 00 47, Fax 67 07 31 82*

TWA: *Via Barberini 59 - 00187 ROMA, ☏ 06/47241, Fax 474 61 25*
Corso Europa 11 - 20122 MILANO, ☏ 02/77961, Fax 76 01 45 83

FOREIGN EXCHANGE

Money can be changed at the Banca d'Italia, other banks and authorised exchange offices (Banks close at 1.30pm and at weekends).

POSTAL SERVICES

Local post offices: *open Monday to Saturday 8.30am to 2.00pm*

General Post Office *(open 24 hours only for telegrams):*
– *Piazza San Silvestro 00187 ROMA – Piazza Cordusio 20123 MILANO*

SHOPPING

In the index of street names those printed in red are where the principal shops are found. In Rome, the main shopping streets are: Via del Babuino, Via Condotti, Via Frattina, Via Vittorio Veneto; in Milan: Via Dante, Via Manzoni, Via Monte Napoleone, Corso Vittorio Emanuele, Via della Spiga.

BREAKDOWN SERVICE

Certain garages in the centre and outskirts of towns operate a 24 hour breakdown service. If you break down the police are usually able to help by indicating the nearest one.
A free car breakdown service (a tax is levied) is operated by the A.C.I. for foreign motorists carrying the fuel card (Carta Carburante). The A.C.I. also offers telephone information in English (24 hours a day) for road and weather conditions and tourist events: 06/4477.

TIPPING

As well as the service charge, it is the custom to tip employees. The amount can vary depending upon the region and the service given.

SPEED LIMITS

On motorways, the maximum permitted speed is 130 km/h - 80 mph for vehicles over 1000 cc, 110 km/h - 68 mph for all other vehicles. On other roads, the speed limit is 90 km/h - 56 mph.

ROME

(ROMA) *00100* 988 ㉖ 430 Q 19 – *Pop. 2 654 187 – alt. 20 –* ✪ *6.*

Distances from Rome are indicated in the text of the other towns listed in this Guide.

ℹ *via Parigi 5* ✉ *00185* ☎ *48 89 92 53, Fax 481 93 16 ; at Termini Station* ☎ *4871270 ; at Fiumicino Airport* ☎ *65956074.*

A.C.I. *via Cristoforo Colombo 261* ✉ *00147* ☎ *514 971 and via Marsala 8* ✉ *00185* ☎ *49981, Telex 610686, Fax 499 82 34.*

⛳18 *Parco de' Medici (closed Tuesday)* ✉ *00148 Roma SW : 4,5 km* ☎ *655 34 77 – Fax 655 33 44.*

⛳18 *(closed Monday) at Acquasanta* ✉ *00178 Roma SE : 12 km.* ☎ *78 34 07, Fax 78 34 62 19.*

⛳18 *and* ⛳18 *Marco Simone (closed Tuesday) at Guidonia Montecelio* ✉ *00012 Roma W : 7 km* ☎ *(0774) 366 469, Fax 366 476.*

⛳18 ⛳9 *Arco di Costantino (closed Tuesday)* ✉ *00188 Roma N : 15 km* ☎ *33 62 44 40, Fax 33 61 29 19*

⛳9 *and* ⛳18 *(closed Monday) at Olgiata* ✉ *00123 Roma NW : 19 km* ☎ *308 89 141, Fax 308 89 968.*

⛳9 *Fioranello (closed Wednesday) at Santa Maria delle Mole* ✉ *00040 Roma SE : 19 km* ☎ *713 80 80, Fax 713 82 12.*

✈ *Ciampino SW : 15 km* ☎ *794941 and Leonardo da Vinci di Fiumicino SE : 26 km* ☎ *65951 – Alitalia, via Bissolati 13* ✉ *00187* ☎ *46881 and via della Magliana 886* ✉ *00148* ☎ *65643.*

🚗 *Termini* ☎ *4775 – Tiburtina* ☎ *47301.*

SIGHTS

Rome's most famous sights are listed p 10. For a more complete visit use the Michelin Green Guide to Rome.

ROMA
NORTH CENTRE

Traffic restricted in the town centre

Altoviti (Lungotevere d.) . . . . . . **JV** 7
Banchi Nuovi (Via d.) . . . . **KV** 13
Banchi Vecchi (Via d.) . . . . **JKX** 15
Banco S. Spirito (Via d.) . . . . **JV** 16
Battisti (Via C.) . . . . NX
Calabria (Via) . . . . PU
Cappellari (Via d.) . . . . KX
Caravita (Via) . . . . MV
Castello (Lungotevere) . . . . KV

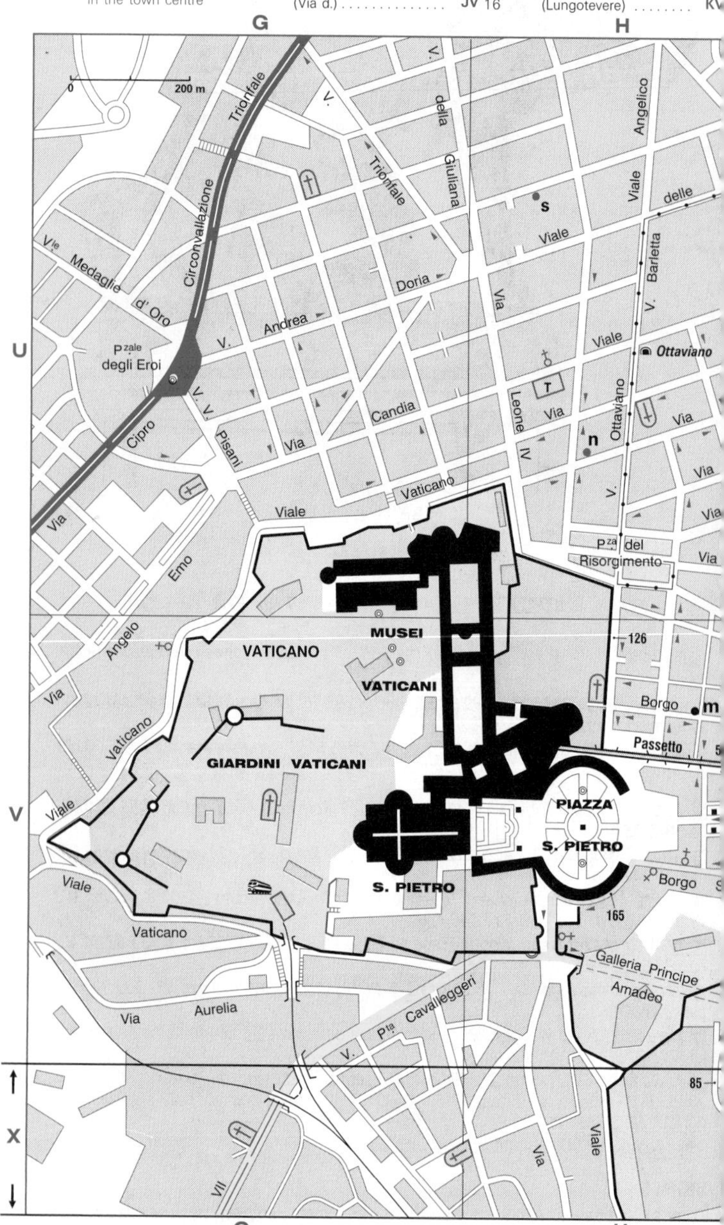

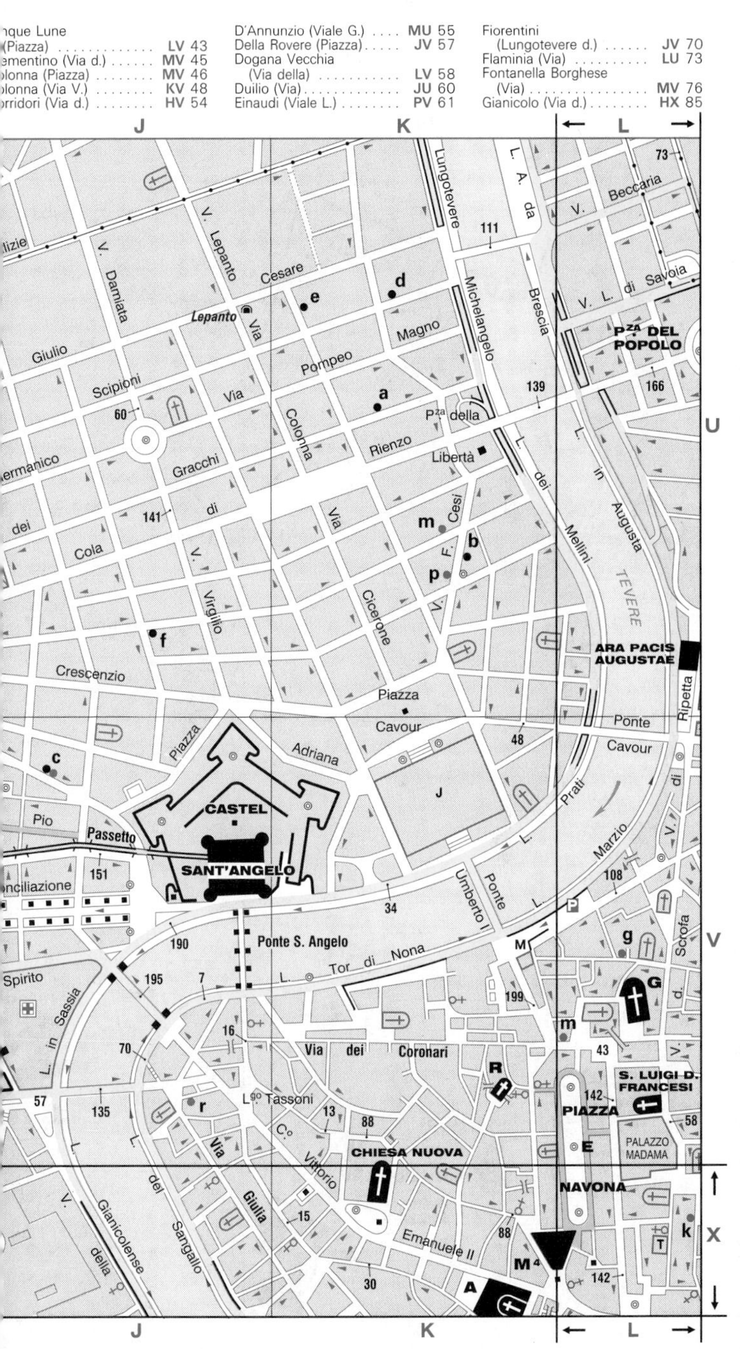

nque Lune
(Piazza) LV 43
ementino (Via d.) MV 45
olonna (Piazza) MV 46
olonna (Via V.) KV 48
orridori (Via d.) HV 54
D'Annunzio (Viale G.) MU 55
Della Rovere (Piazza) JV 57
Dogana Vecchia (Via della) LV 58
Duilio (Via) JU 60
Einaudi (Viale L.) PV 61
Fiorentini (Lungotevere d.) JV 70
Flaminia (Via) LU 73
Fontanella Borghese (Via) MV 76
Gianicolo (Via d.) HX 85
J
K
L
U
V
X
Lungotevere
L. A. da Brescia
V. Lepanto
V. Damiata
Cesare
Lepanto
Via
Giulio
Scipioni
Pompeo
Magno
Michelangelo
V. L. di Savoia
V. Beccaria
Pza DEL POPOLO
Via
Colonna
Pza della Libertà
Rienzo
Gracchi
Germanico
di
dei
Cola
V. Virgilio
Via
Cicerone
V. F. Cesi
L. dei Mellini
L. in Augusta
TEVERE
ARA PACIS AUGUSTAE
Ripetta
Crescenzio
Piazza Cavour
Piazza
Adriana
Ponte Cavour
L. Prati
Marzio
V. di
Scrofa
CASTEL SANT'ANGELO
Pio
Passetto
Conciliazione
Ponte S. Angelo
L. Tor di Nona
Ponte Umberto I
Spirito
L. in Sassia
Via dei Coronari
Lgo Tassoni
Co Vittorio Emanuele II
CHIESA NUOVA
Via Giulia
L. del Sangallo
V. della Gianicolense
S. LUIGI D. FRANCESI
PIAZZA NAVONA
PALAZZO MADAMA
111
73
139
166
60
141
48
108
34
190
195
7
151
16
199
43
142
58
70
57
135
13
88
15
30

Governo Vecchio
(Via d.) . . . . KVX 88
Lucania (Via) . . . . PU 94
Monte Brianzo (Via di) . . . LV 108
Nenni (Ponte P.) . . . . KU 111
Porta Angelica (Via di) . . . HV 126

Prinicpe A. Savoia
Aosta (Ponte . . . . JV 135
Quirinale
(Via d.) . . . . OV 138
Regina Margherita
(Ponte) . . . . KU 139

Regolo (Via A.) . . . . JU 1
Rinascimento
(Corso d.) . . . . LVX 1
Rotonda (Via) . . . . MX 1
S. Angelo (Borgo) . . . . . . JV 1
S. Chiara (Via) . . . . MX 1

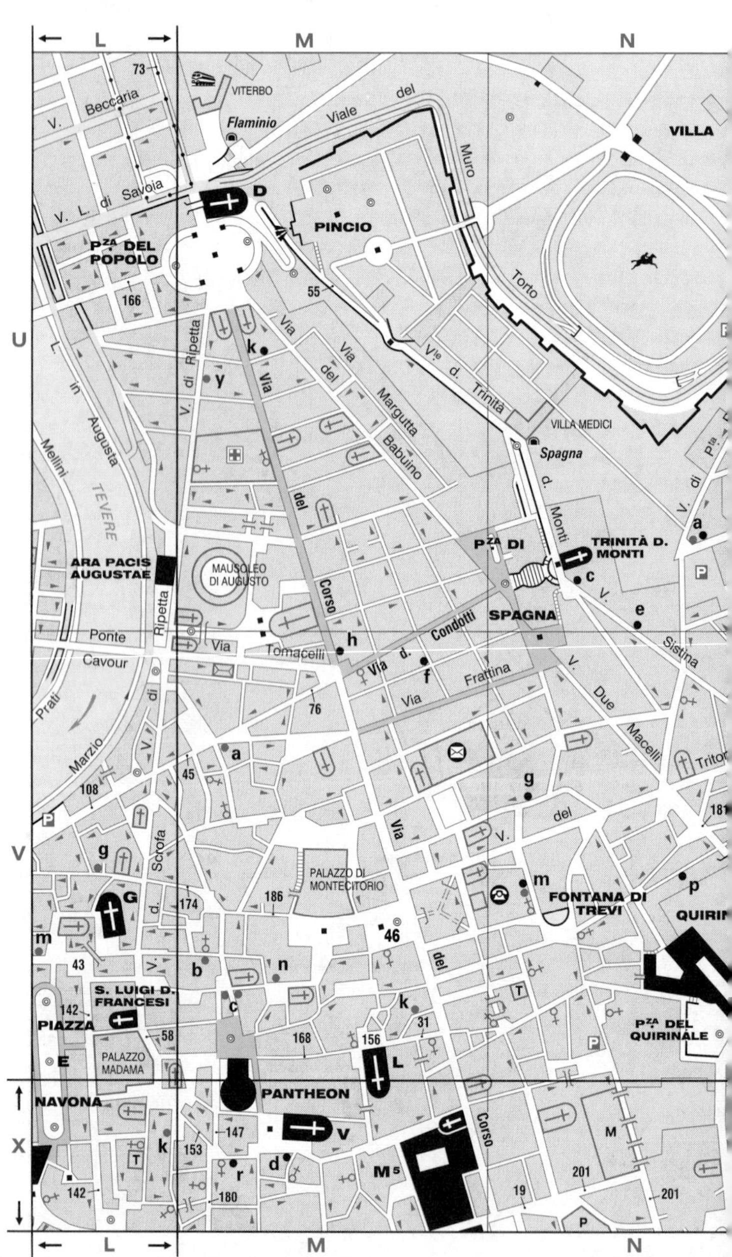

gnazio (Piazza) . . . . . . MV 156
Maria Maggiore
Via) . . . . PX 160
Uffizio (Via d.) . . . . HV 165
voia (Via F. di) . . . . LU 166
minario (Via d.) . . . . . . MV 168

Stelletta (Via d.) . . . . MV 174
Torre Argentina (Via) . . . .MXY 180
Traforo (Via d.) . . . . NV 181
Uffici del Vicario (Via) . . . MV 186
Vaticano
(Lungotevere) . . . . JV 190

Vittorio Emanuelle II
(Ponte) . . . . JV 195
Vittorio Emanuele Orlando (Via) PV 196
Volturno (Via) . . . . PV 198
Zanardelli (Via) . . . . KV 199
4 Novembre (Via) . . . . . . NX 201

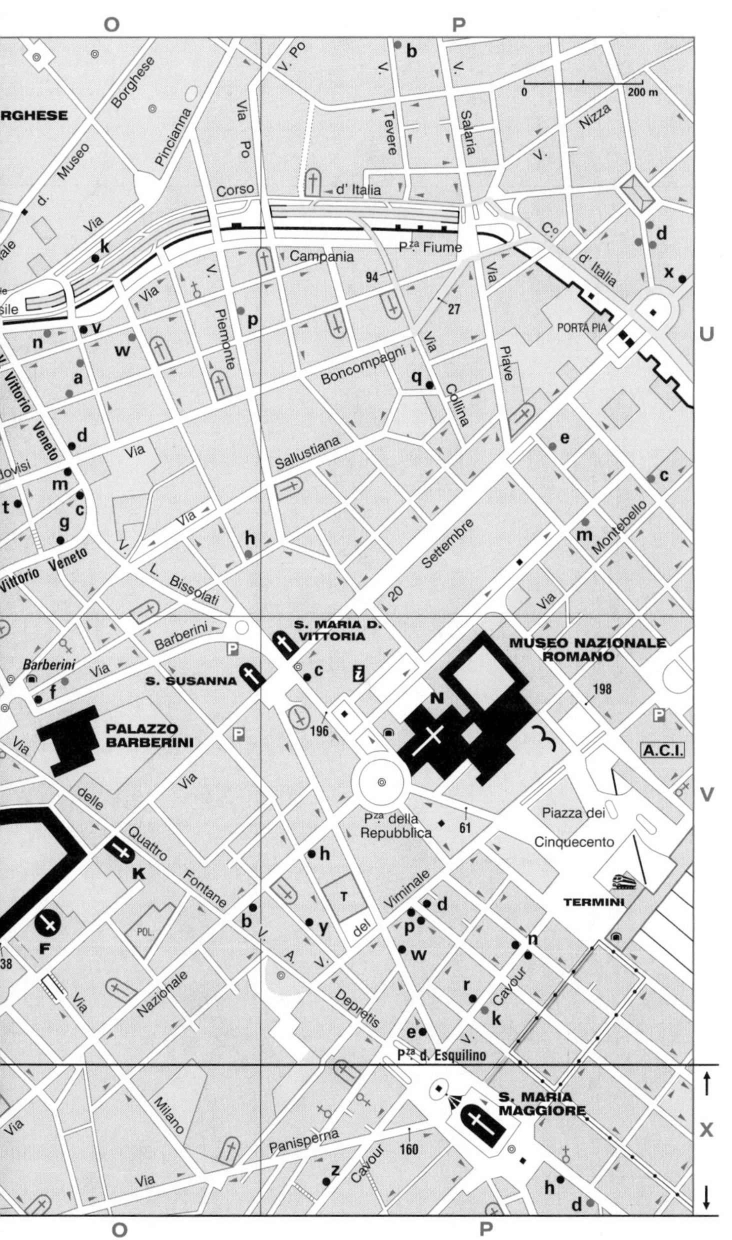

ROMA
SOUTH CENTRE

Traffic restricted
in the town centre

Alberteschi (Lungotevere) . . . . MZ 6
Anguillara (Lungotevere d.) . . . . . . LY 10
Banchi Vecchi (Via d.) . . . . JKX 15
Battisti (Via C.) . . . . NX
Belli (Piazza G. G.) . . . . LYZ
Botteghe Oscure Via d.) . . . . MY
Busiri-Vici (Via A.) . . . . HZ

…mpo dei Fiori (Piazza)	**KY** 28
…ppellari (Via d.)	**KX** 30
…nsolazione (Via d.)	**NY** 49
…riciq (Ponte)	**MY** 64
Florida (Via)	**MY** 75
Foro Olitorio (Via d.)	**MY** 78
Garibaldi (Ponte)	**LY** 81
Gianicolo (Via d.)	**HX** 85
Governo Vecchio (Via d.)	**KVX** 88
Greca (Via d.)	**MZ** 90
Jugario (Vico)	**MY** 91
Lungaretta (Via d.)	**KZ** 96
Mascherone (Via d.)	**KY** 103
Massina (Via A.)	**JZ** 105

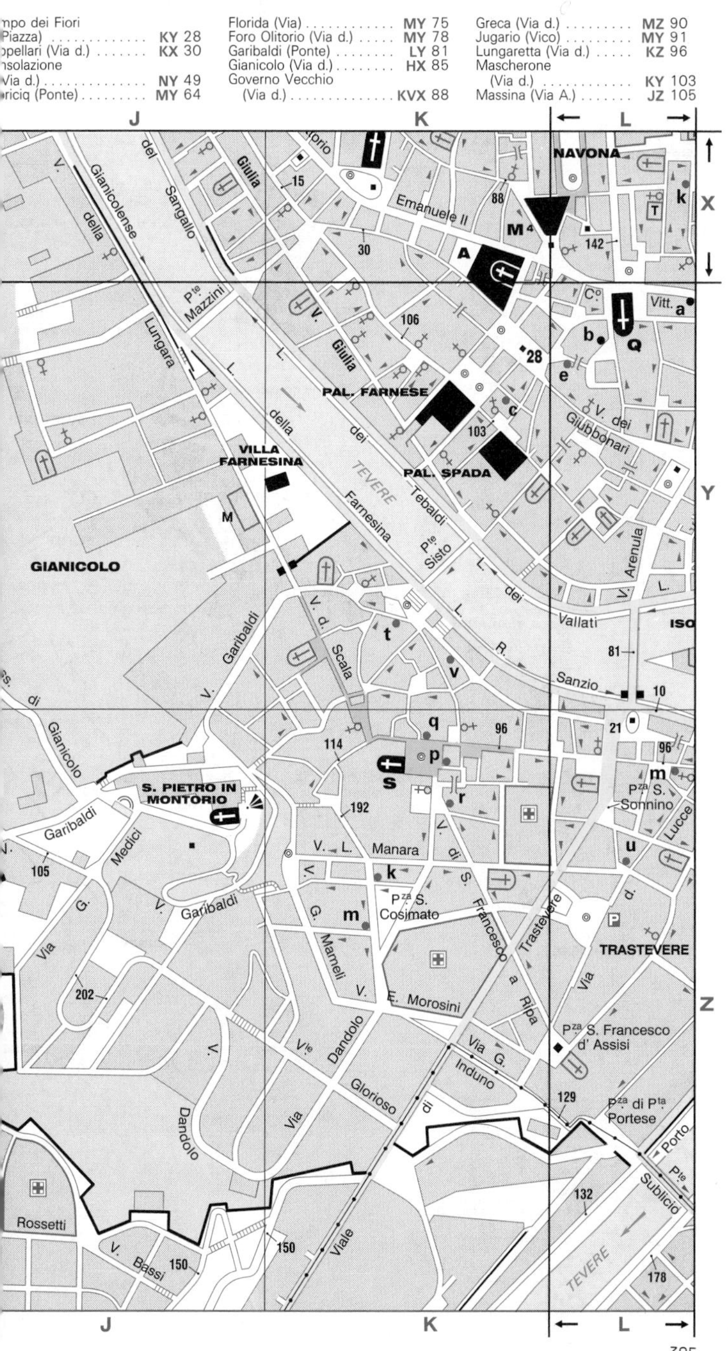

Monserrato		
(Via)	KY	106
Paglia (Via d.)	KZ	114
Pierleoni		
(Lungotevere d.)	MZ	117
Plebiscito (Via d.)	MY	121
Porta Lavernale (Via)	MZ	127
Porta Portese (Via di)	LZ	129
Portico d'Ottavia		
(Via)	MY	130
Portuense		
(Lungotevere)	LZ	132
Publicii		
(Clivo d.)	NZ	1
Rinascimento		
(Corso d.)	LVX	1
Rotonda (Via)	MX	1
Saffi (Viale A.)	JKZ	1

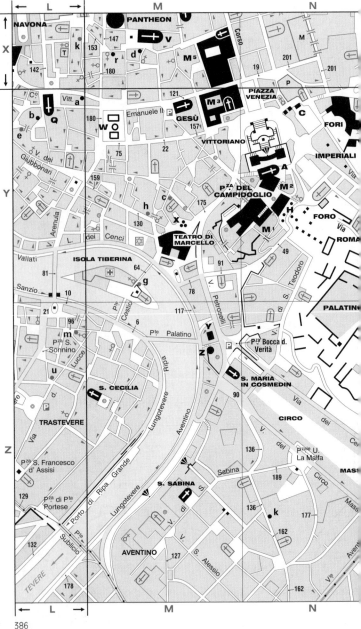

Chiara (Via) .... MX 153
Marco (Via) .... MY 157
Maria del Pianto (Via) .... MY 159
Maria Maggiore (Via) . PX 160
Prisca (Via di) .... NZ 162
Sprovieri (Via F. S.) ..... HZ 171
Teatro di Marcello (Via d.) .... MY 175
Terme Deciane (Via d.) .. NZ 177
Testaccio (Lungotevere) .... LZ 178
Torre Argentina (Via) .... MXY 180
Valle Murcia (Via di) .... NZ 189
Venezian (Via G.) ...... KZ 192
4 Novembre (Via) ...... NX 201
30 Aprile (Viale) .... JZ 202

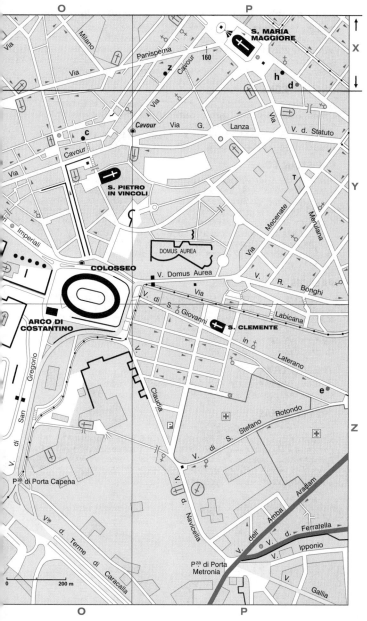

Sights

How to make the most of a trip to Rome – some ideas :

Borghese Museum★★★ – *Villa Giulia*★★★ – *Catacombs*★★★ – *Santa Sabina*★★ MZ – *Villa Borghese*★★ NOU – *Baths of Caracalla*★★ – *St Lawrence Without the Walls*★★ – *St Paul Without the Walls*★★ – *Old Appian Way*★★ – *National Gallery of Modern Art*★ – *Mausoleum of Caius Cestius*★ – *St Paul's Gate*★ – *San'Agnese and Santa Costanza*★ – *Santa Croce in Gerusalemme*★ – *San Saba*★ – *E.U.R.*★ – *Museum of Roman Civilisation*★.

ANCIENT ROME

Colosseum★★★ OYZ – *Roman Forum*★★★ NOY – *Basilica of Maxentius*★★★ OY **B** – *Imperial Fora*★★★ NY – *Trajan's Column*★★★ NY **C** – *Palatine Hill*★★★ NOYZ – *Pantheon*★★★ MVX – *Largo Argentina Sacred Precinct*★★ MY **W** – *Altar of Augustus*★★ LU – *Temple of Apollo Sosianus*★★ MY **X** – Theatre of Marcellus★★ MY – *Tempio della Fortuna Virile*★ MZ **Y** – *Tempio di Vesta*★ MZ **Z** – *Isola Tiberina*★ MY.

CHRISTIAN ROME

Gesù Church★★★ MY – *St Mary Major*★★★ PX – *St John Lateran*★★★ – *Santa Maria d'Aracoeli*★★ NY **A** – *San Luigi dei Francesi*★★ LV – *Sant'Andrea al Quirinale*★★ OV **F** – *St Charles at the Four Fountains*★★ OV **K** – *St Clement's Basilica*★★ PZ – *Sant'Ignazio*★★ MV **L** – *Santa Maria degli Angeli*★★ PV **N** – *Santa Maria della Vittoria*★★ PV – *Santa Susanna*★★ OV – *Santa Maria in Cosmedin*★★ MNZ – *Basilica of St Mary in Trastevere*★★ KZ **S** – *Santa Maria sopra Minerva*★★ MX **V** – *Santa Maria del Popolo*★ MU **D** – *New Church*★ KX – *Sant'Agostino*★ LV **G** – *St Peter in Chains*★ OY – *Santa Cecilia*★ MZ – *San Pietro in Montorio*★ JZ ⋞★★★ – *Sant'Andrea della Valle*★ LY **Q** – *Santa Maria della Pace*★ KV **R**.

PALACES AND MUSEUMS

Conservators' Palace★★★ MNY **M**[1] – *New Palace*★★★ *(Capitoline Museum*★★*)* NY **M**[1] – *Senate House*★★★ NY **H** – *Castel Sant'Angelo*★★★ JKV – *National Roman Museum*★★★ PV – *Chancery Palace*★★ KX **A** – *Palazzo Farnese*★★ KY – *Quirinal Palace*★★ NOV – *Barberini Palace*★★ OV – *Villa Farnesina*★★ KY – *Palazzo Venezia*★ MY **M**[3] – *Palazzo Braschi*★ KX **M**[4] – *Palazzo Doria Pamphili*★ MX **M**[5] – *Palazzo Spada*★ KY – *Museo Napoleanico*★.

THE VATICAN

St Peter's Square★★★ HV – *St Peter's Basilica*★★★ *(Dome* ⋞★★★*)* GV – *Vatican Museums*★★★ *(Sistine Chapel*★★★*)* GHUV – *Vatican Gardens*★★★ GV.

PRETTY AREAS

Pincian Hill ⋞★★★ MU – *Capitol Square*★★★ MNY – *Spanish Square*★★★ MNU – *Piazza Navona*★★★ LVX – *Fountain of the Rivers*★★★ LV **E** – Trevi Fountain★★★ NV – *Victor Emmanuel II Monument (Vittoriano)* ⋞★★ MNY – *Quirinale Square*★★ NV – *Piazza del Popolo*★★ MU – *Gianicolo*★ JY – *Via dei Coronari*★ KV – *Ponte Sant'Angelo*★ JKV – *Piazza Bocca della Verità*★ MNZ – *Piazza Campo dei Fiori*★ KY **28** – *Piazza Colonna*★ MV **46** – *Porta Maggiore*★ – *Piazza Venezia*★ MNY.

Historical Centre corso Vittorio Emanuele, piazza Venezia, Pantheon e Quirinale, piazza di Spagna, piazza Navona

Hassler, piazza Trinità dei Monti 6 ✉ 00187 ☎ 6993401, Telex 610208, Fax 6789991, ≤ City from roof-garden rest. – 70. AE VISA JCB. NU c
Meals *(closed Sunday dinner)* a la carte 140/205000 – 48000 – **85 rm** 470/950000, 15 suites.

Holiday Inn Minerva M, piazza della Minerva 69 ✉ 00186 ☎ 69941888, Telex 620091, Fax 6794165, « Terrace with ≤ » – rm – 120. AE VISA JCB. MX d
Meals a la carte 70/120000 – 34000 – **131 rm** 450/600000, 3 suites.

De la Ville Inter-Continental, via Sistina 69 ✉ 00187 ☎ 67331, Fax 6784213, – 70. AE VISA JCB. NU e
Meals 75/110000 – **169 rm** 540/675000, 23 suites.

D'Inghilterra, via Bocca di Leone 14 ✉ 00187 ☎ 69981, Telex 614552, Fax 69922243, « Former boarding house traditional furnishings » – AE VISA.
Meals a la carte 80/130000 – 30000 – **95 cam** 400/575000, 10 suites. MV f

Dei Borgognoni without rest., via del Bufalo 126 ✉ 00187 ☎ 69941505, Telex 623074, Fax 69941501 – – 70. AE VISA JCB.
20000 – **50 rm** 390/470000. NV g

Plaza without rest., via del Corso 126 ✉ 00186 ☎ 69921111, Telex 624669, Fax 69941575, « Floral terrace with ≤ » – – 60. AE VISA JCB
40000 – **195 rm** 370/540000, 12 suites. MV h

Valadier, via della Fontanella 15 ✉ 00187 ☎ 3611998 and rest. ☎ 3610880, Telex 620873, Fax 3201558, – – 35. AE VISA JCB. rest
Meals ***Valentino*** Rest. a la carte 40/75000 – **38 rm** 390/490000, 4 suites. MU k

Delle Nazioni, via Poli 7 ✉ 00187 ☎ 6792441, Telex 614193, Fax 6782400 – – 50. AE VISA JCB. NV m
Meals (see rest. ***Le Grondici*** below) – 25000 – **83 rm** 320/400000.

White M without rest., via Arcione 77 ✉ 00187 ☎ 6991242, Telex 626065, Fax 6788451 – – 40. AE VISA. NV p
40 rm 280/350000.

Santa Chiara without rest., via Santa Chiara 21 ✉ 00186 ☎ 6872979, Fax 6873144 – – 40. AE VISA JCB. MX r
93 rm 245/340000, 3 suites.

Della Torre Argentina without rest., corso Vittorio Emanuele 102 ✉ 00186 ☎ 6833886, Fax 68801641 – AE VISA JCB. LY a
52 rm 215/305000, suite.

Teatro di Pompeo without rest., largo del Pallaro 8 ✉ 00186 ☎ 68300170, Fax 68805531, « Vaults of Pompeius' theatre » – – 30. AE VISA. LY b
12 rm 200/260000.

El Toulà, via della Lupa 29/b ✉ 00186 ☎ 6873498, Fax 6871115, Elegant rest. – AE VISA JCB. MV a
closed Saturday lunch, Sunday, August and 24 to 26 December – **Meals** (booking essential) a la carte 75/110000 (15 %).

Enoteca Capranica, piazza Capranica 100 ✉ 00186 ☎ 69940992, Fax 69940989 – AE VISA JCB. MV n
closed Saturday lunch and Sunday – **Meals** (booking essential for dinner) 50000 (lunch only) and a la carte 60/80000.

Camponeschi, piazza Farnese 50 ✉ 00186 ☎ 6874927, Fax 6865244, « Summer service with ≤ Farnese palace » – AE VISA. KY c
closed Sunday and 13 to 22 August – **Meals** (dinner only) (booking essential) a la carte 80/110000 (13 %).

Vecchia Roma, via della Tribuna di Campitelli 18 ✉ 00186 ☎ 6864604, , Typical Roman rest. with local and seafood specialities – AE MY c
closed Wednesday and 10 to 25 August – **Meals** a la carte 70/105000 (12 %).

Quinzi Gabrieli, via delle Coppelle 6 ✉ 00186 ☎ 6879389, Fax 6874940, Seafood – AE VISA. MV b
closed Sunday and August – **Meals** (dinner only) (booking essential) a la carte 90/130000
Spec. Carpaccio misto di mare. Spaghetti al granchio peloso. Ombrina al pepe verde e Cerasuolo napoletano.

La Rosetta, via della Rosetta 9 ✉ 00187 ☎ 6861002, Fax 6872852, Seafood – AE VISA JCB MV c
closed Saturday lunch, Sunday and 5 to 25 August – **Meals** (booking essential) a la carte 95/140000.

Le Grondici, via del Mortaro 14 ✉ 00187 ℰ 6795761 – AE E VISA NV
closed Sunday – **Meals** a la carte 50/85000.

Il Convivio, via dell'Orso 44 ✉ 00186 ℰ 6869432, Fax 6869432 – AE E JCB LV
closed Sunday – **Meals** (booking essential) a la carte 90/145000
Spec. Insalata di girello di bue con caciocavallo, ruchetta e tartufo nero. Cavatelli pesce spada affumicato, melanzane e pesto. Rombo in crosta di asparagi con zabaion limone.

Eau Vive, via Monterone 85 ✉ 00186 ℰ 68801095, Fax 68802571, Catholic mis naries, french cuisine, « 16C building » – AE E VISA. LX
closed Sunday and August – **Meals** (booking essential for dinner) 15/30000 and a la ca 45/65000.

Taverna Giulia, vicolo dell'Oro 23 ✉ 00186 ℰ 6869768, Fax 6893720, Ligurian r – AE E VISA JCB. JV
closed Sunday and August – **Meals** (booking essential for dinner) a la carte 50/700

Passetto, via Zanardelli 14 ✉ 00186 ℰ 68806569, Fax 68806569 – AE E JCB. LV
Meals a la carte 70/135000.

Da Pancrazio, piazza del Biscione 92 ✉ 00186 ℰ 6861246, Fax 6861246, « Inn reb on the remains of Pompeius' theatre » – AE E VISA JCB. LY
closed Wednesday, 1 to 20 August and Christmas – **Meals** a la carte 50/80000.

Da Giggetto, via del Portico d'Ottavia 21/a ✉ 00186 ℰ 6861105, Roman tratt – AE E VISA. MY
closed Monday and 15 to 30 July – **Meals** a la carte 50/70000.

Il Falchetto, via del Montecatini 12/14 ✉ 00186 ℰ 6791160, Rustic trattoria – E VISA MV
closed Friday and 5 to 20 August – **Meals** a la carte 45/65000.

La Buca di Ripetta, via di Ripetta 36 ✉ 00186 ℰ 3219391, Habitués rest. – MU
closed Sunday dinner, Monday and August – **Meals** a la carte 40/55000.

Termini Railway Station via Vittorio Veneto, via Nazionale, Viminale, Santa M Maggiore, Porta Pia

Excelsior, via Vittorio Veneto 125 ✉ 00187 ℰ 47081, Telex 610232, Fax 48262 rm – 600. AE E VISA JCB. rest OU
Meals a la carte 85/155000 – 54000 – **282 rm** 465/705000, 45 suites.

Le Grand Hotel, via Vittorio Emanuele Orlando 3 ✉ 00185 ℰ 47091, Telex 6102 Fax 4747307 – 300. AE E VISA JCB. PV
Meals a la carte 125/175000 – 33000 – **134 rm** 465/705000, 36 suites.

Eden, via Ludovisi 49 ✉ 00187 ℰ 478121, Fax 4821584, – 100. AE E VISA JCB. NU
Meals (see rest. **La Terrazza** below) – 45000 – **92 rm** 500/770000, 11 suites.

Majestic, via Vittorio Veneto 50 ✉ 00187 ℰ 486841, Telex 622262, Fax 488098 – 150. AE E VISA JCB. OU
Meals a la carte 70/125000 – **88 rm** 470/560000, 6 suites.

Bernini Bristol, piazza Barberini 23 ✉ 00187 ℰ 4883051, Telex 610554, Fax 4824 – rm – 100. AE E VISA JCB. rest OV
Meals a la carte 85/115000 – 32000 – **110 rm** 400/595000, 16 suites.

Ambasciatori Palace, via Vittorio Veneto 62 ✉ 00187 ℰ 47493, Telex 6102 Fax 4743601, – 200. AE E VISA JCB. rest OU
Meals *(closed Saturday dinner and Sunday)* a la carte 75/115000 – 25000 – **100** 380/550000, 8 suites.

Regina Baglioni, via Vittorio Veneto 72 ✉ 00187 ℰ 476851, Fax 485483 – 40. AE E VISA. OU
Meals *(closed Sunday)* a la carte 60/110000 – **130 rm** 390/560000, 7 suites.

Jolly Vittorio Veneto, corso d'Italia 1 ✉ 00198 ℰ 8495, Telex 612293, Fax 8841 – rm – 400. AE E VISA. rest OU
Meals *(closed Sunday dinner and August)* a la carte 60/110000 – **200 rm** 355/435 3 suites.

Quirinale, via Nazionale 7 ✉ 00184 ℰ 4707, Telex 610332, Fax 4820099, « Sum service rest. in the garden » – 250. AE E VISA PV
Meals a la carte 70/105000 – **198 rm** 300/400000, 3 suites.

Grand Hotel Palace, via Veneto 70 ✉ 00187 ℰ 478719, Fax 47871800 – 200. AE E VISA. OU
Meals a la carte 60/105000 – **92 rm** 420/580000, 3 suites.

Artemide without rest., via Nazionale 22 ✉ 00184 ☎ 489911, Telex 623061, Fax 48991700 – 110. AE VISA JCB. OV b
80 rm 320/460000, 5 suites.

Mecenate Palace Hotel without rest., via Carlo Alberto 3 ✉ 00185 ☎ 44702024, Fax 4461354 – 30. AE VISA JCB. PX h
59 rm 350/470000, 3 suites.

Starhotel Metropole, via Principe Amedeo 3 ✉ 00185 ☎ 4774, Telex 611061, Fax 4740413 – 200. AE VISA JCB. rest PV p
Meals a la carte 65/105000 – **269 rm** 370/480000.

Londra e Cargill, piazza Sallustio 18 ✉ 00187 ☎ 473871, Telex 622227, Fax 4746674 – 200. AE VISA. PU q
Meals *(closed Saturday, Sunday lunch and August)* a la carte 45/65000 – **104 rm** 300/390000, 6 suites.

Victoria, via Campania 41 ✉ 00187 ☎ 473931, Telex 610212, Fax 4871890, « Terrace roof-garden » – 30. AE VISA. rest OU v
Meals 45000 – **108 rm** 250/350000.

Mediterraneo, via Cavour 15 ✉ 00184 ☎ 4884051, Fax 4744105 – 90. AE VISA JCB. PV n
Meals *(closed Saturday) (dinner only)* 40/50000 – **251 rm** 355/470000, 11 suites.

Imperiale, via Vittorio Veneto 24 ✉ 00187 ☎ 4826351, Telex 621071, Fax 4826351 – AE VISA. OV s
Meals 65000 – **95 rm** 370/520000.

Genova without rest., via Cavour 33 ✉ 00184 ☎ 476951, Telex 621599, Fax 4827580 – AE VISA JCB. PV r
91 rm 295/400000.

Universo, via Principe Amedeo 5 ✉ 00185 ☎ 476811, Telex 610342, Fax 4745125 – 300. AE VISA JCB PV p
Meals 55000 – **198 rm** 255/360000.

Sofitel, via Lombardia 47 ✉ 00187 ☎ 478021 and rest. ☎ 4818965, Telex 622247, Fax 4821019 – rm 90. AE VISA JCB. NU s
Meals a la carte 50/80000 – **124 rm** 350/480000.

La Residenza without rest., via Emilia 22 ✉ 00187 ☎ 4880789, Fax 485721 – AE VISA OU t
28 rm 130/295000.

Massimo D'Azeglio, via Cavour 18 ✉ 00184 ☎ 4870270, Telex 610556, Fax 4827386 – 200. AE VISA JCB. PV n
Meals *(closed Sunday)* 40/50000 – **203 rm** 315/420000.

Eliseo without rest., via di Porta Pinciana 30 ✉ 00187 ☎ 4870456, Fax 4819629 – 25. AE VISA JCB. OU u
51 rm 250/400000, 7 suites.

Britannia without rest., via Napoli 64 ✉ 00184 ☎ 4883153, Telex 611292, Fax 4882343 – AE VISA JCB PV y
32 rm 230/330000.

Napoleon without rest., piazza Vittorio Emanuele 105 ✉ 00185 ☎ 4467264, Telex 611069, Fax 4467282 – 80. AE VISA.
79 rm 230/330000. by via Cavour PVX

Rex without rest., via Torino 149 ✉ 00184 ☎ 4824828, Fax 4882743 – 50. AE VISA JCB PV w
50 rm 260/340000, 2 suites.

Barocco without rest., via della Purificazione 4 angolo piazza Barberini ✉ 00187 ☎ 4872001, Fax 485994 – AE VISA JCB. OV a
28 rm 320/420000.

Commodore without rest., via Torino 1 ✉ 00184 ☎ 485656, Telex 612170, Fax 4747562 – 30. AE. PV e
60 rm 275/410000.

Diana, via Principe Amedeo 4 ✉ 00185 ☎ 4827541, Telex 611198, Fax 486998 – 25. AE VISA JCB. PV d
Meals (residents only) 40000 – **183 rm** 205/290000, 2 suites.

Turner without rest., via Nomentana 29 ✉ 00161 ☎ 44250077, Fax 44250165 – AE VISA JCB. PU x
37 rm 245/290000.

La Terrazza - Hotel Eden, via Ludovisi 49 ✉ 00187 ☎ 478121, Fax 4821584, « Roof-garden with ≤ town » – AE VISA JCB. NU a
Meals a la carte 90/160000
Spec. Medaglioni d'astice con favette e radicchio marinato al timo. Risotto "Regina Vittoria" (scampi e champagne). Filetto di rombo al forno con limone e capperi.

XXXX ✿ **Sans Souci,** via Sicilia 20/24 ✉ 00187 ☎ 4821814, Fax 4821771, Elegant tavern, night dinners – ▤. AE ⓢ ⓞ E VISA JCB. ✂ OU
closed Monday and 6 August-3 September – **Meals** (dinner only) (booking essential) carte 90/150000
Spec. Terrina di foie gras tartufata. Spaghetti all'astice e pomodorini freschi. An all'arancia.

XXX **Grappolo d'Oro,** via Palestro 4/10 ✉ 00185 ☎ 4941441, Fax 4452350 – ▤. AE ⓞ E VISA JCB PU
closed Sunday and August – **Meals** 30/50000 (lunch) and a la carte 45/65000.

XX **Agata e Romeo,** via Carlo Alberto 45 ✉ 00185 ☎ 4466115, Fax 4465842 – ▤ ⓢ ⓞ E VISA JCB. ✂ PX
closed Sunday, August and 26 December-6 January – **Meals** (booking essential) a la ca 75/120000.

XX **Edoardo,** via Lucullo 2 ✉ 00187 ☎ 486428, Fax 486428 – ▤. AE ⓢ ⓞ E VISA. OU
closed Sunday and August – **Meals** a la carte 65/85000 (15 %).

XX **Giovanni,** via Marche 64 ✉ 00187 ☎ 4821834, Fax 4817366, Habitués rest. – ▤ ⓢ ⓞ E VISA OU
closed Friday dinner, Saturday and August – **Meals** a la carte 60/90000.

XX **Cicilardone Monte Caruso,** via Farini 12 ✉ 00185 ☎ 483549 – AE ⓢ ⓞ E ✂ PV
closed Sunday, Monday lunch and August – **Meals** a la carte 60/100000.

XX **Cesarina,** via Piemonte 109 ✉ 00187 ☎ 4880073, Fax 4880828, Bolognese rest. – AE ⓢ ⓞ E VISA. ✂ OU
closed Sunday – **Meals** a la carte 45/80000.

XX **Girarrosto Toscano,** via Campania 29 ✉ 00187 ☎ 4823835, Fax 4821899 – ▤ ⓢ ⓞ E VISA JCB. ✂ OU
closed Wednesday – **Meals** a la carte 50/95000.

XX **Dai Toscani,** via Forlè 41 ✉ 00161 ☎ 44231302, Tuscan rest. – ▤. AE ⓢ E V
closed Sunday and August – **Meals** a la carte 50/70000. by via 20 Settembre PU

XX **Mangrovia,** via Milazzo 6/a ✉ 00185 ☎ 4452755, Fax 4959204, Seafood – ▤. AE ⓞ VISA JCB. ✂ by via Volturno PV
Meals a la carte 40/65000.

XX **Tullio,** via San Nicola da Tolentino 26 ✉ 00187 ☎ 4745560, Fax 4818564, Tuscan t toria with spit – ▤. AE ⓢ ⓞ E VISA JCB. ✂ OV
closed Sunday and August – **Meals** a la carte 60/80000.

XX **Papà Baccus,** via Toscana 36 ✉ 00187 ☎ 42742808, Fax 42742808, Tuscan seafood specialities – ▤. AE ⓢ ⓞ E VISA JCB. ✂ OU
closed Saturday lunch, Sunday, 10 to 20 August and 1 to 10 January – **Meals** (book essential) a la carte 60/85000.

XX **Hostaria da Vincenzo,** via Castelfidardo 6 ✉ 00185 ☎ 484596, Fax 4870092 – AE ⓢ ⓞ E VISA PU
closed Sunday and August – **Meals** a la carte 40/70000.

XX **Peppone,** via Emilia 60 ✉ 00187 ☎ 483976, Fax 483976, Traditional rest. – AE ⓢ E VISA. ✂ OU
closed Saturday in August and Sunday – **Meals** a la carte 45/75000 (15 %).

X **Trimani il Wine Bar,** via Cernaia 37/b ✉ 00185 ☎ 4469630, Fax 4468351, Wine with restaurant services quickly meals – ▤. AE ⓢ ⓞ E VISA JCB PU
closed Sunday and 11 to 17 August – **Meals** a la carte 40/60000.

Ancient Rome Colosseo, Fori Imperiali, Aventino, Terme di Caracalla, Porta San Pa Monte Testaccio

🏨 **Forum,** via Tor de' Conti 25 ✉ 00184 ☎ 6792446, Telex 622549, Fax 67864 « Roof-garden rest. with ≤ Imperial Forum » – 🛗 ▤ TV ☎ 🚗 – 🔺 100. AE ⓢ ⓞ VISA JCB. ✂ OY
Meals *(closed Sunday)* a la carte 80/130000 – **81 rm** ☐ 290/440000.

🏨 **Borromeo** without rest., via Cavour 117 ✉ 00184 ☎ 485856, Fax 4882541 – 🛗 TV ☎ ♿. AE ⓢ ⓞ E VISA JCB. ✂ PX
28 rm ☐ 220/290000, suite.

🏨 **Piccadilly** without rest., via Magna Grecia 122 ✉ 00183 ☎ 77207017, Fax 70476 – ⇆ ▤ TV ☎. AE ⓢ ⓞ E VISA. ✂ by via Gallia PZ
55 rm ☐ 170/230000.

🏨 **Duca d'Alba** without rest., via Leonina 12/14 ✉ 00184 ☎ 484471, Telex 6204 Fax 4884840 – 🛗 ▤ TV ☎. AE ⓢ ⓞ E VISA JCB OY
☐ 15000 – **24 rm** 140/190000.

Domus Aventina without rest., via Santa Prisca 11/b 00153 5746135, Fax 57300044 – . AE E VISA JCB. NZ k
26 rm 180/270000.

Nerva without rest., via Tor de' Conti 3/4/4 a 00184 6781835, Fax 69922204 – . AE E VISA JCB. NY h
18000 – **19 rm** 220/325000.

Checchino dal 1887, via Monte Testaccio 30 00153 5743816, Fax 5743816, Historical building, typical Roman cuisine – AE E VISA.
closed August, 24 December-3 January, Sunday dinner and Monday, also Sunday lunch June-September – **Meals** (booking essential) a la carte 65/90000
Spec. Bucatini alla gricia, Coda alla vaccinara, Abbachio alla cacciatora.
by lungotevere Aventino MZ

Charly's Sauciere, via di San Giovanni in Laterano 270 00184 70495666, Fax 70494700, French-Swiss rest. – . AE E VISA JCB PZ e
closed 5 to 20 August, Sunday and lunch of Saturday-Monday – **Meals** (booking essential) a la carte 50/70000.

Mario's Hostaria, piazza del Grillo 9 00184 6793725, – . AE E VISA. NY b
closed Saturday lunch and Sunday – **Meals** (booking essential) a la carte 40/85000.

St. Peter's Basilica (Vatican City) Gianicolo, Monte Mario, Stadio Olimpico

Cavalieri Hilton M, via Cadlolo 101 00136 35091, Telex 625337, Fax 35092241, city, , « Terraces-solarium and park with », – – 2100. AE E VISA JCB. rest by via Trionfale GU
Meals a la carte 70/120000 see also rest. ***La Pergola*** – 37000 – **359 rm** 380/570000, 17 suites.

Jolly Leonardo da Vinci, via dei Gracchi 324 00192 32499, Telex 611182, Fax 3610138 – rm – 220. AE E VISA JCB. rest KU a
Meals 60000 – **256 rm** 350/400000, 2 suites.

Visconti Palace without rest., via Federico Cesi 37 00193 3684, Telex 622489, Fax 3200551 – – 150. AE E VISA JCB. KU b
234 rm 300/400000, 13 suites.

Atlante Star, via Vitelleschi 34 00193 6873233, Telex 622355, Fax 6872300 – – 50. AE E VISA JCB JV c
Meals (see rest. ***Les Etoiles*** below) – **61 rm** 390/490000, 3 suites.

Farnese, without rest., via Alessandro Farnese 30 00192 3212553, Fax 3215129 – KU e
22 rm.

Giulio Cesare without rest., via degli Scipioni 287 00192 3210751, Telex 613010, Fax 3211736, – – 40. AE E VISA JCB. KU d
90 rm 280/380000.

Sant'Anna without rest., borgo Pio 133 00193 68801602, Fax 68308717 – . AE E VISA JCB HV m
20 rm 200/270000.

Arcangelo without rest., via Boezio 15 00192 6874143, Fax 6893050 – . AE E VISA. JU f
33 rm 190/250000.

La Pergola - Hotel Cavalieri Hilton, via Cadlolo 101 00136 35091 – AE E VISA JCB. by via Trionfale GU
closed Sunday, Monday and January – **Meals** (dinner only) a la carte 90/145000.

Les Etoiles - Hotel Atlante Star, via dei Bastioni 1 00193 6893434, « Roof-garden and summer service on terrace with St. Peter's Basilica » – . AE E VISA JCB.
Meals 70/120000 (lunch) 90/170000 (dinner) and a la carte 105/155000. JV c

Lo Squalo Bianco, via Federico Cesi 36 00193 3214700, Seafood – . AE E VISA. KU p
closed Sunday – **Meals** (booking essential) a la carte 45/70000.

Da Enzo, via Ennio Quirino Visconti 39/41 00193 3215743 – . AE E VISA JCB. KU m
closed Sunday and August – **Meals** a la carte 50/80000.

Dal Toscano-al Girarrosto, via Germanico 58 00192 39725717, Habitués rest. and Tuscan specialities – . AE E VISA HU n
closed Monday and August – **Meals** a la carte 45/70000.

Taverna Angelica, piazza delle Vaschette 14/a 00193 6874514, After theatre restaurant, open until late – . AE E VISA. JV t
closed Saturday lunch, Sunday, 10 to 30 August and 23 December-3 January – **Meals** (booking essential) a la carte 45/85000.

Parioli via Flaminia, Villa Borghese, Villa Glori, via Nomentana, via Salaria

Lord Byron, via De Notaris 5 ✉ 00197 ℘ 3220404, Telex 611217, Fax 322(– AE VISA JCB. by lungotevere A. da Brescia K
Meals (see rest. ***Relais le Jardin*** below) – **28 rm** 480/580000, 9 suites.

Aldrovandi Palace Hotel, via Aldrovandi 15 ✉ 00197 ℘ 3223993, Telex 616 Fax 3221435, « Small shaded park » – 350. AE JCB. by via Flaminia L
Meals (see rest. ***Relais La Piscine*** below) – **128 rm** 550/600000, 10 suites.

Parco dei Principi, via Gerolamo Frescobaldi 5 ✉ 00198 ℘ 854421, Telex 610 Fax 8845104, « Small botanical park with » – 1 AE VISA. by via Pinciana O
Meals 60000 – **165 rm** 290/430000, 15 suites.

Albani, via Adda 45 ✉ 00198 ℘ 84991, Telex 625594, Fax 8499399 – 80. AE VISA JCB. by via Salaria P
Meals a la carte 40/75000 – **155 rm** 285/400000.

Polo without rest., piazza Gastaldi 4 ✉ 00197 ℘ 3221041, Telex 623107, Fax 322 – 70. AE VISA. by lungotevere A. da Brescia K
66 rm 375/405000.

Degli Aranci, via Oriani 11 ✉ 00197 ℘ 8070202, Fax 8070704 – AE VISA. by lungotevere A. da Brescia K
Meals 35000 – 15000 – **54 rm** 235/330000.

Villa Glori without rest., via Celentano 11 ✉ 00196 ℘ 3227658, Fax 3219495 – AE VISA JCB. by lungotevere in Augusta KL
38 rm 230/310000.

Villa Florence without rest., via Nomentana 28 ✉ 00161 ℘ 4403036, Telex 624 Fax 4402709, « In a late 19C Patrician villa with a collection of Roman marble remai – AE VISA. by via 20 Settembre P
33 rm 210/25000.

Relais le Jardin - Hotel Lord Byron**,** via De Notaris 5 ✉ 00197 ℘ 3220404, Fax 3220 Elegant rest. – AE VISA JCB. by lungotevere A. da Brescia K
closed Sunday and August – **Meals** (booking essential) a la carte 85/145000
Spec. Savarin di carciofi con guanciale saltato, vellutata di mentuccia e cialda di parmig (autumn-winter). Spigola in crosta di patate al rosmarino con macedonia di verdure. S freddo di fragole e zenzero con salsa di cioccolato bianco (spring-summer).

Relais la Piscine - Hotel Aldrovandi Palace, via Mangili 6 ✉ 00197 ℘ 3216 « Outdoor summer service » – AE VISA JCB.
Meals 70/90000 (lunch) 90/110000 (dinner) and a la carte 90/135000. by lungotevere A. da Brescia K

Al Ceppo, via Panama 2 ✉ 00198 ℘ 8551379, Fax 85301370 – AE
closed Monday and 8 to 30 August – **Meals** (booking essential for dinner) a la c 55/80000. by via Salaria P

Coriolano, via Ancona 14 ✉ 00198 ℘ 44249863, Elegant trattoria – AE VISA P
closed 5 to 30 August, Sunday and Saturday in July – **Meals** (booking essential) a la c 70/105000 (15 %).

Il Caminetto, viale dei Parioli 89 ✉ 00197 ℘ 8083946, – AE VISA
Meals a la carte 50/70000. by lungotevere A. da Brescia K

La Scala, viale dei Parioli 79/d ✉ 00197 ℘ 8083978, – AE by lungotevere A. da Brescia K
closed Wednesday and 2 to 25 August – **Meals** a la carte 45/60000.

Al Fogher, via Tevere 13/b ✉ 00198 ℘ 8417032, Typical Venetian rest. – VISA JCB. P
closed Saturday lunch, Sunday and August – **Meals** a la carte 55/80000.

Al Chianti, via Ancona 17 ✉ 00198 ℘ 44291534, Tuscan trattoria with taverna – AE VISA P
closed Sunday and 6 to 22 August – **Meals** (booking essential) a la carte 40/7500

Al Bersagliere-da Raffone, via Ancona 43 ✉ 00198 ℘ 44249846, Traditional r rest. – AE VISA P
closed Saturday and 5 to 20 August – **Meals** a la carte 40/60000.

Trastevere area (typical district)

Alberto Ciarla, piazza San Cosimato 40 ✉ 00153 ℘ 5818668, Fax 5884377, Seafood – AE VISA JCB. K
closed Sunday, 10 to 20 August and 12 to 19 January – **Meals** (dinner only) (boo essential) 70/90000.

Corsetti-il Galeone, piazza San Cosimato 27 ✉ 00153 ✆ 5816311, Fax 5896255, ☂, Roman seafood rest., « Typical atmosphere » – ▤. AE ⓢ ⓓ E VISA JCB KZ m
Meals a la carte 50/80000.

Sora Lella, via di Ponte Quattro Capi 16 (Isola Tiberina) ✉ 00186 ✆ 6861601, Fax 6861601, Traditional Roman rest. – ▤. AE ⓢ ⓓ E VISA. ✻ MY g
closed Sunday and 10 to 31 August – **Meals** a la carte 45/80000.

Galeassi, piazza di Santa Maria in Trastevere 3 ✉ 00153 ✆ 5803775, ☂, Roman seafood rest. – AE ⓢ ⓓ E VISA KZ q
closed Monday and 20 December-20 January – **Meals** a la carte 50/85000.

Paris, piazza San Callisto 7/a ✉ 00153 ✆ 5815378, ☂ – ▤. AE ⓢ ⓓ E VISA. ✻ KZ r
closed Sunday dinner, Monday and August – **Meals** a la carte 60/90000.

Checco er Carettiere, via Benedetta 10 ✉ 00153 ✆ 5817018, ☂, Roman seafood rest. – ▤. AE ⓢ ⓓ E VISA JCB KY t
closed Sunday dinner, Monday and 11 to 18 August – **Meals** a la carte 60/90000.

Pastarellaro, via di San Crisogono 33 ✉ 00153 ✆ 5810871, Roman seafood rest. – ▤. AE ⓢ ⓓ E VISA. ✻ LZ u
closed Wednesday and August – **Meals** a la carte 50/80000 (12 %).

Taverna Trilussa, via del Politeama 23 ✉ 00153 ✆ 5818918, Fax 5811064, ☂, Typical Roman rest. – ▤. AE ⓢ ⓓ VISA KY v
closed Sunday dinner, Monday and 30 July-28 August – **Meals** a la carte 40/60000.

Gino in Trastevere, via della Lungaretta 85 ✉ 00153 ✆ 5803409, Roman rest. and pizzeria – ▤. AE ⓢ ⓓ E VISA. ✻ LZ m
closed Wednesday – **Meals** (dinner only except holidays) a la carte 35/50000.

North western area via Flaminia, via Cassia, Balduina, Prima Valle, via Aurelia

Jolly Hotel Midas, via Aurelia 800 (al km 8) ✉ 00165 ✆ 66396, Telex 622821, Fax 66418457, ⛱, ⛶, ✂ – ⫼ ⇔ rm ▤ TV ☎ P – 🏛 650. AE ⓢ ⓓ E VISA. ✻ rest by via Aurelia GV
Meals a la carte 60/90000 – **340 rm** ☐ 225/270000, 8 suites.

Forte Agip, via Aurelia al km 8 ✉ 00165 ✆ 66411200, Fax 66414437, ☂, ⛱, ⛶ – ⫼ ⇔ rm ▤ TV ☎ P – 🏛 150. AE ⓢ ⓓ E VISA JCB. ✻ by via Aurelia GV
Meals a la carte 50/80000 – **213 rm** ☐ 250/350000.

Colony Flaminio without rest., via Monterosi 18 ✉ 00191 ✆ 36301843, Fax 36309495 – ⫼ ▤ TV ☎ P – 🏛 90. AE ⓢ ⓓ E VISA JCB OPU
72 rm ☐ 175/215000, suite. by via Po

L'Ortica, via Flaminia Vecchia 573 ✉ 00191 ✆ 3338709, Fax 3338709, ☂, Napolitan rest. – AE ⓢ E VISA JCB OPU
closed Sunday – **Meals** (dinner only) a la carte 60/90000. by via Po

Da Benito, via Flaminia Nuova 230/232 ✉ 00191 ✆ 36307851, Fax 36306079 – ▤ P. AE ⓢ ⓓ E VISA OPU
closed Sunday and 10 to 31 August – **Meals** a la carte 40/80000. by via Po

North eastern area via Salaria, via Nomentana, via Tiburtina

Eurogarden without rest., raccordo anulare Salaria-Flaminia uscita n. 7 ✉ 00138 ✆ 8804507, Fax 8804417, ⛱, ⛶ – ▤ TV ☎ P. AE ⓢ ⓓ E VISA. ✻
48 rm ☐ 165/195000. by via Salaria PU

Southern western area via Aurelia Antica, E.U.R., Città Giardino, via della Magliana, Portuense

Sheraton M, viale del Pattinaggio 100/102 ✉ 00144 ✆ 5453, Telex 626074, Fax 5940689, ≘s, ⛱, ✂ – ⫼ ▤ TV ☎ ♿ 🚗 P – 🏛 1800. AE ⓢ ⓓ E VISA JCB. ✻ by viale Aventino NZ
Meals a la carte 60/95000 – **600 rm** ☐ 455/500000, 22 suites.

Sheraton Golf, viale Parco de Medici 22 ✉ 00148 ✆ 522408, Telex 620297, Fax 52240742, ☂, Fб, ≘s, ⛱, ⛶ – ⫼ ⇔ rm ▤ TV ☎ P – 🏛 500. AE ⓢ ⓓ E VISA JCB. ✻ by viale Trastevere KZ
Meals 75/90000 – **248 rm** ☐ 450/535000, 14 suites.

Villa Pamphili, via della Nocetta 105 ✉ 00164 ✆ 5862, Telex 626539, Fax 66157747, ☂, Fб, ≘s, ⛱ (covered in winter), ⛶, ✂ – ⫼ ⇔ rm ▤ TV ☎ ♿ P – 🏛 500. AE ⓢ ⓓ E VISA. ✻ by via Garibaldi JZ
Meals a la carte 55/85000 – **238 rm** ☐ 320/380000, 10 suites.

Holiday Inn St. Peter's, via Aurelia Antica 415 ✉ 00165 ✆ 6642, Telex 6254 Fax 6637190, ⛲, 🏊, 🌳, 🎾 – 🛗 🚭 rm ▤ 📺 ☎ ♿ 🅿 – 🎤 220 **321 rm.** by via Garibaldi JZ

Holiday Inn-Parco Medici, viale Castello della Magliana 65 ✉ 00148 ✆ 655 Telex 613302, Fax 6557005, 🏊, 🌳, 🎾 – 🛗 🚭 rm ▤ 📺 ☎ ♿ 🅿 – 🎤 650. AE ⓓ E VISA JCB. 🚫 by viale Trastevere KZ
Meals a la carte 70/90000 – **316 rm** ☕ 280/410000.

Shangri Là-Corsetti, viale Algeria 141 ✉ 00144 ✆ 5916441 (will change to 59364 Telex 614664, Fax 5413813, 🏊 heated, 🌳 – ▤ 📺 ☎ 🅿 – 🎤 80. AE $ ⓓ E 🚫 by viale Aventino NZ
Meals (see rest. ***Shangri Là-Corsetti*** below) – **52 rm** ☕ 265/330000, 11 suites.

XXX **Shangri-Là Corsetti,** viale Algeria 141 ✉ 00144 ✆ 5918861 (will change to 59288 🍽, seafood – ▤ 🅿. AE $ ⓓ E VISA JCB by viale Aventino NZ
Meals a la carte 50/90000.

XX **Vecchia America-Corsetti,** piazza Marconi 32 ✉ 00144 ✆ 5926601, Fax 59222 🍽, Typical rest. and ale house – AE $ ⓓ E VISA by viale Aventino NZ
Meals a la carte 45/80000.

XX **La Maielletta,** via Aurelia Antica 270 ✉ 00165 ✆ 39366595, Fax 39366595, Abr rest. – 🅿. AE $ ⓓ E VISA JCB. 🚫 by via Cipro GU
closed Monday and 15 to 30 August – **Meals** a la carte 35/45000.

XX **Pietro al Forte,** via Del Capasso 56/64 ✉ 00164 ✆ 66158531, Fax 66165101, Rest. and pizzeria – AE $ ⓓ E VISA. 🚫 by via Aurelia GV
closed Monday – **Meals** a la carte 35/60000.

Outskirts of Rome

on national road 6 - Casilina :

Myosotis, località Torre Gaia, piazza Pupinia 2 ✉ 00133 ✆ 2054470, Fax 2053671, heated, 🌳 – ▤ 📺 ☎ 🅿 – 🎤 35. AE $ ⓓ E VISA by via Merulana PY
Meals (see rest. ***Villa Marsili*** below) – **18 rm** ☕ 150/200000.

Città 2000 without rest., via della Tenuta di Torrenova 60/68 ✉ 00133 ✆ 20255 Fax 2025539 – 🛗 ▤ 📺 ☎ 🚗 🅿 – 🎤 30. AE $ ⓓ E VISA JCB
54 rm ☕ 90/110000. by via Merulana PY

XX **Villa Marsili,** via Casilina 1604 ✉ 00133 ✆ 2050200, Fax 2055176, « Outdoor sumr service » – ▤ 🅿. AE $ ⓓ E VISA JCB by via Merulana PY
Meals a la carte 30/50000.

at Ciampino *SE : 15 km :*

XX **Da Giacobbe,** via Appia Nuova 1681 ✉ 00179 Ciampino ✆ 79340131, 🍽 – ▤ AE $ ⓓ E VISA. 🚫 by via Labicana PZ
closed Sunday dinner, Monday and 10 to 30 August – **Meals** (booking essential) a la ca 40/60000.

Baschi *05023 Terni* 988 ㉕, 430 N 18 – *pop. 2 726 alt. 165* – ☎ *0744.*
Roma 118 – Orvieto 10 – Terni 70 – Viterbo 46.

XXX ✿✿ **Vissani,** N : 12 km ✉ 05020 Civitella del Lago ✆ 950396, Fax 950396 – 🚭 ▤ 🅿. $ ⓓ E VISA. 🚫
closed Sunday dinner, Wednesday and Thursday lunch – **Meals** (booking essent 100/160000 and a la carte 145/250000 (15 %)
Spec. San Pietro in cocotte con ravioli al grano saraceno e salsa agli asparagi. Carré d'ang al forno con gâteau di zucchine e mentuccia. Anatra con ratatouille di melanzane all'origa fresco, salsa di zucchine al profumo di zenzero.

MICHELIN GREEN GUIDES in English

Austria	Germany	New York City
Belgium Luxemburg	Great Britain	Portugal
Brussels	Greece	Quebec
California	Ireland	Rome
Canada	Italy	Scotland
Chicago	London	Spain
England :	Mexico	Switzerland
The West Country	Netherlands	Tuscany
France	New England	Washington DC

FLORENCE (FIRENZE) *50100* P 988 ⑮, 429 430 K 15 *G. Tuscan – pop. 383 594 alt. 49 – ☎ 055.*

See : *Cathedral*★★★ *(Duomo)* Y : *east end*★★★, *dome*★★★ (✻★★) *Campanile*★★★ YB : ✻★★ *Baptistry*★★★ YC : *doors*★★★, *mosaics*★★★ *Cathedral Museum*★★ Y **M1** – *Piazza della Signoria*★★ Z *Loggia della Signoria*★★ Z **D** : *Perseus*★★★ *by B. Cellini Palazzo Vecchio*★★★ Z H *Uffizi Gallery*★★★ Z – *Bargello Palace and Museum*★★★ Z *San Lorenzo*★★★ Y : *Church*★★, *Laurentian Library*★★, *Medici Tombs*★★★ *in Medicee Chapels*★★ – *Medici-Riccardi Palace*★★ Y : *Chapel*★★★, *Luca Giordano Gallery*★★ – *Church of Santa Maria Novella*★★ Y : *frescoes*★★★ *by Ghirlandaio – Ponte Vecchio*★★ Z *Pitti Palace*★★ DV : *Palatine Gallery*★★★, *Silver Museum*★★, *Works*★★ *by Macchiaioli in Modern Art Gallery*★ – *Boboli Garden*★ DV : ✻★★ *from the Citadel Belvedere Porcelain Museum*★ DV *Monastery and Museum of St. Mark*★★ ET : *works*★★★ *by Beato Angelico – Academy Gallery*★★ ET : *Michelangelo gallery*★★★ *Piazza della Santissima Annunziata*★ ET **168** : *frescoes*★ *in the church, portico*★★ *with corners decorated with terracotta Medallions*★★ *in the Foundling Hospital*★ – *Church of Santa Croce*★★ EU : *Pazzi Chapel*★★ *Excursion to the hills*★★ : ✻★★★ *from Michelangiolo Square* EFV, *Church of San Miniato al Monte*★★ EFV *Strozzi Palace*★★ Z – *Rucellai Palace*★★ Z *Santa Maria del Carmine*★★ DUV *Last Supper of Foligno*★ DT *Last Supper of San Salvi*★ BS **G** *Orsanmichele*★ ZN : *tabernacle*★★ *by Orcagna – La Badia* Z : *campanile*★, *delicate relief sculpture in marble*★★, *tombs*★, *Virgin appearing to St. Bernard*★ *by Filippino Lippi – Sassetti Chapel*★★ *and the Chapel of the Annunciation*★ *in the Holy Trinity Church* Z *Church of the Holy Spirit*★ DUV – *Last Supper*★ *of Sant'Apollonia* ET *All Saints' Church* DU : *Last Supper*★ *by Ghirlandaio Davanzanti Palace*★ Z **M2** *New Market Loggia*★ Z **K** – *Museums : Archaeological*★★ *(Chimera from Arezzo*★★ *Françoise Vase*★★*)* ET, *Science*★ Z **M6** *Marino Marini*★ Z **M7** *Bardini*★ EV *La Specola*★ DV *Casa Buonarroti*★ EU **M3** *Semi-precious Stone Workshop*★ ET **M4.**

Envir. : *Medicee Villas*★ : *villa della Petraia*★, *Villa di Castello*★, *Villa di Poggio a Caiano*★★ *by via P. Toselli* CT : *17 km Galluzzo Carthusian Monastery*★★ *by via Senese* CV.

18 *Dell'Ugolino (closed Monday), to Grassina ✉ 50015 ☎ 2301009, Fax 2301141, S : 12 km* BS.

✈ *of Peretola NW : 4 km by via P. Toselli* CT *☎ 373498 – Alitalia, lungarno Acciaiuoli 10/12 r, ✉ 50123 ☎ 27888.*

🅘 *via Cavour 1 r ✉ 50129 ☎ 290832, Fax 2760383.*

A.C.I. *viale Amendola 36 ✉ 50121 ☎ 24861.*

Roma 277 – Bologna 105 – Milano 298.

Plans on following pages

Excelsior, piazza Ognissanti 3 ✉ 50123 ☎ 264201, Telex 570022, Fax 210278 – 🛗 ▤ TV ☎ ♿ – 🏛 300. AE 🅂 ⓞ E VISA JCB. ✻ rest — DU b
Meals a la carte 100/145000 – ☕ 54000 – **172 rm** 440/705000, 7 suites.

Grand Hotel, piazza Ognissanti 1 ✉ 50123 ☎ 288781, Telex 570055, Fax 217400 – 🛗 ▤ TV ☎ ♿ 🚗 – 🏛 220. AE 🅂 ⓞ E VISA JCB. ✻ rest — DU a
Meals a la carte 110/155000 – ☕ 54000 – **90 rm** 495/825000, 17 suites.

Villa Medici, via Il Prato 42 ✉ 50123 ☎ 2381331, Telex 570179, Fax 2381336, 🌳, 🏊, 🌲 – 🛗 ▤ TV ☎ – 🏛 90. AE 🅂 ⓞ E VISA JCB. ✻ rest — CT c
Meals a la carte 70/100000 – ☕ 36000 – **89 rm** 430/690000, 14 suites.

Regency, piazza Massimo D'Azeglio 3 ✉ 50121 ☎ 245247, Fax 2346735, 🌲 – 🛗 ▤ TV ☎ 🚗. AE 🅂 ⓞ E VISA JCB. ✻ rest — FU a
Meals ***Relais le Jardin*** Rest. *(closed Sunday)* (booking essential) a la carte 70/110000 – **30 rm** ☕ 380/580000, 5 suites.

Helvetia e Bristol, via dei Pescioni 2 ✉ 50123 ☎ 287814, Telex 570696, Fax 288353 – 🛗 ▤ TV ☎. AE 🅂 ⓞ E VISA. ✻ — Z b
Meals a la carte 60/100000 – ☕ 32000 – **37 rm** 380/575000, 15 suites.

Albani, via Fiume 12 ✉ 50123 ☎ 26030, Telex 573316, Fax 211045 – 🛗 ▤ TV ☎ – 🏛 40. AE 🅂 ⓞ E VISA JCB. ✻ — DT a
Meals a la carte 60/90000 – **75 rm** ☕ 380/420000, 4 suites.

Brunelleschi, piazza Santa Elisabetta 3 ✉ 50122 ☎ 562068, Telex 571105, Fax 219653, ≤, « Small private museum in a Byzantine tower » – 🛗 ⇔ rm ▤ TV ☎ – 🏛 100. AE 🅂 ⓞ E VISA JCB. ✻ — Z c
Meals (residents only) a la carte 80/120000 – **88 rm** ☕ 340/460000, 8 suites.

Gd H. Minerva M, piazza Santa Maria Novella 16 ✉ 50123 ☎ 284555, Telex 570414, Fax 268281, 🏊 – 🛗 ▤ TV ☎ – 🏛 90. AE 🅂 ⓞ E VISA JCB. ✻ — Y n
Meals a la carte 45/75000 – **93 rm** ☕ 320/440000, 6 suites.

Astoria Palazzo Gaddi, via del Giglio 9 ✉ 50123 ☎ 2398095, Fax 214632 – 🛗 ▤ TV ☎ ♿ – 🏛 130. AE 🅂 ⓞ E VISA. ✻ rest — Y b
Meals a la carte 50/75000 – **96 rm** ☕ 315/430000, 6 suites.

Plaza Hotel Lucchesi, lungarno della Zecca Vecchia 38 ✉ 50122 ☎ 26236, Telex 570302, Fax 2480921, ≤ – 🛗 ⇔ rm ▤ TV ☎ ♿ 🚗 – 🏛 160. AE 🅂 ⓞ E VISA JCB. ✻ rest — EV b
Meals *(closed Sunday)* (residents only) a la carte 65/100000 – **87 rm** ☕ 340/485000, 10 suites.

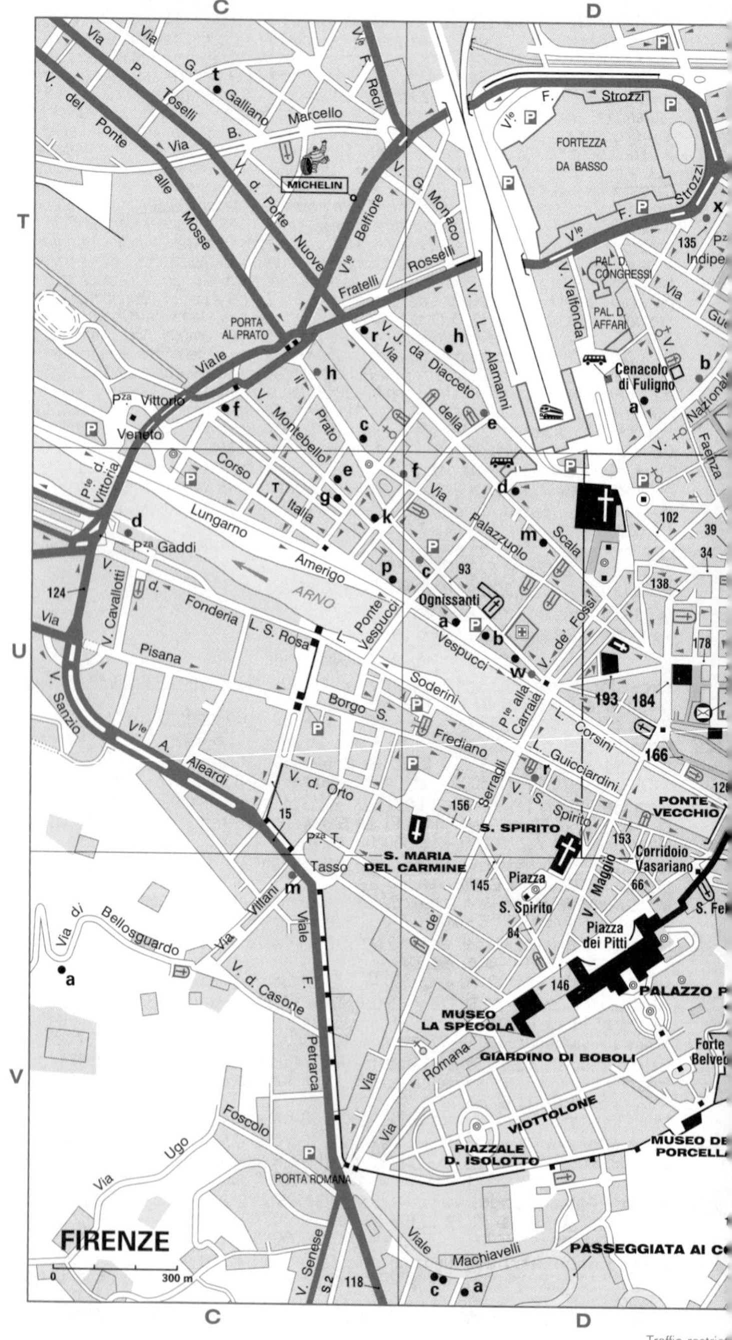

Traffic restric

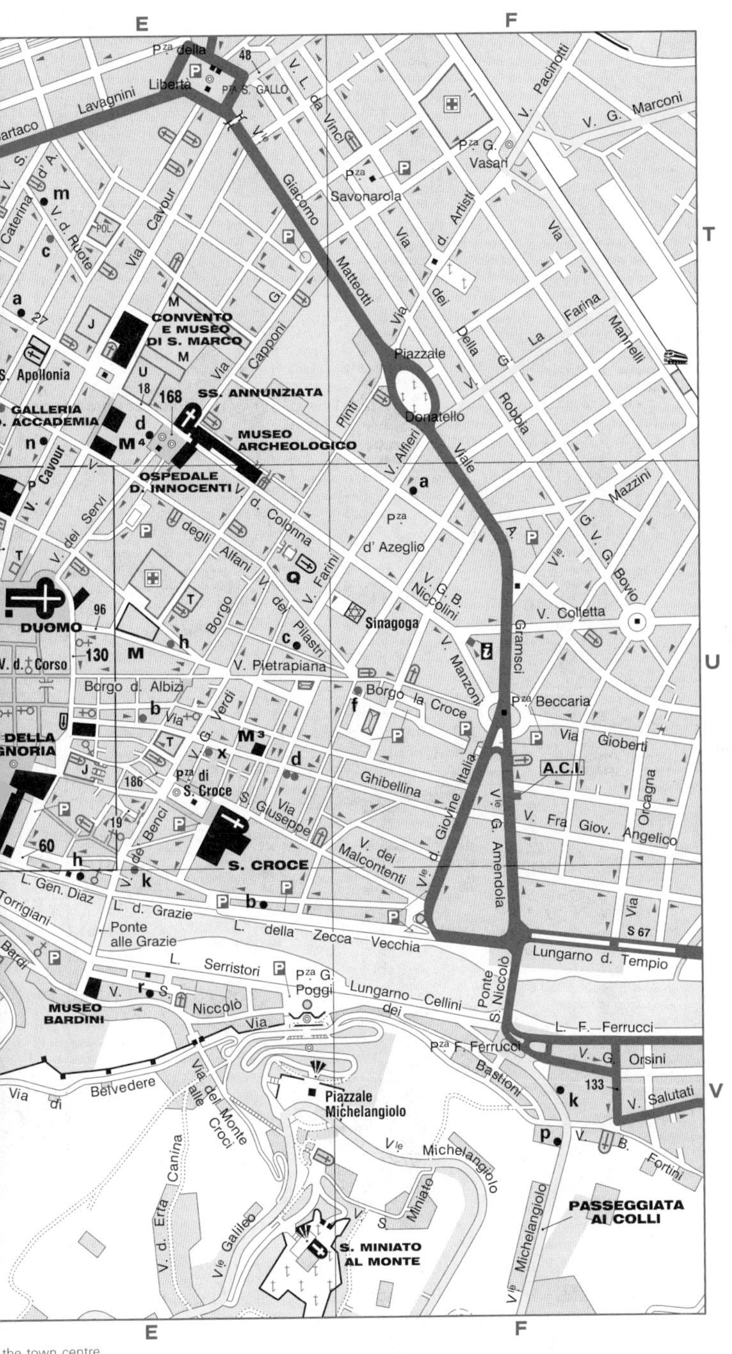
E
F
T
U
V
CONVENTO E MUSEO DI S. MARCO
SS. ANNUNZIATA
MUSEO ARCHEOLOGICO
OSPEDALE D. INNOCENTI
GALLERIA ACCADEMIA
DUOMO
S. CROCE
MUSEO BARDINI
Piazzale Michelangiolo
S. MINIATO AL MONTE
PASSEGGIATA AI COLLI
Sinagoga
A.C.I.
Piazzale Donatello
Pza d' Azeglio
Pza Beccaria
Pza Savonarola
Pza G. Vasari
Pza della Libertà
Pza di S. Croce
Pza G. Poggi
Pza F. Ferrucci
Lungarno d. Tempio
Lungarno Cellini
Ponte alle Grazie
Ponte S. Niccolò
S 67

FIRENZE

Calimala . . . . Z 24
Calzaiuoli (Via dei) . . . . . . YZ
Por S. Maria (Via) . . . . . . Z 126
Porta Rossa (Via) . . . . Z
Roma (Via) . . . . YZ
S. Jacopo (Borgo) . . . . . . Z
Strozzi (Via degli) . . . . Z
Tornabuoni (Via) . . . . Z
Vecchio (Ponte) . . . . Z

Agli (Via degli) . . . . Y 3
Albizi (Vorgo degli) . . . . . Z 7
Antinori (Piazza degli) . . . Y 10
Archibusieri (Lungamo) . . Z 12
Avelli (Via degli) . . . . Y 16
Brunelleschi (Via de) . . . . YZ 22
Canto de' Nelli (Via del) . . T 27
Castellani (Via de') . . . . . . Z 31
Dante Alighieri (Via) . . . . . Z 42
Davanzati (Piazza) . . . . . . Z 43
Faenza (Via) . . . . Y 51
Fiordalisa (Via del) . . . . . . Z 52
Fossi (Via de') . . . . Y 54
Ghibellina (Via) . . . . Z 57
Gondi (Via dei) . . . . Z 61
Guicciardini (Lungarno) . . Z 64
Lambertesca (Via) . . . . . . Z 69
Leoni (Via dei) . . . . Z 70
Madonna degli Aldobrandini (Piazza di) . . . . Y 75
Magazzini (Via dei) . . . . . Z 76
Melarancio (Via del) . . . . . Y 85
Monalda (Via) . . . . Z 88
Nazionale (Via) . . . . Y 90
Oriulo (Via d.) . . . . Y 96
Orsanmichele (Via) . . . . . Z
Parte Guelfa (Piazza di) . . . . Z
Pellicceria (Via) . . . . Z
Pescioni (Via de') . . . . YZ
Rondinelli (Via de') . . . . . Y
S. Giovanni (Piazza) . . . . Y
S. Spirito (Via) . . . . Z
S. Trinità (Piazza) . . . . . . Z
Sassetti (Via de') . . . . Z
Spada (Via della) . . . . Z
Speziali (Via degli) . . . . .
Strozzi (Piazza) . . . . Z
Tavolini (Via dei) . . . .
Terme (Via delle) . . . . . .
Trebbio (Via del) . . . . Y
Uffizi (Piazzale degli) . . . .
Vacchereccia (Via) . . . . . Z
Vigna Nuova (Via della) . Z

Traffic restricted in the town centre

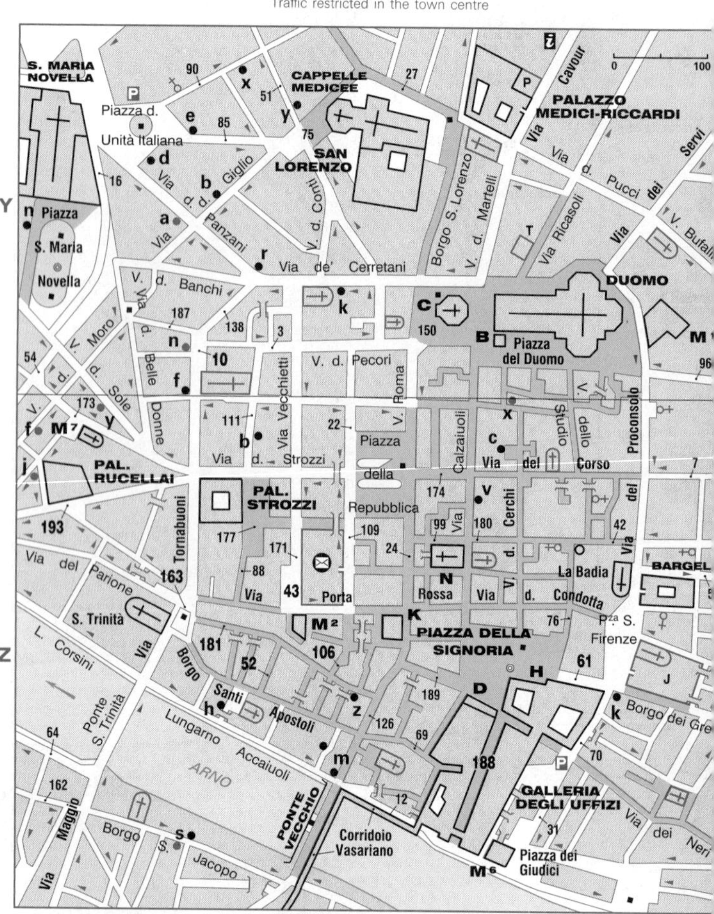

For the quickest route use the MICHELIN Main Road Maps:
970 Europe, 976 Czech Republic-Slovak Republic, 980 Greece, 984 Germany, 985 Scandinavia-Finland, 986 Great Britain and Ireland, 987 Germany-Austria-Benelux, 988 Italy, 989 France, 990 Spain-Portugal *and* 991 Yugoslavia.

mala (Via) Z 24
aiuoli (Via dei) YZ
cciardini (Via de') DV 66
S. Maria (Via) Z
a Rossa (Via) Z
na (Via) DU 136
acopo (Borgo) DU 153
zzi (Via degli) DU 178
nabuoni (Via) DTU 184
chio (Ponte) Z

iaiuoli (Lungarno) Z
(Via degli) Y 3
nanni (Via L.) DT
zi (Borgo degli) Z 7
ardi (Viale A.) CU
ni (Via degli) ETU
eri (Via V.) FTU
endola (Viale G.) FUV
inori (Piazza degli) Y 10
hibusieri (Lungarno) Z 12
osto (Viale F.) CU 15
sti (Via degli) FT
lli (Via degli) Y 16
glio (Piazza d') FU
nchi (Via del) Y
di (Via de) DEV
tioni (Via dei) EFV
tisti (Via C.) ET 18
caria (Piazza) FU
iore (Viale) CT
e Donne (Via delle) Y
osguardo (Via di) CV
vedere (Via di) EV
nci (Via de') EUV
ntaccordi (Via) EU 19
vio (Via G.) FU
nelleschi (Via de') YZ 22
alini (Via) Y
nto de'Nelli (Via del) Y 27
oponi (Via G.) ET
raia (Ponte alla) DU 28
sone (Via del) CV 30
stellani (Via de') Z
vallotti (Via F.) CU
vour (Via) Y
lini (Lungarno) FV
chi (Via de') Z
retani (Via de') DU 34
letta (Via P.) FU
onna (Via della) EU
ndotta (Via della) Z
nti (Via de') DU 39
rsini (Lungarno) Z
so (Via del) Z
ce (Vorgo la) FU
nte Alighieri (Via) Z 42
vanzati (Piazza) Z 43
la Robbia (Via dei) FT
cceto (Via J. da) DT
z (Lungarno Genera- EV
...
n G. Minzoni (Viale) ET 48
natello (Piazzale) FT
omo (Piazza del) Y
nza (Via) Y 51
ina (Via G. La) FT
ini (Via) EFU
rucci (Lungarno F.) FV
rucci (Piazza) FV
rdaliso (Via del) Z 52
nderia (Via della) CU
tini (Via B.) FV
ssi (Via de') Y 54

Fratelli Rosselli (Viale) CDT
Gaddi (Piazza) CU
Galileo (Viale) EV
Galliano (Via G.) CT
Ghibellina (Via) Z 57
Giglio (Via del) Y
Gioberti (Via V.) FU
Giovine Italia (Viale della) FUV
Giudici (Piazza dei) EU 60
Gondi (Via dei) Z 61
Gramsci (Viale) FTU
Grazie (Lungarno delle) EV
Grazie (Ponte alle) EV
Greci (Borgo dei) Z
Guelfa (Via) DET
Guicciardini (Lungarno) Z 64
Indipendenza (Piazza della) DT
Italia (Corso) CU
Lambertesca (Via) Z 69
Lavagnini (Viale S.) DET
Leoni (Via dei) Z 70
Libertà (Piazza della) ET
Madonna degli Aldobrandini (Piazza di) Y 75
Magazzini (Via dei) Z 76
Maggio (Via) Z
Malcontenti (Via dei) fiUV
Mannelli (Via) FT
Manzoni (Via A.) FU
Marcello (Via B.) CT
Marconi (Via G.) FT
Martelli (Via de') EU 82
Matteotti (Viale G/) EFT
Mazzetta (Via) DV 84
Mazzini (Viale G.) FU
Melarancio (Via del) Y 85
Michelangiolo (Piazzale) EFV
Monaco (Via G.) CDT
Monalda (Via) Z 88
Monte alle Croci (Via del) EV
Montebello (Via) CTU
Moro (Via del) Y
Nazionale (Via) Y 90
Neri (Via dei) Z
Niccolini (Via G. B.) FU
Ognissanti (Borgo) DU 93
Orcagna (Via) FUV
Oriuolo (Via d.) Y 96
Orsanmichele (Via) Z 99
Orsine (Via G.) FV
Orto (Via d.) CU
Pacinotti (Via A.) FT
Palazzuolo (Via) DU
Panzani (Via) DU
Parione (Via del) Z
Parte Guelfa (Piazza di) Z 106
Pecori (Via de') Y
Pellicceria (Via) Z 109
Pescioni (Via de') YZ 111
Petrarca (Viale F.) CV
Pietrapiana (Via) EU
Pilastri (Via dei) EFU
Pinti (Borgo) EFTU
Pisana (Via) CU
Pitti (Piazza dei) DV
Poggi (Piazza G.) EV
Poggio Imperiale (Viale del) CV 118
Ponte alle Mosse (Via) CT
Ponte Sospeso (Via del) CU 124
Porte Nuove (Via delle) CT
Prato (il) CT
Proconsolo (Via del) EU 130

Pucci (Via de') Y
Redi (Viale F.) CT
Repubblica (Piazza della) DU 132
Ricasoli (Via) Y
Ricorborli (Via di) FV 133
Ridolfi (Via C.) DT 135
Romana (Via) CDV
Rondinelli (Via de') Y 138
Ruote (Via delle) ET
Saluti (Via C.) FV
S. Agostino (Via) DUV 145
S. Caterina d'Alessandria (Via) ET
S. Croce (Piazza di) EU
S. Firenze (Piazza) Z
S. Frediano (Borgo) CDU
Giorgio (Costa di) EV 148
S. Giovanni (Piazza) Y 150
S. Giuseppe (Via di) EU
S. Leonardo (Via di) DV 154
S. Lorenzo (Borgo) Y
S. Maria Novella (Piazza) Y
S. Monaca (Via) DU 156
S. Niccolò (Ponte) FV
S. Niccolò (Via) EV
S. Rosa (Lungarno di) CU
S. Spirito (Piazza) DV
S. Spirito (Via) Z 162
S. Trinità Z 163
S. Trinità (Ponte) Z 165
Santi Apostoli (Borgo) DU 166

Santissima Annunziata (Piazza della) ET 168
Sanzio (Viale R.) CU
Sasseti (Via de') Z 171
Savonarola (Piazza) FT
Scala (Via della) DTU
Serragli (Via de') DUV
Serristori (Lungarno) EV
Servi (Via dei) Y
Signoria (Piazza della) Z
Soderini (Lungarno) CDU
Sole (Via del) YZ
Spada (via della) Z 173
Speziali (Via degli) Z 174
Strozzi (Piazza) Z 177
Strozzi (Viale F.) DT
Studio (Via dello) YZ
Tasso (Piazza T.) CUV
Tavolini (Via dei) Z 180
Tempio (Lungarno del) FV
Terme (Via delle) Z 181
Torrigiani (Lungarno) EV
Torat (Via) EU 186
Toselli (Via P.) CT
Trebbio (Via del) Y 187
Uffizi (Piazzale degli Z 188
Unità Italiana (Piazza d.) Y
Vacchereccia (Via) Z 189
Valfonda (Via) DT
Vasari (Piazza G.) FT
Vecchietti (Via de') YZ
Veneto (Piazza Vittorio) CT
Verdi (Via G.) EU
Vespucci (Lungarno A.) CDU
Vespucci (Ponte) CU
Vigna Nuova (Via della) Z 193
Villani (Via) CV
Vinci (Via L. da) EFT
Vittoria (Ponte della) CU
Zecca Vecchia (Lungarno della) EFV
27 Aprile (Via) ET

Discover **ITALY** with the **Michelin** Green Guide
Picturesque scenery, buildings
History and geography
Works of art
Touring programmes
Town plans

Grand Hotel Baglioni, piazza Unità Italiana 6 ✉ 50123 ☎ 23580, Telex 5702 Fax 2358895, « Roof-garden rest. with ≤ town » – |$| ▤ TV ☎ ♿ – 🏛 200. AE ⓢ E VISA JCB. ✂ rest Y
Meals a la carte 65/105000 – **190 rm** ☐ 310/420000, 5 suites.

Sofitel, via de' Cerretani 10 ✉ 50123 ☎ 2381301, Telex 574615, Fax 2381312 – ✂ rm ▤ TV ☎ ♿. AE ⓢ ◐ E VISA JCB. ✂ rest Y
Meals a la carte 50/80000 – **84 rm** ☐ 420/490000.

Majestic, via del Melarancio 1 ✉ 50123 ☎ 264021, Telex 570628, Fax 268428 – ▤ TV ☎ ♿ 🚗 – 🏛 80. AE ⓢ ◐ E VISA JCB. ✂ rest Y
Meals 50/55000 – **102 rm** ☐ 330/470000, suite.

Continental without rest., lungarno Acciaiuoli 2 ✉ 50123 ☎ 282392, Telex 5735 Fax 283139, « Floral terrace with ≤ » – |$| ▤ TV ☎ ♿. AE ⓢ ◐ E VISA JCB Z
☐ 25000 – **47 rm** 290/390000, suite.

Bernini Palace without rest., piazza San Firenze 29 ✉ 50122 ☎ 288621, Telex 5736 Fax 268272 – |$| ▤ TV ☎ – 🏛 40. AE ⓢ ◐ E VISA Z
83 rm ☐ 320/450000, 3 suites.

Berchielli without rest., piazza del Limbo 6 r ✉ 50123 ☎ 264061, Fax 218636, – |$| ▤ TV ☎ – 🏛 100. AE ⓢ ◐ E VISA JCB. ✂ Z
73 rm ☐ 390/420000, 3 suites.

Montebello Splendid, via Montebello 60 ✉ 50123 ☎ 2398051, Telex 5740 Fax 211867, 🌳 – |$| ▤ TV ☎ – 🏛 100. AE ⓢ ◐ E VISA JCB. ✂ rest CU
Meals *(closed Sunday)* a la carte 60/105000 – **53 rm** ☐ 315/470000, suite.

Rivoli without rest., via della Scala 33 ✉ 50123 ☎ 282853, Telex 571004, Fax 2940 🌳 – |$| ▤ TV ☎ ♿ – 🏛 100. AE ⓢ ◐ E VISA JCB. ✂ DU
65 rm ☐ 300/400000.

De la Ville, piazza Antinori 1 ✉ 50123 ☎ 2381805, Fax 2381809 – |$| ▤ TV ☎ – 🏛 AE ⓢ ◐ E VISA JCB. ✂ rest Y
Meals (residents only) a la carte 55/70000 – **71 rm** ☐ 345/470000, 4 suites.

Augustus without rest., piazzetta dell'Oro 5 ✉ 50123 ☎ 283054, Telex 5701 Fax 268557 – |$| ▤ TV ☎. AE ⓢ ◐ E VISA JCB Z
53 rm ☐ 370/430000, 8 suites.

J and J without rest., via di Mezzo 20 ✉ 50121 ☎ 2345005, Fax 240282 – ▤ TV AE ⓢ ◐ E VISA. ✂ EU
14 rm ☐ 330/375000, 5 suites.

Lungarno without rest., borgo Sant'Jacopo 14 ✉ 50125 ☎ 264211, Telex 5701 Fax 268437, ≤, « Collection of modern pictures » – |$| ▤ TV ☎ – 🏛 30. AE ⓢ ◐ VISA JCB. ✂ Z
☐ 25000 – **60 rm** 330/380000, 6 suites.

Holiday Inn, viale Europa 205 ✉ 50126 ☎ 6531841, Fax 6531806, 🌳, 🏊 – |$| ✂ ▤ TV ☎ ♿ P – 🏛 120. AE ⓢ ◐ E VISA JCB. ✂ rest BS
Meals 40000 and ***La Tegolaia*** Rest. a la carte 55/70000 – ☐ 25000 – **92 rm** 310/3600

Londra, via Jacopo da Diacceto 18 ✉ 50123 ☎ 2382791, Telex 571152, Fax 2106 🌳 – |$| ▤ TV ☎ ♿ 🚗 – 🏛 200. AE ⓢ ◐ E VISA JCB. ✂ rest DT
Meals a la carte 55/80000 – **158 rm** ☐ 290/390000.

Starhotel Michelangelo, viale Fratelli Rosselli 2 ✉ 50123 ☎ 2784, Telex 5711 Fax 2382232 – |$| ▤ TV ☎ 🚗 – 🏛 250. AE ⓢ ◐ E VISA JCB. ✂ rest CT
Meals (residents only) – **138 rm** ☐ 300/440000.

Executive without rest., via Curtatone 5 ✉ 50123 ☎ 217451, Telex 5745 Fax 268346 – |$| ▤ TV ☎ – 🏛 50. AE ⓢ ◐ E VISA JCB CU
38 rm ☐ 320/420000.

Kraft without rest., via Solferino 2 ✉ 50123 ☎ 284273, Telex 571523, Fax 23982 « Roof garden rest. with ≤ », 🏊 – |$| ▤ TV ☎ – 🏛 50. AE ⓢ ◐ E VISA JCB CU
77 rm ☐ 290/410000.

Principe without rest., lungarno Vespucci 34 ✉ 50123 ☎ 284848, Fax 283458, ≤, – |$| ▤ TV ☎. AE ⓢ ◐ E VISA JCB. ✂ CU
18 rm ☐ 300/400000, 2 suites.

Malaspina without rest., piazza dell'Indipendenza 24 ✉ 50129 ☎ 489869, Fax 4748 – |$| ▤ TV ☎ ♿. AE ⓢ ◐ E VISA. ✂ ET
31 rm ☐ 175/260000.

Il Guelfo Bianco without rest., via Cavour 29 ✉ 50129 ☎ 288330, Fax 295203 – ▤ TV ☎ ♿. AE ⓢ E VISA. ✂ ET
29 rm ☐ 185/260000.

Palazzo Benci without rest., piazza Madonna degli Aldobrandini 3 ✉ 501 ☎ 2382821, Fax 288308 – |$| ▤ TV ☎ – 🏛 30. AE ⓢ ◐ E VISA JCB. ✂ Y
35 rm ☐ 170/240000.

Royal without rest., via delle Ruote 52 ✉ 50129 ☎ 483287, Fax 490976, « Garden » – 🛗 ▤ TV ☎ P. AE ⑤ E VISA ET m
39 rm ☕ 155/260000.

Villa Azalee without rest., viale Fratelli Rosselli 44 ✉ 50123 ☎ 214242, Fax 268264, – ▤ TV ☎. AE ⑤ ⓓ E VISA CT r
24 rm ☕ 155/235000.

Calzaiuoli without rest., via Calzaiuoli 6 ✉ 50122 ☎ 212456, Fax 268310 – 🛗 ▤ TV ☎ ♿. AE ⑤ ⓓ E VISA ZV
45 rm ☕ 180/220000.

Select without rest., via Giuseppe Galliano 24 ✉ 50144 ☎ 330342, Fax 351506 – 🛗 ▤ TV ☎. AE ⑤ ⓓ E VISA JCB CT t
☕ 10000 – **36 rm** 140/170000.

David without rest., viale Michelangiolo 1 ✉ 50125 ☎ 6811695, Fax 680602, – 🛗 ▤ TV ☎ P. AE ⑤ ⓓ E VISA. FV k
☕ 15000 – **26 rm** 115/190000.

Villa Liberty without rest., viale Michelangiolo 40 ✉ 50125 ☎ 6810581, Fax 6812595, – 🛗 ▤ TV ☎ P. AE ⑤ ⓓ E VISA JCB FV p
14 rm ☕ 210/240000, 2 suites.

Laurus without rest., via de' Cerretani 8 ✉ 50123 ☎ 2381752, Fax 268308 – 🛗 ▤ TV ☎. AE ⑤ ⓓ E VISA. Y k
59 rm ☕ 230/330000.

Loggiato dei Serviti without rest., piazza SS. Annunziata 3 ✉ 50122 ☎ 289592, Fax 289595, « 16C building » – 🛗 ▤ TV ☎. AE ⑤ ⓓ E VISA JCB ET d
25 rm ☕ 195/300000, 4 suites.

City without rest., via Sant'Antonino 18 ✉ 50123 ☎ 211543, Fax 295451 – 🛗 ▤ TV ☎. AE ⑤ ⓓ E VISA JCB Y x
18 rm ☕ 185/240000.

Goldoni without rest., via Borgo Ognissanti 8 ✉ 50123 ☎ 284080, Fax 282576 – 🛗 ▤ TV ☎. AE ⑤ E VISA DU w
☕ 10000 – **20 rm** 150/240000.

Balestri without rest., piazza Mentana 7 ✉ 50122 ☎ 214743, Fax 2398042, ← – 🛗 ▤ TV ☎ – 50. AE ⑤ ⓓ E VISA. EUV h
49 rm ☕ 230/260000, suite.

Della Signoria without rest., via delle Terme 1 ✉ 50123 ☎ 214530, Fax 216101 – 🛗 ▤ TV ☎. AE ⑤ ⓓ E VISA JCB Z z
27 rm ☕ 225/280000.

Silla without rest., via dei Renai 5 ✉ 50125 ☎ 2342888, Fax 2341437 – 🛗 ▤ TV ☎. AE ⑤ ⓓ E VISA EV r
32 rm ☕ 160/210000.

Cellai without rest., via 27 Aprile 14 ✉ 50129 ☎ 489291, Fax 470387 – ▤ TV ☎. AE ⑤ ⓓ E VISA ET a
47 rm ☕ 180/230000.

Alba without rest., via della Scala 22 ✉ 50123 ☎ 282610, Fax 288358 – 🛗 ▤ TV ☎. AE ⑤ ⓓ E VISA. DU d
24 rm ☕ 185/260000.

Rapallo, via di Santa Caterina d'Alessandria 7 ✉ 50129 ☎ 472412, Fax 470385 – 🛗 ▤ TV ☎. AE ⑤ ⓓ E VISA. rest ET g
Meals 35000 – ☕ 20000 – **27 rm** 120/190000.

Enoteca Pinchiorri, via Ghibellina 87 ✉ 50122 ☎ 242777, Fax 244983, « Summer service in a cool courtyard » – ▤. AE ⑤ VISA JCB EU x
closed Sunday, Monday-Wednesday lunch, August and 18 to 27 December – **Meals** (booking essential) 90/150000 (lunch) and a la carte 90/210000
Spec. Tortelli di ricotta e mela con crema di parmigiano e buccia di mela fritta. Filetto di triglia con verdure fritte e olive tritate. Costata d i vitello al forno con radicchio, patate e aglio candito all'origano.

Sabatini, via de' Panzani 9/a ✉ 50123 ☎ 211559, Fax 210293, Elegant traditional decor – ▤. AE ⑤ ⓓ E VISA JCB. Y a
closed Monday – **Meals** a la carte 80/125000 (13 %).

Don Chisciotte, via Ridolfi 4 r ✉ 50129 ☎ 475430, Fax 485305 – ▤. AE ⑤ ⓓ E VISA JCB DT x
closed Sunday, Monday lunch and August – **Meals** (booking essential) a la carte 65/105000 (10 %).

Taverna del Bronzino, via delle Ruote 25/27 r ✉ 50129 ☎ 495220 – ▤. AE ⑤ ⓓ E VISA ET c
closed Sunday and August – **Meals** a la carte 60/85000.

XXX **Harry's Bar,** lungarno Vespucci 22 r ✉ 50123 ☎ 2396700, Fax 2396700 – ▤. AE E VISA DU
closed Sunday and 15 December-5 January – **Meals** (booking essential) a la carte 60/95((16 %).

XX **Osteria n. 1,** via del Moro 20 r ✉ 50123 ☎ 284897, Fax 294318 – ▤. AE ⓢ ⓓ VISA JCB Z
closed Sunday, Monday lunch and 3 to 26 August – **Meals** a la carte 60/90000.

XX **Dino,** via Ghibellina 51 r ✉ 50122 ☎ 241452, Fax 241378 – ▤. AE ⓢ ⓓ E VISA
closed Sunday dinner and Monday – **Meals** a la carte 50/70000. EU

XX **Le Fonticine,** via Nazionale 79 r ✉ 50123 ☎ 282106, « Painting collection » – AE ⓓ E VISA JCB. ✈ DT
closed Monday, 22 July-22 August, Christmas and New Year – **Meals** a la carte 50/85(

XX **I 4 Amici,** via degli Orti Oricellari 29 ✉ 50123 ☎ 215413, Fax 289767, seafood – AE ⓢ ⓓ E VISA. ✈ DT
closed Sunday – **Meals** a la carte 45/75000 (12 %).

XX **Cantinetta Antinori,** piazza Antinori 3 ✉ 50123 ☎ 292234, Tuscan rest. – ▤. ⓢ ⓓ VISA JCB. ✈ Y
closed Saturday, Sunday, August and Christmas – **Meals** a la carte 50/80000 (10 %)

XX **Acquerello,** via Ghibellina 156 r ✉ 50122 ☎ 2340554, Fax 2340554 – ▤. AE ⓢ ⓓ E
closed Thursday – **Meals** a la carte 40/60000 (12 %). EU

XX **Mamma Gina,** borgo Sant'Jacopo 37 r ✉ 50125 ☎ 2396009, Fax 213908 – ▤. ⓢ ⓓ E VISA JCB Z
closed Sunday and 7 to 21 August – **Meals** a la carte 50/75000 (12 %).

XX **Ottorino,** via delle Oche 12/16 r ✉ 50122 ☎ 215151, Fax 287140 – ▤. AE ⓢ ⓓ VISA JCB YZ
closed Sunday – **Meals** a la carte 55/80000.

X **Vineria Cibreo-Cibreino,** piazza Ghiberti 35 ✉ 50122 ☎ 2341100, Fax 244966 – AE ⓢ ⓓ E VISA JCB FU
closed Sunday, Monday, 26 July-6 September and 31 December-6 January – **Meals** (book essential) a la carte 35/40000.

X **La Baraonda,** via Ghibellina 67 r ✉ 50122 ☎ 2341171, Fax 2341171 – AE ⓓ
closed Sunday, Monday lunch and August – **Meals** a la carte 40/65000 (10 %). EU

X **Il Cigno,** via Varlungo 3 r ✉ 50136 ☎ 691762, Fax 691762, ☂ – Ⓟ. ⓢ E V ✈ by Lungarno del Tempio FU
closed Monday, 11 to 17 August and November – **Meals** a la carte 40/65000.

X **Il Profeta,** borgo Ognissanti 93 r ✉ 50123 ☎ 212265 – ▤. AE ⓢ ⓓ VISA. ✈
closed Sunday and 15 to 31 August – **Meals** a la carte 45/65000 (12 %). DU

X **La Martinicca,** via del Sole 27 r ✉ 50123 ☎ 218928, Fax 218928 – ▤. AE ⓢ ⓓ VISA Z
closed Sunday and August – **Meals** a la carte 40/65000.

X **Cafaggi,** via Guelfa 35 r ✉ 50129 ☎ 294989 – ▤. ⓢ E VISA ET
closed Sunday and July or August – **Meals** a la carte 40/80000.

X **Trattoria Vittoria,** via della Fonderia 52 r ✉ 50142 ☎ 225657, seafood – ▤. AE ⓓ E VISA JCB CU
closed Wednesday – **Meals** a la carte 70/85000.

X **Angiolino,** via Santo Spirito 36 r ✉ 50125 ☎ 2398976, Typical trattoria – AE ⓢ E VISA. ✈ DU
closed Sunday – **Meals** a la carte 40/55000 (10 %).

X **Cantina Barbagianni,** via Sant'Egidio 13 r ✉ 50122 ☎ 2480508 – ▤. AE ⓢ ⓓ VISA EU
closed Sunday – **Meals** a la carte 35/55000 (10 %).

X **La Carabaccia,** via Palazzuolo 190 r ✉ 50123 ☎ 214782 – AE ⓢ E VISA CDU
closed Sunday, Monday lunch and 13 August-4 September – **Meals** a la carte 45/750(

X **Il Latini,** via dei Palchetti 6 r ✉ 50123 ☎ 210916, Typical trattoria – AE ⓢ ⓓ E V ✈ Z
closed Monday, and 24 December-1 January – **Meals** a la carte 30/55000.

X **Del Fagioli,** corso Tintori 47 r ✉ 50122 ☎ 244285, Typical Tuscan trattoria EV
closed Saturday, Sunday and August – **Meals** a la carte 40/55000.

on the hills *S : 3 km :*

Gd H. Villa Cora ⛱, viale Machiavelli 18 ✉ 50125 ☎ 2298451, Telex 5706(Fax 229086, ☂, « 19C house in floral park with ⛱ » – |‡| ▤ TV ☎ Ⓟ – 🏃 150. ⓢ ⓓ E VISA JCB DV
Meals ***Taverna Machiavelli*** Rest. a la carte 60/90000 – **38 rm** ☕ 420/680000, 10 sui 1000/1800000.

Torre di Bellosguardo without rest., via Roti Michelozzi 2 ✉ 50124 ☏ 2298145, Fax 229008, ≤ town and hills, « Park and terrace with » – . AE ⓢ ① E VISA CV a
25000 – **10 rm** 290/390000, 6 suites 490/590000.

Villa Belvedere without rest., via Benedetto Castelli 3 ✉ 50124 ☏ 222501, Fax 223163, ≤ town and hills, « Garden-park with », – . AE ⓢ ① E VISA. by via Senese CV
March-November – **23 rm** 230/320000, 3 suites.

Villa Carlotta, via Michele di Lando 3 ✉ 50125 ☏ 2336134, Fax 2336147, – . AE ⓢ ① E VISA JCB. rest DV a
Meals (residents only) a la carte 50/80000 – **32 rm** 260/370000.

Classic without rest., viale Machiavelli 25 ✉ 50125 ☏ 229351, Fax 229353, – . AE ⓢ E VISA DV c
10000 – **16 rm** 130/190000, 3 suites.

Arcetri *S : 5 km – ✉ 50125 Firenze :*

Omero, via Pian de' Giullari 11 r ☏ 220053, Country trattoria with ≤, « Summer service dinner on terrace » – AE ⓢ ① E VISA. by viale Machiavelli DV
closed Tuesday and August – **Meals** a la carte 45/60000 (13 %).

Galluzzo *S : 6,5 km – ✉ 50124 Firenze :*

Trattoria Bibe, via delle Bagnese 15 ☏ 2049085, Fax 2047167, « Outdoor summer service » – . AE ⓢ VISA AS c
closed Wednesday, Thursday lunch, 15 to 28 February and 10 to 25 November – **Meals** a la carte 40/55000.

Candeli *E : 7 km – ✉ 50010 :*

Villa La Massa, via La Massa 24 ☏ 6510101, Fax 6510109, ≤, , « 17C house and furnishings », , , – – 120. AE ⓢ ① E VISA. rest
25 March-October – **Meals *Il Verrocchio*** Rest. *(closed Monday)* a la carte 80/105000 – 25000 – **33 rm** 240/480000, 5 suites.

wards Trespiano *N : 7 km :*

Villa le Rondini, via Bolognese Vecchia 224 ✉ 50139 Firenze ☏ 400081, Fax 268212, ≤ town, , « Among the olive trees », , , – rm – 200. AE ⓢ ① E VISA. rest
Meals 45/90000 – **31 rm** 185/270000, 2 suites.

Serpiolle *N : 8 km – ✉ 50141 Firenze :*

Lo Strettoio, via Serpiolle 7 ☏ 4250044, ≤, , « 17C villa among the olive trees » – . AE ⓢ E VISA.
Meals (booking essential) a la carte 60/85000.

the motorway at ring-road A1-A11 *NW : 10 km :*

Forte Agip, ✉ 50013 Campi Bisenzio ☏ 4205081, Fax 4219015 – rm – 200. AE ⓢ ① E VISA JCB.
Meals a la carte 45/70000 – **163 rm** 205/235000.

ose to motorway station A1 Florence South *SE : 6 km :*

Sheraton Firenze Hotel, ✉ 50126 ☏ 64901, Telex 572060, Fax 680747, , – rm – 1500. AE ⓢ ① E VISA JCB.
Meals a la carte 50/80000 – **311 rm** 300/360000, 3 suites.

The video cassette
CHÂTEAUX OF THE LOIRE, from Chambord to Chinon,
is a film to complement the Michelin Green Guide Châteaux of the Loire.
It portrays the Châteaux and the elegant lifestyle of the Touraine.

Available in six versions:
0751 in French SECAM
0752 in French PAL
1752 in English PAL
1753 in English NTSC
2752 in German PAL
3752 in Italian PAL

MILAN 20100 P 988 ③, 428 F 9 *G. Italy – pop. 1 306 494 alt. 122 – ☎ 02.*

See : *Cathedral★★★ (Duomo)* MZ – *Cathedral Museum★★* MZ **M1** – *Via and Piazza Mercanti★* MZ **155** *La Scala Opera House★★* MZ *Manzoni House★* MZ **M7** *Brera Art Gallery★★★* KV *Castle of the Sforzas★★★* JV – *Ambrosian Library★★* MZ : *portraits★ of Gaffurio and Isabella d'Este, Raphael's cartoons★★★ – Poldi-Pezzoli Museum★★* KV M *portrait of a woman★★★ (in profile) by Pollaiolo Palazzo Bagatti Valsecchi★★* KV **L** – *Natural History Museum★* LV **M6** – *Leonardo da Vinci Museum of Science and Technology★* **M4** – *Church of St. Mary of Grace★* HX : *Leonardo da Vinci's Last Supper★★★ – Basilica of St. Ambrose★★* HJX : *altar front★★ – Church of St. Eustorgius★* JY : *Portinari Chapel★★ – General Hospital★* KXY – *Church of St. Satiro★ : dome★* MZ – *Church of St. Maurice★★* JX – *Church of St. Lawrence Major★* JY.

Envir. : *Chiaravalle Abbey★ SE : 7 km by corso Lodi* LY.

18, 9 *(closed Monday) at Monza Park ✉ 20052 Monza ☎ (039) 303081, Fax 3044... by N : 20 km;*

18 *Molinetto (closed Monday) at Cernusco sul Naviglio ✉ 20063 ☎ 921051... Fax 92106635, by NE : 14 km;*

18 *Barlassina (closed Monday) at Birago di Camnago ✉ 20030 ☎ (0362) 5606... Fax 560934, by N : 26 km;*

18 *(closed Monday) at Zoate di Tribiano ✉ 20067 ☎ 90632183, Fax 90631861, SE : 20 k...*

18 *Le Rovedine (closed Monday) at Noverasco di Opera ✉ 20090 5760642... Fax 57606405, by via Ripamonti* BP.

Motor-Racing circuit *at Monza Park by N : 20 km, ☎ (039) 22366.*

✈ *Forlanini of Linate E : 8 km ☎ 74852200 and Malpensa by NW : 45 km ☎ 748522... – Alitalia, corso Como 15 ✉ 20154 62818 and via Albricci 5 ✉ 20122 62817.*

🚗 *675001.*

ℹ *via Marconi 1 ✉ 20123 809662, Fax 72022999 – Central Station ✉ 201... 6690532.*

A.C.I. *corso Venezia 43 ✉ 20121 77451.*

Roma 572 – Genève 323 – Genova 142 – Torino 140.

Plans on following pages

Historical centre Duomo, Scala, Sforza Castle, corso Magenta, via Torino, corso Vittorio Emanuele, via Manzoni

Four Seasons, via Gesù 8 ✉ 20121 ☎ 77088, Fax 77085000, Fō, – |‡| ⇆ TV ☎ ♿ 🚗 – 🏛 280. AE 🅂 ⊙ E VISA JCB. ✻ rest KV
Meals ***Il Teatro*** Rest. *(closed lunch, Sunday and August)* a la carte 75/140000 and ***Veranda*** Rest. a la carte 65/120000 – ☕ 36000 – **82 rm** 815/1015000, 16 suites.

Grand Hotel et de Milan, via Manzoni 29 ✉ 20121 ☎ 723141, Fax 86460861 – ▤ TV ☎ ♿ – 🏛 100. AE 🅂 ⊙ E VISA JCB. ✻ rest KV
Meals ***Caruso*** Rest. *(closed dinner except Sunday)* 60/80000 (lunch) 100/120000 (dinner) and a la carte 85/125000 see also rest ***Don Carlos*** below – ☕ 30000 – **87 r...** 600/715000, 8 suites.

Jolly Hotel President, largo Augusto 10 ✉ 20122 ☎ 77461, Telex 31205... Fax 783449 – |‡| ⇆ rm ▤ TV ☎ – 🏛 100. AE 🅂 ⊙ E VISA JCB. ✻ rest NZ
Meals a la carte 70/115000 – **206 rm** ☕ 445/525000, 13 suite.

Brunelleschi M, via Baracchini 12 ✉ 20123 ☎ 8843, Telex 312256, Fax 804924 |‡| ▤ TV ☎ ♿ – 🏛 50. AE 🅂 ⊙ E VISA JCB. ✻ MZ
Meals (residents only) a la carte 60/90000 – **123 rm** ☕ 360/500000, 5 suites.

Pierre Milano, via Edmondo De Amicis 32 ✉ 20123 ☎ 72000581, Fax 8052157 – ▤ TV ☎. AE 🅂 ⊙ E VISA JCB. ✻ rest JY
Meals 55/85000 – **45 rm** ☕ 330/500000, 4 suites.

Radisson SAS Bonaparte Hotel, via Cusani 13 ✉ 20121 ☎ 8560, Fax 86936... – |‡| ▤ TV ☎ 🚗 – 🏛 25. AE 🅂 ⊙ E VISA JCB. ✻ rest JV
Meals a la carte 55/80000 – **55 rm** ☕ 360/440000, 10 suites.

Sir Edward without rest., via Mazzini 4 ✉ 20123 ☎ 877877, Fax 877844, ≘s – |‡| ▤ TV ☎ ♿. AE 🅂 ⊙ E VISA MZ
38 rm ☕ 290/390000, suite.

Spadari al Duomo M without rest., via Spadari 11 ✉ 20123 ☎ 72002371, Fax 86118... « Collection of modern art » – |‡| ▤ TV ☎. AE 🅂 ⊙ E VISA. ✻ MZ
38 rm ☕ 290/380000.

Grand Hotel Duomo, via San Raffaele 1 ✉ 20121 ☎ 8833, Fax 86462027, ≤ Duomo, – |‡| ▤ TV ☎ – 🏛 100. AE 🅂 ⊙ E VISA JCB. ✻ MZ
Meals a la carte 70/110000 – **132 rm** ☕ 440/605000, 16 suites.

Galileo, corso Europa 9 ✉ 20122 ☎ 7743, Telex 322095, Fax 76020584 – |‡| ▤ ... ☎. AE 🅂 ⊙ E VISA JCB. ✻ NZ
a la carte 60/90000 – **81 rm** ☕ 310/410000, 8 suites.

Regina without rest., via Cesare Correnti 13 ✉ 20123 ✆ 58106913, Fax 58107033, « 18C building » – 40. AE VISA JY a
closed August and 24 December-2 January – **43 rm** 260/340000.

Dei Cavalieri, piazza Missori 1 ✉ 20123 ✆ 88571, Telex 312040, Fax 72021683 – – 60. AE VISA JCB. rest MZ m
Meals 50000 – **171 rm** 150/210000, 7 suites.

Starhotel Rosa without rest., via Pattari 5 ✉ 20122 ✆ 8831, Telex 316067, Fax 8057964 – – 120. AE VISA JCB NZ v
185 rm 390/510000.

De la Ville, via Hoepli 6 ✉ 20121 ✆ 867651, Telex 312642, Fax 866609 – – 60. AE VISA JCB. rest NZ h
Meals see rest. ***Canova*** below – **99 rm** 375/495000, 3 suites.

Ascot without rest., via Lentasio 3/5 ✉ 20122 ✆ 58303300, Fax 58303203 – . AE VISA KY c
closed August and Christmas – **63 rm** 230/320000.

Cavour, via Fatebenefratelli 21 ✉ 20121 ✆ 6572051, Fax 6592263 – – 100. AE VISA JCB. rest KV x
closed 11 to 24 August, Christmas and New Year – **Meals** 55000 and ***Conte Camillo*** Rest. *(closed Sunday)* 35000 (lunch only) and a la carte 50/90000 – 25000 – **111 rm** 255/300000, 2 suites.

Carrobbio without rest., via Medici 3 ✉ 20123 ✆ 89010740, Fax 8053334 – . AE VISA JCB JX d
closed August and 22 December-6 January – **35 rm** 220/310000.

Manzoni without rest., via Santo Spirito 20 ✉ 20121 ✆ 76005700, Fax 784212 – . AE VISA. KV s
20000 – **49 rm** 170/220000, 3 suites.

Lloyd without rest., corso di Porta Romana 48 ✉ 20122 ✆ 58303332, Fax 58303365 – – 100. AE VISA KY c
56 rm 270/370000.

Ambrosiano without rest., via Santa Sofia 9 ✉ 20122 ✆ 58306044, Telex 333872, Fax 58305067, – – 35. AE VISA. KY f
closed 23 December-1 January – **78 rm** 170/250000.

Zurigo without rest., corso Italia 11/a ✉ 20122 ✆ 72022260, Telex 353091, Fax 72000013 – . AE VISA JCB. KY j
closed 24 December-7 January – 8000 – **41 rm** 180/255000.

Casa Svizzera without rest., via San Raffaele 3 ✉ 20121 ✆ 8692246, Fax 72004690 – . AE VISA MZ u
closed 28 July-24 August – **45 rm** 210/260000.

Canada without rest., via Santa Sofia 16 ✉ 20122 ✆ 58304844, Fax 58300282 – . AE VISA KY f
35 rm 190/280000.

Savini, galleria Vittorio Emanuele II ✉ 20121 ✆ 72003433, Fax 86461060, Elegant traditional decor – . AE VISA JCB MZ s
closed Saturday lunch, Sunday, August and 23 December-6 January – **Meals** (booking essential) 65000 b.i. (lunch) 80000 (dinner) and a la carte 75/130000 (12 %).

Don Carlos - Grand Hotel et de Milan**,** vicolo Manzoni ✉ 20121 ✆ 72314640, Late night dinners – . AE VISA JCB. KV g
closed Sunday – **Meals** *(dinner only)* (booking essential) a la carte 85/115000.

Peck, via Victor Hugo 4 ✉ 20123 ✆ 876774, Fax 860408 – . AE VISA JCB. MZ e
closed Sunday, Bank Holidays, 2 to 23 July and 1 to 10 January – **Meals** 60/80000 and a la carte 75/120000
Spec. Insalata d'astice dell'Atlantico all'aceto balsamico. Filetti di rombo con patate, mele e Calvados (autumn-winter). Costolette d'agnello alle primizie con aglio dolce e timo fresco (spring).

Santini, corso Venezia 3 ✉ 20121 ✆ 782010, Fax 76014691, – . AE VISA JCB. NZ n
closed Sunday and 4 to 25 August – **Meals** 60000 (lunch) and a la carte 75/100000.

Canova, via Hoepli 6 ✉ 20121 ✆ 8051231, Fax 860094 – . AE VISA JCB. NZ h
closed Sunday and August – **Meals** (booking essential) a la carte 60/100000

Don Lisander, via Manzoni 12/a ✉ 20121 ✆ 76020130, Fax 784573, « Outdoor summer service » – . AE VISA JCB KV u
closed Sunday, 12 to 22 August and 24 December-10 January – **Meals** (booking essential) a la carte 75/105000.

MILANO

Aurispa (V.) . . . . JY 14
Battisti (V. C.) . . . . KLX 20
Bocchetto (V.) . . . . JX 30
Borgogna (V.) . . . . KX 36
Borgonuovo (V.) . . . . KV 38

Calatafimi (V.) . . . . JY 45
Caradosso (V.) . . . . HX 49
Ceresio (V.) . . . . JU 59
Circo (V.) . . . . JX 63
Col di Lana (Via) . . . . JY 65
Col Moschin (V.) . . . . JY 66
Conça del Naviglio (V.) . . . . JY 69
Copernico (V.) . . . . LT 72

Cordusio (Pza) . . . . KX
Cune (Vie P.M.) . . . . HV
Dugnani (V.) . . . . HY
Fatebenefratelli (V.) . . . . . KV
Gangliano (V.) . . . . KT
Generale Fara (V.) . . . . . . KT
Ghislen (V. A.) . . . . HY
Giardini (V. dei) . . . . KV

Within the green shaded area, the city is divided into zones wich are signposted all the way round. Once entered, it is not possible to drive from one zone into another.

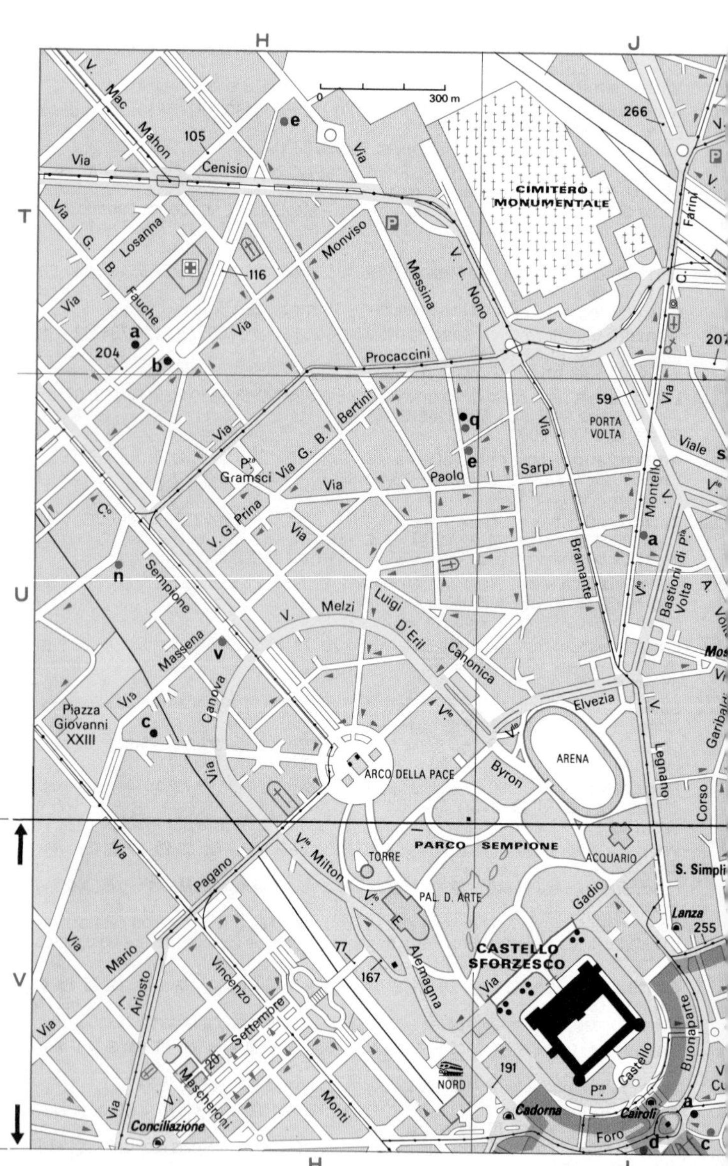

ı S. Bernardo (V.)	HT 105
stalla (V.)	KX 110
ıno (V. Fratelli)	HT 116
ıbertenghi (/.P.)	KT 122
etit (V.)	LTU 128
fei (V. A.)	LY 135
zö (V.)	LU 152
rcato (V.)	JV 158
destino (V.)	HY 165
ière (Vie E.)	HV 167
ıaton (V.L.)	LY 180
Oggiono (V. M. d')	HJY 183
Orseolo (V.)	HY 189
Paleocapa (V.)	JV 191
Pastrengo (V.)	KT 195
Perasto (V.)	KT 198
Poliziano (V.)	HTU 204
Ponte Vetero (V.)	JY 205
Quadrio (V.M.)	JT 207
Restelli (Vie F.)	KT 214
Ruffini (V. Fratelli)	HX 225
S. Babila (Pza)	KX 228
S. Calimero (V.)	KY 230
Savoia (Vie F. di)	KU 243
Tivoli (V.)	HV 255
Torchio (V.)	JX 257
Tornani (V.N.)	LU 258
Trau (V.)	KT 260
Valtellina (V.)	JT 266
Vercelli (Cso)	HX 267
Verdi (V.)	KV 269
Vittono Veneto (Vie)	KLU 278
Zezon (V.)	LU 281

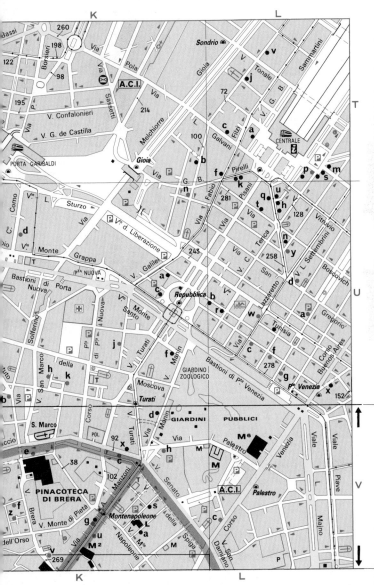

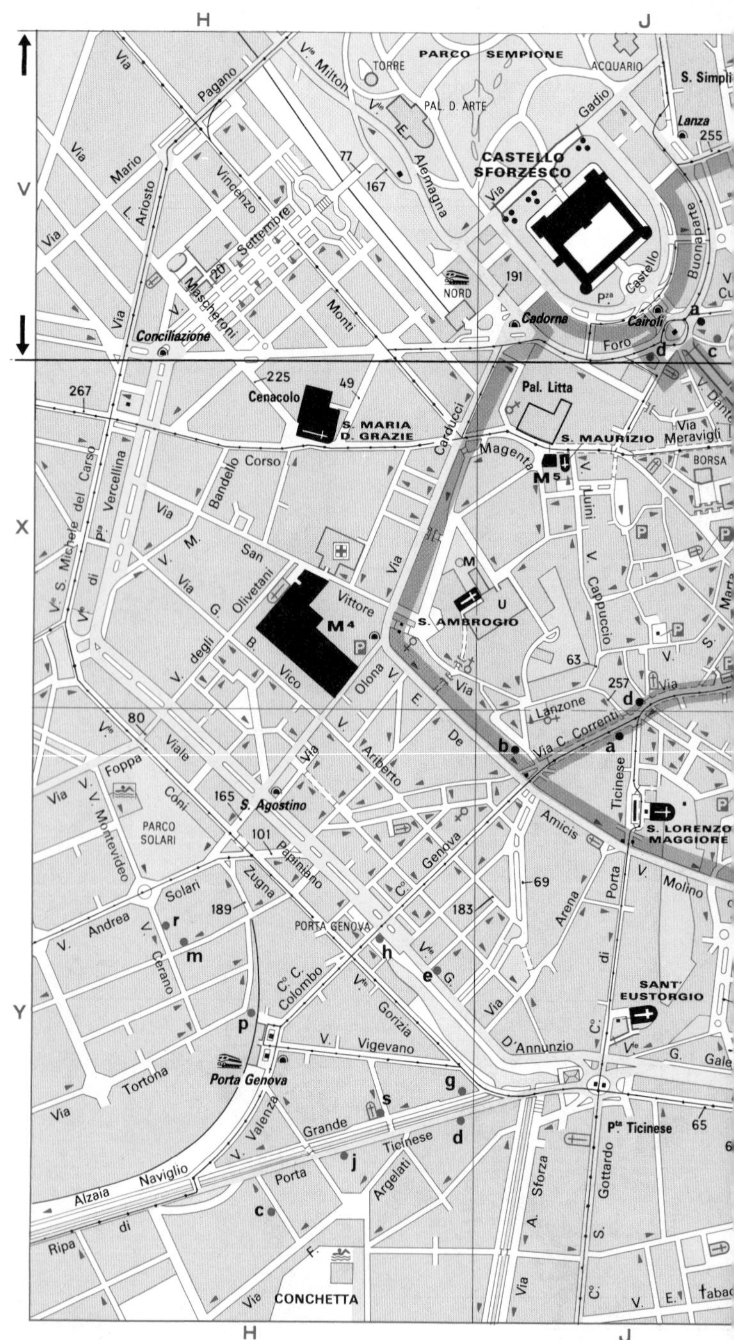

H
J
V
X
Y
PARCO SEMPIONE
TORRE
ACQUARIO
S. Simpli
PAL. D. ARTE
Lanza
255
CASTELLO SFORZESCO
Via Pagano
Via Mario
L. Ariosto
Vincenzo
20 Settembre
Mascheroni
Monti
Alemagna
NORD
191
Cadorna
Cairoli
Foro
Buonaparte
Castello
Gadio
Conciliazione
77
167
225
49
267
Cenacolo
S. MARIA D. GRAZIE
Pal. Litta
S. MAURIZIO
Meravigli
BORSA
Carducci
Magenta
M5
Corso
Bandello
Vercellina
V. S. Michele del Carso
S. AMBROGIO
M4
Vittore
San
Olivetani
V. degli
Olona
Luini
V. Cappuccio
63
257
Lanzone
Via C. Correnti
De
Amicis
Ticinese
S. LORENZO MAGGIORE
80
Viale
Foppa
Coni
PARCO SOLARI
V. Montevideo
165
S. Agostino
101
Papiniano
Zugna
Solari
189
Andrea
Cerano
PORTA GENOVA
Genova
69
183
Arena
Porta
Molino
SANT' EUSTORGIO
Colombo
Gorizia
D'Annunzio
Vigevano
Tortona
Porta Genova
Valenza
Grande
Ticinese
Argelati
Naviglio
Alzaia
Ripa
di
Porta
CONCHETTA
A. Sforza
S. Gottardo
Pta Ticinese
65
Tabac

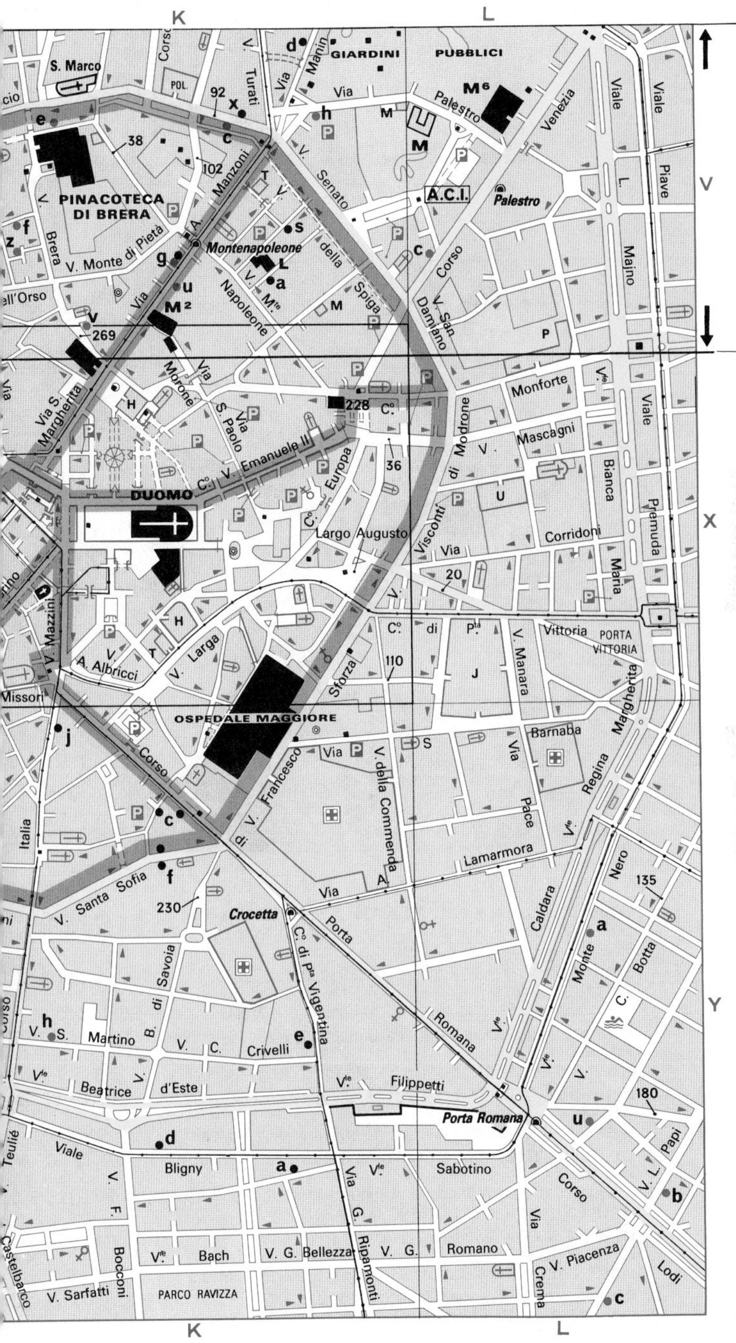
K
L
V
X
Y
GIARDINI
PUBBLICI
S. Marco
PINACOTECA
DI BRERA
Montenapoleone
A.C.I.
Palestro
DUOMO
Largo Augusto
OSPEDALE MAGGIORE
PORTA
VITTORIA
Crocetta
Porta Romana
PARCO RAVIZZA
Missori
Via Manin
Via Palestro
Corso Venezia
Viale Majno
Viale Piave
V. Senato
V. della Spiga
V. Turati
Via Manzoni
V. Monte di Pietà
Brera
Via S. Margherita
Via Morone
Via S. Paolo
C°. V. Emanuele II
C°. Europa
V. Napoleone
Corso V. San Damiano
Monforte
V. Mascagni
Via Visconti di Modrone
Via Corridoni
Viale Bianca Maria
Viale Premuda
C°. di P.ta Vittoria
V. Manara
V. Larga
A. Albricci
V. Mazzini
Via Sforza
V. Francesco
V. della Commenda
Via Barnaba
Via Pace
V.le Regina Margherita
Via Lamarmora
Corso Italia
V. Santa Sofia
Corso di Porta Romana
C°. di P.ta Vigentina
V. di Savoia
V. S. Martino
V. C. Crivelli
V.le Beatrice d'Este
V.le Filippetti
Viale Bligny
V.le Sabotino
Via G. Ripamonti
V. G. Bellezza
V. G. Romano
V.le Bach
V. F. Bocconi
V. Sarfatti
Castelbarco
Teulié
Caldara
V. Monte Nero
V. Botta
V. L. Papi
Corso Lodi
Via Crema
V. Piacenza

MILANO

Street	Grid	No.
Albricci (V.A.)	MZ	3
Arcivescovado (V.)	MNZ	10
Augusto (Largo)	NZ	12
Baracchini (V.)	MZ	17
Bergamini (V.)	NZ	27
Borgogna (V.)	NZ	36
Cantu (V.C.)	MZ	48
Cordusio (Pza)	MZ	73
Edison (Pza)	MZ	83
Festa del Perdono (V.)	NZ	93
Gonzaga (V.)	MZ	104
Laghetto (V.)	NZ	120
Manzoni (V.A.)	MZ	140
Marçoni (V.)	MZ	144
Manno (Pza)	MZ	147
Mengoni (V.)	MZ	153
Mercanti (Pza)	MZ	155
Mercanti (V.)	MZ	156
Misson (Pza)	MZ	162
Monforte (Cso)	NZ	168
Monte Napoleone (V.)	NZ	171
Morone (V.)	MNZ	
Orefici (V.)	MZ	
Pattan (V.)	NZ	
S. Clemente (NZ)	NZ	
S. Radegonda (V.)	MZ	
S. Stefano (Pza)	NZ	
Sforza (V.F.)	NZ	
Unione (V.)	MZ	
Verdi (V.)	MZ	
Verziere (V.)	NZ	
Visconti di Modrone (V.)	NZ	

Within the green shaded area, the city is divided into zones wich are signposted all the way round. Once entered, it is not possible to drive from one zone into another.

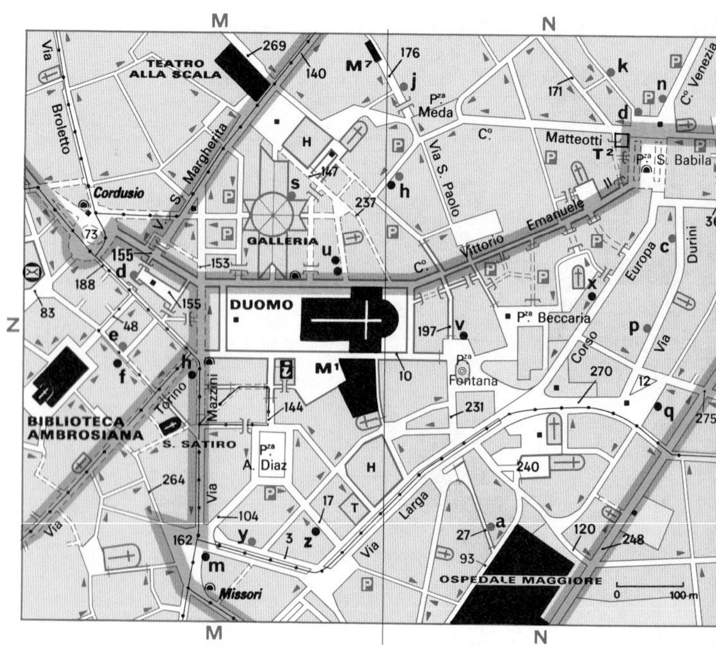

XXX **Boeucc,** piazza Belgioioso 2 ✉ 20121 ✆ 76020224, Fax 796173, « – ▤. AE. ✕
closed Saturday, Sunday lunch, August and 24 December-2 January – **Meals** (booki[ng] essential) a la carte 65/90000. NZ

XXX **Suntory,** via Verdi 6 ✉ 20121 ✆ 8693022, Fax 72023282, Japanese rest. – ▤. AE ⓓ VISA JCB. ✕ KV
closed Sunday, 11 to 22 August and Christmas – **Meals** a la carte 90/110000.

XXX **L'Ulmet,** via Disciplini ang. via Olmetto ✉ 20123 ✆ 86452718 – ▤. AE ⑤ VISA JCB JY
closed Sunday and Monday lunch – **Meals** (booking essential) a la carte 85/115000.

XXX **Peppino,** via Durini 7 ✉ 20122 ✆ 781729, Fax 76002511 – ▤. AE ⑤ ⓓ VISA JCB NZ
closed Friday, Saturday lunch and 10 July-4 August – **Meals** a la carte 50/80000.

XX **La Dolce Vita,** via Bergamini 11 ✉ 20122 ✆ 58307418 – ▤. AE ⑤ ⓓ VISA. ✕ NZ
closed Saturday lunch, Sunday and August – **Meals** (booking essential for dinner) 25/350[00] (lunch only) and a la carte 45/90000 (dinner only).

XX **La Bitta,** via del Carmine 3 ✉ 20121 ✆ 72003185, Fax 72003185, seafood – ▤. [AE] ⑤ ⓓ E VISA KV
closed Saturday lunch, Sunday and 6 to 31 January – **Meals** a la carte 50/70000.

XX **4 Mori,** largo Maria Callas 1 (angolo Largo Cairoli) ✉ 20121 ✆ 878483, « Outdoor summer service » – AE ⑤ ⓓ E VISA JV
closed Saturday lunch and Sunday – **Meals** a la carte 60/80000.

XX **Sogo-Brera,** via Fiori Oscuri 3 ✉ 20121 ℘ 86465367, Japanese rest. – ▤. AE 🅂 ⓞ VISA. 🚫 KV e
closed Sunday and 2 to 27 August – **Meals** 25/40000 (15 %) lunch 80/120000 (15 %) dinner and a la carte 60/100000 (15 %).

XX **Akasaka,** via Durini 23 ✉ 20122 ℘ 76023679, Japanese rest. – ▤. AE 🅂 ⓞ E VISA JCB. 🚫 NZ c
closed Sunday and 10 to 17 August – **Meals** 20/70000 (10 %) lunch 40/100000 (10 %) dinner and a la carte 60/100000 (10 %).

XX **Al Mercante,** piazza Mercanti 17 ✉ 20123 ℘ 8052198, Fax 86465250, « Outdoor summer service » – ▤. AE 🅂 ⓞ E VISA MZ d
closed Sunday and 3 to 28 August – **Meals** a la carte 50/75000.

XX **Moon Fish,** via Bagutta 2 ✉ 20121 ℘ 76005780, ☂, seafood – ▤. 🅂 NZ d
closed Sunday and 7 to 28 August – **Meals** a la carte 65/120000.

XX **Albric,** via Albricci 3 ✉ 20122 ℘ 86461329, Fax 86461329 – ▤. AE 🅂 ⓞ E VISA JCB. 🚫 MZ y
closed Saturday lunch, Sunday and 14 to 28 August – **Meals** a la carte 65/90000.

XX **Rovello,** via Rovello 18 ✉ 20121 ℘ 864396 – ▤. AE ⓞ E VISA. 🚫 JV c
closed Saturday (except dinner September-June) and Sunday – **Meals** a la carte 60/85000.

X **Bagutta,** via Bagutta 14 ✉ 20121 ℘ 76002767, Fax 799613, ☂, Meeting place for artists, « Original paintings and caricatures » – AE 🅂 ⓞ E VISA. 🚫 NZ k
closed Sunday and 23 December-5 January – **Meals** a la carte 70/115000.

X **Ciovassino,** via Ciovassino 5 ✉ 20121 ℘ 8053868, Fax 8053868 – ▤. AE 🅂 ⓞ E VISA KV z
closed Saturday lunch, Sunday and August – **Meals** a la carte 55/80000.

X **La Tavernetta-da Elio,** via Fatebenefratelli 30 ✉ 20121 ℘ 653441, Tuscan rest. – AE 🅂 E VISA KV c
closed Saturday lunch, Sunday and August – **Meals** a la carte 50/70000.

Directional centre via della Moscova, via Solferino, via Melchiorre Gioia, viale Zara, via Carlo Farini

🏨 **Executive,** viale Luigi Sturzo 45 ✉ 20154 ℘ 6294, Telex 310191, Fax 29010238 – 🛗 ▤ TV ☎ – 🎤 800. AE 🅂 ⓞ E VISA JCB. 🚫 KTU e
Meals 30/80000 – **414 rm** ☕ 200/250000, 6 suites.

🏨 Carlyle Brera Hotel without rest., corso Garibaldi 84 ✉ 20121 ℘ 29003888, Fax 29003993 – 🛗 🚭 ▤ TV ☎ ♿ 🚗 JU u
98 rm.

🏨 **Royal Hotel Mercure,** via Cardano 1 ✉ 20124 ℘ 6709151, Fax 6703024 – 🛗 🚭 rm ▤ TV ☎ 🚗 – 🎤 180. AE 🅂 ⓞ E VISA JCB. 🚫 rest KT b
Meals *(closed 1 to 21 August)* 45/55000 – **205 rm** ☕ 335/450000.

XXX **A Riccione,** via Taramelli 70 ✉ 20124 ℘ 6686807, Seafood – ▤. AE 🅂 ⓞ E VISA JCB by via Melchiorre Gioia KLT
closed Monday and August – **Meals** (booking essential) a la carte 80/105000.

XX **Serendib,** via Pontida 2 ✉ 20121 ℘ 6592139, Fax 6592139, Srilanken and Indian Rest. – ▤. 🅂 E VISA JU b
closed Monday and 8 to 27 August – **Meals** (dinner only) (booking essential) a la carte 40/50000.

XX **Al Tronco,** via Thaon di Revel 10 ✉ 20159 ℘ 606072 – ▤. AE 🅂 ⓞ E VISA. 🚫 by via Melchiorre Gioia KLT
closed Saturday lunch, Sunday and August – **Meals** a la carte 40/70000.

XX **Piccolo Teatro-Fuori Porta,** viale Pasubio 8 ✉ 20154 ℘ 6572105 – ▤. AE 🅂 ⓞ E VISA. 🚫 JU m
closed Friday and 25 December-6 January – **Meals** (booking essential) a la carte 60/85000.

XX **Alla Cucina delle Langhe,** corso Como 6 ✉ 20154 ℘ 6554279, Piedmontese rest. – ▤. AE 🅂 ⓞ E VISA. 🚫 KU d
closed Sunday and August – **Meals** a la carte 55/85000.

XX **Casa Fontana-23 Risotti,** piazza Carbonari 5 ✉ 20125 ℘ 6704710 – ▤. AE 🅂 E VISA. 🚫 by via M. Gioia LT
closed 5 to 27 August, Monday, Saturday lunch and Saturday dinner-Sunday in July – **Meals** (booking essential) a la carte 60/95000.

XX **Trattoria della Pesa,** viale Pasubio 10 20154 ℘ 6555741, Fax 29006859, Typical old Milan trattoria, Lombardy rest. – ▤. AE 🅂 ⓞ E VISA. 🚫 JU s
closed Sunday and August – **Meals** a la carte 65/95000.

XX **San Fermo,** via San Fermo della Battaglia 1 ✉ 20121 ℘ 29000901, Spanish rest. – AE 🅂 ⓞ E VISA KU h
closed Saturday lunch and Sunday – **Meals** a la carte 40/60000.

XX **Il Verdi,** piazza Mirabello 5 ✉ 20121 ✆ 6590797 – ▤ KU k
closed Sunday (except December) and 11 to 24 August – **Meals** 20/30000 (lunch) and a la carte 40/60000.

XX **Rigolo,** via Solferino 11 ang. largo Treves ✉ 20121 ✆ 86463220, Fax 86463220, Habitués rest. – ▤. AE ⑤ ⓓ E VISA. ✻ KU b
closed Monday and August – **Meals** a la carte 40/60000.

XX **Da Fumino,** via Bernina 43 ✉ 20158 ✆ 606872, ☂, Tuscan trattoria – ▤. AE ⑤ ⓓ E VISA by via C. Farini JT
closed Saturday lunch, Sunday and August – **Meals** a la carte 45/70000.

X **Fuji,** viale Montello 9 ✉ 20154 ✆ 6552517, Japanese rest. JU a
closed Sunday, Easter, August and Christmas – **Meals** (dinner only) (booking essential) a la carte 65/95000 (12 %).

Central Station corso Buenos Aires, via Vittor Pisani, piazza della Repubblica

Principe di Savoia, piazza della Repubblica 17 ✉ 20124 ✆ 62301 and rest ✆ 62302026, Telex 310052, Fax 6595838, ₺, ≘s, ⛱, ▣ – |♦| ✻ ▤ TV ☎ ♿ ⇔ – 🏛 700. AE ⑤ ⓓ E VISA JCB. ✻ KU a
Meals 90/125000 and ***Galleria*** Rest. *(closed Saturday)* a la carte 95/150000 – ☕ 58500 – **252 rm** 550/690000, 47 suites.

Palace, piazza della Repubblica 20 ✉ 20124 ✆ 6336 and rest ✆ 29000803, Telex 311026, Fax 654485 – |♦| ✻ rm ▤ TV ☎ ♿ ⇔ P – 🏛 250. AE ⑤ ⓓ E VISA JCB. ✻ rest LU b
Meals ***Casanova Grill*** Rest. (booking essential) 100000 – ☕ 32000 – **208 rm** 440/640000, 8 suites.

Excelsior Gallia, piazza Duca d'Aosta 9 ✉ 20124 ✆ 67851, Telex 333653, Fax 66713239, ₺, ≘s – |♦| ✻ rm ▤ TV ☎ – 🏛 500. AE ⑤ ⓓ E VISA JCB. ✻
Meals a la carte 65/120000 – ☕ 38000 – **237 rm** 400/460000, 10 suites. LT a

Milano Hilton, via Galvani 12 ✉ 20124 ✆ 69831, Telex 330433, Fax 66710810 – |♦| ✻ rm ▤ TV ☎ ♿ ⇔ – 🏛 250. AE ⑤ ⓓ E VISA JCB. ✻ rest LT c
Meals a la carte 55/100000 – ☕ 35000 – **321 rm** 450/520000, 2 suites.

Duca di Milano, piazza della Repubblica 13 ✉ 20124 ✆ 6284, Telex 325026, Fax 6555966 – |♦| ▤ TV ☎ ♿ – 🏛 90. AE ⑤ ⓓ E VISA JCB. ✻ rest KU c
closed August – **Meals** a la carte 110/155000 – ☕ 29000 – 99 suites 540/740000.

Michelangelo, via Scarlatti 33 ang. piazza Luigi di Savoia ✉ 20124 ✆ 6755, Telex 340330, Fax 6694232 – |♦| ✻ rm ▤ TV ☎ ♿ ⇔ – 🏛 500. AE ⑤ ⓓ E VISA JCB LTU s
closed August – **Meals** a la carte 85/115000 – **300 rm** ☕ 380/500000, 7 suites.

Jolly Hotel Touring, via Tarchetti 2 ✉ 20121 ✆ 6335, Telex 320118, Fax 6592209 – |♦| ✻ rm ▤ TV ☎ ♿ – 🏛 120. AE ⑤ ⓓ E VISA. ✻ rest KU t
Meals ***Amadeus*** Rest. a la carte 60/80000 – **294 rm** ☕ 380/430000, 11 suites.

Starhotel Ritz, via Spallanzani 40 ✉ 20129 ✆ 2055, Telex 333116, Fax 29518679 – |♦| ✻ rm ▤ TV ☎ ⇔ – 🏛 160. AE ⑤ ⓓ E VISA JCB. ✻ rest
Meals (residents only) – **185 rm** ☕ 370/510000. by Corso Buenos Aires LU

Century Tower Hotel, via Fabio Filzi 25/b ✉ 20124 ✆ 67504, Telex 330557, Fax 66980602 – |♦| ▤ TV ☎ ♿ – 🏛 60. AE ⑤ ⓓ E VISA JCB. ✻ LT t
Meals 50/65000 b.i. – 144 suites ☕ 300/360000.

Doria Grand Hotel, viale Andrea Doria 22 ✉ 20124 ✆ 6696696, Telex 360173, Fax 6696669 – |♦| ✻ ▤ TV ☎ ♿ ⇔ – 🏛 70. AE ⑤ ⓓ E VISA JCB. ✻ rest
Meals *(closed lunch and August)* a la carte 55/95000 – **108 rm** ☕ 360/420000, 2 suites. by corso Buenos Aires LU

Manin, via Manin 7 ✉ 20121 ✆ 6596511, Fax 6552160, ☂ – |♦| ▤ TV ☎ – 🏛 100. AE ⑤ ⓓ E VISA JCB. ✻ rest KV d
closed 1 to 24 August and 24 December-7 January – **Meals** *(closed Saturday)* a la carte 50/85000 – ☕ 24000 – **112 rm** 250/325000, 6 suites.

Bristol without rest., via Scarlatti 32 ✉ 20124 ✆ 6694141, Fax 6702942 – |♦| ▤ TV ☎ – 🏛 50. AE ⑤ ⓓ E VISA LT m
closed August – **68 rm** ☕ 205/300000.

Atlantic without rest., via Napo Torriani 24 ✉ 20124 ✆ 6691941, Telex 321451, Fax 6706533 – |♦| ✻ ▤ TV ☎ ⇔ – 🏛 25. AE ⑤ ⓓ E VISA JCB LU h
62 rm ☕ 210/300000.

Augustus without rest., via Napo Torriani 29 ✉ 20124 ✆ 66988271, Fax 6703096 – |♦| ▤ TV ☎. AE ⑤ ⓓ E VISA JCB LU q
closed 25 July-22 August and 23 to 29 December – **56 rm** ☕ 150/230000.

Mediolanum without rest., via Mauro Macchi 1 ✉ 20124 ✆ 6705312, Telex 310448, Fax 66981921 – |♦| ▤ TV ☎. AE ⑤ ⓓ E VISA JCB LU n
52 rm ☕ 200/305000.

Sanpi without rest., via Lazzaro Palazzi 18 ✉ 20124 ☎ 29513341, Fax 29402451 – 30. AE VISA JCB. LU e
closed 1 to 24 August and 23 December-5 January – **63 rm** 260/360000, 2 suites.

Berna without rest., via Napo Torriani 18 ✉ 20124 ☎ 6691441, Telex 334695, Fax 6693892 – 30. AE VISA JCB. LU h
115 rm 220/305000.

Auriga without rest., via Pirelli 7 ✉ 20124 ☎ 66985851, Fax 66980698 – 25. AE VISA JCB. LTU k
closed August – **54 rm** 220/340000.

Madison without rest., via Gasparotto 8 ✉ 20124 ☎ 67074150, Fax 67075059 – 100. AE VISA LT j
92 rm 185/275000, 8 suites.

Galles, via Ozanam 1 ang. corso Buenos Aires ✉ 20129 ☎ 204841, Telex 322091, Fax 2048422, – 150. AE VISA JCB.
Meals *(closed Sunday)* a la carte 40/65000 – 14000 – **105 rm** 240/340000. by corso Buenos Aires LU

Fenice without rest., corso Buenos Aires 2 ✉ 20124 ☎ 29525541, Fax 29523942 – AE VISA LU x
closed August and 22 December-6 January – **42 rm** 170/230000.

Demidoff without rest., via Plinio 2 ✉ 20129 ☎ 29513889, Fax 29405816 – AE VISA JCB by via Vitruvio LU
closed 2 to 30 August and 24 December-2 January – **36 rm** 140/200000.

New York without rest., via Pirelli 5 ✉ 20124 ☎ 66985551, Fax 6697267 – 50. AE VISA LTU k
closed 1 to 28 August and 24 December-5 January – **69 rm** 160/235000.

City without rest., corso Buenos Aires 42/5 ✉ 20124 ☎ 29523382, Fax 2046957 – AE VISA. by corso Buenos Aires LU
closed 9 to 24 August and 23 December-2 January – **55 rm** 180/255000.

Mini Hotel Aosta without rest., piazza Duca d'Aosta 16 ✉ 20124 ☎ 6691951, Fax 6696215 – AE VISA JCB LT p
63 rm 160/240000.

San Carlo without rest., via Napo Torriani 28 ✉ 20124 ☎ 6693236, Telex 314324, Fax 6703116 – 30. AE VISA JCB LU u
75 rm 150/210000.

Bolzano without rest., via Boscovich 21 ✉ 20124 ☎ 6691451, Fax 6691455, – AE VISA JCB. LU t
15000 – **35 rm** 135/180000.

Sempione, via Finocchiaro Aprile 11 ✉ 20124 ☎ 6570323, Telex 340498, Fax 6575379 – AE VISA JCB LU r
39 rm 170/230000.

Florida without rest., via Lepetit 33 ✉ 20124 ☎ 6705921, Telex 314102, Fax 6692867 – AE VISA LTU s
20000 – **53 rm** 160/215000.

Club Hotel without rest., via Copernico 18 ✉ 20125 ☎ 6707221, Fax 67072050 – AE VISA LT v
53 rm 120/180000.

La Terrazza di Via Palestro, via Palestro 2 ✉ 20121 ☎ 76002186, Fax 76003328, « Summer service on terrace » – AE VISA JCB KV h
closed Sunday and Monday lunch – **Meals** (booking essential) a la carte 65/90000.

Mediterranea, piazza Cincinnato 4 ✉ 20124 ☎ 29522076, Fax 29522076, seafood – AE VISA. LU d
closed Sunday, 5 to 25 August and 1 to 10 January – **Meals** a la carte 50/80000.

Calajunco, via Stoppani 5 ✉ 20129 ☎ 2046003 – VISA.
closed Saturday lunch, Sunday, 10 to 31 August and 23 December-4 January – **Meals** (booking essential) 45/65000 (lunch) 100/120000 (dinner) and a la carte 80/115000. by corso Buenos Aires LU

Cavallini, via Mauro Macchi 2 ✉ 20124 ☎ 6693771, Fax 6693174, « Outdoor summer service » – AE VISA LU y
closed Saturday, Sunday, 3 to 23 August and 22 to 26 December – **Meals** a la carte 55/75000.

Joia, via Panfilo Castaldi 18 ✉ 20124 ☎ 29522124, Vegetarian cuisine – AE VISA JCB LU c
closed Saturday lunch, Sunday, August and 28 December-11 January – **Meals** (booking essential) 20/90000 (lunch) 50/90000 (dinner) and a la carte 60/90000
Spec. Antipasto "Colori gusti e consistenze" con foglia d'oro e tartufo. Riso basmati con tuorlo d'uovo e aneto (December-June). Tortino di patate e asparagi con tartufo nero, salsa di yogurt e sedano rapa (spring).

XX **Buriassi da Lino,** via Lecco 15 ✉ 20124 ☎ 29523227 – ▤ – 35. AE ⓢ E VISA
closed Saturday lunch, Sunday and 7 to 24 August – **Meals** (booking essential for dinner) 35/45000 (lunch) 45/55000 (dinner) a la carte 45/75000. LU

XX **I Malavoglia,** via Lecco 4 ✉ 20124 ☎ 29531387, Sicilian seafood rest. – ▤. AE ⓢ ⓪ E VISA LU
closed Monday and lunch (except Sunday and holidays) – **Meals** (booking essential) a la carte 60/100000.

XX **13 Giugno,** via Goldoni 44 ang. via Uberti ✉ 20129 ☎ 719654, Fax 713875, 🏠, Sicilian rest. – ▤. AE ⓢ ⓪ E VISA by via Mascagni LX
closed Sunday – **Meals** (booking essential) 40/65000 (lunch only) and 65/70000 (dinner only).

XX **La Buca,** via Antonio da Recanate ang. via Napo Torriani 28 ✉ 20124 ☎ 6693774 ▤. AE ⓢ ⓪ E VISA JCB LU
closed Saturday, Sunday lunch, August and 25 December to 6 January – **Meals** a la carte 40/75000.

XX **Le 5 Terre,** via Appiani 9 ✉ 20121 ☎ 6575177, Fax 653034, seafood – ▤. AE ⓢ ⓪ E VISA JCB KU
closed Saturday lunch, Sunday and 10 to 20 August – **Meals** a la carte 50/85000.

XX **Da Bimbi,** viale Abruzzi 33 ✉ 20131 ☎ 29526103, Habituès rest. – ▤. AE ⓢ ⓪ E VISA. ✻ by corso Buenos Aires LU
closed Sunday, Monday lunch, August and 25 December-1 January – **Meals** a la carte 60/95000.

XX **Al Girarrosto da Cesarina,** corso Venezia 31 ✉ 20121 ☎ 76000481 – ▤ LV
closed Saturday, Sunday lunch, August and 25 December-8 January – **Meals** a la carte 60/85000.

XX **Giglio Rosso,** piazza Luigi di Savoia 2 ✉ 20124 ☎ 6692129, Fax 6694174, 🏠 – ▤ AE ⓢ ⓪ E VISA LT
closed Saturday, Sunday lunch, August and 24 December-6 January – **Meals** a la carte 40/75000 (12 %).

XX **Altopascio,** via Gustavo Fara 17 ✉ 20124 ☎ 6702458, Tuscan rest. – ▤. AE ⓢ ⓪ E VISA KU
closed Saturday, Sunday lunch and August – **Meals** a la carte 45/75000.

XX **Osteria la Risacca 2,** viale Regina Giovanna 14 ✉ 20129 ☎ 29531801, seafood ▤. AE ⓢ E VISA. ✻ by corso Buenos Aires LU
closed Saturday lunch, Sunday and August-2 September – **Meals** a la carte 75/90000.

XX **Sukrity,** via Panfilo Castaldi 22 ✉ 20124 ☎ 201315, Indian rest. – AE ⓢ ⓪ E VISA ✻ LU
closed Monday – **Meals** (booking essential for dinner) 20/30000 lunch 35/45000 (10 %) dinner and a la carte 35/50000 (10 %).

Romana-Vittoria corso Porta Romana, corso Lodi, corso XXII Marzo, corso Porta Vittoria

XX **Mistral,** viale Monte Nero 34 ✉ 20135 ☎ 55019104 – ▤. AE ⓢ E VISA LY
closed Sunday – **Meals** (dinner only) (booking essential) a la carte 50/80000.

XX **Hosteria del Cenacolo,** via Archimede 12 ✉ 20129 ☎ 5455536, « Summer service in garden » – AE ⓢ E VISA. ✻ by corso di Porta Vittoria LX
closed Saturday lunch, Sunday and August – **Meals** a la carte 60/80000.

XX **La Risacca 6,** via Marcona 6 ✉ 20129 ☎ 55181658, Fax 55017796, 🏠, seafood ▤. AE ⓢ ⓪ E VISA by corso di Porta Vittoria LX
closed Sunday, Monday lunch, August and Christmas – **Meals** a la carte 75/100000.

XX **I Matteoni,** piazzale 5 Giornate 6 ✉ 20129 ☎ 55188293, Habitués rest. – ▤. AE ⓢ ⓪ E VISA LX
closed Sunday, 1 to 21 August and 1 to 7 January – **Meals** a la carte 40/75000.

X **Masuelli San Marco,** viale Umbria 80 ✉ 20135 ☎ 55184138, Fax 55184138 Lombardy-Piedmontese rest. – ▤. AE ⓢ E VISA by corso di Porta Vittoria LX
closed Sunday, Monday lunch, 16 August-10 September and 25 December-6 January – **Meals** (booking essential for dinner) a la carte 50/75000.

X **Dongiò,** via Corio 3 ✉ 20135 ☎ 5511372 – ▤. AE ⓢ ⓪ E VISA JCB. ✻ LY
closed Saturday lunch, Sunday and August – **Meals** a la carte 45/65000.

X **Da Pietro la Rena,** via Adige 17 ✉ 20135 ☎ 59901232 – ▤. AE ⓢ ⓪ E VISA LY
closed Sunday dinner, Monday and August – **Meals** a la carte 40/60000.

X **Merluzzo Felice,** via Lazzaro Papi 6 ✉ 20135 ☎ 5454711, Sicilian rest. – AE ⓢ ⓪ E VISA LY
closed Sunday – **Meals** (booking essential) a la carte 35/70000.

Navigli via Solari, Ripa di Porta Ticinese, viale Bligny, piazza XXIV Maggio

D'Este without rest., viale Bligny 23 ✉ 20136 ☎ 58321001, Telex 324216, Fax 58321136 – |♦| ▤ TV ☎ – 🏛 80. AE 🅂 ⓓ E VISA. ✂ KY d
☕ 25000 – **79 rm** 230/320000.

Crivi's without rest., corso Porta Vigentina 46 ✉ 20122 ☎ 582891, Fax 58318182 – |♦| ▤ TV ☎ 🚗 – 🏛 120. AE 🅂 ⓓ E VISA JCB KY e
closed August – **83 rm** ☕ 235/335000, 3 suites.

Liberty without rest., viale Bligny 56 ✉ 20136 ☎ 58318562, Fax 58319061 – |♦| ▤ TV ☎ 🚗. AE 🅂 E VISA. ✂ KY a
closed 10 to 25 August – ☕ 20000 – **52 rm** 160/240000.

Sadler, via Ettore Troilo 14 ang. via Conchetta ✉ 20136 ☎ 58104451, Fax 58112343, ⛱ – ▤. 🅂 ⓓ E VISA JCB by corso S. Gottardo JY
closed Sunday, 14 to 28 August and 1 to 21 January – **Meals** (dinner only) (booking essential) 90/120000 and a la carte 75/145000
Spec. Frittelle di fiori di zucchina farciti di mozzarella (spring-summer), Maccheroni al torchio al ragù d'astice, Involtini di pescatrice farciti ai gamberi e avvolti nella melanzana (spring-autumn).

Al Porto, piazzale Generale Cantore ✉ 20123 ☎ 89407425, Fax 8321481, seafood – ▤. AE ⓓ E VISA HY h
closed Sunday, Monday lunch, August and 24 December-3 January – **Meals** (booking essential) a la carte 60/100000.

Osteria di Porta Cicca, ripa di Porta Ticinese 51 ✉ 20143 ☎ 8372763, Fax 8372763 – ▤. AE 🅂 ⓓ VISA. ✂ HY j
closed Saturday lunch and Sunday – **Meals** (booking essential) a la carte 50/85000.

Trattoria Aurora, via Savona 23 ✉ 20144 ☎ 89404978, Fax 89404978, ⛱, Piedmontese rest. – AE 🅂 ⓓ E VISA JCB HY m
closed Monday – **Meals** 30000 b.i. (lunch) and 60000 b.i. (dinner).

Osteria del Binari, via Tortona 1 ✉ 20144 ☎ 89409428, Fax 89407470, ⛱, Old Milan atmosphere – ▤. AE 🅂 ⓓ E VISA HY p
closed Sunday – **Meals** (dinner only) (booking essential) 60000.

Il Torchietto, via Ascanio Sforza 47 ✉ 20136 ☎ 8372910, Fax 8372000, Mantuan rest. – ▤. AE 🅂 ⓓ E VISA. ✂ by via A. Sforza JY
closed Monday, August and 26 December-3 January – **Meals** a la carte 55/75000.

Le Buone Cose, via San Martino 8 ✉ 20122 ☎ 58310589, seafood – ▤. AE 🅂 VISA KY h
closed Saturday lunch, Sunday and August – **Meals** (booking essential) a la carte 55/105000.

Grand Hotel Pub, via Ascanio Sforza 75 ✉ 20141 ☎ 89511586, ⛱ – AE 🅂 VISA
closed Monday – **Meals** (dinner only) a la carte 40/60000. by via A. Sforza JY

Al Capriccio, via Washington 106 ✉ 20146 ☎ 48950655, seafood – ▤. AE 🅂 E VISA. ✂
closed Monday and August – **Meals** a la carte 60/85000. by via Foppa JY

Shri Ganesh, via Lombardini 8 ✉ 20143 ☎ 58110933, Indian rest. – ▤. AE 🅂 ⓓ E VISA. ✂ HY c
closed Sunday and 6 to 21 August – **Meals** (dinner only) 35/50000.

Olivia, viale D'Annunzio 7/9 ✉ 20123 ☎ 89406052 – ▤. AE 🅂 ⓓ E VISA HY e
closed Saturday lunch and Sunday – **Meals** a la carte 50/70000.

Alzaia 26, alzaia Naviglio Grande 26 ✉ 20144 ☎ 8323526, Rest. and bistrot – ▤. AE 🅂 ⓓ VISA HY s
closed Sunday and August – **Meals** (booking essential) a la carte 60/90000.

Posto di Conversazione, alzaia Naviglio Grande 6 ✉ 20144 ☎ 58106646, Fax 58106646 – ▤. AE 🅂 E VISA. ✂ HY g
closed Monday and 30 December-14 January – **Meals** (dinner only) a la carte 50/75000.

Trattoria all'Antica, via Montevideo 4 ✉ 20144 ☎ 58104860, Lombardy rest. – ▤. AE 🅂 E VISA. ✂ HY r
closed Saturday lunch, Sunday, August and 26 December-7 January – **Meals** 25000 b.i. and a la carte 35/55000 (lunch only) 45000 b.i. (dinner only).

Ponte Rosso, Ripa di Porta Ticinese 23 ✉ 20143 ☎ 8373132, Trattoria-bistrot with Triestine and Lombardy specialities HY d
closed Sunday and dinner (except Thursday and Saturday) – **Meals** 30/40000 (lunch) and 40/50000 (dinner).

Fiera-Sempione corso Sempione, piazzale Carlo Magno, via Monte Rosa, via Washington

Hermitage, via Messina 10 ✉ 20154 ☎ 33107700, Fax 33107399, Fₐ – |♦| ▤ TV ☎. ♿ 🚗 – 🏛 200. AE 🅂 ⓓ E VISA. ✂ HJU q
closed August – **Meals** (see rest. ***Il Sambuco*** below) – **123 rm** ☕ 320/420000, 7 suites.

Grand Hotel Ramada M, via Washington 66 ✉ 20146 ☎ 48521, Fax 4818925 – |♦| ⚡ rm ▤ TV ☎ ♿ 🚗 – 🏛 1200. AE 🅂 ⓓ E VISA JCB. ✂ by corso Magenta HX
Meals 50000 and ***La Brasserie*** Rest. a la carte 50/75000 – **322 rm** ☕ 460/590000, suite.

Regency without rest., via Arimondi 12 20155 39216021, Fax 39217734, « In an early 20C noble mansion » – 50. closed August – **57 rm** 240/340000, 2 suites. by corso Sempione HU

Poliziano without rest., via Poliziano 11 20154 33602494, Fax 33106410 – 60. HT closed 9 to 25 August – **98 rm** 250/320000, 2 suites.

Capitol without rest., via Cimarosa 6 20144 48003050, Telex 316150 Fax 4694724 – 60. by corso Magenta HX **95 rm** 260/330000.

Domenichino without rest., via Domenichino 41 20149 48009692, Fax 4800395 – 50. by corso Sempione HU closed 1 to 24 August and 20 December-6 January – **75 rm** 170/235000, 2 suites

Mozart without rest., piazza Gerusalemme 6 20154 33104215, Fax 33103231 – HT **88 rm** 195/285000, 3 suites.

Admiral without rest., via Domodossola 16 20145 3492151, Fax 33106660 – 65. by via Procaccini HTU closed 23 July-28 August – **60 rm** 130/170000.

Berlino without rest., via Plana 33 20155 324141, Fax 39210611 – by corso Sempione HU closed 26 July-25 August and 24 December-3 January – **47 rm** 160/230000.

Lancaster without rest., via Abbondio Sangiorgio 16 20145 344705, Fax 34464 – HU closed August – **30 rm** 160/250000.

Metrò without rest., corso Vercelli 61 20144 468704, Fax 48010295 – 35. by via Ariosto HV **37 rm** 200/300000.

Mini Hotel Portello, via Guglielmo Silva 12 20149 4814944, Fax 4819243 – 100. by Vincenzo Monti HV **96 rm** 160/240000.

Mini Hotel Tiziano without rest., via Tiziano 6 4699035, Fax 4812153, « Little park » – by Vincenzo Monti HV **54 rm** 160/240000.

Il Sambuco - Hotel Hermitage, via Messina 10 20154 33610333, Fax 3319425 – HU closed Saturday lunch, Sunday, 1 to 20 August and 27 December-3 January – **Meals** a la carte 100/120000
Spec. Gallinella di mare con pomodorini, patate e taccole. Sarde ed alici alla napoletana. Zuppa di pesce alla chioggiota.

Alfredo-Gran San Bernardo, via Borgese 14 20154 3319000, Fax 29006859 Milanese rest. – HT closed August, 23 December-9 January, Sunday and Saturday June-July – **Meals** (booking essential) a la carte 75/100000
Spec. Risotto al salto o all'onda. Stracotto al Barbaresco. Foiolo alla milanese.

Trattoria del Ruzante, via Massena 1 20145 316102 – HU closed Saturday lunch, Sunday and August – **Meals** (booking essential) a la carte 60/95000

Taverna della Trisa, via Francesco Ferruccio 1 20145 341304, Trentine rest. – HU closed Monday and August – **Meals** a la carte 45/70000.

Al Vecchio Porco, via Messina 8 20154 313862, Rest. and pizzeria – HU closed Sunday lunch, Monday and August – **Meals** a la carte 40/60000.

Trattoria del Previati, via Gaetano Previati 21 20149 48000064 – by via Vincenzo Monti HV closed Saturday and 10 to 26 August – **Meals** a la carte 45/65000.

Al Vöttantott, corso Sempione 88 20154 33603114 – closed Sunday and August – **Meals** a la carte 35/70000. by corso Sempione HU

Zone periferiche

North-Western area viale Fulvio Testi, Niguarda, viale Fermi, viale Certosa, San Siro, via Novara

Grand Hotel Brun, via Caldera 21 20153 452711, Telex 315370, Fax 48204746 – 500. by corso Sempione HU closed 23 December-7 January – **Meals** a la carte 35/105000 – **306 rm** 370/480000, 24 suites.

Rubens without rest., via Rubens 21 ✉ 20148 ☎ 40302, Telex 353617, Fax 48193114, « Rooms with fresco murals » – AE VISA
87 rm 195/260000. by corso Magenta HX

Accademia without rest., viale Certosa 68 ✉ 20155 ☎ 39211122, Telex 315550, Fax 33103878, « Rooms with fresco murals » – AE VISA
67 rm 250/340000, 2 suites. by corso Sempione HU

Raffaello without rest., viale Certosa 108 ✉ 20156 ☎ 3270146, Fax 3270440 – 120. AE E VISA. by corso Sempione HU
closed 10 to 24 August and 23 December-2 January – **143 rm** 210/320000, 4 suites.

Blaise e Francisc, via Butti 9 ✉ 20158 ☎ 66802366, Fax 66802909 – 200. AE E VISA JCB. rest by via Carlo Farini JT
Meals (residents only) (dinner only) 40/70000 – **110 rm** 280/320000.

Novotel Milano Nord, viale Suzzani 13 ✉ 20162 ☎ 66101861, Telex 331292, Fax 66101961, – rm – 500. AE E VISA. rest
Meals a la carte 55/85000 – **172 rm** 260/300000. by via Valtellina JT

Ibis without rest., viale Suzzani 13/15 ✉ 20162 ☎ 66103000, Fax 66102797 – – 50. AE E VISA by via Valtellina JT
132 rm 140/170000.

Valganna without rest., via Var 32 ✉ 20158 ☎ 39310089, Fax 39312566 – . AE E VISA by via Carlo Farini JT
36 rm 120/170000.

Al Solito Posto, via Bruni 13 ✉ 20158 ☎ 6888310 – AE E VISA.
closed Sunday, 20 July-20 August and 25 December-2 January – **Meals** (dinner only) (booking essential) a la carte 60/80000. by via Carlo Farini JT

Innocenti Evasioni, via privata della Bindellina ✉ 20155 ☎ 33001882, Fax 33001882, – AE E VISA by via Carlo Farini JT
closed Sunday, Monday, August and Christmas – **Meals** (dinner only) a la carte 45/65000.

La Pobbia, via Gallarate 92 ✉ 20151 ☎ 38006641, Fax 38006641, Modern rustic rest., « Outdoor summer service » – 40. AE E VISA by corso Sempione HU
closed Sunday and August – **Meals** a la carte 55/80000 (12 %).

Ribot, via Cremosano 41 ✉ 20148 ☎ 33001646, Fax 39267187, « Summer service in garden » – . AE VISA by corso Sempione HU
closed Monday, 10 to 25 August and Christmas – **Meals** a la carte 50/75000 (10 %).

Al Bimbo, via Marcantonio dal Re 38 ang. via Certosa ✉ 20156 ☎ 3272290, Fax 39216365 – . AE E VISA. by corso Sempione HU
closed Sunday and August – **Meals** a la carte 50/80000.

Northern-Eastern area viale Monza, via Padova, via Porpora, viale Romagna, viale Argonne, viale Forlanini

Concorde without rest., viale Monza 132 ✉ 20125 ☎ 26112020, Telex 315805, Fax 26147879 – – 160. AE E VISA.
120 rm 195/300000. by corso Buenos Aires LU

Starhotel Tourist, viale Fulvio Testi 300 ✉ 20126 ☎ 6437777, Telex 326852, Fax 6472516, – rm – 170. AE E VISA JCB. rest
Meals a la carte 45/60000 – **140 rm** 290/410000. by corso Buenos Aires LU

Lombardia, viale Lombardia 74 ✉ 20131 ☎ 2824938, Fax 2893430 – rm – 100. AE E VISA. by corso Buenos Aires LU
closed 9 to 24 August – **Meals *La Festa*** Rest *(closed Saturday and Sunday) (dinner only)* a la carte 35/70000 – **78 rm** 175/245000, 6 suites.

L'Ami Berton, via Nullo 14 angolo via Goldoni ✉ 20129 ☎ 713669, Elegant rest. – . AE E VISA. by via Mascagni LX
closed Saturday lunch, Sunday, August and 1 to 10 January – **Meals** (booking essential for dinner) a la carte 75/125000
Spec. Gamberi marinati al cipollotto e caviale. Bavette ai filetti di sogliola e taccole. Orata "all'acqua pazza" con porcini.

Osteria Corte Regina, via Rottole 60 ✉ 20132 ☎ 2593377, Fax 2593377, , Elegant rustic rest. – AE E VISA by corso buenos Aires LU
closed Saturday lunch, Sunday and 5 to 25 August open only dinner – **Meals** (booking essential) a la carte 55/85000.

L'Altra Scaletta, viale Zara 116 ✉ 20125 ☎ 6888093, Fax 6888093 – . AE E VISA. by corso Buenos Aires LU
closed Saturday lunch, Sunday and August – **Meals** a la carte 45/65000.

3 Pini, via Tullo Morgagni 19 ✉ 20125 ☎ 66805413, Fax 66801346, « Summer service under pergola » – AE E VISA. by corso Buenos Aires LU
closed Saturday, 5 to 31 August and 25 December-4 January – **Meals** (booking essential) a la carte 55/80000.

XX **Montecatini Alto,** viale Monza 7 ✉ 20125 ☎ 2846773 – ▤
closed Saturday lunch, Sunday and August – **Meals** a la carte 50/60000.
by corso Buenos Aires LU

XX **Da Renzo,** piazza Sire Raul 4 ✉ 20131 ☎ 2846261, Fax 2896634, ☂ – ▤. AE 🅢 ⓞ E VISA
by corso Buenos Aires LU
closed Monday dinner, Tuesday, August and 26 December-2 January – **Meals** a la carte 40/65000.

XX **Baia Chia,** via Bazzini 37 ✉ 20131 ☎ 2361131, ☂, seafood – ▤. 🅢 VISA ✂
by corso Buenos Aires LU
closed Sunday, Easter, August and 24 December-2 January – **Meals** (booking essential) a la carte 45/85000.

X **Mykonos,** via Tofane 5 ✉ 20125 ☎ 2610209, Greek rest.
closed Tuesday and August – **Meals** (dinner only) (booking essential) a la carte 30/40000.
by corso Buenos Aires LU

Southern-Eastern area viale Molise, corso Lodi, via Ripamonti, corso San Gottardo

Quark, via Lampedusa 11/a ✉ 20141 ☎ 84431, Telex 353448, Fax 8464190, ☂ – ▮ ⇔ rm ▤ TV ☎ ⇔ P – 🏛 1100. AE 🅢 ⓞ E VISA JCB ✂ rest
by corso Italia KY
closed 22 July-25 August – **Meals** a la carte 60/110000 – **285 rm** ☕ 365000.

Novotel Milano Est Aeroporto, via Mecenate 121 ✉ 20138 ☎ 58011085 Telex 331237, Fax 58011086, ⛱ – ▮ ⇔ rm ▤ TV ☎ ♿ P – 🏛 350. AE 🅢 ⓞ E VISA. ✂ rest
by corso di Porta Vittoria LX
Meals a la carte 55/85000 – **206 rm** ☕ 275/350000.

XX **Antica Trattoria Monluè,** via Monlu 75 ✉ 20138 ☎ 7610246, Country trattoria with summer service – ▤ P. AE 🅢 ⓞ E VISA. ✂
by corso di Porta Vittoria LX
closed Saturday lunch, Sunday and 4 to 20 August – **Meals** a la carte 50/75000.

XX **La Plancia,** via Cassinis 13 ✉ 20139 ☎ 55211269, Fax 5390558, Seafood and pizzeria – ▤. AE 🅢 ⓞ E VISA. ✂
by corso Lodi LY
closed Sunday and August – **Meals** a la carte 40/65000.

X **Taverna Calabiana,** via Calabiana 3 ✉ 20139 ☎ 55213075, Rest. and pizzeria – ▤ AE 🅢 VISA. ✂
by corso Lodi LY
closed Sunday, Monday, 16 to 21 April, August and 24 December-5 January – **Meals** a la carte 45/65000.

Southern-Western area viale Famagosta, viale Liguria, via Lorenteggio, viale Forze Armate, via Novara

Holiday Inn, via Lorenteggio 278 ✉ 20152 ☎ 410014, Fax 48304729, ⛱ – ▮ ⇔ rm ▤ TV ☎ ♿ ⇔ P – 🏛 70. AE 🅢 ⓞ E VISA JCB. ✂ rest
by via Foppa HY
Meals ***L'Univers Gourmand*** Rest. a la carte 45/70000 – ☕ 34000 – **119 rm** 315/390000.

Green House without rest., viale Famagosta 50 ✉ 20142 ☎ 8132451, Fax 816624 – ▮ ▤ TV ☎ ♿ ⇔. AE 🅢 ⓞ E VISA. ✂
by Ripa di Porta Ticinese HY
☕ 15000 – **45 rm** 130/190000.

XXX ✿✿ **Aimo e Nadia,** via Montecuccoli 6 ✉ 20147 ☎ 416886, Fax 48302005 – ▤. AE 🅢 ⓞ E VISA. ✂
by via Foppa HY
closed Saturday lunch, Sunday, August and 1 to 6 January – **Meals** (booking essential) 60/105000 (lunch) 105000 (dinner) and a la carte 95/140000
Spec. Crema di lenticchie con rossetti e filo d'olio. Fettuccine di farina burattata con alici bottarga di muggine e erbe fini. Copertina di vitello con lardo alle spezie e zafferano (autumn-spring).

on national road 35-Milanofiori *by via Francesco Sforza* JY : *10 km* :

Royal Garden Hotel M ⛱, via Di Vittorio ✉ 20090 Assago ☎ 457811, Fax 4570290 – ▮ ▤ TV ☎ ♿ ⇔ P – 🏛 140. AE 🅢 ⓞ E VISA. ✂ rm
Meals a la carte 60/80000 – **114 rm** ☕ 270/380000, 40 suites.

Jolly Hotel Milanofiori, Strada 2 ✉ 20090 Assago ☎ 82221, Telex 325314, Fax 89200946, 🏋, ≘s, 🎾 – ▮ ⇔ rm ▤ TV ☎ ♿ P – 🏛 120. AE 🅢 ⓞ E VISA. ✂ rest
closed 22 December-7 January – **Meals** 65/90000 – **255 rm** ☕ 285/345000.

at Forlanini Park (West Wide) *by corso di Porta Vittoria* LX : *10 km* :

XX **Osteria i Valtellina,** via Taverna 34 ✉ 20134 Milano ☎ 7561139, Valtellina rest., « Summer service under pergola » – P. AE 🅢 ⓞ E VISA
closed Monday and 4 to 24 August – **Meals** a la carte 60/80000.

on road New Vigevanese-Zingone *by via Foppa HY : 11 km :*

Eur without rest., via Leonardo da Vinci 36 A ✉ 20090 Trezzano sul Naviglio ☎ 4451951, Fax 4451075 – 🛗 ▤ 📺 ☎ 🅿 – 🏛 70. AE 🔒 ⓓ E VISA JCB
39 rm ☕ 140/180000.

Blu Visconti, via Goldoni 49 ✉ 20090 Trezzano sul Naviglio ☎ 48402094, Fax 48403095, – 🛗 ▤ 📺 ☎ ♿ 🚗 🅿 – 🏛 100. AE 🔒 ⓓ E VISA
Meals ***Alla Cava*** Rest. *(closed Monday and 11 to 25 August)* a la carte 35/60000 (12%) – **63 rm** ☕ 110/150000, suite

on national road West-Assago *by via Foppa HY : 11 km :*

Forte Agip, ✉ 20090 Assago ☎ 4880441, Telex 325191, Fax 48843958, – 🛗 rm ▤ 📺 ☎ ♿ 🅿 – 🏛 300. AE 🔒 ⓓ E VISA JCB.
Meals a la carte 45/75000 – **197 rm** ☕ 220/250000.

Abbiategrasso *20081 Milano* 988 ③, 428 F 8 – *pop. 27249 alt. 120 –* ☎ *02.*
Roma 590 – Alessandria 80 – Milano 24 – Novara 29 – Pavia 33.

at Cassinetta di Lugagnano *N : 3 km –* ✉ *20081 :*

XXXX ✿✿ **Antica Osteria del Ponte,** ☎ 9420034, Fax 9420610, – ▤ 🅿. AE 🔒 ⓓ E VISA JCB.
closed Sunday, Monday, August and 25 December-12 January – **Meals** (booking essential) 75000 (lunch) 150000 (dinner) and a la carte 100/185000
Spec. Tagliolini alla chitarra in ragoût di porcini (summer-autumn). Brandade di stoccafisso (winter-summer). Crépinette di capretto alle mandorle (spring).

Bergamo *24100* P 988 ③, 428 E 11 *G. Italy – pop. 116 990 alt. 249 –* ☎ *035.*
, and L'Albenza (closed Monday) at Almenno San Bartolomeo ✉ *24030 640028, Fax 643066;*
La Rossera (closed Tuesday) at Chiuduno ✉ *24060* ☎ *838600, Fax 4427047.*
✈ *Orio al Serio* ☎ *326323, Fax 313432 – Alitalia, via Casalino 5* ☎ *224044, Fax 235127.*
Roma 601 – Brescia 52 – Milano 47.

XXX ✿✿ **Da Vittorio,** viale Papa Giovanni XXIII 21 ✉ 24121 ☎ 218060, Fax 218060 – ▤. AE 🔒 ⓓ E VISA
closed Wednesday and August – **Meals** 60/95000 (lunch) 95/130000 (dinner) and a la carte 90/120000
Spec. Insalata tiepida di pesci al vapore con pesto gentile. Spaghetti ai porcini in bianco. Spiedino di gamberoni e scampi alla "Vittorio".

Canneto sull'Oglio *46013 Mantova* 428 429 *G 13 – pop. 4 564 alt. 35 –* ☎ *0376.*
Roma 493 – Brescia 51 – Cremona 32 – Mantova 38 – Milano 123 – Parma 44.

towards Carzaghetto *NW : 3 km :*

XXXX ✿✿✿ **Dal Pescatore,** ✉ 46013 ☎ 723001, Fax 70304, « Outdoor dinner summer service » – ▤ 🅿. AE 🔒 ⓓ E VISA JCB.
closed Monday, Tuesday, 11 to 31 August, Christmas and 2 to 19 January – **Meals** (booking essential) 135000 and a la carte 100/155000
Spec. Tortelli di zucca. Coscette di rane gratinate alle erbe (March-November). Stracotto di cavallo al Barbera con polenta.

Erbusco *25030 Brescia* 428 429 *F 11 – pop. 6 587 alt. 251 –* ☎ *030.*
Roma 578 – Bergamo 35 – Brescia 22 – Milano 69.

XXXX ✿✿ **Gualtiero Marchesi,** località Bellavista N : 1,5 km ☎ 7760562, Fax 7760379, ≤ lake and mountains, Elegant installation – ▤ 🅿. AE 🔒 ⓓ E VISA JCB.
closed Sunday dinner, Monday, and 12 January-11 February – **Meals** (booking essential) 80000 (lunch) 100/170000 (dinner) and a la carte 100/180000
Spec. Riso, oro e zafferano. Costoletta di vitello alla milanese. Dolce "Montisola".

Ranco *21020 Varese* 428 *E 7,* 219 ⑦ *– pop. 1 097 alt. 214 –* ☎ *0331.*
Roma 644 – Laveno Mombello 21 – Milano 67 – Novara 51 – Sesto Calende 12 – Stresa 37 – Varese 27.

XXX ✿✿ **Il Sole** with rm, ☎ 976507, Fax 976620, ≤, « Summer service under pergola », – ▤ rm 📺 ☎ 🅿. AE 🔒 ⓓ E VISA.
closed December and January – **Meals** (booking essential) (closed Monday dinner except May-September and Tuesday) 70/80000 (10 %) lunch 115/125000 (10 %) dinner and a la carte 90/145000 (10 %) – ☕ 15000 – **9 rm** 210/380000, 6 suites 400/600000
Spec. Tortino d'astice con patate croccanti al basilico. Lasagna multicolore con scampi al Sauternes. Rostin negàa.

Soriso *28018 Novara* 428 E 7, 219 ⑯ – *pop. 747 alt. 452* – ☎ *0322.*
Roma 654 – Arona 20 – Milano 78 – Novara 40 – Stresa 35 – Torino 114 – Varese 46

XXXX ✿✿ **Al Sorriso** with rm, via Roma 18 ☎ 983228, Fax 983328 – ▤ rest TV ☎. AE ⑤ ⓓ E VISA. ✂ rest
closed 5 to 22 August and 8 to 22 January – **Meals** (booking essential) (closed Monday and Tuesday lunch) a la carte 100/140000 – **8 rm** ☐ 150/220000
Spec. Verdure di stagione in casseruola con triglie di scoglio e profumi mediterranei. Lasagnetta di sedano con gamberi di fiume e finferli (May-November). Faraona al granturco con tartufo (September-December).

NAPLES (NAPOLI) *80100* P 988 ㉗, 431 E 24 *G. Italy – pop. 1 050 234 – High Season : April-October* – ☎ *081.*

See : *National Archaeological Museum*★★★ KY – *New Castle*★★ KZ – *Port of Santa Lucia*★★ BU : ≤★★ *of Vesuvius and bay* – ≤★★★ *at night from via Partenope of the Vomero and Posillipo* FX – *San Carlo Theatre*★ KZ **T1** – *Piazza del Plebiscito*★ JKZ – *Royal Palace*★ KZ – *Carthusian Monastery of St. Martin*★★ JZ : ≤★★★ *ofthe Bay of Naples from gallery 25* – *Spacca-Napoli quarter*★★ KY – *Tomb*★★ *of King Robert the Wise in Church of Santa Chiara*★ KY – *Caryatids*★ *by Tino da Camaino in Church of St. Dominic Major* KY – *Sculptures*★ *in Chapel of St. Severo* KY – *Arch*★, *Tomb*★ *of Catherine of Austria, apse*★ *in Church of St. Lawrence Major* LY – *Capodimonte Palace and National Gallery*★★ – *Mergellina*★ : ≤★★ *of the bay* – *Villa Floridiana*★ EVX : ≤★ – *Catacombs of St. Gennaro*★★ – *Church of Santa Maria Donnaregina*★ LY – *Church of St. Giovanni a Carbonara*★ LY – *Capuan Gate*★ LMY – *Como Palace*★ LY – *Sculptures*★ *in the Church of St. Anne of the Lombards* KYZ – *Posillipo*★ – *Marechiaro*★ – ≤★★ *of the Bay from Virgiliano Park(or Rimembranza Park)*.

Exc. : *Bay of Naples*★★★ *road to Campi Flegrei*★★, *to Sorrento Penisula Island of Capri*★★★ *Island of Ischia*★★★.

⛳9 *(closed Tuesday) at Arco Felice* ✉ *80072* ☎ *5264296, W : 19 km.*

✈ *Ugo Niutta of Capodichino NE : 6 km (except Saturday and Sunday)* ☎ *5425333 – Alitalia, via Medina 41* ✉ *80133 5425222.*

⛴ *to Capri (1 h 15 mn), Ischia (1 h 15 mn) e Procida (1 h), daily – Caremar-Travel and Holidays, molo Beverello* ✉ *80133* ☎ *5513882, Fax 5522011; to Cagliari 19 June-17 September Thursday and Saturday, Thursday October-May (15 h 45 mn) and Palermo daily (11 h) – Tirrenia Navigazione, Stazione Marittima, molo Angioino* ✉ *80133* ☎ *5891050, Telex 710030, Fax 7201567 ; to Ischia daily (1 h 15 mn) – Alilauro and Linee Lauro, molo Beverello* ✉ *80133* ☎ *5522838, Fax 5513236 ; to Aeolian Island Wednesday and Friday, 15 June-15 September Monday, Tuesday, Thursday, Friday, Saturday and Sunday (14 h) – Siremar-Genovese Agency, via De Petris 78* ✉ *80133* ☎ *5512112, Telex 710196, Fax 5512114.*

🚤 *to Capri (45 mn), Ischia (45 mn) and Procida (35 mn), daily – Caremar-Travel and Holidays, molo Beverello* ✉ *80133* ☎ *5513882, Fax 5522011; to Ischia (30 mn) and Capri (40 mn), daily – Alilauro, via Caracciolo 11* ✉ *80122* ☎ *7611004, Fax 7614250; to Capri daily (40 mn)Navigazione Libera del Golfo, molo Beverello* ✉ *80133* ☎ *5520763, Telex 722661, Fax 5525589 ; to Capri (45 mn), to Aeolian Island June-September (4 h) and Procida-Ischia daily (35 mn) – Aliscafi SNAV, via Caracciolo 10* ✉ *80122* ☎ *7612348, Telex 720446, Fax 7612141.*

ℹ *piazza dei Martiri 58* ✉ *80121* ☎ *405311 – piazza del Plebiscito (Royal Palace)* ✉ *80132* ☎ *418744, Fax 418619 – Central Station* ✉ *80142* ☎ *268779 - Capodichino Airport* ✉ *80133* ☎ *7805761 – piazza del Gesù Nuovo 7* ✉ *80135* ☎ *5523328 - Passaggio Castel dell'Ovo* ✉ *80132* ☎ *7645688.*

A.C.I. *piazzale Tecchio 49/d* ✉ *80125* ☎ *2394511.*
Roma 219 – Bari 261

Plans on following pages

Grande Albergo Vesuvio, via Partenope 45 ✉ 80121 ☎ 7640044, Telex 710127, Fax 5890380, « Roof-garden rest. with ≤ gulf and Castel dell'Ovo » – 🛗 ⇆ rm ▤ TV ☎ 🚗 – 🎤 400. AE ⑤ ⓓ E VISA JCB. ✂ rest FX r
Meals ***Caruso*** Rest. *(closed Monday)* a la carte 80/115000 – **167 rm** ☐ 370/470000, 16 suites.

Gd H. Parker's, corso Vittorio Emanuele 135 ✉ 80121 ☎ 7612474, Telex 710578, Fax 663527, « Roof-garden rest. with ≤ town and gulf » – 🛗 ▤ TV ☎ 🚗 – 🎤 250. AE ⑤ ⓓ E VISA. ✂ EX
Meals *(closed Sunday dinner)* a la carte 65/115000 – **70 rm** ☐ 250/350000, 10 suites.

Santa Lucia, via Partenope 46 ✉ 80121 ☎ 7640666, Telex 710595, Fax 7648580, ≤ gulf and Castel dell'Ovo – 🛗 ▤ TV ☎ – 🎤 110. AE ⑤ ⓓ E VISA. ✂ GX w
Meals 60/80000 and ***Megaris*** Rest. *(closed Sunday)* a la carte 65/110000 – **97 rm** ☐ 295/410000, 5 suites.

Grand Hotel Terminus M, piazza Garibaldi 91 ✉ 80142 ✆ 7793111, Telex 722270, Fax 206689, – ☎ 300. AE ⓢ ⓓ E VISA. rest MY a
Meals 40000 – **170 rm** ☐ 220/320000, 12 suites.

Holiday Inn M, centro direzionale Isola e/6 ✉ 80143 ✆ 2250111, Telex 720161, Fax 5628074 – rm – 150. AE ⓢ ⓓ E VISA JCB.
Meals 25/55000 and ***Bistrot Victor*** Rest. a la carte 50/75000 – **298** ☐ 310/360000, 32 suites 420000. by corso Meridionale MY

Oriente, via Diaz 44 ✉ 80134 ✆ 5512133, Telex 722398, Fax 5514915 – – 300. AE ⓢ ⓓ E VISA. KZ d
Meals *(closed Friday to Sunday and August)* (dinner only) (residents only) 45/60000 – **130 rm** ☐ 250/380000, 2 suites.

Mercure, without rest., via Depretis 123 ✉ 80133 ✆ 5529500, Fax 5529509 – . AE ⓢ ⓓ E VISA KZ b
85 rm ☐ 220/280000.

Royal, via Partenope 38 ✉ 80121 ✆ 7644800, Fax 7645707, ← gulf, Posillipo and Castel dell'Ovo, – – 180. AE ⓢ ⓓ E VISA JCB. rest FX n
Meals 55/70000 – **259** ☐ 210/340000, 16 suites.

Continental without rest., via Partenope 44 ✉ 80121 ✆ 7644636, Fax 7644661, ← gulf and Castel dell'Ovo – – 600. AE ⓢ ⓓ E VISA JCB FX n
166 rm ☐ 210/340000.

Paradiso, via Catullo 11 ✉ 80122 ✆ 7614161, Fax 7613449, ← gulf, town and Vesuvius, – – 80. AE ⓢ ⓓ E VISA. rest by Riviera di Chiaia EFX
Meals a la carte 55/80000 – **71 rm** ☐ 170/270000.

Villa Capodimonte, via Moiariello 66 ✉ 80131 ✆ 459000, Fax 299344, ←, , – – 50. AE ⓢ ⓓ E VISA JCB. rest by corso Amedeo di Savoia GU
Meals (dinner only) a la carte 45/60000 – **58 rm** ☐ 150/240000.

Miramare without rest., via Nazario Sauro 24 ✉ 80132 ✆ 7647589, Fax 7640775, ← gulf and Vesuvius, « Roof-garden » – . AE ⓢ ⓓ E VISA JCB GX e
30 rm ☐ 240/350000.

Britannique, corso Vittorio Emanuele 133 ✉ 80121 ✆ 7614145, Telex 722281, Fax 660457, ← town and gulf, « Garden » – – 100. AE ⓢ ⓓ E VISA JCB. rest EX r
Meals 40000 – ☐ 15000 – **80 rm** 180/240000, 8 suites.

Majestic, largo Vasto a Chiaia 68 ✉ 80121 ✆ 416500, Telex 720408, Fax 416500 – – 100. AE ⓢ ⓓ E VISA. FX b
Meals *(closed Sunday)* a la carte 35/55000 – **130 rm** ☐ 190/280000.

Nuovo Rebecchino without rest., corso Garibaldi 356 ✉ 80142 ✆ 5535327, Fax 268026 – . AE ⓢ ⓓ E VISA JCB MY b
58 rm ☐ 160/200000.

Executive without rest., via del Cerriglio 10 ✉ 80134 ✆ 5520611, Fax 5520611, – . AE ⓢ ⓓ E VISA JCB KZ c
18 rm ☐ 150/200000, suite.

Belvedere, via Tito Angelini 51 ✉ 80129 ✆ 5788169, Fax 5785417, ← town and gulf, – rm . AE ⓢ ⓓ E VISA. FV a
Meals a la carte 40/60000 – **25 rm** ☐ 150/200000, 2 suites.

Splendid, via Manzoni 96 ✉ 80123 ✆ 7141955, Fax 7146431, ← – . AE ⓢ ⓓ E VISA. rest by Riviera di Chiaia EFX
Meals 35000 – **45 rm** ☐ 150/195000

La Cantinella, via Cuma 42 ✉ 80132 ✆ 7648684, Fax 7648769 – . AE ⓢ ⓓ E VISA JCB. GX v
closed Sunday, 11 to 18 August and 24 to 26 December – **Meals** a la carte 50/95000 (12 %)
Spec. Antipasti alla "Cantinella". Tufoli con fiori di zucchina e cozze. Spigola alla mediterranea.

Ciro a Santa Brigida, via Santa Brigida 73 ✉ 80132 ✆ 5524072, Fax 5528992, Rest. and pizzeria – . AE ⓢ ⓓ E VISA JZ w
closed Sunday and 14 to 29 August – **Meals** a la carte 45/65000.

Giuseppone a Mare, via Ferdinando Russo 13-Capo Posillipo ✉ 80123 ✆ 5756002, seafood with ← – . AE ⓢ ⓓ E VISA by via Caracciolo FX
closed Sunday, 9 to 15 August and 23 to 31 December – **Meals** a la carte 50/70000.

San Carlo, via Cesario Console 18/19 ✉ 80132 ✆ 7649757 – . AE ⓢ ⓓ E VISA JCB. KZ a
closed Sunday and 3 August-3 September – **Meals** (booking essential) a la carte 50/85000 (10 %).

Don Salvatore, strada Mergellina 4 A ✉ 80122 ✆ 681817, Fax 661241, Rest. and pizzeria – . AE ⓢ ⓓ E VISA by Riviera di Chiaia EFX
closed Wednesday – **Meals** a la carte 50/75000.

NAPOLI

Giordano (Via L.) . . . . EV 64
Scarlatti
(Via Alessandro) . . . . . . EV 153

Arcoleo (Via G.) . . . . FX 5
Arena della Sanità (Via) . . . GU 6
Artisti (Piazza degli) . . . . . . EV 9
Bernini (Via G. L.) . . . . EV 12
Bonito (Via G.) . . . . FV 13
Carducci (Via G.) . . . . FX 20
Chiatamone (Via) . . . . FX 25

Cirillo (Via D.) . . . . GU
Colonna (Via Vittoria) . . . . . FX
Crocelle (Via) . . . . GU
D'Auria (Via G.) . . . . FV
Ferraris (Via Galileo) . . . . . . HV
Fontana (Via Domenico) . . EU
Gen. Pignatelli (Via) . . . . . . HU

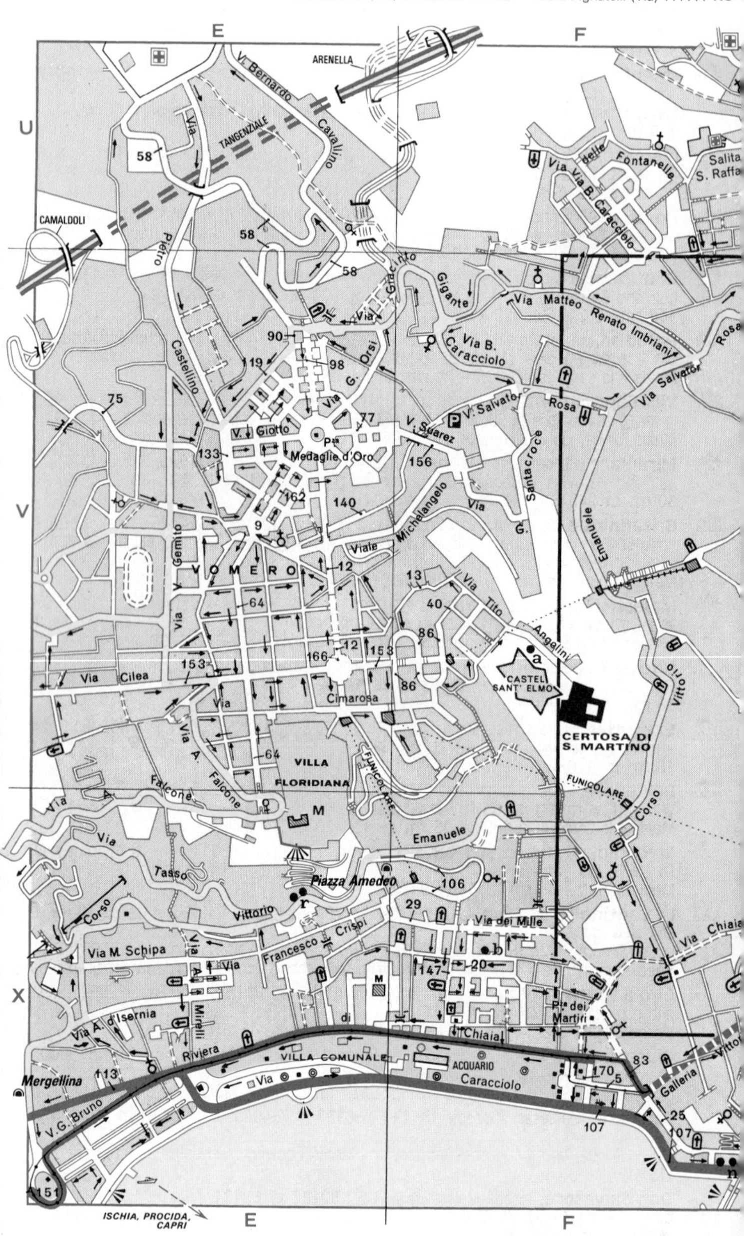

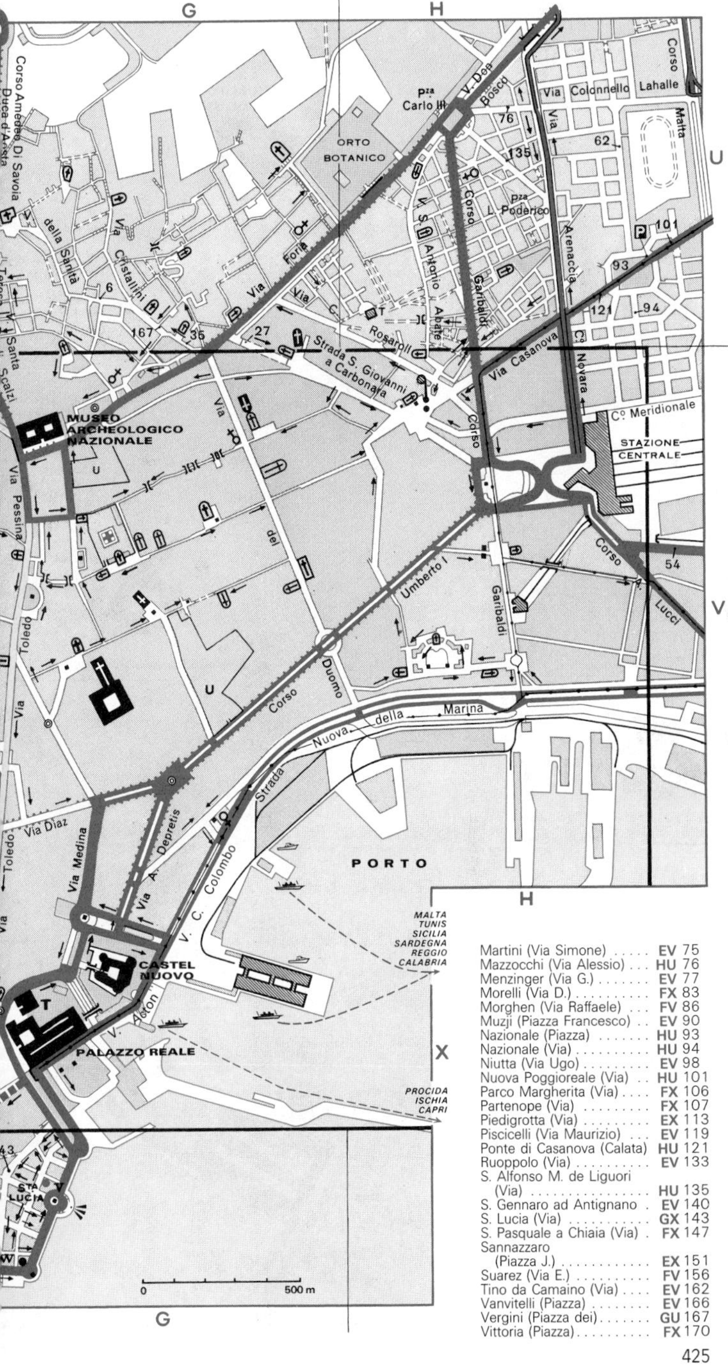

Martini (Via Simone)	EV	75
Mazzocchi (Via Alessio)	HU	76
Menzinger (Via G.)	EV	77
Morelli (Via D.)	FX	83
Morghen (Via Raffaele)	FV	86
Muzji (Piazza Francesco)	EV	90
Nazionale (Piazza)	HU	93
Nazionale (Via)	HU	94
Niutta (Via Ugo)	EV	98
Nuova Poggioreale (Via)	HU	101
Parco Margherita (Via)	FX	106
Partenope (Via)	FX	107
Piedigrotta (Via)	EX	113
Piscicelli (Via Maurizio)	EV	119
Ponte di Casanova (Calata)	HU	121
Ruoppolo (Via)	EV	133
S. Alfonso M. de Liguori (Via)	HU	135
S. Gennaro ad Antignano	EV	140
S. Lucia (Via)	GX	143
S. Pasquale a Chiaia (Via)	FX	147
Sannazzaro (Piazza J.)	EX	151
Suarez (Via E.)	FV	156
Tino da Camaino (Via)	EV	162
Vanvitelli (Piazza)	EV	166
Vergini (Piazza dei)	GU	167
Vittoria (Piazza)	FX	170

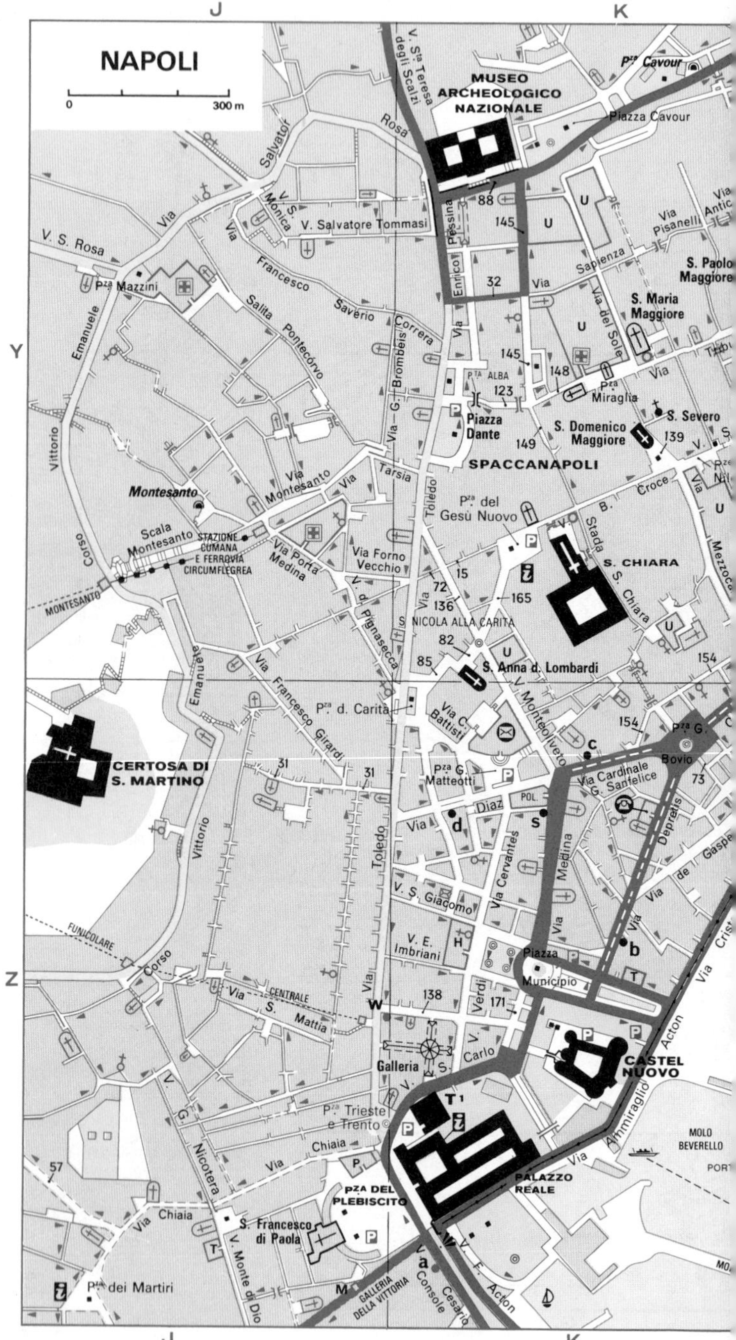
NAPOLI
0
300 m
J
K
Y
Z
MUSEO ARCHEOLOGICO NAZIONALE
Pza Cavour
Piazza Cavour
V. Sta Teresa degli Scalzi
Rosa
Salvator
V. S. Rosa
Pza Mazzini
V. S. Monica
V. Salvatore Tommasi
Via Francesco Saverio Correra
Salita Pontecorvo
Emanuele
Vittorio
Corso
Via Pessina
Enrico
Via G. Brombeis
Via Sapienza
Via Pisanelli
Via Anticaglia
S. Paolo Maggiore
S. Maria Maggiore
Via del Sole
PTA ALBA
Pza Miraglia
Piazza Dante
S. Severo
S. Domenico Maggiore
SPACCANAPOLI
Tarsia
Toledo
Via Montesanto
Montesanto
Scala Montesanto
STAZIONE CUMANA E FERROVIA CIRCUMFLEGREA
MONTESANTO
Via Porta Medina
Via Forno Vecchio
Pza del Gesù Nuovo
B. Croce
Stada S. Chiara
S. CHIARA
Mezzocannone
V. d. Pignasecca
S. NICOLA ALLA CARITÀ
S. Anna d. Lombardi
Via Francesco Girardi
Pza d. Carità
Via C. Battisti
V. Monteoliveto
CERTOSA DI S. MARTINO
Pza G. Matteotti
Pza G. Bovio
Via Cardinale G. Sanfelice
Via Diaz
POL.
Via Cervantes
Via Medina
Via Depretis
Via de Gasperi
V. S. Giacomo
V. E. Imbriani
Piazza Municipio
Via Verdi
FUNICOLARE
Corso
Via CENTRALE S. Mattia
Galleria
V. Carlo
CASTEL NUOVO
Via Acton
Via Cristoforo
Via Ammiraglio
MOLO BEVERELLO
PORTO
PALAZZO REALE
Pza Trieste e Trento
Chiaia
Via Chiaia
Pza DEL PLEBISCITO
S. Francesco di Paola
V. G. Nicotera
V. Monte di Dio
Pza dei Martiri
GALLERIA DELLA VITTORIA
Via Console
Cesario
V. F. Acton

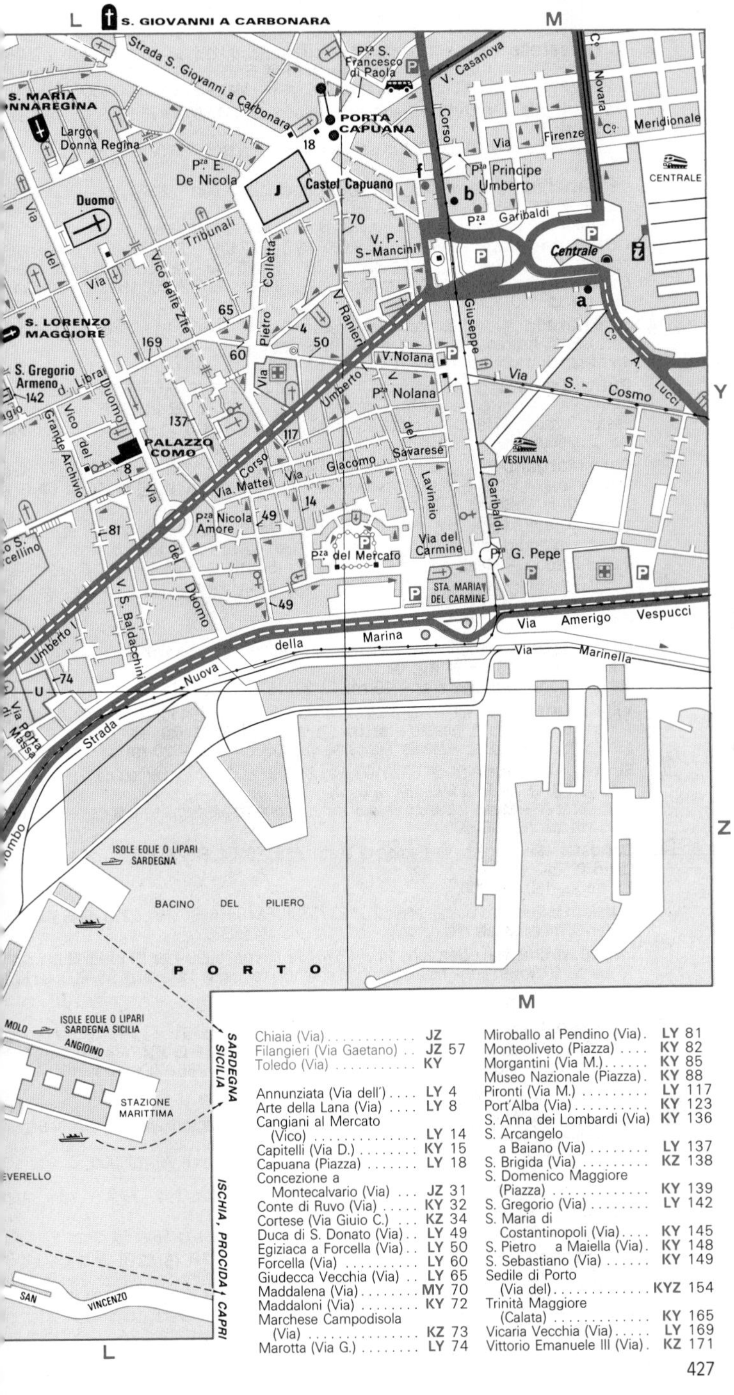

Chiaia (Via) . . . . JZ
Filangieri (Via Gaetano) . . JZ 57
Toledo (Via) . . . . KY

Annunziata (Via dell') . . . . LY 4
Arte della Lana (Via) . . . . LY 8
Cangiani al Mercato (Vico) . . . . LY 14
Capitelli (Via D.) . . . . KY 15
Capuana (Piazza) . . . . LY 18
Concezione a Montecalvario (Via) . . . JZ 31
Conte di Ruvo (Via) . . . . . KY 32
Cortese (Via Giuio C.) . . . KZ 34
Duca di S. Donato (Via) . . LY 49
Egiziaca a Forcella (Via) . . LY 50
Forcella (Via) . . . . LY 60
Giudecca Vecchia (Via) . . LY 65
Maddalena (Via) . . . . MY 70
Maddaloni (Via) . . . . KY 72
Marchese Campodisola (Via) . . . . KZ 73
Marotta (Via G.) . . . . LY 74

Miroballo al Pendino (Via) . LY 81
Monteoliveto (Piazza) . . . . KY 82
Morgantini (Via M.) . . . . . KY 85
Museo Nazionale (Piazza) . KY 88
Pironti (Via M.) . . . . LY 117
Port'Alba (Via) . . . . KY 123
S. Anna dei Lombardi (Via) KY 136
S. Arcangelo a Baiano (Via) . . . . LY 137
S. Brigida (Via) . . . . KZ 138
S. Domenico Maggiore (Piazza) . . . . KY 139
S. Gregorio (Via) . . . . LY 142
S. Maria di Costantinopoli (Via) . . . . KY 145
S. Pietro a Maiella (Via) . KY 148
S. Sebastiano (Via) . . . . . . KY 149
Sedile di Porto (Via del) . . . . KYZ 154
Trinità Maggiore (Calata) . . . . KY 165
Vicaria Vecchia (Via) . . . . . LY 169
Vittorio Emanuele III (Via) . KZ 171

A' Fenestella, calata Ponticello a Marechiaro ✉ 80123 ℘ 7690020, Fax 57506 « Summer service in terrace on sea » – AE VISA by via V. G. Bruno EX
closed 11 to 18 August, Sunday and lunch in August – **Meals** a la carte 40/65000 (15 %).

Da Mimí alla Ferrovia, via Alfonso d'Aragona 21 ✉ 80139 ℘ 5538525 – AE VISA MY
closed Sunday and 10 to 20 August – **Meals** a la carte 35/60000 (12 %).

Island of Capri *80073 Napoli 988 ㉗, 431 F 24 G. Italy – pop. 12 972 alt. – High Season: Easter and June-September – ✆ 081.*

The limitation of motor-vehicles' access is regulated by legislative rules.

Gd H. Quisisana, via Camerelle 2 ℘ 8370788, Telex 710520, Fax 8376080, ≤ sea and Certosa, « Garden with ⛱ », ≘s, – 🏋 550. AE VISA
Easter-October – **Meals *La Colombaia*** Rest. a la carte 70/120000 see also rest. ***Quisi*** – **150 rm** ⊏ 350/750000, 14 suites.

Scalinatella ⛰ without rest., via Tragara 8 ℘ 8370633, Fax 8378291, ≤ sea and Certosa, heated – AE VISA
15 March-5 November – **28 rm** ⊏ 520/670000.

Punta Tragara ⛰, via Tragara 57 ℘ 8370844, Fax 8377790, ≤ Faraglioni and coast, « Panoramic terrace with heated » – AE VISA JCB.
Easter-October – **Meals** a la carte 55/80000 (15 %) – **10 rm** ⊏ 450/520000, 30 suites ⊏ 630/800000.

Casa Morgano M ⛰ without rest., via Tragara 6 ℘ 8370158, Fax 8370681, ≤ sea and Certosa, « Floral terraces in pinewood », heated – AE VISA
15 March-5 November – **28 rm** 320/500000.

Luna ⛰, viale Matteotti 3 ℘ 8370433, Fax 8377459, ≤ sea, Faraglioni and Certosa, « Terraces and garden with » – AE VISA. rest
Easter-October – **Meals** a la carte 60/75000 – **50 rm** ⊏ 350/460000, 4 suites.

La Palma, via Vittorio Emanuele 39 ℘ 8370133, Telex 722015, Fax 8376966, ≘s – 🏋 200
74 rm.

La Pazziella ⛰ without rest., via Giuliani 4 ℘ 8370044, Fax 8370085, « Floral garden » – AE VISA.
March-October and New Year – **19 rm** ⊏ 220/320000, suite.

Villa Brunella ⛰, via Tragara 24 ℘ 8370122, Fax 8370430, ≤ sea and coast, « Floral terraces », heated – rm AE VISA.
19 March-5 November – **Meals** a la carte 40/80000 (12 %) – **20 rm** ⊏ 300/450000

Sirene, via Camerelle 51 ℘ 8370102, Fax 8370957, ≤, « Lemon-garden with » – AE VISA JCB.
April-October – **Meals** *(closed Tuesday except June to September)* a la carte 45/6000 – **35 rm** ⊏ 280/360000.

Canasta without rest., via Campo di Teste ℘ 8370561, Fax 8376675, – AE VISA.
17 rm ⊏ 160/280000.

Quisi, Gd H. Quisisana via Camerelle 2 ℘ 8370788, Fax 8376080 – AE VISA.
Easter-October **Meals** *dinner only – a la carte 80/135000.*

La Capannina, via Le Botteghe 14 ℘ 8370732, Fax 8376990 – AE VISA.
15 March-10 November – **Meals** (booking essential for dinner) a la carte 55/80000 (15 %)

at Anacapri *alt. 275 – ✉ 80071 :*

Europa Palace, via Capodimonte 2 ℘ 8373800, Fax 8373191, ≤, « Floral terraces with », ≘s, – 🏋 200. AE VISA JCB.
April-October – **Meals** a la carte 70/105000 – **90 rm** ⊏ 260/480000, suite.

at Marina Piccola – ✉ *80073 Capri :*

Canzone del Mare, ℘ 8370104, Fax 8370541, ≤ Faraglioni and sea, « Bathing establishment with » – AE VISA.
Easter-October – **Meals** *(lunch only)* 70/80000 and a la carte 70/105000.

Sant'Agata sui due Golfi *80064 Napoli 431 F 25 G. Italy – alt. 391 – High Season: April-September – ✆ 081.*

Roma 266 – Castellammare di Stabia 28 – Napoli 55 – Salerno 56 – Sorrento 9.

Don Alfonso 1890 with rm, ℘ 8780026, Fax 5330226, – AE VISA.
closed 10 January-25 February – **Meals** *(closed Monday June-September and Tuesday October-May)* (booking essential) a la carte 85/135000 – 3 suites ⊏ 160/250000
Spec. Patata novella farcita di ostriche con lenticchie e gamberetti (summer). Casseruola di pesci di scoglio, crostacei e frutti di mare. Faraona picchettata d'aglio spontaneo con tortino di fegato e barbabietole fritte.

PALERMO (Sicily) *90100* **P** 988 ㉟, 432 M 22 *G. Italy – pop. 689 301 –* ☎ *091.*

See : *Palace of the Normans*★★ *: the palatine Chapel*★★★*, mosaics*★★★ AZ – *Regional Gallery of Sicily*★★ *in Abbatellis Palace*★ *: Death Triumphant fresco*★★★ CY – *Piazza Bellini*★ BY *: Martorana Church*★★*, Church of St. Cataldo*★★ – *Church of St. John of the Hermits*★★ AZ – *Capuchin Catacombs*★★ – *Piazza Pretoria*★ BY *: fountain*★★ – *Archaeological Museum*★ *: metopes from the temples at Selinus*★★*, the Ram*★★ BY – *Chiaramonte Palace*★ *: magnolia fig trees*★★ *in Garibaldi Gardens* CY – *Quattro Canti*★ BY – *Cathedral*★ AYZ *Mirto Palace*★ CY **B** *Villa Bonanno*★ AZ *Zisa Palace*★ – *Botanical garden*★ CDZ – *International Museum of Marionettes*★ CY **A** *Sicilian carts*★ *in Ethnographic Museum* **M.**

Envir. : *Monreale*★★★ AZ *by Corso Calatafimi : 8 km – Monte Pellegrino*★★ BX *by via Crispi : 14 km.*

✈ *Punta Raisi E : 30 km* ☎ *591690, Fax 595030 – Alitalia, via Mazzini 59* ✉ *90139* ☎ *6019111.*

⛴ *to Genova daily (20 h) and to Livorno Tuesday, Thursday and Saturday (20 h) – Grandi Navi Veloci, calata Marinai d'italia* ✉ *90133* ☎ *587404, Telex 910098, Fax 6112242; to Napoli daily (11 h), to Genova 18 June-31 December, Monday, Wednesday, Friday and Sunday, Monday, Wednesday and Friday January-May (24 h) and to Cagliari Saturday (14 h 30 mn) – Tirrenia Navigazione, calata Marinai d'Italia* ✉ *90133* ☎ *333300, Telex 910057, Fax 6021221.*

⛴ *to Aeolian Island June-September daily (1 h 50 mn) – SNAV Barbaro Agency, piazza Principe di Belmonte 51/55* ✉ *90139* ☎ *586533, Fax 584830.*

ℹ *piazza Castelnuovo 34* ✉ *90141* ☎ *583847, Telex 910179, Fax 331854 – Punta Raisi Airport at Cinisi* ☎ *591698.*

A.C.I. *via delle Alpi 6* ✉ *90144* ☎ *300468.*

Messina 235.

Plans on following pages

🏨🏨🏨🏨 **Astoria Palace,** via Monte Pellegrino 62 ✉ 90142 ☎ 6371820, Telex 911045, Fax 6372178 – 🛗 ▤ TV ☎ ♿ P – 🎤 800. AE 🅂 ⦿ E VISA. ✂ by via Crispi BX
Meals 55/90000 and ***Il Cedro*** Rest. a la carte 55/90000 – **326 rm** ☕ 220/270000, 8 suites.

🏨🏨🏨 **Jolly,** Foro Italico 22 ✉ 90133 ☎ 6165090, Telex 910076, Fax 6161441, ⛱, 🏊, 🌳 – 🛗 ▤ TV ☎ P – 🎤 300. AE 🅂 ⦿ E VISA. ✂ rest DY s
Meals a la carte 55/85000 – **235 rm** ☕ 185/240000.

🏨🏨🏨 **San Paolo Palace,** via Messina Marine 91 ✉ 90123 ☎ 6211112, Telex 910069, Fax 6215300, <, « Roof-garden rest. », 🏋, ♨, 🏊, 🎾 – 🛗 ▤ TV ☎ ♿ 🚗 P – 🎤 1500. AE 🅂 ⦿ E VISA. ✂ by via Ponte di Mare DZ
Meals 45/55000 – **274 rm** ☕ 160/200000, 9 suites.

🏨🏨🏨 **Centrale Palace Hotel** without rest., corso Vittorio Emanuele 327 ✉ 90134 ☎ 336666, Fax 334881, « In a 17C building » – 🛗 ▤ TV ☎. AE 🅂 ⦿ E VISA JCB. ✂
61 rm ☕ 190/280000, suite. BY b

🏨🏨🏨 **Politeama Palace,** piazza Ruggero Settimo 15 ✉ 90139 ☎ 322777, Telex 911053, Fax 6111589 – 🛗 ▤ TV ☎ – 🎤 130. AE 🅂 ⦿ E VISA. ✂ AX s
Meals a la carte 40/55000 – **102 rm** ☕ 150/200000.

🏨🏨 **Villa d'Amato,** via Messina Marine 180 ✉ 90123 ☎ 6212767, Fax 6212767 – 🛗 ▤ TV ☎ P – 🎤 100. AE 🅂 ⦿ VISA. ✂ rest by via Ponte di Mare DZ
Meals *(closed Sunday)* a la carte 40/50000 – **25 rm** ☕ 110/160000, 12 suites.

🏨🏨 **Forte Agip,** viale della Regione Siciliana 2620 ✉ 90145 ☎ 552033, Fax 408198 – 🛗 ▤ TV ☎ P – 🎤 90. AE 🅂 ⦿ E VISA. ✂ rest by via della Libertà AX
Meals a la carte 40/50000 – **105 rm** ☕ 165/205000.

XXX **La Scuderia,** viale del Fante 9 ✉ 90146 ☎ 520323, Fax 520467 – ▤ P. AE 🅂 ⦿ E VISA. ✂ by via C.A. Dalla Chiesa AX
closed Sunday – **Meals** a la carte 50/80000.

XXX ✿ **L'Approdo Ristorante Renato,** via Messina Marina 224 ✉ 90123 ☎ 6302881, <, ⛱ – AE 🅂 E VISA. ✂ by via Ponte di Mare DZ
closed Monday and 10 to 25 August – **Meals** (booking essential) a la carte 50/90000
Spec. Lonza di porco marinata alle erbe in salsa di prugne e zibibbo. "Tria bastarda ca sarsa murisca Taratatà" (spaghetti in salsa di bottarga, acciughe e peperoncino). Sarago "Sacristanu" in potaggio.

XXX **Gourmand's,** via della Libertà 37/e ✉ 90139 ☎ 323431, Fax 322507 – ▤. AE 🅂 ⦿ E VISA. ✂ AX e
closed Sunday and August – **Meals** a la carte 45/75000.

XX **Friend's Bar,** via Brunelleschi 138 ✉ 90145 ☎ 201401, Fax 201066, ⛱ – ▤. AE 🅂 ⦿. ✂ by via della Libertà AX
closed Monday and 16 to 31 August – **Meals** (booking essential) a la carte 50/70000.

XX **A Cuccagna,** via Principe Granatelli 21/a ✉ 90139 ☎ 587267, Fax 584575, Typical rest. – ▤. AE 🅂 ⦿ E VISA JCB. ✂ BX m
closed 14 to 31 August and Friday (except June-September) – **Meals** a la carte 35/60000.

A
B
X
Y
Z
MUSEO ARCHEOLOGICO
QUATTRO CANTI
Pza PRETORIA
Pza BELLINI
MARTORANA
S. CATALDO
CATTEDRALE
PALAZZO DEI NORMANNI
S. GIOVANNI DEGLI EREMITI
VILLA BONANNO
PORTA NUOVA
AIR TERMINAL
Piazza Indipendenza
PARCO D'ORLÉANS
Via Roma
Via Maqueda
Corso Vittorio Emanuele
Via Volturno
Via Cavour
Via Crispi
Via Ruggero Settimo
Via Dante
Corso Alberto Amedeo
Corso Tukory
Via Porta di Castro
Via A. Mongitore
Via Papireto
Via dei Candelai
Via Sant' Agostino
Via Villafranca
Via Goethe
Via N. Turrisi
Via Libertà
Via Emerico Amari
Via Principe di Belmonte
Via Mariano Stabile
Via Onorato
Via Principe di Scordia
Via R. Pilo
Pza Verdi
Pza S. Oliva
Pza Ballarò
Pza Nasce
S. GIUSEPPE
Via Catania
Via Siracusa
Via Messina
Via Marconi
Via E. Parisi
Via Nicolò Garzilli
Via Isidoro Carini
Via Archimede
Via G. Mazzini
Via La Lumia
Via Puglisi
Via Scinà
Via V. Bandiera
Via Napoli
V. Maggiore Perni
POL.
S 113

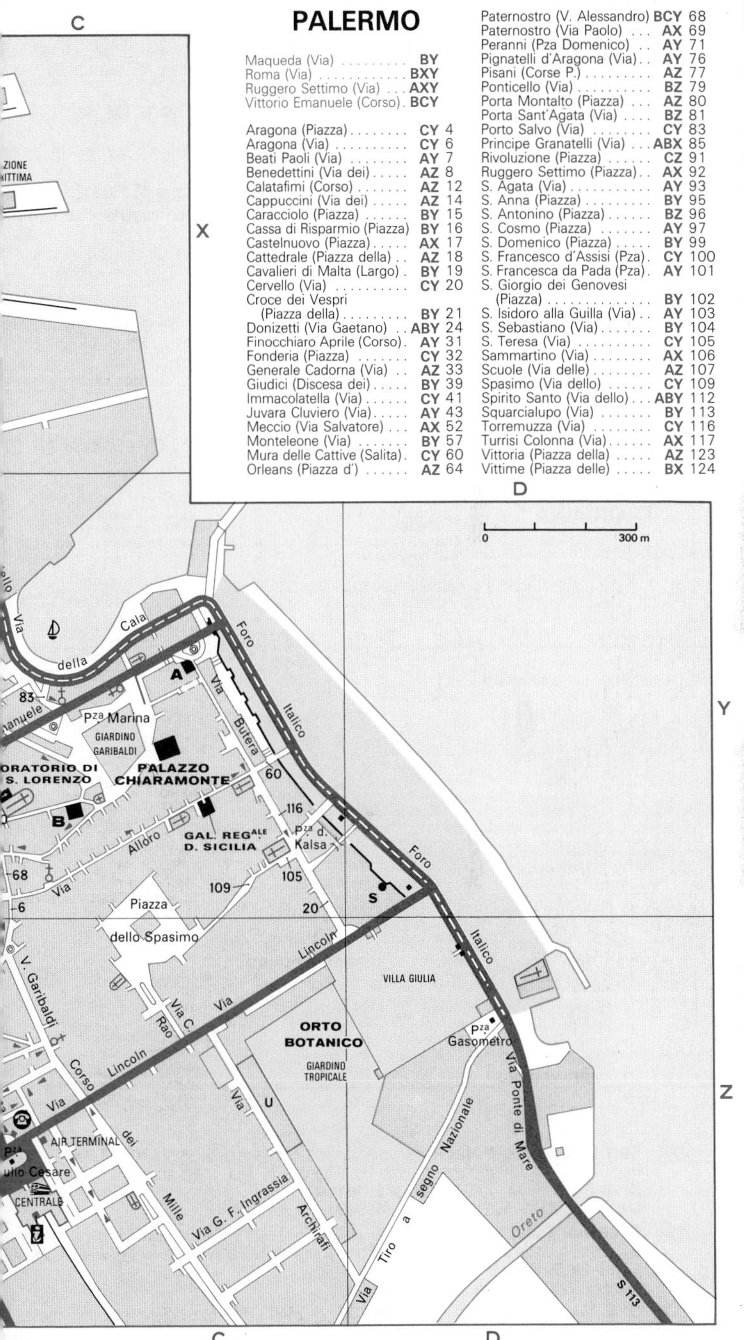
PALERMO
Maqueda (Via) . . . . BY
Roma (Via) . . . . BXY
Ruggero Settimo (Via) . . . AXY
Vittorio Emanuele (Corso) . BCY
Aragona (Piazza) . . . . CY 4
Aragona (Via) . . . . CY 6
Beati Paoli (Via) . . . . AY 7
Benedettini (Via dei) . . . . . AZ 8
Calatafimi (Corso) . . . . AZ 12
Cappuccini (Via dei) . . . . . AZ 14
Caracciolo (Piazza) . . . . . . BY 15
Cassa di Risparmio (Piazza) BY 16
Castelnuovo (Piazza) . . . . . AX 17
Cattedrale (Piazza della) . . AZ 18
Cavalieri di Malta (Largo) . BY 19
Cervello (Via) . . . . CY 20
Croce dei Vespri (Piazza della) . . . . BY 21
Donizetti (Via Gaetano) . . ABY 24
Finocchiaro Aprile (Corso) . AY 31
Fonderia (Piazza) . . . . CY 32
Generale Cadorna (Via) . . AZ 33
Giudici (Discesa dei) . . . . . BY 39
Immacolatella (Via) . . . . . . CY 41
Juvara Cluviero (Via) . . . . . AY 43
Meccio (Via Salvatore) . . . AX 52
Monteleone (Via) . . . . BY 57
Mura delle Cattive (Salita) . CY 60
Orleans (Piazza d') . . . . . . AZ 64
Paternostro (V. Alessandro) BCY 68
Paternostro (Via Paolo) . . . AX 69
Peranni (Pza Domenico) . . AY 71
Pignatelli d'Aragona (Via) . . AY 76
Pisani (Corse P.) . . . . AZ 77
Ponticello (Via) . . . . BZ 79
Porta Montalto (Piazza) . . . AZ 80
Porta Sant'Agata (Via) . . . . BZ 81
Porto Salvo (Via) . . . . CY 83
Principe Granatelli (Via) . . . ABX 85
Rivoluzione (Piazza) . . . . . . CZ 91
Ruggero Settimo (Piazza) . . AX 92
S. Agata (Via) . . . . AY 93
S. Anna (Piazza) . . . . BY 95
S. Antonino (Piazza) . . . . . . BZ 96
S. Cosmo (Piazza) . . . . AY 97
S. Domenico (Piazza) . . . . . BY 99
S. Francesco d'Assisi (Pza) . CY 100
S. Francesca da Pada (Pza) . AY 101
S. Giorgio dei Genovesi (Piazza) . . . . BY 102
S. Isidoro alla Guilla (Via) . . AY 103
S. Sebastiano (Via) . . . . BY 104
S. Teresa (Via) . . . . CY 105
Sammartino (Via) . . . . AX 106
Scuole (Via delle) . . . . AZ 107
Spasimo (Via dello) . . . . CY 109
Spirito Santo (Via dello) . . . ABY 112
Squarcialupo (Via) . . . . BY 113
Torremuzza (Via) . . . . CY 116
Turrisi Colonna (Via) . . . . . . AX 117
Vittoria (Piazza della) . . . . . AZ 123
Vittime (Piazza delle) . . . . . BX 124
C
D
X
Y
Z
0
300 m
Via della Cala
Foro Italico
Via Butera
Pza Marina
GIARDINO GARIBALDI
PALAZZO CHIARAMONTE
ORATORIO DI S. LORENZO
GAL. REGALE D. SICILIA
Pza d. Kalsa
Via Alloro
Piazza dello Spasimo
Via Lincoln
VILLA GIULIA
ORTO BOTANICO
GIARDINO TROPICALE
Pza Gasometro
Via Ponte di Mare
Via Tiro a segno Nazionale
Oreto
S 113
V. Garibaldi
Corso dei Mille
Via C. Rao
AIR TERMINAL
CENTRALE
Via G. F. Ingrassia
Archirafi

XX **Il Ristorantino,** piazza De Gasperi 19 ✉ 90146 ℰ 512861, Fax 6702999, 🏠 – ▤ AE ⓢ ⓓ E VISA. ✂ by via C.A. Dalla Chiesa AX
closed Monday and 5 to 20 August – **Meals** a la carte 50/80000.

XX **Regine,** via Trapani 4/a ✉ 90141 ℰ 586566 – ▤. AE ⓢ ⓓ E VISA. ✂ AX
closed Sunday and August – **Meals** a la carte 50/65000.

X **Trattoria Biondo,** via Carducci 15 ✉ 90141 ℰ 583662 – ▤. AE ⓢ E VISA ✂ AX
closed Wednesday and 15 July-15 September – **Meals** a la carte 35/50000 (15 %).

X **Il Vespro,** via B. D'Acquisto 9 ✉ 90141 ℰ 589932, Rest. and pizzeria – ▤. AE ⓢ ⓓ E VISA. ✂ AX
closed Monday and August – **Meals** a la carte 25/50000.

TAORMINA

TAORMINA (Sicily) *98039 Messina* 988 ㊲, 432 N 27 *G. Italy – pop. 10 537 alt. 250 –* ☎ *094.*

See : *Site★★★ – Greek Theatre★★ : ←★★★* B *– Public garden★★* B *– ★★ from the Square 9 Aprile* A **13** *– Corso Umberto★* A *– Belvedere★* B *– Castle★ : ←★* A.

Exc. : *Etna★★★, SW : for Linguaglossa.*

⛳18 *Picciolo, contrada Rovitello ✉ 95012 Castiglione di Sicilia ℰ 986171, Fax 9865. W : 25 km.*

ℹ *piazza Santa Caterina (Corvaja palace) ℰ 23243, Fax 24941.*

Catania 52 ② – Enna 135 ② – Messina 52 ① – Palermo 255 ② – Siracusa 111 ② Trapani 359 ②

TAORMINA

Umberto (Corso)	A
Cappuccini (Via)	A 2
Crocifisso (Via)	A 3
Dionisio Primo (Via)	A 5
Duomo (Piazza)	A 6
S. Antonio (Piazza)	A 9
Vinci (V. Leonardo da)	A 1
Vittorio Emanuele II (Pza)	B 1
9 Aprile (Piazza)	A 1

Traffic restricted in the town centre from June to September

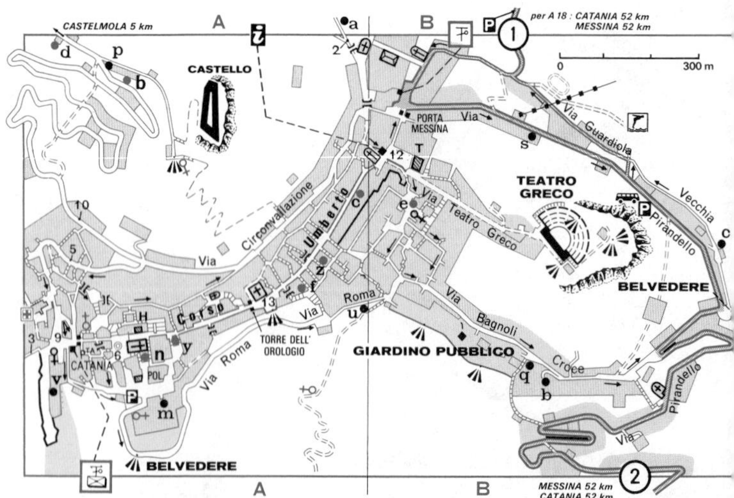

San Domenico Palace ⛱, piazza San Domenico 5 ℰ 23701, Telex 980013 Fax 625506, « 15C monastery with floral garden, ← sea, coast and Etna », ⛱ heated ⎘ ▤ TV ☎ – 🏠 400. AE ⓢ ⓓ E VISA. ✂ A
Meals 100000 – **102 rm** ▭ 400/685000, 6 suites.

Excelsior Palace ⛱, via Toselli 8 ℰ 23975, Telex 980185, Fax 23978, ← sea, coast and Etna, « Little park and ⛱ heated on panoramic terrace » – ⎘ ▤ TV ☎ Ⓟ – 🏠 100 AE ⓢ ⓓ E VISA. ✂ rest A
Meals 65000 – **89 rm** ▭ 180/270000.

Gd H. Miramare, via Guardiola Vecchia 27 ℰ 23401, Fax 626223, ← sea and coast, ⛱ heated, 🌳, ✂ – ⎘ ▤ TV ☎ Ⓟ B
67 rm.

Monte Tauro ⊛, via Madonna delle Grazie 3 ☎ 24402, Telex 980048, Fax 24403, ≤ sea and coast, – – 100. AE VISA JCB. AB u
Meals a la carte 45/70000 – **70 rm** 230/290000.

Jolly Diodoro, via Bagnolo Croci 75 ☎ 23312, Telex 980028, Fax 23391, ≤ sea, coast and Etna, « on panoramic terrace », – – 250 B q
102 rm.

Villa Ducale ⊛ without rest., via Leonardo da Vinci 60 ☎ 28153, Fax 28710, ≤ sea, coast and Etna – . AE E VISA JCB A p
closed 10 January-15 February – **10 rm** 200/320000.

Villa Fiorita without rest., via Pirandello 39 ☎ 24122, Fax 625967, ≤ sea and coast, – . AE E VISA B s
24 rm 160000.

Villa Belvedere without rest., via Bagnoli Croci 79 ☎ 23791, Fax 625830, ≤ gardens, sea and Etna, « Garden with » – rm . E VISA B b
47 rm 155/235000.

Villa Sirina, contrada Sirina ☎ 51776, Fax 51671, – . AE E VISA. 2 km by via Crocifisso A
closed 10 January-20 March – **Meals** (residents only) (dinner only) – **15 rm** 160/190000.

La Giara, vico La Floresta 1 ☎ 23360, Fax 23233, Rest. and piano bar – . AE E VISA JCB. A f
closed Monday except July-September – **Meals** *(dinner only)* a la carte 55/80000.

La Griglia, corso Umberto 54 ☎ 23980, Fax 626047 – . AE E VISA.
closed Tuesday and 20 November-20 December – **Meals** a la carte 40/60000. A c

Al Castello, via Madonna della Rocca 11 ☎ 28158, « Summer service on panoramic terrace with ≤ sea and coast » – AE E VISA. A b
closed Wednesday lunch – **Meals** a la carte 50/70000.

A' Zammara, via Fratelli Bandiera 15 ☎ 24596, Fax 24408, « Summer service in a small shaded garden » – AE E VISA. A z
closed 5 to 20 January and Wednesday except June-September – **Meals** a la carte 40/60000.

Da Lorenzo, via Michele Amari 4 ☎ 23480, Fax 23480, – AE E VISA A n
closed 1 to 15 November and Wednesday except June-September – **Meals** a la carte 40/65000.

Il Ciclope, corso Umberto ☎ 23263, Fax 625910, – . AE E VISA JCB.
closed Wednesday and 10 to 31 January – **Meals** a la carte 35/45000. A y

Il Baccanale, piazzetta Filea 1 ☎ 625390, – . E VISA. B e
closed Thursday except April-September – **Meals** a la carte 30/60000.

La Chioccia d'Oro, via Leonardo da Vinci ☎ 28066, ≤ A d
closed Thursday and November – **Meals** a la carte 30/45000.

t Mazzarò *by ② : 5,5 km – ✉ 98030 :*

Mazzarò Sea Palace, ☎ 24004, Fax 626237, ≤ small bay, – – 90. AE E VISA. rest
April-October – **Meals** 65/120000 – **84 rm** 250/470000, 3 suites.

t Lido di Spisone *by ① : 7 km – ✉ 98030 Mazzarò :*

Lido Caparena, via Nazionale 189 ☎ 652033, Fax 36913, ≤, « Extensive flower garden with outdoor rest. summer service », – – 200. AE E VISA JCB.
Meals a la carte 50/75000 – **88 rm** 230/320000.

Lido Mediterranée, ☎ 24422, Telex 980175, Fax 24774, ≤, – – 100. AE E VISA. rest
22 March-October – **Meals** 60000 – **72 rm** 250/350000.

Bay Palace, via Nazionale ☎ 626200, Fax 626199, « Solarium-terrace with panoramic » – . AE E VISA. rest
Meals (dinner only) 30/65000 – **47 rm** 130/220000.

Pleasant hotels and restaurants
are shown in the Guide by a red sign.
Please send us the names
of any where you have enjoyed your stay.
Your Michelin Guide will be even better.

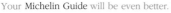

TURIN (TORINO) *10100* 🅿 988 ⑫, 428 G 5 *G. Italy – pop. 923 106 alt. 239 –* ✆ *011.*

See : *Piazza San Carlo*★★ CXY – *Egyptian Museum*★★, *Sabauda Gallery*★★ *in Academy Science* CX **M1** – *Cathedral*★ VX : *relic of the Holy Shroud*★★★ – *Mole Antonelliana*★ : ※ DX – *Madama Palace*★ : *museum of Ancient Art*★ CX **A** – *Royal Palace*★ : *Royal Armoury* CDVX – *Risorgimento Museum*★ *in Carignano Palace* CX **M2** – *Carlo Biscaretti di Ruf Motor Museum*★ – *Model medieval village*★ *in the Valentino Park* CDZ.

Envir. : *Basilica of Superga*★ : ≤★★★, *royal tombs*★ – *Tour to the pass, Colle della Maddalena*★ : ≤★★ *of the city from the route Superga-Pino Torinese,* ≤★ *of the city from the route Colle Colle della Maddalena-Cavoretto.*

18, 9 I Roveri (March-November) at La Mandria ✉ 10070 Fiano ✆ 9235719, Fax 92356 N : 18 km;

18, 18 (closed Monday, January and February), at Fiano Torinese ✉ 10070 ✆ 92354 Fax 9235886, N : 20 km;

18 Le Fronde (closed Tuesday, January and February) at Avigliana ✉ 10051 ✆ 9350 Fax 930928, W : 24 km;

9 Stupinigi (closed Monday), ✆ 3472640, Fax 3978038;

9 (closed Monday and 21 December-9 January) at Vinovo ✉ 10048 ✆ 9653880, F 9623748.

✈ *Turin Airport of Caselle N : 15 km ✆ 5676361, Telex 225119, Fax 5676420 – Alita via Lagrange 35 ✉ 10123 ✆ 57698.*

🚗 *✆ 6651111-int. 2611.*

ℹ *via Roma 226 (piazza C.L.N.) ✉ 10121 ✆ 535901, Fax 530070 – Porta Nuova Railw station ✉ 10125 ✆ 531327.*

A.C.I. *via Giovanni Giolitti 15 ✉ 10123 ✆ 57791.*

Roma 669 – Briançon 108 – Chambéry 209 – Gen ve 252 – Genova 170 – Grenoble 2 – Milano 140 – Nice 220.

Plans on following pages

Turin Palace Hotel, via Sacchi 8 ✉ 10128 ✆ 5625511, Fax 5612187 – ▤ TV ☎ 🚗 – 🏛 200. AE Ⓢ ⓞ E VISA. ✻ rest CY
Meals *(closed August)* a la carte 65/100000 – **121 rm** ☐ 310/390000, 2 suites.

Jolly Principi di Piemonte, via Gobetti 15 ✉ 10123 ✆ 5629693, Telex 2211 Fax 5620270 – ⧉ ▤ TV ☎ – 🏛 300. AE Ⓢ ⓞ E VISA JCB. ✻ rest CY
Meals a la carte 65/115000 – **99 rm** ☐ 420/450000, 8 suites.

Le Meridien Lingotto, via Nizza 262 ✉ 10126 ✆ 6642000, Fax 6642001 – ⧉ ⇹ ▤ TV ☎ ♿ – 🏛 35. AE Ⓢ ⓞ E VISA. ✻ rest by via Nizza CZ
Meals a la carte 55/95000 – **244 rm** ☐ 290/340000.

Gd H. Sitea, via Carlo Alberto 35 ✉ 10123 ✆ 5170171, Fax 548090 – ⧉ ▤ TV – 🏛 100. AE Ⓢ ⓞ E VISA. ✻ rest CY
Meals a la carte 70/95000 – **117 rm** ☐ 290/390000.

Jolly Ambasciatori, corso Vittorio Emanuele II 104 ✉ 10121 ✆ 5752, Telex 2212 Fax 544978 – ⧉ ⇹ rm ▤ TV ☎ 🚗 – 🏛 400. AE Ⓢ ⓞ E VISA. ✻ rest BX
Meals 55/60000 – **195 rm** ☐ 300/360000, 4 suites.

Jolly Hotel Ligure, piazza Carlo Felice 85 ✉ 10123 ✆ 55641, Telex 22016 Fax 535438 – ⧉ ▤ TV ☎ – 🏛 200. AE Ⓢ ⓞ E VISA. ✻ rest CY
Meals a la carte 55/100000 – **167 rm** ☐ 320/380000, 2 suites.

Starhotel Majestic without rest., corso Vittorio Emanuele II 54 ✉ 10123 ✆ 53915 Telex 216260, Fax 534963 – ⧉ ▤ TV ☎. AE Ⓢ ⓞ E VISA JCB CY
152 rm ☐ 330/410000.

City without rest., via Juvarra 25 ✉ 10122 ✆ 540546, Fax 548188 – ⧉ ▤ TV ☎ 🚗 – 🏛 60. AE Ⓢ ⓞ E VISA BV
50 rm ☐ 260/350000, 10 suites.

Victoria without rest., via Nino Costa 4 ✉ 10123 ✆ 5611909, Fax 5611806, « Elega and personal ambience » – ⧉ ▤ TV ☎. AE Ⓢ E VISA. ✻ CY
90 rm ☐ 180/250000.

Holiday Inn Turin City Centre M, via Assietta 3 ✉ 10128 ✆ 5167111, Fax 516769 ⧉ ⇹ rm ▤ TV ☎ ♿ 🚗 – 🏛 40. AE Ⓢ ⓞ E VISA JCB. ✻ rest CY
Meals (dinner only) a la carte 45/65000 – **57 rm** ☐ 250/350000.

Boston without rest., via Massena 70 ✉ 10128 ✆ 500359, Fax 599358, 🌳 – ⧉ TV ☎ 🚗. AE Ⓢ ⓞ E VISA BZ
51 rm ☐ 160/220000, 2 suites.

Genio without rest., corso Vittorio Emanuele II 47 ✉ 10125 ✆ 6505771, Fax 65082 – ⧉ ▤ TV ☎ – 🏛 25. AE Ⓢ ⓞ E VISA JCB CYZ
90 rm ☐ 160/220000.

Concord, via Lagrange 47 ✉ 10123 ✆ 5176756, Telex 221323, Fax 5176305 – ⧉ TV ☎ ♿ – 🏛 180. AE Ⓢ ⓞ E VISA. ✻ rest CY
Meals 40/60000 – **135 rm** ☐ 260/335000, 4 suites.

Royal, corso Regina Margherita 249 ✉ 10144 ☎ 4376777, Fax 4376393 – – 600. BV u
closed 1 to 28 August – **Meals** a la carte 40/70000 – 17000 – **70 rm** 230/300000.

Genova e Stazione without rest., via Sacchi 14/b ✉ 10128 ☎ 5629400, Fax 5629896 – – 60. CZ b
closed 1 to 18 August – **58 rm** 150/220000, suite.

President without rest., via Cecchi 67 ✉ 10152 ☎ 859555, Fax 2480465 – CV s
72 rm 130/170000.

Alexandra without rest., lungo Doria Napoli 14 ✉ 10152 ☎ 858327, Fax 2483805 – CV c
56 rm 130/175000.

Crimea without rest., via Mentana 3 ✉ 10133 ☎ 6604700, Fax 6604912 – DZ e
48 rm 170/220000, suite.

Gran Mogol without rest., via Guarini 2 ✉ 10123 ☎ 5612120, Fax 5623160 – CY r
closed August and 23 December-3 January – **45 rm** 160/220000.

Piemontese without rest., via Berthollet 21 ✉ 10125 ☎ 6698101, Fax 6690571 – CZ x
35 rm 150/195000.

Lancaster without rest., corso Filippo Turati 8 ✉ 10128 ☎ 5681982, Fax 5683019 – BZ r
closed 5 to 31 August – **77 rm** 145/190000.

Venezia without rest., via 20 Settembre 70 ✉ 10122 ☎ 5623384, Fax 5623726 – – 60. CX r
75 rm 130/190000.

Due Mondi without rest., via Saluzzo 3 ✉ 10125 ☎ 6698981, Fax 6699383 – CZ k
closed 10 to 20 August – 15000 – **36 rm** 150/180000.

Villa Sassi-El Toulà with rm, strada al Traforo del Pino 47 ✉ 10132 ☎ 8980556, Fax 8980095, « 18C country house in extensive parkland » – rm – 200. rest by corso Casale DY
closed August – **Meals** *(closed Sunday)* a la carte 70/105000 – **15 rm** 270/400000, suite.

Del Cambio, piazza Carignano 2 ✉ 10123 ☎ 546690, Fax 535282, Historic traditional restaurant, « 19C decor » – CX a
closed Sunday, 8 to 31 August and 1 to 6 January – **Meals** (booking essential) 70/95000 (lunch) 90/105000 (dinner) and a la carte 65/120000 (15 %).

Balbo, via Andrea Doria 11 ✉ 10123 ☎ 8125566, Fax 8127524 –
closed Monday and 25 July-20 August – **Meals** (booking essential) a la carte 75/115000
Spec. Insalata di astice e riso selvaggio. Tagliatelline al rosso d'uovo con intingolo di verdure, pinoli e uvetta. Filetto di vitello piemontese in crosta di patate e salsa al Barbera. CY n

Rendez Vous, corso Vittorio Emanuele II 38 ✉ 10123 ☎ 887666, Fax 889362 – CZ g
closed Saturday lunch and Sunday – **Meals** (booking essential for dinner) 35/50000 (lunch) and a la carte 65/85000.

Villa Somis, strada Val Pattonera 138 ✉ 10133 ☎ 6613086, Fax 6614626, « 18C house with park ; and summer service under a pergola » –
closed 5 to 26 August, 2 to 9 January, Monday and lunch October-May except weekends – **Meals** (booking essential) a la carte 40/65000. HU e

Tiffany, piazza Solferino 16/h ✉ 10121 ☎ 535948 – CX x
closed Saturday lunch, Sunday and August – **Meals** a la carte 40/70000.

Al Gatto Nero, corso Filippo Turati 14 ✉ 10128 ☎ 590414, Fax 502245 – BZ z
closed Sunday and August – **Meals** a la carte 65/85000.

La Cloche, strada al Traforo del Pino 106 ✉ 10132 ☎ 8994213, Fax 8981522 – – 100. by corso Moncalieri CDZ
closed Sunday dinner and Monday – **Meals** (surprise menu)40/60000 and a la carte 65/130000.

Al Bue Rosso, corso Casale 10 ✉ 10131 ☎ 8191393 – DY e
closed Saturday lunch, Monday and August – **Meals** a la carte 60/85000 (10 %).

Perbacco, via Mazzini 31 ✉ 10123 ☎ 882110, Late night dinners – DZ x
closed Sunday and August – **Meals** (dinner only) (booking essential) a la carte 50/70000.

TORINO

Traffic restricted
in the town centre

Carlo Felice (Piazza) .... **CY** 16
Roma (Via)............ **CXY**
S. Carlo (Piazza) .... **CXY**

Alfieri (Via)........... **CY** 6
Cadorna (Lungo Po L.) .. **DY** 10
Carignano (Piazza)...... **CX** 12
Carlo Emanuele II (Pza).. **DY** 13
Casale (Corso)......... **DY** 18
Castello (Piazza) .... **CX** 19
Cesare Augusto (Pza) ... **CV** 23
Consolata (Via della).... **CV** 27
Diaz (Lungo Po A.) ..... **DY** 32
Gran Madre di Dio (Pza) . **DY** 38
Milano (Via)........... **CV** 46
Ponte Vittorio Emanuele I **DY** 55
Repubblica
(Piazza della) .... **CV** 62
S. F. d'Assisi (Via) ...... **CX** 66
Solferino (Piazza)....... **CX** 75
Vitt. Emanuele II (Lgo) .. **BCY** 90
4 Marzo (Via) .... **CX** 93
20 Settembre (Via)..... **CXY** 96

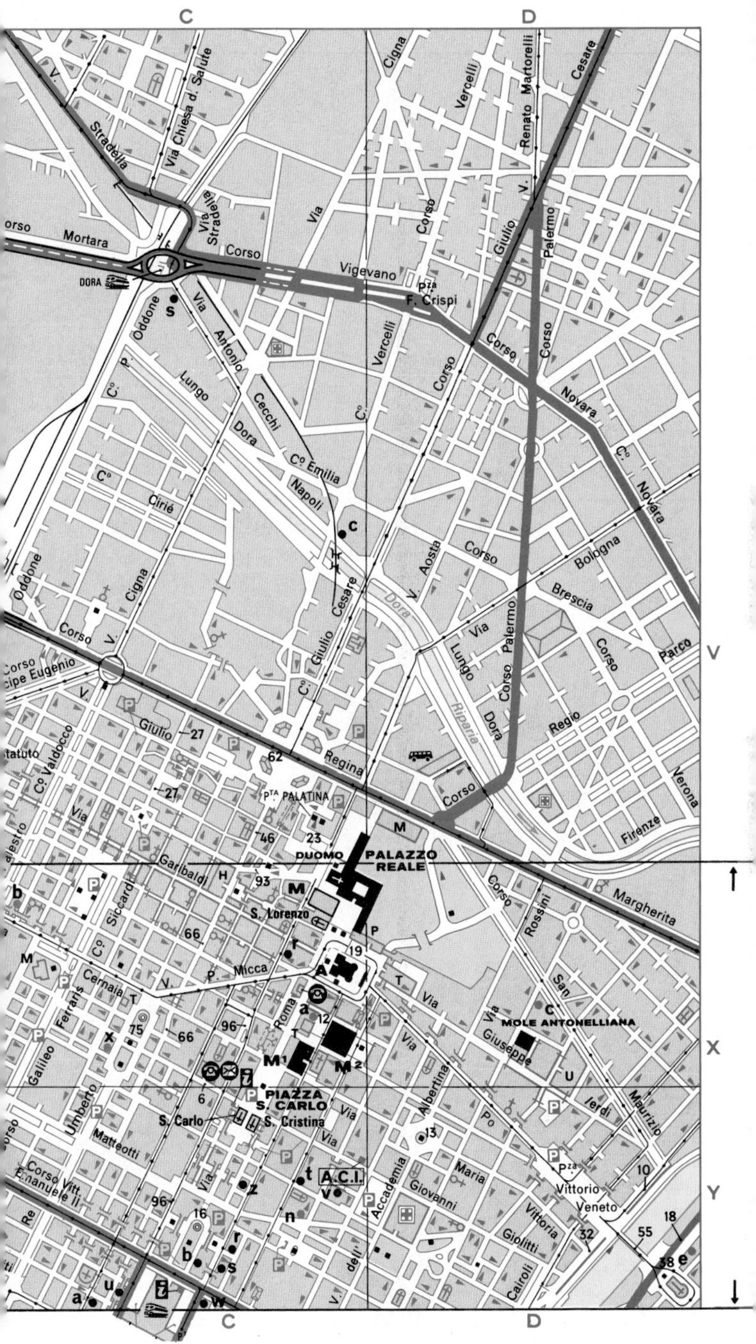

C
D
V
X
Y
DORA
Corso Mortara
Corso Vigevano
Pza F. Crispi
Corso Novara
Corso Giulio Cesare
Corso Palermo
Via Cigna
Corso Vercelli
Corso Regina
Corso Bologna
Corso Brescia
Lungo Dora Riparia
Corso Regio Parco
Corso Verona
Corso Firenze
Corso Margherita
PTA PALATINA
DUOMO
PALAZZO REALE
S. Lorenzo
MOLE ANTONELLIANA
PIAZZA S. CARLO
S. Carlo
S. Cristina
A.C.I.
Via Roma
Via Po
Via Garibaldi
Via Cernaia
Via Pietro Micca
Corso Vitt. Emanuele II
Via Accademia Albertina
Via Maria Vittoria
Via Giolitti
Via Cavour
Pza Vittorio Veneto
Via Giuseppe Verdi
Corso San Maurizio
Corso Rossini
Corso Cairoli
Via Matteotti
Corso Umberto
Via Galileo Ferraris
Corso Siccardi
Corso Valdocco
Corso Principe Eugenio
Corso Ciriè
Corso Napoli
Corso Emilia
Via Cecchi
Via Antonio
Lungo Dora
Via Oddone
Via Chiesa d. Salute
Via Stradella
Via Renato Martorelli
Via Aosta

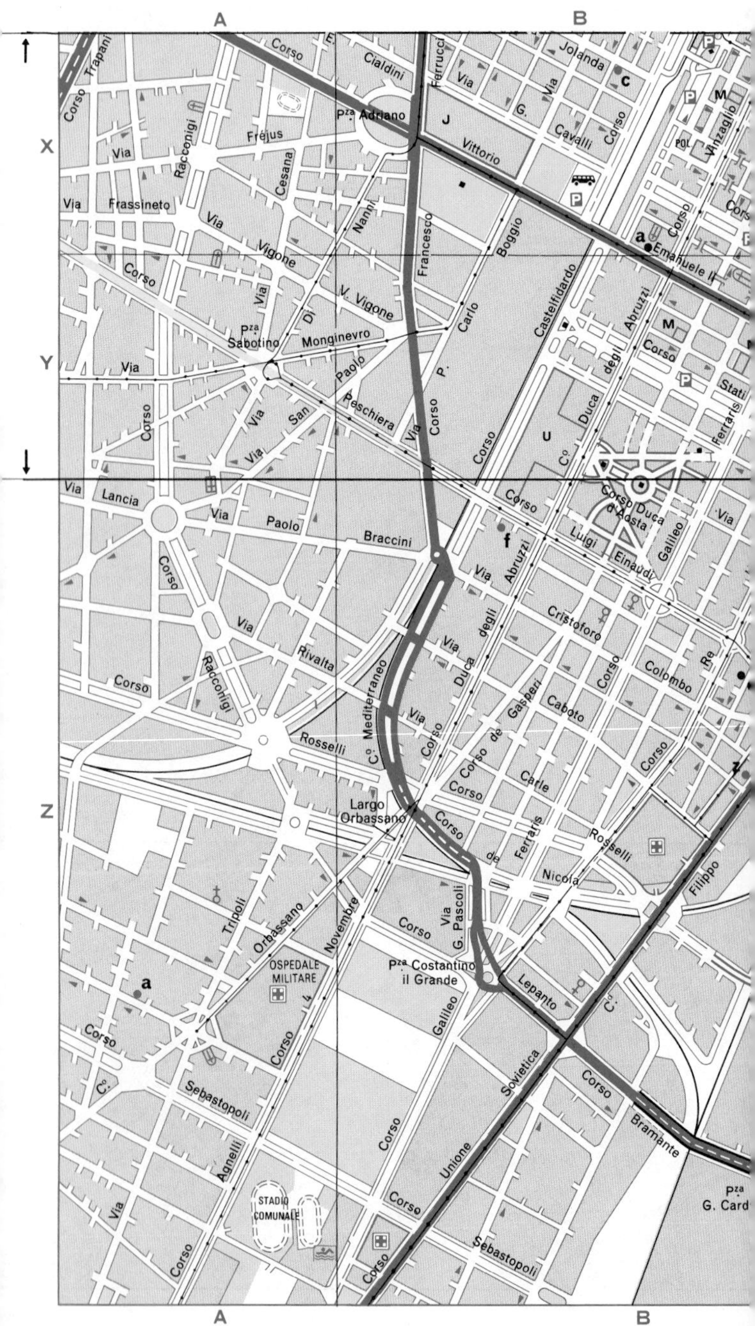
A
B
X
Y
Z
Corso Trapani
Corso Cialdini
Pza Adriano
Ferrucci
Via Jolanda
Via G. Cavalli
Corso Vittorio Emanuele II
Corso Vinzaglio
Fréjus
Via Racconigi
Cesana
Via Frassineto
Via Vigone
Corso
Nanni
Francesco
Boggio
V. Vigone
Di
Pza Sabotino
Monginevro
Via
Paolo
Peschiera
Via San
Corso Castelfidardo
Corso Abruzzi
Duca degli
Corso Stati
Ferraris
Carlo
P.
Corso
Via Lancia
Via Paolo Braccini
Corso Duca d'Aosta
Corso Luigi Einaudi
Galileo
Via Abruzzi
Via Duca degli
Cristoforo Colombo
Re
Via Rivalta
Corso Racconigi
Corso Rosselli
Co Mediterraneo
Via
Corso
Corso de Gasperi
Caboto
Carle
Largo Orbassano
Corso de Nicola
Ferraris
Rosselli
Filippo
Via G. Pascoli
Pza Costantino il Grande
Lepanto
Tripoli
Orbassano
Novembre
OSPEDALE MILITARE
Corso 4
Corso Galileo
Corso Sebastopoli
Agnelli
Sovietica
Corso Unione
Corso Bramante
STADIO COMUNALE
Via
Corso
Pza G. Card
J
U
M
POL.
a
c
f

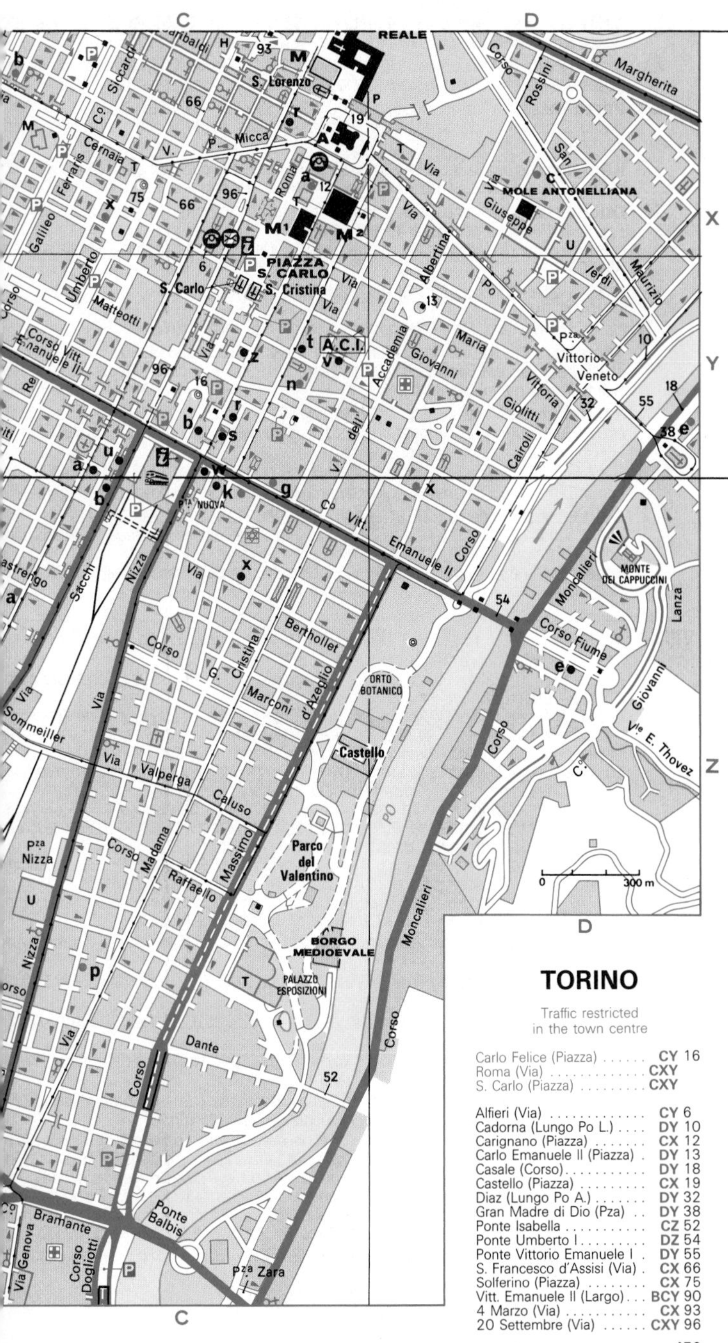

TORINO

Traffic restricted
in the town centre

Carlo Felice (Piazza) ...... CY 16
Roma (Via) .... CXY
S. Carlo (Piazza) .... CXY

Alfieri (Via) .... CY 6
Cadorna (Lungo Po L.) .... DY 10
Carignano (Piazza) .... CX 12
Carlo Emanuele II (Piazza) . DY 13
Casale (Corso) .... DY 18
Castello (Piazza) .... CX 19
Diaz (Lungo Po A.) .... DY 32
Gran Madre di Dio (Pza) .. DY 38
Ponte Isabella .... CZ 52
Ponte Umberto I .... DZ 54
Ponte Vittorio Emanuele I . DY 55
S. Francesco d'Assisi (Via) . CX 66
Solferino (Piazza) .... CX 75
Vitt. Emanuele II (Largo) ... BCY 90
4 Marzo (Via) .... CX 93
20 Settembre (Via) ...... CXY 96

XX **Galante,** corso Palestro 15 ✉ 10122 ✆ 537757 – ▤. AE ⓢ ⦿ E VISA JCB CX
closed Saturday lunch, Sunday and August – **Meals** a la carte 50/85000.

XX **Marco Polo,** via Marco Polo 38 ✉ 10129 ✆ 599900, Fax 500096, Seafood – ▤. AE VIS BZ
closed Monday and lunch (except Sunday) – **Meals** (booking essential) 75000.

XX **Porta Rossa,** via Passalacqua 3/b ✉ 10122 ✆ 530816 – ▤. AE ⓢ ⦿ E VISA. ✂ CV
closed Saturday lunch, Sunday and August – **Meals** 25000 (lunch only) and a la ca 40/80000.

XX **Il Porticciolo,** via Barletta 58 ✉ 10136 ✆ 321601, Seafood – ▤. AE ⓢ E VISA. ✂ AZ
closed Saturday lunch, Sunday and August – **Meals** (booking essential) a la carte 50/800

XX **Duchesse,** via Duchessa Jolanda 7 ang. via Beaumont ✉ 10138 ✆ 43464, Fax 4346494 – ▤. AE ⓢ ⦿ E VISA JCB BX
closed Sunday dinner, Monday, August and 25 December-3 January – **Meals** a la ca 45/80000.

XX **Il 58,** via San Secondo 58 ✉ 10128 ✆ 505566
▤. ⓢ E VISA CZ
closed Monday and 1 to 7 September – **Meals** a la carte 45/65000.

X **Trômlin,** a Cavoretto, via alla Parrocchia 7 ✉ 10133 ✆ 6613050
closed lunch (except Bank Holidays), Monday and 15 July-5 August – **Meals** (booking ess tial) (surprise menu) 50000 b.i.. by corso Moncalieri DZ

X **'l Birichin,** via Monti 16 ✉ 10126 ✆ 657457 – ▤. ⓢ E VISA JCB CZ
closed Sunday, 5 to 25 August and 1 to 7 January – **Meals** a la carte 30/60000.

Costigliole d'Asti *14055 Asti 988 ⑫, 428 H 6 – pop. 5 923 alt. 242 – ☎ 0141.*

Roma 629 – Acqui Terme 34 – Alessandria 51 – Asti 15 – Genova 108 – Torino – 7

XXX **Guido,** piazza Umberto I 27 ✆ 966012, Fax 966012 – AE ⓢ ⦿ E VISA
✿✿ *closed Sunday, Bank Holidays, 1 to 20 August and 23 December-10 January* – **Meals** (din only) (booking essential) 110000
Spec. Peperone farcito al forno (April-September), Zuppa di funghi e tartufi (Septemb December). Capretto di Roccaverano (April-June).

VENICE (VENEZIA) *30100* P *988 ⑤, 429 F 19 G. Venice – pop. 298 915 – ☎ 041.*

See : *St. Marks Square**** KZ :
*Basilica**** LZ – *Doges Palace**** LZ – *Campanile*** : ※** KLZ **Q** – *Correr Museum* KZ **M1** – *Bridge of Sighs*** LZ.
*Grand Canal**** : *Rialto Bridge*** JY – *Ca' d'Oro**** JX – *Academy of Fine Arts**** – *Rezzonico Palace*** BV – *Grassi Palace** BV – *Peggy Guggenheim Collection** *in Pal Venier dei Leoni* DV **M2** – *Vendramin-Calergi Palace** CT – *Cà Pesaro** JX.
*Churches : Santa Maria della Salute*** DV – *St. Giorgio Maggiore** : ※*** *from campa* FV – *St. Zanipolo*** LX – *Santa Maria Gloriosa dei Frari**** BTU – *St. Zaccaria*** – *Interior decoration*** *by Veronese in the Church of St. Sebastiano* ABV – *Ceiling** *the Church of St. Pantaleone* BU – *Santa Maria dei Miracoli** KLX – *St. Francesco d Vigna** FT – *Redentore** *(Giudecca Island)* BV – *Ghetto*** BT.
*Scuola di St. Rocco**** BU – *Scuola di St. Giorgio degli Schiavoni**** FU – *Scuola Carmini** BV – *Facade** *of the Scuola di St. Marco* LX – *Palazzo Labia*** BT.
*The Lido*** – *Murano*** : *Glass Museum**, *Church of Santi Maria e Donato*** – *Burano* - *Torcello*** : *mosaics*** *in the Cathedral of Santa Maria Assunta.*

18 *(closed Monday) at Lido Alberoni ✉ 30011 ✆ 731333, Fax 731339 15 mn by b and 9 km;*

18, 9 *Cà della Nave (closed Tuesday), at Martellago ✉ 30030 ✆ 5401555, Fax 54019 NW : 12 km;*

18, 9 *Villa Condulmer (closed Monday), at Zerman ✉ 31020 ✆ 457062, Fax 457202, 17 km.*

✈ *Marco Polo of Tessera, NE : 13 km ✆ 2609260 – Alitalia, via Sansovino 7 Mes Venezia ✉ 30173 ✆ 2581222.*

⛴ *to Lido-San Nicolò from piazzale Roma (Tronchetto) daily (35 mn); to island of lestrina-Santa Maria del Mare from Lido Alberoni daily (15 mn).*

⛴ *to Punta Sabbioni from Riva degli Schiavoni daily (40 mn) ; to islands of Burano (30 Torcello (40 mn), Murano (1 h 10 mn) from Punta Sabbioni daily ; to islands of Murano (10 Burano (50 mn), Torcello (50 mn) from Fondamenta Nuove daily; to Treporti-Cavallino fr Fondamenta Nuove daily (1 h 10 mn); to Venezia-Fondamenta Nuove from Treporti-Cava (1 h 10 mn), to islands of Murano (1 h), Burano (20 mn), Torcello (25 mn) daily – Informat ACTV-Venetian Trasport Union, piazzale Roma ✉ 30135 ✆ 5287886, Fax 5207135.*

ℹ *Palazzetto Selva-Molo di San Marco 71/c ✉ 30124 ✆ 5226356 – Santa Lucia Rail station ✉ 30121 ✆ 719078.*

Roma 528 – Bologna 152 – Milano 267 – Trieste 158

Plans on following pages

Cipriani, isola della Giudecca 10 ✉ 30133 ✆ 5207744, Fax 5203930, ←, « Floral garden with heated 🏊 », – ▤ TV ☎ – 🏛 80. AE Ⓢ ⓓ E VISA. FV h
closed 10 November-14 March – **Meals** a la carte 130/180000 – **92 rm** ☐ 1100/1300000, 5 suites (**Palazzo Vendramin** 7 apartments closed 7 January-7 February).

Danieli, riva degli Schiavoni 4196 ✉ 30122 ✆ 5226480, Telex 410077, Fax 5200208, ← San Marco Canal, « Hall in a small Venetian style courtyard and summer rest. service on terrace with panoramic view » – ▤ TV ☎ – 🏛 150. AE Ⓢ ⓓ E VISA JCB. LZ a
Meals a la carte 110/160000 – ☐ 36500 – **221 rm** 485/825000, 9 suites.

Gritti Palace, campo Santa Maria del Giglio 2467 ✉ 30124 ✆ 794611, Telex 410125, Fax 5200942, ← Grand Canal, « Outdoor rest. summer service on the Grand Canal » – rm ▤ TV ☎ ♿ – 🏛 50. AE Ⓢ ⓓ E VISA JCB. JZ a
Meals a la carte 120/200000 – **93 rm** ☐ 565/840000, 2 suites.

Bauer Grünwald, campo San Moisè 1459 ✉ 30124 ✆ 5207022, Telex 410075, Fax 5207557, ← Grand Canal, – ▤ TV ☎ – 🏛 150. AE Ⓢ ⓓ E VISA. rest KZ h
Meals a la carte 100/150000 – **214 rm** ☐ 390/750000, 3 suites.

Londra Palace, riva degli Schiavoni 4171 ✉ 30122 ✆ 5200533, Telex 420681, Fax 5225032, ← San Marco Canal – ▤ TV ☎. AE Ⓢ ⓓ E VISA JCB. rest LZ t
Meals *Do Leoni* Rest (Elegant rest., booking essential) a la carte 100/155000 – **53 rm** ☐ 480/580000.

Europa e Regina Cigahotel, calle larga 22 Marzo 2159 ✉ 30124 ✆ 5200477, Telex 410123, Fax 5231533, ← Grand Canal, « Outdoor rest. summer service on the Grand Canal » – ▤ TV ☎ ♿ – 🏛 140. AE Ⓢ ⓓ E VISA JCB. rest KZ d
Meals 85/90000 – ☐ 46000 – **192 rm** 360/540000, 13 suites.

Monaco e Grand Canal, calle Vallaresso 1325 ✉ 30124 ✆ 5200211, Telex 410450, Fax 5200501, ← Grand Canal and Santa Maria della Salute Church, « Outdoor rest. summer service on the Grand Canal » – ▤ TV ☎ ♿ – 🏛 40. AE Ⓢ ⓓ E VISA JCB. KZ e
Meals *Grand Canal* Rest. a la carte 105/155000 – **70 rm** ☐ 420/590000, 2 suites.

Metropole, riva degli Schiavoni 4149 ✉ 30122 ✆ 5205044, Telex 410340, Fax 5223679, ← San Marco Canal, « Collection of period bric-a-brac » – ▤ TV ☎ – 🏛 40. AE Ⓢ ⓓ E VISA JCB FV t
Meals 55000 – **74 rm** ☐ 400/595000.

Luna Hotel Baglioni, calle larga dell'Ascensione 1243 ✉ 30124 ✆ 5289840, Telex 410236, Fax 5287160 – rm ▤ TV ☎ – 🏛 150. AE Ⓢ ⓓ E VISA JCB. rest
Meals 100/120000 and ***Canova*** Rest. a la carte 85/130000 – **87 rm** ☐ 370/640000, 6 suites. KZ p

Sofitel, giardini Papadopoli Santa Croce 245 ✉ 30135 ✆ 710400, Telex 410310, Fax 710394 – rm ▤ TV ☎ – 🏛 60. AE Ⓢ ⓓ E VISA. rest BT k
Meals a la carte 70/115000 – **92 rm** ☐ 460/560000.

Starhotel Splendid-Suisse, San Marco-Mercerie 760 ✉ 30124 ✆ 5200755, Telex 410590, Fax 5286498 – ▤ TV ☎ – 🏛 80. AE Ⓢ ⓓ E VISA JCB. rest
Meals (residents only) – **157 rm** ☐ 440/660000. KY n

Saturnia e International, calle larga 22 Marzo 2398 ✉ 30124 ✆ 5208377, Fax 5207131, « 14C nobleman's town house » – ▤ TV ☎ – 🏛 60. AE Ⓢ E VISA JCB JZ n
Meals (see rest. **La Caravella** below) – **95 rm** ☐ 380/520000.

Bellini without rest., Cannaregio 116-Lista di Spagna ✉ 30121 ✆ 5242488, Fax 715193 – ▤ TV ☎. AE Ⓢ ⓓ E VISA JCB BT f
64 rm ☐ 320/440000, 3 suites.

Amadeus, Lista di Spagna 227 ✉ 30121 ✆ 715300, Telex 420811, Fax 5240841, « Garden » – ▤ TV ☎ – 🏛 150. AE Ⓢ ⓓ E VISA JCB BT b
Meals *Il Papageno* Rest. *(closed Wednesday except May-September)* a la carte 60/80000 (12 %) – **63 rm** ☐ 380/420000.

Cavalletto without rest., calle del Cavalletto 1107 ✉ 30124 ✆ 5200955, Telex 410684, Fax 5238184, ← – ▤ TV ☎. AE Ⓢ ⓓ E VISA JCB KZ f
96 rm ☐ 360/480000.

La Fenice et des Artistes without rest., campiello de la Fenice 1936 ✉ 30124 ✆ 5232333, Fax 5203721 – ▤ TV ☎. AE Ⓢ ⓓ E VISA JZ v
65 rm ☐ 190/300000, 3 suites.

Rialto, riva del Ferro 5149 ✉ 30124 ✆ 5209166, Telex 420809, Fax 5238958, ← Rialto bridge – ▤ TV ☎. AE Ⓢ ⓓ E VISA JCB. KY v
Meals *(closed Thursday and November-20 March)* a la carte 55/85000 (12 %) – **71 rm** ☐ 230/330000.

Concordia without rest., calle larga San Marco 367 ✉ 30124 ✆ 5206866, Telex 411069, Fax 5206775 – ▤ TV ☎. AE Ⓢ ⓓ E VISA JCB LZ r
55 rm ☐ 360/530000.

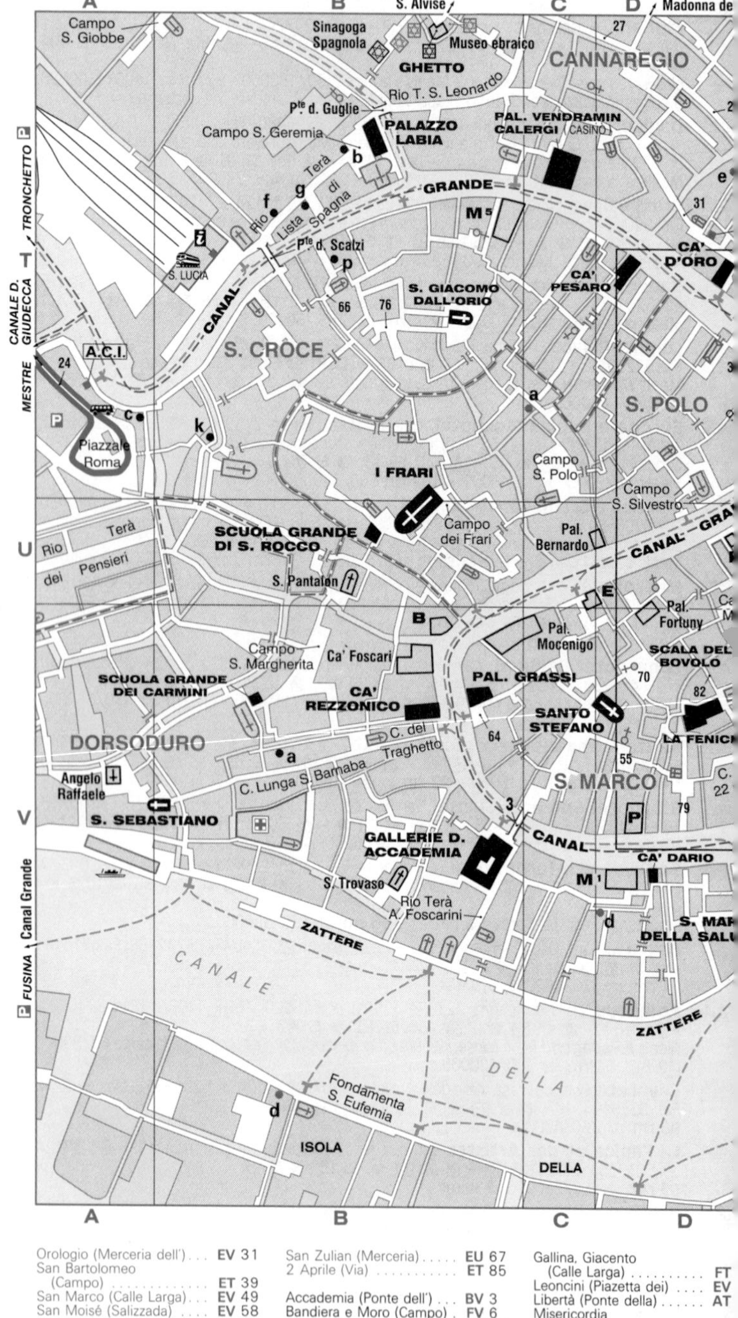

Orologio (Merceria dell') . . . **EV** 31
San Bartolomeo (Campo) . . . . **ET** 39
San Marco (Calle Larga) . . . **EV** 49
San Moisé (Salizzada) . . . . **EV** 58
San Salvador (Merceria) . . . **EU** 61

San Zulian (Merceria) . . . . . **EU** 67
2 Aprile (Via) . . . . **ET** 85

Accademia (Ponte dell') . . . **BV** 3
Bandiera e Moro (Campo) . **FV** 6
Capello (Ramo) . . . . **FT** 10

Gallina, Giacento (Calle Larga) . . . . **FT**
Leoncini (Piazetta dei) . . . . **EV**
Libertà (Ponte della) . . . . . . **AT**
Misericordia (Fondamenta della) . . . . . **DT**

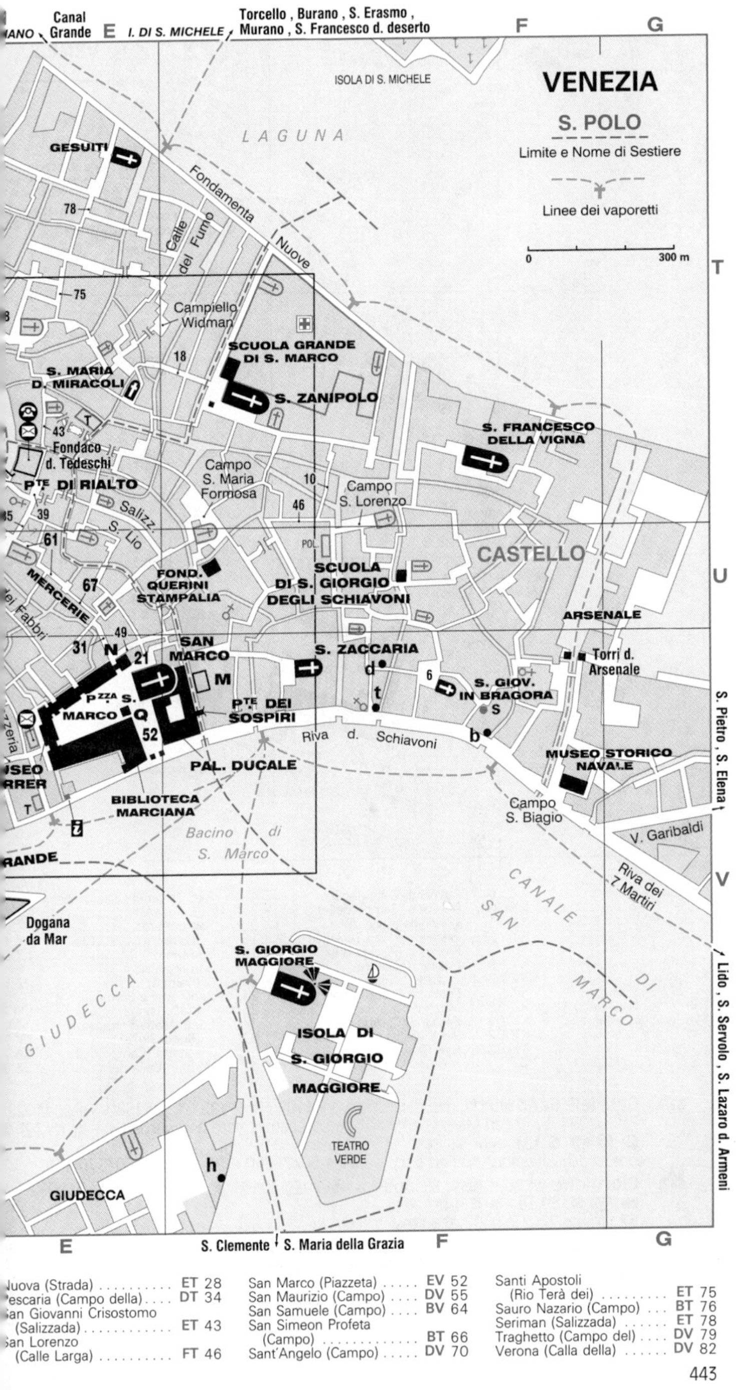

…uova (Strada) . . . . ET 28
…escaria (Campo della) . . . . DT 34
…an Giovanni Crisostomo (Salizzada) . . . . ET 43
…an Lorenzo (Calle Larga) . . . . FT 46
San Marco (Piazzeta) . . . . . EV 52
San Maurizio (Campo) . . . . DV 55
San Samuele (Campo) . . . . BV 64
San Simeon Profeta (Campo) . . . . BT 66
Sant'Angelo (Campo) . . . . . DV 70
Santi Apostoli (Rio Terà dei) . . . . ET 75
Sauro Nazario (Campo) . . . BT 76
Seriman (Salizzada) . . . . . . ET 78
Traghetto (Campo del) . . . . DV 79
Verona (Calla della) . . . . . . DV 82

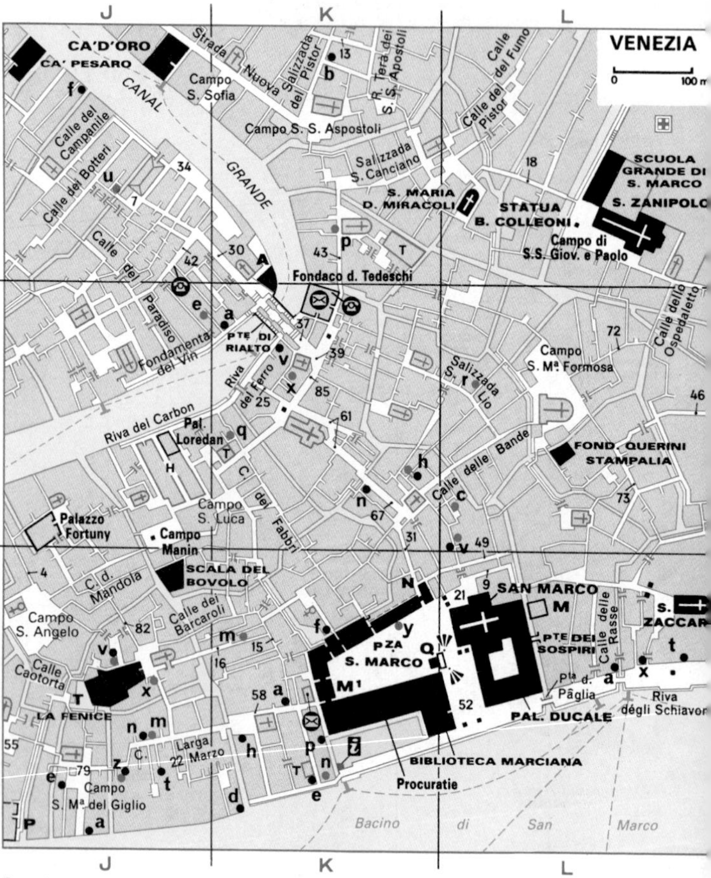

- Frezzeria . . . . KZ 15
- Orefici (Ruga degli) . . . . KX 30
- Orologio (Merceria dell') . . . KY 31
- Rialto (Ponte di) . . . . KY
- San Bartolomeo (Campo) . . . . KY 39
- San Marco (Calle Larga) . . . LYZ 49
- San Marco (Piazza) . . . . KZ
- San Moisé (Salizzada) . . . . KZ 58
- San Salvador (Merceria) . . . KY 61
- San Zulian (Merceria) . . . . . KY 67
- 2 Aprile (Via) . . . . KY 85
- 22 Marzo (Calle Larga) . . . JZ

- Avvocati (Calle degli) . . . . . JZ 4
- Beccarie (Campo delle) . . . JX 7
- Canonica (Calle di) . . . . LZ 9
- Franceschi (Rio Terà dei) . . KX 13
- Frezzeria (Piscina di) . . . . . . KZ 16
- Gallina, Giacento (Calle Larga) . . . . LX 18
- Leoncini (Piazzetta dei) . . . . LZ 21
- Mazzini (Calle Larga) . . . . . KY 25
- Pescaria (Campo della) . . . . JX 34
- Pio X (Salizzada) . . . . KY 37
- San Giovanni (Ruga Vecchia) . . . . JX 42

- San Giovanni Crisostomo (Salizzada) . . . . KX 4
- San Lorenzo (Calle Larga) . . . . LY 4
- San Marco (Piazzetta) . . . . LZ 5
- San Maurizio (Campo) . . . . JZ 5
- Santa Maria Formosa (Calle Lunga) . . . . LY 7
- Santa Maria Formosa (Ruga Giuffa) . . . . LY 7
- Traghetto (Campo del) . . . . JZ 7
- Verona (Calle della) . . . . . . JZ 8

Gabrielli Sandwirth, riva degli Schiavoni 4109 ✉ 30122 ✆ 5231580, Telex 41022, Fax 5209455, ⋞ San Marco Canal, « Little court yard and garden » – AE VISA JCB. rest FV
closed 30 November-12 February – **Meals** 50/75000 – **95 rm** 350/570000.

Giorgione without rest., SS. Apostoli 4587 ✉ 30131 ✆ 5225810, Fax 5239092 – AE VISA. KX
57 rm 220/330000, 6 suites.

Flora without rest., calle larga 22 Marzo 2283/a ✉ 30124 ✆ 5205844, Fax 522821 « Small flower garden » – AE VISA JCB JZ
44 rm 235/320000.

Marconi without rest., San Polo 729 ✉ 30125 ✆ 5222068, Telex 410073, Fax 52297 – AE VISA JCB. KY
26 rm 230/330000.

Ai Due Fanali without rest., Santa Croce 946 ✉ 30135 ☎ 718490, Fax 718344 – AE VISA. BT p
16 rm 220/280000.

Santa Chiara without rest., Santa Croce 548 ✉ 30125 ☎ 5206955, Telex 420690, Fax 5228799 – AE VISA. AT c
28 rm 215/360000.

San Cassiano-Cà Favretto without rest., Santa Croce 2232 ✉ 30135 ☎ 5241768, Telex 420810, Fax 721033, ≤ – AE VISA JCB JX f
35 rm 230/330000.

Spagna without rest., lista di Spagna 184 ✉ 30121 ☎ 715011, Telex 420360, Fax 715318 – AE VISA JCB BT g
19 rm 200/290000.

Firenze without rest., San Marco 1490 ✉ 30124 ☎ 5222858, Fax 5202668 – AE VISA JCB. KZ a
25 rm 300/340000.

Ala without rest., campo Santa Maria del Giglio 2494 ✉ 30124 ☎ 5208333, Telex 410275, Fax 5206390 – AE VISA JCB. JZ e
85 rm 190/280000.

Panada without rest., San Marco-calle dei Specchieri 646 ✉ 30124 ☎ 5209088, Telex 410153, Fax 5209619 – AE VISA JCB. LY v
48 rm 250/350000.

Pausania without rest., Dorsoduro 2824-fondamenta Gherardini ✉ 30123 ☎ 5222083, Telex 420178, Fax 5222989 – AE VISA JCB BV a
23 rm 210/310000.

Savoia e Jolanda, riva degli Schiavoni 4187 ✉ 30122 ☎ 5206644, Telex 410620, Fax 5207494, ≤ San Marco Canal, – AE VISA. rest LZ x
Meals *(closed Tuesday)* 50000 (12 %) – **79 rm** 240/340000.

Bisanzio without rest., calle della Pietà 3651 ✉ 30122 ☎ 5203100, Telex 420099, Fax 5204114 – AE VISA JCB FV d
39 rm 220/300000.

Caffè Quadri, piazza San Marco 120 ✉ 30124 ☎ 5289299, Fax 5208041 – AE VISA JCB. KZ y
closed Monday – **Meals** a la carte 100/150000.

Antico Martini, campo San Fantin 1983 ✉ 30124 ☎ 5224121, Fax 5289857, – AE VISA JCB. JZ x
closed 24 November-March – **Meals** (dinner only) a la carte 85/130000 (15 %).

Harry's Bar, calle Vallaresso 1323 ✉ 30124 ☎ 5285777, Fax 5208822, American bar rest. – AE VISA KZ n
Meals a la carte 140/205000 (10 %)
Spec. Risotto alle seppie. Scampi alla Thermidor. Pasticceria della casa.

La Caravella - Hotel Saturnia-International, calle larga 22 Marzo 2397 ✉ 30124 ☎ 5208901, , Typical rest. – AE VISA JCB. JZ m
closed Wednesday except June-September – **Meals** (booking essential) a la carte 85/140000.

La Colomba, piscina di Frezzeria 1665 ✉ 30124 ☎ 5221175, Fax 5221468, , « Collection of contemporary art » – – 60. AE VISA JCB. KZ m
closed Wednesday except May-June and September-October – **Meals** a la carte 85/150000 (15 %).

Taverna la Fenice, campiello de la Fenice ✉ 30124 ☎ 5223856, Fax 5236866, « Outdoor summer service » – AE VISA JCB. JZ v
closed Sunday, Monday lunch and 10 to 31 January – **Meals** 40/60000 (15 %) lunch 60/80000 (15 %) dinner and a la carte 65/85000 (15 %).

Do Forni, calle dei Specchieri 457/468 ✉ 30124 ☎ 5237729, Fax 5288132 – AE VISA JCB LY c
Meals a la carte 65/95000 (12 %).

Harry's Dolci, Giudecca 773 ✉ 30133 ☎ 5224844, Fax 5222322, « Outdoor summer service on the Giudecca canal » – AE VISA BV d
April-10 November ; closed Tuesday – **Meals** 75/80000 (12 %) and a la carte 85/105000 (12 %).

Osteria da Fiore, San Polo-calle del Scaleter 2202/A ✉ 30125 ☎ 721308, Fax 721343, seafood – AE VISA CT a
closed Sunday, Monday, August and 23 December-11 January – **Meals** (booking essential) a la carte 80/130000
Spec. Risotto agli scampi e porcini (summer-autumn). Filetto di branzino all'aceto balsamico. Rombo al forno in crosta di patate.

XX **Al Covo,** campiello della Pescaria 3968 ✉ 30122 ℘ 5223812 – ⇆. AE Ⓢ VISA
closed Wednesday, Thursday, 10 to 20 August, and January – **Meals** 40000 and a la cart
70/90000. FV

XX **Ai Gondolieri,** Dorsoduro-San Vio 366 ✉ 30123 ℘ 5286396 – AE Ⓢ ⓓ E VISA.
closed Tuesday – **Meals** a la carte 65/100000 (10 %). DV

XX **Ai Mercanti,** San Polo 1588 ✉ 30125 ℘ 5240282, Fax 5240282 – ▤. AE Ⓢ ⓓ
VISA. JX
closed Sunday and Monday lunch – **Meals** a la carte 70/105000 (12 %).

XX **Antico Pignolo,** calle dei Specchieri 451 ✉ 30124 ℘ 5228123, Fax 5209007 –
▤. AE Ⓢ ⓓ E VISA LY
closed Tuesday except May-June and September-October – **Meals** a la carte 60/10500
(12 %).

XX **Al Graspo de Ua,** calle dei Bombaseri 5094 ✉ 30124 ℘ 5200150, Fax 5233917, Typic
taverna – ▤. AE Ⓢ ⓓ E VISA KY
closed 1 to 14 August, 2 to 14 January and Monday April-May and October-November
Meals a la carte 60/95000 (16 %).

XX **Fiaschetteria Toscana,** San Giovanni Crisostomo 5719 ✉ 30121 ℘ 528528
Fax 5285521, – ▤. AE Ⓢ ⓓ E VISA KX
closed Tuesday and 6 July-2 August – **Meals** a la carte 50/85000 (12 %).

XX **Vini da Gigio,** Cannaregio 3628/a-Fondamenta San Felice ✉ 30131 ℘ 5285140 –
Ⓢ ⓓ E VISA DT
closed Monday, 7 to 21 August and 7 to 21 January – **Meals** (booking essential) a la car
45/70000.

XX **Da Raffaele,** calle larga 22 Marzo 2347 ✉ 30124, Fax 5232317, , « Collection
ancient weapons, china and copper pieces » – ▤. AE Ⓢ ⓓ E VISA JCB JZ
closed Thursday and 10 December-25 January – **Meals** a la carte 60/100000 (12 %).

X **Trattoria alla Madonna,** calle della Madonna 594 ✉ 30125 ℘ 522382
Fax 5210167, Venetian trattoria – AE Ⓢ E VISA JCB. JY
closed Wednesday, 4 to 17 August and 24 December-January – **Meals** a la carte 45/7000
(12 %).

X **Al Conte Pescaor,** piscina San Zulian 544 ✉ 30124 ℘ 5221483, Rustic rest. – ▤.
Ⓢ ⓓ E VISA. KY
closed Sunday and 7 January-7 February – **Meals** a la carte 45/75000.

X **Antica Carbonera,** calle Bembo 4648 ✉ 30124 ℘ 5225479, Venetian trattoria –
Ⓢ ⓓ E VISA JCB KY
closed 20 July-10 August, 8 January-2 February, Sunday July-August and Thursday Se
tember-June – **Meals** a la carte 45/75000 (12 %).

in Lido : *15 mn by boat from San Marco* KZ – ✉ *30126 Venezia Lido.*
ℹ *Gran Viale S. M. Elisabetta 6* ℘ *5265721* :

Excelsior, lungomare Marconi 41 ℘ 5260201, Telex 410023, Fax 5267276, ←, ,
, – ▤ TV ☎ ♿ – 🅟 – 600. AE Ⓢ ⓓ E VISA. rest
15 March-15 November – **Meals** 125000 – ☕ 54000 – **191 rm** 540/685000.

Des Bains, lungomare Marconi 17 ℘ 5265921, Telex 410142, Fax 5260113, ←,
« Floral park with heated and », , – ▤ TV ☎ 🅟 – 380. AE Ⓢ
E VISA. rest
April-October – **Meals** 100/120000 – ☕ 32000 – **191 rm** 460/550000, suite.

Villa Mabapa, riviera San Nicolà 16 ℘ 5260590, Telex 410357, Fax 5269441, « Summ
service rest. in garden » – ▤ TV ☎ ♿ – 85. AE Ⓢ ⓓ E VISA JCB. rest
closed 7 to 30 January – **Meals** a la carte 55/80000 – **61 rm** ☕ 270/400000.

Quattro Fontane , via 4 Fontane 16 ℘ 5260227, Telex 411006, Fax 526072
« Summer service rest. in garden », – ▤ TV ☎ 🅟 – 40. AE Ⓢ ⓓ E VISA. re
28 March-3 November – **Meals** a la carte 105/155000 – **62 rm** ☕ 390/430000.

Le Boulevard without rest., Gran Viale S. M. Elisabetta 41 ℘ 5261990, Telex 41018
Fax 5261917 – ▤ TV ☎ 🅟 – 60. AE Ⓢ ⓓ E VISA JCB.
45 rm ☕ 320/430000.

X **Trattoria Favorita,** via Francesco Duodo 33 ℘ 5261626, Fax 5267296, « Outdo
summer service » – AE Ⓢ ⓓ E VISA JCB
closed Monday and 15 January-15 February – **Meals** a la carte 55/85000.

in Murano *10 mn by boat from Fondamenta Nuove* EFT *and 1 h 10 mn by boat from Punta Sabbic*
– ✉ *30121* :

X **Ai Frati,** ℘ 736694, , Seafood – Ⓢ E VISA
closed Thursday and February – **Meals** a la carte 45/70000 (12 %).

Burano *50 mn by boat from Fondamenta Nuove* EFT *and 32 mn by boat from Punta Sabbioni – ✉ 30012 :*

X **Al Gatto Nero-da Ruggero,** ✆ 730120, Fax 735570, Typical trattoria – AE ⑤ ⓪ E VISA
closed Monday, 30 October-15 November and 30 January-10 February – **Meals** a la carte 40/75000.

Torcello *45 mn by boat from Fondamenta Nuove* EFT *and 37 mn by boat from Punta Sabbioni – ✉ 30012 Burano :*

XX **Locanda Cipriani,** ✆ 730150, Fax 735433, « Summer service in garden » – ▤. AE ⑤ ⓪ E VISA
closed Tuesday and January-18 February – **Meals** a la carte 90/125000.

XX **Ostaria al Ponte del Diavolo,** ✆ 730401, Fax 730250, « Outdoor summer service », – AE ⑤ E VISA JCB
closed January, February, Thursday and dinner (except Saturday) – **Meals** a la carte 65/100000 (10 %).

adova *35100* P 988 ⑤, 429 F 17 *G. Italy – pop. 212 731 alt. 12 – ☎ 049.*
18 and 9 Montecchia (closed Monday) at Selvazzano Dentro ✉ 35030 ✆ 8055550, Fax 8055737, W : 8 km;
18 Frassanelle (closed Tuesday except April, May, September and October) ✉ 35030 Frassanelle di Rovolon ✆ 9910722, Fax 9910691, SW : 20 km;
18 (closed Monday and January) at Valsanzibio di Galzignano ✉ 35030 ✆ 9130078, Fax 9131193, E : 21 km.
Central Station ✉ 35131 ✆ 8752077 - Museo Eremitani ✆ 8750655.
A.C.I. *via Enrico degli Scrovegni 19 ✉ 35131 ✆ 654935.*
Roma 491 – Milano 234 – Venezia 42 – Verona 81.

t Rubano *W : 8 km – ✉ 35030 :*

XXX ✿✿ **Le Calandre,** via Liguria 1, località Sarmeola ✆ 630303, Fax 633000 – ▤ P. AE ⑤ ⓪ E VISA.
closed Sunday dinner, except Sunday October-May and Monday lunch – **Meals** (booking essential) a la carte 70/115000
Spec. Fegato di coniglio impanato in salsa (spring). Tortelli con caprino fresco, pomodoro, fagiolini e filetti di triglia (spring-summer). Involtini di scampi fritti in salsa di lattuga.

erona *37100* P 988 ④, 428, 429 F 14 *G. Italy – pop. 254 145 alt. 59 – ☎ 045.*
18 (closed Tuesday) at Sommacampagna ✉ 37066 ✆ 510060, Fax 510242, W : 13 km.
of Villafranca SE : 14 km ✆ 8095666 – Alitalia, corso Porta Nuova 61 ✉ 37122 ✆ 8035700.
✆ 590688.
via Leoncino 61 (Barbieri Palace) ✉ 37121 ✆ 592828, Fax 8003638 – piazza delle Erbe 42 ✉ 37121 ✆ 8030086.
A.C.I. *via della Valverde 34 ✉ 37122 ✆ 595333.*
Roma 503 – Milano 157 – Venezia 114.

XXX ✿✿ **Il Desco,** via Dietro San Sebastiano 7 ✉ 37121 ✆ 595358, Fax 590236 – ▤. AE ⑤ ⓪ E VISA JCB.
closed Sunday, Easter, 17 to 30 June, 25-26 December and 1 to 7 January – **Meals** (booking essential) a la carte 80/120000 (15 %)
Spec. Flan di zucchine con cozze e pomodoro fresco. Zuppa di patate, porcini e tartufo bianco (September-December). Coda di rospo rosolata con fave e lenticchie stufate.

Norway

Norge

PRACTICAL INFORMATION

LOCAL CURRENCY

Norwegian Kroner: *100 NOK = 15.55 USD ($) (Jan. 97)*

TOURIST INFORMATION

The telephone number and address of the Tourist Information office is given in the text under ℹ.

National Holiday in Norway: *17 May.*

FOREIGN EXCHANGE

In the Oslo area banks are usually open between 8.15am and 3.30pm, but in summertime, 15.5 - 31/8, they close at 3pm. Thursdays they are open till 5pm. Saturdays and Sundays closed.

Most large hotels, main airports and railway stations have exchange facilities. At Fornebu Airport the bank is open from 7am to 8pm except Saturdays (7am – 7pm) all the year round.

MEALS

At lunchtime, follow the custom of the country and try the typical buffets of Scandinavian specialities.

At dinner, the a la carte and set menus will offer you more conventional cooking.

SHOPPING IN OSLO

(Knitware - Silver ware)

Your hotel porter should be able to help you with information.

CAR HIRE

The international car hire companies have branches in each major city. Your hotel porter should be able to give details and help you with your arrangements.

TIPPING IN NORWAY

A service charge is included in hotel and restaurant bills and it is up to the customer to give something in addition if he wants to.

The cloakroom is sometimes included in the bill, sometimes an extra charge is made.

Taxi drivers and baggage porters don't expect to be tipped. It is up to you if you want to give a gratuity.

SPEED LIMITS

The maximum permitted speed within built-up areas is 50 km/h - 31mph. Outside these areas it is 80 km/h - 50mph. Where there are other speed limits (lower or higher) they are signposted.

SEAT BELTS

The wearing of seat belts in Norway is compulsory for drivers and all passengers.

OSLO

Norge 985 M 7 – *pop. 458 364.*

Hamburg 888 – København 583 – Stockholm 522.

Norwegian Information Centre Vestbaneplassen 1 ✆ 22 83 00 50, Fax 22 83 81 50 – KNA (Kongelig Norsk Automobilklub) Royal Norwegian Automobile Club, Drammensveien 20C ✆ 22 56 19 00 – NAF (Norges Automobil Forbund), Storg. 2 ✆ 22 34 14 00.

Oslo Golfklubb ✆ 22 50 44 02.
Fornebu SW: 8 km ✆ 67 59 67 16 – SAS Head Office: Oslo City, Stenersg. 1 a ✆ 22 17 41 60 – Air Terminal: Havnegata, main railway station, seaside.
Copenhagen, Frederikshavn, Kiel, Hirtshals : contact tourist information centre (see below).

See: *Bygdøy* ABZ *Viking Ship Museum★★★ (Vikingskipshuset) ; Folk Museum★★★ (Norsk Folkemuseum) ; Fram Museum★★ (Frammuseet) ; Kon-Tiki Museum★★ (Kon-Tiki Museet) ; Maritime Museum★★ (Norsk Sjøfartsmuseum) – Munch Museum★★ (Munch-Museet)* DY *– National Gallery★★ (Nasjonalgalleriet)* CY **M¹** *– Vigelandsparken★ (Vigeland sculptures and museum)* AX *– Akershus Castle★ (Akershus Festning : Resistance Museum★)* CZ **M²** *– Oslo Cathedral (Domkirke: views★★ from steeple)* CY.

Outskirts: *Holmenkollen★ (NW: 10 km): view from ski-jump tower and ski museum* BX *– Sonie Henie-Onstad Art Centre★★ (Sonie Henie-Onstad Kunstsenter) (W: 12 km)* AY

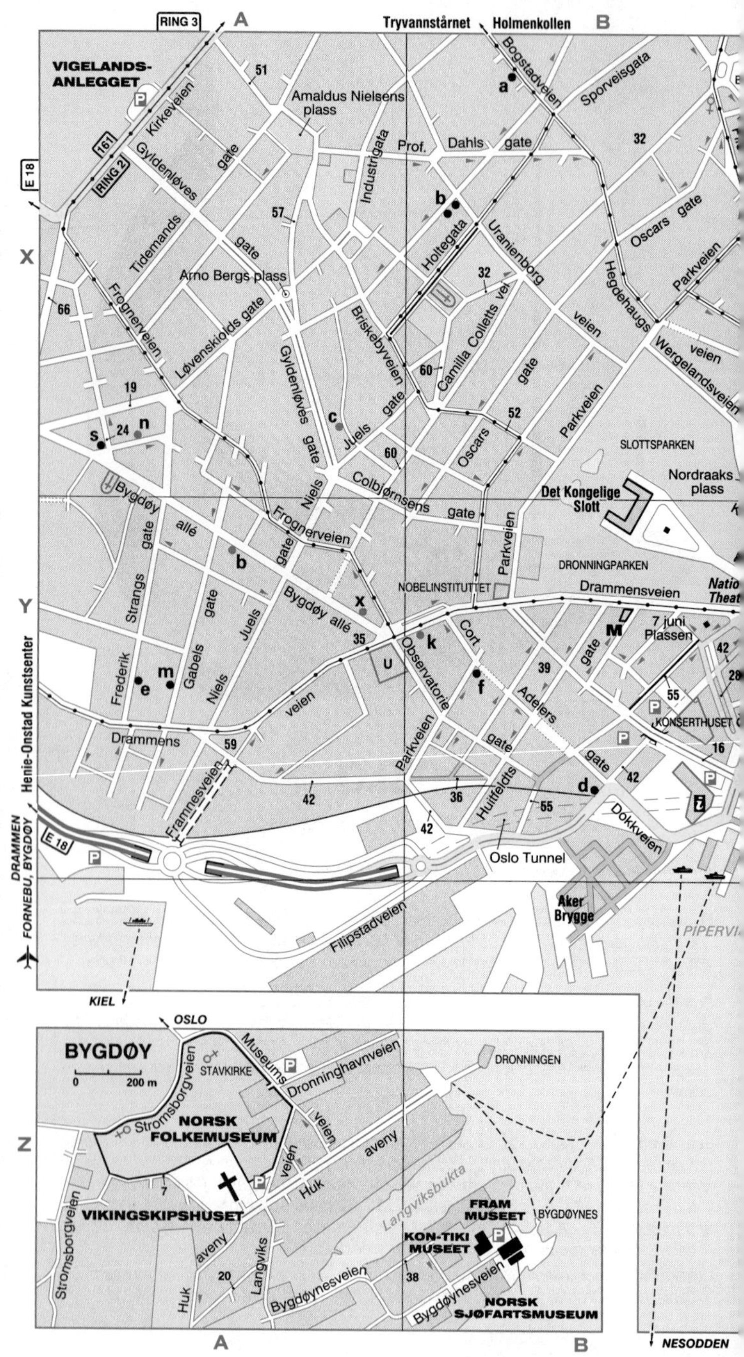

RING 3
Tryvannstårnet
Holmenkollen
VIGELANDS-ANLEGGET
Amaldus Nielsens plass
Prof. Dahls gate
Bogstadveien
Sporveisgata
Kirkeveien
Gyldenløves gate
Industrigata
Holtegata
Uranienborg veien
Oscars gate
Hegdehaugsveien
Parkveien
Wergelandsveien
Tidemands gate
Arno Bergs plass
Frognerveien
Løvenskiolds gate
Gyldenløves gate
Briskebyveien
Camilla Colletts vei
Juels gate
Niels Juels gate
Colbjørnsens gate
SLOTTSPARKEN
Nordraaks plass
Det Kongelige Slott
DRONNINGPARKEN
NOBELINSTITUTTET
Drammensveien
Bygdøy allé
Strangs gate
Frederik Stangs gate
Gabels gate
Observatorie gate
Cort Adelers gate
7 juni Plassen
KONSERTHUSET
Parkveien
Huitfeldts gate
Framnesveien
Dokkveien
Oslo Tunnel
Aker Brygge
Filipstadveien
PIPERVI
Henie-Onstad Kunstsenter
DRAMMEN
FORNEBU, BYGDØY
KIEL
OSLO
BYGDØY
0 200 m
STAVKIRKE
Museumsveien
Dronninghavnveien
Stromsborgveien
NORSK FOLKEMUSEUM
DRONNINGEN
Huk aveny
Langviksbukta
VIKINGSKIPSHUSET
FRAM MUSEET
BYGDØYNES
KON-TIKI MUSEET
Langviksveien
Bygdøynesveien
NORSK SJØFARTSMUSEUM
NESODDEN
A
B
X
Y
Z

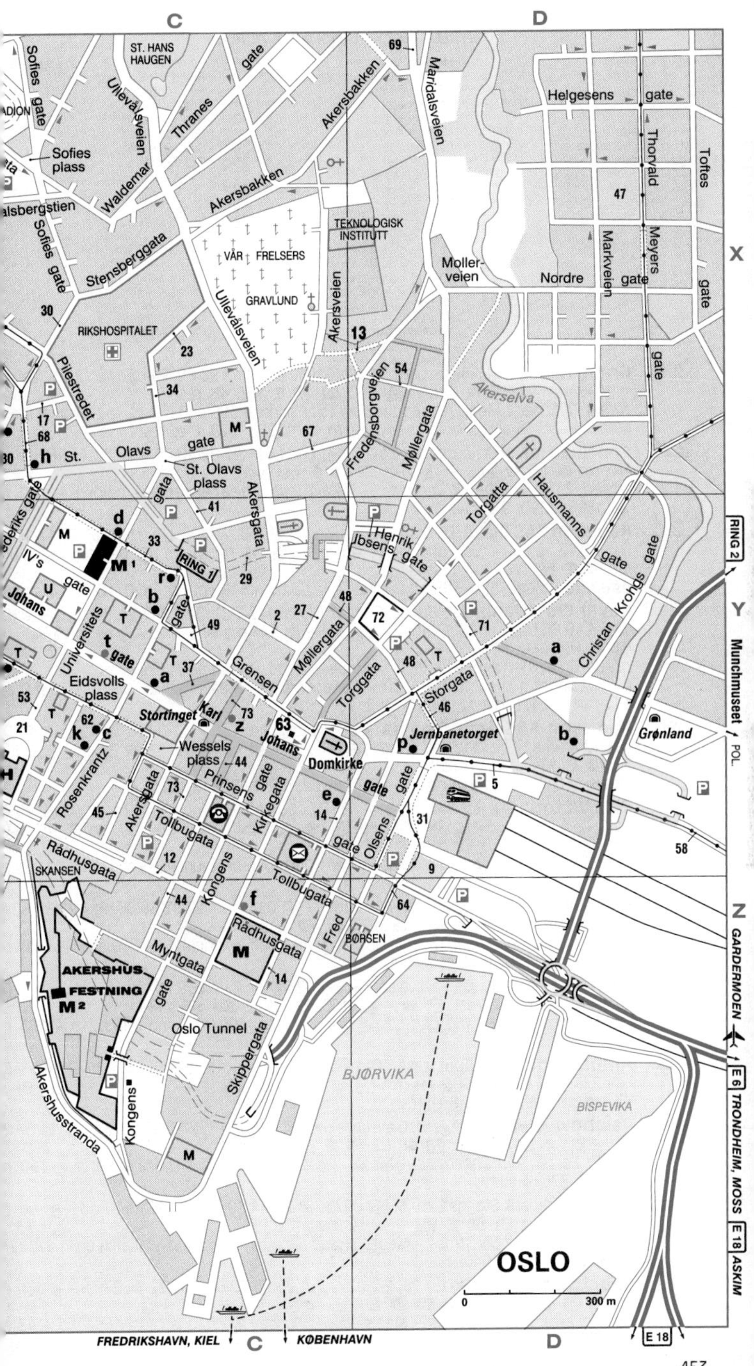
C
D
ST. HANS HAUGEN
Sofies gate
Sofies plass
Ullevålsveien
Thranes gate
Akersbakken
Maridalsveien
Helgesens gate
Thorvald Meyers gate
Toftes gate
Waldemar Thranes gate
Stensberggata
VÅR FRELSERS GRAVLUND
TEKNOLOGISK INSTITUTT
Akersveien
Moller-veien
Nordre gate
Markveien
RIKSHOSPITALET
Pilestredet
Akerselva
Fredensborgveien
Møllergata
St. Olavs gate
St. Olavs plass
Akersgata
Torggata
Hausmanns gate
Henrik Ibsens gate
RING 1
RING 2
Universitetsgata
Grensen
Christian Krongs gate
Munchmuseet
Eidsvolls plass
Stortinget
Karl Johans gate
Domkirke
Storgata
Jernbanetorget
Grønland
Wessels plass
Prinsens gate
Kirkegata
Rosenkrantz gate
Tollbugata
Rådhusgata
SKANSEN
Kongens gate
Myntgata
Fred. Olsens gate
BØRSEN
AKERSHUS FESTNING
Oslo Tunnel
Skippergata
BJØRVIKA
BISPEVIKA
Akershusstranda
GARDERMOEN
E 6 TRONDHEIM, MOSS
E 18 ASKIM
OSLO
0
300 m
FREDRIKSHAVN, KIEL
KØBENHAVN
X
Y
Z

STREET INDEX TO OSLO TOWN PLAN

Karl Johans gate . . . . BCDY
Grensen . . . . CY
Lille Grensen . . . . CY 37
Torggata . . . . CDY

Apotekergata . . . . CY 2
Biskop Gunnerus' gate . . . . DY 5
Bygdøy kappellvei . . . . AZ 7
Christian Frederiks plass . . . DY 9
Christiania torv . . . . CY 12
Damstredet . . . . CDX 13
Dronningens gate . . . . CYZ 14
Dronning Mauds gate . . . . BY 16
Edvard Storms gate . . . . . . CX 17
Elisenbergveien . . . . AX 19
Fredriksborgveien . . . . AZ 20
Fridtjof Nansens plass . . . . CY 21
Frimanns gate . . . . CX 23
Gimleveien . . . . AX 24
Grubbegata . . . . CY 27

Haakon VII's gate . . . . BY 28
Hammersborgtunnelen . . . . CY 29
Holbergs gate . . . . CX 30
Jernbanetorget . . . . DY 31
Josefines gate . . . . ABX 32
Kristian Augusts gate . . . . BCY 33
Langés gate . . . . CX 34
Lapsetorvet . . . . AY 35
Lassons gate . . . . BY 36
Løchenveien . . . . ABZ 38
Løkkeveien . . . . BY 39
Munchs gate . . . . CXY 41
Munkedamsveien . . . . ABY 42
Nedre Slottsgate . . . . CYZ 44
Nedre Vollgate . . . . CY 45
Nygata . . . . DY 46
Olaf Ryes plass . . . . DX 47
Pløens gate . . . . DY 48
Professor Aschehougs pl. . . CY 49
Professor Dahls gate . . . . . AX 51

Riddervolds gate . . . . BX
Roald Amundsens gate . . . CY
Rosteds gate . . . . DX
Ruseløkkveien . . . . ABY
Rådhusplassen . . . . BCY
Schives gate . . . . AX
Schweigaards gate . . . . DY
Skillebekk . . . . AY
Skovveien . . . . ABX
Stortingsgata . . . . CY
Stortorvet . . . . CY
Strandgata . . . . DZ
Sven Bruns gate . . . . BX
Thomas Heftyes gate . . . . . AX
Thor Olsens gate CX
Tullins gate CX
Uelands gate . . . . DX
Vaterlandtunnelen . . . . DY
Youngstorget . . . . DY
Øvre Slottsgate . . . . CY

Grand Hotel, Karl Johans Gate 31, ✉ 0101, ✆ 22 42 93 90, Fax 22 42 12 25, – rm 300. AE VISA. rest CY
Julius Fritzner : **Meals** *(closed Sunday)* (dinner only) 395 and a la carte – ***Grand Caf*** **Meals** 180/348 and a la carte – **269 rm** 1520/1920, 6 suites.

Continental, Stortingsgaten 24-26, ✉ 0161, ✆ 22 82 40 00, Fax 22 42 96 89 – rm 200. AE VISA. CY
closed 23 December-2 January – **Meals** (see ***Theatercaféen*** below) – **150 r** 1585/2290, 8 suites.

Radisson SAS Plaza M, Sonja Henies Plass 3, P.O. Box 9206, ✉ 0134, ✆ 22 17 10 Fax 22 17 73 00, ≤ Oslo and Fjord, – rm rm – 10 AE VISA JCB. rest DY
Abelone : **Meals** 195/398 and dinner a la carte – **648 rm** 1620/1820, 14 suites

Royal Christiania M, Biskop Gunnerus' Gate 3, P.O. Box 768 Sentrum, ✉ 01 ✆ 23 10 80 00, Fax 23 10 80 80, – rm – 400. VISA JCB. DY
closed Christmas and New Year – **Meals** *(closed in summer)* (dinner only and Sund lunch)/dinner a la carte 400/700 – ***Café Atrium :*** **Meals** (buffet lunch) 225/350 a a la carte – **378 rm** 1495/1995, 73 suites.

Radisson SAS Scandinavia M, Holbergsgate 30, ✉ 0166, ✆ 22 11 30 Fax 22 11 30 17, ≤ Oslo and Fjord, – rm – 8 AE VISA JCB. rest CX
Meals 150/480 and a la carte – **479 rm** 1390/1820, 9 suites.

Rica Victoria M, Rosenkrantzgate 13, P.O. Box 1718, Vika, ✉ 0121, ✆ 22 42 99 Fax 22 42 99 43 – rm – 50. AE VISA J CY
closed 23 to 26 December – **Meals** *(closed Sunday)* (buffet lunch) 89 and dinner a la ca 299/382 – **192 rm** 995/1240, 5 suites.

Inter Nor H. Bristol, Kristian IV's Gate 7, ✉ 0164, ✆ 22 82 60 00, Fax 22 82 60 – rm rest – 100. AE VISA JCB. rest CY
Meals *(closed lunch Sunday and Bank Holidays)* (buffet lunch) 185/550 and a la carte **138 rm** 1150/1675, 3 suites.

Scandic H. K.N.A. M, Parkveien 68, ✉ 0254, ✆ 22 44 69 70, Fax 22 44 26 01, – rm rest – 100. AE VISA JCB. BY
Meals *(closed Easter and Christmas)* (buffet lunch) 300/450 and a la carte – **183 r** 895/1495, 2 suites.

Ambassadeur without rest., Camilla Colletts Vei 15, ✉ 0258, ✆ 22 44 18 3 Fax 22 44 47 91, – rm . AE VISA BX
33 rm 1095/1295, 8 suites.

Rainbow H. Europa M, St. Olavsgate 31, ✉ 0166, ✆ 22 20 99 90, Fax 22 11 27 2 – rm rest . AE VISA JCB. CX
closed Easter and Christmas – **Meals** *(closed Sunday)* 165 and a la carte – **160 r** 725/875, 4 suites.

Ritz, Frederik Stangs Gate 3, ✉ 0272, ✆ 22 44 39 60, Fax 22 44 67 13 – – 60. AE VISA JCB. rest AY
closed Easter and Christmas – **Meals** *(closed Saturday and Sunday)* (lunch only) 175/2 – **48 rm** 840/1040.

Gabelshus, Gabelsgate 16, ✉ 0272, ✆ 22 55 22 60, Fax 22 44 27 39 – rm – 70. AE VISA. AY
closed Easter and Christmas – **Meals** *(closed Sunday lunch)* a la carte 160/385 – **43 r** 850/1050.

Rainbow H. Stefan M, Rosenkrantzgate 1, ✉ 0159, ℘ 22 42 92 50, Fax 22 33 70 22 – |♦| ⇔ rm ▤ TV ☎ ♿ – 🏛 50. AE ⓓ E VISA JCB. ✗ CY r
closed Easter and Christmas – **Meals** *(closed Sunday)* (buffet lunch) 175/225 and a la carte – **138 rm** ☐ 495/925.

Rainbow H. Spectrum M without rest., Brugate 7, ✉ 0186, ℘ 22 17 60 30, Fax 22 17 60 80 – |♦| ⇔ TV ♿. AE ⓓ E VISA JCB. ✗ DY a
closed 26 March-1 April and 22 December-2 January – **119 rm** ☐ 580/795.

Rainbow H. Gyldenløve M without rest., Bogstadveien 20, ✉ 0355, ℘ 22 60 10 90, Fax 22 60 33 90 – |♦| ⇔ TV ☎. AE ⓓ E VISA JCB. ✗ BX a
closed 26 March-4 April and 22 December-2 January – **168 rm** ☐ 495/795.

Rainbow Cecil M without rest., Stortingsgaten 8, ✉ 0161, (entrance in Rosenkrantzgate) ℘ 22 42 70 00, Fax 22 42 26 70 – |♦| ⇔ rm TV ☎ ♿. AE ⓓ E VISA. ✗
closed Easter and Christmas – **112 rm** ☐ 795/995. CY c

Norum without rest., Bygdøy Allé 53, ✉ 0265, ℘ 22 44 79 90, Fax 22 44 92 39 – |♦| ⇔ rm ▤ rest TV ☎ – 🏛 30. AE ⓓ E VISA. ✗ AX s
closed 23 December-2 January – **47 rm** ☐ 790/1190.

Norlandia Saga without rest., Eilert Sundtsgt. 39, ✉ 0259, ℘ 22 43 04 85, Fax 22 44 08 63 – ⇔ rm ▤ TV ☎ – 🏛 30. AE ⓓ E VISA JCB. ✗ BX b
closed 23 December-2 January – **37 rm** ☐ 795/995.

Westside without rest., Eilert Sundtsgt. 43, ✉ 0304, ℘ 22 56 87 70, Fax 22 56 63 20, ⌂, – |♦| ⇔ rm ▤ rm TV ☎ P. AE ⓓ E VISA BX b
31 rm ☐ 610/750.

Rainbow Vika Atrium M, Munkedamsveien 45, ✉ 0250, ℘ 22 83 33 00, Fax 22 83 09 57, Fø – |♦| ⇔ rm ▤ TV ☎. AE ⓓ E VISA. ✗ rest BY d
Meals *(closed Friday dinner, Saturday and Sunday)* (buffet lunch) 125 and dinner a la carte 159/253 – **91 rm** ☐ 785/985.

Rainbow H. Astoria M without rest., Dronningensgt. 21, ✉ 0154, ℘ 22 42 00 10, Fax 22 42 57 65 – |♦| ⇔ TV ☎ ♿. AE ⓓ E VISA JCB. ✗ CY e
132 rm ☐ 485/795.

Bagatelle (Hellstrøm), Bygdøy Allé 3, ✉ 0257, ℘ 22 44 63 97, Fax 22 43 64 20 – AE ⓓ E VISA JCB AY x
closed lunch Monday and Saturday, Sunday dinner, Easter and Christmas – **Meals** (booking essential) 350/650 and a la carte 450/670
Spec. Queues de langoustines en beignet, petite salade maraîchère, Coquilles St. Jacques rôties aux échalotes et citrons confits, Homard à la nage en bouillon epicé.

Le Canard, President Harbitz Gate 4, ✉ 0259, ℘ 22 43 40 28, Fax 22 55 65 65, « Tastefully decorated 1900 villa » – AE ⓓ E VISA AX c
closed Sunday, 24 March-1 April and 22 December-5 January – **Meals** (dinner only) 475/495 and a la carte 415/575
Spec. Foie gras and oxtail terrine, light gribiche sauce with cranberries, Lobster and cep sausage with braised endives, horseradish jus, Whole duck served in two ways.

Statholdergaarden, Rådhusgate 11, (entrance by Kirkegate) 1st floor, ✉ 0153, ℘ 22 41 88 00, Fax 22 41 22 24 – ▤. AE ⓓ E VISA CZ f
closed Sunday, 23 March-1 April, 20 July-4 August and 23 December-1 January – **Meals** (booking essential) (dinner only) 425/500 and a la carte.

D'Artagnan, Øvre Slottsgate 16 (1st floor), ✉ 0157, ℘ 22 41 50 62, Fax 22 42 77 41 – ▤. AE ⓓ E VISA JCB CY z
closed Sunday, Easter, 7 July-4 August and 21 December-6 January – **Meals** (dinner only) 425/595 and a la carte.

Spisestedet Feinschmecker, Balchensgate 5, ✉ 0265, ℘ 22 44 17 77, Fax 22 56 11 39, « Tasteful decor » – ▤. AE ⓓ E VISA AX n
closed Sunday, 24 to 31 March, 14 July-3 August and 23 December-4 January – **Meals** (booking essential) (dinner only) 385/465 and a la carte 385/538
Spec. Marinated raw scallops with golden caviar, Herb roasted rack of lamb with sautéed veal sweetbreads, Crème brûlée flavoured with basil.

Det Blå Kjøkken, Drammensveien 30, ✉ 0203, ℘ 22 44 26 50, Fax 22 55 71 56 – ▤. AE ⓓ E VISA JCB BY k
closed Sunday and Bank Holidays – **Meals** (dinner only) 398/520 and a la carte.

Blom, Paléet, Karl Johansgate 41b, ✉ 0162, ℘ 22 42 73 00, Fax 22 42 04 28, « Collection of heraldic shields and paintings » – AE ⓓ E VISA CY t
closed Saturday lunch, Sunday, Christmas and Bank Holidays – **Meals** (buffet lunch) 215/275 and a la carte.

Babette's Gjestehus, 1 Rådhuspassagen, Fridtjof Nansens Pl. 2, ✉ 0160, ℘ 22 41 64 64, « Attractive decor » – ▤. AE ⓓ E VISA BY f
closed Sunday, 4 to 8 April, 24 to 26 December and 31 December-1 January – **Meals** (booking essential) (dinner only) 385/425 and a la carte.

XX **Kastanjen,** Bygdøy Allé 18, ✉ 0262, ✆ 22 43 44 67, Fax 22 55 48 72 – AE ⓓ E V
closed Bank Holiday lunch, Sunday and 26 March-1 April – **Meals** (dinner only) 345/4
and a la carte. AY

XX **Theatercaféen** (at Continental H.), Stortingsgaten 24-26, ✉ 0161, ✆ 22 82 40 5
Fax 22 41 20 94 – ⇆. AE ⓓ E VISA CY
closed 25 December – **Meals** (booking essential) (buffet lunch) 90 and a la carte 305/48

X **A Touch of France,** Øvre Slottsgate 16, ✉ 0157, ✆ 22 42 56 97, Fax 22 42 77
– ▤. AE ⓓ E VISA JCB CY
closed lunch Sunday and Bank Holidays and 22 December-5 January – **Meals** - French st
brasserie - 175/360 and a la carte.

at Fornebu Airport *SW : 8 km by E 18 –* AY *– and Snarøyveien – ☉ 02 Oslo :*

Radisson SAS Park H. Oslo, Fornebuparken, P.O. Box 185, ✉ 1324 Lysak
✆ 67 12 02 20, Fax 67 12 00 11, « Private beach and park », Ⅎ₺, ≘s, ✂ – |✣| ⇆ r
▤ rm ▣ ☎ ♿ – 🏛 150. AE ⓓ E VISA JCB. ✂
Meals (buffet lunch) 225/325 and a la carte – **254 rm** ⊒ 1295/1690.

at Sandvika *SW : 14 km by E 18 –* AY *– exit E 68 – ☉ 02 Oslo :*

Rica H. Oslofjord Ⓜ, Sandviksveien 184, ✉ 1300 Sandvika, ✆ 67 54 57 0
Fax 67 54 27 33, Ⅎ₺, ≘s – |✣| ⇆ rm ▤ ▣ ☎ ♿ ⇔ Ⓟ – 🏛 350. AE ⓓ E VISA.
Orchidee : **Meals** *(closed Sunday and Monday)* 170/410 and a la carte – ***Fontaine :*** **Me**
(buffet lunch) 195/406 and a la carte – **228 rm** ⊒ 1385/2290, 15 suites.

at Holmenkollen *NW : 10 km by Bogstadveien –* BX *– Sørkedalsveien and Holmenkollveien – ☉ (*
Oslo :

Holmenkollen Park H. Rica Ⓜ ⛷, Kongeveien 26, ✉ 0390, ✆ 22 92 20 0
Fax 22 14 61 92, ⩽ Oslo and Fjord, ≘s, ▣ – |✣| ⇆ ▤ ▣ ☎ ♿ ⇔ Ⓟ – 🏛 100.
ⓓ E VISA JCB. ✂ rest
De Fem Stuer : **Meals** *(closed Sunday lunch)* (buffet lunch) 295/450 and dinner a la car
– ***Galleriet :*** **Meals** *(closed Christmas)* (buffet lunch) 215/350 and a la carte – **221 r**
⊒ 1295/1795, 11 suites.

Poland

Polska

Warsaw

PRACTICAL INFORMATION

LOCAL CURRENCY

Zloty : *100 ZT = 35.01 US $ (Jan. 97)*

National Holiday in Poland: *3 May.*

PRICES

Prices may change if goods and service costs in Poland are revised and it is therefore always advisable to confirm rates with the hotelier when making a reservation.

FOREIGN EXCHANGE

It is strongly advised against changing money other than in banks, exchange offices or authorised offices such as large hotels and Kantor. Banks are usually open on weekdays from 8am to 4pm.

HOTEL RESERVATIONS

In case of difficulties in finding a room through our hotel selection, it is always possible to apply to ORBIS, Marszalkowska 142 ☎ (022) 27 80 31, Fax (022) 27 11 23, open on weekdays from 8am to 4pm.

POSTAL SERVICES

Post offices are open from 8am to 8pm on weekdays.

The **General Post Office** *is open 7 days a week and 24 hours a day : Poczta Główna, Świetokryska.*

SHOPPING IN WARSAW

In the index of street names, those printed in red are where the principal shops are found. They are generally open from 10am to 7pm on weekdays and Saturday.

THEATRE BOOKING

Your hotel porter will be able to make your arrangements or direct you to a theatre booking office: Kasy Teatralne, al Jerozolimskie 29 ☎ 621 93 83, open from 11am to 2pm and 3pm to 6pm on weekdays and 11am to 2pm on Saturday.

TIPPING

Hotel, restaurant and café bills include service in the total charge but it is usual to leave the staff a gratuity which will vary depending upon the service given.

CAR HIRE

The international car hire companies have branches in Warsaw. Your hotel porter should be able to give details and help you with your arrangements.

BREAKDOWN SERVICE

A 24 hours breakdown service is operated calling ☎ 981.

SPEED LIMIT

On motorways, the maximum permitted speed is 110 km/h – 68 mph, 90 km/h – 56 mph on other roads and 60 km/h – 37 mph in built up areas.

SEAT BELTS

In Poland, the wearing of seat belts is compulsory for drivers and passengers.

WARSAW

(Warsawa) *Polska* 970 NO 4 - *Pop. 1 700 000* - ☎ *22.*

Berlin 591 - Budapest 670 - Gdansk 345 - Kiev 795 - Moscow 1253 - Zagreb 993.

Warsaw Tourist Information Centre, pl. Zamkowy 1/13, ☎ 635 18 81, Fax 31 04 64.

First Warsaw Golf Club and Country Club, 05110 Jabłonna ☎ 774 06 55.
Okęcie (Warsaw Airport) SW 10 km, by Żwirki i Wigury ☎ 952 or 953.
Bus to airport: from major hotels in the town centre (ask the reception).
Polish Airlines (Lot) al Jerozolmiskie 67, Warsaw ☎ 952 or 953.

SIGHTS

OLD TOWN*** **(STARE MIASTO)** BX
*Castle Square** *(Plac Zamkowy)* BX **33** - *Royal Palace*** *(Zamek Królewski)* BX - *Beer Street (Ulica Piwna)* BX - *Ulica Świętojańska* BX **28** - *St John's Cathedral** *(Katedra Św. Jana)* BX - *Old Town Marketplace**** *(Rynek Starego Miasta)* BX **27** - *Warsaw History Museum** *(Muzeum Historyczne Warsawy)* BX **M1** - *Barbakan* BX **A**.

NEW TOWN* **(NOWE MIASTO)** ABX
New Town Marketplace (Rynek Nowego Miasta) ABX **20** - *Memorial to the Warsaw Uprising (Pomnik Powstania Warzszawskiego)* AX **D**.

ROYAL WAY* **(TRAKT KRÓLEWSKI)**
St Anne's Church (Kościół Św. Anny) BX - *Krakow's District Street (Krakowskie Przedmieście)* BXY - *New World Street (Nowy Świat)* BYZ - *Holy Cross Church (Św. Krzyza)* BY - *National Museum*** *(Muzeum Narodowe)* CZ.

LAZIENKI PARK*** **(PARK ŁAZIENKOWSKI)** *(South)*
*Chopin Memorial (Pomnik Chopina) - Palace-on-the-Water*** *(Pałac na Wodzie) - Belvedere Palace (Belweder).*

WILANOW*** *S. 10 km*

ADDITIONAL SIGHTS
*John Paul II Collection*** *(Muzeum Kolekcji im. Jana Pawla II)* AY - *Palace of Culture and Science (Pałac Kultury i Nauki): view*** *from panoramic gallery* AZ.

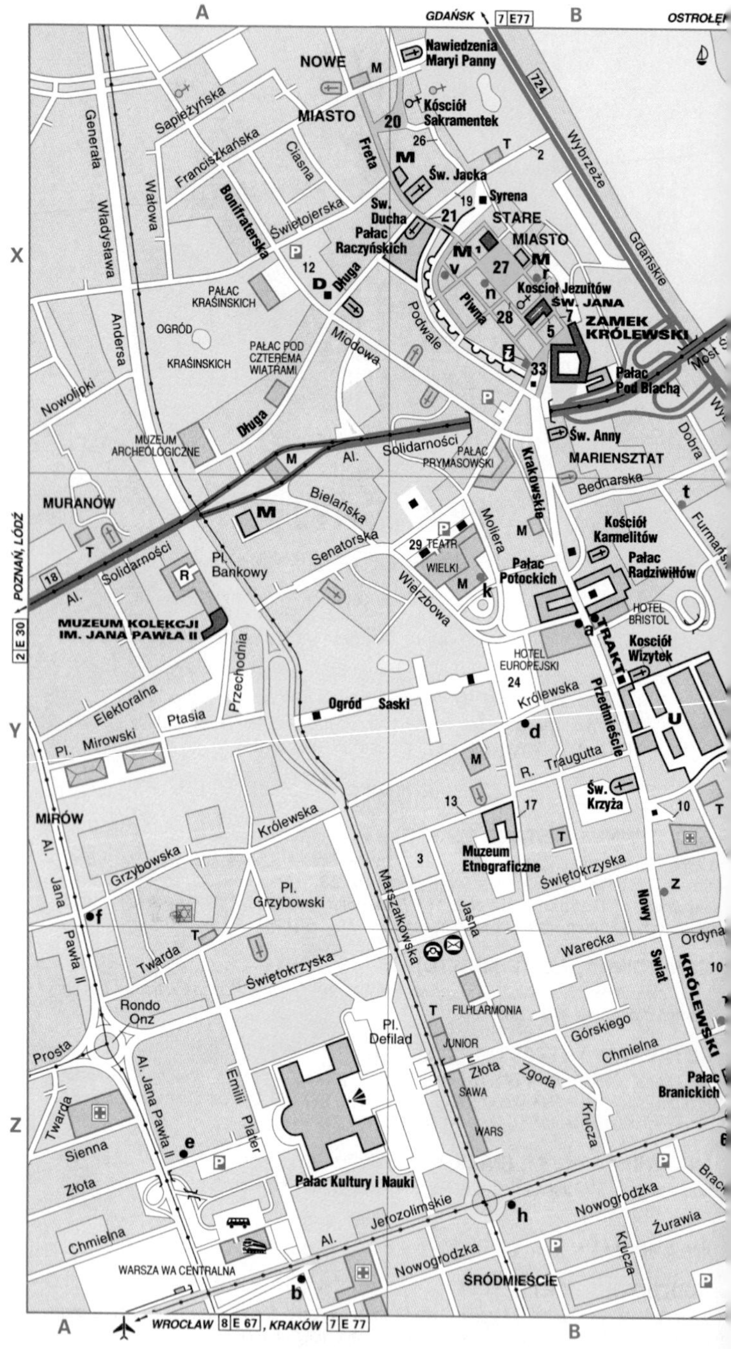

NOWE
MIASTO
STARE
MIASTO
Nawiedzenia Maryi Panny
Kościół Sakramentek
Św. Jacka
Syrena
Św. Ducha
Pałac Raczyńskich
Kościół Jezuitów
ŚW. JANA
ZAMEK KRÓLEWSKI
Pałac Pod Blachą
Św. Anny
MARIENSZTAT
PAŁAC KRAŚINSKICH
OGRÓD KRAŚINSKICH
PAŁAC POD CZTEREMA WIATRAMI
MUZEUM ARCHEOLOGICZNE
PAŁAC PRYMASOWSKI
MURANÓW
MUZEUM KOLEKCJI IM. JANA PAWŁA II
TEATR WIELKI
Kościół Karmelitów
Pałac Radziwiłłów
Pałac Potockich
HOTEL BRISTOL
HOTEL EUROPEJSKI
Kosciół Wizytek
Ogród Saski
Pl. Bankowy
Pl. Mirowski
MIRÓW
Św. Krzyża
Muzeum Etnograficzne
Pl. Grzybowski
Rondo Onz
Pl. Defilad
FILHARMONIA
JUNIOR
SAWA
WARS
Pałac Kultury i Nauki
Pałac Branickich
WARSZA WA CENTRALNA
ŚRÓDMIEŚCIE
TRAKT KRÓLEWSKI
GDAŃSK 7 E77
OSTROŁĘ
POZNAŃ, ŁÓDŹ 2 E 30
WROCŁAW 8 E 67, KRAKÓW 7 E 77

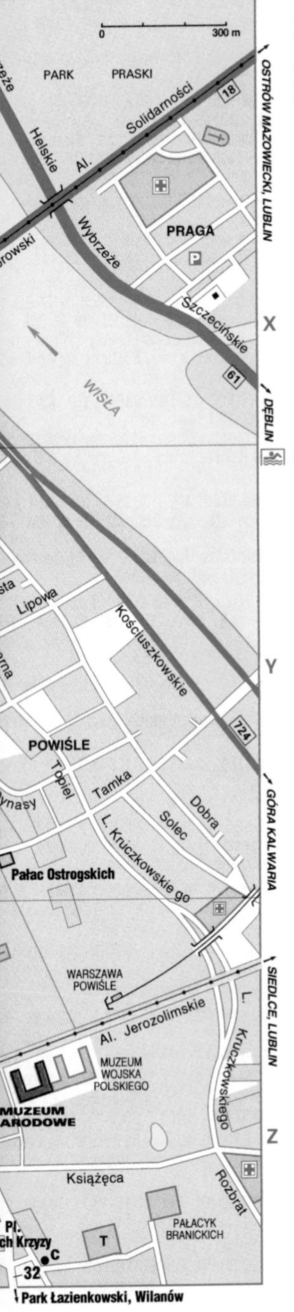

WARSZAWA

Chmielna (ul.) .... **ABZ**
Krakowskie Przedmieście (ul.) . **BXY**
Nowy Świat (ul.) .... **BYZ**
Piwna (ul.) .... **BX**
Świętojańska (ul.) ... **BX** 28

Andersa (ul. Gen. Wł.). **AX**
Bankowy (pl.) .... **AY**
Bednarska (ul.) ...... **BXY**
Bielańska (ul.) ...... **AY**
Boleść (ul.) .... **BX** 2
Bonifraterska (ul.).... **AX**
Bracka (ul.) .... **BZ**
Browarna (ul.) ...... **CY**
Ciasna (ul.) .... **AX**
Dąbrowskiego (pl. J.H.) .... **BY** 3
Defilad (pl.) .... **ABZ**
Długa (ul.) .... **ABX**
Dobra (ul.) .... **BX**
Dynasy (ul.) .... **CY**
Dziekania (ul.) ...... **BX** 5
Elektoralna (ul.) ..... **AY**
Emilii Plater (ul.) .... **AZ**
Franciszkańska (ul.) .... **AX**
Freta (ul.) .... **AX**
Furmańska (ul.) ..... **BY**
Gaulla (Rondo Gen. Ch. de) ..... **BZ** 6
Gęsta (ul.) .... **CY**
Górskiego (ul.) ...... **BZ**
Grzybowska (ul.) .... **AY**
Grzybowski (pl.) ..... **AY**
Jana Pawla II (al.) ... **AYZ**
Jasna (ul.) .... **BYZ**
Jerozolimskie (al.) .... **ABCZ**
Kanonia (ul.) .... **BX** 7
Karowa (ul.) .... **CY** 9
Kopernika .... **BY** 10
Krasińskich (pl.) ..... **AX** 12
Kredytowa (ul.) ..... **BY** 13
Królewska (ul.) ...... **ABY**
Krucza (ul.) .... **BZ**
Kruczkowskiego (ul. L.) .... **CYZ**
Książęca (ul.) .... **CZ**
Leszczyńska (ul.) .... **CY** 14
Lipowa (ul.) .... **CY**
Markiewicza (wiadukt) .... **BY** 16
Marszałkowska (ul.) . **ABYZ**
Mazowiecka (ul.) .... **BY** 17
Miodowa (ul.) ...... **ABX**
Mirowski (pl.) .... **AY**
Moliera (ul.) .... **BY**
Mostowa (ul.) ...... **BX** 19
Nowego Miasta (rynek) .... **ABX** 20
Nowogrodzka (ul.) ... **BZ**
Nowolipki (ul.) ...... **AX**
Nowomiejska (ul.) ... **BX** 21
Oboźna (ul.) .... **BCY** 23
ONZ (rondo) .... **AZ**
Ordynacka (ul.) ..... **BY**
Piłsudskiego (pl. J.) .... **BY** 24
Podwale (ul.) .... **BX**
Powstańców Warszawy (pl.) .... **BYZ** 25
Prosta (ul.) .... **AZ**
Przechodnia (ul.) .... **AY**
Ptasia (ul.) .... **AY**
Rozbrat (ul.) .... **CZ**
Sapieżyńska (ul.) .... **AX**
Senatorska (ul.) ..... **ABY**
Sienna (ul.) .... **AZ**
Solec (ul.) .... **CY**
Solidarności (al.) ... **ACXY**
Stara (ul.) .... **BX** 26
Starego Miasta (rynek) .... **BX** 27
Śląsko-Dąbrowski (most) .... **BCX**
Świętojerska (ul.) .... **AX**
Świętokrzyska (ul.).. **ABYZ**
Tamka (ul.) .... **CY**
Topiel (ul.) .... **CY**
Traugutta (ul. R.) .... **BY**
Twarda (ul.) .... **AYZ**
Wałowa (ul.) .... **AX**
Warecka (ul.) .... **BYZ**
Wierzbowa (ul.) ..... **BY**
Wybrzeże Gdańskie (ul.) .... **BX**
Wybrzeże Helskie (ul.) .... **CX**
Wybrzeże Kosciusz Kowskie (ul.) .... **BCXY**
Wybrzeże Szczecińskie (ul.) .. **CX**
Zgoda (ul.) .... **BZ**
Złota .... **ABZ**
Żurawia .... **BZ**

When in EUROPE never be without:
Michelin Main Road Maps;
Michelin Regional Maps;
Michelin Red Guides:
Benelux, Deutschland, España Portugal, Europe, France, Great Britain and Ireland, Italia, Switzerland
(Hotels and restaurants listed with symbols; preliminary pages in English)
Michelin Green Guides:
Austria, Belgium, Disneyland Paris, England: The West Country, France, Germany, Great Britain, Greece, Ireland, Italy, London, Netherlands, Portugal, Rome, Scotland, Spain, Switzerland, Wales.
Atlantic Coast, Auvergne Rhône Valley, Brittany, Burgundy Jura, Châteaux of the Loire, Dordogne, Flanders Picardy and the Paris region, French Riviera, Normandy, Paris, Provence
(Sights and touring programmes described fully in English; town plans).

Bristol, Krakowskie Przedmieście 42-44, ✉ 00 325, ☎ 625 25 25, Fax 625 25 77, « La 19C facade, partly decorated in Art Nouveau style », ... rm ... - 100. AE ⓓ E VISA JCB. ✻ rest BY
Marconi : **Meals** - Italian - 56/70 and a la carte – (see also ***Malinowa*** below) – **120 r** ☕ 787/913, 43 suites.

Marriott Ⓜ, Al. Jerozolimskie 65-79, ✉ 00 697, ☎ 630 63 06, Fax 830 00 41, ≤ Warsaw, ... - 700. AE ⓓ E VISA JCB. ✻
Chicago Grill : **Meals** (dinner only) 90/260 and a la carte – ***Parmizzano's :*** **Meals** - Italia - *(closed Bank Holiday lunch)* 46/180 and a la carte – ***Lila Weneda :*** **Meals** (buffet lunc 33/123 and a la carte – **488 rm** ☕ 646/767, 34 suites. AZ

Sheraton Ⓜ, Ul. B. Prusa 2, ✉ 00 493, ☎ 657 61 00, Fax 657 62 00, ... - 600. AE ⓓ E VISA. ✻ rest CZ
The Oriental : **Meals** - Oriental - *(closed Saturday lunch and Sunday)* 65/150 and a la car – ***Lalka :*** **Meals** - Central European - (buffet lunch) 75 and a la carte 70/108 – ☕ 44 **331 rm** 650/944, 19 suites.

Victoria Inter-Continental Ⓜ, Ul. Królewska 11, ✉ 00 065, ☎ 657 80 1 Fax 657 80 57, ... rm ... - 500. AE ⓓ E VISA JC
Canaletto : **Meals** 57/104 and a la carte – ***Opera :*** **Meals** *(closed Sunday)* (dinner onl 130/350 and a la carte – ***Hetmańska :*** **Meals** 74 and a la carte – **330 rm** ☕ 464/53 30 suites. BY

Holiday Inn Ⓜ, Ul. Złota 48-54, ✉ 00 120, ☎ 620 03 41, Fax 830 05 69, ... rm ... - 190. AE ⓓ E VISA JCB. ✻ rest AZ
Symfonia : **Meals** a la carte 65/98 – ***Rotisserie :*** **Meals** *(closed Saturday and Sunda* (dinner only) a la carte 51/76 – ***Brasserie :*** **Meals** (buffet only) 51 – ☕ 34 – **326 r** 492/649, 10 suites.

Mercure Fryderyk Chopin Ⓜ, Al. Jana Pawła II 22, ✉ 00 133, ☎ 620 02 0 Fax 620 87 79, ... rm ... - 250. AE ⓓ E VISA JC ✻ rest AY
Balzac : **Meals** - French - 90/150 and a la carte – ***Stanislas :*** **Meals** *(closed 31 Decembe* (buffet lunch) 40/80 and a la carte – **242 rm** ☕ 492/548, 8 suites.

Jan III Sobieski Ⓜ, Plac Artura Zawiszy 1, ✉ 02 025, ☎ 658 44 44, Fax 659 88 2 ... rm ... rm ... - 180. AE ⓓ E VISA JC ✻ rest by Al. Jerozolimskie AZ
Meals 40 (lunch) and a la carte 71/147 – **374 rm** ☕ 421/782, 33 suites.

Forum, Ul. Nowogrodzka 24-26, ✉ 00 511, ☎ 621 02 71, Fax 625 04 76 – ... r ... - 450. AE ⓓ E VISA JCB BZ
Soplica : **Meals** 37/41 and a la carte – ***Maryla :*** **Meals** (buffet lunch only) 30 – **710 r** ☕ 410/471, 23 suites.

Europejski, Ul. Krakowskie Przedmieście 13, ✉ 00 071, ☎ 26 50 51, Fax 26 11 11, ... - 500. AE ⓓ E VISA JCB BY
Meals 46/65 and a la carte – **139 rm** ☕ 237/356, 11 suites.

Vera, Ul. Bitwy Warszawskiej 1920 roku 16, ✉ 02 366, ☎ 22 74 21, Fax 23 62 56 – ... rest ... - 150. AE ⓓ E VISA. ✻ rest by Al. Jerozolimskie AZ
Meals a la carte 33/70 – **150 rm** ☕ 259/332, 6 suites.

M.D.M. without rest., Pl. Konstytucji 1, ✉ 00 647, ☎ 621 41 76, Fax 621 41 73 – ... AE ⓓ E VISA JCB by Marszałkowska BZ
115 rm ☕ 185/252.

Malinowa (at Forte H. Orbis Bristol), Krakowskie Przedmieście 42-44, ✉ 00 32 ☎ 625 25 25, Fax 625 25 77 – ... AE ⓓ E VISA JCB BY
closed August – **Meals** - French - (dinner only) 160 and a la carte.

La Gioconda, Plac Piłsudskiego 9, ✉ 00 078, ☎ 827 94 42, Fax 26 36 13, ... – ... res AE ⓓ E VISA JCB BY
closed Sunday and Monday – **Meals** - Italian - a la carte 137/181.

Belvedere, Ul. Agrykoli 1, ✉ 00 460, ☎ 41 48 06, Fax 41 71 35, ≤, ..., « Late 19 orangery in Łazienkowski park » – ... AE ⓓ E VISA JCB by Al. Ujazdowskie CZ
closed 25 December-15 January – **Meals** 90/200 and a la carte.

Casa Valdemar, Ul. Piękna, kna 7-9, ✉ 00 539, ☎ 628 81 40, Fax 622 88 96, « Elegar Spanish style installation » – ... AE ⓓ E VISA JCB by Al. Ujazdowskie CZ
Meals - Spanish - 79/163 and a la carte.

Fukier, Rynek Starego Miasta 27, ✉ 00 272, ☎ 31 10 13, Fax 31 10 13, « Tradition Polish decor » – ... AE ⓓ E VISA JCB BX
Meals a la carte 66/168.

Kahlenberg, Ul. Koszykowa 54, ✉ 00 675, ☎ 630 88 50, Fax 630 88 50 – ... AE ⓓ E VISA JCB by Marszałkowska BZ
Meals 50/100 and a la carte.

XX **Swiętoszek,** Ul. Jezuicka 6-8, ✉ 00 281, ☎ 31 56 34, Fax 635 59 47, « Vaulted cellar » – AE ⓓ E VISA JCB BX r
closed 15 July-15 August – **Meals** 35/60 and a la carte.

XX **Flik,** Ul. Puławska 43, ✉ 02 508, ☎ 49 44 34, Fax 49 44 34, ☂ – ⇲ ▤. AE ⓓ E VISA JCB by Marszałkowska BZ
closed 25 December – **Meals** (buffet lunch) 33/50 and a la carte 34/69 – ***Petit Flik :*** **Meals** a la carte 23/46.

XX **Tsubame,** Ul. Foksal 16, ✉ 00 372, ☎ 26 51 27, Fax 26 48 51, Japanese decor – ▤. AE ⓓ E VISA JCB BZ s
closed 24-25 December and 1 January – **Meals** - Japanese - 25/48 and a la carte.

XX **Pod Retmanem,** Ul. Bednarska 9, ✉ 00 310, ☎ 26 87 58, Fax 26 87 58, « Fresco depicting the old port of Gdansk » – AE ⓓ E VISA JCB BY t
Meals (music Thursday to Saturday evenings) 50/70 and a la carte.

X **Rycerska,** Ul. Szeroki Dunaj 11, ✉ 00 254, ☎ 31 36 68, Fax 31 47 33, ☂, « Medieval theme » – AE ⓓ E VISA JCB BX v
Meals 45/120 and a la carte.

X **Kuchcik,** Ul. Nowy Świat 64, ✉ 00 357, ☎ 827 39 00, Fax 827 39 00 – ⇲. AE ⓓ E VISA JCB BY z
closed 30 and 31 March – **Meals** 48 (dinner) and a la carte 30/80 – ***Kuchcikiem*** (wine bar in cellar) **:** **Meals** a la carte 15/37.

to the E :

Wawer District *E : 10 km on Lublin road* – CX – ⊛ *22 Warsaw :*

Zajazd Napoleoński, Ul. Płowiecka 83, ✉ 04 501, ☎ 15 30 68, Fax 15 22 16 – ⇲ rest TV ☎ P. AE ⓓ E VISA. ✂
closed 24 December-2 January – **Meals** 60/100 and a la carte – **21 rm** ☕ 242/322, 3 suites.

to the S :

Wilanów *S : 9 km at Palac Wilanowski entrance* – CZ – ⊛ *22 Warsaw :*

XX **Wilanów,** Ul. Wiertnicza 27, ✉ 02 952, ☎ 42 18 52, Fax 42 13 63, « Hunting atmosphere » – AE ⓓ E VISA JCB
Meals a la carte 28/41.

X **Kuźnia Królewska,** Ul. Wiertnicza 24, ☎ 42 31 71, ☂ – AE ⓓ E VISA JCB
Meals a la carte 32/88.

to the SW :

Novotel, Ul. Sierpnia 1, ✉ 02 134, 6 km on airport rd ☎ 846 40 51, Fax 846 36 86, ☂, ⛱, ⛲ – |♦| ⇲ rm ▤ rest TV ☎ ♿ P – 🏛 200. AE ⓓ E VISA JCB. ✂ rest AZ
Meals 37 and a la carte – **146 rm** ☕ 275/331.

Portugal

LISBON

PRACTICAL INFORMATION

LOCAL CURRENCY

Escudo: *100 PTE = 0.64 USD ($) (Jan. 97).*

National Holiday in Portugal: *10 June.*

FOREIGN EXCHANGE

Hotels, restaurants and shops do not always accept foreign currencies and the tourist is therefore advised to change cheques and currency at banks, saving banks and exchange offices - The general opening times are as follows: banks 8.30am to noon and 1 to 3pm (closed on Saturdays and Sundays), money changers 9.30am to 6pm (usually closed on Saturday afternoons and Sundays).

TRANSPORT

Taxis may be hailed when showing the green light or sign "Livre" on the windscreen. Metro (subway) network. In each station complete information and plans will be found.

SHOPPING IN LISBON

Shops and boutiques are generally open from 9am to 1pm and 3 to 7pm - In Lisbon, the main shopping streets are: Rua Augusta, Rua do Carmo, Rua Garrett (Chiado), Rua do Ouro, Rua da Prata, Av. de Roma, Av. da Liberdade, Shopping Center Amoreiras.

TIPPING

A service charge is added to all bills in hotels, restaurants and cafés; it is usual, however, to give an additional tip for personal service; 10 % of the fare or ticket price is also the usual amount given to taxi drivers and cinema and theatre usherettes.

SPEED LIMITS

The speed limit on motorways is 120 km/h - 74 mph, on other roads 90 km/h - 56 mph and in built up areas 50 km/h - 37 mph.

SEAT BELTS

The wearing of seat belts is compulsory for drivers and passengers.

THE FADO

The Lisbon Fado (songs) can be heard in restaurants in old parts of the town such as the Alfama, the Bairro Alto and the Mouraria. A selection of fado cabarets will be found at the end of the Lisbon restaurant list.

LISBON

(LISBOA) 1100 P 440 P 2 - Pop. 662 782 - alt. 111 - ✪ 01.

Madrid 658 - Bilbao/Bilbo 907 - Paris 1820 - Porto 314 - Sevilla 417.

Palácio Foz, Praça dos Restaudores ✉ 1200 ☎ 346 63 07, Fax 346 87 72 and airport ☎ 849 36 89 - A.C.P. Rua Rosa Araújo 24, ✉ 1200, ☎ 356 39 31, Fax 57 47 32.

9, 18 Estoril Golf Club W : 25 km ☎ 468 01 76 - 18 Lisbon Sports Club NW : 20 km ☎ 431 00 77 - 18 Club de Campo da Aroeira S : 15 km ☎ 297 13 14 Aroeira, Monte da Caparica

Lisbon Airport N : 8 km from city centre ☎ 848 11 01 - T.A.P., Praça Marquês de Pombal 3, ✉ 1200, ☎ 386 40 80 and airport ☎ 841 50 00.

Santa Apolónia ☎ 887 75 09 MX.

to Madeira : E.N.M., Rua de São Julião 5-1°, ✉ 1100, ☎ 887 01 21.

SEE

View over the city: ★★ *from the Suspension Bridge (Ponte de 25 Abril),* ★★ *from Christ in Majesty (Cristo-Rei) by Av. da Ponte* EU.

CENTRE

Pombaline Lisbon ★ *(A Baixa Pombalina)* JKXYZ

See: *Rossio (square)*★ KX - *Praça do Comércio*★★ KZ - *Santa Justa lift (Elevador de Santa Justa* ≤★*)* KY.

Chiado and Up town *(Bairro Alto*★*)* JKY - See: *Do Carmo Church (Archaeological Museum)*★ KY **M1** - *Rua Garret*★ KY - *São Roque Church*★ *(São João Baptista chapel*★★*)* JX : *São Roque Arte Sacra Museum*★ *(priestly ornaments*★*)* JKX **M2** - *São Pedro de Alcântara Belvedere*★: ≤★ *(Miradouro de São Pedro de Alcântara)* JX **A**.

Medieval Lisbon★★ LXY - See: *Cathedral*★★ *(Sé: gothic tumulos*★, *grill*★, *tresor*★*)* LY - *Santa Luzia Belvedere:* ≤★ *(Miradouro de Santa Luzia)* LY **C** - *Museum of Decorative Arts (Museu de Artes Decorativas*★: *Fundação Ricardo do Espírito Santo Silva)* LY **M3** - *St. Georges Castle (Castelo de São Jorge)*★★: ≤★★*)* LX - *Alfama*★ LY.

Modern Lisbon - *Avenida da Liberdade*★ JV - *Edward VII Park*★ *(Cold Greenhouse*★*)* FS.

BELÉM★★

W: by Av. 24 de Julho EU.

See: *Hieronymite Monastery*★★ *(Mosteiro dos Jerónimos): Santa Maria Church*★★★ *(Igreja de Santa Maria : crypt*★★, *cloister*★★★, *tresor*★*)* - *Belém Tower*★★ *(Torre de Belém)* - *Monument to the Discoveries*★ *(Padrão dos Descobrimentos).*

MUSEUMS

See: *Museum of Ancient Arts*★★★ *(Museu Nacional de Arte Antiga : polyptych da Adoração de São Vicente*★★★, *Anunciação*★, *Tentação de Santo Antão*★★★, *Twelve Apostles*★, *japanese folding screens*★★, *chapel*★*)* EU **M7** - *Calouste Gulbenkian Museum*★★★ *(Art collection)* FR - *Modern Art Centre*★ FR **M4** - *Maritime Museum*★★ *(Museu da Marinha) W : by Av. 24 de Julho* EU - *Coach Museum*★★ *(Museu Nacional dos Coches) W : by Av. 24 de Julho* EU - *Azulejo Museum*★★ *NE : by Av. Infante D. Henrique* MX - *Water Museum da EPAL*★ *(Museu da Água da EPAL) NE : by Av. Infante D. Henrique* MX - *Costume Museum*★ *(Museu Nacional do Traje) N : by Av. da República* GR - *Military Museum (ceilings*★*)* MY **M10**

OTHER CURIOSITIES

See: *Church of Mother of God*★★ *(Igreja da Madre de Deus : capitulo room*★*) NE : by Av. Infante D. Henrique* MX - *Marquis Fronteira Palace*★★ *(Palácio dos Marqueses de Fronteira: azulejos*★★*)* ER - *Zoological Garden*★ ER - *São Vicente de Fora Church (azulejos*★*)* MX - *Free Waters Aquaduct*★ *(Aqueduto das Águas Livres)* ES - *Botanic Garden*★ JV - *Our Lady Fátima Church (Igreja de Nossa Senhora de Fátima : windows*★*)* FR **K** - *Estrela Basilica (Basílica da Estrela: dome*★, *garden*★*)* EU **L** - *Old Conception Church (Igreja da Conceição Velha : south front*★*)* LZ **V** - *Monsanto Park*★ *(Parque florestal da Monsanto)* ER - *Campo de Santa Clara*★ MX.

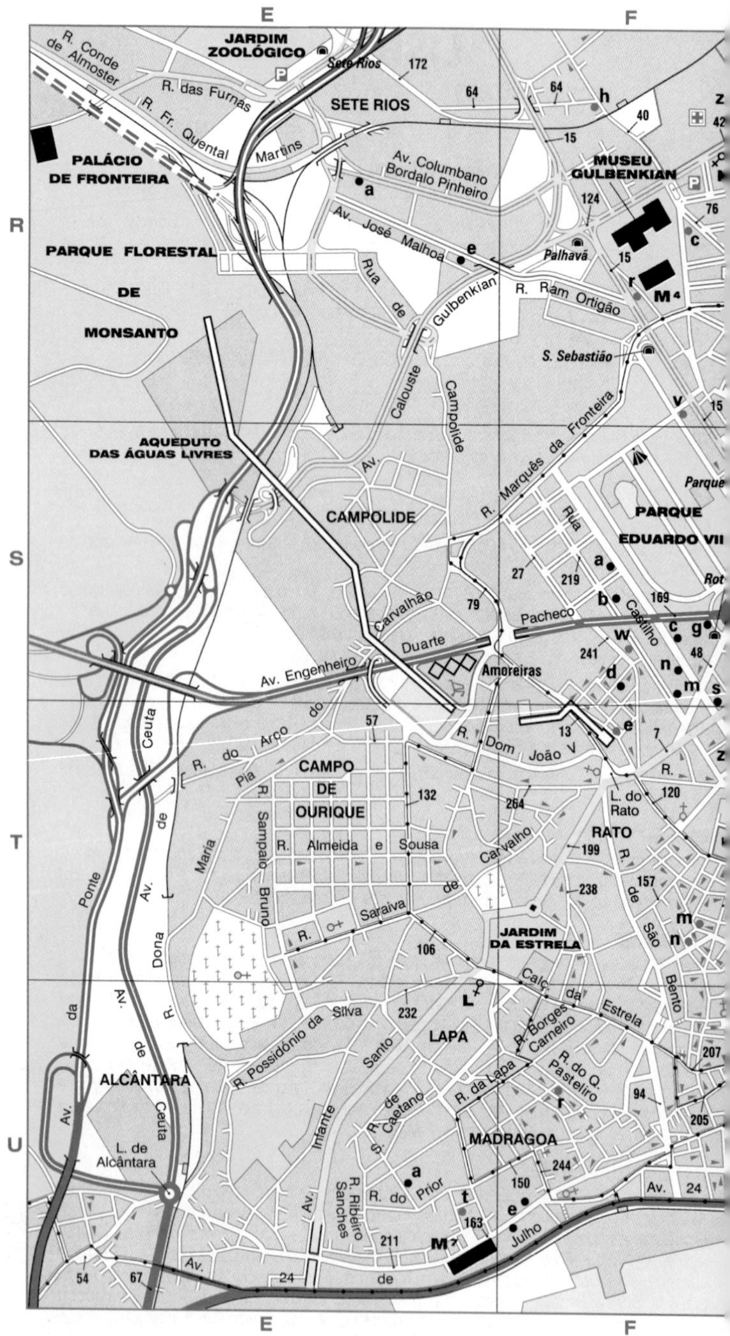

E
F
R
S
T
U
JARDIM ZOOLÓGICO
SETE RIOS
PALÁCIO DE FRONTEIRA
PARQUE FLORESTAL DE MONSANTO
MUSEU GULBENKIAN
Palhavã
S. Sebastião
AQUEDUTO DAS ÁGUAS LIVRES
CAMPOLIDE
PARQUE EDUARDO VII
Amoreiras
CAMPO DE OURIQUE
RATO
JARDIM DA ESTRELA
LAPA
MADRAGOA
ALCÂNTARA
L. de Alcântara
R. Conde de Almoster
R. das Furnas
R. Fr. Quental
Martins
Av. Columbano Bordalo Pinheiro
Av. José Malhoa
Rua de Campolide
Calouste Gulbenkian
R. Ram Ortigão
R. Marquês da Fronteira
Rua Castilho
Pacheco
Carvalhão Duarte
Av. Engenheiro
R. do Arco do
R. Dom João V
L. do Rato
Pia
R. Sampaio Bruno
R. Almeida e Sousa
R. Saraiva de Carvalho
R. de São Bento
Calç. da Estrela
R. Borges Carneiro
R. do Q. Pasteliro
R. da Lapa
R. Possidónio da Silva
Santo
Av. Infante
S. de Caetano
R. do Prior
R. Ribeiro Sanches
Av. de 24 Julho
Ponte da Av.
Av. de Ceuta
Av. Dona Maria
R. de Ceuta

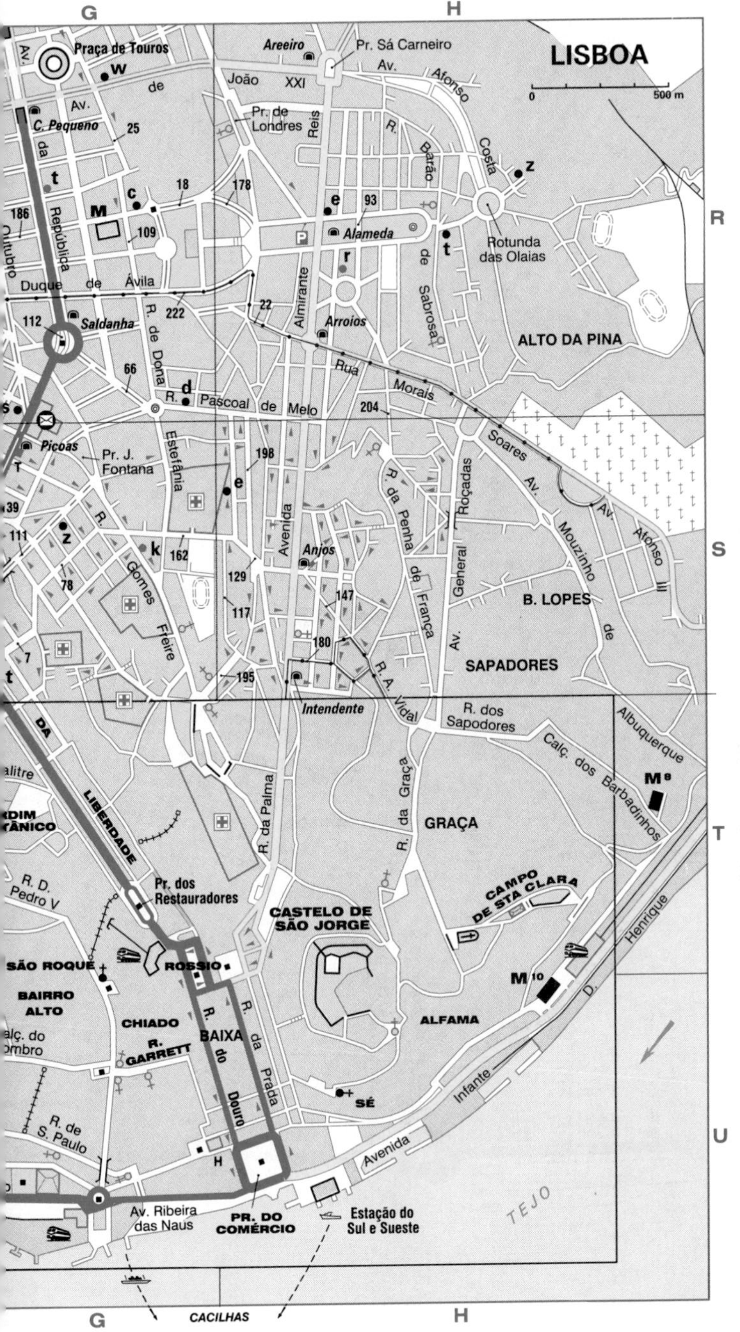
LISBOA
0
500 m
G
H
R
S
T
U
Praça de Touros
Areeiro
Pr. Sá Carneiro
Av. João XXI
Av. Afonso Costa
C. Pequeno
Av. da República
Pr. de Londres
Av. Almirante Reis
R. Barão de Sabrosa
Alameda
Rotunda das Olaias
Duque de Ávila
Saldanha
Arroios
ALTO DA PINA
R. de Dona Estefânia
R. Pascoal de Melo
Rua Morais Soares
Picoas
Pr. J. Fontana
R. da Penha de França
Av. General Roçadas
Av. Afonso
Av. Mouzinho de Albuquerque
R. Gomes Freire
Anjos
B. LOPES
SAPADORES
Intendente
R. A. Vidal
R. dos Sapadores
Calç. dos Barbadinhos
DA LIBERDADE
R. da Palma
R. da Graça
GRAÇA
Pr. dos Restauradores
R. D. Pedro V
CASTELO DE SÃO JORGE
CAMPO DE STA CLARA
SÃO ROQUE
ROSSIO
BAIRRO ALTO
CHIADO
R. GARRETT
BAIXA
R. do Douro
R. da Prada
ALFAMA
Av. Infante D. Henrique
SÉ
R. de S. Paulo
Avenida
TEJO
Av. Ribeira das Naus
PR. DO COMÉRCIO
Estação do Sul e Sueste
CACILHAS

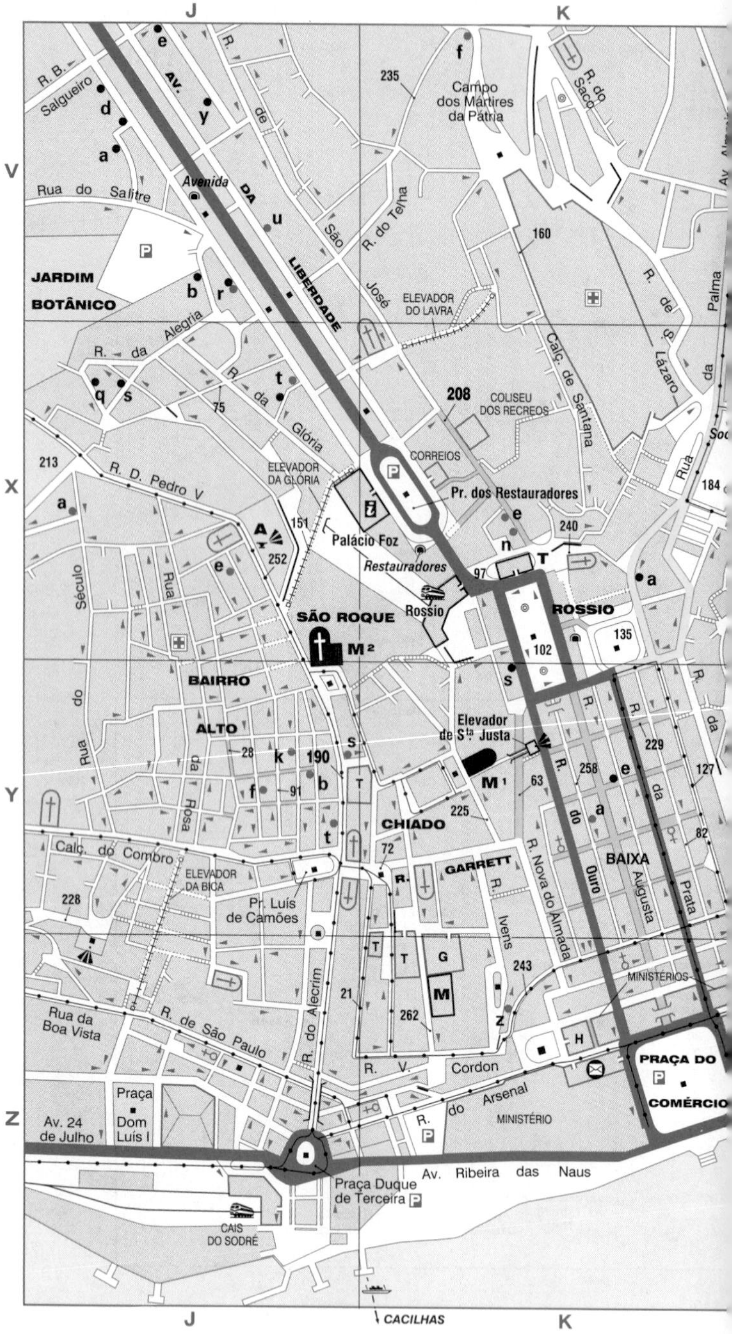

J
K
V
X
Y
Z
Campo dos Mártires da Pátria
R. do Saco
Av. Almirante Reis
R. B. Salgueiro
Rua do Salitre
Avenida DA LIBERDADE
R. de São José
R. do Telha
ELEVADOR DO LAVRA
JARDIM BOTÂNICO
R. da Alegria
R. da Glória
Calç. de Santana
R. de S. Lázaro
Rua da Palma
COLISEU DOS RECREIOS
CORREIOS
ELEVADOR DA GLÓRIA
R. D. Pedro V
Pr. dos Restauradores
Palácio Foz
Restauradores
Rossio
ROSSIO
SÃO ROQUE
BAIRRO ALTO
Rua do Século
Rua da Rosa
Elevador de Sta. Justa
CHIADO
R. GARRETT
R. do Ouro
R. Augusta
R. da Prata
R. Nova do Almada
R. Ivens
BAIXA
Calç. do Combro
ELEVADOR DA BICA
Pr. Luís de Camões
R. do Alecrim
MINISTÉRIOS
Rua da Boa Vista
R. de São Paulo
R. V. Cordon
R. do Arsenal
MINISTÉRIO
PRAÇA DO COMÉRCIO
Praça Dom Luís I
Av. 24 de Julho
Praça Duque de Terceira
Av. Ribeira das Naus
CAIS DO SODRÉ
CACILHAS

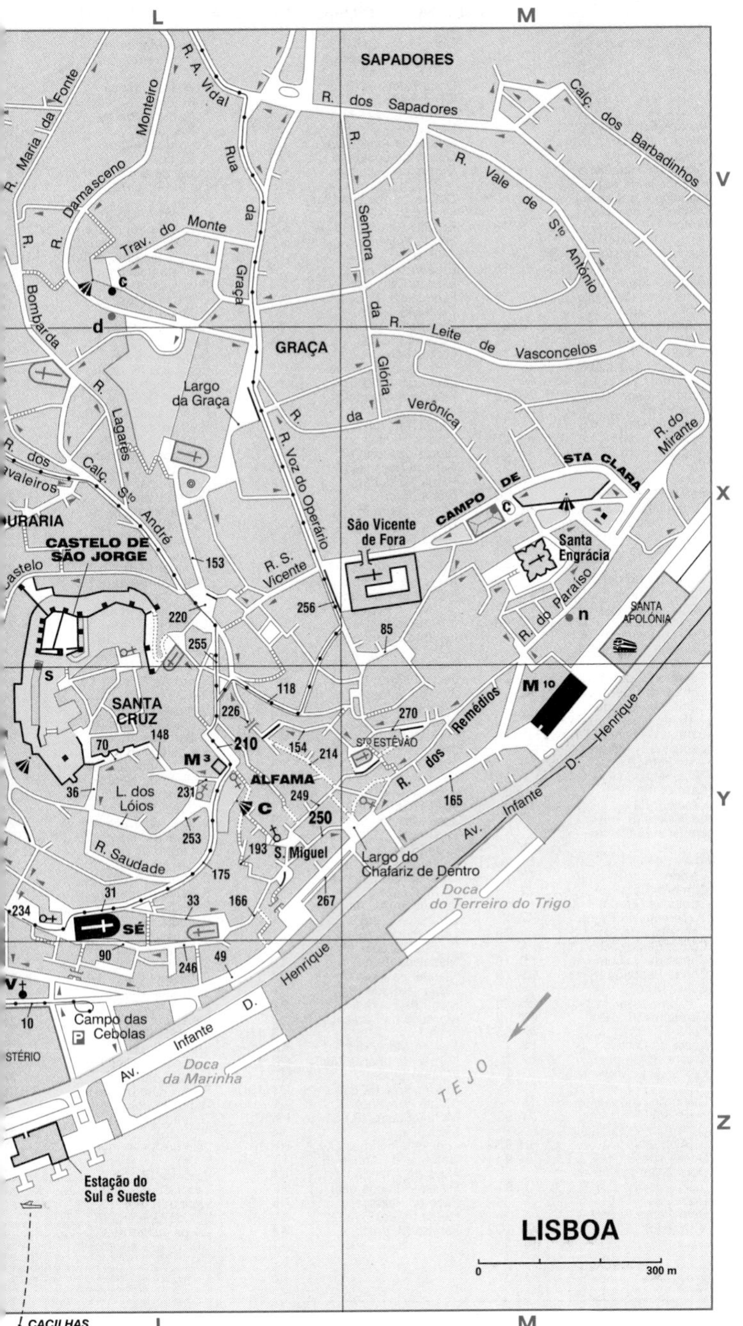
L
M
SAPADORES
GRAÇA
ALFAMA
SANTA CRUZ
CASTELO DE SÃO JORGE
São Vicente de Fora
Santa Engrácia
SANTA APOLÓNIA
Largo da Graça
Largo do Chafariz de Dentro
Doca do Terreiro do Trigo
Doca da Marinha
Campo das Cebolas
Estação do Sul e Sueste
TEJO
CACILHAS
SÉ
S. Miguel
STO ESTÊVÃO
L. dos Lóios
CAMPO DE STA CLARA
V
X
Y
Z
LISBOA
0
300 m

STREET INDEX TO LISBOA TOWN PLANS

Augusta (R.) KY
Carmo (R. do) KY 63
Garrett (R.) (Chiado) KY
Ouro (R. do) KY
Prata (R. da) KY

Afonso Costa (Av.) HR
Alecrim (R. do) JZ
Alegria (R. da) JX
Alexandre Herculano (R.) FT 7
Alfândega (R. da) LZ 10
Almeida e Sousa (R.) ET
Almirante Reis (Av.) HR
Amoreiras (R. das) FT 13
Angelina Vidal (R.) LV
António Augusto de Aguiar (Av.) FR 15
António José de Almeida (Av.) GR 18
António Maria Cardoso (R.) JZ 21
António Pereira Carrilho (R.) HR 22
Arco do Carvalhão (R. do) ET
Arco do Cego (R.) GR 25
Arsenal (R. do) KZ
Artilharia Um (R. da) FS 27
Atalaia (R. da) JY 28
Augusto Rosa (R.) LY 31
Barão (R.) LY 33
Barão de Sabrosa (R.) HR
Barata Salgueiro (R.) FT 34
Barbadinhos (Calç. dos) MV
Bartolomeu de Gusmão (R.) LY 36
Beneficência (R. da) FR 40
Berna (Av. de) FR 42
Boa Vista (R. da) FU 46
Bombarda (R.) LV
Borges Carneiro (R.) FU
Braancamp (R.) FS 48
Cais de Santarém (R.) LZ 49
Calouste Gulbenkian (Av.) ER
Calvário (L. do) EU 54
Campo das Cebolas LZ
Campo de Ourique (R. do) ET 57
Campo de Santa Clara MX
Campo dos Mártires da Pátria KV
Casal Ribeiro (Av.) GR 66
Cascais (R.) EU 67
Castilho (R.) FS
Cavaleiros (R. dos) LX
Chafariz de Dentro (L. do) MY
Chão da Feira (R. do) LY 70
Chiado (L. do) KY 72
Combro (Calç. do) JY
Comércio (Pr. do) (Terreiro do Paço) KZ
Conceição da Gloriá (R.) JX 75
Conde de Almoster (R.) ER
Conde de Valbom (Av.) FR 76
Conde Redondo (R.) GS 78
Conselheiro F. de Sousa (Av.) ES 79
Correeiros (R. dos) KY 82
Corvos (R. dos) MX 85
Costa do Castelo LX
Cruzes da Sé (R.) LZ 90
Damasceno Monteiro (R.) LV
Diário de Notícias (R. do) JY 91
Dom Afonso Henriques (Alameda) HR 93
Dom Carlos I (Av.) FU 94
Dom João da Câmara (Pr.) KX 97
Dom Luis I (Pr.) JZ
Dom Pedro IV (Pr.) (Rossio) KX 102
Dom Pedro V (R.) JX
Domingos Sequeira (R.) ET 106
Dona Estefânia (R. de) GS
Dona Filipa de Vilhena (Av.) GR 109
Dona Maria Pia (R.) ET
Duque de Ávila (Av.) GR
Duque de Loulé (Av.) GS 111
Duque de Saldanha (Pr.) GR 112
Duque de Terceira (Pr.) JZ
Escola do Exército (R.) HS 117
Escolas Gerais (R. das) LY 118
Escola Politécnica (R. da) FT 120
Espanha (Pr. de) FR 124
Estrela (Calç. da) FU
Fanqueiros (R. dos) KY 127
Febo Moniz (R.) HS 129
Ferreira Borges (R.) ET 132
Figueira (Pr. da) KX 135
Fontes Pereira de Melo (Av.) GS 139
Forno do Tijolo (R.) HS 147
Francisco Quental Martins (R.) ER
Funil (Trav. do) LY 148
Furnas (R. das) ER
Garcia da Horta (R.) FU 150
General Roçadas (Av.) HS
Glória (Calç. da) JX 151
Glória (R. da) JX
Gomes Freire (R.) GS
Graça (Calç. da) LX 153
Graça (L. da) LX
Graça (R. da) LV
Guilherme Braga (R.) LY 154
Imprensa Nacional (R.) FT 157
Infante D. Henrique (Av.) MY
Infante Santo (Av.) EU
Instituto Bacteriológico (R.) KV 160
Ivens (R.) KY
Jacinta Marto (R.) GS 162
Janelas Verdes (R. das) EU 163
Jardim do Tabaco (R. do) MY 165
João da Praça (R. de) LY 166
João XXI (Av. de) HR
Joaquim António de Aguiar (R.) FS 169
José Fontana (Pr.) GS
José Malhoa (Av.) ER
Lagares (R.) LX
Lapa (R. da) EU
Laranjeiras (Estr. das) ER 172
Leite de Vasconcelos (R.) MX
Liberdade (Av. da) JV
Limoeiro (L. do) LY 175
Lóios (L. dos) LY
Luís de Camões (Pr.) JY
Madalena (R. da) KY
Manuel da Maia (Av.) HR 178
Maria Andrade (R.) HS 180
Maria da Fonte (R.) LV
Marquês de Pombal (Pr.) FS 183
Martim Moniz (L.) KX 184
Miguel Bombarda (Av.) GR 186
Mirante (R. do) MX
Misericórdia (R. da) JY 190
Monte (Trav. do) LV
Morais Soares (R.) HR
Mouzinho de Albuquerque (Av.) HS
Norberto de Araújo (R.) LY 193
Nova de Almada (R.) KY
Olaias (Rotunda das) HR
Paço da Rainha HS 195
Palma (R. da) KV
Paraíso (R. do) MX
Passos Manuel (R.) HS 1
Pedro Álvares Cabral (Av.) FT 1
Penha de França (R. da) HS
Poço dos Mouros (Calç. do) HR 2
Poço dos Negros (R. do) FU 2
Poiais de S. Bento (R.) FU 2
Ponte (Av. da) ET
Portas de Santo Antão (R.) KX 2
Portas do Sol (L. das) LY 2
Possidónio da Silva (R.) EU
Presidente Arriaga (R.) EU 2
Príncipe Real (Pr. do) JX 2
Prior (R. do) EU
Quelhas Pasteleiro (R. do) FU
Ramalho Ortigão (R.) FR
Rato (L. do) FT
Regueira (R. da) LY 2
Remédios (R. dos) MY
Restauradores (Pr. dos) KX
Ribeira das Naus (Av.) KZ
Ribeiro Sanches (R.) EU
Rodrigo da Fonseca (R.) FS 2
Rodrigues de Freitas (L.) LX 2
Rosa (R. da) JY
Rovisco Pais (Av.) GR 2
Sá Carneiro (Pr.) HR
Saco (R. do) KV
Sacramento (Calç. do) KY 2
Salitre (R. do) JV
Salvador (R. do) LY 2
Sampaio Bruno (R.) ET
Santa Catarina (R. de) JY 2
Santa Justa (R. de) KY 2
Santa Luzia (Trav. de) LY 2
Santana (Calç. de) KX
Santo André (Calç. de) LX
Santo António (R. de) EU 2
Santo António da Sé (L.) LY 2
Santo António dos Capuchos (R.) KV 2
S. Bernardo (R. de) FT 2
S. Caetano (R. de) EU
S. Domingos (L. de) KX 2
S. Filipe de Nery (R.) FS 2
S. Francisco (Calç. de) KZ 2
S. João da Mata (R.) FU 2
S. João da Praça (R.) LZ 2
S. José (R. de) JV
S. Lázaro (R. de) KX
S. Marçal (R. de) FT 2
S. Miguel (R. de) LY 2
S. Paulo (R. de) JZ
S. Pedro (R. de) LY 2
S. Pedro de Alcântara (R. de) JX 2
S. Tiago (R. de) LY 2
S. Tomé (R. de) LX 2
S. Vicente (Calç. de) LX 2
S. Vicente (R.) LX
Sapadores (R. dos) MV
Sapateiros (R. dos) KY 2
Saudade (R.) LY
Século (R. do) JX
Senhora da Glória (R.) MV
Serpa Pinto (R.) KZ 2
Sol ao Rato (R. do) FT 2
Telhal (R. do) KV
Terreiro do Trigo (R. do) LY 2
Vale de Sto António (R.) MV
Verónica (R. da) MX
Victor Cordon (R.) KZ
Vigário (R. do) MY 2
Voz do Operário (R.) LX
24 de Julho (Av.) FU

Don't get lost, use **Michelin Maps** which are updated annually.

Centre : Av. da Liberdade, Rua Augusta, Rua do Ouro, Praça do Comércio, Praça Dom Pedro IV (Rossio), Praça dos Restauradores

Tivoli Lisboa, Av. da Liberdade 185, ✉ 1200, ☎ 353 01 81, Telex 12588, Fax 57 94 61, « Terrace with ≤ town », heated, – 40/200. AE E VISA JCB. JV d
Meals 4800 - ***Grill Terraço :*** **Meals** a la carte 5650/8450 - ***Zodíaco :*** **Meals** a la carte 5100/5300 – **298 rm** ☐ 30000/34000, 29 suites.

Sofitel Lisboa, Av. da Liberdade 125, ✉ 1250, ☎ 342 92 02, Telex 42557, Fax 342 92 22 – – 25/300. AE E VISA JCB JV r
Meals (see rest. ***Cais da Avenida*** below) – ☐ 2500 – **166 rm** 35000, 4 suites.

Lisboa Plaza, Travessa do Salitre 7, ✉ 1250, ☎ 346 39 22, Telex 16402, Fax 347 16 30 – – 25/140. AE E VISA JCB. JV b
Meals 4400 – **94 rm** ☐ 24500/27000, 12 suites.

Tivoli Jardim, Rua Julio Cesar Machado 7, ✉ 1200, ☎ 353 99 71, Telex 12172, Fax 355 65 66, heated, – . AE E VISA JCB. JV a
Meals 4500 – **119 rm** ☐ 23000/27000.

Mundial, Rua D. Duarte 4, ✉ 1100, ☎ 886 31 01, Telex 12308, Fax 887 91 29, ≤ – – 25/120. AE E VISA JCB. KX a
Meals 3950 – **141 rm** ☐ 15750/19000, 6 suites.

Lisboa coffee shop only, Rua Barata Salgueiro 5, ✉ 1150, ☎ 355 41 31, Telex 60228, Fax 355 41 39 – . AE E VISA JCB. JV e
55 rm ☐ 16800/20000, 6 suites.

Veneza without rest, Av. da Liberdade 189, ✉ 1250, ☎ 352 26 18, Fax 352 66 78, « Old palace » – . AE E VISA JCB. JV d
36 rm ☐ 13500/17000.

Príncipe Real, Rua da Alegria 53, ✉ 1250, ☎ 346 01 16, Fax 342 21 04 – . AE E VISA JCB. JX q
Meals 2750 – **24 rm** ☐ 15500/19500.

Britânia without rest, Rua Rodrigues Sampaio 17, ✉ 1150, ☎ 315 50 16, Telex 16402, Fax 315 50 21 – . AE E VISA JCB. JV y
30 rm ☐ 19900/22300.

Metropole without rest, Praça do Rossio 30, ✉ 1100, ☎ 346 91 64, Fax 346 91 66 – . AE E VISA JCB KY s
36 rm ☐ 17000/19000.

Botánico without rest, Rua Mãe de Água 16, ✉ 1250, ☎ 342 03 92, Fax 342 01 25 – . AE E VISA JCB. JX s
30 rm ☐ 10500/13000.

Albergaria Senhora do Monte without rest, Calçada do Monte 39, ✉ 1100, ☎ 886 60 02, Fax 887 77 83, ≤ São Jorge castle, town and river Tejo – . AE E VISA. LV c
28 rm ☐ 14000/17500.

Insulana without rest, Rua da Assunção 52, ✉ 1100, ☎ 342 76 25 – . AE E VISA. KY e
32 rm ☐ 7500/9000.

Tágide, Largo da Académia Nacional de Belas Artes 18, ✉ 1200, ☎ 342 07 20, Fax 347 18 80, ≤ – . AE E VISA JCB. KZ z
closed Saturday lunch and Sunday – **Meals** a la carte 6100/7600.

Clara, Campo dos Mártires da Pátria 49, ✉ 1150, ☎ 885 30 53, Fax 885 20 82, Garden-terrace – . AE E VISA. KV f
closed Saturday lunch, Sunday and 1 to 15 August – **Meals** a la carte approx. 5100.

Tavares, Rua da Misericórdia 37, ✉ 1200, ☎ 342 11 12, Fax 347 81 25, Late 19C decor – . AE E VISA. JY t
closed Saturday and Sunday lunch – **Meals** a la carte approx. 7500.

Bachus, Largo da Trindade 9, ✉ 1200, ☎ 342 28 28, Fax 342 12 60 – . AE E VISA. JY s
closed Saturday lunch and Sunday – **Meals** a la carte approx. 6800.

Gambrinus, Rua das Portas de Santo Antão 25, ✉ 1100, ☎ 342 14 66, Fax 346 50 32 – . AE VISA. KX n
Meals a la carte 11000/14000.

Escorial, Rua das Portas de Santo Antão 47, ✉ 1100, ☎ 346 44 29, Fax 346 37 58 – . AE E VISA JCB. KX e
Meals a la carte approx. 5840.

Cais da Avenida, Av. da Liberdade 123, ✉ 1250, ☎ 342 92 24, Fax 342 92 22 – . AE E VISA JCB JV r
Meals a la carte 3050/5150.

Jardim Tropical with self-service, Av. da Liberdade 144, ✉ 1200, ✆ 342 20 7…, Fax 342 31 24, « Tropical conservatory » – AE E VISA JCB JV
Meals a la carte 3050/8300.

Casa do Leão, Castelo de São Jorge, ✉ 1100, ✆ 887 59 62, Fax 887 63 29, ← – AE E VISA. LXY
Meals a la carte 4450/6950.

Via Graça, Rua Damasceno Monteiro 9 B, ✉ 1170, ✆ 887 08 30, Fax 887 03 0… ← São Jorge castle, town and river Tejo – AE E VISA JCB. LV
closed Saturday lunch and Sunday – **Meals** a la carte 2950/4950.

O Faz Figura, Rua do Paraíso 15 B, ✉ 1100, ✆ 886 89 81, ←, – AE E VISA. MX
closed Sunday and Bank Holidays – **Meals** a la carte approx. 6500.

Sancho, Travessa da Glória 14, ✉ 1250, ✆ 346 97 80
AE E VISA. JX
closed Sunday and Bank Holidays – **Meals** a la carte 2500/3920.

Porta Branca, Rua do Teixeira 35, ✉ 1250, ✆ 342 10 24, Fax 347 92 57 – E VISA JCB. JX
closed Saturday lunch, Sunday, Bank Holidays and August – **Meals** a la carte approx. 391…

Mercado de Santa Clara, Campo de Santa Clara (at market), ✉ 1170, ✆ 887 39 8… Fax 887 39 86, ← – AE E VISA. MX
closed Sunday dinner, Monday and 5 August-6 September – **Meals** a la carte 3300/480…

East : Av. da Liberdade, Av. Almirante Reis, Av. Estados Unidos de América, Av. de Roma, Av. João XXI, Av. da República, Praça Marquês de Pombal

Holiday Inn Crowne Plaza, Av. Marechal Craveiro Lopes 390, ✉ 1700, ✆ 759 96 3… Telex 61170, Fax 758 66 05, – – 25/200. AE E VISA JCB.
Meals 4200 – **205 rm** 31500/33000, 16 suites. N : by Av. da República GR

Holiday Inn Lisboa, Av. António José de Almeida 28 A, ✉ 1000, ✆ 793 52 2… Telex 60330, Fax 793 66 72, – – 25/250. AE E VISA JCB.
Meals 3750 – 1500 – **161 rm** 29000/34000, 8 suites. GR

Altis Park H., Av. Engenheiro Arantes e Oliveira 9, ✉ 1900, ✆ 846 08 66, Fax 846 08 3… – – 25/400. AE E VISA. rest HR
Meals 3650 – **285 rm** 16000/17600, 15 suites.

Lutécia, Av. Frei Miguel Contreiras 52, ✉ 1700, ✆ 840 31 21, Telex 1245… Fax 840 78 18, ← – – 25/100. AE E VISA JCB.
Meals a la carte 3450/5400 – **142 rm** 18000/21000, 8 suites.
N : by Av. Almirante Reis HR

Alif without rest, Campo Pequeno 51, ✉ 1000, ✆ 795 24 64, Telex 6446… Fax 795 41 16 – – 25/40. AE E VISA. GR
107 rm 12900/14500, 8 suites.

Sol Lisboa, Av. Duque de Loulé 45, ✉ 1050, ✆ 353 21 08, Telex 65522, Fax 353 18 6… – AE E VISA JCB. GS
Meals *(closed Sunday)* a la carte 3300/4500 – **80 rm** 24000/26000, 4 suites.

A.S. Lisboa without rest, Av. Almirante Reis 188, ✉ 1000, ✆ 847 30 25, Telex 4425… Fax 847 30 34 – – 25/80. AE E VISA. HR
75 rm 11900/13900.

Presidente coffee shop only, Rua Alexandre Herculano 13, ✉ 1150, ✆ 353 95 0… Fax 352 02 72 – – 25/40. AE E VISA. GS
59 rm 12000/14500.

Dom Carlos without rest, Av. Duque de Loulé 121, ✉ 1050, ✆ 353 90 7… Fax 352 07 28 – – 25/40. AE E VISA. GS
76 rm 13000/15500.

Roma, Av. de Roma 33, ✉ 1700, ✆ 796 77 61, Telex 16586, Fax 793 29 81, ←, – 25/230. AE E VISA JCB. N : by Av. Almirante Reis HR
Meals 2950 – **263 rm** 11500/13500.

Dom João without rest, Rua José Estêvão 43, ✉ 1100, ✆ 52 41 71, Fax 352 45 69 . HS
18 rm 7000/8000.

Antonio Clara-Clube de Empresários, Av. da República 38, ✉ 1050, ✆ 796 63 8… Fax 797 41 44, « Former old palace » – AE E VISA JCB. GR
closed Sunday, Bank Holidays and 15 to 31 August – **Meals** a la carte approx. 6500.

Chez Armand, Rua Carlos Mardel 38, ✉ 1900, ✆ 847 57 70, Fax 316 27 75, French rest – AE E VISA. HR
closed Sunday and August – **Meals** a la carte 3580/4300.

Celta, Rua Gomes Freire 148, ✉ 1150, ✆ 357 30 69 – AE E VISA. GS
closed Sunday – **Meals** a la carte 2950/4660.

West : Av. da Liberdade, Av. 24 de Julho, Av. da India, Av. Infante Santo, Av. de Berna, Av. António Augusto de Aguiar, Largo de Alcântara, Praça Marquês de Pombal, Praça de Espanha

Ritz Inter-Continental, Rua Rodrigo da Fonseca 88, ✉ 1093, ✆ 69 20 20, Telex 12589, Fax 69 17 83, ≤, – 25/600. AE ⓓ E VISA JCB. FS b
Varanda : Meals a la carte 5050/8400 – 2500 – **265 rm** 34000/38000, 20 suites.

Sheraton Lisboa H., Rua Latino Coelho 1, ✉ 1097, ✆ 357 57 57, Telex 12774, Fax 354 71 64, ≤, heated – – 25/550. AE ⓓ E VISA JCB. GR s
Meals 4800 - *Alfama Grill (closed Saturday, Sunday and Bank Holidays)* Meals a la carte 6000/11700 - *Caravela* : Meals a la carte 4950/7600 – 2250 – **377 rm** 35000/38000, 7 suites.

Da Lapa, Rua do Pau de Bandeira 4, ✉ 1200, ✆ 395 00 05, Fax 395 06 65, ≤, « Park with waterfall and » – – 25/225. AE ⓓ E VISA. EU a
Meals a la carte approx. 6500 – 2750 – **78 rm** 42000/44000, 8 suites.

Le Meridien Lisboa, Rua Castilho 149, ✉ 1070, ✆ 383 09 00, Telex 64315, Fax 383 32 31, ≤ – – 25/550. AE ⓓ E VISA JCB. FS a
Meals 4500 - *Brasserie des Amis* : Meals a la carte 6000/6400 – 2300 – **313 rm** 33500/43500, 17 suites.

Alfa Lisboa, Av. Columbano Bordalo Pinheiro, ✉ 1070, ✆ 726 21 21, Telex 18477, Fax 726 30 31, ≤, – – 25/600. AE ⓓ E VISA. ER a
A Aldeia : Meals a la carte 3850/4150 - *Grill Pombalino (closed Saturday, Sunday, Bank Holidays and August)* Meals a la carte 5100/5300 – **440 rm** 25000/30000.

Altis, Rua Castilho 11, ✉ 1200, ✆ 357 92 62, Telex 13314, Fax 354 86 96, – – 25/700. AE ⓓ E VISA. FT z
Meals 4500 - *Girassol* : Meals a la carte 4300/7400 - *Grill Dom Fernando* : Meals a la carte 4300/7400 – **290 rm** 24000/28000, 13 suites.

Novotel Lisboa, Av. José Malhoa 1642, ✉ 1000, ✆ 726 60 22, Telex 40114, Fax 726 64 96, ≤, – – 25/300. AE ⓓ E VISA ER e
Meals 3100 – 1100 – **246 rm** 14500/15750.

Continental, Rua Laura Alves 9, ✉ 1050, ✆ 793 50 05, Telex 65632, Fax 793 42 87 – – 25/180. AE ⓓ E VISA. FR q
D. Miguel (closed Saturday and Sunday) Meals a la carte approx. 5700 - *Coffee Shop Continental* : Meals a la carte approx. 4300 – **210 rm** 23000/26000, 10 suites.

Real Parque, Av. Luís Bívar 67, ✉ 1050, ✆ 357 01 01, Fax 357 07 50 – – 25/100. AE ⓓ E VISA. FR a
Meals 4500 - *Cozinha do Real* : Meals a la carte 4900/6300 – **147 rm** 25000/28000, 6 suites.

Lisboa Penta, Av. dos Combatentes, ✉ 1600, ✆ 726 40 54, Telex 18437, Fax 726 42 81, ≤, – – 25/600. AE ⓓ E VISA JCB. rest NW : by Av. A. Augusto de Aguiar FR
Meals 2700 - *Grill Passarola* : Meals a la carte approx. 7210 - *Verde Pino* : Meals a la carte approx. 3500 – **584 rm** 20000/24000, 4 suites.

Fénix, Praça Marquês de Pombal 8, ✉ 1250, ✆ 386 21 21, Telex 12170, Fax 386 01 31 – – 25/100. AE ⓓ E VISA JCB. FS g
Bodegón : Meals a la carte approx. 6350 – **119 rm** 18500/20500, 4 suites.

Zurique, Rua Ivone Silva 18, ✉ 1050, ✆ 793 71 11, Telex 65349, Fax 793 72 90, – – 25/150. AE ⓓ E VISA. FR s
Meals 3250 – **248 rm** 13000/15000, 4 suites.

Diplomático, Rua Castilho 74, ✉ 1200, ✆ 386 20 41, Telex 13713, Fax 386 21 55 – – 25/60. AE ⓓ E VISA JCB. rest FS c
Meals a la carte 2900/4500 – **73 rm** 10000/17500, 17 suites.

Flórida without rest, Rua Duque de Palmela 32, ✉ 1250, ✆ 357 61 45, Fax 354 35 84 – – 25/100. AE ⓓ E VISA JCB. FS x
108 rm 15000/18000.

Barcelona without rest, Rua Laura Alves 10, ✉ 1000, ✆ 795 42 73, Fax 795 42 81, – – 25/230. AE ⓓ VISA. FR z
120 rm 16500/19500, 5 suites.

Quality H., Campo Grande 7, ✉ 1700, ✆ 795 75 55, Fax 795 75 00 – – 25/50. AE ⓓ E VISA JCB. N : by Av. da República GR
Meals 3500 – **80 rm** 20000/23000, 2 suites.

Executive Inn without rest, Av. Conde Valbom 56, ✉ 1050, ☎ 795 11 57, Telex 6561 Fax 795 11 66 – AE VISA. FR
72 rm 11000/13000.

Amazónia H. coffee shop only, Travessa Fábrica dos Pentes 12, ✉ 1250, ☎ 387 70 0 Telex 66361, Fax 387 90 90, heated – 25/200. AE VISA FS
192 rm 12100/13800.

Dom Manuel I without rest, Av. Duque de Ávila 189, ✉ 1050, ☎ 357 61 6 Telex 43558, Fax 357 69 85, « Tasteful decor » – AE VISA. FR
64 rm 11500/13000.

Dom Rodrigo Suite H. coffee shop only, Rua Rodrigo da Fonseca 44, ✉ 120 ☎ 386 38 00, Fax 386 30 00, – AE VISA. FS
850 – **57 suites** 19500/24000.

Nacional without rest, Rua Castilho 34, ✉ 1250, ☎ 355 44 33, Fax 356 11 22 – AE VISA. FST
59 rm 13200/15400, 2 suites.

York House, Rua das Janelas Verdes 32, ✉ 1200, ☎ 396 25 44, Telex 1679 Fax 397 27 93, « Former 16C convent. Portuguese decor » – AE JCB. FU
Meals a la carte approx. 5000 – **31 rm** 23500/27500, 3 suites.

Miraparque, Av. Sidónio Pais 12, ✉ 1050, ☎ 352 42 86, Telex 16745, Fax 357 89 2 – AE VISA. FS
Meals 3000 – **101 rm** 10700/12800.

As Janelas Verdes without rest, Rua das Janelas Verdes 47, ✉ 1200, ☎ 396 81 4 Telex 164 02, Fax 396 81 44, Late 18C house with attractive courtyard – VISA JCB. FU
17 rm 26000/28500.

Da Torre, Rua dos Jerónimos 8, ✉ 1400, ☎ 363 62 62, Fax 364 59 95 – 25/50. AE VISA JCB. W : by Av. 24 de Julho EU
Meals (see rest. ***São Jerónimo*** below) – **50 rm** 11850/14700.

Flamingo, Rua Castilho 41, ✉ 1250, ☎ 386 21 91, Fax 386 12 16 – VISA. FS
Meals 3000 – **39 rm** 13500/16500.

Berna without rest, Av. António Serpa 13, ✉ 1050, ☎ 793 67 67, Telex 6251 Fax 793 62 78 – 25/140. AE VISA. GR
240 rm 10500/11500.

Eduardo VII, Av. Fontes Pereira de Melo 5, ✉ 1050, ☎ 353 01 41, Fax 353 38 79, – 25/60. AE VISA. FS
Meals a la carte 3500/4500 – **119 rm** 12500/14700, 2 suites.

Imperador without rest, Av. 5 de Outubro 55, ✉ 1050, ☎ 352 48 84, Fax 352 65 3 – AE VISA. GR
43 rm 8000/9000.

Casa da Comida, Travessa das Amoreiras 1, ✉ 1200, ☎ 388 53 76, Fax 387 51 3 « Patio with plants » – AE VISA. FT
closed Saturday lunch and Sunday – **Meals** a la carte 6500/10900.

Pabe, Rua Duque de Palmela 27 A, ✉ 1250, ☎ 353 74 84, Fax 353 64 37, English pu style – AE VISA. FS
Meals a la carte 5700/8300.

Conventual, Praça das Flores 45, ✉ 1200, ☎ 60 91 96, Fax 60 91 96 – AE VISA FT
closed Saturday lunch, Bank Holidays lunch and Sunday – **Meals** a la carte 3800/630
Spec. Concha de mariscos gratinada. Lombo de linguado com molho de marisco. Pato co champagne e pimenta rosa.

São Jerónimo, Rua dos Jerónimos 12, ✉ 1400, ☎ 364 87 97, Fax 363 26 92, Mode decor – AE VISA JCB. W : by Av. 24 de Julho EU
closed Saturday lunch and Sunday – **Meals** a la carte approx. 5200.

Chester, Rua Rodrigo da Fonseca 87 D, ✉ 1250, ☎ 385 73 47, Fax 388 78 11, Mea specialities – AE VISA JCB. FS
closed Sunday – **Meals** a la carte 4650/6980.

Saraiva's, Rua Eng. Canto Resende 3, ✉ 1050, ☎ 354 06 09, Fax 353 19 87, Mode decor – AE VISA JCB. FR
closed Saturday and Bank Holidays – **Meals** a la carte approx. 5300.

Espelho d'Água, Av. de Brasilia, ✉ 1400, ☎ 301 73 73, Fax 363 26 92, ≤, Lakeside setting. Modern decor – AE VISA JCB.
closed Sunday – **Meals** a la carte approx. 5800. W : by Av. 24 de Julho EU

XX **Adega Tía Matilde,** Rua da Beneficéncia 77, ✉ 1600, ✆ 797 21 72, Fax 793 90 00 – ▤. AE ⓞ E VISA. ⚘ FR h
closed Saturday dinner and Sunday – **Meals** a la carte 3500/5400.

XX **O Nobre,** Rua das Mercês 71, ✉ 1300, ✆ 363 38 27, Fax 364 91 07 – ▤. AE E VISA W : by Av. 24 de Julho EU
closed Saturday lunch and Sunday – **Meals** a la carte 4140/5840.

XX **O Polícia,** Rua Marquês Sá da Bandeira 112, ✉ 1050, ✆ 796 35 05, Fax 796 02 19 – ▤. E VISA. ⚘ FR c
closed Saturday dinner and Sunday – **Meals** a la carte 3400/4200.

X **Xêlê Bananas,** Praça das Flores 29, ✉ 1200, ✆ 395 25 15, Tropical style decor – ▤. AE ⓞ E VISA FT n
closed Saturday lunch and Sunday – **Meals** a la carte 3250/5750.

X **Sua Excelência,** Rua do Conde 34, ✉ 1200, ✆ 60 36 14, Fax 396 75 85 – ▤. AE E VISA JCB EU t
closed Saturday lunch, Sunday lunch, Wednesday and September – **Meals** a la carte 4200/7700.

Typical atmosphere :

XX **O Faia,** Rua da Barroca 56, ✉ 1200, ✆ 342 67 42, Fax 342 19 23, Fado cabaret – ▤. AE ⓞ E VISA JCB. ⚘ JY f
closed Sunday – **Meals** (dinner only) a la carte 3850/7300.

XX **Sr. Vinho,** Rua do Meio-à-Lapa 18, ✉ 1200, ✆ 397 74 56, Fax 395 20 72, Fado cabaret – ▤. AE ⓞ E VISA. ⚘ FU r
closed Sunday – **Meals** (dinner only) a la carte approx. 7500.

XX **A Severa,** Rua das Gáveas 51, ✉ 1200, ✆ 342 83 14, Fax 346 40 06, Fados at dinner – ▤. AE ⓞ E VISA JCB. ⚘ JY b
closed Thursday – **Meals** a la carte 5800/7900.

X **Adega Machado,** Rua do Norte 91, ✉ 1200, ✆ 342 87 13, Fax 346 75 07, Fado cabaret – ▤. AE ⓞ E VISA JCB. ⚘ JY k
closed Monday – **Meals** (dinner only) a la carte 7500/9000.

X **D'Avis,** Rua do Grilo 98, ✉ 1900, ✆ 868 13 54, Fax 868 13 54, Alentejo rest, « Typical decor » – ▤. AE ⓞ E VISA JCB E : Av. Infante D. Henrique MX
closed Sunday and August – **Meals** a la carte approx. 2500.

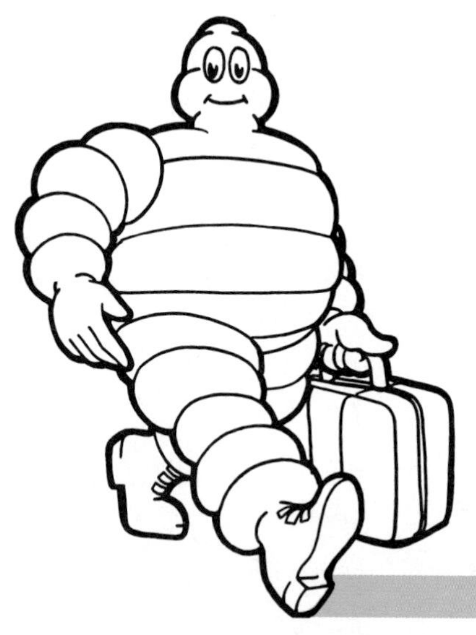

Spain

España

MADRID – BARCELONA – MÁLAGA
MARBELLA – SEVILLA – VALENCIA

PRACTICAL INFORMATION

LOCAL CURRENCY

Peseta: *100 ESP = 0.76 USD ($) (Jan. 97)*

National Holiday in Spain: *12 October*

TOURIST INFORMATION

The telephone number and address of the Tourist Information offices is given in the text of the towns under 🅸.

FOREIGN EXCHANGE

Banks are usually open fron 8.30am to 2pm (closed on Saturdays and Sundays in Summer).
Exchange offices in Sevilla and Valencia airports open from 9am to 2pm, in Barcelona airport from 9am to 2pm and 7 to 11pm. In Madrid and Málaga airports, offices operate a 24-hour service.

TRANSPORT

Taxis may be hailed when showing the green light or sign "Libre" on the windscreen.
Madrid, Barcelona and Valencia have a Metro (subway) network. In each station complete information and plans will be found.

SHOPPING

In the index of street names, those printed in red are where the principal shops are found.
The big stores are easy to find in town centres; they are open from 10am to 9.30pm.
Exclusive shops and boutiques are open from 10am to 2pm and 5 to 8pm - In Madrid they will be found in Serrano, Princesa and the Centre; in Barcelona, Passeig de Gracia, Diagonal and the Rambla de Catalunya.
Second-hand goods and antiques: El Rastro (Flea Market), Las Cortes, Serrano in Madrid; in Barcelona, Les Encantes (Flea Market), Barrio Gótico.

TIPPING

Hotel, restaurant and café bills always include service in the total charge. Nevertheless it is usual to leave the staff a small gratuity which may vary depending upon the district and the service given. Doormen, porters and taxi-drivers are used to being tipped.

SPEED LIMITS

The maximum permitted speed on motorways is 120 km/h - 74 mph, and 90 km/h - 56 mph on other roads.

SEAT BELTS

The wearing of seat belts is compulsory for drivers and passengers.

"TAPAS"

Bars serving "tapas" (typical spanish food to be eaten with a glass of wine or an aperitif) will usually be found in central, busy or old quarters of towns. In Madrid, search out the Calle de Cuchilleros (Plaza Mayor). In Sevilla, search out the Barrio de Santa Cruz, El Arenal and Triana.

MADRID

Madrid 28000 P 444 K 19 - *Pop. 3 084 673 - alt. 646* - ☎ *91.*

Paris (by Irún) 1310 - Barcelona 627 - Bilbao/Bilbo 397 - La Coruña/A Coruña 603 - Lisboa 653 - Málaga 548 - Porto 599 - Sevilla 550 - Valencia 351 - Zaragoza 322.

Princesa 1, ✉ 28008, ☎ 541 23 25, Duque de Medinaceli 2, ✉ 28014, ☎ 429 49 51, Pl. Mayor 3, ☎ 28012, ☎ 366 54 77, Chamartín Station, ✉ 28036, ☎ 315 99 76 and Barajas airport ☎ 305 86 56 - R.A.C.E. José Abascal 10, ✉ 28003, ☎ 447 32 00, Fax 593 20 64.

Racecourse of the Zarzuela ☎ 307 01 40 NW : by Av. Puerta de Hierro DV - 18, 18 *Puerta de Hierro ☎ 316 17 45 NW : by Av. Puerta de Hierro* DV - 9, 18 *Club de Campo ☎ 357 21 32 NW : by Av. Puerta de Hierro* DV - 18 *La Moraleja N : 11 km ☎ 650 07 00* - 9 *Club Barberán SW : 10 km ☎ 509 11 40* - 18 *Las Lomas - El Bosque SW : 18 km ☎ 616 75 00* - 18 *Real Automóvil Club de España N : 28 km ☎ 657 00 11* - 18 *Nuevo Club de Madrid, Las Matas W : 26 km ☎ 630 08 20* - 9 *Somosaguas W : 10 km by Casa de Campo ☎ 352 16 47* - 9 *Club Olivar de la Hinojosa NE by M 30 ☎ 721 18 89.*
✈ *Madrid-Barajas E : 13 km ☎ 393 60 00 - Iberia : Velázquez 130, ✉ 28006, ☎ 329 57 67* HV, *and Aviaco, Maudes 51, ✉ 28003, ✉ 534 42 00* FV.
Chamartín 🚘 *☎ 733 11 22* HR.

See: *The Prado Museum★★★ (Museo del Prado)* NY - *Casón del Buen Retiro★* NY - *The Old Madrid★ : Plaza Mayor★★* KY, *Plaza de la Villa★* KY, *Vistillas Gardens* KYZ. (✳★), *San Francisco El Grande Church (chairs★, sacristy chair★)* KZ - *Oriente Quarter★★ : Royal Palace (Palacio Real★★)* KX *(Palace★ : throne room★, Real Armería★★, Royal Carriage Museum★* DY **M¹**, *Campo del Moro★), Descalzas Reales Monastery★★* KLX *(Monasterio de las Descalzas Reales), Encarnación Royal Monastery★* KX *(Real Monasterio de la Encarnación) From España Building* ⇐★ KV, *University City★ (Ciudad Universitaria)* DV, *Madrid lighthouse (✳★★) (Faro de Madrid)* DV, *West Park★ (Parque del Oeste)* DV, *Country House★ (Casa de Campo)* DX, *Zoo★★ W : by Casa de Campo* DX - *El Madrid de los Borbones★★ : Plaza de la Cibeles★* MNX, *Paseo del Prado★* MNXYZ, *Thyssen-Bornemisza Museum★★★* MY **M⁶**, *Reina Sofía Art Centre National Museum★ (El Guernica★★)* MZ - *Army Museum★ (Museo del Ejército)* NY, *Puerta de Alcalá★* NX, *Parque del Buen Retiro★★* NYZ.

Other Curiosities: *Archaelogical National Museum★★ (Dama de Elche★★★)* NV - *Lázaro Galdiano Museum★★ (collection of enamels and ivories★★★)* HV **M⁴** - *Américan Museum★ (Museo de América : Quimbayas tresor★, Trocortesiano Codex★★★)* DV - *Real Academia de Bellas Artes de San Fernando★* LX **M²** - *San Antonio de la Florida Church (frescos★★)* DX - *Cerralbo Museum★* KV - *Wax Museum★ (Museo de Cera)* NV - *Sorolla Museum★* GV **M⁵** - *Plaza Monumental de las Ventas★* JV **B** - *Museum of the City (Museo de la Ciudad : maquettes★)* HU.

Envir.: *El Pardo (Royal Palace★ : tapestries★) - Capuchins Convent : lying Christ★* NW : *13 km by Av. Arco de la Victoria.*

Centre : Paseo del Prado, Puerta del Sol, Gran Vía, Alcalá, Paseo de Recoletos, Plaza Mayo (plan pp. 6 and 7)

Palace, pl. de las Cortes 7, ✉ 28014, ☏ 429 75 51, Telex 23903, Fax 429 82 66 – 25/600. AE VISA JCB. rest MY
Meals 4450 - ***La Cupola*** *(Italian rest, closed Saturday lunch, Sunday lunch, and August)* Meals a la carte 5900/7000 – 2750 – **436 rm** 38500/46000, 20 suites.

Princesa, Princesa 40, ✉ 28008, ☏ 542 21 00, Fax 542 73 28, – 25/825. AE VISA JCB. plan p. 4 DEV
Meals 2950 – 1950 – **263 rm** 24900/31200, 12 suites.

Villa Real, pl. de las Cortes 10, ✉ 28014, ☏ 420 37 67, Fax 420 25 47, « Tasteful decor » – 35/100. AE VISA. MY
Meals a la carte approx. 5500 – 1700 – **96 rm** 26400/33000, 19 suites.

Holiday Inn Crowne Plaza, pl. de España, ✉ 28013, ☏ 547 12 00, Telex 2738, Fax 548 23 89, ≤ – 25/350. AE VISA JCB. KV
Meals 4200 – 1650 – **295 rm** 26500/29500, 11 suites.

Tryp Ambassador, Cuesta de Santo Domingo 5, ✉ 28013, ☏ 541 67 00, Telex 4953, Fax 559 10 40 – 25/280. AE VISA JCB. KX
Meals 2600 – 1200 – **163 rm** 17475/21900, 18 suites.

Liabeny, Salud 3, ✉ 28013, ☏ 531 90 00, Telex 49024, Fax 532 74 21 – 25/125. AE VISA. LX
Meals 3000 – 1500 – **224 rm** 12000/17500, 5 suites.

Moncloa Garden without rest, Serrano Jover 1, ✉ 28015, ☏ 542 45 8, Fax 542 71 69 – AE VISA JCB. EV
925 – **102 rm** 13200/16400, 19 suites.

Emperador without rest, Gran Vía 53, ✉ 28013, ☏ 547 28 00, Telex 4626, Fax 547 28 17, – 25/150. AE VISA JCB. KX
1575 – **232 rm** 16280/20350.

Arosa coffee shop only, Salud 21, ✉ 28013, ☏ 532 16 00, Telex 43618, Fax 531 31 2 – 25/60. AE VISA JCB LX
1250 – **139 rm** 12125/18745.

G.H. Reina Victoria, pl. de Santa Ana 14, ✉ 28012, ☏ 531 45 00, Telex 4754, Fax 522 03 07 – 25/350. AE VISA JCB. LY
Meals 3625 – 1300 – **195 rm** 17475/21900, 6 suites.

Santo Domingo, pl. de Santo Domingo 13, ✉ 28013, ☏ 547 98 00, Fax 547 59 9 – 25/60. AE VISA JCB. KX
Meals 3475 – 1350 – **120 rm** 15175/21350.

Mayorazgo, Flor Baja 3, ✉ 28013, ☏ 547 26 00, Telex 45647, Fax 541 24 85 – 25/250. AE VISA JCB. KV
Meals 2200 – 1200 – **200 rm** 12500/16500.

El Coloso, Leganitos 13, ✉ 28013, ☏ 559 76 00, Telex 47017, Fax 547 49 68 – 25/200. AE VISA JCB. KX
Meals 2990 – 1300 – **84 rm** 15100/18850.

Suecia, Marqués de Casa Riera 4, ✉ 28014, ☏ 531 69 00, Telex 22313, Fax 521 71 – 25/150. AE VISA JCB. MX
Meals 3500 - ***Bellman*** *(Scandinavian rest)* Meals a la carte 3005/3875 – 1550 – **119 r** 18400/23000, 9 suites.

Gaudí, Gran Vía 9, ✉ 28013, ☏ 531 22 22, Fax 531 54 69, – 25/120. AE VISA JCB. LX
Meals 2500 – 1250 – **88 rm** 15750/18600.

Tryp Menfis, Gran Vía 74, ✉ 28013, ☏ 547 09 00, Telex 48773, Fax 547 51 99 – AE VISA. KV
Meals 1800 – 925 – **115 rm** 13875/17400.

Regina without rest, Alcalá 19, ✉ 28014, ☏ 521 47 25, Telex 27500, Fax 521 47 – AE VISA. LX
750 – **142 rm** 9500/12500.

Casón del Tormes without rest, Río 7, ✉ 28013, ☏ 541 97 46, Fax 541 18 52 – VISA. KV
650 – **63 rm** 8500/12500.

Green El Prado, Prado 11, ✉ 28014, ☏ 369 02 34, Fax 429 28 29 – 25/50. AE VISA. LY
Meals *(closed Sunday dinner)* 1500 – 500 – **47 rm** 11500/18375.

Mercator coffee shop only, Atocha 123, ✉ 28012, ☏ 429 05 00, Telex 4612, Fax 369 12 52 – AE VISA NZ
850 – **89 rm** 8550/11900.

MADRID

aídos de la División Azul . . . . HS 21
apitán Haya . . . . GS 25
omandante Zorita . . . FT 45
osta Rica (Av. de) . . . HS 55
uatro Caminos (Glorieta de) . . . . FU 56
octor Arce (Av. del) . HU 62
octor Fleming . . . . . . GT 63
nrique Larreta . . . . . . HS 76
stébanez Calderón . . . GS 80
ray Bernardino Sahagún . . . . HS 90
en. López Pozas . . . . HS 92
en. Moscardó . . . . . . FT 95
erez . . . . HS 107
edro Teixeira . . . . GT 145
inos Alta . . . . FS 146
intor Juan Gris . . . . . FS 148
residente Carmona . . FT 157
aimundo Fernández Villaverde . . . . FU 162
eina Mercedes . . . . . FT 168
epública Dominicana (Pl.) . . . . HS 172
osa de Silva . . . . FS 177
osario Pino . . . . GS 179
an Amaro (Pl.) . . . . . . FT 183
egre . . . . HT 206
nesio Delgado . . . . . GR 209
or Ángela de la Cruz . GS
eruel . . . . FT 210
íctor Andrés Belaunde . . . . HT 229
íctor de la Serna . . . . HT 231

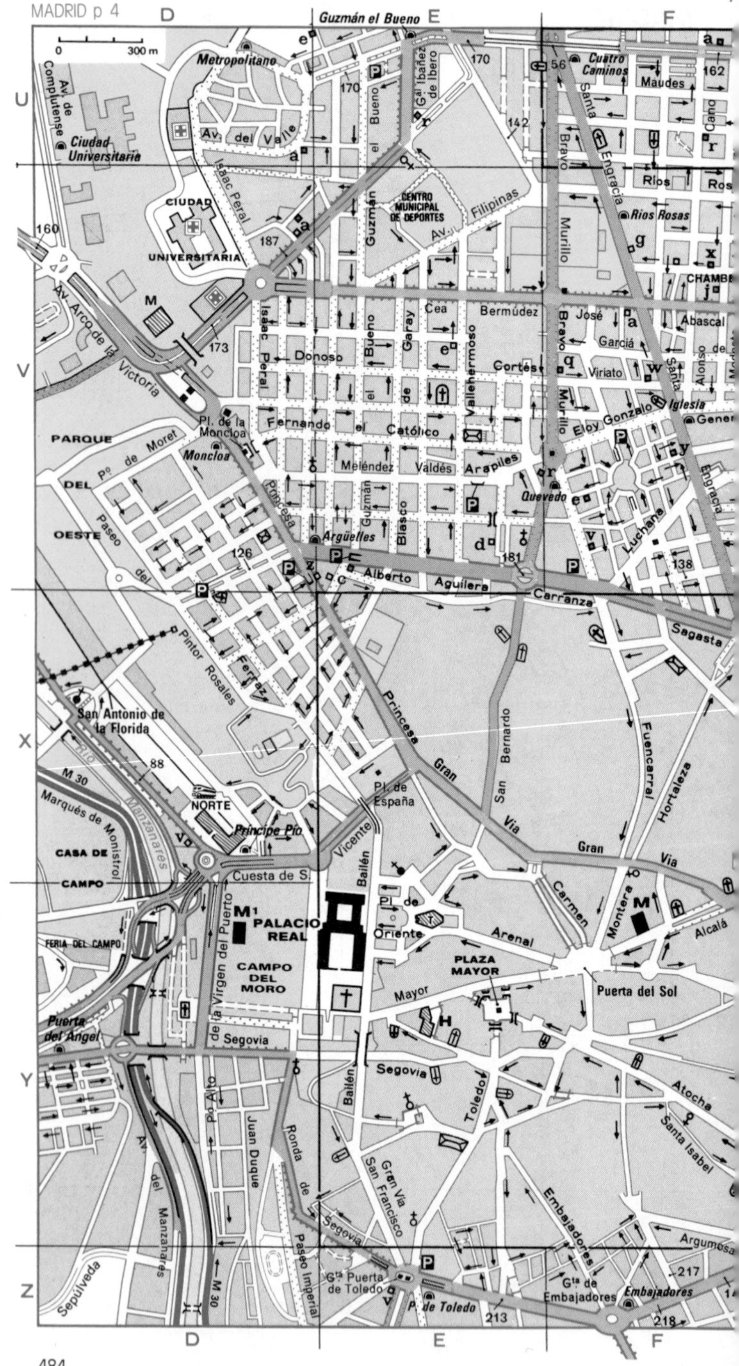
Guzmán el Bueno
Metropolitano
Cuatro Caminos
Ciudad Universitaria
CIUDAD UNIVERSITARIA
CENTRO MUNICIPAL DE DEPORTES
Av. Arco de la Victoria
Pl. de la Moncloa
Moncloa
PARQUE DEL OESTE
Argüelles
Rios Rosas
Iglesia
Quevedo
San Antonio de la Florida
NORTE
Príncipe Pío
CASA DE CAMPO
FERIA DEL CAMPO
PALACIO REAL
CAMPO DEL MORO
PLAZA MAYOR
Puerta del Sol
Puerta del Angel
Gta Puerta de Toledo
P. de Toledo
Gta de Embajadores
Embajadores
Princesa
Gran Vía
San Bernardo
Fuencarral
Hortaleza
Alcalá
Atocha
Santa Isabel
Segovia
Toledo
Bailén
Mayor
Arenal
Carranza
Sagasta
Alberto Aguilera
Fernando el Católico
Meléndez Valdés
Arapiles
Donoso
Cea Bermúdez
Vallehermoso
Bravo Murillo
Santa Engracia
Pintor Rosales
Paseo del Pintor Rosales
Ferraz
Cuesta de S. Vicente
Pl. de España
Pl. de Oriente
Virgen del Puerto
Po Alto
Juan Duque
Ronda de Segovia
Paseo Imperial
Gran Vía de San Francisco
Embajadores
Argumosa
Av. del Manzanares
Sepúlveda
Marqués de Monistrol
Carmen
Montera
Luchana
Eloy Gonzalo
Filipinas
Isaac Peral
Av. de Complutense
Av. del Valle
Maudes
Ríos Rosas
José Abascal
García de Paredes
Cortés
Viriato
Alonso Cano
Gal Ibáñez de Ibero
Pº de Moret
Río Manzanares
M 30
0 300 m

MADRID

Atocha (Ronda de)	FZ	14
Florida (Paseo de la)	DX	88
Lagasca	HVX	116
Marqués de Salamanca (Pl.)	HV	125
Marqués de Urquijo	DV	126
Miguel Ángel	GV	136
Puerta de Hierro (Av.)	DV	160
Reina Cristina (Paseo)	HZ	166
Reina Victoria (Av.)	EU	170
Reyes Católicos (Av.)	DV	173
Ruiz Jiménez (Glorieta)	EV	181
San Francisco de Sales (Pas.)	DV	187
Toledo (Ronda de)	EZ	213
Valencia	FZ	217
Valencia (Ronda de)	FZ	218

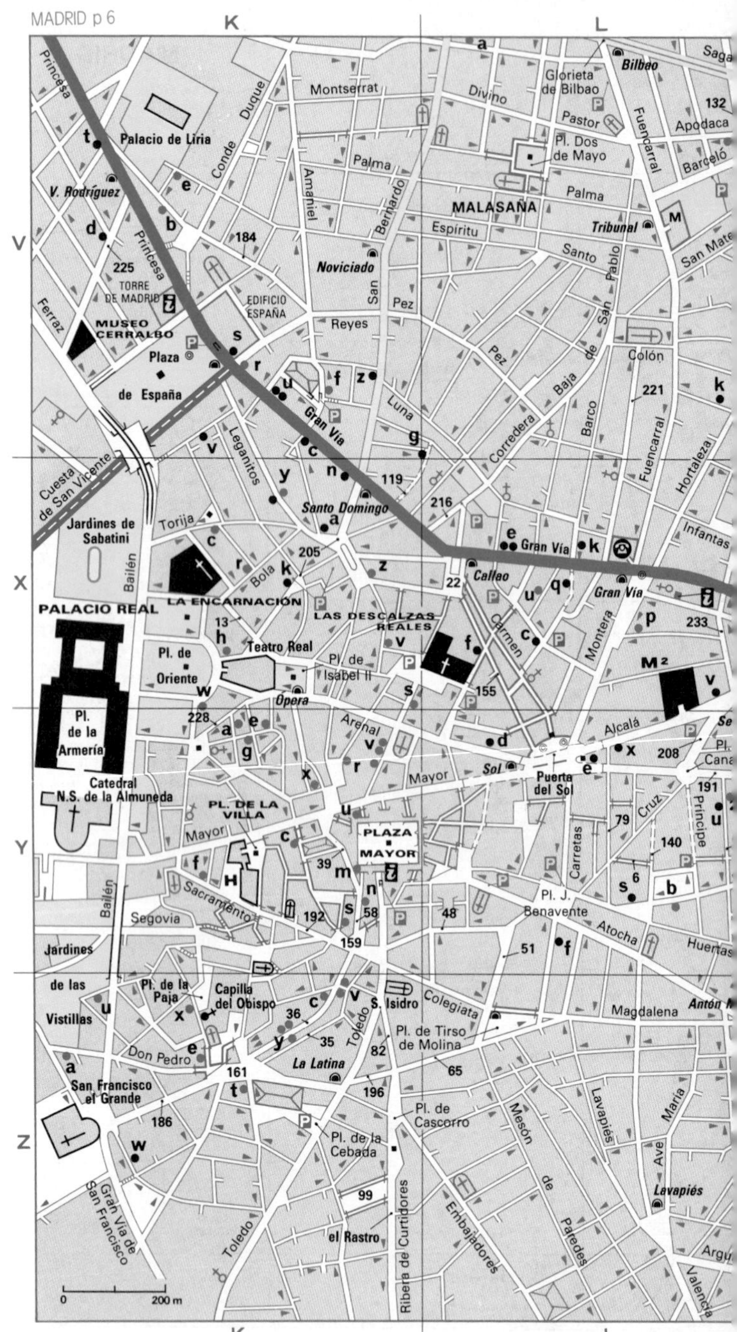
K
L
V
X
Y
Z
Palacio de Liria
V. Rodríguez
Princesa
Conde Duque
Montserrat
Divino
Glorieta de Bilbao
Bilbao
Pastor
Pl. Dos de Mayo
Fuencarral
Apodaca
Barceló
Palma
Amaniel
San Bernardo
MALASAÑA
Espíritu
Tribunal
Santo
San Mateo
Noviciado
TORRE DE MADRID
EDIFICIO ESPAÑA
Ferraz
MUSEO CERRALBO
Reyes
Pez
Baja de San Pablo
Colón
Plaza de España
Gran Vía
Luna
Corredera
Barco
Leganitos
Cuesta de San Vicente
Hortaleza
Santo Domingo
Jardines de Sabatini
Torija
Infantas
Bailén
Bola
Callao
Gran Vía
Montera
PALACIO REAL
LA ENCARNACIÓN
LAS DESCALZAS REALES
Carmen
Teatro Real
Pl. de Oriente
Pl. de Isabel II
Ópera
M²
Pl. de la Armería
Arenal
Alcalá
Sol
Puerta del Sol
Catedral N.S. de la Almuneda
Mayor
PL. DE LA VILLA
PLAZA MAYOR
Cruz
Príncipe
Carretas
Sacramento
Segovia
Pl. J. Benavente
Atocha
Huertas
Jardines de las Vistillas
Pl. de la Paja
Capilla del Obispo
S. Isidro
Colegiata
Magdalena
Antón Martín
Toledo
Pl. de Tirso de Molina
Don Pedro
La Latina
San Francisco el Grande
Pl. de Cascorro
Pl. de la Cebada
Lavapiés
María
Ave
Mesón de Paredes
Embajadores
Ribera de Curtidores
el Rastro
Gran Vía de San Francisco
Argumosa
Valencia
0
200 m

MADRID

Street	Grid	No.
Alcalá	**LMXY**	
Arenal	**KY**	
Carmen	**LX**	
Fuencarral	**LV**	
Gran Vía	**KLX**	
Hortaleza	**LVX**	
Mayor	**KLY**	
Mayor (Plaza)	**KY**	
Montera	**LX**	
Preciados	**LX**	155
Puerta del Sol (Pl.)	**LY**	
San Jerónimo (Carrera de)	**LMY**	191
Álvarez Gato	**LY**	6
Arrieta	**KX**	13
Ayala	**NV**	18
Bárbara de Braganza	**NV**	19
Callao (Pl. de)	**LX**	22
Cava Alta	**KZ**	35
Cava Baja	**KZ**	36
Cava de San Miguel	**KY**	39
Ciudad de Barcelona	**NZ**	41
Colón (Pl. de)	**NV**	44
Concepción Jerónima	**LY**	48
Conde de Romanones	**LY**	51
Cortes (Pl. de las)	**MY**	53
Cuchilleros	**KY**	58
Duque de Alba	**LZ**	65
Echegaray	**LY**	66
Espoz y Mina	**LY**	79
Estudios	**KZ**	82
Fernando el Santo	**NV**	85
Gen. Vara de Rey (Pl.)	**KZ**	99
Goya	**NV**	100
Independencia (Pl. de la)	**NX**	103
Infanta Isabel (Pas.)	**NZ**	105
Libreros	**KX**	119
Madrazo (Los)	**MY**	121
Mejía Lequerica	**LMV**	132
Núñez de Arce	**LY**	140
Puerta Cerrada (Pl.)	**KY**	159
Puerta de Moros (Pl.)	**KZ**	161
Recoletos	**NX**	163
San Bernardino	**KV**	184
San Francisco (Carrera de)	**KZ**	186
San Justo	**KY**	192
San Millán	**KZ**	196
Santa Engracia	**MV**	203
Santo Domingo (Cuesta, Pl. de)	**KX**	205
Sevilla	**LY**	208
Tudescos	**LX**	216
Valverde	**LV**	221
Ventura Rodríguez	**KV**	225
Ventura de la Vega	**LY**	227
Vergara	**KY**	228
Villa de París (Pl.)	**NV**	232
Virgen de los Peligros	**LX**	233

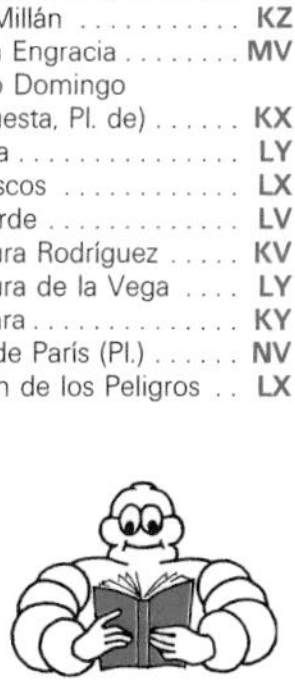

The names of main shopping streets are indicated in red at the beginning of the list of streets.

Carlos V without rest, Maestro Vitoria 5, ✉ 28013, ☎ 531 41 00, Telex 4854
Fax 531 37 61 - |‡| ▤ TV ☎. AE ⓓ E VISA JCB. ✂ LX
67 rm ☕ 10300/12960.

Atlántico without rest, Gran Vía 38-3º, ✉ 28013, ☎ 522 64 80, Telex 4314
Fax 531 02 10 - |‡| ▤ TV ☎. AE ⓓ E VISA JCB. ✂ LX
☕ 750 - **80 rm** 9960/12920.

Tryp Washington, Gran Vía 72, ✉ 28013, ☎ 541 72 27, Telex 48773, Fax 547 51
- |‡| ▤ TV ☎. AE ⓓ E VISA. ✂ KV
Meals (at hotel ***Tryp Menfis*** above) - ☕ 925 - **120 rm** 11800/14800.

Los Condes without rest, Los Libreros 7, ✉ 28004, ☎ 521 54 55, Telex 4273
Fax 521 78 82 - |‡| ▤ TV ☎. AE ⓓ E VISA JCB. ✂ KLV
☕ 600 - **68 rm** 7900/9900.

California without rest, Gran Vía 38, ✉ 28013, ☎ 522 47 03, Fax 531 61 01 - |‡|
TV ☎. AE ⓓ E VISA. ✂ LX
☕ 350 - **26 rm** 6700/8900.

Paradis Madrid, Marqués de Cubas 14, ✉ 28014, ☎ 429 73 03, Fax 429 32 95 -
AE ⓓ E VISA. ✂ MY
closed Saturday lunch, Sunday, Bank Holidays, Holy Week and August - **Meals** a la car
4325/5450.

El Landó, pl. Gabriel Miró 8, ✉ 28005, ☎ 366 76 81, Fax 366 76 81, Tasteful decor
▤. AE ⓓ E VISA. ✂ KZ
closed Sunday, Bank Holidays and August - **Meals** a la carte 3900/5900.

Moaña, Hileras 4, ✉ 28013, ☎ 548 29 14, Fax 541 65 98, Galician rest - ▤ 🚗.
ⓓ E VISA JCB. ✂ KY
closed Sunday - **Meals** a la carte 3440/5600.

Bajamar, Gran Vía 78, ✉ 28013, ☎ 548 48 18, Fax 559 13 26, Seafood - ▤. AE
E VISA JCB. ✂ KV
Meals a la carte 4600/6800.

El Espejo, paseo de Recoletos 31, ✉ 28004, ☎ 308 23 47, Fax 593 22 23, « Old Paris
style café » - ▤. AE ⓓ E VISA. ✂ NV
closed Saturday lunch - **Meals** a la carte approx. 4750.

Errota-Zar, Jovellanos 3-1º, ✉ 28014, ☎ 531 25 64, Fax 531 25 64 - ▤. AE ⓓ E VISA.
closed Sunday and Holy Week - **Meals** a la carte 3700/4150. MY

Ainhoa, Bárbara de Braganza 12, ✉ 28004, ☎ 308 27 26, Basque rest - ▤. AE E VISA.
closed Sunday and August - **Meals** a la carte 4400/5500. NV

Horno de Santa Teresa, Santa Teresa 12, ✉ 28004, ☎ 308 66 98 - ▤. E VISA.
Meals a la carte 3350/3875. MV

Café de Oriente, pl. de Oriente 2, ✉ 28013, ☎ 541 39 74, Fax 547 77 07, In a cel
- ▤. AE ⓓ E VISA. ✂ KXY
Meals a la carte approx. 5550.

La Gastroteca de Stéphane y Arturo, pl. de Chueca 8, ✉ 28004, ☎ 532 25
French rest - ▤. AE ⓓ E VISA. ✂ MV
closed Saturday lunch, Sunday and August - **Meals** a la carte 4300/5840.

Platerías, pl. de Santa Ana 11, ✉ 28012, ☎ 429 70 48, Early 20C style café - ▤.
ⓓ E VISA. ✂ LY
closed Saturday lunch, Sunday, Holy Week and August - **Meals** a la carte approx. 45

El Asador de Aranda, Preciados 44, ✉ 28013, ☎ 547 21 56, Roast lamb, « Castil
decor » - ▤. AE ⓓ E VISA. ✂ KX
closed Monday dinner and 20 July-20 August - **Meals** a la carte approx. 3875.

Arce, Augusto Figueroa 32, ✉ 28004, ☎ 522 04 40, Fax 522 59 13 - ▤. AE ⓓ
VISA MV
closed Saturday lunch, Sunday and 15 to 31 August - **Meals** a la carte 5255/6120.

El Mentidero de la Villa, Santo Tomé 6, ✉ 28004, ☎ 308 12 85, Fax 319 87
« Original decor » - ▤. AE ⓓ E VISA. ✂ MV
closed Saturday lunch and 15 to 31 August - **Meals** a la carte approx. 4500.

Julián de Tolosa, Cava Baja 18, ✉ 28005, ☎ 365 82 10, Neo-rustic decor. Brais
meat specialities - ▤. AE ⓓ VISA JCB KZ
closed Sunday - **Meals** a la carte approx. 4600.

La Taberna de Liria, Duque de Liria 9, ✉ 28015, ☎ 541 45 19 - ▤. AE ⓓ E VISA.
closed Saturday lunch, Sunday, Bank Holidays and last three weeks in August - **Meal**
la carte 4275/5675. KV

Casa Gallega, pl. de San Miguel 8, ✉ 28005, ☎ 547 30 55, Galician rest - ▤. AE
E VISA JCB KY
Meals a la carte 3650/5600.

La Ópera de Madrid, Amnistía 5, ✉ 28013, ☎ 559 50 92 – ▤. AE ⓓ E VISA. ※
closed Sunday, Bank Holidays and August – **Meals** a la carte 3200/4125. KY g

Casa Parrondo, Trujillos 4, ✉ 28013, ☎ 522 62 34, Asturian rest – ▤. AE ⓓ E VISA
Meals a la carte 5800/6100. KX v

El Rincón de Esteban, Santa Catalina 3, ✉ 28014, ☎ 429 25 16, Fax 365 87 70 – ▤. AE ⓓ E VISA. ※ MY a
closed Sunday dinner and August – **Meals** a la carte 3950/5800.

Robata, Reina 31, ✉ 28004, ☎ 521 85 28, Fax 531 30 63, Japanese rest – ▤. AE ⓓ VISA JCB. ※ LX a
closed Tuesday and Christmas – **Meals** a la carte 2000/4000.

Casa Vallejo, San Lorenzo 9 ☎ 308 61 58 – ▤. AE E VISA. ※ LV f
closed Sunday, Monday dinner, Bank Holidays and August – **Meals** a la carte approx. 3500.

Ciao Madrid, Argensola 7, ✉ 28004, ☎ 308 25 19, Italian rest – ▤. AE ⓓ E VISA JCB. ※ MV t
closed Saturday lunch, Sunday and August – **Meals** a la carte 3100/4000.

La Bola, Bola 5, ✉ 28013, ☎ 547 69 30, Fax 547 04 63, Madrid style stew – ▤. ※ KX r
closed Saturday dinner in July-August and Sunday – **Meals** a la carte 3350/4050.

Taberna Carmencita, Libertad 16, ✉ 28004, ☎ 531 66 12, Typical taverna – ▤. AE ⓓ E VISA. ※ MX u
closed Saturday lunch, Sunday and 10 August-10 September – **Meals** a la carte 3100/4200.

Donzoko, Echegaray 3, ✉ 28014, ☎ 429 57 20, Fax 429 57 20, Japanese rest – ▤. AE ⓓ E VISA JCB. ※ LY z
closed Sunday – **Meals** a la carte 2950/6100.

La Esquina del Real, Amnistía 2, ✉ 28013, ☎ 559 43 09 – ▤. AE E VISA. ※ KY e
closed Saturday lunch, Sunday and 11 to 24 August – **Meals** a la carte 4300/4600.

Ciao Madrid, Apodaca 20, ✉ 28004, ☎ 447 00 36, Italian rest – ▤. AE ⓓ E VISA. ※ LV d
closed Saturday lunch, Sunday and September – **Meals** a la carte 3400/3950.

El Ingenio, Leganitos 10, ✉ 28013, ☎ 541 91 33, Fax 547 35 34 – ▤. AE ⓓ E VISA JCB. ※ KX y
closed Sunday and Bank Holidays – **Meals** a la carte 2200/3350.

Typical atmosphere :

Posada de la Villa, Cava Baja 9, ✉ 28005, ☎ 366 18 80, Fax 366 18 80, « Castilian decor » – ▤. ⓓ E VISA. ※ KZ v
closed Sunday dinner and August – **Meals** a la carte 3275/5125.

Botín, Cuchilleros 17, ✉ 28005, ☎ 366 42 17, Fax 366 84 94, Old Madrid decor. Typical cellar – ▤. AE ⓓ E VISA JCB. ※ KY n
Meals a la carte 2915/3860.

Casa Lucio, Cava Baja 35, ✉ 28005, ☎ 365 32 52, Fax 366 48 66, Castilian decor – ▤. AE ⓓ E VISA. ※ KZ y
closed Saturday lunch and August – **Meals** a la carte approx. 5500.

Las Cuevas de Luis Candelas, Cuchilleros 1, ✉ 28005, ☎ 366 54 28, Fax 366 18 80, Old Madrid decor. Staff in bandit costumes – ▤. ⓓ E VISA. ※ KY m
Meals a la carte 3275/5125.

Taberna del Alabardero, Felipe V-6, ✉ 28013, ☎ 547 25 77, Fax 547 77 07, Typical taverna – ▤. AE ⓓ E VISA JCB. ※ KX h
Meals a la carte 3600/5150.

Retiro, Salamanca, Ciudad Lineal : Paseo de la Castellana, Velázquez, Serrano, Goya, Príncipe de Vergara, Narváez (plan p 5 except where otherwise stated)

Ritz, pl. de la Lealtad 5, ✉ 28014, ☎ 521 28 57, Telex 43986, Fax 532 87 76, – ▤ ▤ TV ☎ – 25/280. AE ⓓ E VISA JCB. ※ plan p 7 NY k
Meals a la carte 6400/7900 – ☕ 2750 – **127 rm** 42900/49500, 29 suites.

Villa Magna, paseo de la Castellana 22, ✉ 28046, ☎ 587 12 34, Telex 22914, Fax 575 31 58, – ▤ ▤ TV ☎ – 25/250. AE ⓓ E VISA JCB. ※ rest GV y
Berceo : **Meals** a la carte 5100/8450 – ☕ 2750 – **164 rm** 38000/42000, 18 suites.

Wellington, Velázquez 8, ✉ 28001, ☎ 575 44 00, Telex 22700, Fax 576 41 64, – ▤ ▤ TV ☎ – 25/300. AE ⓓ E VISA. ※ HX t
Meals (see rest. ***El Fogón*** below) – ☕ 2200 – **198 rm** 20750/33250, 25 suites.

Meliá Confort Los Galgos, Claudio Coello 139, ✉ 28006, ☎ 562 66 00, Telex 43957, Fax 561 76 62 – ▤ ▤ TV ☎ – 25/300. AE ⓓ E VISA JCB. ※ HV a
Diábolo *(closed August)* **Meals** a la carte 3225/4975 – ☕ 1450 – **358 rm** 16120/27300.

Tryp Fénix, Hermosilla 2, 28001, 431 67 00, Fax 576 06 61 – 25/100. plan p 7 NV
Meals 2500 – 1700 – **213 rm** 22950/28750, 13 suites.

Meliá Avenida América, Juan Ignacio Luca de Tena 36, 28027, 320 30 Fax 320 14 40, – 25/1200. NE : by Av. de América HV
Meals a la carte 4100/5450 – 1650 – **210 rm** 20800/25600, 18 suites.

Sofitel Madrid-Aeropuerto, Campo de las Naciones, 28042, 721 00 Telex 45008, Fax 721 05 15, – 50/120. NE : by Av. de América HV
Meals a la carte 4600/5750 – 1870 – **175 rm** 24610/27820, 3 suites.

NH Príncipe de Vergara, Príncipe de Vergara 92, 28006, 563 26 Fax 563 72 53 – 25/300. HV
Meals 3150 – 1900 – **167 rm** 20450/28440, 3 suites.

Emperatriz, López de Hoyos 4, 28006, 563 80 88, Fax 563 98 04 – 25/150. GV
Meals 2500 – 1400 – **155 rm** 22000/26000, 3 suites.

NH Sanvy, Goya 3, 28001, 576 08 00, Fax 575 24 43 – 25/1 plan p 7 NV
Meals (see rest. ***Sorolla*** below) – 1900 – **144 rm** 20450/28440, 15 suites.

Agumar coffee shop only, paseo Reina Cristina 7, 28014, 552 69 00, Telex 228 Fax 433 60 95 – 25/150. HZ
1400 – **245 rm** 14750/18500.

Novotel Madrid, Albacete 1, 28027, 405 46 00, Fax 404 11 05, – 25/250. E : by M 30 JY
Meals a la carte 2900/4500 – 1475 – **236 rm** 17655/19100.

Pintor, Goya 79, 28001, 435 75 45, Telex 23281, Fax 576 81 57 – 25/350. HX
Meals 1900 – 1590 – **174 rm** 15460/20500, 2 suites.

Conde de Orgaz, av. Moscatelar 24, 28043, 388 40 99, Fax 388 00 09 – 25/100. NE : by López de Hoyos HU
Meals 2500 – 1150 – **89 rm** 14200/17800.

NH Parque Avenidas, Biarritz 2, 28028, 361 02 88, Fax 361 21 38, – 25/400. JV
Meals 3600 – 1800 – **198 rm** 20875/26100, 1 suite.

NH Lagasca, Lagasca 64, 28001, 575 46 06, Fax 575 16 94 – 25/60. rest HX
Meals *(closed Saturday, Sunday and August)* 1700 – 1500 – **100 rm** 17950/249

NH Alcalá, Alcalá 66, 28009, 435 10 60, Telex 48094, Fax 435 11 05 – 25/100. HX
Meals 2500 – 1900 – **153 rm** 18800/26100.

G.H. Colón, Pez Volador 11, 28007, 573 59 00, Telex 22984, Fax 573 08 09, – 25/250. JY
Meals a la carte approx. 4900 – 1100 – **389 rm** 12100/17600.

Novotel Madrid-Campo de las Naciones, Campo de las Naciones, 280 721 18 18, Fax 721 11 22, – 25/400. NE : by Av. de América HV
Meals 2300 – 1440 – **240 rm** 16800/17850, 6 suites.

Convención coffee shop only, O'Donnell 53, 28009, 574 84 00, Telex 239 Fax 574 56 01 – 25/800. JX
1300 – **739 rm** 11200/14000, 51 suites.

Serrano without rest, Marqués de Villamejor 8, 28006, 435 52 00, Fax 435 48 – GHV
1000 – **30 rm** 12500/15500, 4 suites.

NH Balboa, Núñez de Balboa 112, 28006, 563 03 24, Fax 562 69 80 – 25/30. HV
Meals 2000 – 1500 – **122 rm** 15200/18700.

NH Sur without rest, paseo Infanta Isabel 9, 28014, 539 94 00, Fax 467 09 9 – 25/30. plan p 7 NZ
1300 – **68 rm** 15600/21720.

Abeba without rest, Alcántara 63, 28006, 401 16 50, Fax 402 75 91 – HV
650 – **90 rm** 8500/10500.

XXXX **Club 31,** Alcalá 58, ✉ 28014, ☎ 531 00 92 – ▤. AE ⓓ E VISA. ⚔ plan p. 7 NX e
closed Bank Holidays and August – **Meals** a la carte approx. 8300.

XXXX **El Amparo,** Puigcerdá 8, ✉ 28001, ☎ 431 64 56, Fax 575 54 91, « Original decor » – ▤. AE VISA. ⚔ HX h
✿ *closed Saturday lunch, Sunday and 11 to 17 August* – **Meals** a la carte 7550/8850
Spec. Mousse de ventresca de bonito con bogavante. Rabo de buey guisado al vino tinto. Soufflé caliente de chocolate con crema helada.

XXX **El Fogón,** Villanueva 34, ✉ 28001, ☎ 575 44 00, Telex 22700, Fax 576 41 64 – ▤. AE ⓓ E VISA. ⚔ HX t
closed August – **Meals** a la carte 5900/6900.

XXX **Sorolla,** Hermosilla 4, ✉ 28001, ☎ 431 27 15, Telex 44994, Fax 575 24 43 – ▤. AE ⓓ E VISA JCB. ⚔ plan p. 7 NV r
closed Sunday – **Meals** a la carte approx. 4800.

XXX **Suntory,** paseo de la Castellana 36, ✉ 28046, ☎ 577 37 34, Fax 577 44 55, Japanese rest – ▤ 🚗. AE ⓓ E VISA JCB. ⚔ GV d
closed Sunday and Bank Holidays – **Meals** a la carte approx. 6450.

XXX **Villa y Corte de Madrid,** Serrano 110, ✉ 28006, ☎ 564 50 19, Fax 564 50 19, Tasteful decor – ▤. AE E VISA. ⚔ HV a
closed Sunday and August – **Meals** a la carte 3125/4550.

XXX **El Gran Chambelán,** Ayala 46, ✉ 28001, ☎ 431 77 45 – ▤. AE ⓓ VISA. ⚔
closed Sunday – **Meals** a la carte 3200/3900. HX r

XXX **Balzac,** Moreto 7, ✉ 28014, ☎ 420 01 77, Fax 429 83 70 – ▤. AE ⓓ E VISA. ⚔
closed Sunday and August – **Meals** a la carte 4800/5700. plan p 7 NY a

XXX **Pedro Larumbe,** Serrano 61-top floor, ✉ 28006, ☎ 575 11 12, Fax 562 16 09 – 🛗 ▤. AE ⓓ E VISA. ⚔ HV d
closed Saturday lunch, Sunday and one week in August – **Meals** a la carte approx. 5950.

XXX **Paradis Casa América,** paseo de Recoletos 2, ✉ 28001, ☎ 575 45 40, Fax 576 02 15, 🏖 – ▤. AE ⓓ E VISA. ⚔ NX n
closed Saturday lunch and Sunday – **Meals** a la carte approx. 5500.

XXX **Ponteareas,** Claudio Coello 96, ✉ 28006, ☎ 575 58 73, Fax 541 65 98, Galician rest – ▤ 🚗. AE ⓓ E VISA JCB. ⚔ HV w
closed Sunday, Bank Holidays and August – **Meals** a la carte 3440/5795.

XXX **Castelló 9,** Castelló 9, ✉ 28001, ☎ 435 00 67, Fax 435 91 34 – ▤. AE ⓓ E VISA. ⚔ HX e
closed Sunday and Bank Holidays – **Meals** a la carte 3550/5050.

XX **La Paloma,** Jorge Juan 39, ✉ 28001, ☎ 576 86 92 – ▤. AE E VISA. ⚔ HX g
✿ *closed Sunday, Bank Holidays, Holy Week and August* – **Meals** a la carte 4050/6250
Spec. Lasagña de txangurro y espinacas. Pichón de Las Landas relleno de foie. Tarta fina de hojaldre con manzana.

XX **Viridiana,** Juan de Mena 14, ✉ 28014, ☎ 523 44 78, Fax 532 42 74 – ▤. AE VISA plan p. 7 NY r
✿ *closed Sunday, Holy Week, Chirstmas and August* – **Meals** a la carte 5200/7300
Spec. Arenque marinado y sardina ahumada sobre blinis de trigo. Salteado de avestruz a la hierbabuena. Papaya rellena de flores de naranjo en salsa de almendras.

XX **Al Mounia,** Recoletos 5, ✉ 28001, ☎ 435 08 28, North African rest, « Oriental atmosphere » – ▤. AE ⓓ E VISA plan p 7 NV u
closed Sunday, Monday and August – **Meals** a la carte 4300/4800.

XX **El Chiscón de Castelló,** Castelló 3, ✉ 28001, ☎ 575 56 62, « Welcoming atmosphere » – ▤. AE E VISA. ⚔ HX e
closed Sunday, Bank Holidays and August – **Meals** a la carte 3150/4575.

XX **Rafa,** Narváez 68, ✉ 28009, ☎ 573 10 87, 🏖 – ▤. AE ⓓ E VISA. ⚔ HY a
Meals a la carte 4300/6350.

XX **Casa d'a Troya,** Emiliano Barral 14, ✉ 28043, ☎ 416 44 55, Galician rest – ▤. E VISA. ⚔ E : by M 30 JY
✿ *closed Sunday, Bank Holidays and 15 July-1 September* – **Meals** (booking essential) a la carte approx. 4850
Spec. Pulpo a la gallega. Merluza a la gallega. Tarta de Santiago.

XX **El Asador de Aranda,** Diego de León 9, ✉ 28006, ☎ 563 02 46, Roast lamb – ▤. AE ⓓ E VISA. ⚔ HV s
closed Sunday dinner and August – **Meals** a la carte approx. 4250.

XX **Guisando,** Núñez de Balboa 75, ✉ 28006, ☎ 575 10 10 – ▤. AE ⓓ E VISA. ⚔ HV f
closed Saturday lunch, Sunday, Holy Week and 11 to 24 August – **Meals** a la carte 2500/3950.

XX **St. James,** Juan Bravo 26, ✉ 28006, ☎ 575 00 69, Rice dishes – ▤. AE VISA.
closed Sunday – **Meals** a la carte 5000/6000. HV

XX **Nicolás,** Villalar 4, ✉ 28001, ☎ 431 77 37, Fax 431 77 37 – ▤. AE ⓓ E VISA
closed Sunday, Monday, Holy Week and August – **Meals** a la carte 350
4300. plan p 7 NX

X **La Giralda IV,** Claudio Coello 24, ✉ 28001, ☎ 576 40 69, Andalusian rest – ▤. AE
E VISA. HX
closed Sunday in summer and 15 to 31 August – **Meals** a la carte approx. 5100.

X **Asador Velate,** Jorge Juan 91, ✉ 28009, ☎ 435 10 24, Basque rest – ▤. AE ⓓ
VISA. HJX
closed Sunday and August – **Meals** a la carte 4000/5800.

X **Pelotari,** Recoletos 3, ✉ 28001, ☎ 578 24 97, Fax 431 60 04 – ▤. AE ⓓ E VISA NV
closed Sunday and 15 days in August – **Meals** a la carte approx. 4600.

X ✿ **La Trainera,** Lagasca 60, ✉ 28001, ☎ 576 05 75, Fax 575 06 31, seafood – ▤. AE
VISA. HX
closed Sunday and August – **Meals** a la carte 4300/5600
Spec. Salpicón de mariscos. Delicias de merluza con angulas. Langosta a la americana.

X ✿ **El Pescador,** José Ortega y Gasset 75, ✉ 28006, ☎ 402 12 90, seafood – ▤. E VISA.
closed Sunday, Holy Week and August – **Meals** a la carte 4550/5750 JV
Spec. Angulas de Aguinaga. Lenguado Evaristo. Bogavante a la americana.

Arganzuela, Carabanchel, Villaverde : Antonio López, Paseo de Las Delicias, Pas de Santa María de la Cabeza (plan p 4 to 6 except where otherwise stated)

Rafael Pirámides, paseo de las Acacias 40, ✉ 28005, ☎ 517 18 28, Fax 517 00
– |‡| ▤ TV ☎ ♿ ⇔. AE ⓓ E VISA. rest S : by Gta. Puerta de Toledo EZ
Meals *(closed Saturday, Sunday and August)* 4500 – ☐ 1100 – **84 rm** 11500/1420
9 suites.

Carlton, paseo de las Delicias 26, ✉ 28045, ☎ 539 71 00, Telex 44571, Fax 527 85
– |‡| ▤ TV ☎. AE ⓓ E VISA. plan p 5 GZ
Meals 3150 – ☐ 1400 – **112 rm** 13125/16400.

Praga coffee shop only, Antonio López 65, ✉ 28019, ☎ 469 06 00, Telex 2282
Fax 469 83 25 – |‡| ▤ TV ☎ ⇔ – 🔔 25/350. AE ⓓ E VISA JCB.
☐ 850 – **428 rm** 10100/12800. S : by Gta. Puerta de Toledo EZ

Aramo, paseo Santa María de la Cabeza 73, ✉ 28045, ☎ 473 91 11, Telex 4588
Fax 473 92 14 – |‡| ▤ TV ☎ ⇔. AE ⓓ E VISA. rest
Meals 1500 – ☐ 1000 – **105 rm** 9600/12000. S : by pl. Emperador Carlos V NZ

Puerta de Toledo, glorieta Puerta de Toledo 4, ✉ 28005, ☎ 474 71 00, Telex 2229
Fax 474 07 47 – |‡| ▤ TV ☎ ⇔ – 🔔 25/30. AE ⓓ E VISA JCB. plano p 6 EZ
Meals (see rest. ***Puerta de Toledo*** below) – ☐ 880 – **152 rm** 7500/11400.

XX ✿ **Hontoria,** pl. del General Maroto 2, ✉ 28045, ☎ 473 04 25 – ▤. AE E VI
S : by Gta. de Embajadores FZ
closed Sunday, Bank Holidays and August – **Meals** a la carte 3650/5300
Spec. Ensalada de sardinas (May-October). Salteado de mollejas de ternera con puré espinacas. Biscuit glacé de nueces con salsa de turrón.

XX **Puerta de Toledo,** glorieta Puerta de Toledo 4, ✉ 28005, ☎ 474 76 7
Fax 474 30 35 – ▤. ⓓ VISA – **Meals** a la carte 2150/3775. plan p 6 EZ

Moncloa : Princesa, Paseo del Pintor Rosales, Paseo de la Florida, Casa de Cam (plan p 4 except where otherwise stated)

Meliá Madrid, Princesa 27, ✉ 28008, ☎ 541 82 00, Telex 22537, Fax 541 19 88,
– |‡| ▤ TV ☎ – 🔔 25/200. AE ⓓ E VISA JCB. plan p 6 KV
Meals 3800 – ☐ 2000 – **253 rm** 27500/30900, 23 suites.

Tryp Monte Real , Arroyofresno 17, ✉ 28035, ☎ 316 21 40, Fax 316 39 3
« Garden », – |‡| ▤ TV ☎ ⇔ Ⓟ – 🔔 25/250. AE ⓓ E VISA.
Meals a la carte approx. 4450 – ☐ 1600 – **76 rm** 17475/21900, 4 suites.
NW : 8 km by Av. Puerta de Hierro DV

Florida Norte, paseo de la Florida 5, ✉ 28008, ☎ 542 83 00, Telex 2367
Fax 547 78 33 – |‡| ▤ TV ☎ ⇔. AE ⓓ E VISA JCB. plan p 4 DX
Meals 2600 – ☐ 900 – **399 rm** 12000/17000.

Sofitel-Plaza de España without rest, Tutor 1, ✉ 28008, ☎ 541 98 80, Telex 431
Fax 542 57 36 – |‡| ▤ TV ☎. AE ⓓ E VISA JCB plan p 6 KV
☐ 1700 – **99 rm** 23500/28000.

XX **Sal Gorda,** Beatriz de Bobadilla 9, ✉ 28040, ☎ 553 95 06 – ▤. AE ⓓ E VISA.
closed Sunday and August – **Meals** a la carte 3490/3900. DEU

X **Currito,** Casa de Campo-Pabellón de Vizcaya, ✉ 28011, ☎ 464 57 04, Fax 479 72 5
, Basque rest – ▤ Ⓟ. AE ⓓ E VISA. W : by Feria del Campo DY
closed Sunday dinner – **Meals** a la carte approx. 6000.

Chamberí : San Bernardo, Fuencarral, Alberto Aguilera, Santa Engracia (plan p. 4 to 7)

NH Santo Mauro, Zurbano 36, ✉ 28010, ✆ 319 69 00, Fax 308 54 77, « Elegant palace with garden », – 25/70. AE D E VISA JCB. GV e
Belagua : **Meals** a la carte approx. 6400 – 2100 – **33 rm** 35000/44000, 4 suites.

Miguel Ángel, Miguel Ángel 31, ✉ 28010, ✆ 442 00 22, Telex 44235, Fax 442 53 20, – 25/300. AE D E VISA. GV c
Meals 3300 – 2000 – **251 rm** 28500/35700, 20 suites.

Castellana Inter-Continental, paseo de la Castellana 49, ✉ 28046, ✆ 310 02 00, Telex 27686, Fax 319 58 53, « Garden », – 25/550. AE D E VISA JCB. GV a
Meals a la carte 3520/6600 – 2500 – **278 rm** 34600/41800, 27 suites.

Mindanao, San Francisco de Sales 15, ✉ 28003, ✆ 549 55 00, Telex 22631, Fax 544 55 96, – 25/200. AE D E VISA JCB. DV a
Meals *(closed August)* 3750 – 1600 – **272 rm** 16500/21000, 9 suites.

G.H. Conde Duque coffee shop only, pl. Conde Valle de Suchil 5, ✉ 28015, ✆ 447 70 00, Telex 22058, Fax 448 35 69 – 25/100. AE D E VISA JCB. EV d
1500 – **142 rm** 16600/25000, 1 suite.

Gran Versalles without rest, Covarrubias 4, ✉ 28010, ✆ 447 57 00, Telex 49150, Fax 446 39 87 – 25/120. AE D E VISA. MV a
975 – **143 rm** 15250/21600, 2 suites.

NH Zurbano, Zurbano 79, ✉ 28003, ✆ 441 45 00, Telex 27578, Fax 441 32 24 – 25/100. AE D E VISA JCB. GV x
Meals a la carte approx. 4100 – 1575 – **263 rm** 18850/26200, 1 suite.

NH Embajada, Santa Engracia 5, ✉ 28010, ✆ 594 02 13, Fax 447 33 12, Spanish style building – 25/45. AE D E VISA. MV r
Meals 1900 – 1400 – **101 rm** 15950.

NH Prisma, Santa Engracia 120, ✉ 28003, ✆ 441 93 77, Fax 442 58 51 – 25/70. AE D E VISA. FV g
Meals a la carte approx. 3600 – 1900 – **103 suites** 17600.

NH Argüelles coffee shop only, Vallehermoso 65, ✉ 28015, ✆ 593 97 77, Fax 594 27 39 – AE D E VISA JCB. EV e
1000 – **75 rm** 17375/21720.

Escultor, Miguel Ángel 3, ✉ 28010, ✆ 310 42 03, Telex 44285, Fax 319 25 84 – 25/150. AE D E VISA JCB. GV s
Meals a la carte approx. 3700 – 1350 – **79 rm** 14000/23000, 3 suites.

Sol Alondras coffee shop only, José Abascal 8, ✉ 28003, ✆ 447 40 00, Telex 49454, Fax 593 88 00 – AE D E VISA JCB. FV a
1020 – **72 rm** 15800/19100.

Jockey, Amador de los Ríos 6, ✉ 28010, ✆ 319 24 35, Fax 319 24 35 – AE D E VISA. NV k
closed Saturday lunch, Sunday, Bank Holidays and August – **Meals** a la carte 7500/9600
Spec. Ensalada de atún marinado a la pimienta verde (May-October). Langostinos fritos con verduras y salsa de soja. Costillar de cordero a la provenzal..

Las Cuatro Estaciones, General Ibáñez de Íbero 5, ✉ 28003, ✆ 553 63 05, Fax 553 32 98, Modern decor – AE D E VISA JCB. EU r
closed Saturday except dinner October-March Sunday and August – **Meals** 4500 and a la carte 4260/5830
Spec. Gazpacho con bogavante (Spring-Summer). Arroz negro con chipirones. Foie caliente a las uvas y Pedro Ximénez.

Lur Maitea, Fernando el Santo 4, ✉ 28010, ✆ 308 03 50, Fax 308 03 93, Basque rest – AE D E VISA. MV u
closed Saturday lunch, Sunday, Bank Holidays and August – **Meals** a la carte 4800/5850.

Annapurna, Zurbano 5, ✉ 28010, ✆ 308 32 49, Indian rest – AE D E VISA MV w
closed Saturday lunch, Sunday and Bank Holidays – **Meals** a la carte 3000/4775.

Solchaga, pl. Alonso Martínez 2, ✉ 28004, ✆ 447 14 96, Fax 593 22 23 – AE D E VISA. MV x
closed Saturday lunch, Sunday and August – **Meals** a la carte 4100/5500.

Kulixka, Fuencarral 124, ✉ 28010, ✆ 447 25 38, seafood – AE D E VISA. FV v
closed Sunday and August – **Meals** a la carte 4100/7300.

Polizón, Viriato 39, ✉ 28010, ✆ 593 39 19, seafood – AE D E VISA JCB.
closed Sunday in winter, Sunday dinner the rest of the year and August – **Meals** a la carte 3325/4250. FV w

La Plaza de Chamberí, pl. de Chamberí 10, ✉ 28010, ✆ 446 06 97 – AE D E VISA JCB. – *closed Sunday* – **Meals** a la carte approx. 4525. FV k

XX **La Fuente Quince,** Modesto Lafuente 15, ✉ 28003, ☎ 442 34 53, Fax 441 90 24 – ▤. AE ⓓ E VISA. ✻ FV
closed Saturday lunch, Sunday and August – **Meals** a la carte 2600/3500.

XX **El Corcho,** Zurbano 4, ✉ 28010, ☎ 308 01 36, Fax 310 32 55 – ▤. AE ⓓ E VISA.
closed Saturday lunch, Sunday and August – **Meals** a la carte 3380/4850. NV

XX **O'Xeito,** paseo de la Castellana 49, ✉ 28046, ☎ 308 23 83, Fax 308 35 94, Galician sty decor. seafood – ▤. AE E VISA GV
closed Saturday lunch, Sunday and August – **Meals** a la carte 4200/5200.

XX **Vatel,** Rafael Calvo 40, ✉ 28010, ☎ 310 00 74 – ▤. AE E VISA GV
closed Sunday, Bank Holidays and August – **Meals** a la carte 2950/4425.

X **Pinocchio,** Orfila 2, ✉ 28010, ☎ 308 16 47, Fax 766 98 04, Italian rest – ▤. AE E VISA. ✻ NV
closed Saturday lunch, Sunday and August – **Meals** a la carte 2925/3790.

X **Balear,** Sagunto 18, ✉ 28010, ☎ 447 91 15, Rice dishes – ▤. AE E VISA. ✻
closed dinner Sunday and Monday – **Meals** a la carte approx. 3500. FV

X **La Despensa,** Cardenal Cisneros 6, ✉ 28010, ☎ 446 17 94 – ▤. AE ⓓ E VISA.
closed Monday in summer, Sunday dinner and Monday the rest of the year and Septemb – **Meals** a la carte 2450/2950. FV

Chamartín, Tetuán : Paseo de la Castellana, Capitán Haya, Orense, Alberto Alcoce Paseo de la Habana (plan p 3 except where otherwise stated)

Meliá Castilla, Capitán Haya 43, ✉ 28020, ☎ 567 50 00, Telex 23142, Fax 567 50 5 – ⛀ – 🛗 ▤ TV ☎ ♿ 🚗 – 🏛 25/800. AE ⓓ E VISA JCB. ✻ GS
Meals (see rest. ***L'Albufera*** and rest. ***La Fragata*** below) – ☕ 2300 – **896 r** 26900/30900, 14 suites.

Holiday Inn, pl. Carlos Trías Beltrán 4 (entrance by Orense 22-24), ✉ 2802 ☎ 456 80 00, Telex 44709, Fax 456 80 01, Fā, ⛀ – 🛗 ▤ TV ☎ ♿ – 🏛 25/400. ⓓ E VISA JCB. ✻ rest GT
La Terraza : **Meals** a la carte 3450/6425 - ***La Tasca*** *(buffet only, closed Saturday, Sund and August)* **Meals** 3200 – ☕ 2050 – **282 rm** 25650/28650, 31 suites.

Eurobuilding, Padre Damián 23, ✉ 28036, ☎ 345 45 00, Telex 22548, Fax 345 45 7 – « Garden and terrace with ⛀ », Fā – 🛗 ▤ TV ☎ 🚗 – 🏛 25/900. AE ⓓ E VI JCB. ✻ HS
La Taberna : **Meals** a la carte 4200/5500 - ***Le Relais :*** **Meals** a la carte 3025/4100 – 1975 – **416 rm** 24500/29950, 84 suites.

Cuzco coffee shop only, paseo de la Castellana 133, ✉ 28046, ☎ 556 06 0 Telex 22464, Fax 556 03 72, Fā – 🛗 ▤ TV ☎ 🚗 🅟 – 🏛 25/450. AE ⓓ E VISA. ✻ ☕ 1190 – **320 rm** 18500/22500, 8 suites. GS

Augusta Club 143, López de Hoyos 143, ✉ 28002, ☎ 519 91 91, Fax 519 67 73 – 🛗 ▤ TV ☎ 🚗 – 🏛 25/80. AE E VISA. ✻ NE : by López de Hoyos HU
Meals 1800 – ☕ 1000 – **120 suites** 13500/16000.

Chamartín without rest, Chamartín railway station, ✉ 28036, ☎ 323 18 3 Telex 49201, Fax 733 02 14 – 🛗 ▤ TV ☎ – 🏛 25/500. AE ⓓ VISA. ✻ HR
☕ 1200 – **360 rm** 14300/16600, 18 suites.

NH La Habana, paseo de la Habana 73, ✉ 28036, ☎ 345 82 84, Fax 457 75 79 – ▤ TV ☎ 🚗 – 🏛 25/250. AE ⓓ E VISA JCB. ✻ HT
Meals 3700 – ☕ 1900 – **157 rm** 18800/26100.

Orense 38, Pedro Teixeira 5, ✉ 28020, ☎ 597 15 68, Fax 597 12 95, Fā – 🛗 ▤ ☎ 🚗. AE ⓓ E VISA. ✻ GT
Meals a la carte 2900/4800 – ☕ 1100 – **140 rm** 15520/18700.

Foxá 32, Agustín de Foxá 32, ✉ 28036, ☎ 733 10 60, Fax 314 11 65 – 🛗 ▤ TV 🚗 – 🏛 25/250. AE ⓓ E VISA. ✻ HR
Meals 1500 – ☕ 1100 – **63 rm** 12500, 98 suites.

Foxá 25, Agustín de Foxá 25, ✉ 28036, ☎ 323 11 19, Fax 314 53 11 – 🛗 ▤ TV 🚗. AE ⓓ E VISA. ✻ HR
Meals 1500 – ☕ 1100 – **121 suites** 12500.

Castilla Plaza, paseo de la Castellana 220, ✉ 28046, ☎ 323 11 86, Fax 315 54 06 – 🛗 ▤ TV ☎ 🚗 – 🏛 25/150. AE ⓓ VISA GS
Meals 2000 – ☕ 1450 – **147 rm** 17700/19700.

El Gran Atlanta without rest, Comandante Zorita 34, ✉ 28020, ☎ 553 59 0 Fax 533 08 58, Fā – 🛗 ▤ TV ☎ 🚗 – 🏛 25/120. AE ⓓ E VISA. ✻ FT
☕ 1200 – **180 rm** 16250/22500.

El Jardín without rest, carret. N I-km 5'7 (entrance by M 40-Service road), ✉ 2805 ☎ 302 83 36, Fax 766 86 91, ⛀, 🌳, 🎾 – 🛗 ▤ TV ☎ 🚗 🅟. AE ⓓ E VISA. ✻
41 suites ☕ 11000/12500. N : by M 30 HR

Aristos, av. Pío XII-34, ✉ 28016, ☎ 345 04 50, Fax 345 10 23 – AE ⓓ E VISA. HS d
Meals (see rest. ***El Chaflán*** below) – ☕ 900 – **24 rm** 14250/19000, 1 suite.

La Residencia de El Viso without rest, Nervión 8, ✉ 28002, ☎ 564 03 70, Fax 564 19 65 – AE ⓓ E VISA. HU c
☕ 750 – **12 rm** 9000/14000.

Zalacaín, Álvarez de Baena 4, ✉ 28006, ☎ 561 48 40, Fax 561 47 32, – AE ⓓ E VISA JCB. plan p 5 GV b
closed Saturday lunch, Sunday, Bank Holidays, Holy Week and August – **Meals** 6950 and a la carte 6200/9200
Spec. Ensalada de bogavante. Merluza a la flor de tomillo. Crujiente de chocolate con piña templada.

Príncipe y Serrano, Serrano 240, ✉ 28016, ☎ 458 62 31, Fax 458 86 76 – AE ⓓ E VISA. HT a
closed Saturday lunch, Sunday, Bank Holidays and August – **Meals** a la carte 5200/7300.

La Máquina, Sor Ángela de la Cruz 22, ✉ 28020, ☎ 572 33 18, Fax 570 13 04 – AE ⓓ VISA. FS e
closed Sunday – **Meals** a la carte 4200/5050.

El Bodegón, Pinar 15, ✉ 28006, ☎ 562 88 44 – AE ⓓ E VISA. plan p 5 GV q
closed Saturday lunch, Sunday, Bank Holidays and August – **Meals** a la carte 5850/7950.

Príncipe de Viana, Manuel de Falla 5, ✉ 28036, ☎ 457 15 49, Fax 457 52 83, Basque rest – AE ⓓ E VISA JCB. GT c
closed Saturday lunch, Sunday, Bank Holidays, Holy Week and August – **Meals** a la carte 4950/5875
Spec. Crema montada de bacalao y ventresca en ensalada. Salmonetes a la vinagreta de trufas. Pichón guisado al jengibre.

Nicolasa, Velázquez 150, ✉ 28002, ☎ 563 17 35, Fax 564 32 75 – AE ⓓ E VISA. HU a
closed Holy Week and August – **Meals** a la carte 4150/6050.

O'Pazo, Reina Mercedes 20, ✉ 28020, ☎ 553 23 33, Fax 554 90 72, seafood – E VISA. FT p
closed Sunday and August – **Meals** a la carte 4550/5650.

L'Albufera, Capitán Haya 43, ✉ 28020, ☎ 567 51 97, Fax 567 50 51, Rice dishes – AE ⓓ E VISA JCB. GS c
Meals a la carte 4500/5650.

La Fragata, Capitán Haya 43, ✉ 28020, ☎ 567 51 96 – AE ⓓ E VISA. GS c
closed August – **Meals** a la carte approx. 5500.

José Luis, Rafael Salgado 11, ✉ 28036, ☎ 457 50 36, Fax 344 18 37 – AE ⓓ E VISA. GT m
closed Sunday and August – **Meals** a la carte approx. 6000.

Bogavante, Capitán Haya 20, ✉ 28020, ☎ 556 21 14, Fax 597 00 79, seafood – AE ⓓ E VISA JCB. GT d
closed Sunday dinner – **Meals** a la carte 3100/7400.

Señorío de Alcocer, Alberto Alcocer 1, ✉ 28036, ☎ 345 16 96 – AE ⓓ E VISA. GS e
closed Saturday lunch, Sunday, Bank Holidays and August – **Meals** a la carte approx. 6500.

El Olivo, General Gallegos 1, ✉ 28036, ☎ 359 15 35, Fax 345 91 83 – AE ⓓ E VISA JCB. HS c
closed Sunday, Monday and 15 to 30 August – **Meals** 5600 and a la carte 4650/5900
Spec. Milhojas de emperador con vinagreta y verduras. Foie con salsa de Pedro Ximénez. Bonito sobre compota de tomate y cebolla confitada (season).

Goizeko Kabi, Comandante Zorita 37, ✉ 28020, ☎ 533 01 85, Fax 533 02 14, Basque rest – AE ⓓ E VISA. FT a
closed Saturday lunch 15 June-15 September and Sunday – **Meals** a la carte 5750/6900
Spec. Parrillada de trigueros y xixas (April-June). Talos de bacalao. Becada asada al viejo brandy (November-March).

Cabo Mayor, Juan Ramón Jiménez 37, ✉ 28036, ☎ 350 87 76, Fax 359 16 21 – AE ⓓ E VISA. GHS r
closed Saturday lunch, Sunday, Holy Week and 15 to 31 August – **Meals** a la carte 5900/7700.

Blanca de Navarra, av. de Brasil 13, ✉ 28020, ☎ 555 10 29 – AE ⓓ E VISA GT q
closed Sunday and August – **Meals** a la carte approx. 6000.

XXXX **Lutecia,** Corazón de María 78, ✉ 28002, ☎ 519 34 15 – ▤. AE ⓓ E VISA. ⚡
closed Saturday lunch, Sunday, Bank Holidays and August – **Meals** a la carte 295(
3550. NE : by López de Hoyos HU

XXXX **Aldaba,** Alberto Alcocer 5, ✉ 28036, ☎ 345 21 93 – ▤. AE ⓓ E VISA. ⚡ GS
closed Saturday lunch, Sunday and August – **Meals** a la carte 4350/6025.

XXXX **El Foque,** Suero de Quiñones 22, ✉ 28002, ☎ 519 25 72, Fax 519 52 61, Cod dish
– ▤. AE ⓓ E VISA. ⚡ HU
closed Sunday – **Meals** a la carte 4450/5150.

XX **Combarro,** Reina Mercedes 12, ✉ 28020, ☎ 554 77 84, Fax 534 25 01, seafood –
AE ⓓ E VISA JCB. ⚡ FT
closed Sunday dinner and August – **Meals** a la carte 4650/7955.

XX **La Tahona,** Capitán Haya 21 (side), ✉ 28020, ☎ 555 04 41, Roast lamb, « Castilia
medieval decor » – ▤. AE ⓓ E VISA. ⚡ GT
closed Sunday dinner and August – **Meals** a la carte 3400/3975.

XX **De Funy,** Serrano 213, ✉ 28016, ☎ 457 95 22, Fax 458 85 84, 🏠, Lebanese rest
▤. AE ⓓ E VISA. ⚡ HT
Meals a la carte 3600/4150.

XX **Gaztelupe,** Comandante Zorita 32, ✉ 28020, ☎ 534 90 28, Basque rest – ▤. AE
E VISA. ⚡ FT
closed Sunday 15 June-15 September and Sunday dinner the rest of the year – **Meals**
la carte 4600/5100.

XX **Asador Errota-Zar,** Corazón de María 32, ✉ 28002, ☎ 413 52 24, Fax 519 30 84
▤. AE ⓓ E VISA. ⚡ NE : by Cartagena HV
closed Sunday, Holy Week and August – **Meals** a la carte approx. 4700.

XX **Carta Marina,** Padre Damián 40, ✉ 28036, ☎ 458 68 26, Fax 350 78 83 – ▤. AE
E VISA. ⚡ HS
closed Sunday, Holy Week and August – **Meals** a la carte 3850/5650.

XX **Serramar,** Rosario Pino 12, ✉ 28020, ☎ 570 07 90, Fax 570 48 09, seafood – ▤.
ⓓ E VISA GS
closed Sunday – **Meals** a la carte 3800/4900.

XX **Sacha,** Juan Hurtado de Mendoza 11 (back), ✉ 28036, ☎ 345 59 52, 🏠 – ▤. AE
E VISA. ⚡ GHS
closed Sunday, Bank Holidays, Holy Week and 10 to 31 August – **Meals** a la carte appro
5000.

XX **Rianxo,** Oruro 11, ✉ 28016, ☎ 457 10 06, Galician rest – ▤. AE ⓓ E VISA. ⚡
closed Sunday dinner – **Meals** a la carte 4100/6300. HT

XX **El Chaflán,** av. Pío XII-34, ✉ 28016, ☎ 350 61 93, Fax 345 10 23, 🏠 – ▤. AE ⓓ
VISA. ⚡ HS
closed Sunday dinner and Holy Week – **Meals** a la carte 4075/4925.

XX **Asador de Roa,** Pintor Juan Gris 5, ✉ 28020, ☎ 555 39 28, Fax 555 78 13 – ▤.
ⓓ E VISA GT
Meals a la carte approx. 3500.

XX **House of Ming,** paseo de la Castellana 74, ✉ 28046, ☎ 561 10 13, Fax 561 98 2
Chinese rest – ▤. AE ⓓ E VISA. ⚡ plan p 5 GV
Meals a la carte 2805/3565.

X **La Ancha,** Príncipe de Vergara 204, ✉ 28002, ☎ 563 89 77, 🏠 – ▤. AE ⓓ E VIS
⚡ HT
closed Sunday, Bank Holidays, Holy Week and Christmas – **Meals** a la carte 3400/
4900.

X **El Asador de Aranda,** pl. de Castilla 3, ✉ 28046, ☎ 733 87 02, Roast lamb. Castilia
decor – ▤. AE ⓓ E VISA. ⚡ GS
closed Sunday dinner and 15 August-10 September – Meals a la carte approx. 4250.

X **Zacarías de Santander,** Rosario Pino 17, ✉ 28020, ☎ 571 28 86, 🏠 – ▤. AE ⓓ
E VISA. ⚡ GS
Meals a la carte 5150/7400.

X **Casa Benigna,** Benigno Soto 9, ✉ 28002, ☎ 413 33 56, Fax 416 93 57 – ▤. AE ⓓ
E VISA HT
Meals a la carte 3650/4950.

Environs

on the road to the airport *E : 12,5 km – ✉ 28042 Madrid – ☎ 91 :*

Tryp Diana, Galeón 27 (Alameda de Osuna) ☎ 747 13 55, Telex 45688, Fax 747 97 97
– |‡| ▤ 📺 ☎ – 🏛 25/220. AE ⓓ E VISA
Meals 1800 - ***Asador Duque de Osuna*** *(closed Sunday)* **Meals** a la carte 2900/4000
☕ 1100 – **220 rm** 10000/12500, 40 suites.

y motorway N VI – ✉ *28023 Madrid* – ☎ *91* :

XXX **Gaztelubide,** Sopelana 13 - La Florida : 12,8 km ☎ 372 85 44, Fax 372 84 19, 🏕, Basque rest – 🛗 ▤ 🅿. AE ⓓ E VISA. 🚫
closed Sunday dinner – **Meals** a la carte approx. 5000.

XX **Los Remos,** La Florida : 13 km ☎ 307 72 30, Fax 372 84 35, Seafood – ▤ 🅿. AE E VISA
Meals a la carte 4500/5700.

y motorway N I *N : 13 km* – ✉ *28100 Alcobendas* – ☎ *91* :

La Moraleja without rest, av. de Europa 17 - parque empresarial La Moraleja ☎ 661 80 55, Fax 661 21 88, 🏋, 🏊 – 🛗 ▤ 📺 ☎ 🚗 🅿. AE ⓓ E VISA. 🚫
☕ 1350 – **37 suites** 22000.

t Barajas *E : 14 km* – ✉ *28042 Madrid* – ☎ *91* :

Barajas, av. de Logroño 305 ☎ 747 77 00, Telex 22255, Fax 747 87 17, 🏕, 🏋, 🏊, 🌳 – 🛗 ▤ 📺 ☎ 🅿 – 🏛 25/675. AE ⓓ E VISA JCB. 🚫 rest
Meals 4350 – ☕ 1850 – **218 rm** 22800/28500, 12 suites.

Alameda, av. de Logroño 100 ☎ 747 48 00, Telex 43809, Fax 747 89 28, 🏊 – 🛗 ▤ 📺 ☎ 🅿 – 🏛 25/280. AE ⓓ E VISA JCB. 🚫 rest
Meals 3950 – ☕ 1300 – **136 rm** 18000/22500, 9 suites.

loralzarzal *28411 Madrid* 444 J 18 – *pop. 2 248 alt. 979* – ☎ *91.*
Madrid 42.

XXX **El Cenador de Salvador,** av. de España 30 ☎ 857 77 22, Fax 857 77 80, 🏕, « Garden terrace » – ▤ 🅿. AE ⓓ E VISA. 🚫
✿ *closed Sunday dinner, Monday and 15 to 31 October* – **Meals** a la carte 6000/8100
Spec. Foie macerado al vino de Oporto con láminas de manzana. Solomillo de rape "coup de feu" en nabiza. Breseado de carrillera de buey con patatas revolcona.

Ask your bookseller for the catalogue of **Michelin publications.**

ARCELONA *08000* P 443 H36 – *pop. 1 681 132* – ☎ *93.*

See : *Gothic Quarter★★ (Barrio Gótico) : Cathedral★* MX, *Casa de l'Ardiaca★* MX **A,** *Plaça del Rei★★* MX **149,** *Museum of the City's History★* MX **M1,** *Santa Ágata Chapel★* MX *F, Rei Martí Belvedere ≤★★* MX **K,** *Frederic Marès Museum★* MX **M2** – *La Rambla★★* LX MY : *Atarazanas and Maritim Museum★★* MY, *Contemporary Art Barcelona Museum★★* HX **M10,** *Plaça Reial★★* MY, *Güell Palace★★* LY, *Liceu Great Theater★* LY, *Santa Maria del Pi Church★* LX – *Vicereine Palace★* LX, *Montcada st★ (carrer de Montcada)* NX **122** : *Picasso Museum★* NV, *Santa Maria del Mar Church★★* NX – *Montjüic★ ≤★ by Av. Reina María Cristina* GY : *Mies van der Rohe Pavilion★★, Catalonian Art Museum★★★, Spanish Village★ (Poble Espanyol), Olympic Ring★ (Olympic Stadium★, Palau Sant Jordi★★), Joan Miró Foundation★★, Greek Theater★, Archaeological Museum★* – *El Eixample★★ : Rambla de Catalunya★* HVX, *Holy Family★★★ (Sagrada Familia)* JU, *Sant Pau Hospital★ N : by Padilla* JU – *Passeig de Gràcia★★* HV *(streetlamps★, Lleó i Morera House★* HV **Y,** *Amatller House★* HV **Y,** *Batlló House★★* HV **Y,** *La Pedrera or Milà House★★★* HV **P),** *Terrades House (les Punxes★)* HV **Q** – *Güell Park★★ N : by Padilla* JU, *Catalonian Music Palace★★ (Palau de la Música Catalana)* MV, *Antoni Tàpies Foundation★★* HV **S** – *The Maritim Front★ (La Fachada Marítima) : Port Vell★* NY, *Basílica de la Mercè★* NY, *La Llotja★* NX, *França Station★* NVX, *Ciutadella Park★* NV KX *(Three Dragons Castell★★* NV **M7,** *Zoology Museum★* NV **M7,** *Zoo★* KX) – *La Barceloneta★* KXY , *Vila Olímpica★ (pleasure harbour★★, twin towers ✲★★★) E : by Av. d'Icària* KX.

Other curiosities : *Tibidabo (✲★★) NW : by Balmes* FU, *Pedralbes Monastery★★ (Sant Miquel chapel frescos★★★, Thyssen Bornemisza Collection★) W : by Av. de Pedralbes* EV *Pedralbes Palace (Ceramic Museum★)* EX, *Güell Pavilions★* EX, *Trade Towers★* EX.

⛳, ⛳ *Prat SW : 16 km* ☎ *379 02 78* – ⛳ *Sant Cugat NW : 20 km* ☎ *674 39 08, Fax 675 51 52.*

✈ *Barcelona SW : 12 km* ☎ *298 38 38 – Iberia : Passeig de Gràcia 30,* ✉ *08007,* ☎ *412 56 67* HV – *and Aviaco : Airport* ☎ *478 24 11.*

🚆 *Sants* ☎ *490 75 91.*

⛴ *to the Balearic Islands : Cía. Trasmediterránea, Moll de Barcelona - Estació Marítima,* ✉ *08039,* ☎ *443 25 32 Fax 443 27 81.*

ℹ *Gran Vía de les Corts Catalanes 658,* ✉ *08010,* ☎ *301 74 43 Fax 412 25 70, Sants Estació,* ☎ *491 44 31 and at Airport 478 47 04* – **R.A.C.C.** *Santaló 8,* ✉ *08021,* ☎ *200 33 11 Fax 414 31 63.*

Madrid 627 – Bilbao/Bilbo 607 – Lérida/Lleida 169 – Perpignan 187 – Tarragona 109 – Toulouse 388 – Valencia 361 – Zaragoza 307.

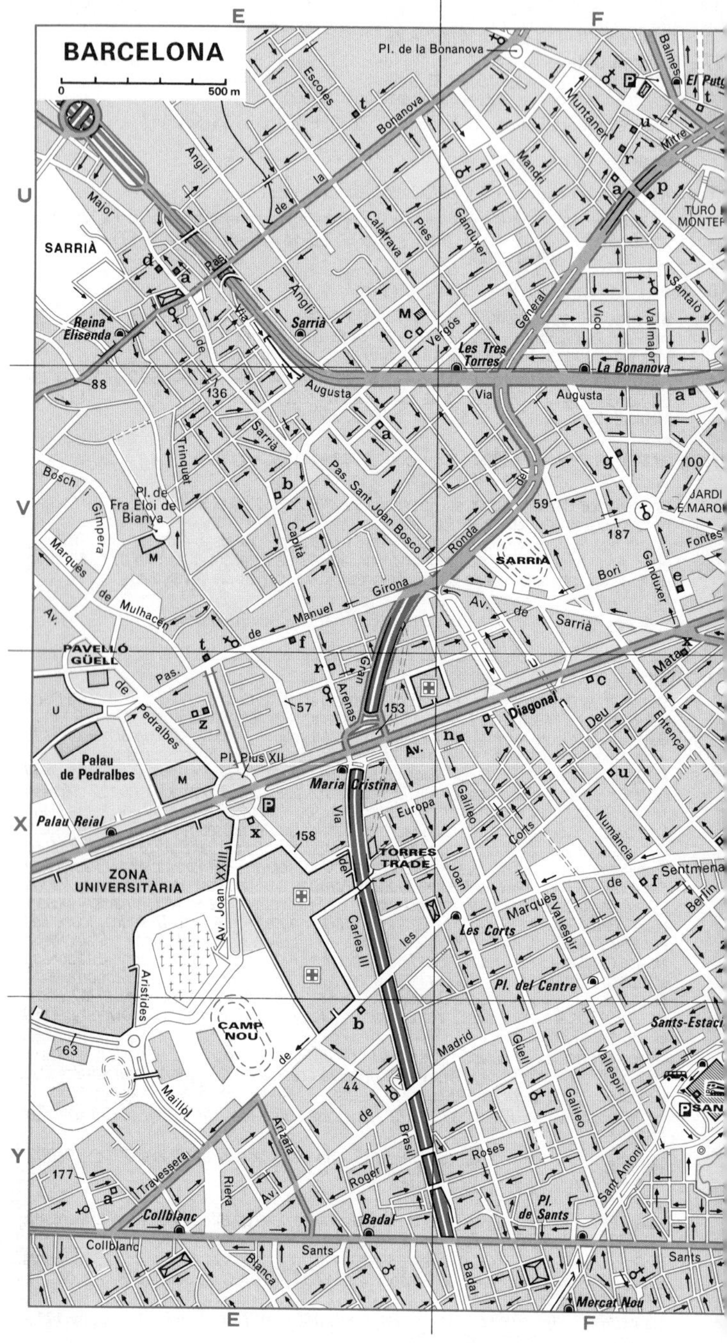
BARCELONA
0
500 m
E
F
U
V
X
Y
Pl. de la Bonanova
SARRIÀ
Reina Elisenda
Sarrià
Les Tres Torres
La Bonanova
Augusta
Via Augusta
Bonanova
Escoles
Angli
Major
Calatrava
Pies
Ganduxer
Muntaner
Mandri
Balmes
El Putget
Mitre
TURÓ MONTERO
Santaló
Vico
Valmajor
General
Vergós
Pas.
Via
Sarrià
Trinquet
Bosch
Gimpera
Pl. de Fra Eloi de Bianya
Marquès
de Mulhacén
Capità
Pas. Sant Joan Bosco
Ronda del
Girona
Manuel
Av. de Sarrià
Bori
Fontes
JARDI E.MARQ
SARRIÀ
PAVELLÓ GÜELL
Pas. de Pedralbes
Gran
Arenas
Diagonal
Mata
Entença
Deu
Palau de Pedralbes
Pl. Pius XII
Maria Cristina
Av.
Galileo
Europa
Corts
Numància
Sentmenat
Berlin
Palau Reial
ZONA UNIVERSITÀRIA
Av. Joan XXIII
Via de Carles III
TORRES TRADE
Joan
les
Les Corts
Marquès de
Vallespir
Pl. del Centre
Sants-Estació
Aristides
CAMP NOU
Maillol
Travessera de
Madrid
Güell
Galileo
Vallespir
Arizala
Riera
Av.
Roger de
Brasil
Roses
Sant Antoni
Pl. de Sants
Collblanc
Badal
Sants
Blanca
Mercat Nou
88
136
100
59
187
57
153
158
63
44
177

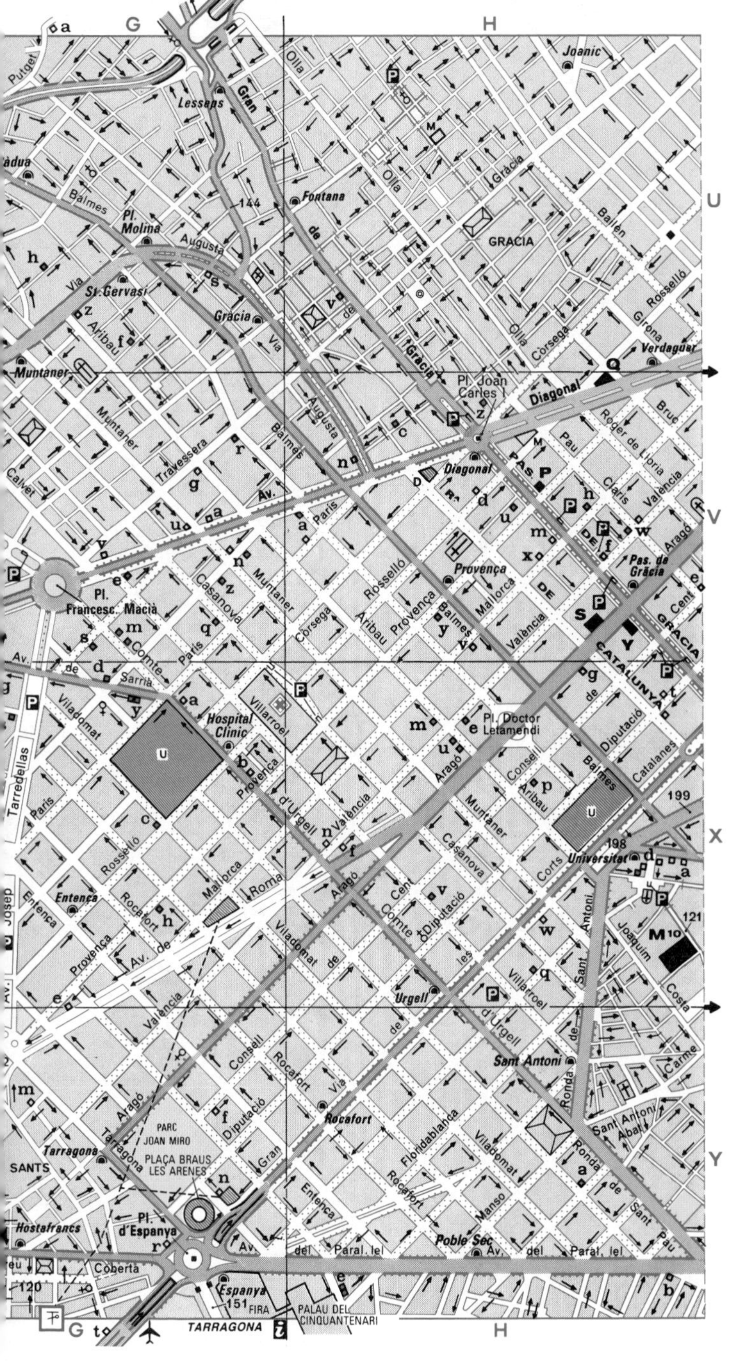
G
H
U
V
X
Y
GRACIA
Pl. Molina
Sant Gervasi
Pl. Francesc. Macià
Hospital Clínic
Pl. Joan Carles I
Pl. Doctor Letamendi
PARC JOAN MIRO
PLAÇA BRAUS LES ARENES
Pl. d'Espanya
SANTS
PALAU DEL CINQUANTENARI
FIRA
TARRAGONA

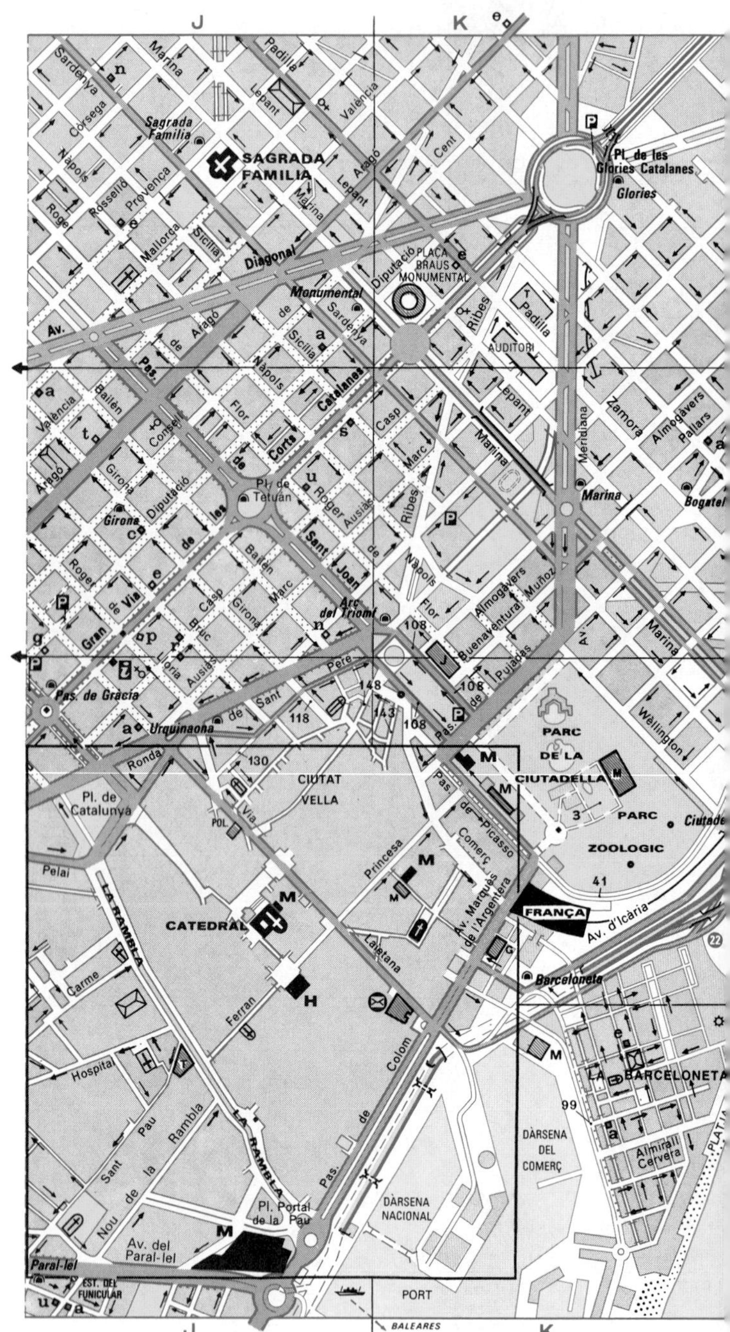
J
K
SAGRADA FAMILIA
Sagrada Familia
Pl. de les Glories Catalanes
Glories
PLAÇA BRAUS MONUMENTAL
Monumental
Diagonal
AUDITORI
Pl. de Tetuan
Arc del Triomf
Urquinaona
Pas. de Gràcia
PARC DE LA CIUTADELLA
PARC ZOOLOGIC
CIUTAT VELLA
Pl. de Catalunya
CATEDRAL
FRANÇA
Av. d'Icària
Barceloneta
LA BARCELONETA
DÀRSENA DEL COMERÇ
DÀRSENA NACIONAL
Pl. Portal de la Pau
Av. del Paral-lel
Paral-lel
EST. DEL FUNICULAR
PORT
BALEARES
LA RAMBLA
Marina
Bogatell
Ciutadella

STREET INDEX TO BARCELONA TOWN PLAN

utxins (Rambla dels) MY 35
alunya (Pl. de) LV
alunya (Rambla de) HX
ts Catalanes
Gran Via de les) HX
udis (Rambla dels) LX
cia (Pas. de) HV
i LV
t Josep (Rambla de) LX 168
ta Mónica
Rambla de) MY
versitat (Pl. de la) HX 198
versitat (Ronda de la) LV 199

irall Cervera KY
ogàvers KV
ple MY
el (Pl. de l') MX
els LX
gli EU
oni López (Pl. d') MY
oni Maura (Pl. d') MV
gó HX
enteria NX
au HX
stides Maillol EY
ala EY
es (Pl.) KX 3
aonadors NV
gusta (Via) FV
sias Marc JV
nyó MY
ardí (Pas.) MY 4
al FY
én JV
mes HV
ys Nous MX 7
gara LV 10
lín FX
pe Irurita MX 15
anova (Pas. de la) EU
anova (Pl. de la) FU
queria (Pl. de la) LY
ia MV 18
í i Fontestà FV
n (Pas. de) NX 20
sch i Alsina
Moll de) NY
sch i Gimpera EV
ers MX 23
sil EY
c HV
naventura Muñoz KV
atrava EU
vet GV
naletes (Rambla de) LV 27
nonge Colom (Pl.) LY 28
nuda LX
nvís Vells NX 32
pità Arenas EV
rdenal Casañas LX 36
rders NV
rles I (Pas. de) KV
rles III (Gran Via de) EX
rme LX
sanova HX
sp JV
tedral (Av. de la) MV 40
cumval·lació (Pas. de) KX 41
tat MX 43
llblanc EY
om (Pas. de) NY
mandant Benítez EY 44
merç NV
mercial (Pl.) NV 45
mte d'Urgell HX
nsell de Cent HX
rsega HU
rts (Travessera de les) EY
eu Coberta GY
curulla LX 55

Déu i Mata FX
Diagonal (Av.) HV
Diputació HX
Doctor Ferran EX 57
Doctor Fleming FV 59
Doctor Joaquim Pou MV 61
Doctor Letamendi (Pl.) HX
Doctor Marañón (Av. del) EY 63
Drassanes (Av. de les) LY
Duc de Medinaceli
(Pl. del) NY
Elísabets LX
Entença GX
Escoles Pies EU
Escudellers MY
Espanya (Moll d') NY
Espanya (Pl. d') GY
Europa EX
Ferran MY
Floridablanca HY
Fontanella LV
Fra Eloi de Bianya (Pl. de) EV
Francesc Cambó (Av.) MV 79
Francesc. Macià (Pl. de) GV
Galileo FX
Ganduxer FV
Garriga i Bach MX 81
General Mitre (Ronda del) FU
Girona JV
Glòries Catalanes
(Pl. de les) KU
Gràcia (Travessera de) HU
Gran de Gràcia HU
Hospital LY
Icària (Av. d') KX
Isabel II (Pas. d') NX 98
Joan Carles (Pl. de) HV
Joan de Borbó (Pas.) KY
Joan Güell FY
Joan XXIII (Av.) EX
Joaquim Costa HX
Johann Sebastian Bach FV 99
Josep Anselm Clavé MY
Laietana (Via) MX
Lepant JU
Lleida HY
Lluís Companys (Pas. de) KX 108
Madrid (Av. de) EFY
Major de Sarrià EV
Mallorca HV
Mandri FU
Manso HY
Manuel Girona (Pas. de) EVX
Marina JU
Marquès de l'Argentera
(Av.) NX
Marquès de Mulhacén EV
Marquès de Sentmenat FX
Mata FX
Méndez Núñez JX 118
Mereaders MV
Meridiana (Av.) KV
Mirallers NX
Moianés GY 120
Montalegre HX 121
Montcada NX 122
Montjuïc del Bisbe MX 123
Muntaner GV
Nàpols JU
Nou de la Rambla LY
Nou de Sant Francesc MY 126
Nova (Pl.) MX 128
Numància FX
Olla HU
Ortigosa JX 130
Padilla KU
Països Catalans (Pl.) FY
Palau (Pl. del) NX 132
Palla MX
Pallars KV
Paradís MX 135

Paral·lel (Av. del) HJY
París GX
Pau Claris HV
Pau Villa (Pl. de) NY
Pedralbes (Av. de) EX
Pedró de la Creu EV 136
Pi (Pl. del) LX 137
Picasso (Pas. de) NV
Pintor Fortuny LX 140
Pius XII (Pl.) EX
Portaferrissa LX
Portal de l'Àngel (Av.) LV
Portal de la Pau (Pl.) MY
Portal de Santa Madrona MY 142
Portal Nou KX 143
Príncep d'Astúries (Av. del) GU 144
Princesa NV
Provença GX
Pujades (Pas. de) KX
Putget GU
Ramón Berenguer
el Gran (Pl. de) MX 147
Rec Comtal JX 148
Rei (Pl. del) MX 149
Reial (Pl.) MY
Reina Elisenda de
Montcada (Pas. de la) EUV 150
Reina Maria Cristina (Av.) GY 151
Reina Maria Cristina (Pl.) EX 153
Ribes KV
Rocafort HY
Roger EY
Roger de Flor JU
Roger de Llúria HV
Roma (Av. de) GX
Roses FY
Rosselló HV
Sabino de Arana EX 158
Sant Antoni FY
Sant Antoni (Ronda de) HXY
Sant Antoni Abat HY
Sant Rafael LY
Sant Felip Neri (Pl.) MX 163
Sant Jaume (Pl.) MX
Sant Joan (Pas. de) JV
Sant Joan Bosco (Pas. de) EV
Sant Josep Oriol LX 167
Sant Lu (Pl. de) MX 170
Sant Miquel (Pl. de) MX 173
Sant Pau LY
Sant Pau (Ronda de) HY
Sant Pere mès alt MV
Sant Pere més baix MV
Sant Pere (Ronda de) JX
Sant Ramon Nonat (Av. de) EY 177
Sant Sever MX 181
Santa Anna LV 182
Santa Fe de Nou Mèxic FV 187
Santa Maria (Pl.) NX 189
Santaló FU
Sants FY
Sardenya JU
Sarrià (Av. de) FV
Serra MY
Seu (Pl. de la) MX 192
Sicília JU
Tapineria MX 193
Tarragona GY
Teatre (Pl. del) MY
Tetuàn (Pl. de) JV
Trinquet EV
Urquinaona (Pl.) JX
València HX
Vallespir FY
Vallmajor FU
Vergós FU
Vico FU
Viladomat HY
Villarroel GX
Wellington KX
Zamora KV

EUROPE on a single sheet
Michelin map n° 970

BARCELONA

Caputxins (Rambla dels) . . . . **MY** 35
Catalunya (Pl. de) . . . . **LV**
Estudis (Rambla dels) . . . . . **LX**
Sant Josep (Rambla de) . . **LX** 168
Santa Mònica (Rambla de) . . . . **MY**
Universitat (Ronda de la) . . . . **LV** 199

Bacardí (Pas.) . . . . **MY** 4
Banys Nous . . . . **MX** 7
Bergara . . . . **LV** 10
Bisbe Irurita . . . . **MX** 15
Bòria . . . . **MV** 18
Born (Pas. del) . . . . **NX** 20
Boters . . . . **MX** 23
Canaletes (Rambla de) . . . . **LV** 27
Canonge Colom (Pl.) . . . . . **LY** 28
Canvis Vells . . . . **NX** 32
Cardenal Casañas . . . . **LX** 36
Catedral (Av.) . . . . **MV** 40
Ciutat . . . . **MX** 43
Comercial (Pl.) . . . . **NV** 45
Cucurella . . . . **LX** 55
Doctor Joaquim Pou . . . . . **MV** 61
Escudellers . . . . **MY**
Francesc Cambó (Av.) . . . . **MV** 79
Garriga i Bach . . . . **MX** 81
Isabel II (Pas. d') . . . . **NX** 98
Montcada . . . . **NX** 122
Montjuïc del Bisbe . . . . . . **MX** 123
Nou de Sant Francesc . . . . **MY** 126
Nova (Pl.) . . . . **MX** 128
Paradís . . . . **MX** 135
Pi (Pl. del) . . . . **LX** 137
Pintor Fortuny . . . . **LX** 140
Portal de Santa Madrona . . . . **MY** 142
Ramon Berenguer el Gran (Pl.) . . . . **MX** 147
Rei (Plaça del) . . . . **MX** 149
Sant Felip Neri (Pl.) . . . . . . **MX** 163
Sant Miquel (Pl. de) . . . . . . **MX** 173
Sant Sever . . . . **MX** 181
Santa Anna . . . . **LV** 182
Santa Maria (Pl.) . . . . **NX** 189

We suggest:

For a successful tour, that you prepare it in advance.
***Michelin maps** and **guides** will give you much useful information on route planning, places of interest, accommodation, prices, etc.*

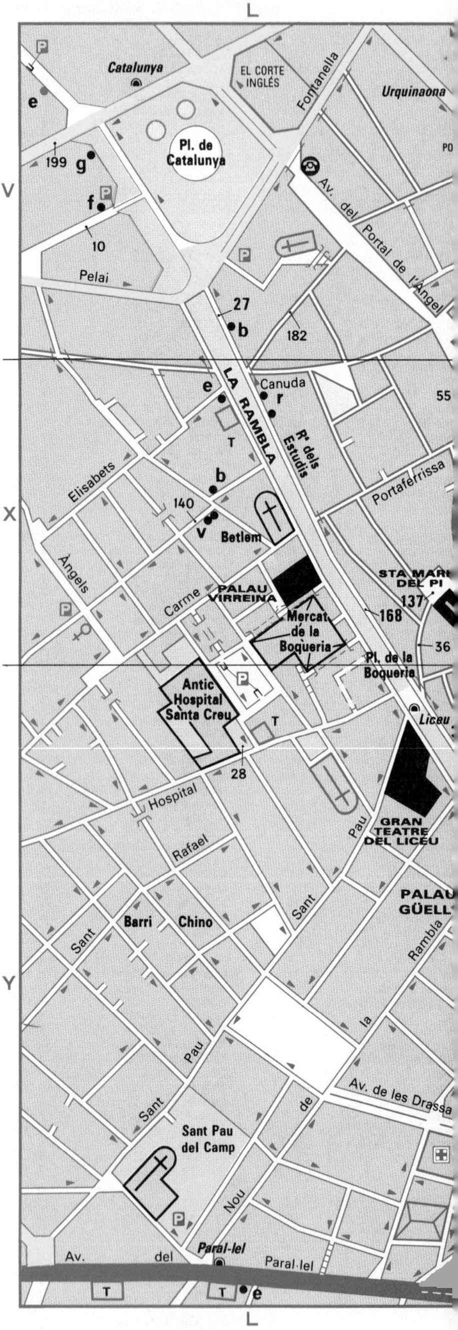

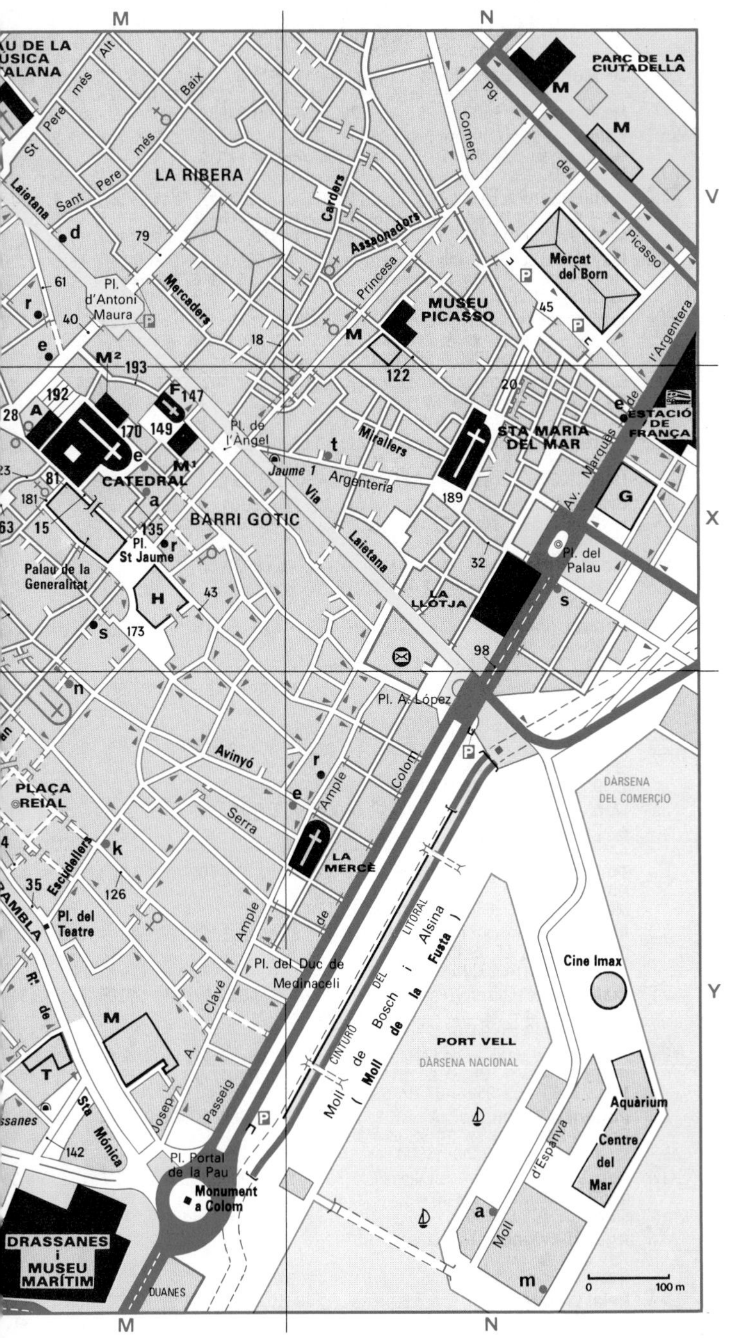
M
N
PARC DE LA CIUTADELLA
LA RIBERA
Cardera
Assaonadors
Princesa
Mercaders
Mercat del Born
MUSEU PICASSO
Picasso
Pl. d'Antoni Maura
CATEDRAL
Pl. de l'Àngel
Miralles
STA MARIA DEL MAR
ESTACIÓ DE FRANÇA
Argenteria
Via Laietana
BARRI GOTIC
Pl. St Jaume
Palau de la Generalitat
LA LLOTJA
Pl. del Palau
Pl. A. López
Avinyó
PLAÇA REIAL
Escudellers
LA MERCÈ
Pl. del Teatre
DÀRSENA DEL COMERÇIO
Pl. del Duc de Medinaceli
Moll de Bosch i Alsina (Moll de la Fusta)
CINTURÓ DEL LITORAL
Cine Imax
PORT VELL
DÀRSENA NACIONAL
Aquàrium
Centre del Mar
Moll d'Espanya
Pl. Portal de la Pau
Monument a Colom
DRASSANES i MUSEU MARÍTIM
DUANES
V
X
Y
0
100 m

Old Town and the Gothic Quarter : Ramblas, Pl. S. Jaume, Via Laietana, Passeig de Joan Borbó de Barcelona, Passeig de Colom

Le Meridien Barcelona, La Rambla 111, ✉ 08002, ✆ 318 62 00, Telex 5463, Fax 301 77 76 – 🛗 ▤ TV ☎ ♿ 🚗 – 🏛 25/200. AE ⓓ E VISA JCB. ✗ LX
Meals a la carte 3500/5325 – ☕ 2250 – **198 rm** 24000/30000, 7 suites.

Colón, av. de la Catedral 7, ✉ 08002, ✆ 301 14 04, Telex 52654, Fax 317 29 15 – ▤ TV ☎ ♿ – 🏛 25/120. AE ⓓ E VISA JCB. ✗ rest MV
Meals 3500 – ☕ 1600 – **138 rm** 14750/22000, 9 suites.

Rivoli Rambla, La Rambla 128, ✉ 08002, ✆ 302 66 43, Telex 99222, Fax 317 20 3 Lδ – 🛗 ▤ TV ☎ ♿ – 🏛 25/180. AE ⓓ E VISA JCB. ✗ LX
Meals (lunch only) 3500 – ☕ 1900 – **81 rm** 19000/24000, 9 suites.

Royal coffee shop only, La Rambla 117, ✉ 08002, ✆ 301 94 00, Telex 9756 Fax 317 31 79 – 🛗 ▤ TV ☎ 🚗 – 🏛 25/100. AE ⓓ E VISA JCB. ✗ LX
☕ 1500 – **108 rm** 13800/17500.

Ambassador, Pintor Fortuny 13, ✉ 08001, ✆ 412 05 30, Telex 99222, Fax 317 20 3 Lδ, 🏊 – 🛗 ▤ TV ☎ ♿ 🚗 – 🏛 25/200. AE ⓓ E VISA JCB. ✗ LX
Meals 2800 – ☕ 1900 – **96 rm** 15900/19900, 9 suites.

G.H. Barcino without rest, Jaume I-6, ✉ 08002, ✆ 302 20 12, Fax 301 42 42 – 🛗 TV ☎ ♿. AE ⓓ E VISA. ✗ MX
☕ 1700 – **53 rm** 16300/23500.

Guitart Almirante, Via Laietana 42, ✉ 08003, ✆ 268 30 20, Fax 268 31 92 – 🛗 TV ☎ 🚗 – 🏛 25/40. AE ⓓ E VISA JCB. ✗ MV
Meals 3000 – ☕ 1300 – **73 rm** 11250/15000, 3 suites.

Gravina coffee shop only, Gravina 12, ✉ 08001, ✆ 301 68 68, Telex 9937 Fax 317 28 38 – 🛗 ▤ TV ☎ – 🏛 25/50. AE ⓓ E VISA. ✗ HX
☕ 1000 – **60 rm** 10900/15900.

Montecarlo without rest, La Rambla 124, ✉ 08002, ✆ 412 04 04, Fax 318 73 23 🛗 ▤ TV ☎ ♿ 🚗. AE ⓓ E VISA. ✗ LX
☕ 1100 – **80 rm** 8900/12500.

Reding, Gravina 5, ✉ 08001, ✆ 412 10 97, Fax 268 34 82 – 🛗 ▤ TV ☎ 🚗. AE E VISA JCB. ✗ HX
Meals 1075 – ☕ 1100 – **44 rm** 13500/16200.

Atlantis without rest, Pelai 20, ✉ 08001, ✆ 318 90 12, Fax 412 09 14 – 🛗 ▤ TV AE ⓓ E VISA. ✗ HX
☕ 900 – **42 rm** 8000/10000.

Metropol without rest, Ample 31, ✉ 08002, ✆ 310 51 00, Fax 319 12 76 – 🛗 ▤ ☎. AE ⓓ E VISA. ✗ NY
☕ 995 – **68 rm** 10400/11600.

Lleó coffee shop only, Pelai 22, ✉ 08001, ✆ 318 13 12, Fax 412 26 57 – 🛗 ▤ TV ♿. AE E VISA JCB HX
☕ 975 – **75 rm** 8500/11000.

Turín, Pintor Fortuny 9, ✉ 08001, ✆ 302 48 12, Fax 302 10 05 – 🛗 ▤ TV ☎ ♿. ⓓ E VISA LX
Meals 1000 – ☕ 850 – **60 rm** 8900/13500.

Ramblas H. without rest, Rambles 33, ✉ 08002, ✆ 301 57 00, Fax 412 25 07 – 🛗 TV ☎ ♿ – 🏛 25. E VISA. ✗ MY
☕ 975 – **70 rm** 10225/12750.

Rialto coffee shop only, Ferran 42, ✉ 08002, ✆ 318 52 12, Telex 97206, Fax 318 53 – 🛗 ▤ TV ☎ – 🏛 25/50. AE ⓓ E VISA JCB MX
☕ 700 – **149 rm** 9470/12360.

Park H., av. Marquès de l'Argentera 11, ✉ 08003, ✆ 319 60 00, Fax 319 45 19 – ▤ TV ☎ ♿ 🚗. AE ⓓ E VISA JCB. ✗ NX
Meals 2500 – ☕ 950 – **87 rm** 8500/11500.

Regencia Colón without rest, Sagristans 13, ✉ 08002, ✆ 318 98 58, Telex 9817 Fax 317 28 22 – 🛗 ▤ TV ☎. AE ⓓ E VISA MV
☕ 1000 – **55 rm** 7900/13500.

Continental without rest, Rambles 138-2º, ✉ 08002, ✆ 301 25 70, Fax 302 73 60 🛗 TV ☎. AE ⓓ E VISA JCB LV
35 rm ☕ 6950/9900.

Agut d'Avignon, Trinitat 3, ✉ 08002, ✆ 302 60 34, Fax 302 53 18 – ▤. AE ⓓ VISA JCB. ✗ MY
Meals a la carte 3970/5385.

Reial Club Marítim, Moll d'Espanya, ✉ 08039, ✆ 221 71 43, Fax 221 44 12, ≤, – ▤. E VISA JCB NY
Meals a la carte 3200/4675.

Senyor Parellada, Argenteria 37, ✉ 08003, ☎ 310 50 94 – ▤. AE ⓓ E VISA JCB. ✗ NX t
closed Sunday and Bank Holidays – **Meals** a la carte 2525/3700.

7 Portes, passeig d'Isabel II-14, ✉ 08003, ☎ 319 30 33, Fax 319 30 46 – ▤. AE ⓓ VISA NX s
Meals a la carte 3100/5900.

Can Ramonet, Maquinista 17, ✉ 08003, ☎ 319 30 64, Fax 319 70 14, seafood – ▤. AE ⓓ E VISA JCB KY e
closed 5 August-5 September – **Meals** a la carte 2800/4150.

Pitarra, Avinyó 56, ✉ 08002, ☎ 301 16 47, Fax 301 16 47, Period decor with memorabilia of the poet Pitarra – ▤. AE ⓓ E VISA NY e
closed Sunday, Bank Holidays and August – **Meals** a la carte 2125/3275.

Can Solé, Sant Carles 4, ✉ 08003, ☎ 221 58 15, Fax 221 58 15, seafood – ▤. AE E VISA KY a
closed Sunday dinner and Monday – **Meals** a la carte 2925/4975.

Ca la María, Tallers 76 bis, ✉ 08001, ☎ 318 89 93
▤. AE ⓓ E VISA JCB HX d
closed Sunday dinner, Monday and August – **Meals** a la carte 2500/3200.

South of Av. Diagonal : Pl. de Catalunya, Gran Via de les Corts Catalanes, Passeig de Gràcia, Balmes, Muntaner, Aragó

Rey Juan Carlos I ⛯, av. Diagonal 661, ✉ 08028, ☎ 448 08 08, Fax 448 06 07, ← *city*, ☂, « Modern facilities, park with lake and ⛱ », Fá, ⛱, ⛱ – |♦| ▤ TV ☎ ♿ ⇔ Ⓟ – 🔬 25/1000. AE ⓓ E VISA. ✗ W : by Av. Diagonal EX
Chez Vous *(closed Saturday lunch and Sunday)* **Meals** a la carte 4300/5850 - ***Café Polo :*** **Meals** a la carte 2100/4900 – ☕ 2100 – **375 rm** 27000/36000, 37 suites.

Arts ⛯, Marina 19, ✉ 08005, ☎ 221 10 00, Fax 221 10 70, ←, ⛱ – |♦| ▤ TV ☎ ♿ ⇔ – 🔬 25/900. AE ⓓ VISA JCB. ✗ E : by Av. d'Icària KX
Newport *(dinner only, closed Sunday, Monday and August)* **Meals** a la carte 4950/7100 – ☕ 2500 – **397 rm** 27000, 58 suites.

Palace, Gran Via de les Corts Catalanes 668, ✉ 08010, ☎ 318 52 00, Telex 52739, Fax 318 01 48, ☂ – |♦| ▤ TV ☎ – 🔬 25/350. AE ⓓ E VISA. ✗ JV p
Meals a la carte 5500/6600 – ☕ 2300 – **148 rm** 29500/43000, 13 suites.

Claris ⛯, Pau Claris 150, ✉ 08009, ☎ 487 62 62, Fax 215 79 70, « Modern facilities with antiques, archaeological museum », ⛱ – |♦| ▤ TV ☎ ⇔ – 🔬 25/60. AE ⓓ E VISA JCB. ✗ rest HV w
Meals 6000 - ***Beluga*** *(dinner only, closed Sunday)* **Meals** a la carte 6000/9000 – ☕ 2100 – **106 rm** 25500/31850, 18 suites.

Barcelona Hilton, av. Diagonal 589, ✉ 08014, ☎ 419 22 33, Telex 99623, Fax 405 25 73, ☂ – |♦| ▤ TV ☎ ♿ ⇔ – 🔬 25/800. AE ⓓ E VISA JCB FX v
Meals 2800 – ☕ 2100 – **285 rm** 24000/29000, 2 suites.

Meliá Barcelona, av. de Sarrià 50, ✉ 08029, ☎ 410 60 60, Telex 51638, Fax 321 51 79, ← – |♦| ▤ TV ☎ ⇔ – 🔬 25/500. AE ⓓ E VISA JCB. ✗ FV n
Meals 6000 – ☕ 2000 – **308 rm** 23500/30500, 4 suites.

Princesa Sofía Inter-Continental, pl. Pius XII-4, ✉ 08028, ☎ 330 71 11, Telex 51032, Fax 330 76 21, ←, Fá, ⛱ – |♦| ▤ TV ☎ ⇔ – 🔬 25/1200. AE ⓓ E VISA
Meals 3900 - ***L'Empordà*** *(closed Saturday, Sunday and 15 July-15 August)* **Meals** a la carte 4100/6500 – ☕ 1800 – **481 rm** 20000/25000, 24 suites. EX x

G.H. Havana, Gran Via de les Corts Catalanes 647, ✉ 08010, ☎ 412 11 15, Fax 412 26 11 – |♦| ▤ TV ☎ ⇔ – 🔬 25/200. AE ⓓ E VISA JCB. ✗ rest JV e
Meals 2650 – ☕ 1350 – **141 rm** 17500/19500, 4 suites.

Fira Palace, av. Rius i Taulet 1, ✉ 08004, ☎ 426 22 23, Telex 97588, Fax 424 86 79, Fá, ⛱ – |♦| ▤ TV ☎ ♿ ⇔ – 🔬 25/1300. AE ⓓ E VISA JCB. ✗
Meals 3000 - ***El Mall :*** **Meals** a la carte 3100/3700 – ☕ 1400 – **260 rm** 18000/22500, 16 suites. S : by Lleida HY

Barcelona Plaza H., pl. d'Espanya 6, ✉ 08014, ☎ 426 26 00, Fax 426 04 00, Fá, ⛱ – |♦| ▤ TV ☎ ♿ ⇔ – 🔬 25/600. AE ⓓ E VISA JCB. ✗ GY r
Meals 3000 - ***Gourmet Plaza :*** **Meals** a la carte 3600/5100 – ☕ 1400 – **338 rm** 15500/17000, 9 suites.

Majestic, passeig de Gràcia 70, ✉ 08008, ☎ 488 17 17, Telex 52211, Fax 488 18 80, ⛱ – |♦| ▤ TV ☎ – 🔬 25/600. AE ⓓ E VISA JCB. ✗ HV f
Meals 2600 – ☕ 1900 – **328 rm** 20000/25000, 1 suite.

Diplomatic, Pau Claris 122, ✉ 08009, ☎ 488 02 00, Telex 54701, Fax 488 12 22, ⛱ – |♦| ▤ TV ☎ ⇔ – 🔬 25/250. AE ⓓ E VISA JCB. ✗ HV e
La Salsa : **Meals** a la carte 3400/4550 – ☕ 1500 – **210 rm** 16800/21000, 7 suites.

NH Calderón, Rambla de Catalunya 26, ⊠ 08007, ℰ 301 00 00, Fax 317 31 57, [pool] – [lift] [air-con] [TV] ☎ [garage] – [meeting] 25/200. AE ① E VISA JCB. ⌧ rest HX
Meals a la carte 3300/4400 – ☕ 1800 – **245 rm** 18000/25000, 17 suites.

Barceló Sants, pl. dels Països Catalans (Barcelona Sants railway station), ⊠ 0801 ℰ 490 95 95, Telex 97568, Fax 490 60 45, ≤ – [lift] [air-con] [TV] ☎ ♿ [P] – [meeting] 25/1500. AE ① E VISA JCB. ⌧ FY
Meals 3250 – ☕ 1650 – **364 rm** 14100/17300, 13 suites.

G.H. Catalonia, Balmes 142, ⊠ 08008, ℰ 415 90 90, Telex 98718, Fax 415 22 09 [lift] [air-con] [TV] ☎ ♿ [garage] – [meeting] 50/260. AE ① E VISA JCB. ⌧ HV
Meals 2700 – ☕ 1500 – **82 rm** 15750/17490, 2 suites.

Condes de Barcelona *(Monument and Centre)*, passeig de Gràcia 75, ⊠ 0800 ℰ 488 22 00, Telex 51531, Fax 487 14 42, [pool] – [lift] [air-con] [TV] ☎ [garage] – [meeting] 25/300. AE ① E VISA. ⌧ HV
Meals 3500 – ☕ 1500 – **180 rm** 23000/29000, 2 suites.

L'Illa without rest, av. Diagonal 555, ⊠ 08029, ℰ 410 33 00, Fax 410 88 92 – [lift] [air-con] ☎ ♿ – [meeting] 25/100. AE ① E VISA. ⌧ FX
☕ 1300 – **103 rm** 19900/24500, 10 suites.

Gallery H., Rosselló 249, ⊠ 08008, ℰ 415 99 11, Telex 97518, Fax 415 91 84, [terrace], – [lift] [air-con] [TV] ☎ ♿ [garage] – [meeting] 25/200. AE ① E VISA. ⌧ HV
Meals 2250 – ☕ 1750 – **110 rm** 19400/23500, 5 suites.

Meliá Confort Apolo without rest, av. del Paral.lel 57, ⊠ 08004, ℰ 443 11 2 Fax 443 00 59 – [lift] [air-con] [TV] ☎ ♿ [P] – [meeting] 25/500. AE ① E VISA JCB LY
☕ 950 – **303 rm** 14500/17500.

St. Moritz, Diputació 262, ⊠ 08007, ℰ 412 15 00, Telex 97340, Fax 412 12 36 – [air-con] [TV] ☎ ♿ [garage] – [meeting] 25/140. AE ① E VISA JCB. ⌧ rest JV
Meals 2300 – ☕ 1750 – **92 rm** 15400/18000.

Gran Derby without rest, Loreto 28, ⊠ 08029, ℰ 322 20 62, Telex 9742 Fax 419 68 20 – [lift] [air-con] [TV] ☎ [garage] – [meeting] 25/100. AE ① E VISA JCB GX
☕ 1700 – **31 rm** 16200/17850, 12 suites.

Balmes, Mallorca 216, ⊠ 08008, ℰ 451 19 14, Fax 451 00 49, « Terrace with [pool] » [lift] [air-con] [TV] ☎ [garage] – [meeting] 25/70. AE ① E VISA JCB. ⌧ rest HV
Meals 1700 – ☕ 1400 – **92 rm** 15500/17350, 8 suites.

City Park H., Nicaragua 47, ⊠ 08029, ℰ 419 95 00, Fax 419 71 63 – [lift] [air-con] [TV] ☎ [garage] – [meeting] 25/40. AE ① E VISA JCB. ⌧ FX
Meals 2500 – ☕ 1100 – **80 rm** 14500/20500.

NH Podium, Bailén 4, ⊠ 08010, ℰ 265 02 02, Fax 265 05 06, [gym], [pool] – [lift] [air-con] [TV] ♿ [garage] – [meeting] 25/240. AE ① E VISA JCB. ⌧ JV
Meals 2700 – ☕ 1600 – **140 rm** 15000/21000, 5 suites.

Derby coffee shop only, Loreto 21, ⊠ 08029, ℰ 322 32 15, Telex 97429, Fax 410 08 6 – [lift] [air-con] [TV] ☎ [garage] – [meeting] 25/100. AE ① E VISA JCB FX
☕ 1500 – **107 rm** 15500/17350, 4 suites.

Alexandra, Mallorca 251, ⊠ 08008, ℰ 487 05 05, Telex 81107, Fax 488 02 58 – [air-con] [TV] ☎ ♿ [garage] – [meeting] 25/100. AE ① E VISA JCB. ⌧ HV
Meals 2300 – ☕ 1700 – **73 rm** 15000/19000, 2 suites.

Astoria without rest, París 203, ⊠ 08036, ℰ 209 83 11, Telex 81129, Fax 202 30 – [lift] [air-con] [TV] ☎ – [meeting] 25/30. AE ① E VISA JCB HV
☕ 1200 – **114 rm** 14200/16200, 3 suites.

NH Master, València 105, ⊠ 08011, ℰ 323 62 15, Telex 81258, Fax 323 43 89 – [air-con] [TV] ☎ [garage] – [meeting] 25/170. AE ① E VISA JCB. ⌧ rest HX
Meals 2400 – ☕ 1100 – **80 rm** 11880/16500, 1 suite.

Cristal, Diputació 257, ⊠ 08007, ℰ 487 87 78, Telex 54560, Fax 487 90 30 – [lift] [TV] ☎ [garage] – [meeting] 25/70. AE ① E VISA JCB. ⌧ rest HX
Meals 1400 – **148 rm** ☕ 14900/22400.

NH Numància, Numància 74, ⊠ 08029, ℰ 322 44 51, Fax 410 76 42 – [lift] [air-con] [TV] [garage] – [meeting] 25/70. AE ① E VISA JCB. ⌧ FX
Meals a la carte approx. 3500 – ☕ 1200 – **140 rm** 13600/17000.

NH Sant Angelo coffe shop dinner only, Consell de Cent 74, ⊠ 08015, ℰ 423 46 4 Fax 423 88 40 – [lift] [air-con] [TV] ☎ ♿ [garage] – [meeting] 25. AE ① E VISA JCB. ⌧ GY
☕ 1200 – **50 rm** 13600/17000.

Guitart Grand Passage, Muntaner 212, ⊠ 08036, ℰ 201 03 06, Telex 9831 Fax 201 00 04 – [lift] [air-con] [TV] ☎ – [meeting] 25/80. AE ① E VISA. ⌧ rest GV
Meals *(closed August)* a la carte approx. 3700 – ☕ 1200 – **40 suites** 16000/20000.

Núñez Urgel without rest, Comte d'Urgell 232, ⊠ 08036, ℰ 322 41 53, Fax 419 01 0 – [lift] [air-con] [TV] ☎ [garage] – [meeting] 25/100. AE ① E VISA JCB GX
☕ 1300 – **120 rm** 9500/12000, 2 suites.

Expo H., Mallorca 1, ✉ 08014, ☎ 325 12 12, Telex 54147, Fax 325 11 44, – 25/900. AE VISA. GY m
Meals 1900 – 1000 – **435 rm** 12000.

Duques de Bergara, Bergara 11, ✉ 08002, ☎ 301 51 51, Fax 317 34 42 – – 25/80. AE E VISA JCB. LV f
Meals 1800 – 1200 – **51 rm** 14850/16400.

Caledonian without rest, Gran Via de les Corts Catalanes 574, ✉ 08011, ☎ 453 02 00, Fax 451 77 03 – AE E VISA. HX w
44 rm 10200/16600.

Abbot without rest, av. de Roma 23, ✉ 08029, ☎ 430 04 05, Fax 419 57 41 – – 25/100. AE E VISA. GXY e
1100 – **39 rm** 10500/13500.

NH Forum, Ecuador 20, ✉ 08029, ☎ 419 36 36, Fax 419 89 10 – – 25/50. AE E VISA JCB. FX t
Meals 2500 – 1200 – **47 rm** 14000/18000, 1 suite.

NH Rallye, Travessera de les Corts 150, ✉ 08028, ☎ 339 90 50, Fax 411 07 90, – – 25/200. AE VISA JCB. EY b
Meals *(closed August)* 2400 – 1300 – **106 rm** 13500.

NH Les Corts, Travessera de les Corts 292, ✉ 08029, ☎ 322 08 11, Fax 322 09 08 – – 25/80. AE E VISA JCB. rest FX u
Meals (dinner only) 1900 – 1200 – **80 rm** 10350/11000, 1 suite.

Catalunya Plaza without rest, pl. de Catalunya 7, ✉ 08002, ☎ 317 71 71, Fax 317 78 55 – – 25. AE E VISA. LV g
1000 – **46 rm** 13000/15000.

Onix without rest, Llansà 30, ✉ 08015, ☎ 426 00 87, Fax 426 19 81, – – 25/150. AE VISA. GY n
1000 – **80 rm** 11200/14000.

Beltxenea, Mallorca 275, ✉ 08008, ☎ 215 30 24, Fax 487 00 81, , « Garden terrace » – . AE VISA. HV h
closed Saturday lunch, Sunday and August – **Meals** a la carte 5300/6600.

La Dama, av. Diagonal 423, ✉ 08036, ☎ 202 06 86, Fax 200 72 99 – . AE E VISA. HV a
Meals 5975 and a la carte 4950/6875
Spec. Ensalada tibia de salmonetes con patatas al caviar. Medallones de rape Costa Brava. Carro de pastelería.

Finisterre, av. Diagonal 469, ✉ 08036, ☎ 439 55 76, Fax 439 99 41 – . AE E VISA. GV e
Meals a la carte approx. 7000.

Oliver y Hardy, av. Diagonal 593, ✉ 08014, ☎ 419 31 81, Fax 419 18 99, – . AE E VISA. FX n
Meals a la carte 4250/5600.

Casa Calvet, Casp 48, ✉ 08010, ☎ 412 40 12, Fax 412 43 36 – . AE E VISA. JVX r
closed Sunday, Bank Holidays and 11 to 24 August – **Meals** a la carte 4300/5700.

Jaume de Provença, Provença 88, ✉ 08029, ☎ 430 00 29, Fax 439 29 50 – . AE E VISA JCB. GX h
closed Sunday dinner, Monday, Holy Week, August and Christmas – **Meals** 7000 and a la carte 4900/5500
Spec. Arroz Basmati a la catalana con mariscos. Milhojas de bacalao al all i oli de canela y almendras. Suprema de turbot a la plancha en salsa virgen.

Talaia Mar, Marina 16, ✉ 08005, ☎ 221 90 90, Fax 221 89 89, ← – . AE E VISA. E : by Av. d'Icària KX
Meals a la carte 4950/6150.

El Tragaluz, passatge de la Concepció 5-1º, ✉ 08008, ☎ 487 01 96, Fax 217 01 19, « Original decor with glass roof » – . AE E VISA JCB. HV u
Meals a la carte 2900/4500.

Tikal, Rambla de Catalunya 5, ✉ 08007, ☎ 302 22 21 – . AE E VISA JCB. LV e
Meals a la carte approx. 3480.

El Asador de Aranda, Londres 94, ✉ 08036, ☎ 414 67 90, Fax 414 67 90, Roast lamb – . AE E VISA. GV n
closed Sunday dinner and 16 to 31 August – **Meals** a la carte approx. 4000.

Els Pescadors, pl. Prim 1, ✉ 08005, ☎ 225 20 18, Fax 225 20 18, , seafood – . AE E VISA E : by Av. d'Icària KX
closed Holy Week and Christmas – **Meals** a la carte 3325/4600.

Rías de Galicia, Lleida 7, 08004, 424 81 52, Fax 426 13 07, seafood – HY
Meals a la carte 3900/5700.

Vinya Rosa-Magí, av. de Sarrià 17, 08029, 430 00 03, Fax 430 00 41 – GX
closed Saturday lunch and Sunday – **Meals** a la carte approx. 4420.

Gorría, Diputació 421, 08013, 245 11 64, Fax 232 78 57, Basque rest – JU
closed Sunday, Bank Holidays dinner, Holy Week and August – **Meals** a la carte 4525/530[illegible]

La Provença, Provença 242, 08008, 323 23 67, Fax 451 23 89 – HV
Meals a la carte 2470/3330.

Sibarit, Aribau 65, 08011, 453 93 03 – HX
closed Saturday lunch, Sunday, Bank Holidays, Holy Week and 15 to 31 August – **Meal[s]** a la carte approx. 5000.

Casa Darío, Consell de Cent 256, 08011, 453 31 35, Fax 451 33 95 – HX
closed Sunday and August – **Meals** a la carte 3900/5750.

El Túnel del Port, moll de Gregal 12 (Port Olímpic), 08005, 221 03 2[illegible] Fax 221 35 86, – E : by Av. d'Icària KX
closed Sunday dinner – **Meals** a la carte 3100/4400.

El Celler de Casa Jordi, Rita Bonnat 3, 08029, 430 10 45 – GX
closed Sunday and August – **Meals** a la carte 2200/3025.

Rosamar, Sepúlveda 159, 08011, 453 31 92 – HX
closed Sunday dinner, Monday, Holy Week and August – **Meals** a la carte 2700/3800.

El Pescador, Mallorca 314, 08037, 207 10 24, seafood – JV
closed Monday – **Meals** a la carte 4000/5350.

Elche, Vila i Vilà 71, 08004, 329 68 46, Fax 329 40 12, Rice dishes – JY
closed Sunday dinner – **Meals** a la carte 2500/3500.

Chicoa, Aribau 73, 08036, 453 11 23 – HX
closed Sunday, Bank Holidays and August – **Meals** a la carte approx. 4000.

Els Perols de l'Empordà, Villarroel 88, 08011, 323 10 33, Ampurdan rest – HX
closed Sunday dinner, Holy Week and 15 days in August – **Meals** a la carte 2850/425[illegible]

Azpiolea, Casanova 167, 08036, 430 90 30, Basque rest – GV
closed Sunday, Bank Holiday dinner, Holy Week and August – **Meals** a la carte 3425/485[illegible]

Cañota, Lleida 7, 08004, 325 91 71, Fax 426 13 07, Braised meat specialities – HY
Meals a la carte approx. 2500.

North of Av. Diagonal : Via Augusta, Capità Arenas, Ronda General Mitre, Passeig d[e] la Bonanova, Av. de Pedralbes

Tryp Presidente, av. Diagonal 570, 08021, 200 21 11, Fax 209 51 06 – 25/420. GV
Meals 2500 – 1350 – **155 rm** 14500/18500.

Alimara, Berruguete 126, 08035, 427 00 00, Fax 427 92 92 – 25/470. rest N : by Padilla JU
Meals 1950 – 1100 – **156 rm** 13500/15600.

Hesperia coffee shop only, Vergós 20, 08017, 204 55 51, Telex 98403 Fax 204 43 92 – 25/150. EU
1300 – **139 rm** 17000/19000.

Suite H., Muntaner 505, 08022, 212 80 12, Telex 99077, Fax 211 23 17 – 25/90. FU
Meals 1900 – 1200 – **77 suites** 12650/14190.

Balmoral without rest, Via Augusta 5, 08006, 217 87 00, Fax 415 14 21 – 25/250. HV
1050 – **94 rm** 11100/13600.

NH Cóndor, Via Augusta 127, 08006, 209 45 11, Telex 52925, Fax 202 27 13 – 25/50. rest GU
Meals 2000 – 1100 – **78 rm** 11500/17000, 12 suites.

Arenas coffee shop only, Capità Arenas 20, ✉ 08034, ☎ 280 03 03, Fax 280 33 92 – EX r
1000 – **58 rm** 14000/17000, 1 suite.

Victoria, av. de Pedralbes 16 bis, ✉ 08034, ☎ 280 15 15, Fax 280 52 67, rest EX z
Meals 1650 – 1350 – **74 suites** 14400/18000.

Park Putxet, Putxet 68, ✉ 08023, ☎ 212 51 58, Telex 98718, Fax 418 58 17 – 25/200. GU a
Meals 1800 – 950 – **141 rm** 8700/9750.

NH Belagua, Via Augusta 89, ✉ 08006, ☎ 237 39 40, Fax 415 30 62 – 25/90. rest GU s
Meals *(closed Saturday and 2 to 24 August)* (dinner only) 2400 – 1200 – **72 rm** 12250/17000.

Mitre without rest, Bertràn 9, ✉ 08023, ☎ 212 11 04, Fax 418 94 81 – FU t
775 – **57 rm** 11000/14000.

Condado without rest, Aribau 201, ✉ 08021, ☎ 200 23 11, Fax 200 25 86 – GV g
1100 – **88 rm** 11115/12335.

NH Pedralbes coffee shop dinner only, Fontcuberta 4, ✉ 08034, ☎ 203 71 12, Fax 205 70 65 – 25. EV b
1200 – **30 rm** 13600/17000.

Covadonga without rest, av. Diagonal 596, ✉ 08021, ☎ 209 55 11, Fax 209 58 33 – GV v
650 – **85 rm** 8300/14000.

Albéniz without rest, Aragó 591, ✉ 08026, ☎ 265 26 26, Fax 265 40 07 – 25/50. NE : by G.V. de les Corts Catalanes HX
950 – **47 rm** 9400/10900.

Via Veneto, Ganduxer 10, ✉ 08021, ☎ 200 72 44, Fax 201 60 95, « Early 20C style » – FV e
closed Saturday lunch, Sunday and 1 to 20 August – **Meals** a la carte 5480/7680
Spec. Lasaña con hígado de pato fresco y setas al perfume de albahaca. Raya asada con verduras a la salsa de almendras. Espuma de limón con salsa de maracuyá.

Reno, Tuset 27, ✉ 08006, ☎ 200 91 29, Fax 414 41 14 – GV r
closed Saturday lunch – **Meals** a la carte 5600/6650.

Neichel, Beltran i Rózpide 16 bis, ✉ 08034, ☎ 203 84 08, Fax 205 63 69 – EX z
closed Saturday lunch, Sunday, Holy Week, August and 1 to 6 January – **Meals** 7300 and a la carte 6300/7200
Spec. Rapet de playa con piperrada al tomillo y olivada de anchoas. Caneton en dos sabores y cocciones. Mousse de ruibarbo y fresas con helado de regaliz.

Jean Luc Figueras, Santa Teresa 10, ✉ 08012, ☎ 415 28 77, Fax 218 92 62, Tasteful decor – HV z
closed Saturday lunch, Sunday and 15 to 31 August – **Meals** a la carte 5400/6600
Spec. Filloa de caviar con bogavante, queso y membrillo. Pescado de playa con parmentier de berenjenas (summer). Pintada del Gers rustida con cardamomo y canela.

Botafumeiro, Gran de Gràcia 81, ✉ 08012, ☎ 218 42 30, Fax 415 58 48, seafood – HU v
closed 5 to 25 August – **Meals** a la carte 4850/6500.

Roncesvalles, Via Augusta 201, ✉ 08021, ☎ 209 01 25, Fax 209 12 95 – FV a
closed Saturday lunch and Sunday dinner – **Meals** a la carte approx. 4000.

El Trapío, Esperanza 25, ✉ 08017, ☎ 211 58 17, Fax 417 10 37, « Terrace » – EU t
closed Sunday dinner – **Meals** a la carte 3000/4500.

La Petite Marmite, Madrazo 68, ✉ 08006, ☎ 201 48 79 – GU f
closed Sunday, Bank Holidays, Holy Week and August – **Meals** a la carte 2800/4050.

Tiró Mimet, Sant Màrius 22, ✉ 08022, ☎ 211 77 66, Fax 211 77 66 – FU r
closed Saturday lunch, Sunday, 2 to 7 January, Holy Week and three weeks in August – **Meals** a la carte 3650/5050.

Can Cortada, av. de l'Estatut de Catalunya, ✉ 08035, ☎ 427 23 15, Fax 427 02 94, « 16C farm » – N : by Padilla JU
Meals a la carte 2975/5350.

XX **El Asador de Aranda,** av. del Tibidabo 31, ✉ 08022, ☎ 417 01 15, Fax 212 24 8
, Roast lamb, « Former palace » – AE ⓓ E VISA. NW : by Balmes FU
closed Sunday dinner – **Meals** a la carte approx. 4000.

XX **El Racó d'en Freixa,** Sant Elíes 22, ✉ 08006, ☎ 209 75 59, Fax 209 79 18 – ▤.
ⓓ E VISA. GU
closed Sunday dinner, Monday, Holy Week and August – **Meals** a la carte 4500/6075
Spec. El huevo poché con crema de trufas (winter). Escabeche de codornices y pies cerdo. El pescado de Palamós a la cocotte con setas (October-December).

XX **Gaig,** passeig de Maragall 402, ✉ 08031, ☎ 429 10 17, Fax 429 70 02, – ▤. AE
E VISA N : by Travessera de Gràcia HU
closed Monday, Bank Holidays dinner, Holy Week and 2 August-1 September – **Meals** a carte 4200/6505
Spec. Arroz de pichón y ceps. Rodaballo y percebes al jengibre. Perdiz asada con toci de Jabugo (October-January).

XX **Roig Robí,** Séneca 20, ✉ 08006, ☎ 218 92 22, Fax 415 78 42, , « Garden terrace
– ▤. AE ⓓ E VISA JCB. HV
closed Saturday lunch, Sunday and two weeks in August – **Meals** a la carte 4150/630

XX **Tram-Tram,** Major de Sarrià 121, ✉ 08017, ☎ 204 85 18, – ▤. AE E VISA.
closed Saturday lunch, Sunday, Holy Week, 7 to 17 August and 24 December-2 Janua – **Meals** a la carte 4150/5800. EU

X **Vivanda,** Major de Sarrià 134, ✉ 08017, ☎ 205 47 17, Fax 203 19 18, – ▤.
E VISA. EU
closed Sunday and Monday lunch – **Meals** a la carte approx. 3500.

X **Sal i Pebre,** Alfambra 14, ✉ 08034, ☎ 205 36 58, Fax 205 56 72 – ▤. AE ⓓ VIS
W : by Pas. de Manuel Girona EX
Meals a la carte 2575/3050.

X **La Yaya Amelia,** Sardenya 364, ✉ 08025, ☎ 456 45 73
▤. AE E VISA JCB. JU
closed Sunday, Holy Week and 15 days in August – **Meals** a la carte 2850/3925.

Typical atmosphere :

XX **Font del Gat,** passeig Santa Madrona (Montjuïc), ✉ 08004, ☎ 424 02 2
Fax 207 10 26, , Regional decor – Ⓟ. AE ⓓ E VISA.
closed Sunday dinner and Monday except Bank Holidays – **Meals** a la carte 270C 3450. S : by Av. Reina María Cristina GY

X **La Cuineta,** Paradís 4, ✉ 08002, ☎ 315 01 11, Fax 315 07 98, Typical rest, « In a 17 cellar » – ▤. AE ⓓ E VISA JCB. MX
Meals a la carte 2360/4560.

X **Can Culleretes,** Quintana 5, ✉ 08002, ☎ 317 64 85, Fax 317 64 85, Typical rest
▤. AE ⓓ E VISA JCB MY
closed Sunday dinner, Monday and 1 to 22 July – **Meals** a la carte 2150/3200.

X **Los Caracoles,** Escudellers 14, ✉ 08002, ☎ 302 31 85, Fax 302 07 43, Typical res
Rustic regional decor – ▤. AE ⓓ E VISA JCB. MY
Meals a la carte 2975/4725.

X **Pá i Trago,** Parlament 41, ✉ 08015, ☎ 441 13 20, Fax 441 13 20, Typical rest – ▤. E VI
closed Monday and 24 June-7 July – **Meals** a la carte 2400/4350. HY

X **A la Menta,** passeig Manuel Girona 50, ✉ 08034, ☎ 204 15 49, Typical taverna – ▤
AE ⓓ E VISA. EV
closed Sunday dinner – **Meals** a la carte 3500/4600.

Environs

at Esplugues de Llobregat *W : 5 km – ✉ 08950 Esplugues de Llobregat – ☎ 93 :*

XXX **La Masía,** av. Països Catalans 58 ☎ 371 00 09, Fax 372 84 00, , « Terrace under pir trees » – ▤ Ⓟ. AE ⓓ E VISA JCB.
closed Sunday dinner – **Meals** a la carte 3750/5650.

X **Quirze,** Laureà Miró 202 ☎ 371 10 84, Fax 371 65 12, – ▤ Ⓟ. AE E VISA.
closed Saturday dinner and Sunday – **Meals** a la carte 3400/4400.

at Sant Just Desvern *W : 6 km – ✉ 08960 Sant Just Desvern – ☎ 93 :*

Sant Just, Frederic Mompou 1 ☎ 473 25 17, Fax 473 24 50, – |‡| ▤ TV ☎
– 25/450. AE ⓓ E VISA.
Alambí : **Meals** a la carte 3150/4650 – 1300 – **138 rm** 13900/14900, 12 suites

at Sant Cugat del Vallés *NW : 18 km – ✉ 08190 Sant Cugat del Vallés – ☎ 93 :*

Novotel Barcelona-Sant Cugat , pl. Xavier Cugat, ✉ 08190 apartado 12
☎ 589 41 41, Fax 589 30 31, <, , – |‡| ▤ TV ☎ Ⓟ – 25/300. AE ⓓ E VIS
Meals a la carte approx. 4500 – 1450 – **146 rm** 12900/16000, 4 suites.

...n Celoni o **Sant Celoni** *08470 Barcelona* 443 *G37 – pop. 11937 alt. 152 – ☎ 93.*
Envir.: NO: Sierra de Montseny★: itinerary★★ from San Celoni to Santa Fé del Montseny – Road★ from San Celoni to Tona by Montseny.
Madrid 662 – Barcelona 49 – Gerona/Girona 57.

XXX ✿✿ **El Racó de Can Fabes,** Sant Joan 6 ✆ 867 28 51, Fax 867 38 61, Rustic decor – ▤ ⛟. AE ⓓ E VISA JCB
closed Sunday dinner, Monday, 27 January-10 February and 23 June-7 July – **Meals** 12500 and a la carte 9000/11000
Spec. Espardenyes con tocino confitado. Royal de bogavante. Paletilla de ciervo al enebro (season).

For the quickest route use the MICHELIN Main Road Maps:
970 Europe, 976 Czech Republic-Slovak Republic, 980 Greece, 984 Germany, 985 Scandinavia-Finland, 986 Great Britain and Ireland, 987 Germany-Austria-Benelux, 988 Italy, 989 France, 990 Spain-Portugal and 991 Yugoslavia.

...ÁLAGA - MARBELLA

...álaga *29000* 446 *V 16 – pop. 534683 – ☎ 95 – Seaside resort.*
See: Gibralfaro: ≤★★ DY – Alcazaba★ (museum ★) DY.
Envir.: Finca de la Concepción★ N: 7 km.
Málaga SW: 9 km ✆ 237 66 77, Fax 237 66 12 – El Candado E: 5 km ✆ 229 93 40 Fax 229 08 45.
Málaga SW: 9 km ✆ 204 84 84 – Iberia: Molina Larios 13, ✉ 29015, ✆ 213 61 47 CY and – Aviaco: Airport ✆ 223 08 63.
✆ 231 13 96.
to Melilla: Cía Trasmediterránea, Estación Marítima, Local E-1 ✉ 29016 CZ, ✆ 222 43 91 Fax 222 48 83.
Pasaje de Chinitas 4, ✉ 29015, ✆ 221 34 45 Fax 222 94 21 – R.A.C.E. *Calderería 1, ✉ 29008, ✆ 221 42 60 Fax 221 20 32.*
Madrid 548 – Algeciras 133 – Córdoba 175 – Sevilla 217 – Valencia 651.

Plan on next page

Parador de Málaga-Gibralfaro ⊗, Castillo de Gibralfaro, ✉ 29016, ✆ 222 19 02, Fax 222 19 04, « Magnificent setting with ≤ Málaga and sea », ⛱ – |‡| ▤ TV ☎ ♿ P – 🏛 25/60. AE ⓓ E VISA JCB. ✂ DY
Meals 3500 – ☕ 1200 – **38 rm** 18000.

Málaga Palacio without rest, av. Cortina del Muelle 1, ✉ 29015, ✆ 221 51 85, Fax 221 51 85, ≤, ⛱ – |‡| ▤ TV ☎ – 🏛 25/300. AE ⓓ E VISA. ✂ CZ b
☕ 1000 – **221 rm** 17850/25500.

Larios coffee shop only, Marqués de Larios 2, ✉ 29005, ✆ 222 22 00, Fax 222 24 07 – |‡| ▤ TV ☎ – 🏛 25/150. AE ⓓ E VISA. ✂ CY s
☕ 1250 – **39 rm** 13500/17000.

Don Curro coffee shop only, Sancha de Lara 7, ✉ 29015, ✆ 222 72 00, Fax 221 59 46 – |‡| ▤ TV ☎. AE ⓓ E VISA JCB CZ e
☕ 625 – **103 rm** 9100/13300.

Los Naranjos without rest, paseo de Sancha 35, ✉ 29016, ✆ 222 43 19, Fax 222 59 75 – |‡| ▤ TV ☎ ⛟. AE ⓓ E VISA. ✂ E: by Pas. Cánovas del Castillo DZ
☕ 900 – **40 rm** 10800/14800, 1 suite.

XXX **Café de París,** Vélez Málaga 8, ✉ 29016, ✆ 222 50 43, Fax 260 38 64 – ▤. AE ⓓ E VISA JCB. ✂ E: by Pas. Cánovas del Castillo DZ
closed Sunday and 15 June-15 July – **Meals** a la carte 2475/4400.

XX **Adolfo,** paseo Marítimo Pablo Ruiz Picasso 12, ✉ 29016, ✆ 260 19 14 – ▤. AE ⓓ E VISA. ✂ E: by Pas. Cánovas del Castillo DZ
closed Sunday – **Meals** a la carte 2800/4800.

X **Refectorium,** Cervantes 8, ✉ 29016, ✆ 221 89 90 – ▤. AE ⓓ E VISA
closed Sunday and 15 to 30 June – **Meals** a la carte approx. 4200. E: by Pas. Cánovas del Castillo DZ

...t Club de Campo *SW: 9 km – ✉ 29000 Málaga – ☎ 95:*

Parador de Málaga del Golf, at the golf course, ✉ 29080 apartado 324 Málaga, ✆ 238 12 55, Fax 238 89 63, ≤, ⛱, « Overlooking the golf course », ⛱, ✂, 18 – ▤ TV ☎ P – 🏛 25/70. AE ⓓ E VISA. ✂
Meals 3500 – ☕ 1200 – **56 rm** 16500, 4 suites.

MÁLAGA

Constitución . . . . CY 40
Granada . . . . CDY
Marqués de Larios . . . . . CYZ 84
Nueva . . . . CYZ
Santa Lucía . . . . CY 123

Aduana (Pl. de la) . . . . . . DY 2
Arriola (Pl. de la) . . . . CZ 5
Atocha (Pasillo) . . . . CZ 8

Calderería . . . . CY 13
Cánovas del Castillo (Pas.) . DZ 18
Cárcer . . . . CY 27
Casapalma . . . . CY 30
Colón (Alameda de) . . . . . . CZ 32
Comandante Benítez
(Av. del) . . . . CZ 35
Compañía . . . . CY 37
Cortina del Muelle . . . . CZ 42
Especerías . . . . CY 56
Frailes . . . . CDY 61
Huerto del Conde . . . . DY 67

Mariblanca . . . . CY 7
Martínez . . . . CZ 8
Molina Larios . . . . CYZ 9
Postigo de los Abades . . . CDZ 1
Reding (Paseo de) . . . . . . DY 1
Santa Isabel (Pasillo de) . . CYZ 1
Santa María . . . . CY 1
Sebastián Souvirón . . . . . CZ 1
Strachan . . . . CZ 1
Teatro (Pl. del) . . . . CY 1
Tejón y Rodríguez . . . . . . CY 1
Tetuán (Puente de) . . . . . CZ 1

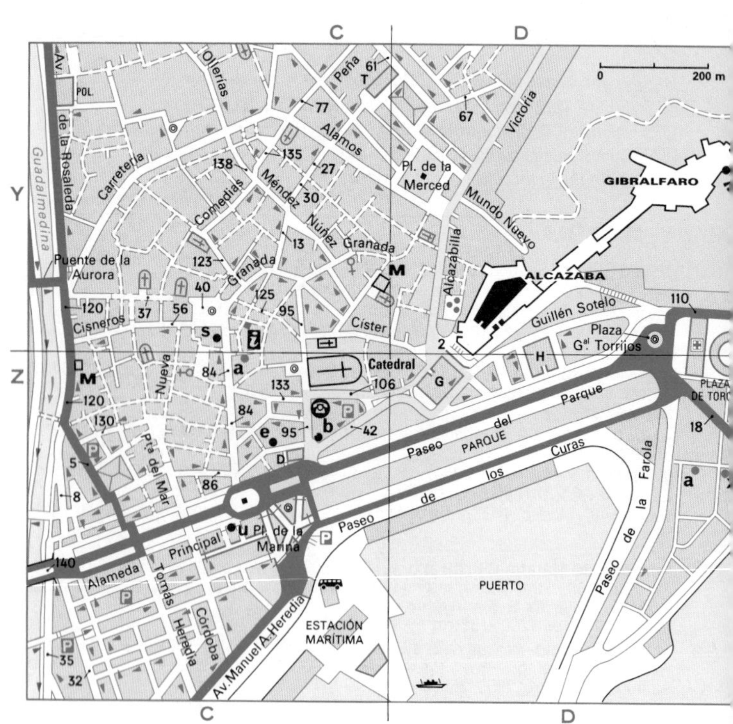

at Urbanización Mijas Golf *by N 340 - SW : 30 km - ✉ 29640 Fuengirola - ☎ 95 :*

Byblos Andaluz, ☎ 247 30 50, Telex 79713, Fax 247 67 83, ≤ golf course and moun tains, , Thalassotherapy facilities, « Tasteful Andalusian style situated between two go courses », - - 20/170. AE ① E VISA. ✻
Le Nailhac *(dinner only, closed Wednesday)* **Meals** a la carte approx. 7100 - ***El Andalu*** *(dinner only)* **Meals** a la carte approx. 4600 - ☐ 2250 - **108 rm** 31500/37500, 36 suite

Marbella *29600 Málaga* 446 W 15 *- pop. 84 410 - ☎ 95 - Beach.*
Envir. : *Puerto Banús (Pleasure harbour★) by ② : 8 km.*
18 Río Real by ① : 5 km ☎ 277 95 09 Fax 277 21 40 - 18 Los Naranjos by ② : 7 k ☎ 281 24 28 - 18 Aloha, urb. Aloha by ② : 8 km ☎ 281 23 88 - 18 Las Brisas, Nuev Andalucía by ② : 11 km, ☎ 281 08 75.
Glorieta de la Fontanilla ☎ 277 14 42 Fax 277 94 57 and Pl. de los Naranjos ☎ 282 35 5 Fax 277 36 21.
Madrid 602 ① - Algeciras 77 ② - Cádiz 201 ② - Málaga 56 ①

Plan opposite

Gran Meliá Don Pepe, José Meliá ☎ 277 03 00, Telex 77055, Fax 277 99 54, *sea and mountains*, , « Subtropical plants », - 25/300. AE ① E VISA JCB. ✻ rest by
Meals 5600 - ***Grill La Farola*** *(dinner only)* **Meals** a la carte 6300/7800 - ☐ 2300 - **198 r** 24400/36500, 6 suites.

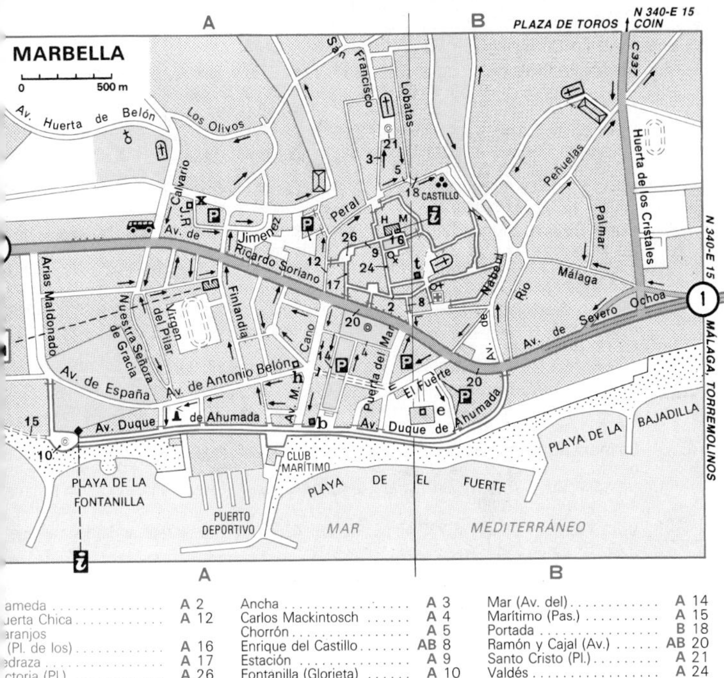

(Pl. de los)	A 16	Ancha	A 3	Mar (Av. del)	A 14
ctoria (Pl.)	A 26	Carlos Mackintosch	A 4	Marítimo (Pas.)	A 15
		Chorrón	A 5	Portada	B 18
		Enrique del Castillo	AB 8	Ramón y Cajal (Av.)	AB 20
		Estación	A 9	Santo Cristo (Pl.)	A 21
		Fontanilla (Glorieta)	A 10	Valdés	A 24

El Fuerte, av. del Fuerte ✆ 286 15 00, Telex 77523, Fax 282 44 11, ≤, « Terraces with garden and palm trees », heated, – 25/500. rest AB e
Meals 3800 – 1500 – **244 rm** 10900/19800, 19 suites.

Marbella Inn coffee shop only, Jacinto Benavente - bloque 6 ✆ 282 54 87, Fax 282 54 87, heated – A x
700 – **40 suites** 9100/11350.

Lima without rest, av. Antonio Belón 2 ✆ 277 05 00, Fax 286 30 91 – A h
495 – **64 rm** 7160/8950.

Santiago, av. Duque de Ahumada 5 ✆ 277 43 39, Fax 282 45 03, seafood – A b
closed November – **Meals** a la carte 4200/5700.

Triana, Gloria 11 ✆ 277 99 62, Rice dishes – B t
closed Monday and 12 January-5 March – **Meals** a la carte 2800/3750.

Cenicienta, av. Cánovas del Castillo 52 (by pass) ✆ 277 43 18, –
closed January – **Meals** (dinner only) a la carte 2950/4250. by ②

on the road to Málaga *by ① – ✉ 29600 Marbella – 95 :*

Don Carlos , 10 km ✆ 283 11 40, Telex 77015, Fax 283 34 29, ≤, « Large garden », heated, – – 25/1200.
Meals 4700 - ***Los Naranjos*** *(dinner only)* **Meals** a la carte 4495/9250 – 1400 – **223 rm** 27000/32000, 15 suites.

Artola without rest, 12,5 km ✆ 283 13 90, Fax 283 04 50, ≤, « On a golf course », –
900 – **29 rm** 7000/11000, 2 suites.

La Hacienda, 11,5 km and detour 1,5 km ✆ 283 12 67, Fax 283 33 28, « Rustic decor, patio » –
closed Monday except August, Tuesday except July-August and 15 November-15 December – **Meals** (dinner only in August) a la carte 5425/7895.

Las Banderas, 9,5 km and detour 0,5 km ✆ 283 18 19, –
closed Wednesday – **Meals** a la carte 2600/3800.

on the road to Cádiz *by ② – ✉ 29600 Marbella – ☎ 95 :*

Marbella Club ⛱, 3 km ☎ 282 22 11, Telex 77319, Fax 282 98 84, ⛱, heated, ⛱, ⛱, 🎾 – 🛗 ▤ 📺 ☎ 🅟 – 🏔 25/180. AE ⓓ E VISA. ✗
Meals 5600 – ☕ 2300 – **83 rm** 34000/42000, 46 suites.

Puente Romano ⛱, 3,5 km ☎ 282 09 00, Telex 77399, Fax 277 57 66, ⛱, « Elegant Andalusian complex in attractive garden », heated, ⛱, 🎾 – 🛗 ▤ 📺 ☎ 🅟 – 🏔 25/170. AE ⓓ E VISA
Meals 5800 - ***La Plaza*** *(dinner only)* **Meals** a la carte approx. 5725 – ☕ 1900 – **142 rm** 33000/45000, 77 suites.

Coral Beach, 5 km ☎ 282 45 00, Telex 79816, Fax 282 62 57, Lš, ⛱, ⛱ – 🛗 ▤ 📺 ☎ ♿ 🚗 🅟 – 🏔 25/200. AE ⓓ E VISA. ✗
15 March-October – ***Florencia*** *(dinner only)* **Meals** a la carte approx. 6400 – ☕ 1800 – **148 rm** 26000/31000, 22 suites.

Rincón Andaluz, 8 km, ✉ 29660 Nueva Andalucía, ☎ 281 15 17, Fax 281 41 80, « In the style of an Andalusian village », heated, ⛱, ⛱ – ▤ 📺 ☎ 🅟 – 🏔 25/100. AE ⓓ E VISA. ✗
15 March-October – **Meals** 3200 – ☕ 1300 – **222 rm** 17500/29500.

Tryp Marbella Dinamar, 6 km, ✉ 29660 Nueva Andalucía, ☎ 281 05 00, Fax 281 23 46, ⋞, ⛱, « Garden with ⛱ », ⛱, 🎾 – 🛗 ▤ 📺 ☎ 🅟 – 🏔 25/150. AE ⓓ E VISA. ✗
Meals 3200 – **116 rm** ☕ 19200/25000.

La Meridiana, camino de la Cruz - 3,5 km ☎ 277 61 90, Fax 282 60 24, ⋞, ⛱, « Garden terrace » – ▤ 🅟. AE ⓓ E VISA. ✗
closed Monday, Tuesday lunch and 7 January-February – **Meals** (dinner only in summer) a la carte 6100/7200.

Villa Tiberio, 2,5 km ☎ 277 17 99, Fax 282 47 72, ⛱, Italian rest, « Garden terrace » – 🅟. AE ⓓ E VISA. ✗
closed Sunday – **Meals** (dinner only) a la carte 4600/5500.

El Portalón, 3 km ☎ 282 78 80, Fax 277 71 04, Braised meat specialities – ▤ 🅟. AE ⓓ E VISA. ✗
Meals a la carte 4400/6200.

at Puerto Banús *W : 8 km – ✉ 29660 Nueva Andalucía – ☎ 95 :*

Cipriano, av. Playas del Duque - edificio Sevilla ☎ 281 10 77, Fax 281 10 77, ⛱ – ▤ 🅟. AE ⓓ E VISA
Meals a la carte 4200/6550

Taberna del Alabardero, muelle Benabola ☎ 281 27 94, Fax 281 86 30, ⛱ – ▤ AE ⓓ E VISA. ✗
Meals a la carte 5075/6100.

SEVILLA *41000* 🅿 446 T 11 y 12 – *pop. 704 857 alt. 12 – ☎ 95.*

See : *La Giralda★★★ (※★★)* BX – *Cathedral★★★ (Capilla Mayor altarpiece★★★, Capilla Real★★)* BX – *Reales Alcázares★★★* BXY *(Admiral Apartment : Virgin of the Mareantes altarpiece★ ; Pedro el Cruel Palace★★★ : Ambassadors room vault★★ ; – Carlos V Palace tapestries★★, gardens★) – Santa Cruz Quarter★★* BCX *(Venerables Hospital★) – Fine Arts Museum★★ (room V★★★, room X★★)* AV – *Pilate's House★★ (Azulejos★★, staircase★ cupule★)* CX – *María Luisa Park★★ (España Square★, – Archaelogical Museum : Carambolo tresor★) S : by Paseo de las Delicias* BY.

Other Curiosities : Charity Hospital★ BY *Santa Paula Convent★* CV *(front★ church) – Salvador Church★* BX *(baroque altarpieces★★) – Sant Josep Chappel★* BX – *Town Hall (Ayuntamiento) : east front★* BX.

Pineda SE : 3 km ☎ 461 14 00.

Sevilla - San Pablo NE : 14 km ☎ 444 90 00 – Iberia : Almirante Lobo 2, ✉ 41001 ☎ 422 89 01 BX.

Santa Justa ☎ 453 86 86.

Av. de la Constitución 21 B ✉ 41004, ☎ 422 14 04 Fax 422 97 53 and Paseo de las Delicias ✉ 41012, ☎ 423 44 65 – R.A.C.E. *Av. Eduardo Dato 22, ✉ 41002, ☎ 463 13 50 Fax 465 96 04.*

Madrid 550 – La Coruña/A Coruña 950 – Lisboa 417 – Málaga 217 – Valencia 682.

Plans on following pages

Alfonso XIII, San Fernando 2, ✉ 41004, ☎ 422 28 50, Telex 72725, Fax 421 60 33, ⛱, « Magnificent Andalusian building », ⛱, ⛱ – 🛗 ▤ 📺 ☎ 🚗 🅟 – 🏔 25/500. AE ⓓ E VISA JCB BY
Meals a la carte 4600/6200 – ☕ 2500 – **127 rm** 49500/61600, 19 suites.

Príncipe de Asturias ⛱, Isla de La Cartuja, ✉ 41092, ☎ 446 22 22, Fax 446 04 28, ⛱ – 🛗 ▤ 📺 ☎ 🚗 – 🏔 25/900. AE ⓓ E VISA. ✗ N : by Torneo AV
Meals 4000 – **288 rm** ☕ 21000/26500, 7 suites.

Tryp Colón, Canalejas 1, ✉ 41001, ☎ 422 29 00, Telex 72726, Fax 422 09 38, – AE VISA JCB. AX s
Meals (see rest. ***El Burladero*** below) – 1600 – **204 rm** 17850/22050, 14 suites.

Occidental Porta Coeli, av. Eduardo Dato 49, ✉ 41018, ☎ 453 35 00, Telex 72913, Fax 453 23 42, – 25/600. AE E VISA.
Meals (see rest. ***Florencia*** below) – 1500 – **241 rm** 15000/19000, 3 suites.
E : by Demetrio de los Ríos CXY

Meliá Lebreros, Luis Morales 2, ✉ 41005, ☎ 457 94 00, Fax 458 27 26, – 25/600. AE E VISA JCB. E : by Luis Montoto CX
Meals (see rest. ***La Dehesa*** below) 4300 – 1500 – **431 rm** 14400/17500, 6 suites.

Meliá Sevilla, Doctor Pedro de Castro 1, ✉ 41004, ☎ 442 15 11, Fax 442 16 08, – 25/1000. AE E VISA JCB. SE : by Av. de Portugal CY
closed July and August – **Meals** 3500 – 1500 – **361 rm** 20500/23800, 5 suites.

Meliá Confort Macarena, San Juan de Ribera 2, ✉ 41009, ☎ 437 58 00, Fax 438 18 03, – 25/700. AE E VISA.
Meals 3500 – 1500 – **317 rm** 12300/15200, 10 suites. N : by María Auxiliadora CV

Occidental Sevilla coffee shop only, av. Kansas City, ✉ 41018, ☎ 458 20 00, Fax 458 46 15, – 25/320. AE E VISA JCB.
1400 – **228 rm** 22000/27000, 14 suites. E : by Luis Montoto CX

Inglaterra, pl. Nueva 7, ✉ 41001, ☎ 422 49 70, Fax 456 13 36 – 25/200. AE E VISA JCB. rest AX r
Meals 3000 – 1200 – **109 rm** 16500/21000, 4 suites.

Los Seises, Segovias 6, ✉ 41004, ☎ 422 94 95, Fax 422 43 34, « On the 3rd patio of the Archbishop's Palace », – 25/100. AE E VISA. BX f
Meals *(closed August)* a la carte 4400/5500 – 1500 – **43 rm** 20000/25000.

Al-Andalus Palace, av. de la Palmera, ✉ 41012, ☎ 423 06 00, Fax 423 02 00, – 25/1100. AE E VISA.
Meals 3000 - ***El Patio* :** **Meals** a la carte 2350/4100 – 1500 – **327 rm** 14000/17500, 1 suite. SE : by Paseo de las Delicias BY

NH Ciudad de Sevilla, av. Manuel Siurot 25, ✉ 41013, ☎ 423 05 05, Fax 423 85 39, – 25/300. AE E VISA JCB. SE : by Paseo de las Delicias BY
Meals 3000 – 1250 – **90 rm** 13800/16000, 3 suites.

Pasarela without rest, av. de la Borbolla 11, ✉ 41004, ☎ 441 55 11, Fax 442 07 27 – 25. AE E VISA. SE : by Av. de Portugal CY
1000 – **77 rm** 11000/18000, 5 suites.

G.H. Lar, pl. Carmen Benítez 3, ✉ 41003, ☎ 441 03 61, Fax 441 04 52 – 25/300. AE E VISA. CX f
Meals 2600 – 1000 – **129 rm** 11500/16500, 8 suites.

Husa Sevilla, Pagés del Corro 90, ✉ 41010, ☎ 434 24 12, Fax 434 27 07 – 25/220. AE E VISA. AY a
Meals 2650 – 1100 – **114 rm** 12500/18500, 14 suites.

NH Plaza de Armas, av. Marqués de Paradas, ✉ 41001, ☎ 490 19 92, Fax 490 12 32, – 25/250. AE E VISA. AV c
Meals a la carte approx. 3910 – 1300 – **260 rm** 12100/15200, 2 suites.

Sevilla Congresos, Alcalde Luis Uruñuela, ✉ 41020, ☎ 425 90 00, Fax 425 95 00, – 25/270. AE E VISA. rest NE : by Luis Montoto CX
Meals a la carte approx. 4575 – **202 rm** 10000/12500, 1 suite.

Bécquer coffee shop only, Reyes Católicos 4, ✉ 41001, ☎ 422 89 00, Fax 421 44 00 – 25/45. AE E VISA AX v
1000 – **120 rm** 7000/12000.

Emperador Trajano, José Laguillo 8, ✉ 41003, ☎ 441 11 11, Fax 453 57 02 – 25/150. AE E VISA JCB. CV a
Meals 1900 – 1000 – **77 rm** 10850/13000.

San Gil without rest, Parras 28, ✉ 41002, ☎ 490 68 11, Fax 490 69 39, « Early 20C partially converted typical Sevilian building, patio with garden », – . AE E VISA JCB. N : by María Auxiliadora CV
800 – **4 rm** 11300/13200, 35 suites.

Álvarez Quintero coffee shop only, Álvarez Quintero 9, ✉ 41004, ☎ 422 12 98, Fax 456 41 41 – . AE E VISA. BX c
850 – **43 rm** 10000/15000.

Giralda, Sierra Nevada 3, ✉ 41003, ☎ 441 66 61, Fax 441 93 52 – 25/250. AE E VISA JCB. CX e
Meals 1500 – 1000 – **98 rm** 10830/13000.

SEVILLA

Francos . . . . BX
Sierpes . . . . BVX
Tetuán . . . . BX

Alemanes . . . . BX 12
Alfaro (Pl.) . . . . CXY 15
Almirante Apodaca . . . . CV 20
Almirante Lobo . . . . BY 22
Álvarez Quintero . . . . . . BX 23
Amparo . . . . BV 25
Aposentadores . . . . BV 28
Argote de Molina . . . . . . BX 30
Armas (Pl. de) . . . . AX 31
Banderas (Patio de) . . . BXY 35
Capitán Vigueras . . . . . . CY 42
Cardenal Spínola . . . . . . AV 47
Castelar . . . . AX 55
Chapina (Puente) . . . . . . AX 59
Cruces . . . . CX 75
Doña Elvira . . . . BX 95
Doña Guiomar . . . . AX 97
Escuelas Pías . . . . CV 114
Farmacéutico E.
Murillo Herrera . . . . . . AY 115
Feria . . . . BV 123
Francisco Carrión
Mejías . . . . CV 126
Fray Ceferino
González . . . . BX 127
García de Vinuesa . . . . . BX 130
General Polavieja . . . . . . BX 135
Jesús de la Vera Cruz . . AV 147
José María Martínez
Sánchez Arjona . . . . . AY 150
Julio César . . . . AX 152
Luis Montoto . . . . CX 160
Marcelino Champagnat . AY 172
Martín Villa . . . . BV 190
Mateos Gago . . . . BX 192
Murillo . . . . AV 202
Museo (Pl.) . . . . AV 205
Navarros . . . . CVX 207
O'Donnell . . . . BV 210
Pascual de Gayangos . . . AV 220
Pastor y Landero . . . . . . AX 222
Pedro del Toro . . . . AV 227
Ponce de León (Pl.) . . . . CV 234
Puente y Pellón . . . . BV 239
Puerta de Jerez . . . . BY 242
República Argentina
(Av.) . . . . AY 255
Reyes Católicos . . . . AX 260
San Gregorio . . . . BY 272
San Juan
de la Palma . . . . BV 277
San Pedro (Pl.) . . . . BV 286
San Sebastián (Pl.) . . . . . CY 287
Santa María
la Blanca . . . . CX 297
Santander . . . . BY 300
Saturno . . . . CV 302
Triunfo (Pl.) . . . . BX 307
Velázquez . . . . BV 310
Venerables (Pl.) . . . . BX 312
Viriato . . . . BV 329

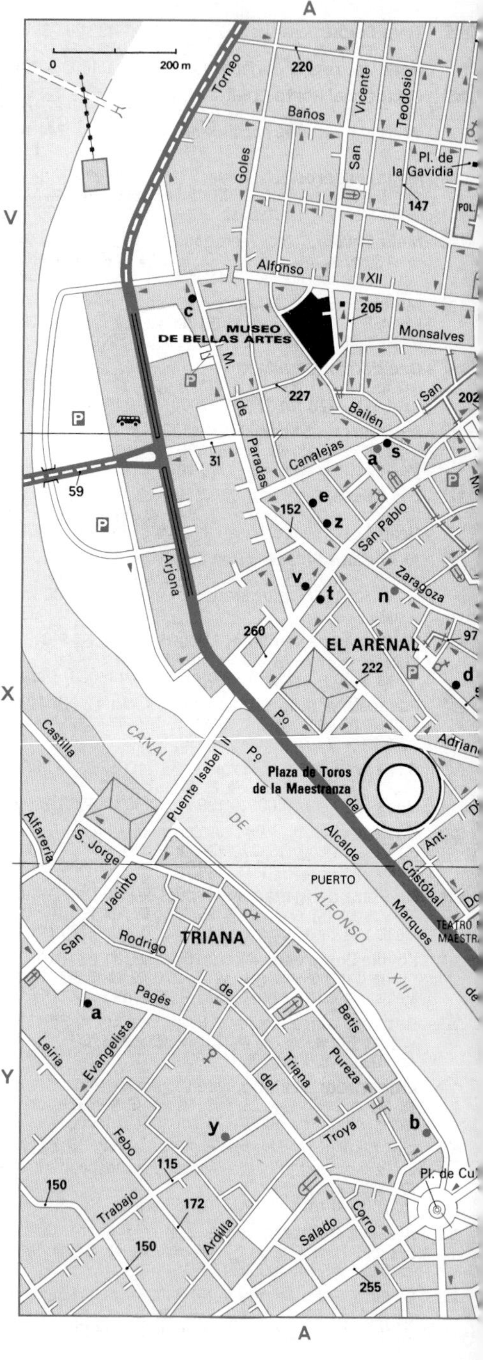

Inclusion in the
Michelin Guide
cannot be achieved
by pulling strings
or by offering favours.

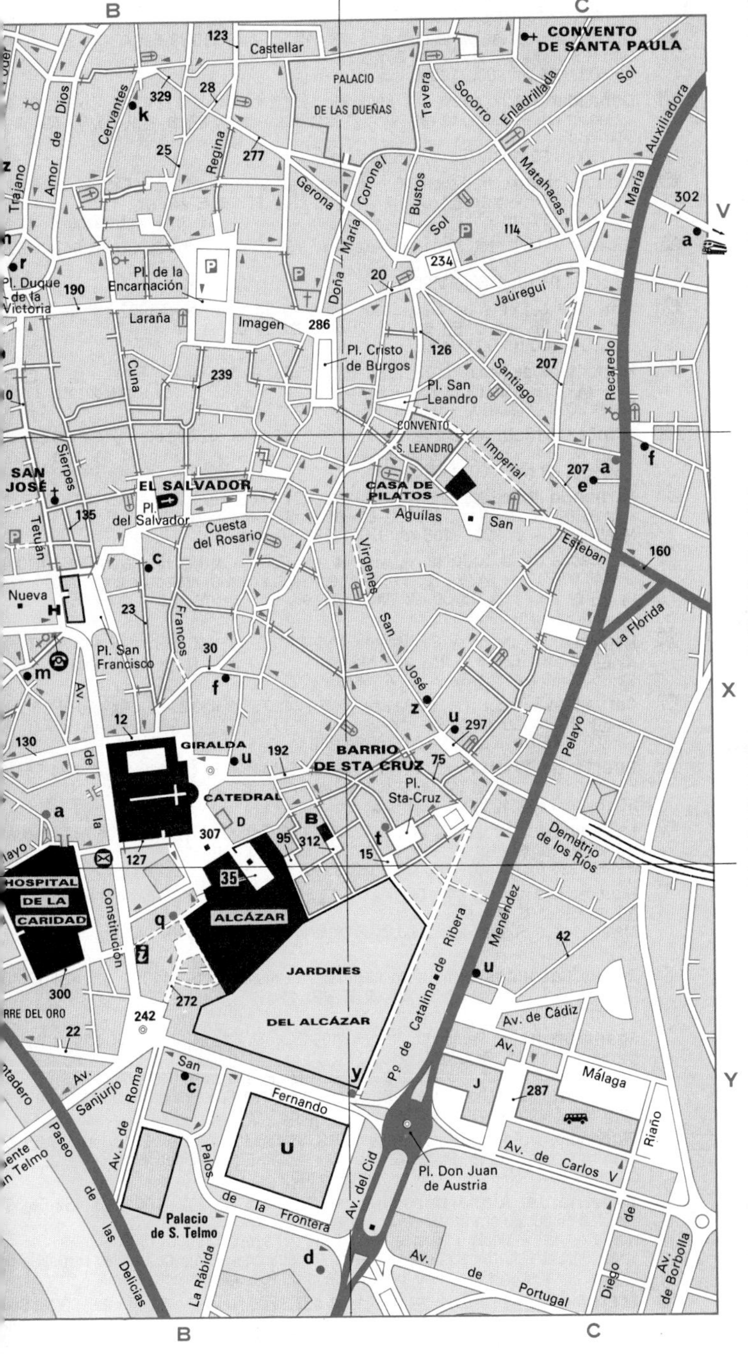
B
C
123
Castellar
CONVENTO DE SANTA PAULA
PALACIO DE LAS DUEÑAS
Amor de Dios
Cervantes
329
28
k
Regina
277
25
Trajano
Tavera
Socorro
Enladrillada
Sol
Auxiliadora
María
Matahacas
Gerona
Coronel
Bustos
302
V
a
114
Sol
234
Pl. Duque de la Victoria
190
Pl. de la Encarnación
Doña María Coronel
20
Jaúregui
Laraña
Imagen
286
Pl. Cristo de Burgos
126
Santiago
207
Recaredo
Cuna
239
Pl. San Leandro
CONVENTO S. LEANDRO
Imperial
f
207
a
e
SAN JOSÉ
Sierpes
EL SALVADOR
Pl. del Salvador
CASA DE PILATOS
Aguilas
San Esteban
135
Tetuán
Cuesta del Rosario
Vírgenes
160
c
Nueva
H
23
Francos
San José
La Florida
Pl. San Francisco
30
f
m
X
z
u
297
Pelayo
12
GIRALDA
u
192
BARRIO DE STA CRUZ
75
130
Av. de la Constitución
CATEDRAL
Pl. Sta-Cruz
a
D
B
307
312
95
t
Demetrio de los Ríos
127
15
HOSPITAL DE LA CARIDAD
35
ALCÁZAR
q
Menéndez Pelayo
42
JARDINES DEL ALCÁZAR
Pº de Catalina de Ribera
u
300
272
TORRE DEL ORO
242
Av. de Cádiz
22
Av.
San
c
Málaga
Y
Av. Sanjurjo
Av. de Roma
Fernando
y
J
287
Paseo de las Delicias
U
Av. del Cid
Pl. Don Juan de Austria
Av. de Carlos V
Riaño
Palos de la Frontera
Palacio de S. Telmo
d
Av. de Portugal
Diego de Riaño
Av. de Borbolla
La Rábida
B
C

Derby without rest, pl. del Duque 13, ✉ 41002, ☎ 456 10 88, Fax 421 33 91, Terrac with ≤ - . AE E VISA. BV
800 - **75 rm** 9000/10000.

Doña María without rest, Don Remondo 19, ✉ 41004, ☎ 422 49 90, Fax 421 95 4 « Elegant classic decor, terrace with and ≤ » - 25/40. AE VISA. BX
1300 - **59 rm** 10500/17000, 2 suites.

Monte Triana coffee shop only, Clara de Jesús Montero 24, ✉ 41010, ☎ 434 31 1 Fax 434 33 28 - - 25/100. AE E VISA.
750 - **117 rm** 9200/11500. W : by Puente Isabel II AX

Alcázar without rest, Menéndez Pelayo 10, ✉ 41004, ☎ 441 20 11, Fax 442 16 59 . AE E VISA. CY
500 - **93 rm** 13000/16000.

América coffee shop only, Jesús del Gran Poder 2, ✉ 41002, ☎ 422 09 5 Fax 421 06 26 - - 25/150. AE E VISA. BV
800 - **100 rm** 9000/10000.

Hispalis, av. de Andalucía 52, ✉ 41006, ☎ 452 94 33, Fax 467 53 13 - - 25/50. AE E VISA JCB. E : by Luis Montoto CX
Meals 2000 - 1000 - **67 rm** 9750/11550, 1 suite.

Monte Carmelo without rest, Turia 7, ✉ 41011, ☎ 427 90 00, Fax 427 10 04 - - 25/35. AE E VISA S : by Pl. de Cuba AY
700 - **68 rm** 7000/11000.

Fernando III, San José 21, ✉ 41004, ☎ 421 77 08, Telex 72491, Fax 422 02 46, - - 25/250. AE E VISA. CX
Meals 2300 - 990 - **156 rm** 8785/11800, 1 suite.

Las Casas de la Judería without rest, Callejón de Dos Hermanas 7, ✉ 4100 ☎ 441 51 50, Fax 442 21 70, « Ancient stately home with attractive courtyards » - - 25/50. AE E VISA. CX
950 - **53 rm** 9000/11500.

Regina coffee shop only, San Vicente 97, ✉ 41002, ☎ 490 75 75, Fax 490 75 62 - . AE E VISA JCB. N : by San Vincente AV
950 - **68 rm** 11000/18000, 4 suites.

Cervantes without rest, Cervantes 10, ✉ 41003, ☎ 490 05 52, Fax 490 05 36 - . AE E VISA. BV
600 - **46 rm** 10000/12500.

Puerta de Triana without rest, Reyes Católicos 5, ✉ 41001, ☎ 421 54 0 Fax 421 54 01 - . AE E VISA JCB. AX
65 rm 7500/10000.

La Rábida, Castelar 24, ✉ 41001, ☎ 422 09 60, Telex 73062, Fax 422 43 75 - rr . AE E VISA. rest AX
Meals 1925 - 400 - **100 rm** 5500/8500.

Montecarlo (annexe), Gravina 51, ✉ 41001, ☎ 421 75 03, Fax 421 68 25 - . AE E VISA. AX
Meals *(closed Sunday and January-February)* 1900 - 600 - **47 rm** 6500/950 4 suites.

Reyes Católicos without rest. no , Gravina 57, ✉ 41001, ☎ 421 12 0 Fax 421 63 12 - . AE E VISA. AX
27 rm 6500/9500.

Egaña Oriza, San Fernando 41, ✉ 41004, ☎ 422 72 54, Fax 421 04 29, « Winte garden » - . AE E VISA. BY
closed Saturday lunch, Sunday and August - **Meals** a la carte 5400/6650
Spec. Langostinos al bacon con salsa de ajos y azafrán. Suprema de lubina asada en sals de trufas. Muslo de pato estofado con mano de ternera.

Florencia, av. Eduardo Dato 49, ✉ 41018, ☎ 453 35 00, Telex 72913, Fax 453 23 4 Tasteful decor - . AE E VISA. E : by Demetrio de los Ríos CXY
closed August - **Meals** a la carte approx. 5100.

Taberna del Alabardero with rm, Zaragoza 20, ✉ 41001, ☎ 456 06 3 Fax 456 36 66, « Former palace » - . AE E VISA. AX
closed August - **Meals** a la carte 4000/6750 - **7 rm** 12000/16000
Spec. Ensalada de tomate, queso fresco y boquerones. Lomo de bacalao con salsa d pimientos choriceros. Solomillo ibérico relleno de foie a la pimienta verde.

El Burladero, Canalejas 1, ✉ 41001, ☎ 422 29 00, Telex 72726, Fax 422 09 38, Bull fighting theme - . AE E VISA JCB. AX
closed 15 June-August - **Meals** a la carte 4050/5650.

XXX **La Dehesa,** Luis Morales 2, ✉ 41005, ✆ 457 94 00, Fax 458 23 09, ☂, Typical Andalusian decor. Braised meat specialities – ▤. AE ⓓ E VISA. ✂
closed August – **Meals** a la carte approx. 4500. E : by Luis Montoto CX

XX **Pello Roteta,** Farmacéutico Murillo Herrera 10, ✉ 41010, ✆ 427 84 17, Basque rest – ▤. AE ⓓ E VISA. ✂ AY y
closed Holy Week and August – **Meals** a la carte approx. 3900.

XX **Al-Mutamid,** Alfonso XI-1, ✉ 41005, ✆ 492 55 04, Fax 492 25 02, ☂ – ▤. AE ⓓ E VISA JCB. ✂ E : by Demetrio de los Ríos CXY
closed Sunday July-August – **Meals** a la carte 3200/4950.

XX **La Albahaca,** pl. Santa Cruz 12, ✉ 41004, ✆ 422 07 14, Fax 456 12 04, ☂, « Former manor house » – ▤. AE ⓓ E VISA. ✂ CX t
closed August – **Meals** a la carte 4400/5400.

XX **Rincón de Curro,** Virgen de Luján 45, ✉ 41011, ✆ 445 02 38, Fax 445 02 38 – ▤. AE ⓓ E VISA. ✂ S : by Pl. de Cuba AY
closed Sunday dinner – **Meals** a la carte 3100/4500.

XX **Rincón de Casana,** Santo Domingo de la Calzada 13, ✉ 41018, ✆ 453 17 10, Fax 464 49 74, Regional decor – ▤. AE ⓓ E VISA. ✂ E : by Demetrio de los Ríos CXY
closed Sunday July-August – **Meals** a la carte 3900/4800.

XX **La Isla,** Arfe 25, ✉ 41001, ✆ 421 26 31, Fax 456 22 19 – ▤. AE ⓓ VISA. ✂
closed Monday and August – **Meals** a la carte 4800/6000. BX a

XX **Ox's,** Betis 61, ✉ 41010, ✆ 427 95 85, Fax 427 84 65, Basque rest – ▤. AE ⓓ E VISA. ✂ AY b
closed Saturday and Sunday in August and Sunday dinner the rest of the year – **Meals** a la carte 3900/5300.

XX **Horacio,** Antonia Díaz 9, ✉ 41001, ✆ 422 53 85 – ▤. AE ⓓ E VISA. ✂ AX c
closed 10 days in August – **Meals** a la carte 3325/4500.

X **El Cantábrico,** Jesús del Gran Poder 20, ✉ 41002, ✆ 438 73 03 – ▤. AE E VISA. ✂ BV z
closed Sunday, Bank Holidays dinner and August – **Meals** a la carte 3075/4100.

X **Los Alcázares,** Miguel de Mañara 10, ✉ 41004, ✆ 421 31 03, Fax 456 18 29, ☂, Regional decor – ▤. E VISA. ✂ BY q
closed Sunday – **Meals** a la carte 2925/4325.

at San Juan de Aznalfarache *W : 4 km – ✉ 41920 San Juan de Aznalfarache – ☎ 95 :*

Alcora ⚘ coffee shop only, carret. de Tomares ✆ 476 94 00, Fax 476 94 98, ≤, « Patio with plants », Lб, ⛱ – |‡| ▤ TV ☎ ♿ ⇔ P – 🚶 25/1200. AE ⓓ E VISA. ✂
☕ 1400 – **331 rm** 14000/17500, 70 suites.

at Castilleja de la Cuesta *W : 5 km – ✉ 41950 Castilleja de la Cuesta – ☎ 95 :*

Hacienda San Ygnacio, Real 194 ✆ 416 04 30, Fax 416 14 37, ☂, « In an old rustic inn », ⛱, ⌂ – ▤ TV ☎ P – 🚶 25/200. AE ⓓ E VISA JCB. ✂ rest
Almazara *(closed Sunday dinner and Monday)* **Meals** a la carte 3100/4600 – ☕ 1100 – **16 rm** 14000/19000.

at Benacazón *W : 23 km – ✉ 41805 Benacazón – ☎ 95 :*

Andalusi Park H., autopista A 49 - salida 6 ✆ 570 56 00, Fax 570 50 79, « Arabian style building, garden », Lб, ⛱ – |‡| ▤ TV ☎ ♿ P – 🚶 25/500. AE ⓓ E VISA. ✂
Los Olivos : **Meals** a la carte approx. 4000 - ***Al'Mutamid :*** **Meals** a la carte approx. 5500 – ☕ 1500 – **189 rm** 12800/16000, 11 suites.

at Sanlúcar la Mayor *W : 27 km – ✉ 41800 Sanlúcar la Mayor – ☎ 95 :*

Hacienda Benazuza ⚘, Virgen de las Nieves ✆ 570 33 44, Fax 570 34 10, ≤, « In a 10C Arabian farmhouse », ⛱, ⌂, 🎾 – |‡| ▤ TV ☎ P – 🚶 25/400. AE ⓓ E VISA. ✂ rest
closed 15 July-August – **Meals** 6000 - ***La Alquería :*** **Meals** a la carte 5600/6200 – ☕ 1500 – **26 rm** 33500/41500, 18 suites.

at Carmona *E : 33 km – ✉ 41410 Carmona – ☎ 95 :*

Parador de Carmona ⚘, ✆ 414 10 10, Telex 72992, Fax 414 17 12, ≤ Corbones fertile plain, « Mudéjar style », ⛱ – |‡| ▤ TV ☎ P – 🚶 25/250. AE ⓓ E VISA. ✂
Meals 3500 – ☕ 1200 – **63 rm** 18000.

EUROPE on a single sheet Michelin Map no 970.

VALENCIA *46000* 445 N 28 y 29 – *pop. 777 427 alt. 13 – ☎ 96.*

See : *The Old town★ : Cathedral★ (El Miguelete★)* EX – *Palacio de la Generalidad★ (golden room : ceiling★)* EX **D** – *Lonja★ (silkhall★★, Maritime consulate hall : ceiling★)* DY.

Other curiosities : *Ceramic Museum★★ (Palacio del Marqués de Dos Aguas★)* EY **M1** *San Pío V Museum★ (valencian primitifs★★)* FX – *Patriarch College or of the Corpus Christi★ (Passion triptych★)* EY **N** – *Serranos Towers★* EX.

Manises E : 12 km, ☎ 152 38 04 – Escorpión NW : 19 km ☎ 160 12 11 – El Saler, Parador Luis Vives-SE : 15 km ☎ 161 11 86.

Valencia - Manises Airport E : 9,5 km ☎ 370 95 00 – Iberia : Paz 14, ✉ 46003, ☎ 352 75 52 EFY.

To the Balearic Islands : Estación Marítima ✉ 46024 ☎ 367 65 12 Fax 367 06 44 by Av. Regne de València FZ.

Pl. del Ayuntamiento 1, ✉ 46002 ☎ 351 04 17, Av. Cataluña 1, ✉ 46010 ☎ 369 79 32 and Paz 48 ✉ 46003 ☎ 394 22 22 – R.A.C.E. *(R.A.C. de València) Av. Regne de València 64, ✉ 46005, ☎ 374 94 05.*

Madrid 351 – Albacete 183 – Alicante/Alacant (by coast) 174 – Barcelona 361 – Bilbao/Bilbo 606 – Castellón de la Plana/Castelló de la Plana 75 – Málaga 651 – Sevilla 682 – Zaragoza 330.

Plans on following pages

Meliá Valencia Palace, paseo de la Alameda 32, ✉ 46023, ☎ 337 50 37, Fax 337 55 32, ≤, – ☎ – 25/800. AE VISA JCB. E : by Puente de Aragón FZ
Meals 3600 – ☐ 1500 – **183 rm** 23500/29500, 16 suites.

Meliá Rey Don Jaime, av. Baleares 2, ✉ 46023, ☎ 337 50 30, Fax 337 15 72, – ☎ – 25/250. AE E VISA. E : by Puente de Aragón FZ
Meals 4000 – ☐ 1450 – **312 rm** 18200/22800, 2 suites.

Astoria Palace, pl. Rodrigo Botet 5, ✉ 46002, ☎ 352 67 37, Telex 62733, Fax 352 80 78 – ☎ – 25/500. AE E VISA JCB. EY p
Meals 3500 - ***Vinatea :*** **Meals** a la carte 3550/4500 – ☐ 1500 – **196 rm** 19500/24500, 7 suites.

Turia, Profesor Beltrán Baguena 2, ✉ 46009, ☎ 347 00 00, Fax 347 32 44 – ☎ – 25/300. E VISA. NW : by G.V. Fernando el Católico DY
Meals 3000 – ☐ 600 – **160 rm** 10150/14600, 10 suites.

Acteón Plaza, Islas Canarias 102, ✉ 46023, ☎ 331 07 07, Fax 330 22 30 – ☎ – 25/400. AE E VISA. E : by Av. Regne de València FZ
Meals 1150 – ☐ 1400 – **182 rm** 18400/23000, 5 suites.

Conqueridor, Cervantes 9, ✉ 46007, ☎ 352 29 10, Fax 352 28 83 – ☎ – 25/80. AE E VISA. DZ b
Meals 2700 – ☐ 1400 – **55 rm** 13900/21800, 4 suites.

Dimar coffee shop only, Gran Vía Marqués del Turia 80, ✉ 46005, ☎ 395 10 30, Fax 395 19 26 – ☎ – 25/50. AE E VISA JCB FZ q
☐ 1300 – **103 rm** 13000/21000, 1 suite.

Reina Victoria, Barcas 4, ✉ 46002, ☎ 352 04 87, Telex 64755, Fax 352 04 87 – ☎ – 25/75. AE E VISA. EY s
Meals 3800 – ☐ 1200 – **94 rm** 12500/20000, 3 suites.

NH Center, Ricardo Micó 1, ✉ 46009, ☎ 347 50 00, Fax 347 62 52, heated – ☎ – 25/400. AE E VISA JCB. N : by Gran Vía Fernando el Católico DY
Meals 3000 – ☐ 1300 – **193 rm** 15000/22000, 3 suites.

NH Ciudad de Valencia, av. del Puerto 214, ✉ 46023, ☎ 330 75 00, Fax 330 98 64 – ☎ – 30/80. AE E VISA JCB.
Meals 2900 – ☐ 1000 – **147 rm** 11500, 2 suites. E : by Puente de Aragón FZ

NH Abashiri, av. Ausias March 59, ✉ 46013, ☎ 373 28 52, Fax 373 49 66 – ☎ – 30/250. AE E VISA JCB. S : by Av. Regne de València FZ
Meals 3000 – ☐ 1100 – **105 rm** 10500/12000.

NH Villacarlos without rest, av. del Puerto 60, ✉ 46023, ☎ 337 50 25, Fax 337 50 74 – ☎ . AE E VISA JCB. E : by Puente de Aragón FZ
☐ 1000 – **51 rm** 12000/17000.

Cónsul del Mar, av. del Puerto 39, ✉ 46021, ☎ 362 54 32, Fax 362 16 25, Old stately home – ☎ . AE E VISA. E : by Puente de Aragón FZ
Meals 1100 – ☐ 700 – **40 rm** 16000.

Ad-Hoc, Boix 4, ✉ 46003, ☎ 391 91 40, Fax 391 36 67, « Attractive 19C building » – ☎. AE E VISA FX a
Meals (see rest. ***Chust Godoy*** below) – ☐ 775 – **28 rm** 11300/15950.

Renasa coffee shop only, av. de Cataluña 5, ✉ 46010, ☎ 369 24 50, Fax 393 18 24 – ☎ – 25/75. AE E VISA E : by Puente del Real FX
☐ 600 – **69 rm** 7000/11500, 4 suites.

Llar without rest, Colón 46, ✉ 46004, ☎ 352 84 60, Fax 351 90 00 - 25/30. AE ⓓ E VISA FZ u
1100 - **50 rm** 9200/12000.

Sorolla without rest., no, Convento de Santa Clara 5, ✉ 46002, ☎ 352 33 92, Fax 352 14 65 - AE ⓓ E VISA. EZ z
50 rm 5900/10700.

Chambelán, Chile 4, ✉ 46021, ☎ 393 37 74, Fax 393 37 72 - AE ⓓ E VISA. E : by Puente de Aragón FZ
closed Saturday lunch, Sunday and Holy Week - **Meals** a la carte 4700/6800.

Eladio, Chiva 40, ✉ 46018, ☎ 384 22 44, Fax 384 22 44 - AE ⓓ E VISA.
closed Sunday and August - **Meals** a la carte approx. 5150. W : by Ángel Guimerá DY

Óscar Torrijos, Dr. Sumsi 4, ✉ 46005, ☎ 373 29 49 - AE ⓓ E VISA.
closed Sunday and 15 August-15 September - **Meals** a la carte 4500/5400 FZ h
Spec. Arroz de rape y alcachofas. Muslo y pechuga de pato en dos cocciones con salsa de naranja. Frambuesas calientes con helado de vainilla.

Rías Gallegas, Cirilo Amorós 4, ✉ 46004, ☎ 352 51 11, Fax 351 99 10, Galician rest - AE ⓓ E VISA EZ r
closed Sunday and 11 to 24 August - **Meals** 4650 and a la carte 3900/6550
Spec. Lamprea estilo Arbo (January-March). Abadejo con grelos y ajos confitados. Solomillo al queso de Cabrales.

Albacar, Sorní 35, ✉ 46004, ☎ 395 10 05 - AE ⓓ E VISA. FY s
closed Saturday lunch, Sunday, Holy Week and 9 August-9 September - **Meals** a la carte approx. 4850.

El Ángel Azul, Conde de Altea 33, ✉ 46005, ☎ 374 56 56 - AE ⓓ VISA. FZ e
closed Sunday, Monday, Holy Week and 1 to 21 September - **Meals** a la carte approx. 4100.

Kailuze, Gregorio Mayáns 5, ✉ 46005, ☎ 374 39 99, Basque rest - AE VISA.
closed Saturday lunch, Sunday, Bank Holidays, Holy Week and August - **Meals** a la carte 3750/4450. FZ d

El Gastrónomo, av. Primado Reig 149, ✉ 46020, ☎ 369 70 36 - AE E VISA. NE : by Puente del Real FX
closed Sunday and August - **Meals** a la carte 3550/4500.

Joaquín Schmidt, Visitación 7 ☎ 340 17 10, Fax 340 17 10, - AE ⓓ VISA.
closed Sunday, Monday lunch, 31 March-10 April and 10 August-4 September - **Meals** a la carte 4350/4950. N : by Cronista Rivelles EX

El Gourmet, Taquígrafo Martí 3, ✉ 46005, ☎ 395 25 09
AE ⓓ E VISA FZ b
closed Sunday, Holy Week and August - **Meals** a la carte 2700/3800.

Civera, Lérida 11, ✉ 46009, ☎ 347 59 17, Fax 348 46 38, Seafood - AE ⓓ E VISA. N : by Cronista Rivelles EX
closed Sunday dinner, Monday and August - **Meals** a la carte 4300/6600.

El Cabanyal, Reina 128, ✉ 46011, ☎ 356 15 03 - AE ⓓ E VISA.
closed Sunday and 15 August-15 September - **Meals** a la carte 4000/5200. E : by Puente de Aragón FZ

El Asador de Aranda, Félix Pizcueta 9, ✉ 46004, ☎ 352 97 91, Fax 352 97 91, Roast lamb - AE ⓓ E VISA. EZ t
closed Sunday dinner - **Meals** a la carte approx. 4400.

Chust Godoy, Boix 4, ✉ 46003, ☎ 391 38 15, Fax 391 36 67 - AE E VISA.
closed Saturday lunch, Sunday and August - **Meals** a la carte 3100/3900. FX a

José Mari, Estación Marítima 1º, ✉ 46024, ☎ 367 20 15, ←, Basque rest - AE ⓓ E VISA. SE : by Puente de Aragón FZ
closed Sunday and August - **Meals** a la carte 2500/4000.

Alghero, Burriana 52, ✉ 46005, ☎ 333 35 79 - AE E VISA FZ m
Meals a la carte approx. 4000.

Montes, pl. Obispo Amigó 5, ✉ 46007, ☎ 385 50 25
AE ⓓ E VISA. DZ v
closed Sunday dinner, Monday and August - **Meals** a la carte 2635/4165.

Mey Mey, Historiador Diago 19, ✉ 46007, ☎ 384 07 47, Chinese rest - AE VISA DZ e
closed Holy Week and the last three weeks in August - **Meals** a la carte 1900/2430.

El Plat, Císcar 3, ✉ 46005, ☎ 374 12 54
AE E VISA JCB FZ w
closed Monday except Bank Holidays - **Meals** a la carte 3100/5050.

Eguzki, av. Baleares 1, ✉ 46023, ☎ 337 50 33, Basque rest - E VISA.
closed Sunday and August - **Meals** a la carte 3500/5100. E : by Puente de Aragón FZ

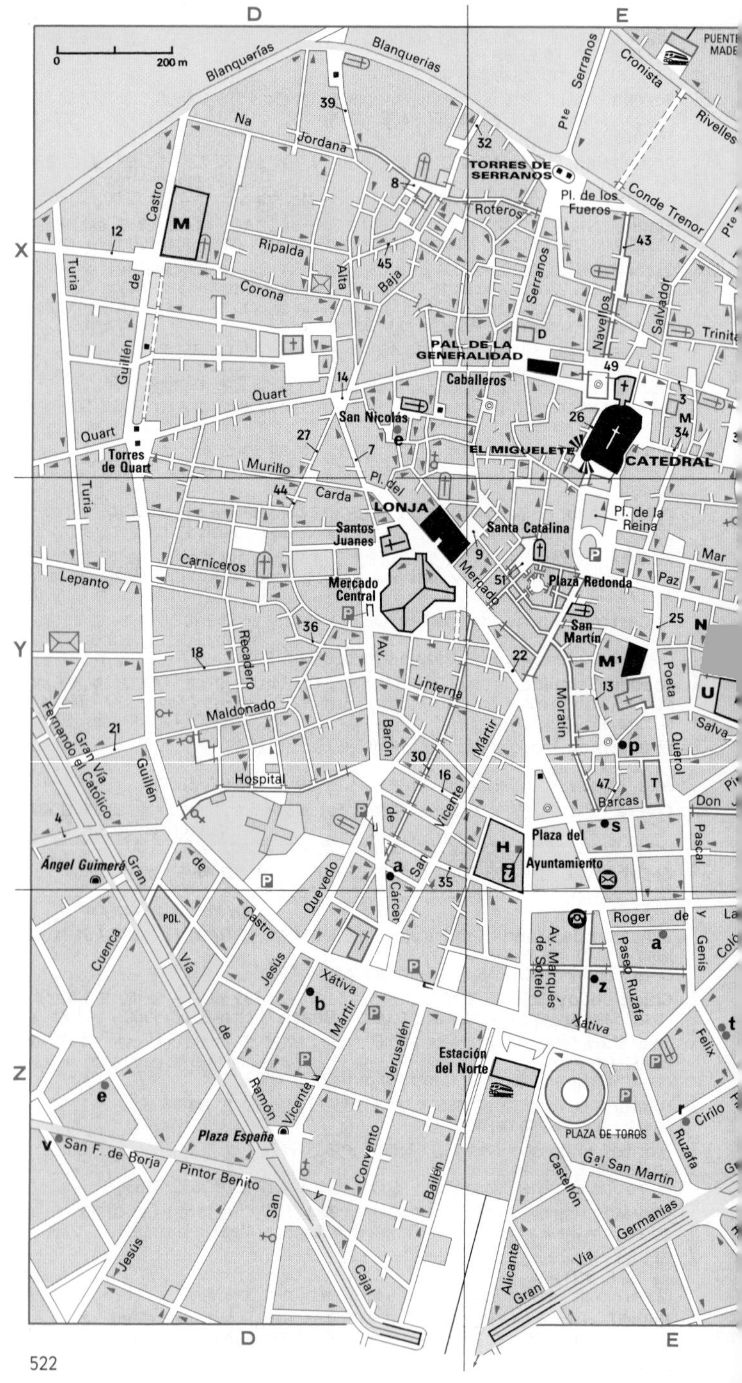

D
E
0
200 m
Blanquerías
Na Jordana
Castro
Turia
Guillén
Ripalda
Corona
Alta
Baja
Quart
Torres de Quart
San Nicolás
Murillo
Carda
Pl. del
LONJA
Santos Juanes
Mercado Central
Carniceros
Lepanto
Recadero
Maldonado
Hospital
Gran Vía Fernando el Católico
Ángel Guimerá
TORRES DE SERRANOS
Serranos
Roteros
Pl. de los Fueros
Conde Trenor
Cronista Rivelles
PAL. DE LA GENERALIDAD
Caballeros
EL MIGUELETE
CATEDRAL
Navellos
Salvador
Pl. de la Reina
Santa Catalina
Plaza Redonda
Mercado
Mar
Paz
San Martín
Linterna
Barón
Mártir
San Vicente
Moratín
Poeta Querol
Salva
Barcas
Pascual
Plaza del Ayuntamiento
Roger de Lauria
Av. Marqués de Sotelo
Paseo Ruzafa
Xátiva
Quevedo
Cárcel
Jesús
Estación del Norte
PLAZA DE TOROS
Cuenca
Vía
Ramón
Plaza España
Convento Jerusalén
Bailén
San F. de Borja
Pintor Benito
Cajal
Gran Vía Germanías
Alicante
Castellón
Gl San Martín
Cirilo
Félix
Ruzafa
Genís
POL.
X
Y
Z

VALENCIA

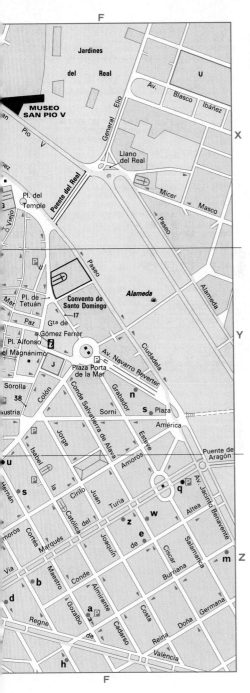

Ayuntamiento (Pl. del)	EY	
Marqués de Sotelo (Av.)	EZ	
Pascual y Genís	EYZ	
Paz	EFY	
San Vicente Mártir	DY	
Almirante	EX	2
Almudín	EX	3
Ángel Guimerà	DY	4
Bolsería	DX	7
Carmen (Pl. del)	DX	8
Dr. Collado (Pl.)	EY	9
Dr. Sanchís Bergón	DX	12
Embajador Vich	EY	13
Esparto (Pl. del)	DX	14
Garrigues	DY	16
General Palanca	FY	17
Guillém Sorolla	DY	18
Maestres	FX	20
Maestro Palau	DY	21
María Cristina (Av.)	EY	22
Marqués de Dos Aguas	EY	25
Micalet	EX	26
Moro Zeit	DX	27
Músico Peydro	DY	30
Nápoles y Sicilia (Pl.)	EX	31
Padre Huérfanos	EX	32
Palau	EX	34
Periodista Azzati	DY	35
Pie de la Cruz	DY	36
Poeta Quintana	FY	38
Salvador Giner	DX	39
San Vicente Ferrer (Pl.)	EY	40
Santa Ana (Muro)	EX	43
Santa Teresa	DY	44
Santo Tomás	DX	45
Transits	EY	47
Universidad	EY	48
Virgen (Pl. de la)	EX	49
Virgen de la Paz (Pl.)	EY	51

We suggest:

For a successful tour, that you prepare it in advance.
Michelin maps** and **guides
will give you much useful information on route planning, places of interest, accommodation, prices, etc.

Palace Fesol, Hernán Cortés 7, ✉ 46004, ☎ 352 93 23, Fax 352 93 23, « Regio
decor » – ▤. AE ⓓ E VISA. ✻ FZ
closed Saturday and Sunday in summer and Holy Week – **Meals** a la carte 2800/42C

Bazterretxe, Maestro Gozalbo 25, ✉ 46005, ☎ 395 18 94, Basque rest – ▤.
VISA FZ
closed Sunday dinner and August – **Meals** a la carte 2100/3200.

El Romeral, Gran Vía Marqués del Turia 62, ✉ 46005, ☎ 395 15 17 – ▤. AE ⓓ
VISA. ✻ FZ
closed Monday, Holy Week and August – **Meals** a la carte 3150/4050.

Olabarrieta, La Barraca 35, ✉ 46011, ☎ 367 07 79 – ▤. VISA. ✻
closed Sunday and 15 to 31 August – **Meals** a la carte approx. 3500.
E : by Puente de Aragón FZ

by road C 234 *NW : 8,5 km – ✉ 46035 Valencia – ☎ 96 :*

Feria, av. de las Ferias 2 ☎ 364 44 11, Fax 364 54 83 – ▤ TV ☎ – 25/2C
AE ⓓ E VISA. ✻ rest NO : by G.V. Fernando el Católico DY
Meals a la carte 3650/4900 – **136 suites** ☐ 15950/25500.

at El Saler *S : 8 km – ✉ 46012 Valencia – ☎ 96 :*

Sidi Saler ⑤, playa - 3 km ☎ 161 04 11, Fax 161 08 38, ≤, ...
– ▤ TV ☎ P – 25/300. AE ⓓ E VISA JCB. ✻ rest
Meals 3500 - ***Grill Bendinat :*** **Meals** a la carte 3500/4600 – ☐ 1500 – **260**
19300/24000, 17 suites.

Parador de El Saler ⑤, 7 km ☎ 161 11 86, Fax 162 70 16, ≤, « In the middle
the golf course », ..., 18 – ▤ TV ☎ P – 25/60. AE ⓓ E VISA. ✻
Meals 3500 – ☐ 1200 – **58 rm** 19000.

at Manises *on the airport road E : 9,5 km – ✉ 46940 Manises – ☎ 96 :*

Meliá Confort Azafata, autopista del aeropuerto 15 ☎ 154 61 00, Fax 153 20
– ▤ TV ☎ P – 25/300. AE ⓓ E VISA. ✻ rest
Meals 2580 – ☐ 1150 – **126 rm** 12100/15100, 4 suites.

at Puçol *N : 25 km by motorway A 7 – ✉ 46760 Puçol – ☎ 96 :*

Monte Picayo ⑤, urb. Monte Picayo ☎ 142 01 00, Telex 62087, Fax 142 21 68,
« On a hillside with ≤ », ... – ▤ TV ☎ P – 25/800. AE ⓓ E VISA.
Meals 3500 – ☐ 1350 – **79 rm** 18350/22950, 4 suites.

Sweden

Sverige

STOCKHOLM – GOTHENBURG

PRACTICAL INFORMATION

LOCAL CURRENCY

Swedish Kronor: *100 SEK = 14.52 US $ (Jan. 97).*

TOURIST INFORMATION

In Stockholm, the Tourist Centre is situated in Sweden House, entrance from Kungsträdgården at Hamngatan. Open Mon-Fri 9am-6pm. Sat. and Sun. 9am-3pm. Telephone weekdays 08/789 24 00, weekends to Excursion Shop and Tourist Centre. For Gothenburg, see information in the text of the town under **i***.*

National Holiday in Sweden: *6 June.*

FOREIGN EXCHANGE

Banks are open between 9.30am and 3pm on weekdays only. Some banks in the centre of the city are usually open weekdays 9am to 6pm. Most large hotels and the Tourist Centre have exchange facilities. Arlanda airport has banking facilities between 7am to 10pm seven days a week.

MEALS

At lunchtime, follow the custom of the country and try the typical buffets of Scandinavian specialities.
At dinner, the a la carte and set menus will offer you more conventional cooking.

SHOPPING

In the index of street names, those printed in red are where the principal shops are found.
The main shopping streets in the centre of Stockholm are: Hamngatan, Biblioteksgatan, Drottninggatan.
In the Old Town mainly Västerlånggatan.

THEATRE BOOKINGS

Your hotel porter will be able to make your arrangements or direct you to Theatre Booking Agents.

CAR HIRE

The international car hire companies have branches in Stockholm, Gothenburg, Arlanda and Landvetter airports. Your hotel porter should be able to give details and help you with your arrangements.

TIPPING

Hotels and restaurants normally include a service charge of 15 per cent. Doormen, baggage porters etc. are generally given a gratuity.
Taxis include 10 % tip in the amount shown on the meter.

SPEED LIMITS - SEAT BELTS

The maximum permitted speed on motorways and dual carriageways is 110 km/h - 68 mph and 90 km/h - 56 mph on other roads except where a lower speed limit is indicated.
The wearing of seat belts is compulsory for drivers and passengers.
In Sweden, drivers must not drink alcoholic beverage at all.

STOCKHOLM

Sverige 985 M 15 – *pop. 674 459 Greater Stockholm 1 491 726* – ☎ *8.*

Hamburg 935 – Copenhagen 630 – Oslo 522.

Stockholm Information Service, Tourist Centre, Sverigehuset, Hamngatan 27 ☎ 789 24 00 – Motormännens Riksförbund ☎ 690 38 00 – Kungliga. Automobilklubben (Royal Automobile Club) Gyllenstiernsgatan 4 ☎ 660 00 55.

Svenska Golfförbundet (Swedish Golf Federation) ☎ 622 15 00.

Stockholm-Arlanda N : 41 km ☎ 797 61 00 – SAS : Flygcity, Stureplan 8 ☎ 797 41 75, Reservations 020/727 727 – Air-Terminal : opposite main railway station.

Motorail for Southern Europe : Ticket Travel-Agency, Kungsgatan 60 ☎ 24 00 90.

To Finland : contact Silja Line ☎ 22 21 40 or Viking Line ☎ 714 57 70 – Excursions by boat : contact Stockholm Information Service (see below).

See: *Old Town★★★ (Gamla Stan)* AZ – *Vasa Museum★★★ (Vasamuseet)* DY – *Skansen Open-Air Museum★★★* DY.
Royal Palace★★ (Kungliga Slottet) AZ ; *Royal Apartments★★ ; Royal Armoury★ ; Royal Tresury★★ – Stockholm Cathedral★★ (Storkyrkan)* AZ – *City Hall★★ (Stadhuset) : Blue Hall★★★, Golden Hall★★★ ; ☼★★★* BY **H** – *Prins Eugens Waldemarsudde★★ (house and gallery)* DY – *Thiel Gallery★★ (Thielska Galleriet)* DZ.
House of the Nobility★ (Riddarhuset) AZ **R** – *Riddarholmen Church★ (Riddarholmskyrkan)* AZ – *Österlånggatan★* AZ.
Kaknäs TV Tower (Kaknästornet) ☼★★★ DY – *Stigberget : Fjällgatan ☼★* DZ – *Skinnerviksberget : ☼★* BZ.

Museums: *National Art Gallery★★ (Nationalmuseum)* DY **M5** – *Nordic Museum★★ (Nordiska Museet)* DY – *Museum of National Antiquities★★ (Historiska Museet)* DY – *Museum of Medieval Stockholm★★ (Stockholms Medeltidsmuseet)* CY **M1** – *Museum of Far Eastern Antiquities★ (Östasiatiska Museet)* DY **M6** – *Hallwyl Collection★ (Hallwylska Museet)* CY **M3** – *Strindberg Museum★ (Strindbergsmuseet)* BX **M2**.

Outskirts : *Drottningholm Palace★★★ (Drottningholm Slott) W : 12 km* BY – *Stockholm Archipelago★★★ – Millesgården★★ (house and gallery) E : 4 km* BX – *Skogskyrkogården (UNESCO World Heritage Site).*

Excursions : *Gripsholms Slott★★ – Skokloster★★ – Ulriksdal★ – Birka★ – Strängnas★ – Sigtuna★.*

STOCKHOLM

Biblioteksgatan	CY 2
Drottninggatan	BX, CY 10
Gallerian	CY 14
Grev Turegatan	CY 18
Hamngatan	CY
Kungsgatan	BCY
Sergelgatan	CY 53
Västerlånggatan	AZ
Österlånggatan	AZ

Birger Jarlsgatan	CXY 3
Brunkebergstorg	CY 5
Brunnsgränd	AZ 6
Bryggargatan	BY 7
Brända Tomten	AZ 8
Djurgårdsbron	DY 9
Evert Taubes Terrass	AZ 13
Gustav Adolfs Torg	CY 16
Herkulesgatan	CY 19
Hötorget	CY 20
Järntorget	AZ 21
Järntorgsgatan	AZ 23
Kindstugatan	AZ 24
Klarabergsgatan	CY 25
Klarabergsviadukten	BY 27
Kornhamnstorg	AZ 28
Kungsträdgårdsgatan	CY 32
Köpmangatan	AZ 35
Lilla Nygatan	AZ 36
Mosebacke Torg	CZ 39
Munkbrogatan	AZ 40
Master Mikaels Gata	DZ 41
Myntgatan	AZ 42
Norrbro	CY 43
Norrlandsgatan	CY 44
Nybroplan	CY 45
Olof Palmes Gata	BY 47
Prästgatan	AZ 48
Riddarhusgränd	AZ 49
Riddarhustorget	AZ 50
Rådhusgränd	AZ 52
Sergels Torg	CY 54
Sista Styverns Trappor	DZ 55
Slottskajen	AZ 56
Slussplan	AZ 57
Stallgatan	CY 59
Stigbergsgatan	DZ 60
Storkyrkobrinken	AZ 61
Strömbron	CY 62
Strömgatan	CY 63
Södermalmstorg	CZ 64
Södra Blasieholmshamnen	CY 66
Tegelbacken	CY 67
Tegnérlunden	BX 69
Triewaldsgränd	AZ 70
Tyska Brinken	AZ 73
Urvädersgränd	CZ 74
Östermalmstorg	DY 76
Östra Järnvägsgatan	BY 78

GAMLA STAN

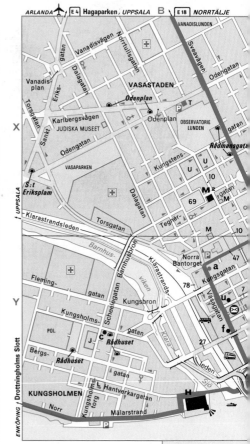

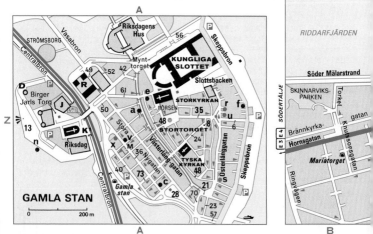

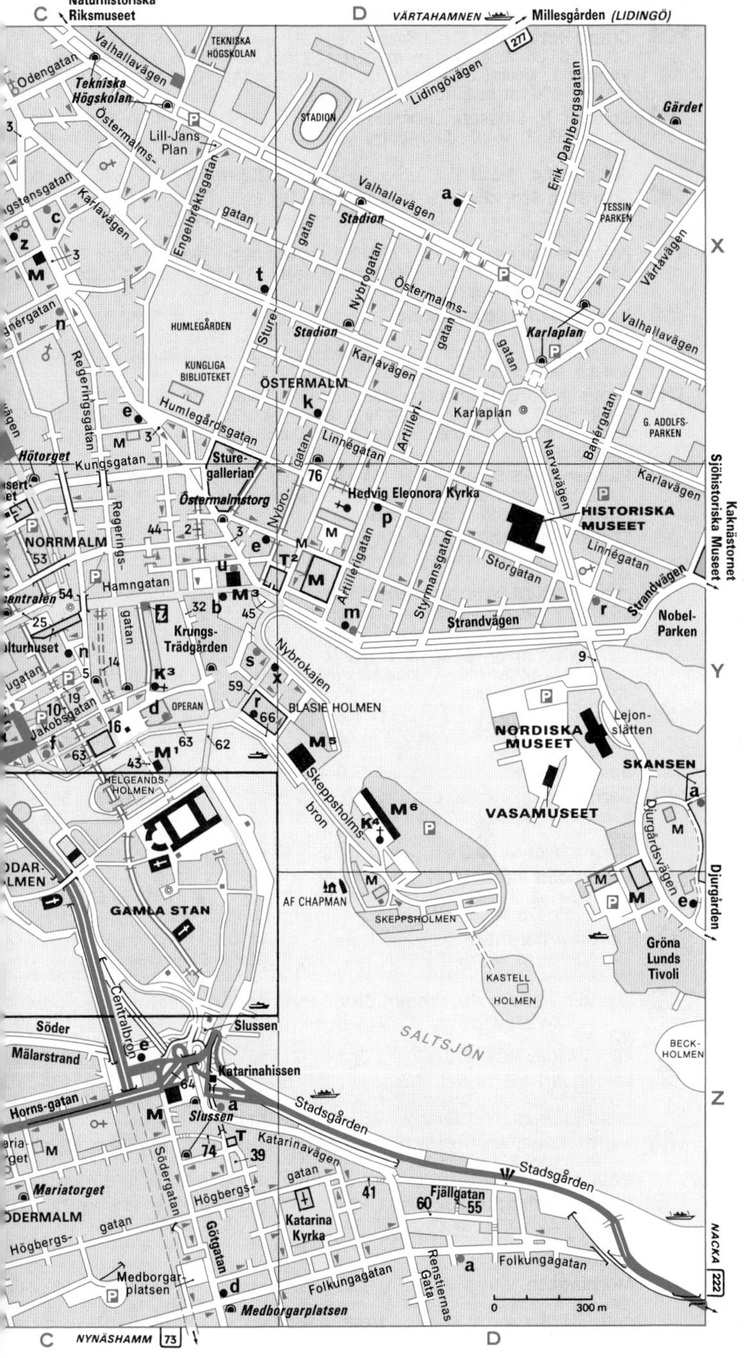

C
Naturhistoriska Riksmuseet
D
VÄRTAHAMNEN
Millesgården (LIDINGÖ)
277
TEKNISKA HÖGSKOLAN
Valhallavägen
Odengatan
Tekniska Högskolan
Lidingövägen
STADION
Erik Dahlbergsgatan
Gärdet
Östermalms-
Lill-Jans Plan
Engelbrektsgatan
Karlavägen
Valhallavägen
Stadion
TESSIN PARKEN
Värtavägen
X
HUMLEGÅRDEN
Sture-
Nybrogatan
Östermalms-gatan
Karlaplan
KUNGLIGA BIBLIOTEKET
ÖSTERMALM
Regeringsgatan
Humlegårdsgatan
Linnégatan
Artillerigatan
Karlaplan
Banérgatan
G. ADOLFS-PARKEN
Hötorget
Kungsgatan
Sture-gallerian
Östermalmstorg
Hedvig Eleonora Kyrka
Narvavägen
Karlavägen
HISTORISKA MUSEET
Kaknästornet
Sjöhistoriska Museet
NORRMALM
Nybro-gatan
Linnégatan
Storgatan
Strandvägen
Styrmansgatan
Hamngatan
Centralen
Krungs-Trädgården
Strandvägen
Nobel-Parken
Kulturhuset
Nybrokajen
Y
OPERAN
BLASIE HOLMEN
Jakobsgatan
NORDISKA MUSEET
Lejon-slätten
SKANSEN
HELGEANDSHOLMEN
Skeppsholmsbron
VASAMUSEET
Djurgårdsvägen
RIDDARHOLMEN
AF CHAPMAN
SKEPPSHOLMEN
Djurgården
GAMLA STAN
Gröna Lunds Tivoli
KASTELL HOLMEN
Centralbron
Söder Mälarstrand
Slussen
SALTSJÖN
BECK-HOLMEN
Katarinahissen
Z
Horns-gatan
Slussen
Stadsgården
Katarinavägen
Stadsgården
Mariatorget
Södergatan
Högbergsgatan
Katarina Kyrka
Fjällgatan
SÖDERMALM
Götgatan
NACKA
Högbergsgatan
Renstiernas Gata
Folkungagatan
222
Medborgarplatsen
Folkungagatan
0
300 m
Medborgarplatsen
C
NYNÄSHAMM
73
D

Grand Hotel, Södra Blasieholmshamnen 8, P.O. Box 16424, ✉ S-103 27, ☎ 679 35 0 Fax 611 86 86, ≤, – rm rest – 600. AE VISA JCB. **Verandan :** **Meals** (buffet lunch) 225/395 and a la carte – (see also ***Franska Matsal*** below) – **280 rm** 2075/3180, 20 suites. CY

Scandic H. Slussen, Guldgränd 8, P.O. Box 15270, ✉ S-104 65, ☎ 702 25 0 Fax 642 83 58, ≤, – rm – 285. AE VISA JCB. CZ
Guldgränd 4 **:** **Meals** 150/425 and a la carte – **253 rm** 1490/1695, 11 suites.

Sheraton Stockholm H. and Towers, Tegelbacken 6, P.O. Box 195, ✉ S-101 2 ☎ 14 26 00, Fax 21 70 26, ≤, – rm rest – 200. E VISA JCB. rest CY
Premiere **:** **Meals** - Seafood - 370/575 and a la carte – ***Bistro*** **:** **Meals** (buffet lunc 188/335 and a la carte – ***Die Ecke*** **:** **Meals** 215/385 and a la carte – **453 r** 1790/2490, 6 suites.

Radisson SAS Royal Viking, Vasagatan 1, ✉ S-101 24, ☎ 14 10 00, Fax 10 81 8 – rm – 130. AE E VISA JCB. BY
closed December – **Meals** - Italian - *(closed lunch Saturday and Sunday)* (buffet lunch) 1 and a la carte 301/367 – **315 rm** 1395/2195, 4 suites.

Provobis Sergel Plaza, Brunkebergstorg 9, P.O. Box 16411, ✉ S-103 27, ☎ 22 66 0 Fax 21 50 70 – rm – 200. AE E VISA JCB. rest
Anna Rella **:** **Meals** *(closed Sunday)* 190/360 and a la carte – **394 rm** 1545/209 12 suites. CY

Radisson SAS Strand, Nybrokajen 9, P.O. Box 16396, ✉ S-103 27, ☎ 678 78 0 Fax 611 24 36, ≤, – rm – 70. AE E VISA JCB.
Meals a la carte 192/388 – **120 rm** 1590/2440, 18 suites. CDY

Stockholm Globe, Arenaslingan 7, P.O. Box 10004, ✉ S-121 26, S : 1 ½ km by Rd ☎ 725 90 00, Fax 649 08 80, – rm – 220. AE E VI
closed 23 to 28 December – ***Arena*** **:** **Meals** *(closed Saturday and Sunday)* (lunch on 295/410 – ***Tabac*** **:** **Meals** a la carte approx. 165 – **279 rm** 995/1195, 8 suites.

Diplomat, Strandvägen 7c, P.O. Box 14059, ✉ S-104 40, ☎ 663 58 00, Fax 783 66 3 – rm AE E VISA. DY
closed 22 to 27 December – **Meals** *(closed Bank Holidays)* 177/304 and a la carte – **131 r** 1465/2195, 2 suites.

Silja H. Ariadne, Sodra Kajen 37, ✉ S-115 74, NE : 3 km by Värtavägen and Teg luddsvägen ☎ 665 78 00, Fax 662 76 70, ≤, – rm – 25 AE E VISA.
Meals (buffet lunch) 168/395 and dinner a la carte – **283 rm** 1220/1445.

Berns, Näckströmsgatan 8, Berzelii Park, ✉ S-111 47, ☎ 614 07 00, Fax 611 51 75, « Restaurant in 19C ballroom » – rm rm – 180. AE E V JCB. CY
Meals 309 (dinner) and a la carte 213/395 – **62 rm** 1690/2440, 1 suite.

Stockholm Plaza, Birger Jarlsgatan 29, P.O. Box 7707, ✉ S-103 95, ☎ 14 51 2 Fax 10 34 92, – rm rest – 45. AE E VISA.
Meals 295/325 and dinner a la carte – **151 rm** 1225/1425. CX

First H. Amaranten, Kungsholmsgatan 31, ✉ S-104 20, ☎ 654 10 60, Fax 662 62 4 – rm rest – 85. AE E VISA JCB. BY
Meals *(closed Sunday)* (dinner only) a la carte 154/260 – **409 rm** 1055/1855, 1 sui

Scandic H. Park Stockholm City, Karlavägen 43, P.O. Box 5255, ✉ S-102 4 ☎ 22 96 20, Fax 21 62 68, – rm – 120. AE VISA. CX
Park Village **:** **Meals** 210/270 and dinner a la carte – **199 rm** 1365/1969, 3 suite

Birger Jarl without rest., Tulegatan 8, P.O. Box 19016, ✉ S-104 32, ☎ 674 10 0 Fax 673 73 66, – – 150. AE E VISA. CX
closed 23 December-3 January – **225 rm** 995/1440.

Tapto Home, Jungfrugatan 57, ✉ S-115 31, ☎ 664 50 00, Fax 664 07 00, – rm – 25. AE E VISA. DX
Meals (buffet dinner residents only) – **86 rm** (dinner included) 1200/1320.

City H. Slöjdgatan, Slöjdgatan 7, Hötorget, P.O. Box 1132, ✉ S-111 81, ☎ 723 72 0 Fax 723 72 09, – rm rest – 90. AE E VISA. CY
Meals *(closed Saturday and Sunday)* (lunch only) (unlicensed) a la carte 54/58 – **293 r** 1040/1260.

Mornington, Nybrogatan 53, P.O. Box 5197, ✉ S-114 40, ☎ 663 12 40, Fax 662 21 7 – rm rest – 100. AE E VISA. DX
closed 23 December-2 January – **Meals** *(closed Saturday and Sunday)* 175 (dinner) a a la carte 240/320 – **139 rm** 1195/1495.

Scandic H. Malmen, Götgatan 49-51, ✉ S-102 66, ✆ 22 60 80, Fax 641 11 48, – rm – 90. rest CZ d
Meals (dinner only) 215/260 – **283 rm** 1085/1388.

Wellington, Storgatan 6, ✉ S-114 51, ✆ 667 09 10, Fax 667 12 54, – rm . DY p
Meals *(closed Saturday dinner and Sunday)* 145/185 and a la carte – **49 rm** 1095/1295.

Castle without rest., Riddargatan 14, ✉ S-114 34, ✆ 679 57 00, Fax 611 20 22, – rest – 120. . CY e
48 rm 1075/1300, 2 suites.

Freys, Bryggargatan 12b, ✉ S-101 31, ✆ 20 13 00, Fax 24 22 24 – rm rm . rest – *closed 20 to 26 December* – **Meals** *(closed Saturday and Sunday lunch)* 136/250 and a la carte – **107 rm** 1060/1260. BY u

Franska Matsalen (at Grand Hotel), Södra Blasieholmshamnen 8, P.O. Box 16424, ✉ S-103 27, ✆ 679 35 84, Fax 611 86 86, ← – . CY r
closed Saturday, Sunday and July – **Meals** (dinner only) 685/895 and a la carte.

Operakällaren (at Opera House), Operahuset, Karl XII's Torg, P.O. Box 1616, ✉ S-111 86, ✆ 676 58 00, Fax 20 95 92, ←, « Opulent classical decor » – . CY d
closed July – **Meals** (dinner only) 415/485 and a la carte.

Videgård, Regeringsgatan 111, ✉ S-111 39, ✆ 411 61 53, Fax 10 76 35 – . – *closed Saturday lunch, Sunday, 24 June-15 August, 22 December-12 January and Bank Holidays* – **Meals** 150/458 and a la carte. CX n

Paul and Norbert (Lang), Strandvägen 9, ✉ S-114 56, ✆ 663 81 83, Fax 661 72 36 – DY m
closed Saturday, Sunday, July, 23 December-6 January and Bank Holidays – **Meals** (booking essential) 345/440 and a la carte 500/605
Spec. Fried sea bass tartar with bleak roe and caviar, oyster sauce with vodka, Elk's fillet stuffed with marinated goose liver, lingonberry sauce, Cloudberry parfait with warm cloudberries, port wine and almond biscuit.

Gondolen, Stadsgården 6, P.O. Box 15155, ✉ S-104 56, ✆ 641 70 90, Fax 641 11 40, ← Saltsjön – . – *closed July lunch, Sunday, Easter, Christmas and Bank Holidays* – **Meals** 195/450 and a la carte. CZ a

Nils Emil, Folkungagatan 122, ✉ S-116 30, ✆ 640 72 09, Fax 640 37 25 – .
closed Saturday and Sunday lunch and July – **Meals** (booking essential) 175/375 and a la carte. DZ a

Clas På Hörnet with rm, Surbrunnsgatan 20, P.O. Box 19156, ✉ S-113 48, ✆ 16 51 30, Fax 612 53 15, « 18C atmosphere » – . . CX f
Meals *(closed 22 December-7 January)* 195/280 and a la carte – **10 rm** 890/1190.

Stallmästaregården, Norrtull, ✉ S-113 47, N : 2 km by Sveavägen (at beginning of E 4) ✆ 610 13 00, Fax 32 27 40, ←, , « 17C inn, waterside setting », – .
closed Sunday, 30 June-31 July and Bank Holidays – **Meals** (buffet lunch) 195/220 and a la carte.

Wedholms Fisk (Wedholm), Nybrokajen 17, ✉ S-111 48, ✆ 611 78 74 – . CY s
closed Sunday, July and Bank Holidays – **Meals** - Seafood - (dinner only) a la carte 330/620
Spec. Tartar of salmon and salmon roe with crème fraîche, Boiled turbot with melted butter and horseradish, Fricassee of sole, turbot, lobster and scallops with a Champagne sauce.

Fredsgatan 12, Fredsgatan 12, ✉ S-111 52, ✆ 24 80 52, Fax 411 73 48, « Modern decor » – CY f
closed Saturday lunch, Sunday, Christmas and New Year – **Meals** (booking essential) (light lunch) 165/285 and a la carte.

Frednick's Bistro, Kungstensgatan 9, ✉ S-114 25, ✆ 21 61 69, Fax 20 34 46 – – *closed Sunday* – **Meals** (dinner only) a la carte 160/333. CX c

KB (Klein), Smålandsgatan 7, ✉ S-111 46, ✆ 679 60 32, Fax 611 82 83 –
closed Saturday lunch, Sunday, 20 June-4 August and Bank Holidays – **Meals** (booking essential) 125/450 and a la carte 250/520 CY u
Spec. Assorted marinated herring and Baltic herring, Roasted milk-fed lamb with pettle and morel dumplings, Arctic raspberry and yoghurt mousse with raspberry marmelad.

Gässlingen, Brännkyrkagatan 93, ✉ S-117 26, ✆ 669 54 95, Fax 84 89 90 – BZ
closed 20 June-4 August – **Meals** (booking essential) (dinner only) 385/550 and a la carte.

Eriks Bakficka, Frederikshovsgatan 4, ✉ S-115 23, ✆ 660 15 99, Fax 663 25 67, – . – *closed Saturday and Sunday lunch, 28 to 31 March, 20 to 22 June and 23 December-2 January* – **Meals** - Bistro - 185/445 and a la carte. DY r

Greitz, Vasagatan 50, ✉ S-111 20, ✆ 23 48 20, Fax 24 20 93 – BY a
closed Saturday lunch, Sunday and July – **Meals** 185/475 and a la carte.

Gamla Stan (Old Stockholm) :

First H. Reisen, Skeppsbron 12-14, ✉ S-111 30, ☏ 22 32 60, Fax 20 15 59, « Original maritime decor », – rm rest – 60. AE E VISA.
Meals *(closed Sunday)* (dinner only) 395/510 and a la carte – **111 rm** 1325/19 3 suites. AZ

Victory, Lilla Nygatan 5, ✉ S-111 28, ☏ 14 30 90, Fax 20 21 77, « Swedish ru furnishings, maritime antiques », – rm – 90. AE E VISA AZ
closed 20 December-6 January – **Meals** – (see ***Leijontornet*** below) – **45** 1760/2280, 3 suites.

Gamla Stan without rest., Lilla Nygatan 25, ✉ S-111 28, ☏ 24 44 50, Fax 21 64 – – 35. AE E VISA JCB AZ
50 rm 1040/1350, 1 suite.

Lady Hamilton without rest., Storkyrkobrinken 5, ✉ S-111 28, ☏ 23 46 Fax 411 11 48, « Swedish rural antiques », – . AE E VISA AZ
34 rm 1460/2040.

Lord Nelson without rest., Västerlånggatan 22, ✉ S-111 29, ☏ 23 23 90, Fax 10 10 « Ship style installation, maritime antiques », – . AE E VISA.
closed Christmas and New Year – **31 rm** 1220/1770. AZ

Mälardrottningen, Riddarholmen, ✉ S-111 28, ☏ 24 36 00, Fax 24 36 « Formerly Barbara Hutton's yacht », – rm . AE E VISA JCB.
closed 23 to 28 December – **Meals** *(closed lunch Saturday, Sunday and Bank Holidays)* (dinner) and a la carte 264/451 – **58 rm (cabins)** 790/950, 1 suite. AZ

Eriks (Lallerstedt), Österlånggatan 17, ✉ S-111 31, ☏ 23 85 00, Fax 796 60 69 – re AE E VISA JCB AZ
closed Sunday, July, Christmas and New Year – **Meals** - Seafood - (booking essent 185/595 and a la carte 513/627
Spec. Scandinavian specialities, Fish and shellfish, Dessert soufflés.

Leijontornet (at Victory H.), Lilla Nygatan 5, ✉ S-111 28, ☏ 14 23 55, Fax 406 08 , « Remains of a 14C fortification tower in the dining room » – . AE E VISA
closed Saturday lunch, Sunday, July, 23 December-7 January and Bank Holidays
Meals (booking essential) (restricted lunch) 180/540 and a la carte 365/565 AZ
Spec. Cold saffron lasagne with trout roe and crab, Veal cutlet in basil sauce with goat's cheese and beetroot strudel, Parfait of arctic raspberries served on a brownie w a cloudberry sherbet.

Den Gyldene Freden, Österlånggatan 51, ✉ S-103 17, ☏ 24 97 60, Fax 21 38 – . AE E VISA AZ
closed Sunday and July – **Meals** (dinner only and Saturday lunch)/dinner 245/365 a a la carte.

Källaren Aurora, Munkbron 11, ✉ S-111 28, ☏ 21 93 59, Fax 411 16 22, « In t cellars of a 17C house » – AE E VISA JCB AZ
closed 24 and 25 December – **Meals** (dinner only) 350/475 and a la carte.

Fem Små Hus, Nygränd 10, ✉ S-111 30, ☏ 10 87 75, Fax 14 96 95, « 17C cella antiques » – . AE E VISA JCB AZ
Meals 130/360 and a la carte.

to the E :

at Djurgården – *08 Stockholm :*

Arctia H. Hasselbacken, Hazeliusbacken 20, ✉ S-100 55, ☏ 670 50 Fax 663 84 10, , – rm – 250. AE E V DZ
Meals (booking essential) 200/420 and a la carte – **109 rm** 1290/1690, 2 suites

Källhagens Wärdshus, Djurgårdsbrunnsvägen 10, ✉ S-115 27, E : 3 km by Stra vägen ☏ 665 03 00, Fax 665 03 99, <, , « Waterside setting, garden », , – rm – 60. AE E VISA. rest
closed 2 days Christmas – **Meals** 215/650 and a la carte – **18 rm** 1420/1630, 2 suit

Ulla Winbladh, Rosendalsvägen 8, ✉ S-115 21, ☏ 663 05 71, Fax 663 05 73, AE E VISA DY
Meals (booking essential) a la carte 245/345.

at Fjäderholmarna Island *25 mn by boat, departure every hour from Nybroplan* – CY – *Stockholm :*

Fjäderholmarnas Krog, P.O. Box 14046, ✉ S-104 40, ☏ 718 33 55, Fax 716 39 , « Waterside setting on Archipelago Island with < neighbouring islands and sea » AE E VISA
closed 1 January-30 April and 1 October-30 November – **Meals** 180/450 and a la car

to the W :

Bromma W : 10 km by Norr Mälarstrand – BY – and Drottningholmsvägen – 08 Stockholm :

XX **Sjöpaviljongen,** Tranebergs Strand 4, ✉ 167 40, E : 1 ½ km ☎ 704 04 24, Fax 704 82 40, ≤, «Waterside setting» – P. AE ① E VISA JCB
closed Saturday lunch, Sunday, 23 December-7 January and Bank Holidays – **Meals** 160/400 and a la carte.

to the NW :

Solna NW : 5 km by Sveavägen – BX – and E 4 – 08 Stockholm :

Radisson SAS Royal Park, Frösundaviks Allé 15, ✉ S-171 03, Exit Frösunda by E 4 and Frösundavik rd ☎ 624 55 00, Fax 85 85 66, ≤, park – rm TV ☎ & P – 200. AE ① E VISA. rest
Meals 160/500 and a la carte – **190 rm** 1410/1630, 9 suites.

XXX **Ulriksdals Wärdshus,** , ✉ 170 71, Exit E 18/E 3 from E 4 ☎ 85 08 15, Fax 85 08 58, ≤, «Former inn in Royal Park», – P. AE ① E VISA
closed dinner Sunday and Bank Holidays and 24 to 26 December – **Meals** (booking essential) (buffet lunch) 320/450 and a la carte 415/595.

XX **Finsmakaren,** Råsundavägen 9, ✉ 171 52, ☎ 27 67 71, Fax 83 30 08 – AE ① E VISA JCB
Meals 315/410 and a la carte 315/410.

Sollentuna NW : 15 km by Sveavägen – BX – and E 4 – 08 Stockholm :

XX ✿ **Edsbacka Krog** (Lingström), Sollentunavägen 220, ✉ 191 35, ☎ 96 33 00, Fax 96 40 19, «17C inn» – P. AE ① E VISA JCB
closed Saturday lunch, Monday dinner, Sunday, Easter, Whitsun, midsummer and 4 weeks July-August – **Meals** 425 (dinner) and a la carte 330/698
Spec. Truffled fricassee of white cabbage with grilled duck liver, Angler fish with finely cut vegetables and a veal and balsamic gravy, Banana galette filled with coconut cream served with a cherry sorbet.

Upplands Väsby NW : 29 km by Sveavägen – BX – and E 4 – 08 Stockholm :

Scandic H. Infra City, Kanalvägen 10, ✉ S-194 61, E 4 - Bredden Exit ☎ 590 955 00, Fax 590 955 10, – rm TV ☎ & – 350. AE ① E VISA. rest
Meals 165 (lunch) and a la carte 250/328 – **228 rm** 1198/1472, 8 suites.

Arlanda Airport NW : 40 km by Sveavägen – BX – and E 4 – ✉ Arlanda – 08 Stockholm :

Radisson SAS Sky City, P.O. Box 82, ✉ 190 45 Stockholm-Arlanda, between Terminal 4 and 5 ☎ 590 773 00, Fax 593 781 00, – rm TV ☎ & – 350. AE ① E VISA.
closed Christmas – **Meals** (buffet lunch) 150/350 and a la carte – **230 rm** 1595/1695.

Radisson SAS Arlandia, P.O. Box 103, ✉ 190 45 Stockholm-Arlanda, SE : 1 km ☎ 593 618 00, Fax 593 601 25, – rm rest TV ☎ & P – 245. AE ① E VISA.
Meals 280/350 and a la carte – **335 rm** 1270/1470, 2 suites.

GOTHENBURG (Göteborg) Sverige 985 O 8 – pop. 437 313 – 031.

See : *Art Gallery★★ (Göteborgs Konstmuseet)* CX **M1** – *Castle Park★★ (Slottsskogen)* AX – *Botanical Gardens★★ (Botaniska Trädgården)* AX – *East India House★★ (Ostindiska Huset : Göteborgs stadmuseum)* BU **M2** *Museum of Arts and Crafts★★ (Röhsska Konstlojdmuseet)* BV **M3** – *Liseberg Amusement Park★★ (Liseberg Nöjespark)* DX *Horticultural Gardens★★ (Trädgårdsföreningen)* CU – *Natural History Museum★ (Naturhistoriska museet)* AX – *Maritime Museum★ (Sjöfartsmuseet)* AV – *Kungsportsavenyn★* BCVX **22** – *Götaplatsen (Carl Milles Poseidon★★)* CX – *Seaman's Tower (Sjömanstornet) (※★★)* AV *Göteborgs-Utkiken (※★★)* BT – *Masthugg Church (Masthuggskyrkan) (interior★)* AV.

Envir. : *Öckerö Archipelago★ by boat or by car : N : 17 km by E 6 and road 155 – New Älvsborg Fortress★ (Nya Älvsborgs Fästning)* AU – *Bohuslan★★ (The Golden Coast) N : - Halland coast to the south : Äskhult Open-Air Museum★ ; Tjolöholms Slott★* AX.

18 Albatross, Lillhagsvägen Hisings Backa ☎ 55 19 01 – 18 Delsjö, Kallebäck ☎ 40 69 59 – 18 Göteborgs, Golfbanevägen, Hovås ☎ 28 24 44.

Scandinavian Airlines System : Svenska Mässan (vid Korsvägen) ☎ 94 20 00 Landvetter Airport : ☎ 94 10 00.

To Denmark : contact Stena Line A/B ☎ 775 00 00, Fax 85 85 95 - Color SeaCat ☎ 775 08 00 – To Continent : contact Scandinavian Seaways ☎ 65 06 50, Fax 53 23 09.

Kungsportplatsen 2 ☎ 10 07 40, Fax 13 21 84.

Copenhagen 279 – Oslo 322 – Stockholm 500.

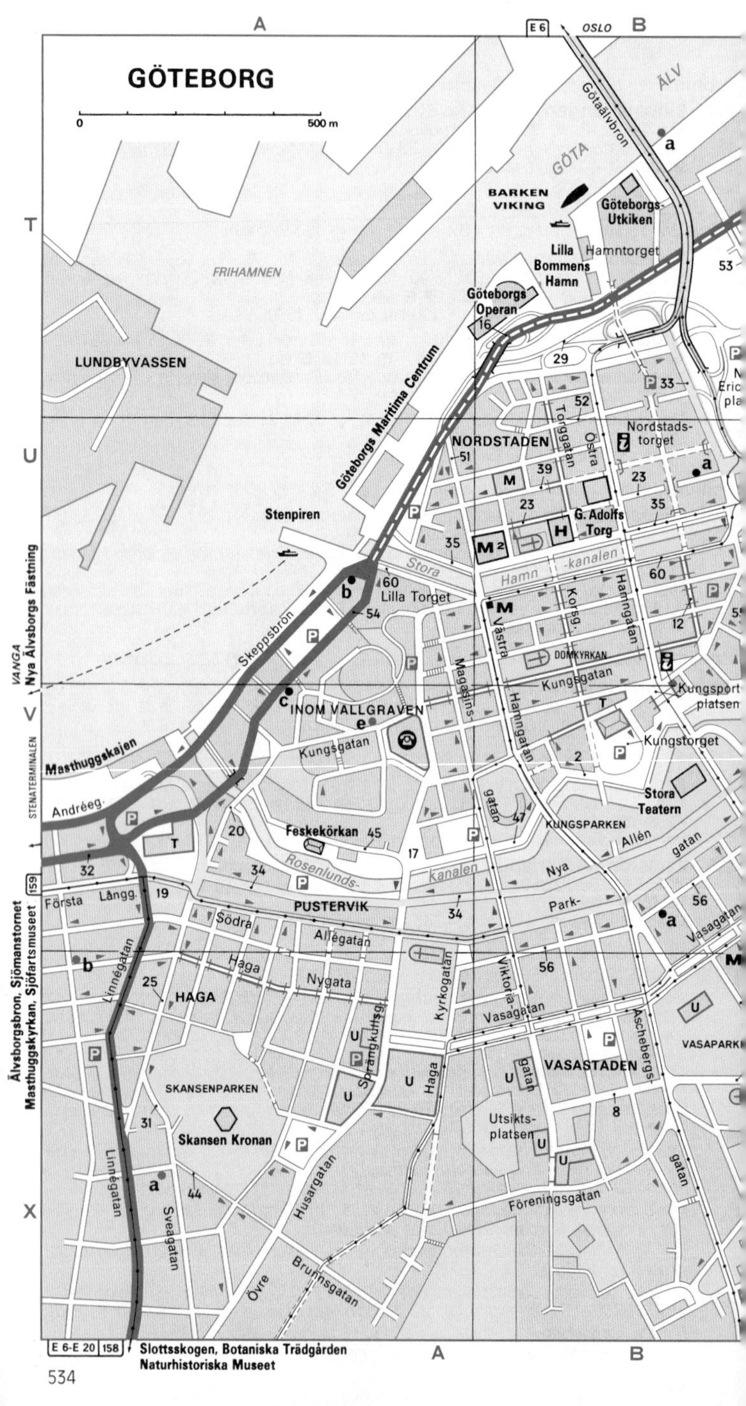
GÖTEBORG
0
500 m
E 6
OSLO
GÖTA
ÄLV
Götaälvbron
FRIHAMNEN
LUNDBYVASSEN
BARKEN VIKING
Göteborgs-Utkiken
Lilla Bommens Hamn
Hamntorget
Göteborgs Operan
Göteborgs Maritima Centrum
Stenpiren
NORDSTADEN
Nordstads-torget
G. Adolfs Torg
Stora Hamn -kanalen
Lilla Torget
Skeppsbron
INOM VALLGRAVEN
Kungsgatan
Västra Hamngatan
Östra Hamngatan
Torggatan
Korsg.
DOMKYRKAN
Magasinsgatan
Kungsportsplatsen
Kungstorget
Stora Teatern
KUNGSPARKEN
Nya Allén
Masthuggskajen
Andréeg.
STENATERMINALEN
Feskekörkan
Rosenlunds-kanalen
PUSTERVIK
Första Långg.
Södra Allégatan
Haga Nygata
Linnégatan
HAGA
Sprängkullsg.
Kyrkogatan
Viktoriagatan
Vasagatan
Park-gatan
Aschebergsgatan
VASASTADEN
VASAPARK
SKANSENPARKEN
Skansen Kronan
Utsikts-platsen
Föreningsgatan
Husargatan
Sveagatan
Övre Husargatan
Brunnsgatan
VANGA
Nya Älvsborgs Fästning
Älvsborgsbron, Sjömanstornet
Masthuggskyrkan, Sjöfartsmuseet
E 6-E 20
158
159
Slottsskogen, Botaniska Trädgården
Naturhistoriska Museet

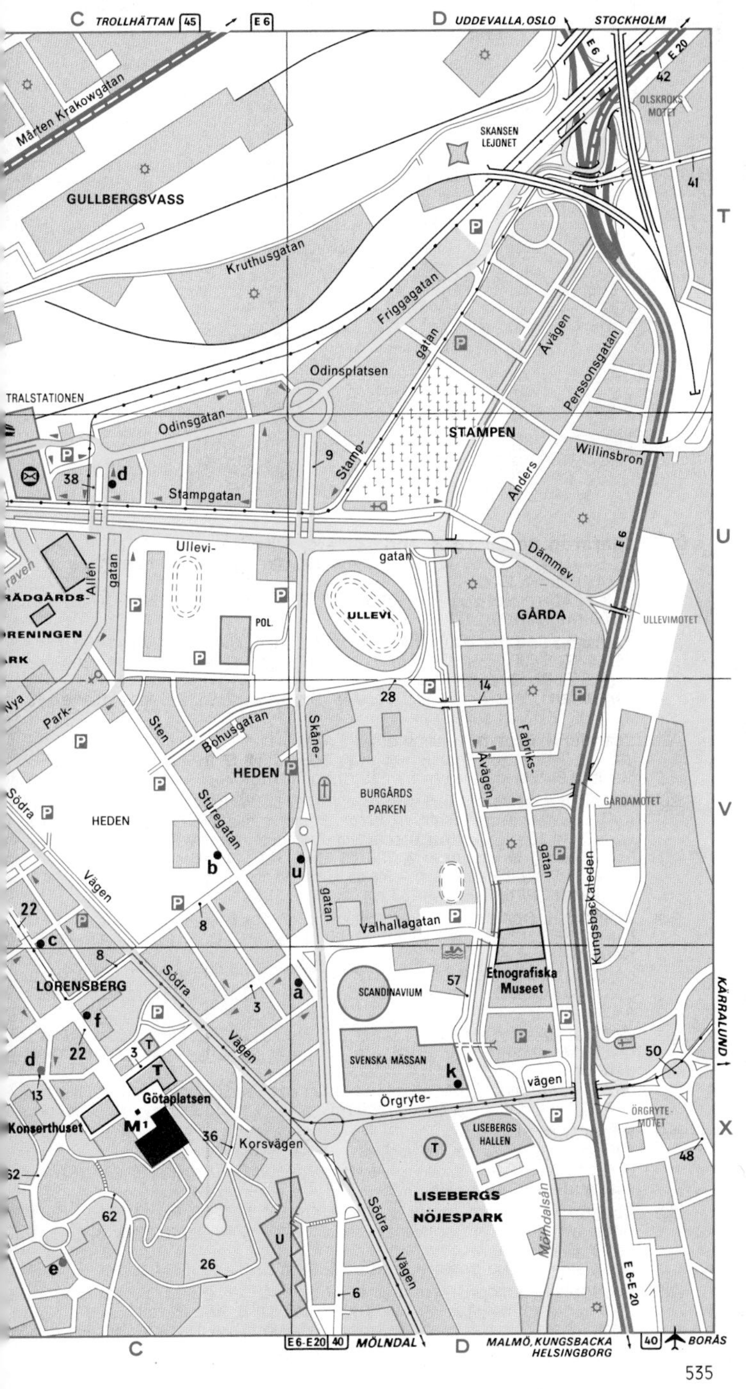

C TROLLHÄTTAN 45 E 6
D UDDEVALLA, OSLO
STOCKHOLM
E 6
E 20
42
OLSKROKSMOTET
SKANSEN LEJONET
41
T
Mårten Krakowgatan
GULLBERGSVASS
Kruthusgatan
Friggagatan
Odinsplatsen
TRALSTATIONEN
Odinsgatan
STAMPEN
Åvägen
Perssonsgatan
Willinsbron
9
Stamp-
gatan
38
d
Stampgatan
Anders
U
Ullevi-
gatan
Dämmev.
E 6
Allén
gatan
ULLEVI
POL.
GÅRDA
ULLEVIMOTET
RÄDGÅRDS-
RENINGEN
ARK
Nya
Park-
Sten
Bohusgatan
Skåne-
28
14
Fabriks-
HEDEN
BURGÅRDS PARKEN
Åvägen
GÅRDAMOTET
V
Södra
HEDEN
Sturegatan
b
u
gatan
gatan
Kungsbackaleden
Vägen
22
8
Valhallagatan
c
8
LORENSBERG
Södra
3
a
SCANDINAVIUM
57
Etnografiska Museet
KÄRRALUND
f
22
Vägen
SVENSKA MÄSSAN
k
50
d
3
13
Götaplatsen
Örgryte-
vägen
ÖRGRYTEMOTET
Konserthuset
M1
36
Korsvägen
LISEBERGS HALLEN
X
48
62
62
LISEBERGS NÖJESPARK
Södra
Vägen
Mölndalsån
U
26
e
6
E 6-E 20
E6-E20 40 MÖLNDAL
C
D
MALMÖ, KUNGSBACKA HELSINGBORG
40 BORÅS

STREET INDEX TO GÖTEBORG TOWN PLAN

Fredsgatan .... BU 12
Korsgatan .... BU
Kungsgatan .... ABV
Köpmansgatan .... BU 23
Postgatan .... BU 39
Spannmålsgatan .... BTU 52
Torggatan .... BTU

Anders Perssonsgatan ... DTU
Andréegatan .... AV
Basargatan .... BV 2
Berzeliigatan .... CX 3
Bohusgatan CV
Brunnsgatan .... AX
Drottningtorget .... BU 5
Dämmevägen .... DU
Eklandagatan .... DX 6
Engelbrektsgatan ...... BCVX 8
Fabriksgatan .... DV
Folkungagatan .... DU 9
Friggagatan .... DT
Föreningsgatan .... BX
Första Långgatan .... AV
Geijersgatan .... CX 13
Gustaf Adolfs Torg .... BU
Gårdavägen .... DV 14
Götabergsgatan .... BX 15
Götaleden .... BT 16
Götaplatsen CX
Götaälvbron .... BT

Haga Kyrkogata .... AX
Haga Nygata .... AX
Hvitfeldtsplatsen .... AV 17
Järntorget .... AV 19
Järntorgsgatan .... AV 20
Korsvägen .... CDX
Kruthusgatan .... CT
Kungsbackaleden .... DV
Kungsportsavenyn ..... BCUX 22
Kungsportsplatsen .... BV
Kungstorget .... BV
Landsvägsgatan .... AX 25
Lennart
Torstenssonsgatan ..... CX 26
Levgrensvägen .... DV 28
Lilla Bommen .... BT 29
Lilla Risåsgatan .... AX 31
Lilla Torget .... AU
Magasinsgatan .... ABV
Masthamnsgatan .... AV 32
Mårten Krakowgatan ..... CT
Nils Ericsonsgatan .... BT 33
Nils Ericsonsplatsen .... BT
Norra Allégatan .... AV 34
Norra Hamngatan .... ABU 35
Nya Allén .... BCV
Odinsgatan .... CU
Odinsplatsen .... DT
Olof Wijksgatan .... CX 36
Parkgatan .... BCV

Polhemsplatsen .... CU
Redbergsvägen .... DT
Riddaregatan .... DT
Risåsgatan .... AX
Rosenlundsgatan .... AV
Sahlgrensgatan .... BV
Sankt Sigfridsgatan .... DX
Sankt Sigfrids Plan .... DX
Skeppsbron .... AU
Skånegatan .... DV
Smedjegatan .... AU
Stadstjänaregatan .... BT
Stampgatan .... CDU
Sten Sturegatan CV
Stora Badhusgatan .... AU
Stora Nygatan .... BU
Storgatan .... BVX
Sveagatan .... AX
Sven Rydells Gata .... DX
Södra Allégatan .... AV
Södra Hamngatan ...... ABU
Södra Vägen .... CDX
Ullevigatan .... CDU
Valhallagatan .... DV
Viktor Rydbergsgatan CX
Willinsbron .... DU
Västra Hamngatan ...... BUV
Åvägen .... DTV
Örgrytevägen .... DX
Östra Hamngatan .... BU

Sheraton Göteborg H. and Towers, Södra Hamngatan 59-65, P.O. Box 28
S-401 24, 80 60 00, Fax 15 98 88, - rm
450. BU
closed 22 December-2 January – ***Frascati :*** **Meals** (buffet lunch) 215/420 and a la car
– **300 rm** 1920/2120, 11 suites.

Radisson SAS Park Avenue H. Gothenburg, Kungsportsavenyn 36-38, P.O. B
53233, S-400 16, 17 65 20, Fax 16 95 68, - rm rest
– 550. CX
Parkbaren : **Meals** *(closed Sunday and 15 June-5 August)* 95/210 and a la carte – **301 r**
1495/2045, 17 suites.

Scandic H. Crown, Polhemsplatsen 3, S-411 11, 80 09 00, Fax 15 45 88,
– rm – 300. rest CU
Meals 168/180 and a la carte – **315 rm** 1170/1570, 5 suites.

Hotel 11, Maskingatan 11, Eriksberg, S-417 64, W : 6 km by Götaälvbron follow sig
for Torslanda and turn left at Shell garage, or boat from Lilla Bommens Hamn 779 11 1
Fax 779 11 10, « Former shipbuilding warehouse, modern interior design », –
rm – 200. rest
closed 21 December-2 January – **Meals** (in bar) (dinner only) 230/370 and a la carte (s
also ***Westra Piren*** below) – **133 rm** 1100/1238.

Scandic H. Opalen, Engelbrektsgatan 73, P.O. Box 5106, S-402 23, 81 03 C
Fax 18 76 22, – rm – 180.
rest DV
closed Christmas – **Meals** *(closed Sunday lunch)* (buffet lunch) (dancing Tuesday to Saturd
evenings except in summer) 195/350 and a la carte – **237 rm** 1085/155
4 suites.

Gothia, Mässans Gata 24, S-402 26, 40 93 00, Fax 18 98 04, « Panoran
restaurant on 18th floor », – rm – 1500.
DX
18 : E Våningen : **Meals** *(closed Saturday and Sunday lunch)* (buffet lunch)/dinn
267/327 and dinner a la carte – **288 rm** 1150/1650, 2 suites.

Panorama, Eklandagatan 51-53, S-400 22, 81 08 80, Fax 81 42 37, –
rm – 120. rest DX
closed 19 December-7 January – **Meals** *(closed Saturday lunch and Sunday)* 217/299 a
a la carte – **339 rm** 990/1290.

Riverton, Stora Badhusgatan 26, S-411 21, 10 12 00, Fax 13 08 66, « 12th flo
restaurant with Göta Älv river and docks », – rm – 3C
AV
Meals 225/425 and dinner a la carte – **190 rm** 975/1375, 4 suites.

Provobis H. Europa, Köpmansgatan 38, S-404 29, 80 12 80, Fax 15 47 55,
– rm – 60. rest BU
Meals *(closed Saturday lunch and Sunday)* 175 (lunch) and a la carte 250/401 – **453 r**
1090/1550, 7 suites.

Scandic H. Rubinen, Kungsportsavenyn 24, ✉ S-400 14, ✆ 81 08 00, Fax 16 75 86 - 🛗 ⇆ rm ▤ TV ☎ - 🏠 60. AE ⓓ E VISA. ✗ rest CV c
Meals 175/415 and dinner a la carte - **189 rm** ☐ 1085/2621, 1 suite.

Victors, Skeppsbroplatsen 1, ✉ S-411 18, ✆ 17 41 80, Fax 13 96 10, ≤ Göta Älv river and harbour, ≘ - 🛗 ⇆ rm TV ☎ ♿ - 🏠 40. AE ⓓ E VISA. ✗ rest AU b
Meals *(closed Friday to Sunday except in December)* 125/290 and dinner a la carte - **31 rm** ☐ 1050/1450, 13 suites.

Mornington, Kungsportsavenyn 6, ✉ S-411 36, ✆ 17 65 40, Fax 711 34 39, ≘ - 🛗 ⇆ rm ▤ TV ☎ 🚗 - 🏠 35. AE ⓓ E VISA JCB. ✗ CV e
closed 20 December-6 January - ***Brasserie Lipp :*** **Meals** *(closed Sunday)* 265 (dinner) and a la carte 299/393 - **91 rm** ☐ 920/1495.

Novotel Göteborg, Klippan 1, ✉ S-414 51, SW : 3 ½ km by Andréeg or boat from Lilla Bommens Hamn ✆ 14 90 00, Fax 42 22 32, ≤, 🍽, « Converted brewery on waterfront », ≘ - 🛗 ⇆ rm ▤ TV ☎ ♿ Ⓟ - 🏠 150. AE ⓓ E VISA. ✗
Meals (buffet lunch) 185 and a la carte 283/351 - **144 rm** ☐ 970/1100, 4 suites.

Tidbloms, Olskroksgatan 23, ✉ S-416 66, NE : 2 ½ km by E 20 ✆ 19 20 70, Fax 19 78 35, ≘ - 🛗 ⇆ rm TV ☎ Ⓟ - 🏠 80. AE ⓓ E VISA. ✗
closed 20 December-6 January - **Meals** *(closed Sunday)* a la carte 185/284 - **42 rm** ☐ 940/1100.

Eggers, Drottningtorget, P.O. Box 323, ✉ S-401 25, ✆ 80 60 70, Fax 15 42 43 - 🛗 ⇆ rm TV ☎ - 🏠 30. AE ⓓ E VISA JCB. ✗ BU e
closed 23 to 27 December - **Meals** *(closed Saturday lunch and Sunday)* 225 (dinner) and a la carte 240/330 - **67 rm** ☐ 1085/1610.

Liseberg Heden 🐎, Sten Sturegatan, ✉ S-411 38, ✆ 20 02 80, Fax 16 52 83, ≘, 🌳 - 🛗 ⇆ rm TV ☎ ♿ Ⓟ - 🏠 70. AE ⓓ E VISA JCB. ✗ rest CV b
closed Christmas and New Year - **Meals** *(closed Saturday and Sunday lunch)* (buffet lunch) 195/350 and a la carte - **156 rm** ☐ 975/1650, 3 suites.

Onyxen without rest., Sten Sturegatan 23, ✉ S-412 52, ✆ 81 08 45, Fax 16 56 72 - 🛗 ⇆ rm TV ☎ Ⓟ. AE ⓓ E VISA DX a
closed Christmas - **34 rm** ☐ 895/1250.

Poseidon without rest., Storgatan 33, ✉ S-411 38, ✆ 10 05 50, Fax 13 83 91, ≘ - 🛗 ⇆ TV ☎. AE ⓓ E VISA JCB. ✗ BV a
closed Christmas-New Year - **49 rm** ☐ 840/1100.

Westra Piren (Öster), Eriksberg, Dockepiren, (on Pier No. 4), ✉ S-417 64, W : 6 km by Götaälvbron, follow signs for Torslanda and turn left at Shell garage, or boat from Lilla Bommens Hamn ✆ 51 95 55, Fax 23 99 40, « Dockside setting, overlooking Göta Älv river and harbour » - Ⓟ. AE ⓓ E VISA JCB
closed Sunday, 7 July-4 August, 20 December-12 January and Bank Holidays - **Meals** (booking essential) (dinner only) 425/640 and a la carte 440/610
Spec. Croustillant de pommes de terre au saumon et cabillaud, jus de cerfeuil, Homard noir en médallions sur un lit de risotto, beurre blanc au champagne, Mousse glacée aux framboises et fromage blanc, tartelette au chocolat.

Brasserie, 🍽
closed 19 to 22 June, 22 to 27 December and 31 December-1 January - **Meals** 195/375 and a la carte.

Mannerström, Arkivgatan 7, ✉ S-411 34, ✆ 16 03 33, Fax 16 78 54 - AE ⓓ E VISA JCB CX d
closed Sunday - **Meals** (buffet lunch)/dinner 295 and a la carte 195/395.

28 + (Lyxell), Götabergsgatan 28, ✉ S-411 32, ✆ 20 21 61, Fax 81 97 57, « Cellar » - AE ⓓ E VISA JCB BX n
closed Saturday and Monday lunch, Sunday except dinner in December, 28 March-1 April, 21 June-11 August and 23 December-6 January - **Meals** 235/510 and a la carte 308/554
Spec. Grilled duck liver with apple filled brioche and Calvados juice, Lightly smoked fillet of roe deer, lingonberry sauce and pear tarte Tatin, Warm arctic bramble berry soup with savarin and vanilla ice cream.

St. Yves, Teknologgatan 3, ✉ 411 32, ✆ 16 20 66, Fax 69 46 66 - ▤. AE ⓓ E VISA CX e
closed Sunday - **Meals** (booking essential) 180/650 and a la carte.

Sjömagasinet, Klippans Kulturreservat 5, ✉ S-414 51, SW : 3 ½ km by Andréeg or boat from Lilla Bommens Hamn ✆ 24 65 10, Fax 24 55 39, ≤, 🍽, « Former East India company warehouse » - Ⓟ. AE ⓓ E VISA
Meals - Seafood - 310/495 and a la carte.

XX **Le Village,** Tredje Långgatan 13, ✉ S-413 03, ☎ 24 20 03, Fax 24 20 69, « Antique shop in the cellar » – AE ⓓ E VISA JCB AX
Meals 195/595 and a la carte.

X **KB** (Klein), Smålandsgatan 7, ✉ S-111 46, ☎ 679 60 32, Fax 611 82 83 – AE AE ⓓ VISA CY
✿ *closed Saturday lunch, Sunday, 20 June-4 August and Bank Holidays* – **Meals** (booking essential) 125/450 and a la carte 250/520.
Spec. Assorted marinated herring and Baltic herring. Roasted milk-fed lamb with nettle and morel dumplings. Arctic raspberry and yoghurt mousse with raspberry marmalade.

X **Hos Pelle,** Djupedalsgatan 2, ✉ S-413 07, ☎ 12 10 31, Fax 775 38 32 – AE ⓓ E VISA JCB AX
closed Sunday – **Meals** (dinner only) 300/450 and a la carte.

X **Bröderna Dahlbom,** Kungsgatan 12, ✉ S-411 19, ☎ 701 77 84, Fax 701 77 8 « Bistro restaurant, original decor » – AE ⓓ E VISA JCB AV
closed Saturday lunch, Sunday, July and Christmas – **Meals** 225/465 and a la carte

at Landvetter Airport *E : 30 km by Rd 40* – DX – ✉ *S-438 02 Landvetter :*

Landvetter Airport H., P.O. Box 2103, ✉ S-438 13, ☎ 97 75 50, Fax 94 64 70, – |‡| ⇆ rm TV ☎ ♿ P – 🎤 25. AE ⓓ E VISA. ✂
closed 24 and 25 December – **Meals** *(closed Saturday and Sunday)* (residents only) 245 (dinner) and a la carte 245/335 – **41 rm** ☐ 995/1190, 3 suites.

Switzerland

Suisse
Schweiz
Svizzera

BERNE – BASLE – GENEVA – ZÜRICH

PRACTICAL INFORMATION

LOCAL CURRENCY – PRICES

Swiss Franc: *100 CHF = 74.09 USD ($) (Jan. 97).*

National Holiday in Switzerland: *1st August.*

LANGUAGES SPOKEN

German, French and Italian are usually spoken in all administrative departments, shops, hotels and restaurants.

AIRLINES

SWISSAIR: *P.O. Box 316, 1215 Genève 15, ✆ 022/799 59 99, Fax 022/799 31 38. Hirschengraben 84, 8058 Zürich, ✆ 01/258 34 34, Fax 01/258 34 40.*

AIR FRANCE: *IBC, 24 Pré-Bois, 1201 Genève, ✆ 022/798 05 05, Fax 022/788 50 40. Talstr. 70, 8001 Zürich, ✆ 01/211 13 77, Fax 01/212 01 35.*

ALITALIA: *rue Lausanne 36, 1201 Genève, ✆ 022/731 66 50, Fax 022/732 40 29. Thurgauerstr. 39, 8050 Zürich, ✆ 01/306 93 33, Fax 01/306 91 44.*

AMERICAN AIRLINES: *Lintheschergasse 15, 8001 Zürich, ✆ 01/225 16 16, Fax 01/212 04 21.*

BRITISH AIRWAYS: *Chantepoulet 13, 1201 Genève, ✆ 155 69 69, Talacker 42, 8023 Zürich, ✆ 01/215 66 66.*

LUFTHANSA: *Chantepoulet 1-3, 1201 Genève, ✆ 022/908 01 80, Fax 022/908 01 88. Gutenbergstr. 10, 8027 Zürich, ✆ 01/286 70 00, Fax 01/286 72 07.*

POSTAL SERVICES

In large towns, post offices are open from 7.30am to noon and 1.45pm to 6pm, and Saturdays until 11am. The telephone system is fully automatic.
Many public phones are equipped with phone card facilities. Prepaid phone cards are available from post offices, railway stations and tobacconist's shops.

SHOPPING

Department stores are generally open from 8.30am to 6pm, except on Saturdays when they close at 4 or 5pm. They close on Monday mornings.
In the index of street names, those printed in red are where the principal shops are found.

TIPPING

In hotels, restaurants and cafés the service charge is generally included in the prices.

SPEED LIMITS – MOTORWAYS

The speed limit on motorways is 120 km/h - 74 mph, on other roads 80 km/h - 50 mph, and in built up areas 50 km/h - 31 mph.
Driving on Swiss motorways is subject to the purchase of a single rate annual road tax (vignette) obtainable from frontier posts, tourist offices and post offices.

SEAT BELTS

The wearing of seat belts is compulsory in all Swiss cantons for drivers and all passengers.

Town plans of Berne, Basle, Geneva and Zürich : with the permission of Federal directorate for cadastral surveys.

BERNE

3000 Bern 427 ⑬, 217 ⑥ – *pop. 130 069 – alt. 548 –* ✪ *31.*

Basle 100 – Lyons 315 – Munich 435 – Paris 556 – Strasbourg 235 – Turin 311.

Tourist Office, Railway Station ✆ 311 66 11, Fax 312 12 33 – T.C.S., Thunstr. 63, ✆ 352 22 22, Fax 352 22 29 – A.C.S., Theaterplatz 13, ✆ 311 38 13, Fax 311 26 37.

18 *Blumisberg, ✉ 3184 Wünnewil (16 March-11 November), ✆ 026/496 34 38, Fax 026/496 35 23, SW : 18 km.*

✈ *Bern-Belp, ✆ 960 21 11, Fax 960 21 12.*

See: *Old Berne★★ : Marktgasse★* DZ ; *Clock Tower★* EZ **C** ; *Kramgasse★* EZ ; *views★ from the Nydegg Bridge* FY ; *Bear Pit★* FZ ; *Cathedral of St Vincent★* EZ : *tympanum★★, panorama★★ from the tower* EZ – *Rosengarden* FY : *view★ of the Old Berne – Botanical Garden★* DY – *Dählhölzli Zoo★ – Church of St Nicholas★.*

Museums: *Fine Arts Museum★★* DY – *Natural History Museum★★* EZ – *Bernese Historical Museum★★* EZ – *Alpine Museum★★* EZ – *Swiss Postal Museum★* EZ.

Excursions: *The Gurten★★.*

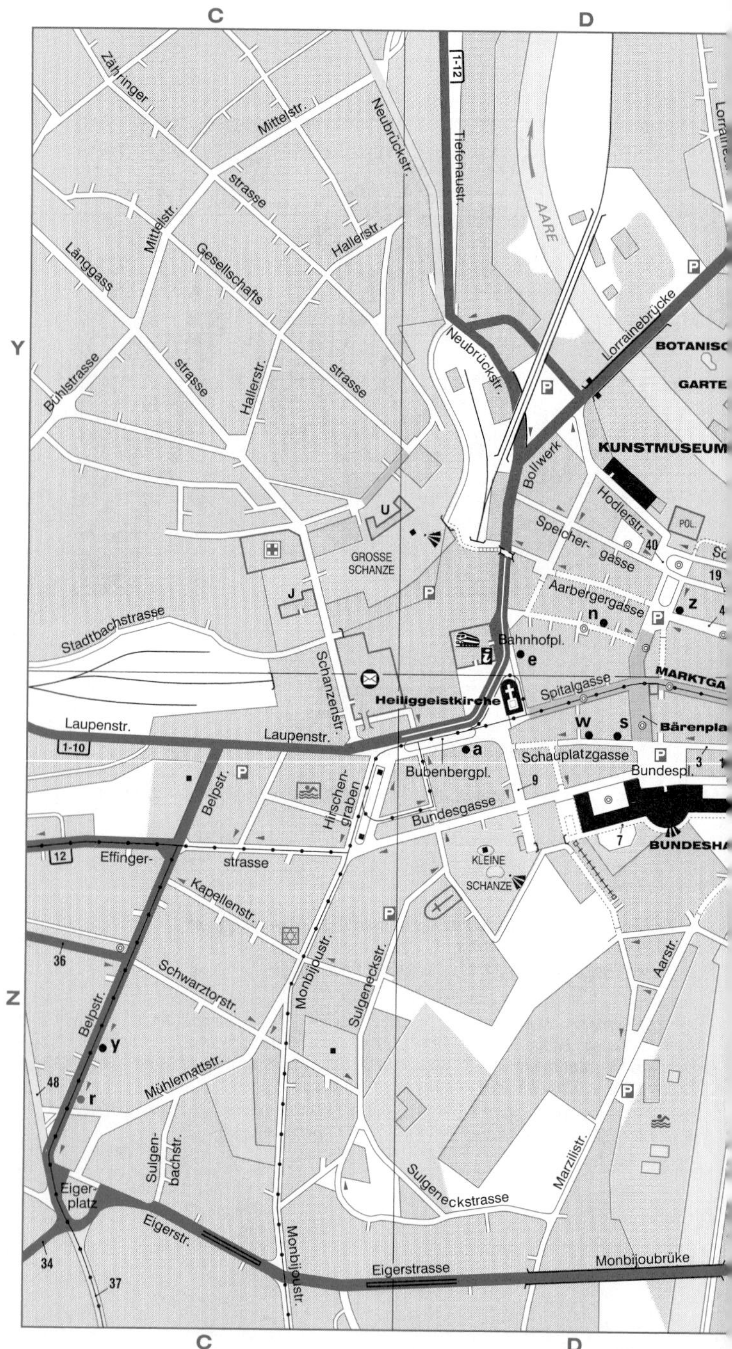
C
D
Y
Z
Zähringer
Mittelstr.
Neubrückstr.
Tiefenaustr.
1-12
AARE
Lorrainestr.
strasse
Mittelstr.
Hallerstr.
Länggass
Gesellschafts
Lorrainebrücke
BOTANISC
GARTE
Bühlstrasse
strasse
Hallerstr.
strasse
Neubrückstr.
KUNSTMUSEUM
Bollwerk
Hodlerstr.
U
Speicher-
gasse
POL.
40
19
GROSSE
SCHANZE
J
Aarbergergasse
Z
n
Stadtbachstrasse
Bahnhofpl.
e
Schanzenstr.
MARKTGA
Spitalgasse
Heiliggeistkirche
Laupenstr.
Laupenstr.
W
S
Bärenpla
1-10
a
Schauplatzgasse
Bundespl.
3
Belpstr.
Hirschen-
graben
Bubenbergpl.
9
Bundesgasse
7
BUNDESHA
12
Effinger-
strasse
KLEINE
SCHANZE
Kapellenstr.
36
Aarstr.
Schwarztorstr.
Monbijoustr.
Sulgeneckstr.
Belpstr.
y
48
r
Mühlemattstr.
Sulgen-
bachstr.
Marzilistr.
Eiger-
platz
Sulgeneckstrasse
Eigerstr.
34
Monbijoustr.
37
Eigerstrasse
Monbijoubrüke
C
D

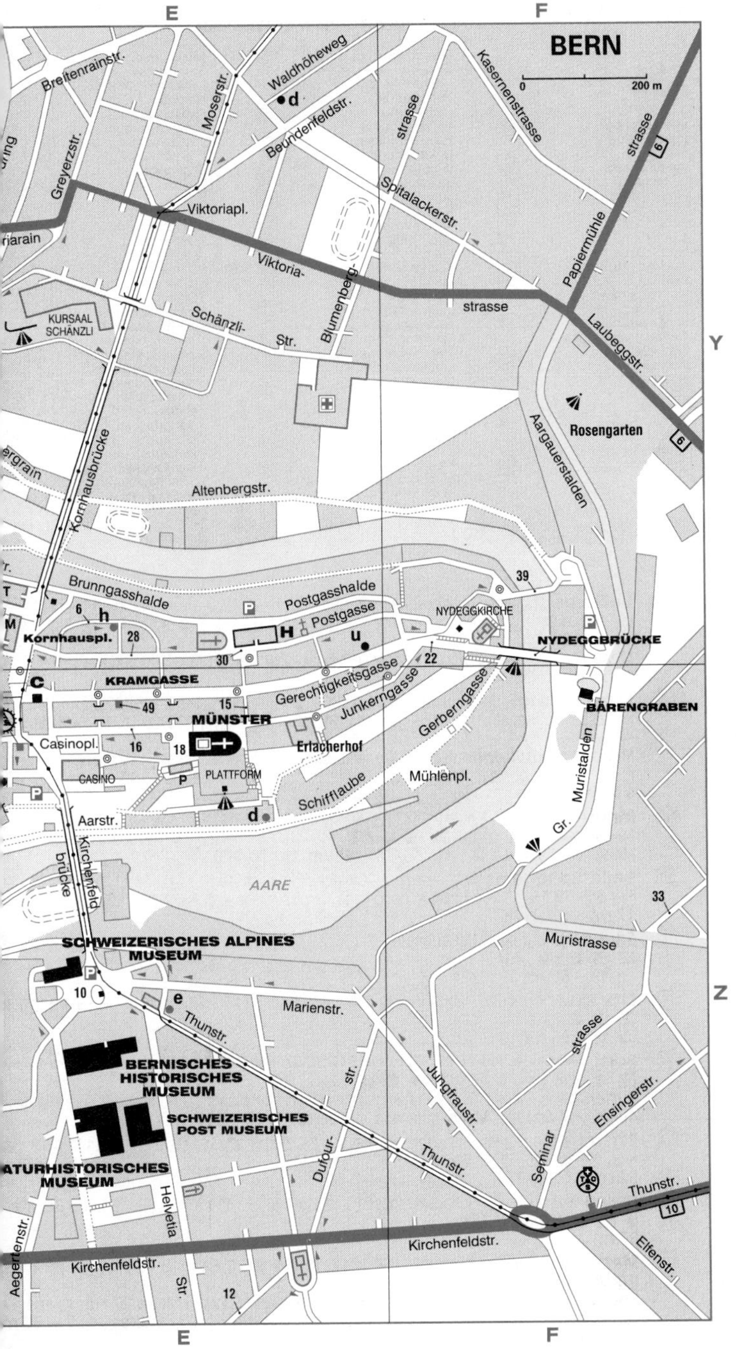
BERN
0
200 m
E
F
Y
Z
Breitenrainstr.
Moserstr.
Waldhöheweg
Beundenfeldstr.
Kasernenstrasse
Greyerzstr.
Viktoriapl.
Viktoria-
strasse
Spitalackerstr.
Papiermühle
Laubeggstr.
KURSAAL SCHÄNZLI
Schänzli-
Str.
Blumenberg-
Rosengarten
Aargauerstalden
Kornhausbrücke
Altenbergstr.
Brunngasshalde
Postgasshalde
Postgasse
NYDEGGKIRCHE
NYDEGGBRÜCKE
Kornhauspl.
KRAMGASSE
Gerechtigkeitsgasse
Junkerngasse
Gerberngasse
BÄRENGRABEN
MÜNSTER
Erlacherhof
Casinopl.
CASINO
PLATTFORM
Mühlenpl.
Schifflaube
Muristalden
Aarstr.
Kirchenfeld-
brücke
AARE
Gr.
Muristrasse
SCHWEIZERISCHES ALPINES MUSEUM
Marienstr.
Thunstr.
BERNISCHES HISTORISCHES MUSEUM
SCHWEIZERISCHES POST MUSEUM
NATURHISTORISCHES MUSEUM
Jungfraustr.
Dufour-
str.
Seminar
strasse
Ensingerstr.
Helvetia
Str.
Aegertenstr.
Kirchenfeldstr.
Elfenstr.
12
10
33
39
22
15
49
16
18
28
30
6

STREET INDEX TO BERN TOWN PLAN

Street	Grid	No.
Bärenplatz	DZ	
Kramgasse	EZ	
Marktgasse	DEZ	
Spitalgasse	DZ	
Aarbergergasse	DY	
Aargauerstalden	FY	
Aarstrasse	DEZ	
Aegertenstrasse	EZ	
Altenbergrain	DEY	
Altenbergstrasse	EFY	
Amthausgasse	DEZ	3
Bahnhofplatz	DY	
Belpstrasse	CZ	
Beundenfeldstrasse	EFY	
Blumenbergstrasse	EFY	
Bollwerk	DY	
Breitenrainstrasse	EY	
Brunngasse	EY	6
Brunngasshalde	EY	
Bubenbergplatz	DZ	
Bühlstrasse	CY	
Bundesgasse	DZ	
Bundesplatz	DZ	
Bundesterrasse	DZ	7
Casinoplatz	EZ	
Christoffelgasse	DZ	9
Dalmaziquai	DZ	
Dufourstrasse	EZ	
Effingerstrasse	CZ	
Eigerplatz	CZ	
Eigerstrasse	CDZ	
Elfenstrasse	FZ	
Ensingerstrasse	FZ	
Gerberngasse	FZ	
Gerechtigkeitsgasse	EYZ	
Gesellschaftsstrasse	CY	
Greyerstrasse	EY	
Hallerstrasse	CY	
Helvetiaplatz	EZ	10
Helvetiastrasse	EZ	
Hirschengraben	CZ	
Holderstrasse	DY	
Jubiläumsstrasse	EZ	12
Jungfraustrasse	FZ	
Junkerngasse	EFZ	
Kapellenstrasse	CZ	
Kasernenstrasse	FY	
Kirchenfeldbrücke	EZ	
Kirchenfeldstrasse	EFZ	
Kochergasse	DEZ	13
Kornhausbrücke	EY	
Kreuzgasse	EZ	15
Langassstrasse	CY	
Laubeggstrasse	FY	
Laupenstrasse	CZ	
Lorrainebrücke	DY	
Lorrainestrasse	DY	
Luisenstrasse	EZ	
Marienstrasse	EZ	
Marzilistrasse	DZ	
Mittelstrasse	CY	
Monbijoubrücke	DZ	
Monbijoustrasse	CZ	
Moserstrasse	EY	
Mühlemattstrasse	CZ	
Mühlenplatz	FZ	
Münstergasse	EZ	16
Münsterplatz	EZ	18
Muristalden	FZ	
Muristrasse	FZ	
Nägeligasse	DY	
Neubrückstrasse	CDY	
Nordring	EY	
Nydeggasse	FY	
Papiermühlestrasse	FY	
Postgasse	EY	
Postgasshalde	EY	
Rathausgasse	EY	
Rathausplatz	EY	
Schanzenstrasse	CYZ	
Schänzlistrasse	EY	
Schauplatzgasse	DZ	
Schifflaube	EY	
Schosshaldenstrasse	FZ	
Schüttestrasse	DEY	
Schwarztorstrasse	CZ	
Seftigenstrasse	CZ	
Seminarstrasse	FZ	
Speichergasse	DY	
Spitalackerstrasse	EFY	
Stadtbachstrasse	CY	
Sulgenbachstrasse	CZ	
Sulgeneckstrasse	CDZ	
Thunstrasse	EFZ	
Tiefenaustrasse	DY	
Untertorbrücke	FY	
Viktoriaplatz	EY	
Viktoriarain	EY	
Viktoriastrasse	EFY	
Waisenhausplatz	DY	
Waldhöheweg	EY	
Zähringerstrasse	CY	
Zeughausgasse	DY	
Zieglerstrasse	CZ	

Bellevue Palace, Kochergasse 3, ⊠ 3001, ℰ 320 45 45, Fax 311 47 43, « Terrace with views over the Aare » – |♦| ▤ rest TV video ☎ ♿ – 🏛 25/150. AE ⓓ E VISA JCB. ⚘ rest EZ
Meals see ***Bellevue-Grill/La Terrasse*** below – ***Zur Münz* :** Meals *20* and a la carte 53/9 – **131 rm** ☕ 350/430, 14 suites.

Schweizerhof, Bahnhofplatz 11, ⊠ 3001, ℰ 311 45 01, Telex 911782, Fax 312 21 7 « Tasteful installation » – |♦| ▤ TV ☎ – 🏛 25/140. AE ⓓ E VIS ⚘ rest DY
Meals see ***Schultenheissenstube*** and ***Jack's Brasserie*** below – ***Yamato*** - Japanes rest. - *(closed Sunday and Monday) (dinner only)* **Meals** 52/92 – **89 rm** ☕ 260/45 3 suites.

Innere Enge 🐎, Engestr. 54, ⊠ 3012, ℰ 309 61 11, Fax 309 61 12, 🏡, park – ⊭ rm ▤ rm TV ☎ 🅿. AE ⓓ E VISA by Tiefenaustrasse DY
Meals *17* - 29 and a la carte 33/76 – **26 rm** ☕ 170/260.

Belle Epoque Ⓜ without rest, Gerechtigkeitsgasse 18, ⊠ 3011, ℰ 311 43 3 Fax 311 39 36, « Belle Epoque decor and furnishings » – |♦| ⊭ TV ☎. AE ⓓ E VISA. ⚘ **17 rm** ☕ 200/285. EY

Savoy without rest, Neuengasse 26, ⊠ 3011, ℰ 311 44 05, Fax 312 19 78 – |♦| TV ☎ AE ⓓ E VISA JCB DY
☕ 18 – **56 rm** 127/224.

City Ⓜ without rest, Bahnhofplatz 7, ⊠ 3007, ℰ 311 53 77, Fax 311 06 36 – |♦| TV ☎ AE ⓓ E VISA DZ
☕ 16 – **58 rm** 105/175.

Bern, Zeughausgasse 9, ⊠ 3011, ℰ 312 10 21, Fax 312 11 47, 🏡 – |♦| ⊭ rm ▤ res TV ☎ ♿ – 🏛 25/160. AE ⓓ E VISA JCB EY
Kurierstube *(closed 6 July - 3 August and Sunday)* **Meals** 29 (lunch)/60 and a la cart 49/99 – ***7 Stube* :** **Meals** *15.50* and a la carte 27/75 – **100 rm** ☕ 200/260.

Bristol without rest, Schauplatzgasse 10, ⊠ 3011, ℰ 311 01 01, Fax 311 94 79, ≘s – |♦| TV ☎. AE ⓓ E VISA JCB DZ
92 rm ☕ 165/230.

Bären without rest, Schauplatzgasse 4, ⊠ 3011, ℰ 311 33 67, Fax 311 69 83, ≘s |♦| TV ☎. AE ⓓ E VISA JCB DZ
57 rm ☕ 170/275.

Metropole, Zeughausgasse 28, ⊠ 3011, ℰ 311 50 21, Fax 312 11 53, 🏡 – |♦| ⊭ rm TV ☎ – 🏛 25/100. AE ⓓ E VISA DY
Rôtisserie Vieux Moulin *(closed Saturday lunch and Sunday)* **Meals** 27 (lunch) and a l carte 41/91 – ***Brasserie* :** **Meals** *16.50* and a la carte 34/65, children 21.50 – **58 rm** ☕ 150/220.

Waldhorn without rest, Waldhöheweg 2, ✉ 3013, ☎ 332 23 43, Fax 332 18 69 – AE E VISA EY d
46 rm ☐ 118/192.

Pergola without rest, Belpstr. 43, ✉ 3007, ☎ 381 91 46, Fax 381 50 54 – E VISA CZ y
closed 23 December - 1st January – **55 rm** ☐ 135/180.

XXX **Bellevue Grill / Bellevue Terrasse** - Hotel Bellevue Palace, Kochergasse 3, ✉ 3001, ☎ 320 45 45, Fax 311 47 43, «, Terrace with views over the Aare » – AE E VISA JCB EZ p
Grill : closed June - September and lunch ; Terrasse : closed dinner in winter – **Meals** *38* - 66/114 and a la carte 78/135.

XXX **Schultheissenstube** - Hotel Schweizerhof, Bahnhofplatz 11 (1st floor), ✉ 3001, ☎ 311 45 01, Telex 911782, Fax 312 21 79 – AE E VISA DY e
closed Sunday – **Meals** *48* - 75 and a la carte 72/118.

XX **Jack's Brasserie** - Hotel Schweizerhof, Bahnhofplatz 11, ✉ 3001, ☎ 311 45 01, Telex 911782, Fax 312 21 79 – AE E VISA DY e
Meals *39* - 74/92 and a la carte 40/110.

XX **Ermitage,** Marktgasse 15, ✉ 3011, ☎ 311 35 41, Fax 311 35 42 – AE E VISA EZ g
closed Sunday – **Meals** *17.50* - 27 (lunch)/69 and a la carte 38/71.

X **Kirchenfeld,** Thunstr. 5, ✉ 3005, ☎ 351 02 78, Fax 351 84 16, – AE E VISA EZ e
closed 2 weeks in July, Sunday and Monday – **Meals** *16* - 35 (lunch)/55 and a la carte 40/78.

X **Zum Zähringer,** Badgasse 1, ✉ 3013, ☎ 311 32 70, – AE E VISA EZ d
closed January - February, Sunday and Monday – **Meals** *17.50* and a la carte 43/78.

X **Frohegg,** Belpstr.51, ✉ 3007, ☎ 382 25 24, – AE E VISA CZ r
closed Sunday – **Meals** *16.50* - 49 (lunch) and a la carte 37/87.

X **Zimmermania,** Brunngasse 19, ✉ 3011, ☎ 311 15 42, Fax 312 28 22, Old Bernese bistro – AE E VISA EY h
closed 6 July - 4 August, Sunday and Monday – **Meals** (booking essential) *17.50* - 37 (lunch)/75 and a la carte 41/90.

at Muri *SE : 3,5 km by Thunstrasse – ✉ 3074 Muri bei Bern – ☎ 031 :*

Sternen, Thunstr. 80, ☎ 950 71 11, Fax 950 71 00, – TV – 25/120. AE E VISA
Läubli : **Meals** 39 (lunch)/65 and a la carte 42/79 – ***Da Pietro*** - Italian rest. - *(closed July - August, and dinner Saturday and Sunday)* **Meals** *18* and a la carte 37/80 – **44 rm** ☐ 195/255.

at Wabern *S : 5 km direction Belp – ✉ 3084 Wabern – ☎ 031 :*

XX **Maygut** with rm, Seftigenstr. 370, ☎ 961 39 81, – P. AE E VISA
closed Sunday and Monday – ***Kreidolfstube :*** **Meals** 68/95 and a la carte 66/110 – ***Gaststube :*** **Meals** *15.50* and a la carte 44/87 – ☐ 9 – **3 rm** 110/120.

at Liebefeld *SW : 3 km direction Schwarzenburg – ✉ 3097 Liebefeld – ☎ 031 :*

XX **Landhaus,** Schwarzenburgstr. 134, ☎ 971 07 58, Fax 972 02 49, – P. AE E VISA
closed Sunday and Bank Holidays – ***Rôtisserie :*** **Meals** 54 (lunch)/120 and a la carte 61/107 – ***Taverne Alsacienne :*** **Meals** *15.50* and a la carte 40/75.

BASLE (BASEL) *4000 Basel-Stadt* 427 ④, 216 ④, 66 ⑩ – *175 510 – alt. 273 – ☎ Basle and environs ; from France 19-41-61 from Switzerland 061.*

See : *Old town★ : Cathedral★★ (Münster) : ≤★ CY – Fish Market Fountain★ (Fischmarkt-brunnen) BY – Old Streets★ BY – Zoological Garden★★★ AZ – The Port (Hafen) ★, "From Basle to the High Seas"★ Exhibition.*

Museums : *Fine Arts★★★ (Kunstmuseum) CY – Historical★ (Historisches Museum) BY – Ethnographic★ (Museum für Völkerkunde) BY* **M**[1] – *Antiquities★ (Antikenmuseum) CY – Paper Museum★ (Basler Papiermühle) DY* **M**[6] – *Haus zum Kirschgarten★ BZ.*

Envir : *★ from Bruderholz Water Tower S : 3,5 km – Chapel of St.-Chrischona★ NE : 8 km – Augst Roman Ruins★★ SE : 11 km.*

18 *at Hagenthal-le-Bas, ✉ F-68220 (March - November), SW : 10 km, ☎ (0033) 389 68 50 91, Fax (0033) 389 68 55 66.*

Euro-Airport, ☎ 325 31 11, Basle (Switzerland) by Flughafenstrasse 8 km and – at Saint-Louis (France), ☎ (0033) 389 90 31 11.

Tourist Office, Schifflände 5, ☎ 268 68 68, Fax 268 68 70 – T.C.S., Steinentorstr. 13, ☎ 205 99 99, Fax 205 99 70 – A.C.S., Birsigstr. 4, ☎ 272 39 33, Fax 281 36 57.

Berne 100 – Freiburg im Breisgau 72 – Lyons 401 – Mulhouse 35 – Paris 554 – Strasbourg 145.

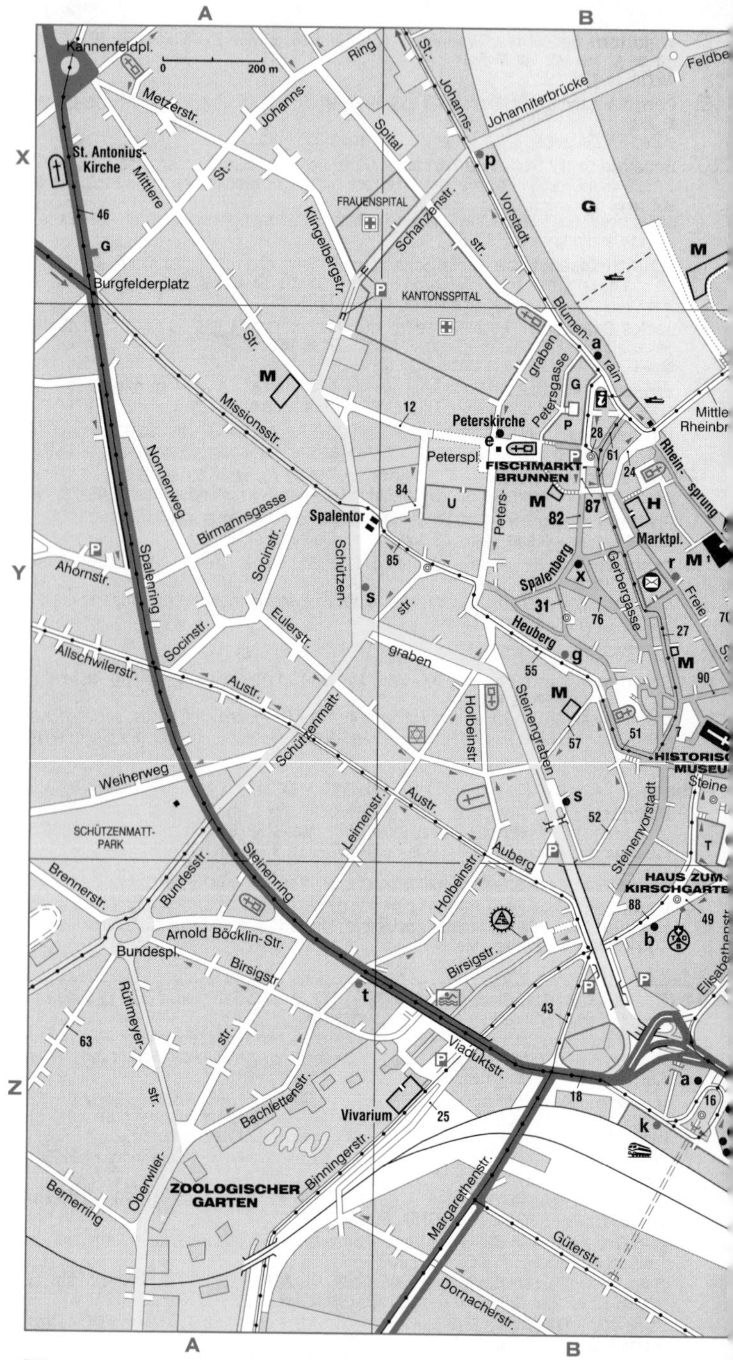
Kannenfeldpl.
St. Antonius-Kirche
Burgfelderplatz
Metzerstr.
Mittlere
St.-Johanns-Ring
Spital
Klingelbergstr.
FRAUENSPITAL
Schanzenstr.
KANTONSSPITAL
St.-Johanns-Vorstadt
Johanniterbrücke
Blumenrain
Petersgraben
Petersgasse
Peterskirche
Peterspl.
FISCHMARKT-BRUNNEN
Mittlere Rheinbr
Rheinsprung
Marktpl.
Freie
Gerbergasse
Spalenberg
Heuberg
Missionsstr.
Spalentor
Schützengraben
Nonnenweg
Birmannsgasse
Socinstr.
Ahornstr.
Spalenring
Eulerstr.
Allschwilerstr.
Austr.
Schützenmattstr.
Holbeinstr.
Steinengraben
HISTORISCHES MUSEUM
Steinenvorstadt
HAUS ZUM KIRSCHGARTEN
Elisabethenstr.
Weiherweg
SCHÜTZENMATT-PARK
Leimenstr.
Auberg
Steinenring
Bundesstr.
Brennerstr.
Bundespl.
Arnold Böcklin-Str.
Birsigstr.
Rütimeyerstr.
Viaduktstr.
Bachlettenstr.
Vivarium
Binningerstr.
Margarethenstr.
Oberwilerstr.
ZOOLOGISCHER GARTEN
Bernerring
Güterstr.
Dornacherstr.
Feldbe
A
B
X
Y
Z
200 m

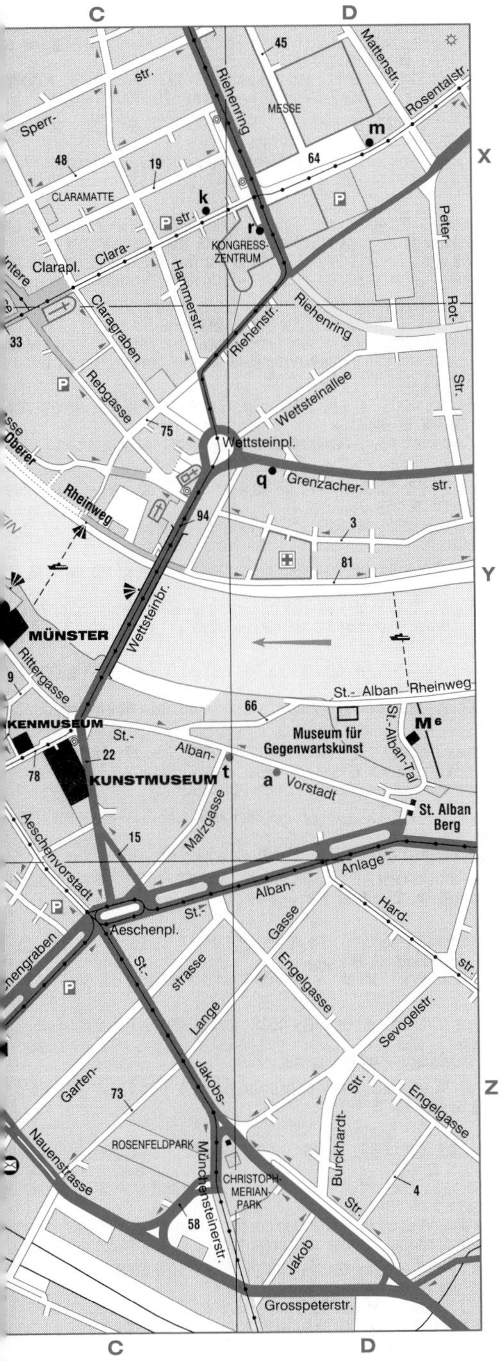

BASEL

Aeschenvorstadt	**CYZ**
Barfüsserplatz	**BY** 7
Centralbahnplatz	**BZ** 16
Claraplatz	**CX**
Eisengasse	**BY** 24
Falknerstrasse	**BY** 27
Freie Strasse	**BY**
Gerbergasse	**BY**
Greifengasse	**BCY** 33
Marktplatz	**BY**
Steinenvorstadt	**BYZ**

Alemannengasse	**DY** 3
Andreas Heusler-Strasse	**DZ** 4
Augustinergasse	**BY** 6
Bäumleingasse	**CY** 9
Bernoullistrasse	**ABY** 12
Brunngässlein	**CYZ** 15
Centralbahnstrasse	**BZ** 18
Drahtzugstrasse	**CX** 19
Dufourstrasse	**CY** 22
Erdbeergraben	**BZ** 25
Fischmarkt	**BY** 28
Gemsberg	**BY** 31
Innere Margarethenstrasse	**BZ** 43
Isteinerstrasse	**DX** 45
Kannenfeldstrasse	**AX** 46
Klingentalstrasse	**CX** 48
Klosterberg	**BZ** 49
Kohlenberg	**BY** 51
Kohlenberggasse	**BY** 52
Leonhardsgraben	**BY** 55
Leonhardsstrasse	**BY** 57
Lindenhofstrasse	**CZ** 58
Luftgässlein	**CY** 60
Marktgasse	**BY** 61
Marschalkenstrasse	**AZ** 63
Messeplatz	**DX** 64
Mühlenberg	**CDY** 66
Münsterberg	**BY** 69
Münsterplatz	**BY** 70
Peter Merian-Strasse	**CZ** 73
Riehentorstrasse	**CY** 75
Rümelingsplatz	**BY** 76
St.Alban-Graben	**CY** 78
Schaffhauserrheinweg	**DY** 81
Schneidergasse	**BY** 82
Spalengraben	**BY** 84
Spalenvorstadt	**BY** 85
Stadthausgasse	**BY** 87
Steinentorstrasse	**BZ** 88
Streitgasse	**BY** 90
Wettsteinstrasse	**CY** 94

The names of main shopping streets are printed in red at the beginning of the list of streets.

Drei Könige, Blumenrain 8, ✉ 4001, ✆ 261 52 52, Fax 261 21 53, ≤, 🏞 - 🛗 ⇆ r ▤ rm TV ☎ P - 🏛 25/80. AE ① E VISA JCB BY
Rôtisserie des Rois : **Meals** 52 (lunch)/112 and a la carte 65/122, children 25 - ***König brasserie :*** **Meals** *19* and a la carte 40/73 - ☕ 29 - **82 rm** 320/590, 6 suites.

Plaza M, Messeplatz 25, ✉ 4021, ✆ 690 33 33, Fax 690 39 70, ≘s, 🏊 - 🛗 ⇆ r ▤ TV ☎ 🚗 - 🏛 35. AE ① E VISA JCB. ✱ rest DX
Le Monet *(closed beginning of July - mid August)* **Meals** 48 (lunch)/66 and a la carte 57/9 - ***Le Provence :*** **Meals** *16* - 24.50 (lunch) and a la carte 47/90 - **238 rm** ☕ 379/538 ½ P 30.

Hilton M, Aeschengraben 31, ✉ 4002, ✆ 275 66 00, Telex 965555, Fax 275 66 50, ≘ 🏊 - 🛗 ⇆ rm ▤ TV video ☎ ♿ - 🏛 25/300. AE ① E VISA JCB. ✱ rest CZ
Le Wettstein : **Meals** 52 and a la carte 54/105 - ***Café Marine Suisse*** *(closed Saturda and Sunday)* **Meals** *18* and a la carte 30/80 - ☕ 25 - **204 rm** 295/495, 10 suites.

International, Steinentorstr. 25, ✉ 4001, ✆ 281 75 85, Fax 281 76 27, 🏋, ≘s, 🏊 - 🛗 ⇆ ▤ rm TV ☎ ♿ 🚗 - 🏛 25/150. AE ① E VISA JCB. ✱ rest BZ
Rôtisserie Charolaise *(closed beginning of July - mid August and Saturday lunch)* **Mea** 41 (lunch)/80 and a la carte 48/107 - ***Steinenpick*** (Brasserie) **Meals** *23* and a la cart 37/94, children 10 - **202 rm** ☕ 335/480, 5 suites.

Europe M, Clarastr. 43, ✉ 4005, ✆ 690 80 80, Fax 690 88 80 - 🛗 ⇆ ▤ TV vide ☎ 🚗 - 🏛 25/180. AE ① E VISA JCB CX
Meals see ***Les Quatre Saisons*** below - ***Bajazzo*** (Brasserie) **Meals** *19* and a la carte 30/7 - **166 rm** ☕ 295/395.

Euler, Centralbahnplatz 14, ✉ 4002, ✆ 272 45 00, Fax 271 50 00, 🏞 - 🛗 TV vide ☎ 🚗 - 🏛 25/80. AE ① E VISA JCB. ✱ BZ
Le Bonheur *(closed Saturday lunch)* **Meals** *37* - 58/118 and a la carte 52/140 - ☕ 28.5 - **61 rm** 320/550, 3 suites.

Basel M, Münzgasse 12, ✉ 4051, ✆ 264 68 00, Fax 264 68 11 - 🛗 TV ☎ - 🏛 2 AE ① E VISA JCB BY
Basler Keller *(closed 5 July - 4 August, Saturday lunch and Sunday)* **Meals** 36 (lunch)/7 and a la carte 53/112 - ***Brasserie Münz :*** **Meals** *19.50* and a la carte 33/79 - **72 r** ☕ 220/315.

Merian M, Rheingasse 2, ✉ 4005, ✆ 681 00 00, Fax 681 11 01, ≤, 🏞 - 🛗 TV ☎ 🚗 - 🏛 25/100. AE ① E VISA JCB BY
Café Spitz - Fish specialities - **Meals** *17* - 43/75 and a la carte 46/88 - **65 rm** ☕ 200/27 - ½ P 35.

Schweizerhof, Centralbahnplatz 1, ✉ 4002, ✆ 271 28 33, Fax 271 29 19, 🏞 - ▤ rm TV ☎ P - 🏛 25/80. AE ① E VISA. ✱ rest BZ
Meals *27* - 43/67 and a la carte 48/107 - **75 rm** ☕ 200/350.

Victoria, Centralbahnplatz 3, ✉ 4002, ✆ 271 55 66, Fax 271 55 01 - 🛗 ▤ rest TV - 🏛 25/80. AE ① E VISA JCB BZ
Meals *19* and a la carte 39/90, children 15 - **95 rm** ☕ 230/310.

St. Gotthard M without rest, Centralbahnstr. 13, ✉ 4002, ✆ 271 52 5 Fax 271 52 14 - 🛗 ⇆ TV ☎. AE ① E VISA JCB BZ
64 rm ☕ 220/320.

Admiral, Rosentalstr. 5 (on Messeplatz), ✉ 4021, ✆ 691 77 77, Fax 691 77 89, 🏊 🛗 ⇆ rm TV ☎ - 🏛 25. AE ① E VISA JCB DX
closed 22 December - 6 January - **Meals** *16.50* - 30/60 and a la carte 30/86 - **136 r** ☕ 200/350 - ½ P 30.

Wettstein without rest., Grenzacherstr. 8, ✉ 4058, ✆ 690 69 69, Fax 691 05 45 - ⇆ TV ☎. AE ① E VISA DY
closed 22 December - 2 January - **44 rm** ☕ 180/270.

Steinenschanze without rest, Steinengraben 69, ✉ 4051, ✆ 272 53 5 Fax 272 45 73 - 🛗 TV ☎. AE ① E VISA BY
53 rm ☕ 180/250.

Stucki, Bruderholzallee 42, ✉ 4059, ✆ 361 82 22, Fax 361 82 03, 🏞, « Flowere garden », 🏞 - P. AE ① E VISA by Münchensteinerstrasse CDZ
✿✿ *closed 16 to 24 February, 22 December - 6 January, Sunday and Monday* - **Meals** 8 (lunch)/185 and a la carte 125/194
Spec. Langoustines aux amandes, curry et mangue confite au gingembre. Rognon de vea aux échalotes grises et à la sauge. Strudel au fromage blanc et aux fruits de saison.

Les Quatre Saisons - Hotel Europe, Clarastr. 43 (1st floor), ✉ 4005, ✆ 690 87 2 Fax 690 88 80 - ▤. AE ① E VISA JCB. ✱ CX
✿ *closed July - August and Sunday* - **Meals** 55 (lunch)/165 and a la carte 90/158
Spec. Strudel à la truffe noire. Caneton braisé sur risotto au raifort. Soupe froide d'orang soufflée et glace au chocolat amer.

XXX **Der Teufelhof** with rm, Leonhardsgraben 47, ✉ 4051, ☎ 261 10 10, Fax 261 10 04, – AE E VISA BY g
Meals (1st floor) *(closed 28 September - 20 October, 17 February - 10 March, Sunday and Monday)* 98/180 and a la carte 94/160 – ***Weinstube :*** **Meals** 70 and a la carte 58/97 – **33 rm** 145/290
Spec. Nanteser Entenwurst in Schalottenjus. Steinbuttfilet mit Périgord-Trüffeln im Mangoldblatt. Holunderblütensülze mit Kirschenkompott.

XXX **Chez Donati,** St. Johanns-Vorstadt 48, ✉ 4056, ☎ 322 09 19, Fax 322 09 81, Typical bistro installation from the turn of the century BX p
closed mid July - mid August, Monday and Tuesday – **Meals** - Italian rest. - a la carte 58/114.

XXX **Le Bourguignon,** Bachlettenstr. 1, ✉ 4054, ☎ 281 14 10, Fax 281 14 20 – AE E VISA JCB. AZ t
closed 21 July - 10 August, 17 to 23 February, Saturday (except dinner in winter) and Sunday – **Meals** *34* - 45 (lunch)/120 and a la carte 42/112.

XX **Schlüsselzunft,** Freie Strasse 25, ✉ 4001, ☎ 261 20 46, Fax 261 20 56, « 15C house » – AE E VISA BY r
closed Sunday and Bank Holidays – **Meals** 68 (dinner) and a la carte 56/112 – ***Höfli :*** **Meals** *19.50* and a la carte 40/54, children 8.50.

XX **St. Alban-Eck,** St. Alban-Vorstadt 60, ✉ 4052, ☎ 271 03 20 – AE E VISA.
closed 12 July - 10 August, Saturday except dinner from mid September - June, Sunday and Bank Holidays – **Meals** *28* - 37 (lunch)/76 and a la carte 66/107. CDY t

XX **Charon,** Schützengraben 62, ✉ 4051, ☎ 261 99 80, Fax 261 99 09, Bistro atmosphere – AE E VISA JCB AY s
closed Easter, July, Christmas, Sunday - Monday from November - April and Saturday - Sunday from May - October – **Meals** *30* - 85 (dinner) and a la carte 62/104.

XX **Sakura,** Centralbahnstr. 14, ✉ 4051, ☎ 272 05 05, Fax 295 39 90, Japanese rest. – AE E VISA JCB BZ k
closed 13 July - 10 August, Saturday lunch and Sunday – ***Teppanyaki :*** **Meals** 52/94 and a la carte 40/91 – ***Yakitori*** (Grill) **Meals** *16.50* -28/52 and a la carte 31/66.

X **St. Alban-Stübli,** St. Ablan-Vorstadt 74, ✉ 4052, ☎ 272 54 15, – AE E VISA
closed 21 December - 13 January, Saturday lunch and Sunday – **Meals** *21* and a la carte 35/90. DY a

at Binningen *S : 2 km by Oberwilerstrasse* AZ – ✉ *4102 Binningen* – ☎ *061 :*

Schlüssel, Schlüsselgasse 1, ☎ 421 25 66, Fax 421 66 62, – TV ☎ P. AE E VISA
Meals *(closed Sunday dinner and Saturday) 20* and a la carte 32/81, children 15 – **26 rm** 120/180.

XXX **Schloss Binningen,** Schlossgasse 5, ☎ 421 20 55, Fax 421 06 35, « Old mansion, antique furniture, park » – P. AE VISA JCB
closed 9 to 23 February, Sunday and Monday – **Meals** *22.50* - 45 (lunch)/95 and a la carte 51/112.

XX **Gasthof Neubad** with rm, Neubadrain 4, ☎ 302 07 05, Fax 302 81 16, – TV ☎ P. E VISA
closed 8 to 26 February and Wednesday – **Meals** *21* - 52 and a la carte 39/96 – **6 rm** 90/170.

at Euro-Airport *NW : 8 km by Kannenfeldstrasse* AX :

XX **Euroairport,** 5th floor of the airport, ✉ 4030 Basel, ☎ 325 32 32, Fax 325 32 65, – AE E VISA
Grill : **Meals** 45 and a la carte 41/69 – ***Brasserie :*** **Meals** 25 and a la carte 29/47, children 8.50.

MICHELIN GREEN GUIDES in English

Austria
Belgium Luxemburg
Brussels
California
Canada
Chicago
England :
The West Country
France
Germany
Great Britain
Greece
Ireland
Italy
London
Mexico
Netherlands
New England
New York City
Portugal
Quebec
Rome
Scotland
Spain
Switzerland
Tuscany
Washington DC

GENEVA 1200 Genève 427 ⑪, 217 ⑪, 74 ⑥ – 170 189 – alt. 375 – Geneva, environs : fro
France 19-41-22, from Switzerland 022.

See : The Shores of the lake★★ : ←★★★ FGY – Parks★★ : Mon Repos GX, La Perle du La and Villa Barton – Botanical Garden★ : alpine rock-garden★★ – Cathedral St-Pierre★ : nort Tower ✻★★ FZ – Old Town★ : Reformation Monument★ FZ **D** ; Archaeological Site★ Palais des Nations★★ – Parc de la Grange★ – Parc des Eaux-Vives★ – Nave★ of Churc of Christ the King – Woodwork★ in the Historical Museum of the Swiss Abroad – Bau Collection★ (in 19C mansion) GZ – Maison Tavel★ FZ.

Museums : Ariana★★ – Art and History★★ GZ – Natural History★★ GZ – Internation Automobile Museum★ – Petit Palais : Modern Art★★ GZ – International Red Cross and Re Crescent Museum★.

Excursions : by boat on the lake, Information : Cie Gén. de Nav., Jardin Angla ℘ 311 25 21- Mouettes genevoises, 8 quai du Mont-Blanc, ℘ 732 29 44 - Swiss Boa 4 quai du Mont-Blanc, ℘ 736 79 35.

18 at Cologny ✉ 1223 (March - December), ℘ 735 75 40, Fax 735 71 05 ; 18 at Bosse ✉ F-74160 (March - December), ℘ (0033) 450 43 95 50, Fax (0033) 450 95 32 57 b road to Troinex ; 18 at Esery ✉ F-74930 Reignier (March - December ℘ (0033) 450 36 58 70, Fax (0033) 450 36 57 62,.

SE : 15 km ; 18 Maison Blanche at Echenevex-Gex ✉ F-01170 (March - mid December ℘ (0033) 450 42 44 42, Fax (0033) 450 42 44 43, NW : 17 km.

✈ Genève-Cointrin, ℘ 717 71 11.

Tourist Office, Place du Molard, ℘ 311 98 27, Fax 311 80 52 and 3 r. du Mont Blan ℘ 909 70 00, Fax 909 70 11 – T.C.S., 9 r. Pierre-Fatio, ℘ 737 12 12, Fax 786 09 92 A.C.S., 21 r. de la Fontenette ✉ 1227 Carouge, ℘ 342 22 33, Fax 301 37 11.

Berne 164 – Bourg-en-B. 101 – Lausanne 60 – Lyons 151 – Paris 538 – Turin 252.

Plans on following pages

Right Bank (Cornavin Railway Station - Les Quais) :

Le Richemond, Jardin Brunswick, ✉ 1201, ℘ 731 14 00, Fax 731 67 09, ←, – video ☎ – 25/230. AE ⓓ E VISA JCB FY
Meals see ***Le Gentilhomme*** below – ***Le Jardin :*** **Meals** 24 - 40 (lunch) and a la carte 64/10 – 34 – **68 rm** 390/720, 31 suites.

Des Bergues, 33 quai des Bergues, ✉ 1201, ℘ 731 50 50, Telex 41254 Fax 732 19 89 – rm video ☎ ♿ – 25/350. AE ⓓ E VISA JCB FY
Meals see ***Amphitryon*** below – ***Le Pavillon :*** **Meals** 31 -45 (lunch)/53 and a la carte 46/9 – 35 – **113 rm** 410/695, 10 suites – ½ P 65.

Rhône, 1 quai Turrettini, ✉ 1201, ℘ 731 98 31, Telex 412559, Fax 732 45 58, ←, – rm video ☎ – 25/150. AE ⓓ E VISA JCB. rest FY
Meals see ***Le Neptune*** below – ***Café Rafael :*** **Meals** 29 - 44 (lunch) and a la carte 57/9 – 30 – **194 rm** 350/775, 20 suites.

Noga Hilton, 19 quai du Mont-Blanc, ✉ 1201, ℘ 908 90 81, Telex 41233 Fax 908 90 90, ←, – rm video ☎ ♿ – 25/850. AE E VISA JCB GY
Meals see ***Le Cygne*** below – ***La Grignotière :*** **Meals** a la carte 41/77, children 15 – 31 – **374 rm** 340/655, 36 suites.

Président Wilson M, 47 quai Wilson, ✉ 1205, ℘ 906 66 66, Fax 906 66 67, ← lak – rm ☎ – 25/1100. AE ⓓ E VISA JCB rest GX
Le Cirque : **Meals** 28 -45 (lunch) and a la carte 60/100 – ***L'Arabesque*** - Oriental rest. **Meals** 60/95 and a la carte 42/86 – 32 – **227 rm** 530/800, 24 suites – ½ P 52.

Beau-Rivage, 13 quai du Mont-Blanc, ✉ 1201, ℘ 716 66 66, Telex 41253 Fax 716 60 60, ←, – rm rm video ☎ – 25/250. AE ⓓ E VIS JCB. FY
Meals see ***Le Chat Botté*** below – ***Le Quai 13,*** ℘ 716 69 25 **Meals** 21 and a la carte 34/9 – 34 – **89 rm** 375/570, 8 suites.

Angleterre M, 17 quai du Mont-Blanc, ✉ 1201, ℘ 906 55 55, Fax 906 55 56, « Tasteful installation », – ☎ – 35. AE ⓓ E VIS JCB FGY
Bertie's : **Meals** 21 -35 (lunch)/45 and a la carte 48/94 – 28 – **45 rm** 450/700.

Forum, 19 r. de Zurich, ✉ 1201, ℘ 731 02 41, Telex 412557, Fax 738 75 14 – rm video ☎ – 25/110. AE ⓓ E VISA JCB FX
The Taj - Indian and International rest. - *(closed Sunday lunch)* **Meals** 18 - 60 and a la cart 39/87 – ***Le Refuge*** - "fondues" speciality - **Meals** 36 and a la carte 36/71 – 26 **196 rm** 280/380, 11 suites.

Bristol, 10 r. du Mont-Blanc, ✉ 1201, ℘ 732 38 00, Telex 412544, Fax 738 90 39, – ☎ – 25/90. AE ⓓ E VISA JCB. rest FY
Meals 19 - 41 and a la carte 41/87 – 27 – **93 rm** 275/450, 5 suites.

Warwick, 14 r. de Lausanne, ✉ 1201, ☎ 731 62 50, Telex 412731, Fax 738 99 35 – rm – 25/300. AE ① E VISA JCB. FY c
Les 4 Saisons *(closed 19 July - 9 August, Saturday lunch and Sunday)* **Meals** 27-46 (lunch)/55 and a la carte 53/99 – ***La Bonne Brasserie :*** **Meals** 15-22 (lunch)/31 and a la carte 36/73, children 13 – ☕ 26 – **169 rm** 352/442 – ½ P 35.

Sofitel, 18 r. du Cendrier, ✉ 1201, ☎ 731 52 00, Telex 412704, Fax 731 91 69, – rm rest TV ☎. AE ① E VISA JCB FY t
Meals *(closed 21 December - 5 January, Saturday and Sunday)* 19 - 43 and a la carte 48/98 – ☕ 29 – **85 rm** 360/400, 10 suites.

Cornavin without rest, 23 bd James-Fazy, ✉ 1201, ☎ 732 21 00, Fax 732 88 43 – TV ☎. AE ① E VISA JCB FY a
☕ 16 – **118 rm** 150/265, 3 suites.

Grand Pré without rest, 35 r. du Grand-Pré, ✉ 1202, ☎ 918 11 11, Telex 414210, Fax 734 76 91 – TV ☎ – 25. AE ① E VISA by rue du Fort-Barreau FX
89 rm ☕ 210/300.

Eden, 135 r. de Lausanne, ✉ 1202, ☎ 732 65 40, Fax 731 52 60 – rm TV ☎. AE ① E VISA JCB CU t
closed Saturday and Sunday – **Meals** 17 - 30 and a la carte 30/59 – **54 rm** ☕ 180/240 – ½ P 28.

Carlton, 22 r. Amat, ✉ 1202, ☎ 908 68 50, Telex 412546, Fax 908 68 68 – TV ☎. AE ① E VISA JCB FX a
Meals *(closed 1 to 7 January, Sunday lunch and Saturday)* 15.50 and a la carte 28/51 – **123 rm** ☕ 225/295 – ½ P 27.

Strasbourg - Univers without rest, 10 r. Pradier, ✉ 1201, ☎ 906 58 00, Fax 738 42 08 – TV ☎. AE ① E VISA. FY q
51 rm ☕ 150/210.

Du Midi, 4 pl. Chevelu, ✉ 1211, ☎ 731 78 00, Telex 412552, Fax 731 00 20 – TV ☎. AE ① E VISA FY v
Meals *(closed Saturday and Sunday)* 23 - 29 (lunch) and a la carte 42/61 – ☕ 12 – **88 rm** 175/250.

Le Cygne - Hotel Noga Hilton, 19 quai du Mont-Blanc, ✉ 1201, ☎ 908 90 85, Fax 908 90 90, ← – . AE ① E VISA JCB. GY y
closed 31 March - 7 April, 30 June - 21 July and 2 to 6 January – **Meals** 59 (lunch)/145 and a la carte 67/136
Spec. Bar de ligne cuit à la fumée de bois et vinaigrette aux truffes. Pigeonneau du Haut-Anjou rôti aux jeunes oignons, risotto crémeux et lard croustillant. Chariots de desserts.

Le Chat Botté - Hotel Beau-Rivage, 13 quai du Mont-Blanc, ✉ 1201, ☎ 716 66 66, Telex 412539, Fax 716 60 60, – AE ① E VISA JCB. FY d
closed Easter, Christmas - New Year, Saturday, Sunday and Bank Holidays – **Meals** 60 (lunch)/135 and a la carte 74/135
Spec. Filets de perche à la vinaigrette aux appétits (summer). Homard breton rôti et pommes de terre au four. Eventail de truffes glacées en coffret de nougatine.

Le Neptune - Hotel du Rhône, quai Turrettini, ✉ 1201, ☎ 738 74 89, Fax 732 45 58 – . AE ① E VISA JCB. FY r
closed 21 July - 10 August, Saturday, Sunday and Bank Holidays – **Meals** 65 (lunch)/125 and a la carte 88/137
Spec. Tempura de queues de langoustines et coulis de gaspacho (summer), Darne de sole bardée d'herbes, raidie en maraîchère, Pigeon du Haut-Anjou rôti en cocotte, millefeuille de polenta au confit de toma.

Le Gentilhomme - Hotel Richemond, Jardin Brunswick, ✉ 1201, ☎ 731 14 00, Fax 731 67 09, « Elegant decor » – . AE ① E VISA JCB FY u
closed 15 June - 14 September, Saturday and Sunday – **Meals** *(dinner only)* 95/120 and a la carte 77/173.

Amphitryon - Hotel Des Bergues, 33 quai des Bergues, ✉ 1201, ☎ 731 50 50, Telex 412540, Fax 732 19 89 – AE ① E VISA JCB FY k
closed July - August, Saturday, Sunday and Bank Holidays – **Meals** 65 (lunch)/105 and a la carte 67/129.

Tsé Yang, 19 quai du Mont-Blanc, ✉ 1201, ☎ 732 50 81, Fax 908 90 90, ←, « Elegant installation » – . AE ① E VISA JCB GY e
Meals - Chinese rest. - 38 (lunch)/125 and a la carte 57/123.

La Fenice, 78 av. de Châtelaine, ✉ 1219, ☎ 797 03 70, Fax 797 01 79, – AE ① E VISA
closed 3 to 25 August, 22 December - 2 January, Sunday and Monday – **Meals** - Italian rest. - a la carte 57/101. BU a

Bœuf Rouge, 17 r. Alfred-Vincent, ✉ 1201, ☎ 732 75 37, Fax 731 46 84 – AE ① E VISA
closed Saturday and Sunday – **Meals** - Specialities of Lyons - 16 - 33 (lunch) and a la carte 46/86. FY z

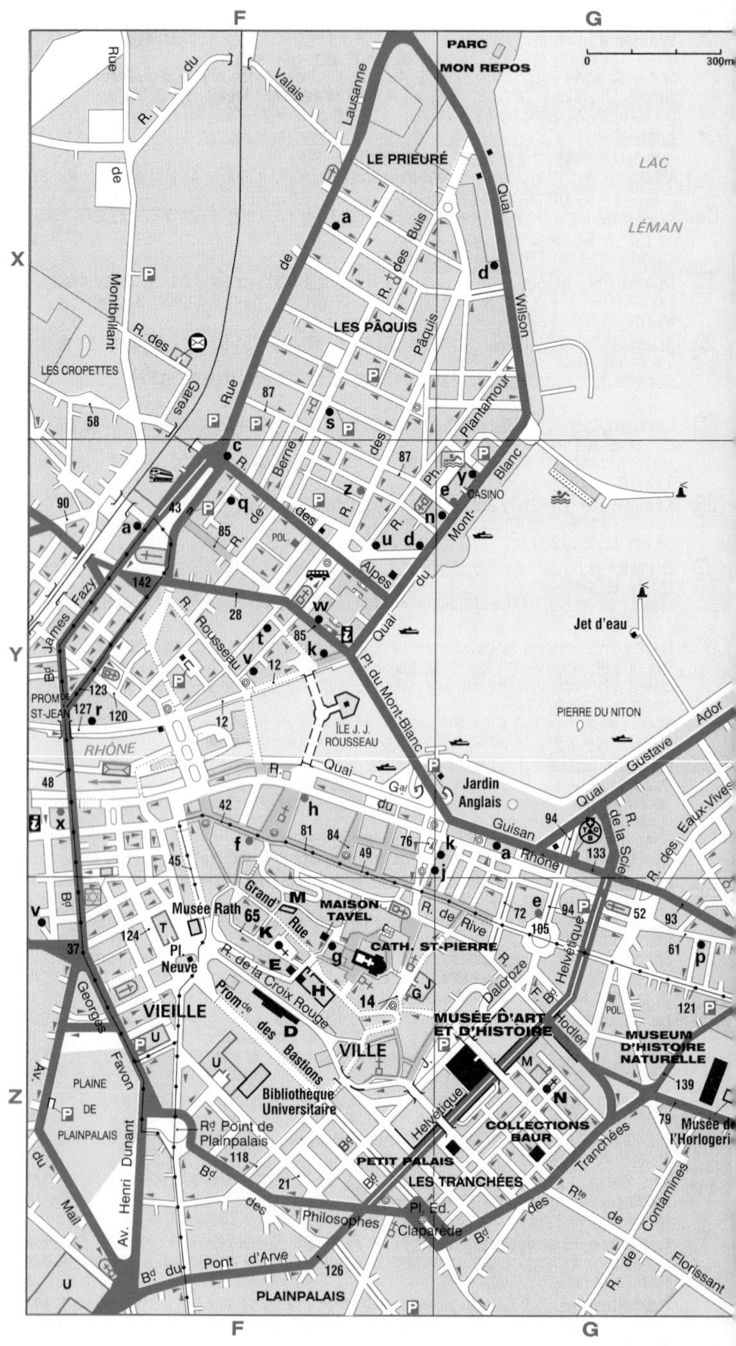
PARC
MON REPOS
LE PRIEURÉ
LAC
LÉMAN
LES PÂQUIS
LES CROPETTES
CASINO
Jet d'eau
PIERRE DU NITON
ÎLE J. J. ROUSSEAU
RHÔNE
Jardin Anglais
MAISON TAVEL
CATH. ST-PIERRE
Musée Rath
VIEILLE
VILLE
MUSÉE D'ART ET D'HISTOIRE
MUSEUM D'HISTOIRE NATURELLE
Bibliothèque Universitaire
COLLECTIONS BAUR
PETIT PALAIS
LES TRANCHÉES
PLAINE DE PLAINPALAIS
Rd Point de Plainpalais
Pl. Ed. Claparède
Musée de l'Horlogerie
PLAINPALAIS
Pl. Neuve
Quai Wilson
Quai du Mont-Blanc
Pt du Mont-Blanc
Quai Gustave Ador
Quai Gal Guisan
R. de Lausanne
R. de Berne
R. des Alpes
R. Rousseau
R. de Rive
R. du Rhône
R. des Eaux-Vives
Bd James Fazy
Bd Georges Favon
Av. Henri Dunant
Av. du Mail
Bd du Pont d'Arve
Bd des Philosophes
Bd Helvétique
Rte de Florissant
R. de Contamines
Grand' Rue
R. de la Croix Rouge
Promde des Bastions
Rue de Montbrillant
R. des Gares
PROMde ST-JEAN
0
300m
F
G
X
Y
Z

STREET INDEX TO GENEVE TOWN PLAN

nfédération
(R. de la) . . . . FY 42
arché (R. du) . . . . FY 81
ont-Blanc (R. du) . . . . FY 85
ône (R. du) . . . . FGY
/e (R. de) . . . . FGZ
oes (R. des) . . . . FY
stions (Prom. des) . . . . . . FZ
l-Air (Pl.) . . . . FY 10
rgues (Quai des) . . . . FY 12
rne (R. de) . . . . FY
urg-de-Four (Pl. du) . . . . . FZ 14
is (R. des) . . . . FX
ndolle (R. de) . . . . FZ 21
antepoulet (R. de) . . . . . . FY 28
que (Pl. du) . . . . FZ 37
ntamines (R. de) . . . . GZ
rnavin (Pl. de) . . . . FY 43
rraterie (R. de la) . . . . . . FY 45
ulouvrenière
(Pont de la) . . . . FY 48
oix-d'Or (R. de la) . . . . . . FY 49
oix-Rouge (R. de la) . . . . . FZ
ux-Vives (Pl. des) . . . . . . GZ 52
ux-Vives (R. des) . . . . GY

Edouard-Claparède (Pl.) . . . FGZ
Ferdinand-Hodler (R.) . . . . GZ
Fort-Barreau (R. du) . . . . . FX 58
Frontenex (Av. de) . . . . . . GZ 61
Gares (R. des) . . . . FX
Général-Guisan (Quai) . . . . FGY
Georges-Favon (Bd) . . . . . . FZ
Grange (R. de la) . . . . FZ 65
Grand'Rue . . . . FZ
Gustave-Ador (Quai) . . . . . GY
Helvétique (Bd) . . . . FGZ
Henri-Dunant (Av.) . . . . . . FZ
Italie (R. d') . . . . GZ 72
Jacques-Dalcroze (Bd) . . . . FGZ
James-Fazy (Bd) . . . . FY
Lausanne (R. de) . . . . FX
Longemalle (Pl.) . . . . FY 76
Mail (Av. du) . . . . FZ
Malagnou (Rte de) . . . . . . GZ 79
Molard (Pl. du) . . . . FY 84
Mont-Blanc (Pont du) . . . . FY
Mont-Blanc (Quai du) . . . . FGY
Montbrillant (R. de) . . . . . FX
Monthoux (R. de) . . . . FXY 87
Neuve (Pl.) . . . . FZ
Pâquis (R. des) . . . . FXY

Pépinière (R. de la) . . . . . FY 90
Philippe-Plantamour (R.) . GX
Philosophes (Bd des) . . . . FZ
Pictet-de-Rochemont
(Av.) . . . . GZ 93
Pierre-Fatio (R.) . . . . GYZ 94
Plainpalais
(Rond-Point de) . . . . FZ
Pont-d'Arve (Bd du) . . . . . FZ
Rive (Rond-Point de) . . . . . GZ 105
Rousseau (R.) . . . . FY
Scie (R. de la) . . . . GY
St-Léger (R.) . . . . FZ 118
Temple (R. du) . . . . FY 120
Terrassière (R. de la) . . . . . GZ 121
Terreaux-du-Temple
(R. des) . . . . FY 123
Théâtre (Bd du) . . . . FZ 124
Tour (Bd de la) . . . . FZ 126
Tranchées (Bd des) . . . . . . GZ
Turrettini (Quai) . . . . FY 127
Valais (R. du) . . . . FX
Versonnex (R.) . . . . GY 133
Villereuse (R. de) . . . . GZ 139
Wilson (Quai) . . . . GX
22-Cantons (Pl. des) . . . . . FY 142

eft Bank (Commercial Centre) :

Métropole, 34 quai Général-Guisan, ✉ 1204, ☎ 318 32 00, Telex 421550, Fax 318 33 00, ☂ – |‡| ▤ TV video ☎ – 🔗 25/200. AE ⓓ E VISA. ✗ rest GY a
Meals see ***L'Arlequin*** below – ***Le Grand Quai :*** **Meals** *24.50* and a la carte 47/95 – ☕ 20 – **121 rm** 290/455, 6 suites.

La Cigogne, 17 pl. Longemalle, ✉ 1204, ☎ 818 40 40, Fax 818 40 50, « Tastefully decorated and furnished » – |‡| ▤ TV video ☎. AE ⓓ E VISA. ✗ rest FGY j
Meals *35* - 55 (lunch)/85 and a la carte 68/95 – **45 rm** ☕ 315/495, 7 suites.

Les Armures ⛭, 1 r. du Puits-Saint-Pierre, ✉ 1204, ☎ 310 91 72, Fax 310 98 46, ☂, « Attractive rustic furnishings in a 17C house » – |‡| ▤ rm TV video ☎ – 🔗 25. AE ⓓ E VISA FZ g
Meals *(closed Christmas and New Year)* *17* - 45 and a la carte 32/78, children 17 – **28 rm** ☕ 280/440.

Century without rest, 24 av. de Frontenex, ✉ 1207, ☎ 736 80 95, Telex 413246, Fax 786 52 74 – |‡| ⇆ TV ☎ Ⓟ – 🔗 35. AE ⓓ E VISA JCB GZ p
118 rm ☕ 165/350, 14 suites.

Tiffany Ⓜ, 18 r. de l'Arquebuse, ✉ 1204, ☎ 329 33 11, Fax 320 89 91 – |‡| ▤ rm TV video ☎. AE ⓓ E VISA JCB FZ v
Meals *(closed Christmas and New Year)* *19* - 48 (dinner) and a la carte 35/75 – **28 rm** ☕ 195/300 – ½ P 38.

XXXX **Parc des Eaux-Vives,** 82 quai G.-Ador, ✉ 1207, ☎ 735 41 40, Fax 786 87 65, ≤, ☂, « Pleasant setting in extensive park » – Ⓟ. AE E VISA JCB by quai G. Ador GY
closed 31 March - 15 April, 18 October - 4 November, 24 December - 10 January, Sunday except lunch May - September and Monday – **Meals** 56/60 and a la carte 73/165.

XXXX **L'Arlequin** - Hotel Métropole, 34 quai Général-Guisan, ✉ 1204, ☎ 318 32 00, Telex 421550, Fax 318 33 00 – ▤. AE ⓓ E VISA JCB. ✗ GY a
closed 15 July - 25 August, Saturday, Sunday and Bank Holidays – **Meals** *38* - 58 (lunch)/100 and a la carte 52/134.

XXX ✿✿ **Le Béarn** (Goddard), 4 quai de la Poste, ✉ 1204, ☎ 321 00 28, Fax 781 31 15 – ▤. AE ⓓ E VISA FY x
closed 18 July - 21 August, 9 to 16 February, Saturday except dinner October - May and Sunday – **Meals** 58 (lunch)/155 and a la carte 88/164
Spec. Soufflé de truffe fraîche (winter), Morilles fraîches à la truffe et pointes d'asperges (spring), Saint-Pierre rôti à la feuille de laurier, pomme verte et céleri (summer).

XXX **Baron de la Mouette (Mövenpick Fusterie),** 40 r. du Rhône, ✉ 1204, ☎ 311 88 55, Fax 310 93 22 – AE ⓓ E VISA FY h
closed Saturday - Sunday and dinner from July to August, Monday dinner, Tuesday dinner and Sunday from September to June – **Meals** *35* - 55 and a la carte 46/101.

XX **Roberto,** 10 r. Pierre-Fatio, ✉ 1204, ☎ 311 80 33, Fax 311 84 66 – ▤. AE E VISA GZ e
closed Saturday dinner and Sunday – **Meals** - Italian rest. - a la carte 52/109.

X **Brasserie Lipp,** 8 r. de la Confédération (2nd floor), ✉ 1204, ☎ 311 10 11, Fax 312 01 04, ☂ – ⇆ ▤. AE ⓓ E VISA FY f
Meals 20.50 and a la carte 35/79.

Environs

to the N :

Palais des Nations : *by quai Wilson* FGX :

Intercontinental M, 7 chemin du Petit-Saconnex, ✉ 1209, ☎ 919 39 3 Telex 412921, Fax 919 38 38, ≤, ☂, Ƒ₅, ⛱ - |‡| ▤ TV ☎ ⇔ P - 🏛 25/600. AE ⓓ E VISA JCB. ✗ rest
Meals see *Les Continents* below – *La Pergola :* **Meals** *25* and a la carte 64/96 – ☐ – **285 rm** 420/500, 60 suites.

Les Continents - Hotel Intercontinental, 7 chemin du Petit-Saconnex, ✉ 120 ☎ 919 33 50, Telex 412921, Fax 919 38 38 – ▤ P. AE ⓓ E VISA JCB. ✗
closed Easter, Christmas, New Year, Saturday and Sunday – **Meals** 55 (lunch)/92 and la carte 74/158
Spec. Eventail d'omble chevalier croustillant, crème à la livèche et pleurotes sautées, Fil de St. Pierre poêlé en feuille d'algue et sésame, Suprême de canette au miel et gingembr confit de navets.

La Perle du Lac, 128 r. de Lausanne, ✉ 1202, ☎ 731 79 35, Fax 731 49 79, ☂ « Chalet in a park ≤ lake » – P. AE ⓓ E VISA JCB. ✗
closed 22 December - 1 February and Monday – **Meals** 58 (lunch)/145 and a la carte 72/13

at Palais des Expositions : *by quai Wilson* FGX *: 5 km – ✉ 1218 Le Grand-Saconnex – ☎ 02.*

Holiday Inn Crowne Plaza M, 26 voie de Moëns, ☎ 791 00 11, Fax 798 92 73, Ƒ ≘s, ⛱ – |‡| ✗ rm ▤ TV video ☎ ♿ ⇔ – 🏛 25/140. AE ⓓ E VISA JCB
Meals *22* - 42 and a la carte 58/112 – ☐ 25 – **305 rm** 340/395.

at Chambésy *5 km* - CT – *✉ 1292 Chambésy – ☎ 022 :*

Relais de Chambésy, 8 pl. de Chambésy, ☎ 758 11 05, Fax 758 02 30, ☂ – AE ⓓ E VISA CT
closed Saturday lunch and Sunday – **Meals** *17.50* - 29 (lunch)/50 and a la carte 39/73.

at Bellevue : *by road to Lausanne* FX *: 6 km – ✉ 1293 Bellevue – ☎ 022 :*

La Réserve, 301 rte de Lausanne, ☎ 774 17 41, Fax 774 25 71, ≤, ☂, Park, Ƒ₅, ≘s ⛱, ⛱, ✗, ⚓ – ▤ TV ☎ ⇔ P – 🏛 25/80. AE ⓓ E VISA JCB
Meals see *Tsé Fung* below – *Mikado* - Japanese rest. - *(closed Sunday lunch except summer and Saturday lunch)* **Meals** 45 (lunch)/95 and a la carte 41/112 – *Chez Gianni* - Italia rest. - *(dinner only)* **Meals** a la carte 66/94 – *La Closerie :* **Meals** 48/75 and a la cart 72/146 – ☐ 28 – **108 rm** 295/495, 6 suites.

Tsé Fung - Hotel La Réserve, 301 rte de Lausanne, ☎ 774 17 41, Fax 774 25 71, ☂ – ▤ P. AE ⓓ E VISA JCB
Meals - Chinese rest. - 50 (lunch)/125 and a la carte 66/125.

to the E by road to Evian :

at Cologny : *by Quai Gustave Ador* GY *: 3,5 km – ✉ 1223 Cologny – ☎ 022 :*

Aub. du Lion d'Or (Byrne/Dupont), 5 pl. Pierre-Gautier, ☎ 736 44 32, Fax 786 74 6 ≤, ☂, « Overlooking the lake and Geneva » – P. AE ⓓ E VISA
closed January, Saturday and Sunday – **Meals** 56 (lunch)/110 and a la carte 94/133
Bistro de Cologny : **Meals** *22* -39 (lunch) and a la carte 52/87
Spec. Millefeuille Parmentier de homard et mesclun, Assiette royale de l'Atlantique au herbes thaï, Filet de veau rôti, macaroni aux primeurs de l'été et parmesan.

to the E by road to Annemasse :

at Thônex : *by rte de Chêne* GZ *: 5 km – ✉ 1226 Thônex – ☎ 022 :*

Chez Cigalon (Bessire), 39 rte d'Ambilly, at the customs border of Pierre-à-Boche ☎ 349 97 33, Fax 349 97 33, ☂ – P. AE E VISA. ✗
closed 15 June - 8 July, 9 to 16 February, Saturday lunch, Sunday dinner and Monday
Meals *22* - 42 (lunch)/78 and a la carte 61/99
Spec. Filet de loup rôti en écailles aux asperges vertes, Magret de canard au four et ju aux kumquats, Médaillons de lotte de Roscoff au curry doux.

to the S :

at Conches : *by rte de Florissant* GZ *: 5 km – ✉ 1234 Conches – ☎ 022 :*

Le Vallon, 182 rte de Florissant, ☎ 347 11 04, Fax 347 63 81, ☂, Bistro-style deco
closed 29 March - 7 April, 23 June - 14 July, 24 December - 6 January, Saturday and Sunda – **Meals** *30* and a la carte 53/86.

at Vessy : *by road to Veyrier : 4 km – ✉ 1234 Vessy – ☎ 022 :*

Alain Lavergnat, 130 rte de Veyrier, ☎ 784 26 26, Fax 784 13 34, ☂ – P. AE E VIS
closed 20 July - 10 August, 22 December - 6 January, Monday from September to June Saturday from July to August and Sunday – **Meals** *17* - 48 (lunch)/90 and a la carte 70/11

at Carouge : *by Av. Henri-Dunant FZ : 3 km – ✉ 1227 Carouge – ☎ 022 :*

XXX **Aub. de Pinchat** with rm, 33 chemin de Pinchat, ☎ 342 30 77, Fax 300 22 19, 🌳 – TV ☎ P. E VISA
closed 23 March - 1st April, 21 October - 3 November, 21 December - 7 January, Sunday and Monday – **Meals** 45 (lunch)/94 and a la carte 64/108 – **5 rm** ☕ 120/140.

XX **Olivier de Provence,** 13 r. Jacques-Dalphin, ☎ 342 04 50, Fax 342 88 80, 🌳 – AE ① E VISA CV a
closed 2 to 17 August, 1st to 8 January, Saturday lunch, Sunday and Bank Holidays – **Meals** *16.50* - 41 (lunch)/98 and a la carte 60/102.

at Petit-Lancy : *by Av. Henri-Dunant FZ : 3 km – ✉ 1213 Petit-Lancy – ☎ 022 :*

Host. de la Vendée, 28 chemin de la Vendée, ☎ 792 04 11, Fax 792 05 46, 🌳, Wintergarden – |⇕| ▤ TV ☎ 🚗 – 🧑‍🏫 40. AE ① E VISA
✿ *closed Easter and 22 December - 6 January* – **Meals** *(closed Saturday lunch and Sunday)* 50 (lunch)/120 and a la carte 72/124 – ***Bistro*** *(closed Saturday lunch and Sunday)* – **Meals** *24* -36 and a la carte 39/82 – **33 rm** ☕ 155/265 – ½ P 40
Spec. Millefeuille de homard aux herbes du potager (spring - summer), Carré d'agneau rôti, mogettes vendéennes, Rosace de pêche au Beaumes de Venise, crème glacée à la menthe.

at Lully *SW : 8 km by road to Bernex – ✉ 1233 Bernex – ☎ 022 :*

XX **La Colombière** (Lonati), 122 rte de Soral, ☎ 757 10 27, Fax 757 65 49, 🌳 – AE E
✿ VISA AV b
closed 22 September - 22 October, 22 December - 15 January, Saturday and Sunday – **Meals** (booking essential) 42 (lunch)/82 and a la carte 67/101
Spec. Foie gras de canard aux Fruits confits, épices et Banyuls, Pavé de saumon d'Ecosse aux cèpes, jus au vin jaune, Désossé de pigeon rôti aux pois gourmands, risotto d'oignons doux à la truffe noire.

to the W :

at Peney-Dessus : *by road to Satigny and private lane : 10 km – ✉ 1242 Satigny – ☎ 022 :*

XXX **Domaine de Châteauvieux** (Chevrier) 🐟 with rm, ☎ 753 15 11, Fax 753 19 24, ≤,
✿✿ 🌳, « Beautiful country inn, in a former farm » – TV ☎ P. AE E VISA
closed 3 to 18 August, 22 December - 7 January – **Meals** *(closed Sunday and Monday)* 65 (lunch)/160 and a la carte 100/162 – **20 rm** ☕ 145/235
Spec. Sauté de gros turbot à l'effilochée d'araignée de mer parfumé à la citronnelle, Bécassine des marais rôtie aux salsifis et truffes noires, Biscuit coulant au chocolat chaud, crème glacée à la vanille.

at Cointrin : *by road to Lyons : 4 km – ✉ 1216 Cointrin – ☎ 022 :*

Mövenpick Genève M, 20 rte Pré-Bois, ✉ 1215, ☎ 798 75 75, Telex 415701, Fax 791 02 84 – |⇕| ⇹ rm ▤ TV ☎ ♿ P – 🧑‍🏫 25/400. AE ① E VISA JCB
La Brasserie : **Meals** *18* and a la carte 41/80 – ***Japanese rest.*** *(closed Sunday and Monday)* **Meals** *12.50* - 40/98 and a la carte 42/90, children 20 – ☕ 24 – **346 rm** 275/390, 4 suites.

Penta, 75 av. Louis-Casaï, ☎ 798 47 00, Telex 415571, Fax 798 77 58, 🌳, Fб, ≘s – |⇕| ⇹ rm ▤ rm TV ☎ ♿ P – 🧑‍🏫 25/700. AE ① E VISA JCB. ⛔ rest
La Récolte : **Meals** *16* -29 and a la carte 48/95 – ☕ 25.50 – **302 rm** 265/360, 6 suites.

XX **Canonica,** 2nd floor at the airport, ☎ 717 76 76, Fax 798 77 68, ≤, Restaurants arranged around an aircraft cabin – ▤. AE ① E VISA
Plein Ciel *(closed Sunday except lunch in summer and Saturday)* **Meals** 53 and a la carte 72/123 – ***L'Avion*** (Brasserie) **Meals** *14.50* and a la carte 36/77, children 12.50.

Lausanne *1000 Vaud* 427 ⑪, 217 ③ ⑬ *– 117 571 – alt. 455 – ☎ 021.*
Genève 60.

XXX **La Grappe d'Or** (Baermann), 3 Cheneau de Bourg, ✉ 1003, ☎ 323 07 60,
✿ Fax 323 22 30 – ▤. AE VISA. ⛔
closed Saturday lunch and Sunday – **Meals** 58 (lunch) and a la carte 91/133
Spec. Ravioli cantonais au basilic thaï, citronnelle et épices, Blanc de Saint-Pierre aux graines de chanvre et à l'oseille, Filet d'agneau en galette de riz au cumin du Maroc.

at Crissier : *NW by road to Vallorbe : 5 km – ✉ 1023 Crissier – ☎ 021 :*

XXXX **Girardet** (Rochat), 1 r. d'Yverdon, ☎ 634 05 05, « Elegant decor » – ▤
✿✿ *closed 27 July - 20 August, 23 December - 16 January, Sunday and Monday* – **Meals** 185/200 and a la carte 115/215
Spec. Timbale de macaroni aux morilles et friolée de grenouilles (March - April), Omble du Haut-Lac en sabayon d'épices (May - September), Dodine de truite du lac à l'aneth, sauce verjutée (June - August).

Montreux *1820 Vaud 427 ⑫, 217 ⑭ – 21 362 – alt. 398 – ☎ 021.*
Genève 91.

at Brent : *NW : 7 km – ✉ 1817 Brent – ☎ 021 :*

XXXX ✿✿ **Le Pont de Brent** (Rabaey), ☎ 964 52 30, Fax 964 55 30, « Elegant decor » – ▤ P E VISA
closed 20 July - 4 August, 22 December - 6 January, Sunday and Monday – **Meals** *38* - 65 (lunch)/165 and a la carte 90/166
Spec. Cabillaud rôti, tagliatelles au citron, Saltimbocca de ris de veau aux oignons confits, Conversation aux abricots (June - August).

at Clarens : *W : 1,5 km – ✉ 1815 Clarens – ☎ 021 :*

XXX ✿ **L'Ermitage** (Krebs) with rm, 75 r. du Lac, ☎ 964 44 11, Fax 964 70 02, ≤ lake, « Garden on the lakeside » – TV ☎. AE O E VISA
closed 22 December - 22 January – **Meals** *(closed Sunday except Bank Holidays and Monday)* 58 (lunch)/145 and a la carte 92/128 – ***Le Jardin*** *(mid May - September)* **Meals** *28* -52/95 and a la carte 65/109 – **7 rm** ☐ 220/360
Spec. Foie gras en deux manières, Carré et ris d'agneau braisés aux fleurs de courgettes, pistou de tomates confites (June - July), Bouchons vaudois aux fraises des bois et crème de pralin (June - July).

Vufflens-le-Château *1134 Vaud 427 ⑪, 217 ② – 554 – alt. 471 – ☎ 021.*
Genève 51.

XXXX ✿✿ **L'Ermitage** (Ravet) with rm, ☎ 802 21 91, Fax 802 22 40, « Beautiful residence in a garden, pond » – TV ☎ P. O E VISA
closed 27 July - 20 August, 22 December - 13 January, Sunday and Monday – **Meals** 78 (lunch)/175 and a la carte 128/197 – **9 rm** ☐ 300/400
Spec. Homard breton à la broche, Composition de poissons du lac (April - October), Jarret de veau rôti entier à l'os.

ZÜRICH *8000 Zürich 427 ⑥, 216 ⑱ – 345 235 – alt. 409 – ☎ 01.*

See : *The Quays★★ : ≤★ FZ ; Mythenquai : ≤★ CX – Fraumünster cloisters★ (Alter Kreuzgang des Fraumünsters), windows★ EZ – Church of SS. Felix and Regula★ – Cathedral★ (Grossmünster) – Fine Arts Museum★★ (Kunsthaus) FZ – Zoological Gardens★ (Zoo Dolder) – Bührle Collection★★ (Sammlung Bührle).*

Museums : *Swiss National Museum★★ (Schweizerisches Landesmuseum) EY – Rietberg Museum★★ CX* **M²**.

Envir : *Uetliberg★★ SW : by rail – Albis Pass Road★ SW by the Bederstrasse – Former Abbey of Kappel★ SW : 22 km – Eglisau : site★ N : 27 km.*

Excursions : *Boat Trips, Information : Zürichsee-Schiffahrtsgesellschaft, Bürkliplatz 10, ☎ 482 10 33.*

Dolder (April - 15 Nov.), ☎ 261 50 45, Fax 261 53 02 ; at Zumikon, ✉ 8126 (April - October), ☎ 918 00 50, Fax 918 00 37, SE : 9 km ; at Hittnau, ✉ 8335 (April - Nov.), ☎ 950 24 42, Fax 951 01 66 E : 33 km, at Breitenloo, ✉ 8309 Nürensdorf (April - Oct.), ☎ 836 40 80, N : 22 km.

Zürich-Kloten, ☎ 816 22 11.

Tourist Office, Im Hauptbahnhof, ☎ 211 40 00, Fax 212 01 41 – T.C.S., Alfred Escher-Str. 38, ☎ 286 86 86, Fax 286 86 87 – A.C.S., Forchstr. 95, ☎ 422 15 00, Fax 422 15 37.

Berne 125 – Basle 109 – Geneva 278 – Innsbruck 288 – Milan 304.

Plans on following pages

On the right bank of river Limmat (University, Fine Arts Museum) :

Dolder Grand Hotel, Kurhausstr. 65, ✉ 8032, ☎ 251 62 31, Telex 816416, Fax 251 88 29, Park, « Overlooking the Zurich lake, town and mountains », – ▤ rest TV ☎ – 25/120. AE O E VISA JCB. rest by Gloriastrasse DV
La Rotonde : **Meals** 80 (dinner) and a la carte 65/141 – **172 rm** ☐ 400/560, 11 suites.

Zürich and La Résidence, Neumühlequai 42, ✉ 8001, ☎ 363 63 63, Telex 817587, Fax 363 60 15, ≤, – rm ▤ TV video ☎ – 25/250. AE O E VISA. rest EY c
Scala *(closed Sunday lunch)* **Meals** *36* -54 (lunch)/85 and a la carte 66/111 – ***White Elephant*** - Thaï rest. - *(closed 22 December - 20 January, Sunday and Monday)* **Meals** 36 (lunch)/85 and a la carte 51/86 – ***La Brasserie :*** **Meals** *21* -39 and a la carte 39/86 – **264 rm** ☐ 380/430, 7 suites.

Eden au Lac, Utoquai 45, ✉ 8023, ☎ 261 94 04, Fax 261 94 09, ≤, – ▤ TV ☎ P. AE O E VISA JCB. rest DX a
Meals *42* - 105 and a la carte 65/134 – **56 rm** ☐ 300/570.

Waldhaus Dolder ⛰, Kurhausstr. 20, ✉ 8032, ✆ 251 93 60, Telex 816460, Fax 251 00 29, ← Zürich and lake, 🏊, 9, 🏊, 🎾, ✗ – 🛗 ▤ rest 📺 ☎ 🚗 🅿 – 🏃 35. AE ◐ E VISA JCB by Gloriastrasse DV
Meals *22* and a la carte 47/109, children 16 – ☕ 16 – **65 rm** 220/440.

Sofitel, Stampfenbachstr. 60, ✉ 8035, ✆ 363 33 63, Fax 363 33 18 – 🛗 ⊁ rm ▤ 📺 ☎ 🚗 – 🏃 25/70. AE ◐ E VISA. ⊁ rest FY b
Diff : Meals *32* and a la carte 57/125 – ☕ 29 – **176 rm** 300/360.

Central Plaza Ⓜ, Central 1, ✉ 8001, ✆ 251 55 55, Telex 817152, Fax 251 85 35 – 🛗 ▤ 📺 video ☎ – 🏃 35. AE ◐ E VISA JCB FY z
Cascade : Meals *34.50* and a la carte 48/100 – ☕ 24 – **94 rm** 270/362, 4 suites.

Florhof Ⓜ ⛰, Florhofgasse 4, ✉ 8001, ✆ 261 44 70, Fax 261 46 11, 🏊, « Tasteful installation » – 🛗 ⊁ rm 📺 ☎. AE ◐ E VISA JCB FZ k
Meals *(closed 19 to 26 April, 6 to 12 October, 21 December - 12 January, Saturday and Sunday) 27* - 43 (lunch)/68 and a la carte 54/100 – **33 rm** ☕ 220/330.

Europe without rest, Dufourstr. 4, ✉ 8008, ✆ 261 10 30, Fax 251 03 67 – 🛗 ▤ 📺 ☎. AE ◐ E VISA FZ u
☕ 20 – **40 rm** 200/300.

Opera without rest, Dufourstr. 5, ✉ 8008, ✆ 251 90 90, Fax 251 90 01 – 🛗 ▤ 📺 video ☎. AE ◐ E VISA JCB FZ b
closed 21 December - 5 January – **66 rm** ☕ 220/320.

Ambassador, Falkenstr. 6, ✉ 8008, ✆ 261 76 00, Fax 251 23 94 – 🛗 ▤ 📺 video ☎. AE ◐ E VISA JCB FZ a
Meals 23 and a la carte 44/110 – **46 rm** ☕ 220/320.

Krone Unterstrass, Schaffhauserstr. 1, ✉ 8006, ✆ 361 16 88, Fax 361 19 67 – 🛗 ▤ rm 📺 ☎ 🅿 – 🏃 25/90. AE ◐ E VISA CV b
Grill : Meals a la carte 40/76 – ***Wirtschaft :*** Meals *17* and a la carte 29/63 – **57 rm** ☕ 145/215.

Tiefenau, Steinwiesstr. 8, ✉ 8032, ✆ 251 24 09, Fax 251 24 76, 🏊 – 🛗 📺 video ☎. AE ◐ E VISA JCB FZ h
closed 20 December - 5 January – ***Züri-Stube :*** Meals *24* and a la carte 46/88 – ☕ 19.50 – **30 rm** 240/400 – ½ P 40.

Wellenberg Ⓜ without rest, Niederdorfstr. 10, ✉ 8001, ✆ 262 43 00, Fax 251 31 30 – 🛗 ⊁ 📺 ☎. AE ◐ E VISA FZ s
closed 24 December to 1st January – **45 rm** ☕ 240/330.

Helmhaus without rest, Schifflände 30, ✉ 8001, ✆ 251 88 10, Fax 251 04 30 – 🛗 ⊁ ▤ 📺 ☎. AE ◐ E VISA JCB FZ v
25 rm ☕ 210/315.

Rütli without rest, Zähringerstr. 43, ✉ 8001, ✆ 251 54 26, Fax 261 21 53 – 🛗 📺 ☎. AE ◐ E VISA FY a
62 rm ☕ 180/260.

Seegarten, Seegartenstr. 14, ✉ 8008, ✆ 383 37 37, Fax 383 37 38, 🏊 – 🛗 📺 video ☎. AE ◐ E VISA DX b
Latino - Italian rest. - *(closed lunch Saturday and Sunday)* **Meals** *22* and a la carte 46/80 – **28 rm** ☕ 175/260.

Rex Ⓜ, Weinbergstr. 92, ✉ 8006, ✆ 360 25 25, Fax 360 25 52, 🏊 – 🛗 📺 ☎ 🅿. AE ◐ E VISA DV a
Blauer Apfel *(closed Sunday)* **Meals** *16.50* and a la carte 36/78 – **37 rm** ☕ 125/225 – ½ P 20.

Tübli, Hottingerstr. 5, ✉ 8032, ✆ 251 26 26, Fax 252 50 62 – AE ◐ E VISA FZ d
closed Sunday lunch – **Meals** (booking essential) 56 (lunch)/140 and a la carte 78/129.

Zunfthaus zur Schmiden, Marktgasse 20, ✉ 8001, ✆ 251 52 87, Fax 261 12 67, « 15C blacksmith's guild house » – ▤. AE ◐ E VISA JCB FZ f
closed Easter, Pentecost, mid July - mid August and Christmas – **Meals** *24.50* and a la carte 50/107.

Kronenhalle, Rämistr. 4, ✉ 8001, ✆ 251 66 69, Fax 251 66 81, « Collection of exceptional works of art » – ▤. AE ◐ E VISA FZ t
Meals *30* and a la carte 52/123.

Haus zum Rüden, Limmatquai 42 (1st floor), ✉ 8001, ✆ 261 95 66, Fax 261 18 04, « 13C guild house » – ▤. AE ◐ E VISA JCB FZ c
closed Saturday and Sunday – **Meals** 52 (lunch)/92 and a la carte 61/115.

Zunfthaus zur Zimmerleuten, Limmatquai 40 (1st floor), ✉ 8001, ✆ 252 08 34, Fax 252 08 48, « 18C guild house » – AE ◐ E VISA FZ z
closed 22 July - 18 August and Sunday – **Meals** *22* and a la carte 42/99.

ZÜRICH

Bahnhofstrasse . . . . EYZ
Bellevueplatz . . . . FZ
Limmatquai . . . . FYZ
Löwenstrasse . . . . EY
Paradeplatz . . . . EZ
Poststrasse . . . . EZ 58
Rennweg . . . . EYZ 63
Storchengasse . . . . EZ 85
Strehlgasse . . . . EZ 87
Uraniastrasse . . . . EYZ

Allmendstrasse . . . . CX 6
Augustinergasse . . . . EZ 9
Bärengasse . . . . EZ 10
Beethovenstrasse . . . . EZ 12
Birmensdorferstrasse . . . . . CX 15
Claridenstrasse . . . . EZ 18
Clausiusstrasse . . . . FY 19
Culmannstrasse . . . . FY 21
Dufourstrasse . . . . DX 24
Feldstrasse . . . . CV 27
Fraumünsterstrasse . . . . . . EZ 28
Freiestrasse . . . . DVX 30
Gablerstrasse . . . . CX 31
General Wille-Strasse . . . . CX 33
Hafnerstrasse . . . . EY 36
Kantonsschulstrasse . . . . . FZ 39
Konradstrasse . . . . EY 40
Kreuzstrasse . . . . DX 42
Manessestrasse . . . . CX 45
Marktgasse . . . . FZ 46
Münsterhof . . . . EZ 48
Museumstrasse . . . . EY 49
Nelkenstrasse . . . . FY 52
Neumarkt . . . . FZ 54
Nordstrasse . . . . DV 55
Rathausbrücke . . . . EFZ 60
Rindermarkt . . . . FZ 64
Schimmelstrasse . . . . CX 69
Seebahnstrasse . . . . CX 72
Selnaustrasse . . . . CX 75
Sihlhölzlistrasse . . . . CX 76
Stadelhoferstrasse . . . . FZ 78
Stampfenbachplatz . . . . . . FY 79
Stampfenbachstrasse . . . . EFY 81
Stauffacherplatz . . . . CX 82
Stauffacherstrasse . . . . . . CVX 84
Sumatrastrasse . . . . FY 88
Talacker . . . . EZ 90
Tannenstrasse . . . . FY 91
Theaterstrasse . . . . FZ 93
Toblerstrasse . . . . DV 96
Tunnelstrasse . . . . CX 97
Usteristrasse . . . . EY 100
Waffenplatzstrasse . . . . . . CX 102
Weinbergfussweg . . . . FY 103
Zollikerstrasse . . . . DX 108

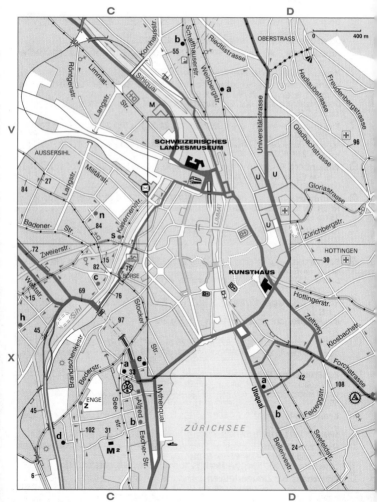

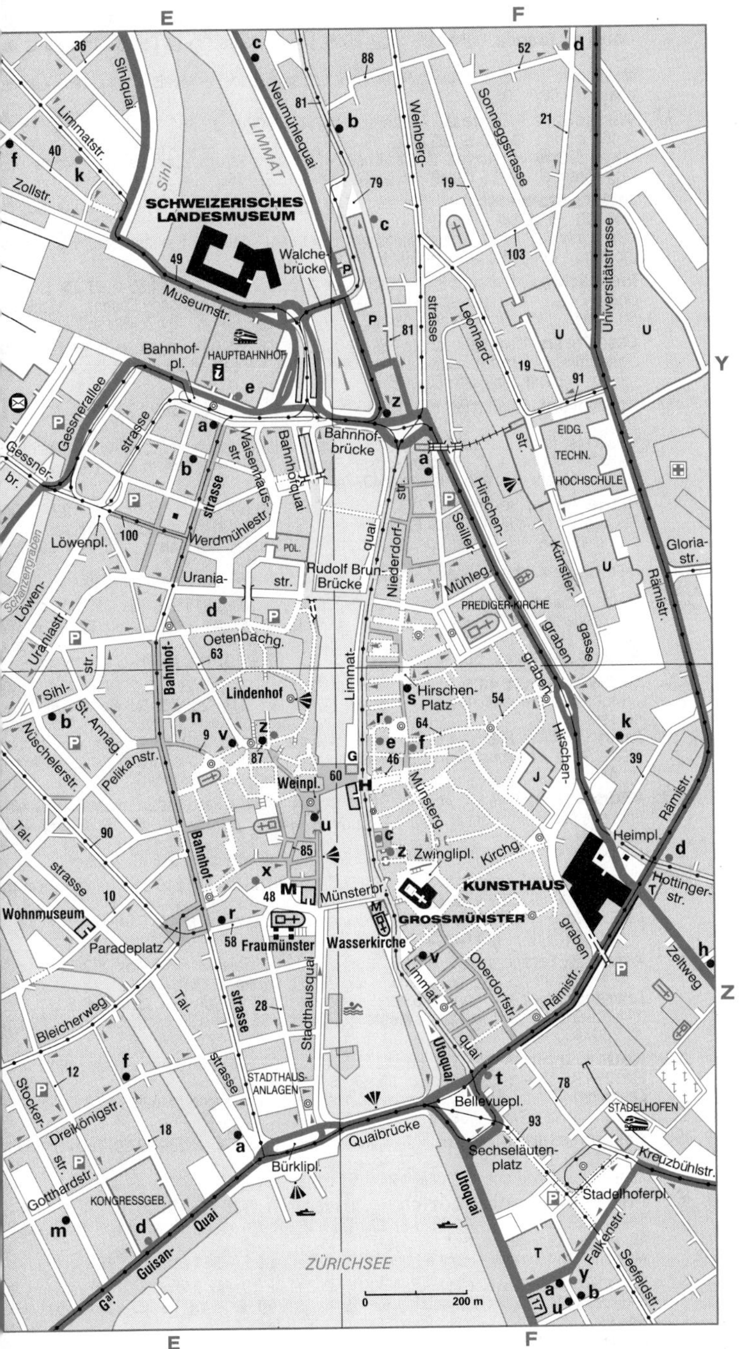
SCHWEIZERISCHES LANDESMUSEUM
HAUPTBAHNHOF
EIDG. TECHN. HOCHSCHULE
PREDIGER-KIRCHE
Lindenhof
KUNSTHAUS
GROSSMÜNSTER
Fraumünster
Wasserkirche
Wohnmuseum
Paradeplatz
STADTHAUS-ANLAGEN
KONGRESSGEB.
STADELHOFEN
ZÜRICHSEE
LIMMAT
Sihl
Bahnhofbrücke
Rudolf Brun-Brücke
Münsterbr.
Quaibrücke
Walchebrücke
Bellevuepl.
Sechseläutenplatz
Stadelhoferpl.
Bürklipl.
Weinpl.
Hirschen-Platz
Zwinglipl.
Heimpl.
Löwenpl.
Bahnhofpl.
200 m

XX **Conti-da Bianca,** Dufourstr. 1, ✉ 8008, ✆ 251 06 66, Fax 251 06 67 – AE ⓓ E VISA FZ
closed mid July - mid August, Saturday lunch and Sunday – **Meals** - Italian rest. - *23* and a la carte 58/100.

XX **Wirtschaft Flühgass,** Zollikerstr. 214, ✉ 8008, ✆ 381 12 15, Fax 422 75 32 « 16C inn » – Ⓟ. AE E VISA by Zollikerstrasse DX
closed 12 July - 10 August, 21 December - 2 January, Saturday and Sunday – **Meals** (booking essential) *22* - 55 (lunch)/95 and a la carte 55/115.

XX **Jacky's Stapferstube,** Culmannstr. 45, ✉ 8006, ✆ 361 37 48, Fax 364 00 60, – Ⓟ. AE ⓓ E VISA FY
closed mid July - mid August, Sunday and Monday – **Meals** - veal and beef specialities (booking essential) a la carte 69/150.

XX **Riesbächli,** Zollikerstr. 157, ✉ 8008, ✆ 422 23 24, Fax 422 34 35 – AE ⓓ E VISA
closed 24 July - 18 August, 23 December - 5 January, Saturday and Sunday – **Meals** *28* 50 (lunch)/135 and a la carte 59/137. by Zollikerstrasse DX

XX **Casa Ferlin,** Stampfenbachstr. 38, ✉ 8006, ✆ 362 35 09 – ▤. AE ⓓ E VISA FY
closed mid July - mid August, Saturday and Sunday – **Meals** - Italian rest. - (booking essential) *27* - 48 and a la carte 60/113.

XX **Königstuhl,** Stüssihofstatt 3, ✉ 8001, ✆ 261 76 18, Fax 262 71 23, – AE ⓓ E VISA FZ
Meals (1st floor) *(closed 15 July - 17 August, Saturday lunch and Sunday)* 45 (lunch)/95 and a la carte 56/107 – ***Bistro*** *: (closed Saturday lunch except from June to August and Sunday)* **Meals** *17.50* and a la carte 40/74.

X **Blaue Ente,** Seefeldstr. 223 (Mühle Tiefenbrunnen), ✉ 8008, ✆ 422 77 06, Fax 422 77 41, – AE ⓓ E VISA by Zollikerstrasse DX
closed 13 July - 4 August and 24 December - 5 January – **Meals** a la carte 47/98.

On the left bank of the river Limmat *(Main railway station, Business centre) :*

Baur au Lac, Talstr. 1, ✉ 8022, ✆ 220 50 20, Telex 813567, Fax 220 50 44, « Lakeside setting and garden », – |‡| ▤ TV ☎ ♿ – 🔬 25/60. AE ⓓ E VISA JCB. ✻ EZ
Pavillon : **Meals** *45* - 68/84 and a la carte 70/167 – **107 rm** ⊐ 410/720, 18 suites.

Savoy Baur en Ville Ⓜ, am Paradeplatz, ✉ 8022, ✆ 215 25 25, Fax 215 25 00, « Modern - elegant decor » – |‡| ▤ TV ☎ ♿ – 🔬 25/70. AE ⓓ E VISA JCB ✻ rest EZ
Savoy (1st floor) **Meals** *39* -64 (lunch)/92 and a la carte 65/140 – ***Orsini*** (am Münsterhof) - Italian rest. - *(booking essential)* **Meals** *37* - 57 (lunch)/74 and a la carte 61/122 – **104 rm** ⊐ 430/630, 8 suites.

Widder Ⓜ, Rennweg 7, ✆ 224 25 26, Fax 224 24 24, « Restored old town houses with contemporary interiors » – |‡| ▤ TV ☎ ♿ – 🔬 25/170. AE ⓓ E VISA JCB ✻ rest EZ
Meals *38* - 58 (lunch)/85 and a la carte 58/115 – **42 rm** ⊐ 400/630, 7 suites.

Schweizerhof, Bahnhofplatz 7, ✉ 8023, ✆ 218 88 88, Fax 218 81 81 – |‡| ⇔ rm ▤ TV ☎ – 🔬 40. AE ⓓ E VISA JCB. ✻ rest EY
La Soupière (1st floor) *(closed Saturday lunch and Sunday)* **Meals** 64 (lunch)/89 and a la carte 67/122 – **115 rm** ⊐ 360/530.

Ascot Ⓜ, Tessinerplatz 9, ✉ 8002, ✆ 201 18 00, Telex 815454, Fax 202 72 10, – |‡| ⇔ rm ▤ rest TV ☎ ♿ – 🔬 25/50. AE ⓓ E VISA JCB CX
Lawrence : **Meals** 48 (lunch)/68 and a la carte 55/89 – ***Fujiya of Japan*** ✆ 201 11 55 *(closed Sunday and Monday)* **Meals** 48 (lunch)/85 and a la carte 56/92 – **72 rm** ⊐ 280/400 – ½ P 42.

Neues Schloss Ⓜ, Stockerstr. 17, ✉ 8022, ✆ 286 94 00, Telex 815560, Fax 286 94 45 – |‡| TV video ☎. AE ⓓ E VISA. ✻ rest EZ
Le Jardin *(Sunday and Bank Holidays dinner only for residents)* **Meals** *35* -48 (lunch)/89 and a la carte 57/97 – **58 rm** ⊐ 270/400.

Splügenschloss, Splügenstr. 2 / Genferstrasse, ✉ 8002, ✆ 289 99 99, Telex 815553, Fax 289 99 98 – |‡| ⇔ rm ▤ TV ☎ Ⓟ. AE ⓓ E VISA JCB CX
Meals *28* - 69 and a la carte 68/126 – **51 rm** ⊐ 290/530.

Inter-Continental Zürich Ⓜ, Badenerstr. 420, ✉ 8040, ✆ 404 44 44, Telex 822822, Fax 404 44 40, – |‡| ⇔ rm ▤ TV ☎ ♿ – 🔬 25/400. AE ⓓ E VISA JCB. ✻ rest AT
Meals *(closed Sunday lunch)* a la carte 45/93 – ⊐ 21 – **364 rm** 245/375.

Zum Storchen, Weinplatz 2, ✉ 8001, ✆ 211 55 10, Fax 211 64 51, ≤ River Limmat and City, , « Riverside setting » – |‡| ⇔ rm TV ☎ – 🔬 25. AE ⓓ E VISA JCB. ✻ rest EZ
Rôtisserie : **Meals** *38* and a la carte 64/101 – **73 rm** ⊐ 295/530.

St. Gotthard, Bahnhofstr. 87, ✉ 8023, ☎ 211 55 00, Fax 211 24 19, – AE ⓓ E VISA JCB EY b
La Bouillabaisse - Fish specialities - **Meals** *30* -38 (lunch) and a la carte 56/136 – ***Hummerbar :*** **Meals** a la carte 88/141 – ***Prime Grill :*** **Meals** a la carte 35/83 – ☕ 27 – **135 rm** 285/480.

Stoller Ⓜ, Badenerstr. 357, ✉ 8040, ☎ 492 65 00, Fax 492 65 01, – rm – 25. AE ⓓ E VISA JCB by Badenerstrasse CV
Meals 25/49 – **79 rm** ☕ 220/390 – ½ P 28.

Glärnischhof Ⓜ, Claridenstr. 30, ✉ 8022, ☎ 286 22 22, Fax 286 22 86 – rm rest – 30. AE ⓓ E VISA JCB EZ f
Vivace : **Meals** *23* and a la carte 41/78 – ***Le Poisson*** *(closed Saturday and Sunday)* **Meals** *25* -48/75 and a la carte 59/101 – **63 rm** ☕ 250/420.

Glockenhof, Sihlstr. 31, ✉ 8023, ☎ 211 56 50, Fax 211 56 60, – rm rest . AE ⓓ E VISA JCB EZ b
Meals *21* and a la carte 49/84 – **106 rm** ☕ 250/350.

Engematthof, Engimattstr. 14, ✉ 8002, ☎ 284 16 16, Fax 201 25 16, , – . AE ⓓ E VISA JCB CX d
Meals *19* and a la carte 40/99, children 15 – **79 rm** ☕ 170/300 – ½ P 35.

Kindli Ⓜ, Pfalzgasse 1, ✉ 8001, ☎ 211 59 17, Fax 211 65 28, , « English country house style installation » – . AE ⓓ E VISA EZ z
Opus *(closed Sunday)* **Meals** a la carte 46/99 – **21 rm** ☕ 180/290.

Montana, Konradstr. 39, ✉ 8005, ☎ 271 69 00, Telex 822640, Fax 272 30 70, – . AE ⓓ E VISA JCB EY f
Bistrot le Lyonnais *(closed Saturday lunch and Sunday)* **Meals** *20* -40 and a la carte 46/87 – **74 rm** ☕ 220/290 – ½ P 30.

Sukhothai, Erlachstr. 46, ✉ 8003, ☎ 462 66 22, Fax 462 66 54 – . AE E VISA.
closed Easter, 15 July - 11 August, Saturday except September - May and Sunday – **Meals** - Thai rest. - a la carte 75/135. CX h

Giangrossi (Rosa Tschudi), Rebgasse 8, ✉ 8004, ☎ 241 20 64, Fax 241 20 84, – AE ⓓ E VISA CV s
closed 25 December - 3 January, 15 to 28 February, Sunday and Monday – **Meals** (booking essential) *32* and a la carte 85/134
Spec. Eglifilets gebacken Sauce Mousseline, Kalbskopf in Balsamicovinaigrette, Sauerbraten mit Kartoffelstock.

Accademia Piccoli, Rotwandstr. 48, ✉ 8004, ☎ 241 62 43 – . AE E VISA.
closed Saturday except dinner September - April and Sunday – **Meals** - Italian rest. - a la carte 72/117. CV n

Intermezzo - Kongresshaus Zürich, Gotthardstr. 5, ✉ 8022, ☎ 206 36 36, Fax 206 36 59 – . AE ⓓ E VISA. EZ d
closed 12 July - 3 August, Saturday and Sunday – **Meals** 48 and a la carte 41/81.

Zunfthaus zur Waag, Münsterhof 8, ✉ 8001, ☎ 211 07 30, Fax 212 01 69, Linen weaver's and hatter's guildhall – AE ⓓ E VISA EZ x
Meals *24* and a la carte 61/108.

Sala of Tokyo, Limmatstr. 29, ✉ 8005, ☎ 271 52 90, Fax 271 78 07, – AE ⓓ E VISA JCB EY k
closed 20 July - 11 August, 22 December - 6 January, Sunday and Monday – **Meals** - Japanese rest. - 58/110 and a la carte 47/110.

da Bernasconi, Lavaterstr. 87, ✉ 8002, ☎ 201 16 13, Fax 201 16 49, – AE ⓓ E VISA CX b
Meals - Italian rest. - *30* and a la carte 49/94.

Il Giglio, Weberstr. 14, ✉ 8004, ☎ 242 85 97, Fax 291 01 83 – AE ⓓ E VISA
closed mid July - mid August, 1st to 8 January, Saturday lunch and Sunday – **Meals** - Italian rest. - *24* - 38 (lunch)/95 and a la carte 51/97. CX c

Brasserie Lipp, Uraniastr. 9, ✉ 8001, ☎ 211 11 55, Fax 212 17 26, – . AE ⓓ E VISA EY d
closed Sunday July - August – **Meals** *20* and a la carte 37/94.

L'Hexagone, Kuttelgasse 15, ✉ 8001, ☎ 211 94 11, Fax 212 70 38, – AE E VISA
closed 26 July - 10 August, 21 December - 12 January, Saturday and Sunday – **Meals** *(lunch only)* 23. EZ n

at Zürich-Oerlikon : *N : by Universitätstrasse DV : 5 km – ✉ 8050 Zürich-Oerlikon – 01 :*

Swissôtel Zürich Ⓜ, Am Marktplatz, ☎ 311 43 41, Telex 823251, Fax 312 44 68, ≤, , , – rm rm video – 25/500. AE ⓓ E VISA JCB
Szenario : **Meals** *19* and a la carte 36/111 – ☕ 23 – **336 rm** 260/380, 11 suites.

at Glattbrugg : *N : by Universitätstrasse* DV *: 8 km – ✉ 8152 Glattbrugg – ☎ 01 :*

Renaissance Ⓜ, Talackerstr. 1, ✆ 810 85 00, Telex 825003, Fax 810 87 55, ... – ... rm ... – 25/300. AE ① E VISA JCB. rest
Asian Place - Asian rest. - *(closed mid July - mid August, Saturday lunch and Sunday lunch)* **Meals** a la carte 49/137 – ***Brasserie La Noblesse*** *(closed mid July - mid August, Saturday and Sunday)* **Meals** 43 (lunch) and a la carte 47/96, children 12 – ☕ 28 – **196 rm** 250/344, 8 suites – ½ P 48.

Hilton, Hohenbühlstr. 10, ✆ 810 31 31, Fax 810 93 66, ..., ... – ... rm ... – 25/280. AE ① E VISA
Harvest Grill *(closed July - August, Saturday lunch and Sunday lunch)* **Meals** 45 (lunch)/79 and a la carte 56/113 – ***Taverne*** *(closed Saturday except dinner from June - September, and Sunday)* **Meals** *19* and a la carte 33/86 – ☕ 30 – **278 rm** 270/410, 8 suites.

Mövenpick Ⓜ, Walter Mittelholzerstr. 8, ✆ 808 88 88, Fax 808 88 77 – ... rm ... – 25/220. AE ① E VISA JCB
Appenzeller Stube *(closed mid July - mid August and Saturday lunch)* **Meals** a la carte 47/117 – ***Mövenpick Rest.*** *:* **Meals** *16.50* and a la carte 30/83 – ***Dim Sum*** - Chinese rest. - *(closed 3 weeks late July - early August, Saturday lunch and Sunday lunch)* **Meals** *25*-58 and a la carte 47/106 – ☕ 23 – **335 rm** 295/345.

Novotel Zürich Airport, Talackerstr. 21, ✆ 810 31 11, Fax 810 81 85, ... – ... rm ... – 25/150. AE ① E VISA
Meals *20* and a la carte 33/70, children 16 – ☕ 19 – **257 rm** 180/210.

Airport, Oberhauserstr. 30, ✆ 810 44 44, Fax 810 97 08 – ... AE ① E VISA JCB. rest
Edo Garden : **Meals** 60/78 and a la carte 49/83 – ***Fujiya of Japan :*** **Meals** 75/95 and a la carte 49/96 – **44 rm** ☕ 180/235 – ½ P 35.

Bruno's Rest., Europastr. 2, ✆ 811 03 01, Fax 811 03 21, ..., Modern - elegant decor – ... AE E VISA.
closed 28 July - 11 August, 23 December - 15 January, Sunday and Monday – **Meals** 59 (lunch)/98 and a la carte 59/122, children 20.

at Kloten : *N : by Universitätstrasse* DV *: 12 km – ✉ 8302 Kloten – ☎ 01 :*

Fly Away Ⓜ, Marktgasse 19, ✆ 813 66 13, Fax 813 51 25, ... – ... rm ... AE ① E VISA
Meals - Italian rest. - *17* and a la carte 41/72 – ☕ 14 – **42 rm** 150/200.

Top-Air, at the airport (Terminal A), ✆ 816 60 60, Fax 816 41 91, ≤ – ... AE ① E VISA
Meals *37*- 49 and a la carte 45/121, children 18.50.

at Küsnacht : *SE : by Bellerivestrasse* DX *: 8 km – ✉ 8700 Küsnacht – ☎ 01 :*

Ermitage am See Ⓜ with rm, Seestr. 80, ✆ 910 52 22, Fax 910 52 44, ≤ Zurich lake, ..., « Lakeside setting, terrace and garden », ... – ... AE ① E VISA. rest
Meals 59 (lunch)/144 and a la carte 77/135 – ☕ 17 – **20 rm** 170/340, 6 suites
Spec. Rougets à la tapenade, millefeuille d'artichauts et tomates confites, Pêche du lac meunière, beurre au citron, aux câpres et févettes, Agneau de Sisteron au pistou, ratatouille niçoise et socca croustillante.

Petermann's Kunststuben, Seestr. 160, ✆ 910 07 15, Fax 910 04 95, ... – ... AE ① E VISA
closed 17 August - 1st September, 9 to 24 February, Sunday and Monday – **Meals** 98/170 and a la carte 84/175
Spec. Huîtres en gelée de betterave et caviar (September - February), Ecrevisses et mangetout, vinaigrette de truffes noires (May - August), Selle de lapin au chutney de mangue et pommes vertes.

at Unterengstringen : *NW : by Sihlquai* CV *: 10 km – ✉ 8103 Unterengstringen – ☎ 01 :*

Witschi's, Zürcherstr. 55, ✆ 750 44 60, Fax 750 19 68, ..., « Modern - elegant installation » – ... AE ① E VISA JCB
closed 27 July - 11 August, 22 December - 6 January, Sunday and Monday – **Meals** 69 (lunch)/190 and a la carte 80/156
Spec. Homard de l'Atlantique mi-cuit au carpaccio de fenouil (spring - summer), Pigeon poêlé aux fèves et aux truffes noires (winter), Millefeuille de pommes sautées, sauce caramel et miel de lavande (autumn).

United Kingdom

LONDON – BIRMINGHAM – EDINBURGH
GLASGOW – LEEDS – LIVERPOOL
MANCHESTER

The town plans in the Great Britain Section of this Guide are based upon the Ordnance Survey of Great Britain with the permission of the Controller of Her Majesty's Stationery Office. Crown Copyright reserved.

PRACTICAL INFORMATION

LOCAL CURRENCY

Pound Sterling: *1 GBP = 1.70 US $ (Jan. 97).*

TOURIST INFORMATION

Tourist information offices exist in each city included in the Guide. The telephone number and address is given in each text under 🛈

FOREIGN EXCHANGE

Banks are open between 9.30am and 3pm on weekdays only and some open on Saturdays. Most large hotels have exchange facilities. Heathrow and Gatwick Airports have 24-hour banking facilities.

SHOPPING

In London: *Oxford St./Regent St. (department stores, exclusive shops) Bond St. (exclusive shops, antiques)*

Knightsbridge area (department stores, exclusive shops, boutiques)

For other towns see the index of street names: those printed in red are where the principal shops are found.

THEATRE BOOKINGS IN LONDON

Your hotel porter will be able to make your arrangements or direct you to Theatre Booking Agents.

In addition there is a kiosk in Leicester Square selling tickets for the same day's performances at half price plus a booking fee. It is open 12 noon-6.30pm.

CAR HIRE

The international car hire companies have branches in each major city. Your hotel porter should be able to give details and help you with your arrangements.

TIPPING

Many hotels and restaurants include a service charge but where this is not the case an amount equivalent to between 10 and 15 per cent of the bill is customary. Additionally doormen, baggage porters and cloakroom attendants are generally given a gratuity.

Taxi drivers are customarily tipped between 10 and 15 per cent of the amount shown on the meter in addition to the fare.

SPEED LIMITS

The maximum permitted speed on motorways and dual carriageways is 70 mph (113 km/h.) and 60 mph (97 km/h.) on other roads except where a lower speed limit is indicated.

SEAT BELTS

The wearing of seat belts in the United Kingdom is compulsory for drivers, front seat passengers and rear seat passengers where seat belts are fitted. It is illegal for front seat passengers to carry children on their lap.

ANIMALS

It is forbidden to bring domestic animals (dogs, cats...) into the United Kingdom.

LONDON

404 *folds* ㊷ *to* ㊹ *– pop. 6 679 699 –* ✪ *0171 or 0181 : see heading of each area.*

Major sights in London and the outskirts	p 2
Alphabetical list of areas included	p 2
Maps	pp 4 to 11 and 12 to 17
Central London	pp 4 to 11
Detailed maps of :	
Mayfair, Soho, St. James's, Marylebone	pp 12 and 13
South Kensington, Chelsea, Belgravia	pp 14 and 15
Victoria, Strand, Bayswater, Kensington	pp 16 and 17
Hotels and Restaurants	
Establishments with stars and Meals	p 18
Restaurants classified according to type	pp 19 to 21
Hotels and Restaurants listed by boroughs	pp 22 to 44

British Travel Centre, 12 Regent St. Piccadilly Circus, SW1Y 4 PQ, ✆ (0171) 971 0026. Victoria Station Forecourt, SW1, ✆ (0171) 730 3488.

Heathrow, ✆ (0181) 759 4321 – **Terminal** *: Airbus (A1) from Victoria, Airbus (A2) from Paddington – Underground (Piccadilly line) frequent service daily.*

Gatwick, ✆ (01293) 535353, and ✆ (0181) 763 2020, by A 23 and M 23 – **Terminal** *: Coach service from Victoria Coach Station (Flightline 777, hourly service) – Railink (Gatwick Express) from Victoria (24 h service).*

London City Airport, ✆ (0171) 474 5555.

Stansted, at Bishop's Stortford, ✆ (01279) 680500, Fax 66 20 66, NE : 34 m. off M 11 and A 120.

British Airways, Victoria Air Terminal *: 115 Buckingham Palace Rd., SW1, ✆ (0171) 834 9411, Fax 828 7142, p. 16.*

The maps in this section of the Guide are based upon the Ordnance Survey of Great Britain with the permission of the Controller of Her Majesty's Stationery Office. Crown Copyright reserved.

SIGHTS

HISTORIC BUILDINGS AND MONUMENTS

Palace of Westminster★★★ p. 10 LY – *Tower of London*★★★ p. 11 PVX – *Banqueting House*★★ p. 10 LX – *Buckingham Palace*★★ p. 16 BVX – *Kensington Palace*★★ p. 8 FX – *Lincoln's Inn*★★ p. 17 EV – *Lloyds Building*★★ p. 7 PV – *London Bridge*★ p. 11 PVX – *Royal Hospital Chelsea*★★ p. 15 FU – *St. James's Palace*★★ p. 13 EP – *Somerset House*★★ p. 17 EXY – *South Bank Arts Centre*★★ p. 10 MX – *Spencer House*★★ p. 13 DP – *The Temple*★★ p. 6 MV – *Tower Bridge*★★ p. 11 PX – *Albert Memorial*★ p. 14 CQ – *Apsley House*★ p. 12 BP – *George Inn*★, *Southwark* p. 11 PX – *Guildhall*★ p. 7 OU – *International Shakespeare Globe Centre*★ p. 11 OX – *Dr Johnson's House*★ p. 6 NUV **A** – *Leighton House*★ p. 8 EY – *The Monument*★ (✻★) p. 7 PV **G** – *Royal Albert Hall*★ p. 14 CQ – *Royal Opera Arcade*★ p. 13 FGN – *Staple Inn*★ p. 6 MU **Y** – *Theatre Royal*★ *(Haymarket)* p. 13 GM.

CHURCHES

The City Churches – *St. Paul's Cathedral*★★★ p. 7 NOV – *St. Bartholomew the Great*★★ p. 7 OU **K** – *St. Mary-at-Hill*★★ p. 7 PV **B** – *Temple Church*★★ p. 6 MV – *All Hallows-by-the-Tower (font cover*★★, *brasses*★*)* p. 7 PV **Y** – *St. Bride*★ *(steeple*★★*)* p. 7 NV **J** – *St. Giles Cripplegate*★ p. 7 OU **N** – *St. Helen Bishopsgate*★ *(monuments*★★*)* p. 7 PUV **R** – *St. James Garlickhythe (tower and spire*★, *sword rest*★*)* p. 7 OV **R** – *St. Margaret Lothbury* p. 7 PU **S** – *St. Margaret Pattens (woodwork*★*)* p. 7 PV **N** – *St. Mary Abchurch*★ p. 7 PV **X** – *St. Mary-le-Bow (tower and steeple*★★*)* p. 7 OV **G** – *St. Michael Paternoster Royal (tower and spire*★*)* p. 7 OV **D** – *St. Olave*★ p. 7 PV **S**.

Other Churches – *Westminster Abbey*★★★ p. 10 LY – *Southwark Cathedral*★★ p. 11 PX – *Queen's Chapel*★ p. 13 EP – *St. Clement Danes*★ p. 17 EX – *St. James's*★ p. 13 EM – *St. Margaret's*★ p. 10 LY **A** – *St. Martin in-the-Fields*★ p. 17 DY – *St. Paul's*★ *(Covent Garden)* p. 17 DX – *Westminster Roman Catholic Cathedral*★ p. 10 KY **B**.

STREETS – SQUARES – PARKS

The City★★★ p. 7 NV – *Regent's Park*★★★ *(Terraces*★★, *Zoo*★★*)* p. 5 HIT – *Belgrave Square*★★ p. 16 AVX – *Burlington Arcade*★★ p. 13 DM – *Covent Garden*★★ *(The Piazza*★★*)* p. 17 DX – *Hyde Park*★★ p. 9 GHVX – *The Mall*★★ p. 13 FP – *St. James's Park*★★ p. 10 KXY – *Trafalgar Square*★★ p. 17 DY – *Whitehall*★★ *(Horse Guards*★*)* p. 10 LX – *Barbican*★ p. 7 OU – *Bloomsbury*★ p. 6 LMU – *Bond Street*★ pp. 12-13 CK-DM – *Charing Cross*★ p. 17 DY – *Cheyne Walk*★ p. 9 GHZ – *Jermyn Street*★ p. 13 EN – *Leicester Square*★ p. 13 GM – *Neal's Yard*★ p. 17 DV – *Piccadilly Arcade*★ p. 13 DEN – *Piccadilly Circus*★ p. 13 FM – *Queen Anne's Gate*★ p. 10 KY – *Regent Street*★ p. 13 EM – *St. James's Square*★ p. 13 FN – *St. James's Street*★ p. 13 EN – *Shepherd Market*★ p. 12 CN – *Soho*★ p. 13 FKL – *Strand*★ p. 17 DY – *Victoria Embankment*★ p. 17 DEXY – *Waterloo Place*★ p. 13 FN.

MUSEUMS

British Museum★★★ p. 6 LU – *National Gallery*★★★ p. 13 GM – *Science Museum*★★★ p. 14 CR – *Tate Gallery*★★★ p. 10 LZ – *Victoria and Albert Museum*★★★ p. 15 DR – *Wallace Collection*★★★ p. 12 AH – *Courtauld Institute Galleries*★★ p. 6 KLU **M** – *Museum of London*★★ p. 7 OU **M** – *National Portrait Gallery*★★ p. 13 GM – *Natural History Museum*★★ p. 14 CS – *Sir John Soane's Museum*★★ p. 6 MU **M** – *Queen's Gallery*★★ p. 16 BV – *Imperial War Museum*★ p. 10 NY – *London Transport Museum*★ p. 17 DX – *Madame Tussaud's*★ p. 5 IU **M** – *Planetarium*★ p. 5 IU **M** – *Wellington Museum*★ *(Apsley House)* p. 12 BP.

Alphabetical list of areas included

Area	Page
Battersea	33
Bayswater and Maida Vale	38
Belgravia	34
Bermondsey	32
Bloomsbury	23
Chelsea	26
City of London	25
Dulwich	32
Euston	24
Finsbury	26
Fulham	25
Gatwick Airport	22
Hammersmith	25
Hampstead	24
Heathrow Airport	22
Holborn	24
Hyde Park and Knightsbridge	34
Islington	26
Kensington	28
Mayfair	35
North Kensington	30
Putney	33
Regent's Park	24
Regent's Park and Marylebone	38
Rotherhithe	32
St. James's	40
Soho	41
South Kensington	30
Southwark	32
Strand and Covent Garden	42
Swiss Cottage	24
Victoria	43
Waterloo	32
Wandsworth	33
Wimbledon	32

LONDON CENTRE

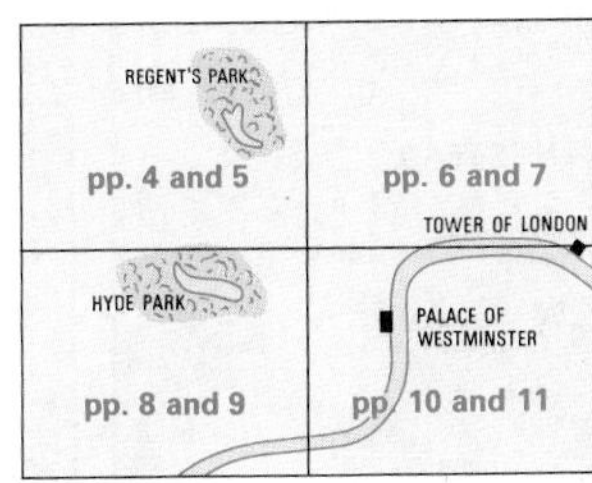

STREET INDEX TO LONDON CENTRE TOWN PLANS

Street	Grid	No.
Beauchamp Place	ER	
Brompton Road	DS	
Burlington Arcade	DM	
Camden Passage	NS	70
Carnaby Street	EK	
Jermyn Street	EN	
Kensington High Street	EY	
King's Road	DU	
Knigntsbridge	EQ	
Middlesex Street	PU	
New Bond Street	CK	
Old Bond Street	DM	
Oxford Street	BK	
Piccadilly	EM	
Portobello Road	EV	
Regent Street	EM	
Sloane Street	FR	
Abingdon Rd	EY	2
Addison Crescent	EY	3
Allsop Pl.	HU	4
Appold St.	PU	5
Atterbury St.	LZ	9
Bartholomew Rd	KS	16
Battersea Park Rd	JS	19
Belsize Crescent	ES	22
Belvedere Rd	MX	23
Bernard St.	LT	25
Bessborough St.	KZ	30
Bethnal Green Rd	PT	32
Bevis Marks	PU	34
Bishopsgate	PU	36
Blackfriars Bridge	NV	38
Bloomsbury St.	LU	39
Bowling Green Lane	NT	43
Bridgefoot	LZ	49
Broad Sanctuary	LY	52
Byward St.	PV	62
Calthorpe St.	MT	65
Camomile St.	PU	71
Carriage Drive North	IZ	75
Charlbert St.	HT	79
Charterhouse Square	OU	81
Charterhouse St.	NU	83
Churton St.	KZ	91
Constantine Rd	ES	106
Cornwall Crescent	EV	107
Cornwall Rd	MX	108
Corporation Row	NT	110
Cowcross St.	NU	113
Crawford Pl.	HU	116
Cromwell Crescent	EZ	119
Crucifix Lane	PX	125
Curtain Rd	PT	126
Dante Rd	NZ	129
Downshire Hill	ES	139
Dufferin St.	OT	141
Duke's Pl.	PV	145
Durham St.	MZ	150
Eardley Crescent	EZ	151
Eastcheap	PV	154
Ebury Bridge	IZ	156
Edwardes Square	EY	158
Elephant Rd	OZ	163
Fann St.	OU	166
Farringdon St.	NU	168
Fetter Lane	NU	169
Frognal Rise	ES	171
Garden Row	NY	173
Giltspur St.	OU	178
Gliddon Rd	EZ	182
Goodge St.	KU	184
Gracechurch St.	PV	187
Great Eastern St.	PT	192
Great George St.	LY	193
Great Smith St.	LY	196
Great Tower St.	PV	197
Greycoat Pl.	KY	200
Gunter Grove	FZ	202
Gunterstone Rd	EZ	203
Hampstead Grove	ES	208
Hampstead High St.	ES	209
Harleyford St.	MZ	211
Herbrand St.	LT	218
Hercules Rd	MY	219
Holland Park Gardens	EX	224
Holland Walk	EY	225
Hollybush Hill	ES	227
Horseguards Av.	LX	228
Hornton St.	FY	229
Howland St.	KU	232
Hunter St.	LT	233
Hyde Rd	PS	235
Keat's Grove	ES	236
Kenway Rd	FZ	245
King Edward St.	OU	247
King William St.	PV	250
Leadenhall St.	PV	260
Little Britain	OU	264
Lloyd Baker St.	MT	265
Lombard St.	PV	268
Long Lane CITY	OU	270
Lothbury	PU	273
Lower Marsh	MY	277
Lower Thames St.	PV	278
Mansell St.	PV	282
Miles St.	LZ	290
Moreland St.	OT	293
Myddelton St.	NT	296
Nassington St.	ES	297
Nevern Pl.	ES	298
Nevern Square	EZ	299
New Bridge St.	NV	301
New Change	OV	304
New End Square	ES	305
Newington Butts	OZ	306
Newington Causeway	OY	307
Northumberland Av.	LX	317
Old Bailey	NV	318
Old Broad St.	PU	319
Old Marylebone Rd	HU	324
Olympia Way	EY	326
Ornan Rd	ES	331
Paddington St.	IU	333
Park Crescent	IU	337
Parliament St.	LY	340
Parry St.	LZ	341
Pembroke Gardens	EY	342
Penn St.	PS	343
Penton Rise	MT	344
Penton St.	MT	345
Penywern Rd	FZ	347
Philbeach Gardens	EZ	348
Pilgrimage St.	PY	349
Poole St.	PS	350
Porchester Rd	FU	351
Poultry	OV	352
Princes St.	PV	357
Queen's Circus	IZ	361
Queen St.	OV	365
Randolph St.	KS	366
Rossmore Rd	HT	369
Royal Crescent	EX	371
St. Andrew St.	NU	372
St. Bride St.	NV	376
St. John's Wood High St.	GT	378
St. John's Wood Park	GS	379
St. Martin's-le-Grand	OU	380
Shoreditch High St.	PT	384
Sidmouth St.	LT	385
Snows Fields	PX	386
Southampton Row	LU	387
South Hill	ES	390
South Pl.	PU	391
Southwark Bridge	OV	395
Spencer St.	NT	398
Spital Square	PU	399
Storeys Gate	LY	402
Tabard St.	OY	408
Tavistock Square	LT	409
Templeton Pl.	EZ	410
Threadneedle St.	PV	417
Throgmorton St.	PU	418
Tower Hill	PV	425
Trebovir Rd	FZ	426
Upper Ground	NX	428
Upper Thames St.	OV	431
Upper Woburn Pl.	LT	432
Vincent St.	LZ	436
Warwick Av.	FU	441
Westbourne Park Villas	FU	449
Westbourne Terrace Rd	FU	452
West Smithfield	NU	454
Wharfdale Rd	LS	455
Whitechapel High St.	PU	456
Whitehall Court	LX	460
Whitehall Pl.	LX	462
Whitmore Rd	PS	464
Willoughby Rd	ES	470
Wormwood St.	PU	472

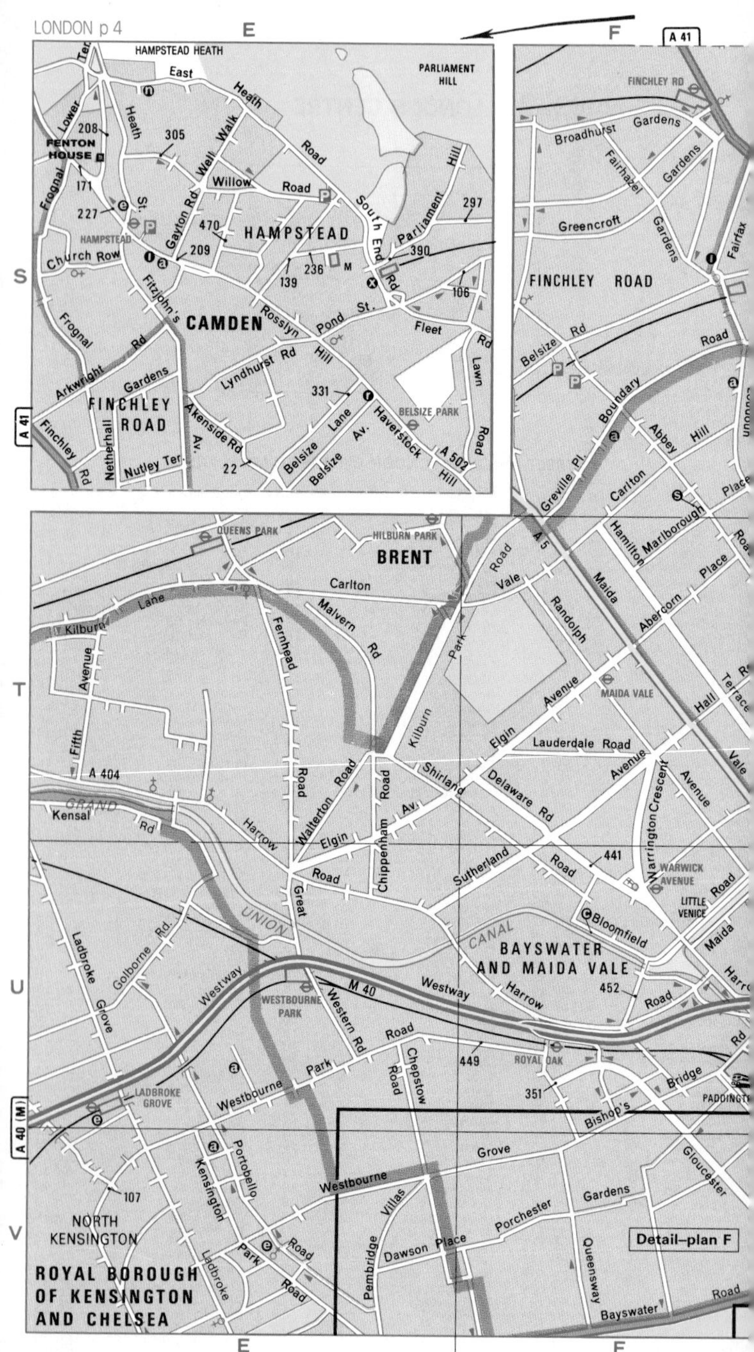

HAMPSTEAD HEATH
PARLIAMENT HILL
FENTON HOUSE
HAMPSTEAD
CAMDEN
FINCHLEY ROAD
BELSIZE PARK
BRENT
QUEENS PARK
KILBURN PARK
MAIDA VALE
WARWICK AVENUE
LITTLE VENICE
BAYSWATER AND MAIDA VALE
WESTBOURNE PARK
ROYAL OAK
LADBROKE GROVE
NORTH KENSINGTON
ROYAL BOROUGH OF KENSINGTON AND CHELSEA
GRAND UNION CANAL
Detail–plan F
A 41
A 40 (M)
M 40
A 404
A 502
A 5

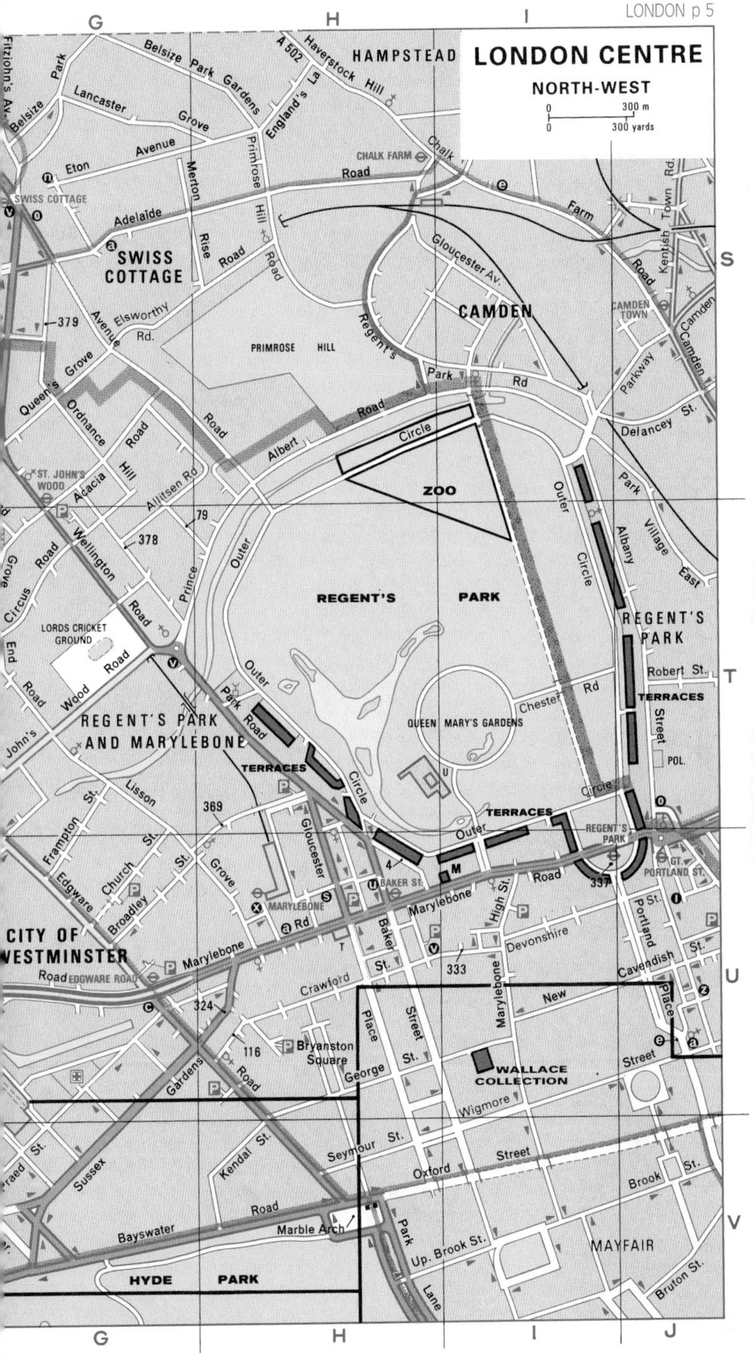
LONDON CENTRE
NORTH-WEST
HAMPSTEAD
SWISS COTTAGE
CAMDEN
PRIMROSE HILL
ZOO
REGENT'S PARK
QUEEN MARY'S GARDENS
LORDS CRICKET GROUND
REGENT'S PARK AND MARYLEBONE
TERRACES
CITY OF WESTMINSTER
WALLACE COLLECTION
HYDE PARK
MAYFAIR
ST. JOHN'S WOOD
CHALK FARM
CAMDEN TOWN
BAKER ST.
MARYLEBONE
EDGWARE ROAD
GT. PORTLAND ST.
Marble Arch

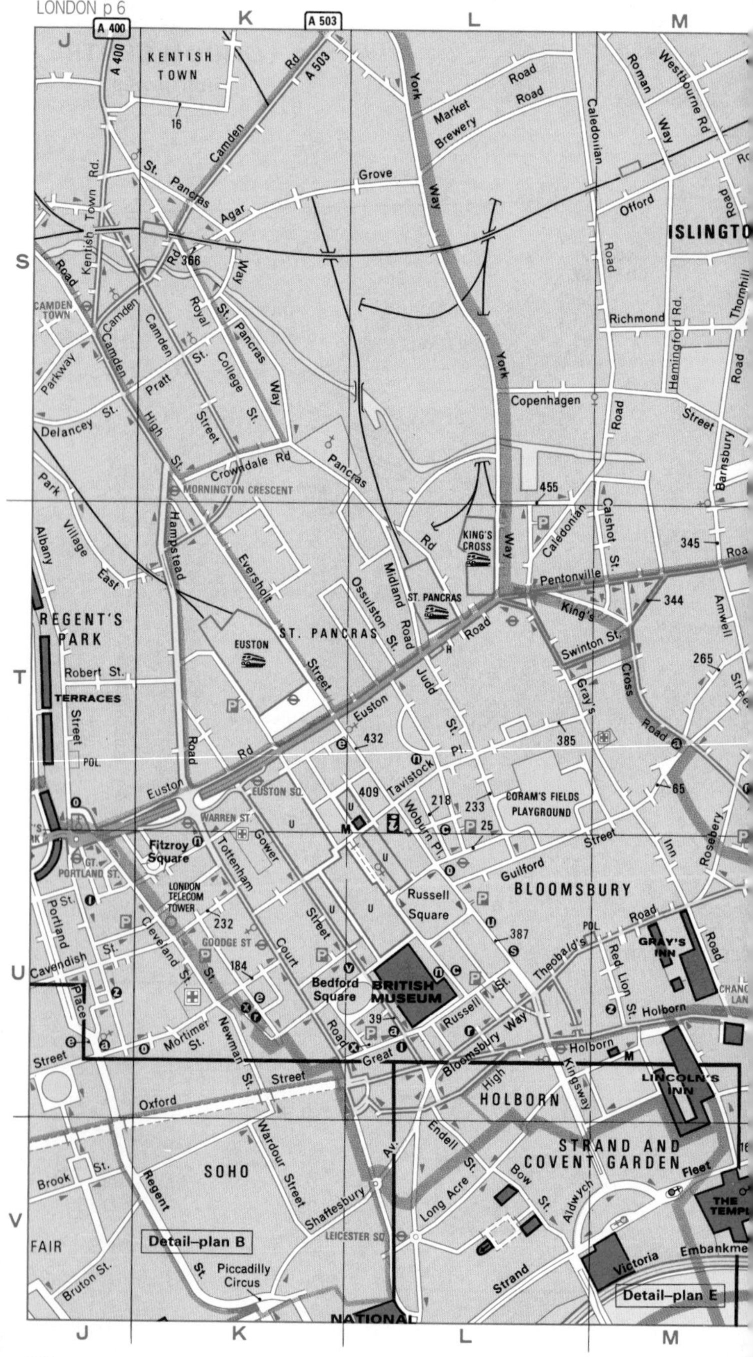

A 400
A 503
J
K
L
M
KENTISH TOWN
ISLINGTON
CAMDEN TOWN
REGENT'S PARK
TERRACES
MORNINGTON CRESCENT
EUSTON
ST. PANCRAS
KING'S CROSS
EUSTON SQ.
WARREN ST.
Fitzroy Square
LONDON TELECOM TOWER
GT. PORTLAND ST.
GOODGE ST
CORAM'S FIELDS PLAYGROUND
BLOOMSBURY
Russell Square
Bedford Square
BRITISH MUSEUM
GRAY'S INN
LINCOLN'S INN
HOLBORN
STRAND AND COVENT GARDEN
SOHO
LEICESTER SQ
Piccadilly Circus
NATIONAL
THE TEMPLE
Detail-plan B
Detail-plan E
FAIR
S
T
U
V

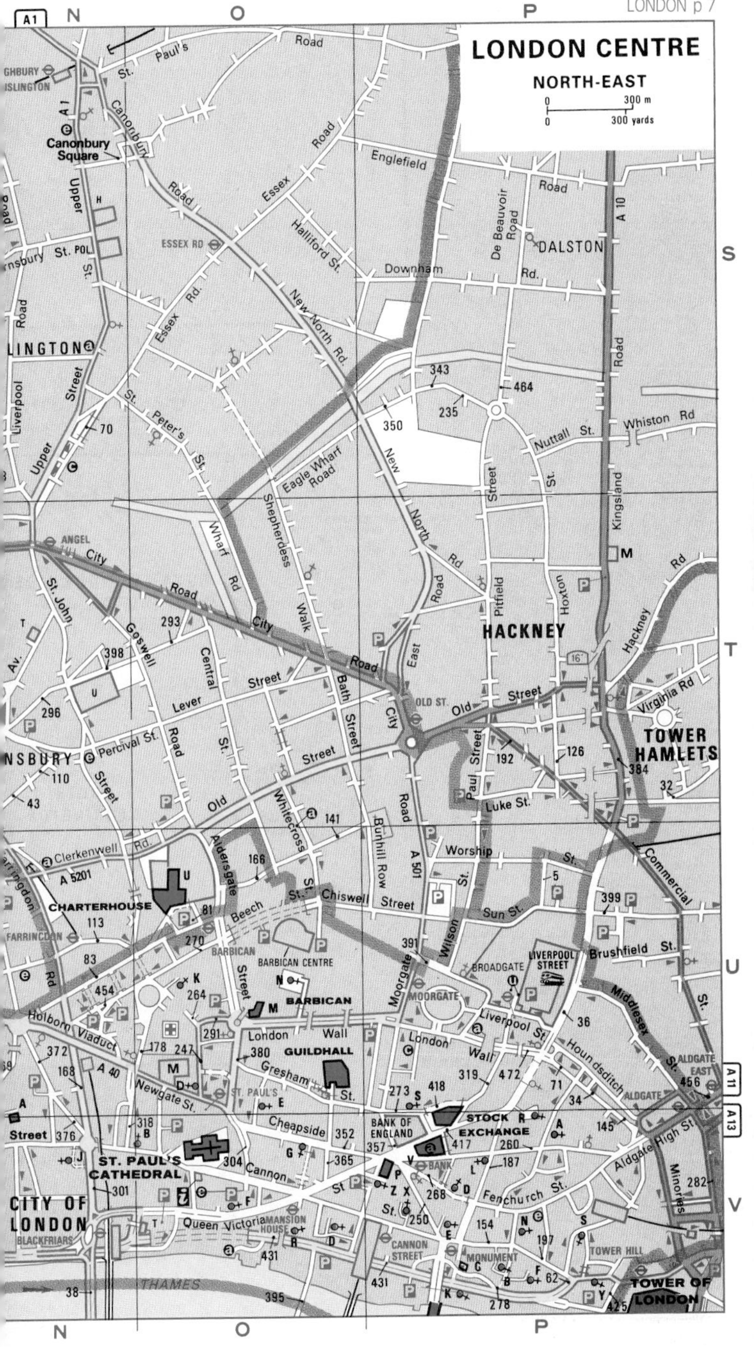
LONDON CENTRE
NORTH-EAST
0 300 m
0 300 yards
CANONBURY SQUARE
HACKNEY
TOWER HAMLETS
CITY OF LONDON
DALSTON
BARBICAN
BARBICAN CENTRE
GUILDHALL
ST. PAUL'S CATHEDRAL
BANK OF ENGLAND
STOCK EXCHANGE
CHARTERHOUSE
TOWER OF LONDON
THAMES

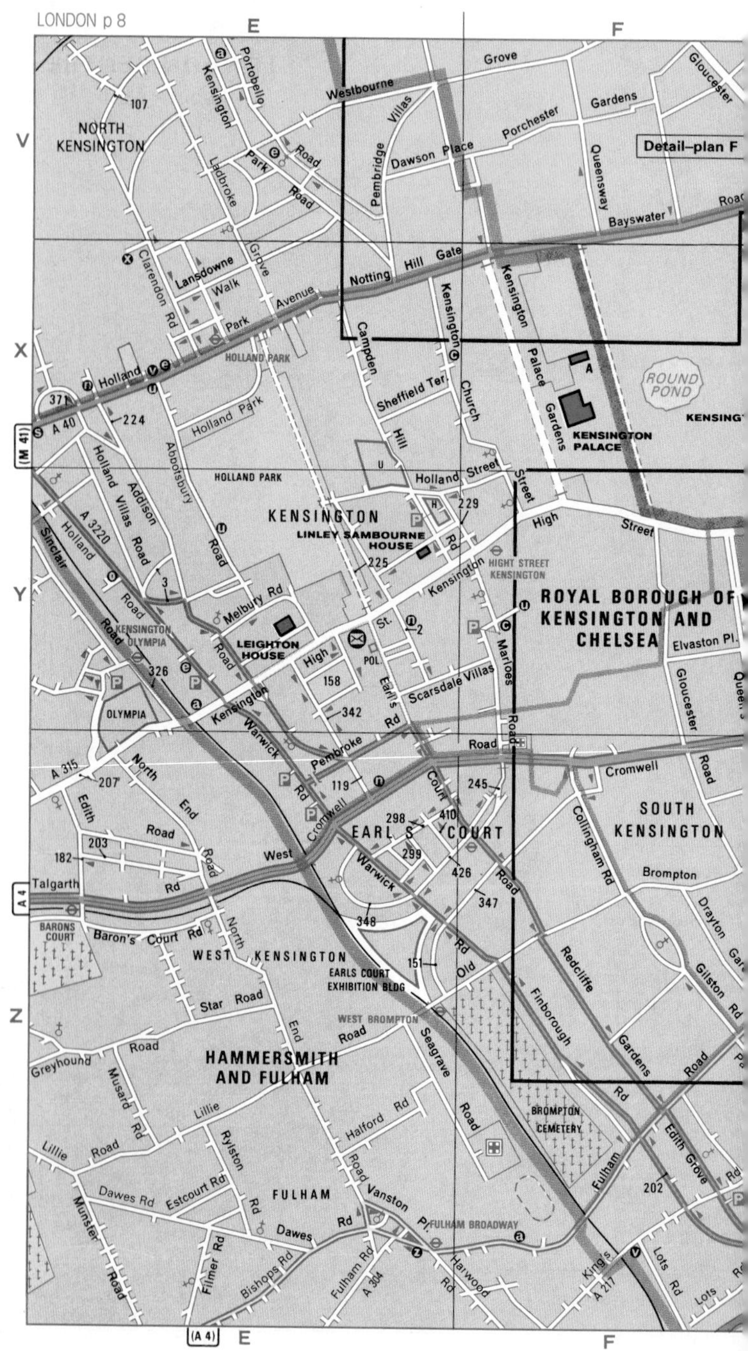

NORTH KENSINGTON
KENSINGTON
HOLLAND PARK
LINLEY SAMBOURNE HOUSE
LEIGHTON HOUSE
KENSINGTON PALACE
ROUND POND
ROYAL BOROUGH OF KENSINGTON AND CHELSEA
EARL'S COURT
SOUTH KENSINGTON
WEST KENSINGTON
EARLS COURT EXHIBITION BLDG
HAMMERSMITH AND FULHAM
FULHAM
BROMPTON CEMETERY
OLYMPIA
Detail–plan F

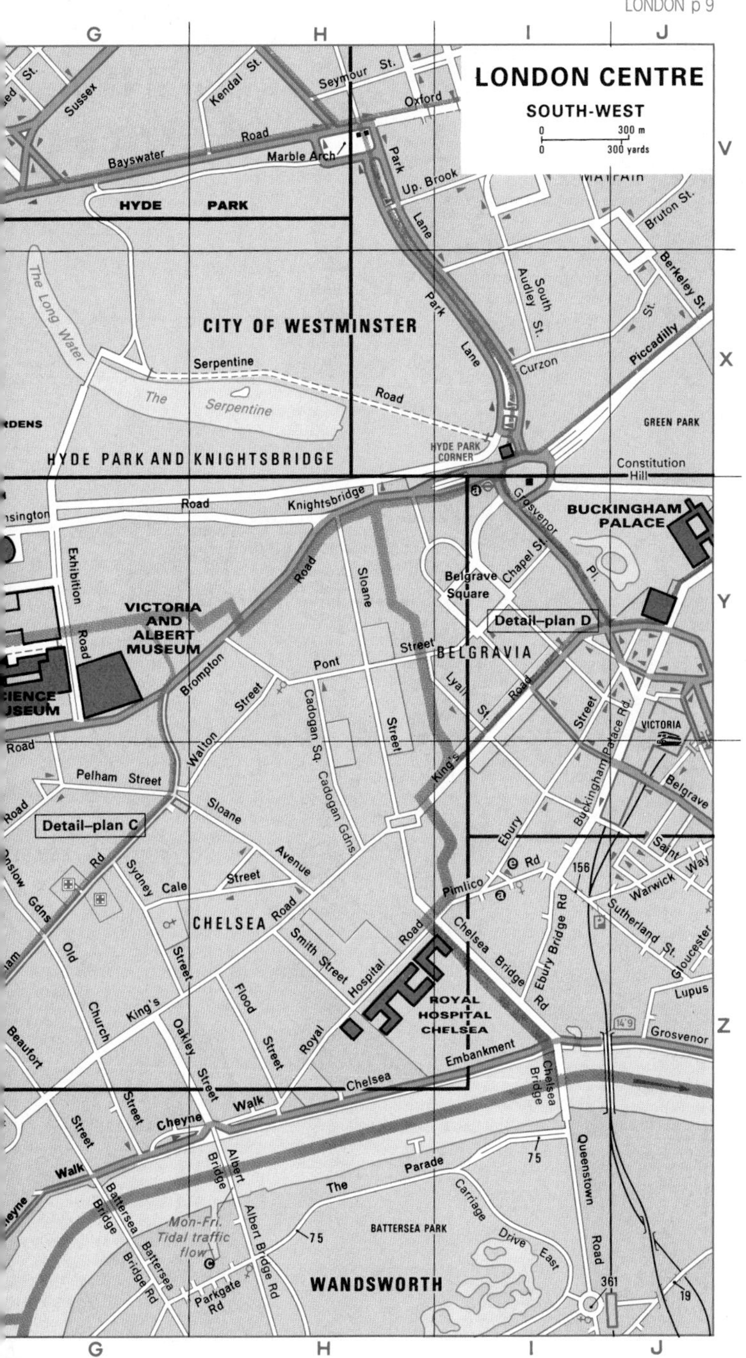
LONDON CENTRE
SOUTH-WEST
0 300 m
0 300 yards
G
H
I
J
V
X
Y
Z
HYDE PARK
CITY OF WESTMINSTER
The Long Water
The Serpentine
Serpentine
Road
HYDE PARK AND KNIGHTSBRIDGE
HYDE PARK CORNER
GREEN PARK
Constitution Hill
BUCKINGHAM PALACE
Bayswater Road
Marble Arch
Oxford
Seymour St.
Kendal St.
Sussex
Park Lane
Up. Brook
MAYFAIR
Bruton St.
Berkeley St.
South Audley St.
Curzon
Piccadilly
Knightsbridge
Road
Grosvenor Pl.
Chapel St.
Belgrave Square
Detail-plan D
BELGRAVIA
Exhibition Road
VICTORIA AND ALBERT MUSEUM
SCIENCE MUSEUM
Brompton Road
Sloane Street
Pont Street
Lyall St.
Cadogan Sq.
Cadogan Gdns
Walton Street
Pelham Street
Detail-plan C
Sloane Avenue
Cale Street
Sydney
Onslow Gdns
CHELSEA
King's Road
Eaton Rd
Ebury
Buckingham Palace Rd.
VICTORIA
Belgrave
Warwick Way
Saint
Sutherland St.
Gloucester
Lupus
Grosvenor
156
Pimlico Road
Chelsea Bridge Rd
Ebury Bridge Rd
Smith Street
Royal Hospital Road
ROYAL HOSPITAL CHELSEA
Flood Street
Oakley Street
Old Church Street
Beaufort Street
Chelsea Embankment
Chelsea Bridge
Cheyne Walk
Albert Bridge
Battersea Bridge
Battersea Bridge Rd
Albert Bridge Rd
Parkgate Rd
Mon-Fri. Tidal traffic flow
The Parade
Carriage Drive East
BATTERSEA PARK
WANDSWORTH
Queenstown Road
75
361
19
14'9

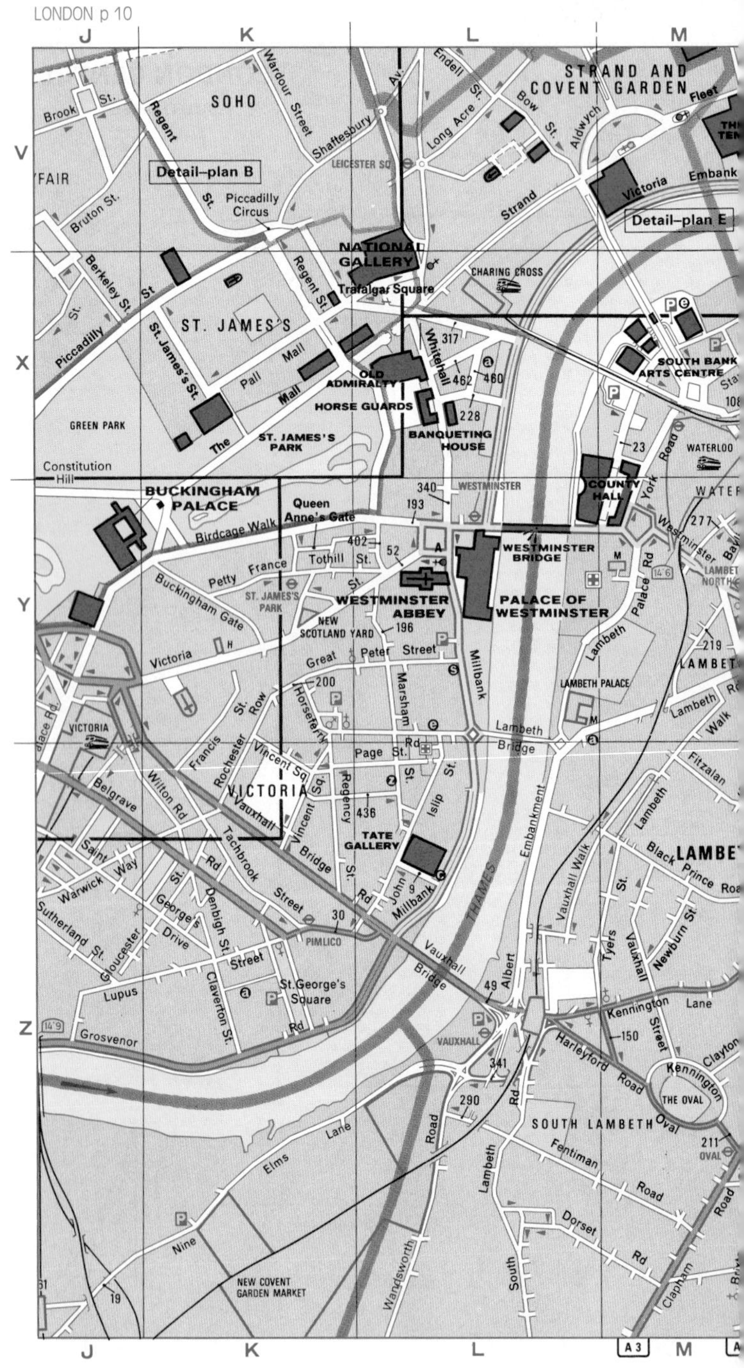
J
K
L
M
V
X
Y
Z
SOHO
STRAND AND COVENT GARDEN
Detail–plan B
Detail–plan E
Piccadilly Circus
LEICESTER SQ.
NATIONAL GALLERY
Trafalgar Square
CHARING CROSS
ST. JAMES'S
OLD ADMIRALTY
HORSE GUARDS
BANQUETING HOUSE
SOUTH BANK ARTS CENTRE
GREEN PARK
ST. JAMES'S PARK
Constitution Hill
BUCKINGHAM PALACE
Queen Anne's Gate
WESTMINSTER
WESTMINSTER BRIDGE
COUNTY HALL
WATERLOO
WESTMINSTER ABBEY
PALACE OF WESTMINSTER
NEW SCOTLAND YARD
LAMBETH PALACE
VICTORIA
TATE GALLERY
PIMLICO
St.George's Square
VAUXHALL
THAMES
SOUTH LAMBETH
THE OVAL
OVAL
NEW COVENT GARDEN MARKET
A 3

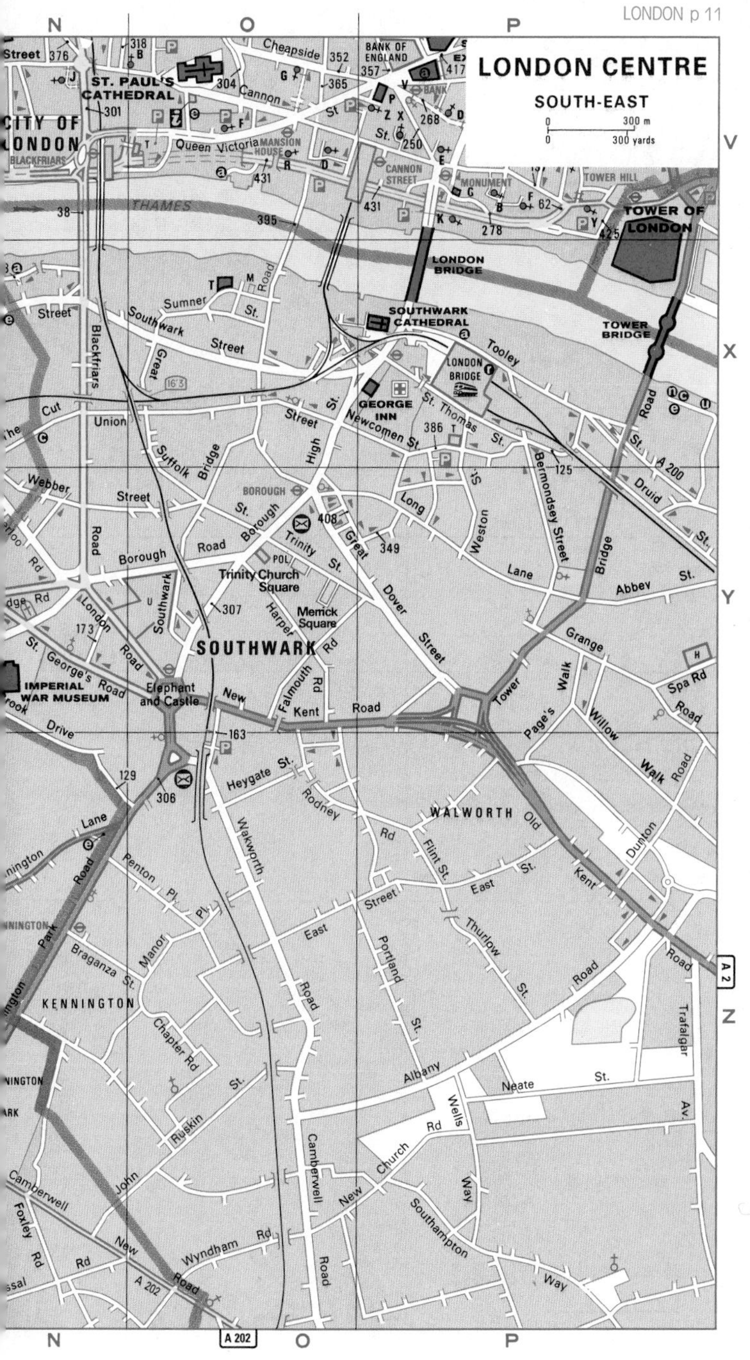

LONDON CENTRE
SOUTH-EAST
300 m
300 yards
ST. PAUL'S CATHEDRAL
CITY OF LONDON
BLACKFRIARS
Cheapside
Cannon St.
Queen Victoria
MANSION HOUSE
BANK OF ENGLAND
BANK
CANNON STREET
MONUMENT
TOWER HILL
THAMES
TOWER OF LONDON
LONDON BRIDGE
TOWER BRIDGE
SOUTHWARK CATHEDRAL
Southwark Street
Sumner St.
Tooley
LONDON BRIDGE
GEORGE INN
St. Thomas St.
Newcomen St.
Union Street
Blackfriars
Great
Suffolk
Bridge
BOROUGH
Borough High St.
Borough Road
Long Lane
Weston St.
Bermondsey Street
Druid St.
Webber Street
Trinity St.
Trinity Church Square
Merrick Square
Harper Rd
Great Dover Street
Abbey St.
Grange
SOUTHWARK
London Road
St. George's Road
IMPERIAL WAR MUSEUM
Elephant and Castle
New Kent Road
Falmouth Rd
Tower Bridge
Page's Walk
Willow Walk
Spa Rd
Heygate St.
Rodney Rd
WALWORTH
Old Kent Road
Dunton
Flint St.
East St.
East Street
Penton Pl.
Wakworth Road
Portland St.
Thurlow St.
Braganza St.
Manor Pl.
KENNINGTON
Kennington Park Road
Chapter Rd
Albany Road
Neate St.
Trafalgar Av.
Wells Way
Ruskin
John
New Church Rd
Camberwell Road
Southampton Way
Wyndham Rd
Camberwell New Road
Foxley Rd
A 202
A 200
A 2
N
O
P
V
X
Y
Z

B
A
B
C
H
J
K
L
M
N
P
WALLACE COLLECTION
REGENT'S PARK AND MARYLEBONE
Portman Square
Cavendish Sq.
MARBLE ARCH
Grosvenor Square
CITY OF WESTMINSTER
MAYFAIR
Berkeley Square
HYDE PARK
HYDE PARK AND KNIGHTSBRIDGE
Shepherd Market
GREEN PARK
APSLEY HOUSE WELLINGTON MUSEUM
Oxford Street
Park Lane
Piccadilly
Serpentine Road
0 200 m
0 200 yards

Street	Grid	No.
ʌrlington Street	DN	6
ʌvery Row	CL	12
ʒateman Street	FK	18
ʒerwick Street	FK	26
ʒinney Street	BL	35
ʻarlton Gardens	FP	74
)eanery Street	BN	132
)enman Street	FM	133
)enmark Street	GJ	134
)uke of York Street	EN	143
)uke Street ST. JAMES	EN	146
Dunraven Street	AL	149
Gerrard Street	GL	174
Gilbert Street	BL	175
Glasshouse Street	EM	179
Granville Place	AK	188
Great Castle Street	DJ	189
Greek Street	GK	198
Hamilton Place	BP	205
Hanover Square	CK	210
Hertford Street	BP	220
Leicester Square	GM	261
Manchester Square	AJ	281
Market Place	DJ	286
Marylebone Lane	BJ	287
North Audley Street	AK	314
Old Burlington Street	DM	322
Old Compton Street	GK	323
Panton Street	FM	336
Romilly Street	GL	368
Thayer Street	BJ	413
Tilney Street	BN	421
Warwick Street	EM	444

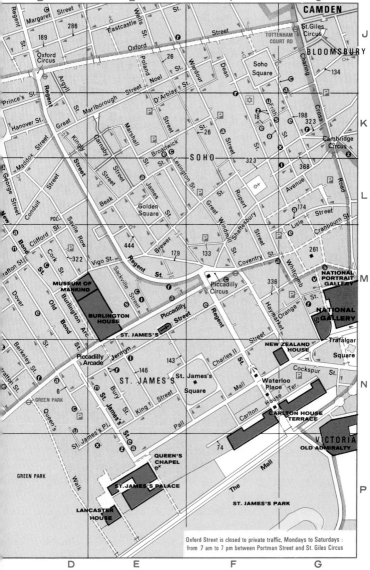

Oxford Street is closed to private traffic, Mondays to Saturdays : from 7 am to 7 pm between Portman Street and St. Giles Circus

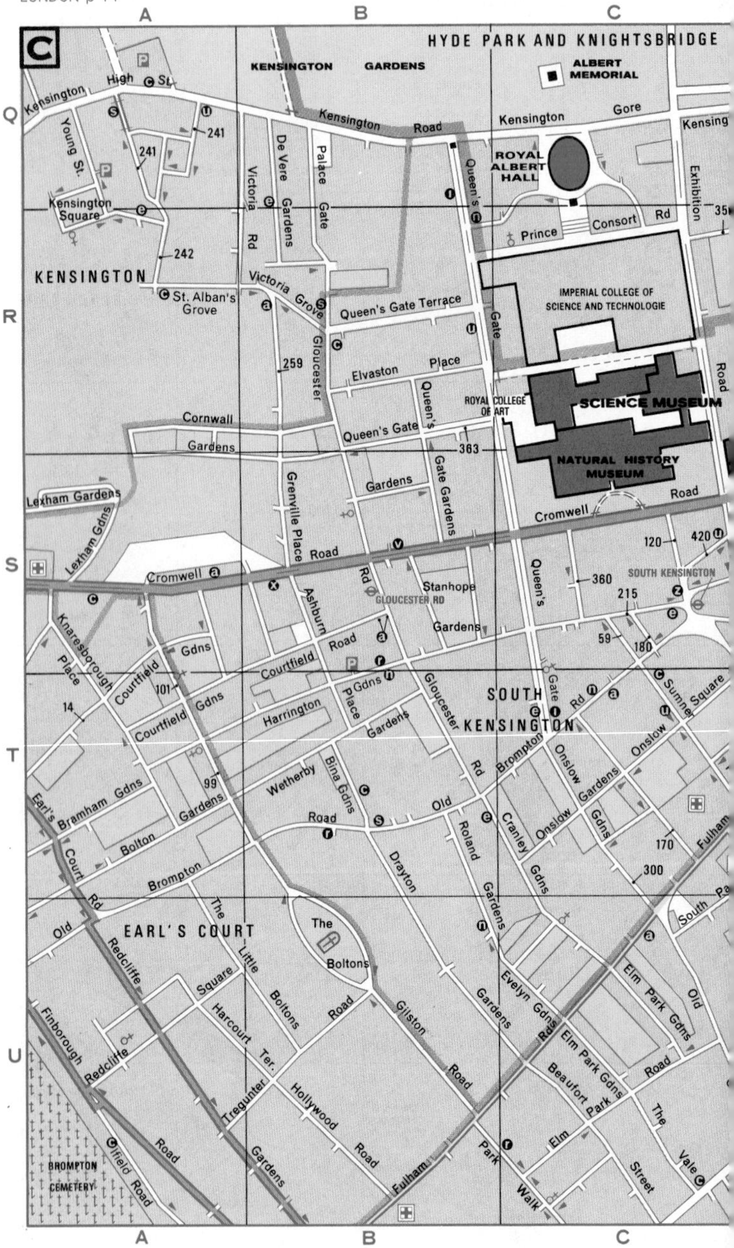

C

HYDE PARK AND KNIGHTSBRIDGE

Barkston Gardens . . . . AT 14
Bray Place . . . . ET 45
Bute Street . . . . CS 59
Collingham Gardens . . . . . AT 99
Collingham Road . . . . AT 101
Cromwell Place . . . . CS 120
Egerton Gardens . . . . DS 160
Egerton Terrace . . . . DR 161
Egerton Gardens Mews . . . . ER 162
Foulis Terrace . . . . CT 17
Glendower Place . . . . CS 18
Harriet Street . . . . FQ 21
Harrington Road . . . . CS 21
Holbein Mews . . . . FT 22

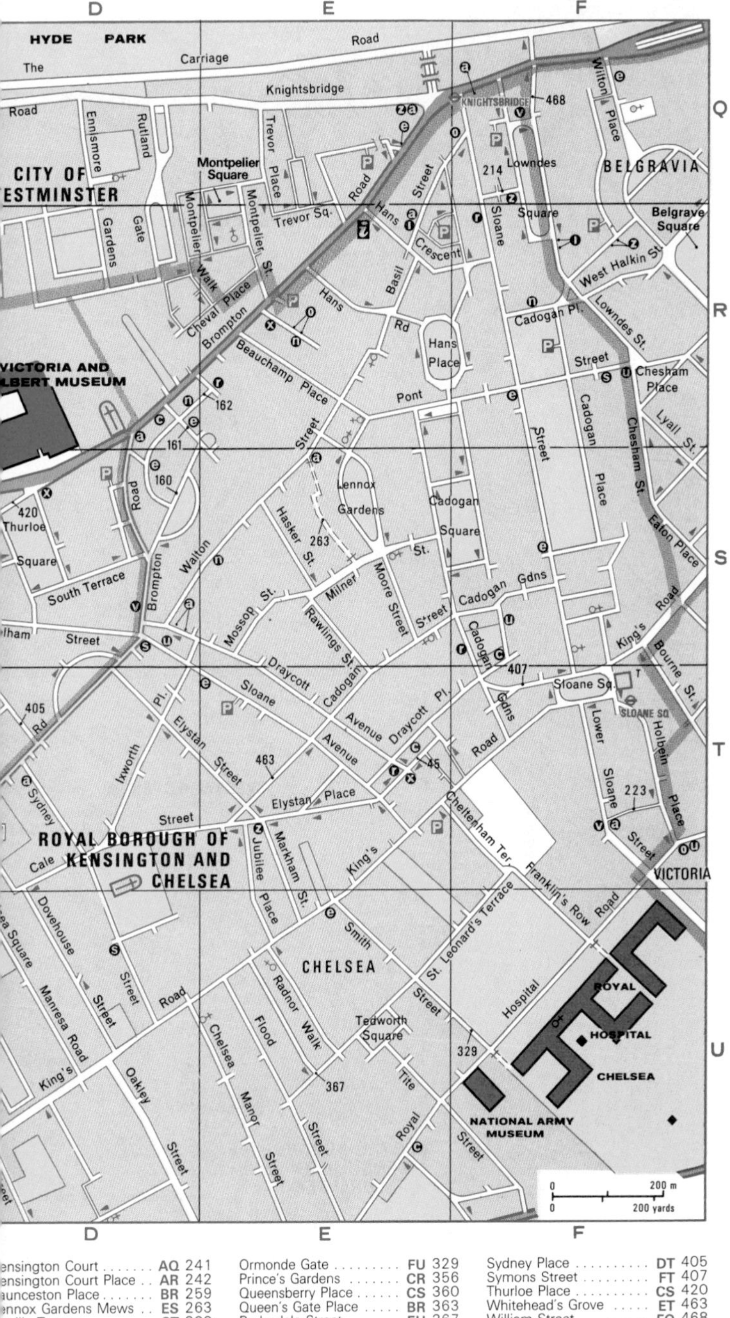

ensington Court . . . . AQ 241
ensington Court Place . . AR 242
aunceston Place . . . . BR 259
ennox Gardens Mews . . ES 263
eville Terrace . . . . CT 300

Ormonde Gate . . . . FU 329
Prince's Gardens . . . . CR 356
Queensberry Place . . . . . . CS 360
Queen's Gate Place . . . . . BR 363
Redesdale Street . . . . EU 367

Sydney Place . . . . DT 405
Symons Street . . . . FT 407
Thurloe Place . . . . CS 420
Whitehead's Grove . . . . . ET 463
William Street . . . . FQ 468

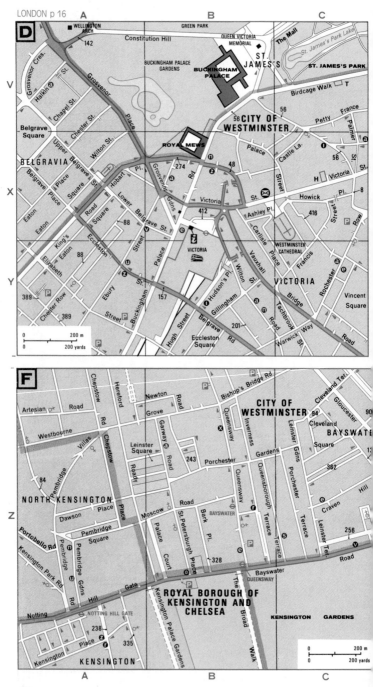

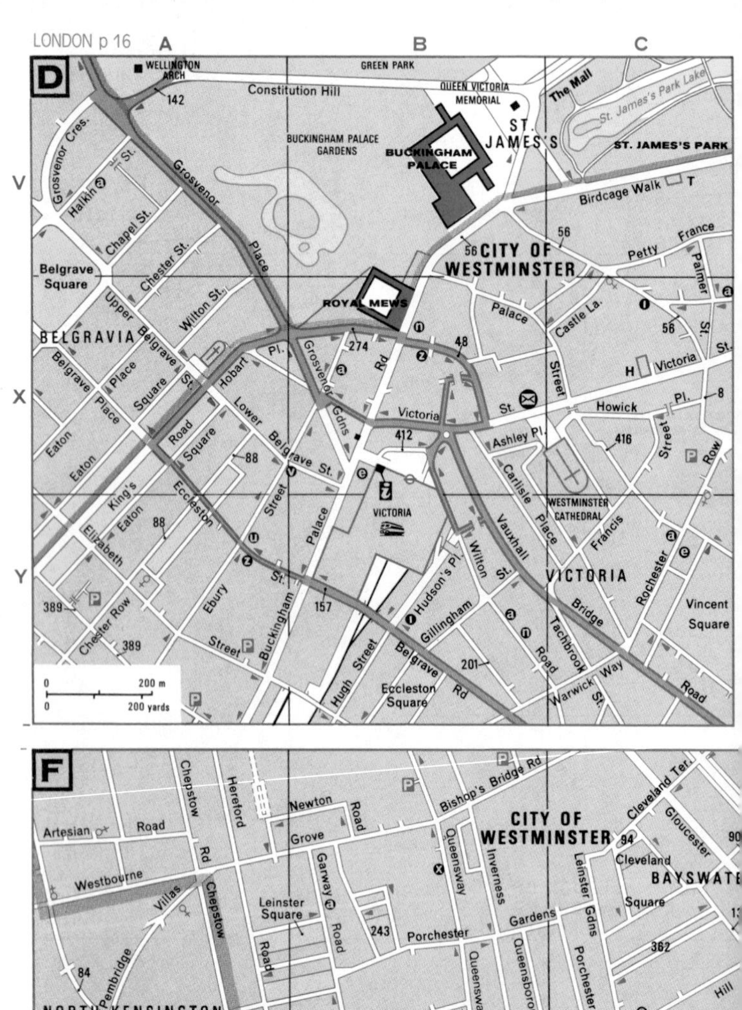
D
A
B
C
WELLINGTON ARCH
GREEN PARK
Constitution Hill
142
QUEEN VICTORIA MEMORIAL
The Mall
St. James's Park Lake
ST. JAMES'S
ST. JAMES'S PARK
BUCKINGHAM PALACE GARDENS
BUCKINGHAM PALACE
Birdcage Walk
Grosvenor Cres.
Halkin St.
Chapel St.
Grosvenor Place
Belgrave Square
Chester St.
CITY OF WESTMINSTER
Petty France
Palmer St.
ROYAL MEWS
Upper Belgrave St.
Wilton St.
Palace St.
Castle La.
BELGRAVIA
Hobart Pl.
Grosvenor Gdns
274
Rd
48
56
Belgrave Place
Square
Lower Belgrave St.
Victoria St.
Street
Victoria St.
H
Howick Pl.
8
Eaton Square
Road
Square
88
412
Ashley Pl.
416
Street
Row
Eaton Place
Eccleston
Street
VICTORIA
Carlisle Place
WESTMINSTER CATHEDRAL
King's Road
Eaton
88
Palace
Vauxhall
Francis
Elizabeth
Wilton
Rochester
St.
VICTORIA
Ebury
Buckingham
157
Hudson's Pl.
Bridge
Vincent Square
389
Chester Row
389
Street
Gillingham
Tachbrook
Hugh Street
Belgrave Rd
201
Road
Warwick Way
St.
Eccleston Square
Rd
0 200 m
0 200 yards
F
Chepstow Rd
Hereford
Newton Road
Bishop's Bridge Rd
Cleveland Ter.
Artesian Road
Grove
CITY OF WESTMINSTER
Gloucester
94
Westbourne
Queensway
Inverness
Leinster Gdns
Cleveland Square
BAYSWATER
Villas
Chepstow
Garway Road
Leinster Square
243
Porchester
Gardens
Road
362
Pembridge
Queensway
Queensborough Terrace
Porchester Terrace
Hill
84
NORTH KENSINGTON
Place
Place
Moscow Road
BAYSWATER
Craven
Dawson
St.Petersburgh Place
Bark Pl.
Leinster Ter.
256
Pembridge Square
Palace Court
Terrace
Portobello Rd
Pembridge
Pembridge Gdns
328
Road
Kensington Park Rd
Rd
Bayswater
QUEENSWAY
Gate
The Broad Walk
ROYAL BOROUGH OF KENSINGTON AND CHELSEA
Kensington Palace Gardens
Hill
Notting
NOTTING HILL GATE
KENSINGTON GARDENS
238
Place
335
Kensington
KENSINGTON
0 200 m
0 200 yards
A
B
C

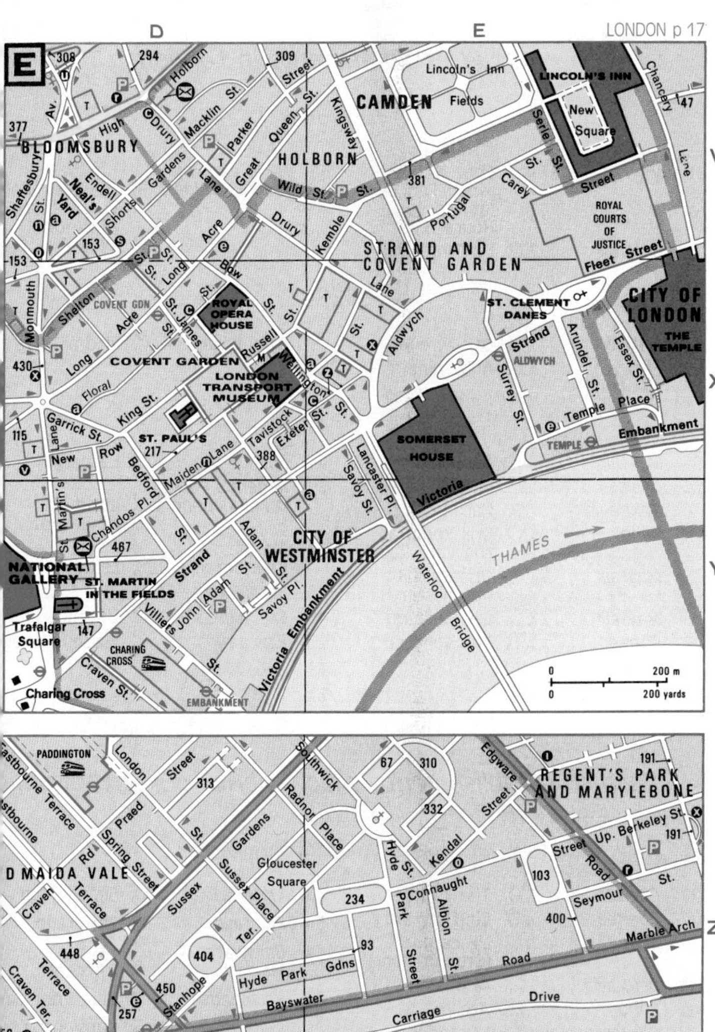

ɪtillery Row . . . . CVX 8	Eccleston Bridge . . . . BY 157	Orme Court . . . . BZ 328
ɜam's Building . . . . EV 47	Great Cumberland Place . EZ 191	Oxford Square . . . . EZ 332
essenden Place . . . . BX 48	Guildhouse Street . . . . . . BY 201	Palace Gardens Terrace . . AZ 335
ɪckingham Gate . . . . CV 56	Henrietta Street . . . . DX 217	Queen's Gardens . . . . CZ 362
ɪmbridge Square . . . . . . EZ 67	Hyde Park Square . . . . . EZ 234	St. Giles High Street . . . . DV 377
epstow Crescent . . . . . AZ 84	Kensington Church Street . AZ 238	Sardinia Street . . . . EV 381
ester Square . . . . AX 88	Kensington Gardens Square . . . . BZ 243	Southampton Street . . . . DX 388
ilworth Street . . . . CZ 90	Lancaster Gate . . . . CDZ 256	South Eaton Place . . . . . AY 389
ɜrendon Place . . . . EZ 93	Lancaster Terrace . . . . . . DZ 257	Stanhope Place . . . . EZ 400
ɜveland Gardens . . . . . . CZ 94	Lower Grosvenor Place . . BX 274	Sussex Square . . . . DZ 404
nnaught Square . . . . . . EZ 103	Museum Street . . . . DV 294	Terminus Place . . . . BX 412
ɜnbourn Street . . . . DX 115	New Oxford Street . . . . . DV 308	Thirleby Road . . . . CX 416
vonshire Terrace . . . . . CZ 136	Newton Street . . . . DV 309	Upper St. Martin's Lane . . DX 430
ɪke of Wellington Place . AV 142	Norfolk Crescent . . . . EZ 310	Westbourne Crescent . . . DZ 448
ɪncannon Street . . . . . . DY 147	Norfolk Square . . . . DZ 313	Westbourne Street . . . . . DZ 450
ɪlham Street . . . . DV 153		William IV Street . . . . DY 467

Starred establishments in London

36	*Mayfair*	XXXXX	Chez Nico at Ninety Park Lane (at Grosvenor House H.)
27	*Chelsea*	XXXX	La Tante Claire
35	*Hyde Park & Knightsbridge*	XXXX	The Restauran Marco Pierre White (at Hyde Park H.)

✿✿

36	*Mayfair*	XXXX	Le Gavroche
27	*Chelsea*	XXX	Aubergine
23	*Bloomsbury*	XX	Pied à Terre

✿

35	*Mayfair*		Connaught
26	*Chelsea*		Capital
34	*Belgravia*		Halkin
41	*Soho*	XXXX	Grill Room at the Café Royal
36	*Mayfair*	XXXX	Oriental (at Dorchester H.)
37	*Mayfair*	XXXX	Les Saveurs
27	*Chelsea*	XXX	The Canteen
41	*Soho*	XXX	L'Escargot
39	*Regent's Park & Marylebone*	XXX	Interlude de Chavot
30	*North Kensington*	XXX	Leith's
40	*St. James's*	XXX	The Square
40	*St. James's*	XX	L'Oranger
26	*Finsbury*	XX	Maison Novelli

Further establishments which merit your attention

Meals

27	*Chelsea*	XXX	The Canteen
27	*Chelsea*	XXX	Chutney Mary
41	*Soho*	XXX	L'Escargot (Ground Floor)
34	*Belgravia*	XX	Al Bustan
41	*Soho*	XX	Atelier
40	*St. James's*	XX	L'Oranger
39	*Regent's Park & Marylebone*	XX	Nico Central
43	*Victoria*	XX	Simply Nico
34	*Belgravia*	XX	Zafferano
34	*Bayswater & Maida Vale*	X	L'Accento
32	*Bermondsey*	X	Blue Print Caf
29	*Kensington*	X	Kensington Place
29	*Kensington*	X	Malabar

Restaurants classified according to type

eafood

7	*Mayfair*	XXX	Scotts
7	*Mayfair*	XX	Bentley's
1	*South Kensington*	XX	Downstairs at One Ninety
34	*Bayswater & Maida Vale*	XX	Jason's
28	*Chelsea*	XX	Poissonnerie de l'Avenue
42	*Strand & Covent Garden*	XX	Sheekey's

rgentinian

7	*Mayfair*	XX	Gaucho Grill

hinese

6	*Mayfair*	XXXX	✿ Oriental
5	*Hyde Park & Knightsbridge*	XXX	Mr Chow
5	*Hyde Park & Knightsbridge*	XXX	Pearl
7	*Mayfair*	XXX	Princess Garden
2	*Strand & Covent Garden*	XXX	WestZENders
7	*Mayfair*	XXX	Zen Central
8	*Chelsea*	XX	Good Earth
4	*Victoria*	XX	Hunan
5	*City of London*	XX	Imperial City
4	*Victoria*	XX	Joyful
44	*Victoria*	XX	Ken Lo's Memories of China
25	*Fulham*	XX	Mao Tai
34	*Bayswater & Maida Vale*	XX	Poons
28	*Chelsea*	XX	Red
34	*Bayswater & Maida Vale*	XX	Royal China
33	*Putney*	XX	Royal China
24	*Hampstead*	XX	ZeNW3
42	*Soho*	X	Fung Shing
42	*Soho*	X	Poons

nglish

7	*Mayfair*	XXXX	Grill Room (at Dorchester H.)
3	*Victoria*	XXX	Shepherd's
3	*Chelsea*	XX	English Garden
42	*Strand & Covent Garden*	XX	Rules
44	*Victoria*	XX	Tate Gallery
24	*Bloomsbury*	X	Alfred

rench

6	*Mayfair*	XXXXX	✿✿✿ Chez Nico at Ninety Park Lane
5	*Mayfair*	XXXXX	Oak Room
6	*Mayfair*	XXXX	✿✿ Gavroche (Le)
7	*Mayfair*	XXXX	✿ Saveurs (Les)
7	*Chelsea*	XXXX	✿✿✿ Tante Claire (La)
3	*Victoria*	XXX	Auberge de Provence
9	*Regent's Park & Marylebone*	XXX	✿ Interlude de Chavot
	Soho	XXX	Jardin des Gourmets (Au)
3	*Chelsea*	XX	Brasserie St. Quentin
	North Kensington	XX	Chez Moi
	Kensington	XX	Escargot Doré (L')
42	*Stand & Covent Garden*	XX	Estaminet (L')
26	*Finsbury*	XX	✿ Maison Novelli
24	*Bloomsbury*	XX	Mon Plaisir
28	*Chelsea*	XX	Poissonnerie de l'Avenue
29	*Kensington*	XX	Pomme d'Amour (La)
25	*City of London*	XX	Quai (Le)
32	*Southwark*	XX	Truffe Noire (La)
34	*Belgravia*	XX	Vong (French/Thai)
39	*Regent's Park & Marylebone*	X	Aventure (L')
49	*Strand & Covent Garden*	X	Magno's Brasserie
39	*Regent's Park & Marylebone*	X	Muscadet (Le)
44	*Victoria*	X	Poule au Pot (La)

Hungarian

41 *Soho* XX Gay Hussar

Indian & Pakistani

32 *Bermondsey* XXX Bengal Clipper
31 *South Kensington* XXX Bombay Brasserie
27 *Chelsea* XXX Chutney Mary (Anglo-Indian)
31 *South Kensington* XX Café Lazeez
31 *South Kensington* XX Delhi Brasserie
39 *Regent's Park & Marylebone* XX Gaylord
41 *Soho* XX Gopal's
31 *South Kensington* XX Khan's of Kensington
24 *Bloomsbury* XX Malabar Junction
31 *South Kensington* XX Memories of India
39 *Regent's Park & Marylebone* XX Porte des Indes (L
41 *Soho* XX Red Fort
31 *South Kensington* XX Star of India
33 *Wandsworth* XX Tabaq
37 *Mayfair* XX Tamarind
25 *Hammersmith* XX Tandoori Nigh
33 *Wandsworth* X Bombay Bicycl Club
29 *Kensington* X Malabar

Irish

37 *Mayfair* XX Mulligans

Italian

34 *Belgravia* ✿ Halkin
43 *Victoria* XXX Incontro (L')
43 *Victoria* XXX Santini
44 *Victoria* XX Amico (L')
42 *Strand & Covent Garden* XX Bertorelli's
39 *Regent's Park & Marylebone* XX Caldesi
28 *Chelsea* XX Caraffini
28 *Chelsea* XX Daphne's
33 *Putney* XX Del Buongustaio
29 *Kensington* XX Fenice (La)
28 *Chelsea* XX Finezza (La)
44 *Victoria* XX Gran Paradiso
32 *Dulwich* XX Luigi's
30 *North Kensington* XX Orsino
42 *Strand & Covent Garden* XX Orso
28 *Chelsea* XX Osteria Le Fat
25 *Hammersmith* XX River Café
34 *Bayswater & Maida Vale* XX San Vincenzo (
39 *Regent's Park & Marylebone* XX Sol e Stella
28 *Chelsea* XX Toto's
34 *Belgravia* XX Zafferano
34 *Bayswater & Maida Vale* X Accento (L')
32 *Bermondsey* X Cantina Del Ponte
29 *Kensington* X Cibo
44 *Victoria* X Olivo

Japanese

28 *Chelsea* XXX Benihana
40 *St. James's* XXX Suntory
25 *City of London* XXX Tatsuso
39 *Regent's Park & Marylebone* XX Asuka
24 *Hampstead* XX Benihana
37 *Mayfair* XX Benihana
41 *St. James's* XX Matsuri
25 *City of London* XX Miyama
37 *Mayfair* XX Shogun
39 *Regent's Park & Marylebone* X Nakamura

ebanese

4	*Belgravia*	XX	Bustan (Al)
9	*Regent's Park & Marylebone*	XX	Maroush III
29	*Kensington*	XX	Phoenicia

iddle Eastern

2	*Soho*	X	Bruno Soho

panish

7	*Chelsea*	XXX	Albero & Grana

hai

5	*Fulham*	XX	Blue Elephant
8	*Chelsea*	XX	Busabong Too
3	*Battersea*	XX	Chada
4	*Bayswater & Maida Vale*	XX	Nipa
25	*City of London*	XX	Sri Siam City
31	*South Kensington*	XX	Tui
34	*Belgravia*	XX	Vong (French/Thai)
41	*Soho*	X	Sri Siam

ietnamese

2	*Soho*	X	Saigon

Greater London *is divided, for administrative purposes, into 32 boroughs plus the City; thes sub-divide naturally into minor areas, usually grouped around former villages or quarters, whic often maintain a distinctive character.*

of Greater London: ***0171*** *or* ***0181*** *except special cases.*

LONDON AIRPORTS

Heathrow *Middx. W : 17 m. by A 4, M 4* **Underground** *Piccadilly line direct – 0181.*
759 4321 – **Terminal :** Airbus (A 1) from Victoria, Airbus (A 2) from Paddingto
Underground Station Concourse, Heathrow Airport, TW6 2JA (0171) 824 8844.

Radisson Edwardian, 140 Bath Rd, Hayes, UB3 5AW, 759 6311, Fax 759 4559, – rm – 500. AE VISA JCB
Henleys : **Meals** a la carte 32.00/44.00 **st.** 8.00 – ***Brasserie :*** **Meals** a la cart 16.00/27.00 **st.** 8.00 – 14.00 – **442 rm** 175.00 **st.**, 17 suites.

Holiday Inn Crowne Plaza Heathrow London, Stockley Rd, West Drayton, UE 9NA, (01895) 445555, Fax 445122, – rm – 20 AE VISA
Marlowe : **Meals** *(closed Sunday and 24 December-2 January)* (dinner only) 23.95 **st.** ar a la carte 6.50 – ***Cafe Galleria :*** **Meals** 15.95/17.50 **st.** and a la carte 6.50 – 11.5 – **372 rm** 115.00/160.00 **st.**, 2 suites – SB.

Sheraton Skyline, Bath Rd, Hayes, UB3 5BP, 759 2535, Fax 750 9150, rm – 500. AE VISA
Colony Room : **Meals** (dinner only) 32.00 **t.** and a la carte 7.50 – ***Cafe Jardin*** **Meals** 18.50 **t.** and a la carte 7.50 – 12.50 – **347 rm** 220.00/230.00 **st** 5 suites.

London Heathrow Hilton, Terminal 4, TW6 3AF, 759 7755, Fax 759 7579, – rm – 240. AE VISA JCB.
Brasserie : **Meals** 17.95/20.50 **t.** and a la carte 7.95 – ***Zen Oriental :*** **Meals** - Chines - 28.80 **st.** (dinner) and a la carte 16.00 – 12.95 – **390 rm** 176.00/201.00 **st.**, 5 suit – SB.

Excelsior Heathrow (Forte), Bath Rd, West Drayton, UB7 0DU, 759 661 Fax 759 3421, – rm – 700. AE VISA JC
Meals (carving rest.) 17.50 **st.** and a la carte 7.75 – ***Wheeler's :*** **Meals** - Seafood - (close lunch Saturday and Sunday and Bank Holidays) a la carte 17.85/31.95 **st.** 7.95 – 11.4 – **822 rm** 110.00/120.00 **st.**, 10 suites – SB.

Ramada H. Heathrow, Bath Rd, TW6 2AQ, 897 6363, Fax 897 1113, rm – 550. AE VISA JCB.
Meals 16.50/19.50 **st.** and a la carte 6.00 – 10.50 – **633 rm** 125.00 **st.**, 7 suite

Forte Crest, Sipson Rd, West Drayton, UB7 0JU, 759 2323, Fax 897 8659 – r – 100. AE VISA JCB.
Meals (carving rest.) 17.50 **st.** 10.00 – ***Sampans :*** **Meals** - Chinese - (dinner onl 17.95 **st.** and a la carte 12.00 – ***Tutto :*** **Meals** - Italian - 13.50/17.50 **st.** and a la carte 10.00 – 11.95 – **567 rm** 120.00/140.00 **st.**, 2 suites – SB.

Sheraton Heathrow, Colnbrook bypass, West Drayton, UB7 0HJ, 759 242 Fax 759 2091 – rm – 50. AE VISA JCB.
Meals 18.50 **t.** and a la carte 9.50 – 13.50 – **426 rm** 170.00/180.00 **st.**, 4 suite

Forte Posthouse Heathrow, Bath Rd, Hayes, UB3 5AJ, 759 2552, Fax 564 92 – rm – 45. AE VISA JCB.
Meals 17.95 **st.** (dinner) and a la carte approx 18.05 **st.** – 10.95 – **186 rm** 99.00 s

Gatwick *W. Sussex S : 28 m. by A 23 and M 23* - **Train** *from Victoria : Gatwick Express* 404 T
– *Crawley – 01293.*
535353.
International Arrivals Concourse, South Terminal, RH6 0NP 560108.

London Gatwick Airport Hilton, South Terminal, RH6 0LL, 518080, Fax 52898 – rm – 500. AE VISA.
Meals 22.75 **t.** and a la carte 7.50 – 12.95 – **547 rm** 178.00 **t.**, 3 suites.

Ramada H. Gatwick, Povey Cross Rd, RH6 0BE, 820169, Fax 820259, squash – rm – 180. AE VISA.
Meals *(closed lunch Saturday and Sunday)* 14.50/16.50 **t.** and a la carte 5.50 – 10. – **250 rm** 80.00 **st.**, 5 suites.

Forte Crest, Gatwick Airport (North Terminal), RH6 0PH, ☎ 567070, Fax 567739, ≘s, – |☰| ⇔ rm ☰ TV ☎ ♿ P – 🏛 350. MC AE ① VISA JCB
New Fortune : **Meals** - Chinese - 25.00 **t.** and a la carte 8.00 – ***Brasserie :*** **Meals** *(closed Saturday lunch)* 13.95/18.95 **st.** and dinner a la carte 8.50 – ☐ 10.50 – **450 rm** 135.00 **st.**, 6 suites – SB .

Forte Posthouse Gatwick, Povey Cross Rd, RH6 0BA, ☎ 771621, Fax 771054 – |☰| ⇔ rm ☰ rest TV ☎ P – 🏛 120. MC AE ① VISA
Meals a la carte 16.85/21.25 **st.** 7.95 – ☐ 9.95 – **210 rm** 79.00 **st.** – SB .

CAMDEN *Except where otherwise stated see pp 4-7.*

Bloomsbury – ✉ *NW1/W1/WC1* – ☎ *0171.*
34-37 Woburn Pl. WC1H 0JR ☎ 580 4599.

Holiday Inn Kings Cross, 1 Kings Cross Rd, WC1X 9HX, ☎ 833 3900, Fax 917 6163, ≘s, squash – |☰| ⇔ rm ☰ TV ☎ ♿ – 🏛 220. MC AE ① VISA JCB.
Meals *(closed lunch Saturday and Sunday)* 17.95 **st.** and a la carte 6.00 – ☐ 9.75 – **402 rm** 140.00/150.00 **st.**, 3 suites. MT a

Marlborough (Radisson Edwardian), 9-14 Bloomsbury St., WC1B 3QD, ☎ 636 5601, Fax 636 0532 – |☰| ☰ rest TV ☎ ♿ – 🏛 200. MC AE ① VISA JCB LU i
Meals a la carte 17.00/23.00 **st.** 8.00 – ☐ 14.00 – **167 rm** 150.00/195.00 **st.**, 2 suites.

Russell (Forte), Russell Sq., WC1B 5BE, ☎ 837 6470, Fax 837 2857 – |☰| ⇔ rm ☰ rest TV ☎ – 🏛 400. MC AE ① VISA JCB. LU o
Meals a la carte 13.50/18.50 **st.** – ☐ 10.50 – **327 rm** 140.00/150.00 **st.**, 2 suites – SB .

Grafton (Radisson Edwardian), 130 Tottenham Court Rd, W1P 9HP, ☎ 388 4131, Fax 387 7394 – |☰| ⇔ rm ☰ rest TV ☎ – 🏛 100. MC AE ① VISA JCB KU n
Meals a la carte 20.00/31.00 **st.** 8.00 – ☐ 11.00 – **319 rm** 125.00/160.00 **st.**, 5 suites.

Mountbatten (Radisson Edwardian), 20 Monmouth St., WC2H 9HD, ☎ 836 4300, Fax 240 3540 – |☰| ⇔ rm ☰ rest TV ☎ – 🏛 75. MC AE ① VISA JCB p. 17 DV o
Meals a la carte 18.00/29.00 **st.** 8.00 – ☐ 14.00 – **120 rm** 175.00/225.00 **st.**, 7 suites.

Montague, 15 Montague St., WC1B 5BJ, ☎ 637 1001, Fax 637 2516 – |☰| ⇔ rm ☰ rest TV ☎ ♿ – 🏛 120. MC AE ① VISA JCB. LU c
Meals *(closed Sunday lunch)* 12.50 **t.** and a la carte 11.20 – ☐ 10.00 – **107 rm** 110.00/145.00 **s.**, 2 suites.

Covent Garden H., 10 Monmouth St., WC2H 9HB, ☎ 806 1000, Fax 806 1100, – |☰| ☰ TV ☎. MC AE VISA. p. 17 DV n
Meals a la carte approx. 16.50 **t.** – ☐ 13.00 – **48 rm** 150.00/195.00 **s.**, 2 suites.

Kingsley (Thistle), Bloomsbury Way, WC1A 2SD, ☎ 242 5881, Fax 831 0225 – |☰| ⇔ rm TV ☎ – 🏛 90. MC AE ① VISA JCB. LU r
Meals *(closed lunch Saturday, Sunday and Bank Holidays)* 15.25 **t.** and a la carte 5.10 – ☐ 9.95 – **130 rm** 115.00/210.00 **st.**

Forte Posthouse Bloomsbury, Coram St., WC1N 1HT, ☎ 837 1200, Fax 837 5374 – |☰| ⇔ rm ☰ rest TV ☎ ♿ P – 🏛 750. MC AE ① VISA JCB. LT c
Meals 16.95 **st.** (dinner) and a la carte 12.00/20.00 **st.** 6.00 – ☐ 10.95 – **282 rm** 130.00/140.00 **st.**, 2 suites – SB .

Kenilworth (Radisson Edwardian), 97 Great Russell St., WC1B 3LB, ☎ 637 3477, Fax 631 3133 – |☰| ⇔ rm ☰ rest TV ☎ – 🏛 65. MC AE ① VISA JCB LU a
Meals a la carte 16.00/23.00 **st.** 8.00 – ☐ 11.00 – **187 rm** 130.00/170.00 **st.**

Blooms without rest., 7 Montague St., WC1B 5BP, ☎ 323 1717, Fax 636 6498 – |☰| TV ☎. MC AE ① VISA JCB. LU n
27 rm ☐ 110.00/180.00 **st.**

Bonnington, 92 Southampton Row, WC1B 4BH, ☎ 242 2828, Fax 831 9170 – |☰| ⇔ rm ☰ rest TV ☎ ♿ – 🏛 250. MC AE ① VISA JCB LU s
Meals *(closed lunch Saturday and Sunday)* 10.50/18.50 **st.** and a la carte – **215 rm** ☐ 93.00/118.00 **st.**

Bloomsbury Park (Mount Charlotte), 126 Southampton Row, WC1B 5AD, ☎ 430 0434, Fax 242 0665 – |☰| ⇔ rm TV ☎ – 🏛 25. MC AE ① VISA JCB. LU u
Meals *(closed Sunday)* (dinner only) 13.95 **t.** and a la carte 4.50 – ☐ 8.95 – **95 rm** 89.00/140.00 **st.**

Pied à Terre, 34 Charlotte St., W1P 1HJ, ☎ 636 1178, Fax 916 1171 – ☰. MC AE ① VISA JCB KU e
closed Saturday lunch, Sunday, last 2 weeks August, 2 weeks Christmas and Bank Holidays – **Meals** 22.00/33.00-46.00 **t.** 8.00
Spec. Langoustine salad, truffled potato and langoustine vinaigrette, Ballotine of duck confit and foie gras, Charlotte of rhubarb with caramelised pears and rhubarb sorbet.

XX **Neal Street,** 26 Neal St., WC2H 9PS, ✆ 836 8368, Fax 497 1361 – MC AE ① VISA p 17 DV
closed Sunday, 1 week Christmas and Bank Holidays – **Meals** a la carte 25.00/37.00 **t.**

XX **Malabar Junction,** 107 Great Russell St., WC1B 3NA, ✆ 580 5230 – ▤. MC AE VISA LU
closed 25 December – **Meals** - South Indian - 7.95/15.00 **st.** and a la carte 🍷 6.00.

XX **Mon Plaisir,** 21 Monmouth St., WC2H 9DD, ✆ 836 7243, Fax 379 0121 – MC AE ① VISA JCB p 17 DV
closed Saturday lunch, Sunday, 1 week Christmas-New Year, Easter and Bank Holidays – **Meals** - French - 13.95/19.95 **st.** and a la carte 🍷 5.95.

XX **Bleeding Heart,** Bleeding Heart Yard, EC1N 8SJ, off Greville St., Hatton Garden ✆ 242 2056, Fax 831 1402, 🏠 – MC AE ① VISA JCB NU
closed Saturday, Sunday and 24 December-6 January – **Meals** a la carte 17.90/24.15 **t.** 🍷 4.25.

X **Chiaroscuro,** 24 Coptic St., WC1A 1NT, ✆ 636 2731 – MC AE ① VISA p. 17 DV
closed Saturday lunch and Sunday – **Meals** a la carte 15.50/27.50 **t.** 🍷 8.00.

X **Alfred,** 245 Shaftesbury Av., WC2H 8EH, ✆ 240 2566, Fax 497 0672, 🏠 – ▤. MC AE ① VISA JCB p 17 DV
closed Saturday lunch, Sunday and Christmas-New Year – **Meals** - English - 15.90 **t.** and a la carte 🍷 6.00.

Euston – ✉ *WC1* – ☎ *0171.*

🏨 **Euston Plaza,** 17/18 Upper Woburn Pl., WC1H 0HT, ✆ 383 4105, Fax 383 4106, Fø, ≘s – 🛗 ⇔ rm ▤ 📺 ☎ ♿ – 🏛 150. MC AE ① VISA JCB. ✗ KLT
Meals 16.95 **st.** and dinner a la carte 🍷 6.95 – ☕ 9.50 – **150 rm** 119.00/135.00 **st.**

Hampstead – ✉ *NW3* – ☎ *0171.*

⛳ *Winnington Rd, Hampstead* ✆ *455 0203.*

🏨 **Swiss Cottage** without rest., 4 Adamson Rd, NW3 3HP, ✆ 722 2281, Fax 483 4588 « Antique furniture » – 🛗 📺 ☎ – 🏛 50. MC AE ① VISA. ✗ GS
55 rm ☕ 75.00/140.00 **st.**, 5 suites.

🏨 **Forte Posthouse Hampstead,** 215 Haverstock Hill, NW3 4RB, ✆ 794 8121, Fax 435 5586 – 🛗 ⇔ rm ▤ rest 📺 ☎ 🅿 – 🏛 30. MC AE ① VISA JCB ES
Meals 10.00 **t.** and a la carte 🍷 6.75 – ☕ 9.95 – **140 rm** 99.00 **st.** – SB.

XX **ZeNW3,** 83-84 Hampstead High St., NW3 1RE, ✆ 794 7863, Fax 794 6956 – ▤. MC AE ① VISA JCB ES
closed Christmas – **Meals** - Chinese - 12.50/26.50 **t.** and a la carte.

XX **Benihana,** 100 Avenue Rd, NW3 3HF, ✆ 586 9508, Fax 586 6740 – ▤. MC AE ① VISA JCB GS
closed 25 December – **Meals** - Japanese (Teppan-Yaki) - a la carte 15.20/25.00 **t.**

Holborn – ✉ *WC2* – ☎ *0171.*

🏨 **Drury Lane Moat House** (Q.M.H.), 10 Drury Lane, High Holborn, WC2B 5RE ✆ 208 9988, Fax 831 1548 – 🛗 ⇔ rm ▤ 📺 ☎ ♿ 🅿 – 🏛 60. MC AE ① VISA JCB p 17 DV
Meals 15.80 **st.** and a la carte 🍷 6.00 – ☕ 10.25 – **163 rm** 125.00/197.00 **st.** – SB.

Regent's Park – ✉ *NW1* – ☎ *0171.*

🏨 **White House,** Albany St., NW1 3UP, ✆ 387 1200, Fax 388 0091, Fø, ≘s – 🛗 ⇔ rm ▤ rest 📺 ☎ – 🏛 110. MC AE ① VISA JCB. ✗ JT
The Restaurant : **Meals** *(closed Saturday lunch and Sunday)* 22.00/26.00 **t.** and dinner a la carte 🍷 15.00 – ***Garden Cafe*** : **Meals** 15.00 **t.** (dinner) and a la carte 12.50/29.00 **t.** 🍷 7.00 – ☕ 10.75 – **582 rm** 132.00/159.00 **st.**, 2 suites.

XX **Odette's,** 130 Regent's Park Rd, NW1 8XL, ✆ 586 5486 – MC AE ① VISA HS
closed 1 week Christmas – **Meals** 10.00 **t.** (lunch) and a la carte 22.50/33.50 **t.**

Swiss Cottage – ✉ *NW3* – ☎ *0171.*

🏨 **Regents Park Marriott,** 128 King Henry's Rd, NW3 3ST, ✆ 722 7711, Fax 586 5822, Fø, ≘s, 🏊 – 🛗 ⇔ rm ▤ 📺 ☎ ♿ 🅿 – 🏛 400. MC AE ① VISA JCB. ✗ GS
Meals 18.95/15.95 **t.** and a la carte – ☕ 12.95 – **298 rm** 165.00/185.00 **s.**, 5 suites SB.

XX **Peter's Chateaubriand,** 65 Fairfax Rd, NW6 4EE, ✆ 624 5804 – ▤. MC AE ① VISA JCB FS
closed Saturday lunch, 1-2 January and 26-27 December – **Meals** 12.95 **t.** and a la carte

ITY OF LONDON – 0171 Except where otherwise stated see p. 7.

XXXX **Tatsuso,** 32 Broadgate Circle, EC2M 2QS, 638 5863, Fax 638 5864 – ▤. MC AE ◑ VISA JCB PU u
closed Saturday and Sunday – **Meals** - Japanese - (booking essential) 38.00/43.00 **st.** and a la carte.

XXXX **Gladwins,** Minister Court, Mark Lane, EC3R 7AA, 444 0004, Fax 444 0001 – ▤. MC AE VISA JCB PV e
closed Saturday, Sunday, 2 weeks August, 2 weeks Christmas and Bank Holidays – **Meals** (lunch only) 32.00 **t.**

XX **Brasserie Rocque,** 37 Broadgate Circle, EC2M 2QS, 638 7919, Fax 628 5899, – ▤. MC AE ◑ VISA PU u
closed Saturday, Sunday, Christmas and Bank Holidays – **Meals** (lunch only) 27.50 **t.** and a la carte 5.00.

XX **Le Quai,** Riverside Walkway, 1 Broken Wharf, High Timber St., EC4V 3QQ, 236 6480, Fax 236 6479 – ▤. MC AE ◑ VISA JCB OV a
closed Saturday, Sunday, 2 weeks Christmas and Bank Holidays – **Meals** - French - (dinner booking essential) 32.50 **t.**

XX **Miyama,** 17 Godliman St., EC4V 5BD, 489 1937, Fax 236 0325 – ▤. MC AE ◑ VISA JCB OV e
closed Saturday dinner, Sunday and Christmas-New Year – **Meals** - Japanese - 20.00/35.00 **t.** and a la carte 8.50.

XX **Imperial City,** Royal Exchange, Cornhill, EC3V 3LL, 626 3437, Fax 338 0125 – ▤. MC AE ◑ VISA PV a
closed Saturday, Sunday and Bank Holidays – **Meals** - Chinese - 14.95/24.95 **t.** and a la carte.

XX **Sri Siam City,** 85 London Wall, EC2M 7AD, 628 5772 – ▤. MC AE ◑ VISA PU a
closed Saturday, Sunday and Bank Holidays – **Meals** - Thai - 14.95/24.95 **t.** and a la carte.

HAMMERSMITH AND FULHAM *p. 8.*

Fulham – ✉ *SW6* – *0171.*

La Reserve, 422-428 Fulham Rd, SW6 1DU, 385 8561, Fax 385 7662, « Contemporary decor » – rm TV ☎. MC AE ◑ VISA JCB. FZ a
Meals a la carte 12.00/17.20 5.90 – 3.50 – **41 rm** 75.00/110.00 **st.** – SB.

XX **Blue Elephant,** 4-6 Fulham Broadway, SW6 1AA, 385 6595, Fax 386 7665 – ▤. MC AE ◑ VISA EZ z
closed Saturday lunch and 24 to 27 December – **Meals** - Thai - (booking essential) 29.00/34.00 **st.** and a la carte.

XX **Fables,** 839 Fulham Rd, SW6 5HQ, 371 5445, Fax 371 5545 – ▤. MC AE ◑ VISA
Meals 22.00 **t.** and a la carte.

XX **755,** 755 Fulham Rd, SW6 5UU, 371 0755, Fax 371 0695 – ▤. MC AE VISA
closed Monday lunch and 25 to 31 December – **Meals** 14.00/22.00 **t.** and a la carte 6.95.

XX **Mao Tai,** 58 New Kings Rd., Parsons Green, SW6 4UG, 731 2520 – ▤. MC AE ◑ VISA JCB
closed 24 to 26 December – **Meals** - Chinese (Szechuan) - 17.50 **t.** and a la carte.

Hammersmith – ✉ *W6/W12/W14* – *0181.*

XX **River Café,** Thames Wharf, Rainville Rd, W6 9HA, (0171) 381 8824, Fax 381 6217, – MC AE VISA
closed Sunday dinner, Christmas-New Year and Bank Holidays – **Meals** - Italian - a la carte approx. 31.50 **t.**

XX **Tandoori Nights,** 319-321 King St., W6 9NH, 741 4328, Fax 741 4328 – ▤. MC AE ◑ VISA JCB
closed 25 and 26 December – **Meals** - Indian - 10.95/11.95 **st.** and a la carte 5.95.

X **Snows on the Green,** 166 Shepherd's Bush Rd, Brook Green, W6 7PB, (0171) 603 2142, Fax 602 7553 – MC AE ◑ VISA
closed Saturday lunch, Sunday dinner and 24 December-1 January – **Meals** 15.00 **t.** (lunch) and a la carte 19.00/23.25 **t.** 7.50.

X **Brackenbury,** 129-131 Brackenbury Rd, W6 0BQ, 748 0107, Fax 741 0905 – MC AE VISA JCB
closed lunch Monday and Saturday, Sunday dinner and 1 week Christmas – **Meals** a la carte 13.00/17.50 **t.**

ISLINGTON *p 7.*

Finsbury – ✉ *WC1/EC1/EC2* – *0171.*

Maison Novelli (Novelli), 29 Clerkenwell Green, EC1R 0DU, 251 6606, Fax 490 108 – VISA NU
closed Saturday and Sunday – **Meals** 27.00 **t.** and a la carte 27.00/32.00 **t.**
Spec. Steamed mixed wild mushroom, poppy seed pancake and Parmesan crackling, Swe onion Tatin, roast pigeon gigolette and fried pancetta, Hot and cold, dark and whi chocolate plate.

Brasserie : Meals *(closed Saturday and Sunday)* 13.95 **t.** and a la carte.

Islington – ✉ *N1* – *0171.*

Frederick's, Camden Passage, N1 8EG, 359 2888, Fax 359 5173, – . VISA JCB NS
closed Sunday, 25 December and Bank Holidays – **Meals** a la carte 21.75/27.75 **st.** 6.8

KENSINGTON and CHELSEA *(Royal Borough of).*

Chelsea – ✉ *SW1/SW3/SW10* – *0171 – Except where otherwise stated see pp 14 and 1.*

Hyatt Carlton Tower, 2 Cadogan Pl., SW1X 9PY, 235 1234, Fax 235 9129, – rm – 150. VISA JCB. FR
Rib Room *(824 7053)* **: Meals** 25.00/32.00 **t.** and a la carte 8.50 – 15.50 – **191 r** 220.00/245.00 **s.**, 29 suites.

Sheraton Park Tower, 101 Knightsbridge, SW1X 7RN, 235 8050, Fax 235 823 – rm – 60. VISA JCB. FQ
101 Knightsbridge **: Meals** 22.50/34.00 **t.** and a la carte 9.50 – 16.00 – **267 r** 250.00/270.00 **s.**, 22 suites.

Conrad International London, Chelsea Harbour, SW10 0XG, 823 300 Fax 351 6525, – rm – 200. VISA JC
Meals 9.50/22.50 **t.** and a la carte 8.00 – 17.00, **159 suites** 250.00/270.00 **s.**

Capital, 22-24 Basil St., SW3 1AT, 589 5171, Fax 225 0011 – – 2 VISA. ER
Meals 25.00/55.00 **st.** and a la carte 40.00/54.00 **st.** – 16.50 – **48 rm** 167.00/290.00
Spec. Three vegetable crème brûlées, Grilled scallops on a caviar sabayon, anchovy mous and red pepper oil, Assiette of vanilla.

Durley House, 115 Sloane St., SW1X 9PJ, 235 5537, Fax 259 6977, « Tasteful furnished Georgian town house », – . VISA. FS
Meals (room service only) a la carte approx. 22.50 **t.** 9.95 – 12.50 – **11 suite** 195.00/325.00 **s.**

Cliveden Town House, 24-26 Cadogan Gdns., SW3 2RP, 730 6466, Fax 730 023 – rm . VISA FS
Meals (room service only) – 17.50 – **24 rm** 110.00/250.00 **s.**, 1 suite.

Cadogan, 75 Sloane St., SW1X 9SG, 235 7141, Fax 245 0994, – r rest – 40. VISA. FR
Meals *(closed Saturday lunch)* 16.90/23.90 **t.** and a la carte 6.25 – 13.50 – **60 r** 135.00/195.00 **st.**, 5 suites – SB .

Franklin, 28 Egerton Gdns., SW3 2DB, 584 5533, Fax 584 5449, « Tastefull furnished Victorian town house », – . VISA. DS
Meals (room service only) a la carte approx. 20.00 **st.** 6.00 – 14.00 – **46 r** 125.00/240.00, 1 suite.

Basil Street, 8 Basil St., SW3 1AH, 581 3311, Fax 581 3693 – – 5 VISA JCB. FQ
Meals (carving lunch Saturday) 16.50/22.00 **t.** 6.50 – 13.25 – **93 r** 135.00/195.00 **t.**

Chelsea, 17-25 Sloane St., SW1X 9NU, 235 4377, Fax 235 3705 – rm – 100. VISA JCB. FR
Meals *(closed Sunday dinner)* a la carte 16.50/30.85 **t.** – 13.50 – **219 r** 150.00/180.00 **s.**, 5 suites.

Sydney House, 9-11 Sydney St., SW3 6PU, 376 7711, Fax 376 4233, « Tastefull furnished Victorian town house » – . VISA DT
Meals (room service only) – 12.50 – **21 rm** 130.00/200.00 **s.**

Egerton House, 17-19 Egerton Terr., SW3 2BX, 589 2412, Fax 584 6540, « Tastefull furnished Victorian town house », – . VISA. DR
Meals (room service only) a la carte 17.00/37.00 **t.** 6.50 – 14.00 – **27 r** 125.00/190.00 **s.**, 1 suite.

Sloane, 29 Draycott Pl., SW3 2SH, ☏ 581 5757, Fax 584 1348, « Victorian town house, antiques » – ☎. MC AE VISA. ET c
Meals (room service only) – 11.00 – **12 rm** 120.00/225.00.

Eleven Cadogan Gardens, 11 Cadogan Gdns., SW3 2RJ, ☏ 730 3426, Fax 730 5217, – ☎. MC AE VISA JCB. FS u
Meals (room service only) a la carte 17.00/20.00 6.00 – 10.00 – **55 rm** 108.00/208.00 **st.**, 5 suites.

The London Outpost of the Carnegie Club without rest., 69 Cadogan Gdns., SW3 2RB, ☏ 589 7333, Fax 581 4958, – ☎. MC AE VISA. FS r
14.75 – **11 rm** 150.00/235.00.

Beaufort without rest., 33 Beaufort Gdns., SW3 1PP, ☏ 584 5252, Fax 589 2834, « English floral watercolour collection » – ☎. MC AE VISA JCB. ER n
28 rm 110.00/240.00 **s.**

Parkes without rest., 41 Beaufort Gdns., SW3 1PW, ☏ 581 9944, Fax 581 1999 – ☎. MC AE VISA. ER x
18 rm 115.00/160.00 **s.**, 15 suites 190.00/250.00 **s.**

Claverley without rest., 13-14 Beaufort Gdns., SW3 1PS, ☏ 589 8541, Fax 584 3410 – ☎. MC AE VISA. ER o
30 rm 60.00/195.00 **t.**

Knightsbridge, 12 Beaufort Gdns., SW3 1PT, ☏ 589 9271, Fax 823 9692, – ☎. MC AE VISA JCB. ER o
Meals (room service only) – **44 rm** 85.00/135.00 **st.**, 6 suites.

L'Hotel, 28 Basil St., SW3 1AT, ☏ 589 6286, Fax 225 0011 – ☎. MC AE VISA. ER i
***Le Metro* : Meals** *(closed Sunday)* a la carte 14.70/17.00 **t.** – 6.50 – **12 rm** 145.00/165.00 **st.**

La Tante Claire (Koffmann), 68-69 Royal Hospital Rd, SW3 4HP, ☏ 352 6045, Fax 352 3257 – MC AE VISA EU c
closed Saturday, Sunday, 1 week Easter, 3 weeks August and 10 days Christmas – **Meals** - French - (booking essential) 27.00 **st.** (lunch) and a la carte 53.00/59.00 **st.** 11.00
Spec. Coquilles St. Jacques à la planche, sauce encre, Pied de cochon aux morilles, Croustade de pommes caramélisées à l'Armagnac.

Waltons, 121 Walton St., SW3 2HP, ☏ 584 0204, Fax 581 2848 – MC AE VISA JCB DS a
closed 25 December dinner and 26 December – **Meals** 15.75/22.50 **t.** and a la carte 5.50.

Bibendum, Michelin House, 81 Fulham Rd, SW3 6RD, ☏ 581 5817, Fax 823 7925 – MC AE VISA DS s
closed 25 and 26 December – **Meals** 27.00 **t.** (lunch) and dinner a la carte 26.00/50.00 **t.** 4.75.

The Canteen, Harbour Yard, Chelsea Harbour, SW10 0XD, ☏ 351 7330, Fax 351 6189 – MC AE VISA
closed Saturday lunch and Sunday dinner – **Meals** 19.50/24.85 and a la carte 23.85/33.40
Spec. Warm salad of sea scallops, apple and cashew nuts, Pappardelle with field mushrooms and truffle oil, Roast sea bass, potato confit, bouillabaisse sauce.

Aubergine (Ramsay), 11 Park Walk, SW10 0AJ, ☏ 352 3449, Fax 351 1770 – MC AE VISA CU r
closed Saturday lunch, Sunday, 2 weeks August, 2 weeks Christmas and Bank Holidays – **Meals** (booking essential) 22.00/40.00-50.00 **t.** 9.00
Spec. Foie gras three ways, Roasted sea bass with crushed new potatoes and tomato confit, Saveur de chocolat with mandarin sorbet.

Fifth Floor (at Harvey Nichols), Knightsbridge, SW1X 7RJ, ☏ 235 5250, Fax 823 2207 – MC AE VISA JCB FQ a
closed dinner Sunday and Monday, 25 December and Bank Holiday Mondays – **Meals** 22.50 **t.** (lunch) and dinner a la carte 23.75/33.00 **t.** 7.50.

Turner's, 87-89 Walton St., SW3 2HP, ☏ 584 6711, Fax 584 4441 – MC AE VISA JCB ES n
closed Saturday lunch, 25 to 30 December and Bank Holidays – **Meals** 13.50/26.50 **t.** and a la carte.

Chutney Mary, 535 King's Rd, SW10 0SZ, ☏ 351 3113, Fax 351 7694 – MC AE VISA JCB p. 8 FZ v
closed 25 December dinner and 26 December – **Meals** - Anglo-Indian - 15.00 **t.** (lunch) and a la carte 21.60/27.65 **t.** 8.25.

Albero & Grana, Chelsea Cloisters, 89 Sloane Av., SW3 3DX, ☏ 225 1048, Fax 581 3259 – MC AE VISA JCB ET e
closed Sunday – **Meals** - Spanish - (dinner only) a la carte 28.50/47.00 **t.**

XXX **Benihana,** 77 King's Rd, SW3 4NX, ✆ 376 7799, Fax 376 7377 – ▤. MC AE ⓓ VISA JCB
closed 25 December – **Meals** - Japanese (Teppan-Yaki) - a la carte 20.00/32.50 **t.** EU

XX **Fulham Road,** 257-259 Fulham Rd, SW3 6HY, ✆ 351 7823, Fax 376 4971 – MC AE VISA
closed Saturday lunch, 1 week Christmas and Bank Holidays – **Meals** 20.00 **t.** (lunch) and a la carte 26.50/37.50 **t.** CU

XX **English Garden,** 10 Lincoln St., SW3 2TS, ✆ 584 7272, Fax 581 2848 – ▤. MC AE ⓓ VISA JCB ET
closed 25 and 26 December – **Meals** - English - 15.75 **t.** (lunch) and a la carte 20.25/36.75 🍷 5.50.

XX **Brasserie St. Quentin,** 243 Brompton Rd, SW3 2EP, ✆ 589 8005, Fax 584 6064 ▤. MC AE ⓓ VISA JCB DR
Meals - French - a la carte 18.90/27.20 **t.** 🍷 4.60.

XX **Poissonnerie de l'Avenue,** 82 Sloane Av., SW3 3DZ, ✆ 589 2457, Fax 581 3360 ▤. MC AE ⓓ VISA JCB DS
closed Sunday, Christmas-New Year and Bank Holidays – **Meals** - French Seafood - 16.50 (lunch) and a la carte 23.00/31.50 **t.** 🍷 6.50.

XX **Daphne's,** 112 Draycott Av., SW3 3AE, ✆ 589 4257, Fax 581 2232 – ▤. MC AE ⓓ VISA
closed 25 and 26 December – **Meals** - Italian - a la carte 19.75/35.75 **t.** DS

XX **La Finezza,** 62-64 Lower Sloane St., SW1N 8BP, ✆ 730 8639 – ▤. MC AE ⓓ VISA
closed Saturday lunch, Sunday, Easter and 25-26 December – **Meals** - Italian - a la carte 17.50/43.00 **t.** 🍷 8.50. FT

XX **The Collection,** 264 Brompton Rd, SW3 2AS, ✆ 225 1212, Fax 225 1050 – ▤. MC AE ⓓ VISA DS
closed Sunday July-October and 1 week Christmas – **Meals** a la carte 14.50/23.00 **t.**

XX **Caraffini,** 61-63 Lower Sloane St., SW1W 8DH, ✆ 259 0235 – ▤. MC AE VISA FT
closed Sunday and Bank Holidays – **Meals** - Italian - a la carte 16.20/25.70 **t.** 🍷 4.75.

XX **Osteria Le Fate,** 5 Draycott Av., SW3, ✆ 591 0071 – MC AE VISA JCB ET
closed Sunday and Bank Holidays – **Meals** - Italian - 17.50/20.50 **t.** and a la carte.

XX **Grill St. Quentin,** 3 Yeoman's Row, SW3 2AL, ✆ 581 8377, Fax 584 6064 – ▤. MC AE ⓓ VISA JCB ER
Meals a la carte 16.40/30.90 **t.** 🍷 4.60.

XX **Busabong Too,** 1a Langton St., SW10 0JL, ✆ 352 7414 – ▤. MC AE ⓓ VISA JCB
closed 24 to 26 December – **Meals** - Thai - (dinner only) 25.95 **t.** and a la carte. p. 8 FZ

XX **Toto's,** Walton House, Walton St., SW3 2JH, ✆ 589 0075, Fax 581 9668 – MC AE ⓓ VISA JCB ES
closed 24 to 26 December – **Meals** - Italian - 17.50/30.00 **st.** and a la carte 🍷 6.75.

XX **Red,** 8 Egerton Garden Mews, SW3 2EH, ✆ 584 7007 – MC AE ⓓ VISA JCB DR
Meals - Chinese - 12.50/15.00 **t.** and a la carte 🍷 4.50.

XX **Good Earth,** 233 Brompton Rd, SW3 2EP, ✆ 584 3658, Fax 823 8769 – ▤. MC AE ⓓ VISA JCB DR
closed 23 to 27 December – **Meals** - Chinese - 12.95/18.95 **t.** and a la carte.

XX **Dan's,** 119 Sydney St., SW3 6NR, ✆ 352 2718, Fax 352 3265 – MC AE VISA DU
closed Saturday lunch, Sunday, Christmas-New Year and Bank Holidays – **Meals** a la carte 14.50/27.00 **t.** 🍷 5.00.

XX **Beit Eddine,** 8 Harriet St., SW1X 9JW, ✆ 235 3969, Fax 245 6335 – MC AE ⓓ VISA
Meals - Lebanese - a la carte 15.50/25.25 **t.** 🍷 6.50. FQ

X **Drones of Pont Street,** 1 Pont St., SW1X 9EJ, ✆ 259 6166, Fax 259 6177 – ▤. MC AE ⓓ VISA FR
Meals 12.95 **t.** (lunch) and a la carte 19.40/35.45.

Kensington – ✉ SW7/W8/W11/W14 – ☎ 0171 – *Except where otherwise stated see pp. 8-1*

🏨 **Royal Garden,** 2-24 Kensington High St., W8 4PT, ✆ 937 8000, Fax 938 4532, ← – |‡| ⇔ rm ▤ TV ☎ ♿ P – 🏛 600. MC AE ⓓ VISA JCB p. 14 AQ
The Tenth : **Meals** *(closed Saturday lunch, Sunday and Bank Holidays)* 19.95 **t.** and a la carte – ***Park Terrace*** : **Meals** 14.95 **t.** (lunch) and a la carte 15.95/27.15 **t.** – ☕ 15.5 – **385 rm** 145.00/215.00, 15 suites.

🏨 **Copthorne Tara,** Scarsdale Pl., W8 5SR, ✆ 937 7211, Fax 937 7100 – |‡| ⇔ rm ▤ TV ☎ ♿ P – 🏛 500. MC AE ⓓ VISA JCB. ✗ FY
Brasserie : **Meals** 17.50 **t.** and a la carte 🍷 5.90 – ***Jerome K. Jerome*** : **Meals** *(closed Sunday)* (dinner only) a la carte 22.10/36.60 **t.** 🍷 5.90 – ☕ 12.25 – **815 rm** 160.00/200.00 **st.**, 10 suites.

🏨 **Halcyon,** 81 Holland Park, W11 3RZ, ✆ 727 7288, Fax 229 8516 – |‡| ▤ TV ☎. MC AE ⓓ VISA JCB. ✗ EX
closed 26 to 31 December – **Meals** (see ***The Room*** below) – ☕ 13.50 – **40 rm** 165.00/250.00 **st.**, 3 suites.

The Milestone without rest., 1-2 Kensington Court, W8 5DL, ☎ 917 1000, Fax 917 1010, – – MO AE VISA. p 14 AQ u
15.00 – **47 rm** 220.00/270.00 **st.**, 6 suites.

London Kensington Hilton, 179-199 Holland Park Av., W11 4UL, ☎ 603 3355, Fax 602 9397 – rm – 300. MO AE VISA JCB. EX s
Meals *(closed January and February)* 15.95 **t.** (lunch) and dinner a la carte 15.00/30.00 9.50 – ***Hiroko :*** **Meals** - Japanese - *(closed Monday)* 15.00/32.00 7.00 – 13.00 – **602 rm** 160.00/180.00 **st.**, 1 suite.

Kensington Park Thistle, 16-32 De Vere Gdns., W8 5AG, ☎ 937 8080, Fax 937 7616 – rm rest – 120. MO AE VISA. p 14 BQ e
Moniques Brasserie : **Meals** a la carte 16.40/19.40 **t.** 6.95 – ***Cairngorm Grill :*** **Meals** *(closed Sunday and Monday)* (dinner only) 19.95 **t.** and a la carte 9.00 – 11.25 – **326 rm** 135.00/180.00 **st.**, 6 suites – SB.

Hilton National London Olympia, 380 Kensington High St., W14 8NL, ☎ 603 3333, Fax 603 4846, – rm rest – 450. MO AE VISA. EY a
Meals 16.50 **st.** and a la carte 6.50 – 12.95 – **395 rm** 140.00/150.00 **st.**, 10 suites.

Kensington Close (Forte), Wrights Lane, W8 5SP, ☎ 937 8170, Fax 937 8289, , squash – rm rest – 180. MO AE VISA JCB. FY c
Meals a la carte 13.65/25.85 – 11.00 – **531 rm** 115.00/200.00 **st.**

Holland Court without rest., 31 Holland Rd, W14 8HJ, ☎ 371 1133, Fax 602 9114, – MO AE VISA JCB. EY e
22 rm 75.00/105.00 **st.**

The Room (at Halcyon H.), 129 Holland Park Av., W11 3UT, ☎ 221 5411, Fax 229 8516, – MO AE VISA JCB EX u
closed Saturday lunch and 26 to 31 December – **Meals** a la carte approx. 35.00 5.50.

Clarke's, 124 Kensington Church St., W8 4BH, ☎ 221 9225, Fax 229 4564 – MO AE VISA
closed Saturday and Sunday – **Meals** 26.00/37.00 **st.** 9.25. EX c

Launceston Place, 1a Launceston Pl., W8 5RL, ☎ 937 6912, Fax 938 2412 – MO AE VISA p 14 BR a
closed Saturday lunch, Sunday dinner, 25-26 December, 1 January and Bank Holidays – **Meals** a la carte 26.00/31.00 **t.** 5.50.

Belvedere in Holland Park, Holland House, off Abbotsbury Rd, W8 6LU, ☎ 602 1238, Fax 610 4382, « 19C orangery in park » – MO AE VISA JCB EY u
closed Sunday dinner, 25 December and 1 January – **Meals** a la carte 17.50/27.00 **t.** 8.50.

Arcadia, Kensington Court, 35 Kensington High St., W8 5EB, ☎ 937 4294, Fax 937 4393 – MO AE VISA p 14 AQ s
closed lunch Saturday and Sunday, 25-26 December and 1 January – **Meals** 15.95 **t.** and dinner a la carte 6.75.

Boyd's, 135 Kensington Church St., W8 7LP, ☎ 727 5452, Fax 221 0615 – MO AE VISA p 16 AZ r
closed Sunday, 2 weeks Christmas-New Year and Bank Holidays – **Meals** 15.00 **t.** (lunch) and a la carte 21.45/30.75 **t.**

La Pomme d'Amour, 128 Holland Park Av., W11 4UE, ☎ 229 8532, Fax 221 4096 – MO AE VISA EX e
closed Saturday lunch, Sunday, 25 December and Bank Holidays – **Meals** - French - 10.75/14.50 **t.** and a la carte 5.50.

L'Escargot Doré, 2-4 Thackeray St., W8 5ET, ☎ 937 8508, Fax 937 8508 – MO AE VISA JCB p 14 AQR e
closed Saturday lunch, Sunday and last 2 weeks August – **Meals** 16.00 **t.** and a la carte 5.80.

La Fenice, 148 Holland Park Av., W11 4UE, ☎ 221 6090, Fax 221 4096 – MO AE VISA
closed Saturday lunch, Monday, 25 December and Bank Holidays – **Meals** - Italian - 11.40/14.75 **t.** and a la carte 4.25. EX v

Phoenicia, 11-13 Abingdon Rd, W8 6AH, ☎ 937 0120, Fax 937 7668 – MO AE VISA JCB EY n
closed 24 and 25 December – **Meals** - Lebanese - (buffet lunch) a la carte 12.85/18.20 **t.** 5.00.

Kensington Place, 201 Kensington Church St., W8 7LX, ☎ 727 3184, Fax 229 2025 – MO AE VISA JCB p 16 AZ z
closed 25-26 December and 1 January – **Meals** 14.50 **t.** (lunch) and a la carte 18.50/30.50 **t.** 4.50.

Cibo, 3 Russell Gdns., W14 8EZ, ☎ 371 6271, Fax 602 1371 – MO AE VISA JCB
closed Saturday lunch, Sunday dinner, 24 to 26 December and Easter Sunday – **Meals** - Italian - 12.50 **t.** (lunch) and a la carte 19.95/32.25 **t.** 5.95. EY o

Malabar, 27 Uxbridge St., W8 7TQ, ☎ 727 8800 – MO VISA p 16 AZ e
closed last week August and 4 days Christmas – **Meals** - Indian - (booking essential) (buffet lunch Sunday) 15.75 **st.** and a la carte 14.95/28.30 **st.** 4.75.

North Kensington – ✉ *W2/W10/W11* – ☎ *0171* – *Except where otherwise stated se pp 4-7.*

Pembridge Court, 34 Pembridge Gdns, W2 4DX, ☎ 229 9977, Fax 727 498 « Collection of antique clothing » – rest. p 16 AZ
Meals (residents only) (restricted menu) (dinner only) a la carte 13.40/21.40 **st.** 4.95 **20 rm** 105.00/165.00 **t.**

Abbey Court without rest., 20 Pembridge Gdns, W2 4DU, ☎ 221 7518, Fax 792 085 « Tastefully furnished Victorian town house » – **22 rm** 88.00/175.00 **t.** p 16 AZ

Leith's, 92 Kensington Park Rd, W11 2PN, ☎ 229 4481 – *closed lunch Saturday to Monday, Sunday dinner, 10 to 26 August and 24 December 4 January* – **Meals** 19.50/35.00 **t.** and a la carte 34.50/44.25 **t.** 7.75 EV
Spec. Roast scallops, spiced lemon couscous, artichokes and light curry butter, Braise saddle of rabbit with tortellini of morels, Fillet of sea bass with crab, saffron risotto an clear gazpacho.

Chez Moi, 1 Addison Av., Holland Park, W11 4QS, ☎ 603 8267, Fax 603 3898 – p 8 EX
closed Saturday lunch, Sunday and Bank Holidays – **Meals** - French - 15.00 **t.** (lunch) an a la carte 21.25/31.50 **t.** 5.00.

Orsino, 119 Portland Rd, W11 4LN, ☎ 221 3299, Fax 229 9414 – *closed 24 and 25 December* – **Meals** - Italian - 15.50 **t.** (lunch) and a la carte 16.50/28.50 t 5.50. p 8 EX

Sugar Club, 33a All Saints Rd, W11 1HE, ☎ 221 3844, – EU
closed 1 week Christmas and August Bank Holiday – **Meals** 15.50 **t.** (lunch) and a la cart 22.50/26.20 **t.** 5.25.

Alastair Little Lancaster Road, 136a Lancaster Rd, W11 1QU, ☎ 243 2220 – EU
closed Sunday and Bank Holidays – **Meals** 20.00 **t.** 10.00.

South Kensington – ✉ *SW5/SW7/W8* – ☎ *0171* – *pp 14 and 15.*

Gloucester, 4-18 Harrington Gdns., SW7 4LH, ☎ 373 6030, Fax 373 0409, – rm – 400. BS
Meals *(closed Saturday lunch)* (carving lunch) a la carte 15.50/26.20 **t.** 7.00 – 14.9 – **542 rm** 176.25/193.90 **st.**, 6 suites.

Harrington Hall, 5-25 Harrington Gdns., SW7 4JW, ☎ 396 9696, Fax 396 9090, – rm – 250. BT
Wetherby's : **Meals** 18.00/19.25 **st.** and a la carte 6.50 – 12.50 – **200 rm** 140.00/175.00 **st.**

Pelham, 15 Cromwell Pl., SW7 2LA, ☎ 589 8288, Fax 584 8444, « Tastefully furnishe Victorian town house » – CS
Kemps : **Meals** *(closed Saturday)* 12.95/15.50 **t.** and a la carte 18.70/22.20 **t.** – 12.5 – **38 rm** 120.00/185.00 **s.**, 3 suites.

Blakes, 33 Roland Gdns, SW7 3PF, ☎ 370 6701, Fax 373 0442, « Antique orienta furnishings » – rest. BU
Meals a la carte approx. 45.75 **t.** 9.50 – 17.00 – **45 rm** 135.00/520.00 **st.**, 6 suites

Rembrandt, 11 Thurloe Pl., SW7 2RS, ☎ 589 8100, Fax 225 3363, – rm rest – 250. DS
Meals 15.95 **st.** and a la carte 5.40 – 9.75 – **195 rm** 115.00/140.00 **st.** – SB.

Swallow International, Cromwell Rd, SW5 0TH, ☎ 973 1000, Fax 244 8194, – rm – 200. AS
Meals 16.00/20.00 **st.** and a la carte – 11.50 – **414 rm** 115.00/130.00 **st.**, 2 suite – SB.

Jury's Kensington, 109-113 Queen's Gate, SW7 5LR, ☎ 589 6300, Fax 581 1492 – rm rest – 80. CT
closed Christmas – **Meals** (bar lunch)/dinner 20.00 **st.** and a la carte 5.50 – 9.50 – **171 rm** 125.00 **st.**

Vanderbilt (Radisson Edwardian), 68-86 Cromwell Rd, SW7 5BT, ☎ 589 2424 Fax 225 2293 – rest – 120. BS
Meals a la carte 21.00/27.00 **st.** 8.00 – 11.00 – **223 rm** 105.00/135.00 **st.**

Forum (Inter-Con), 97 Cromwell Rd, SW7 4DN, ☎ 370 5757, Fax 373 1448, – rm – 400. BS
Meals a la carte 13.45/23.00 **st.** 6.50 – 11.50 – **906 rm** 150.00/170.00 **st.**, 4 suites

Regency, 100 Queen's Gate, SW7 5AC, ☎ 370 4595, Fax 370 5555, – rm – 100. CT
Meals *(closed lunch Saturday and Sunday)* 15.00/19.00 **st.** and a la carte 6.00 – 12.00 – **192 rm** 123.00 **s.**, 6 suites.

Bailey's, 140 Gloucester Rd, SW7 4QH, 373 6000, Fax 370 3760 – rm rm AE VISA JCB. BS a
Meals a la carte 17.00/25.00 **st.** 7.00 – 13.00 – **213 rm** 85.00/250.00 **s.**

Gore, 189 Queen's Gate, SW7 5EX, 584 6601, Fax 589 8127, « Attractive decor » – rm AE VISA JCB BR n
closed 25 and 26 December – ***Bistrot 190 :*** **Meals** (only members and residents may book) a la carte 14.85/24.15 **t.** 4.00 – (see also ***Downstairs at One Ninety*** below) – 8.50 – **54 rm** 117.00/233.00 **st.**

Jarvis Embassy House, 31-33 Queen's Gate, SW7 5JA, 584 7222, Fax 589 3910 – rm – 60. AE VISA JCB. BR u
Meals 14.50/17.50 **st.** and dinner a la carte 5.75 – 10.75 – **69 rm** 89.00/99.00 **t.**, 1 suite – SB.

John Howard, 4 Queen's Gate, SW7 5EH, 581 3011, Fax 589 8403 – AE VISA JCB. BQ i
Meals *(closed Sunday)* (dinner only) 20.00 **st.** and a la carte 6.00 – 11.50 – **43 rm** 79.00/109.00 **st.**, 9 suites.

Cranley, 10-12 Bina Gdns., SW5 0LA, 373 0123, Fax 373 9497, « Antiques » – rm AE VISA. BT c
Meals (room service only) – 12.50 – **32 rm** 120.00/140.00 **st.**, 4 suites.

Cranley Gardens without rest., 8 Cranley Gdns., SW7 3DB, 373 3232, Fax 373 7944 – AE VISA JCB – 5.50 – **85 rm** 75.00/105.00 **st.** BT e

Number Sixteen without rest., 16 Sumner Pl., SW7 3EG, 589 5232, Fax 584 8615, « Attractively furnished Victorian town houses », – AE VISA. 8.00 – **36 rm** 80.00/170.00 **st.** CT c

Five Sumner Place without rest., 5 Sumner Pl., SW7 3EE, 584 7586, Fax 823 9962 – AE VISA JCB. CT u
13 rm 81.00/120.00 **st.**

Aster House without rest., 3 Sumner Pl., SW7 3EE, 581 5888, Fax 584 4925, – VISA. CT u
12 rm 70.00/118.00 **st.**

Hotel 167 without rest., 167 Old Brompton Rd, SW5 0AN, 373 3221, Fax 373 3360 – AE VISA. BT r
18 rm 66.00/90.00 **st.**

Bombay Brasserie, Courtfield Close, 140 Gloucester Rd, SW7 4UH, 370 4040, Fax 835 1669, « Raj-style decor, conservatory garden » – VISA BS a
closed 25 and 26 December – **Meals** - Indian - (buffet lunch) 14.95/25.00 **t.** and dinner a la carte 6.95.

Hilaire, 68 Old Brompton Rd, SW7 3LQ, 584 8993, Fax 581 2949 – AE VISA JCB
closed Saturday lunch, Sunday and Bank Holidays – **Meals** (booking essential) 29.50 **t.** (dinner) and a la carte 24.00/32.50 **t.** CT n

Shaw's, 119 Old Brompton Rd, SW7 3RN, 373 7774, Fax 370 5102 – AE VISA
closed Saturday lunch, Sunday, 1 week August, 1 week Christmas-New Year and Bank Holidays – **Meals** 19.50/34.95 **t.** 9.50. BT v

Downstairs at One Ninety, 190 Queen's Gate, SW7 5EU, 581 5666, Fax 581 8172 – AE VISA JCB BR n
closed Sunday – **Meals** - Seafood - (booking essential) (dinner only) 27.50 **t.** and a la carte.

Khan's of Kensington, 3 Harrington Rd, SW7 3ES, 581 2900, Fax 581 2900 – AE VISA CS e
closed 25 and 26 December – **Meals** - Indian - 7.95/14.50 **t.** and a la carte 4.95.

Café Lazeez, 93-95 Old Brompton Rd, SW7 3LD, 581 9993, Fax 581 8200 – AE VISA JCB CT a
Restaurant : **Meals** - North Indian - 7.50 **t.** (lunch) and a la carte 15.40/25.55 **t.** 4.40.
Cafe : Meals 7.50 **t.** (lunch) and a la carte 10.85/19.25 **t.** 4.40.

Tui, 19 Exhibition Rd, SW7 2HE, 584 8359 – AE VISA JCB CS u
closed 5 days at Christmas and Bank Holiday Mondays – **Meals** - Thai - a la carte 14.45/21.10 **t.** 4.50.

Star of India, 154 Old Brompton Rd, SW5 0BE, 373 2901, Fax 373 5664 – AE VISA JCB BT s
closed 25 December and Bank Holidays – **Meals** - Indian - a la carte 21.50/29.70 **t.**

Delhi Brasserie, 134 Cromwell Rd, SW7 4HA, 370 7617, Fax 244 8639 – AE VISA AS a
closed 25 and 26 December – **Meals** - Indian - 6.95/15.95 **t.** and a la carte 8.95.

Memories of India, 18 Gloucester Rd, SW7 4RB, 589 6450, Fax 584 4438 – AE VISA JCB BR s
closed 25 and 26 December – **Meals** - Indian - 7.95/14.50 **t.** and a la carte.

LAMBETH pp. 10 and 11.

Waterloo – ✉ SE1 – ☎ 0171.

XX **People's Palace,** Level 3, The Royal Festival Hall, SE1 8XX, ☎ 928 9999, Fax 928 235 ≤ Victoria Embankment and River Thames – ▤. MC AE ⓓ VISA MX closed 25 December and Bank Holidays – **Meals** 14.50 **t.** (lunch) and a la carte 16.50/26.0 🍾 6.00.

XX **RSJ,** 13a Coin St., SE1 8YQ, ☎ 928 4554 – ▤. MC AE ⓓ VISA NX *closed Saturday lunch, Sunday, 25 December and Bank Holidays* – **Meals** 15.95 **t.** an a la carte 🍾 5.95.

MERTON

Wimbledon – ✉ SW19 – ☎ 0181.

Cannizaro House (Thistle) ⚓, West Side, Wimbledon Common, SW19 4UF ☎ 879 1464, Fax 879 7338, ≤, « 18C country house in Cannizaro Park », – |‡| ⇹ r TV ☎ P – 🏛 45. MC AE ⓓ VISA JCB. ✂ **Meals** 25.75 **t.** and a la carte 🍾 9.35 – ☕ 11.25 – **44 rm** 135.00/220.00 **t.**, 2 suites – SB

SOUTHWARK p 11.

Bermondsey – ✉ SE1 – ☎ 0171.

XXX **Le Pont de la Tour,** 36d Shad Thames, Butlers Wharf, SE1 2YE, ☎ 403 840 Fax 403 0267, ≤, 🏖, « Riverside setting » – ▤. MC AE ⓓ VISA PX *closed Saturday lunch and 25-26 December* – **Meals** 27.50 **t.** (lunch) and dinner a la cart 29.75/42.25 **t.** 🍾 7.95.

XXX **Bengal Clipper,** Cardamom Building, Shad Thames, Butlers Wharf, SE1 2YR ☎ 357 9001, Fax 357 9002 – ▤. MC AE ⓓ VISA JCB PX *closed 25 and 26 December* – **Meals** - Indian - a la carte 13.45/19.85 **t.**

X **Blue Print Café,** Design Museum, Shad Thames, Butlers Wharf, SE1 2YD, ☎ 378 703 Fax 378 6540, ≤, 🏖, « Riverside setting » – MC AE ⓓ VISA JCB PX *closed Sunday dinner* – **Meals** a la carte 22.95/26.50 **t.**

X **Cantina Del Ponte,** 36c Shad Thames, Butlers Wharf, SE1 2YE, ☎ 403 540 Fax 403 0267, ≤, 🏖, « Riverside setting » – MC AE ⓓ VISA PX *closed Sunday dinner and 25-26 December* – **Meals** - Italian-Mediterranean - a la cart 19.65/26.95 **t.**

X **Butlers Wharf Chop House,** 36e Shad Thames, Butlers Wharf, SE1 2YE, ☎ 403 340 Fax 403 3414, « Riverside setting, ≤Tower Bridge » – MC AE ⓓ VISA PX *closed Saturday lunch, Sunday dinner and first week January* – **Meals** 22.75 **t.** (lunch) an dinner a la carte 21.75/31.50 **t.**

Dulwich – ✉ SE19 – ☎ 0181.

XX **Luigi's,** 129 Gipsy Hill, SE19 1QS, ☎ 670 1843 – ▤. MC AE ⓓ VISA JCB *closed Saturday lunch, Sunday and Bank Holidays* – **Meals** - Italian - a la carte 15.20/23.20 t

Rotherhithe – ✉ SE16 – ☎ 0171.

Holiday Inn at Nelson Dock, 265 Rotherhithe St., Nelson Dock, SE16 1EJ ☎ 231 1001, Fax 231 0599, ≤, 🏖, « Riverside setting », Fō, ≘s, 🏊, 🎾 – |‡| ⇹ rn ▤ rest TV ☎ ♿ P – 🏛 350. MC AE ⓓ VISA JCB. ✂ *closed 23 to 29 December* – **Meals** 21.50 **st.** and dinner a la carte 🍾 10.50 – ☕ 10.5 – **366 rm** 105.00/125.00 **st.**, 2 suites.

Southwark – ✉ SE1 – ☎ 0171.

XXX **Oxo Tower** (8th floor), Oxo Tower Wharf, Barge House St., SE1 9PH, ☎ 803 3888 Fax 803 3838, ≤ London skyline and River Thames, 🏖 – |‡| ▤. MC AE ⓓ VISA JCB *closed dinner 24 to 26 December* – **Meals** 23.50 (lunch) and dinner a la carte 25.00/35.5 🍾 8.00. NX

X **Brasserie : Meals** *(closed dinner 24 to 26 December)* a la carte 18.75/21.25 **t.** 🍾 8.00

XX **La Truffe Noire,** 29 Tooley St., SE1 2QF, ☎ 378 0621, Fax 403 0689 – ▤. MC AE ⓓ VISA JCB PX *closed Saturday, Sunday, 2 weeks from 24 December-early January and Bank Holidays* – **Meals** - French - 20.00 **t.** and a la carte 🍾 4.50.

X **Café dell'Ugo,** 56-58 Tooley St., SE1 2SZ, ☎ 407 6001, Fax 357 8806 – ▤. MC AE ⓓ VISA PX *closed Saturday lunch, Sunday and Bank Holidays* – **Meals** 12.95 **t.** (dinner) and a la carte 17.15/25.15 **t.**

WANDSWORTH

Battersea – ✉ SW8/SW11 – ☎ 0171.

XX **Ransome's Dock,** 35-37 Parkgate Rd, SW11 4NP, ✆ 223 1611, Fax 924 2614, – MC AE D VISA HZ c
closed Sunday dinner, Christmas and August Bank Holiday – **Meals** 11.50 **t.** (lunch) and a la carte 17.75/27.00 **t.** 6.00.

XX **Chada,** 208-210 Battersea Park Rd, SW11 4ND, ✆ 622 2209, Fax 924 2178 – ▤. MC AE D VISA JCB
closed Saturday lunch and Bank Holidays – **Meals** - Thai - a la carte 12.90/22.45 **st.**

Putney – ✉ SW15 – ☎ 0181.

XX **Royal China,** 3 Chelverton Rd, SW15 1RN, ✆ 788 0907 – ▤. MC AE D VISA
Meals - Chinese - 20.00/26.00 **st.** and a la carte 4.50.

XX **Del Buongustaio,** 283 Putney Bridge Rd, SW15 2PT, ✆ 780 9361, Fax 789 9659 – ▤. MC AE VISA
closed lunch Saturday and Sunday June-mid September and 10 days Christmas-New Year – **Meals** - Italian - a la carte 17.60/20.50 **t.** 5.95.

Wandsworth – ✉ SW12/SW17/SW18 – ☎ 0181.

XX **Tabaq,** 47 Balham Hill, SW12 9DR, ✆ 673 7820, Fax 673 2701 – ▤. MC AE D VISA
closed Sunday and 25 December – **Meals** - Indian - a la carte 14.95/29.95 **t.** 4.75.

XX **Chez Bruce,** 2 Bellevue Rd, SW17 7EG, ✆ 672 0114, Fax 767 6648 – ▤. MC AE D VISA JCB
closed Sunday dinner, 1 week Christmas and Bank Holidays – **Meals** 17.50/24.50 **t.**

X **Bombay Bicycle Club,** 95 Nightingale Lane, SW12 8NX, ✆ 673 6217 – MC AE D VISA
closed Sunday, 1 week Christmas and Bank Holidays – **Meals** - Indian - (dinner only) a la carte 16.75/25.00 **t.** 6.50.

WESTMINSTER (City of).

Bayswater and Maida Vale – ✉ W2/W9 – ☎ 0171 – *Except where otherwise stated see pp 16 and 17.*

Royal Lancaster, Lancaster Terr., W2 2TY, ✆ 262 6737, Fax 724 3191, ← – ▯ ⇔ rm ▤ TV ☎ P – 1400. MC AE D VISA JCB. ✻ DZ e
Park : **Meals** *(closed Saturday lunch and Sunday dinner)* 23.50 **st.** and a la carte 8.50 – ***Pavement Cafe :*** **Meals** a la carte 13.30/20.40 **st.** 7.00 – (see also ***Nipa*** below) – ☐ 14.50 – **398 rm** 195.00/235.00 **st.** – 20 suites.

London Metropole, Edgware Rd, W2 1JU, ✆ 402 4141, Fax 724 8866, ←, Fб, ≘s, ▢ – ▯ ⇔ rm ▤ TV ☎ – 1200. MC AE D VISA JCB. ✻ p 5 GU c
Meals (buffet rest.) 19.95 **st.** (see also ***Aspects*** below) – ☐ 14.95 – **716 rm** 145.00/270.00 **st.**, 26 suites – SB.

Whites (Thistle), Bayswater Rd, 90-92 Lancaster Gate, W2 3NR, ✆ 262 2711, Fax 262 2147 – ▯ ⇔ rm ▤ TV ☎. MC AE D VISA JCB. ✻ CZ v
Meals *(closed Saturday lunch)* 17.50/21.00 **t.** and a la carte 7.00 – ☐ 11.25 – **52 rm** 165.00/230.00 **st.**, 2 suites – SB.

London Embassy (Jarvis), 150 Bayswater Rd, W2 4RT, ✆ 229 1212, Fax 229 2623 – ▯ ⇔ rm ▤ rest TV ☎ P – 60. MC AE D VISA BZ o
Meals (carving rest.) 15.95 **st.** and a la carte 5.75 – ☐ 9.50 – **193 rm** 99.00/135.00 **st.**, 1 suite – SB.

Plaza on Hyde Park (Hilton), 1-7 Lancaster Gate, W2 3LG, ✆ 262 5022, Fax 724 8666 – ▯ ⇔ rm TV ☎ – 30. MC AE D VISA JCB. ✻ DZ r
Meals 14.95 **st.** and a la carte 6.95 – ☐ 9.80 – **402 rm** 105.00/120.00 **st.** – SB.

Stakis London Coburg, 129 Bayswater Rd, W2 4RJ, ✆ 221 2217, Fax 229 0557 – ▯ ⇔ rm ▤ rest TV ☎ – 100. MC AE D VISA. ✻ BZ c
Meals (dinner only) 16.50 **st.** and a la carte 4.95 – ☐ 9.95 – **131 rm** 95.00/115.00 **st.**, 1 suite – SB.

Hyde Park Towers, 41-51 Inverness Terr., W2 3JN, ✆ 221 8484, Fax 792 3201 – ▯ ▤ rest TV ☎ – 45. MC AE D VISA. ✻ BZ r
Meals *(closed Sunday lunch)* 13.95 **t.** and a la carte 4.50 – ☐ 7.50 – **114 rm** 96.00/106.00 **t.**

Queen's Park, 48 Queensborough Terr., W2 3SS, ✆ 229 8080, Fax 792 1330 – ▯ ▤ rest TV ☎ – 80. MC AE D VISA JCB. ✻ CZ s
Meals (dinner only) 13.00 and a la carte – ☐ 7.50 – **86 rm** 90.00/130.00 **st.** – SB.

Mornington without rest., 12 Lancaster Gate, W2 3LG, ✆ 262 7361, Fax 706 1028 – rm. ⓜ AE ⓓ VISA – **68 rm** 95.00/125.00 **st.** DZ

Aspects (at London Metropole H.), Edgware Rd, W2 1JU, ✆ 402 4141, Fax 724 8866 ≤ London – ▤. ⓜ AE ⓓ VISA JCB p. 5 GU
closed Saturday lunch, Sunday and Bank Holidays – **Meals** 20.95/30.50 **st.** and a la carte

Nipa (at Royal Lancaster H.), Lancaster Terr., W2 2TY, ✆ 262 6737, Fax 724 3191 – ▤ Ⓟ. ⓜ AE ⓓ VISA JCB DZ
closed Saturday lunch and Sunday – **Meals** - Thai - 22.00 **st.** and a la carte 11.00.

Poons, Unit 205, Whiteleys, Queensway, W2 4YN, ✆ 792 2884 – ▤. ⓜ AE ⓓ VISA
closed 24 to 27 December – **Meals** - Chinese - 15.00/25.00 **t.** and a la carte. BZ

Al San Vincenzo, 30 Connaught St., W2 2AE, ✆ 262 9623 – ⓜ VISA EZ
closed Saturday lunch and Sunday – **Meals** - Italian - (booking essential) a la carte 22.00/34.00 **t.** 7.50.

Jason's, Blomfield Rd, Little Venice, W9 2PD, ✆ 286 6752, Fax 266 4332, « Canalside setting » – ⓜ AE VISA JCB p 4 FU
closed Sunday dinner and 25 December – **Meals** - Seafood - 18.95/21.00 **t.** and a la carte

Royal China, 13 Queensway, W2 4QJ, ✆ 221 2535 – ▤ p 16 BZ
Meals - Chinese rest.

L'Accento, 16 Garway Rd, W2 4NH, ✆ 243 2201, Fax 243 2201 ⓜ VISA BZ
closed Bank Holidays – **Meals** - Italian - 15.50 **t.** and a la carte 17.50/22.00 **t.**

Belgravia – ✉ *SW1* – ☎ *0171* – *Except where otherwise stated see pp. 14 and 15.*

Lanesborough, 1 Lanesborough Pl., SW1X 7TA, ✆ 259 5599, Fax 259 5606, – rm ▤ ☎ & Ⓟ – 90. ⓜ AE ⓓ VISA JCB p 9 IY
The Conservatory : **Meals** 23.50/28.50 **st.** and a la carte – 16.50 – **86 rm** 195.00/375.00 **s.**, 9 suites.

The Berkeley, Wilton Pl., SW1X 7RL, ✆ 235 6000, Fax 235 4330, – rm ▤ ☎ – 220. ⓜ AE ⓓ VISA JCB. FQ
Restaurant : **Meals** 24.00/27.50 **st.** and a la carte 9.75 – (see also ***Vong*** below) – 17.00 – **130 rm** 210.00/395.00 **s.**, 26 suites.

Halkin, 5 Halkin St., SW1X 7DJ, ✆ 333 1000, Fax 333 1100, « Contemporary interior design » – rm ▤ ☎ Ⓟ – 25. ⓜ AE ⓓ VISA JCB. p 16 AV
Meals - Italian - *(closed lunch Saturday and Sunday)* 24.00 **st.** (lunch) and a la carte 38.00/46.00 **st.** 8.50 – 14.25 – **36 rm** 240.00/275.00 **s.**, 5 suites – SB
Spec. Salad of langoustine and asparagus with shellfish vinaigrette, Rabbit raviole with crayfish and courgettes, Monkfish casserole with vegetables, poached quail eggs and black truffle.

Sheraton Belgravia, 20 Chesham Pl., SW1X 8HQ, ✆ 235 6040, Fax 259 6243 – rm ▤ ☎ Ⓟ – 50. ⓜ AE ⓓ VISA JCB. FR
closed 21 December-6 January – **Meals** *(closed Saturday lunch)* 19.50 **t.** (lunch) and a la carte 21.85/30.40 **t.** 6.00 – 13.50 – **82 rm** 250.00/270.00 **s.**, 7 suites.

Lowndes (Hyatt), 21 Lowndes St., SW1X 9ES, ✆ 823 1234, Fax 235 1154, – rm ▤ ☎ Ⓟ – 25. ⓜ AE ⓓ VISA JCB. FR
Brasserie 21 : **Meals** 14.50 **st.** and a la carte 9.50 – 13.50 – **77 rm** 205.00/225.00 **s.**, 1 suite – SB.

Zafferano, 15 Lowndes St., SW1X 9ES, ✆ 235 5800, Fax 235 1971 – ▤. ⓜ AE VISA
closed Sunday, 2 weeks August, 1 week Christmas and Bank Holidays – **Meals** - Italian 17.50/22.50 **t.** and a la carte. FR

Vong (at The Berkeley H.), Wilton Pl., SW1X 7RL, ✆ 235 1010, Fax 235 1011 – ⓜ AE ⓓ VISA JCB FQ
closed Sunday lunch – **Meals** - French-Thai - 21.00 **st.** (lunch) and a la carte 25.00/47.25 **st**

Al Bustan, 27 Motcomb St., SW1X 8JU, ✆ 235 8277, Fax 235 1668 – ▤. ⓜ AE ⓓ VISA
closed 24 to 26 and 31 December and 1 January – **Meals** - Lebanese - a la carte 15.75/20.00 **t.** 6.00. FR

Motcombs, 26 Motcomb St., SW1X 8JU, ✆ 235 6382, Fax 245 6351 – ▤. ⓜ AE ⓓ VISA
closed Saturday lunch, Sunday, Easter, 25 December and Bank Holidays – **Meals** 14.75 **t.** (lunch) and a la carte 20.25/32.00 **t.** 9.95. FR

Hyde Park and Knightsbridge – ✉ *SW1/SW7* – ☎ *0171* – *pp. 14 and 15.*

Hyde Park (Forte), 66 Knightsbridge, SW1X 7LA, ✆ 235 2000, Fax 235 4552, ≤, – rm ▤ ☎ & – 250. ⓜ AE ⓓ VISA JCB. FQ
Park Room : **Meals** 25.00/35.00 **t.** and a la carte 19.00 (see also ***The Restaurant, Marco Pierre White*** below) – 16.50 – **168 rm** 260.00/290.00 **s.**, 17 suites

Knightsbridge Green without rest., 159 Knightsbridge, SW1X 7PD, ✆ 584 6274, Fax 225 1635 – ▤ ☎. ⓜ AE ⓓ VISA. EQ
closed 24 to 27 December – 9.50 – **13 rm** 85.00/120.00 **st.**, 12 suites 135.00 **st**

XXXX ✿✿✿ **The Restaurant, Marco Pierre White,** (at Hyde Park H.), 66 Knightsbridge, SW1X 7LA, ☎ 259 5380, Fax 235 4552 – ▤. MC AE ◑ VISA FQ x
closed Saturday lunch, Sunday, last 2 weeks August, last week December and first week January – **Meals** (booking essential) 29.00/70.00 **t.** 17.00
Spec. Terrine of foie gras with green peppercorns, Sauternes jelly, Escalope of sea bass with caviar, beignets of oyster, Champagne velouté, Tarte Tatin of pears with spices.

XXX **Pearl,** 22 Brompton Rd, SW1X 7QN, ☎ 225 3888, Fax 225 0252 – ▤. MC AE ◑ VISA
closed 25 and 26 December – **Meals** - Chinese - 10.00 **t.** (lunch) and a la carte 18.50/23.00 **t.** EQ e

XXX **Mr. Chow,** 151 Knightsbridge, SW1X 7PA, ☎ 589 7347, Fax 584 5780 – ▤. MC AE ◑ VISA JCB EQ a
closed 25 December, 1 January and Bank Holidays – **Meals** - Chinese - 13.00 **t.** (lunch) and a la carte 20.00/28.00 **t.** 8.50.

Mayfair – ✉ *W1* – ☎ *0171 – pp 12 and 13.*

Dorchester, Park Lane, W1A 2HJ, ☎ 629 8888, Fax 409 0114, Fā, ≘s – ⫼ ⇔ rm ▤ TV ☎ ♿ 🚗 – 🎤 550. MC AE ◑ VISA JCB. ✱ BN a
Meals – (see ***Oriental*** and ***Grill Room*** below) – ☕ 18.50 – **197 rm** 240.00/295.00 **s.**, 47 suites – SB.

Claridge's, Brook St., W1A 2JQ, ☎ 629 8860, Fax 499 2210 – ⫼ ⇔ rm ▤ TV ☎ ♿ – 🎤 200. MC AE ◑ VISA JCB. ✱ BL c
Restaurant : **Meals** 29.00/38.00 **st.** and a la carte 10.50 – ***Causerie :*** **Meals** *(closed Saturday and Sunday)* 28.00 **st.** (dinner) and a la carte 27.50/55.50 **st.** 10.50 – ☕ 16.50 – **134 rm** 210.00/330.00 **s.**, 58 suites – SB.

Four Seasons, Hamilton Pl., Park Lane, W1A 1AZ, ☎ 499 0888, Fax 493 1895, Fā – ⫼ ⇔ rm ▤ TV ☎ 🚗 – 🎤 500. MC AE ◑ VISA JCB. ✱ BP a
Lanes : **Meals** 25.00/28.00 **st.** and dinner a la carte – (see also ***Four Seasons*** below) – ☕ 16.00 – **201 rm** 240.00/295.00 **s.**, 26 suites.

Le Meridien Piccadilly (Forte), 21 Piccadilly, W1V 0BH, ☎ 734 8000, Fax 437 3574, Fā, ≘s, ▣, squash – ⫼ ⇔ rm ▤ TV ☎ ♿ – 🎤 250. MC AE ◑ VISA JCB. ✱
Terrace Garden : **Meals** 14.50 and a la carte 14.50 – (see also ***Oak Room*** below) – ☕ 14.50 – **248 rm** 230.00/270.00 **s.**, 18 suites – SB. EM a

Grosvenor House (Forte), Park Lane, W1A 3AA, ☎ 499 6363, Fax 493 3341, Fā, ≘s, ▣ – ⫼ ⇔ rm ▤ TV ☎ ♿ 🚗 – 🎤 1500. MC AE ◑ VISA JCB. ✱ AM a
Café Nico : **Meals** 26.00 **st.** and a la carte 9.00 – ***Pasta Vino :*** **Meals** - Italian - *(closed Saturday lunch and Sunday)* a la carte 26.50/38.50 **t.** 9.00 – (see also ***Chez Nico at Ninety Park Lane*** below) – ☕ 16.50 – **382 rm** 210.00/225.00 **s.**, 72 suites.

London Hilton on Park Lane, 22 Park Lane, W1Y 4BE, ☎ 493 8000, Fax 493 4957, « Panoramic ≤ of London », Fā – ⫼ ⇔ rm ▤ TV ☎ ♿ – 🎤 1000. MC AE ◑ VISA JCB. ✱
Trader Vics (☎ *208 4113)* **: Meals** (dinner only) a la carte approx. 25.00 **t.** – ***Park Brasserie :*** **Meals** 19.75 **t.** and a la carte – (see also ***Windows*** below) – ☕ 14.50 – **394 rm** 210.00/285.00 **s.**, 52 suites. BP e

✿ **Connaught,** Carlos Pl., W1Y 6AL, ☎ 499 7070, Fax 495 3262 – ⫼ ▤ TV ☎. MC AE ◑ VISA. ✱ BM e
The Restaurant : **Meals** (booking essential) 25.00/55.00 **t.** and a la carte 25.80/48.60 **t.** 11.50 – ***Grill Room :*** **Meals** *(closed Saturday lunch and Bank Holidays)* (booking essential) 25.00/35.00 **t.** and a la carte 25.80/48.60 **t.** 11.50 – **66 rm** 215.00/285.00 **s.**, 24 suites
Spec. Sole "Jubilee", Prelude gourmande Connaught, Sherry trifle "Wally Ladd".

47 Park Street, 47 Park St., W1Y 4EB, ☎ 491 7282, Fax 491 7281 – ⫼ ▤ TV ☎. MC AE ◑ VISA JCB. ✱ AM c
Meals (room service) – (see also ***Le Gavroche*** below) – ☕ 19.00 – **52 suites** 250.00/560.00 **s.**

Brown's (Forte), 29-34 Albemarle St., W1X 4BP, ☎ 493 6020, Fax 493 9381 – ⫼ ⇔ rm TV ☎ – 🎤 70. MC AE ◑ VISA JCB. ✱ DM e
Meals *(closed Saturday lunch)* 26.50 **t.** and a la carte 11.00 – ☕ 16.50 – **110 rm** 225.00/310.00, 6 suites – SB.

Park Lane, Piccadilly, W1Y 8BX, ☎ 499 6321, Fax 499 1965, Fā – ⫼ ⇔ rm TV ☎ 🅿 – 🎤 300. MC AE ◑ VISA JCB CP x
Brasserie on the Park : **Meals** 15.00 **st.** and a la carte 5.00 – (see also ***Bracewells*** below) – ☕ 12.00 – **273 rm** 210.00/230.00 **s.**, 30 suites.

Britannia, Grosvenor Sq., W1A 3AN, ☎ 629 9400, Fax 629 7736, Fā – ⫼ ⇔ rm ▤ TV ☎ – 🎤 100. MC AE ◑ VISA JCB. ✱ BM x
Adams : **Meals** 25.00 **t.** and a la carte 7.95 – ***Best of Both Worlds :*** **Meals** 19.00 **t.** and a la carte 7.95 – (see also ***Shogun*** below) – ☕ 15.95 – **306 rm** 155.00/250.00 **s.**, 12 suites.

UNITED KINGDOM

Westbury (Forte), Bond St., W1A 4UH, ☎ 629 7755, Fax 495 1163 – rm – 110. AE VISA JCB DM a
La Mediterranée 19.00 **st.** and a la carte 8.00 – 14.75 – **231 rm** 160.00/230.00 **s.**, 13 suites.

May Fair Inter-Continental, Stratton St., W1A 2AN, ☎ 629 7777, Fax 629 1459, – rm – 290. AE VISA JCB. DN z
May Fair Café *(☎ 915 2842)* **: Meals** 15.00 **t.** and a la carte – (see also ***The Chateau*** below) – 14.00 – **262 rm** 175.00/280.00, 25 suites.

Inter-Continental, 1 Hamilton Pl., Hyde Park Corner, W1V 0QY, ☎ 409 3131, Fax 409 7460, – rm – 1000. AE VISA JCB.
Meals 20.00/23.50 **t.** and a la carte 10.00 – (see also ***Le Soufflé*** below) – 17.95 – **412 rm** 210.00 **s.**, 48 suites. BP o

Athenaeum, 116 Piccadilly, W1V 0BJ, ☎ 499 3464, Fax 493 1860, – rm – 55. AE VISA. CP s
Bulloch's at 116 **: Meals** *(closed lunch Saturday and Sunday)* 24.50 **t.** and a la carte 9.50 – 15.50 – **121 rm** 215.00/295.00 **s.**, 35 suites.

London Marriott, Duke St., Grosvenor Sq., W1A 4AW, ☎ 493 1232, Fax 491 3201, – rm – 600. AE VISA JCB. BL a
Diplomat **: Meals** 19.50 **t.** (lunch) and a la carte 17.15/34.45 **t.** 12.25 – 12.25 – **210 rm** 215.00, 11 suites – SB.

Chesterfield, 35 Charles St., W1X 8LX, ☎ 491 2622, Fax 491 4793 – rm rest – 110. AE VISA JCB. CN c
Butlers **: Meals** *(closed Saturday lunch)* 8.50/22.50 **t.** and a la carte 7.95 – 14.00 – **106 rm** 130.00/180.00 **s.**, 4 suites.

Washington, 5-7 Curzon St., W1Y 8DT, ☎ 499 7000, Fax 495 6172 – rm – 80. AE VISA JCB CN s
Meals 19.95 **st.** (dinner) and a la carte 7.75 – 12.95 – **169 rm** 175.00/195.00 **st.**, 4 suites.

Holiday Inn Mayfair, 3 Berkeley St., W1X 6NE, ☎ 493 8282, Fax 629 2827 – rm – 60 DN r
179 rm, 6 suites.

Flemings, 7-12 Half Moon St., W1Y 7RA, ☎ 499 2964, Fax 629 4063 – rest – 45. AE VISA JCB. CN z
Meals 10.50/23.50 **st.** and a la carte 9.00 – 10.50 – **120 rm** 130.00/195.00 **st.**, 10 suites.

Green Park, Half Moon St., W1Y 8BP, ☎ 629 7522, Fax 491 8971 – rm rest – 70. AE VISA JCB. CN a
Meals *(closed lunch Saturday and Sunday)* 14.50 **st.** (lunch) and a la carte 18.65/29.65 **st.** 6.25 – 10.75 – **160 rm** 135.00/180.00 **st.**, 1 suite.

London Mews Hilton, 2 Stanhope Row, W1Y 7HE, ☎ 493 7222, Fax 629 9423 – rm – 50. AE VISA JCB. BP u
Meals (light lunch)/dinner 18.50 **t.** and a la carte – 13.50 – **71 rm** 164.00/221.00 **st.**, 1 suite.

Oak Room (at Le Meridien Piccadilly H.), 21 Piccadilly, W1V 0BH, ☎ 465 1640, Fax 437 3574 – . AE VISA JCB EM a
closed Saturday lunch and Sunday – **Meals** - French - 24.00/28.00 **st.** and a la carte.

Chez Nico at Ninety Park Lane (Ladenis) (at Grosvenor House H.), Park Lane, W1A 3AA, ☎ 409 1290, Fax 355 4877 – . AE VISA AM e
closed Saturday lunch, Sunday, 4 days at Easter, 10 days at Christmas and Bank Holiday Mondays – **Meals** - French - (booking essential) 29.00/60.00 **st.**
Spec. Rosette of grilled scallops, Saddle of lamb with a herb crust, Assiette gourmande.

Le Gavroche (Roux), 43 Upper Brook St., W1Y 1PF, ☎ 408 0881, Fax 409 0939 – . AE VISA AM c
closed Saturday, Sunday and Bank Holidays – **Meals** - French - (booking essential) 38.00/60.00 **st.** and a la carte 56.70/100.50 **st.**
Spec. Rouelle de homard sur ragoût de girolles à la sauge, Foie gras de canard rôti aux raisins, Bar en papillote farci au fenouil.

Oriental (at Dorchester H.), Park Lane, W1A 2HJ, ☎ 317 6328, Fax 409 0114 – . AE VISA JCB BN a
closed Saturday lunch, Sunday, August and Bank Holidays – **Meals** - Chinese (Canton) - 27.50/35.50 **st.** and a la carte 35.00/45.50 **st.** 8.50
Spec. Pan fried slices of goose liver with five-spice, Grilled fresh eel in honey barbecue sauce, Steamed chicken dumplings with crabmeat sauce.

Four Seasons (at Four Seasons H.), Hamilton Pl., Park Lane, W1A 1AZ, ☎ 499 0888, Fax 493 1895 – . AE VISA JCB BP a
Meals 25.00/45.00 **st.** and a la carte.

XXXX **Windows** (at London Hilton on Park Lane), 22 Park Lane, W1Y 4BE, ✆ 493 8000, « Panoramic ≤ of London » – ▤. MC AE DC VISA JCB BP e
closed Sunday dinner – **Meals** 35.95/33.50 **t.** and a la carte.

XXXX ✿ **Les Saveurs,** 37a Curzon St., W1Y 7AF, ✆ 491 8919, Fax 491 3658 – ▤. MC AE DC VISA JCB BN o
closed Saturday, Sunday and Bank Holidays – **Meals** - French - 22.00/47.00 **t.** 🍷 17.00
Spec. Soupe de rouget au saffran avec rouille, Noisettes d'agneau avec salpicon, câpres et persil, Soufflé au chocolat amer.

XXXX **Le Soufflé** (at Inter-Continental H.), 1 Hamilton Pl., Hyde Park Corner, W1V 0QY, ✆ 409 3131, Fax 409 7460 – ▤ 🚗. MC AE DC VISA JCB BP o
closed Sunday dinner and Monday – **Meals** 28.50/47.00 **t.** and a la carte 🍷 10.00.

XXX **Goode's at Thomas Goode,** 19 South Audley St., W1Y 6BN, ✆ 409 7242, Fax 629 4230 – ▤. MC AE DC VISA BM c
closed Saturday, Sunday, first 3 weeks August and Bank Holidays – **Meals** (lunch only) 37.50 **st.** 🍷 7.00.

XXX **Grill Room** (at Dorchester H.), Park Lane, W1A 2HJ, ✆ 317 6336, Fax 409 0114 – ▤. MC AE DC VISA JCB BN a
Meals - English - 27.50/35.50 **st.** and a la carte 31.50/43.50 **st.** 🍷 8.50.

XXX **Princess Garden,** 8-10 North Audley St., W1Y 1WF, ✆ 493 3223, Fax 629 3130 – ▤. MC AE DC VISA JCB AL z
closed 4 days Christmas – **Meals** - Chinese (Peking, Szechuan) - 40.00 **t.** (dinner) and a la carte 25.50/42.50 **t.** 🍷 8.00.

XXX **Bracewells** (at Park Lane H.), Piccadilly, W1Y 8BX, ✆ 753 6725, Fax 499 1965 – **P**. MC AE DC VISA JCB CP x
closed Saturday lunch, Sunday and Bank Holidays – **Meals** 26.00 **st.** (lunch) and a la carte 31.00/40.00 **st.** 🍷 6.00.

XXX **The Chateau** (at May Fair Inter-Continental H.), Stratton St., W1A 2AN, ✆ 915 2842, Fax 629 1459 – ▤. MC AE DC VISA JCB DN z
closed Saturday lunch – **Meals** a la carte 20.00/40.50 **t.**

XXX **Scotts,** 20 Mount St., W1Y 6HE, ✆ 629 5248, Fax 499 8246 – ▤. MC AE DC VISA JCB
closed Saturday lunch, 25-26 December and 1 January – **Meals** - Seafood - a la carte 22.00/44.00 **t.** BM a

XXX **Zen Central,** 20 Queen St., W1X 7PJ, ✆ 629 8089, Fax 493 6181 – ▤. MC AE DC VISA
Meals - Chinese - 28.00/42.00 **st.** and a la carte. CN x

XX **L'Odéon,** 65 Regent St., W1R 7HH, ✆ 287 1400, Fax 287 1300 – ▤. MC AE DC VISA JCB
closed Saturday lunch, 25-26 December and 1 January – **Meals** 16.50 **t.** (lunch) and dinner a la carte approx. 30.45 **t.** EM r

XX **Tamarind,** 20 Queen St., W1X 7PJ, ✆ 629 3561, Fax 499 5034 – MC AE DC VISA JCB
closed Saturday lunch, 25 December, 1 January and Bank Holidays – **Meals** - Indian - 16.50 **t.** (lunch) and a la carte 22.50/35.50 **t.** 🍷 9.50. CN e

XX **Greenhouse,** 27a Hay's Mews, W1X 7RJ, ✆ 499 3331, Fax 499 5368 – ▤. MC AE DC VISA JCB BN e
closed Saturday lunch, Christmas and Bank Holidays – **Meals** a la carte 27.90/36.30 **t.**

XX **Bentley's,** 11-15 Swallow St., W1R 7HD, ✆ 734 4756, Fax 287 2972 – ▤. MC AE DC VISA JCB EM i
closed Sunday – **Meals** - Seafood - 19.50 **t.** and a la carte 🍷 8.50.

XX **Nicole's,** 158 New Bond St., W1V 9PA, ✆ 499 8408, Fax 499 7522 – ▤. MC AE DC VISA
closed Saturday dinner, Sunday, 25 December and Bank Holidays – **Meals** a la carte 19.85/28.85 **t.** DM n

XX **Langan's Brasserie,** Stratton St., W1X 5FD, ✆ 491 8822 – ▤. MC AE DC VISA
closed Saturday lunch, Sunday, Good Friday, 25 December and Bank Holidays – **Meals** (booking essential) a la carte 21.50/28.00 **t.** DN e

XX **Benihana,** 37 Sackville St., Piccadilly, W1X 2DQ, ✆ 494 2525, Fax 494 1456 – ▤. MC AE DC VISA JCB EM s
Meals - Japanese (Teppan-Yaki) - a la carte 16.80/27.00.

XX **Gaucho Grill,** 19 Swallow St., W1R 7HD, ✆ 734 4040, Fax 734 1076 – ▤. MC AE DC VISA
closed 25-26 December and 1 January – **Meals** - Argentinian - a la carte 18.50/28.85 🍷 5.95. EM c

XX **Mulligans,** 13-14 Cork St., W1X 1PF, ✆ 409 1370, Fax 409 2732 – MC AE DC VISA JCB
closed Saturday lunch and Sunday – **Meals** - Irish - 17.95 **t.** (lunch) and a la carte 19.00/28.00 **t.** 🍷 6.50. DM c

XX **Shogun** (at Britannia H.), Adams Row, W1Y 5DE, ✆ 493 1255 – ▤. MC AE DC VISA JCB BM x
closed Monday – **Meals** - Japanese - (dinner only) 32.00 and a la carte.

Regent's Park and Marylebone - ✉ *NW1/NW6/NW8/W1* - *0171 - Except wher otherwise stated see pp. 12 and 13.*

Basement Services Arcade, Selfridges Store, Oxford St., W1 ℘ 824 8844.

Landmark London, 222 Marylebone Rd, NW1 6JQ, ℘ 631 8000, Fax 631 8092 « Victorian Gothic architecture, atrium and winter garden », - rm - 350. VISA JCB. p 5 HU
The Dining Room : **Meals** *(closed Sunday dinner)* 21.00 **st.** (lunch) and a la cart 28.00/39.50 13.75 - 15.95 - **294 rm** 225.00 **s.**, 10 suites.

Churchill Inter-Continental, 30 Portman Sq., W1A 4ZX, ℘ 486 5800, Fax 486 1255 - rm - 200. VISA JCB. AJ
Meals *(closed Saturday lunch)* 21.50 **t.** and a la carte 8.25 - 16.50 - **415 rr** 195.00/240.00, 33 suites.

Langham Hilton, 1 Portland Pl., Regent St., W1N 4JA, ℘ 636 1000, Fax 323 2340, - rm - 250. VISA JCB. p 5 JU
Memories : **Meals** 23.00/29.75 **st.** and dinner a la carte 8.75 - ***Tsar's :*** **Meals** *(close Sunday)* 20.75 8.75 - 16.50 - **359 rm** 230.00/450.00 **s.**, 20 suites.

Selfridge (Thistle), Orchard St., W1H 0JS, ℘ 408 2080, Fax 629 8849 - rm - 220. VISA JCB. AK
Fletchers : **Meals** *(closed Saturday lunch and Sunday)* 19.50 **t.** and a la carte - ***Orchard*** **Meals** 11.00 **t.** and a la carte - 12.50 - **290 rm** 170.00/220.00 **st.**, 4 suites - SB

The Leonard, 15 Seymour St., W1H 5AA, ℘ 935 2010, Fax 935 6700, « Attractivel furnished Georgian town houses » - - 30. VISA. AK
Meals (room service only) - 12.50 - **6 rm** 150.00 **s.**, **20 suites** 200.00/345.00 **s.**

Radisson SAS Portman, 22 Portman Sq., W1H 9FL, ℘ 208 6000, Fax 208 6001, - rm - 350. VISA JCB. AJ
Meals 16.50 **st.** (lunch) and a la carte 20.00/31.00 **st.** 10.00 - 15.50 - **272 rn** 208.00/288.00 **st.**, 7 suites.

Berkshire (Radisson Edwardian), 350 Oxford St., W1N 0BY, ℘ 629 7474, Fax 629 815 - rm - 40. VISA JCB BK
Meals *(closed Saturday and Sunday)* a la carte 16.00/27.00 **st.** 8.00 - 14.00 - **145 rn** 175.00/255.00 **st.**, 2 suites.

London Regent's Park Hilton, 18 Lodge Rd, NW8 7JT, ℘ 722 7722, Fax 483 240 - rm - 150. VISA JCB. p 5 GT
Minsky's : **Meals** 19.95 **st.** and a la carte 9.75 - ***Kashinoki :*** **Meals** - Japanese - *(close Monday)* 17.50/32.00 **t.** and a la carte 8.00 - 14.50 - **374 rm** 140.00/160.00 **st.** 3 suites.

Clifton Ford, 47 Welbeck St., W1M 8DN, ℘ 486 6600, Fax 486 7492 - - 150. VISA. BH
Meals a la carte approx. 25.00 **t.** 3.80 - 13.50 - **191 rm** 185.00/195.00 **s.**, 2 suites

Montcalm, Great Cumberland Pl., W1A 2LF, ℘ 402 4288, Fax 724 9180 - rm - 80. VISA JCB. p 17 EZ
Crescent : **Meals** *(closed lunch Saturday and Sunday)* 25.00 **st.** and a la carte 6.00 - 14.95 - **110 rm** 170.00/215.00, 10 suites.

Marble Arch Marriott, 134 George St., W1H 6DN, ℘ 723 1277, Fax 402 0666, - rm rest - 150. VISA JCB. p 17 EZ
Meals 19.95/23.95 **t.** and a la carte 7.95 - 12.95 - **240 rm** 155.00/175.00.

Berners, 10 Berners St., W1A 3BE, ℘ 636 1629, Fax 580 3972 - rm rest - 150. VISA JCB. EJ
Meals 16.95 **t.** and a la carte 7.50 - 13.75 - **214 rm** 140.00/210.00 **st.**, 3 suites

Forte Posthouse Regent's Park, Carburton St., W1P 8EE, ℘ 388 2300, Fax 387 280 - rm rest - 220. VISA JCB. p 5 JU
Meals 14.50/16.95 **t.** and a la carte - 10.95 - **315 rm** 125.00/140.00 **st.**, 2 suites - SB

St. George's (Forte), Langham Pl., W1N 8QS, ℘ 580 0111, Fax 436 7997, - rm - 25. VISA JCB. p 5 JU
Meals - (see ***The Heights*** below) - 12.95 - **83 rm** 150.00/180.00 **st.**, 3 suites - SB

Dorset Square, 39-40 Dorset Sq., NW1 6QN, ℘ 723 7874, Fax 724 3328, « Attractivel furnished Regency town houses », - . VISA. p 5 HU
Meals *(closed Sunday lunch and Saturday)* 15.95 and a la carte - 12.50 - **37 rr** 95.00/170.00 **s.**

Rathbone without rest., Rathbone St., W1P 2LB, ℘ 636 2001, Fax 636 3882 - . VISA JCB. p 6 KU
13.50 - **72 rm** 130.00/170.00 **st.**

Durrants, 26-32 George St., W1H 6BJ, ℘ 935 8131, Fax 487 3510, « Converted Georgian houses with Regency façade » - - 100. VISA. AH
Meals 18.00 **t.** and a la carte - 9.50 - **90 rm** 87.50/110.00 **st.**, 3 suites.

Savoy Court (Radisson Edwardian), Granville Pl., W1H 0EH, ✆ 408 0130, Fax 493 2070 – rest. AE VISA JCB AK i
Meals a la carte 21.00/27.00 **st.** 8.00 – 11.00 – **95 rm** 105.00/135.00 **st.**

Langham Court, 31-35 Langham St., W1N 5RE, ✆ 436 6622, Fax 436 2303 – – 80. AE VISA JCB. p 5 JU z
Meals *(closed lunch Saturday and Sunday)* 17.95 **st.** and a la carte – 9.50 – **56 rm** 105.00/135.00 **st.**

Stakis London Harewood, Harewood Row, NW1 6SE, ✆ 262 2707, Fax 262 2975 – rm rest. AE VISA. p 5 HU x
Meals (dinner only) 16.50 **t.** and a la carte 10.00 – 9.50 – **92 rm** 85.00/115.00 **st.** – SB.

Interlude de Chavot (Chavot), 5 Charlotte St., W1P 1HD, ✆ 637 0222, Fax 637 0224 – AE VISA p 6 KU r
closed Saturday lunch, Sunday, 2 weeks August and 2 weeks Christmas – **Meals** - French - a la carte 31.00/40.00 **t.** 11.00
Spec. Pan fried foie gras with a Tatin of caramelised endive, Stuffed rabbit leg with squid, pearl barley risotto, Sauternes and grapefruit jelly, chocolate and Grand Marnier samosa.

The Heights (at St. George's H.) (16th floor), Langham Pl., W1N 8QS, ✆ 636 1939, Fax 753 0259, ≤ London – AE VISA JCB p 5 JU a
restricted opening Christmas-New Year, closed Saturday lunch, Sunday and Bank Holidays – **Meals** 24.50 **st.** (lunch) and a la carte 30.00/39.00 **st.** 7.85.

Nico Central, 35 Great Portland St., W1N 5DD, ✆ 436 8846, Fax 436 3455 – AE VISA JCB DJ c
closed Saturday lunch, Sunday, 10 days Christmas and Bank Holidays – Meals 25.50/27.00 **st.** 8.00.

La Porte des Indes, 32 Bryanston St., W1H 7AE, ✆ 224 0055, Fax 224 1144 – AE VISA AK r
closed 25 and 26 December – **Meals** - Indian - 15.00/18.00 **t.** and a la carte.

Caldesi, 15-17 Marylebone Lane, W1M 5FE, ✆ 935 9226, Fax 929 0924 – AE VISA JCB BJ e
closed Saturday lunch, Sunday, 25 December and Bank Holidays – **Meals** - Italian - a la carte 17.40/28.35 **t.** 4.75.

Gaylord, 79-81 Mortimer St., W1N 7TB, ✆ 580 3615, Fax 631 5077 – AE VISA JCB p 6 KU o
Meals - Indian - 14.95 **t.** and a la carte 4.95.

Maroush III, 62 Seymour St., W1H 5AF, ✆ 724 5024, Fax 706 3493 – p. 17 EZ r
Meals - Lebanese rest.

Stephen Bull, 5-7 Blandford St., W1H 3AA, ✆ 486 9696, Fax 490 3128 – AE VISA
closed Saturday lunch, Sunday, 1 week Christmas and Bank Holidays – **Meals** a la carte 19.00/30.00 **t.** BH e

Sol e Stella, 43 Blandford St., W1H 3AE, ✆ 487 3336, Fax 486 3340 – AE VISA JCB. AH s
closed Saturday, Sunday, 25-26 December and 1 January – **Meals** - Italian - 8.95/11.95 **t.** and a la carte.

Asuka, Berkeley Arcade, 209a Baker St., NW1 6AB, ✆ 486 5026, Fax 224 1741 – AE VISA JCB p 5 HU u
closed Saturday lunch, Sunday and Bank Holidays – **Meals** - Japanese - 13.50/23.90 **t.** and a la carte.

The Blenheim, 21 Loudoun Rd, NW8 0NB, ✆ 625 1222, Fax 328 1593, – AE VISA p 4 FS a
closed Monday lunch and 5 days Christmas – **Meals** a la carte 13.15/29.10 **t.** 6.50.

Le Muscadet, 25 Paddington St., W1M 3RF, ✆ 935 2883 – VISA JCB
closed Saturday lunch, Sunday, last 3 weeks August, 1 week Christmas-New Year and Bank Holidays – **Meals** - French - a la carte 21.10/26.30 **t.** p 5 HU v

L'Aventure, 3 Blenheim Terr., NW8 0EH, ✆ 624 6232, Fax 625 5548 – AE VISA
closed Saturday lunch, 4 days Easter and 1 week Christmas – **Meals** - French - 18.50/25.00 **t.** 7.25. p 4 FS s

Nakamura, 31 Marylebone Lane, W1M 5FH, ✆ 935 2931, Fax 935 2931 – AE VISA JCB BJ i
closed lunch Sunday and Bank Holidays, Saturday, 2 weeks in summer and 25 December – **Meals** - Japanese - 12.50/26.90 **t.** and a la carte.

Zoe, 3-5 Barrett St., St. Christopher's Pl., W1M 5HH, ✆ 224 1122, Fax 935 5444 – AE VISA BJ a
closed Saturday lunch, Sunday and Bank Holidays – **Meals** a la carte 16.15/29.40 **t.**

Union Café, 96 Marylebone Lane, W1M 5FP, ✆ 486 4860 – VISA BH c
closed Saturday, Sunday, last week August and 2 weeks Christmas – **Meals** a la carte 16.50/24.75 **t.**

St. James's - ✉ W1/SW1/WC2 - ☎ 0171 - pp. 12 and 13.

Ritz, 150 Piccadilly, W1V 9DG, ☎ 493 8181, Fax 493 2687, – rm – 50. AE VISA JCB.
DN
Italian Garden : **Meals** (summer only) 28.00 **st.** (lunch) and a la carte 35.00/56.00 **st.** (see also ***The Restaurant*** below) – 17.75 – **116 rm** 215.00/285.00 **s.**, 14 suites – SB

Dukes, 35 St. James's Pl., SW1A 1NY, ☎ 491 4840, Fax 493 1264 – 50. AE VISA JCB.
EP
Meals *(closed Saturday lunch)* (residents only) a la carte 24.45/31.45 6.75 – 14.0
– **55 rm** 165.00/215.00 **s.**, 9 suites.

22 Jermyn Street, 22 Jermyn St., SW1Y 6HL, ☎ 734 2353, Fax 734 0750 – ☎. AE VISA JCB.
FM
Meals (restricted room service only) – 16.50 – **5 rm** 185.00 **s.**, **13 suite** 235.00/270.00 **s.**

Stafford, 16-18 St. James's Pl., SW1A 1NJ, ☎ 493 0111, Fax 493 7121 – ☎ – 35. AE VISA.
DN
Meals *(closed Saturday lunch)* 22.50/25.00 **s.** and a la carte 8.00 – 15.50 – **75 rm** 170.00/215.00 **s.**, 5 suites.

Cavendish (Forte), 81 Jermyn St., SW1Y 6JF, ☎ 930 2111, Fax 839 2125 – rm rest ☎ – 80. AE VISA JCB.
EN
Meals 17.50 **st.** (lunch) and dinner a la carte 20.00/29.00 **st.** 6.95 – 13.95 – **252 rm** 135.00/155.00 **s.**, 3 suites – SB.

Pastoria (Radisson Edwardian), 3-6 St. Martin's St., off Leicester Sq., WC2H 7HL ☎ 930 8641, Fax 925 0551 – rm rest ☎ – 60. AE VISA JCB
Meals 11.00 **st.** 8.00 – 11.00 – **58 rm** 145.00/185.00 **st.**
GM

Royal Trafalgar Thistle, Whitcomb St., WC2H 7HG, ☎ 930 4477, Fax 925 2149 – rm ☎. AE VISA JCB.
GM
Meals 12.50/14.50 **st.** and a la carte 5.50 – 11.25 – **108 rm** 120.00/155.00 **st.** SB.

Hospitality Inn Piccadilly (Mount Charlotte) without rest., 39 Coventry St., W1V 8EL ☎ 930 4033, Fax 925 2586 – ☎. AE VISA JCB.
FGM
11.25 – **92 rm** 125.00/155.00 **st.**

The Restaurant (at Ritz H.), 150 Piccadilly, W1V 9DG, ☎ 493 8181, Fax 493 2687,
« Elegant restaurant in Louis XVI style » – . AE VISA JCB
DN
Meals (dancing Friday and Saturday evenings) 28.00/36.50 **st.** and a la carte 35.00/56.00 **st.**

Quaglino's, 16 Bury St., SW1Y 6AL, ☎ 930 6767, Fax 839 2866 – . AE VISA
EN
closed 25 and 26 December – **Meals** (booking essential) 13.95 **t.** (lunch) and a la carte 24.00/76.00 **t.** 6.00.

Suntory, 72-73 St. James's St., SW1A 1PH, ☎ 409 0201, Fax 499 0208 – . AE VISA JCB
EP
closed Sunday and Bank Holidays – **Meals** - Japanese - 20.00/49.80 **st.** and a la carte 35.00/89.20 **st.** 12.00.

The Square, 32 King St., SW1Y 6RJ, *(expected move during 1997 to 10 Bruton St., Mayfair ☎ 495 7100)* ☎ 495 7100, Fax 495 7150 – . AE VISA
CM
closed lunch Saturday and Sunday, 25 December and 1 January – **Meals** 39.50 **t** 9.50
Spec. Crisp red mullet, lasagne of sardines and tomato, Thinly sliced rump of veal, purée of artichokes, fondant potatoes, Warm salad of duck, deep fried vegetables and balsamic vinegar.

33, 33 St. James's St., SW1A 1HD, ☎ 930 4272, Fax 930 7618 – . AE VISA
closed Saturday lunch and Sunday – **Meals** 21.90 **t.** (lunch) and a la carte 22.85/36.85 **t** 11.00.
EN

L'Oranger, 5 St. James's St., SW1A 1EF, ☎ 839 3774, Fax 839 4330, – . AE VISA
EP
closed Sunday lunch – **Meals** 19.50/22.00 **t.**
Spec. Ravioli of duck confit, cep consommé, Pan fried cod with wild mushroom duxelle, Fine plum tart with vanilla ice cream.

Criterion Brasserie Marco Pierre White, 224 Piccadilly, W1V 9LB, ☎ 930 0488, Fax 930 8190, « 19C Neo-Byzantine decor » – AE VISA
FM
Meals 14.00 **t.** (lunch) and a la carte 20.00/28.95 **t.** 6.25.

Le Caprice, Arlington House, Arlington St., SW1A 1RT, ☎ 629 2239, Fax 493 9040 – . AE VISA
DN
closed 24-26 December and 1 January – **Meals** a la carte 22.50/35.75 **t.**

XX **The Avenue,** 7-9 St. James's St., SW1A 1EE, ✆ 321 2111, Fax 321 2500 – ▤. MC AE ⓓ VISA EP e
closed 25-26 December and 1 January – **Meals** 19.50 **t.** (lunch) and dinner a la carte 24.25/34.75 **t.**

XX **Matsuri,** 15 Bury St., SW1Y 6AL, ✆ 839 1101, Fax 930 7010 – ▤. MC AE ⓓ VISA JCB
closed Sunday and Bank Holidays – **Meals** - Japanese (Teppan-Yaki, Sushi) - a la carte 21.00/26.00 **t.** 🍷 10.50. EN r

Soho – ✉ *W1/WC2* – ☎ *0171 – pp 12 and 13.*

Hampshire (Radisson Edwardian), Leicester Sq., WC2H 7LH, ✆ 839 9399, Fax 930 8122 – |♦| ⇴ rm ▤ TV ☎ – 🎪 80. MC AE ⓓ VISA JCB GM s
Meals a la carte 15.00/26.00 **st.** 🍷 9.00 – ☕ 14.00 – **120 rm** 230.00/265.00 **st.**, 4 suites.

Hazlitt's without rest., 6 Frith St., W1V 5TZ, ✆ 434 1771, Fax 439 1524 – TV ☎. MC AE ⓓ VISA JCB. ✻ FK u
closed 25 and 26 December – **22 rm** 115.00/145.00 **s.**, 1 suite.

XXXXX ✿ **Grill Room at the Café Royal,** 68 Regent St., W1R 6EL, ✆ 437 9090, Fax 439 7672, « Rococo decoration » – ▤. MC AE ⓓ VISA JCB EM e
closed Saturday lunch, Sunday, 26 to 30 December and Bank Holidays – **Meals** 24.50/39.00 **st.** and a la carte 39.50/51.00 **st.** 🍷 7.25
Spec. Carpaccio of tuna and scallops, Tournedos of Angus beef, gratin of parsnips, foie gras and truffles, Iced prune and Armagnac soufflé with candied orange peel.

XXX **Au Jardin des Gourmets,** 5 Greek St., W1V 6NA, ✆ 437 1816, Fax 437 0043 – ▤. MC AE ⓓ VISA JCB GJ a
closed Saturday lunch, Sunday, 25 December and Bank Holidays – **Meals** - French - 23.00 **t.** and a la carte 🍷 4.90.

XXX **Lindsay House,** 21 Romilly St., W1V 5TG, ✆ 439 0450, Fax 581 2848 – ▤. MC AE ⓓ VISA JCB GL i
closed 25 and 26 December – **Meals** 16.75 **t.** (lunch) and a la carte 23.50/37.25 **t.** 🍷 5.50.

XXX ✿ **L'Escargot,** 48 Greek St., W1V 5LQ, ✆ 437 2679, Fax 437 0790 – ▤. MC AE ⓓ VISA JCB GK e
Ground Floor : **Meals** *(closed Saturday lunch and Sunday)* 23.85 **t.** – ***First Floor :*** **Meals** *(closed Saturday lunch, Sunday, Monday, August and Bank Holidays)* 28.00/38.00 **t.**
Spec. Tartlet of snails, smoked bacon and morels, Sea bass, vermouth cream, Cornfed chicken, sauce vessie, purée of herbs.

XX **Red Fort,** 77 Dean St., W1V 5HA, ✆ 437 2115, Fax 434 0721 – ▤. MC AE ⓓ VISA
Meals - Indian - (buffet lunch) 12.50 **t.** (lunch) and a la carte 22.95/32.50 🍷 7.50. FJK r

XX **Mezzo,** Lower ground floor, 100 Wardour St., W1V 3LE, ✆ 314 4000, Fax 314 4040 – ▤. MC AE ⓓ VISA FK a
closed Saturday lunch – **Meals** 19.50 **t.** (lunch) and a la carte 19.50/39.50 **t.**

XX **Soho Soho,** (first floor), 11-13 Frith St., W1V 5TS, ✆ 494 3491, Fax 437 3091 – ▤. MC AE ⓓ VISA FK s
closed Saturday lunch, Sunday, 25 December and Bank Holidays – **Meals** 17.95 **t.** (dinner) and a la carte 19.25/24.70 **t.** 🍷 9.25.

XX **Brasserie at the Café Royal,** 68 Regent St., W1R 6EL, ✆ 437 9090, Fax 439 7672 – ▤. MC AE ⓓ VISA JCB EM e
closed Sunday dinner – **Meals** 13.50/16.50 **st.** and a la carte 🍷 7.75.

XX **Lexington,** 45 Lexington St., W1R 3LG, ✆ 434 3401, Fax 287 2997 – ▤. MC AE ⓓ VISA
closed Saturday lunch, Sunday, 1 week Christmas-New Year and Bank Holidays – **Meals** a la carte 18.00/25.25 **t.** EK e

XX **Gopal's,** 12 Bateman St., W1V 5TD, ✆ 434 0840 – ▤. MC AE VISA FK e
Meals - Indian - a la carte 16.20/26.05 **t.**

XX **Gay Hussar,** 2 Greek St., W1V 6NB, ✆ 437 0973, Fax 437 4631 – ▤. MC AE ⓓ VISA GJ c
closed Sunday and Bank Holidays – **Meals** - Hungarian - 16.00 **t.** (lunch) and a la carte 18.10/26.30 🍷 7.50.

XX **Atelier,** 41 Beak St., W1R 3LE, ✆ 287 2057, Fax 287 1767 – MC AE ⓓ VISA EL a
closed Saturday lunch, Sunday, 2 weeks August, 2 weeks Christmas-New Year and Bank Holidays – **Meals** 19.50 **t.** and a la carte 23.00/28.25 **t.**

X **dell'Ugo,** 56 Frith St., W1V 5TA, ✆ 734 8300, Fax 734 8784 – MC AE ⓓ VISA FK z
closed Sunday and Bank Holidays – **Meals** 12.95 **t.** (lunch) and a la carte 16.75/26.25 **t.**

X **Sri Siam,** 16 Old Compton St., W1V 5PE, ✆ 434 3544, Fax 287 1311 – ▤. MC AE ⓓ VISA GK r
closed Sunday lunch, 25-26 December and 1 January – **Meals** - Thai - 11.00/14.95 **t.** and a la carte.

Alastair Little, 49 Frith St., W1V 5TE, ✆ 734 5183 – MC AE VISA JCB FK c
closed Saturday lunch, Sunday and Bank Holidays – **Meals** (booking essential) 15.00/28.00 **t.**

Bruno Soho, 63 Frith St., W1V 5TA, ✆ 734 4545, Fax 287 1027 – ▤. MC AE ⓓ VISA
closed Sunday, Christmas-New Year and Bank Holidays – **Meals** - Middle Eastern - 16.50 **t.** (lunch) and a la carte 18.50/29.50 **t.** ₰ 4.50. FK z

Poons, 4 Leicester St., Leicester Sq., WC2H 7BL, ✆ 437 1528 – ▤. MC AE VISA JCB
closed 24 to 26 December – **Meals** - Chinese - 14.00/17.00 **t.** and a la carte. GM e

Andrew Edmunds, 46 Lexington St., W1R 3LH, ✆ 437 5708, Fax 439 2551 – MC AE VISA EK c
closed Easter Bank Holiday and Christmas-New Year – **Meals** a la carte 12.15/18.15 **t.**

Fung Shing, 15 Lisle St., WC2H 7BE, ✆ 734 0284, Fax 734 0284 – ▤. MC AE ⓓ VISA GL a
closed 24 to 26 December – **Meals** - Chinese (Canton) - 14.50 **t.** and a la carte ₰ 5.00

Saigon, 45 Frith St., W1V 5TE, ✆ 437 7109, Fax 734 1668 – ▤. MC AE ⓓ VISA FGK x
closed Sunday and Bank Holidays – **Meals** - Vietnamese - a la carte 11.60/17.80 ₰ 8.50

Strand and Covent Garden – ✉ *WC2* – ☎ *0171* – *p 17.*

The Savoy, Strand, WC2R 0EU, ✆ 836 4343, Fax 240 6040, ₣₺, ≘s, ▣ – ▮ ⇔ rm ▤ TV ☎ 🚗 – 🏛 500. MC AE ⓓ VISA JCB. ✂ DEY a
Grill : **Meals** *(closed Saturday lunch, Sunday, August and Bank Holidays)* a la carte 35.50/44.25 **t.** ₰ 9.00 – ***River :*** **Meals** 27.50/32.90 **st.** and a la carte ₰ 9.00 – ☐ 16.25 – **154 rm** 195.00/320.00 **s.**, 48 suites – SB.

Waldorf Meridien (Forte), Aldwych, WC2B 4DD, ✆ 836 2400, Fax 836 7244 – ▮ ⇔ rm ▤ rm TV ☎ – 🏛 450. MC AE ⓓ VISA JCB. ✂ EX x
Meals *(closed lunch Saturday and Sunday)* 26.00 **st.** (lunch) and a la carte 25.00/35.00 **st.** – ***Aldwych Brasserie :*** **Meals** a la carte 14.45/20.40 **st.** ₰ 7.50 – ☐ 15.00 – **286 rm** 190.00/210.00 **s.**, 6 suites – SB.

The Howard, Temple Pl., WC2R 2PR, ✆ 836 3555, Fax 379 4547, ← – ▮ ⇔ rm ▤ TV ☎ 🚗 – 🏛 100. MC AE ⓓ VISA JCB. ✂ EX e
Meals 25.00 **st.** and a la carte – ☐ 17.00 – **133 rm** 220.00/240.00 **st.**, 2 suites.

Ivy, 1 West St., WC2H 9NE, ✆ 836 4751, Fax 497 3644 – ▤. MC AE ⓓ VISA
closed dinner 24 to 26 December and lunch Bank Holidays – **Meals** a la carte 22.50/35.75 **t.** p 13 GK z

WestZENders, 4a Upper St. Martin's Lane, WC2H 9EA, ✆ 497 0376, Fax 497 0378 – ▤. MC AE ⓓ VISA DX x
closed 25 and 26 December – **Meals** - Chinese - 10.80/18.80 **t.** and a la carte.

Rules, 35 Maiden Lane, WC2E 7LB, ✆ 836 5314, Fax 497 1081, « London's oldest restaurant with collection of antique cartoons, drawings and paintings » – MC AE ⓓ VISA
closed 23 to 26 December – **Meals** - English - a la carte 23.15/31.40 **t.** ₰ 5.25. DX n

Christopher's, 18 Wellington St., WC2E 7DD, ✆ 240 4222, Fax 240 3357 – MC AE ⓓ VISA JCB EX z
closed Saturday lunch, Sunday, Christmas and Bank Holidays – **Meals** a la carte 15.50/30.75 **t.**

Orso, 27 Wellington St., WC2E 7DA, ✆ 240 5269, Fax 497 2148 – ▤. MC AE VISA EX z
closed 24 and 25 December – **Meals** - Italian - (booking essential) a la carte 16.00/28.50 **t.** ₰ 5.50.

L'Estaminet, 14 Garrick St., off Floral St., WC2 9BJ, ✆ 379 1432 – MC AE VISA JCB
closed Sunday, Easter, Christmas and Bank Holidays – **Meals** - French - a la carte 16.90/26.30 **t.** ₰ 4.60. DX a

Sheekey's, 28-32 St. Martin's Court, WC2N 4AL, ✆ 240 2565, Fax 240 8114 – ▤. MC AE ⓓ VISA DX v
closed Sunday, Easter, 25 December and Bank Holidays – **Meals** - Seafood - 18.75 **t.** and a la carte.

Bertorelli's, 44a Floral St., WC2E 9DA, ✆ 836 3969, Fax 836 1868 – ▤. MC AE ⓓ VISA JCB DX c
closed Sunday – **Meals** - Italian - a la carte 13.60/20.65 **t.**

Le Café du Jardin, 28 Wellington St., WC2E 7BD, ✆ 836 8769, Fax 836 4123 – ▤. MC AE ⓓ VISA EX a
closed 25 December – **Meals** 13.50 **t.** and a la carte.

Magno's Brasserie, 65a Long Acre, WC2E 9JH, ✆ 836 6077, Fax 379 6184 – ▤. MC AE ⓓ VISA JCB DV e
closed Saturday lunch and Sunday – **Meals** - French - 16.95 **t.** and a la carte ₰ 7.95.

Joe Allen, 13 Exeter St., WC2E 7DT, ✆ 836 0651, Fax 497 2148 – ▤. MC AE VISA EX c
closed 24 and 25 December – **Meals** 13.00 **t.** (lunch) and a la carte 17.00/24.00 **t.** ₰ 5.50.

Victoria - SW1 - 0171 - *Except where otherwise stated see p 16.*
Victoria Station Forecourt, SW1V 1JU 824 8844.

St. James Court, 45 Buckingham Gate, SW1E 6AF, 834 6655, Fax 630 7587, - rm - 180. MC AE DC VISA JCB. CX i
Café Mediterranée : **Meals** 15.00 **t.** (lunch) and a la carte 17.90/30.75 **t.** 8.50 – ***Inn of Happiness :*** **Meals** - Chinese - 15.00/23.00 **st.** and a la carte – (see also ***Auberge de Provence*** below) – 14.00 – **372 rm** 150.00/165.00 **s.**, 18 suites.

Royal Horseguards Thistle, 2 Whitehall Court, SW1A 2EJ, 839 3400, Fax 925 2263 – rm rest – 60. MC AE DC VISA JCB. p 10 LX a
Meals *(closed Saturday lunch and Sunday)* 22.50 **st.** and a la carte 8.75 – 11.50 – **304 rm** 150.00/210.00 **st.**, 6 suites.

Stakis London St. Ermin's, Caxton St., SW1H 0QW, 222 7888, Fax 222 6914 – rm rest – 250. MC AE DC VISA. CX a
Meals *(closed lunch Saturday and Sunday)* (carving rest.) 19.95 and a la carte – ***Caxton Grill :*** **Meals** *(closed Saturday lunch and Sunday)* 18.95/21.95 **t.** and dinner a la carte – 10.95 – **288 rm** 135.00/155.00 **st.**, 2 suites – SB .

Goring, 15 Beeston Pl., Grosvenor Gdns., SW1W 0JW, 396 9000, Fax 834 4393 – rm – 50. MC AE DC VISA. BX a
Meals 22.00/30.00 **t.** 8.00 – 13.00 – **72 rm** 148.00/205.00 **s.**, 4 suites.

Royal Westminster Thistle, 49 Buckingham Palace Rd, SW1W 0QT, 834 1821, Fax 931 7542 – rm – 180. MC AE DC VISA JCB. BX z
Meals 13.60/23.00 **st.** and a la carte 8.00 – 11.25 – **134 rm** 140.00/290.00 **st.**

Grosvenor Thistle, 101 Buckingham Palace Rd, SW1W 0SJ, 834 9494, Fax 630 1978 – rm – 200. MC AE DC VISA JCB. BX e
Meals (carving rest.) 16.35 **t.** and a la carte 6.00 – 9.95 – **363 rm** 115.00/175.00 **t.**, 3 suites.

Dolphin Square, Dolphin Sq., SW1V 3LX, 834 3800, Fax 798 8735, squash – rest – 50. MC AE DC VISA. p 10 KZ a
Meals 13.95/16.95 **st.** and a la carte 7.50 – 12.50 – **14 rm** 99.00/132.00 **st.**, **137 suites** 144.00/170.00 **st.**

Rubens, 39-41 Buckingham Palace Rd, SW1W 0PS, 834 6600, Fax 828 5401 – rm rest – 75. MC AE DC VISA JCB. BX n
Meals (carving lunch) 15.95 **st.** and a la carte 6.95 – 9.95 – **178 rm** 110.00/150.00 **st.**, 1 suite.

Holiday Inn Victoria, 2 Bridge Pl., SW1V 1QA, 834 8123, Fax 828 1099, – rm – 150. MC AE DC VISA JCB. BY i
Meals 17.95/18.50 **st.** and dinner a la carte 6.50 – 11.50 – **212 rm** 140.00/250.00 **st.** – SB .

Rochester, 69 Vincent Sq., SW1P 2PA, 828 6611, Fax 233 6724 – rest – 60. MC AE DC VISA JCB. CY e
Meals 17.95 **st.** and a la carte – 9.50 – **80 rm** 109.00/149.00 **st.**

Auberge de Provence (at St. James Court H.), 45 Buckingham Gate, SW1E 6AF, 821 1899, Fax 630 7587 – . MC AE DC VISA JCB CX i
closed Saturday lunch, Sunday and Bank Holidays – **Meals** - French - 25.50/32.50 **t.** and dinner a la carte 12.50.

L'Incontro, 87 Pimlico Rd, SW1W 8PH, 730 6327, Fax 730 5062 – . MC AE DC VISA JCB p 15 FT u
closed lunch Saturday and Sunday and 25-26 December – **Meals** - Italian - 18.50 **t.** (lunch) and a la carte 28.00/46.00 **t.** 11.50.

Santini, 29 Ebury St., SW1W 0NZ, 730 4094, Fax 730 0544 – . MC AE DC VISA JCB ABX v
closed lunch Saturday and Sunday and 25-26 December – **Meals** - Italian - 18.75 **t.** (lunch) and a la carte 25.50/43.00 **t.** 8.00.

Shepherd's, Marsham Court, Marsham St., SW1P 4LA, 834 9552, Fax 233 6047 – . MC AE DC VISA p 10 LZ z
closed Saturday, Sunday, Good Friday, 25 December and Bank Holidays – **Meals** - English - (booking essential) 21.95 **t.**

Simply Nico, 48a Rochester Row, SW1P 1JU, 630 8061 – . MC AE DC VISA JCB CY a
closed Saturday lunch, Sunday, 2 weeks Christmas and Bank Holidays – **Meals** (booking essential) 25.00/27.00 **st.** 10.00.

Atrium, 4 Millbank, SW1P 3JA, 233 0032, Fax 233 0010 – . MC AE DC VISA p 10 LY s
closed Saturday lunch, Sunday, 25-26 December and 1 January – 19.95 **t.** 4.50.

XX **Ken Lo's Memories of China,** 67-69 Ebury St., SW1W 0NZ, ✆ 730 7734 Fax 730 2992 – ▤. MC AE ◑ VISA JCB AY
closed Sunday lunch and Bank Holidays – **Meals** - Chinese - 19.50/23.80 **t.** and a la carte.

XX **L'Amico,** 44 Horseferry Rd, SW1P 2AF, ✆ 222 4680 – MC AE ◑ VISA p 10 LY
closed Saturday, Sunday, Easter, Christmas and Bank Holidays – **Meals** - Italian - (booking essential) 16.50/18.50 **t.** and a la carte.

XX **Hunan,** 51 Pimlico Rd, SW1W 8NE, ✆ 730 5712 – MC AE VISA p 9 IZ
closed Sunday lunch, Christmas-New Year and Bank Holidays – **Meals** - Chinese (Hunan) 22.00 **t.** (dinner) and a la carte 23.00/40.00 **t.**

XX **Tate Gallery,** Tate Gallery, Millbank, SW1P 4RG, ✆ 887 8877, Fax 887 8007 « Rex Whistler murals » – ▤. MC AE VISA p. 10 LZ
closed Sunday – **Meals** (booking essential) (lunch only) 23.00 **st.** and a la carte.

XX **Gran Paradiso,** 52 Wilton Rd, SW1V 1DE, ✆ 828 5818, Fax 828 3608 – MC AE ◑ VISA JCB BY
closed Saturday lunch, Sunday and Bank Holidays – **Meals** - Italian - a la carte 17.00/21.50 **t** 🍷 5.00.

XX **Joyful,** 72-73 Wilton Rd, SW1V 1DE, ✆ 828 9300, Fax 630 8481 – ▤. MC AE ◑ VISA BY
closed Monday and 24 to 28 December – **Meals** - Chinese (Peking, Canton) - 14.50 **t.** and a la carte 🍷 4.00.

X **Olivo,** 21 Eccleston St., SW1W 9LX, ✆ 730 2505, Fax 824 8190 – ▤. MC AE VISA
closed Saturday lunch and Bank Holidays – **Meals** - Italian - 15.50 **t.** (lunch) and dinner a la carte 17.00/24.00. AY

X **La Poule au Pot,** 231 Ebury St., SW1W 8UT, ✆ 730 7763, Fax 259 9651, 🏡 – ▤ MC AE ◑ VISA p 9 IZ
Meals - French - 13.75 **t.** (lunch) and a la carte 23.25/36.00 **t.** 🍷 5.50.

Bray-on-Thames

Berks. W : 34 m. by M 4 (junction 8-9) and A 308 404 *R 29 – pop. 8 121 –* ✉ *Maidenhead –* ☎ *01628.*

XXXX ✿✿✿ **Waterside Inn** (Roux) with rm, Ferry Rd, SL6 2AT, ✆ 20691, Fax 784710, « ≤ Thames-side setting » – ▤ rest TV ☎ P. MC AE ◑ VISA JCB. ✂
closed 26 December-31 January – **Meals** - French - (closed Tuesday lunch, Sunday dinner from mid October-mid April, Monday and Bank Holidays) 29.50/68.50 **st.** and a la carte 58.80/88.60 **st.** 🍷 10.00 – **6 rm** 135.00/165.00 **st.**, 1 suite
Spec. Tronçonnettes de homard poêlées minute au Porto blanc, Filets de lapereau grillés aux marrons glacés, Soufflé chaud aux framboises.

Reading

Berks. at Shinfield W : 43 m. by M 4 and A 329 on A 327 403 404 *Q 29 – pop. 213 474 –* ☎ *0118 9.*
🅱 *Town Hall, Blagrave St., RG1 1QH* ✆ *566226.*

XXX ✿✿ **L'Ortolan** (Burton-Race), The Old Vicarage, Church Lane, RG2 9BY, ✆ 883783, Fax 885391, 🏡 – P. MC AE ◑ VISA
closed Sunday dinner, Monday and last 2 weeks February – **Meals** - French - 29.50/39.50 **t.** and a la carte 60.00/82.50 **t.** 🍷 10.00
Spec. Assiette de foie gras, Escalope de turbot étuvé au basilic, au coulis de tomate, sauce vierge, Assiette framboisière.

Oxford

Oxon. at Great Milton NW : 49 m. by M 40 (junction 7) and A 329 403 404 *Q 28 – pop. 118 795 –* ✉ *Great Milton –* ☎ *01865.*
🅱 *The Old School, Gloucester Green, OX1 2DA* ✆ *726871.*

🏰 ✿✿ **Le Manoir aux Quat' Saisons** (Blanc) 🐌, Church Rd, OX44 7PD, ✆ 278881, Fax 278847, ≤, « Part 15C and 16C manor house, gardens », 🏊 heated, *park*, 🎾 – ⇆ rest ▤ rest TV ☎ P – 🏛 35. MC AE ◑ VISA JCB. ✂
Meals 29.50/69.00 **t.** and a la carte 65.00/76.00 **t.** – ☕ 14.50 – **16 rm** 185.00/285.00 **t.**, 3 suites – SB
Spec. Foie gras de canard poêlé aux pommes, boudin noir, cannelle et noisettes, Nage de poissons et coquillages à la noix de coco, Le Café Crème.

Send us your comments on the restaurants we recommend and your opinion on the specialities and local wines they offer.

IRMINGHAM W. Mids. 403 404 O 26 **Great Britain G.** – pop. 965 928 – ☎ 0121.

See : City★ – Museum and Art Gallery★★ JZ **M2** – Barber Institute of Fine Arts★★ (at Birmingham University) EX – Museum of Science and Industry★ JY **M3** – Cathedral of St. Philip (stained glass portrayals★) KYZ.

Envir. : Aston Hall★★ FV **M.**

Exc. : Black Country Museum★, Dudley, NW : 10 m. by A 456 and A 4123.

⛳18 Edgbaston, Church Rd ℘ 454 1736 FX – ⛳18 Hilltop, Park Lane, Handsworth ℘ 554 4463 – ⛳18 Hatchford Brook, Coventry Rd, Sheldon ℘ 743 9821 HX – ⛳18 Brand Hall, Heron Rd, Oldbury, Warley ℘ 552 2195 – ⛳9 Harborne Church Farm, Vicarage Rd, Harborne ℘ 427 1204 EX.

✈ Birmingham International Airport : ℘ 767 5511, E : 6 ½ m. by A 45.

ℹ Convention Visitor Bureau, 2 City Arcade, B2 4TX ℘ 643 2514, Fax 616 1038 – Convention Visitor Bureau, National Exhibition Centre, B40 1NT ℘ 780 4321 – Birmingham Airport, Information Desk, B26 3QJ, ℘ 767 7145/7146.

London 122 – Bristol 91 – Liverpool 103 – Manchester 86 – Nottingham 50.

Plans on following pages

Hyatt Regency, 2 Bridge St., B1 2JZ, ℘ 643 1234, Fax 616 2323, ≤, Ƒ₆, ≘s, ☒ – |♯| ⇔ rm ▤ TV ☎ ⇔ – ♣ 250. MC AE ◑ VISA JCB. ✻ JZ a
Meals – (see ***Number 282*** below) – ☕ 12.00 – **308 rm** 108.00 **st.**, 11 suites.

Swallow, 12 Hagley Rd, B16 8SJ, ℘ 452 1144, Fax 456 3442, Ƒ₆, ☒ – |♯| ⇔ rm ▤ TV ☎ ♿ P – ♣ 25. MC AE ◑ VISA FX c
Langtrys : Meals *(closed Sunday)* a la carte 18.00/26.95 **st.** 🍷 8.00 – (see also ***Sir Edward Elgar's*** below) – **94 rm** ☕ 135.00/190.00 **st.**, 4 suites – SB.

Holiday Inn Crowne Plaza, Central Sq., Holliday St., B1 1HH, ℘ 631 2000, Fax 643 9018, Ƒ₆, ≘s, ☒ – |♯| ⇔ rm ▤ TV ☎ ♿ P – ♣ 150. MC AE ◑ VISA JCB
Meals *(closed Saturday lunch)* (carving lunch) 14.95/18.50 **st.** and dinner a la carte 🍷 6.95 – ☕ 10.95 – **281 rm** 108.00/118.00 **st.**, 3 suites – SB. JZ z

Copthorne, Paradise Circus, B3 3HJ, ℘ 200 2727, Fax 200 1197, Ƒ₆, ≘s, ☒ – |♯| ⇔ rm ▤ rest TV ☎ ♿ P – ♣ 180. MC AE ◑ VISA. ✻ JZ e
Meals 13.95 **st.** (lunch) and a la carte 16.20/22.00 **st.** – ☕ 11.00 – **209 rm** 110.00/120.00, 3 suites – SB.

Jonathan's, 16-24 Wolverhampton Rd, Oldbury, B68 0LH, W : 4 m. by A 456 ℘ 429 3757, Fax 434 3107, « Authentic Victorian furnishings and memorabilia » – ⇔ rest TV ☎ P. MC AE ◑ VISA
closed 1 January – **Meals** - English - 15.00/24.50 **t.** and a la carte 🍷 6.75 – **21 rm** ☕ 69.00/80.00 **st.**, 11 suites 118.00/150.00 **st.** – SB.

Grand (Q.M.H.), Colmore Row, B3 2DA, ℘ 607 9955, Fax 233 1465 – |♯| ⇔ rm ▤ rest TV ☎ – ♣ 500. MC AE ◑ VISA JKY c
Meals 12.95/21.20 **st.** and a la carte. 🍷 7.05 – ☕ 10.50 – **170 rm** 105.00/125.00 **st.**, 2 suites – SB.

Plough and Harrow (Regal), 135 Hagley Rd, Edgbaston, B16 8LS, ℘ 454 4111, Fax 454 1868, 🌳 – |♯| ⇔ TV ☎ P – ♣ 70. MC AE ◑ VISA JCB. ✻ EX a
Meals *(closed Saturday lunch)* 14.95 **st.** (lunch) and a la carte 15.90/27.85 **st.** 🍷 6.05 – ☕ 8.50 – **42 rm** 79.00/89.00 **st.**, 2 suites – SB.

Forte Posthouse Birmingham City, Smallbrook, Queensway, B5 4EW, ℘ 643 8171, Fax 631 2528, Ƒ₆, ≘s, ☒, *squash* – |♯| ⇔ rm ▤ TV ☎ P – ♣ 630. MC AE ◑ VISA JCB. ✻ KZ o
Meals 12.95/14.95 **st.** and a la carte 🍷 6.50 – ☕ 9.95 – **252 rm** 89.00/99.00 **st.**, 1 suite – SB.

Strathallan Thistle, 225 Hagley Rd, Edgbaston, B16 9RY, ℘ 455 9777, Fax 454 9432 – |♯| ⇔ rm ▤ rest TV ☎ P – ♣ 170. MC AE ◑ VISA JCB. ✻ EX i
Meals *(closed Saturday lunch)* a la carte 19.00/25.40 **st.** 🍷 5.75 – ☕ 9.50 – **163 rm** 85.00/112.00 **st.**, 4 suites.

Apollo (Mount Charlotte), 243 Hagley Rd, Edgbaston, B16 9RA, ℘ 455 0271, Fax 456 2394 – |♯| ⇔ rm ▤ rest TV ☎ P – ♣ 150. MC AE ◑ VISA JCB EX o
Meals *(closed Saturday lunch)* (carving lunch) 12.50/13.50 **st.** and a la carte 🍷 5.30 – ☕ 8.95 – **124 rm** 69.00/99.00 **st.**, 2 suites – SB.

Quality Norfolk (Friendly), 267 Hagley Rd, B16 9NA, ℘ 454 8071, Fax 455 6149 – |♯| ⇔ rm ▤ rest TV ☎ P – ♣ 100. MC AE ◑ VISA JCB EX n
Meals *(closed Sunday lunch)* (carving rest.) 8.50/13.50 **t.** and dinner a la carte 🍷 4.25 – ☕ 7.75 – **168 rm** 57.50/77.50 **st.** – SB.

Novotel, 70 Broad St., B1 2HT, ℘ 643 2000, Fax 643 9796, Ƒ₆, ≘s – |♯| ⇔ rm ▤ rest TV ☎ ♿ P – ♣ 250. MC AE ◑ VISA JCB. ✻ FV a
Meals 17.00 **st.** (dinner) and a la carte 9.50/17.50 **st.** – ☕ 8.50 – **148 rm** 73.00/83.00 **st.**

Chamberlain, Alcester St., B12 0PJ, ℘ 606 9000, Fax 606 9001 – |♯| ⇔ ▤ rest TV ☎ ⇔ – ♣ 400. MC AE ◑ VISA JCB. ✻ FX r
Meals (carving rest.) 6.00/9.00 **t.** – **250 rm** ☕ 35.00/40.00 **t.**

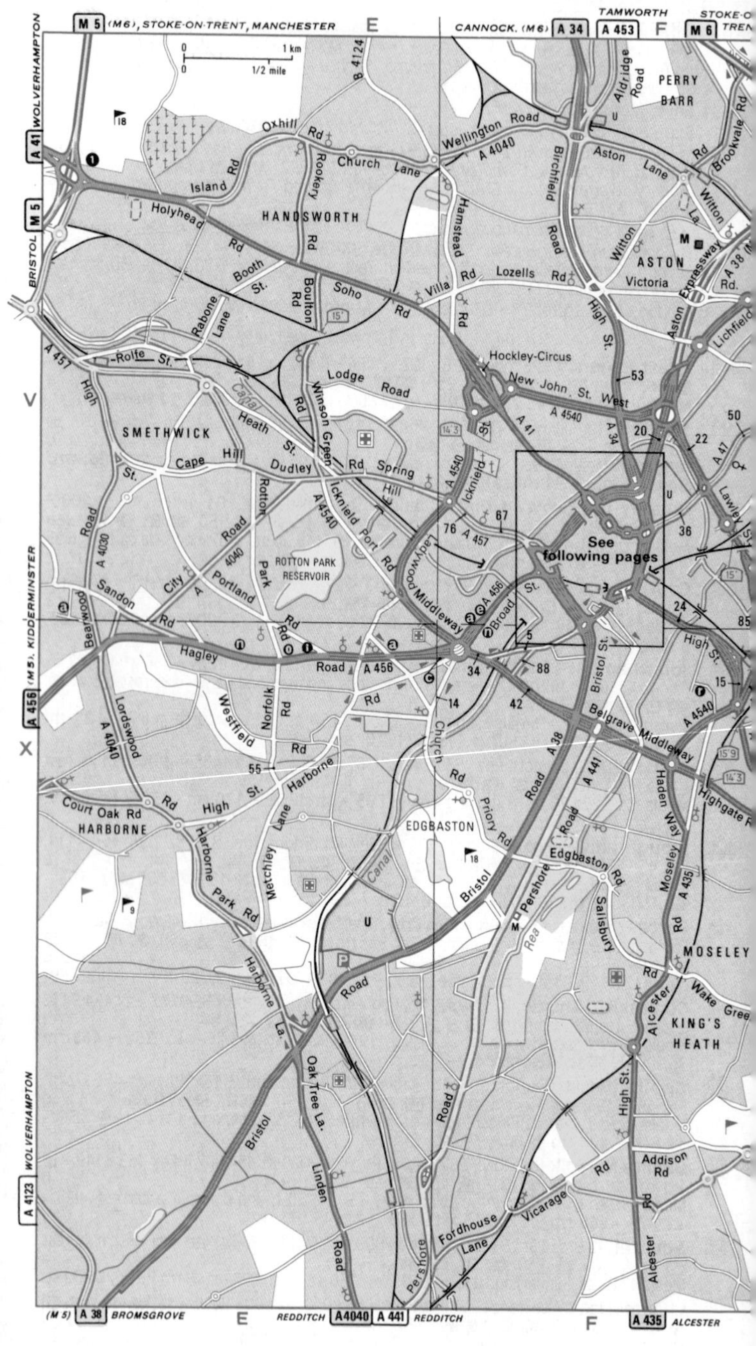

M 5 (M6), STOKE-ON-TRENT, MANCHESTER
CANNOCK, (M6) A 34
TAMWORTH A 453
STOKE-ON-TRENT M 6
E
F
V
X
0 1 km
0 1/2 mile
A 41 WOLVERHAMPTON
M 5 BRISTOL
A 456 (M5), KIDDERMINSTER
A 4123 WOLVERHAMPTON
(M 5) A 38 BROMSGROVE
REDDITCH A4040 A 441 REDDITCH
A 435 ALCESTER
PERRY BARR
HANDSWORTH
ASTON
SMETHWICK
HARBORNE
EDGBASTON
MOSELEY
KING'S HEATH
ROTTON PARK RESERVOIR
See following pages
Oxhill Rd
Church Lane
Rookery Rd
Island Rd
Holyhead Rd
Wellington Road
A 4040
Aldridge Road
Birchfield Road
Aston Lane
Brookvale Rd
Witton La.
Witton Rd
Aston Expressway
Victoria Rd.
Hamstead Rd
Lozells Rd
Villa Rd
Booth St.
Soho Rd
Boulton Rd
Rabone Lane
Rolfe St.
A 457
High St.
Lodge Road
Winson Green Rd
Hockley-Circus
New John St. West
A 4540
A 41
A 34
Lichfield
A 47
Lawley St.
Canal
Heath St.
Cape Hill
Dudley Rd
Spring Hill
Icknield St.
Icknield Port Rd
A 4540
Rotton Park Rd
City Road
A 4040
Portland Rd
Sandon Rd
Bearwood Rd
A 4030
Ladywood Middleway
A 456
Broad St.
Hagley Road
Norfolk Rd
Westfield Rd
Lordswood Rd
A 4040
Church Rd
Bristol St.
Belgrave Middleway
A 4540
Highgate
High St.
A 38
Bristol Road
A 441
Haden Way
Court Oak Rd
High St.
Harborne Park Rd
Metchley Lane
Priory Rd
Pershore Road
Edgbaston Rd
Salisbury Rd
Moseley Rd
A 435
Wake Green
Alcester Rd
Rea
Harborne La.
Oak Tree La.
Linden Road
Bristol Road
Pershore Road
Fordhouse Lane
Vicarage Rd
Addison Rd
High St.
Alcester Rd

BIRMINGHAM
BUILT UP AREA

Bath Row .... FX 5
Bordesley Middleway ...... FX 10
Calthorpe Rd ...... FX 14
Camp Hill .... FX 15
Corporation St ..... FV 20
Darmouth Middleway ...... FV 22
Digbeth .... FV 24
Dudley Park Rd .... GX 25
High St .... GV 31
Islington Row Middleway ...... FX 34
Jennen's Rd .... FV 36
Lee Bank Middleway ...... FX 42
Nechell's Parkway .... FV 50
New Town Row ... FV 53
Nursery Rd .... EX 55
Saltley Rd .... GV 66
Sand Pits Parade .... FV 67
Solihull Lane ...... GX 74
Summer Hill Rd .... FV 76
Watery Lane ...... FV 85
Westley Rd .... GX 87
Wheeley's Lane .... FX 88

BIRMINGHAM
CENTRE

Street	Grid	No.
Albert St.	KZ	2
Bull St.	KY	13
Dale End	KZ	21
Hall St.	JY	29
Holloway Circus	JZ	32
James Watt Queensway	KY	35
Jennen's Rd	KY	36
Lancaster Circus	KY	39
Lancaster St.	KY	41
Masshouse Circus	KY	43
Moor St. Queensway	KZ	46
Navigation St.	JZ	49
Newton St.	KY	52
Paradise Circus	JZ	56
Priory Queensway	KY	57
St. Chads Circus	JKY	62
St. Chads Ringway	KY	63
St. Martin's Circus	KZ	64
Shadwell St.	KY	70
Smallbrook Queensway	KZ	71
Snow Hill Queensway	KY	73
Summer Row	JY	77
Temple Row	KZ	80
Waterloo St.	JZ	84

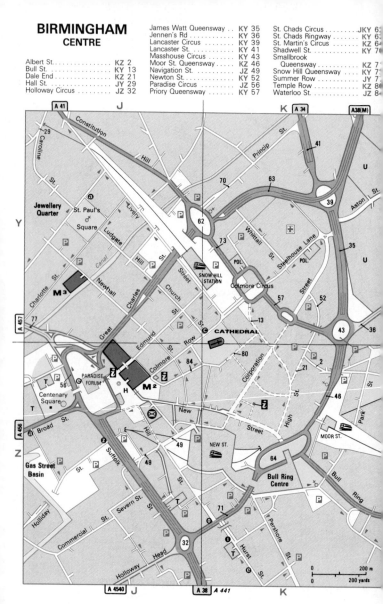

GREEN TOURIST GUIDES

Picturesque scenery, buildings
Attractive route
Touring programmes
Plans of towns and buildings.

STREET INDEX TO BIRMINGHAM TOWN PLANS

Bull Ring Centre KZ
Corporation St. KYZ
New St. JKZ
Paradise Forum Shopping Centre JZ

Addison Rd FX
Albert St. KZ 2
Alcester Rd FX
Aldridge Rd FV
Alum Rock Rd GV
Aston Church Rd GV
Aston Expressway FV
Aston Lane FV
Aston St. KY
Bath Row FX 5
Bearwood Rd EV
Belgrave Middleway FX
Birchfield Rd FV
Booth St. EV
Bordesley Green GV
Bordesley Green Rd GV
Bordesley Middleway FX 10
Boulton Rd EV
Bowyer Rd GV
Bradford Rd HV
Bristol Rd EX
Bristol St. FX
Broad St. FV
Bromford Lane GV
Bromford Rd HV
Brook Lane GX
Brookvale Rd FV
Bull Ring KZ
Bull Ring Centre KZ
Bull St. KY 13
Calthorpe Rd FX 14
Camp Hill FX 15
Cape Hill EV
Caroline St. JY
Cattell Rd GV
Centenary Square JZ
Charlotte St. JY
Chester Rd HV
Church Lane EV
Church Rd EDGBASTON FX
Church Rd SHELDON HX
Church Rd YARDLEY HX
Church St. JY
City Rd EV
Coleshill Rd HV
College Rd GX
Colmore Circus KY
Colmore Row JZ
Commercial St. JZ
Constitution Hill JY
Corporation St. FV 20
Court Oak Rd EX
Coventry Rd GX
Dale End KZ 21
Darmouth Middleway FV 22
Digbeth FV 24
Dudley Park Rd GX 25
Dudley Rd EV
Edgbaston Rd FX
Edmund St. JYZ
Fordhouse Lane FX
Fox Hollies Rd GX
Golden Hillock Rd GX
Gravelly Hill GV
Gravelly Hill Junction GV
Great Charles St. JY
Hadden Way FX
Hagley Rd EX
Hall St. JY 29
Hampstead Rd FV
Harborne Lane EX
Harborne Park Rd EX
Harborne Rd EX
Heath St. EV
Highfield Rd GX
Highfield Rd SALTLEY GV
Highgate Rd FX
High St. KZ
High St. ASTON FV
High St. BORDESLEY FX
High St. HARBORNE EX
High St. KING'S HEATH FX
High St. SALTLEY GV 31
High St. SMETHWICK EV
Hill St. JZ
Hob's Moat Rd HX
Hockley Circus FV
Hockley Hill JY
Holliday St. JZ
Holloway Circus JZ 32
Holloway Head JZ
Holyhead Rd EV
Hurst St. KZ
Icknield Port Rd EV
Icknield St. FV
Island Rd EV
Islington Row Middleway FX 34
James Watt Queensay KY 35
Jennen's Rd FV 36
Kingsbury Rd HV
Ladywood Middleway EV
Lancaster Circus KY 39
Lancaster St. KY 41
Lawley St. FV
Lee Bank Middleway FX 42
Lichfield Rd FV
Linden Rd EX
Livery St. JY
Lodge Rd EV
Lordswood Rd EX
Lozells Rd FV
Ludgate Hill JY
Masshouse Circus KY 43
Metchley Lane EX
Moor St. Queensway KZ 46
Moseley Rd FX
Navigation St. JZ 49
Nechell's Parkway FV 50
Newhall St. JY
New John St. West FV
Newport Rd HV
New St. JZ
Newton St. KY 52
New Town Row FV 53
Norfolk Rd EX
Nursery Rd EX 55
Oak Tree Lane EX
Olton Bd East GX
Oxhill Rd EV
Paradise Circus JZ 56
Park St. KZ
Pershore Rd FX
Pershore St. KZ
Portland Rd EV
Princip St. KY
Priory Queensway KY 57
Priory Rd FX
Rabone Lane EV
Richmond Rd HX
Robin Hood Lane GX
Rolfe St. EV
Rookery Rd EV
Rotton Park Rd EV
St. Chads Circus JY 62
St. Chads Ringway KY 63
St. Martin's Circus KZ 64
St. Paul's Square JY
Salisbury Rd FX
Saltley Rd GV 66
Sandon Rd EV
Sand Pits Parade FV 67
Severn St. JZ
Shadwell St. KY 70
Shaftmoor Lane GX
Sheaf Lane HX
Sheldon Heath Rd HX
Shirley Rd GX
Smallbrook Queensway KZ 71
Small Heath Highway GX
Snow Hill Queensway KY 73
Soho Rd EV
Solihull Lane GX 74
Spring Hill EV
Station Rd HV
Stechford Lane HV
Steelhouse Lane KY
Stockfield Rd GX
Stoney La MOSELEY GX
Stoney La SHELDON HX
Stratford Rd GX
Suffolk St. JZ
Summer Hill Rd FV 76
Summer Row JY 77
Temple Row KZ 80
Tyburn Rd GV
Vicarage Rd FX
Victoria Rd FV
Villa Rd FV
Wagon Lane HX
Wake Green Rd FX
Warwick Rd GX
Washwood Heath Rd GV
Waterloo St. JZ 84
Watery Lane FX 85
Wellington Rd FV
Westfield Rd EX
Westley Rd GX 87
Wheeley's Lane FX 88
Whittal St. KY
Winson Green Rd EV
Witton Lane FV
Witton Rd FV
Wood End Rd GV
Yardley Rd HX
Yardley Wood Rd GX

Pleasant hotels and restaurants
are shown in the Guide by a red sign.

Please send us the names
of any where you have enjoyed your stay.

Your **Michelin Guide** will be even better.

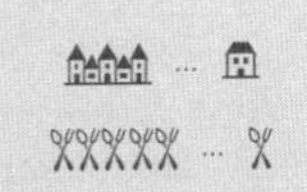

XXXX **Sir Edward Elgar's** (at Swallow H.), 12 Hagley Rd, B16 8SJ, 452 1144, Fax 456 344 – P. VISA FX
closed Saturday lunch – **Meals** 21.50/26.00 **st.** and a la carte 8.00.

XX **Leftbank,** 79 Broad St., B15 1QA, 643 4464, Fax 643 4464 – VISA JC
closed Saturday lunch, Sunday, 24 to 30 December, early January and Bank Holidays – **Meals** 12.50 **t.** (lunch) and a la carte 18.90/25.90 **t.** 5.50. FV

XX **Number 282** (at Hyatt Regency H.), 2 Bridge St., B1 2JZ, 643 1234, Fax 616 232 – VISA JCB JZ
closed Saturday and Sunday lunch – **Meals** 14.75/16.75 **st.** and a la carte 3.90.

XX **Shimla Pinks,** 214 Broad St., B15 1AY, 633 0366, Fax 633 0366 – VIS
closed lunch Saturday and Sunday and 25 December – **Meals** - Indian - 6.95/12.95 **st.** an a la carte. FX

XX **Henry's,** 27 St. Paul's Sq., B3 1RB, 200 1136, Fax 200 1190 – VISA JY
closed Sunday and Bank Holidays – **Meals** - Chinese (Canton) - 14.00 **t.** and a la carte.

XX **Dynasty,** 93-103 Hurst St., B5 4TE, 622 1410 – VISA JCB KZ
closed Christmas and Bank Holiday Mondays – **Meals** - Chinese - (lunch b arrangement)/dinner a la carte 14.50/24.00 **t.** 7.90.

XX **Maharaja,** 23-25 Hurst St., B5 4AS, 622 2641, Fax 662 4021 – VIS
closed Sunday, last week July and Bank Holidays – **Meals** - North Indian - a la cart 12.40/15.15 **t.** 6.25. KZ

XX **Franzl's,** 151 Milcote Rd, Bearwood, Smethwick, B67 5BN, 429 7920, Fax 429 161 – VISA JCB EV
closed Sunday, Monday, 26 December and 3 weeks August – **Meals** - Austrian - (dinne only) 13.45/19.45 **t.** 4.50.

at Hall Green *SE : 5 ¾ m. by A 41 on A 34 – Birmingham – 0121 :*

Robin Hood (Toby), Stratford Rd, B28 9ES, 745 9900, Fax 733 1075 – P. VISA GX
Meals (grill rest.) a la carte approx. 10.95 **t.** – **30 rm** 65.00/75.00 **st.** – SB.

at Birmingham Airport *SE : 9 m. by A 45* – HX – *Birmingham – 0121 :*

Novotel, Passenger Terminal, B26 3QL, 782 7000, Fax 782 0445 – rm res – 35. VISA
closed 25 December – **Meals** 16.00 **t.** and a la carte 4.75 – 7.95 – **195 rm** 80.00/99.00 **st.** – SB.

Forte Posthouse Birmingham Airport, Coventry Rd, B26 3QW, on A 4 782 8141, Fax 782 2476 – rm – 130. VISA JCB
Meals a la carte 10.70/22.15 **st.** 5.75 – 7.95 – **136 rm** 56.00 **st.** – SB.

at National Exhibition Centre *SE : 9 ½ m. on A 45* – HX – *Birmingham – 0121 :*

Birmingham Metropole, Bickenhill, B40 1PP, 780 4242, Fax 780 3923, – rm – 2000. VISA
closed 25 and 26 December – **Meals** (carving rest.) 24.50 **t.** 8.50 – ***Primavera :*** **Meal** - Italian - (closed Saturday lunch and Sunday) a la carte 25.00/34.50 **t.** 8.50 – **787 rm** 156.00/235.00 **t.**, 15 suites – SB.

Arden, Coventry Rd, B92 0EH, (01675) 443221, Fax 443221, – rm – 170. VISA JCB.
Meals 13.10 **t.** and a la carte 5.20 – 8.50 – **146 rm** 69.00/79.00 **t.** – SB.

Mill House, 180 Lifford Lane, B30 3NT, 459 5800, Fax 459 8553, – 120. VISA.
closed first 2 weeks January – **Meals** – (see ***Lombard Room*** below) – **8 rm** 85.00/95.00 **t.**, 1 suite – SB.

XXX **Lombard Room,** 180 Lifford Lane, B30 3NT, 459 5800, Fax 459 8553, P. VISA
closed Sunday dinner, Monday and first 2 weeks January – **Meals** 15.00/19.50 **t.** 7.00

at Great Barr *NW : 6 m. on A 34* – FV – *Birmingham – 0121 :*

Forte Posthouse Birmingham, Chapel Lane, B43 7BG, 357 7444, Fax 357 7503 – rm – 120. VISA JCB.
Meals a la carte 16.10/24.35 **st.** – 9.95 – **192 rm** 79.00 **st.** – SB.

at West Bromwich *NW : 6 m. on A 41* – EV – *Birmingham – 0121 :*

Moat House Birmingham (Q.M.H.), Birmingham Rd, B70 6RS, 609 9988 Fax 525 7403, – rm rest – 180. VISA JCB
Meals 13.95 **st.** and a la carte 6.00 – 8.50 – **168 rm** 90.00/105.00 **st.** – SB.

BRISTOL *Bristol* 403 404 M 29 – *pop. 407 992* – ☎ *0117.*

St. Nicholas Church, St. Nicholas St., BS1 1UE ☎ 926 0767.

Manchester 121 – Birmingham 91.

XX ✿✿ **Lettonie** (Blunos), 9 Druid Hill, Stoke Bishop, BS9 1EW, (possibly relocating during 1997) ☎ 968 6456, Fax 968 6943 – MC AE ◑ VISA
closed Sunday, Monday, 2 weeks August and 1 week Christmas – **Meals** - French - (booking essential) 19.95/36.50 **t.**
Spec. Aubergine and mackerel mille-feuille, scallops and red pepper purée, Squab pigeon breasts and sausage, dill scented broth, Vanilla cream raviolis, pink grapefruit and toasted almonds.

EDINBURGH *Edinburgh City* 401 K 16 **Scotland G.** – *pop. 418 914* – ☎ *0131.*

See : *City★★★ Edinburgh International Festival★★★ (August) – National Gallery of Scotland★★* DY **M4** *Royal Botanic Garden★★★ The Castle★★* DYZ*: site★★★ – Palace Block (Honours of Scotland★★★) St. Margaret's Chapel (✳★★★) Great Hall (Hammerbeam Roof★★) ≤★★ from Argyle and Mill's Mount* DZ *– Abbey and Palace of Holyroodhouse★★ (Plasterwork Ceilings★★★, ✳★★ from Arthur's Seat) – Royal Mile★★ : St. Giles' Cathedral★★ (Crown Spire★★★)* EYZ *Gladstone's Land★* EYZ **A** *– Canongate Talbooth★* EY **B** *– New Town★★ (Charlotte Square★★★* CY **14** *Royal Museum of Scotland (Antiquities)★★* EZ **M2** *– The Georgian House ★* CY **D** *National Portrait Gallery★* EY **M3** *Dundas House★* EY **E***) – Victoria Street★* EZ **84** *Scott Monument★ (≤★)* EY **F** *– Craigmillar Castle★ Calton Hill (✳★★★ from Nelson's Monument)* EY.

Envir. : *Edinburgh Zoo★★ – Hill End Ski Centre (✳★★), S : 5 ½ m. by A 702 – The Royal Observatory (West Tower ≤★) – Ingleston, Scottish Agricultural Museum★, W : 6 ½m. by A 8.*

Exc. : *Rosslyn Chapel★★ (Apprentice Pillar★★★) S : 7 ½ m. by A 701 and B 7006 – Forth Bridges★★, NW : 9 ½ m. by A 90 – Hopetoun House★★ , NW : 11 ½ m. by A 90 and A 904 – Dalmeny★ (Dalmeny House★, St. Cuthbert's Church★ - Norman South Doorway★★) NW : 7 m. by A 90 – Crichton Castle (Italianate Courtyard range★), SE : 10 m. by A 7 and B 6372.*

18, 18 Braid Hills, Braid Hills Rd ☎ 447 6666 – 18 Craigmillar Park, 1 Observatory Rd ☎ 667 2837 – 18 Carrick Knowe, Glendevon Park ☎ 337 1096 – 18 Duddingston Road West ☎ 661 1005 – 18 Silverknowes, Parkway ☎ 336 3843 – 18 Liberton, 297 Gilmerton Rd ☎ 664 8580 9 Portobello, Stanley St. ☎ 669 4361 – 18, 18 Dalmahoy Hotel C.C., Kirknewton ☎ 333 4105/1845.

✈ *Edinburgh Airport : ☎ 333 1000, W : 6 m. by A 8 –* **Terminal :** *Waverley Bridge.*

Edinburgh Scotland Information Centre, 3 Princes St., EH2 2QP ☎ 557 1700 – Edinburgh Airport, Tourist Information Desk ☎ 333 2167.

Glasgow 46 – Newcastle upon Tyne 105.

Plan on next page

Balmoral (Forte), Princes St., EH2 2EQ, ☎ 556 2414, Fax 557 3747, Fб, ≘s, ⊠ – |‡| ⇎ rm ▤ rest ▣ ☎ ♿ ⇔ – 🎓 350. MC AE ◑ VISA JCB. ✂ EY n
Brasserie : **Meals** 14.50 **st.** (lunch) and a la carte 13.45/18.10 **st.** 🍷 7.00 – (see also ***The Restaurant, No. 1 Princes Street*** below) – ☕ 14.50 – **165 rm** 140.00/235.00 **st.**, 21 suites – SB.

Caledonian (Q.M.H.), Princes St., EH1 2AB, ☎ 459 9988, Fax 225 6632 – |‡| ⇎ rm ▤ rest ▣ ☎ ♿ Ⓟ – 🎓 300. MC AE ◑ VISA. ✂ CY n
Carriages : **Meals** 20.00 **t.** and a la carte 🍷 9.40 – (see also ***Pompadour*** below) – ☕ 16.75 – **223 rm** 134.00/290.00 **t.**, 11 suites – SB.

Sheraton Grand, 1 Festival Sq., EH3 9SR, ☎ 229 9131, Fax 229 6254, Fб, ≘s, ⊠ – |‡| ⇎ rm ▤ ▣ ☎ ♿ Ⓟ – 🎓 500. MC AE ◑ VISA JCB. ✂ CDZ v
Terrace : **Meals** 17.50 **st.** and a la carte – (see also ***Grill Room*** below) – ☕ 14.00 – **244 rm** 140.00/205.00 **st.**, 17 suites.

George Inter-Continental, 19-21 George St., EH2 2PB, ☎ 225 1251, Fax 226 5644 – |‡| ⇎ rm ▣ ☎ Ⓟ – 🎓 200. MC AE ◑ VISA JCB. ✂ DY z
Le Chambertin : **Meals** 21.00/21.50 **t.** and a la carte 🍷 6.00 – ***Carvers*** *(☎ 459 2305) :* **Meals** 17.95 **t.** and a la carte – ☕ 12.95 – **193 rm** 140.00/190.00 **st.**, 2 suites – SB.

Marriott Dalmahoy H. Country Club ⛰, Kirknewton, EH27 8EB, SW : 7 m. on A 71 ☎ 333 1845, Fax 335 3203, ≤, Fб, ≘s, ⊠, 18, ⛱, *park*, ✂, squash – |‡| ⇎ ▣ ☎ ♿ Ⓟ – 🎓 400. MC AE ◑ VISA. ✂
Pentland : **Meals** 14.50/23.50 **t.** and dinner a la carte – ***Terrace :*** **Meals** (grill rest.) 7.75 **t.** and a la carte – **150 rm** ☕ 125.00/135.00 **t.**, 1 suite – SB.

Carlton Highland, North Bridge St., EH1 1SD, ☎ 556 7277, Fax 556 2691, Fб, ≘s, ⊠, squash – |‡| ⇎ rm ▤ rest ▣ ☎ ♿ Ⓟ – 🎓 280. MC AE ◑ VISA EY s
Quills : **Meals** *(closed Sunday lunch)* 14.95/21.50 **t.** 🍷 6.50 – ***Courts :*** **Meals** (carving rest.) 9.95/17.00 **t.** and a la carte 🍷 5.00 – **193 rm** ☕ 107.00/166.00 **st.**, 4 suites – SB.

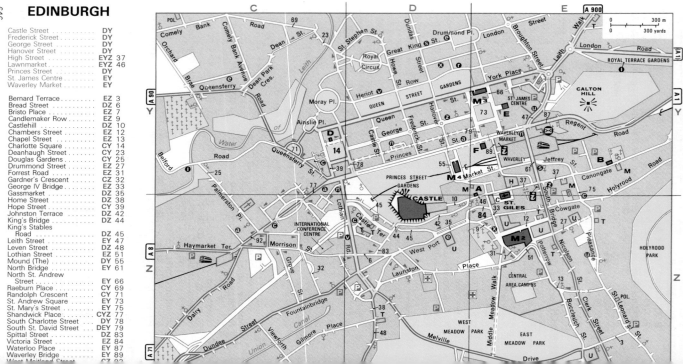

EDINBURGH

Street	Grid	No.
Castle Street	DY	
Frederick Street	DY	
George Street	DY	
Hanover Street	DY	
High Street	EYZ	37
Lawnmarket	EYZ	46
Princes Street	DY	
St. James Centre	EY	
Waverley Market	EY	
Bernard Terrace	EZ	3
Bread Street	DZ	6
Bristo Place	EZ	7
Candlemaker Row	EZ	9
Castlehill	DZ	10
Chambers Street	EZ	12
Chapel Street	EZ	13
Charlotte Square	CY	14
Deanhaugh Street	CY	23
Douglas Gardens	CY	25
Drummond Street	EZ	27
Forrest Road	EZ	31
Gardner's Crescent	CZ	32
George IV Bridge	EZ	33
Gassmarket	DZ	35
Home Street	DZ	38
Hope Street	CY	39
Johnston Terrace	DZ	42
King's Bridge	DZ	44
King's Stables Road	DZ	45
Leith Street	EY	47
Leven Street	DZ	48
Lothian Street	EZ	51
Mound (The)	DY	55
North Bridge	EY	61
North St. Andrew Street	EY	66
Raeburn Place	CY	69
Randolph Crescent	CY	71
St. Andrew Square	EY	73
St. Mary's Street	EY	75
Shandwick Place	CYZ	77
South Charlotte Street	DY	78
South St. David Street	DEY	79
Spittal Street	DZ	83
Victoria Street	EZ	84
Waterloo Place	EY	87
Waverley Bridge	EY	89

Swallow Royal Scot, 111 Glasgow Rd, EH12 8NF, W : 4 ½ m. on A 8 ✆ 334 9191, Fax 316 4507, – rm – 300. VISA
Meals 16.50/21.50 **st.** and a la carte – **255 rm** 115.00/145.00 **st.**, 4 suites – SB.

Howard, 34 Gt. King St., EH3 6QH, ✆ 557 3500, Fax 557 6515, « Georgian town houses » – 40. VISA. DY s
Meals – (see **36** below) – **15 rm** 110.00/275.00 **st.**

Holiday Inn Crowne Plaza, 80 High St., EH1 1TH, ✆ 557 9797, Fax 557 9789, – rm – 200. VISA JCB. EY z
closed 24 to 27 December – **Meals** 15.50/21.50 **st.** and a la carte – 12.50 – **229 rm** 130.00/195.00 **st.**, 9 suites – SB.

Hilton National, 69 Belford Rd, EH4 3DG, ✆ 332 2545, Fax 332 3805 – rm – 130. VISA JCB CY i
Meals 13.50/17.50 **st.** and dinner a la carte – 11.50 – **144 rm** 130.00/250.00 **t.**

Channings, South Learmonth Gdns., EH4 1EZ, ✆ 315 2226, Fax 332 9631, – rest – 35. VISA JCB. CY e
closed 23 to 25 December – **Meals** *(closed lunch Saturday and Sunday)* 9.95/21.00 **st.** – **48 rm** 102.00/190.00 **st.** – SB.

Malmaison, 1 Tower Pl., Leith, EH6 7DB, NE : 2 m. by A 900 ✆ 555 6868, Fax 555 6999, « Contemporary interior » – rm rest – 100. VISA.
Meals - Brasserie - a la carte 19.05/24.00 **t.** 8.50 – 10.00 – **19 rm** 90.00/110.00 **t.**, 6 suites.

King James Thistle, 107 Leith St., EH1 3SW, ✆ 556 0111, Fax 557 5333 – rm – 250. VISA JCB. EY u
Meals *(closed Sunday lunch)* 10.50/19.75 **st.** 5.15 – ***Saint Jacques :*** **Meals** (dinner only) a la carte 18.50/34.45 **st.** – 9.95 – **140 rm** 110.00/150.00 **st.**, 5 suites – SB.

Royal Terrace, 18 Royal Terr., EH7 5AQ, ✆ 557 3222, Fax 557 5334, – 80. VISA. EY i
Meals 17.75 **st.** and a la carte 5.95 – 9.95 – **92 rm** 115.00/180.00 **st.**, 1 suite – SB.

Stakis Edinburgh Grosvenor, Grosvenor St., EH12 5EF, ✆ 226 6001, Fax 220 2387 – 500. VISA JCB CZ a
Meals *(closed lunch Saturday and Sunday)* 9.95/15.75 **t.** and a la carte 7.00 – 8.50 – **186 rm** 97.00/107.00 **t.**, 1 suite – SB.

Edinburgh Capital Moat House (Q.M.H.), Clermiston Rd, EH12 6UG, ✆ 535 9988, Fax 334 9712, – – 300. VISA. by A 8 CZ
Meals 10.50/16.50 **t.** and a la carte – 10.50 – **111 rm** 79.00/145.00 **t.** – SB.

Mount Royal (Jarvis), 53 Princes St., EH2 2DG, ✆ 225 7161, Fax 220 4671, – – 50. VISA. DY a
Meals 6.00/14.95 **st.** and dinner a la carte – 8.75 – **158 rm** 99.00/145.00 **st.** – SB.

Holiday Inn Garden Court, 107 Queensferry Rd, EH4 3HL, ✆ 332 2442, Fax 332 3408, – rm rest – 60. VISA JCB
Meals (bar lunch Monday to Saturday)/dinner 14.95 **st.** and a la carte 5.25 – 8.45 – **118 rm** 79.00/89.00 **st.**, 1 suite – SB. by A 90 CY

Forte Posthouse Edinburgh, Corstorphine Rd, EH12 6UA, W : 3 m. on A 8 ✆ 334 0390, Fax 334 9237 – rm rest – 120. VISA JCB.
Meals a la carte 19.40/27.25 **st.** – 9.95 – **204 rm** 79.00 **st.** – SB.

Jarvis Ellersly House, 4 Ellersly Rd, EH12 6HZ, ✆ 337 6888, Fax 313 2543, – rm – 70. VISA by A 8 CZ
Meals *(closed Saturday lunch)* 10.95/14.00 **t.** and a la carte 5.95 – 8.50 – **57 rm** 99.00/125.00 **t.** – SB.

Apex International, 31-35 Grassmarket, EH1 2HS, ✆ 300 3456, Fax 220 5345 – rm rest . VISA. DZ e
Meals (carving rest.) (bar lunch)/dinner 12.95 **st.** 4.95 – 6.95 – **99 rm** 64.95 **st.**

Maitland without rest., 25a Shandwick Pl., EH2 4RG, ✆ 229 1467, Fax 229 7549 – . VISA JCB. CY a
closed 22 to 28 December – **65 rm** 65.00/120.00 **st.**

Drummond House without rest., 17 Drummond Pl., EH3 6PL, ✆ 557 9189, Fax 557 9189, « Georgian town house » – . VISA. DY e
closed Christmas – **3 rm** 85.00/90.00 **t.**

17 Abercromby Place without rest., 17 Abercromby Pl., EH3 6LB, ✆ 557 8036, Fax 558 3453, « Georgian town house » – . VISA. DY r
closed Christmas – **8 rm** 70.00/90.00 **st.**

Sibbet House without rest., 26 Northumberland St., EH3 6LS, ✆ 556 1078, Fax 557 9445, « Georgian town house » – . VISA. DY x
5 rm 60.00/100.00 **st.**

27 Heriot Row, 27 Heriot Row, EH3 6EN, ☎ 220 1699, Fax 225 9474, « Georgian town house », – TV ☎. MC VISA. DY v
Meals (by arrangement) (communal dining) 25.00 **st.** – **3 rm** 50.00/80.00 **st.**

The Restaurant, No. 1 Princes Street (at Balmoral H.), 1 Princes St., EH2 2EQ, ☎ 556 6727, Fax 557 3747 – ▤. MC AE ⓓ VISA JCB EY n
closed lunch Saturday and Sunday – **Meals** 19.75/29.50 **st.** and a la carte 8.00.

Pompadour (at Caledonian H.), Princes St., EH1 2AB, ☎ 459 9988, Fax 225 6632 – P. MC AE ⓓ VISA CY n
closed Sunday and Monday – **Meals** (dinner only) 45.00 **t.** and a la carte 9.40.

Grill Room (at Sheraton Grand H.), 1 Festival Sq., EH3 9SR, ☎ 229 9131, Fax 229 6254 – ▤ P. MC AE ⓓ VISA JCB CDZ v
closed Saturday lunch and Sunday – **Meals** 22.50/28.50 **st.** and a la carte 12.50.

L'Auberge, 56 St. Mary's St., EH1 1SX, ☎ 556 5888, Fax 556 2588 – ▤. MC AE ⓓ VISA JCB
closed 25-26 December and 1-2 January – **Meals** - French - 14.50/24.50 **t.** and a la carte 6.50. EYZ c

36 (at Howard H.), 36 Great King St., EH3 6QH, ☎ 556 3636, Fax 556 3663, « Contemporary decor » – ▤. MC AE ⓓ VISA DY s
Meals a la carte 17.95/28.75 **st.**

Martins, 70 Rose St., North Lane, EH2 3DX, ☎ 225 3106 – . MC AE ⓓ VISA JCB
closed Saturday lunch, Sunday, Monday, 1 week May-June, 1 week September-October and 24 December-22 January – **Meals** (booking essential) 17.75 **t.** (lunch) and a la carte 25.75/30.30 **t.** DY n

(fitz)Henry, 19 Shore Pl., Leith, EH6 6SW, ☎ 555 6625, Fax 554 6216, « Part 17C warehouse » – MC AE VISA
closed Sunday, 25 December and 1 January – Meals 13.50/22.00 **t.** 7.90.

Raffaelli, 10 Randolph Pl., EH3 7TA, ☎ 225 6060, Fax 225 8830 – MC AE ⓓ VISA
closed Saturday lunch, Sunday, 25-26 December, 1-2 January and Bank Holidays – **Meals** - Italian - a la carte 13.95/25.05 **t.** 5.25. CY c

Indian Cavalry Club, 3 Atholl Pl., EH3 8HP, ☎ 228 3282, Fax 225 1911 – MC AE ⓓ VISA
Meals - Indian - 6.95/15.95 **t.** and a la carte. CZ c

Vintners Room, The Vaults, 87 Giles St., Leith, EH6 6BZ, ☎ 554 6767, Fax 467 7130 – . MC AE VISA by A 900 EY
closed Sunday and 2 weeks Christmas-New Year – **Meals** 12.00 **t.** (lunch) and a la carte 22.75/30.75 **t.** 5.00.

Yumi, 2 West Coates, EH12 5JQ, ☎ 337 2173 – P. MC VISA
closed Sunday, Christmas and New Year – **Meals** - Japanese - (dinner only) 30.00 **t.** 5.00.

Denzler's 121, 121 Constitution St., EH6 7AE, ☎ 554 3268, Fax 467 7239 – MC AE ⓓ VISA JCB on A 900 EY
closed Sunday, Monday, 25 and 26 December, 1 and 2 January and last 2 weeks July – **Meals** 18.50 **st.** (dinner) and a la carte 12.50/22.65 **st.** 5.65.

Merchants, 17 Merchant St., EH1 2QD, off Candlemaker Row, (under bridge) ☎ 225 4009, Fax 557 9318 – MC AE ⓓ VISA JCB EZ x
closed Sunday – **Meals** (booking essential) 10.50/17.50 **t.** and a la carte 6.00.

Kelly's, 46 West Richmond St., EH8 9DZ, ☎ 668 3847 – MC AE VISA EZ u
closed Sunday to Tuesday, first week January and October – **Meals** (dinner only) 24.00 **t.** 6.00.

Atrium, 10 Cambridge St., EH1 2ED, ☎ 228 8882, Fax 228 8808 – ▤. MC AE VISA
closed Saturday lunch, Sunday and 1 week Christmas-New Year – Meals a la carte 11.50/26.50 **t.** 6.50. DZ c

Dalhousie Castle, , EH19 3JB, *SE : 1 ¼ m. on B 704* ☎ 820153, Fax 821936, ≤, « Part 13C and 15C castle with Victorian additions », – TV ☎ P – 120. MC AE ⓓ VISA JCB
closed 3 weeks January – **Meals** 25.00 **st.** (dinner) and lunch a la carte 6.80 – **28 rm** 90.00/205.00 **st.** – SB.

at Edinburgh International Airport *W : 7 ½ m. by A 8 – CZ – ✉ Edinburgh – ☎ 0131 :*

Stakis Edinburgh Airport, , EH28 8LL, ☎ 519 4400, Fax 519 4422 – rm ▤ rest TV ☎ P – 220. MC AE ⓓ VISA.
Meals (grill rest.) 7.25 **st.** (lunch) and a la carte 11.60/23.05 **st.** 4.00 – 8.50 – **134 rm** 99.00/149.00 **st.** – SB.

at Ingliston *W : 7 ¾ m. on A 8 – CZ – ✉ Edinburgh – ☎ 0131 :*

Norton House (Virgin) , EH28 8LX, *on A 8* ☎ 333 1275, Fax 333 5305, ≤, – rm TV ☎ P – 300. MC AE ⓓ VISA.
Meals *(closed Saturday lunch)* 28.00 **t.** (dinner) and a la carte 27.50/33.25 **t.** – **46 rm** 105.00/130.00 **t.**, 1 suite – SB.

UNITED KINGDOM

GLASGOW *Glasgow City* 401 402 H 16 **Scotland G.** – *pop. 662 853* – ☎ *0141.*

See : *City★★★ – Cathedral★★★ (≤★)* DZ – *The Burrell Collection★★★ – Hunterian Art Gallery★★ (Whistler Collection★★★ – Mackintosh Wing★★★)* CY **M4** – *Museum of Transport★★ (Scottish Built Cars★★★, The Clyde Room of Ship Models★★★) – Art Gallery and Museum Kelvingrove★★* CY – *Pollok House★ (The Paintings★★) – Tolbooth Steeple★* DZ **A** – *Hunterian Museum (Coin and Medal Collection★)* CY **M1** – *City Chambers★* DZ **C** – *Glasgow School of Art★* CY **B** – *Necropolis (≤★ of Cathedral)* DYZ

Exc. : *The Trossachs★★★, N : 31 m. by A 879, A 81 and A 821 – Loch Lomond★★, NW : 19 m. by A 82.*

18 Littlehill, Auchinairn Rd ☎ 772 1916 – 18 Deaconsbank, Rouken Glen Park, Stewarton Rd, Eastwood ☎ 638 7044 – 18 Linn Park, Simshill Rd ☎ 637 5871 – 18 Lethamhill, Cumbernauld Rd ☎ 770 6220 – 9 Alexandra Park, Dennistown ☎ 556 3991 – 9 King's Park, 150a Croftpark Av., Croftfoot ☎ 634 4745 – 9 Knightswood, Lincoln Av. ☎ 959 2131 9 Ruchill, Brassey St. ☎ 946 7676.

Access to Oban by helicopter.

Erskine Bridge (toll).

Glasgow Airport : ☎ 887 1111, W : 8 m. by M 8 – **Terminal :** *Coach service from Glasgow Central and Queen Street main line Railway Stations and from Anderston Cross and Buchanan Bus Stations Prestwick International Airport : ☎ (01292) 479822* **Terminal :** *Buchanan Bus Station.*

11 George Sq., G2 1DY ☎ 204 4480 – Glasgow Airport, Tourist Information Desk, Paisley ☎ 848 4440.

Edinburgh 46 – Manchester 221.

Plans on following pages

Glasgow Hilton, 1 William St., G3 8HT, ☎ 204 5555, Fax 204 5004, ≤, Fδ, ≘s, ⊠ – |≑| ⇔ rm ▤ TV ☎ ♿ P – 🏛 1000. MC AE ⓓ VISA JCB. ✻ CZ s
Minsky's : **Meals** 18.50 **st.** and a la carte 🍷 7.95 – (see also ***Camerons*** below) – ☕ 14.75 – **315 rm** 150.00/175.00 **st.**, 4 suites – SB .

One Devonshire Gardens, 1 Devonshire Gdns., G12 0UX, ☎ 339 2001, Fax 337 1663, « Victorian town houses, opulent interior design » – ⇔ rest TV ☎ – 🏛 50. MC AE ⓓ VISA by A 82 CY
Meals *(closed Saturday lunch)* 25.00/40.00 **st.** 🍷 8.50 – ☕ 13.50 – **25 rm** 145.00/170.00 **st.**, 2 suites
Spec. Roasted king scallops with sweet carrot and Thai spiced sauce, Fillet of Aberdeen Angus beef with basil and shallot butter, red wine jus, White chocolate and coconut mousse with dark chocolate sorbet.

Glasgow Moat House (Q.M.H.), Congress Rd, G3 8QT, ☎ 306 9988, Fax 221 2022, ≤, Fδ, ≘s, ⊠ – |≑| ⇔ rm ▤ TV ☎ ♿ P – 🏛 800. MC AE ⓓ VISA. ✻ CZ r
Mariners : **Meals** *(closed Saturday lunch and Sunday)* 16.50 **s.** (lunch) and dinner a la carte 19.00/30.00 **s.** 🍷 8.75 – ***Pointhouse :*** **Meals** 16.95/19.95 **s.** and a la carte 🍷 8.75 – ☕ 10.95 – **267 rm** 115.00 **st.**, 16 suites – SB .

Glasgow Marriott, 500 Argyle St., Anderston, G3 8RR, ☎ 226 5577, Fax 221 7676, Fδ, ≘s, ⊠, *squash* – |≑| ⇔ rm ▤ TV ☎ ♿ P – 🏛 720. MC AE ⓓ VISA CZ a
Terrace : **Meals** 17.50 **st.** (dinner) and a la carte 17.50/22.50 **st.** 🍷 6.25 – ***L'Academie :*** **Meals** 17.50 **st.** (dinner) and a la carte 17.50/22.50 **st.** 🍷 6.25 – ☕ 10.25 – **293 rm** 94.00/110.00 **st.**, 5 suites – SB .

Glasgow Thistle, 36 Cambridge St., G2 3HN, ☎ 332 3311, Fax 332 4050 – |≑| ⇔ rm ▤ rest TV ☎ ♿ P – 🏛 1500. MC AE ⓓ VISA JCB DY z
Garden Cafe : **Meals** (carving rest.) 12.50/17.50 **st.** and a la carte – ***Prince of Wales :*** **Meals** *(closed Saturday lunch and Sunday)* 17.50/25.00 **st.** and a la carte – ☕ 11.50 – **299 rm** 97.00/150.00 **st.**, 3 suites – SB .

Forte Posthouse Glasgow City, Bothwell St., G2 7EN, ☎ 248 2656, Fax 221 8986, ≤ – |≑| ⇔ rm ▤ TV ☎ P – 🏛 800. MC AE ⓓ VISA JCB CZ z
closed 24 to 26 December – ***The Carvery :*** **Meals** 15.75 **t.** 🍷 6.75 – ***Jules :*** **Meals** 14.50/15.95 **st.** and a la carte 🍷 6.75 – ☕ 10.95 – **246 rm** 99.00 **st.**, 1 suite – SB .

Devonshire, 5 Devonshire Gdns., G12 0UX, ☎ 339 7878, Fax 339 3980 – TV ☎ – 🏛 50. MC AE ⓓ VISA. ✻ by A 82 CY
Meals (residents only Sunday lunch) a la carte 22.50/30.95 **t.** 🍷 7.95 – ☕ 10.75 – **14 rm** 90.00/150.00 **t.** – SB .

Malmaison, 278 West George St., G2 4LL, ☎ 221 6400, Fax 221 6411, « Contemporary interior » – TV ☎. MC AE ⓓ VISA. ✻ CY c
Meals - Brasserie - a la carte 17.55/24.25 **t.** 🍷 8.50 – ☕ 7.50 – **17 rm** 80.00 **t.**, 4 suites.

Copthorne Glasgow, George Sq., G2 1DS, ☎ 332 6711, Fax 332 4264 – |≑| ⇔ rm TV ☎ – 🏛 100. MC AE ⓓ VISA DZ n
closed 25 and 26 December – **Meals** *(closed Saturday and Sunday lunch)* 14.95/16.95 **t.** and a la carte 🍷 7.50 – ☕ 10.50 – **136 rm** 108.00/127.00 **t.**, 5 suites – SB .

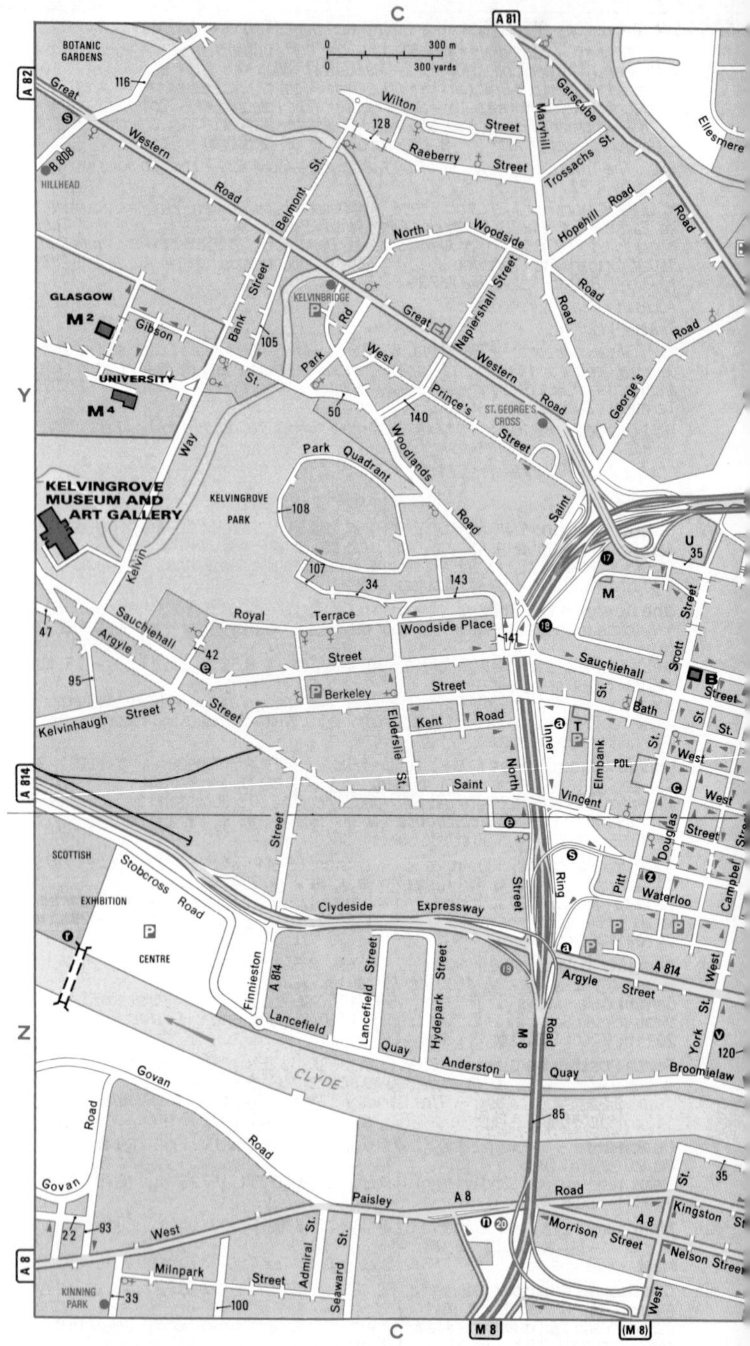
C
A 81
BOTANIC GARDENS
0 300 m
0 300 yards
A 82
Great Western Road
116
B 808
HILLHEAD
Wilton Street
128
Raeberry Street
Belmont St.
Maryhill Road
Garscube Road
Trossachs St.
Ellesmere
Hopehill Road
North Woodside Road
Napiershall Street
GLASGOW
M²
UNIVERSITY
M⁴
Y
Gibson St.
Bank Street
105
KELVINBRIDGE
Park Rd
West Prince's Street
50
140
ST. GEORGE'S CROSS
St. George's Road
Woodlands Road
Park Quadrant
KELVINGROVE MUSEUM AND ART GALLERY
Kelvin Way
KELVINGROVE PARK
108
107
34
143
Royal Terrace
Woodside Place
141
Saint George's Road
U 35
M
B
Sauchiehall Street
Argyle Street
47
42
95
Berkeley Street
Elderslie St.
Kent Road
Kelvinhaugh Street
Scott Street
Bath St.
Inner Ring Road
T
Elmbank St.
POL.
West Regent St.
West George St.
A 814
Saint Vincent Street
North Street
Douglas St.
Pitt St.
Waterloo St.
Campbell St.
SCOTTISH EXHIBITION CENTRE
Stobcross Road
Finnieston Street
Clydeside Expressway
Lancefield Street
Hydepark Street
Lancefield Quay
Anderston Quay
Argyle Street
A 814
West St.
York St.
120
Broomielaw
Z
CLYDE
M 8
85
Govan Road
Govan Road
Paisley Road
A 8
West St.
35
Kingston St.
Morrison Street
Nelson Street
West St.
22
93
West
Milnpark Street
Admiral St.
Seaward St.
KINNING PARK
39
100
A 8
M 8
(M 8)
C

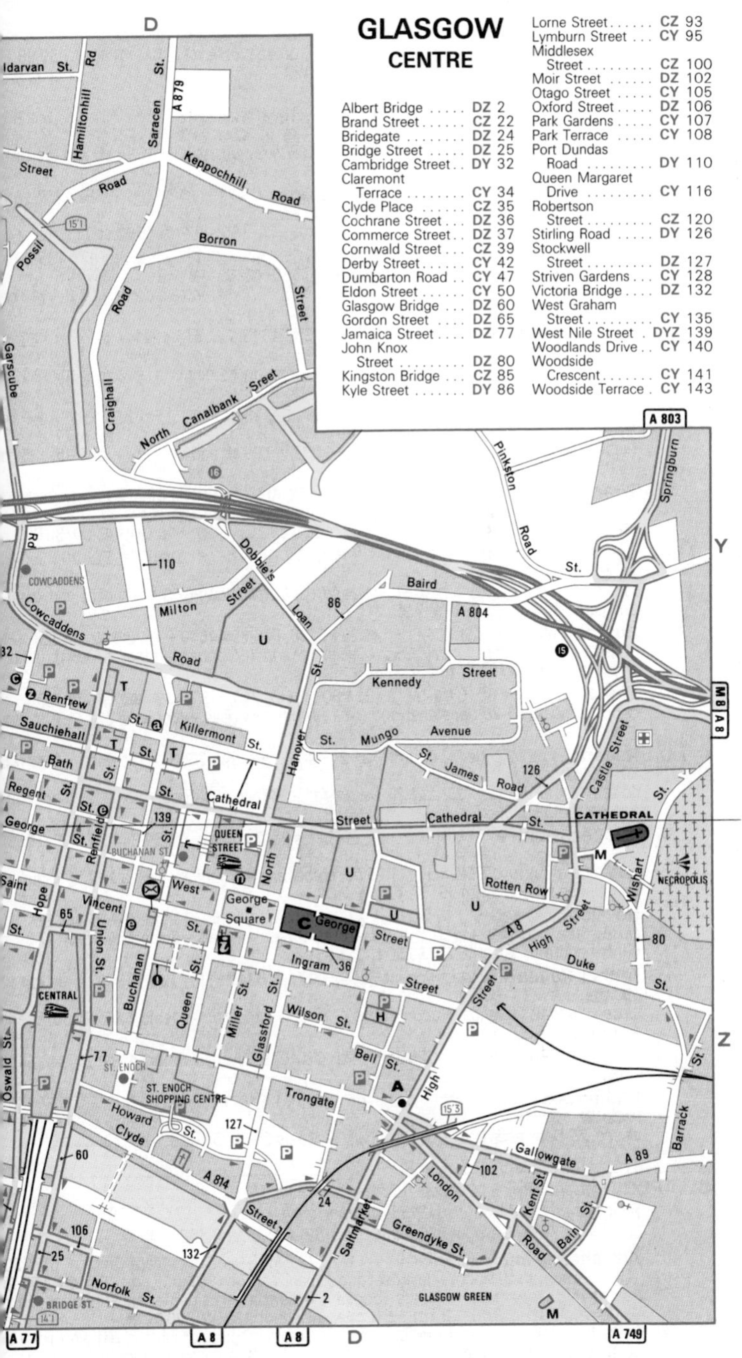
GLASGOW
CENTRE
Albert Bridge . . . . . DZ 2
Brand Street . . . . . . CZ 22
Bridegate . . . . DZ 24
Bridge Street . . . . . . DZ 25
Cambridge Street . . DY 32
Claremont Terrace . . . . CY 34
Clyde Place . . . . . . CZ 35
Cochrane Street . . . DZ 36
Commerce Street . . DZ 37
Cornwald Street . . . CZ 39
Derby Street . . . . . . CY 42
Dumbarton Road . . CY 47
Eldon Street . . . . . . CY 50
Glasgow Bridge . . . DZ 60
Gordon Street . . . . DZ 65
Jamaica Street . . . . DZ 77
John Knox Street . . . . DZ 80
Kingston Bridge . . . CZ 85
Kyle Street . . . . DY 86
Lorne Street . . . . . . CZ 93
Lymburn Street . . . CY 95
Middlesex Street . . . . CZ 100
Moir Street . . . . . . DZ 102
Otago Street . . . . . CY 105
Oxford Street . . . . . DZ 106
Park Gardens . . . . . CY 107
Park Terrace . . . . . CY 108
Port Dundas Road . . . . DY 110
Queen Margaret Drive . . . . CY 116
Robertson Street . . . . CZ 120
Stirling Road . . . . . DY 126
Stockwell Street . . . . DZ 127
Striven Gardens . . . CY 128
Victoria Bridge . . . . DZ 132
West Graham Street . . . . CY 135
West Nile Street . DYZ 139
Woodlands Drive . . CY 140
Woodside Crescent . . . . . . CY 141
Woodside Terrace . CY 143
D
Y
Z
A 803
M 8
A 8
A 77
A 749
A 879
A 804
A 814
A 89
CATHEDRAL
NECROPOLIS
QUEEN STREET
CENTRAL
BUCHANAN ST.
COWCADDENS
ST. ENOCH
ST. ENOCH SHOPPING CENTRE
BRIDGE ST.
GLASGOW GREEN
George Square
Sauchiehall St.
Cathedral St.
Trongate
Gallowgate
Saltmarket
High Street
Duke St.
Argyle St.
Renfrew St.
Bath St.
Regent St.
West George St.
Saint Vincent St.
Ingram Street
Wilson St.
Bell St.
Howard St.
Clyde St.
Norfolk St.
Greendyke St.
London Road
Rotten Row
Castle Street
Springburn Road
Pinkston Road
Baird St.
Kennedy Street
St. Mungo Avenue
St. James Road
Dobbie's Loan
Milton Street
Cowcaddens Road
Killermont St.
North Canalbank Street
Borron Street
Possil Road
Craighall Road
Garscube Rd
Saracen St.
Keppochhill Road
Hamiltonhill Rd
Hanover St.
Buchanan St.
Queen St.
Miller St.
Glassford St.
Union St.
Hope St.
Renfield St.
Oswald St.
Wishart St.
Kent St.
Bain St.
Barrack St.

Stakis Glasgow Grosvenor, Grosvenor Terr., Great Western Rd, G12 0TA, 339 8811 Fax 334 0710 – rm – 450 CY
94 rm, 2 suites.

Holiday Inn Garden Court Glasgow, Theatreland, 161 West Nile St., G1 2RL 353 2595, Fax 332 7447 – rm – 80. DY
La Bonne Auberge Brasserie : **Meals** *(closed Sunday lunch)* 7.95/16.95 **st.** and a la carte 4.75 – 7.95 – **80 rm** 64.75 **st.** – SB.

Kelvin Park Lorne (Q.M.H.), 923 Sauchiehall St., G3 7TE, 314 9955, Fax 337 1659 – rm – 300. CY
Meals (bar lunch)/dinner 17.95 **st.** and a la carte – 9.50 – **97 rm** 75.00 **st.**, 1 suite – SB

Swallow Glasgow, 517 Paisley Road West, G51 1RW, 427 3146, Fax 427 4059, – rm rest – 350. by A 8 CZ
Meals *(closed Saturday lunch)* (carving lunch) 7.95/16.75 **st.** and a la carte 5.50 – **117 rm** 90.00/135.00 **st.** – SB.

Stakis Glasgow City, Hill St., G3 6PR, 333 1515, Fax 333 1221 – rm – 35. DY
closed 24 to 26 December – **Meals** (grill rest.) (bar lunch)/dinner a la carte 9.40/19.10 **t.** – 7.50 – **93 rm** 54.00/64.00 **t.**

Tinto Firs Thistle, 470 Kilmarnock Rd, G43 2BB, 637 2353, Fax 633 1340 – rm – 200. by A 77 DZ
Meals *(closed lunch Monday and Saturday)* 12.95/19.95 **st.** and a la carte – 8.95 – **25 rm** 79.00/99.00 **st.**, 2 suites – SB.

Charing Cross Tower, Elmbank Gdns., G2 4PP, pedestrianised area off Bath St 221 1000, Fax 248 1000, – rm . CY
Meals (bar lunch)/dinner a la carte 8.25/15.20 **t.** – 5.90 – **281 rm** 43.00/50.00 **t.**

Camerons (at Glasgow Hilton H.), 1 William St., G3 8HT, 204 5511, Fax 204 5004 CZ
Meals *(closed Saturday lunch, Sunday and Bank Holidays)* 16.50 **st.** (lunch) and dinner a la carte 32.70/49.50 **st.** 7.95.

Buttery, 652 Argyle St., G3 8UF, 221 8188, Fax 204 4639 –
closed Saturday lunch, Sunday, 25-26 December and 1-2 January – **Meals** 14.85 **st.** (lunch) and a la carte 24.70/31.45 **t.** CZ

Yes, 22 West Nile St., G1 2PW, 221 8044, Fax 248 9159 –
closed Sunday, 25-26 December and Bank Holiday Mondays – **Meals** 14.95/24.50 **t.** and a la carte. DZ

Rogano, 11 Exchange Pl., G1 3AN, 248 4055, Fax 248 2608, « Art Deco » – DZ
closed 1 to 3 January, 25 and 26 December – **Meals** - Seafood - 16.50 **t.** (lunch) and a la carte 13.50/31.25 **t.**

Puppet Theatre, 11 Ruthven Lane, off Byres Rd, G12 9BG, 339 8444, Fax 339 7666 –
closed Saturday lunch, Monday, 25-26 December and 1-2 January – **Meals** 14.50 **t.** (lunch) and dinner a la carte 24.95/30.45 **t.** 7.00.

Ho Wong, 82 York St., G2 8LE, 221 3550, Fax 248 5330 –
closed Sunday dinner and 3 days Chinese New Year – **Meals** - Chinese (Peking) - 7.90 **t.** (lunch) and a la carte 18.20/29.50 **t.** 5.95. CZ

Amber Regent, 50 West Regent St., G2 2QZ, 331 1655, Fax 353 3398 – DY
closed Sunday, 1 January and 3 days Chinese New Year – **Meals** 6.95/24.00 **t.** and a la carte 5.95.

Killermont Polo Club, 2022 Maryhill Rd, G20 0AB, NW : 3 m. on A 81 946 5412 –

Ubiquitous Chip, 12 Ashton Lane, off Byres Rd, G12 8SJ, 334 5007, Fax 337 1302 – by A 808 CY
closed 25 December and 1 to 2 January – **Meals** 23.00/31.00 **t.** and a la carte.

ULLAPOOL *Highland* 401 E 10 – *pop. 1 231* – *01854.*
Argyle St., IV26 2UR 612135 (summer only).
Edinburgh 215 – Glasgow 225 – Inverness 59 – Aberdeen 168.

Altnaharrie Inn (Gunn Eriksen) ,, IV26 2SS, *SW : ½ m. by private ferry* 633230 Loch Broom and Ullapool, « Idyllic setting on banks of Loch Broom », – .
Easter-mid November – **Meals** (booking essential) (residents only) (dinner only) 65.00/75.00 **st.** 6.00 – **8 rm** (dinner included) 225.00/390.00 **st.**
Spec. Mousseline of scallops inlaid with crab, Creamy "soup" of lobster with vermicelli of cucumber, Saddle of lamb with asparagus and morels, asparagus sauce.

LEEDS *W. Yorks.* 402 P 22 **Great Britain G.** – *pop. 424 194* – *0113.*

See : *City* ★ – *City Art Gallery* ★ DZ **M.**

Envir. : *Kirkstall Abbey* ★ , *NW : 3 m. by A 65* – *Templenewsam* ★ *(decorative arts* ★*), E : 5 m. by A 64 and A 63.*

Exc. : *Harewood House* ★★ *(The Gallery* ★*) , N : 8 m. by A 61.*

18, 18 Temple Newsam, Temple Newsam Rd, Halton 264 5624 – 18 Cotts Park, Armley Ridge Rd, 234 2019 – 18 Middleton Park, Ring Rd, Beeston Park, Middleton 270 9506 – 18, 9 Moor Allerton, Coal Rd, Wike 266 1154 – 18 Howley Hall, Scotchman Lane, Morley (01924) 472432 – 9 Roundhay, Park Lane 266 2695.

Leeds - Bradford Airport : 250 9696, NW : 8 m. by A 65 and A 658.

The Arcade, City Station, LS1 1PL 242 5242.

London 204 – Liverpool 75 – Manchester 43 – Newcastle upon Tyne 95 – Nottingham 74.

Plan on next page

Oulton Hall (De Vere), Rothwell Lane, Oulton, LS26 8HN, SE : 5 ½ m. by A 61 and A 639 282 1000, Fax 282 8066, 18, 9, squash – rest – 330.
***Bronte* :** **Meals** *(closed Saturday lunch)* 13.00/21.50 **t.** and dinner a la carte 6.50 – **150 rm** 115.00/125.00 **st.**, 2 suites – SB.

Leeds Marriott, 4 Trevelyan Sq., Boar Lane, LS1 6ET, 236 6366, Fax 236 6367, – rm – 350. DZ x
Dyson's *(236 6444)* **: Meals** *(closed Saturday lunch and Sunday dinner)* 15.95 **st.** and a la carte 4.50 – 10.95 – **240 rm** 89.00/111.00 **st.**, 4 suites – SB.

42 The Calls, 42 The Calls, LS2 7EW, 244 0099, Fax 234 4100, « Converted riverside grain mill » – rm – 55. DZ z
closed 1 week Christmas – **Meals** – (see ***Pool Court at 42*** below) (see also ***Brasserie Forty Four*** below) – 11.50 – **38 rm** 95.00/145.00 **st.**, 3 suites.

Holiday Inn Crown Plaza, Wellington St., LS1 4DL, 244 2200, Fax 244 0460, – rm – 200. CZ c
Meals *(closed Saturday lunch)* 12.50/16.50 **st.** and dinner a la carte 8.95 – 11.50 – **120 rm** 115.00 **st.**, 5 suites – SB.

Hilton National Leeds, Neville St., LS1 4BX, 244 2000, Fax 243 3577, – rm – 400. DZ r
Meals 12.95/16.95 **st.** and a la carte 6.50 – 11.95 – **186 rm** 99.00 **st.**, 20 suites – SB.

Queen's (Forte), City Sq., LS1 1PL, 243 1323, Fax 242 5154 – rm – 600. DZ a
Meals (carving rest.) 12.50/17.50 **st.** and a la carte 7.50 – ***Harewood* : Meals** *(closed Saturday lunch and Bank Holidays)* 13.50/17.50 **st.** and a la carte 7.50 – 11.50 – **184 rm** 82.00/92.00 **st.**, 6 suites – SB.

Weetwood Hall, Otley Rd, LS16 5PS, NW : 4 m. on A 660 230 6000, Fax 230 6095, – rest – 150.
Meals 11.95/14.25 **st.** and a la carte 6.50 – 7.95 – **108 rm** 67.50/110.00 **st.**

Haley's (Virgin), Shire Oak Rd, Headingley, LS6 2DE, NW : 2 m. off Otley Rd (A 660) 278 4446, Fax 275 3342 – – 25.
accommodation closed 26 to 30 December – **Meals** *(closed Sunday dinner to non-residents)* (dinner only and Sunday lunch)/dinner a la carte 18.45/25.85 **st.** 5.10 – **22 rm** 95.00/112.00 **st.** – SB.

Merrion Thistle, Merrion Centre, 17 Wade Lane, LS2 8NH, 243 9191, Fax 242 3527 – rest – 80. DZ e
Meals 16.50 **st.** (dinner) and a la carte 17.45/25.45 **st.** 6.00 – 9.50 – **108 rm** 89.00/109.00 **st.**, 1 suite.

Metropole, King St., LS1 2HQ, 245 0841, Fax 242 5156 – – 200. CZ e
Meals *(closed Saturday lunch and Bank Holidays)* 9.95/17.95 **t.** and dinner a la carte 6.50 – 9.95 – **104 rm** 79.00 **t.**, 1 suite – SB.

Golden Lion (Mount Charlotte), 2 Lower Briggate, LS1 4AE, 243 6454, Fax 242 9327 – rm – 120. DZ v
Meals *(closed lunch Saturday and Sunday)* 15.50 **st.** and a la carte 4.80 – **89 rm** 85.00/100.00 **st.** – SB.

Pool Court at 42 (at 42 The Calls H.), 44 The Calls, LS2 7EW, 244 4242, Fax 234 3332, « Riverside setting » – . DZ z
closed Saturday lunch, Sunday, 1 week Christmas and Bank Holidays – **Meals** 17.00/27.50 **t.** 8.95
Spec. Tarte Tatin of foie gras, balsamic vinegar dressing, Chargrilled fillet of beef, potato crust, soubise and Morgon sauce, Saltburn sea bass roasted on salt, crab mayonnaise and lobster oil.

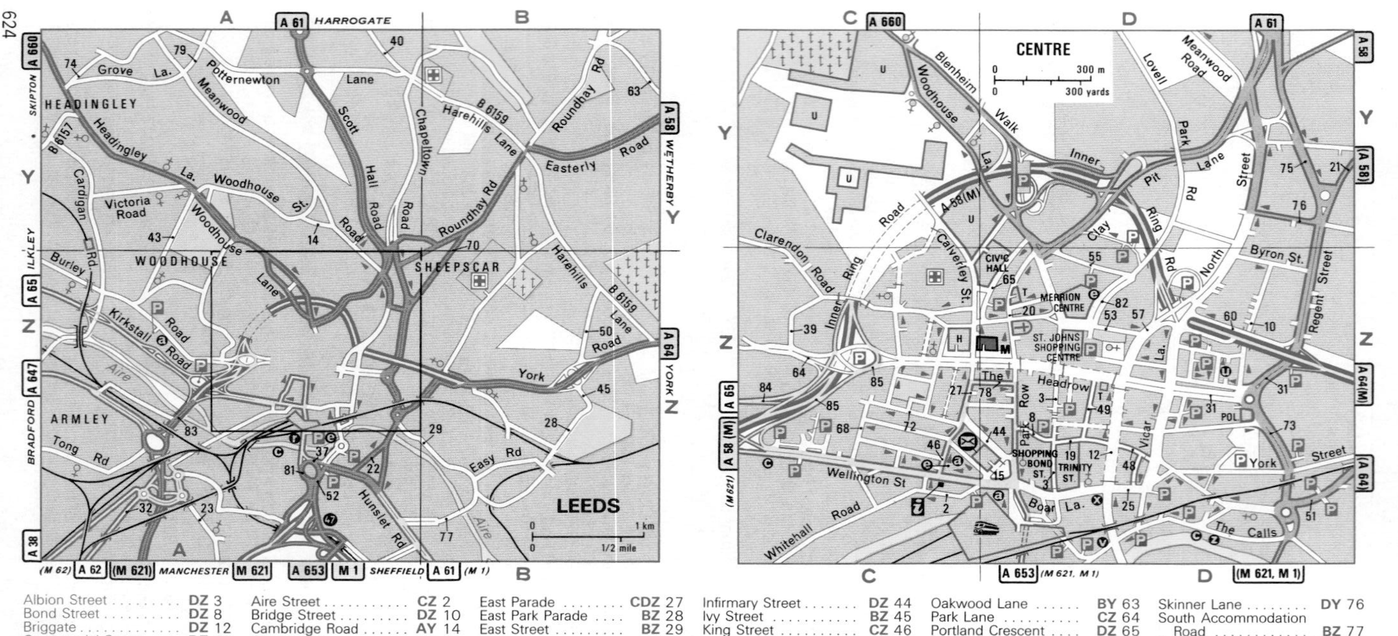

Albion Street	DZ 3	Aire Street	CZ 2	East Parade	CDZ 27	Infirmary Street	DZ 44	Oakwood Lane	BY 63	Skinner Lane	DY 76
Bond Street	DZ 8	Bridge Street	DZ 10	East Park Parade	BZ 28	Ivy Street	BZ 45	Park Lane	CZ 64	South Accommodation Road	BZ 77
Briggate	DZ 12	Cambridge Road	AY 14	East Street	BZ 29	King Street	CZ 46	Portland Crescent	DZ 65	South Parade	CDZ 78
Commercial Street	DZ 19	City Square	DZ 15	Eastgate	DZ 31	Lupton Avenue	BZ 50	Queen Street	CZ 68	Stainbeck Road	AY 79
Headrow (The)	DZ	Cookridge Street	DZ 20	Gelderd Road	AZ 32	Marsh Lane	DZ 51	Roseville Road	BYZ 70	Victoria Road	AZ 81
Kirkgate	DZ 48	Cross Stamford Street	DY 21	Great Wilson Street	AZ 37	Meadow Lane	AZ 52	St. Paul's Street	CZ 72	Wade Lane	DZ 82
Lands Lane	DZ 49	Crown Point Road	AZ 22	Hanover Way	CZ 39	Merrion Street	DZ 53	St. Peter's Street	DZ 73	Wellington Road	AZ 83
Merrion Centre	DZ	Domestic Street	AZ 23	Harrogate Road	AY 40	Merrion Way	DZ 55	Shaw Lane	AY 74	West Street	CZ 84
St John's Centre	DZ					New Briggate	DZ 57	Sheepscar Street			

Rascasse (Gueller), Canal Wharf, Water Lane, LS11 5BB, ☎ 244 6611, Fax 244 0736, <, « Converted grain warehouse, canalside setting » – ▤. MC AE ① VISA AZ c
closed Saturday lunch, Sunday, Bank Holiday Monday and 1 week after Christmas – Meals 14.00 **t.** (lunch) and a la carte 22.00/27.50 **t.** 6.50
Spec. Chicken, veal sweetbread and foie gras terrine, sauce gribiche, Medallions of lamb, truffled potatoes, peas and tarragon jus, Lemon tart.

Leodis, Victoria Mill, Sovereign St., LS1 4BJ, ☎ 242 1010, Fax 243 0432, « Converted riverside warehouse » – ▤. MC AE ① VISA AZ e
closed Saturday and Bank Holiday Monday lunch, Sunday, 25-26 December and 1 January – **Meals** 12.95 **t.** and a la carte 15.80/30.90 **t.** 5.00.

Brasserie Forty Four (at 42 The Calls H.), 42-44 The Calls, LS2 8AQ, ☎ 234 3232, Fax 234 3332 – ▤. MC AE ① VISA DZ z
closed Saturday lunch, Sunday, 25-26 December and Bank Holidays – **Meals** 11.95 **t.** (lunch) and dinner a la carte 15.90/22.10 **t.** 7.70.

Maxi's, 6 Bingley St., LS3 1LX, *off Kirkstall Rd* ☎ 244 0552, Fax 234 3902, « Pagoda, ornate decor » – ▤ P. MC AE ① VISA JCB AZ a
Meals - Chinese (Canton, Peking) - a la carte 11.40/13.40 **st.**

Lucky Dragon, Templar Lane, LS2 7LP, ☎ 245 0520, Fax 245 0520 – ▤. MC AE ① VISA JCB DZ u
closed 25 and 26 December – **Meals** - Chinese (Cantonese) - a la carte 8.80/13.00 **t.** 4.25.

Hereford Beefstouw, Calls Landing, 38 The Calls, LS2 7EW, ☎ 245 3870, Fax 243 9035, « Converted riverside warehouse » – ▤ P. MC AE ① VISA DZ c
closed Sunday lunch and 24 December-2 January – **Meals** (grill rest.) a la carte 10.50/23.40 **t.** 5.75.

Sous le nez en ville, Quebec House, Quebec St., LS1 2HA, ☎ 244 0108, Fax 245 0240 – MC AE VISA CZ a
closed Sunday and Bank Holidays – **Meals** 14.95 **st.** (dinner) and a la carte.

at Seacroft *NE : 5 ½ m. at junction of A 64 with A 6120* – BZ – ✉ *Leeds* – ☎ *0113 :*

Stakis Leeds, Ring Rd, LS14 5QF, ☎ 273 2323, Fax 232 3018 – |‡| ⇔ rm TV ☎ P – 250. MC AE ① VISA JCB
Meals *(closed Saturday lunch)* 9.95/16.45 **st.** and a la carte – ☐ 8.50 – **100 rm** 79.00/111.00 **st.** – SB.

at Garforth *E : 6 m. by A 63 at junction with A 642* – BZ – ✉ *Leeds* – ☎ *0113 :*

Hilton National, Wakefield Rd, LS25 1LH, ☎ 286 6556, Fax 286 8326, Lδ, ≘s, ☒ – ⇔ rm ▤ rest TV ☎ ♿ P – 350. MC AE ① VISA JCB
Meals *(closed Saturday lunch)* (carving lunch) 10.50/17.00 **st.** and a la carte 5.35 – ☐ 10.25 – **144 rm** 82.50/105.00 **st.** – SB.

Aagrah, Aberford Rd, LS25 1BA, *on A 642* ☎ 287 6606 – P. MC AE VISA JCB
closed 25 December – **Meals** - Indian - (dinner only) a la carte 11.15/13.80 **st.**

Aagrah, 483 Bradford Rd, LS28 8ED, *on A 647* ☎ 668818, Fax 669803 – P. MC AE VISA
closed 25 December – **Meals** - Indian - (dinner only and Sunday lunch)/dinner a la carte 11.15/13.80 **st.**

at Horsforth *NW : 5 m. by A 65* – AZ – *off A 6120* – ✉ *Leeds* – ☎ *0113 :*

Paris, Calverley Bridge, Calverley Lane, Rodley, LS13 1NP, SW : 1 m. by A 6120 ☎ 258 1885, Fax 239 0651 – ▤ P – 40. MC ① VISA
closed Saturday lunch – **Meals** 10.95 **t.** and a la carte.

at Bramhope *NW : 8 m. on A 660* – AY – ✉ *Leeds* – ☎ *0113 :*

Forte Posthouse Leeds/Bradford, Leeds Rd, LS16 9JJ, ☎ 284 2911, Fax 284 3451, <, Lδ, ≘s, ☒, *park* – |‡| ⇔ rm TV ☎ P – 160. MC AE ① VISA JCB
Meals 7.95 **st.** and a la carte – ☐ 9.95 – **123 rm** 79.00 **st.**, 1 suite – SB.

Jarvis Parkway H. and Country Club, Otley Rd, LS16 8AC, S : 2 m. on A 660 ☎ 267 2551, Fax 267 4410, Lδ, ≘s, ☒, ✂ – |‡| ⇔ rm TV ☎ ♿ P – 300. MC AE ① VISA
Meals (bar lunch Monday to Saturday)/dinner 16.80 **st.** and a la carte – ☐ 9.50 – **105 rm** 99.00 **st.** – SB.

In this Guide,
a symbol or a character, printed in red or black,
does not have the same meaning.
Please read the explanatory pages carefully.

LIVERPOOL
CENTRE

Street	Grid	No.
Bold St.	DZ	
Church St.	DY	
Lime St.	DY	
London Rd	DEY	
Lord St.	CDY	
Parker St.	DY	103
Ranelagh St.	DY	108
Renshaw St.	DEZ	
St. Johns Centre	DY	
Argyle St.	DZ	6
Blackburne Pl.	EZ	11
Brunswick Rd	EY	19
Canning Pl.	CZ	23
Churchill Way	DY	25
Clarence St.	EYZ	26
College Lane	DZ	28
Commutation Row	DY	30
Cook St.	CY	32
Crosshall St.	DY	36
Daulby St.	EY	40
Erskine St.	EY	45
Fontenoy St.	DY	48
Forrest St.	DZ	49
George's Dock Gate	CY	51
Grafton St.	DZ	53
Great Charlotte St.	DY	54
Great Howard St.	CY	56
Hatton Garden	DY	57
Haymarket	DY	58
Hood St.	DY	62
Houghton St.	DY	65
Huskisson St.	EZ	66
James St.	CY	68
King Edward St.	CY	69
Knight St.	EZ	72
Leece St.	EZ	73
Liver St.	CZ	76
Mansfield St.	DEY	80
Mathew St.	CDY	81
Moss St.	EY	86
Mount St.	EZ	88
Myrtle St.	EZ	89
Newington	DZ	92
New Quay	CY	93
North John St.	CY	96
Norton St.	EY	97
Prescot St.	EY	105
Prince's Rd	EZ	107
Richmond St.	DY	109
Roe St.	DY	114
St. James Pl.	EZ	117
St. John's Lane	DY	118
School Lane	DYZ	122
Scotland Pl.	DY	123
Setton St.	DZ	129
Seymour St.	EY	130
Skelhorne St.	DY	133
Stanley St.	CDY	135
Suffolk St.	DZ	137
Tarleton St.	DY	139
Victoria St.	DY	143
Water St.	CY	150
William Brown St.	DY	156
York St.	DZ	157

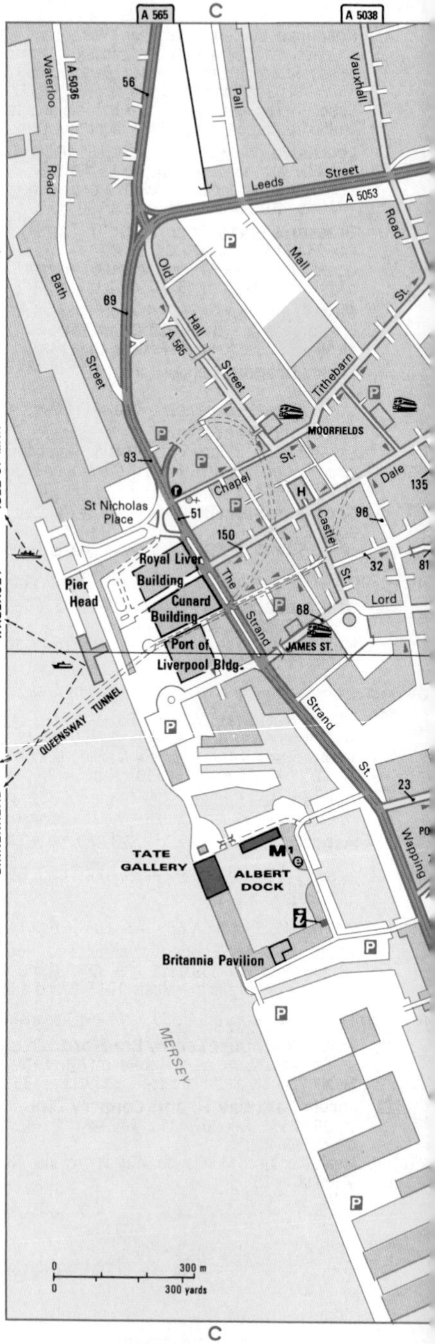

Great Britain and *Ireland* is now covered by an *Atlas* at a scale of 1 inch to 4.75 miles.

Three easy to use versions: Paperback, Spiralbound, Hardback.

A 565
C
A 5038
Waterloo Road
A 5036
Pall
Vauxhall Road
Leeds Street
A 5053
Mall
Old Hall Street
A 565
Bath Street
Tithebarn St.
MOORFIELDS
Chapel St.
Dale St.
Castle St.
Lord St.
St Nicholas Place
Royal Liver Building
Cunard Building
Port of Liverpool Bldg.
Pier Head
The Strand
Strand St.
JAMES ST.
QUEENSWAY TUNNEL
ISLE OF MAN
WALLASEY
BIRKENHEAD
TATE GALLERY
ALBERT DOCK
Britannia Pavilion
Wapping
MERSEY
Y
Z
300 m
300 yards

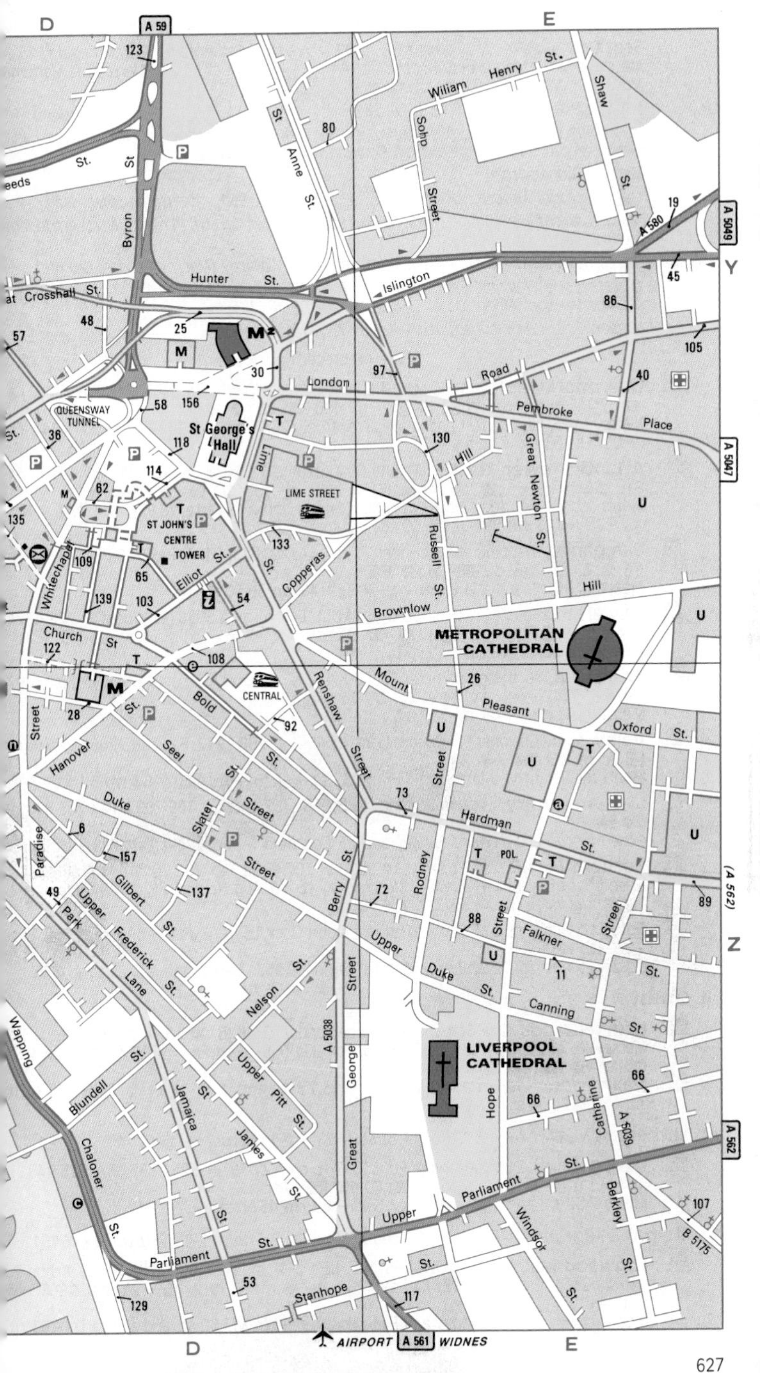
D
E
Y
Z
A 59
A 5049
A 5047
A 562
(A 562)
A 580
A 5038
A 5039
B 5175
AIRPORT A 561 WIDNES
Leeds St.
Byron St.
Anne St.
Soho Street
William Henry St.
Shaw St.
Hunter St.
Islington
Crosshall St.
London Road
Pembroke Place
QUEENSWAY TUNNEL
St George's Hall
Lime St.
LIME STREET
Great Newton St.
Russell St.
Hill
ST JOHN'S CENTRE TOWER
Whitechapel
Elliot St.
Copperas Hill
Brownlow Hill
METROPOLITAN CATHEDRAL
Church St
CENTRAL
Renshaw Street
Mount Pleasant
Oxford St.
Bold St.
Hanover St.
Seel St.
Slater St.
Duke Street
Hardman St.
Paradise Street
Gilbert St.
Berry St.
Rodney Street
Hope Street
Falkner St.
Upper Duke St.
Canning St.
Upper Park Lane
Upper Frederick St.
Nelson St.
Great George Street
LIVERPOOL CATHEDRAL
Catharine Street
Wapping
Blundell St.
Jamaica St.
Upper Pitt St.
James St.
Chaloner St.
Upper Parliament St.
Parliament St.
Windsor St.
Berkley St.
Stanhope St.
POL.

LIVERPOOL *Mersey.* 402 403 L 23 **Great Britain G.** – *pop. 481 786* – ☎ *0151.*

See : *City★ - Walker Art Gallery★★* DY **M2** – *Liverpool Cathedral★★ (Lady Chapel★)* EZ – *Metropolitan Cathedral of Christ the King★★* EY – *Albert Dock★* CZ – *(Merseyside Maritime Museum★* **M1** - *Tate Gallery Liverpool★).*

Exc. : *Speke Hall★ , SE : 8 m. by A 561.*

Allerton Municipal, Allerton Rd ☎ 428 1046 – Liverpool Municipal, Ingoe Lane, Kirkby ☎ 546 5435 – Bowring, Bowring Park, Roby Rd, Huyton ☎ 489 1901.

Mersey Tunnels (toll).

Liverpool Airport : ☎ 486 8877, SE : 6 m. by A 561 – **Terminal** : *Pier Head.*

to Isle of Man (Douglas) (Isle of Man Steam Packet Co. Ltd) (4 h) – to Northern Ireland (Belfast) (Norse Irish Ferries Ltd) (11 h).

to Birkenhead (Mersey Ferries) (10 mn) – to Wallasey (Mersey Ferries) (20 mn).

Merseyside Welcome Centre, Clayton Square Shopping Centre, L1 1QR ☎ 709 3631 – Atlantic Pavilion, Albert Dock, L3 4AA ☎ 708 8854.

London 219 – Birmingham 103 – Leeds 75 – Manchester 35.

Plans on preceding pages

Liverpool Moat House (Q.M.H.), Paradise St., L1 8JD, ☎ 471 9988, Fax 709 2706, – rm – 400. AE VISA DZ
Meals 14.95 **st.** (dinner) and a la carte 11.40/26.95 **st.** 6.25 – 9.50 – **244 rm** 98.00/115.00 **st.**, 7 suites – SB.

Atlantic Tower Thistle (Mount Charlotte), 30 Chapel St., L3 9RE, ☎ 227 4444, Fax 236 3973, ← – rm – 100. AE VISA JCB CY
Meals *(closed Saturday lunch)* 16.50 **t.** (dinner) and a la carte 18.95/33.00 **t.** 4.90 – 9.25 – **223 rm** 89.00/106.00 **st.**, 3 suites – SB.

Campanile, Wapping and Chaloner St., L3 4AJ, ☎ 709 8104, Fax 709 8725 – rm – 30. AE VISA CZ
Meals 10.55 **st.** and a la carte – 4.50 – **78 rm** 36.50 **st.**

Travel Inn, Queens Dr., West Derby, L13 0DL, E : 4 m. on A 5058 (Ringroad) ☎ 228 4724, Fax 220 7610 – rm. AE VISA. by A 5049 EY
Meals (grill rest.) – **40 rm** 35.50 **t.**

Travel Inn, Northern Perimeter Rd, L30 7PT, N : 6 m. by A 59 on A 5036 ☎ 531 1497, Fax 520 1842 – rm. AE VISA.
Meals (grill rest.) – **43 rm** 35.50 **t.**

Dolby, 36-42 Chaloner St., Queens Dock, L3 4DE, ☎ 708 7272, Fax 708 7266, ← – rm. VISA JCB. DZ
Meals (dinner only) a la carte 11.05/15.35 **st.** 5.75 – 4.50 – **64 rm** 30.50.

Lyceum Library, Lyceum Building, 1a Bold St., L1 4DD, ☎ 709 7097, Fax 708 8751 – VISA DYZ
closed lunch Saturday and Sunday and 25 December – **Meals** a la carte 19.85/30.85 **t.**

Becher's Brook, 29a Hope St., L1 9BQ, ☎ 707 0005, Fax 708 7011 – . AE VISA
closed Saturday lunch, Sunday, Monday, 15 to 30 August and 25 to 28 December – **Meals** a la carte 12.00/32.00 **t.** 6.75. EZ

Est, Est, Est , Unit 5-6, Edward Pavilion, Albert Dock, L3 4AA, ☎ 708 6969, Fax 709 4912 – . AE VISA CZ
closed 25 and 26 December – **Meals** - Italian - 9.95/12.95 **t.** and a la carte 4.75.

at Crosby *N : 5 ½ m. by A 565 – CY – ☎ 0151 :*

Blundellsands, The Serpentine, Blundellsands, L23 6YB, W : 1 ¼ m. via College Rd, Mersey Rd and Agnes Rd ☎ 924 6515, Fax 931 5364 – rm – 250. AE VISA.
Meals *(closed Saturday lunch)* 7.75/13.75 **t.** and a la carte 7.75 – **37 rm** 65.00/75.00 **st.** – SB.

at Netherton *N : 6 m. by A 5038 off A 5036 – CY – ✉ Liverpool – ☎ 0151 :*

Park (Premier), Dunningsbridge Rd, L30 6YN, *on A 5036* ☎ 525 7555, Fax 525 2481 – rm – 100. AE VISA.
Meals 7.50 **st.** and a la carte – 6.95 – **62 rm** 43.50 **st.** – SB.

at Huyton *E : 8 ¼ m. by A5047 – EY – and A 5080 on B 5199 – ✉ Liverpool – ☎ 0151 :*

Logwood Mill, Fallows Way, L35 1RZ, SE : 3 ¼ m. by A 5080 off Windy Arbor Rd ☎ 449 2341, Fax 449 3832, – rm – 200. AE VISA.
Meals *(closed lunch Saturday and Bank Holidays)* 15.00/17.50 **st.** and a la carte – **63 rm** 75.00/85.00 **st.** – SB.

Derby Lodge, Roby Rd, L36 4HD, SW : 1 m. on A 5080 ✆ 480 4440, Fax 480 8132, – TV ☎ P – 150. AE VISA JCB.
Meals *(closed Saturday lunch and Bank Holidays)* 15.50 **t.** (dinner) and a la carte 17.45/40.45 **t.** 7.50 – **19 rm** 55.00/65.00 **st.**

Travel Inn, Wilson Rd, Tarbock, L36 6AD, SE : 2 ¼ m. on A 5080 ✆ 480 9614, Fax 480 9361 – rm TV P. AE VISA.
Meals (grill rest.) – **40 rm** 35.50 **t.**

at Grassendale *SE : 4 ½ m. on A 561 – EZ – ✉ Liverpool – 0151 :*

Gulshan, 544-548 Aigburth Rd, L19 3QG, on A 561 ✆ 427 2273 – . AE VISA
Meals - Indian - (dinner only) a la carte 16.80/24.55 **t.** 6.50.

at Woolton *SE : 6 m. by A 562 – EZ –, A 5058 and Woolton Rd – ✉ Liverpool – 0151 :*

Woolton Redbourne, Acrefield Rd, L25 5JN, ✆ 428 2152, Fax 421 1501, « Victorian house, antiques », – TV ☎ P. AE VISA JCB
Meals (residents only) (dinner only) 22.95 **st.** 6.00 – **25 rm** 65.00/98.00 **st.**, 1 suite – SB.

MANCHESTER *Gtr. Manchester* 402 403 404 N 23 **Great Britain G.** – *pop. 402 889 – 0161.*

See : *City★ – Castlefield Heritage Park★* CZ – *Town Hall★* CZ – *City Art Gallery★* CZ **M2** – *Cathedral★ (Stalls and Canopies★)* CY.

Heaton Park, Prestwick ✆ 798 0295 – Houldsworth Park, Houldsworth St., Reddish, Stockport ✆ 442 9611 – Chorlton-cum-Hardy, Barlow Hall, Barlow Hall Rd ✆ 881 3139 – William Wroe, Pennybridge Lane, Flixton ✆ 748 8680.

Manchester International Airport : ✆ 489 3000, S : 10 m. by A 5103 and M 56 – **Terminal :** *Coach service from Victoria Station.*

Town Hall, Lloyd St., M60 2LA ✆ 234 3157/8 – Manchester Airport, International Arrivals Hall, Terminal 1, M90 3NY ✆ 436 3344.

Manchester Airport, International Arrivals Hall, Terminal 2, M90 4TU ✆ 489 6412.

London 202 – Birmingham 86 – Glasgow 221 – Leeds 43 – Liverpool 35 – Nottingham 72.

Plan on next page

Victoria and Albert, Water St., M3 4JQ, ✆ 832 1188, Fax 834 2484, « Converted 19C warehouse, television themed interior », – rm TV ☎ P – 250. AE VISA. by Quay St. CZ
Cafe Maigret : **Meals** *(closed Saturday lunch and Sunday)* 18.95 **st.** (dinner) and lunch a la carte 17.20/23.70 **st.** – (see also ***Sherlock Holmes*** below) – 11.95 – **152 rm** 135.00 **st.**, 4 suites – SB.

Holiday Inn Crowne Plaza Midland, Peter St., M60 2DS, ✆ 236 3333, Fax 932 4100, squash – rm TV ☎ P – 600. AE VISA JCB. CZ x
French rest. : **Meals** *(closed Sunday)* (dinner only) 32.50 **t.** and a la carte 6.75 – ***Trafford Room :*** **Meals** *(closed Saturday lunch)* (carving rest.) 18.95 **t.** and a la carte 6.75 – ***Wyvern :*** **Meals** *(closed Sunday)* a la carte 13.00/24.00 **t.** 6.75 – 11.50 – **296 rm** 120.00 **t.**, 7 suites – SB.

Ramada, Blackfriars St., Deansgate, M3 2EQ, ✆ 835 2555, Fax 835 3077 – rm rest TV ☎ P – 400. AE VISA. CY v
Meals *(closed Saturday lunch and Sunday)* 9.95/19.50 **st.** and dinner a la carte 5.95 – 10.20 – **196 rm** 120.00 **st.**, 5 suites.

Copthorne Manchester, Clippers Quay, Salford Quays, M5 2XP, ✆ 873 7321, Fax 873 7318, – rm rest TV ☎ P – 150. AE VISA. by A 56 CZ
Meals 17.50/18.50 **st.** and a la carte – 11.75 – **166 rm** 120.00/150.00 **st.** – SB.

Portland Thistle, 3-5 Portland St., Piccadilly Gdns., M1 6DP, ✆ 228 3400, Fax 228 6347, – rm rest TV ☎ P – 270. AE VISA JCB
Meals *(closed Saturday lunch and Sunday)* 16.45/20.45 **st.** and a la carte 6.95 – 10.25 – **204 rm** 102.00/136.00 **st.**, 1 suite – SB. CZ a

Castlefield, Liverpool Rd, M3 4JR, ✆ 832 7073, Fax 839 0326, – rest TV ☎ P – 65. AE VISA JCB by Quay St. CZ
closed 24 to 26 December – **Meals** (bar lunch)/dinner 13.95 **t.** and a la carte 4.50 – **48 rm** 72.00/78.00 **st.** – SB.

Sherlock Holmes (at Victoria and Albert H.), Water St., M3 4JQ, ✆ 832 1188, Fax 832 2484 – P. AE VISA by Quay St. CZ
Meals *(closed Saturday lunch and Sunday)* 16.95/25.00 **st.**

Brasserie St Pierre, 57-63 Princess St., M2 4EQ, ✆ 228 0231, Fax 228 0231 – AE VISA CZ s
closed Saturday lunch, Monday dinner, Sunday and 24 December-2 January – **Meals** 13.95 **t.** and a la carte 8.95.

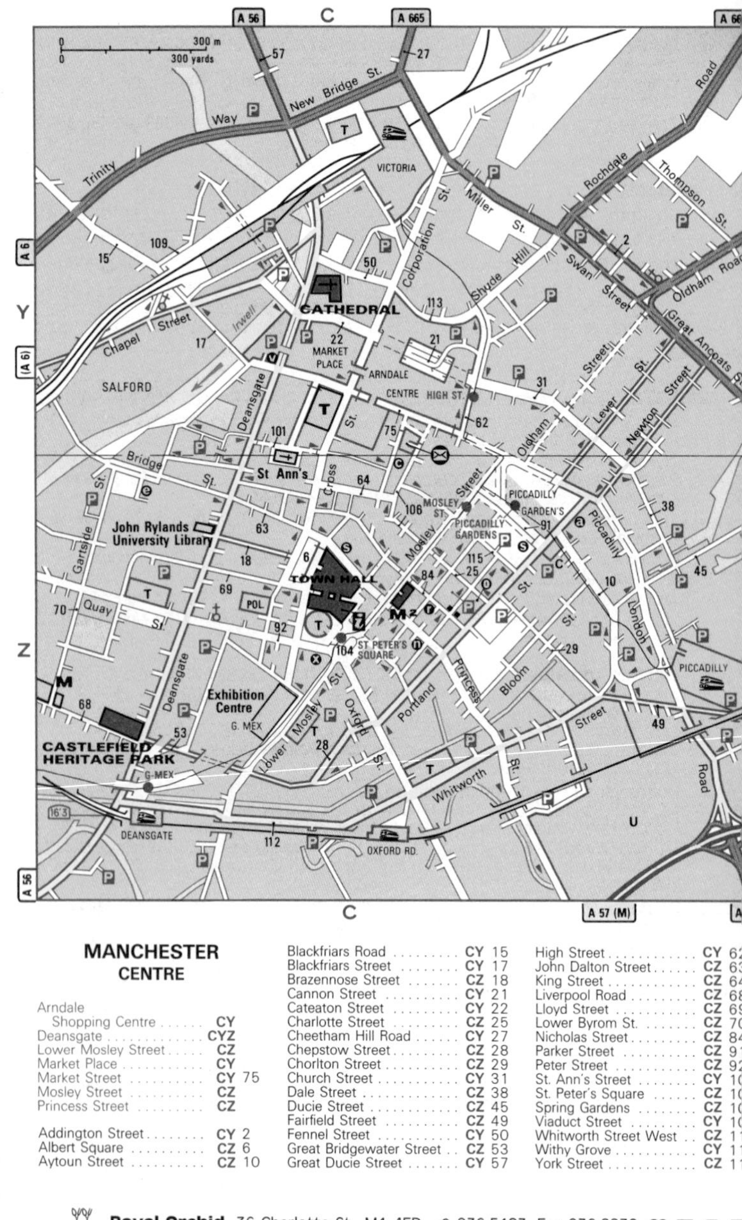

MANCHESTER
CENTRE

Arndale Shopping Centre ...... CY
Deansgate .... CYZ
Lower Mosley Street ..... CZ
Market Place .... CY
Market Street .... CY 75
Mosley Street .... CZ
Princess Street .... CZ

Addington Street .... CY 2
Albert Square .... CZ 6
Aytoun Street .... CZ 10
Blackfriars Road .... CY 15
Blackfriars Street .... CY 17
Brazennose Street .... CZ 18
Cannon Street .... CY 21
Cateaton Street .... CY 22
Charlotte Street .... CZ 25
Cheetham Hill Road .... CY 27
Chepstow Street .... CZ 28
Chorlton Street .... CZ 29
Church Street .... CY 31
Dale Street .... CZ 38
Ducie Street .... CZ 45
Fairfield Street .... CZ 49
Fennel Street .... CY 50
Great Bridgewater Street .. CZ 53
Great Ducie Street .... CY 57
High Street .... CY 6
John Dalton Street ...... CZ 6
King Street .... CZ 6
Liverpool Road .... CZ 6
Lloyd Street .... CZ 6
Lower Byrom St. .... CZ 7
Nicholas Street .... CZ 8
Parker Street .... CZ 9
Peter Street .... CZ 9
St. Ann's Street .... CY 1
St. Peter's Square ...... CZ 1
Spring Gardens .... CZ 1
Viaduct Street .... CY 1
Whitworth Street West .. CZ 1
Withy Grove .... CY 1
York Street .... CZ 1

XX **Royal Orchid,** 36 Charlotte St., M1 4FD, ✆ 236 5183, Fax 236 8830. MC AE ① VI
closed Monday lunch, Sunday and 25 December – **Meals** - Thai - 7.00/16.00 **t.** ar
a la carte. CZ

XX **Isola Bella,** Dolefield, Crown Sq., M3 3EN, ✆ 831 7099, Fax 839 1561 – ▤. MC
VISA CZ
closed Sunday, 25-26 December and Bank Holidays – **Meals** - Italian - 9.50 **t.** and a la car
🍷 5.50.

XX **Giulio's Terrazza,** 14 Nicholas St., M1 4EJ, ✆ 236 4033, Fax 228 6501 – ▤. MC AE ⓓ VISA JCB CZ r
closed Sunday, 25 December and Bank Holidays – **Meals** - Italian - 9.50/12.50 **t.** and a la carte 🍷 6.50.

XX **Gaylord,** Amethyst House, Marriott's Court, Spring Gdns, M2 1EA, ✆ 832 4866, Fax 832 6037 – ▤. MC AE ⓓ VISA CZ c
closed 25 December and 1 January – **Meals** - Indian - 5.95/11.95 **t.** and a la carte 🍷 5.60.

X **Yang Sing,** 34 Princess St., M1 4JY, ✆ 236 2200, Fax 236 5934 – ▤. MC AE VISA CZ n
closed 25 December – **Meals** - Chinese (Canton) - (booking essential) 14.00 **t.** and a la carte.

at Northenden *S : 5 ¼ m. by A 57 (M) – CZ – and A 5103 – ✉ Manchester – ☎ 0161 :*

Forte Posthouse Manchester, Palatine Rd, M22 4FH, ✆ 998 7090, Fax 946 0139 – |‡| ⇔ rm TV ☎ P – 🏛 150. MC AE ⓓ VISA JCB. ✻
closed 22 December-2 January – **Meals** *(closed Saturday lunch)* 7.95/12.95 **st.** and a la carte 🍷 6.95 – ☕ 8.95 – **190 rm** 69.00/79.00 **st.** – SB.

at Manchester Airport *S : 9 m. by Lower Mosley St. – CZ – and A 5103 off M 56 – ✉ Manchester – ☎ 0161 :*

Manchester Airport Hilton, Outwood Lane, Ringway, M90 4WP, ✆ 435 3000, Fax 435 3040, Fϭ, ≘s, ⛶ – |‡| ⇔ rm ▤ TV ☎ ♿ P – 🏛 250. MC AE ⓓ VISA. ✻
Meals 18.50 **st.** and a la carte 🍷 6.50 – ***Lowry's :*** **Meals** 18.50 **st.** 🍷 6.50 – ☕ 13.50 – **222 rm** 130.00/177.00 **st.**

Forte Posthouse Manchester Airport, Ringway Rd, Wythenshawe, M90 3NS, ✆ 437 5811, Fax 436 2340, Fϭ, ≘s, ⛶ – |‡| ⇔ rm ▤ TV ☎ P – 🏛 45. MC AE ⓓ VISA JCB. ✻
Meals 9.95/16.95 **t.** and dinner a la carte 🍷 6.95 – ☕ 9.95 – **283 rm** 79.00/89.00 **t.**, 2 suites – SB.

Holiday Inn Garden Court, Outwood Lane, M90 4HL, ✆ 498 0333, Fax 498 0222 – |‡| ⇔ rm ▤ rm TV ☎ ♿ P. MC AE ⓓ VISA JCB. ✻
Meals (dinner only) a la carte approx. 12.60 **t.** 🍷 4.50 – ☕ 5.50 – **163 rm** 50.00 **t.**

Etrop Grange (Regal), Thorley Lane, M90 4EG, ✆ 499 0500, Fax 499 0790 – ⇔ rm TV ☎ ♿ P – 🏛 40. MC AE ⓓ VISA JCB
Meals *(closed Saturday lunch)* 16.50/27.50 **st.** 🍷 6.00 – ☕ 10.00 – **37 rm** 103.00/135.00 **st.**, 2 suites.

XXX **Moss Nook,** Ringway Rd, Moss Nook, M22 5WD, ✆ 437 4778, Fax 498 8089 – P. MC AE ⓓ VISA
closed Saturday lunch, Sunday, Monday and 2 weeks Christmas – **Meals** 16.75/29.50 **st.** and a la carte 🍷 6.50.

at Worsley *W : 7 ¼ m. by A 6 – CY, – A 5063, M 602 and M 62 (eastbound) on A 572 – ✉ Manchester – ☎ 0161 :*

Novotel Manchester West, Worsley Brow, M28 2YA, at junction 13 of M 62 ✆ 799 3535, Fax 703 8207, ⛶ heated – |‡| ⇔ rm ▤ rest TV ☎ ♿ P – 🏛 220. MC AE ⓓ VISA
Meals 16.00 **st.** and a la carte 🍷 9.75 – ☕ 7.50 – **119 rm** 65.00 **st.**

XX **Tung Fong,** 2 Worsley Rd, M28 4NL, *on A 572* ✆ 794 5331, Fax 727 9598 – ▤. MC AE VISA
Meals - Chinese (Peking) - 5.80/15.50 **st.** and a la carte 🍷 5.00.

at Pendlebury *NW : 4 m. by A 6 – CY – on A 666 – ✉ Manchester – ☎ 0161 :*

Henry Boddington, 219 Bolton Rd, M27 8TG, ✆ 736 5143, Fax 737 2786 – TV ☎ ♿ P. MC AE ⓓ VISA JCB. ✻
Meals (grill rest.) 7.50/12.50 **t.** and a la carte – ☕ 4.95 – **30 rm** 41.50 **st.** – SB.

at Swinton *NW : 4 m. by A 6 – CY –, A 580 and A 572 on B 5231 – ✉ Manchester – ☎ 0161 :*

New Ellesmere Lodge (Premier), East Lancs Rd, M27 8AA, SW : ½ m. on A 580 ✆ 728 2791, Fax 794 8222 – ⇔ rm TV ☎ ♿ P. MC AE ⓓ VISA. ✻
Meals (grill rest.) 8.50/14.50 **st.** 🍷 3.95 – ☕ 4.95 – **27 rm** 41.50 **st.** – SB.

LONGRIDGE *Lancs.* 402 M 22 – *pop. 7 351* – ☎ *01772.*
Manchester 36 – Liverpool 42.

XXX ✿✿ **Paul Heathcote's** (Heathcote), 104-106 Higher Rd, PR3 3SY, NE : ½ m. by B 5269 following signs for Jeffrey Hill ✆ 784969, Fax 785713 – ⇔. MC AE ⓓ VISA
closed Monday – **Meals** (dinner only and lunch Friday and Sunday) 22.50/38.00 **t.** and dinner a la carte 30.00/43.00 **t.** 🍷 10.00
Spec. Baked fillet of cod in hot pot potatoes, rosemary lamb juice, Goosnargh duckling with fondant potatoes and mead scented juices, Baked egg custard with rose-water.

Calendar of main tradefairs and other international events in 1997

AUSTRIA

Vienna	*Wiener Festwochen*	*8 May to 22 June*
Salzburg	*Salzburg Festival (Festspiele)*	*22 to 31 March* *26 July to 31 August*

BENELUX

Amsterdam	*Holland Festival*	*June*
Bruges	*Ascension Day Procession*	*Ascension*
Brussels	*Guild Procession (Ommegang)*	*first Thursday of July and the previous Tuesday*
	Holiday and Leisure Activities International Show	*Late March 98*
	Belgian Antique Dealers Fair	*Late Jan. to early Feb. 98*
	Eurantica (Antiques Show)	*Late March 98*

CZECH REPUBLIC

Prague	*Prague's Spring International Music Festival*	*12 May to 6 June*

DENMARK

Copenhagen	*Scandinavian Furniture Fair*	*5 to 9 March*
	International Fashion Fair	*16 to 19 August*

FINLAND

Helsinki	*International Fashion Fair*	*17 to 19 August*
	Helsinki Festival	*20 to 31 August*
	International Horse Show	*17 to 19 October*
	Helsinki Motor Show	*12 to 14 December*

FRANCE

Paris	*Paris Fair*	*26 April to 8 May*
	Motorcycle Show	*27 Sept. to 6 October*
Cannes	*International Film Festival*	*7 to 18 May*
Lyons	*Lyons Fair*	*5 to 14 April*
Marseilles	*Marseilles Fair*	*26 Sept. to 6 Oct.*

GERMANY

Berlin	*Berlin Fair (Grüne Woche)*	*17 to 26 January*
Frankfurt	*International Fair*	*14 to 18 February* *23 to 27 August*
	Frankfurt Book Fair	*15 to 20 October*
Hanover	*Hanover Fair*	*14 to 19 April*
Leipzig	*International Book Fair*	*20 to 23 March*
Munich	*Beer Festival (Oktoberfest)*	*20 Sept. to 5 Oct.*

GREECE

Athens	*Athens Festival*	*Early June to late Sept.*

HUNGARY

Budapest	*Spring Festival (Music, Arts)*	*Mid to late March*
	International Fashion Fair	*30 March,* *31 August to 2 Sept.,* *30 September*
	International Motor Exhibition	*1 to 5 October*

IRELAND

Dublin	*Dublin Horse Show*	*6 to 10 August*

ITALY

Milan	*Fashion Fair (Moda Milano)*	*28 February to 4 March* *3 to 7 October*
	Bit (International Tourism Exchange)	*26 February* *to 2 March*
	SMAU (International Exhibition of Information and Communication Technology)	*2 to 6 October*
Florence	*Fashion Fair (Pitti Immagine Uomo)*	*26 to 29 June*
Turin	*International Industrial and Commercial Vehicle show*	*23 to 27 April*
	International Book Fair	*22 to 27 May*
Venice	*International Film Festival*	*27 August to 6 September*
	The Carnival	*31 January to 11 February*

NORWAY

Oslo	*Fashion Fair*	*23 to 25 August*
	International Book Fair	*30 October to 2 Nov.*

POLAND

Warsaw	*International Book Fair*	*20 to 25 May*
	Mozart Festival	*9 June to 27 July*
	Jazz Festival	*October 97*

PORTUGAL

Lisbon	*Handicraft fair (Fia Lisboa)*	*5 to 13 July*
	Motorexpo	*29 Nov. to 7 Dec.*

SPAIN

Madrid	*Fitur*	*29 Jan. to 2 Feb.*
	International Fashion Week	*13 to 16 Feb.*
	Feriarte	*22 to 30 Nov.*
Barcelona	*Fashion Barcelona*	*8 to 10 Feb.*
	International Motor Show	*17 to 15 May*
Sevilla	*April Fair*	*15 to 20 April*
Valencia	*International Fair*	*21 Dec. to 2 Jan.*
	Fallas	*15 to 19 March*

SWEDEN

Stockholm	*Stockholm Water Festival*	*1 to 9 August*
	International Fashion Fair	*23 to 25 August*
	International Boat Show	*1 to 9 March*
	International Art Fair	*14 to 16 February*
Gothenburg	*International Horse Show*	*29 April to 4 May*
	International Book & Library Fair	*30 October to 2 November*
	International Boat Show	*31 Jan. to 9 February*
	International Film Festival	*February 98*

SWITZERLAND

Berne	*BEA : Exhibition for Handicraft, Agriculture, Trade and Industry*	*3 to 12 May*
Basle	*European Watch, Clock and Jewellery Fair*	*10 to 17 April*
Geneva	*International Motor Show*	*5 to 15 March 98*
	International exhibition of inventions, new technologies and products	*11 to 20 April*
	International fair for travel, languages and cultures	*30 April to 4 May*
Zürich	*Züspa : Zurich Autumn Show for Home and Living, Sport and Fashion*	*25 Sept. to 5 Oct.*

UNITED KINGDOM

London	*Fine Art and Antiques Fair*	*5 to 15 June*
	International Motor Show	*15 to 26 October*
	London International Boat Show	*January 98*
	London International Bookfair	*22 to 24 March 98*
Birmingham	*Automative Trade Show*	*27 to 30 April*
	Classic and Sportscar Show	*3 to 5 May*
	International Motorcycle Show	*8 to 16 November*
	National Classic Motor Show	*15 and 16 November*
Edinburgh	*Book Festival*	*9 to 25 August*
	Arts Festival	*10 to 30 August*
	International Film Festival	*August*
Glasgow	*May Festival*	*1 to 24 May*
Leeds	*International Film Festival*	*16 to 31 October*

International Dialling Codes

Indicatifs Téléphoniques Internationaux

Internationale Telefon-Vorwahlnummern

国際電話国別番号

from / to	Ⓐ A	B	CH	CZ	D	DK	E	FIN	F	GB	GR
AUSTRIA	–	0032	0041	0042	0049	0045	0034	00358	0033	0044	0030
BELGIUM	0043	–	0041	0042	0049	0045	0034	00358	0033	0044	0030
CZECH REPUBLIC	0043	0032	0041	–	0049	0045	0034	00358	0033	0044	0030
DENMARK	0043	0032	0041	0042	0049	–	0034	00358	0033	0044	0030
FINLAND	0043	0032	0041	0042	0049	0045	0034	–	0033	0044	0030
FRANCE	0043	0032	0041	0042	0049	0045	0034	00358	–	0044	0030
GERMANY	0043	0032	0041	0042	–	0045	0034	00358	0033	0044	0030
GREECE	0043	0032	0041	0042	0049	0045	0034	00358	0033	0044	–
HUNGARY	0043	0032	0041	0042	0049	0045	0034	00358	0033	0044	0030
IRELAND	0043	0032	0041	0042	0049	0045	0034	00358	0033	0044	0030
ITALY	0043	0032	0041	0042	0049	0045	0034	00358	0033	0044	0030
JAPAN	00143	00132	00141	00142	00149	00145	00134	001358	00133	00144	00130
LUXEMBOURG	0043	0032	0041	0042	05	0045	0034	00358	0033	0044	0030
NORWAY	0043	0032	0041	0042	0049	0045	0034	0358	0033	0044	0030
NETHERLANDS	0043	0032	0041	0042	0049	0045	0034	00358	0033	0044	0030
POLAND	0043	0032	0041	0042	0049	0045	0034	00358	0033	0044	0030
PORTUGAL	0043	0032	0041	0042	0049	0045	0034	00358	0033	0044	0030
SPAIN	0743	0732	0741	0742	0749	0745	–	07358	0733	0744	0730
SWEDEN	00943	00932	00941	00942	00949	00945	00934	009358	00933	00944	00930
SWITZERLAND	0043	0032	–	0042	0049	0045	0034	00358	0033	0044	0030
UNITED KINGDOM	0043	0032	0041	0042	0049	0045	0034	00358	0033	–	0030
USA	01143	01132	01141	01142	01149	01145	01134	011358	01133	01144	01130

(H)	(I)	(IRL)	(J)	(L)	(N)	(NL)	(P)	(PL)	(S)	(USA)	
0036	0039	00353	0081	00352	0047	0031	00351	0048	0046	001	**AUSTRIA**
0036	0039	00353	0081	00352	0047	0031	00351	0048	0046	001	**BELGIUM**
0036	0039	00353	0081	00352	0047	0031	00351	0048	0046	001	**CZECH REPUBLIC**
0036	0039	00353	0081	00352	0047	0031	00351	0048	0046	001	**DENMARK**
0036	0039	00353	0081	00352	0047	0031	00351	0048	0046	001	**FINLAND**
0036	0039	00353	0081	00352	0047	0031	00351	0048	0046	191	**FRANCE**
0036	0039	00353	0081	00352	0047	0031	00351	0048	0046	001	**GERMANY**
0036	0039	00353	0081	00352	0047	0031	00351	0048	0046	001	**GREECE**
–	0039	00353	0081	00352	0047	0031	00351	0048	0046	001	**HUNGARY**
0036	0039	–	0081	00352	0047	0031	00351	0048	0046	001	**IRELAND**
0036	–	00353	0081	00352	0047	0031	00351	0048	0046	001	**ITALY**
00136	00139	001353	–	001352	00147	00131	001351	00148	00146	0011	**JAPAN**
0036	0039	00353	0081	–	0047	0031	00351	0048	0046	001	**LUXEMBOURG**
0036	0039	00353	0081	00352	–	0031	00351	0048	0046	001	**NORWAY**
0036	0039	00353	0081	00352	0047	–	00351	0048	0046	001	**NETHERLANDS**
0036	0039	00353	0081	00352	0047	0031	00351	–	0046	001	**POLAND**
0036	0039	00353	0081	00352	0047	0031	–	0048	0046	001	**PORTUGAL**
0736	0739	07353	0781	07352	0747	0731	07351	0748	0746	071	**SPAIN**
00936	00939	009353	00981	009352	00947	00931	009351	00948	–	0091	**SWEDEN**
0036	0039	00353	0081	00352	0047	0031	00351	0048	0046	001	**SWITZERLAND**
0036	0039	00353	0081	00352	0047	0031	00351	0048	0046	001	**UNITED KINGDOM**
01136	01139	011353	01181	011352	01147	01131	011351	01148	01146	–	**USA**

Manufacture française des pneumatiques Michelin
Société en commandite par actions au capital de 2 000 000 000 de francs
Place des Carmes-Déchaux – 63 Clermont-Ferrand (France)
R.C.S. Clermont-Fd B 855 200 507

Michelin et Cie, propriétaires-éditeurs, 1997
Dépôt légal : mars 97 – ISBN 2.06.007079-1

No part of this publication may be reproduced in any form without the prior permission of the publisher.

Printed in the EU – 3.1997
Photocomposition : MAURY Imprimeur S.A., Malesherbes
Impression : MAURY Imprimeur S.A., Malesherbes – KAPP LAHURE JOMBART, Evreux
Reliure : S.I.R.C., Marigny-le-Châtel

Illustrations : Nathalie Benavides, Patricia Haubert, Cécile Imbert/MICHELIN
Narratif Systèmes/Genclo p. 61, p. 111, p. 177 – Rodolphe Corbel p. 459